MW00340420

Corporations and Other Business Associations

ASPEN CASEBOOK SERIES

Corporations and Other Business Associations

Cases and Materials

Seventh Edition

Charles R.T. O'Kelley

Professor and Director
Adolf A. Berle, Jr. Center on Corporations, Law and Society
Seattle University

Robert B. Thompson

Peter P. Weidenbruch Jr. Professor of Business Law
Georgetown University Law Center

Wolters Kluwer
Law & Business

Published by Wolters Kluwer Law & Business in New York.

Wolters Kluwer Law & Business serves customers worldwide with CCH, Aspen Publishers, and Kluwer Law International products. (www.wolterskluwerlb.com)

To contact Customer Service, e-mail customer.service@wolterskluwer.com, call 1-800-234-1660, fax 1-800-901-9075, or mail correspondence to:

Wolters Kluwer Law & Business
Attn: Order Department
PO Box 990
Frederick, MD 21705

Printed in the United States of America.

2 3 4 5 6 7 8 9 0

ISBN 978-1-4548-3762-6

Library of Congress Cataloging-in-Publication Data

O'Kelley, Charles R. (Charles Rogers), 1946- author.
   Corporations and other business associations : cases and materials / Charles R.T. O'Kelley, Professor and Director, Adolf A. Berle, Jr. Center on Corporations, Law and Society, Seattle University; Robert B. Thompson, Peter P. Weidenbruch Jr. Professor of Business Law, Georgetown University Law Center.—Seventh edition.
       pages cm.— (Aspen casebook series)
   Includes bibliographical references and index.
   ISBN 978-1-4548-3762-6 (alk. paper)
 1. Corporation law—United States. 2. Business enterprises—Law and legislation—United States. I. Thompson, Robert B., 1949- author. II. Title.
   KF1414.O39 2014
   346.73'066—dc23

                                                        2013046713

About Wolters Kluwer Law & Business

Wolters Kluwer Law & Business is a leading global provider of intelligent information and digital solutions for legal and business professionals in key specialty areas, and respected educational resources for professors and law students. Wolters Kluwer Law & Business connects legal and business professionals as well as those in the education market with timely, specialized authoritative content and information-enabled solutions to support success through productivity, accuracy and mobility.

Serving customers worldwide, Wolters Kluwer Law & Business products include those under the Aspen Publishers, CCH, Kluwer Law International, Loislaw, ftwilliam.com and MediRegs family of products.

CCH products have been a trusted resource since 1913, and are highly regarded resources for legal, securities, antitrust and trade regulation, government contracting, banking, pension, payroll, employment and labor, and healthcare reimbursement and compliance professionals.

Aspen Publishers products provide essential information to attorneys, business professionals and law students. Written by preeminent authorities, the product line offers analytical and practical information in a range of specialty practice areas from securities law and intellectual property to mergers and acquisitions and pension/benefits. Aspen's trusted legal education resources provide professors and students with high-quality, up-to-date and effective resources for successful instruction and study in all areas of the law.

Kluwer Law International products provide the global business community with reliable international legal information in English. Legal practitioners, corporate counsel and business executives around the world rely on Kluwer Law journals, looseleafs, books, and electronic products for comprehensive information in many areas of international legal practice.

Loislaw is a comprehensive online legal research product providing legal content to law firm practitioners of various specializations. Loislaw provides attorneys with the ability to quickly and efficiently find the necessary legal information they need, when and where they need it, by facilitating access to primary law as well as state-specific law, records, forms and treatises.

ftwilliam.com offers employee benefits professionals the highest quality plan documents (retirement, welfare and non-qualified) and government forms (5500/PBGC, 1099 and IRS) software at highly competitive prices.

MediRegs products provide integrated health care compliance content and software solutions for professionals in healthcare, higher education and life sciences, including professionals in accounting, law and consulting.

Wolters Kluwer Law & Business, a division of Wolters Kluwer, is headquartered in New York. Wolters Kluwer is a market-leading global information services company focused on professionals.

Summary of Contents

Contents

2   *Partnerships*   49

5   *Protecting Participants' Expectations in Closely Held Corporations*   **451**

10 *Disclosure and Corporate Governance*   947

Preface

This book provides material for the basic course in corporations and other business associations. There is more than one way to teach any course, and the paths multiply for the business associations survey course, in which teachers divide among those who emphasize closely held businesses, those who emphasize the public corporation, and those who spend about the same amount of time on both. This book can be adapted to any one of these approaches with ease. We have structured the chapters so that most topics can be moved and used effectively out of their original order. The book can also be adapted to a one- or two-semester course. Nonetheless, the current organization reflects a coherent combination of material ordered in a way that will be helpful to someone who is approaching corporations and other business associations for the first time.

One of our goals when we began this project more than 25 years ago was to provide a casebook that could grow and change with the subject it addresses while providing continuity to users. Thus, the core structure was designed not to reflect current fancy but rather to illustrate what we believe are central, recurring issues and themes. Each edition, therefore, continues to feel like an old friend to continuing users, though it contains new materials reflective of the constant changes in law, business enterprise, and society. This edition continues that tradition. As with the sixth edition, continuing users will notice new material reflective of our fast evolving securities markets and the relationship of those markets to corporate governance and society. The new millennium has seen two severe shocks to the stock markets: the collapse of the dot-com bubble and the financial meltdown in 2008. The fallout from these financial difficulties has caused some policy makers, lawmakers, and academics to question the extent to which we leave organization of collective business behavior only to markets. Renewed government regulation of executive compensation (e.g., say on pay) and shareholder rights reflect these concerns. At the same time, dramatic changes in the makeup of the market—particularly the growth of share ownership by institutional investors, the expanding role of independent directors, and the rise of activist shareholders—illustrate the vibrancy of private-sector responses. Chapter 3 in particular seeks to capture these recent movements in a context that lets students see how the regulation of publicly held companies is different from that of the closely held enterprise.

The introduction to the corporate form in Chapter 3 can be taught either as a follow-on to Chapter 2 or as a freestanding beginning to the study of the corporate form. In a succinct footprint, the chapter provides the essentials for forming a corporation and includes a business planning exercise for those who wish to pursue experiential learning. At the same time, this chapter provides the necessary overview for students to understand how a publicly held corporation is a different type of business entity. In turn, this leads to the extensive discussion in Chapter 4 on director and shareholder roles in the corporation.

Any examination of the law of American business enterprises must provide an overview of the interaction of our national and state legal systems. As with many other parts of our national life, the presence of the federal government continues to grow as the law provider in corporate law, a trend exacerbated in the post-Enron, post-financial meltdown environment. In Chapters 10-12 we provide the detail to fill out the initial survey of federal law contained in Chapter 3, including the issue of insider trading, which remains one of the most visible and accessible contexts for viewing the impact of law on corporate behavior. Mergers and other corporate acquisitions provide the most recurring context for federal law covered in this book. In putting most of the federal material after the presentation of the state law structure of these transactions in Chapters 8 and 9, we hope that students will better understand the factual setting and can better evaluate the legal rules.

Despite this growth of federal law, state law (and in particular Delaware law) remains the dominant source for legal rules for corporations. State law reflects a strong preference for private ordering; this law continues to be built around trusting directors to govern corporations and permitting them to make use of a variety of incentives and monitoring devices made available in the private sector and by government regulation. Under this view, the government's role is focused on providing essential background rules and a judicial forum for shareholders to bring fiduciary duties claims as a check on the broad power given directors to control "other people's money." This essentially common law process is visible throughout the book, but Chapter 4 is particularly designed to introduce this theme. It includes materials to cover, for example, narrowing the independent use of good faith and the increasing variety of contexts in which judicial review occurs through special litigation committees.

The seventh edition continues our separate discussion of limited liability companies within what we believe is an innovative chapter. LLCs have been growing since the mid-1990s and now exceed the number of new corporations. The legal principles governing this entity are similar to what students will have seen in earlier parts of the book addressing corporations and partnership. In this chapter we develop a distinctive part of LLC law that is particularly visible in Delaware. That state and its judiciary have focused on legal rules seemingly aimed at sophisticated entities, as contrasted with, for example, the traditional "mom-and-pop" enterprise, whose participants are willing to take the time and pay the costs of developing a specialized template to govern their business relationship. Thus, in Chapter 6 we have picked cases to illustrate the extent to which parties can waive the fiduciary duties provided by law or the ability for investors to seek involuntary dissolution from courts. This in turn reintroduces, in a new context, the question of markets versus government regulation discussed at the beginning of this preface.

Unlike many of the "private" law courses found in the traditional first-year law school curriculum, corporation law does not respond to problems commonly experienced in discrete transactions or interactions between "strangers." Instead, the law of corporations and other business associations addresses the governance of a collective, relational enterprise. For example, the key recurring issue is the ongoing relationship of shareholders to directors and officers, and the extent to which any individual or group can speak for or direct the enterprise. The corporations or business associations course is many law students' first extended contact with the intricacies of business relationships. Thus, it is especially important to help students grasp new terminology, develop an understanding of what motivates individuals to invest their human or money capital in a cooperative business venture, and recognize how law and private ordering interact to protect participants' reasonable expectations. Economic learning advances the discussion of these issues. An understanding of how markets work and of the incentives that commonly motivate people in economic transactions enriches students' ability to interpret and use the law, so we discuss these concepts in the early chapters. Understanding the economic concepts of "collective action" and "rational apathy" can help to explain why legal rules will be different for an enterprise with many dispersed passive participants than for one with a few close-knit investors.

Although we provide economic-based tools for understanding, the thematic framework of this book is how the law shapes collective business relationships. In the first few chapters, we compare the various forms of doing business: sole proprietorships, partnerships, limited partnerships, limited liability companies, close corporations, and publicly held corporations. A comparative analysis of these forms continues throughout the book in a variety of legal contexts.

We ask students to recognize the various methods used by law to regulate collective business relationships. In examining what legal constraints there should be on the behavior of those who control corporations, a student who has read this book will have considered:

- Voting and other governance rules imposed by law before any transaction has occurred
- Fiduciary duty applied by courts to specific transactions after they have occurred
- Disclosure rules mandating information to be provided in corporate relationships
- Specific legal remedies like appraisals or buyouts

This examination is designed to give students an appreciation for the different ways that law works and the relative advantage of each method as it is applied in particular circumstances, with consideration given to the possible market or private ordering alternatives. Is law supplemental or mandatory? Does it seek to provide the rules that the parties would have agreed to if they had thought carefully about the situation, or does it seek to impose a penalty or an incentive to encourage one side or the other?

At the beginning of each relevant part, section, or subsection, we have noted the statutory or regulatory material to which students should refer when studying that segment. This reflects our view that this material is best studied in close relation to the statutory law. Our comparative approach asks students to think about how the Delaware statute differs from the Model Business Corporation Act, the two most commonly referenced statutory guideposts for corporation law in this country. Referenced statutory and regulatory material appears in the statutory supplement to this book, also published by Wolters Kluwer, which currently includes, for example, new statutory material on benefit corporations and an actual complaint that permits discussion of judicial review in the Disney cases. Throughout the casebook we use the Model Business Corporation Act to refer to the current version of that Act.

Many case, statutory, and other citations have been omitted from quoted material without indication. Most footnotes have also been omitted from quoted material without indication, but those that remain retain their original numbers. Bracketed material in a quoted source indicates transitional or summary materials that we have provided.

Charles R.T. O'Kelley
Robert B. Thompson

November 2013

*Corporations
and Other
Business Associations*

1 Economic and Legal Aspects of the Firm

A. Some Basic Concepts and Terminology

1. The Classical Firm

a. Introductory Note

The classical firm[1] is a business owned and managed by one person. In law, the classical firm is referred to as a sole proprietorship, and the owner as the sole proprietor. Traditionally, economists have examined the classical firm as a starting point for understanding the nature of more complex firms that are organized with multiple owners. In this part and throughout this chapter, we will highlight the most important insights and issues economists have uncovered. We begin with a look at how economists analyze and describe the classical firm.

b. The Entrepreneur

The central actor in the economic conception of the firm is the entrepreneur.[2] As Frank Knight described, the entrepreneur is the person who does two critical tasks.[3] First, the entrepreneur *directs* the business and exercises the ultimate *business judgment*. The entrepreneur decides what to make and how to make it. In the real world, this does not involve simply reacting to what consumers want. Rather, it involves forecasting whether, at what price, and in what quantities consumers would be willing to buy a particular product or service *if* it were produced and made available to the market. It involves forecasting whether and how a *team* of employees can be hired and organized

---

1. The modifier "classical" has two connotations. First, the owner-managed firm dominated the economic landscape at the outset of the industrial revolution—the heyday, or "classical" period, of capitalism. Second, the owner-managed firm represents the purest, or most classical, form of economic organization because it avoids the problems of misaligned incentives that arise when authority and responsibility are divided between and among multiple owners, a problem that you will observe in different forms throughout your study of corporations and other business associations.

2. The sole proprietor is in economic parlance the firm's entrepreneur.

3. For the seminal analysis of the entrepreneur, see Frank Knight, Risk, Uncertainty, and Profit (1921).

to produce the product or service at a cost that will produce a profit. In other words, it involves managing in the shadow of *uncertainty*.

The entrepreneur's second task is accepting full *responsibility* for his or her business decisions by being the residual guarantor and claimant. If the entrepreneur's business judgment proves faulty, and the business operates at a loss, the entrepreneur stands ready to draw on his or her personal wealth to satisfy the claims of the firm's employees and creditors. The entrepreneur is a fully responsible owner; stated in legal terms, the entrepreneur has *unlimited liability*. On the other hand, if the entrepreneur's judgment proves sound, and profits result, even immense profits, these rewards all belong to the entrepreneur. They are his or her just deserts for taking the risks of *responsible ownership*.

Consider the example of Mary, who decides to start a new business—a wholesale bakery, which she will own and operate as a sole proprietorship. Mary will be the bakery firm's entrepreneur. In deciding to start her business, and thereafter in running the business from day to day, Mary must solve innumerable problems. Being able to solve these problems, and being responsible if the problems are not solved, is the essence of being an entrepreneur. Some problems will be routine, but many will be complex and require forecasting. Mary must determine what bakery products her business can profitably offer to the market. She must determine how to house, equip, staff, supply, and finance her business. To solve each of these problems a certain amount of knowledge, business judgment, and skill is required. Moreover, solving these problems often involves convincing others (prospective employees, lenders, or suppliers) to invest their human or money capital in the bakery venture. Thus, Mary must be willing to demonstrate that she is a *responsible owner* who will make good on her promises. To do this, Mary, as a classical entrepreneur, must be confident enough in her own ability and judgment that she will be willing to be the firm's *residual claimant*. In other words, Mary will agree that she will pay herself last, and only if the bakery is profitable. Moreover, Mary will agree that if the bakery venture is a failure, she will use her own wealth to make good on the promises she has made to employers, suppliers, and lenders.

c. *The Coasean Firm: Differentiating the Market and the Firm*

Economist R.H. Coase[4] identifies a "firm" as the antithesis of the market with respect to the means by which economic resources are allocated. In the idealized market economy often identified with Adam Smith, each producer and consumer separately calculates her own self-interest and chooses what to make and what to buy based on price signals received in the market. As a result, resources are allocated to their highest and best use, not in response to governmental orders or other communicated commands, but as if by an invisible hand, through the separate, self-interested choices of all producers and consumers. By contrast, inside a firm resources are allocated pursuant to conscious orders or directions from the entrepreneur to her employees.

Return to our bakery hypothetical. Mary handles most of the baking, writes advertising copy, deals with customers, and so on. However, for certain parts of the

---

4. See Ronald H. Coase, The Nature of the Firm, 4 Economica, 386-405 (1937).

production and sales process Mary uses the market. For example, Mary cannot efficiently produce the raw materials she uses. Instead she buys eggs, flour, and butter from a supplier. Likewise, she purchases transport services from a trucking firm, accounting services from a local certified public accountant, and electricity from a utility company. But Mary does not rely solely on market transactions for the materials and services that she cannot self-produce. She also hires employees and directs them to perform the tasks—waiting on customers, keeping the premises clean, handling baking on weekends—that cannot as efficiently be handled via market transactions or by Mary herself.

From this Coasean perspective, the "firm" is what we call the set of relations that arise when the entrepreneur allocates resources via commands to her employees, rather than the set of relations that arise when an entrepreneur allocates resources via market transactions with outsiders. Thus, depicted as a circle and using Mary, the classical owner/entrepreneur, as an example, the Coasean firm includes Mary and her employees, but excludes the customers, suppliers, and creditors with whom Mary does business via contract or market exchanges.

From the Coasean perspective, the essence of the firm is the entrepreneur's management and conscious direction of resource allocation decisions. Thus, a firm is identified with an internal decision-making hierarchy. The entrepreneur is the responsible owner/manager who sits at the top of the hierarchy. All decisional authority resides in the entrepreneur, and is either exercised by the entrepreneur or delegated to employees to exercise. Decisions within the firm are made, not in response to price signals, but via conscious direction and command. Each employee surrenders the autonomy he would possess as a sole proprietor and agrees, instead, to follow the commands and directions of the entrepreneur.

2. The Business Association

Recall our simple bakery example, discussed above. Mary's firm is a sole proprietorship. She is the only owner; she is the entrepreneur. She and she alone has the authority to make and carry out business policies, including hiring, firing, and directing employees. Suppose, however, that Mary needs not only to hire employees and use market transactions to run her bakery, but also to obtain a substantial infusion of capital and management expertise to expand the bakery to serve a larger geographic area. Suppose, further, that the preferred way to obtain these new resources is to combine Mary's bakery with the bakery of a competitor, John, into one firm that will be jointly owned by Mary and John. Joining ownership will result in the functions of the classical owner/entrepreneur being divided between Mary and John in some fashion. The jointly owned firm that Mary and John will create is commonly referred to as a "business association." Most business associations are organized as a partnership, corporation, or limited liability company (LLC), which business forms are the primary focus of this book.

Business associations run the gamut from firms jointly owned by two persons to multinational organizations whose owners number in the tens of thousands. Firms with a very small number of owners are commonly called "closely held." At the opposite extreme, firms with thousands of owners are commonly called "publicly traded" because the ownership interests in such firms are widely traded via stock exchange markets or electronic trading markets that are accessible to the public.

3.   The Modern Corporation and the Berle-Means Critique

At the beginning of the nineteenth century, the American economy was dominated by sole proprietorships, and thus, by the classical entrepreneur. By the end of the nineteenth century, a profound transformation was well under way. The ownership of a substantial and increasing percentage of America's industrial wealth was in the hands of business firms organized as corporations, whose owners numbered in the hundreds and thousands.

Writing in 1932,[5] Adolf Berle and Gardiner Means correctly predicted that the power of the modern corporation would continue to grow and that eventually in every industrial sector, ownership of the means of production would reside in an increasingly small number of corporations. Importantly, Berle and Means identified the key attributes of the "modern corporation" that thereafter would dominate the American economy. Unlike the sole proprietorship, or the closely held firm whose owners usually operated similarly to a sole proprietorship in terms of control of the firm's business, the modern corporation was characterized by a complete separation of ownership from control. In the modern corporation, the firm's managers did not own a controlling amount of the corporation's stock; instead, a great majority of the corporation's stock was in the hands of a large number of passive, geographically dispersed shareholders, who had neither the means nor the will to monitor managers or engage in the process of electing the corporation's directors.[6] As a result, managers perpetuated themselves in office, and enjoyed almost total discretion in the operation of the firm.

Berle and Means described the separation of ownership from control in the modern corporation as presenting a fundamental challenge to America's governing ideology. Free market ideology, rooted in the work of Adam Smith, viewed the individual entrepreneur—the sole proprietor who owned and managed her own firm—as the primary motor driving the economy from the producer side of the equation. In turn, private property in the means of production was justified as central to a system depending on the voluntary actions of each market participant. Private property in the means of production allows and creates incentives for the entrepreneur to use her talents and capital in an effort to maximize her own wealth and happiness. The entrepreneur's selfish use of her property—her effort to make a profit and accumulate wealth—results in the best possible allocation of resources and the maximization of all citizens' wealth and happiness.

---

5. Adolph A. Berle, Jr., and Gardiner C. Means, The Modern Corporation and Private Property, 340-341 (Macmillan, 1933) (hereinafter "Berle and Means").

6. Berle and Means, at 5. Berle and Means found that in more than half of the 200 largest publicly traded corporations, management's stock ownership constituted such a small percentage of the voting stock as to be irrelevant in the election of directors. Id. at 94, 114, 117.

In Berle and Means's view, the modern corporation destroyed the theoretical underpinnings of the free enterprise system.

> It has been assumed that, if the individual is protected in the right both to use his own property as he sees fit and to receive the full fruits of its use, his desire for personal gain, for profits, can be relied upon as an effective incentive to his efficient use of any industrial property he may possess.
>
> In the [modern] corporation, such an assumption no longer holds. As we have seen, it is no longer the individual, himself, who uses his wealth. Those in control of that wealth, and therefore in a position to secure industrial efficiency and produce profits, are no longer as owners entitled to the bulk of such profits. . . . The explosion of the atom of property destroys the basis of the old assumption that the quest for profits will spur the owner of industrial property to its effective use.[7]

Berle and Means clearly worried about the agency cost problem associated with separation of ownership and control that became the center of subsequent developments by contractarian-oriented scholars described below. More broadly, however, Berle and Means were concerned about the problem of power. They identified the modern corporation, and the larger corporate system, as new institutions that compete with and threaten to supplant the nation-state as the dominant form of social organization. They worried because the modern corporation "involves a concentration of power in the economic field comparable to the concentration of economic power in the mediaeval church or of political power in the modern state."[8] Significantly, Berle and Means concluded that the corporation should now be analyzed as a social organization, and with a view to determining how managers' power should be constrained for the public good.[9]

Berle and Means categorized three types of possible responses to the economic power of the modern corporation and its managers. Society could bend the modern corporation and its managers to the will of the shareholders, so that shareholders, collectively, would act as real owners. Alternatively, society could recognize that corporate managers have absolute power, constrained only by their sense of morality and public duty. A third possibility would be to treat the interests of both managers and shareholders as subordinate to the paramount claims of society.

From the New Deal onward for nearly 50 years, federal law and policy makers often chose to pursue the third approach identified by Berle and Means—subordinating private property in the means of production to the legitimate claims of the larger society. The institution of private property that had given the entrepreneur almost total control over his business—the right to hire and fire whomever he wanted for whatever reason, the right to set wages and working conditions, the right to pollute air and water rather than incur costs for less environmentally harmful methods of production—would yield to competing interests within the larger society.

---

7. Berle and Means, at 8-9.
8. Berle and Means, at 352.
9. Berle and Means, at 353-357.

4.   The Return of Free Market Ideology: The Firm as a Nexus of Contracts

By 1980, the New Deal ideology and its preference for government regulation of business gave way to a more deregulatory approach. Advocates of free markets, individualism, and elimination of government regulation recaptured political and intellectual influence in America, England, and within a decade, most of the first-world countries. Within corporation law, a similar ideological shift occurred.

The new dominant view of the firm traced its origins to the work of economists working out the implications of the principal-agent problem. These theorists, including prominently Michael Jensen and William Meckling,[10] emphasized the contractual nature of the firm rather than the distinction between the firm and the market. From this perspective, a firm is described as a nexus of contracts between the various claimants to a share of the gross profits generated by the business. Thus, depicted as a circle, and using Mary's bakery as an example, the firm includes not only the contractual relations between Mary and her employees, but also Mary's contractual relationships with customers, suppliers, lenders, independent contractors, communities in which plants are located, and others with whom Mary contracts in conducting business.

Strong-form proponents of the nexus-of-contracts view of the firm emphasize that the firm does not exist apart from its constituent relationships. To speak of a corporation as having social responsibility would reify the corporation in a way inconsistent with that view. Significantly, this contractarian view of the firm tends to focus attention away from the corporation as a social institution. Moreover, by its very nature, this microeconomic focus on the individual as the appropriate unit of analysis does not often lead to reform proposals advocating greater government regulation of the corporation or the economy.

5.   Separation of Ownership and Control and Agency Costs

Principal-agent theorists provided new tools for understanding the relationship between passive shareholders and managers. First, theorists identified shareholders as the owners, or in agency terms, principals, of the modern corporation; managers are viewed as the shareholders' agents. This economic usage of the terms "principal" and "agent" differs from legal usage of these terms. In law, principals have legal rights of control and direction and agents have legal obligations of obedience. As economists use these terms, however, principals have no inherent right of control and agents have no inherent obligation of obedience. Instead, principals and agents contract with each other to determine how much control the principal will retain, and how much control will be ceded to the agent. From this view of the principal-agent relationship, the modern corporation represents a consensual choice by shareholders and managers to cede authority and power over the modern corporation almost entirely to managers. However, the power ceded is accompanied by the use of various contractual devices that, in the view of principal-agent theorists, operate to limit the ability of managers to *shirk*—to use

---

10. See Michael C. Jensen and William H. Meckling, Theory of the Firm: Managerial Behavior, Agency Costs and Ownership Structure, 3 J. Fin. Econ. 305 (1976).

corporate resources in ways that diverge from the best interests of shareholders. These agency-cost-limiting devices include (1) direct monitoring of managers' actions, (2) bonding agreements by managers that will result in the imposition of penalties or other costs if certain objectively verifiable events do or do not occur, and (3) incentive schemes to align managers' interests with those of shareholders. All of these devices to limit agency costs involve expenses that reduce the net value of the return from operation of the modern corporation. Moreover, some amount of shirking — the *residual loss* — will occur despite the implementation of agency-cost-limiting mechanisms. Thus, the gains for the shareholders/principals from operating as a modern corporation will be reduced by the sum of (1) the cost of agency-cost-limiting mechanisms and (2) the residual loss. At the margin, agency-cost-limiting mechanisms are justified only to the extent that the net return to shareholders is greater than would be the case without such expenditures.

Thus, from the principal-agent perspective that came to dominate policy-maker views in the last three decades of the twentieth century, separation of ownership and control is not the central problem posed by the modern corporation. Rather, separation of ownership and control is the optimal state of affairs — the contractual allocation of rights and responsibilities for which owners and managers have bargained. Writ large, the contractarian view sees the corporation as a consensual association of value maximizing individuals whose contractual autonomy must be acknowledged and protected. In this ideological and theoretical rethinking of the modern corporation, the role of government as regulator, and the interests of non-shareholder constituents and society as a whole, take a backseat to the goal of shareholder wealth maximization.

6.   The New Millennium: Corporate Scandal, Financial Crises, Corporate Governance, and Government Regulation

The new millennium saw two significant shocks to the American economy and, particularly, to the nation's faith in corporate executives and in the wisdom of investing in corporate stock. The first shock, in 2001, commonly identified with the collapse of Enron, involved fraudulent accounting by numerous corporations for the purpose of artificially inflating the value of corporate stock. The second, commencing in 2008, involved the collapse of major financial and industrial institutions that had undertaken excessive risk. These events reinvigorated debate about the nature of firms and the role of government regulation. While insights from the contractarian view of the corporation and the principal-agent theorists have not been discarded, these views are now placed in a broader context. As you journey through this book, you will have many occasions to evaluate the various theories of the firm, and assess their strengths and weaknesses. Clearly, however, there is renewed interest in exploring two topics — governance and government regulation — and clearly there is more awareness of the fundamental insights of Berle and Means.

The renewed emphasis on governance builds on Berle and Means's insight that the modern corporation does not have a traditional entrepreneur/owner. Rather, the corporation has managers who in most cases own a very small percentage of the corporation's stock. The renewed emphasis on governance takes seriously the power of the modern corporation highlighted by Berle and Means, and both the potential for good and the threat to society that this power poses. In addition to concern for wealth maximization and protection of shareholders, the current debate includes the influence of the modern corporation on broader issues—human health and happiness, climate change, global poverty, and women's role in male-dominated societies.

The current focus on governance addresses central questions, whose answers are of interest not only to shareholders but also to other corporate constituents, and to society as a whole. How is the modern corporation governed? How should it be governed? How will decisions be made concerning the allocation of resources within the firm? Who will decide whether to locate a new plant in America or Uganda? Who will decide whether to dedicate 1 percent of the firm's gross revenue to charitable contributions, improve health and safety standards, or increase dividends to shareholders? Who will decide the short- and long-term goals of the firm? What structures, systems, and processes will yield the optimum operation of the firm for the benefit of owners, managers, employees, and society as a whole?

The new millennium also has seen an increased emphasis on government regulation of the modern corporation, both in the United States and abroad. More so than in prior periods, the federal government has exercised its legislative and regulatory authority to shape how American corporations are governed. These changes include requirements that corporate boards of directors be more independent, federal bailout of troubled financial and industrial firms, limits on the amount and structure of executive pay, creation of costly new accounting regimes, increased financial disclosure requirements, and expansion of shareholders' rights to initiate changes in corporate governance structures. Not since the New Deal have we seen government so active in the regulation of the modern corporation.

B.   Organizing the Firm: Selecting a Value-Maximizing Governance Structure

1.   Business Planning: The Role of the Corporate Lawyer in Organizing a Firm

Where do firms come from? How are they created? In order to understand the modern corporation (which will be a primary focus of much of this book), you must understand how a basic business association is created and governed. You must also understand the fundamental, creative, value-maximizing role played by the corporate lawyer.

The corporate lawyer is a planner. At the birth of a firm, she will assist the prospective venture in the creation of an appropriate initial governance structure, and as the venture grows she will assist in adapting the organization as required by changed circumstances. The experienced corporate lawyer will understand and apply several concepts that will be introduced in the remainder of this section B. First and foremost she will be a transaction-cost engineer. She will understand that human beings are cognitively limited, usually seek to promote their own self-interest, and have a propensity to act opportunistically in certain circumstances. Necessarily, then, the planner must understand when opportunism is likely, and suggest an organizational structure that will minimize the expected costs of future opportunistic behavior by employees, managers, or owners. However, to students steeped in law school's emphasis on litigation, we stress an important point that all experienced corporate lawyers keep in mind: owners and managers of firms have a strong, usually rational, preference for private ordering over court ordering. That is, when a firm encounters a need, or asserted need, to adapt to changed circumstances, it is usually more efficient, and often more consistent with the pre-dispute expectations of owners and managers, for those disputes to be resolved pursuant to the internal decision-making processes of the firm, rather than by resort to litigation and a judicially imposed solution. Accordingly, the corporate lawyer must understand how to select and modify governance structures so as to optimally minimize the use of litigation as a governance tool, while preserving the availability of litigation to deal with circumstances that cannot be appropriately governed solely by private ordering. Moreover, the good corporate lawyer must understand the governance role of markets and intra-firm culture. To the extent these extra-legal institutions can be expected to give managers and employees strong incentives to voluntarily use their best efforts on behalf of the firm, the experienced corporate lawyer will recommend organizational structures that de-emphasize governance via court ordering.

2. The Goal of Informed Rational Choice Between Competing Investment Options

a. Comparative Search for Best Investment

Participants in our market economy are constantly faced with investment decisions. Every participant has a store of human capital—a set of skills or an ability to render services. And many participants also have money capital—cash, cash equivalents, or other investment property that can be valued in terms of money. Economists assume that a rational person chooses her career, and adjusts that choice as circumstances change, in order to maximize the value of her human capital. Likewise, rational individuals with money capital deploy and redeploy those resources in a search for maximum value.

The search for maximum value requires rational investors to take both a comparative and an ex ante perspective.[11] The perspective is comparative because a determination of the best investment decision involves a weighing of plausible alternatives. The perspective is ex ante because the goal is to predict which investment strategy will yield the optimal result. It may turn out afterwards, from an ex post perspective, that some road other than the one actually taken would have been more advantageous. Nevertheless, all of us must make our investment decisions before actual outcomes are known.

Consider the investment situations of Sharon and Jake. Sharon is a sales representative for a national brewery. Jake, a friend of Sharon, is the head brewmaster at

---

11. *Ex ante* literally means "from before." The choice of heads or tails before a coin is flipped is a decision made from an ex ante perspective—that is, before we know the outcome. *Ex post* literally means "from after." Once the coin is flipped, we know the outcome. Any decisions related to that outcome are made from an ex post perspective.

a different firm. Jake and Sharon have discussed the possibility of joining forces in a brewing venture. Jake's role would be to manufacture a high-quality beer with a unique and pleasing taste. Sharon's role would be to develop a substantial market for this product. Recently, Sharon inherited $200,000. She is now considering the following three alternative uses of her human capital and the inherited money capital.

Alternative 1.   Sharon can continue to work for her current employer and invest $200,000 in U.S. Government bonds, maturing in one year and paying interest at the rate of 8 percent per year. At the maturity date Sharon would be entitled to receive $216,000.

Alternative 2.   Sharon can continue to work for her current employer and invest $200,000 in bonds issued by the Atomic Energy Corporation, which mature in one year and promise to pay interest at the rate of 20 percent per year. At the maturity date, Sharon would be entitled to receive $240,000.

Alternative 3.   Sharon can quit her job and invest both her human and newly acquired money capital in the brewery venture with Jake. Sharon believes that a $200,000 investment in the brewery could be worth $500,000 in one year, but realizes that less favorable outcomes are quite possible.

In the following sections we will identify the economic factors that might influence Sharon's investment decision. Keep in mind that should Sharon favor Alternative 3, she will be able to pursue it only if Jake also believes that the proposed venture is the best use of his capital.

b. *Risk and Return*

In comparing investment options, individuals attempt to determine the likely return from alternative investment choices. Financial theorists describe this process as a determination and comparison of "expected return." For some investments a rational person might foresee only one possible outcome. In such cases, the one foreseeable outcome is also the expected return from the investment. But for most investments there will be a range of possible outcomes. The expected return for these investments is determined by first multiplying each possible return by its probability, and by then summing these products.

For example, as hypothesized above, Sharon is considering three investment options. Alternatives 1 and 2 have different promised outcomes: Alternative 1 promises to pay Sharon $216,000 in one year, while Alternative 2 promises to pay Sharon $240,000 in one year. Under the assumptions outlined below, however, each of these investments has an expected return of $216,000.

Alternative 1

(Investment of $200,000 with Promised Return of $216,000)

Possible Return	Probability	Possible Return × Probability
$216,000	1.00	$216,000
		Expected Return = $216,000

Alternative 2

(Investment of $200,000 with Promised Return of $240,000)

Possible Return	Probability	Possible Return × Probability
$240,000	0.90	$216,000
-0-	0.10	-0-
		Expected Return = $216,000

While Alternatives 1 and 2 have the same expected return, Alternative 2 is "riskier" than Alternative 1 (which, in fact, would be described as a "risk-free" investment). As used here, "risk" means the degree to which the various possible outcomes will differ from the expected return. When the range of possible returns is zero, as in Alternative 1, the investment is risk-free. If Sharon purchases the Atomic Energy Corporation bonds, she runs a greater risk of receiving less than the expected return. On the other hand, the Atomic Energy Corporation bonds hold out the promise of a higher return than the U.S. Government bonds 90 percent of the time. Thus, risk is not necessarily bad, for with it comes the chance of greater reward.

Whether Sharon will prefer Alternative 1 or 2 depends on her taste or preference for risk. To some extent that preference may be a deeply ingrained behavioral characteristic over which Sharon has no control. Nonetheless, Sharon's risk preference is likely to be affected by the magnitude of a particular risk in relation to her existing wealth, and by the effect of this new investment on the riskiness of her existing portfolio.

Investors are generally characterized as "risk averse," "risk neutral," or "risk preferring." If Sharon is risk averse, then she will prefer the risk-free government bonds to the riskier corporate bonds. If Sharon is risk neutral, then she will be indifferent to a choice between Alternatives 1 and 2. Each promises the same return, and, since Sharon is risk neutral, she is unaffected by the greater risk presented by Alternative 2. If Sharon is risk preferring, then she will choose Alternative 2, gambling in effect that she will avoid the 10 percent chance of no return and receive the greater return promised, but not guaranteed, by Alternative 2.

An investor's risk preference will likely differ according to the circumstances. For example, if a relatively small amount is at stake, normally risk-averse individuals may actually be risk preferrers, or at least less risk averse. A good example is a $1 lottery ticket. Many normally risk-averse investors might prefer lottery ticket A, which has one chance in one thousand of paying $600, to lottery ticket B, which has one chance in two of paying $1.20, even though both tickets have an expected return of $0.60. Likewise, Sharon is likely to have a greater taste for risk if the $200,000 she is investing is but a small part of her wealth than if she is investing a significant portion of her money capital.

Risk-averse investors often minimize risk by diversifying their portfolios. For example, suppose that Sharon has a total of $400,000 in money capital—the recently inherited $200,000 and a $200,000 investment in bonds of United Airlines Corporation. Furthermore, assume that the United Airlines bonds and the Atomic Energy

Corporation bonds Sharon is considering buying have an identical expected return and riskiness. Finally, assume that the events that will cause either of these bonds to deliver a $0 payout can be identified and will not overlap. In such circumstances, a risk-averse Sharon would actually prefer Alternative 2 because such investment will decrease the overall riskiness of her portfolio.

If a $0 return occurs with respect to Sharon's investment in United Airlines bonds, it will be partially offset by a $240,000 return on the Atomic Energy Corporation bonds. If, instead, Sharon invests her inherited funds in U.S. Government bonds (Alternative 1), a $0 return on the United Airlines bonds will be offset by only the $216,000 return promised by Alternative 1. In the described circumstances, Alternative 2 is actually a less risky investment for Sharon than is Alternative 1, the so-called risk-free investment.

In technical terms, Sharon is able to achieve a less risky portfolio by diversifying her holdings so that the range of possible outcomes varies less from the expected return—or mean of possible outcomes—than before. In other words, the more diversified the portfolio becomes, the less will be the possible disparity between actual and expected total returns.

Of course, Sharon will only pursue a portfolio diversification strategy if she is risk averse. Moreover, such a strategy depends for its success on being able to discover that the events that will cause one investment to produce a lower than expected return will cause another investment to produce a higher than expected return.

The foregoing analysis draws on Sharon's options for investing her money capital. However, the same analysis is appropriate for human capital investments. Sharon must not only consider the expected return from various uses of her human capital but also the riskiness of such paths. Her current job may offer a lower expected return on her human capital than does the contemplated venture with Jake (Alternative 3), but it also may offer a much more certain return. Moreover, since it is impossible to own another human being, it will be difficult for Sharon to diversify against risks inherent in certain uses of her human capital.

3. Transaction Costs and Choice of Organizational Form

a. Introduction

As we bring Alternative 3 into focus, the proposed brewery venture with Jake, the complexity of the ex ante investment selection process increases. If Sharon and Jake choose to pursue the brewery venture, they must agree on how to structure their relationship.

We can assume that at the outset of their venture Sharon and Jake share two expectations: (1) that both will use their best efforts to make the venture successful, and (2) that profits will be divided according to their relative contributions. To maximize the probability that these expectations will be fulfilled, Sharon and Jake could embody their understanding in a long-term contract. Alternatively, they could structure their relationship as sole proprietor and agent, a partnership, a limited liability company, or a corporation. This section introduces the role of transaction costs in determining the most efficient solution.

b. Transaction Cost Factors

Transaction cost economists, principally Ronald Coase, Armen Alchian, and Oliver Williamson, have identified the behavioral and economic factors that explain why particular transactions are most efficiently organized in a particular way. In discussing transaction costs, economists commonly use three terms that will be helpful to your study of corporations and other business associations. These terms, discussed below, are *bounded rationality, opportunism,* and *team-specific investment.*

Bounded rationality. While individuals intend to act rationally, there are cognitive limits, or bounds, on their ability to do so. There are simply too many variables to be considered. Thus, Sharon will intend to value accurately Alternative C, the brewery venture, and will intend to structure her relationship with Jake in a value-maximizing way. Nonetheless, bounds on her rationality will limit the accuracy of her judgments.

Opportunism. Economists assume that individuals pursue their own self-interest in economic matters. However, there are two categories of self-interest seeking. In simple, or open, self-interest seeking, economic actors prefer their own interests to those of other economic actors, but do so while being honest and aboveboard in their dealings. Opportunism is self-interest seeking with guile: individuals who act opportunistically seek to further their own ends by taking advantage of the information deficits of those with whom they deal. An opportunistic actor seeks to extract an advantage that would be denied him if the party with whom he deals had full information. As Oliver Williamson puts it, "opportunism refers to the incomplete or distorted disclosure of information, especially to calculated efforts to mislead, distort, disguise, obfuscate, or otherwise confuse."[12]

Team-specific investment. If Sharon and Jake pursue the brewery venture, they may usefully be described as a team, and their collective activities in making and marketing beer may be described as team production. When a person or asset has a higher value in its current team use than its value in its next best use, the person or asset is said to have team-specific value.

Suppose, for example, that Sharon owns and operates a generic beer distributing business and that Jake owns and operates a generic beer brewery. Sharon buys generic beer for resale to grocery stores. She currently buys from Jake, but there are other brewers who would supply generic beer on similar terms. Likewise, Jake currently sells his product to Sharon, but there are other distributors who would purchase his output on similar terms. If Jake and Sharon stopped dealing with each other, thereby terminating their team, neither would experience any loss in the value of their human or money capital because they could continue to earn the same return by dealing with others. Accordingly, neither Jake's nor Sharon's investments are team-specific.

On the other hand, suppose that Sharon is in the business of distributing only the special beer that Jake produces and that there are no other suppliers who can give her an equivalent product on similar terms. Further, suppose that Jake distributes his beer only through Sharon and that there are no replacement distributors who

---

12. Williamson, The Economic Institutions of Capitalism: Firms, Markets, Relational Contracting 47 (1985).

would purchase the same volume or pay the same price as Sharon. If Jake and Sharon stopped dealing with each other, thereby terminating their team, both would experience a loss in the value of their human or money capital. Thus, Jake's and Sharon's investments would be described as having team-specific value.

c. *Discrete and Relational Contracting*

One response to the problem of opportunism is to negotiate and execute a contract that specifies the rights and duties of the parties, thereby creating an explicit team. The appropriate contractual strategy depends on the team's expected duration and need to adapt.

In *discrete contracting*, the parties have no preexisting obligations to each other. As they approach a contemplated venture, they negotiate a contract that anticipates and provides a rule governing all contingencies. Nothing is left to be worked out in the future. For example, Sharon and Jake might enter into a long-term contract specifying both their initial obligations and how, if at all, such obligations will be affected by future events. Jake might be required to produce a certain quantity and quality of beer, which Sharon is required to purchase at a set price. However, the contract might specify, in detail, what objective factors would entitle either party to a price or quantity change.

Discrete contracting is most likely to be successful when the team's expected duration is short and the number of exchanges between team members will be few. As the duration and frequency of exchange increase, bounded rationality makes it increasingly more likely that the parties will specify an inappropriate rule for a particular contingency, or that the parties will fail to identify and specify a result for a relevant contingency.

Relational contracting is a response to the defects of discrete contracting. In relational contracting, parties do not attempt to provide an answer to all contingencies at the time the relation commences. Instead, they attempt to build a governance structure that will allow them to solve problems when, and if, they arise. The goal of relational contracting is to reinforce the relation itself. The hope is that cooperation and harmony will become ingrained norms of the relationship, and that the parties will continue to deal with each other in good faith even when facing difficult adjustment problems.

Contracts that contain relation-reinforcing provisions will not eliminate the threat of opportunism. By giving parties express permission to seek renegotiation, the risk of opportunistic refusal to renegotiate may be less than in a discrete contract, but the threat of opportunistic requests for readjustment may be greater. Moreover, because of bounded rationality, courts may find that a contract is discrete when the parties intended it to be relational, and vice versa.

d. *Deciding to Organize as a Firm*

When a team is organized via contract, team members retain ownership and control over the productive assets used to produce their part of the team's goods or services. The autonomy of each team member makes it difficult for a team to adjust to changed circumstances and exposes the team to the costs of opportunistic threats of withdrawal. If a team member becomes less valuable than was expected ex ante, he may be reluctant to agree to a readjustment of his contract that accurately reflects his current value to the team. Likewise, if a team member becomes more valuable than was expected ex ante, other team members may be equally reluctant to grant an upward adjustment in the payment that team member will receive. Additionally, team members may request adjustments when an omniscient observer, but not other team members, would be able to see that the request is unjustified. As a result, teams organized via contract will experience substantial costs from having team members' compensation and incentives misaligned and from the haggling to correct these misalignments that results.

The advantage of organizing as a firm is the avoidance of these haggling costs. As Coase noted, a key aspect of a firm is the allocation of resources at the direction of the entrepreneur. The owner's power to make unilaterally all management decisions—what is made, how it is made, who is hired and fired, and who is paid what—allows the firm to adapt quickly to changed circumstances.

The potential disadvantage of organizing as a firm for an employee is that in surrendering autonomous control over her own business she becomes subject to the employer's opportunism. Thus, a key organizational problem for all firms is how to optimally minimize the risk to which the employee is so exposed. A key organizational problem for jointly owned firms is how to allocate management rights and responsibilities between and among co-owners and how to ensure that the entrepreneurial function carried out by the entrepreneur in the classic firm is carried out efficiently in a firm where ownership power is not united in one person.

4.   State-Provided Governance Structures

a.   Entity and Employment Law as Standard Form Contracts

When individuals choose to organize their business relationship by assuming roles within a firm, they do so with certain reasonable expectations in mind. It may be necessary to protect some of these expectations by contract, but it will not be necessary to draft contracts from scratch to cover every possible expectation or concern. Instead, by structuring the relationship as that between employer and employee, or as a corporation, partnership, or LLC, the parties receive the benefit of state-provided rules and dispute resolution processes. Thus, the employer-employee relationship, the corporation, the partnership, and the LLC are often described as state-provided standard form contracts.

b.   Default Versus Immutable Rules

Most of the off-the-rack rules found in each state-provided standard form are "enabling" in the sense that they provide parties with default rules that govern the relationship if the parties do not provide otherwise. To the extent that parties prefer, they may modify or change these default rules.

In some instances, however, the rules provided by law are immutable and cannot be "trumped" by private ordering. Some such mandatory rules exist because lawmakers fear the negative effect on third parties of allowing firms to adopt a different rule.

Other immutable rules may be designed to protect firm members from their own contracting mistakes.

Every good business lawyer must know the standard form rules—the legal bargain—that are provided by the employment relationship and by corporate, partnership, and limited liability company law. However, it is critically important to understand which of these rules are default in nature, how the default rules of each form differ, and what makes these rules efficient or inefficient for a particular set of prospective team members. It is equally crucial to understand which rules are immutable, and whether these immutable rules will serve the interests of a particular member of the firm.

As you proceed through this book, be sure to determine whether a rule falls into the default or immutable category. And do not be surprised if you encounter some rules that are partially default and partially immutable. For each rule consider what economic or legal factors explain both its content and its immutable or default character. And be ever on the lookout for misguided paternalism.

c. *Tailored, Majoritarian, and Penalty Default Rules*

If lawmakers are efficiency-minded,[13] they will set default rules so as to maximize team members' ability to adapt to changed circumstances while minimizing their exposure to opportunism. To choose the appropriate rule, lawmakers must appreciate the difference between tailored, majoritarian, and penalty default rules.

Tailored rules are designed to give contracting parties the exact rule that they would themselves have chosen if they had been able to bargain costlessly over the matter in dispute. The availability of tailored results via ex post judging allows parties to avoid the costs of negotiating and executing a contract specifically covering all possible contingencies. However, providing tailored rules is a very problematic undertaking because of bounded rationality. How is a lawmaker to know what rule the particular parties would themselves select?

Any default rule could be said to be a tailored rule for parties that do not vary the rule by contract. But how do we know that their failure to vary was not the product of ignorance? How do we know that they did not simply trust each other's good faith and assume that the default rules would be adjusted as, and if, appropriate?

If the tailored result is to be provided by ex post judging, then bounds on the knowledge of judge and jury will make it difficult to determine the rule for which the parties would have bargained if transaction costs had been zero. Each party will have her own, perhaps opportunistic, account of the past. Each party will be represented by counsel who seeks to persuade the court of the merits of her own case.

Even if courts are able to arrive at "tailored" results, such an achievement may often be hollow. Society and the parties themselves bear substantial litigation costs in arriving at the tailored result. Since no two firms or set of team members are exactly the same, the availability of tailored results to be provided by ex post judging may discourage settlement of disputes because there is no "normal" rule that the parties can

---

13. Credit for coining the wonderful term "efficiency-minded lawmakers" goes to Ayres and Gertner, Filling Gaps in Incomplete Contracts: An Economic Theory of Default Rules, 99 Yale L.J. 87 (1989).

expect will apply to their unique case. Moreover, the availability of tailored rules to be provided by ex post judging may discourage ex ante contracting because it is not clear what rule is to be contracted around.

Majoritarian rules are designed to provide investors with the result that most similarly situated parties would prefer. By abandoning the search for tailored rules, lawmakers may make assumptions about the contracting needs of prospective members of a firm and provide rules that will suit a large number of them. Those who do not like the rules provided may vary them or simply choose another business form that has a more suitable set of rules.

Both tailored and majoritarian rules can be described as designed to provide contracting parties with the rule that they would have bargained for in a cost-free environment. However, advocates of tailored rules are speaking literally. They seek the result each particular litigant actually would have chosen. Advocates of majoritarian rules speak metaphorically. In essence they seek the rule that will best protect the rational ex ante expectations of parties similarly situated to the contracting parties.

Penalty default rules are designed to motivate one or more contracting parties to contract around the default. The goal of penalty defaults is not to economize on ex ante transaction costs. Instead, the goal is to force the parties to specify their own rules ex ante, instead of relying on a default rule provided by law. For example, a default rule might be intentionally set so as to penalize some or all of the parties as a means of forcing them to negotiate a rule that they prefer. Such a rule may be motivated by a desire to force the parties to share information with each other about their true intentions, rather than allowing the parties to simply adopt a set of standard form rules without revealing their true intentions. Or it may be motivated by lawmakers' desire to avoid the social cost of providing rules to parties via ex post judging, the cost of which is partially subsidized by society.

As you encounter the state-provided default rules for each form of business association, consider whether they can best be explained as an attempt to provide tailored, majoritarian, or penalty default rules. If possible, identify the factors that explain why the particular rule is so structured.

5. Nonjudicial Mechanisms That Supplement and Reinforce Private Ordering

a. *The Governance Role of Markets*

A variety of markets play an important role in the governance of firms and in how efficiency-minded lawmakers design the rules of business associations. These markets act to ensure that team members perform their services diligently and loyally, and otherwise to protect the reasonable expectations of investors in jointly owned firms. In so doing they make it less necessary for team members to engage in costly private ordering and make it less necessary for lawmakers to intercede.

The product market. Firms compete against each other in the production and sale of goods and services. If team members perform without sufficient skill and diligence, the firm will be at a competitive disadvantage. If the lack of skill and diligence is extreme, the firm may actually go out of existence.

The capital market.   From time to time firms need to raise additional capital. To do so, they must compete with other firms who also seek capital. Prospective capital providers will seek the best return on their investment. Firms that are not well run will find that their costs of capital, in the form of interest charges, for example, are higher than the costs of efficiently run companies.

The national securities markets.   The ownership rights (commonly called stock) of most larger firms will be frequently traded in one or more of our national securities exchanges. These markets provide liquidity to investors by permitting them a rapid and near costless means of buying or selling their investments. As discussed in more detail in Chapter 3, these markets are thought to provide a constantly changing, accurate measure of the relative value of publicly traded firms, and by extension, an accurate measure of the value of their managers. To the extent that this is true, the need for judicial and regulatory checks on managers' conduct may be lessened.

The labor markets (including the market for managerial services).   Most individuals realize the value of their human capital by selling their services in the labor market. Once they obtain employment, they cooperatively compete with other employees for various rewards, including the good reputations that will make it possible to advance within the firm or change jobs. If an employee is not considered to be diligent and loyal, he is unlikely to advance within the firm and is unlikely to receive good evaluations while employed or good recommendations upon departing. If his performance is sufficiently unacceptable, he may be discharged from the firm—imposing a costly reputational mark. But even if a team member is not identified by other team members as a slacker or worse, the team member's reputation may suffer if the firm, as a whole, is doing poorly.

Thus, the discipline of the labor markets may significantly reduce the need for ex ante contracting or the setting up of costly monitoring systems. For senior executives, this discipline is supplemented by the valuations made by the stock markets. Moreover, the reputational costs imposed by exposure as a negligent or dishonest team member may deter such conduct more effectively than fear of legal action.

b.   The Role of Trust

Trust and trustworthiness are factors that economists generally leave out in analyzing why firms serve, or can be structured to serve, the interests of team members better than organization via contracts between autonomous producers. Consider the comments of Professors Blair and Stout:

> Social scientists have long argued that evolution can favor the development of a capacity for altruism in social organisms such as *homo sapiens*. This is because "irrationally" cooperative behavior within a particular group (including but not limited to trust and trustworthiness) often enhances the group's overall welfare. If the group does well, members of the group on average also do well. . . .
>
> For similar reasons, cooperative behavior can be an important factor in the evolution not just of social organisms but also of social *institutions*. This is because groups whose members cooperate with each other can often thrive and grow at the expense of groups whose members do not

cooperate. Social institutions that can promote and support trust among their participants can, as a result, have an evolutionary advantage over institutions that cannot.

Margaret M. Blair & Lynn A. Stout, Trust, Trustworthiness, and the Behavioral Foundations of Corporation Law, 149 Pa. L. Rev. 1735, 1753-1754 (2001). How best to foster trust between employees and the entrepreneur in the classic firm, and between all participants in the more complex publicly traded firm, is obviously a key issue for both lawmakers and business planners.

c. The Role of Norms

Most activity within a firm is governed not by judicially enforceable contracts, but by norms—non-legally enforceable rules and standards (NLERS). Firms that have effective NLERS get more loyal and diligent performance from team members than firms that do not, and, therefore, are more likely to succeed than firms with less effective NLERS.

> What are the NLERS? To some extent, this will depend on the individual firm. For example, the famous dress code of IBM in the 1960s requiring white shirts, ties, and dark suits was an IBM-specific NLERS. Most everyone did it, you were expected to do it, and you were sanctioned, either formally or informally, if you did not. Less trivially, the promotion of teamwork is an NLERS practiced in many firms. Other firms, however, may promote individual effort.
>
> One useful way of thinking of NLERS is that they form a great part of what is sometimes referred to as the firm's "corporate culture." Corporate culture can serve a coordinating function, making it more likely that employees will do what they are supposed to do when they are supposed to do it. NLERS play the intrafirm coordinating role that contracts play in market activity. Those that live up to or outperform the contract or NLERS expectations are credited, while those who do not are penalized with a range of sanctions including demotion, suspension, or dismissal. A principal difference, however, between NLERS and contracts is that when the parties disagree as to whether performance has been satisfied, courts can impose penalties in the latter case, but only the parties can do so in the former. . . .
>
> Within a firm, NLERS operate at many different levels. . . . For example, "discharge only for cause" in a world of employment-at-will is one of the prime NLERS that protects employees. Promotion from within to reward outstanding performance or seniority is another employment NLERS.
>
> Other NLERS involve the manner in which the firm determines whether an investment project should be undertaken. The use of discounted present value for this purpose is an NLERS observed in many firms. . . .
>
> NLERS also are not invariably efficient, socially beneficial, or conducive to the success of the firm. Some seem to help the firm succeed, like the NLERS of high-tech firms that lead engineers to work intensely on critical projects. Others may interfere with success, like the NLERS of not working too hard that emerges in some industrial work places. In historically regulated industries, all types of suboptimal, cost inefficient practices thrived and were protected and reinforced by the suppliers, unions, and others that benefited from them. These NLERS were sanctioned by the firms but were not socially efficient. For decades, racial, religious, and ethnic discrimination was an NLERS openly practiced by blue-chip firms. In some boardrooms, an NLERS is to accede to the wishes of the CEO regardless of her value to the firm. The decision by the board of Occidental Petroleum to build the Armand Hammer museum to house the CEO's unremarkable art collection was the result of such an NLERS. This type of NLERS is supportive of the executive officers but not the shareholders.

Edward B. Rock & Michael L. Wachter, Islands of Conscious Power: Law, Norms, and the Self-Governing Corporation, 149 U. Pa. L. Rev. 1619, 1642-1643 (2001).

C. The Firm and the Law of Agency

1. Introduction

In this section, we examine the role of agency law in the governance of the firm. Agency law may be thought of as a set of standard form rules that provide a backdrop for contracts or market transactions among team members. Agency law governs both relations between team members in a firm and relations between the firm and outsiders. Our examination of both the sole proprietorship and agency law is limited. We focus only on the fundamental factors that affect the decision to operate as a firm, and on those elements of agency law that have direct relevance for both the sole proprietorship and the jointly owned firm. We will then be ready to begin our study of the partnership and corporate forms.

2. Agency Law and the Choice of Sole Proprietorship Form

Restatement (Third) of Agency §§1.01, 1.02, 1.03

A firm is created simply by unifying the ownership and control of the team in the hands of one or more owners, referred to in agency law as the principal, while other team members agree to serve as employees, generally referred to as agents. A principal signals her entry into the firm by investing her own money capital to acquire assets needed by the team, and by agreeing to employ one or more agents to carry out, under the principal's control, a portion of the team's work. Other team members signal their entry into the firm simply by agreeing to provide services to the firm subject to the dictates and control of the owner. At common law this mutual assent creates the relationship of principal and agent—the owner being the principal, the employees being the agents. Unless otherwise agreed, this relationship may also be terminated at will by either the principal or agent. However, so long as the relationship exists, the agent is subject to the principal's control with respect to the services that the agent has agreed to perform.

In a world where organization as a firm is legally indistinguishable from organization via contract, the firm would appear to pose the same risks and transaction costs as does organization via contract. The principal's power to discharge an agent at will gives the principal substantial power opportunistically to discharge, or threaten to discharge, an employee. Likewise, an employee can opportunistically threaten to withdraw, or can withdraw and thereafter convert to personal use information or skills acquired while in the firm's employ. Thus, in contemplating organization as a firm in this hypothetical world, it would often be necessary for principal and agent to enter a discrete contract specifying in detail what their various rights and duties will be.

In all jurisdictions, however, there is a significant difference between organization as a firm and organization outside of a firm via long-term contract. The right of selfish action by proprietor and agent is not absolute. The law of agency imposes a fiduciary duty on agents, and other legal doctrines impose some limits on the principal's right to discharge an employee. Thus, the need to limit contractually the right of action of either the proprietor or her agents depends, in part, on the extent to which adequate protection will be provided by ex post judicial enforcement of these state-provided rules. We examine these judicially supplied limits in the next two sections. To the extent these limitations obviate the need for contractual protection, organization as a firm may be less costly than organization via contract.

3.   Fiduciary Limits on Agent's Right of Action

Organizing team production via market exchange between autonomous individuals maximizes the ability of individual team members to adapt to changed circumstances. However, team members will have minimal incentive to make team-specific investments. For example, suppose that Sharon and Jake organize a brewery venture as an implicit team — Sharon owns and operates a beer distributorship, and Jake owns and operates a brewery. Initially, Jake sells all of his product to Sharon, and Sharon develops a network of dealers to whom she sells Jake's beer. After the distributor network is well established, Jake may be tempted to deal directly with Sharon's customers, thereby appropriating the profit attributable to Sharon's sales efforts. Because there is no contractual relationship between Sharon and Jake, Sharon may have no legal remedy. Consequently, Sharon will be unlikely to develop the distributorship in the first place without obtaining contractual protection for her investment.

Suppose, instead, that the brewery venture is organized as a sole proprietorship, with Sharon serving as owner and Jake as an employee. Under the common law of agency, Jake now owes a fiduciary duty to Sharon. He must deal with her in total candor, must account to her for all profits flowing from information he receives in her service, must not use or disclose Sharon's trade secrets, and may not carry on a competing business until after the agency relationship is terminated. In short, Jake, as an agent, is required to prefer Sharon's, his principal's, interests to his own.

It is easy to look at fiduciary duty from a moralistic standpoint. After all, Sharon *owns* the brewery business. It is only *right* and *fair* that Jake be required to submerge his own self-interest in favor of Sharon's good. But this view may tend to obfuscate the function of fiduciary duty.

In part, if not completely, fiduciary duty is a contractual device supplied to Sharon and Jake by the state. As such, fiduciary duty substitutes for an express contractual specification of exactly what an agent may or may not do. A rational person in Jake's shoes might wish to make the promises inherent in fiduciary duty in order to convince Sharon that he will not act opportunistically during the course of the venture and, thereby, to induce Sharon to make a needed investment. Thus, we might say that in agreeing to become Sharon's agent Jake has impliedly acquiesced to the restrictions imposed by fiduciary duty. If Jake does act opportunistically, he runs the risk that a court will find that Jake has violated his fiduciary duty.

What, then, is the substantive content or meaning of fiduciary duty? You should begin to answer that question as you read the following cases. Since fiduciary duty is a central feature of both partnership and corporate law, you will have many occasions to revisit this question.

Community Counselling Service, Inc. v. Reilly
United States Court of Appeals, Fourth Circuit, 1963
317 F.2d 239

HAYNSWORTH, CIRCUIT JUDGE.

Community Counselling Service, Inc. sought an accounting from a former sales-man-employee based upon allegations of disloyal promotion of his conflicting interests prior to the termination of his employment. The defendant, Reilly, filed a counter-claim seeking the recovery of salary and commission payments which the employer had withheld as an offset against its claim. . . .

CCS is a professional fund raising organization, working principally for Catholic parishes and institutions. Reilly, without prior experience in this type of professional fund raising, was employed by CCS in March 1957. Assigned as an associate director, he assisted in the conduct of a campaign and later, as a director, conducted campaigns to which he was assigned by CCS. In 1959, Reilly indicated an interest in a transfer from the operations division to the sales division of CCS. The transfer was effected, and, on July 1, 1959, Reilly became regional sales representative of CCS for the area between the northern boundary of Maryland and Georgia. As such, he was expected to seek out likely prospects and to convince them of the desirability of use of the services of CCS. He worked under the direction of CCS's sales manager in New York, to whom he was required to submit daily reports. He was assisted by his employer's distribution in the area of promotional materials and advertisements which featured Reilly as its regional representative who should be contacted by interested persons.

Campaigns for which Reilly secured contracts were not conducted by him or any-one in the sales division, but by the employees in the operations division.

For his services as regional representative, Reilly received a salary of $140 per week, plus commissions on an ascending scale, based upon sales in his area cumulated over the period of each year.

For a period of three weeks in November 1959, Reilly was temporarily assigned to operational work in Florida. Upon his return to the District of Columbia area and his resumption of his duties as Regional Representative, he failed to submit the written daily reports of his activities which were required of him.[1] The plaintiff's sales manager requested the resumption of daily reporting, but such reports were not forthcoming.

On January 4, 1960, Reilly presented himself at the New York office of CCS, and there informed the Vice President in charge of sales that he intended to resign. As the reason for his resignation, he stated that he wished to earn more money, that he wanted to do less travelling, and that his wife was ill. He stated that he thought he would go back to work for the federal government or into teaching, in which he had experience. The next day he wrote a formal letter of resignation, in which he stated that he was acting because of "urgent personal reasons."

---

1. There were some telephone conversations with his superior about his work. His last written report was dated October 30, 1959. While engaged in the conduct of the campaign in Florida during November no reports were required of him. After termination of his employment, Reilly submitted a cumulative sales report containing references to his contacts with St. Ambrose Parish. Before that report was made, however, the defendant had firmly secured the St. Ambrose campaign for himself, as will later appear.

The contract of employment required thirty days' notice of termination, but it was agreed on January 4, 1960 that Reilly's resignation would be effective as of January 29, a Friday.

Before the end of January 1960, a letter from the Archbishop of the Roman Catholic Archdiocese of Washington was received by CCS in its New York office. In this letter, the Archbishop stated that St. Ambrose Parish had already engaged the services of CCS for a campaign, and that two other campaigns were in the offing, and, if those eventuated, they would be in touch with Reilly as Regional Representative of CCS. Because the New York office had heard nothing from Reilly of the St. Ambrose Parish campaign, it asked Reilly to come to New York on January 25.

CCS's Vice President in charge of sales testified that at the conference in New York on January 25, he inquired of Reilly about St. Ambrose Parish. Reilly responded by saying that Monsignor Brown of St. Ambrose did not want the services of CCS but he wished those of Reilly. To the suggestion that until the end of the month he was obligated to undertake to sell the services of CCS rather than his own, he responded, according to the Vice President, "Do you expect me to walk out of here next Friday and not have a job?"

According to the Vice President, during the January 25th conference in New York Reilly also stated that Father Cahill and Monsignor Kennedy, pastors, respectively, of Our Lady of Mercy Parish and the Parish of St. John the Evangelist, wished him to run campaigns for their parishes.

There is no doubt but that Reilly actually conducted a campaign for Monsignor Brown's St. Ambrose Parish, commencing on February 8, 1960 and lasting into March. Reilly conducted a campaign for Our Lady of Mercy beginning in March 1960 and lasting until April. He conducted a campaign for St. John the Evangelist beginning in May 1960. For these three campaigns, respectively, he received fees of $6,720, $3,840, $6,720.

Though the campaign for St. Ambrose Parish actually began on February 8, 1960, Reilly, at the trial, testified he had not reached an agreement with Monsignor Brown, of St. Ambrose, until sometime after January 30. In his pretrial deposition, he had clearly and unequivocally testified that he had agreed to run the St. Ambrose campaign on some date between January 10 and January 29. Monsignor Brown, as a witness at the trial, testified that he had agreed with Reilly in January that Reilly would conduct the St. Ambrose campaign after the first of February or "at such time as he would be free to do it," or "after he got rid of the contract with the CCS people."

Reilly, as CCS's sales representative, had been in touch with Father Cahill, of Our Lady of Mercy, in October 1959. Father Cahill was undertaking the formation of a new parish and was interested in procuring the services of CCS. Because of conflicting campaigns, however, he did not obtain permission of the Archbishop to actually conduct the campaign until sometime after the end of January 1960. Meanwhile, he remained in touch with Reilly. Father Cahill testified that early in 1960 he learned from Reilly of Reilly's intention to leave the employ of CCS. He testified that there may have been discussions between him and Reilly regarding Reilly's availability to conduct the campaign for Our Lady of Mercy.

According to the testimony for CCS, Reilly spoke on January 25th of the fact that Father Cahill wished him to conduct the imminent campaign for Our Lady of Mercy.

Reilly had also been in touch with Monsignor Kennedy and Father Gillen, of St. John the Evangelist. The priests had decided upon a campaign which in October, 1959 was tentatively planned from February 1 to April 8, 1960. Reilly's report of October 6, 1959 indicated that CCS's success in conducting a campaign for Monsignor Russell, at Wheaton, Maryland, had sold the priests upon CCS and upon the effectiveness of its services.

Father Gillen, the Assistant Pastor of St. John's, testified that in October of 1959 they had sought to have Reilly, himself, conduct the campaign; Reilly then explained he was exclusively engaged in sales work and could not conduct it himself, but that a good director would be furnished for that purpose. Father Gillen testified that he did not know Reilly had left the employ of CCS until sometime after January 1960, but the Pastor of the Parish, Monsignor Kennedy, did not testify, and there is the actual fact that Reilly did conduct the campaign when the Archbishop authorized St. John's to proceed and the testimony of CCS that on January 25, 1960 Reilly stated that Monsignor Kennedy wanted him, not CCS, to conduct the campaign. More importantly, in his deposition Reilly admitted that "it is possible" that prior to January 29, 1960, he entered into a firm agreement with Monsignor Kennedy to run the campaign for St. John's. . . .

Considering Reilly's deposition with all of the other testimony, it is unmistakable that, before termination of his employment by CCS, Reilly not only formed the intention of engaging in fund raising activities on his own account, but he actively sought employment for himself and entered into firm agreements on his own account, with the result that there was no substantial hiatus between the termination of his employment by CCS and the commencement of the first of the three campaigns that he had lined up for himself.

There is no claim here that there was any inhibition upon Reilly's engagement in competitive activities after the termination of his employment with CCS. The usual rule is that a former employee, after termination of his employment, may compete with his former employer, the only restraint being that he may not use confidential information or trade secrets obtained from the former employer, appropriating, in effect, to his competitive advantage what rightfully belongs to his employer. There is no suggestion here that CCS had any trade secrets which ought not to be utilized by Reilly in competing with it, and, since there was no covenant not to compete, Reilly had a clear and unrestricted right to compete after January 29, 1960.

Though it is plain that Reilly after January 1960 could have solicited for himself the business of St. Ambrose, Our Lady of Mercy and St. John's, he had absolutely no right to do that before January 29, 1960, when he was employed by CCS to solicit the business of those and other parishes for CCS and not for himself. That was the sole purpose of Reilly's employment. His great and primary duty as an employee was to sell the services of CCS and to promote its interest, and, when, during his employment, he solicited the business of the three parishes for himself, he was untrue to his employment obligation and was disloyal to his employer.

Employment as a sales representative demands of the employee the highest duty of loyalty. It is not without its difficulties when the employment continues after the employee has arrived at a fixed determination to leave his employment, for then his interests and those of his employer have lost their identity and may have become conflicting. Until the employment relationship is finally severed however, the employee must prefer the interests of his employer to his own. During such a period, he cannot solicit for himself future business which his employment requires him to solicit for his employer. If prospective customers undertake the opening of negotiations which the employee could not initiate, he must decline to participate in them. Above all, he should be candid with his employer and should withhold no information which would be useful to the employer in the protection and promotion of its interests.

Reilly's conduct was far short of the standards by which he should have governed himself.

It is quite irrelevant that the three parishes may not have been in position to actually commence their campaigns before the effective date of Reilly's resignation from his employment by CCS. The substantial fees which he collected for the conduct of the three campaigns were not the fruit solely of his efforts in aid of the campaigns after they commenced, but the fruit also of his disloyal conduct during his employment in soliciting the valuable contracts for himself when he owed an unequivocal duty to solicit those contracts for his employer. The fruit of that disloyal conduct Reilly may not retain.

It thus appears that CCS was clearly entitled to the accounting it sought of its former employee and it was improper on this record for the Court to have entered a judgment in Reilly's favor. The judgment below is reversed and the cause remanded for further proceedings consistent with this opinion. . . .

Hamburger v. Hamburger

Superior Court of Massachusetts, Suffolk County, 1995
1995 WL 579679

FINDINGS, RULINGS AND ORDER FOR JUDGMENT

THAYER FREMONT-SMITH, JUSTICE.

These consolidated actions were heard jury-waived on September 19-September 27, 1995. Based upon all of the credible evidence, the Court makes the following findings, rulings and order for judgment.

David Hamburger (David), son of Joseph Hamburger (Joseph) and nephew of Jacob (Ted), began working at Ace Wire and Burlap, Inc. (Ace) and A. Hamburger & Sons (A. Hamburger) summers as a high school student beginning in 1978. His work was primarily that of a warehouseman, loading and unloading trucks, assisting in delivering wire and picking up wool and other manual labor.

In November, 1984, after graduating from the University of Bridgeport, David began working at Ace full time. His responsibilities were similar to the work he had done during preceding summers, i.e. general warehouse work for both the wire and wool business. At the time he began full-time employment at Ace, David was aware of a strained relationship between his father, Joe, and uncle, Ted. Nevertheless, both brothers agreed to his employment and welcomed him into the business.

David continued to work, primarily as a warehouseman. Beginning around 1986, however, he began to become involved in the sales activities of Ace. He increasingly began to call on customers and to learn from his father about the pricing and uses for different types of wire. His father also introduced him to customers and suppliers. In subsequent years, David built the business of Ace from about 300 suppliers and $500,000 in sales to over 700 accounts and over $1,000,000 in sales.

Although Ted had originally welcomed David as a general helper and warehouseman, he became increasingly resentful of David's gradual ascent to the role of sales manager and general manager of the wire business which resulted in a further deterioration of the relationship between Ted and Joseph. Heated and sometimes physical altercations between the brothers ensued, into which David was sometimes drawn on the side of his father. Periodically, Ted attempted to fire David from the business but Joe successfully resisted these efforts. In 1987, Ted went so far as to retain an attorney and brought suit to remove his nephew from the business, but this effort also failed. Things deteriorated to the point where Ted would berate and insult David in front of other employees, and David, on at least one occasion, responded in kind.

In early 1992 David, concerned about his long-term future at Ace, consulted with Ted to inquire about his prospects in the business. Ted rejected David's request for increased compensation or a commission on sales and told him words to the effect that "in 10 years your father or I will probably die; when that happens you'll know what your future is." David, not unreasonably, understood this to signify that he could expect to be fired if his father died before Ted.

In February or March of 1993, David had a dinner meeting with Robert Yates, Jr. of Eastern Wire Products, Inc. (Eastern Wire), one of Ace's four suppliers of wire. At this meeting David expressed his unhappiness at Ace and told Yates that he was contemplating going into business for himself. He inquired whether Yates would be willing to help finance a wire company that David would start. Yates subsequently agreed to loan David $50,000 in order to start his new company, $30,000 of which David received and deposited in an account under the name of his new company, New England Baling Wire, Inc. (NEBW), in early May, 1993. He also leased space for his new company in Avon, Massachusetts.

On May 13, 1993, David resigned without prior notice, formally incorporated NEBW and commenced work the following day at his new quarters in Avon, Massachusetts. He also immediately hired Ace's book-keeper, Ray Brennan, who had resigned a week earlier, and Ace's truck driver was employed on May 20, 1993. Beginning on May 13, David and Brennan began to actively solicit, by telephone, many of Ace's customers, with the result that several hundred of them are now customers of David's NEBW.

Ted contends that David's arrangement for financing and leasehold arrangements for NEBW and his solicitation of Ace's customers were wrongful because they not only had commenced while he was still an Ace employee, but because the customer solicitation was facilitated by David's wrongful appropriation of confidential customer lists and pricing information of Ace, which David is alleged to have obtained with Joseph's connivance, in violation of David's and Joseph's fiduciary obligations to Ace and to Ted. See Chelsea Industries, Inc. v. Gaffney, 389 Mass. 1 (1983); Cardullo v. Landau, 329 Mass. 5, 8 (1952).

The Court rules, however, that David's having arranged financing and leased space for NEBW while he was still an Ace employee was not illegal, as an employee is free to make such logistical arrangements while still an employee. See Chelsea Industries, supra, at 10; Meehan v. Shaughnessey; Cohen, 404 Mass. 419, 435 (1989).

With respect to David's solicitation of Ace customers, there was no evidence that this had commenced, in any significant way, prior to his May 13, 1993 resignation. As Ace's sales manager, he had been intimately familiar with its customers and pricing, so that he was familiar with such information when he left Ace's employ. He was entitled to use his general knowledge, experience, memory and skill in establishing NEBW, including "remembered information." J.T. Healy & Son, Inc. v. James A. Murphy & Son, Inc., 357 Mass. 728, 740 (1970). Although he was certainly a key employee, an employer who wishes to restrict the post-employment competitive activities of a key employee, where the activities do not entail misuse of proprietary information, must protect that goal through a non-competition agreement. Augat, Inc. v. Aegis, Inc., 409 Mass. 165, 172 (1991). This the plaintiff neglected to do. Moreover, while David may have made some use of personal notes relating to Ace customers, customer lists are not considered trade secrets if the information is readily available from published sources, such as business directories. Such directories were in fact available to him and were used by him and Brennan to contact customers on and after May 13. While Ted suspected that Joseph was providing David with such information from Ace, there was no hard evidence of this such as would convince the Court that this occurred to any significant extent. And, while Ted and Joseph were certainly at logger-heads with respect to customer pricing after David left, the Court concludes that Joseph's contradiction of Ted's quoted prices to customers resulted from their divergent views as to what was best for the company, rather than from any attempt by Joseph to sabotage the wire business for the benefit of his son.[1]

By the same token, the Court is not convinced that Ted, on his part, acted in bad faith in his conduct of the business or in filing this lawsuit. Ted's views were so colored by his animosity for his brother and nephew that Ted suspected the worst of them and reacted accordingly in bringing the lawsuit.

The sad and ironic thing about this case is that this festering hatred between two brothers caused the ruination of a good family business, by driving away the very person who had built the business up since 1984 and who was the only person around who had the energy, personality, knowledge and love for the business that could have preserved it for the long run. Under the circumstances in which he found himself, David took the only reasonable course open to him and did so in a way which the court finds did not violate any legal obligation to Ted or Ace.

NOTES AND QUESTIONS

1. Fiduciary duty can be described as a device for economizing on transaction costs. Instead of specifying in advance *exactly* what the agent can and cannot do, fiduciary duty imposes a general obligation to act fairly. But how should a court determine whether an act is fair or unfair? Are the following two formulations helpful? How do they differ?

---

1. Ted testified that he believed Ace should meet the lower price competition of NEBW even if this meant selling wire at below fully-accounted cost, whereas Joseph testified that he believed that sales should only be made at prices which could return a net profit to the company.

a. Fiduciary duty obliges "the fiduciary to act in the best interests of his client or beneficiary and to refrain from self-interested behavior not specifically allowed by the
employment contract." Anderson, Conflicts of Interest: Efficiency, Fairness and
Corporate Structure, 25 UCLA L. Rev. 738, 760 (1978).

b. "Socially optimal fiduciary rules approximate the bargain that investors and agents
would strike if they were able to dicker at no cost." Easterbrook and Fischel, Corporate
Control Transactions, 91 Yale L.J. 698, 702 (1982).

2. As an alternative to relying solely on fiduciary duty, principals may contract for
greater protection from postemployment competition. Courts will enforce noncompetition agreements if they are reasonable given the duration, geographical coverage, and
the nature of the employer's risk from such competition. In effect, courts will balance
the legitimate interests of the employer in protecting her business against the legitimate
interest of the employee in seeking to redeploy her human capital. Such covenants will
not be enforced if the employee has no ability to seize team-specific value to which the
employer has a fair claim. Consider the court's analysis in Robbins v. Finlay, 645 P.2d 623,
628 (Utah 1982), in refusing to enforce a noncompetition agreement that prohibited
defendant Finlay, a hearing aid salesman, from competing with plaintiff Robbins (doing
business as Beltone of Utah) for a period of one year:

> The record shows that Finlay's job required little training and is not unlike the job of many
> other types of salesmen. The company's investment in training him was small. . . . Furthermore,
> there is no showing that his services were special, unique, or extraordinary, even if their value to his
> employer was high. Thus, this case is similar to Columbia Ribbon & Carbon Mfg. Co. v. A-1-A Corp.,
> 42 N.Y.2d 496, 398 N.Y.S.2d 1004, 369 N.E.2d 4 (1977), where the court stated:
>
>> It is clear that [the covenant's] broadsweeping language is unrestrained by any limitations
>> keyed to uniqueness [of the employee's services], trade secrets, confidentiality or even com-
>> petitive unfairness. It does no more than baldly restrain competition. . . .
>
> It is of no moment that defendant may have been especially proficient in his work. General
> knowledge or expertise acquired through employment in a common calling cannot be appropri-
> ated as a trade secret. "The efficiency and skills which an employee develops through his work
> belong to him and not to his former employer." Hallmark Personnel of Texas, Inc. v. Franks, Tex.
> Ct. App., 562 S.W.2d 933, 936 (1978). The same principles apply to the covenant here. We hold that
> the covenant not to compete had the effect of preventing the defendant from exploiting skills and
> experience which he had a right to exploit.

3. In *Community Counselling Service*, Reilly unfairly competed with his principal during the course of his employment. What steps should Reilly have taken to avoid liability? If Reilly and his employer had entered into a noncompetition agreement, would
it have been enforceable?

4. Limits on the Firm's Right to Discharge an Employee at Will

Although the firm may have the power to discharge a valued employee without cause,
it usually will not be in the firm's best interest to do so in bad faith. If the firm terminates an employee unfairly, other employees may become less diligent or may leave. In
other words, the employer's costs in lost reputation and in being subsequently served
by a less skilled or diligent work force should usually deter such unfair conduct.

Of course firms may not always act rationally, and there may be circumstances where those acting for the firm may have personal reasons for dismissing an employee that are not based on the firm's best interests. In response to this risk, some courts and legislatures have created exceptions to the at-will doctrine in order to protect employees from irrational or opportunistic discharge.

As you read the following case, consider not only where the line should be drawn between protecting employees from harsh treatment and preserving the employment-at-will doctrine, but also who should draw that line—the parties, the courts, or the legislature. Note carefully how the court interprets the contract between employer and employee. Does it use an appropriate interpretational strategy?

Foley v. Interactive Data Corp.
California Supreme Court, 1988
47 Cal. 3d 654, 254 Cal. Rptr. 211, 765 P.2d 373

LUCAS, CHIEF JUSTICE.

After Interactive Data Corporation (defendant) fired plaintiff Daniel D. Foley, an executive employee, he filed this action seeking compensatory and punitive damages for wrongful discharge. . . .

FACTS

. . . According to the complaint, plaintiff is a former employee of defendant, a wholly owned subsidiary of Chase Manhattan Bank that markets computer-based decision-support services. Defendant hired plaintiff in June 1976 as an assistant product manager at a starting salary of $18,500. . . .

Over the next six years and nine months, plaintiff received a steady series of salary increases, promotions, bonuses, awards and superior performance evaluations. In 1979 defendant named him consultant manager of the year and in 1981 promoted him to branch manager of its Los Angeles office. His annual salary rose to $56,164 and he received an additional $6,762 merit bonus two days before his discharge in March 1983. He alleges defendant's officers made repeated oral assurances of job security so long as his performance remained adequate.

Plaintiff also alleged that during his employment, defendant maintained written "Termination Guidelines" that set forth express grounds for discharge and a mandatory seven-step pretermination procedure. Plaintiff understood that these guidelines applied not only to employees under plaintiff's supervision, but to him as well. On the basis of these representations, plaintiff alleged that he reasonably believed defendant would not discharge him except for good cause, and therefore he refrained from accepting or pursuing other job opportunities.

The event that led to plaintiff's discharge was a private conversation in January 1983 with his former supervisor, vice president Richard Earnest. During the previous year defendant had hired Robert Kuhne and subsequently named Kuhne to replace Earnest as plaintiff's immediate supervisor. Plaintiff learned that Kuhne was currently under investigation by the Federal Bureau of Investigation for embezzlement from his former employer, Bank of America.[1] Plaintiff reported what he knew about Kuhne to Earnest, because he was "worried about working for Kuhne and having him in a supervisory position . . . , in view of Kuhne's suspected criminal conduct." Plaintiff asserted he "made this disclosure in the interest and for the benefit of his employer," allegedly because he believed that because defendant and its parent do business with the financial community on a confidential basis, the company would have a legitimate interest in knowing about a high executive's alleged prior criminal conduct.

In response, Earnest allegedly told plaintiff not to discuss "rumors" and to "forget what he heard" about Kuhne's past. In early March, Kuhne informed plaintiff that defendant had decided to replace him for "performance reasons" and that he could transfer to a position in another division in Waltham, Massachusetts. Plaintiff was told that if he did not accept a transfer, he might be demoted but not fired. One week later, in Waltham, Earnest informed plaintiff he was not doing a good job, and six days later, he notified plaintiff he could continue as branch manager if he "agreed to go on a 'performance plan.'" Plaintiff asserts he agreed to consider such an arrangement. The next day, when Kuhne met with plaintiff, purportedly to present him with a written "performance plan" proposal, Kuhne instead informed plaintiff he had the choice of resigning or being fired. Kuhne offered neither a performance plan nor an option to transfer to another position. . . .

I.   TORTIOUS DISCHARGE IN CONTRAVENTION OF PUBLIC POLICY

We turn first to plaintiff's cause of action alleging he was discharged in violation of public policy. Labor Code §2922 provides in relevant part, "An employment, having no specified term, may be terminated at the will of either party on notice to the other. . . ." This presumption may be superseded by a contract, express or implied, limiting the employer's right to discharge the employee. Absent any contract, however, the employment is "at will," and the employee can be fired with or without good cause. But the employer's right to discharge an "at will" employee is still subject to limits imposed by public policy, since otherwise the threat of discharge could be used to coerce employees into committing crimes, concealing wrongdoing, or taking other action harmful to the public weal. . . .

In the present case, plaintiff alleges that defendant discharged him in "sharp derogation" of a substantial public policy that imposes a legal duty on employees to report relevant business information to management. An employee is an agent, and as such "is required to disclose to [his] principal all information he has relevant to the subject matter of the agency." (2 Watkin, Summary of Cal. Law (9th ed. 1987) Agency & Employment §41.) Thus, plaintiff asserts, if he discovered information that might

---

1. In September 1983, after plaintiff's discharge, Kuhne pleaded guilty in federal court to a felony count of embezzlement.

lead his employer to conclude that an employee was an embezzler, and should not be retained, plaintiff had a duty to communicate that information to his principal.

It is unclear whether the alleged duty is one founded in statute. . . .

Whether or not there is a statutory duty requiring an employee to report information relevant to his employer's interest, we do not find a substantial public policy prohibiting an employer from discharging an employee for performing that duty. Past decisions recognizing a tort action for discharge in violation of public policy seek to protect the public, by protecting the employee who refuses to commit a crime (*Tameny* [v. Atlantic Richfield Co. (1980)], 27 Cal. 3d 167, 164 Cal. Rptr. 839, 610 P.2d 1330), who reports criminal activity to proper authorities, or who discloses other illegal, unethical, or unsafe practices. No equivalent public interest bars the discharge of the present plaintiff. When the duty of an employee to disclose information to his employer serves only the private interest of the employer, the rationale underlying the *Tameny* cause of action is not implicated.

We conclude that the Court of Appeal properly upheld the trial court's ruling sustaining the demurrer without leave to amend to plaintiff's first cause of action.

II.   BREACH OF EMPLOYMENT CONTRACT

Plaintiff's second cause of action alleged that over the course of his nearly seven years of employment with defendant, the company's own conduct and personnel policies gave rise to an "oral contract" not to fire him without good cause. . . .

B. SUFFICIENCY OF THE ALLEGATIONS
OF ORAL OR IMPLIED CONTRACT

Although plaintiff describes his cause of action as one for breach of an oral contract, he does not allege explicit words by which the parties agreed that he would not be terminated without good cause. Instead he alleges that a course of conduct, including various oral representations, created a reasonable expectation to that effect. Thus, his cause of action is more properly described as one for breach of an implied-in-fact contract.[20] . . .

We begin by acknowledging the fundamental principle of freedom of contract: employer and employee are free to agree to a contract terminable at will or subject to limitations. Their agreement will be enforced so long as it does not violate legal strictures external to the contract, such as laws affecting union membership and activity, prohibitions on indentured servitude, or the many other legal restrictions already described which place certain restraints on the employment arrangement. . . .

---

20. Plaintiff alleges defendant maintained written "Guidelines for Termination" that required good cause for the discharge of an employee, and that plaintiff understood these guidelines applied to him. If he had further alleged that the parties expressly agreed that these guidelines covered his employment, he could state a cause of action for breach of an express oral contract. He has made no such allegation.

The absence of an express written or oral contract term concerning termination of employment does not necessarily indicate that the employment is actually intended by the parties to be "at will," because the presumption of at-will employment may be overcome by evidence of contrary intent. Generally, courts seek to enforce the actual understanding of the parties to a contract, and in so doing may inquire into the parties' conduct to determine if it demonstrates an implied contract. . . .

The limitations on employment security terms on which defendant relies were developed during a period when courts were generally reluctant to look beyond explicit promises of the parties to a contract. "The court-imposed presumption that the employment contract is terminable at will relies upon the formalistic approach to contract interpretation predominant in late nineteenth century legal thought: manifestations of assent must be evidenced by definite, express terms if promises are to be enforceable." (Note, Protecting At Will Employees, [1980] 93 Harv. L. Rev. at p. 1825.) In the intervening decades, however, courts increasingly demonstrated their willingness to examine the entire relationship of the parties to commercial contracts to ascertain their actual intent, and this trend has been reflected in the body of law guiding contract interpretation. (See, Goetz & Scott, The Limits of Expanded Choice: An Analysis of the Interactions Between Express and Implied Contract Terms (1985) 73 Cal. L. Rev. 261, 273-276 ("The [Uniform Commercial] Code, now joined by the Second Restatement of Contracts, effectively reverses the common law presumption that the parties' writing and the official law of contract are the definitive elements of the agreement. Evidence derived from experience and practice can now trigger the incorporation of additional, implied terms").)

Similarly, 20 years ago, Professor Blumrosen observed that during the decades preceding his analysis, courts had demonstrated an increasing willingness to "consider the entire relationship of the parties, and to find that facts and circumstances establish a contract which cannot be terminated by the employer without cause." (Blumrosen, Settlement of Disputes Concerning the Exercise of Employer Disciplinary Power: United States Report [1964], 18 Rutgers L. Rev. at p. 432, fn. omitted.) "This approach has been recognized as consistent with customary interpretation techniques of commercial contracts permitting 'gap filling' by implication of reasonable terms." (Miller & Estes, Recent Judicial Limitations on the Right to Discharge: A California Trilogy (1982) 16 U. C. Davis L. Rev. 65, 101, fn. omitted.)

In the employment context, factors apart from consideration and express terms may be used to ascertain the existence and content of an employment agreement, including "the personnel policies or practices of the employer, the employee's longevity of service, actions or communications by the employer reflecting assurances of continued employment, and the practices of the industry in which the employee is engaged." [Pugh v. See's Candies, Inc. (1981) 116 Cal. App. 3d 311, 327, 171 Cal. Rptr. 917.] Pursuant to Labor Code §2922, if the parties reach no express or implied agreement to the contrary, the relationship is terminable at any time without cause. But when the parties have enforceable expectations concerning either the term of employment or the grounds or manner of termination, Labor Code §2922 does not diminish the force of such contractual or legal obligations. The presumption that an employment relationship of indefinite duration is intended to be terminable at will is therefore "subject, like any presumption, to contrary evidence. This may take the form of an agreement, express or implied, that . . . the employment relationship will continue indefinitely, pending the occurrence of some event such as the employer's dissatisfaction with the employee's services or the existence of some 'cause' for termination." (*Pugh*, supra, 116 Cal. App. 3d at pp. 324-325.)

Finally, we do not agree with the Court of Appeal that employment security agreements are so inherently harmful or unfair to employers, who do not receive equivalent guarantees of continued service, as to merit treatment different from that accorded other contracts. On the contrary, employers may benefit from the increased loyalty and productivity that such agreements may inspire. Permitting proof of and reliance on implied-in-fact contract terms does not nullify the at-will rule, it merely treats such contracts in a manner in keeping with general contract law. . . .

Defendant's remaining argument is that even if a promise to discharge "for good cause only" could be implied in fact, the evidentiary factors . . . relied on by plaintiff, are inadequate as a matter of law. This contention fails on several grounds.

First, defendant overemphasizes the fact that plaintiff was employed for "only" six years and nine months. Length of employment is a relevant consideration but six years and nine months is sufficient time for conduct to occur on which a trier of fact could find the existence of an implied contract. As to establishing the requisite promise, "oblique language will not, standing alone, be sufficient to establish agreement" instead, the totality of the circumstances determines the nature of the contract. Agreement may be "'shown by the acts and conduct of the parties, interpreted in the light of the subject matter and of the surrounding circumstances.'" (*Pugh*, supra, 116 Cal. App. 3d at p. 329.) Plaintiff here alleged repeated oral assurances of job security and consistent promotions, salary increases and bonuses during the term of his employment contributing to his reasonable expectation that he would not be discharged except for good cause.

Second, an allegation of breach of written "Termination Guidelines" implying self-imposed limitations on the employer's power to discharge at will may be sufficient to state a cause of action for breach of an employment contract. *Pugh*, supra, 116 Cal. App. 3d 311, 171 Cal. Rptr. 917, is not alone in holding that the trier of fact can infer an agreement to limit the grounds for termination based on the employee's reasonable reliance on the company's personnel manual or policies.

Finally, plaintiff alleges that he supplied the company valuable and separate consideration by signing an agreement whereby he promised not to compete or conceal any computer-related information from defendant for one year after termination. The noncompetition agreement may be probative evidence that "it is more probable that the parties intended a continuing relationship, with limitations upon the employer's dismissal authority [because the] employee has provided some benefit to the employer, or suffers some detriment, beyond the usual rendition of service." (*Pugh*, supra, 116 Cal. App. 3d at p. 326.)

In sum, plaintiff has pleaded facts which, if proved, may be sufficient for a jury to find an implied-in-fact contract limiting defendant's right to discharge him arbitrarily—facts sufficient to overcome the presumption of Labor Code §2922. On demurrer, we must assume these facts to be true. In other words, plaintiff has pleaded an implied-in-fact contract and its breach, and is entitled to his opportunity to prove those allegations.

III. Breach of the Implied Covenant
of Good Faith and Fair Dealing

We turn now to plaintiff's cause of action for tortious breach of the implied covenant of good faith and fair dealing. . . .

The distinction between tort and contract is well grounded in common law, and divergent objectives underlie the remedies created in the two areas. Whereas contract actions are created to enforce the intentions of the parties to the agreement, tort law is primarily designed to vindicate "social policy." The covenant of good faith and fair dealing was developed in the contract arena and is aimed at making effective the agreement's promises. Plaintiff asks that we find that the breach of the implied covenant in employment contracts also gives rise to an action seeking an award of tort damages.

In this instance, where an extension of tort remedies is sought for a duty whose breach previously has been compensable by contractual remedies, it is helpful to consider certain principles relevant to contract law. First, predictability about the cost of contractual relationships plays an important role in our commercial system. Moreover, "Courts traditionally have awarded damages for breach of contract to compensate the aggrieved party rather than to punish the breaching party." (Note, (1985) 60 Notre Dame L. Rev. 510, 526.) With these concepts in mind, we turn to analyze the role of the implied covenant of good faith and fair dealing and the propriety of the extension of remedies urged by plaintiff.

"Every contract imposes upon each party a duty of good faith and fair dealing in its performance and its enforcement." (Rest. 2d Contracts, §205.) This duty has been recognized in the majority of American jurisdictions, the Restatement, and the Uniform Commercial Code. (Burton, Breach of Contract and the Common Law Duty to Perform in Good Faith (1980) 94 Harv. L. Rev. 369.) Because the covenant is a contract term, however, compensation for its breach has almost always been limited to contract rather than tort remedies. As to the scope of the covenant, "'[t]he precise nature and extent of the duty imposed by such an implied promise will depend on the contractual purposes.'" (Egan v. Mutual of Omaha Ins. Co. (1979) 24 Cal. 3d 809, 818, 169 Cal. Rptr. 691, 620 P.2d 141.) Initially, the concept of a duty of good faith developed in contract law as "a kind of 'safety valve' to which judges may turn to fill gaps and qualify or limit rights and duties otherwise arising under rules of law and specific contract language." (Summers, The General Duty of Good Faith—Its Recognition and Conceptualization (1982) 67 Cornell L. Rev. 810, 812, fn. omitted; see also Burton, supra, 94 Harv. L. Rev. 369, 371 ("the courts employ the good faith doctrine to effectuate the intentions of parties, or to protect their reasonable expectations").) As a contract concept, breach of the duty led to imposition of contract damages determined by the nature of the breach and standard contract principles.

An exception to this general rule has developed in the context of insurance contracts where, for a variety of policy reasons, courts have held that breach of the implied covenant will provide the basis for an action in tort. . . . We explained in Gruenberg v. Aetna Ins. Co. (1973) 9 Cal. 3d 566, 108 Cal. Rptr. 480, 510 P.2d 1032, that "[t]he duty [to comport with the implied covenant of good faith and fair dealing] is immanent in the contract whether the company is attending [on the insured's behalf] to the claims of third persons against the insured or the claims of the insured itself. Accordingly, when the insurer unreasonably and in bad faith withholds payment of the claim of its insured, it is subject to liability in tort."

In Egan v. Mutual of Omaha Ins. Co., supra, 24 Cal. 3d 809, 169 Cal. Rptr. 691, 620 P.2d 141, we described some of the bases for permitting tort recovery for breach of the implied covenant in the insurance context. "The insured in a contract like the one before us does not seek to obtain a commercial advantage by purchasing the policy—rather, he seeks protection against calamity." (Id. at p. 819.) Thus, "As one commentary has noted, 'The insurers' obligations are . . . rooted in their status as purveyors of a vital service labeled quasi-public in nature. Suppliers of services affected with a public interest must take the public's interest seriously, where necessary placing it before their interest in maximizing gains and limiting disbursements. . . . [A]s a supplier of a public service rather than a manufactured product, the obligations of insurers go beyond meeting reasonable expectations of coverage. The obligations of good faith and fair dealing encompass qualities of decency and humanity inherent in the responsibilities of a fiduciary.' (Goodman & Seaton, Foreword: Ripe for Decision, Internal Workings and Current Concerns of the California Supreme Court (1974) 62 Cal. L. Rev. 309, 346-347)." (24 Cal. 3d at p. 820.)

In addition, the *Egan* court emphasized that "the relationship of insurer and insured is inherently unbalanced: the adhesive nature of insurance contracts places the insurer in a superior bargaining position." (24 Cal. 3d at p. 820.) This emphasis on the "special relationship" of insurer and insured has been echoed in arguments and analysis in subsequent scholarly commentary and cases which urge the availability of tort remedies in the employment context. . . .

In our view, the underlying problem in the line of cases relied on by plaintiff lies in the decisions' uncritical incorporation of the insurance model into the employment context, without careful consideration of the fundamental policies underlying the development of tort and contract law in general or of significant differences between the insurer/insured and employer/employee relationships. When a court enforces the implied covenant it is in essence acting to protect "the interest in having promises performed" (Prosser, Law of Torts (4th ed. 1971) p. 613)—the traditional realm of a contract action—rather than to protect some general duty to society which the law places on an employer without regard to the substance of its contractual obligations to its employee. An allegation of breach of the implied covenant of good faith and fair dealing is an allegation of breach of an "ex contractu" obligation, namely one arising out of the contract itself. The covenant of good faith is read into contracts in order to protect the express covenants or promises of the contract, not to protect some general public policy interest not directly tied to the contract's purposes. The insurance cases thus were a major departure from traditional principles of contract law. . . .

After review of the various commentators, and independent consideration of the similarities between the two areas, we are not convinced that a "special relationship" analogous to that between insurer and insured should be deemed to exist in the usual employment relationship which would warrant recognition of a tort action for breach of the implied covenant. Even if we were to assume that the special relationship model is an appropriate one to follow in determining whether to expand tort recovery, a breach in the employment context does not place the employee in the same economic dilemma that an insured faces when an insurer in bad faith refuses to pay a claim or to accept a settlement offer within policy limits. When an insurer takes such actions, the insured cannot turn to the marketplace to find another insurance company willing to pay for the loss already incurred. The wrongfully terminated employee, on the other hand, can (and must, in order to mitigate damages) make reasonable efforts to seek alternative employment. . . .

We therefore conclude that the employment relationship is not sufficiently similar to that of insurer and insured to warrant judicial extension of the proposed additional tort remedies in view of the countervailing concerns about economic policy and stability, the traditional separation of tort and contract law, and finally, the numerous protections against improper terminations already afforded employees. . . .

PANELLI, ARGUELLES and EAGLESON, J.J., concur. [The concurring and dissenting opinions of Justices Broussard and Kaufman are omitted.]

NOTES AND QUESTIONS

1. The employment-at-will doctrine has been a central feature of American law for well over a century. It sprang seemingly out of nowhere, and governed employer-employee relationships without challenge until the Great Depression. The following excerpt from Fitzgerald v. Salsbury Chemical, 613 N.W.2d 275 (Ia. 2000), describes the genesis of the doctrine, and its subsequent evolution in one American jurisdiction.

The roots of the at-will employment doctrine are more than a century old. It is said to have originated in an 1877 treatise by Horace Gray Wood, which articulated the rule in clear and appealing terms:

> With us, the rule is inflexible, that a general or indefinite hiring is, prima facie, a hiring at will, and if the servant seeks to make it out a yearly hiring, the burden is upon him to establish it by proof. . . . [I]t is an indefinite hiring and is determinable at the will of either party.

Horace G. Wood, A Treatise on the Law of Master & Servant §134, at 272 (1877). Despite its direct contradiction to the traditional English rule, the at-will rule was judicially adopted in New York, see Martin v. New York Life Ins. Co., 148 N.Y. 117, 42 N.E. 416, 417 (1895), and quickly became the prevailing rule throughout the country.

Fitzgerald, 613 N.W.2d 275, 280.

As early as 1562, the English common law presumed employment was for a one-year term. See Gary E. Murg & Clifford Scharman, ("Employment at Will: Do the Exceptions Overwhelm the Rule?," 23 B.C.L.Rev. 329, 332 (1982) [hereinafter Murg & Scharman]. This was for the protection of the seasonal worker, as the presumption was difficult to overcome. English courts held an employer liable for a breach of the employment contract for terminations prior to the expiration of the one-year term absent proof of a "reasonable cause to do so." Wagenseller v. Scottsdale Mem'l Hosp., 147 Ariz. 370, 710 P.2d 1025, 1030 (1985) (citing 1 W. Blackstone, Commentaries at 413). Initially American courts adopted this English rule; however with the Industrial Revolution came the rise of a more impersonal employer-employee relationship and so went the traditional master-servant relationship and the protections that came with it. Murg & Scharman, 23 B.C.L.Rev. at 334.

Fitzgerald, 613 N.W.2d 275, 280 at fn.1.

The United States Supreme Court gave the doctrine a boost in 1908 in Adair v. United States, when it found a federal law making it a crime to discharge an employee for being a member of a union violated due process guarantees of freedom of contract. Adair v. United States, 208 U.S. 161, 174-75, 28 S.Ct. 277, 280, 52 L.Ed. 436, 442 (1908) ("the right of the employee to quit the service of the employer, for whatever reason, is the same as the right of the employer, for whatever reason, to dispense with the services of the employee").

The *Martin* court, and those which followed, adopted the at-will doctrine advocated by Woods without a thorough analysis of the underlying authority. Legal scholars have since criticized the basis for the rule. See Christopher L. Pennington, "The Public Policy Exception to the Employment-at-Will Doctrine: Its Inconsistencies in Application," 68 Tul. L.Rev. 1583, 1586 n. 13 (1994) [hereinafter Pennington] (the four American cases Woods cited in support of his rule were far off the mark, no policy grounds were offered).

We too have long recognized that "indefinite employment may be abandoned at will by either party without incurring any liability." Harrod v. Wineman, 146 Iowa 718, 719, 125 N.W. 812, 813 (1910). Yet, the passage of time has begun to weaken this once powerful rule. The at-will employment doctrine first began to give way in 1937 when the United States Supreme Court abandoned the Adair holding and upheld the National Labor Relations Act which made it an unfair labor practice for an employer to consider membership in a union as a basis for hiring an employee. NLRB v. Jones & Laughlin Steel Corp., 301 U.S. 1, 45-46, 57 S.Ct. 615, 628, 81 L.Ed. 893, 916 (1937). After this case, courts began to scrutinize the common law doctrine, and the erosion began. See Pennington, 68 Tul. L.Rev. at 1589-90. As one court put it, "[t]he at will presumption, the citadel that once governed the field with such predictability, has been eroded of late by piecemeal attacks on both the contract and tort fronts and the entire field seems precariously perched on the brink of change." Scott v. Extracorporeal Inc., 376 Pa.Super. 90, 545 A.2d 334, 336 (1988) (quoting Martin v. Capital Cities Media, Inc., 354 Pa.Super. 199, 511 A.2d 830, 834 (1986)).

In recent years three exceptions to the at-will employment doctrine have surfaced to add employee protections to the employer/employee relationship. Generally, these exceptions fall into three categories: (1) discharges in violation of public policy, (2) discharges in violation of employee handbooks which constitute a unilateral contract, and (3) discharges in violation of a covenant of good faith and fair dealing. See *Anderson*, 540 N.W.2d at 282 (citing Stephen F. Befort, ("Employee Handbooks & the Legal Effect of Disclaimers," 13 Indus. Rel. L.J. 326, 333-34 (1991/1992)).

We have only adopted the first two recognized exceptions to the doctrine. See Abrisz v. Pulley Freight Lines, Inc., 270 N.W.2d 454, 455 (Iowa 1978) (we first recognized the possibility of public policy exception); Springer v. Weeks & Leo Co., 429 N.W.2d 558, 560 (Iowa 1988) (narrow public policy exception adopted); French v. Foods, Inc., 495 N.W.2d 768, 769-71 (Iowa 1993) (employee handbook may create unilateral contract). We have consistently refused to adopt a covenant of good faith and fair dealing with respect to at-will employment relationships. See Huegerich v. IBP, Inc., 547 N.W.2d 216, 220 (Iowa 1996). Thus, the traditional doctrine of termination "at any time, for any reason, or no reason at all," *Phipps,* 558 N.W.2d at 202, is now more properly stated as permitting "termination at any time for any lawful reason." Lockhart v. Cedar Rapids Community Sch. Dist., 577 N.W.2d 845, 846 (Iowa 1998).

Fitzgerald, 613 N.W.2d 275, 280-281.

2. Suppose that Jake, a brewer, hires Sharon to sell beer for him. Their agreement assigns Sharon an exclusive territory and provides that she will be compensated by receiving: (1) a 15 percent commission on all beer sold in her territory; and (2) an additional 5 percent bonus commission on such sales if she is still assigned to that territory when the beer is delivered to the purchaser. The contract provides that it is terminable at will and without cause by either party. What results if shortly after Sharon obtains a $5,000,000 order, Jake discharges Sharon, allegedly to avoid paying her the 5 percent delivery bonus? Should a court find that every contract has an implied covenant of good faith? Should a court find that this particular contract has an implied covenant of good faith?

In a case with similar facts, the Supreme Judicial Court of Massachusetts upheld the trial court's award of damages for breach of the duty of good faith and fair dealing:

> We believe that the holding in [Monge v. Beebe Rubber Co.] merely extends to employment contracts the rule that " . . . in *every* contract there exists an implied covenant of good faith and fair dealing." . . . In the instant case, we need not pronounce our adherence to so broad a policy nor need we speculate as to whether the good faith requirement is implicit in every contract for employment at will. It is clear, however, that, on the facts before us, a finding is warranted that a breach of the contract occurred. Where the principal seeks to deprive the agent of all compensation by terminating the contractual relationship when the agent is on the brink of successfully completing the sale, the principal has acted in bad faith and the ensuing transaction between the principal and the buyer is to be regarded as having been accomplished by the agent. . . . The same result obtains where the principal attempts to deprive the agent of any portion of a commission due the agent.

Fortune v. National Cash Register Co., 373 Mass. 96, 104-105, 364 N.E.2d 1251, 1257 (1977).

3. Does the court in Foley v. Interactive Data Corp. treat the employment contract as relational or discrete? How could the employer have insured that a court would not find that the employment agreement was subject to a good cause termination requirement?

4. Is the court in *Foley* correct in refusing to create a tort remedy for bad faith breach? Is its principal reason that the legislature is more competent to determine the proper approach? Is that a sufficient reason?

5. For an economic analysis and defense of the employment-at-will doctrine, see Epstein, In Defense of the Contract at Will, 51 U. Chi. L. Rev. 947 (1984).

5. Agency Law and Relations with Creditors

Restatement (Third) of Agency §§2.01-2.06, 3.01, 3.03

In addition to creating a need for internal governance rules, the decision to operate as a firm creates a need for rules allowing creditors and others to know with whom they are dealing. Does the agent speak for the firm or only for herself? Again, the law of agency provides standard form rules on which creditors may rely.

Suppose that Jake operates a brewery as a sole proprietor and employs Sharon as a sales representative. He orally instructs Sharon to offer volume discounts of up to 10 percent. Despite these instructions, Sharon, purporting to act as Jake's agent, enters into a contract with Sam for 10,000 cases of beer at a 25 percent discount. Is Jake bound by this contract?

Traditional common law rules are designed to protect a principal's property interests. A third party who deals with an agent does so at his peril. The agent's actions will bind the principal only if the principal has manifested his or its assent to such actions. Such manifestations of consent can take two forms—actual authority or apparent authority (sometimes called ostensible authority).

Actual authority occurs when the principal manifests his consent directly to the agent. The consent may be expressly manifested, as when the principal instructs the agent in writing or orally as to the scope of the agent's authority. Alternatively, the manifestation of consent may be implied from the conduct of the principal. For example, Jake, the principal, may not have expressly authorized Sharon, his agent, to offer more than a 10 percent discount. However, if she has done so several times in the past, and Jake has silently acquiesced to such transactions, then Jake may be deemed to have impliedly authorized Sharon to make such offers in the future. If actual authority exists, the principal is bound by the agent's authorized actions, even if the party with whom the agent deals is unaware that the agent has actual authority, and even if it would be unusual for an agent to have such authority.

Apparent authority, sometimes called ostensible authority, arises when an agent is without actual authority, but the principal manifests his consent directly to the third party who is dealing with the agent. As with actual authority, apparent authority may be created expressly or impliedly. A third party will be able to bind the principal on the basis of apparent authority only if the third party reasonably believed that the agent was authorized. Thus, if the third party knows that an agent is without actual authority, or if the manifestations made by the principal constitute an insufficient foundation for forming a reasonable belief that the agent is authorized, then the agent's unauthorized actions will not bind the principal.

The traditional common law rules were ill-suited for the needs of modern commerce. Accordingly, courts increasingly strained to protect the expectations of third parties even when the principal's manifestations of consent were illusory at best. The result of this struggle to protect third parties was both an increasingly flexible application of the concept of apparent authority and the growing recognition of a new category of authority—inherent authority.

Inherent authority does not arise from manifestations of consent of the type contemplated by traditional common law authority rules, but rather springs from a desire to protect the reasonable expectations of outsiders who deal with an agent. Perhaps inherent authority is best viewed as an implied term in the contract between a principal and all who deal with his agents. As such, inherent authority is a gap-filling device used by courts to achieve a fair and efficient allocation of the losses from an agent's unauthorized actions.

Judge Learned Hand explained the need for this new concept, or at least for a flexible application of the doctrine of apparent authority, in Kidd v. Thomas A. Edison, Inc., 239 F. 405, 408 (S.D.N.Y.), aff'd., 242 F. 923 (2d Cir. 1917):

> If a man select another to act for him with some discretion, he has by that fact vouched to some extent for his reliability. While it may not be fair to impose upon him the results of a total departure from the general subject of his confidence, the detailed execution of his mandate stands on a different footing. The very purpose of delegated authority is to avoid constant recourse by third persons to the principal, which would be a corollary of denying the agent any latitude beyond his exact instructions. Once a third person has assured himself widely of the character of the agent's mandate, the very purpose of the relation demands the possibility of the principal's being bound through the agent's minor deviations.

Disputes between principals and third parties over the authority of agents can be divided into two categories: (1) cases in which an agent exceeds her authority in an attempt to further the interests of the principal, and (2) cases involving totally opportunistic action, where the agent intentionally misleads both the principal and the third party. Into which category does the following case fall?

Blackburn v. Witter
California District Court of Appeal, 1962
201 Cal. App. 2d 518, 19 Cal. Rptr. 842

STONE, JUSTICE.

Respondent is the widow of a dairy farmer who died in 1954. That same year she was introduced to a Mr. Long, an employee of Walston & Company. Respondent was without business experience, and she had no family to advise her. She selected Long as her investment advisor. He called upon her approximately once a month, and suggested stocks to buy and when to buy them, and told her which stocks to sell and when to sell. Long ceased working for Walston & Company February 28, 1957. He became a representative of Dean Witter & Company March 4, 1957, and continued to act as financial counselor for respondent until he was discharged by Dean Witter February 14, 1958.

During the year 1957, while employed by Walston & Company, Long persuaded Mrs. Blackburn to invest in a nonexistent company which he called American Commercial Investment Company. Long told Mrs. Blackburn that she could get a higher rate of interest from American Commercial than she had realized from stocks which she had purchased in the past. Long represented that the American Commercial Investment Company was a large, growing concern engaged in heavy construction, and that the company was both willing and able to pay 10% interest. She obtained the money to invest by selling some of her stock through Long acting as agent for his employer. For the money "invested" Long gave respondent commercial "rediform" receipts, which he later supplemented by promissory notes bearing 10% interest. When respondent asked Long why the receipts and the notes were not written on company stationery, Long replied that the company was new and that its stationery was being printed.

Respondent, on cross-examination, admitted that for other stock purchased from Walston & Company she had received a different type of receipt than the "rediform" given her by Long, that checks to purchase stock were made payable to Walston & Company or Dean Witter & Company, and that the stock was issued to her directly by Walston & Company or Dean Witter & Company. Mrs. Blackburn also admitted that each month she received a summary or transaction sheet from Walston & Company or Dean Witter, setting forth all transactions between her and the brokerage house for the preceding month. None of the transactions between her and Long concerning the American Commercial Investment Company appeared on any of the monthly reports.

Mrs. Blackburn testified that she had confidence in Long, that he had been a trustworthy counselor up to the time of the American Commercial transaction, and that she did not doubt his statements. Respondent also testified that she believed Long's representation that he was acting for his employer and that the investment was recommended as the result of research conducted by the brokerage companies.

Appellants presented testimony by officials of Walston & Company and Dean Witter & Company concerning the limitations placed upon the authority of their account executives or investment representatives, and the limitations imposed by the New York Stock Exchange and the Securities [and] Exchange Commission. However, it was not shown that these limitations were made known to respondent.

The trial court, on the theory of ostensible authority, entered judgment in favor of respondent and against appellants Dean Witter & Company and its bonding agency, Firemans Fund Insurance Company, and against appellants Walston & Company, Inc. and its bonding agency, Massachusetts Bonding & Insurance Company.

If there is liability, it must rest on the theory of ostensible agency since Long clearly had no authority as an employee of either Walston & Company or Dean Witter & Company to borrow money for his personal use, or to take money from a client and give his personal note rather than a security for it. Ostensible authority is defined by Civil Code, §2317, as follows: "Ostensible authority is such as a principal, intentionally or by want of ordinary care, causes or allows a third person to believe the agent to possess."

The conditions under which a principal is bound by the acts of his agent under the theory of ostensible or apparent agency are delineated in Civil Code, §2334, which provides: "A principal is bound by acts of his agent, under a merely ostensible authority, to those persons only who have in good faith, and without want of ordinary care, incurred a liability or parted with value, upon the faith thereof."

In applying the foregoing provisions of the Civil Code, the courts of California have adopted the principle expressed in §261 of the Restatement of the Law of Agency. In Rutherford v. Rideout Bank, 11 Cal. 2d 479, at pages 483-484, 80 P.2d 978, at page 981, 117 A.L.R. 383, it is said:

> The rule is clearly stated in the Restatement of the Law of Agency, §§261 and 262.
> Section 261: "A principal who puts an agent in a position that enables the agent, while apparently acting within his authority, to commit a fraud upon third persons is subject to liability to such third persons for the fraud."
> The illustrations and the comment found under these two sections are convincing. Under §261 it is said: "The principal is subject to liability under the rule stated in this section although he is entirely innocent, although he has received no benefit from the transaction, and, as stated in §262, although the agent acts solely for his own purposes. Liability is based upon the fact that the agent's position facilitates the consummation of the fraud, in that from the point of view of the third person the transaction seems regular on its face and the agent appears to be acting in the ordinary course of the business confided to him."

Appellants argue that the facts of this case do not bring it within the rationale of Civil Code, §2334 or the Restatement of Agency quoted above, because respondent, as a reasonable person of ordinary prudence, should not have been misled by Long. It is contended that the transaction whereby respondent gave Long the money and took back a receipt and a note, differed so radically from the stock purchase and sale transactions previously had with Long, that it cannot be said that respondent was misled. Appellants ably argue that as a reasonable person, respondent must have known that Long was acting for himself and not on behalf of either brokerage house when he took her money for investment. However, the trial court found to the contrary, and the familiar rule that the trier of fact is the sole judge of the credibility of the witness and of the weight of the evidence, is applicable. . . . Substantial evidence to support the finding of the trial court can be found in the record. Long testified:

Q. And didn't you advise her that Walston & Company and Dean Witter and Company had research divisions that told when to buy and when to sell stock?

A. Yes, I think I did.

Q. And didn't you tell her that the stock that she sold at that time, it was the proper time to sell the stock?

A. More than likely I did.

Q. And that she could get a better investment this way—

A. (Inter'g) Yes.

Q. (Cont'g)—through the note? And that, as far as you know, when you said to buy the note, that that would also be inferred that it was from the research division?

A. Yes.

This bit of testimony serves to show that the research services which appellants' brokerage houses used to induce customers to rely upon them for advice, contributed to the fraud in this case. It also presents the rather nice question of how appellants can concede that the part of the transaction by which respondent sold her stock through Long and the brokerage house to obtain the money was within the scope of Long's agency, while the part of the transaction whereby Long received the proceeds of the stock sale was not within the scope of his apparent authority. In short, it is difficult to see how appellants can accept the benefits of the sale of the stock by Long as their agent and deny liability for the fraudulent misuses of the money obtained by the sale of the stock. (Gift v. Ahrnke, 107 Cal. App. 2d 614, 623, 237 P.2d 706.)

Perhaps the evidence which we deem substantial in support of the judgment can best be expressed by quoting from the written opinion of the trial court, wherein the evidence is summarized thusly:

> A review of the testimony will indicate that plaintiff was an elderly widow who depended largely for her livelihood on her investments. She is not versed in business nor business transactions. She had been referred to Mr. Long by a friend, and Mr. Long visited her and discussed stock transactions. In regular stock transactions plaintiff would receive immediate confirmation from Walston and Company or Dean Witter and Company, as the case might be, would receive stock certificates from Walston or Dean Witter, would receive checks of Walston and Company or Dean Witter and Company, or would receive monthly statements from said companies. In the transactions at hand no such documents were received by plaintiff. Defendant Long gave plaintiff "promissory notes" signed by Long or plain receipts. In the regular transactions he would give a company receipt or the check would be made out to the particular stock brokerage house. Plaintiff inquired of defendant Long regarding these discrepancies and defendant stated that the new receipts or the new documents had not been printed. He stated that he was the new trustee and was acting for Walston and Company or Dean Witter and Company. She was justified in believing Long. In fact, Mr. Morrison of Dean Witter and Company said it was easy to have faith and confidence in Mr. Long, and that he did not believe that Long would defraud anyone. Mr. Smith of Walston and Company stated that Walston and Company knew Long was drinking in excess, gambling heavily, and encouraging customers to buy and sell stock merely for the purpose of promoting volume so that his commissions would be greater. Walston and Company did nothing to advise the customers of this nor of any stock exchange, customer or agent regulations. Walston and Company and Dean Witter and Company knew that this is a highly specialized and technical business, and customers rely on their employees for advice, guidance and consultation. In this case, brokerage houses placed defendant Long in position to defraud their customers. It is the finding of the Court that plaintiff acted with ordinary care.

. . . The judgment is affirmed.

CONLEY, P.J., and BROWN, J., concur.

Sennott v. Rodman & Renshaw
United States Court of Appeals, Seventh Circuit
474 F.2d 32 (1973)

PELL, CIRCUIT JUDGE.

Appellant Rodman & Renshaw, a securities brokerage house and member of the New York Stock Exchange, appeals from an adverse judgment in the district court awarding appellees Richard and Joan Sennott damages of $99,600 plus prejudgment interest. Appellant was found vicariously liable for the damage caused Sennott and his wife by the fraudulent securities manipulations of Jordan Rothbart, a former associate of Rodman & Renshaw and son of a partner in the firm. Judgments were also entered against Jordan Rothbart and his father, William Rothbart. Only Rodman & Renshaw (Rodman) appealed.

Jordan Rothbart, a commodities speculator and securities dealer apparently possessed of persuasive sales ability but a lesser standard of integrity, had at one time but not subsequent to 1958, been an employee of Rodman. No express authority to act on behalf of that firm existed subsequent to 1958; indeed it fairly appears that he was at the times here involved persona non grata to Rodman notwithstanding his father's status as a partner therein. In 1962, the Securities and Exchange Commission in an order had held that Jordan had between 1955 and 1957, while employed by another broker-dealer, violated certain anti-fraud provisions of the Securities Act. In 1958, his registration as a representative of a member of the National Association of Securities Dealers, Inc. had been revoked because of deceptive practices in the sale of securities. The Sennotts were unacquainted with this background at any material time here involved.

Jordan became a member of the Chicago Board of Trade in 1960 and engaged thereafter as a trader for his own account in commodities. Through his dealings at the Board of Trade, Jordan became acquainted with Richard Sennott who was also an active trader. Sennott traded both for himself and for the Honeymead Trading Corporation of which he was an officer.

As their relationship developed, Sennott, a more experienced commodities trader, recommended various transactions to Jordan who reciprocated by encouraging Sennott to take advantage of Jordan's father's expertise in the securities market. Specifically, Jordan told Sennott that his father had made money in the stock market for several members of the Board of Trade and that if Sennott ever wished to open a stock trading account Jordan would have one opened for him at Rodman & Renshaw. Initially Sennott declined to act on Jordan's recommendations, but in January 1964, in response to Jordan's assertion that his father thought a particular stock was a good buy, Sennott asked Jordan to purchase a limited number of shares for him. Jordan immediately went to the special Rodman telephone located on the floor of the Board of Trade and arranged for the purchase of Sennott's order through Rodman.

In the same month Jordan arranged for Sennott to open a trading account with Rodman in the name of his, Sennott's, wife. Trading through that account and six others which he subsequently opened, Sennott's trading volume with Rodman for the two-year period between 1964 and 1966 totalled more than $2,000,000. Approximately seventy per cent of this trading was done through accounts opened by Jordan Rothbart, and much of it was done on the recommendation of Jordan or his father. A typical transaction involved Jordan advising Sennott that his father believed a particular stock should be bought or sold, Sennott indicating a desire to purchase, and Jordan going to the Rodman phone on the Board of Trade floor and calling in the order. Shortly thereafter Sennott would receive a mailed confirmation slip from Rodman. Sennott, of course, paid brokerage fees on all of these transactions.

In February, 1964, Jordan and Sennott had a conversation on the floor of the Board of Trade during which Jordan told him that Skyline Homes, Inc. (Skyline) was about to be listed on the New York Stock Exchange but that the company needed more shares to be eligible. In an effort to meet the requirement, Skyline stock was made a secondary offering through Rodman & Renshaw at approximately $40 per share. Jordan's offer to procure a portion of this offering for Sennott was accepted, and it was agreed that Jordan would place an order with Rodman for 2,000 shares of Skyline. Sennott received the shares in April and went immediately to the offices of Rodman & Renshaw to deliver a check for the shares. It was on this occasion that Sennott first met William Rothbart.

While there was nothing fraudulent or improper about this or the previous sales, it was the precursor for the deception which followed. In March 1964, shortly after the order for 2,000 shares of Skyline was placed but before Sennott met William Rothbart, Jordan approached Sennott with respect to the purchase of additional shares of Skyline stock, this time through stock options which allegedly had been made available to Jordan through his father's dealings with Skyline. The district court's Finding of Fact Number 9 correctly sets forth the representations made by Jordan Rothbart:

> . . . Rothbart told Sennott that a number of options for the purchase of Skyline Homes, Inc. stock had been made available to him, that the options had initially been offered to his father William Rothbart, a partner in Rodman & Renshaw, in return for services his father had rendered Skyline Homes, Inc. in the secondary public offering referred to above and also for helping Skyline Homes, Inc. become listed on the American Stock Exchange, but that, when Rothbart's father turned down the offer because SEC regulations forbid such transactions on the part of broker-dealers, the options had been made available to him. Jordan Rothbart said that he was willing to exercise some of the options on behalf of Sennott. Jordan Rothbart also told Sennott that he was going to exercise some of the options for himself and that all the money for the options would be held in escrow in New York City until the time came for the exercise of the option rights. He told Sennott that the options would be exercised for shares of Skyline Homes, Inc. stock within seven months and that he would then deliver shares of said stock to Sennott at a price of $26.50 per share.

At the time these representations were made, Skyline was selling for approximately $40 per share. Lured by a discount of that magnitude, Sennott agreed to purchase Skyline stock through the option plan. On seven separate occasions between March 18 and October 2, 1964, Sennott placed orders and delivered checks to Jordan Rothbart for Skyline stock at the option price. Payments for these orders totalled approximately $142,000. No stock options of the type described by Jordan ever existed and the representations were obviously designed to defraud Sennott. Instead of depositing the payments in an escrow account in New York, Jordan placed each check in his wife's personal checking account at the First National Bank of Highland Park and subsequently used the money to pay his own substantial trading losses.

When Jordan Rothbart first proposed the purchase of Skyline stock through the option arrangement, it was agreed that neither party would divulge the nature of their dealings. In accordance with that agreement each of the seven payments was recorded only by handwritten cash receipts prepared by Sennott and signed by Jordan Rothbart.

When the stock which had been set for delivery on October 18, 1964, did not materialize, Sennott inquired as to the reason for the delay. He was told by Jordan that there was no reason for concern, that the temporary delay was caused by the S.E.C.'s refusal to list Skyline on the New York Stock Exchange until the company had more shareholders. Satisfied with this explanation and with Jordan's assurance that the stock would be forthcoming soon, Sennott took no further action with respect to the Skyline options until early November 1964 when he was summoned to a meeting with the managing partner of Rodman & Renshaw, Vernon Carroll.

The circumstances of this meeting warrant detailed scrutiny. In October or early November, Jordan Rothbart approached Sennott on the floor of the Board of Trade and asked him to accompany him to a public phone to speak with William Rothbart. In the course of their conversation, William Rothbart told Sennott that Mr. Carroll wanted to meet with him to discuss the Skyline options but that the matters which Mr. Carroll wished to discuss were none of his business. Sennott was then advised not to cooperate with Carroll. Accompanied by Jordan, Sennott went to the offices of Rodman & Renshaw that afternoon to meet with Carroll. Jordan's father met them at the door and again told Sennott the option transactions were none of Carroll's business. At this time, he also added that Sennott should not worry, he would get his stock options. All three men then went to Carroll's office where Carroll produced several of the checks Sennott had given Jordan Rothbart for the options. Carroll then sought to question Sennott with respect to how the checks happened to have been endorsed by Dolores Rothbart (Jordan's wife) and deposited in her account in the First National Bank of Highland Park. Sennott, while admittedly shocked by this revelation, told Carroll it was none of his business and refused to disclose the nature of his dealings with Jordan. Immediately after the conference, Sennott asked Jordan Rothbart about the checks and was told that they were deposited in the Rothbart account so Jordan, who asserted he was purchasing equal amounts of Skyline stock, could pay for the total stock purchase with a single check. Apparently this explanation satisfied Sennott since he made no further inquiries on the matter. Indeed, when again summoned to Carroll's office a few weeks later, he voluntarily signed a letter of indemnity protecting Rodman & Renshaw from liability for any failure on their part to investigate fully the signatures on the checks.

However, when several months had passed without delivery, Sennott again pressed Jordan for an explanation. On February 26, 1965, as a result of this inquiry, Jordan delivered 1,000 shares of Skyline common stock in street name to Sennott. This stock was purchased through Jordan's own broker, not Rodman & Renshaw, on the open market and merely signed over to Sennott in an effort to deceive him into believing he was receiving part of his "stock options." The deception was effective for, although Sennott continued his requests for the balance of the stock, he made no further inquiry into the actual facts surrounding the late options.

Between February 26, 1965, and January 20, 1966, Jordan delivered an additional 2,200 shares of Skyline common stock to Sennott. Delivery of this stock was made in six installments. As before, each delivery consisted of stock purchased on the open market for the market price. . . . [T]he value of the shares at the time received totalled $82,600.

In the spring of 1966, Sennott, who apparently had been oblivious to the waving banners of suspect practices of which he was the victim, learned that another member of the Board of Trade had filed a $75,000 claim against Jordan Rothbart with the Board of Directors alleging a fraudulent scheme remarkably similar to the circumstances of Sennott's own transactions with Jordan. At approximately the same time, Sennott also learned that Jordan Rothbart had previously been expelled from the securities market. Until that time, Sennott had been unaware of Jordan's prior fraudulent practices or his dismissal from Rodman. In spite of these revelations, however, Sennott clung to the hope that the stock would be delivered, and, in an effort to facilitate that vain hope, when summoned before the Business Conduct Committee investigating Jordan Rothbart, he refused to cooperate or disclose his dealings. Indeed, not until May 1966, after numerous delivery dates had passed without receipt of further shares of stock, did Sennott go to William Rothbart to inquire about the stock options. Sennott described his meeting with William Rothbart at the Rodman office. "I let Bill know exactly what was going on as far as no delivery of the Skyline Homes, that he [Jordan] was probably going to be expelled from the Chicago Board of Trade, at which time Bill Rothbart told me there was nothing he could do about it."

Jordan was expelled from the Board of Trade in June 1966 for refusing to turn his financial records over to the Business Conduct Committee. At that point he ceased coming to the floor of the Board of Trade and Sennott discontinued his unsuccessful efforts to procure delivery of the stock by telephone. Only after all else had failed did Sennott approach Rodman with evidence of the scheme.

At the conclusion of a bench trial on the merits, the trial judge found Rodman vicariously liable for the losses caused the Sennotts. Liability was based upon several theories set forth in the court's conclusions of law. First, the court concluded that William Rothbart "knowingly assisted and participated in the efforts of Jordan Rothbart to defraud plaintiffs," in violation of Section 10(b) of the Securities Exchange Act of 1934 and Rule 10b-5 adopted by the Securities and Exchange Commission thereunder, Section 9(a)(4) of the Securities Exchange Act of 1934, and Section 17(a) of the Securities Act of 1933. The court then held that not only William Rothbart's knowledge of the solicitation of stock business by Jordan at the Board of Trade but also his knowledge of the false representations to Sennott regarding Skyline was acquired within the scope of the Rodman partnership business and therefore was imputed to and binding upon Rodman. In addition, the judge concluded that because Rodman "knew or should have known" of the illegal conduct of William and Jordan Rothbart, it was equally liable with them for the false representations. . . .

The ground rules for our review are well-established and need not be repeated here. . . . Assigning the matter of credibility to the district court we turn therefore to a determination of whether there is substantial evidence to support the findings of fact and whether the court erred as to the applicable law.

Taking the agency questions first, it is clear that Rodman must be deemed to have had knowledge of all of the securities transactions which Jordan solicited for his father prior to the inception of the fraudulent stock option scheme. In that situation, the knowledge of William Rothbart is, under general principles of agency, imputed to the partnership. Had plaintiff been defrauded in one of those transactions, Rodman's liability would seem to be unquestionable. Those transactions, however, do not comprise the substance of this lawsuit. On the contrary, the facts upon which liability must be established in this case, if at all, are critically different. While the evidence leaves no doubt that William Rothbart, having processed the orders and his firm having received a broker's fee, had knowledge of the solicitations of Jordan in the prior transactions, the record is silent as to a basis upon which the district court could properly have inferred that William had knowledge at any pertinent time of his son's stock option deception.

We are at a loss as to the basis in the record for the district court's conclusion that William Rothbart "knowingly assisted and participated" in the fraud. Indeed, the first contact the plaintiff had with William respecting the options took place in November 1964, after all of the payments for the stock had been made. This is not a pertinent time. There is no evidence that prior to the Carroll meeting William Rothbart did anything to induce Sennott to subject himself to Jordan's defalcations, nor that he had any knowledge of what was transpiring until after the fact.

Further, we find no reason to believe that Sennott considered William Rothbart to be any part of the transaction other than that he had been the original offeree of the mythical options. In fact, Sennott himself indicated that his understanding of Jordan's stricture of confidentiality to be he should not say a word about the transaction to anybody including William Rothbart. Sennott also testified that it was never his understanding that the option shares were coming from or through Rodman but he imagined they would be coming from the Skyline corporation itself. Finally, Sennott admitted on cross-examination that he had testified in his deposition that when asked by investigators for the Illinois Securities Commission, which was looking into his complaint against Jordan, whether William Rothbart had ever participated or conspired with Jordan to perpetrate the option fraud, he had replied, "[N]o, not to my knowledge."[4]

Citing Crittendon v. State Oil Company, 78 Ill. App. 2d 112, 115, 222 N.E.2d 561, 563-564 (1966), Sennott contends on this appeal that Rodman & Renshaw is estopped by its conduct from claiming that Jordan was not its representative. Again, we do not disagree as to the transactions handled through that firm, but those are not the ones with which we are now concerned. Sennott also speaks of "apparent agency" established by Rodman. Without becoming involved in the semantic niceties of distinctions, if any, between ostensible agency, apparent agency, and agency by estoppel, we note that Crittendon (78 Ill. App. 2d at 116, 222 N.E.2d at 564) states that "[i]t is essential to the application of the doctrine of estoppel that such conduct or representations be relied and acted upon. . . ."

---

4. This would seem consistent with Sennott's description of his May 1966 meeting with William Rothbart at which he "let Bill know exactly what was going on as far as no delivery of the Skyline Homes. . . ." When questioned about that meeting, Sennott stated in deposition:

"And at this particular time is when I said, 'Well, you know, Bill, whether you realize it or not, it was supposedly offered to you and that because you were a senior partner in Rodman & Renshaw, Jordie told me, under the SEC rules you couldn't accept it.'"

"He said, 'Well, that's not true.' He said, 'I knew nothing of the stock options in Skyline.'"

"And again I asked him, 'Why did you tell me before going to Carroll's office not to worry? I'd get my stock options in Skyline.'"

"He said, 'Because Jordie had assured me that you would.'"

Under Sennott's theory of apparent authority or estoppel, therefore, plaintiff would be required to prove that he was relying upon Jordan's apparent authority, and hence on Rodman, when he decided to purchase the Skyline options. Reliance is not evident from the record before us. Indeed, the converse is clearly demonstrated, for not only did the fraudulent representations never involve Rodman but both Sennott and Jordan Rothbart actively sought to prevent Rodman from discovering the option transactions. Sennott agreed to keep the option plan secret, including from Rodman, and intentionally used personal payment receipts to record Sennott's payments. The strongest evidence of the plaintiffs' lack of reliance upon Rodman, however, is seen in Sennott's refusal to cooperate with Carroll's inquiry into the endorsements on Sennott's checks. Had Sennott been relying on Rodman's participation in the option plan, it is unlikely that he would have refused even to discuss the matter with a representative of Rodman. On the contrary, Sennott's own statements belie such reliance. Responding to an inquiry by defendant's attorney, Sennott observed, "[W]ith regard to this money that had been invested, I really felt that this thing would have completely gone undetected by Rodman & Renshaw had not that check been made out of the profit sharing."

The Sennotts also place considerable reliance on Blackburn v. Dean Witter, 201 Cal. App. 2d 518, 19 Cal. Rptr. 842 (5th Dist. Ct. App. 1962), a case which they assert is "squarely in point." There, a registered representative of the defendant brokerage house persuaded the plaintiff to invest in stock of a nonexistent company. The plaintiff then, as Sennott did here, sold some stock through the brokerage house to finance the purchase of the nonexistent stock. The brokerage house was subsequently found liable for the fraudulent acts of its representative. While *Blackburn* is factually similar to this case, a major distinction exists. The plaintiff in the *Blackburn* case was a customer who believed that he was purchasing stock through the brokerage house in the same manner as he had previously made purchases, and, as such, was relying on the expertise and integrity of the brokerage. Both the agency and the reliance elements were unquestionably present. Here, however, while some type of implied agency may well have existed as to other transactions, there was no reliance upon this agency in the transactions in question. Simply stated, the damage Jordan Rothbart inflicted upon the plaintiffs was a result of Sennott's misplaced reliance upon Jordan Rothbart and not upon Rodman & Renshaw.

Having reviewed the record at length and found that the evidence supports neither plaintiffs' theory that William Rothbart had knowledge of his son's reprehensible scheme which was imputable to Rodman nor their theory of apparent authority, we are forced to reject the trial court's factual findings and legal conclusions with respect to these issues. . . .

Reversed and remanded.

2 *Partnerships*

A. Introduction

1. Traditional Noncorporate Business Associations

a. The General Partnership

UPA (1997) §§103, 202, 301, 306, 401, 601, 801

Partnership law, both judicial and statutory, provides a set of standard form, off-the-rack rules for persons who wish jointly to own and operate a firm. These partnership rules are an amalgam of well-developed common law and equitable doctrines, now largely codified. Every state except Louisiana bases its partnership law on the Uniform Partnership Act ("UPA (1914)") or the Uniform Partnership Act (1997) ("UPA (1997)"). However, these statutory provisions contemplate that courts will continue to provide particularized rules via ex post adjudication to enforce fiduciary duties or otherwise ensure equitable results.

It is quite easy to adopt the standard form rules provided by general partnership law. All that is required is formation of a general partnership. Similar to formation of the principal-agent relationship, formation of a general partnership requires no written agreement or governmental action. All that is required is a statutorily specified mutual manifestation of consent. Under partnership law norms, the association of two or more persons to carry on as co-owners a business for profit creates a partnership.

The standard form rules provided by general partnership law will not be ideal for all general partnerships. Thus, it will be important to develop an understanding of which rules can be varied, and what factors would cause rational persons to expend the resources necessary to accomplish such modifications.

At the same time, the immutable and default rules of partnership law do provide an ideal governance structure for certain jointly owned firms. Therefore, it is helpful to think of general partnership law in relation to an archetypical general partnership. Presumably, many of the provisions of general partnership law save transaction costs for the archetypical general partnership because the standard form rules are those that the partners would themselves select if they could rationally and without cost bargain for a fully contingent contract.

The archetypical general partnership, for which general partnership law's default and immutable rules are ideal, is a small, intimate firm in which each partner participates in all aspects of the business and has substantial confidence in the trustworthiness and skill of fellow partners. The defining characteristics of general partnership form, discussed below, are consistent with and reinforce the typical partner's expectations.

Equal sharing of ownership and management functions.   A sole proprietor usually performs three ownership and management functions. First, she is the residual claimant and ultimate risk bearer—the person who takes what is left, if anything, after all employees and other creditors have been paid. Second, she oversees the business and affairs of her firm, developing business policies and directing their implementation. Third, the sole proprietor sits at the top of the firm's day-to-day operational hierarchy, empowered to act on behalf of the firm in interactions with the firm's employees, customers, suppliers, and creditors.

General partnership norms distribute these ownership and management functions equally either to each partner or to the partners as a group. Thus, each partner is a residual claimant, has a full and equal right to participate in management of the firm, and has an equal right to act as an agent of the partnership. Partnership law norms also assign to each partner an equal share of profits and an equal responsibility for losses.

Because partners have equal rights in management and profits, general partnership law norms will be most efficient if partners make similar contributions of services and capital. Conversely, tension might develop if some partners contribute only money capital while others contribute only services, or if substantial differences exist in the quality or character of the partners' contributions.

Individual partner's adaptability to changed circumstances favored over firm's continuity and adaptability.   In a sole proprietorship, agency and employment law default rules allow the proprietor to adapt to changed circumstances by hiring and firing agents at will, by changing the course or nature of the business at will, and by terminating the firm at will. Normally, a proprietor may so adapt without risk of liability to an agent or employee damaged by the adaptive action.

Under general partnership law default rules, if the partnership wishes to terminate its association with a partner, it may do so only by dissolving the partnership and paying the expelled partner the value of her interest in cash. Thus, adaptation by changing the makeup of the team comes at a price: lack of stability and continuity. For small, unspecialized firms, this is an acceptable price. For firms with more specialized capital, continuity may hold a higher value.

Likewise, general partnership law's decision-making norms sacrifice somewhat the firm's adaptability in favor of each partner's participatory rights. Ordinary decisions may be made by majority vote of the partners. However, extraordinary decisions and changes in the partnership agreement require unanimity. Again, these rules may be modified by private ordering.

Unlimited personal liability.   Under general partnership norms, all partners are jointly and severally liable for all obligations of the partnership and there is no limit on this potential personal liability. Thus, the misconduct of one partner could result in financial ruin for fellow partners. Unlimited liability is most palatable when each partner will easily be able to monitor the activities of other partners and agents.

Fiduciary duty. Fiduciary duty reduces the likelihood that one or more partners will misuse their ownership powers or rights. Under well-established equitable doctrines, each partner owes a fiduciary duty to other partners. This mutual duty to act fairly and honestly reinforces the notion that the archetypical general partnership is an intimate relation among equals who have combined forces in pursuit of a common good. Many commentators have described fiduciary duty as the defining characteristic of general partnership law. We will have a number of occasions to consider that proposition throughout this chapter.

b. Joint Ventures

Common law courts distinguished between general partnerships, wherein associates carry on a business as co-owners, and joint ventures, wherein associates join to exploit a particular opportunity.

While the line between general partnership and joint venture is not bright, the label "joint venture" continues to connote a less permanent and less complete merging of assets and interests than does the label "general partnership." For example, a joint venture is defined in Florida Tomato Packers, Inc. v. Wilson, 296 So.2d 536, 539 (Fla. Dist. Ct. App. 1974), as the legal relationship between "two or more persons, who, in some specific venture, seek a profit jointly without the existence between them of any actual partnership, corporation, or other business entity."

At common law, partnerships and joint ventures were governed by similar, if not identical, rules of law. This continues to be true even though the Uniform Partnership Acts literally apply only to partnerships. However, there may be subtle differences between the rules applied to a joint venture that relate to the less permanent and complete merging of interests in such associations. For instance, third parties may not be able to assume that joint venturers have agency powers equal to those of general partners. And joint venturers may have greater room to prefer their own interests than fiduciary duty allows to general partners.

An important current use of joint ventures is by larger corporate firms that unite for a single purpose, such as a joint research project or a joint marketing effort. The terms of such relationships are carefully negotiated and specified in written agreements that preserve the separate identity and purposes of the venturers. As you proceed through this chapter, consider why and how two such firms uniting to pursue a joint venture would choose to vary the normal rules provided by general partnership law. Later, as you study corporate law, consider why corporate form is not selected for such single-purpose ventures.

c. The Limited Partnership

Uniform Limited Partnership Act (2001)
§§102(8)-(13), 107, 110, 301-303, 401-404, 603, 604

A limited partnership is a business association composed of one or more general partners and one or more limited partners. A limited partnership is formed by filing a certificate of limited partnership with the secretary of state in the jurisdiction chosen by the parties. The defining characteristics of the limited partnership differ markedly from those of the general partnership.

Separation of ownership and management functions.   In a limited partnership, ownership and management functions are divided among the firm's general and limited partners. Under statutory default norms, limited partners have essentially no management power and no authority to act as agents in carrying out the partnership's business. General partners are the active participants in the firm, empowered to make and carry out the firm's business policies.

Limited liability.   Limited partners are not personally liable for the limited partnership's obligations. General partners, as in a general partnership, are jointly and severally liable for the firm's obligations.

Firm's continuity and adaptability to changed circumstances favored over individual's adaptability.   Under limited partnership default rules, general partners may withdraw from the partnership at will, but limited partners may not. Unlike in a general partnership, however, such withdrawal does not automatically or necessarily trigger dissolution and liquidation of the limited partnership. Decision-making rules also favor the firm's adaptability. As in general partnership law, general partners make ordinary decisions by majority vote and extraordinary decisions unanimously.

2. Emergence of Additional Limited Liability Entities as the Norm

a. Impetus for New Forms

The 1980s saw a substantial increase in malpractice litigation aimed at accountants, lawyers, and other professionals, most of whose firms were then organized as general partnerships. This phenomenon caused increasing disenchantment with a central feature of general partnership form—its requirement that all partners be jointly and severally liable for the firm's obligations, including claims arising out of another partner's negligence or misconduct. Dissatisfaction with the risks associated with partnership form led smaller firms to adopt corporate form (often under a separate professional corporation code available in many states).

However, for medium- and large-sized professional firms, the corporation was not a desirable alternative. Although corporate form would provide protection from vicarious liability, only smaller firms could adopt S corporation status or otherwise avoid the entity level tax imposed on incorporated enterprises under Subchapter C of the Internal Revenue Code. Accordingly, planners and policy makers considered and debated alternative means to provide the favorable tax treatment of general partnership form while avoiding its unfavorable limited liability rules. At the forefront of the overlapping lobbying and law reform effort were members of the accounting and legal professions. Largely because of the intense special interest efforts of these two groups, the 1990s saw the remarkably rapid acceptance of two new "limited liability entities": the limited liability company and the registered limited liability partnership.

b. The Limited Liability Partnership

UPA (1997) §§306, 1001
ULPA (2001) §§102(9), 404(c)

From the standpoint of sophisticated business venturers, the traditional general partnership and limited partnership business forms have a central drawback—general partners are personally liable for the firm's obligations. In the 1990s the landscape changed dramatically. A new business form, the limited liability company (LLC), was authorized in every American state. Chapter 6 provides a detailed look at this relatively new business entity. One of the characteristics of the LLC is "limited liability." In other words, if an LLC were unable to satisfy its obligations, its owners (members) would lose only the capital they had actually invested in the company; LLC members would not be personally liable for the debts and obligations of the LLC that could not be satisfied out of the firm's assets.

The nationwide acceptance of the LLC was accompanied by a rethinking of the traditional liability rules of general and limited partnership law. As a result, by the beginning of the twenty-first century every American state had recognized two new business entities—the limited liability partnership (LLP) and the limited liability limited partnership (LLLP). The sole purpose of the two new entities was to make limited liability available as an opt-in default rule for firms operating as a general or limited partnership.

To become an LLP an existing or newly created general partnership simply registers with the secretary of state as an LLP. A limited partnership follows the same registration procedure to become an LLLP. Most states require a nominal initial and annual renewal fee. Once created, an LLP is governed by general partnership law in all respects except for special statutory liability and asset-distribution-limiting provisions designed to protect third parties. An LLLP is similarly governed by limited partnership law.

The early LLP statutes were adopted in response to demands by large professional partnerships; principals in these firms felt that it was fundamentally unfair that they faced vicarious liability for the misdeeds of a fellow partner, when owners of corporations and LLCs did not. Accordingly, the norm in early LLP statutes was to eliminate the general partners' vicarious liability for professional negligence, but not to eliminate liability for ordinary contract claims. However, the trend in later LLP and LLLP statutes has been to protect general partners fully from personal liability, thereby giving general partners the same security as members in an LLC or shareholders in a corporation.

3. Determining the Legal Nature of the Relationship

UPA (1997) §§202, 203

Carrying out a business venture as partners may result in very different risks and rewards than would ensue from carrying out the same venture as employer and employee, lender and borrower, or through other contractual arrangements. Unfortunately, determining whether one is or is not in a partnership is not always easy. If the business relationship sours, the legal nature of that relationship may become a prime focus of litigation between the parties, and the label placed on the relationship by the parties is not controlling. Accordingly, participants in a business venture will sometimes discover to their surprise that they are not partners (or joint venturers) when they had always thought they were, or that they are partners (or joint venturers) despite their contrary assumption.

Byker v. Mannes
Supreme Court of Michigan, 2002
641 N.W.2d 210

MARKMAN, J. . . .

I. FACTS AND PROCEEDINGS

This case arises out of an alleged partnership between plaintiff David Byker and defendant Tom Mannes. In 1985, plaintiff was doing accounting work for defendant. The two individuals talked about going into business together because they had complementary business skills—defendant could locate certain properties because of his real estate background and plaintiff could raise money for their property purchases. Indeed, the parties stipulated the following:

> [T]he Plaintiff . . . and Defendant . . . agreed to engage in an ongoing business enterprise, to furnish capital, labor and/or skill to such enterprise, to raise investment funds and to share equally in the profits, losses and expenses of such enterprise. . . . In order to facilitate investment of limited partners, Byker and Mannes created separate entities wherein they were general partners or shareholders for the purposes of operating each separate entity.

Over a period of several years, the parties pursued various business enterprises. They have stipulated that the following business entities were created during this time:

a. A 100% general partner interest in M & B Properties Limited Partnership, a Michigan limited partnership, which limited partnership owns a 50% partnership interest in Hall Street Partners, a Michigan partnership.

b. A 100% general partner interest in M & B Properties Limited Partnership II, a Michigan limited partnership, which limited partnership owns a 50% partnership interest in Breton Commercial Properties, a Michigan partnership.

c. A 66-2/3% of the issued and outstanding shares of the common stock of JTD Properties, Inc., a Michigan corporation, which is the general partner of JTD Properties Limited Partnership I, a Michigan limited partnership, and which is also the general partner of M & B Properties Limited Partnership III, a Michigan limited partnership. The interest was later increased to 100% when John Noel left the partnership.

d. A 66-2/3% of the issued and outstanding shares of the common stock of Pier 1000 Ltd., a Michigan corporation. The interest was later increased to 100% when John Noel left the partnership.

e. A 66-2/3% general partner interest in BMW Properties, a Michigan partnership.

With regard to these entities, the parties shared equally in the commissions, financing fees, and termination costs. The parties also personally guaranteed loans from several financial institutions.

The business relationship between the parties began to deteriorate after the creation of Pier 1000 Ltd., which was created to own and manage a marina. Shortly after the creation of Pier 1000 Ltd., the marina encountered serious financial difficulties. To address these difficulties, the parties placed their profits from M & B Limited Partnership II into Pier 1000 Ltd. and borrowed money from several financial institutions.

Eventually, defendant refused to make any additional monetary contributions. Plaintiff, however, continued to make loan payments and incurred accounting fees on behalf of Pier 1000 Ltd., as well as on behalf of other business entities. Plaintiff also entered into several individual loans for the benefit of Pier 1000 Ltd. These business transactions were performed without defendant's knowledge.

The marina was eventually returned to its previous owners in exchange for their assumption of plaintiff's and defendant's business obligations. At this point, the business ventures between plaintiff and defendant ceased.

Plaintiff then approached defendant with regard to equalizing payments as a result of the losses incurred from the various entities. Defendant testified that this was the first time that he had received notice from plaintiff concerning any outstanding payments, and that he was "absolutely dumbfounded" by plaintiff's request for money.

After unsuccessfully seeking reimbursement from defendant, plaintiff filed suit for the recovery of the money on the basis that the parties had entered into a partnership.[1] Specifically, plaintiff asserted that the obligations between him and defendant were not limited to their formal business relationships established by the individual partnerships and corporate entities, but that there was a "general" partnership underlying all their business affairs. In response, defendant asserted that he merely invested in separate business ventures with plaintiff and that there were no other understandings between them.

The case proceeded to a bench trial where the trial court determined that the parties had created a general partnership.[2] The court observed that, although Michigan had not formally adopted §202 of the 1994 Uniform Partnership Act (1994 UPA),[3] the law in Michigan is that parties must merely have an intent to carry on a business for profit, not a subjective intent to create a partnership. On this basis, the trial court concluded that the parties had maintained a business relationship that constituted a partnership. It stated:

> Having weighed the credibility of the witnesses, principally plaintiff and defendant, we conclude that they began their relationship with a general agreement that they were partners and would share profits and losses equally. Whether understood or not they had a general or super partnership. The evidence supports that both understood it.

1. The parties stipulated that the alleged partnership was never memorialized in a written partnership agreement, had no formal name, no tax identification number, and no income tax filings.

2. The trial court and the Court of Appeals termed the alleged partnership at issue a "super" partnership. The trial court defined such a partnership as one that, although not entailing a formal business relationship by the parties, is a "general partnership between them underlying all of their business affairs." Because the statutory and case law merely define a "partnership," this Court will simply use that term without embellishment.

3. The Uniform Partnership Act, originally adopted in 1914, is a statement of partnership law drafted by the National Conference of Commissioners on Uniform State Laws and is intended to contribute to the uniformity of state laws.

Defendant appealed to the Court of Appeals, which reversed. Unpublished opinion per curiam, issued February 1, 2000 (Docket No. 205266). In part, the Court of Appeals stated that the trial court incorrectly relied on §202 "for the proposition that 'the association of two or more persons to carry on as co-owners of business for profit forms a partnership, *whether or not the persons intend to form a partnership.*" Slip op at 2 (emphasis in original). Further, it stated that "[t]he absence of intent to form a partnership contradicts the established law in this state that the *mutual* intent of the parties is of *prime* importance in ascertaining whether a partnership exists." Id. (emphasis in original). Upon review of the facts, the Court of Appeals determined that the parties clearly did not intend to form a partnership.[4] Id. at 3. . . .

II. STANDARD OF REVIEW

Whether Michigan partnership law, M.C.L. §449.6(1), requires a subjective intent to form a partnership or merely an intent to carry on as co-owners a business for profit is a question of law. This Court reviews questions of law under a de novo standard of review.

III. DISCUSSION

UNIFORM PARTNERSHIP ACTS

In 1917, the Michigan Legislature drafted the Michigan Uniform Partnership Act. In this act, a partnership was defined as "an association of two [2] or more persons to carry on as co-owners a business for profit. . . ." Id. at §6. Over the years, the definition has remained essentially constant. At present, partnership is defined as "an association of 2 or more persons, which may consist of husband and wife, to carry on as co-owners a business for profit. . . ." M.C.L. §449.6(1). This definition, as well as its predecessors, was modeled after the definition of partnership set forth in the 1914 UPA. In 1914, the UPA had defined a partnership as "an association of two or more persons to carry on as owners a business for profit." Uniform Partnership Act of 1914, §6. In construing §6, courts had "universal[ly]" determined that a partnership was formed by "the association of persons whose intent is to carry on as co-owners a business for profit, regardless of their subjective intention to be 'partners.'" See Uniform Partnership Act of 1994, §202, Comment 1.

In 1994, however, the UPA definition of partnership was amended by the National Conference of Commissioners. The amended definition stated that "the association of two or more persons to carry on as co-owners a business for profit forms a partnership, whether or not the persons intend to form a partnership." Section 202 (emphasis added). Although the commissioners were apparently satisfied with the existing judicial construction of the definition of partnership, the commissioners added the

---

4. A significant factor in the Court of Appeals finding was the fact that the parties were unaware that they had formed a partnership until nine years after the parties entered into their informal relationship.

new language "whether or not the persons intend to form a partnership" in order to "codif[y] the universal judicial construction of UPA Section 6(1) that a partnership is created by the association of persons whose intent is to carry on as co-owners a business for profit, regardless of their subjective intention to be 'partners.'" Section 202 (Comment 1). The commissioners emphasized that "[n]o substantive change in the law" was intended by the amendment of §6. Id. To date, Michigan has not adopted the amended definition of partnership.

B. MCL 449.6(1)

Although Michigan has not adopted the amended definition of partnership as set forth in §202 of the Uniform Partnership Act of 1994, we believe nonetheless that M.C.L. §449.6 is consistent with that amendment. As stated numerous times by this Court, it is essential that this Court discern and give effect to the Legislature's intent. In doing so, we must examine the language contained within the applicable statutory provision. If the language is clear and unambiguous, this Court will presume that the Legislature intended the meaning plainly expressed and will enforce the statute as written. Wickens v. Oakwood Healthcare System, 465 Mich. 53, 60, 631 N.W.2d 686 (2001).

As already noted, a partnership in Michigan is statutorily defined as "an association of 2 or more persons, which may consist of husband and wife, to carry on as co-owners a business for profit. . . ." M.C.L. §449.6(1). That is, if the parties associate themselves to "carry on" as co-owners a business for profit, they will be deemed to have formed a partnership relationship regardless of their subjective intent to form such a legal relationship. The statutory language is devoid of any requirement that the individuals have the subjective intent to create a partnership. Stated more plainly, the statute does not require "partners" to be aware of their status as partners in order to have a legal partnership. . . .

C. COMMON LAW

Although the provisions of M.C.L. §449.6(1) set forth the standard for determining whether a partnership has been formed, we note that the Court of Appeals relied heavily on several of our earlier cases that, in the Court's view, focused this inquiry on whether the parties mutually intended to form a partnership. However, upon further examination of these cases, we respectfully disagree with the Court of Appeals. Rather, we find that, despite language that could potentially lead to such a conclusion, these cases, in fact, contemplated an examination of all the parties' acts and conduct in determining the existence of a partnership. . . .

Accordingly, we believe that our prior case law has, consistent with M.C.L. §449.6(1), properly examined the requirements of a legal partnership by focusing on whether the parties intentionally acted as co-owners of a business for profit, and not on whether they consciously intended to create the legal relationship of "partnership." We emphasize, however, that any future development of case law regarding partnership in our state must take place in accord with the provisions of the Michigan Partnership Act.

IV. CONCLUSION

With the language of the statute as our focal point, we conclude that . . . in ascertaining the existence of a partnership, the proper focus is on whether the parties intended to, and in fact did, "carry on as co-owners a business for profit" and not on whether the parties subjectively intended to form a partnership. . . . Accordingly, we remand this matter to the Court of Appeals for analysis under the proper test for determining the existence of a partnership under the Michigan Uniform Partnership Act.

Hynansky v. Vietri
Delaware Court of Chancery, 2003
2003 WL 21976031

NOBLE, VICE CHANCELLOR.

I.

Plaintiff John Hynansky ("Hynansky") and Defendant Albert A. Vietri ("Vietri") entered into a business venture in 1988 to purchase and develop a parcel of land in Delaware County, Pennsylvania (the "Parcel"). Because of zoning obstacles, the Parcel could not be rezoned as the parties had intended and eventually it was sold at a substantial loss. Hynansky brings this action to obtain payment by Vietri of his initial capital contribution, which Vietri never made, and Vietri's pro rata share of the business venture's losses.

II.

During the closing on the acquisition of the Parcel on January 9, 1989, Vietri and Hynansky executed a document (the "Agreement") that purportedly established "JHV Associates" (the "Partnership") and provided in part:

PARTNERSHIP AGREEMENT
JHV ASSOCIATES

THIS PARTNERSHIP AGREEMENT is made effective as of January 9, 1989, by and between two parties: John Hynansky and Albert Vietri, being sometimes individually referred to herein as a "Partner" and collectively as the "Partners."

1. Formation. A partnership (the "Partnership") is hereby formed under and pursuant to the provisions of the Delaware Uniform Partnership Law, 6 Del. C. S 1501 et seq. (the "Delaware Act").

2. Name. The business of the Partnership shall be conducted under the name "JHV Associates" . . .

3. Purpose. The purpose of the Partnership is to own, develop and lease real property in Delaware County, Pennsylvania.

4. Partners. The Partners of the Partnership shall consist of the parties hereto. . . .

5. Principal Office. The principal office of the Partnership shall be maintained. . . . .

6. Term. The Partnership shall continue for a term of fifty (50) years from and after the date hereof, unless earlier terminated pursuant to Section 17 hereof.

7. Capital Contributions. The initial capital of the Partnership, contributed in cash by the Partners, is as follows:

> Hynansky $34,555.15
> Vietri $33,200.03

8. Capital Accounts. A separate capital account shall be maintained for each Partner. . . . .

Thus, even the most cursory review of the Agreement would have revealed that it had been drafted to create a partnership. In addition, the documents contemporaneously executed by Vietri to acquire the Parcel and to finance its acquisition clearly indicated that the acquiring entity was a partnership and that Vietri was executing the closing documents, including, specifically, the note and the mortgage, as a "Partner."[5]

Although Vietri acknowledges that he signed the various documents, including the Agreement, and that he saw the term "Partner," he now asserts that he did not read the Agreement. Instead, he contends that he relied upon his attorney (who was also representing Hynansky and the Partnership) to implement the business arrangement in accordance with his understanding that the business would be conducted under some type of limited liability entity.[6] Vietri also maintains that he was not to become an equity participant in the venture until the Parcel had been successfully rezoned.[7] When he raised this issue with the attorney, the attorney, according to Vietri, told him that he was receiving his equity interest at closing on the acquisition of the Parcel in order to avoid a subsequent transfer tax that otherwise would have been paid at the time Vietri became entitled to his equity interest.[8] Because of their inability to obtain a favorable rezoning, Hynansky and Vietri agreed to sell the Parcel in 1994 for a price significantly below the purchase price paid in 1989.

III.

Hynansky has moved for summary judgment.[9] His motion presents several issues. First, Hynansky asserts that the business venture was a Delaware general partnership known as JHV Associates. Second, Hynansky, assuming that the formation of a partnership will be confirmed, seeks dissolution of that partnership because it no longer has any useful purpose. Third, because Vietri never made any monetary contributions to the Partnership, Hynansky seeks payment by Vietri of his required capital contribution and reimbursement from Vietri of his proportionate share of the Partnership's losses which Hynansky absorbed from Vietri's share of the venture.

---

5. Both the note and the mortgage identify the borrower as "JHV Associates, a Delaware general partnership."

6. The contract of sale for the Parcel, negotiated by Hynansky, identified the purchaser as "JHV Inc."

7. Aff. of Albert A. Vietri P 3.

8. Id. P 5.

9. Vietri has also moved for summary judgment and sought sanctions under Court of Chancery Rule 11 against Hynansky.

Vietri concedes that he and Hynansky both executed a "partnership agreement"—the Agreement, which clearly and unambiguously purported to establish a general partnership. Vietri, however, contends that he understood that the business venture would be conducted through a corporation or limited partnership and that his contribution to the venture would not be cash but, instead, would be his experience and expertise in the real estate business.[10] Vietri also asserts that he was not to become an equity participant unless and until he obtained the rezoning. Vietri recognizes that his efforts to tender such assertions implicate the parol evidence rule. . . .

IV.

The cross-motions for summary judgment are, of course, governed by the familiar standard of Court of Chancery Rule 56: a party seeking summary judgment may obtain that relief if there are no material facts in dispute and he is entitled to judgment as a matter of law.

V.

A. THE PAROL EVIDENCE RULE

Initially, I undertake a brief review of the parol evidence rule, which the parties agree is critical to the resolution of this matter. "The parol evidence rule . . . prevents the use of extrinsic evidence of an oral agreement to vary a fully integrated agreement that the parties have reduced to writing. . . ."

C. FULLY INTEGRATED AGREEMENT

In order for the parol evidence rule to apply in all its splendor, one must first present a "fully integrated agreement." The factors to be assessed in ascertaining whether a contract is fully integrated include: "whether the writing was carefully and formally drafted, whether the writing addresses the questions that would naturally arise out of the subject matter, and whether it expresses the final intentions of the parties." Here, the Agreement was a formal document, evidencing the typical degree of care associated with establishing a relatively straightforward partnership arrangement. The questions, material for present purposes, of the nature of the business venture, and the parties' immediate rights in the venture, were clearly answered by explicit language creating a partnership, without any suggestion that it was anything other than a general partnership, and by the clear expression that Vietri became a partner upon execution of the Agreement without any suggestion that any other condition precedent, such as obtaining the rezoning, controlled the vesting.

---

10. By 1988, Vietri had been engaged in real estate development or sales for almost two decades. Vietri Dep., Pl.'s Mot., Tab 2 at 9-10.

The intentions of the parties are best expressed by the language of the Agreement; Paragraph 21 provides:

> 21. *Entire Agreement/Amendments.* This Agreement contains the entire understanding between the parties with respect to the Partnership and supercedes all prior written and oral agreements between them. There are no representations, agreements, arrangements or understandings, oral or written, between the Partners relating to the subject matter of this Agreement which are not fully expressed herein. This Agreement may not be amended or modified except by written instrument executed by all of the Partners.

Thus, through the integration clause of Paragraph 21 of the Agreement, Hynansky and Vietri "clearly assented to the Agreement as their complete understanding as evidenced by the integration clause." Indeed, the text of the Agreement demonstrates that it was the intention of the parties to execute an integrated agreement. Accordingly, the Agreement is to be interpreted in light of the parol evidence rule and extrinsic evidence of an oral agreement contradicting the terms of the Agreement may not be considered, unless one of the exceptions to the application of the parol evidence rule is present.

Vietri maintains that, by seeking to impose a condition precedent on his ascension to partner status, he is not seeking to "vary" the Agreement. That, however, is exactly what he seeks. He asks for an interpretation of the Agreement that is the direct opposite of the Agreement's plain and unambiguous language and meaning. This integrated agreement, signed by both Hynansky and Vietri, clearly provided that Vietri became a general partner in a general partnership known as JHV Associates upon execution of that agreement. Vietri, however, wants to vary its meaning, through extrinsic evidence of an oral agreement or negotiations leading up to the execution of the Agreement, to reach a conclusion that he is not a general partner in JHV Associates and that JHV Associates was not formed as a general partnership. Deviation from the plain meaning of an integrated agreement, such as Vietri advocates here, is precisely the result that the parol evidence rule is designed to preclude. . . .

D. FRAUD OR MUTUAL MISTAKE

Even though the parol evidence rule generally prevents consideration of evidence of an oral agreement to vary the terms of a fully integrated agreement that has been reduced to writing, there are exceptions to this rule. One of these exceptions is "where fraud or misrepresentation is alleged." Another is where mutual mistake occurred.

As part of any successful claim based on fraud or misrepresentation, there must be a showing that a false statement was made and that the complaining party's conduct was in justifiable reliance upon the misrepresentation.

Here, Vietri cannot, under the standard of Court of Chancery Rule 56, demonstrate that he relied upon any misrepresentation of Hynansky. First, he saw the Agreement and, although he may not have read it, he concedes that he realized that he was signing the Agreement as a "Partner." Thus, any reliance would not have been reasonable. Second, he contends that he relied upon the statement of the attorney who formed the Partnership and handled the closing on the Parcel—not upon any representation of Hynansky. Vietri contends that his attorney misled him by telling him when he would "really" receive his partnership interest and that he would not have any personal liability. If the attorney misled him, Vietri has not provided a basis for attributing the attorney's statement to Hynansky. Indeed, Vietri emphasizes that the attorney was representing not only Hynansky and the business venture but also him.

Vietri also has failed to provide any basis for a conclusion that the Agreement was the product of mutual mistake. For summary judgment purposes, Vietri may have demonstrated that as he went to closing he did not anticipate that the business venture would be conducted as a general partnership. However, he signed the Agreement, after having had fair opportunity to review it and after having noted the word "Partner" in the Agreement. In addition, at about the same time, he signed loan closing documents as "Partner." To find mutual mistake in the face of this conduct would be to allow the disappointed party to assert mutual mistake whenever events did not unfold as anticipated. More specifically, there is no reason to believe that the mistake, if any, was mutual. Hynansky signed the Agreement; it clearly and unambiguously memorialized his understanding to establish a general partnership. In sum, the argued exceptions to the parol evidence rule are of no help to Vietri.

VI.

The previous issues, regarding the application and effect of the parol evidence rule upon certain evidence sought to be introduced by Vietri, are a subset of the more weighty dispute between the parties: whether a partnership was created. A "partnership" is defined by the relevant statutory authority as "an association of two or more persons to carry on as co-owners a business for profit."[11] The creation of a partnership is a question of intent. To prove the existence of a partnership, one must show the intent to divide the profits of the venture. In demonstrating that a partnership exists, the acts, dealings, conduct, admissions and declarations of the purported partners, in addition to other direct evidence, may be utilized. When the controversy is between two partners, as it is here, stricter proof of the intention to create a partnership is required.

In support of his argument that a partnership was created, Hynansky principally relies upon the existence of the Agreement. The Agreement, as previously noted, unambiguously sought to create a Delaware general partnership named JHV Associates. However, because the fundamental inquiry in determining whether the parties created a general partnership is the intention of those parties, evidence in the form of a partnership agreement is strong but not conclusive proof of such an intention. Indeed, "the entire agreement and all the attendant circumstances must be taken into consideration in reaching a determination that a partnership has actually materialized." Thus, in determining whether Hynansky and Vietri intended to create a partnership, I must not confine my analysis solely to the terms of the Agreement.

In light of the standard of review at this stage in the proceedings, the broad scope of the intensely factual review of "all the attendant circumstances" that I am obliged

---

11. 6 Del. C. §1506(a).

to undertake, and the stricter standard of proof applying to disputes between two partners as to the creation of a partnership, I deny Hynansky's motion for summary judgment upon the issue of whether a partnership exists. I note that Vietri has proffered evidence that Hynansky treated the assets, and in particular the losses, of JHV Associates as his own for tax purposes,[12] and that Hynansky identified JHV Associates as a corporation on the contract of sale for the Parcel. Because any conclusion as to the parties' intent to form a partnership would require me to balance the conflicting evidence, I may not grant summary judgment on the question of whether JHV Associates is a Delaware general partnership. Furthermore, I deny Hynansky's motion for summary judgment upon all his other claims as they are premised upon a finding that JHV Associates is a general partnership existing between Hynansky and Vietri.

NOTES AND QUESTIONS

1. In some jurisdictions, most prominently New York, an agreement to share losses appears indispensable to the existence of a partnership. See, for example, Bailey v. Broder, 1998 WL 13827, *4 (S.D.N.Y.) ("individuals must agree to share the losses as well as the profits if their agreement is to be regarded in law as a partnership"). In many jurisdictions an agreement to share losses also is indispensable to the existence of a joint venture. See, for example, Mallis v. Bankers Trust Co., 717 F.2d 683, 690 (2d Cir. 1983) ("Under New York law, the crucial element of a joint venture is the existence of a "mutual promise or undertaking of the parties to share in the profits . . . and *submit to the burden of making good the losses*") (internal citations omitted).

2. UPA (1997) §401(a)(2) and its predecessor UPA (1914) §18(a) both provide that, unless otherwise agreed, partners share partnership losses in the same proportion as they share partnership profits. As a matter of statutory construction, how can an actual agreement to share losses be essential to the characterization of a business association as a partnership, if the statute implies an agreement to share losses in the absence of an actual agreement?

3. One circumstance in which an actual agreement to share losses has been found unnecessary to the characterization of a business relationship as a joint venture or partnership is when one person has provided services and the other capital to a common enterprise. See, for example, Florida Tomato Packers, Inc. v. Wilson, 296 So. 2d 536 (Fla. 3d Dist. Ct. App. 1974), in which the court found that "a partnership and/or joint venture relationship . . . existed between George F. Lytton and Florida Tomato . . ." despite the lack of an actual agreement to share losses, because "a duty to share in losses actually and impliedly exists as a matter of law in a situation where one party supplies the labor, experience and skill, and the other the necessary capital since in the event of a loss, the party supplying the knowhow would have exercised his skill in vain

---

12. Specifically, Hynansky admittedly never sent a K-1 partnership tax form to Vietri for Vietri's share of any of the partnership's losses. Rather, Hynansky deducted on his personal income tax returns all of the losses of the partnership as losses suffered on personal, versus partnership, property. See Hynansky Dep. at 190, 200-02.

and the party supplying the capital investment would have suffered a diminishment thereof." Id. at 539.

4. Some jurisdictions determine whether a joint venture has been formed without relying on specific indispensable factors. See, for example, Nagle v. Gokey, 799 A.2d 1225, 1227:

> "A joint venture is an association between two or more individuals or entities who agree to pool their efforts and resources to jointly seek profits." Nancy W. Bayley, Inc. v. Employment Sec. Comm'n, 472 A.2d 1374, 1377 (Me. 1984). Moreover, a joint venture can be found "where persons embark on an undertaking without entering on the prosecution of the business as partners strictly but engage in a common enterprise for their mutual benefit." Simpson v. Richmond Worsted Spinning Co., 128 Me. 22, 29, 145 A. 250, 253-54 (1929) (quoting Hey v. Duncan, 13 F.2d 794, 795 (7th Cir. 1926). Like a partnership, whether a joint venture exists depends upon the circumstances surrounding the partie's relationship. Id. at 30, 145 A. at 254. Therefore, although very similar to a partnership, a joint venture is "generally more limited in scope and duration." Nancy W. Bayley, Inc., 472 A.2d at 1377.

5. Some jurisdictions are quite strict in the factors that must be present to support a finding that a joint venture was formed. For example, see Harriman v. United Dominion Industries, Inc., 693 N.W.2d 44, 50 (S.D. 2005) (internal citations omitted):

> We recently set forth six elements necessary to establish a joint venture. These six elements include:
>
> (1) an intent to enter into a joint venture;
> (2) an agreement, express or implied, among members of the group;
> (3) a common purpose to be carried out by the group;
> (4) a joint pecuniary interest in that purpose;
> (5) an equal right to a voice in the direction and control of the group; and
> (6) a right to share in the profits and a duty to share in any losses.
>
> All six elements must be met in order to establish the existence of a joint venture.

6. Akin to the question of whether a partnership has been created is the question of whether a particular person is a partner or, instead, stands in a different relationship to the partnership. Consider a question likely to be of some interest to law students: is a "junior partner" in a law firm who possesses no vote on major decisions really a glorified employee or a legitimate "owner" of the firm? This question comes up in a variety of circumstances, including whether a particular person is entitled to the employment discrimination protection afforded by Title VII. Consider the implications of the following discussion of how to distinguish between a partner who is akin to a proprietor and a partner who is akin to an employee.

> In large, the critical attributes of proprietary status involve three broad, overlapping categories: ownership, remuneration, and management. . . . [A]lthough myriad factors may influence a court's ultimate decision in a given case, we recount a non-exclusive list of factors that frequently will bear upon such determinations.
>
> Under the first category, relevant factors include investment in the firm, ownership of firm assets, and liability for firm debts and obligations. To the extent that these factors exist, they indicate a proprietary role; to the extent that they do not exist, they indicate a status more akin to that of an employee.
>
> Under the second category, the most relevant factor is whether (and if so, to what extent) the individual's compensation is based on the firm's profits. To the extent that a partner's remuneration

is subject to the vagaries of the firm's economic fortunes, her status more closely resembles that of a proprietor; conversely, to the extent that a partner is paid on a straight salary basis, the argument for treating her as an ordinary employee will gain strength. . . .

Under the third category, relevant factors include the right to engage in policymaking; participation in, and voting power with regard to, firm governance; the ability to assign work and to direct the activities of employees within the firm; and the ability to act for the firm and its principals. Once again, to the extent that these factors exist, they indicate a proprietary role.

Serapion v. Martinez, 119 F.3d 982, 990 (1st Cir. 1997).

PROBLEM 2-1

Shady entered a bid with the Metro Sewer District ("MSD") to dispose of excess limestone ("spoil") generated by various MSD tunnel projects. While the bid was pending, Shady discovered that Dale had a twenty-acre site suitable for disposal of the spoil. Shady proposed a business arrangement. Dale would allow the spoil to be stored on her land; Dale and Shady would split the profits upon sale of the spoil.

Dale hired an attorney, Harv. At a subsequent meeting at Harv's office, Shady and Dale discussed entering into a partnership. During the discussions, Shady revealed that he was being investigated for a felony—transporting hazardous waste without a license—and that he intended to pay "grease" payments to MSD to ensure winning the bid. After the meeting Harv advised Dale not to do business with Shady, but, if she must, to do so without forming a partnership.

Despite Harv's advice, Dale agreed to allow Shady to store spoil on her land. The parties did not enter into a written agreement. Dale and Shady soon had a falling out. Thereafter, Dale prevented Shady from storing spoil on her land and granted one of Shady's competitors the right to use her land for spoil storage. As a result MSD cancelled its contract with Shady. Shady sued Dale for damages, asserting that Shady and Dale were partners, and that Shady had violated her obligations under the partnership agreement.

At trial, Dale testified that she considered herself to be a sole proprietor in the business of storing and selling spoil and that she considered Shady to be an independent contractor who "sold" spoil to her in exchange for half of the profits upon the eventual resale of the spoil. She denied any intent to form a partnership. Shady testified that before the meeting with Harv: (1) Dale indicated "that she was interested in partnering up with me," that they "needed to get rolling," and that she would "hire an attorney to legalize the agreement"; and (2) Dale and Shady "came to an agreement that [Shady] would deliver the spoil and Dale would pay the MSD invoices if [Shady] had trouble getting a loan," and that "whatever monies we put into the operation to make it go, we'd get it back when we sold the spoil, and then we'd split the profits 50/50." Shady also testified that after the meeting with Harv: (1) he asked Dale "dozens of times" to finalize a written partnership agreement, but "she always came up with something she needed to clear with her attorney"; (2) both he and Dale referred to each other as "partner"; (3) he was involved in negotiations to sell the spoil and had vetoed one potential sale because "the price was way too low"; and (4) he generally was on site to accept delivery of the spoil.

The trial court determined that Dale and Shady were either partners or joint venturers and awarded damages to Shady. Dale appealed. Should the appeals court affirm the trial court's ruling?

PROBLEM 2-2

In April 2010, Gary entered into an agreement to sell his restaurant business to Nova. Under the terms of the agreement Nova was required to pay Gary $2,000 per week for a period of six years. The contract provided Gary with the right to control all business decisions made during the six-year payment period.

Nova took over operation of the restaurant on May 1, 2010, but because of her inexperience ran into numerous difficulties. On May 15, 2010, Gary agreed to help Nova with the day-to-day operations for six months. At all times during the six-year payment period, Gary kept close tabs on the restaurant, maintained access to the books and records, occasionally advanced funds needed for restaurant improvements, and frequently consulted with Nova concerning business decisions. In 2012, Nova secretly obtained a line of credit from the First Metro Bank ("FMB"); Nova represented to the bank that the funds were being used for improvements to the restaurant, but, in fact, Nova used the funds personally. In 2014, Nova filed for personal bankruptcy reporting no assets and substantial debt. She listed the loan from FMB as "a joint obligation with Gary, my partner in the restaurant business."

Ultimately FMB filed suit against Gary to recover the sums borrowed by Nova. The trial court determined that Gary and Nova were either partners or joint venturers and awarded damages to FMB. Gary appealed. Should the appeals court affirm the trial court's ruling?

4. Sharing Profits and Losses

UPA (1997) §§101(11), 401

The common law and the Uniform Partnership Act each provide default rules governing a partner's right to share in profits, to be paid for services, or to receive interest on contributed capital or money loaned to the firm. Likewise the common law and the Uniform Partnership Act provide fallback rules governing a partner's responsibility to share in any losses experienced by the partnership. In the archetypal general partnership, where two persons each contribute equal amounts of money and services to the business, the default rules are consonant with what most persons would presumably have bargained for—an equal sharing of profits and losses. Moreover, the default rule that a partner is not entitled to receive compensation for her services or interest on her contributed capital is of little importance; each partner is contributing equally and will share equally in the expected profits from the venture.

The fair result is less clear when partners' contributions are less obviously equal. For example, if one partner contributes only her expertise and future services, while the other partner agrees to contribute money but no services, should the partner contributing services be entitled to compensation for her services even if the partners have never discussed it? Should her contribution of services be treated as a type of contribution of capital? If so, how should that contribution be valued? The following two cases explore the application of the statutory and common law default rules in nonarchetypal settings.

Kovacik v. Reed
California Supreme Court, 1957
49 Cal. 2d 166, 315 P.2d 314

SCHAUER, JUSTICE.

In this suit for dissolution of a joint venture and for an accounting, defendant appeals from a judgment that plaintiff recover from defendant one half the losses of the venture. We have concluded that inasmuch as the parties agreed the plaintiff was to supply the money and defendant the labor to carry on the venture, defendant is correct in his contention that the trial court erred in holding him liable for one half the monetary losses, and that the judgment should therefore be reversed.

The appeal is taken upon a settled statement. . . . From the "condensed statement of the oral proceedings" included in the settled statement, it appears that plaintiff, a licensed building contractor in San Francisco, operated his contracting business as a sole proprietorship under the fictitious name of "Asbestos Siding Company." Defendant had for a number of years worked for various building contractors in that city as a job superintendent and estimator.

Early in November, 1952, Kovacik (plaintiff) told Reed (defendant) that Kovacik had an opportunity to do kitchen remodeling work for Sears Roebuck Company in San Francisco and asked Reed to become his job superintendent and estimator in this venture. Kovacik said that he had about $10,000.00 to invest in the venture and that, if Reed would superintend and estimate the jobs, Kovacik would share the profits with Reed on a 50-50 basis. Kovacik did not ask Reed to agree to share any loss that might result and Reed did not offer to share any such loss. The subject of a possible loss was not discussed in the inception of this venture. Reed accepted Kovacik's proposal and commenced work for the venture shortly after November 1, 1952. . . . Reed's only contribution was his own labor. Kovacik provided all of the venture's financing through the credit of Asbestos Siding Company, although at times Reed purchased materials for the jobs in his own name or on his account for which he was reimbursed. . . .

"The venture bid on and was awarded a number of . . . remodeling jobs . . . in San Francisco. Reed worked on all of the jobs as job superintendent. . . . During . . . August, 1953, Kovacik, who at that time had had all of the financial records of the venture in his possession, . . . informed Reed that the venture had been unprofitable and demanded contribution from Reed as to amounts which Kovacik claimed to have advanced in excess of the income received from the venture. Reed at no time promised, represented or agreed that he was liable for any of the venture's losses and he consistently and without exception refused to contribute to or pay any of the loss resulting from the venture. . . . The venture was terminated on August 31, 1953."

Kovacik thereafter instituted this proceeding, seeking an accounting of the affairs of the venture and to recover from Reed one half of the losses. Despite the evidence above set forth from the statement of the oral proceedings, showing that at no time had defendant agreed to be liable for any of the losses, the trial court "found"—more accurately, we think, concluded as a matter of law—that "plaintiff and defendant were to share equally all their joint venture profits and losses between them," and that defendant "agreed to share equally in the profits and losses of said joint venture." Following an accounting taken by a referee appointed by the court, judgment was rendered awarding plaintiff recovery against defendant of some $4,340, as one half the monetary losses[1] found by the referee to have been sustained by the joint venture.

It is the general rule that in the absence of an agreement to the contrary the law presumes that partners and joint adventurers intended to participate equally in the profits and losses of the common enterprise, irrespective of any inequality in the amounts each contributed to the capital employed in the venture, with the losses being shared by them in the same proportions as they share the profits.

However, it appears that in the cases in which the above stated general rule has been applied, each of the parties had contributed capital consisting of either money or land or other tangible property, or else was to receive compensation for services rendered to the common undertaking which was to be paid before computation of the profits or losses. Where, however, as in the present case, one partner or joint adventurer contributes the money capital as against the other's skill and labor, all the cases cited, and which our research has discovered, hold that neither party is liable to the other for contribution for any loss sustained. Thus, upon loss of the money the party who contributed it is not entitled to recover any part of it from the party who contributed only services. The rationale of this rule, as expressed in Heran v. Hall, 40 Ky. 159 (1840), and Meadows v. Mocquot, 110 Ky. 220 (1901), is that where one party contributes money and the other contributes services, then in the event of a loss each would lose his own capital the one his money and the other his labor. Another view would be that in such a situation the parties have, by their agreement to share equally in profits, agreed that the value of their contributions the money on the one hand and the labor on the other were likewise equal; it would follow that upon the loss, as here, of both money and labor, the parties have shared equally in the losses. Actually, of course, plaintiff here lost only some $8,680 or somewhat less than the $10,000 which he originally proposed and agreed to invest. . . .

It follows that the conclusion of law upon which the judgment in favor of plaintiff for recovery from defendant of one half the monetary losses depends is untenable, and that the judgment should be reversed.

---

1. The record is silent as to the factors taken into account by the referee in determining the "loss" suffered by the venture. However, there is no contention that defendant's services were ascribed any value whatsoever. It may also be noted that the trial court "found" that "neither plaintiff nor defendant was to receive compensation for their services rendered to said joint venture, but plaintiff and defendant were to share equally all their joint venture profits and losses between them." Neither party suggests that plaintiff actually rendered services to the venture in the same sense that defendant did. And, as is clear from the settled statement, plaintiff's proposition to defendant was that plaintiff would provide the money as against defendant's contribution of services as estimator and superintendent.

Shamloo v. Ladd

California Court of Appeal, Second District
2003 WL 68054

TURNER, PRESIDING JUDGE

I. INTRODUCTION

Defendant and cross-complainant, Rick Ladd, individually and doing business as Inner Circle Graphics, appeals from a judgment entered on dissolution of a partnership, known as Ginnytex Company, Inc. ("Ginnytex"). The partnership was between Mr. Ladd and plaintiff and cross-defendant, Farhad Shamloo.

II. BACKGROUND

On November 30, 1999, Mr. Shamloo filed a complaint for: partnership contract breach (first); fiduciary duty breach (second); conversion (third); partnership dissolution; accounting (fourth); and appointment of receiver (fifth). The complaint alleged that around July 1995, Mr. Shamloo and Mr. Ladd formed Ginnytex, which was to be incorporated in California but was not active. The parties did not complete all required formalities to conduct business under Ginnytex as a corporation. Accordingly, the corporation operated under an oral partnership agreement. The complaint further alleged that: the business purpose of Ginnytex was to manufacture yarn into fabric for resale; the conversion or manufacturing of the yarn was to be performed by third parties for which Ginnytex would pay the market rate for their services; Mr. Shamloo's own facilities could also be used for the processing of the yarn; and Mr. Shamloo would be paid for the use of such facilities according to the market rate. In addition, the complaint alleged that Mr. Ladd contributed $75,000 as a capital investment to the partnership and another $75,000 in the form of an interest free loan. Mr. Shamloo contributed, in the words of his complaint, "sweat equity," which was in the form of labor, knowledge, and expertise in the industry. Mr. Shamloo devoted approximately 50 percent of his time and energy to running the enterprise. . . . Mr. Ladd was alleged to have breached the partnership agreement by: failing to pay Mr. Shamloo his share of partnership assets; converting partnership assets; failing to pay creditors of Ginnytex. . . .

III. DISCUSSION

SUMMARY OF CONTENTIONS AND STANDARD OF REVIEW

Mr. Ladd argues the trial court erred in: (1) awarding Mr. Shamloo $41,700 in compensation for his services rendered to the enterprise, which was reduced to $27,344.96 in the amended judgment due to lack of partnership assets . . . and (4) denying interest on the balance of the loan made by Mr. Ladd to Ginnytex. . . .

A. MR. SHAMLOO'S CAPITAL ACCOUNT

Mr. Ladd contends the trial court erred in awarding over $40,000 in "sweat equity" to Mr. Shamloo. As noted previously, Mr. Shamloo alleged he made a capital contribution in the form of services. Mr. Shamloo counters that the trial court's award was not based on his service. Rather, Mr. Shamloo argues the award was reimbursement for a capital contribution. Mr. Shamloo further argues that there was evidence introduced that he contributed 15 years of "know how," as well as his facilities, equipment, and the services of his staff. Based on this evidence, the trial court could reasonably value $40,000 as his equitable contribution to the enterprise.

The evidence established that the parties initially agreed to form a corporation but failed to comply with the requisite procedures to incorporate. It was undisputed that, as a result of the failure to incorporate, Ginnytex was a de facto partnership, which is governed by the applicable version of the California Uniform Partnership Act located in former section 15001 et seq. of the Corporations Code. . . . Former section 15018, provides in part:

> The rights and duties of the partners in relation to the partnership shall be determined, subject to any agreement between them, by the following rules:
>
>> (a) Each partner shall be repaid his or her contributions, whether by way of capital or advances to the partnership property and share equally in the profits and surplus remaining after all liabilities, including those to partners, are satisfied. . . .
>>
>> (f) No partner is entitled to remuneration for acting in the partnership business, except that a surviving partner is entitled to reasonable compensation for his or her services in winding up the partnership affairs.

In Tiffany v. Short (1943) 22 Cal.2d 531, 139 P.2d 939, the California Supreme Court explained the manner in which partnership assets may be distributed upon dissolution as follows.

> The general rule applicable to dissolution in such cases is that in the absence of an express agreement to the contrary, the person advancing capital is entitled to its return before there is a division of income or profits. . . . "Upon dissolution of a firm the capital remaining after payment of the debts should be divided in accordance with the respective interests of the partners. While it has been said that, in the absence of any evidence showing a contrary intent, capital will be divided equally, the general rule is that each partner is entitled to the amount of capital that he contributed, this being regarded as a debt of the firm to be repaid in whole if the firm assets are sufficient, and pro rata if firm assets are insufficient." It is further stated . . . that a partner contributing only services is ordinarily not entitled to a share of capital on dissolution. [Citations.] (Id. at pp. 533-534, 139 P.2d 939; see Kovacik v. Reed (1957) 49 Cal.2d 166, 169, 315 P.2d 314.)

Thus, the rule is that, absent an agreement, a partner is not entitled to compensation for rendering services for the partnership other than profits. A partner is only entitled to compensation where the evidence discloses an express or implied agreement that such partner will be compensated.

There is no substantial evidence that the . . . agreement between the parties contemplated, much less resolved, the issue of whether Mr. Shamloo was to be compensated upon dissolution of the partnership for his contribution of services to the enterprise in lieu of an actual capital contribution. When asked to explain his understanding of the agreement, Mr. Shamloo testified that Mr. Ladd would contribute the money. According to Mr. Shamloo, he would be contributing his expertise. Also, Mr. Shamloo would provide the facilities to support the partnership operations. Mr. Shamloo testified that the profits would be split evenly. Mr. Shamloo testified that there was an understanding that Mr. Ladd would complete the paperwork for the incorporation of Ginnytex. A similar understanding was reached in connection with the formalities for a partnership. Once the business was formed, Mr. Ladd contributed $75,000 in capital and $75,000 as a loan. Other than a $450 to $500 cash payment for what Mr. Shamloo described as a "corporation cost fee," he only contributed his "expertise in this business." Mr. Ladd testified that Mr. Shamloo's contribution of his expertise did not represent 50 percent of the enterprise's capital. Mr. Ladd categorically denied that there was ever a understanding that his expertise would be treated as a percentage of capital. As can be noted, there was no testimony that the parties agreed that Mr. Shamloo's contribution of services, expertise, and use of his plant would be treated as capital which would be compensable upon dissolution of the enterprise. Therefore, under the controlling authority of Tiffany v. Short, supra, 22 Cal.2d at pages 533-534, 139 P.2d 939, the $27,344.96 award to Mr. Shamloo is reversed. . . .

D. THE INTEREST ON THE $75,000 LOAN TO GINNYTEX

Mr. Ladd argues that the trial court failed to award any interest on the loan in the amount of $75,000 by him to Ginnytex. The evidence shows Mr. Ladd agreed to contribute $75,000 as capital. Mr. Ladd also agreed to loan $75,000 to Ginnytex. The record also shows that Mr. Ladd unilaterally withdrew $61,496.05 from a Ginnytex account. The trial court awarded Mr. Ladd $13,503.95 as the remaining balance on the loan to Ginnytex but denied his interest claim. Mr. Ladd claims he is entitled to $29,430.30, which includes interest calculated from the date of the advance.

Former section 15018, subdivision (c) provides, that subject to any agreement between the parties: "A partner, who in aid of the partnership makes any payment or advance beyond the amount of the capital which he agreed to contribute, shall be paid interest from the date of the payment or advance." This statute clearly and unequivocally states that a partner should be paid interest from the date of an advance.

Mr. Shamloo nevertheless argues that there was no evidence that the parties expressly or impliedly agreed to pay interest on the loan. Mr. Shamloo's argument is based on a number of authorities which have concluded that a partner is not entitled to interest on capital contributions. However a distinction must be made between interest payable on a loan or advance from the interest payable on a capital contribution. An advance is not a capital contribution but is treated as a loan or obligation to the partnership requiring the payment of interest. Pursuant to former section 15018, subdivision (c), interest is payable on an advance unless there is a contrary agreement.

By contrast, former section 15018, subdivision (d) provides: "A partner shall receive interest on the capital contributed by him only from the date when repayment should be made." Accordingly, interest is not due on a capital contribution unless the parties agree otherwise or until payment of the capital is due. Mr. Ladd did not request interest on his capital contribution nor would he have been entitled to interest in the absence of an agreement.

While Mr. Ladd is not entitled to interest on his capital contribution, he is entitled to interest on the loan unless the evidence establishes the parties agreed to the contrary. No evidence was introduced that the parties agreed not to pay Mr. Ladd interest on the loan to Ginnytex. Accordingly, he is entitled to interest on the loan from the date of the advance. . . .

NOTES AND QUESTIONS

1. Is the reasoning in the two principal cases sound? The policy rational? What are the incentive effects? Would it have made more sense to decide Kovacik v. Reed by terming the relationship as one between a sole proprietor and an independent contractor?

2. Reconsider Note 1, page 68. Could it be argued that the relationship between Kovacik and Reed was not a joint venture because the parties had no express or implied agreement to share losses? Consider the implications of the following analysis: "a duty to share in losses actually and impliedly exists as a matter of law in a situation where one party supplies the labor, experience and skill, and the other the necessary capital since in the event of a loss, the party supplying the knowhow would have exercised his skill in vain and the party supplying the capital investment would have suffered a diminishment thereof." Florida Tomato Packers, Inc. v. Wilson, 296 So.2d. 536, 539 (Fla. 3d DCA 1974).

3. For a recent case explicitly following Kovacik v. Reed, see Kessler v. Antinora, 653 A.2d. 579 (N.J. Super. A.D. 1995).

PROBLEM 2-3

Full-Time, Part-Time, and None agreed to own and operate a coffee shop. None contributed $50,000 in cash; Part-Time contributed $25,000 in cash and the use of the premises on which the coffee shop was to be operated. Full-Time made no contribution of money, but agreed to and did devote her full time and efforts in managing the coffee shop. Part-Time served as the bookkeeper for the business, devoting approximately ten hours per week to this task. None provided no services to the venture, other than occasionally discussing the status of the business with Part-Time and Full-Time. The coffee shop operated for six months, but was forced to close when the owner of the property terminated Part-Time's lease. Rather than find a new location, the venturers decided to settle accounts and go their separate ways. After reducing the firm's assets to cash, Part-Time was able to pay off all claims by third parties. At no time was any money withdrawn from the business by None, Part-Time, or Full-Time, either as compensation for services, as a loan, or as a share of profits. What are None's, Part-Time's, and Full-Time's rights and obligations if the residual cash totals:

(a) $0?
(b) $75,000?
(c) $100,000?

PROBLEM 2-4

Reconsider the facts in Problem 2-3. What are None's, Part-Time's, and Full-Time's rights and obligations if after reducing the firm's assets to cash, the claims of third parties exceed the available cash by $90,000?

B.   *The Partner as Fiduciary*

UPA (1997) §§103, 403, 404

1.   The Common Law Duty of Loyalty

In jointly owned firms, owners usually manifest their shared expectations by choosing a state-provided business form and by executing contractual agreements that appropriately supplement that form's normal rules. However, contracting may be inadequate at the outset. Even if done well, the resulting contractual and relational framework may provide insufficient protection of owners' expectations.

In the partnership setting, the traditional judicial response is to demand that partners deal with one another as fiduciaries in all matters affecting the partnership. Imposition of fiduciary duties recognizes that in many cases, judicial exercise of equitable discretion is the only effective means of protecting partners' expectations. The following case typifies the traditional judicial approach to fiduciary duty cases and contains the most widely cited description of partners' fiduciary duty of loyalty.

Meinhard v. Salmon
New York Court of Appeals, 1928
164 N.E. 545

Cardozo, Circuit Judge.

On April 10, 1902, Louisa M. Gerry leased to the defendant Walter J. Salmon the premises known as the Hotel Bristol at the northwest corner of Forty-Second street and Fifth avenue in the city of New York. The lease was for a term of 20 years, commencing May 1, 1902, and ending April 30, 1922. The lessee undertook to change the hotel building for use as shops and offices at a cost of $200,000. Alterations and additions were to be accretions to the land.

Salmon, while in course of treaty with the lessor as to the execution of the lease, was in course of treaty with Meinhard, the plaintiff, for the necessary funds. The result was a joint venture with terms embodied in a writing. Meinhard was to pay to Salmon half of the moneys requisite to reconstruct, alter, manage, and operate the property. Salmon was to pay to Meinhard 40 percent of the net profits for the first five years of the lease and 50 percent for the years thereafter. If there were losses, each party was to bear them equally. Salmon, however, was to have sole power to "manage, lease, underlet and operate" the building. There were to be certain pre-emptive rights for each in the contingency of death.

The two were coadventurers, subject to fiduciary duties akin to those of partners. As to this we are all agreed. The heavier weight of duty rested, however, upon Salmon. He was a coadventurer with Meinhard, but he was manager as well. During the early years of the enterprise, the building, reconstructed, was operated at a loss. If the relation had then ended, Meinhard as well as Salmon would have carried a heavy burden. Later the profits became large with the result that for each of the investors there came a rich return. For each the venture had its phases of fair weather and of foul. The two were in it jointly, for better or for worse.

When the lease was near its end, Elbridge T. Gerry had become the owner of the reversion. He owned much other property in the neighborhood, one lot adjoining the Bristol building on Fifth avenue and four lots on Forty-Second street. He had a plan to lease the entire tract for a long term to some one who would destroy the buildings then existing and put up another in their place. In the latter part of 1921, he submitted such a project to several capitalists and dealers. He was unable to carry it through with any of them. Then, in January, 1922, with less than four months of the lease to run, he approached the defendant Salmon. The result was a new lease to the Midpoint Realty Company, which is owned and controlled by Salmon, a lease covering the whole tract, and involving a huge outlay. The term is to be 20 years, but successive covenants for renewal will extend it to a maximum of 80 years at the will of either party. The existing buildings may remain unchanged for seven years. They are then to be torn down, and a new building to cost $3,000,000 is to be placed upon the site. The rental, which under the Bristol lease was only $55,000, is to be from $350,000 to $475,000 for the properties so combined. Salmon personally guaranteed the performance by the lessee of the covenants of the new lease until such time as the new building had been completed and fully paid for.

The lease between Gerry and the Midpoint Realty Company was signed and delivered on January 25, 1922. Salmon had not told Meinhard anything about it. Whatever his motive may have been, he had kept the negotiations to himself. Meinhard was not informed even of the bare existence of a project. The first that he knew of it was in February, when the lease was an accomplished fact. He then made demand on the defendants that the lease be held in trust as an asset of the venture, making offer upon the trial to share the personal obligations incidental to the guaranty. The demand was followed by refusal, and later by this suit. A referee gave judgment for the plaintiff, limiting the plaintiff's interest in the lease, however, to 25 percent. The limitation was on the theory that the plaintiff's equity was to be restricted to one-half of so much of the value of the lease as was contributed or represented by the occupation of the Bristol site. Upon cross-appeals to the Appellate Division, the judgment was modified so as to enlarge the equitable interest to one-half of the whole lease. With this enlargement of plaintiff's interest, there went, of course, a corresponding enlargement of his attendant obligations. The case is now here on an appeal by the defendants.

Joint adventurers, like copartners, owe to one another, while the enterprise continues, the duty of the finest loyalty. Many forms of conduct permissible in a workaday world for those acting at arm's length, are forbidden to those bound by fiduciary ties. A trustee is held to something stricter than the morals of the market place. Not honesty alone, but the punctilio of an honor the most sensitive, is then the standard of behavior. As to this there has developed a tradition that is unbending and inveterate.

Uncompromising rigidity has been the attitude of courts of equity when petitioned to undermine the rule of undivided loyalty by the "disintegrating erosion" of particular exceptions. Only thus has the level of conduct for fiduciaries been kept at a level higher than that trodden by the crowd. It will not consciously be lowered by any judgment of this court.

The owner of the reversion, Mr. Gerry, had vainly striven to find a tenant who would favor his ambitious scheme of demolition and construction. Baffled in the search, he turned to the defendant Salmon in possession of the Bristol, the keystone of the project. He figured to himself beyond a doubt that the man in possession would prove a likely customer. To the eye of an observer, Salmon held the lease as owner in his own right, for himself and no one else. In fact he held it as a fiduciary, for himself and another, sharers in a common venture. If this fact had been proclaimed, if the lease by its terms had run in favor of a partnership, Mr. Gerry, we may fairly assume, would have laid before the partners, and not merely before one of them, his plan of reconstruction. The pre-emptive privilege, or, better, the pre-emptive opportunity, that was thus an incident of the enterprise, Salmon appropriated to himself in secrecy and silence. He might have warned Meinhard that the plan had been submitted, and that either would be free to compete for the award. If he had done this, we do not need to say whether he would have been under a duty, if successful in the competition, to hold the lease so acquired for the benefit of a venture then about to end, and thus prolong by indirection its responsibilities and duties. The trouble about his conduct is that he excluded his coadventurer from any chance to compete, from any chance to enjoy the opportunity for benefit that had come to him alone by virtue of his agency. This chance, if nothing more, he was under a duty to concede. The price of its denial is an extension of the trust at the option and for the benefit of the one whom he excluded.

No answer is it to say that the chance would have been of little value even if seasonably offered. Such a calculus of probabilities is beyond the science of the chancery. Salmon, the real estate operator, might have been preferred to Meinhard, the woolen merchant. On the other hand, Meinhard might have offered better terms, or reinforced his offer by alliance with the wealth of others. Perhaps he might even have persuaded the lessor to renew the Bristol lease alone, postponing for a time, in return for higher rentals, the improvement of adjoining lots. We know that even under the lease as made the time for the enlargement of the building was delayed for seven years. All these opportunities were cut away from him through another's intervention. He knew that Salmon was the manager. As the time drew near for the expiration of the lease, he would naturally assume from silence, if from nothing else, that the lessor was willing to extend it for a term of years, or at least to let it stand as a lease from year to year. Not impossibly the lessor would have done so, whatever his protestations of unwillingness, if Salmon had not given assent to a project more attractive. At all events, notice of termination, even if not necessary, might seem, not unreasonably, to be something to be looked for, if the business was over and another tenant was to enter. In the absence of such notice, the matter of an extension was one that would naturally be attended to by the manager of the enterprise, and not neglected altogether. At least, there was nothing in the situation to give warning to any one that while the lease was still in being, there had come to the manager an offer of extension which he had locked within his breast to be utilized by himself alone. The very fact that Salmon was in control with exclusive powers of direction charged him the more obviously with the duty of disclosure, since only through disclosure could opportunity be equalized. If he might cut off renewal by a purchase for his own benefit when four months were to pass before the lease would have an end, he might do so with equal right while there remained as many years. He might steal a march on his comrade under cover of the darkness, and then hold the captured ground. Loyalty and comradeship are not so easily abjured.

Little profit will come from a dissection of the precedents. None precisely similar is cited in the briefs of counsel. What is similar in many, or so it seems to us, is the animating principle. Authority is, of course, abundant that one partner may not appropriate to his own use a renewal of a lease, though its term is to begin at the expiration of the partnership. . . . Certain it is also that there may be no abuse of special opportunities growing out of a special trust as manager or agent. If conflicting inferences are possible as to abuse or opportunity, the trier of the facts must make the choice between them. There can be no revision in this court unless the choice is clearly wrong. It is no answer for the fiduciary to say "that he was not bound to risk his money as he did, or to go into the enterprise at all." Beatty v. Guggenheim Exploration Co., 225 N.Y. 380, 385, 122 N.E. 378, 380. "He might have kept out of it altogether, but if he went in, he could not withhold from his employer the benefit of the bargain." Beatty v. Guggenheim Exploration Co., supra. A constructive trust is, then, the remedial device through which preference of self is made subordinate to loyalty to others. . . .

We have no thought to hold that Salmon was guilty of a conscious purpose to defraud. Very likely he assumed in all good faith that with the approaching end of the venture he might ignore his coadventurer and take the extension for himself. He had given to the enterprise time and labor as well as money. He had made it a success. Meinhard, who had given money, but neither time nor labor, had already been richly paid. There might seem to be something grasping in his insistence upon more. Such recriminations are not unusual when coadventurers fall out. They are not without their force if conduct is to be judged by the common standards of competitors. That is not to say that they have pertinency here. Salmon had put himself in a position in which thought of self was to be renounced, however hard the abnegation. He was much more than a coadventurer. He was a managing coadventurer. For him and for those like him the rule of undivided loyalty is relentless and supreme. A different question would be here if there were lacking any nexus of relation between the business conducted by the manager and the opportunity brought to him as an incident of management. For this problem, as for most, there are distinctions of degree. If Salmon had received from Gerry a proposition to lease a building at a location far removed, he might have held for himself the privilege thus acquired, or so we shall assume. Here the subject-matter of the new lease was an extension and enlargement of the subject-matter of the old one. A managing coadventurer appropriating the benefit of such a lease without warning to his partner might fairly expect to be reproached with conduct that was underhand, or lacking, to say the least, in reasonable candor, if the partner were to surprise him in the act of signing the new instrument. Conduct subject to that reproach does not receive from equity a healing benediction.

A question remains as to the form and extent of the equitable interest to be allotted to the plaintiff. The trust as declared has been held to attach to the lease which was in the name of the defendant corporation. We think it ought to attach at the option of the defendant Salmon to the shares of stock which were owned by him or were under his control. The difference may be important if the lessee shall wish to execute an assignment of the lease, as it ought to be free to do with the consent of the lessor. On the other hand, an equal division of the shares might lead to other hardships. It might take away from Salmon the power of control and management which under the plan of the joint venture he was to have from first to last. The number of shares to be allotted to the plaintiff should, therefore, be reduced to such an extent as may be necessary to preserve to the defendant Salmon the expected measure of dominion. To that end an extra share should be added to his half.

Subject to this adjustment, we agree with the Appellate Division that the plaintiff's equitable interest is to be measured by the value of half of the entire lease, and not merely by half of some undivided part. A single building covers the whole area. Physical division is impracticable along the lines of the Bristol site, the keystone of the whole. Division of interests and burdens is equally impracticable. Salmon, as tenant under the new lease, or as guarantor of the performance of the tenant's obligations, might well protest if Meinhard, claiming an equitable interest, had offered to assume a liability not equal to Salmon's, but only half as great. He might justly insist that the lease must be accepted by his coadventurer in such form as it had been given, and not constructively divided into imaginary fragments. What must be yielded to the one may be demanded by the other. The lease as it has been executed is single and entire. If confusion has resulted from the union of adjoining parcels, the trustee who consented to the union must bear the inconvenience. . . .

ANDREWS, J. (dissenting).

. . . I am of the opinion that the issue here is simple. Was the transaction, in view of all the circumstances surrounding it, unfair and inequitable? I reach this conclusion for two reasons. There was no general partnership, merely a joint venture for a limited object, to end at a fixed time. The new lease, covering additional property, containing many new and unusual terms and conditions, with a possible duration of 80 years, was more nearly the purchase of the reversion than the ordinary renewal with which the authorities are concerned. . . .

This lease is valuable. In making it Mr. Gerry acted in good faith without any collusion with Mr. Salmon and with no purpose to deprive Mr. Meinhard of any equities he might have. But as to the negotiations leading to it or as to the execution of the lease itself Mr. Meinhard knew nothing. Mr. Salmon acted for himself to acquire the lease for his own benefit.

. . . I assume that where parties engage in a joint enterprise each owes to the other the duty of the utmost good faith in all that relates to their common venture. Within its scope they stand in a fiduciary relationship. I assume prima facie that even as between joint adventurers one may not secretly obtain a renewal of the lease of property actually used in the joint adventure where the possibility of renewal is expressly or impliedly involved in the enterprise. I assume also that Mr. Meinhard had an equitable interest in the Bristol Hotel lease. Further, that an expectancy of renewal inhered in that lease. Two questions then arise. Under his contract did he share in that expectancy? And if so, did that expectancy mature into a graft of the original lease? To both questions my answer is "No."

The one complaint made is that Mr. Salmon obtained the new lease without informing Mr. Meinhard of his intention. Nothing else. There is no claim of actual fraud. No claim of misrepresentation to any one. . . . Here was a refusal of the landlord to renew the Bristol lease on any terms; a proposal made by him, not sought by Mr. Salmon, and a choice by him and by the original lessor of the person with whom they wished to deal shown by the covenants against assignment or under-letting, and by their ignorance of the arrangement with Mr. Meinhard.

What then was the scope of the adventure into which the two men entered? It is to be remembered that before their contract was signed Mr. Salmon had obtained the lease of the Bristol property. Very likely the matter had been earlier discussed between them. The $5,000 advance by Mr. Meinhard indicates that fact. But it has been held that the written contract defines their rights and duties. Having the lease, Mr. Salmon assigns no interest in it to Mr. Meinhard. He is to manage the property. It is for him to decide what alterations shall be made and to fix the rents. But for 20 years from May 1, 1902, Salmon is to make all advances from his own funds and Meinhard is to pay him personally on demand one-half of all expenses incurred and all losses sustained "during the full term of said lease," and during the same period Salmon is to pay him a part of the net profits. There was no joint capital provided.

It seems to me that the venture so inaugurated had in view a limited object and was to end at a limited time. There was no intent to expand it into a far greater undertaking lasting for many years. The design was to exploit a particular lease. Doubtless in it Mr. Meinhard had an equitable interest, but in it alone. This interest terminated when the joint adventure terminated. . . . Mr. Salmon has done all he promised to do in return for Mr. Meinhard's undertaking when he distributed profits up to May 1, 1922. Suppose this lease, nonassignable without the consent of the lessor, had contained a renewal option. Could Mr. Meinhard have exercised it? Could he have insisted that Mr. Salmon do so? Had Mr. Salmon done so could he insist that the agreement to share losses still existed, or could Mr. Meinhard have claimed that the joint adventure was still to continue for 20 or 80 years? I do not think so. The adventure by its express terms ended on May 1, 1922. The contract by its language and by its whole import excluded the idea that the tenant's expectancy was to subsist for the benefit of the plaintiff. On that date whatever there was left of value in the lease reverted to Mr. Salmon, as it would had the lease been for thirty years instead of twenty. Any equity which Mr. Meinhard possessed was in the particular lease itself, not in any possibility of renewal. There was nothing unfair in Mr. Salmon's conduct. . . .

NOTES AND QUESTIONS

1. Even today, judges often quote Cardozo's description of a partner's fiduciary duty in Meinhard v. Salmon. Moreover, its exhortatory, sermon-like rhetoric ("Not honesty alone, but the punctilio of an honor the most sensitive"), as well as its suggestion that partners are analogous to trustees, is typical of the most modern cases. Does such language serve the primary function of reinforcing the importance of trust and honesty in relations?

2. Meinhard and Salmon did not specify what rights either of them would have with respect to a new lease covering both the leased and adjacent property. If they had bargained over this contingency, can we predict with confidence what specific terms they would have adopted? If Meinhard and Salmon contemplated that Meinhard would have only the right to profit from this specific lease, that expectation could have been expressed ex ante. In the absence of such express limitation of Meinhard's rights, is there a gap in the venturers' contract? If so, how should a court fill that gap? From a contract interpretation perspective, how do the majority and dissenting opinions in Meinhard v. Salmon differ? Is the result best described as an attempt to give the parties the result for which they would have bargained? Is it possible to describe the result as imposing a penalty default rule whose purpose is to penalize the contracting party who has failed to disclose to the other party information as to his true intentions?

3. UPA (1997) §405 recognizes a partner's right to a formal accounting to enforce fiduciary duties or contractual rights. A formal accounting is an equitable proceeding. The court, usually acting through a master, has power to determine the true facts about partnership affairs, to settle disputes about the proper interpretation of partnership agreements, and to determine the relative rights and duties of the partners. The court may grant a money judgment in favor of a partner, if appropriate, and may grant injunctive or other equitable relief. At common law an accounting was available only in connection with dissolution of a partnership.

4. UPA (1997) §403 requires a partner, on demand, to furnish the requesting partner with full and complete information about partnership affairs. Do statutes similar to UPA (1997) §403 abrogate the common law fiduciary duty of disclosure imposed in Meinhard v. Salmon? The answer is clearly no, as explained in Appletree Square I Limited Partnership v. Investmark, Inc., 494 N.W.2d 889, 892-893 (Minn. Ct. App. 1993):

> The trial court held that the Uniform Limited Partnership Act changed the common law duties of disclosure. Minn. Stat. §322A.28(2) (1990) states that limited partners have the right, "upon reasonable demand," to obtain information from the general partners. This statute mirrors the disclosure requirement in the Uniform Partnership Act and should be interpreted similarly. See Minn. Stat. §323.19 (1990). The trial court held that because appellants did not demand information about asbestos, respondents had no obligation to disclose the information.
>
> The trial court's holding is contradicted by a proper interpretation of the disclosure statute. Minn. Stat. §322A.28(2) addresses the narrow duty of partners to respond to requests for information. It does not negate a partner's broad common law duty to disclose all material facts. See H. Reuschlein and W. Gregory, Handbook on the Law of Agency and Partnership, 285 (1979) (the duty to render information is not the same as the duty to disclose). This view has been accepted by other jurisdictions that have adopted the uniform acts governing general and limited partnerships. See Band v. Livonia Assocs., 439 N.W.2d 285, 294 (Mich. App. 1989) ("section 20 [of the Uniform Partnership Act] has been broadly interpreted as imposing a duty to disclose all known information that is significant and material to the affairs or property of the partnership"), appeal denied (Mich. Dec. 28, 1989); Peskin v. Deutsch, 134 Ill. App. 3d 48, 89 Ill. Dec. 28, 32, 479 N.E.2d 1034, 1038 (1985) (partners owe each other the "duty to make full and fair disclosure"), appeal denied (Ill. Dec. 4, 1985); Covalt v. High, 100 N.M. 700, 675 P.2d 999, 1001 (App. 1983) ("[a]s a fiduciary, each partner has a duty to fully disclose to the other, all material facts which may affect the business of the partnership"), cert. denied, 100 N.M. 631, 674 P.2d 521 (1984). Minn. Stat. §322A.28(2) did not eliminate respondents' common law duty to disclose material information to their partners.

5. An important aspect of fiduciary duty is its impact on litigants' burdens of proof. Under the normal rule, fiduciaries must carry the burden of proving by clear and

convincing evidence that they have fulfilled their fiduciary obligations. See Oakhill Associates v. D'Amato, 638 A.2d 31, 33 (Conn. 1994). Does the assignment of burden of proof explain the result in Meinhard v. Salmon?

PROBLEM 2-5

Jane, a partner in a small law firm, was recently approached by the firm's landlord, a personal friend, for advice on who might be interested in buying the office building and the attached leases. Without informing her partners, Jane negotiated an agreement to buy the building for her own account. Did Jane breach her fiduciary duty to her partners? Would it affect your answer if the building in question were a 20-story office building in which the partnership occupied less than a floor? Would it affect your answer if before joining the firm, Jane notified each partner in writing that she could only accept their offer of partnership if it was agreeable for her to continue to pursue outside business ventures with her personal friend, the owner of the building, and no partner raised an objection?

2. Self-Dealing

Vigneau v. Storch Engineers
Superior Court of Connecticut, 1995
1995 WL 767984

MEMORANDUM OF DECISION

SATTER, JUDGE TRIAL REFEREE

Plaintiff sues to recover the value of his partnership interest pursuant to the retirement provisions of a partnership agreement. Defendant defends and counterclaims on the grounds of plaintiff's breach of fiduciary duty, breach of contract, fraud, violation of Connecticut Unfair Trade Practices Act (CUTPA), and negligence.... The primary issue presented is the consequences flowing from plaintiff violating the fiduciary duty owed to the defendant partnership by his self-dealing.

The facts are as follows:

Defendant Storch Engineers (sometimes hereinafter Storch) is a consulting engineering firm, operating as a partnership, with its principal place of business in New Jersey and offices also in Connecticut and other northeastern states. Plaintiff was hired by defendant as an architect for its Hartford office in 1980 and became a partner in 1983 when he acquired one partnership point or a one percent interest in the partnership. Plaintiff funded additional partnership points by executing promissory notes in favor of Herbert Storch, the managing partner, and the partnership. Eventually, he accumulated 3.071 points of ownership in the partnership....

Plaintiff functioned as the sole architect in the defendant's Hartford office. In the period from 1983, when plaintiff became a partner, until 1987, when plaintiff resigned, defendant's net billings in Connecticut increased from $884,523 to $2,014,661.

The partnership agreement between plaintiff and Storch (hereinafter the Agreement) provides at paragraph 13 that each partner shall

> (c) diligently attend to the business of the partnership and devote his whole time and attention thereto unless otherwise determined and authorized by the Managing Partner.
>
> (d) be just and faithful to the other partners and at all times give to the other partners full information and truthful explanations of all matters relating to the affairs of the partnership and afford every assistance in his power to carry on the business for the mutual advantage of his partners.

In 1983, Joseph Merluzzo, head of defendant's Connecticut operations, recruited plaintiff to invest with him in a real estate development partnership known as Highview Condominium Associates (hereinafter HCA) to build condominiums in Cromwell. Merluzzo became the managing partner of HCA and plaintiff a general partner with a 22% interest. The arrangement was kept secret from Storch. HCA hired Storch to do the architectural and engineering work for its project and plaintiff was Storch's architect-in-charge. Plaintiff appeared before a Cromwell zoning and planning board to seek approval of the plans for the project.

The fees for Storch's services to HCA were negotiated by Merluzzo and plaintiff acting in dual roles as secret partners of HCA and as representative of Storch. Although a witness for Storch testified the fees of $34,000 charged for Storch's services were low by $19,000, the court believes plaintiff's testimony that those fees were reasonable and in accordance with market rates.

Plaintiff made a profit in 1984 from his interest in HCA of $28,059, which he never revealed or accounted for to his partners at Storch.

In June 1984 Merluzzo initiated another real estate partnership, called Grandford Associates, to build an office building in Hartford. Plaintiff became a general partner in that partnership with an 8.33% share.

Merluzzo and plaintiff posted a job announcement with Storch Engineers that Storch would do the architectural and engineering work on the Grandford project. The announcement was designed to conceal Merluzzo's and plaintiff's interest in Grandford.

Merluzzo and plaintiff negotiated secretly with themselves to establish the fees Storch was to charge Grandford for Storch's services. Although defendant's witness testified those fees were low by $120,000, the court believed plaintiff's testimony that those fees were reasonable and in accordance with market rates.

Grandford suffered reverses and was unable to pay Storch's bills totalling $114,000. Plaintiff participated in decisions of Grandford to pay other creditors rather than Storch. Grandford's debt caused considerable concern to Storch. Merluzzo and plaintiff falsely assured Storch the bill would be paid by Grandford's "professional" partners obtaining bank financing.

In January 1986 plaintiff, in his capacity as Storch's architect-in-charge, wrote to Grandford formally requesting payment of Storch's long-overdue bill. This was a calculated deception by which plaintiff was concealing his Grandford involvement, in effect dunning himself and giving the illusion of an arm's-length transaction between Storch and Grandford. Eventually, Grandford was taken over by another firm and in October 1986 the Storch bill was fully paid with interest.

Plaintiff lost $22,000 on the Grandford deal.

Merluzzo resigned from Storch in July 1986 when his participation in Grandford was discovered by Storch. At that time he told Storch that plaintiff's involvement in Grandford was "minimal." Plaintiff promised Storch to divest himself of his entire interest in Grandford. He attempted to do so but could find no takers. Storch demanded plaintiff produce the Grandford partnership agreement. Not until February 1989 did plaintiff do so and also reveal his role in HCA. Only then did Storch get the full and true picture of plaintiff's self-dealing in those two projects.

The Agreement provides at paragraph 22 that the partnership "shall purchase for the price and in the manner hereinafter set forth, the interest of (a) any partner desiring to sell his interest, or (b) any . . . retired partner. . . ."

Plaintiff resigned from Storch by letter dated May 1, 1987, effective as of June 30, 1987. The reasons for the resignation was poor health and dissatisfaction with the direction of the partnership. . . . Plaintiff duly demanded that his partnership interest be purchased and paid for by the partnership pursuant to the Agreement. Storch has refused to do so. . . . The parties have stipulated that the plaintiff's 3.071% partnership interest had a value at the time of his resignation of $167,794.50. . . . The defendant, while conceding the value of plaintiff's partnership interest, argues that it is not obligated to pay it because plaintiff violated the partnership agreement and its fiduciary duty to the partnership. . . .

[Under the governing law, whether it be that of New Jersey or that of Connecticut] a partner bears a fiduciary relationship to his partners. Justice Benjamin Cardozo in Meinhard v. Salmon, 249 N.Y. 458, 464 (1928), equated partners with trustees and stated the oft-quoted words: "A trustee is held to something stricter than the morals of the marketplace. Not honesty alone, but the punctilio of an honor the most sensitive, is then the standard of behavior." That standard is incorporated in Connecticut law, Konover Dev. Corp. v. Zeller, 228 Conn. 206, 218 n. 9 (1994), and in New Jersey law, Heller v. Hartz Mountain Industries, 636 A.2d 599, 603 (N.J. Super. App. 1993).

The one absolute taboo is that a fiduciary may not engage in self-dealing. As stated in Shepard, Law of Fiduciaries at 156-57 (1981), "[T]he basic rule is a strong prohibition against self-dealing. The idea is that the fiduciary should not be acting as both vendor and purchaser, whether for goods or services." See also Bromberg and Ribstein on Partnership §6.07 at 6:74. A partner is also obligated to his partners to render "true accounts and full information about everything which affects the partnership." Weidlich v. Weidlich, 147 Conn. 160, 164 (1960). The Agreement between this plaintiff and defendant specifically imposes that requirement at paragraph 13(d).

The facts of this case clearly establish that plaintiff violated his fiduciary duty to the defendant by self-dealing in the HCA and Grandford projects and by concealing from the defendant those activities. Plaintiff argues that defendant suffered no harm and in fact benefitted from those two projects because defendant realized substantial fees from them. The fact that defendant suffered no injury as a result of the plaintiff's disloyalty is of no consequence and acts as no excuse. As stated in Bromberg and Ribstein on Partnership, §6.07 at 6:94, the rule is "prophylactic in nature, based on the need not only to compensate but to deter conduct that poses a risk of damage to the partnership."

In Cogan v. Kedder, Matthew & Senger, Inc., 648 P.2d 875, 878 (Wash. 1982), the court held that when an agent has dual responsibilities and serves interests adverse to the principal, it is of no consequence that his disloyalty did not injure the principal. "Not only does harm not define the scope of fiduciary duty, it also is not determinative of damages." Id. at 886. It further stated that strong public policy reasons justify the rule: "If damages were measured solely by the loss to the principal, often there would be little disincentive to the agent for assuming conflicting responsibilities without disclosure." Id.

The real issue here is whether plaintiff's violation of his fiduciary duty deprives him of his right to be paid for his vested partnership interest. . . . While neither Connecticut nor New Jersey have cases on the point, other jurisdictions have clearly held that a disloyal partner is entitled to reimbursement for his vested interest or capital contributions.

In Meechan v. Shaughnessy, 535 N.E.2d 1255 (Mass. 1989), where law partners were found to have breached their fiduciary duty to their firm, the firm argued they thereby forfeited all rights to their capital contributions. The court expressly rejected that contention, holding the disloyal partners were entitled to their interest in the partnership's reserve and capital accounts and in the partnership income earned but not distributed. The court said capital contributions "are not a form of liquidated damages to which partners can resort in the event of breach." Id. at 1266. . . . Thus, this court holds that, despite plaintiff's breach of fiduciary duty owed to Storch, he is entitled to the value of his vested partnership interest, stipulated to amount to $167,794.50. . . .

As to defendant's counterclaim of breach of fiduciary duty, the court recognizes the rule that once a fiduciary relationship is established, as is the fact here, the burden of proof of fair dealing shifts to the plaintiff and he must meet that burden by clear and convincing evidence. Konover Dev. Corp. v. Zeller, 228 Conn. 206, 229-30 (1994). Clearly plaintiff has failed to do so, and the court finds that plaintiff's hidden participation in the Grandford and HCA projects constituted a violation of the fiduciary obligations he owed Storch.

One consequence of such a violation is Storch is entitled to recover from plaintiff the secret profit of $28,059 plaintiff realized on the HCA deal. As stated in Bromberg and Ribstein on Partnership, §6.07, p. 6:93 (1994), "The measure of damages for fiduciary breach clearly includes any profits earned as a result of the breach." C.G.S. §34-59(1) provides that the breaching partner holds unauthorized profits "as trustee."

Pursuant to §37-3a this court awards interest at 10% per annum on the profit of $28,059 from 1984 to 1995, amounting to interest of $30,864, for a total of $58,923. . . .

Storch claims damages for all compensation and profit-sharing paid to plaintiff during the period of disloyalty, amounting to $164,105. The Restatement of Agency, Second at §469 provides that "[a]n agent is entitled to no compensation for conduct . . . which is a breach of his duty of loyalty; if such conduct constitutes a willful and deliberate breach of his contract of service, he is not entitled to compensation even for properly performed services for which no compensation is apportioned." Hegman

v. Kline, 344 F.Supp. 1110, 1114 (D.Conn. 1979), rev'd on other grounds, 456 F.2d 125 (2nd Cir. 1972), interpreted that section to mean, "when a disloyal employee is paid without [the principal's] knowledge of his disloyalty, he may be compelled to return what he has improperly received."

However, other courts have examined the reasoning behind the provisions of the Restatements of Agency and Trusts, and "find the basis for refusal of compensation to a trustee, not in the theory of a penalty, but in the theory that payment is not due for services not properly performed." Lydia E. Pinkhorn Medicine Co. v. Gove, 20 N.E.2d 482, 486 (1939). Thus, the rule that a failed fiduciary may be denied compensation or be required to return compensation paid is "not inflexible and generally rests with the discretion of the court." Williams v. Queen Fisheries, Inc., 469 P.2d 583, 585 (Wash. App. 1970); Cogan v. Kidder Matthews & Signer, Inc., 648 P.2d 875, 890 (Wash. 1982); Welles v. Van Wog, 20 So.2d 690 (Fla. 1945).

In the instant case, apart from his disloyal participation in the HCA and Grandford projects, plaintiff performed his architectural services for Storch competently and contributed substantially to the success of the firm over the period 1980 to 1987. Requiring him to repay his entire compensation would constitute undue enrichment to Storch and amount to an unjust penalty. This court exercises its discretion to deny such a result.

Storch would be entitled to the losses resulting from plaintiff negotiating Storch's fees for services to HCA and Grandford lower than the market, but this court finds those fees were reasonable and in line with market rates.

[Editors' note: The Court further determined that plaintiff's conduct constituted a breach of CUPTA, for which breach the Court imposed punitive damages in the amount of $50,000 and awarded defendant its reasonable attorney's fees in the amount of $110,000.]

3.   Fiduciary Duty and Management of the Partnership's Business and Affairs

UPA (1997) §401(f) and (j)

Under UPA (1997) §401(f), each partner has equal rights in the management and conduct of partnership business. Under UPA (1997) §401(j), differences as to ordinary matters connected with partnership business may be decided by a majority of the partners. However, no act in contravention of an agreement between the partners may be done rightfully without the consent of all partners. Thus, if partners have agreed to deal with even an ordinary matter in a certain way, such agreement will control until changed by subsequent consent of all the partners. UPA (1997) §401(j) also requires that disagreements about extraordinary matters be decided unanimously.

In effect, §401(j) provides that business decisions are decided by a vote of the partners. Partners who are unable to muster the required vote must be content with the result. But what is the recourse of a partner who feels that the majority is opportunistically refusing to adapt to changed circumstances? Must she withdraw or threaten to withdraw from the partnership, or does she have a judicial remedy? The principal case, below, explores the extent to which fiduciary duty or other equitable considerations may constrain the majority's opportunistic refusal to "vote" for needed changes in partnership policies.

Covalt v. High
New Mexico Court of Appeals, 1983
675 P.2d 999

DONNELLY, JUDGE.

... The plaintiff, Louis E. Covalt, filed suit against defendant, William L. High, seeking (1) the sale of real property in lieu of partition, (2) an accounting as to former partnership property, and (3) seeking both actual and punitive damages. . . .

The trial court ordered that Covalt's claim for loss of rental income, allegedly owed by defendant to the former partnership, be bifurcated from the remaining issues and tried separately to the court. Following trial thereon, Covalt was awarded judgment against William L. High, individually, in the sum of $9,500, plus prejudgment interest in the sum of $2,269.

High appeals the partial judgment entered solely against him. The single issue presented on appeal is whether the trial court erred by ruling that High breached a fiduciary duty of fairness to his former partner Covalt by failing to negotiate and obtain an increase in the amount of rental for the partnership realty.

FACTS

Covalt and High were corporate officers and shareholders in CSI. Covalt owned 25% of the stock and High owned the remaining 75% of the stock. Both men received remuneration from the corporation in the form of salaries and bonuses. In late 1971, after both High and Covalt had become corporate officers, they orally agreed to the formation of a partnership. The partnership bought real estate and constructed an office and warehouse building on the land. In February, 1973, CSI leased the building from the partnership for a five-year term. Following the expiration of the initial term of the lease, CSI remained a tenant of the building; the corporation and the partnership orally agreed to certain rental increases. The corporation made substantial improvements to the leasehold. Under the original lease any improvements to the premises were to accrue to the partnership upon termination of the lease.

In December, 1978, Covalt resigned his corporate position and was employed by a competitor of CSI. Covalt, however, remained a partner with High in the ownership of the land and the building rented to CSI. On January 9, 1979, Covalt wrote to High demanding that the monthly rent for the partnership real estate leased to CSI be increased from $1,850 to $2,850 per month. Upon receipt of the letter, High informed Covalt he would determine if the rent could be increased. Thereafter, however, High did not agree to the increased rent and took no action to renegotiate the amount of the monthly rent payable.

At the trial, High testified that he felt CSI could not afford a higher rent and that the corporation had a poor financial status. The trial court, however, adopted findings that CSI could afford the requested rental increase and that High's failure to assent to his partner's demand was a breach of his fiduciary duty. The trial court also found that at the time of Covalt's demand, a reasonable monthly rental would have been $2,850 per month or more. . . .

Based on the foregoing findings, the trial court concluded that High breached his fiduciary duty to Covalt, resulting in damage to Covalt in the sum of $9,500 as lost rentals, plus prejudgment interest through April 30, 1982, in the amount of $2,269.66.

FIDUCIARY DUTY AS A PARTNER

Did High breach a fiduciary partnership duty to Covalt warranting an award of damages?

The status resulting from the formation of a partnership creates a fiduciary relationship between partners. The status of partnership requires of each member an obligation of good faith and fairness in their dealings with one another, and a duty to act in furtherance of the common benefit of all partners in transactions conducted within the ambit of partnership affairs. . . .

The problems which have arisen between the parties herein, emphasize the importance of formulating written partnership agreements detailing the rights and obligations of the partners. Here, at the time of Covalt's demand for an increase in rents, both he and High simultaneously occupied the positions of corporate shareholders in CSI and as partners engaged in the ownership and rental of real property to the same corporation. Prior to Covalt's resignation as a corporate officer, he also served as vice president of CSI. The trial court found that High occupied the position of managing partner of the partnership.

Except where the partners expressly agree to the contrary, it is a fundamental principle of the law of partnership that all partners have equal rights in the management and conduct of the business of the partnership. As specified in the Uniform Partnership Act adopted by New Mexico, where there is a difference of opinion between the partners as to the management or conduct of the partnership business, the decision of the majority must govern.

Under [UPA §18(h)], Covalt was legally invested with an equal voice in the management of the partnership affairs. Assuming, but not deciding, that High's status as a managing partner is not to be considered, neither partner had the right to impose his will or decision concerning the operation of the partnership business upon the other. The fact that a proposal may in fact benefit the partnership does not mandate acceptance by all the partners. As specified in [UPA §18(h)], "any difference arising as to ordinary matters connected with the partnership business may be decided by a majority of the partners; but no act in contravention of any agreement between the partners may be done rightfully without the consent of all the partners."

As stated in Lindley on the Law of Partnership, Chapter 14 at 354 (E. Scamell 12th ed. 1962) (hereinafter referred to as *Lindley*), as to differences arising in the ordinary scope of the partnership business: "[I]f the partners are equally divided, those who forbid a change must have their way. . . . [O]ne partner cannot either engage a new or dismiss an old servant against the will of his co-partner; nor, if the lease of the partnership place of business expires, insist on renewing the lease and continuing the business at the old place."

In Summers v. Dooley, 94 Idaho 87, 481 P.2d 318 (1971), the Supreme Court of Idaho was confronted with a similar problem arising out of a partnership of two individuals. There, the partners were engaged in a trash collection business and each contributed to the necessary labor. Over the objection of one partner, the other hired an additional employee. The disagreement over the hiring and compensation of the new employee resulted in a suit between the partners. The one partner sought to compel his co-partner to contribute to the expenses for hiring the additional man. The court held that, based upon the Idaho statute, mirroring the Uniform Partnership Act and identical to that adopted by New Mexico, the statutory language that any differences between partners as to the ordinary course of partnership business "may be decided by a majority of the partners," is mandatory rather than permissive in nature. 94 Idaho at 89, 481 P.2d at 320.

In keeping with *Lindley* and *Summers,* as between the partners themselves, in the absence of an agreement of a majority of the partners—an act involving the partnership business may not be compelled by the co-partner. If the parties are evenly divided as to a business decision affecting the partnership, and in the absence of a written provision in the partnership agreement providing for such contingency, then, as between the partners, the power to exercise discretion on behalf of the partners is suspended so long as the division continues. . . .

Similarly, it is observed in 1 J. Barrett & E. Seago, Partners and Partnerships Law and Taxation, Chapter 5, §7 at 484 (1956): "Where the partnership consists of only two partners there is ordinarily no question of one partner controlling the other and there is no majority. The rights of each of the two partners are equal. If the partners are unable to agree and if the partnership agreement does not provide an acceptable means for settlement of this disagreement, the only course of action is to dissolve the partnership."

At the time of the formation of the partnership, both Covalt and High were officers and shareholders of CSI. Each was aware of the potential for conflict between their duties as corporate officers to further the business of the corporation, and that of their role as partners in leasing realty to the corporation for the benefit of the partnership business. In the posture of being both a landlord and representatives of the tenant they had conflicting loyalties and fiduciary duties. After Covalt's resignation as an officer of the corporation he continued to remain a shareholder of the corporation. Each party's conflict of interest was known to the other and was acquiesced in when the partnership was formed.

Under the facts herein, in the absence of a mutual agreement between the partners to increase the rent of the partnership realty, we hold that one partner may not recover damages for the failure of the co-partner to acquiesce in a demand by the plaintiff that High negotiate and execute an increase in the monthly rentals of partnership property with CSI. Thus, there was no breach of a fiduciary duty. In the absence of a mutual agreement, or a written instrument detailing the rights of the parties, the remedy for such an impasse is a dissolution of the partnership. . . .

4. Contracting for Absolute Discretion

UPA (1997) §§103(a)(3), 404

The relationship of fiduciary duty and private ordering is controversial. At one end of the spectrum is the view that fiduciary duty is an immutable feature of partnership law, empowering judges to ensure that partners exercise the utmost honesty, candor, and good faith in deals with, or that affect, the partnership. At the opposite extreme is the view that fiduciary duty is a fully mutable feature of partnership law that must yield to contractual agreements that limit or eliminate a role for ex post judicial intervention. The compromise position, reflected in case law and UPA (1997) §§103(a)(3) and 404, views fiduciary duty as partly mutable, but with an irreducible core.

Not uncommonly, a subset of partners will contract for near or absolute discretion in managing the partnership's business. For example, a large law firm may give to a managing partner or an executive committee absolute discretion to set the profit shares of the members of the firm from year to year. Should courts review these self-interested decisions when disgruntled partners assert that the partners with absolute discretion have unfairly favored themselves?

Starr v. Fordham
Supreme Judicial Court of Massachusetts, 1995
648 N.E.2d 1261

Before LIACOS, C.J., and ABRAMS, NOLAN, LYNCH and GREANEY, JJ., NOLAN, JUSTICE.

The plaintiff, Ian M. Starr, was a partner in the Boston law firm Fordham & Starrett (firm). After the plaintiff withdrew from the firm, he commenced this action to recover amounts to which he claimed that he was entitled under the partnership agreement. The plaintiff also sought damages for breach of fiduciary duty and fraudulent misrepresentation. . . . After a jury-waived trial, a Superior Court judge concluded that [the founding partners, Fordham and Starrett], had violated their fiduciary duties to the plaintiff as well as the implied covenant of good faith and fair dealing in the partnership agreement when they determined the plaintiff's share of the firm's profits for 1986. The judge awarded the plaintiff damages of $75,538.48, plus interest from the date on which the plaintiff filed his complaint. . . .

1. *Facts.* We summarize the judge's findings of fact. In 1984, the plaintiff was a partner in the Boston law firm Foley, Hoag & Eliot (Foley Hoag). The plaintiff specialized in corporate and business law. Although the plaintiff had become a partner at Foley Hoag in 1982, he was actively seeking to leave the firm in early 1984. During this time, the founding partners were also partners at Foley Hoag. Both men enjoyed outstanding professional reputations among their colleagues. Nevertheless, they agreed that they would withdraw from Foley Hoag in early 1985 in order to establish a new law firm with another established Boston attorney, Frank W. Kilburn. Fordham invited the plaintiff to join the new law firm Kilburn, Fordham & Starrett in January, 1985. At first, the plaintiff was somewhat hesitant to accept the offer because he was not known as a "rainmaker" (i.e., an attorney responsible for significant client origination) at

Foley Hoag. Fordham, however, assured the plaintiff that business origination would not be a significant factor for allocating the profits among the partners. Relying on this representation, the plaintiff withdrew from Foley Hoag on March 1, 1985. The founding partners and another attorney, the defendant Brian W. LeClair, withdrew from Foley Hoag on March 4, 1985.

Prior to executing the partnership agreement, the plaintiff informed Fordham that certain provisions in the agreement disturbed him. The source of the plaintiff's disquiet was Paragraph 1 of the partnership agreement which vested in the founding partners and Kilburn, the authority to determine, both prospectively and retrospectively, each partner's share of the firm's profits. Despite his concern, the plaintiff did not claim at this time that the agreement contradicted Fordham's representations to him that rainmaking would not be a significant factor in distributing the firm's profits. Fordham summarily dismissed the plaintiff's concerns, telling him, in effect, to "take it or leave it." On March 5, 1985, the founding partners, Kilburn, and LeClair each executed the partnership agreement for Kilburn, Fordham & Starrett. The plaintiff also signed the agreement without objection and without making any revisions. The defendant Barry A. Guryan joined the new firm on March 11, 1985.

In August of 1985, Kilburn withdrew from the firm. Subsequently, the firm assumed the name Fordham & Starrett. . . .

The founding partners had divided the firm's profits equally among the partners in 1985. Each of the five partners received $11,602. In 1986, the firm's financial fortunes improved significantly. On December 31, 1986, the firm's profits were $1,605,128. In addition, the firm had $1,844,366.59 in accounts receivable and work in progress.

The plaintiff withdrew from the firm on December 31, 1986. The partners remaining in the firm were the founding partners, LeClair, and Guryan. . . . The founding partners determined the plaintiff's share of the firm's profits for 1986 to be 6.3% of the total profits. . . .

3. *1986 profits.* . . . The founding partners assert several arguments on appeal from the judge's finding that they violated their fiduciary duties and the implied covenant of good faith and fair dealing when they allocated to the plaintiff only 6.3% of the firm's profits for 1986. We address each in turn.

A.   The Burden of Proof

The founding partners claim that the judge erroneously imposed on them the burden of proving the fairness of their profit distribution to the plaintiff. We disagree.

Partners owe each other a fiduciary duty of the highest degree of good faith and fair dealing. Cardullo v. Landau, 329 Mass. 5, 8, 105 N.E.2d 843 (1952). Shelley v. Smith, 271 Mass. 106, 115, 170 N.E. 826 (1930). When a partner has engaged in self-dealing, that partner has the burden to prove the fairness of his actions and to prove that his actions did not result in harm to the partnership. See Meehan v. Shaughnessy, 404 Mass. 419, 441, 535 N.E.2d 1255 (1989). In the present case, it is clear that the judge concluded that the founding partners had engaged in self-dealing. The judge found that the founding partners' determination of the plaintiff's share of the profits "positioned them on both sides of the transaction" because the percentage of the profits which they had assigned to the plaintiff had a direct impact on their own share of the profits. We cannot say that this conclusion was clearly erroneous. The founding partners were responsible for dividing the partnership's profits and assigning to each partner his respective share of the profits. Thus, the founding partners had some self-interest in designating each partner's respective share of the profits because the percentage of profits which they were assigning to the other partners had a direct effect on their own percentage of the profits. See Sagalyn v. Meekins, Packard & Wheat, Inc., 290 Mass. 434, 439, 195 N.E. 769 (1935). As a result, we conclude that there was no error in the judge's imposing on the founding partners the burden of proving that their distribution of the firm's profits to the plaintiff was fair and reasonable. See Meehan v. Shaughnessy, supra.

B.   THE BUSINESS JUDGMENT RULE

The founding partners argue next that the judge erred in concluding that the business judgment rule does not preclude judicial review of their determination of the plaintiff's share of the 1986 profits. There was no error.

The test to be applied when one partner alleges that another partner has violated his duty of strict faith is whether the allegedly violating partner can demonstrate a legitimate business purpose for his action. See Zimmerman v. Bogoff, 402 Mass. 650, 657, 524 N.E.2d 849 (1988). Nevertheless, the business judgment rule does not apply if the plaintiff can demonstrate self-dealing on the part of the allegedly wrongdoing partner. See Johnson v. Witkowski, 30 Mass. App. Ct. 697, 711-712, 573 N.E.2d 513 (1991). Having properly concluded that the founding partners had engaged in self-dealing when they assigned to the plaintiff his share of the profit, the judge made no error in concluding that the business judgment rule did not apply to the founding partners' actions.

C.   FIDUCIARY DUTIES AND COVENANT OF GOOD FAITH

The founding partners argue that the judge's conclusion that they had violated both their fiduciary duties and the implied covenant of good faith and fair dealing when they allocated only 6.3% of the firm's profits for 1986 to the plaintiff was clearly erroneous. We disagree.

An implied covenant of good faith and fair dealing exists in every contract. See Druker v. Roland Wm. Jutras Assocs., 370 Mass. 383, 385, 348 N.E.2d 763 (1976), quoting Uproar Co. v. National Broadcasting Co., 81 F.2d 373, 377 (1st Cir.), cert. denied, 298 U.S. 670, 56 S.Ct. 835, 80 L.Ed. 1393 (1936). Thus, an unfair determination of a partner's respective share of a partnership's earnings is a breach not only of one's fiduciary duty, see Stratis v. Andreson, 254 Mass. 536, 539, 150 N.E. 832 (1926), but also of the implied covenant of good faith and fair dealing. See Druker v. Roland Wm. Jutras Assocs., supra at 385, 348 N.E.2d 763. A court has the power to determine whether a partner's share of the profits is fair and equitable as a matter of law. Noble

v. Joseph Burnett Co., 208 Mass. 75, 82, 94 N.E. 289 (1911). In the present case, the judge "vigorously scrutinized" the founding partners' determination of the plaintiff's share of the profits. See Houle v. Low, 407 Mass. 810, 824, 556 N.E.2d 51 (1990). The judge then made extensive findings concerning the fairness of the plaintiff's share of the profit distribution. The judge found that the plaintiff had produced billable hour and billable dollar amounts that constituted 16.4% and 15%, respectively, of the total billable hour and billable dollar amounts for all of the partners as a group. The judge noted, however, that the founding partners distributed only 6.3% of the firm's 1986 profits to the plaintiff. Meanwhile, the other partners received substantially greater shares of the profits. The judge concluded, therefore, that the founding partners had decided to exclude billable hour and billable dollar totals as a factor in determining compensation. The judge determined that this decision to exclude billable hour figures was unfair to the plaintiff and indicated that the founding partners had selected performance criteria in order to justify the lowest possible payment to the plaintiff.[1] The judge also noted that Fordham had fabricated a list of negative factors that the founding partners had used in determining the plaintiff's share of the firm's profits. As a result, the judge concluded that the founding partners had violated their respective fiduciary duties to the plaintiff as well as the implied covenant of good faith and fair dealing. The judge also concluded that the plaintiff was entitled to 11% of the firm's profits for 1986 and awarded the plaintiff $75,538.48 in damages.[2]

Having examined the record, all 127 exhibits, and the judge's own findings of fact and rulings of law, we conclude that the judge's ultimate finding of liability was not clearly erroneous. We note that "[t]he authority of an appellate court, when reviewing the findings of a judge as well as those of a jury, is circumscribed by the deference it must give to decisions of the trier of fact, who is usually in a superior position to appraise and weigh the evidence. The question for the appellate court under Rule 52(a) is not whether it would have made the findings the trial court did, but whether 'on the entire evidence [it] is left with the definite and firm conviction that a mistake has been committed.' " First Pa. Mortgage Trust v. Dorchester Sav. Bank, 395 Mass. 614, 621, 481 N.E.2d 1132 (1985), quoting Zenith Radio Corp. v. Hazeltine Research, Inc., 395 U.S. 100, 123, 89 S.Ct. 1562, 1576, 23 L.Ed.2d 129 (1969). We cannot conclude that the judge committed a mistake in finding that the founding partners had violated both their fiduciary duties to the plaintiff and the implied covenant of good faith and fair dealing.

---

1. The judge compared the plaintiff's work performance directly to the work performance of the defendants Guryan and LeClair. The judge concluded that the plaintiff's "billable hours by working attorney" were 85% of the total billable hours that Guryan had worked and 77% of the total billable hours that LeClair had worked. The plaintiff's share of the profits, however, was only 34% of the amount which Guryan and LeClair each had received.

2. The judge found that 11% of the profits was a more accurate reflection of the plaintiff's contribution to the firm's 1986 profits after considering the plaintiff's billable hour and billable dollar totals. In addition, the judge noted that Starrett had recommended that the plaintiff receive an 11% profit share in the fall of 1986 when the plaintiff first had informed his partners of his intention to withdraw from the firm. Eleven percent of the firm's total profits for 1986 amounted to $176,564.08. The judge then subtracted the 6.3% of the profits, which the plaintiff had already received, from $176,564.08 to arrive at $75,538.48.

NOTES AND QUESTIONS

1. Should the decision in Starr v. Fordham be the same in a jurisdiction that had adopted the provisions of UPA (1997)?

2. Should the court intervene in cases like Starr v. Fordham only with respect to decisions made after a complaining partner has decided to leave her partnership? Suppose, for example, that a partner is unhappy about profit allocations, but does not want to leave the firm. Should the partner be able to bring suit for breach of fiduciary duty, while continuing in the partnership?

3. To what extent should a partner be able to contract away his right to demand full information about all things affecting the partnership? Consider the following answer:

> Under Alaska law, a general partner stands in a fiduciary relationship with the limited partnership and thereby owes "a fiduciary duty . . . to disclose information concerning partnership affairs." Parker v. Northern Mixing Co., 756 P.2d 881, 894 (Alaska 1988); Alaska Stat. §32.05.150 ("Partners shall provide on demand true and full information of all things affecting the partnership to any partner. . . ."). The partnership agreement, however, will determine the extent of disclosure required between partners and whether a failure of disclosure constitutes fraud or breach of the agreement.
>
> "Partner fiduciary duties are aspects of the 'standard form' of partnership. As with respect to the other rights and duties among the partners, the partners may alter the standard form fiduciary duties to suit their particular relationship." 2 Alan R. Bromberg & Larry E. Ribstein, Bromberg and Ribstein on Partnership §6.07(h), at 6:89 (1991); id. §6.06, at 6:67 (arguing that "parties could at least circumscribe the right to information"); id. §6.05(d), at 6:59 (partners can bargain over access to information).
>
> Courts should allow parties to define the means of disclosure as the management of a partnership necessarily involves "the weighing and balancing of disparate considerations to which the court does not have access." Betz v. Chena Hot Springs Group, 657 P.2d 831, 835 (Alaska 1982).

Exxon Corp. v. Burglin, 4 F.3d 1294, 1299 (5th Cir. 1993).

5. The Duty of Care

UPA (1997) §404(c)

Restatement (Second) of Agency §379(1) (1958) provides: "Unless otherwise agreed, a paid agent is subject to a duty to the principal to act with standard care and with the skill which is standard in the locality for the kind of work which he is employed to perform. . . ." Thus, in any business association a nonowner agent, including a managerial agent, owes a fiduciary duty of care to her principal.

Since each partner is an agent of the partnership for purpose of carrying out its business, it might seem appropriate that a general partner's negligent performance of services would likewise give other general partners a cause of action for damages. However, the statutory and limited case law on this point is contradictory.

Older partnership statutes are silent concerning a duty of care. Statutes following UPA §404(c) impose a duty of care on general partners. Limited partnership statutes are also silent, but most provide that general partners have the same powers, and are subject to the same restrictions, as partners in a general partnership.

Though case law is scant, the better view in the limited partnership setting is that general partners owe limited partners a fiduciary duty of loyalty and care in the exercise of management functions. The imposition of a duty of care arguably is necessary to protect limited partners, who have no right to manage and control the partnership business and, thus, have little ability to monitor general partners' conduct. However, cases holding managers liable for breach of duty of care are very rare. As a result, we learn what the duty of care is mainly by reference to cases finding that there has been no breach of duty. Cincinnati Bell Cellular Systems Co. v. Ameritech Mobile Phone Service of Cincinnati, Inc., 1996 WL 506906 (Del. Ch.) is a typical case. Cincinnati Bell, a 40 percent owner in a limited partnership, sued Ameritech and its subsidiary AMCI (collectively the general partner), for breach of duty of care in managing the firm's business.

> Cincinnati Bell characterizes AMCI's conduct over the years as gross negligence and gross mismanagement. Under Delaware law, therefore, it is Cincinnati Bell's burden to plead and to prove that AMCI was "recklessly uninformed" or acted "outside the bounds of reason." Tomczak v. Morton Thiokol, Inc., Del. Ch., C.A. No. 7861, Hartnett, V.C. (April 5, 1990), Mem.Op. at 31-32; Rabkin v. Philip A. Hunt Chemical Corp., Del. Ch., 547 A.2d 963, 970 (1986). . . .
>
> Most of the disputed evidence . . . centers around conflicting opinions by experts concerning the wisdom of a particular business strategy undertaken by AMCI on behalf of the Partnership (for example, the D2000 initiative; the switch from analog to digital equipment; the absence of a Kotler-type marketing plan; the failure to partner with other wireless carriers in a national consortium; the structure for awarding incentive bonuses). Ameritech counters each charge of mismanagement with an arsenal of statistics and expert opinion justifying the business decisions undertaken on behalf of the Partnership. None of this disputed evidence, however, is a basis for denying summary judgment because the material facts are in agreement—all of the questioned acts or decisions were business decisions undertaken in good faith by the managing partner to meet a strong competitor in the Ohio market (CCI), often on the advice of consultants and experts hired by the managing partner specifically for the purpose of making such decisions. Thus, in the D2000 initiative example, the uncontested facts reveal that Ameritech adopted it on the recommendation of qualified outside consultants and implemented the plan to the consultants' satisfaction. So even though Cincinnati Bell now points to opinions post hoc from its experts that the initiative was poorly conceived or implemented, it cannot show that Ameritech's conduct represents gross negligence. The evidence is and would be that Ameritech adopted D2000 after soliciting advice from recognized experts. As a matter of law, on those undisputed facts, I cannot conclude that Ameritech acted in a recklessly uninformed manner.

1996 WL 506906 at *14-18.

The better answer in the general partnership setting is less clear, as the following case illustrates. On the one hand, general partners can participate actively in management and may be as responsible as other general partners for loss from lack of care. On the other hand, general partners can be passive investors who depend on other general partners' management expertise.

Ferguson v. Williams
Texas Court of Appeals, 1984
670 S.W.2d 327

BRADY, JUSTICE.
Appellee Williams brought suit to recover funds invested and expended by him in a joint venture with appellants Ferguson and Welborn. In a bench trial, the trial court

rendered judgment for Williams against appellants jointly and severally in the sum of $30,518.53 damages, plus $5,000.00 exemplary damages and attorney fees of $20,719.00. The trial court filed findings of fact and conclusions of law holding that Williams' interest in the venture was an "investment contract" and thus a security; that the same was not registered with the State Securities Board; that the same was sold by Ferguson and Welborn by means of false representations; that appellants were also negligent in the management of the venture; and that appellee Williams was entitled to rescind and recover all funds invested or expended by him in the venture. . . .

On March 1, 1979, Ferguson and Welborn, doing business as the F & W Development Company, purchased two apartment buildings containing thirty-two two-bedroom units located near Bergstrom Air Force Base from the U.S. Corps of Engineers. The buildings were to be removed to a new location, rehabilitated, leased to tenants, and then sold at a profit by the partners. Two months later, the appellants, running low on cash, contacted appellee Williams and sold him a one-fourth interest in the venture for $15,000.00. With the infusion of this additional capital, the appellants purchased land near Bergstrom, depositing $5,000.00 as earnest money. Appellants used the balance of Williams' money to secure a $300,000.00 permanent mortgage loan commitment. However, because of their inability to obtain interim or construction financing, the venture failed and the buildings eventually were dismantled and materials sold to pay debts. . . .

In our view, Williams played a significant role in the actual business of the partnership. Appellee volunteered his employees to help get the buildings ready to move, sending an overseer for the job. Appellee volunteered the use of his front-end loader to clean up the building site, kept in touch with the progress of the work, and, according to the evidence, talked to Ferguson at least once or twice a week from May, 1979 until January, 1980. When the partnership bank account needed money, Williams advanced an additional $5,000.00 to help get this project "rolling." Williams aided the business in obtaining an $11,000.00 loan from the Bank of Austin. He also signed a loan application with Ryan Mortgage Company for a permanent loan commitment for the partnership. He participated in preparation of a brochure, paid bills of the firm, and inspected the site chosen to relocate the buildings. We agree with appellants' argument that Williams' conduct was that of a partner and "not that of a passive investor." . . .

As to the findings by the trial court that appellants Ferguson and Welborn were guilty of negligence in the management of the affairs of the business and that such negligence was the proximate cause of Williams' loss of his invested funds, we hold as a matter of law that negligence in the management of the affairs of a general partnership or joint venture does not create any right of action against that partner by other members of the partnership. It is only when there is a breach of trust, such as when one partner or joint venturer holds property or assets belonging to the partnership or venture, and converts such to his own use, would such action lie. In the ordinary management and operation of a general partnership or joint venture there is no liability to the other partners or joint venturers for the negligence in the management or operation of the affairs of the enterprise, such as the six acts of "negligence" found by the trial court. The six findings of "negligence" by the trial court were that appellants were negligent: (1) "in the manner in which they sought construction and permanent financing for the venture"; (2) "in failing to promptly retain a house moving firm to move the condemned buildings";

(3) "in failing to adequately capitalize the venture"; (4) "in failing to promptly secure the necessary real property for the project"; (5) "in failing to diligently pursue completion of the venture's responsibility under its contract with the U.S. Army Corps of Engineers"; and (6) "in failing to truthfully and fully disclose to Williams all details of the venture." Appellee cites us no authority, and we have found none, to support his theory of this case. None of the "negligence" findings involve any breach of trust or fiduciary duty of Ferguson and Welborn to Williams. . . .

NOTES AND QUESTIONS

1. Why is case law virtually silent on the question of a partner's duty of care in a general partnership setting? Is there something about the archetypical general partnership that makes such a duty inappropriate? Is it more efficient to have partners collectively bear the risk of loss from choosing to associate with a partner who proves to be negligent or unskilled, than to have negligence deterred by judicial enforcement of a fiduciary duty of care? If partners should owe a duty of care, why would a gross negligence standard be appropriate instead of a more stringent standard such as an obligation to use either reasonable care or the care that would be used by an ordinarily prudent person in like circumstance?

2. Ferguson v. Williams has been followed in both the joint venture and limited partnership setting. See Duffy v. Piazza Construction, Inc., 815 P.2d 267 (Wash. App. 1991) (joint venturer does not owe other venturers a duty of care), and Johnson v. Weber, 803 P.2d 939 (Ariz. App. 1990) (general partner does not owe limited partner duty of care).

3. For the proposition that general partners do owe limited partners a fiduciary duty of care, see Roper v. Thomas, 298 S.E.2d 424 (N.C. App. 1982); Wyler v. Feurer, 85 Cal. App. 3d 392, 149 Cal. Rptr. 626 (1978); Boxer v. Husky Oil Co., 1983 WL 17937 (Del. Ch.); and Shinn v. Thrust IV, Inc., 786 P.2d 285 (Wash. App. 1990).

PROBLEM 2-6

In January, Sharon and Ruth formed a limited liability partnership, BHD, Ltd., to purchase and renovate dilapidated residences in the Barrow Historic District. As per the agreement, Sharon was in charge of supervising renovation and marketing. Ruth was only responsible for providing needed capital. BHD acquired two Victorian houses in February. Ruth then left town to spend six months on active duty with the Marine Corps. While Sharon had many years experience as a builder, she had never worked on renovation of older structures. She chose workmen and materials that were totally unsuited for the project. Upon completion, Sharon spent lavishly for radio and television ads trumpeting the two projects. BHD was unable to sell the two houses for more than the original purchase price, resulting in a loss of all of the capital invested in renovation and advertising.

Ruth has asked your advice concerning BHD's losses. Do you recommend that she sue Sharon for breach of her fiduciary duty of care?

C. *Dissolution and Dissociation*

1. The Basic Framework

UPA (1997) §§103(b)(6), 601, 603, 701, 801-803
UPA (1914) §§29-31, 38, 42

The law governing a partner's dissociation and the partnership's dissolution is complex and often misunderstood even by experienced practitioners. Therefore, we begin with an examination of the dissolution framework as it applies to the so-called at-will partnership—a partnership formed without agreement that the partnership shall continue for a specified term or undertaking.

Under partnership law norms, the general partnership is an at-will relationship that can continue only as long as every member assents. The at-will characteristic ensures that any partner will be able to adapt to changed circumstances by dissociating from the partnership and redeploying his talents and capital elsewhere. However, a general partnership relationship is more difficult to untangle than the relation of proprietor and agent. The relationship must first be dissolved and then the business of the partnership must be wound up.

In an at-will general partnership, any partner may "dissociate" and thereby cause a "dissolution" of the partnership by simply expressing his will to cease association with the partnership. Under partnership law norms, once dissolution occurs, the partnership must wind up its business, pay off its debts, and settle accounts with partners. This process may be quite lengthy. For example, if the partnership's business is still viable, the partners may wish to continue operating the business until it can be sold to third parties. On the other hand, a partnership might be wound up almost immediately if all partners are in agreement that the partnership's business is to be taken over by a subset of the partners. In any event, as soon as partnership affairs are wound up, the partnership terminates.

Under UPA (1914), upon the non-wrongful dissolution of a partnership, whether caused by a partner's death or dissociation, or otherwise, any partner normally has the right to require that the partnership's assets be liquidated via a judicially supervised auction, with any cash remaining after satisfaction of superior claims being distributed to the partners in accordance with their respective profit shares. However, partners may avoid the normal rule by agreement entered into either before or after dissolution.

Under UPA (1997), any partner normally has the right to require that the partnership's assets be liquidated via a judicially supervised auction only if the partnership is at will and has been dissolved by a partner's expression of will to dissociate. As under UPA (1914), partners may avoid such a forced sale by ex ante or ex post agreement. A partner's death or non-wrongful dissociation by any means other than her expression of will does not give any partner the right to force a liquidating sale as was the case under UPA (1914). Instead, the partnership interest of a deceased or otherwise dissociating partner will be purchased by the partnership for a "buyout price" based on the greater of the partnership's liquidating or going-concern value.

The normal rule found in UPA (1914) and UPA (1997) can be viewed as a device whereby upon dissolution any partner or partner's representative may force a competition for the right to continue the firm, with the winner being the party that submits the highest cash bid at the judicial sale of the partnership's assets. So viewed, the statutory norms reflect a policy judgment that disputes concerning who should continue a partnership's business post-dissolution should be decided by the parties themselves through ex ante or ex post negotiation or, if negotiations fail, in a neutral auction. As you read the following cases, consider to what extent this policy judgment should control judges' discretion.

As the case below reveals, under certain circumstances courts will be tempted to avoid the normal rules of UPA (1914) and UPA (1997) by fashioning a buy out right for the continuing partners not provided by statute or by ordering an in-kind distribution of assets. As you read the following case, consider what interests the judicial and statutory rules are protecting when they choose not to allow liquidation via judicially supervised auction.

McCormick v. Brevig
Supreme Court of Montana, 2004
322 Mont. 112, 96 P.3d 697

Justice JIM RICE delivered the Opinion of the Court.

¶1. This case involves a protracted dispute between a brother and sister concerning their respective interests in a ranching partnership that is before the Court a second time. The litigation began in 1995 when Joan McCormick ("Joan") brought this action against her brother, Clark Brevig ("Clark"), and their Partnership, Brevig Land Live and Lumber (hereinafter, "the Partnership"), seeking a Partnership accounting and dissolution. . . .

¶3. . . . A bench trial was held January 18 through 21, 2000. On April 3, 2000, the District Court entered findings of fact and conclusions of law, dissolving the Partnership, and ordering its business wound up, pending a hearing before a special master and a determination of the proper method for dissolution.

¶4. A limited accounting by a special master was thereafter performed. On December 27, 2001, the District Court concluded that the parties' Partnership agreement did not apply, and that a judicial dissolution of the Partnership was warranted pursuant to §35-10-624(5), MCA. The court further recognized that §35-10-629, MCA, explicitly required any surplus assets after paying creditors to be paid to the partners in cash in accordance with their right to distribution. Nonetheless, the court found that it would be inequitable to order the liquidation of the Partnership assets in order to satisfy Joan's interest in the Partnership. Therefore, in keeping with its desire to preserve the family farm, the Court ordered Joan to sell her interest in the Partnership to her brother following an appraisal and determination of the value of her share. With the assistance of a special master, and following an accounting of Partnership assets, the District Court eventually fixed a price of $1,107,672 on Joan's 50 percent interest in the Partnership. Joan appeals from the District Court's accounting and order requiring her to sell her interest in the Partnership to her brother, and Clark cross-appeals from the court's determination regarding certain Partnership assets, as well as from an evidentiary ruling made at trial. We affirm in part, reverse in part, and remand for further proceedings.

FACTUAL AND PROCEDURAL BACKGROUND

¶12. Joan and Clark are the children of Charles and Helen Brevig (hereinafter, "Charles" and "Helen"). In 1960 Charles purchased the Brevig Ranch outside of Lewistown from his parents. In 1971, Charles transferred his sole interest in the ranch by warranty deed to himself and Helen as joint tenants. The following year, Charles and Helen conveyed the ranch to Clark and Helen as joint tenants.

¶13. When Charles and Helen divorced in 1977, Helen conveyed her interest in the ranch to Charles in the property settlement agreement. Thereafter, Clark and his father owned the ranch in equal shares, and began operating the ranch as Brevig Land, Live & Lumber, a partnership, pursuant to a written agreement.

¶14. Although she was not a partner in the ranch operation, Joan lived on the ranch and assisted in ranch operations from 1975 until 1981. In 1981, with the ranch facing severe financial hardship, Joan left the ranch to work as an oil and gas "landman," in order to generate outside income to enable the ranch to meet its financial obligations. . . .

¶15. In 1982, Charles and Clark sought to refinance the farm debt in the amount of $422,000 with the Federal Land Bank. Because the ranch operation did not generate sufficient cash flow to meet the projected debt payment, the bank required Joan to sign the mortgage which was secured by the ranch real estate. Joan's income as a landman became committed to assist in repayment of the ranch debt.

¶16. During the time of Joan's employment as a landman from 1981 through 1986, it was Joan's practice to contribute all of her income, less expenses, to the support of the ranch operation. In 1983, Joan closed her personal bank account and began to deposit all of her income into the partnership bank account. From this account, Joan would pay her personal expenses and the balance would be applied to the obligations of Charles and Clark's partnership. After she married in 1986, Joan made payments directly to the banks for the ranch obligations rather than to deposit the money in the ranch operating account. Joan also made direct payments for taxes and insurance.

¶17. On October 28, 1982, Charles died unexpectedly after a short illness. Thereafter, pursuant to Charles' Last Will and Testament, Clark and Joan were appointed co-personal representatives and probated Charles' estate. Clark and Joan each received one-half of Charles' estate, which principally consisted of his 50 percent interest in the ranch and Partnership. As a result of the distributions, Clark then owned 75 percent of the ranch assets, and Joan 25 percent. A written partnership agreement was thereafter executed by Clark and Joan reflecting their respective 75/25 percent interests in the Partnership. Except for these ownership percentages, the written agreement was identical to the one executed between Charles and Clark in 1978.

¶18. After Charles' death, Joan continued her work as a landman, and made financial contributions to the new Partnership. She also maintained the Partnership's books and records. Meanwhile, Clark assumed responsibility for the day-to-day affairs of the ranch. Clark and Joan made management decisions together.

¶19. In 1984, Joan obtained an additional 25 percent in the Partnership, fully paying for this interest by the following year. . . . From 1984 to 1993, Joan was listed as a 50/50 partner on all the tax returns for the Partnership. . . .

¶21. Disagreements concerning management of the ranch, and particularly, management of the debt load on the ranch, caused Clark and Joan's relationship to deteriorate. By the early 1990s, cooperation between Clark and Joan regarding the operation of the ranch and securing of loans necessary to fund the ranch had essentially ceased, and they began looking for ways to dissolve the Partnership.

¶22. In 1995, Joan brought suit against Clark and the Partnership, alleging that Clark had converted Partnership assets to his own personal use, and sought an accounting of the Partnership's affairs. She also requested a determination that Clark had engaged in conduct warranting a decree of expulsion. Alternatively, Joan sought an order dissolving and winding up the Partnership. . . .

¶25. On April 3, 2000, the District Court issued findings of fact and conclusions of law, finding that neither Clark nor Joan had dissociated from the Partnership, that Joan was a 50 percent partner and should be credited for any excess capital contributions she made to the Partnership, and that Clark was not entitled to receive compensation as a partner. The court further concluded that the Partnership should be dissolved and its business wound up, and reasoned that appointment of a special master was appropriate in order to determine the amount of the parties' respective capital contributions and Partnership assets.

¶26. On February 7, 2001, following the appointment and discharge of the two previous masters, Larry Blakely, CPA, ("Blakely") was appointed special master. Blakely was vested with the authority to inquire into all pertinent matters of record and charged with determining the amount, if any, of Joan's excess capital contributions to the Partnership as well as to resolve disputes concerning Partnership assets. . . .

¶28. Joan objected to Blakely's report, arguing that he had improperly limited himself to draft and unfiled tax returns previously prepared by Russ Spika, CPA ("Spika"), and had failed to consider evidence which Joan had presented showing significant contributions to the Partnership. Joan further argued that Blakely had failed to follow the historical methods of accounting that had been used by the Partnership up through 1993, which Clark was estopped from challenging pursuant to the court's April 3, 2000 order.

¶30. A real estate appraiser was subsequently appointed by the court, and a new series of disputes concerning the appraisal process began. On August 7, 2002, the court entered an order appointing additional real estate appraisers to assist in the appraisal process, and reenlisted the services of special master Blakely to review the revised Partnership income tax returns prepared by Spika for the 1994 through 2001 tax years. . . .

¶31. On December 12, 2002, Blakely filed his final report with the court, accepting Spika's tax returns, and valuing Joan's interest in the Partnership at $795,629. Joan objected to Blakely's findings and a hearing followed. On January 29, 2003, the District Court entered findings of fact and conclusions of law, accepting Blakely's findings and valuing Joan's interest in the Partnership at $1,107,672. Clark thereafter tendered this amount to Joan for the purchase of her interest, which Joan rejected. This appeal followed.

DISCUSSION

¶33. After ordering dissolution of the Partnership, did the District Court err by failing to order liquidation of the Partnership assets, and instead granting Clark the right to purchase Joan's Partnership interest at a price determined by the court?

¶34. Joan contends that when a partnership is dissolved by judicial decree, Montana's Revised Uniform Partnership Act, §35-10-101 et seq., MCA (2001), requires liquidation by sale of partnership assets and distribution in cash of any surplus to the partners. In response, Clark asserts that there are other judicially acceptable methods of distributing partnership assets upon dissolution besides liquidating assets through a forced sale. For the reasons set forth below, we conclude that the Revised Uniform Partnership Act requires liquidation of partnership assets and distribution of the net surplus in cash to the partners upon dissolution entered by judicial decree when it is no longer reasonably practicable to carry on the business of the partnership. . . .

¶36. Partnership law in Montana and throughout the United States has been primarily derived from the Uniform Partnership Act ("UPA"), which was originally promulgated by the Uniform Law Commissioners in 1914. Under the UPA, the law of partnership breakups was couched in terms of dissolution. A partnership was dissolved and its assets liquidated upon the happening of specific events, the most significant of which was the death of a partner or any partner expressing a will to leave the partnership. Montana adopted the UPA in 1947.

¶37. In 1993, our legislature significantly amended the UPA by adopting the Revised Uniform Partnership Act, or RUPA. Unlike the UPA, RUPA now provides two separate tracks for the exiting partner. The first track applies to the dissociating partner, and does not result in a dissolution, but in a buy-out of the dissociating partner's interest in the partnership. See §35-10-616, MCA. The term "dissociation" is new to the act, and occurs upon the happening of any one of ten events specified in §35-10-616, MCA. Examples of events leading to dissociation include bankruptcy of a partner and death, see §35-10-616(6)(a) and (7)(a), MCA, but does not include a judicially ordered dissolution of the partnership.

¶38. The second track for the exiting partner does involve dissolution and winding up of the partnership's affairs. Section 35-10-624, MCA, sets forth the events causing dissolution and winding up of a partnership, and includes the following:

Events causing dissolution and winding up of partnership business. . . .
(5) a judicial decree, issued upon application by a partner, that:
    (a) the economic purpose of the partnership is likely to be unreasonably frustrated;
    (b) another partner has engaged in conduct relating to the partnership business that makes it not reasonably practicable to carry on the business in partnership with that partner; or
    (c) it is not otherwise reasonably practicable to carry on the partnership business in conformity with the partnership agreement. . . .

¶39. In this case, the District Court dissolved the Partnership pursuant to §35-10-624(5), MCA. In so doing, it recognized that, in the absence of a partnership agreement to the contrary, the only possible result under RUPA was for the partnership assets to be liquidated and the proceeds distributed between the partners proportionately. The court reasoned, however, that the term "liquidate" had a variety of possible meanings, one of which was "to assemble and mobilize the assets, settle with the creditors and debtors and apportion the remaining assets, if any, among the stockholders or owners." Applying this definition, which the court had obtained from Black's Law Dictionary, the court concluded that a judicially ordered buy-out of Joan's interest in the Partnership by Clark was an acceptable alternative to liquidation of the partnership assets through a compelled sale. . . .

¶41. It is true that this Court has previously utilized dictionaries when seeking to define the common use and meaning of terms. However, in this case, we conclude that it was not necessary for the District Court to resort to such devices. Section 35-10-629(1), MCA, clearly provides that "[i]n winding up a partnership's business, the assets of the partnership must be applied to discharge its obligations to creditors, including partners who are creditors. Any surplus must be applied to pay in cash the net amount distributable to partners in accordance with their right to distributions pursuant to subsection (2)." (Emphasis added.) Furthermore, subsection (2) of the statute provides:

> Each partner is entitled to a settlement of all partnership accounts upon winding up the partnership business. In settling accounts among the partners, the profits and losses that result from the *liquidation of the partnership assets* must be credited and charged to the partners' accounts. The partnership shall make a distribution to a partner in an amount equal to that partner's positive account balance. (Emphasis added.)

Thus, the common purpose and plain meaning of the term "liquidation," as it is used in §35-10-629(2), MCA, is to reduce the partnership assets to cash, pay creditors, and distribute to partners the value of their respective interest. See also 59A Am.Jur.2d Partnership §1100 (2003). This is all part of the process of "winding up" the business of a partnership and terminating its affairs.

¶42. Clark invites this Court to take a liberal reading of §35-10-629, MCA, and cites Creel v. Lilly (1999), 354 Md. 77, 729 A.2d 385, in support of the proposition that judicially acceptable alternatives exist to compelled liquidation in a dissolution situation. At issue in *Creel* was whether the surviving partners of a partnership had a duty to liquidate all partnership assets because there was no provision in the partnership agreement providing for the continuation of the partnership upon a partner's death, and the estate had not consented to the continuation of business. *Creel*, 729 A.2d at 387. After examining cases in which other courts had elected to order an in-kind distribution rather than a compelled liquidation, or had allowed the remaining partners to purchase the withdrawing partner's interest in the partnership, the court concluded that the UPA did not mandate a forced sale of all partnership assets in order to ascertain the true value of the business, and that "winding up" was not always synonymous with liquidation. *Creel*, 729 A.2d at 403. The court further noted that it would have reached the same conclusion regardless of whether the UPA or RUPA governed since, under RUPA, the remaining partners could have elected to continue business following the death of one of the partners. *Creel*, 729 A.2d at 397.

¶43. However, of critical distinction between the facts in *Creel* and the case subjudice is the manner in which the partners exited the entity. In *Creel* one of the partners had died. Here, Joan sought a court-ordered dissolution of the Partnership. Under RUPA, the death of a partner triggers the provisions of §35-10-619, MCA, which allows for the purchase of the dissociated partner's interest in the partnership, much like what was ordered in *Creel*. Conversely, a court-ordered dissolution pursuant to §35-10-624(5), MCA, as in this case, results in the dissolution and winding up of the partnership. Thus, *Creel* is both legally and factually distinguishable.

¶44. Furthermore, the cases relied upon by the court in *Creel* in reaching its conclusion that liquidation of assets was not always mandated upon dissolution, Nicholes v. Hunt (1975), 273 Or. 255, 541 P.2d 820, Logoluso v. Logoluso (1965), 233 Cal.App.2d 523, 43 Cal.Rptr. 678, Gregg v. Bernards (1968), 250 Or. 458, 443 P.2d 166, Goergen v. Nebrich (1958), 12 Misc.2d 1011, 174 N.Y.S.2d 366, and Fortugno v. Hudson Manure Co. (1958), 51 N.J.Super. 482, 144 A.2d 207, are likewise pre-RUPA holdings, which are inapposite to the facts at issue in this case.

¶45. Accordingly, we conclude that when a partnership's dissolution is court ordered pursuant to §35-10-624(5), MCA, the partnership assets necessarily must be reduced to cash in order to satisfy the obligations of the partnership and distribute any net surplus in cash to the remaining partners in accordance with their respective interests. By adopting a judicially created alternative to this statutorily mandated requirement, the District Court erred.

¶46. Did the District Court err by failing to grant Joan's petition for an accounting of the Partnership's business affairs?

¶47. Joan maintains that the accounting performed by special master Blakely was inadequate. . . .

¶48. Every partner is generally entitled to have an accounting of the partnership's affairs, even in the absence of an express contract so providing. 59A Am. Jur.2d Partnership §617. Moreover, RUPA provides that a partner may maintain an action against the partnership or another partner for legal or equitable relief, including an accounting as to partnership business, or to enforce a right to compel a dissolution and winding up of the partnership business under §35-10-624, MCA. See §35-10-409(2) (b)(iii), MCA.

¶49. The purpose of an accounting is to determine the rights and liabilities of the partners, and to ascertain the value of the partners' interests in the partnership as of a particular date, such as the date of dissolution. 59A Am. Jur. 2d Partnership at §667. "When an action for an accounting is being used to wind up the partnership's affairs, the court is obligated to provide 'for a full accounting of the partnership assets and obligations and distribution of any remaining assets or liabilities to the partners in accordance with their interests in the partnership.'" Guntle v. Barnett (1994), 73 Wash.App. 825, 871 P.2d 627, 630. This is often accomplished through the appointment of a special master subject to court review, who conducts a comprehensive investigation of the transactions of the partnership and the partners. *Guntle*, 871 P.2d at 630. In rendering the accounting, mere summaries or lump listings of types of items, or schedules of cash to be distributed without detailing the firm's transactions, are generally insufficient, as are mere tax returns. 59A Am. Jur. 2d Partnership at §621; Juliano v. Rea (1982), 89 A.D.2d 618, 452 N.Y.S.2d 668, 669.

¶50. In this case, special master Blakely was charged with determining the amount of Joan's excess capital contributions and resolving disputes concerning ownership of Partnership assets. In this regard, Blakely performed a detailed accounting of the assets, liabilities, and capital contributions of each of the partners. While he accomplished much of this by reviewing the partnership tax returns from 1985 to 2001, some of which were apparently in draft form, Blakely also held several extensive meetings with the parties in which he heard oral arguments and received evidence. From these meetings, and information obtained from the partnership tax returns, Blakely prepared and submitted two reports to the District Court, detailing the partners' respective capital contributions and withdrawals, as well as partnership assets and liabilities. These reports further itemized transactions occurring within the Partnership from 1995 through 2001, and included a break-down for Blakely's determination of the suggested purchase price for Joan's interest in the Partnership. This was sufficient given the issues which were presented for Blakely's review, and given the fact that he testified before the District Court and was subject to cross-examination concerning his findings.

¶51. Because we conclude, however, that the Partnership's assets must be liquidated in order to satisfy the Partnership's obligations to its creditors and distribute the net surplus of any assets in cash to the partners, on remand it will become necessary for the District Court to perform a full accounting of the Partnership's affairs. Once again, this requires a detailed accounting of all the Partnership's assets and liabilities, as well as distributions of assets and liabilities to the partners in accordance with their respective interests in the Partnership. Blakely's reports may very well be of assistance in this process. . . .

NOTES AND QUESTIONS

1. Although a majority of courts have interpreted UPA (1914) §38 as giving a non-wrongfully dissociating partner the right to force a liquidating sale of the partnership's assets, a number of courts have found exceptions to that rule. One such case is Nicholes v. Hunt, 541 P.2d 820 (Or. 1975). Hunt operated a business as a sole proprietorship. In order to obtain needed additional capital and services, Hunt contributed the business to a new partnership in which he and Nicholes were equal partners. The new venture was a financial success but subject to considerable dissension. One year after formation, Hunt notified Nicholes that he was dissolving the partnership and that he intended to continue the partnership's business as sole proprietor. Nicholes sought judicial relief to protect his rights under UPA §38(1) so that he might bid against Hunt for control of the partnership's assets. The trial court found the dissolution non-wrongful but refused to order a public sale. Instead, it apportioned and distributed the assets in-kind, giving the partnership's operating assets to Hunt and giving to Nicholes the value of his partnership interest in cash.

Nicholes appealed, arguing that under UPA §38(1) the assets must be sold at public sale unless all parties consent to some other method of liquidation. The Oregon Supreme Court affirmed the trial court's decision:

We conclude, as defendant contends and as the trial court found, that the equities lie with the defendant in this case. Further, since there was no evidence regarding the value which the partnership assets might command on the market, it is difficult for us to determine whether a sale would be beneficial or prejudicial to the respective parties. As earlier described, this is a unique, or unusual, business which required particular knowledge of the remanufacturing process and ability to repair and operate the necessary machinery. Plaintiff argues that he is entitled to purchase the 50 percent share of the defendant but this is no answer to the problem that confronted the trial court. The defendant conceived and designed the machinery and the method of operation, which was successfully operated for a number of years before formation of the partnership at will. Plaintiff is not precluded from engaging in a like or similar business.

541 P.2d at 828.

2. A recent case also rejecting a strict interpretation of UPA (1914) §38, is Disotell v. Stiltner, 100 P.3d 890 (AK 2004).

Disotell argues that the superior court failed to follow the Act when the court gave Stiltner the option to purchase Disotell's partnership interest for $73,213.50, the value of Disotell's interest as calculated by the court. . . .

We decline to follow the line of cases holding that the statute requires liquidation. We hold that the superior court did not err in reading subsection .330(a) to allow it to permit Stiltner to buy out Disotell's partnership interest. Careful reading of the text of AS 32.05.330(a) does not convince us that this subsection absolutely compels liquidation and forbids a buyout. Under appropriate, although perhaps limited, circumstances, a buyout seems a justifiable way of winding up a partnership. The superior court reasoned that a buyout would reduce economic waste by avoiding the cost of appointing a receiver and conducting a sale. Even though there was no ongoing business, the superior court noted that the expense of a sale could total as much as twelve percent of the property's value. This was a valid reason and potentially benefitted both partners. The potential savings were significant. The court's effort to avoid further loss to both partners justifies its decision to offer Stiltner the buyout option. Further, properly conducted, a buyout guaranteed Disotell a fair value for his partnership interest. Liquidation exposed Disotell to the risk that no buyer would offer to pay fair market value for the property. A liquidation sale in which no other buyers participated might have given Stiltner an opportunity to buy the property for less than fair market value, to Disotell's disadvantage. . . .

Although it was not error to grant Stiltner the option to buy out Disotell's partnership interest, it was error to permit the buyout without requiring some objective determination of the value of all of the partnership assets, particularly the land and building Stiltner contributed. The superior court used tax appraisals to establish the value of the hotel property and parking lot. The court relied on a report by an expert witness who, to explain the accounting methodology set out in AS 32.05.350, "assume[d], for illustrative purposes only," that the hotel property and parking lot would sell for their tax-appraised values. The tax appraisals were not introduced into evidence. The expert discussed them only hypothetically to illustrate an entirely different point, not as support for an opinion of property values. Neither party introduced evidence of any appraisal. Disotell and Stiltner both acknowledge that neither offered any evidence of value of the partnership assets.

Because a buyout is appropriate only if it is for fair market value, and there was no admissible evidence of fair market value, we must remand. It will be necessary on remand to determine the value of the assets before Stiltner attempts to buy out Disotell. The parties may offer any evidence relevant to the value of the partnership property. The partnership assets include both the hotel property and the parking lot.

Contemporaneous appraisals of both will be necessary so that neither party is prejudiced by a fluctuation in the value of one asset. On appeal, Disotell claims that he had no pretrial notice that the superior court would establish a value for the partnership property. The remand will provide Disotell full opportunity to introduce evidence or otherwise address the issue.

Id. at 892-893. Is the court's reasoning persuasive?

PROBLEM 2-7

Alpha, Beta, Charlie, and Delta formed an oral, at-will partnership in Nirvana several years ago. Nirvana adopted the UPA (1914) in 1937 and the UPA (1997) in 1999. It is unclear which version of the UPA governs the ABCD partnership. In each of the following circumstances, determine whether the dissociated partner(s) or her successors in interest have a right to demand a wind-up and liquidating sale of the business. If not, then determine how the value of the dissociated partner's interest will be determined, whether payment must be made in cash, and whether payment may be made in installments over some period of time. If your answer is dependent in some circumstances on a determination of which version of the UPA governs, explain how your answer would change.

Circumstance #1. At the partnership's monthly luncheon meeting, Alpha announces that he is withdrawing from the partnership effective immediately, and that he will insist that the partnership be liquidated.

Circumstance #2. Alpha dies; Helen is Alpha's sole heir and the executor of Alpha's estate. Several weeks after Alpha's death, Beta, Charlie, Delta, and Helen meet to discuss what to do in the wake of Alpha's death. Beta, Charlie, and Delta indicate their desire to continue the business and to pay Alpha's estate the value of Alpha's interest over the next few years out of future profits. Helen consents to this plan.

Circumstance #3. Alpha dies; Helen is Alpha's sole heir and the executor of Alpha's estate. Several weeks after Alpha's death, Beta, Charlie, Delta, and Helen meet to discuss what to do in the wake of Alpha's death. Beta, Charlie, and Delta indicate their desire to continue the business and to pay Alpha's estate the value of Alpha's interest over the next few years out of future profits. Helen refuses to consent to the continuance of the business. She demands that the business be liquidated and the value of Alpha's interest paid to Alpha's estate in cash.

Circumstance #4. Alpha dies. Four weeks later Beta notifies Charlie and Delta that she is withdrawing from the partnership effective immediately.

PROBLEM 2-8

Jillian has owned and operated Jillian Motors, a car dealership, as a sole proprietorship for 30 years. Short on funds for a planned renovation and expansion of the dealership facilities, Jillian turned to Sam, who recently inherited a great deal of money. Subsequently, Sam and Jillian formed an oral, at-will partnership to which Jillian contributed her car dealership and Sam contributed $10 million. The partners agreed that Jillian would receive 75 percent of the profits and Sam 25 percent. The partners' shared expectation was that Sam would be an active participant in the business. However, several weeks into the relationship, Jillian and Sam had a serious falling out over the extent of Sam's authority. Several days later, Sam delivered a written notice to Jillian, expressing his will to withdraw from the partnership. In the letter, Sam demanded that the dealership be liquidated, and the cash remaining after payment of creditors be distributed to the partners.

Jillian has consulted your firm for advice. She believes that Sam is entitled to no more than the return of the $10 million that he invested in the partnership, most of which is still in the partnership's account at a local bank. What is your advice assuming that UPA (1997) governs? Would your advice be different if UPA (1914) applies?

2. Wrongful Dissociation

UPA (1997) §§601, 602, 701, 801
UPA (1914) §§31, 32, 38

The rules governing partner dissociation and partnership dissolution necessarily must strike a balance between the individual partners' ability to adapt to changed circumstances and the firm's desire for stability and continuity. Partnership law default norms emphasize individual adaptability. Normally, any partner can withdraw from the partnership at will, force a liquidating judicial sale, and receive the net value of her partnership interest in cash. Partners wishing to continue the business, absent agreement, must purchase the partnership's assets for cash at the judicial sale. Conversely, a majority group of partners may force out another partner by collectively dissociating themselves from the unwanted partner. Again, however, partners wishing to continue the business must purchase it at the resulting judicial sale.

The value of the individual partner's unilateral right to exit and the dominant group of partners' unilateral right to expel an unwanted partner must be weighed against the costs. From the standpoint of partners wishing to continue the business, it may be costly to replace the human and money capital of a valuable departing partner. Moreover, the continuing partners may be subject to opportunistic threats of exit by a strong partner who seeks to obtain unfair concessions from the other partners. From the standpoint of a minority partner, the easy exit and expulsion rights present the risk of opportunism by a dominant group having specialized skills or unique commercial ties with the partnership. The dominant group may use expulsion rights or react to the minority partner's exit by purchasing or threatening to purchase the partnerships assets at an unfairly low price.

Partners can easily shift the balance between adaptability and continuity by agreeing that the partnership will continue for a fixed term or particular undertaking. So doing brings into play the wrongful dissociation provisions of partnership law. If a partner dissociates from the partnership before completion of the agreed term or undertaking, such dissociation will be wrongful. Nondissociating partners have the option of continuing the partnership's business without the consent of the wrongfully dissociating partner. Additionally, the wrongfully dissociating partner must compensate other partners for damages resulting from the wrongful dissociation.

The consequences of wrongful dissociation are potentially devastating. Moreover, as partnership relations deteriorate, or the interests of partners begin to diverge, partners may unwittingly take actions that put them at risk in later court proceedings. Often unclear to the partners and their advisers are the answers to two questions. First, is their partnership at will or for a term or undertaking? Second, have they already conducted themselves in a way that will be labeled wrongful?

Drashner v. Sorenson

Supreme Court of South Dakota, 1954

75 S.D. 247, 63 N.W.2d 255

SMITH, PRESIDING JUDGE.

In January 1951 the plaintiff, C. H. Drashner, and defendants, A. D. Sorenson and Jacob P. Deis, associated themselves as co-owners in the real estate, loan and insurance business at Rapid City. For a consideration of $7500 they purchased the real estate and insurance agency known as J. Schumacher Co. located in an office room on the ground floor of the Alex Johnson Hotel building. The entire purchase price was advanced for the partnership by the defendants, but at the time of trial $3,000 of that sum had been repaid to them by the partnership. Although, as will appear from facts presently to be outlined, their operations were not unsuccessful, differences arose and on June 15, 1951 plaintiff commenced this action in which he sought an accounting, dissolution and winding up of the partnership. The answer and counterclaim of defendants prayed for like relief.

The cause came on for trial September 4, 1951. The court among others made the following findings.

VII. "That thereafter the plaintiff violated the terms of said partnership agreement, in that he demanded a larger share of the income of the said partnership than he was entitled to receive under the terms of said partnership agreement; that the plaintiff was arrested for reckless driving and served a term in jail for said offense; that the plaintiff demanded that the defendants permit him to draw money for his own personal use out of the moneys held in escrow by the partnership; that the plaintiff spent a large amount of time during business hours in the Brass Rail Bar in Rapid City, South Dakota, and other bars, and neglected his duties in connection with the business of the said partnership. . . . That the plaintiff, by his actions hereinbefore set forth, has made it impossible to carry on the partnership."

The conclusions adopted read as follows:

I. "That the defendants are entitled to continue the partnership and have the value of the plaintiff's interest in the partnership business determined, upon the filing and approval of a good and sufficient bond, conditioned upon the release of the plaintiff from any liability arising out of the said partnership, and further conditioned upon the payment by the defendants to the plaintiff of the value of plaintiff's interest in the partnership as determined by the Court."

II. "That in computing the value of the plaintiff's interest in the said partnership, the value of the good will of the business shall not be considered."

III. "That the value of the partnership shall be finally determined upon a hearing before this Court, . . ." and

IV. "That the plaintiff shall be entitled to receive one-third of the value of the partnership property owned by the partnership on the 12th day of September, 1951, not including the good will of the business, after the payment of the liabilities of the partnership and the payment to the defendants of the invested capital in the sum of $4,500.00."

Judgment was accordingly entered dissolving the partnership as of September 12, 1951.

After hearing at a later date the court found . . . "[t]hat there is not sufficient partnership property to reimburse the defendants for their invested capital." Thereupon the court decree "[t]hat the plaintiff had no interest in the property of the said partnership," and that the defendants were the sole owners thereof. . . .

The agreement of the parties contemplated an association which would continue at least until the $7500 advance of defendants had been repaid from the gross earnings of the business. Hence, it was not a partnership at will. Vangel v. Vangel, 116 Cal.App.2d 615, 254 P.2d 919; Zeibak v. Nasser, 12 Cal.2d 1, 82 P.2d 375. In apparent recognition of that fact, both plaintiff and defendants sought dissolution in contravention of the partnership agreement, see SDC 49.0603(2) under SDC 49.0604(1)d) on the ground that the adverse party had caused the dissolution wrongfully by willfully and persistently committing a breach of the partnership agreement, and by so conducting himself in matters relating to the partnership business as to render impracticable the carrying on of the business in partnership with him.

By SDC 49.0610(2) of the Uniform Partnership Act it is provided:

> When dissolution is caused in contravention of the partnership agreement the rights of the partners shall be as follows:
>
> (b) The partners who have not caused the dissolution wrongfully, if they all desire to continue the business in the same name, either by themselves or jointly with others, may do so, during the agreed term for the partnership and for that purpose may possess the partnership property, provided they secure the payment by bond approved by the Court, or pay to any partner who has caused the dissolution wrongfully, the value of his interest in the partnership at the dissolution less any damages recoverable under clause (2)(a)(2) of this section and in like manner indemnify him against all present or future partnership liabilities. . . .

From this background we turn to a consideration of the evidence from which the trial court inferred that plaintiff caused the dissolution wrongfully.

The breach between the parties resulted from a continuing controversy over the right of plaintiff to withdraw sufficient money from the partnership to defray his living expenses. Plaintiff was dependent upon his earnings for the support of his family. The defendants had other resources. Plaintiff claimed that he was to be permitted to draw from the earnings of the partnership a sufficient amount to support himself and family. The defendants asserted that there was a definite arrangement for the allocation of the income of the partnership and there was no agreement for withdrawal by plaintiff of more than his allotment under that plan. Defendants' version of the facts was corroborated by a written admission of plaintiff offered in evidence.

From evidence thus sharply in conflict, the trial court made a finding, reading as follows:

> That the oral partnership agreement between the parties provided that each of the three partners were to draw as compensation one-third of one-half of the commissions earned upon sales made by the partners; that the other one-half of the commissions earned on sales made by the partners and one-half of the commissions earned upon sales made by salesmen employed by the partnership, together with the earnings from the insurance business carried on by the partnership, was to be placed in a fund to be used for the payment of the operating expenses of the partnership, and after the payment of such operating expenses to be used to reimburse the defendants for the capital advanced in the purchase of the Julius Schumacher business and the capital advanced in the sum of Eight Hundred Dollars ($800.00) for the operating expenses of the business.

As an outgrowth of this crucial difference, there was evidence from which a court could reasonably believe that plaintiff neglected the business and spent too much time in a nearby bar during business hours. At a time when plaintiff had overdrawn his partners and was also indebted to one of defendants for personal advances, he requested $100 and his request was refused. In substance he then said, according to the testimony of the defendant Deis, that he would see that he "gets some money to run on," and if they "didn't give it to him he was going to dissolve the partnership and see that he got it." Thereafter plaintiff pressed his claims through counsel, and eventually brought this action to dissolve the partnership. The claim so persistently asserted was contrary to the partnership agreement found by the court.

The foregoing picture of the widening breach between the parties is drawn almost entirely from the evidence of defendants. Of course, plaintiff's version of the agreement of the parties, and of the ensuing differences, if believed, would have supported findings of a different order by the trier of the fact. It cannot be said, we think, that the trial court acted unreasonably in believing defendants, and we think it equally clear the court could reasonably conclude that the insistent and continuing demands of the plaintiff and his attendant conduct rendered it reasonably impracticable to carry on the business in partnership with him. It follows, we are of the opinion, the evidence supports the finding that plaintiff caused the dissolution wrongfully. Zeibak v. Nasser, 12 Cal.2d 1, 82 P.2d 375; Owen v. Cohen, 19 Cal.2d 147, 119 P.2d 713; Meherin v. Meherin, 93 Cal.App.2d 459, 209 P.2d 36; and Vangel v. Vangel, 116 Cal.App.2d 615, 254 P.2d 919. . . .

The judgment of the trial court is affirmed.

McCormick v. Brevig
Supreme Court of Montana, 2004
322 Mont. 112, 96 P.3d 697

[The facts of this case are set forth supra, beginning at page 97.]

57. Did the District Court err in ruling that Clark did not dissociate by withdrawing from the Partnership?

58. In her amended complaint, Joan petitioned the District Court for an order expelling Clark from the Partnership pursuant to §35-10-616, MCA, as a result of his allegedly wrongful conduct of converting Partnership assets to his own personal use. Following a non-jury trial, the District Court concluded that neither party had dissociated from the Partnership, and denied Joan's request for an order of expulsion.

59. On appeal, Joan contends that the District Court failed to consider evidence showing that Clark had dissociated from the Partnership pursuant to §35-10-616(5), MCA. She argues that the court failed to consider evidence that Clark had denied the existence of the Partnership and had taken steps to transfer legal title of the Partnership's primary asset—the ranch—to his name, and had converted over $400,000 of Partnership funds to his own personal use. She further maintains that the court erred in denying her request for expulsion in light of the fact that Clark had instigated criminal theft charges against her in 1994, which later proved frivolous. In response, Clark asserts that the District Court adequately considered each of the events leading to dissociation under §35-10-616, MCA, and properly denied Joan's request for expulsion.

60. Section 35-10-616, MCA, delineates ten events causing a partner's dissociation from a partnership. Pursuant to §35-10-616(5), MCA, one of the ways a partner may be

dissociated is expulsion by judicial decree, made upon the application by the partnership or another partner, because:

> (a) the partner engaged in wrongful conduct that adversely and materially affected the partnership business;
> (b) the partner willfully or persistently committed a material breach of the partnership agreement or of a duty owed to the partnership or other partners under §35-10-405, MCA;
> (c) the partner engaged in conduct relating to the partnership business that made it not reasonably practical to carry on business in partnership with that partner. . . .

Dissociation under §35-10-616(5), MCA, is considered wrongful. Section 35-10-617(1)(b)(ii), MCA.

61. In this case, Joan's amended complaint did not specifically request relief pursuant to §35-10-616(5), MCA, and it is evident from the record that the District Court considered her claim generally under §35-10-616, MCA. In so doing, the District Court found that Clark had not given notice of his express will to withdraw as a partner, that the partnership agreement did not apply, and that Clark had continued to work the ranch since his alleged dissociation in 1994, which Joan and the Partnership had benefitted from. The court further noted that, although Clark had obtained loans in his individual name from 1994 forward, this did not constitute dissociation since it was a necessary action in light of the parties' inability to communicate about ranch finances. . . .

62. Based upon these findings, which Joan does not dispute, we cannot disagree with the District Court's conclusion that Clark did not dissociate from the Partnership. While Joan contends that the District Court failed to consider evidence that Clark wrongfully converted over $400,000 of Partnership funds to his personal use, it does not appear from the record that Joan raised this argument before the District Court in a timely fashion. Rather, the record shows that these allegations first surfaced following trial and the appointment of a special master.

63. Additionally, Joan's contention that Clark dissociated from the Partnership by instigating criminal theft charges against her fails. The District Court weighed this evidence at trial and rejected it, finding that both parties were at least partially at fault for the deterioration of the Partnership. The court also noted that the act of taking alternate legal positions during the course of the dispute did not amount to dissociation. Because Joan has not established that the District Court's findings were clearly erroneous, we conclude the court did not err in concluding that Clark did not dissociate from the Partnership pursuant to §35-10-616, MCA. . . .

NOTES AND QUESTIONS

1. Was it fair for the Court to determine that Drashner had caused the dissolution of the partnership wrongfully? Would it have been better to conclude, as did the Court in *Brevig*, that both sides of the intra-partnership dispute bore some of the blame?

2. When a court concludes, as in *Drashner*, that a partner's conduct over a period of time has caused a dissolution of the partnership, it will also be necessary to determine *when* dissolution occurred. In such circumstances, will the date of dissolution be the date on which the first such act occurred? The date the civil action was filed? Every case stands

on its own facts and a "court has broad powers to act in equity to determine the date of dissolution (citation omitted)." Brown v. Hallisey, 2004 WL 3218003, *5 (Mass. Super.).

PROBLEM 2-9

Alpha, Beta, Charlie, and Delta formed a partnership in Nirvana several years ago. Nirvana adopted the UPA (1914) in 1937 and the UPA (1997) in 1999. It is unclear which version of the UPA governs the ABCD partnership. The ABCD partnership is governed by a written agreement that provides in relevant part as follows:

Article 3. Duration. The partnership shall continue until December 31, 2025.

Relations between Beta and the other partners have been deteriorating for months due to Beta's insistence that she be given a larger share of partnership profits to reflect her highly successful "rainmaking." In each of the following circumstances, determine whether Beta has "wrongfully" dissociated or caused dissolution "wrongfully." Then determine what rights she and the other partners have as a result of her dissociation.

Circumstance #1. On January 10, 2014, Beta delivers written notice to the other partners that she is withdrawing from the partnership effective immediately.

Circumstance #2. On January 10, 2014, Beta instigates litigation in Nirvana Superior Court, seeking judicial dissolution of the partnership on the grounds that relations are irrevocably broken, that the other partners have in bad faith refused to allocate profits according to the relative value of each partner's contributions, and that it is impractical to continue in business together.

Circumstance #3. Alpha dies in an industrial accident on January 7, 2014.

Circumstance #4. Alpha and Charlie die in an industrial accident on January 7, 2014. On January 10, 2014, Beta delivers written notice to Delta that she is withdrawing from the partnership effective immediately.

3. Fiduciary Limits on Dissolution "At Will"

The archetypical general partnership is an at-will relationship. If the association becomes unwanted by any partner, then that partner may dissolve the relationship at will. Moreover, in most circumstances, after dissolution of an at-will partnership, any former partner may force a liquidating sale of the business. Are there, or should there be, any fiduciary limits on this right to cause dissolution and liquidation of an at-will partnership?

Page v. Page
California Supreme Court, 1961
359 P.2d 41

TRAYNOR, JUSTICE.

Plaintiff and defendant are partners in a linen supply business in Santa Maria, California. Plaintiff appeals from a judgment declaring the partnership to be for a term rather than at will.

The partners entered into an oral partnership agreement in 1949. Within the first two years each partner contributed approximately $43,000 for the purchase of land, machinery, and linen needed to begin the business. From 1949 to 1957 the enterprise was unprofitable, losing approximately $62,000. The partnership's major creditor is a corporation, wholly owned by plaintiff, that supplies the linen and machinery necessary for the day-to-day operation of the business. This corporation holds a $47,000 demand note of the partnership. The partnership operations began to improve in 1958. The partnership earned $3,824.41 in that year and $2,282.30 in the first three months of 1959. Despite this improvement plaintiff wishes to terminate the partnership.

The Uniform Partnership Act provides that a partnership may be dissolved "[b]y the express will of any partner when no definite term or particular undertaking is specified." The trial court found that the partnership is for a term, namely, "such reasonable time as is necessary to enable said partnership to repay from partnership profits, indebtedness incurred for the purchase of land, buildings, laundry and delivery equipment and linen for the operation of such business. . . ." Plaintiff correctly contends that this finding is without support in the evidence.

Defendant testified that the terms of the partnership were to be similar to former partnerships of plaintiff and defendant, and that the understanding of these partnerships was that "we went into partnership to start the business and let the business operation pay for itself, — put in so much money, and let the business pay itself out." There was also testimony that one of the former partnership agreements provided in writing that the profits were to be retained until all obligations were paid.

Upon cross-examination defendant admitted that the former partnership in which the earnings were to be retained until the obligations were repaid was substantially different from the present partnership. The former partnership was a limited partnership and provided for a definite term of five years and a partnership at will thereafter. Defendant insists, however, that the method of operation of the former partnership showed an understanding that all obligations were to be repaid from profits. He nevertheless concedes that there was no understanding as to the term of the present partnership in the event of losses. He was asked: "(W)as there any discussion with reference to the continuation of the business in the event of losses?" He replied, "Not that I can remember." He was then asked, "Did you have any understanding with Mr. Page, your brother, the plaintiff in this action, as to how the obligations were to be paid if there were losses?" He replied, "Not that I can remember. I can't remember discussing that at all. We never figured on losing, I guess."

Viewing this evidence most favorably for defendant, it proves only that the partners expected to meet current expenses from current income and to recoup their investment if the business were successful.

Defendant contends that such an expectation is sufficient to create a partnership for a term under the rule of Owen v. Cohen, 19 Cal. 2d 147, 150, 119 P.2d 713. In that case we held that when a partner advances a sum of money to a partnership with the understanding that the amount contributed was to be a loan to the partnership and was to be repaid as soon as feasible from the prospective profits of the business, the partnership is for the term reasonably required to repay the loan. It is true that Owen v. Cohen, supra, and other cases hold that partners may impliedly agree to continue in business until a certain sum of money is earned, or one or more partners recoup their investments, or until certain debts are paid, or until certain property could be disposed of on favorable terms. In each of these cases, however, the implied agreement found support in the evidence.

In Owen v. Cohen, supra, the partners borrowed substantial amounts of money to launch the enterprise and there was an understanding that the loans would be repaid from partnership profits. In Vangel v. Vangel [116 Cal. App. 2d 615, 254 P.2d 919], one partner loaned his co-partner money to invest in the partnership with the understanding that the money would be repaid from partnership profits. In Mervyn Investment Co. v. Biber [184 Cal. 637, 194 P. 1037], one partner contributed all the capital, the other contributed his services, and it was understood that upon the repayment of the contributed capital from partnership profits the partner who contributed his services would receive a one-third interest in the partnership assets. In each of these cases the court properly held that the partners impliedly promised to continue the partnership for a term reasonably required to allow the partnership to earn sufficient money to accomplish the understood objective. In Shannon v. Hudson [161 Cal. App. 2d 44, 325 P.2d 1022], the parties entered into a joint venture to build and operate a motel until it could be sold upon favorable and mutually satisfactory terms, and the court held that the joint venture was for a reasonable term sufficient to accomplish the purpose of the joint venture.

In the instant case, however, defendant failed to prove any facts from which an agreement to continue the partnership for a term may be implied. The understanding to which defendant testified was no more than a common hope that the partnership earnings would pay for all the necessary expenses. Such a hope does not establish even by implication a "definite term or particular undertaking" as required by [UPA §31(1)(b)]. All partnerships are ordinarily entered into with the hope that they will be profitable, but that alone does not make them all partnerships for a term and obligate the partners to continue in the partnerships until all of the losses over a period of many years have been recovered.

Defendant contends that plaintiff is acting in bad faith and is attempting to use his superior financial position to appropriate the now profitable business of the partnership. Defendant has invested $43,000 in the firm, and owing to the long period of losses his interest in the partnership assets is very small. The fact that plaintiff's wholly-owned corporation holds a $47,000 demand note of the partnership may make it difficult to sell the business as a going concern. Defendant fears that upon dissolution he will receive very little and that plaintiff, who is the managing partner and knows how to conduct the operations of the partnership, will receive a business that has become very profitable because of the establishment of Vandenberg Air Force Base in its vicinity. Defendant charges that plaintiff has been content to share the losses but now that the business has become profitable he wishes to keep all the gains.

There is no showing in the record of bad faith or that the improved profit situation is more than temporary. In any event these contentions are irrelevant to the issue whether the partnership is for a term or at will. Since, however, this action is for a declaratory judgment and will be the basis for future action by the parties, it is appropriate to point out that defendant is amply protected by the fiduciary duties of co-partners.

Even though the Uniform Partnership Act provides that a partnership at will may be dissolved by the express will of any partner, this power, like any other power held by a fiduciary, must be exercised in good faith.

We have often stated that "partners are trustees for each other, and in all proceedings connected with the conduct of the partnership every partner is bound to act in the highest good faith to his copartner, and may not obtain any advantage over him in the partnership affairs by the slightest misrepresentation, concealment, threat, or adverse pressure of any kind." . . .

A partner at will is not bound to remain in a partnership, regardless of whether the business is profitable or unprofitable. A partner may not, however, by use of adverse pressure "freeze out" a co-partner and appropriate the business to his own use. A partner may not dissolve a partnership to gain the benefits of the business for himself, unless he fully compensates his co-partner for his share of the prospective business opportunity. In this regard his fiduciary duties are at least as great as those of a shareholder of a corporation.

In the case of In re Security Finance Co., 49 Cal. 2d 370, 376-377, 317 P.2d 1, 5, we stated that although shareholders representing 50 percent of the voting power have a right . . . to dissolve a corporation, they may not exercise such right in order "to defraud the other shareholders, to "freeze out" minority shareholders, or to sell the assets of the dissolved corporation at an inadequate price."

Likewise in the instant case, plaintiff has the power to dissolve the partnership by express notice to defendant. If, however, it is proved that plaintiff acted in bad faith and violated his fiduciary duties by attempting to appropriate to his own use the new prosperity of the partnership without adequate compensation to his co-partner, the dissolution would be wrongful and the plaintiff would be liable as provided by [UPA §38(2)(a)] . . . for violation of the implied agreement not to exclude defendant wrongfully from the partnership business opportunity.

The judgment is reversed. . . .

NOTES AND QUESTIONS

1. Does Page v. Page strike a proper balance between two conflicting goals— protecting a partner's ability to adapt to changed circumstances and deterring opportunistic withdrawal or threats of withdrawal?

2. Page v. Page has been criticized. The views of Professor Hillman summarize the concerns.

> The weaker partner in *Page* could have bargained for a definite term, but he did not. Fairness under such circumstances does not require the stronger partner to carry the weaker partner indefinitely.

Hillman, The Dissatisfied Participant in the Solvent Business Venture: A Consideration of the Relative Permanence of Partnerships and Close Corporations, 67 Minn. L. Rev. 1, 33 (1982).

Professor O'Kelley suggests that the line drawn should not be so bright.

> Some commentators assert that *Page* unduly restricts the adaptability of majority partners. These commentators argue that if the parties had wished to fetter the majority partner's withdrawal

rights, they would have specified a durational term. This view overlooks the longstanding role of fiduciary duty in partnership law and the significance of the parties' selection of partnership form instead of sole proprietorship form. Assuming rational actors, selection of general partnership form instead of sole proprietorship form signals to an efficiency-minded judge that the parties desired that more stringent judicial constraints be placed on the majority partner's adaptability than would be the case if the majority partner were the firm's sole proprietor. Consistent with this expectation, *Page* recognizes that majority partners have substantially less adaptability than do sole proprietors.

O'Kelley, Filling Gaps in the Close Corporation Contract: A Transaction Cost Analysis, 87 Nw. U. L. Rev. 216, 237 (1992).

3. Cude v. Couch, 588 S.W. 2d 554 (Tenn. 1979), presents a fact pattern similar to Page v. Page. Couch and Cude formed a partnership to operate a laundromat. The partnership leased its premises from Couch on a month-to-month basis. Couch obtained a judicial dissolution of the partnership, and the partnership's assets were subsequently auctioned at a public sale. At the time of sale Couch announced that he would not lease the premises to anyone wishing to operate a laundromat on the premises. As a result, the partnership's assets were worth more to Couch, who could leave them in place, than to any other buyer, and Couch, through an undisclosed agent, was the successful bidder. Cude moved to set aside the sale on the grounds that Couch's actions breached his fiduciary duty. The court by majority opinion refused to grant relief:

> From the beginning of the partnership, Couch made it clear that he would not permit a lease of the property, in part to insure that the operation of the laundromat would not interfere with that of his car dealership, operating in the same building. . . . Unquestionably, Couch had an advantage, divorced from the partnership, that made it more practicable for him to carry on the business of the partnership after dissolution than for others. However, the fact that Couch benefitted from that circumstance harmed neither Cude nor the partnership, and breached his duty to neither.

588 S.W.2d at 556.

PROBLEM 2-10

Harv Hansen, Stan Simpson, and Bill Brock have been equal partners for two years. Their partnership owns and operates a specialty sporting goods store, under the name World Cup Soccer Shop. Harv and Stan provide day-to-day management services, but no capital, to the partnership. Bill, a prominent physician, provides capital, but no services, to the partnership. The partners' original goal was to develop a national chain of soccer shops, but so far they have been unable to attract franchisees. The partnership broke even each of its first two years.

Bill Brock believes that as the next World Cup approaches, the partnership will realize its franchising goal and become extremely profitable. Bill recently approached Stan and suggested that the existing partnership be terminated and a new one formed, excluding Harv. Stan is agreeable.

Bill has retained your services in connection with the above plan of action. How would you advise him to proceed? What questions would you ask before giving your advice?

4. Fiduciary Limits on Expulsion of Unwanted Partners

UPA (1997) §§601(3), 701, 801(1)

Partnerships are often bound together by shared values and expectations as to effort, collegiality, and professionalism. If a partner does not measure up to the shared values and expectations, the other partners may wish to expel the deficient partner. In a term partnership, if the majority ousts the deficient partner, this dissociation could be deemed "wrongful," exposing the ousting partners to substantial liability. Accordingly, partners will often negotiate in advance for terms governing expulsion. To the extent the partners do not so agree, the right to expel will be governed by the dictates of partnership law, including fiduciary duty.

Bohatch v. Butler & Binion
Supreme Court of Texas, 1998
977 S.W.2d 543

ENOCH, JUSTICE.

I. FACTS

[Colette] Bohatch became an associate in the Washington, D.C., office of Butler & Binion in 1986 after working for several years as Deputy Assistant General Counsel at the Federal Energy Regulatory Commission. John McDonald, the managing partner of the office, and Richard Powers, a partner, were the only other attorneys in the Washington office. The office did work for Pennzoil almost exclusively.

Bohatch was made partner in February 1990. She then began receiving internal firm reports showing the number of hours each attorney worked, billed, and collected. From her review of these reports, Bohatch became concerned that McDonald was overbilling Pennzoil and discussed the matter with Powers. Together they reviewed and copied portions of McDonald's time diary. Bohatch's review of McDonald's time entries increased her concern.

On July 15, 1990, Bohatch met with Louis Paine, the firm's managing partner, to report her concern that McDonald was overbilling Pennzoil. Paine said he would investigate. Later that day, Bohatch told Powers about her conversation with Paine.

The following day, McDonald met with Bohatch and informed her that Pennzoil was not satisfied with her work and wanted her work to be supervised. Bohatch testified that this was the first time she had ever heard criticism of her work for Pennzoil.

The next day, Bohatch repeated her concerns to Paine and to R. Hayden Burns and Marion E. McDaniel, two other members of the firm's management committee, in a telephone conversation. Over the next month, Paine and Burns investigated Bohatch's complaint. They reviewed the Pennzoil bills and supporting computer print-outs for those bills. They then discussed the allegations with Pennzoil in-house counsel John Chapman, the firm's primary contact with Pennzoil. Chapman, who had a long-standing relationship with McDonald, responded that Pennzoil was satisfied that the bills were reasonable.

In August, Paine met with Bohatch and told her that the firm's investigation revealed no basis for her contentions. He added that she should begin looking for other employment, but that the firm would continue to provide her a monthly draw, insurance coverage, office space, and a secretary. After this meeting, Bohatch received no further work assignments from the firm.

In January 1991, the firm denied Bohatch a year-end partnership distribution for 1990 and reduced her tentative distribution share for 1991 to zero. In June, the firm paid Bohatch her monthly draw and told her that this draw would be her last. Finally, in August, the firm gave Bohatch until November to vacate her office.

By September, Bohatch had found new employment. She filed this suit on October 18, 1991, and the firm voted formally to expel her from the partnership three days later, October 21, 1991. . . .

The breach of fiduciary duty claim and a breach of contract claim were tried to a jury. The jury found that the firm breached the partnership agreement and its fiduciary duty. It awarded Bohatch $57,000 for past lost wages, $250,000 for past mental anguish, $4,000,000 total in punitive damages (this amount was apportioned against several defendants), and attorney's fees. The trial court rendered judgment for Bohatch in the amounts found by the jury, except it disallowed attorney's fees because the judgment was based in tort. After suggesting remittitur, which Bohatch accepted, the trial court reduced the punitive damages to around $237,000.

All parties appealed. The court of appeals held that the firm's only duty to Bohatch was not to expel her in bad faith. 905 S.W.2d at 602. The court of appeals stated that "'[b]ad faith' in this context means only that partners cannot expel another partner for self-gain." Id. Finding no evidence that the firm expelled Bohatch for self-gain, the court concluded that Bohatch could not recover for breach of fiduciary duty. Id. at 604. However, the court concluded that the firm breached the partnership agreement when it reduced Bohatch's tentative partnership distribution for 1991 to zero without notice, and when it terminated her draw three months before she left. Id. at 606. The court concluded that Bohatch was entitled to recover $35,000 in lost earnings for 1991 but none for 1990, and no mental anguish damages. Id. at 606-607. Accordingly, the court rendered judgment for Bohatch for $35,000 plus $225,000 in attorney's fees. Id. at 608.

II. Breach of Fiduciary Duty

We have long recognized as a matter of common law that "[t]he relationship between . . . partners . . . is fiduciary in character, and imposes upon all the participants the obligation of loyalty to the joint concern and of the utmost good faith, fairness, and honesty in their dealings with each other with respect to matters pertaining to the enterprise." Fitz-Gerald v. Hull, 150 Tex. 39, 237 S.W.2d 256, 264 (1951) (quotation omitted). Yet, partners have no obligation to remain partners; "at the heart of the partnership concept is the principle that partners may choose with whom they wish to be associated." Gelder Med. Group v. Webber, 41 N.Y.2d 680, 394 N.Y.S.2d 867, 870-871, 363 N.E.2d 573, 577

(1977). The issue presented, one of first impression, is whether the fiduciary relationship between and among partners creates an exception to the at-will nature of partnerships; that is, in this case, whether it gives rise to a duty not to expel a partner who reports suspected overbilling by another partner. . . .

[N]either statutory nor contract law principles answer the question of whether the firm owed Bohatch a duty not to expel her. The Texas Uniform Partnership Act, Tex. Rev. Civ. Stat. Ann. art. 6701b, addresses expulsion of a partner only in the context of dissolution of the partnership. See id. §§31, 38. In this case, as provided by the partnership agreement, Bohatch's expulsion did not dissolve the partnership. . . . Finally, the partnership agreement contemplates expulsion of a partner and prescribes procedures to be followed, but it does not specify or limit the grounds for expulsion. Thus, while Bohatch's claim that she was expelled in an improper way is governed by the partnership agreement, her claim that she was expelled for an improper reason is not. Therefore, we look to the common law to find the principles governing Bohatch's claim that the firm breached a duty when it expelled her.

Courts in other states have held that a partnership may expel a partner for purely business reasons. See St. Joseph's Reg'l Health Ctr. v. Munos, 326 Ark. 605, 934 S.W.2d 192, 197 (1996) (holding that partner's termination of another partner's contract to manage services performed by medical partnership was not breach of fiduciary duty because termination was for business purpose); Waite v. Sylvester, 131 N.H. 663, 560 A.2d 619, 622-623 (1989) (holding that removal of a partner as managing partner of limited partnership was not breach of fiduciary duty because it was based on legitimate business purpose); Leigh v. Crescent Square, Ltd., 80 Ohio App. 3d 231, 608 N.E.2d 1166, 1170 (1992) ("Taking into account the general partners' past problems and the previous litigation wherein Leigh was found to have acted in contravention of the partnership's best interests, the ouster was instituted in good faith and for legitimate business purposes."). Further, courts recognize that a law firm can expel a partner to protect relationships both within the firm and with clients. See Lawlis v. Kightlinger & Gray, 562 N.E.2d 435, 442 (Ind. App. 1990) (holding that law firm did not breach fiduciary duty by expelling partner after partner's successful struggle against alcoholism because "if a partner's propensity toward alcohol has the potential to damage his firm's good will or reputation for astuteness in the practice of law, simple prudence dictates the exercise of corrective action . . . since the survival of the partnership itself potentially is at stake"); Holman v. Coie, 11 Wash. App. 195, 522 P.2d 515, 523 (1974) (finding no breach of fiduciary duty where law firm expelled two partners because of their contentious behavior during executive committee meetings and because one, as state senator, made speech offensive to major client). Finally, many courts have held that a partnership can expel a partner without breaching any duty in order to resolve a "fundamental schism." See Waite, 560 A.2d at 623 (concluding that in removing a partner as managing partner "the partners acted in good faith to resolve the 'fundamental schism' between them"); Heller v. Pillsbury Madison & Sutro, 50 Cal. App. 4th 1367, 58 Cal. Rptr.2d 336, 348 (1996) (holding that law firm did not breach fiduciary duty when it expelled partner who was not as productive as firm expected and who was offensive to some of firm's major clients); Levy v. Nassau Queens Med. Group, 102 A.D.2d 845, 476 N.Y.S.2d 613, 614 (1984) (concluding that expelling partner because of "[p]olicy disagreements" is not "bad faith").

The fiduciary duty that partners owe one another does not encompass a duty to remain partners or else answer in tort damages. Nonetheless, *Bohatch* and several distinguished legal scholars urge this Court to recognize that public policy requires a limited duty to remain partners—i.e., a partnership must retain a whistleblower partner. They argue that such an extension of a partner's fiduciary duty is necessary because permitting a law firm to retaliate against a partner who in good faith reports suspected overbilling would discourage compliance with rules of professional conduct and thereby hurt clients.

While this argument is not without some force, we must reject it. A partnership exists solely because the partners choose to place personal confidence and trust in one another. See *Holman,* 522 P.2d at 524 ("The foundation of a professional relationship is personal confidence and trust."). Just as a partner can be expelled, without a breach of any common law duty, over disagreements about firm policy or to resolve some other "fundamental schism," a partner can be expelled for accusing another partner of overbilling without subjecting the partnership to tort damages. Such charges, whether true or not, may have a profound effect on the personal confidence and trust essential to the partner relationship. Once such charges are made, partners may find it impossible to continue to work together to their mutual benefit and the benefit of their clients.

We are sensitive to the concern expressed by the dissenting Justices that "retaliation against a partner who tries in good faith to correct or report perceived misconduct virtually assures that others will not take these appropriate steps in the future."—S.W.2d at— (Spector, J., dissenting). However, the dissenting Justices do not explain how the trust relationship necessary both for the firm's existence and for representing clients can survive such serious accusations by one partner against another. The threat of tort liability for expulsion would tend to force partners to remain in untenable circumstance—suspicious of and angry with each other—to their own detriment and that of their clients whose matters are neglected by lawyers distracted with intra-firm frictions. . . .

We emphasize that our refusal to create an exception to the at-will nature of partnerships in no way obviates the ethical duties of lawyers. Such duties sometimes necessitate difficult decisions, as when a lawyer suspects overbilling by a colleague. The fact that the ethical duty to report may create an irreparable schism between partners neither excuses failure to report nor transforms expulsion as a means of resolving that schism into a tort.

We hold that the firm did not owe Bohatch a duty not to expel her for reporting suspected overbilling by another partner.

III. BREACH OF THE PARTNERSHIP AGREEMENT

The court of appeals concluded that the firm breached the partnership agreement by reducing Bohatch's tentative distribution for 1991 to zero without the requisite notice. 905 S.W.2d at 606. The firm contests this finding on the ground that the management committee had the right to set tentative and year-end bonuses. However, the partnership agreement guarantees a monthly draw of $7,500 per month regardless of the tentative distribution. Moreover, the firm's right to reduce the bonus was contingent upon providing proper notice to Bohatch. The firm does not dispute that it did not give Bohatch notice that the firm was reducing her tentative distribution. Accordingly, the court of appeals did not err in finding the firm liable for breach of the partnership agreement. Moreover, because Bohatch's damages sound in contract, and because she sought attorney's fees at trial under section 38.001(8) of the Texas Civil Practice and Remedies Code, we affirm the court of appeals' award of Bohatch's attorney's fees. . . .

SPECTOR, joined by PHILLIPS, CHIEF JUSTICE, dissenting.

> [W]hat's the use you learning to do right when it's troublesome to do right and ain't no trouble to
> do wrong, and the wages is just the same?
>
> —The Adventures of Huckleberry Finn

The issue in this appeal is whether law partners violate a fiduciary duty by retaliating against one partner for questioning the billing practices of another partner. I would hold that partners violate their fiduciary duty to one another by punishing compliance with the Disciplinary Rules of Professional Conduct. Accordingly, I dissent. . . .

II.

The majority views the partnership relationship among lawyers as strictly business. I disagree. The practice of law is a profession first, then a business. Moreover, it is a self-regulated profession subject to the Rules promulgated by this Court.

As attorneys, we take an oath to "honestly demean [ourselves] in the practice of law; and . . . discharge [our] duty to [our] client[s] to the best of [our] ability." Tex. Gov't Code §82.037. This oath of honesty and duty is not mere "self-adulatory bombast" but mandated by the Legislature. See Schware v. Board of Bar Exam'rs, 353 U.S. 232, 247, 77 S.Ct. 752, 760-761, 1 L.Ed.2d 796 (Frankfurter, J. concurring) (noting that the rhetoric used to describe the esteemed role of the legal profession has real meaning). As attorneys, we bear responsibilities to our clients and the bar itself that transcend ordinary business relationships.

Certain requirements imposed by the Rules have particular relevance in this case. Lawyers may not charge unconscionable fees. TEX. DISCIPLINARY R. PROF'L CONDUCT 1.04(a), reprinted in TEX. GOV'T CODE, tit. 2, subtit. G app. A (TEX. STATE BAR R. art. X, §9); see D.C. R. PROF'L CONDUCT 1.5(a)(1) (West 1997). Partners and supervisory attorneys have a duty to take reasonable remedial action to avoid or mitigate the consequences of known violations by other lawyers in their firm. TEX. DISCIPLINARY R. PROF'L CONDUCT 5.01; see D.C. R. PROF'L CONDUCT 5.1. Lawyers who know that another lawyer has violated a rule of professional conduct in a way that raises a substantial question as to that lawyer's honesty or fitness as a lawyer must report that violation. TEX. DISCIPLINARY R. PROF'L CONDUCT 8.03(a); D.C. R. Prof'l Conduct 8.3. In Texas, Rules 5.01 and 8.03 are essential to the self-regulatory nature of the practice of law and the honor of our profession itself. . . .

III.

The few cases that provide guidance here do so with conflicting results, but each case highlights the grave implications of those decisions for a self-regulated profession. Ultimately, agreements to practice law may not by their terms or effect circumvent the ethical obligations of attorneys established by law. See Southwestern Bell Tel. Co. v. DeLanney, 809 S.W.2d 493, 494 n. 1 (Tex. 1991); Central Educ. Agency v. George West Indep. Sch. Dist., 783 S.W.2d 200, 202 (Tex. 1989).

A.

In Wieder v. Skala, the New York Court of Appeals held in an at-will employment context that an associate terminated for reporting another associate's misconduct had a valid claim for breach of contract against his law firm based on an implied-in-law obligation to comply with the rules of the profession. 80 N.Y.2d 628, 593 N.Y.S.2d 752, 757, 609 N.E.2d 105, 110 (1992). The court recognized that "[i]ntrinsic to [the hiring of an attorney to practice law] . . . was the unstated but essential compact that in conducting the firm's legal practice both plaintiff and the firm would do so in compliance with the prevailing rules of conduct and ethical standards of the profession." Id. 593 N.Y.S.2d at 756-757, 609 N.E.2d at 109-110. To find otherwise would amount to "nothing less than a frustration of the only legitimate purpose of the employment relationship," id. 593 N.Y.S.2d at 757, 609 N.E.2d at 110, that is, "the lawful and ethical practice of law." Id. 593 N.Y.S.2d at 755, 609 N.E.2d at 108. See also Seymour Moskowitz, Employment-at-Will and Codes of Ethics: The Professional's Dilemma, 23 Val. U.L. Rev. 33, 56-66 (1988) (arguing for a public policy exception to at-will employment for professional codes of ethics). The plaintiff was not just an employee, but also an "independent officer of the court responsible in a broader public sense for [his] professional obligations." Wieder, 593 N.Y.S.2d at 755, 609 N.E.2d at 108. . . .

B.

I believe that the fiduciary relationship among law partners should incorporate the rules of the profession promulgated by this Court. See Central Educ. Agency, 783 S.W.2d at 202 (noting that employment contracts incorporate existing law). Although the evidence put on by Bohatch is by no means conclusive, applying the proper presumptions of a no-evidence review, this trial testimony amounts to some evidence that Bohatch made a good-faith report of suspected overbilling in an effort to comply with her professional duty. Further, it provides some evidence that the partners of Butler & Binion began a retaliatory course of action before any investigation of the allegation had begun.

In light of this Court's role in setting standards to govern attorneys' conduct, it is particularly inappropriate for the Court to deny recourse to attorneys wronged for adhering to the Disciplinary Rules. See Blackwell, supra, at 44-48. I would hold that in this case the law partners violated their fiduciary duty by retaliating against a fellow partner who made a good-faith effort to alert her partners to the possible overbilling of a client.

C.

The duty to prevent overbilling and other misconduct exists for the protection of the client. Even if a report turns out to be mistaken or a client ultimately consents to the behavior in question, as in this case, retaliation against a partner who tries in good faith to correct or report perceived misconduct virtually assures that others will not take these appropriate steps in the future. Although I agree with the majority that partners have a right not to continue a partnership with someone against their will, they may still be liable for damages directly resulting from terminating that relationship. See Woodruff v. Bryant, 558 S.W.2d 535, 539 (Tex.Civ.App. — Corpus Christi 1977, writ ref'd n.r.e.).

III.

The Court's writing in this case sends an inappropriate signal to lawyers and to the public that the rules of professional responsibility are subordinate to a law firm's other interests. Under the majority opinion's vision for the legal profession, the wages would not even be the same for "doing right"; they diminish considerably and leave an attorney who acts ethically and in good faith without recourse. Accordingly, I respectfully dissent.

PROBLEM 2-11

Baker and Smith is a partnership engaged in the practice of law. In 1993, Frank Wesson, then 60 years old, was admitted to the partnership, following a one-year trial period in which he was employed as a litigator. Previously, Wesson had enjoyed a career as a high-profile civil rights attorney. The Baker and Smith partnership agreement, to which Wesson assented, provided that "any partner may be expelled without notice or cause by a vote of a majority of the partners."

Wesson's association turned out to be unsatisfactory to his partners. He accepted several high-profile cases on a pro bono basis, including advocacy on behalf of a controversial gay rights organization. This caused a negative reaction from several important clients. Additionally, some partners viewed Wesson as abrasive, both professionally and personally. In December 2002, the partners voted unanimously to expel Wesson from the partnership, effective December 31, 2002.

What are Wesson's rights under UPA (1997)?

5. Contracting to Prevent Opportunistic Withdrawal: The Fiduciary Duties Owed by Withdrawing Partners

UPA (1997) §§601, 602, 701, 801

In service partnerships, it is common for one or more partners to dissociate, form a new firm that carries on a similar business, and then attract a number of their former firm's clients to the new firm. It is also common for partners to contract in advance concerning the rights and obligations of continuing and withdrawing partners. As you read the following case, consider what the parties' rights would have been absent the partnership agreement. Also consider whether the partnership agreement was fair and efficient. Finally, consider the role of fiduciary duty in protecting a partnership from opportunistic withdrawal by one or more partners.

Meehan v. Shaughnessy
Massachusetts Supreme Judicial Court, 1989
535 N.E.2d 1255

HENNESSEY, CHIEF JUSTICE.

The plaintiffs, James F. Meehan (Meehan) and Leo V. Boyle (Boyle), were partners of the law firm, Parker, Coulter, Daley & White (Parker Coulter). After Meehan and Boyle terminated their relationship with Parker Coulter to start their own firm, they commenced this action both to recover amounts they claim the defendants, their former partners, owed them under the partnership agreement, and to obtain a declaration as to amounts they owed the defendants for work done at Parker Coulter on cases they removed to their new firm. The defendants (hereinafter collectively Parker Coulter) counterclaimed that Meehan and Boyle violated their fiduciary duties, breached the partnership agreement, and tortiously interfered with their advantageous business and contractual relationships. . . .

We summarize the facts as found by the judge. . . . Parker, Coulter, Daley & White is a large partnership which specializes in litigation on behalf of both defendants and plaintiffs. Meehan joined the firm in 1959, and became a partner in 1963; his practice focuses primarily on complex tort litigation, such as product liability and aviation defense work. Boyle joined Parker Coulter in 1971, and became a partner in 1980; he has concentrated on plaintiffs' work. Both have developed outstanding reputations as trial lawyers in the Commonwealth. Meehan and Boyle each were active in the management of Parker Coulter. They each served, for example, on the partnership's executive committee and, as members of this committee, were responsible for considering and making policy recommendations to the general partnership. Boyle was also in charge of the "plaintiffs department" within the firm, which managed approximately 350 cases. At the time of their leaving, Meehan's interest in the partnership was 6% and Boyle's interest was 4.8%.

Meehan and Boyle had become dissatisfied at Parker Coulter. On June 27, 1984, after unsuccessfully opposing the adoption of a firm-wide pension plan, the two first discussed the possibility of leaving Parker Coulter. . . . On July 1, Meehan and Boyle decided to leave Parker Coulter and form their own partnership.

[The court then describes Meehan's and Boyle's actions between July 1 and December 1 in planning for their departure. During this period, four other attorneys—Cohen, Schafer, Black, and Fitzgerald—agreed to leave Parker Coulter to join Meehan's and Boyle's new firm (MBC). Although the partnership agreement required a notice period of three months, Meehan and Boyle decided to give only thirty days' notice.]

Toward the end of November, Boyle prepared form letters to send to clients and referring attorneys as soon as Parker Coulter was notified of the separation. He also drafted a form for the clients to return to him at his home address authorizing him to remove cases to MBC. . . .

While they were planning their departure, from July to approximately December, Meehan, Boyle, Cohen, Schafer, Black, and Fitzgerald all continued to work full schedules. They settled cases appropriately, made reasonable efforts to avoid continuances, tried cases, and worked on discovery. Each generally maintained his or her usual standard of performance.

Meehan and Boyle had originally intended to give notice to Parker Coulter on December 1, 1984. Rumors of their leaving, however, began to circulate before then. During the period from July to early fall, different Parker Coulter partners approached Meehan individually on three separate occasions and asked him if the rumors about his leaving were true. On each occasion, Meehan denied that he was leaving. On November 30, 1984, a partner, Maurice F. Shaughnessy (Shaughnessy), approached Boyle and asked him whether Meehan and Boyle intended to leave the firm. Shaughnessy interpreted Boyle's evasive response as an affirmation of the rumors. Meehan and Boyle then decided to distribute their notice that afternoon, which stated, as their proposed date for leaving, December 31, 1984. A notice was left on the desk of each partner. When Meehan, Boyle, and Cohen gave their notice, the atmosphere at Parker Coulter became "tense, emotional and unpleasant, if not adversarial."

On December 3, the Parker Coulter partners appointed a separation committee and decided to communicate with "important sources of business" to tell them of the separation and of Parker Coulter's desire to continue representing them. Meehan and Boyle asked their partners for financial information about the firm, discussed cases and clients with them, and stated that they intended to communicate with clients and referring attorneys on the cases in which they were involved. Sometime during the week of December 3, the partners sent Boyle a list of cases and requested that he identify the cases he intended to take with him.

Boyle had begun to make telephone calls to referring attorneys on Saturday morning, December 1. He had spoken with three referring attorneys by that date and told them of his departure from Parker Coulter and his wish to continue handling their cases. On December 3, he mailed his previously typed letters and authorization forms, and by the end of the first two weeks of December he had spoken with a majority of referring attorneys, and had obtained authorizations from a majority of clients whose cases he planned to remove to MBC.

Although the partners previously were aware of Boyle's intention to communicate with clients, they did not become aware of the extent of his communications until December 12 or 13. Boyle did not provide his partners with the list they requested of cases he intended to remove until December 17. . . . On December 19, 1984, one of the partners accepted on behalf of Parker Coulter the December 31 departure date and waived the three-month notice period provided for by the partnership agreement. Meehan, Boyle, and Cohen formalized their arrangement as a professional corporation on January 1, 1985.

MBC removed a number of cases from Parker Coulter. Of the roughly 350 contingent fee cases pending at Parker Coulter in 1984, Boyle, Schafer, and Meehan removed approximately 142 to MBC. . . .

1. STATUTORY CONSIDERATIONS;
THE PARTNERSHIP AGREEMENT

Before we address Parker Coulter's claims of wrongdoing, we first review the statutory right a partner has to cease his or her association with a partnership, and the statutory right the partner has to assets of the partnership upon leaving. We then examine how the partners in this case have modified these statutory rights in their partnership agreement.

[Here the court reviews the UPA's dissolution rules.]

The Parker Coulter partnership agreement provided for rights on a dissolution caused by the will of a partner which are different from those [provided by the UPA default provisions]. . . . The agreement provides for an allocation to the departing partner of a share of the firm's current net income, and a return of his or her capital contributions. In addition, the agreement also recognizes that a major asset of a law firm is the expected fees it will receive from unfinished business currently being transacted. Instead of assigning a value to the departing partner's interest in this unfinished business, or waiting for the unfinished business to be "wound up" and liquidated, which is the method of division [the UPA] provides, the agreement gives the partner the right to remove any case which came to the firm "through the personal effort or connection" of the partner, if the partner compensates the dissolved partnership "for the services to and expenditures for the client." Once the partner has removed a case, the agreement provides that the partner is entitled to retain all future fees in the case, with the exception of the "fair charge" owed to the dissolved firm.[9]

Although the provision in the partnership agreement which divides the dissolved firm's unfinished business does not expressly apply to the removal of cases which did not come to Parker Coulter through the efforts of the departing partner, we believe that the parties intended this provision to apply to these cases also. . . . Therefore, based on the partners' intent, and on the prohibition against restrictive covenants between attorneys, we interpret the agreement to provide that, upon the payment of a fair charge, any case may be removed regardless of whether the case came to the firm through the personal efforts of the departing partner. This privilege to remove, as is shown in our later discussion, is of course dependent upon the partner's compliance with fiduciary obligations.

Under the agreement, therefore, a partner who separates his or her practice from that of the firm receives (1) the right to his or her capital contribution, (2) the right to a share of the net income to which the dissolved partnership is currently entitled, and (3) the right to a portion of the firm's unfinished business, and in exchange gives up all other rights in the dissolved firm's remaining assets. As to (3) above, "unfinished

---

9. The agreement provides that this "fair charge" is a "receivable account of the earlier partnership . . . and [is] divided between the remaining partners and the retiring partner on the basis of which they share in the profits of the firm at the time of the withdrawal." This fair charge is thus treated as an asset of the former partnership. Because the partnership, upon the receipt of the fair charge, gives up all future rights to income from the removed case, the partnership's collective interest in the case is effectively "wound up." The fair charge, therefore, is a method of valuing the partnership's unfinished business as it relates to the removed case.

business," the partner gives up all right to proceeds from any unfinished business of the dissolved firm which the new, surviving firm retains. Under the agreement, the old firm's unfinished business is, in effect, "wound up" immediately; the departing partner takes certain of the unfinished business of the old, dissolved Parker Coulter on the payment of a "fair charge," and the new, surviving Parker Coulter takes the remainder of the old partnership's unfinished business.[11] The two entities surviving after the dissolution possess "new business," unconnected with that of the old firm, and the former partners no longer have a continuing fiduciary obligation to wind up for the benefit of each other the business they shared in their former partnerships.

In sum, the statute gives a partner the power to dissolve a partnership at any time. Under the statute, the assets of the dissolved partnership are divided among the former partners through the process of liquidation and windup. The statute, however, allows partners to design their own methods of dividing assets and, provided the dissolution is not premature, expressly states that the partners' method controls. Here, the partners have fashioned a division method which immediately winds up unfinished business, allows for a quick separation of the surviving practices, and minimizes the disruptive impact of a dissolution.

2. FIDUCIARY DUTIES; BREACH

We now consider Parker Coulter's claims of wrongdoing. Parker Coulter claims that the judge erred in finding that Meehan, Boyle, Cohen, and Schafer fulfilled their fiduciary duties to the former partnership. In particular, Parker Coulter argues that these attorneys breached their duties (1) by improperly handling cases for their own, and not the partnership's benefit, (2) by secretly competing with the partnership, and (3) by unfairly acquiring from clients and referring attorneys consent to withdraw cases to MBC.[12] We do not agree with Parker Coulter's first two arguments but agree with the third. We first address the claims against Meehan and Boyle, and then turn to those against Cohen and Schafer. . . .

Parker Coulter next argues that the judge's findings compel the conclusion that Meehan and Boyle breached their fiduciary duty not to compete with their partners by secretly setting up a new firm during their tenure at Parker Coulter. We disagree. We have stated that fiduciaries may plan to compete with the entity to which they owe allegiance, "provided that in the course of such arrangements they [do] not otherwise act

---

11. A more equitable provision would require that the new, surviving partnership also pay a "fair charge" on the cases it takes from the dissolved partnership. This "fair charge" from the new firm, as is the "fair charge" from the departing partner, would be an asset of the dissolved partnership, in which the departing partner has an interest.

12. Parker Coulter does not claim that Meehan and Boyle wrongfully dissolved the partnership by leaving prematurely. The partnership agreement, although providing that the firm "shall continue indefinitely," required that a partner who leaves to continue practicing elsewhere give three-months' advance notice. This, therefore, may not have been a purely "at will" partnership which a partner has a right to dissolve at any time without triggering the remedies of [UPA] §38(2). Here, Parker Coulter waived compliance with the agreement's three-month notice provision. Meehan and Boyle, therefore, dissolved the partnership "[w]ithout violation of the agreement between the partners." [UPA] §31.

in violation of their fiduciary duties." Here, the judge found that Meehan and Boyle made certain logistical arrangements for the establishment of MBC. These arrangements included executing a lease for MBC's office, preparing lists of clients expected to leave Parker Coulter for MBC, and obtaining financing on the basis of these lists. We believe these logistical arrangements to establish a physical plant for the new firm were permissible . . . , especially in light of the attorney's obligation to represent adequately any clients who might continue to retain them on their departure from Parker Coulter. . . .

Lastly, Parker Coulter argues that the judge's findings compel the conclusion that Meehan and Boyle breached their fiduciary duties by unfairly acquiring consent from clients to remove cases from Parker Coulter. We agree that Meehan and Boyle, through their preparation for obtaining clients' consent, their secrecy concerning which clients they intended to take, and the substance and method of their communications with clients, obtained an unfair advantage over their former partners in breach of their fiduciary duties.

A partner has an obligation to "render on demand true and full information of all things affecting the partnership to any partner." G.L. c.108A, §20. On three separate occasions Meehan affirmatively denied to his partners, on their demand, that he had any plans for leaving the partnership. During this period of secrecy, Meehan and Boyle made preparations for obtaining removal authorizations from clients. Meehan traveled to New York to meet with a representative of [U.S. Aviation Underwriters] and interest him in the new firm. Boyle prepared form letters on Parker Coulter's letterhead for authorizations from prospective MBC clients. Thus, they were "ready to move" the instant they gave notice to their partners.

On giving their notice, Meehan and Boyle continued to use their position of trust and confidence to the disadvantage of Parker Coulter. The two immediately began communicating with clients and referring attorneys. Boyle delayed providing his partners with a list of clients he intended to solicit until mid-December, by which time he had obtained authorization from a majority of the clients.

Finally, the content of the letter sent to the clients was unfairly prejudicial to Parker Coulter. The ABA Committee on Ethics and Professional Responsibility, in Informal Opinion 1457 (April 29, 1980), set forth ethical standards for attorneys announcing a change in professional association.[15] Because this standard is intended primarily to protect clients, proof by Parker Coulter of a technical violation of this standard does not aid them in their claims. We will, however, look to this standard for general guidelines as to what partners are entitled to expect from each other concerning their joint

---

15. These standards provide the following guidelines for notice to clients: "(a) the notice is mailed; (b) the notice is sent only to persons with whom the lawyer had an active lawyer-client relationship immediately before the change in the lawyer's professional association; (c) the notice is clearly related to open and pending matters for which the lawyer had direct professional responsibility to the client immediately before the change; (d) the notice is sent promptly after the change; (e) the notice does not urge the client to sever a relationship with the lawyer's former firm and does not recommend the lawyer's employment (although it indicates the lawyer's willingness to continue his responsibility for the matters); (f) the notice makes it clear that the client has the right to decide who will complete or continue the matters; and (g) the notice is brief, dignified, and not disparaging of the lawyer's former firm."

clients on the division of their practice. The ethical standard provides that any notice explain to a client that he or she has the right to decide who will continue the representation. Here, the judge found that the notice did not "clearly present to the clients the choice they had between remaining at Parker Coulter or moving to the new firm." By sending a one-sided announcement, on Parker Coulter letterhead, so soon after notice of their departure, Meehan and Boyle excluded their partners from effectively presenting their services as an alternative to those of Meehan and Boyle.

Meehan and Boyle could have foreseen that the news of their departure would cause a certain amount of confusion and disruption among their partners. The speed and pre-emptive character of their campaign to acquire clients' consent took advantage of their partners' confusion. By engaging in these pre-emptive tactics, Meehan and Boyle violated the duty of utmost good faith and loyalty which they owed their partners. Therefore, we conclude that the judge erred in deciding that Meehan and Boyle acted properly in acquiring consent to remove cases to MBC. . . .

3. Consequences of Breach

Before we examine the consequences of the MBC attorneys' breach of duty, we briefly outline what is at stake. If there had been no breach of duty, the assets of the partnership upon dissolution would be divided strictly according to the partnership agreement. Under the agreement, Meehan and Boyle would be entitled to the return of their capital contributions and their share of the dissolved firm's profits. They would also possess the right to remove cases from the old partnership, and to retain all future fees generated by these cases in excess of the fair charge owed to the partnership for work performed there on the removed cases. Because the fair charge is an asset of the dissolved firm under the agreement, Meehan and Boyle would share in this amount according to their respective interests in the former partnership. Thus, of the fair charges returned to their former partnership, Meehan and Boyle would receive their combined 10.8% partnership share, and their former partners would receive the remainder. . . .

For Parker Coulter to recover any amount in addition to what it would be entitled to receive upon dissolution under the partnership agreement or the statute, there must be a causal connection between its claimed losses and the breach of duty on the part of the MBC attorneys. We have concluded that the MBC attorneys unfairly acquired consent from clients. Parker Coulter, therefore, is entitled to recover only those amounts which flow from this breach of duty.

There is no conceivable connection between the attorneys' breach of duty and Parker Coulter's claims to the capital contributions and profit shares of Meehan and Boyle. We have ruled that a partner does not forfeit his or her right to the accrued profits of a partnership by simply breaching the partnership agreement. The same rule applies to a partner's capital contributions. These amounts are not a form of liquidated damages to which partners can resort in the event of a breach. We conclude, therefore, that Parker Coulter is not entitled to recover these amounts. The judge correctly found that Meehan and Boyle are entitled to a return of their capital contributions (their interest, as determined by the judge, in the partners' reserve account and the partners' capital account), and to the receipt of a portion of the old firm's profits (their interest in the income earned but not distributed account).

We similarly reject Parker Coulter's claims that the MBC attorneys should be required to forfeit all compensation during the period of their breach. Parker Coulter is correct in stating that a fiduciary "can be required to forfeit the right to retain or receive his compensation for conduct in violation of his fiduciary duties." Parker Coulter fails to consider, however, that a fiduciary may be required "to repay only that portion of his compensation, if any, that was in excess of the worth of his services to his employer." Here, the judge found that throughout the period in question the MBC attorneys worked as hard, and were as productive as they had always been. This finding was warranted, and is unchallenged by Parker Coulter. In these circumstances, we conclude that the value of the MBC attorneys' services was equal to their compensation. Parker Coulter, therefore, is not entitled to this relief.

Parker Coulter's claim that it is entitled to all fees from removed cases, however, rests on a different footing from its claims to compensation, capital contributions, and profit shares. We therefore examine more closely Parker Coulter's allegations of a causal connection between the breach of duty and its loss of clients.

Although the judge found that the MBC attorneys did not breach their fiduciary duties in acquiring consent from clients, he nonetheless stated, as an alternative ground for denying relief on this claim, that Parker Coulter had shown no causal connection between the departing attorneys' acts and its loss of clients. He ruled that Parker Coulter failed to show that clients who left the firm would have remained had the plaintiffs and third-party defendants acted properly. Parker Coulter argues that the standard of causation the judge imposed was too strict. We agree that the judge's ruling placed an inappropriate burden on Parker Coulter.

In these circumstances, it is appropriate to place on the party who improperly removed the case the burden of proving that the client would have consented to removal in the absence of any breach of duty. We have recognized that shifting the burden of proof may be justified on policy grounds because it encourages a defendant both to preserve information concerning the circumstances of the plaintiff's injury and to use best efforts to fulfill any duty he or she may owe the plaintiff. Based on similar reasoning, courts in other jurisdictions have shifted the burden of proof in cases involving a breach of fiduciary duty. Once it is established that a partner or corporate manager has engaged in self-dealing, or has acquired a corporate or partnership opportunity, these courts require the fiduciary to prove that his or her actions were intrinsically fair, and did not result in harm to the corporation or partnership.

We conclude that Meehan and Boyle had the burden of proving no causal connection between their breach of duty and Parker Coulter's loss of clients. Proof of the circumstances of the preparations for obtaining authorizations and of the actual communications with clients was more accessible to Meehan and Boyle than to Parker Coulter. Furthermore, requiring these partners to disprove causation will encourage partners in the future to disclose seasonably and fully any plans to remove cases. This disclosure will allow the partnership and the departing partner an equal opportunity to present to clients the option of continuing with the partnership or retaining the departing partner individually.

We remand the case to the Superior Court for findings consistent with our conclusion that the MBC attorneys bear the burden of proof. . . .

4. CONCLUSION AND ORDER

In sum, we conclude that the MBC attorneys' breach of duty consisted of their method of acquiring consent from clients to remove cases. We therefore limit Parker Coulter's recovery to only those losses which were caused by this breach of duty, but place on the MBC attorneys the burden of disproving causation. On remand, the judge is to determine, based on the record and his findings as they now stand, whether the MBC attorneys have met their burden as to each case removed from Parker Coulter. A constructive trust for the benefit of the former partnership is to be imposed on any profits which Meehan, Boyle, Cohen, or Schafer receive on cases which the judge determines they unfairly removed. Because the fair charge which Meehan and Boyle owe on all removed cases is an asset of the former partnership, and because the constructive trust we impose is for the benefit of the former partnership, each former partner is entitled to his or her partnership share of these amounts. The Parker Coulter defendants are thus entitled to 89.2% of the fair charges on all removed cases, and 89.2% of the profits from the unfairly removed cases; Meehan and Boyle are entitled to 6% and 4.8%, respectively, of these amounts. Additionally, under the agreement's terms, Meehan and Boyle are to receive the return of their capital contributions and their profit shares. . . .

NOTES AND QUESTIONS

1. Did the partnership agreement in Meehan v. Shaughnessy increase the value of the partners' investments ex ante? Did it provide a proper incentive for majority interests to accommodate Meehan's and Boyle's complaints? Did it adequately prevent opportunistic withdrawal or threats of withdrawal? For a somewhat similar case, governed solely by the UPA default provisions, see Rosenfeld, Meyer & Susman v. Cohen, 146 Cal. App. 3d 200, 194 Cal. Rptr. 180 (1983).

2. For an excellent discussion of the problem presented by Meehan v. Shaughnessy, see Hillman, Law Firms and Their Partners: The Law and Ethics of Grabbing and Leaving, 67 Tex. L. Rev. 1 (1988).

3. If a partner is considering leaving a law firm to join another firm, or set up a new firm, may she secretly recruit other partners to leave with her? Consider the following analysis.

Initially, the "solicitation" of one's own partners to make a joint move simply does not qualify as a breach of fiduciary duty. . . . Merely approaching another partner, in order to broach and explore the subject of a joint move to another firm, even to attempt to convince him of the advantages of such a joint move, simply cannot serve as the foundation for liability to the firm.

Furthermore, should the two partners finally agree on a move, and ultimately arrive at an arrangement with another firm acceptable to both, the "orchestration" of the move cannot serve as a basis for liability in the absence of a type of sneaky or malicious conduct present in Kantor v.

Bernstein, 225 A.D.2d 500, 640 N.Y.S.2d 40, and Graubard Mollen Dannett & Horowitz v. Moskovitz, 653 N.E.2d 1179 (N.Y. 1995), but absent here.

The observation of the trial court that plaintiffs' joint departure "denuded" Breed, Abbott's trusts and estates department is irrelevant to the issue of breach of fiduciary duty. Where a department of a law firm contains two active partners, a few associates and support staff, a decision by the two partners to withdraw from the firm will of necessity "denude" the department, and may indeed even "cripple" it, at least temporarily. However, it does not follow that the departure violates the duty owed by the departing partners to the firm. Partners' freedom to withdraw from a firm simply cannot be reconciled with a requirement that their departure be arranged in such a way as to protect the integrity of the department, and ensure its continued profit levels.

Gibbs v. Breed, Abbott & Morgan, 710 N.Y.S.2d 578, 586, 588-589 (S. Ct. 2000) (Saxe, concurring in part, dissenting in part).

PROBLEM 2-12

Six individuals have been equal partners in the practice of law for several years. Two of these lawyers are handling a complex antitrust case on a contingent fee basis. They have produced very little revenue for the firm recently and probably will spend most of their time on this case for several years. The other partners have not been troubled by this because the firm is doing well and, if the suit is successful, the firm will reap a bonanza. Recently, however, the two antitrust lawyers have been complaining that their share of firm profits is too low. The partners are all interested in preventing further deterioration of their relationship. To that end, they have scheduled a firm retreat to draft a partnership provision that will deal fairly with partner withdrawal from the firm. You have been hired to mediate the retreat and help draft the "withdrawing partner" provision. What do you think would be a fair and efficient provision?

D. Partners as Agents — Allocating the Risk of Loss in Transactions with Third Parties

1. A Partner's Apparent and Inherent Authority

UPA (1997) §§102, 301, 303, 306, 603

Partnerships face a contractual risk common to all agency relationships: under some circumstances they may be accountable to third parties for a partner's unauthorized action. In a partnership setting, the question centers on the extent of a general partner's agency authority.

State partnership statutes provide specific rules delineating a general partner's authority. Such statutes incorporate by reference the law of agency, and should be interpreted in light of the law of agency, including the principles of actual, apparent, and inherent authority (see discussion of these principles in Chapter 1 at pages 38-40).

Under agency law, authority comes from the principal's manifestations of consent to either the agent or the third party. The extent of a particular agent's authority thus depends on a case-by-case analysis to determine what manifestations have been made and whether these manifestations are sufficient to create authority in a particular case. The broadest possible grant of agency power is the general agency power granted to one who is the general manager in charge of the entire business. However, the existence of that authority must be traceable to a manifestation of consent by the principal, requiring application of agency principles.

As explained in 1 A. Bromberg and L. Ribstein, Bromberg and Ribstein on Partnership 4:4 (1988), UPA (1997) §301 and its predecessor UPA (1914) §9 make this case-by-case inquiry and application of agency doctrines unnecessary to determine the nature of a particular partner's actual agency power:

> If §9(1) went no further than providing that the partner is an agent of the partnership, it would be left to general agency law to determine the consequences of the partner's status. . . . The effect of §9(1) is to characterize a partner as a particular type of agent, at least in the absence of contrary evidence. A partner's actual or apparent authority, or inherent agency power, is equivalent in scope to the authority that can be implied from the position of a general managerial agent, as distinguished from one who engages in merely ministerial acts or acts only in connection with a particular phase of the business.

P.A. Properties, Inc. v. B.S. Moss' Criterion Center Corp.
United States District Court, S.D.N.Y., 2004
2004 WL 2979984

SWAIN, J.

In this breach of contract action, Plaintiff P.A. Properties, Inc. ("PAP"), seeks to recover from Defendant B.S. Moss's Criterion Center Corporation ("Moss") amounts PAP claims are due and owing under a consulting agreement entered into in 1992 by PAP and United Artists Theatre Circuit, Inc. ("UA"), which was at the time Moss' partner in a joint venture. . . .

BACKGROUND

THE MOSS/UA JOINT VENTURE

On or about February 1, 1988, UA entered into a joint venture agreement with the Moss Venturers, a group of entities consisting of the Yonkers Joint Venture, the Movieland 8th Street Joint Venture and B & E Concessions Corporation. Defendant Moss is the successor in interest to the Moss Venturers under the JV Agreement. Moss and UA agreed to operate the joint venture (which is hereinafter referred to as the "Joint Venture") under the working name "Moss/United Artists Joint Venture," with termination of the venture scheduled for July 31, 2034. The JV Agreement was governed by New York partnership law and provided that the members of the Joint Venture were "liable for all debts, liabilities and obligations of the Joint Venture in proportion to their Allocable Shares."

The stated purpose of the Joint Venture was to "manage, operate, lease, deal with and . . . dispose of, the [movie] Theatres" operated by the joint venturers, which included Movieland Yonkers, Movieland 8th Street and the theatre pertinent to the instant controversy, Movieworld Douglaston. Under the JV Agreement, UA was designated Managing Venturer and by the express terms of that agreement had the "complete authority and responsibility to manage the Joint Venture, to operate the Theatres and to make all decisions regarding the day-to-day business of the Joint Venture." These broad duties included, "without limitation, . . . maintenance of the Theatres, compliance with the terms of the leases for the Theatres, [and] payment of real property taxes." Further, UA as Managing Venturer was required to "devote such time and personnel to the management and operation of the Theatres as may be necessary to ensure that the Theatres are operated in a first class manner. . . ."

THE 1992 AGREEMENT BETWEEN UA AND PAP

On or about September 15, 1992, UA and PAP entered into a written agreement ("Consulting Agreement") whereby PAP would provide consulting and lease recovery services to discover possible overcharges on the Movieworld Douglaston lease. . . . The only entities named as parties to the Consulting Agreement were PAP and UA; the Joint Venture was not mentioned in the Agreement. At the time the Consulting Agreement was executed, UA was the Managing Venturer of the Joint Venture.

The Consulting Agreement provided that PAP's duties thereunder were principally to consist of the "Identification of Overpayments" by "analyz[ing]" relevant records and source documents in order to identify opportunities for claiming Lease Charge Recoveries. . . ."

On December 28, 1998, PAP filed suit against UA in an Illinois state court, for breach of contract, seeking compensation due for its lease recovery services. . . .

On September 5, 2000, UA filed a Chapter 11 bankruptcy petition in the United States Bankruptcy Court for the District of Delaware. . . . PAP filed a proof of claim on November 9, 2000, in the approximate amount of $1,059,716.40 and, in February of 2002, entered into an agreement with UA pursuant to which its claim was allowed in the amount of $600,000.00, "in full and complete satisfaction of all prepetition claims held by PAP against UA," without prejudice to PAP's ability to seek to recover the monies from Moss. PAP has received approximately $35,000.00 through the UA bankruptcy in respect of its allowed $600,000.00 claim. . . .

In the instant litigation, PAP seeks to hold Moss liable for the unpaid amount of its claim for compensation under the Consulting Agreement. . . .

DISCUSSION

THE CONSULTING AGREEMENT WAS AN OBLIGATION
OF THE JOINT VENTURE

The first issue to be decided on these motions for summary judgment is whether UA's Consulting Agreement with PAP was an obligation of the Joint Venture, such that the remaining solvent co-venturer, Moss, is liable thereon. The Court finds that it was such an obligation.

The JV Agreement, entered into in 1988, provided that the entity formed was to be a "joint venture general partnership under and pursuant to the provisions of the [New York Uniform Partnership] Act," and that "[t]he rights and liabilities of the Joint Venturers [would] be as provided in th[at] Act except as herein expressly provided." The JV Agreement appointed UA as Managing Venturer, with "complete authority and responsibility to manage the Joint Venture . . . and to make all decisions regarding the day-to-day business of the Joint Venture," including "compliance with the terms of the leases for the Theatres . . . , preparing or causing to be prepared financial statements and reports for the Joint Venture and managing financial matters for the Joint Venture."

The Uniform Partnership Act, adopted as New York's Partnership Law, provides in pertinent part that "[e]very partner is an agent of the partnership for the purpose of its business, and the act of every partner, . . . for apparently carrying on in the usual way the business of the partnership of which he is a member binds the partnership." NY Partnership Law §20(1) (McKinney 1988). Partners are "liable . . . jointly for all debts . . . and obligations of the partnership," *id.* §26(a)(2), and the general law of agency applies to partnerships governed by the statute. Id. §4(3).

Under the general law of agency, a principal may be liable to a third party on a transaction conducted by its agent if the agent was actually or apparently authorized to enter into the transaction, "or . . . the agent had a power arising from the agency relation and not dependent upon authority or apparent authority." Restatement (Second) Agency §140 (1958) (the "Restatement"). Section 194 of the Restatement provides that

> [a] general agent for an undisclosed principal authorized to conduct transactions subjects his principal to liability for acts done on his account, if usual or necessary in such transactions, although forbidden by the principal to do them.

Id. §194. The commentary to Section 194 describes this as "inherent agency power," and explains that the liability of the undisclosed principal turns on the intent of the agent in entering into the transaction:

> The undisclosed principal is not in general liable for acts by the agent intended by him to be wholly for his own account, since the principal becomes a party to a transaction conducted by the agent only because the agent so intends. Thus, if a general buying agent for a menagerie, directed to buy no more horses, were to buy one for himself, and by a separate contract, one for his employer, the principal would not be liable for the former. He would, however, be liable for the one purchased for the menagerie; in such case the agent, although knowingly disobedient, was intending to do an act of the sort he was employed to do, one normally done by such agents and one intended by him for his principal's business. If the agent intends the transaction to be part of the principal's business, . . . the principal is liable on the contract to the other party to the transaction, although the prevailing motive of the agent was his own benefit and he knowingly disregarded his principal's interests.

Id. cmt. b. Such an agent is termed a "general agent" under the Restatement and is defined as one who is "authorized to conduct a series of transactions involving a continuity of service." Id. §3(1).

New York case law likewise recognizes the power of general agents to bind their undisclosed principals as to matters within the general scope of the agency. See Indus.

Mfrs., Inc. v. Bangor Mills, Inc., 126 N.Y.S.2d 508, 511 (1st Dep't 1953) ("The general rule is recognized that an undisclosed principal is liable to third parties on contracts made in his behalf by his agent acting within his actual authority."); Garrett v. McAllister, 244 N.Y.S. 283, 285-86 (N.Y. Sup. Ct. 1930) (party can be liable as principal or co-adventurer on contract made in individual name of agent); Harder v. Cont'l Printing & Playing Card Co., 117 N.Y.S. 1001, 1004 (N.Y. App. Term. 1909) ("The rule of agency, where the principal is undisclosed, is as follows: If the agent buy in his own name, but for the benefit of his principal, without disclosing the name of the principal, the latter as well as the former will be bound, provided that the goods are received by the principal, and the agent, in making the purchase, acted within his power as agent."); see also 2A N.Y. Jur.2d, Agency and Independent Contractors ("N.Y. Jur. Agency"), §§348, 351-52, 356 (1998).

Here, it is undisputed that the Consulting Agreement was entered into during the life of the Joint Venture, at a time when UA served as Managing Venturer and the Douglaston theatre was being operated for the benefit of the Joint Venture. It is equally undisputed that UA executed the Consulting Agreement in its own name, that neither the agreement nor the Douglaston lease itself mentions the Joint Venture at all, and that PAP was unaware of the existence of the Joint Venture when it contracted to perform its services. Moss thus contends, correctly, that it is not a party to the Consulting Agreement as a matter of contract law. Nor is there any basis for holding the Joint Venture, or Moss, responsible for the payment of liabilities under the contract on the agency law principle of apparent authority, as no conduct of Moss or of the Joint Venture led PAP to believe that UA was authorized to bind the Joint Venture. Cf. Ford v. Unity Hosp., 32 N.Y.2d 464, 473 (1973) ("The very basis of the doctrine of apparent authority indicates that the principal can be held liable under the doctrine only where he was responsible for the appearance of authority in the agent to conduct the transaction in question." (quoting 2 N.Y. Jur. Agency §89)).

The undisputed facts do make it clear, however, that the Consulting Agreement is an obligation of the Joint Venture (and thus of its component partners) by virtue of the doctrine of inherent liability of an undisclosed principal for acts within the scope of a general agency, at least with respect to PAP's claims relating to periods during which the Douglaston theatre was operated by and for the benefit of the Joint Venture. UA was the Managing Venturer of the Joint Venture at the time it entered into the Consulting Agreement. That agreement was clearly for the benefit of the Joint Venture, which operated the Douglaston theatre at that time. The contract was well within the scope of the broad powers granted to UA as Managing Venturer, as it related to the day-to-day operations of the theatre, compliance with the lease under which the theatre was operated, and the management of the Joint Venture's financial matters. The undisputed facts of record also show that UA intended to benefit the Joint Venture by virtue of the arrangement, the goal being to reduce the Joint Venture's lease payments, and that UA indeed withheld, on the basis of issues identified by PAP, substantial amounts of rent otherwise payable under the lease. Moss argues that, even if the matters contemplated by the Consulting Agreement were within the general scope of UA's powers as agent, PAP's claim is defeated by a provision of the JV Agreement denying UA unilateral authority to "retain or replace independent accountants to review and audit the books and records of the Joint Venture and the Theatres." (*JV Agreement§5.2(m).*)

This argument is unavailing for, as shown above, the doctrine of inherent authority is operative as to matters within the broad scope of a general agency even if, as between principal and agent, the particular action has been forbidden.

CONCLUSION

For the foregoing reasons, PAP's motion for summary judgment is denied. . . .

Haymond v. Lundy
United States District Court, E.D. Pennsylvania, 2002
2002 WL 1972101

SHAPIRO, S.J.

MEMORANDUM AND ORDER

The Philadelphia law firm of Haymond & Lundy, LLP ("H & L") was formed on October 13, 1997 and dissolved on October 8, 1999. There were three founding partners: John Haymond ("Haymond"), Marvin Lundy ("Lundy") and Robert Hochberg ("Hochberg"). [After the dissolution of the firm, the parties were unable to reach agreement on their relative rights and responsibilities with respect to a number of matters, including a referral fee agreed to and paid by Lundy on behalf of the firm. The court appointed a receiver, Martin Heller, Esq. ("Heller" or the "Receiver"), to evaluate the parties' various contentions.]

THE FITZPATRICK REFERRAL FEE

Haymond objects to the Receiver's proposed treatment of a $150,000 "partnership expense," paid in the form of a referral fee to F. Emmett Fitzpatrick, Esq. ("Fitzpatrick").

On February 3, 1997, John Kelly ("Kelly") was hurt in an accident at the Bellevue Hotel, and retained Fitzpatrick's firm to represent him in a subsequent personal injury action. Fitzpatrick did what was necessary to file a complaint. On May 29, 1998, Kelly told Fitzpatrick that he wanted to retain Lundy, through H & L, instead of Fitzpatrick. This decision was "final and [Kelly did not] wish to be contacted by [Fitzpatrick]."

Lundy promised Fitzpatrick reimbursement for his costs and he also offered to pay a customary referral fee to retain Fitzpatrick's good will if Lundy were successful: this unsolicited action was allegedly the customary practice of members of the Philadelphia personal injury bar. Lundy, writing to Fitzpatrick on June 5, 1998, memorialized this agreement. Lundy first reimbursed Fitzpatrick's costs, and then stated: "This matter will of course be handled on a referral basis and I would appreciate your participation in the case."

In December, 2000, the Kelly case settled for $2,468,750: the attorney's fees portion of the settlement was $996,500. One third of this sum, the "referral fee" claimed by Fitzpatrick, was $332,166.66. Lundy, after negotiating with Fitzpatrick, agreed to pay him $150,000. . . .

Lundy's ability to create partnership expenses was limited by the partnership agreement. The Partnership Agreement, at §5.01, states that partners may bind the partnership without approval of a majority of the partners only in a limited number of circumstances; if a partner "purchases or disposes of any material asset," he must get the permission of a majority of the partners if the asset's value exceeds $10,000. Partnership Agreement, §5.01(iv).

Lundy argues that §5.01(iv) does not apply because: (1) it was not the custom of the partnership to treat referral fees as material assets. . . .

There is no other evidence of record establishing the partnership's customary practice respecting referral fees. In the absence of such evidence, it is inappropriate to disregard the plain language of the governing contract regarding attorney's fees from settlements, material assets of the firm, by holding that the referral fee portion of a settlement is an exception to §5.01(iv). . . .

The issue is whether Lundy's oral (and later written) commitment to pay a standard referral fee exceeded his authority to bind H & L under the Partnership Agreement. It did. Later, Lundy mitigated this error by settling with Fitzpatrick to pay a lesser sum. This agreement was an accord and satisfaction of the underlying contractual obligation, not a new agreement (a novation). . . .

Lundy's agreement to pay the referral fee to Fitzpatrick was a decision by a partner of H & L and bound the partnership to pay Fitzpatrick 1/3 of fees received when the Kelly matter settled. It disposed of a material asset of the partnership (the undivided right to a contingent fee in the Kelly matter) exceeding $10,000. Absent persuasive evidence that undivided rights to contingent fees are not "assets," Lundy exceeded his authority under §5.01(iv) by not obtaining his partners' consent before making this agreement. Therefore, only $10,000 of the $150,000 referral fee should be attributable to the partnership. . . .

NOTE: AUTHORITY OF JOINT VENTURERS

A number of cases suggest that the apparent or inherent agency power of a joint venturer may be less than that of a general partner. Properly analyzed, the difference in agency power is a function of the fundamental difference between a joint venture and a general partnership.

A joint venture is for a limited purpose and normally involves a less than total merging of the interests and assets of the venturers. Thus, it is not reasonable to assume that the venturers have granted each other the authority of a general manager. Of course, in a particular case, the venturers may grant such authority to one or more of their number. But the common law does not assume that such grant of general agency power has been made. Instead, the party seeking to bind the joint venture must establish the extent of the agent's actual authority. If that actual authority is limited, then the apparent or inherent authority of the joint venturer may also be less than would accompany a more general grant of authority.

In contrast, a general partnership normally involves a complete merging of interests and assets to carry on a business. It is reasonable to believe that partners in such ventures would usually grant each other the agency power appropriate for a general managerial agent. Consistent with that reasoning, UPA §9 creates a presumption on which third parties without knowledge to the contrary may rely—that all general partners have the actual authority of a general managerial agent.

An instructive case is Matanuska Valley Bank v. Arnold, 223 F.2d 778 (9th Cir. 1955). Irene Arnold and Willard Davis entered a joint venture for the purpose of completing one construction contract. Arnold's part of the bargain was to provide the needed capital, thought to be $10,000. She did this by borrowing the money from her bank, which knew the details of the venture. Later, Davis borrowed money from Arnold's bank in the name of the venture and used the proceeds for personal purposes. The court refused to hold Arnold responsible for the note as a co-venturer:

> Davis, as a joint adventurer, did not have the general implied authority of a partner in an ordinary trading or commercial partnership.
>
> The power of one joint venturer to bind another must be derived from express authority or by implication from the nature of the agreement in the particular circumstances of each case.
>
> In the instant case we find no evidence of express authority having been given Davis to execute the notes on behalf of the firm, nor can authority be implied. We have a situation where the parties were contemplating no long range operation which might carry with it future financing by means of borrowing. The parties must have contemplated that the contract price would finance the job; that the necessary preliminary financing would be taken care of by the $10,000 advanced by the bank and secured by Mrs. Arnold's notes. . . . It seems clear that the proper implication to be drawn from all the circumstances is that if future borrowing became necessary the manner in which it would be accomplished was a matter for future agreement.

223 F.2d at 780.

There are a number of cases in accord with Matanuska Valley Bank v. Arnold. However, there are also a number of jurisdictions that do not recognize a distinction between the authority of a joint venturer and a general partner. For a discussion of the different judicial approaches, see Comment, Apparent Authority and the Joint Venture: Narrowing the Scope of Agency Between Business Associates, 13 U.C. Davis L. Rev. 831 (1980).

PROBLEM 2-13

John Harris, an investment broker, contacted the law firm of Watts & Watts for assistance in obtaining a divorce. The attorney to whom he first spoke referred him to Susan Armor, representing that "she's our best partner in the domestic relations area." Armor represented Harris in the divorce, in connection with which she met with him numerous times at Watts & Watts' law office. Several months after the divorce, Armor had lunch with Harris, who lamented the lack of good investments to sell clients wanting high return and low risk. Armor told Harris that Watts & Watts was making lucrative foreign investments and was eager to take money in $100,000 units for one year at a time and pay 15 percent interest, a rate double the then prime lending rate. Later that afternoon, Armor visited Harris' office, where he gave her a $1.5 million check made out in her name. In return Harris received 15 promissory notes naming Watts

& Watts as the promisor, and executed by "Susan Armor, partner in charge of overseas investments."

Armor disappeared one week later, and it is rumored that her assets were transferred to unreachable foreign bank accounts. Watts & Watts was completely unaware of Armor's fraudulent representations or actions. Is Watts & Watts liable to Harris for the $1.5 million that Harris "loaned the firm"?

PROBLEM 2-14

Jones and Investor formed a partnership to own and operate a sporting goods store. Investor agreed to contribute needed capital, and Jones agreed to manage the sporting goods store. Investor and Jones agreed to share profits and losses equally. After one year of operation, Investor asked Jones to stop making inventory purchases on credit. Jones refused. Thereafter, Investor wrote the partnership's principal suppliers demanding that they cease selling goods to the firm on credit and stating that Investor would not be personally responsible for any additional credit extended to the partnership. Thereafter, Dense, one of the suppliers so notified, at the request of Jones sold and delivered sporting goods to the firm on credit. Are the partnership and Investor liable for the sums owed Dense?

2.   Partnership Authority and the Limited Liability Partnership

UPA (1997) §306

The LLP changes the balance of risk between innocent partners and third parties. In an ordinary general partnership, a finding that the partnership is liable for the unauthorized actions of a partner exposes every partner to potential liability with respect to the unauthorized act. In an LLP, a finding that the partnership is liable for the unauthorized actions of a partner will normally not expose other partners to the risk of personal liability. How, if at all, should this change in the balance of risks affect the law concerning the apparent or inherent authority of a partner?

Dow v. Jones
United States District Court, Maryland, 2004
311 F. Supp. 2d 461

MEMORANDUM

BLAKE, DISTRICT JUDGE.
Now pending before the court is a motion for summary judgment filed by the defendant, Seals Jones Wilson Garrow & Evans, L.L.P., against the plaintiff, Jeffrey Dow. . . . For the reasons stated below, the motion for summary judgment will be denied.

BACKGROUND

This case involves claims of legal malpractice arising from the representation of the plaintiff, Jeffrey Dow ("Dow"), in a criminal trial in Maryland state court.

On October 3, 1996, Dow was charged with various criminal offenses in the Circuit Court for Wicomico County, Maryland, arising from an alleged sexual assault of a minor. At the time, Dow was a radio disc jockey and a candidate for mayor of Berlin, Maryland. Although Dow had been appointed counsel from the Office of the Public Defender for Wicomico County, he also sought private counsel to represent him. On November 15, 1996, Dow and his wife met at the Washington, D.C. office of the law firm Seals Jones Wilson Garrow & Evans, L.L.P. ("SJWGE") with two partners, James Benny Jones ("Jones") and Robert Wilson. Dow states that Jones agreed at that meeting to represent Dow, on behalf of himself and the firm SJWGE. On January 15, 1997, Dow paid a $1,000.00 retainer to Jones and executed a criminal retainer agreement, agreeing to pay a flat fee of $12,500.00 for the representation. The retainer agreement is printed on SJWGE letterhead, and states that Dow agrees "to retain the legal services of Attorney James Benny Jones to provide representation" in his pending criminal case.[1]

At some time between January 15 and March 26, 1997, Dow also retained attorney Edwin H. Harvey ("Harvey") to assist Jones as co-counsel in the case. On March 11, Jones sent a letter to the Assistant State's Attorney, copied to the Office of the Public Defender, stating that he represented Dow in the pending criminal case and that he would be entering his appearance. The letter is printed on SJWGE letterhead, but refers only to "my representation" of Dow. On March 26, Harvey sent a notice entering the appearances of James Benny Jones and Edwin H. Harvey as attorneys of record for Dow in the pending criminal case. This notice does not reference the firm of SJWGE, but lists Jones's business address as 1010 Massachusetts Avenue, NW, Washington, D.C., which is the address for SJWGE.

According to Dow, Jones advised him that he would leave the investigation of the case to the Office of the Public Defender, explaining to Dow that this was standard criminal defense practice. Dow states that the defendants "conducted only a cursory, one day investigation" and failed to interview key defense witnesses. According to Dow, Jones and Harvey also failed to move for a change of venue despite substantial pretrial publicity, did not question potential jurors about this pretrial publicity, did not object to the presentation of inadmissible testimony at his trial, and failed to call available defense witnesses, including alibi witnesses.

Dow was tried before a jury on July 30 and 31, 1997, and was found guilty of second degree sex offense, third degree sex offense, and perverted sexual practice. Dow was sentenced to 15 years of imprisonment, all but seven years suspended, and 36

---

1. SJWGE believes that Dow paid the retainer by a check made out to Jones, rather than to the firm SJWGE. (Def.'s Reply at 2.) SJWGE states that although the defendants have requested a copy of the canceled check, Dow has not provided it. (Id.) Without further documentary proof, and drawing all reasonable inferences in favor of the nonmoving plaintiff, this is not sufficient evidence to conclude that Dow made out the check to Jones personally.

months of supervised probation. The trial court denied a motion for new trial, and Dow's direct appeal was dismissed by the Office of Public Defender. In March 1999, Dow filed a petition for post-conviction relief, alleging ineffective assistance of counsel at his criminal trial. On March 6, 2000, the Circuit Court for Wicomico County vacated Dow's convictions and granted a new trial. On November 26, 2001 the Circuit Court for Wicomico County entered a nolle prosequi in the pending criminal case against Dow.

SJWGE was organized as a registered limited liability partnership ("LLP") in the District of Columbia in May 1994. Dow states that the five named partners of SJWGE held themselves out to the public generally, and to Dow specifically, as partners operating a law firm under the name of Seals Jones Wilson Garrow & Evans, L.L.P. On June 27, 1997, approximately one month before Dow's criminal trial, SJWGE received a certificate from the District of Columbia government formally canceling the firm's status as a limited liability partnership. The firm states that SJWGE actually had dissolved as of May 1, 1997. Dow states that he was not notified and was not aware of SJWGE's dissolution, or that Jones might not have the authority to act for SJWGE, or that Jones might not be a partner of SJWGE.[2]

Dow originally filed this suit in the Circuit Court for Wicomico County on July 28, 2000 against Jones, Harvey, SJWGE, and the four individual partners of SJWGE other than Jones. On December 28, 2000 the Circuit Court entered summary judgment in favor of the individual partners other than Jones, but denied defendant SJWGE's motion for summary judgment. The remaining defendants removed the case to this court on August 3, 2001. . . .

ANALYSIS . . .

II. . . .

A.

In general partnerships, all partners are jointly and severally liable for all debts and obligations of the partnership, including any wrongful acts or omissions by another partner. See, e.g., D.C. Code §33-103.06 (2001). By registering with the state, paying a fee, and carrying a specified amount of liability insurance, registered LLPs are granted a special statutory shield which limits the liability of individual partners for the misconduct of other partners. See Carter G. Bishop & Daniel S. Kleinberger, Limited Liability Companies: Tax & Business Law §§15.01(1), 15.02(3)(b),(e) (2004). This does not relieve partners who are personally culpable of their individual liability to

---

2. Jones is listed as a partner in SJWGE's May 1994 application for a limited liability partnership and in its June 1997 cancellation of the limited liability partnership. (Pl.'s Opp. Mem. at Exs. B, G.) However, in its response to the plaintiff's request for admissions in this case, SJWGE denied a statement that Jones was a partner in SJWGE as of January 15, 1997 and as of March 11, 1997. (Id. at Ex. F, at P 7.) There is no other evidence in the record regarding Jones's partnership status. Drawing all reasonable inferences in favor of the nonmoving plaintiff for purposes of this summary judgment motion, the court cannot conclude that Jones was not a partner in SJWGE.

third parties, and partnership assets also remain available to satisfy third-party claims. See id. §§15.02(1),(3).

SJWGE was formed under the Registered Limited Liability Partnership Amendment Act of 1993 ("RLLPAA"), which was adopted by the District of Columbia to amend provisions of the Uniform Partnership Act of 1962 ("UPA").[3] The law provides for the registration and naming of LLPs, and requires registered LLPs to carry liability insurance. See D.C. Code Ann. §§41-143 to 41-145 (1981). Importantly, the RLLPAA limits the liability of individual partners in registered LLPs:

> A partner in a registered limited liability partnership is not individually liable for debts and obligations of the partnership arising from errors, omissions, negligence, incompetence, or malfeasance committed in the course of the partnership business by a second partner or a representative of the partnership not working under the supervision or direction of the first partner at the time the errors, omissions, negligence, incompetence, or malfeasance occurred.

Id. §41-146(a). Exceptions are provided if a partner was directly involved in or had written notice or knowledge of the specific conduct at issue. Id. In addition, these provisions do not limit "the liability of partnership assets for partnership debts and obligations." Id. §41-146(c). The RLLPAA also specifies that the liability of partners in an LLP properly registered in the District of Columbia for the debts and obligations of the LLP "shall at all time be determined solely and exclusively" by the provisions of the District of Columbia's UPA. Id. §41-148(c).[4]

B.

The malpractice claims against SJWGE rely on Dow's subjective belief that an attorney-client relationship had been formed between the firm and himself, based on representations allegedly made by Jones and SJWGE itself. SJWGE first argues that because the liability of partners in registered LLPs for the acts of other partners is governed by an objective standard under the RLLPAA, the court also should apply an objective analysis to determine LLP liability for the acts of partners. SJWGE thus would have the court apply an objective analysis to the question of whether an attorney-client relationship was formed with the LLP. SJWGE admits that a subjective analysis would govern under general partnership law, but argues that general partnership law is inapplicable to registered LLPs, and notes that no provision in the RLLPAA specifically provides for partnership liability for the acts of partners. If SJWGE were correct, then Dow's subjective beliefs that he was represented by SJWGE would be irrelevant.

---

3. The Uniform Partnership Act has been adopted by the District of Columbia and all states except for Louisiana, and thus provides a uniform body of general partnership law in the United States. The RLLPAA, originally codified at D.C. Code §§41-143 through 41-148, was repealed effective January 1, 1998 with the adoption of the revised Uniform Partnership Act of 1996. The parties do not dispute that the repealed provisions govern this case, because Dow's injury accrued in 1997. See D.C. Code Ann. §§33-112.02, 33-112.04 (2001).

4. Such choice-of-law provisions are common in registered LLP statutes, and are generally followed by courts in other jurisdictions. See Bishop & Kleinberger, supra, §15.02(1); see also, e.g., Md. Code Ann., *Corps. & Ass'ns* §9A-106. Both parties agree that the provisions of the RLLPAA should govern this case. As discussed infra, the RLLPAA also incorporates the provisions of the UPA on general partnership law, which in turn incorporates principles of agency law.

This argument fails, however, because general principles of agency and partnership law continue to govern registered LLPs. The RLLPAA provides that, "[u]nless otherwise specifically provided by other provisions of this chapter, the registered limited liability partnership shall be subject to all the provisions of this chapter," referring to the provisions governing general partnerships under the District of Columbia's UPA. D.C. Code Ann. §41-143(g)(1981). Courts in jurisdictions with similar provisions have recognized that general partnership law continues to govern LLPs, and have applied provisions of their UPA statutes to LLPs. See Canada Life Assurance Co. v. Estate of Lebowitz, 185 F.3d 231, 236 n. 4 (4th Cir. 1999); Mudge Rose Guthrie Alexander & Ferdon v. Pickett, 11 F. Supp. 2d 449, 452 (S.D.N.Y. 1998); First Am. Title Ins. Co. v. Lawson, 177 N.J. 125, 827 A.2d 230, 236-37 (2003); see also Shenandoah Assocs. Ltd. P'ship v. Tirana, 182 F.Supp.2d 14, 19-20 (D.D.C. 2001) (noting that the UPA governs general partnerships and registered LLPs under D.C. law, whereas a separate chapter governs limited partnerships).

Pursuant to the provisions of the UPA, as in effect in the District of Columbia in 1997, every partner of an LLP has the power to bind the partnership as an agent:

> Every partner is an agent of the partnership for the purpose of its business, and the act of every partner, including the execution in the partnership name of any instrument, for apparently carrying on in the usual way the business of the partnership of which he is a member binds the partnership, unless the partner so acting has in fact no authority to act for the partnership in the particular matter, and the person with whom he is dealing has knowledge of the fact that he has no such authority.

D.C. Code Ann. §41-108(a) (1981); see also *id.* §41-103(c) (noting that the "law of agency" applies under the UPA); cf. *First Am. Title Ins. Co.*, 827 A.2d at 236-37 (indicating that a limited liability partnership law firm is governed by a similar statutory provision under the New Jersey UPA). Under these provisions and basic principles of agency law, a partner of an LLP who is acting within the actual or apparent authority of the partnership can bind the partnership to an agreement with a third party. See *Restatement (Second) of Agency* §§7-8, 27, 140, 159. Apparent authority is created when a principal represents that a party is his agent, and a third party actually and reasonably relies on this representation. For example, if a law firm publicly represents that a person is a partner, and a third party actually and reasonably relies on this representation, then that person has apparent authority to perform all acts that a partner in a law firm ordinarily would. Cf. id. §27 cmt. a. (noting that "apparent authority can be created by appointing a person to a position, such as manager or treasurer, which carries with it generally recognized duties").[5]

Following this general reasoning, courts in other jurisdictions have applied their UPA statutes and these general principles of agency law to determine a law firm's

---

5. This does not require a showing that Dow was familiar with the extent of powers that a partner in a law firm ordinarily would possess. See Restatement (Second) of Agency S 27 cmt. d. ("Thus, a manager has apparent authority to do those things which managers in that business at that time and place customarily do, as to persons who know that he is a manager, although they do not know what powers managers in such businesses have.").

liability for the acts of its individual partners. See, e.g., *In re Summit Airlines, Inc.*, 160 B.R. 911, 917-20 (Bankr. E.D. Pa. 1993) (embezzling client funds); Blackmon v. Hale, 1 Cal. 3d 548, 83 Cal. Rptr. 194, 463 P.2d 418, 422-23 (1970) (misappropriating client funds); Podolan v. Idaho Legal Aid Services, Inc., 123 Idaho 937, 854 P.2d 280, 286-87 (Ct. App. 1993) (entering into representation on behalf of firm); Homa v. Friendly Mobile Manor, Inc., 93 Md. App. 337, 612 A.2d 322, 332-35 (Ct. Spec. App. 1992) (engaging client on behalf of firm); Kansallis Fin. Ltd. v. Fern, 421 Mass. 659, 659 N.E.2d 731, 736-37 (1996) (issuing fraudulent opinion letter); Staron v. Weinstein, 305 N.J. Super. 236, 701 A.2d 1325, 1327-28 (Super. Ct. App. Div. 1997) (entering into retainer agreement on behalf of firm); Heath v. Craighill, Rendleman, Ingle & Blythe, P.A., 97 N.C. App. 236, 388 S.E.2d 178, 181-83 (1990) (soliciting investments).

Dow has raised genuine issues of material fact as to whether Jones had apparent authority to enter into a retainer agreement on behalf of SJWGE, as a partner of the firm.[6] SJWGE listed Jones as a partner in its application for a limited liability partnership and included his last name and the designation of "partnership" in the firm's operating name. SJWGE does not dispute Dow's assertions that he met with Jones and another partner of SJWGE at the firm's office in November 1996 "to discuss the firm's representation of me," and that Jones agreed at that meeting to represent Dow "on behalf of himself and SJWGE."[7] Dow states that he never received any information suggesting that Jones did not have authority to enter into the retainer agreement on behalf of the firm, and the agreement itself was printed on firm letterhead. By holding Jones out publicly as a partner in SJWGE, and by Robert Wilson's conduct in so representing Jones, the firm may have vested Jones with apparent authority to perform those acts customarily performed by law firm partners. Jones, by entering into the retainer agreement with Dow, was "apparently carrying on in the usual way the business of the partnership." D.C. Code Ann. §41-108(a). This evidence raises a genuine factual issue as to whether Jones had apparent authority to act as a partner of SJWGE and thus to enter into representation agreements on behalf of the firm, and whether Dow actually and reasonably relied on this apparent authority.

Even if Jones was not a partner of SJWGE, the UPA provides that a person who represents himself or is represented by others as a partner in an existing partnership "is an agent of the persons consenting to such representation to bind them to the same extent and in the same manner as though he were a partner in fact, with respect to persons who rely upon the representation." D.C. Code Ann. §41-115(b). Courts have applied similar statutory provisions in other jurisdictions and general principles of partnership by estoppel to hold entities apparently operating as law firms responsible

---

6. As stated, although SJWGE apparently denies that Jones was a partner of the firm as of January 15, 1997, the date of the retainer agreement, there is sufficient evidence in the record to raise a genuine factual issue on this point. Drawing all reasonable inferences in favor of the nonmoving plaintiff, the court cannot conclude that Jones was not a partner in SJWGE. However, SJWGE also claims that Jones did not have actual authority to enter into retainer agreements with clients, and because Dow has not disputed this factual contention his claim must rest on Jones's apparent authority.

7. Importantly, any representations made by Robert Wilson, the other partner of SJWGE at the November 1996 meeting, can be attributed to the partnership, and thus can serve as a manifestation by the firm to a third party that Jones was its agent, thus creating apparent authority. *See* D.C. Code Ann. §§41-108, -110; *Restatement (Second) of Agency* §8 & cmt. a.

for malpractice committed by non-partners who were held out to the public as partners. Dow also has presented sufficient evidence to raise genuine factual issues as to whether SJWGE made public representations that Jones was a partner, such that Jones could create obligations that were binding on the partnership as if he were a partner. As noted, Jones was listed as a partner in SJWGE's LLP application and the firm's operating name included Jones's last name and the designation of "partnership." Dow met with Jones and another named partner at SJWGE's office, signed a retainer agreement on firm letterhead, and received at least one letter on firm letterhead. Dow states that he never received any information suggesting that Jones was not a partner of SJWGE, or that SJWGE was not a partnership. In cases involving similar public indicia of partnership and no contrary representations, courts have relied on the doctrine of partnership by estoppel to impose liability on entities that appeared to be operating as law firm partnerships. See *Bonavire*, 779 F.2d at 1016-17 (meetings at shared office space, public designation of "law firm," use of firm letterhead); *Atlas Tack*, 637 N.E.2d at 232 (shared office space, public designation of "professional association," use of firm letterhead); *Royal Bank & Trust*, 506 N.Y.S.2d 151, 497 N.E.2d at 290-91 (shared office space, public designation of law firm, use of firm letterhead).

C.

SJWGE next argues that the firm cannot be held liable for Jones's alleged malpractice, because the firm had dissolved as of May 1, 1997, several months prior to Dow's criminal trial. Without citing any authority, SJWGE argues that the UPA provisions regarding the dissolution of general partnerships should not apply to registered LLPs. SJWGE's argument fails for many of the reasons stated above. SJWGE's premise that the UPA provisions governing dissolution of general partnerships do not apply to registered LLPs is incorrect. See D.C. Code Ann. 41-143(g) (1981) (noting that provisions of the UPA are applicable to registered LLPs); see also *Mudge Rose*, 11 F. Supp. 2d at 452-53 (applying UPA provisions in New York to winding up and dissolution of LLP law firm).

Under the governing UPA provisions, an LLP does not terminate immediately upon dissolution, but instead "continues until the winding up of partnership affairs is completed." D.C. Code Ann. §41-129 (1981). After dissolution a partner still can bind the partnership "by any act appropriate for winding up partnership affairs or completing transactions unfinished at dissolution." Id. §41-134(a)(1); see also Pottash Bros. v. Burnet, 50 F.2d 317, 319 (D.C. Cir. 1931).[8] A partner also can bind the partnership after dissolution:

> [B]y any transaction which would bind the partnership if dissolution had not taken place, provided the other party to the transaction . . . had nevertheless known of the partnership prior to dissolution, and, having no knowledge or notice of dissolution, the fact of dissolution had not been

---

8. Even if the partner has no actual authority to wind up partnership affairs, the partnership will be bound if the third party to the transaction had no knowledge or notice that the partner lacked such authority, and the lack of authority was not advertised in a newspaper of general circulation in the place at which the partnership business was regularly carried on. See D.C. Code Ann. §41-134(c)(3)(B) (1981).

advertised in a newspaper of general circulation in the place . . . at which the partnership business was regularly carried on.

D.C. Code Ann. §41-134(a)(2)(B) (1981); see also *Pottash Bros.*, 50 F.2d at 319 (enforcing a waiver executed without proper authority by a former partner after dissolution, because the partnership had not provided notice of its dissolution).

In some cases, it may be appropriate to impose liability for legal malpractice claims arising after dissolution because the conduct at issue is appropriate for winding up the law partnership. See, e.g., Majer v. Schmidt, 169 A.D.2d 501, 564 N.Y.S.2d 722, 724 (1991) (misappropriating client funds to pay a pre-dissolution liability of the law firm partnership). A number of courts have held that cases that are pending at the time of a law firm's dissolution are matters that must be wound up. See Robinson v. Nussbaum, 11 F. Supp. 2d 1, 5-6 (D.D.C. 1997) (holding that fees from hourly billing after dissolution for cases pending at dissolution are partnership property); Grossman v. Davis, 28 Cal. App. 4th 1833, 34 Cal. Rptr. 2d 355, 356-57 (1994) (same for proceeds of contingency fee agreement); Beckman v. Farmer, 579 A.2d 618, 636 (D.C. 1990) (same); Gast v. Peters, 267 Neb. 18, 671 N.W.2d 758, 762-63 (2003) (same). Applying this reasoning and the UPA provisions regarding partnership liability during the winding-up period, a former partner's malpractice which occurs after dissolution but in a case that was pending prior to dissolution still can bind a dissolved law firm partnership, because the former partner's conduct is appropriate for winding up partnership affairs. See Redman v. Walters, 88 Cal. App. 3d 448, 152 Cal. Rptr. 42, 44-45 (1979); cf. Thompson v. Gilmore, 888 S.W.2d 715, 716-17 (Mo. Ct. App. 1994) (noting that the UPA provisions are not inconsistent with the long-standing rule that dissolution does not relieve partners from liability for pending partnership contracts). In other cases, courts may apply the UPA rule cited above on notice of dissolution to impose liability for post-dissolution malpractice by a former partner, if the client previously had dealt with the partnership and had no knowledge of the partnership's dissolution. *See* Palomba v. Barish, 626 F. Supp. 722, 724-25 (E.D. Pa. 1985); *Blackmon* 83 Cal. Rptr. 194, 463 P.2d at 424 n. 3; Vollgraff v. Block, 117 Misc. 2d 489, 458 N.Y.S. 2d 437, 439-40 (Spec. Term 1982); cf. *Staron*, 701 A.2d at 1328 (noting that a law firm's failure to give notice of dissolution may result in continuing responsibility for client matters).

SJWGE correctly states that the partnership's liability for Jones's malpractice depends on the state of partnership affairs at the time of the alleged malpractice, in July 1997. Cf. In re Keck, Mahin & Cate, 274 B.R. 740, 745-46 (Bankr. N.D. Ill. 2002) (noting that vicarious liability for a partner's legal malpractice arises at the time of the malpractice). Even if the partnership had dissolved as of July 1997, SJWGE nonetheless may be liable for Jones's malpractice under two different theories. First, Dow can argue that his representation was a pending client matter that had to be wound up following the dissolution of the partnership. Jones's conduct in representing Dow in July 1997 thus would be appropriate for winding up partnership affairs, and binding on the partnership under former D.C.Code §41-134(a)(1). Second, Dow can argue that Jones's power to bind the partnership under ordinary agency and partnership law, as described supra, continued after the firm's dissolution with respect to Dow, because Dow did not receive proper notice of SJWGE's dissolution. Dow alleges that he never received notice or otherwise became aware of SJWGE's dissolution, and there is no evidence in the record that SJWGE provided any public notice of its dissolution. Jones's conduct in representing Dow, which would have bound the partnership if dissolution had not taken place, thus continued to bind the partnership under former D.C.Code §41-134(a)(2)(B). Dow has presented sufficient evidence to raise genuine factual issues under either of these two theories as to SJWGE's continuing liability after the firm's dissolution for Jones's alleged malpractice.

D.

Finally, SJWGE argues that Dow's lawsuit is a thinly-disguised attempt to circumvent the statutory shield under the RLLPAA and hold the individual partners of SJWGE liable for another partner's misconduct. SJWGE asserts, and Dow apparently does not dispute, that the firm has no assets that can be attached or levied to satisfy any judgment against the firm. SJWGE argues that the only purpose that could be served by winning a judgment against the firm would be to provide grounds for piercing the veil of the former LLP and pursuing the assets of the individual partners. However, the parties' filings suggest an alternative and legitimate purpose that may be served by winning a judgment against SJWGE. Under the RLLPAA, the firm was required to maintain a liability insurance policy of at least $100,000 to cover "the kind of errors, omissions, negligence, incompetence, or malfeasance" for which the liability of the individual partners is limited. D.C. Code Ann. §41-145 (1981). Although SJWGE states that its insurance policy did not cover matters handled by Jones outside of the scope of the LLP, which SJWGE asserts would include Dow's case, this argument assumes the answer to the issues in dispute. Dow is entitled to pursue a judgment against SJWGE and then to pursue any available relief under the firm's insurance policy. . . .

IV.

Dow has presented specific evidence that raises genuine issues as to material facts governing SJGWE's liability for any legal malpractice committed by James Benny Jones. Dow has raised genuine factual disputes as to whether SJGWE formed an attorney-client relationship with Dow, under a theory of apparent authority or partnership by estoppel. Dow also has raised genuine factual disputes as to whether SJGWE remained liable for any malpractice that occurred after the LLP's dissolution, based on the rules governing winding up of partnership affairs and providing notice of dissolution. For the reasons stated above, the defendant SJGWE's motion for summary judgment will be denied.

3   The Corporate Form and the Specialized Roles of Shareholders, Directors, and Officers

A.   The Corporate Form

1.   Overview

MBCA §§2.06, 8.01, 8.40, 10.01-10.04, 10.20
Delaware G.C.L. §§109, 141(a), 142, 242

State corporation law, both judicial and statutory, provides a set of standard form, off-the-rack rules for persons wishing to own and operate a firm. As defined by corporations statutes, the archetypical corporation separates ownership and management functions into three specialized roles: directors, officers, and shareholders. Thus, three discrete bundles of rights are created, each having distinct powers and responsibilities that, in a sole proprietorship, would belong to one participant and in a general partnership would be shared equally by the partners. Essentially, shareholders provide capital and elect directors. Directors make major policy decisions. Officers execute those policies and provide day-to-day management. Of course, other constituents are important to the enterprise—for example, employees, creditors, suppliers, customers, and others—but as to these relationships corporate law defers to other areas of law, markets, and norms.

While the corporate form assumes separation of these functions, it does not require it, and this can be a source of confusion for one new to corporate law. The same individual may occupy more than one realm and simultaneously serve as a shareholder, director, and officer. This often occurs, for example, in a closely held corporation. Thus, the same legal form serves a spectrum of business firms, ranging from "mom and pop" enterprises, which make little use of the specialization provided in the legal form, to industrial giants requiring extremely specialized human and fiscal capital.

The corporate form provides a hierarchical form for decision making that permits the enterprise to adapt easily to changed circumstances. By statute, all corporate powers are exercised by, or under the authority of, a centralized group—the board of directors. In addition, day-to-day management operations are delegated to the corporation's officers and other agents. No direct management role is left to the shareholders.

149

Additionally, under state corporate law, the board acts as a unit via majority rule, as do voting shareholders. Thus, the corporate form favors adaptability and decisive but reasoned decision making, permitting minimal potential for individual participants to hold up collective action. On the other hand, as you will see throughout Chapters 4, 5, 8, and 9, centralization of power and majority rule enable opportunistic behavior by the majority against minority investors.

As you explore the following subparts, which flesh out the respective roles of corporate actors, bear in mind that law recognizes the corporation as an entity separate from the directors, officers, and shareholders who make it up. In fact, in most respects a corporation will be granted the same legal rights and responsibilities as would any person. Thus, the enterprise itself may own property, assert legal rights, and continue even if one participant dies, retires, quits, or is fired (assuming, of course, other participants are able to pick up the work that needs to be done and the assets to be provided). A corporation has the potential of perpetual duration, at least until a majority of directors and shareholders decide to end its existence.

2.   Directors

The board of directors is the locus of all legal power and authority exercised by the corporation. See, e.g., Delaware G.C.L. §141 and MBCA §8.01. Collectively, directors determine basic corporate policies, appoint and monitor the corporate officers, and determine when and if dividends—periodic distributions of profit—are to be paid to shareholders. Directors are entitled to compensation for their services, but do not share in the firm's residual profits (except by virtue of any shares they may own in their personal capacity). As discussed above, directors' management power must be exercised collectively and by majority rule, and individual directors are not given general agency power to deal with outsiders.

With this much power in the directors you ought to ask what incentives directors have to do the right thing and what monitoring we might expect of how they do their job. Incentives come from private ordering, for example, providing directors with share ownership such that their financial interests are aligned with those of shareholders. Law imposes constraints on director behavior to the extent that directors owe fiduciary duties to the corporation and its shareholders, a topic that is the center of our discussion in Chapter 4. Commentators have provided structural and theoretical reasons why directors should take into account other constituents, such as employees, creditors, suppliers, and the communities in which corporations operate. See, e.g., Margaret Blair and Lynn Stout, A Team Production Theory of Corporation Law, 85 Va. L. Rev. 249 (1999). This debate continues to evolve. What you should be clear on at the moment is the centralized role that the law gives to directors. In addition to the statutes already mentioned, this is reflected in the deference courts and regulators give to the business judgments of the board. You will see this characteristic in many of the cases and federal securities regulations in the remainder of this chapter. If a shareholder challenges a decision by the board, the reviewing court will likely begin its analysis by applying the "business judgment rule" (discussed in Chapter 4 and reappearing in Chapters 5, 8, and 9), which is a judicial presumption that directors acted properly. Put simply, courts and regulators prefer not to substitute their own judgment for that of the board of directors.

Who are directors? In a closely held corporation, the major shareholders generally comprise the board of directors. In a publicly traded corporation, the size of the typical board ranges up to the upper teens and occasionally even larger. A recent and important development is the move of publicly held corporations to have a majority of independent outside directors, a move that is not required by the corporations statutes, but by listing standards of our national stock exchanges. The typical publicly traded corporation thus has a few "inside" directors (generally the chief executive officer and her principal subordinate officers) and a balance of "outside" directors (who usually are employed full time as chief executives or financial officers of other corporations, or are lawyers, accountants, or investment bankers, and therefore have the skill, integrity, and political insight to oversee the business and affairs of their corporations).

While corporations statutes entrust management power to the board of directors collectively without identifying distinct roles for particular directors, inside and outside directors now perform de facto specialized roles. These roles are shaped and reinforced by judicial rulings (see Chapter 4), the stock exchange rules mentioned above, and corporate norms. Inside directors are intimately familiar with the corporation's business, personnel, and markets. As a result, inside directors serve as an informational link between the corporation and the board of directors. Normally, inside directors also develop business plans and policies for the corporation, subject only to the oversight and advice of the outside directors.

3. Officers

State corporation law norms contemplate that a corporation will have various officers responsible for day-to-day operation of the corporation's business affairs, although most statutes are remarkably silent about specifying duties for these officers. Instead, corporate law considers officers as agents and the corporation as principal (acting through its board of directors) and leaves it to the board to work out the oversight that it desires as to its agents. More recently, federal law, as opposed to the laws of the 50 states that are the source of corporate law mentioned above, has begun to play a role in the specification of officers' duties. For example, the Sarbanes-Oxley Act of 2002 requires that the chief executive officer and the chief financial officer of a corporation certify the financial reports of the corporation that are made pursuant to disclosure rules of the federal securities laws. Like directors, officers receive compensation for services they perform, but do not share in the corporation's residual profit unless they also own shares.

The term "officer" connotes a corporate employee who ranks above other corporate employees in a corporation's management hierarchy. In older statutes, corporations were required to have a president, secretary, and treasurer. Modern statutes simply allow corporations to have the officers specified in the bylaws or determined by the board. See MBCA §8.40 and Delaware G.C.L. §142. The only remaining requirement in most codes is that the corporation designate an individual to be responsible for keeping and verifying corporate records, a duty often identified with the title "corporate secretary." A corporation's principal officer is often termed the chief executive officer, or "CEO," but that designation does not come from the corporations statute. In the run-up to the enactment of new federal legislation in 2002, former Federal Reserve Chairman Alan Greenspan was quoted as saying that CEOs are the "fulcrum" of corporate governance in American corporations today, a statement that is not obvious from the relationship contemplated by the corporations statutes, but nevertheless undoubtedly true. Often this person serves as chair of the board of directors, a combination that has been controversial to the extent that it impedes the monitoring or oversight of the CEO by the board of directors.

4. Shareholders

Corporate ownership interests are represented by shares—fungible ownership units—that typically entitle the holder to a pro rata share of the firm's profits and net assets when the corporation dissolves and winds up its business. Thus, the holders of those shares are the corporation's risk bearers and residual claimants. Shareholders collectively have the power to elect annually the corporation's directors and approve fundamental changes in the corporation's governing rules or structure. An individual shareholder, however, has very limited rights or power to participate directly in the management or operation of the corporation's business.

Shares are treated like other fungible property interests and are freely transferable by their owners. The purchaser of shares receives all voting power and other rights possessed by the selling shareholder. The unstated complement to this ability to freely transfer stock is the expectation that a shareholder will in fact recover the value of her investment via transfer to a third party, rather than forcing the corporation to provide liquidity by converting its assets to cash as would a dissolving partnership.

Normally, a shareholder has no obligation or liability to the corporation or its creditors beyond the amount she paid for the shares. This concept, known as "limited liability," allows a shareholder to risk only a predetermined amount of capital in each corporate investment, instead of potentially risking her entire wealth as would be the case if shareholders were personally liable for a corporation's debts. Likewise, directors and officers are not liable for the debts of the enterprise, although as will be seen in Chapter 7, they may incur liability if they commit torts or breach their duty to the corporation or its shareholders.

Limited liability also reduces the transaction costs in connection with the resale of shares, particularly when there are a large number of shareholders. If shareholders were personally liable for corporate debts, a potential purchaser would require information about the wealth and investment decisions of other shareholders in order to assess fully the risk that he would assume by becoming a shareholder. For example, consider two corporations—Corporation A and Corporation B—with identical businesses and assets. Corporation A's shareholders are collectively worth $1 billion, while Corporation B's shareholders are judgment-proof. Corporation B would present a much greater investment risk for a potential investor with assets that could be reached by creditors.

The governance role of shareholders may seem surprisingly limited given their financial interest in the entity. In this book we will see that shareholders do three things—vote, sell, and sue—but all in carefully measured doses. The statutory norms provide for annual and special shareholders' meetings and sometimes actions by written consent. Shareholders may use such a forum to elect (and possibly remove) directors and to vote on certain fundamental corporate actions such as mergers or amendments to the articles of incorporation, but only if such items have first been submitted by the directors acting as a gatekeeper. Additionally, shareholders can make some changes to the bylaws without prior approval by the directors. Despite shareholder power to vote, attend annual meetings, and (in some circumstances) call special meetings, even a majority of the shareholders may be unable to make business decisions for the corporation or require the directors to make changes in policies or procedures. Instead, as discussed above, corporate law statutory norms entrust management of corporate affairs to the directors. Continental Securities Co. v. Belmont, 206 N.Y. 7, 16-17, 99 N.E. 138, 141 (1912), contains a classic summary of shareholders' normal governance status:

> As a general rule, stockholders cannot act in relation to the ordinary business of a corporation. The body of stockholders have certain authority conferred by statute which must be exercised to enable the corporation to act in specific cases, but except for certain authority conferred by statute, which is mainly permissive or confirmatory . . . they have no express power given by statute. They are not by any statute in this state given general power of initiative in corporate affairs. Any action by them relating to the details of the corporate business is necessarily in the form of an assent, request, or recommendation. Recommendations by a body of stockholders can only be enforced through the board of directors, and indirectly by the authority of the stockholders to change the personnel of the directors at a meeting for the election of directors.

Almost all state corporation codes now provide that the business of a corporation shall be entrusted to directors, *except as otherwise provided in the articles of incorporation*. Thus, the original articles of incorporation can give shareholders a right to control, or participate in control of, ordinary business matters. But that is not often done. If shareholders in a corporation that has not made advance provision for direct shareholder management become disillusioned with some corporate policy or practice, how might they attempt to change corporate policies or affect the ordinary business decisions of the corporation? One obvious route would be to amend the articles of incorporation to give shareholders the right to make a business decision or to prescribe directly whatever change is desired. Apart from the difficulty in gaining the necessary votes, however, shareholders run head-on into the normal corporate law rule that only the directors may initiate an amendment to the articles. MBCA §8.01 and Delaware G.C.L. §141(a) are, in form, default rules. However, both sections limit the methods of opting out of or contracting around their default rules to provisions contained in the articles of incorporation. Since the MBCA and the Delaware G.C.L. require that the board of directors initiates amendments to the articles, and since directors will not initiate an amendment curbing their own powers, §§8.01 and 141(a) effectively are immutable rules for corporations that do not opt out in the initial articles of incorporation.

Most states do allow shareholders to initiate a change in the corporation's bylaws. See, e.g., Del. §109. However, shareholders normally may not amend the bylaws to make ordinary business decisions or to establish corporate policies. That power belongs to the directors and can be taken away from them only by contrary provision in the articles of incorporation. See, e.g., Del. §141. There is some overlap and tension between these statutory provisions. In CA, Inc. v. AFSMCE Employees Pension Plan, 953 A.2d 227 (Del. 2008), excerpted later in this chapter, the Delaware Supreme Court upheld the right of shareholders to pass bylaws on "the process for electing directors—a subject in which shareholders of Delaware corporations have a legitimate and protected interest." The court contrasted this "proper function of bylaws" from bylaws that would mandate how a board should decide specific substantive business decisions. This tension, particularly visible in public corporations, is explored in more detail later in this chapter.

The directors' management authority extends to chairing and controlling the agenda of shareholders' meetings. Therefore, in the exercise of such authority, management normally may rule out of order any shareholder's attempt to propose an amendment to the articles or bylaws that would intrude on management's authority to make ordinary business decisions or to establish corporate policies. Shareholders have no authority to act for the corporation in such matters, unless empowered by a preexisting provision in the articles of incorporation.

Despite their inability to make management decisions, shareholders do have the right to suggest that the directors take a particular action or adopt a new policy. See, e.g., Auer v. Dressel, 306 N.Y. 427, 118 N.E.2d 590 (1954) (shareholders may call meeting to support ousted president and urge his reinstatement, even though they have no power to force his reappointment). This right to communicate with fellow shareholders at any meeting and, in so doing, to attempt to persuade management to change its policies is discussed in more detail later in this chapter.

PROBLEM 3-1

A central governance issue addressed by corporate law is how power and authority are allocated among the board of directors, officers, and shareholders. Take a brief tour through the MBCA or the Delaware General Corporation Law and begin your study of the statute by identifying the key sections that describe the role for each group and what the statute says is the power allocated to each group.

PROBLEM 3-2

Joan owns approximately 10 percent of the outstanding voting shares of Northwest Timber Company, a Delaware corporation. Since her retirement in 2010 as a senior executive of Northwest, Joan has become active in environmental issues. She is concerned about the rate at which the corporation is cutting old-growth timber on company-owned land. She does not think it prudent for the corporation to exceed a sustainable yield, nor does she want to be a party to the ecological consequences associated with overcutting. Joan is also concerned about the impact on Timber City, Northwest's principal place of business, of the corporation's recent decision to move its banking business from a locally owned and operated bank to a New York-based bank with branches throughout the world.

1. Assuming that Northwest Timber has no special provisions in its articles or bylaws, may Joan make the following proposals at Northwest's next annual shareholders' meeting?
   a. That the articles or bylaws be amended to require that the corporation locate its principal banking operations in Timber City.
   b. That the articles or bylaws be amended to state that the purpose of the corporation is to conduct all lawful business for a profit, but with due consideration for ensuring that forests are managed to maximize long-term profitability.
   c. That the articles or bylaws be amended to create the office of vice president for ecology, with such officer having the responsibility to monitor the corporation's timber-cutting programs and report quarterly to the shareholders as to the short- and long-term economic and ecological effects of such programs.
   d. That the articles or bylaws be amended to provide for annual election by the shareholders of all corporate officers.
   e. That the corporation pay a dividend in the amount of $5 for each share.
   f. That the corporation merge with a firm in the industry that follows timber-cutting policies that Joan thinks are in line with the origins of Northwest and the interest of the community.
2. Would any of your answers change if Northwest Timber were incorporated in an MBCA jurisdiction?

B. The Formation of the Corporation and the Governance Expectations of the Initial Participants

1. Where to Incorporate: State Corporation Laws as Competing Sets of Standard Form Rules

Business participants choose the rules they want for their enterprise by selecting the state of incorporation. Corporations incorporated in one state are recognized by other states. Under traditional choice-of-law rules, termed the "internal affairs doctrine," courts look to the laws of the incorporating state to determine the basic rights and duties applicable to a particular corporation. As a result, the owners of a firm may shop around and choose to incorporate (or reincorporate) in whichever state offers the most attractive rules. A state has an incentive to provide attractive rules because it can collect fees and taxes directly from firms incorporating under its laws. In extremely limited circumstances, the interests of a nonincorporating state may be so great that its law will be applied to regulate a foreign corporation or to determine the relative rights of its shareholders. For a discussion of these cases, see Beveridge, The Internal Affairs Doctrine: The Proper Law of a Corporation, 44 Bus. Law. 693, 702-709 (1989).

We place special emphasis on two statutes — the Model Business Corporation Act (MBCA) and the Delaware General Corporation Law (Delaware G.C.L.). Most states base their corporation code on, or draw heavily from, some version of the MBCA, which was developed (and is frequently updated) by the American Bar Association Section of Business Law, Committee on Corporate Laws. Delaware, one of the states that does not follow the MBCA, is the preeminent American corporate law jurisdiction. More than half of the country's largest corporations are incorporated in that small, mid-Atlantic state, forty-ninth in size and forty-fifth in population among American states.

Differences among the states are not as great as they once were. Successful Delaware innovations are quickly copied by the MBCA, and vice versa. In addition, there is substantial uniformity in the so-called common law of corporations. Courts in one state may borrow freely from the jurisprudence developed by courts in other states. Delaware, as the home of so many publicly traded corporations, again plays a dominant role. Delaware courts are frequently called on to decide major questions of corporate law and have developed a large body of judicial rules and precedent on major corporate law issues, and courts in other jurisdictions routinely cite their decisions. Indeed, Delaware case law frames much of the debate about the structure of corporate law. For this reason, you will see Delaware cases dominate the discussion in Chapters 3, 4, 8, and 9, which focus on publicly held corporations.

While we examine the MBCA and Delaware law, we will also draw your attention to other states' statutory and judicial innovations. In addition, we will discuss the American Law Institute's Principles of Corporate Governance: Analysis and Recommendations (hereafter Principles). The Principles are the product of the ALI Corporate Governance Project, begun in the 1970s and completed in 1992. The project involved a thorough examination of the fundamentals of corporate governance.

In addition to state law, we study two other law-givers for corporate governance. Federal law, particularly the Securities Exchange Act of 1934 (discussed later in this chapter and in Chapter 10), sometimes regulates particular aspects of governance such as proxy solicitation, usually by rules that focus on disclosure. These rules have a mandatory impact in that they apply to all public companies. Since the Enron-related crisis in 2002, federal law has expanded to require CEOs and CFOs to certify financial statements and to ban corporate loans to senior officers and directors. The federal Dodd-Frank legislation in 2010 added additional governance requirements, such as "say on pay." Important governance requirements are also found in the listing standards of the national stock exchanges. For example, the New York Stock Exchange and NASDAQ require that a majority of a corporation's directors be independent, as defined in their standards, and that a board have three committees — audit, compensation, and nominating/governance — made up entirely of independent directors. The rules ostensibly come from these quasi-private self-regulatory organizations, but they are an important example of federal-influenced limitations on the usual rules provided by state corporation law.

NOTES ON THE DEVELOPMENT OF AMERICAN CORPORATE LAW

1. During the latter part of the eighteenth century and continuing into the first half of the nineteenth century, corporation law was a blend of special state legislation

and common law principles. Persons seeking to operate as a corporation could do so only by obtaining a special legislative charter. Charters were usually granted to private firms engaged in quasi-public functions, such as operation of a public utility or provision of banking or insurance services. The rules and regulations governing such specially chartered corporations were a mixture of the legislatively determined charter provisions, common law doctrines, and private contracts.

During the nineteenth century, special chartering fell into disrepute. By the beginning of the twentieth century, most states had both constitutional provisions prohibiting legislatures from creating corporations by special charters and corporation codes specifying simple administrative steps to be followed by individuals wishing to conduct business as a corporation. These "general" corporation codes made corporate status available to all persons, not just those able to obtain legislative favor.

2. The shift from special chartering to general corporation codes was accompanied by a change in legal conceptualization of the corporation. At the height of special chartering, the corporation was described as an artificial entity created by the state. By the end of the nineteenth century, the corporation was more often described as a natural entity created by private contract. During the twentieth century, theories of corporate form continued to evolve.

3. The early general corporation codes contained many immutable rules. Some such rules were apparently intended to protect the interests of individuals investing money capital as shareholders. Others, such as limits on the size and duration of incorporated firms, were clearly designed to protect the larger community from the risks believed to be posed by excessive concentration of capital. However, these immutable features began to disappear rapidly at the beginning of the twentieth century because of open competition among several states determined to "steal" incorporation business from one another. Delaware soon emerged as the leader in this ongoing competition for charters, and remains so today.

The long-dominant story about state charter competition described Delaware as winning a race to the bottom. Delaware, claimed critics, unfairly skewed its corporation laws in favor of management interests at the expense of shareholders in order to capture charter business. The ongoing competition prevented Delaware or other states from altering this status quo in order to offer more equitable corporation laws. Thus, according to the critics, the only hope for eventual equity is a federal corporations code. See William Cary's article in favor of federal regulation, Federalism and Corporate Law: Reflections upon Delaware, 83 Yale L.J. 663 (1974).

This theory, however, was strongly challenged by scholars versed in economics. Since investors choose, ex ante, whether to invest in a corporation chartered in Delaware or elsewhere, economic theory suggests that shareholders would demand a premium to invest in corporations with laws that allowed management excessive room to act opportunistically. Indeed, say many of these scholars, economic theory suggests that management should incorporate in a jurisdiction that provides laws that optimally balance the sometimes conflicting interests of management and shareholders. Under this view, Delaware obtains corporation business because its laws best achieve this balance.

For theoretical analysis from an economic perspective, see Winter, State Law, Shareholder Protection and the Theory of the Corporation, 6 J. Legal Stud. 251 (1977);

Romano, The State Competition Debate in Corporate Law, 8 Cardozo L. Rev. 709 (1987). For statistical studies and discussion, see Dodd & Leftwich, The Market for Corporate Charters: "Unhealthy Competition" versus Federal Regulation, 53 J. Bus. L. 259 (1980) (empirical study finding that shareholders of firms reincorporating in Delaware earn statistically significant positive abnormal returns over the 25-month period preceding reincorporation); Weiss & White, Of Econometrics and Indeterminacy: A Study of Investors' Reactions to "Changes" in Corporate Law, 75 Cal. L. Rev. 551 (1987) (reviewing several studies and concluding that methodology is too weak or flawed to resolve the issue); Daines, Does Delaware Law Improve Firm Value?, 62 J. Fin. Econ. 559 (2001) (finding Delaware firms generally worth more than firms incorporated elsewhere using Tobin's Q, a financial measure of company performance); Subrahmanian, The Disappearing Delaware Effect, 20 J.L. Econ. & Org. 32 (2004) (finding the difference did not continue outside the original time period and for larger firms). In any event, Delaware is winning this race, in whatever direction it appears to be going. The choice is almost always between Delaware and the state where the corporation is headquartered. No state other than Delaware has a significant share of the market for those corporations that leave their home state to incorporate. See Bebchuk and Cohen, Firms' Decisions Where to Incorporate, 48 J.L. & Econ. 383 (2003).

4. Delaware does not maintain its lead in the competition for charters simply by virtue of the substantive content of its corporation code. While other states quickly copy its statutory innovations, they have proved unable to emulate either Delaware's reliability of adapting its laws to changed circumstances or the predictability provided by its well-developed body of case law. Delaware's court system is a core part of Delaware's continuing advantage. All corporate law cases are heard by its Chancery Court, which gives those judges (and the Delaware Supreme Court, which hears appeals) an expertise in corporate law matters unrivaled elsewhere. For explanations of the advantages provided by Delaware law and the interests served by these advantages, see Macey & Miller, Toward an Interest-Group Theory of Delaware Corporate Law, 65 Tex. L. Rev. 469 (1987); Branson, Indeterminacy: The Final Ingredient in an Interest Group Analysis of Corporate Law, 43 Vand. L. Rev. 85 (1990); Rock, Saints and Sinners: How Does Delaware Corporate Law Work?, 44 UCLA L. Rev. 1009 (1997).

5. For a suggestion that the main competition to Delaware comes not from any other state, but from the federal government, see Roe, Delaware's Competition, 117 Harv. L. Rev. 588 (2003).

2. Formation: The Articles of Incorporation

MBCA §§2.01-2.06; 3.01
Delaware G.C.L. §§101, 102, 361-368

The process of forming a corporation is fairly simple. Participants complete the articles of incorporation and file them with the appropriate state official in the chosen state, often a designee of the secretary of state. How will you as an attorney for the participants know what to include in the articles? The most direct constraints are that you have to satisfy the statute and your clients. The state requirements are now fairly minimal—certain basic facts (see MBCA §2.01), including the corporation's name, its registered office and agent for service of process, and the number of shares it is authorized to issue. After the articles are filed, there is usually an initial organizational meeting at which directors are elected, shares are issued in exchange for consideration that the corporation receives to undertake its business, and bylaws governing corporate procedures are adopted.

Under the Model Act, the corporation's purpose may but need not be stated in the articles and every corporation is declared to have the purpose of engaging in any lawful business unless a more limited purpose is set forth in the articles, Delaware requires a purpose to be stated in the certificate and provides it will be sufficient to state the purpose is to engage in any lawful act or activity, which is the common language in Delaware charters. Many states, including Delaware (and by suggested language from the MBCA), now permit public benefit corporations or a similar designation to PBC, which identifies a corporation that has included a public benefit purpose in its articles. Chapter 4 includes a discussion on how this purpose affects governance and the powers of directors.

PROBLEM 3-3

The Soft Drink Association is incorporated in Delaware. Management is considering reincorporating in a state that has adopted the MBCA. As Soft Drink's in-house counsel, you have been asked whether this change will impose any problems. Begin your analysis by determining what changes, if any, will be required in Soft Drink's current Articles of Incorporation, which provide as follows:

Article One. The name of the company is The Soft Drink Association.

Article Two. The corporation's registered agent is Barbara Smith, 101 Browning Street, Wilmington, Delaware.

Article Three. The purpose of the corporation is to engage in any lawful act or activity for which corporations may be organized under the Delaware G.C.L.

Article Four. The corporation has authority to issue 5 million shares having a par value of $10 per share.

Article Five. The directors of the corporation are hereby exculpated from liability for breach of the duty of care to the maximum extent allowed by Delaware law.

3. Determining Shares to Issue

MBCA §6.01
Delaware G.C.L. §151

A corporation may have several types or classes of shares with characteristics as specified in the articles of incorporation. Corporate norms specify that there must be a class of shares that carry authority to elect directors and exercise all other shareholder voting rights. There must also be a class that entitles the bearer to receive the corporation's net assets upon dissolution. Shares that combine both residual claimant status and voting rights are called "common shares." Corporate norms contemplate that all shares of a given class will be fungible—that is, they will have identical rights, preferences, and limitations (see MBCA §6.01)—which supports an expectation that the common shares of all corporations will possess similar rights. This, in turn, supports a uniform expectation that minimizes transaction costs for a purchaser and bolsters the functioning of a national market for shares.

Where a corporation or its promoters find that there are different groups of investors with risk preferences that require a different set of incentives in order to get the investors to part with their money, the corporation may issue other classes of stock with different rights. For example, "preferred shares" might be granted a dividend or liquidation preference over common shares. Not uncommonly, however, the financial preference granted to preferred shares is coupled with a limitation or denial of voting rights. Preferred shares of the same class have identical rights, but preferred shares do not have identical rights across classes or from corporation to corporation. Accordingly, purchasers and sellers of preferred shares may be unable to rely upon national market valuation and instead may face research costs in ascertaining exactly what rights attach to shares, making preferred shares a more sophisticated investment option.

PROBLEM 3-4

Charlotte is a recent graduate of MIT, where she majored in computer science. Since her junior year in high school Charlotte has formed a number of small, software/computer/Internet-related businesses.

Angela, also a recent graduate of MIT, has a degree in computer science. Angela's passion is music. She plays several instruments and has been a radio DJ since her high school years.

Davis, a good friend of Angela's, is a recent graduate of Tufts, where he majored in history. Davis's passion is the entrepreneurial side of show business. His father produces motion pictures in Los Angeles. Davis has promoted rock concerts since high school.

For several years, Angela and Davis have been discussing forming an Internet-related entertainment business upon graduation. Recently they invited Charlotte to join the endeavor because they believed that Charlotte possessed essential technology and business start-up expertise that neither Angela nor Davis possessed. In early August, Charlotte, Angela, and Davis (hereafter sometimes collectively referred to as "the Venturers") agreed to join forces to form an entertainment business under the name Hip-Hop.com. The business will be headquartered in Boston.

Each of the Venturers initially expects to be actively involved in most aspects of the business. Charlotte and Davis are both strong willed and each privately believes her/himself to be the appropriate overall leader of the venture. Despite Angela's close friendship with Davis, Angela believes that Charlotte should be the overall leader. However, Angela is concerned that Charlotte is too much of a loner and could lack the interpersonal skills to head a larger organization. Angela, who likes to be liked by everyone, has not communicated her impressions and concerns to either Charlotte or Davis.

Charlotte has obtained the agreement of her grandfather, "Pop," to invest $50,000 in the business in return for 2.5 percent of the company's stock. Davis has obtained the agreement of Bermuda, a California-based investor who is the parent of a woman Davis once dated, to invest $150,000 in return for 7.5 percent of the company's stock. The agreements with Pop and Bermuda are "tentative" and "informal" and subject to each investor's consultations with personal advisors about legal and other ramifications. Angela and Davis both expect their parents to make small investments within the next two months. Other friends and relatives of the Venturers are also likely to make investments in the $10,000 to $20,000 range.

The Venturers reached the following understandings at an informal meeting on August 25, 2014:

1. They will form a corporation named Hip-Hop.com. Charlotte has volunteered you, her older sibling, to do the legal work for free.

2. Charlotte will use the title Chief Operating Officer and/or Chief Technology Officer. Angela will use the title President and/or Chief Financial Officer. Davis will use the title Vice President for Corporate Planning and/or Managing Director of the Music Division. The Venturers will constitute the corporation's initial board of directors.

3. Among the three Venturers, the stock of Hip-Hop.com initially will be divided as follows: Charlotte will own 40 percent; Davis will own 30 percent; Angela will own 20 percent. [Charlotte's comment to you: Davis is bitter about this allocation. Originally shares were to be divided equally. Charlotte subsequently demanded 50 percent, but agreed to accept 40 percent after Angela intervened. Charlotte is worried about Davis teaming up with Angela at some future date.] The stock will be sold to the Venturers in return for the expenses they have each incurred in promoting the business—costs of business phone calls, trips, etc.—which for each Venturer is more than $200, but less than $500. The Venturers expect that they will then need to raise additional capital every three months or so by selling stock to additional investors. They realize that such sales will dilute the ownership percentages of initial investors.

4. The Venturers expect that it will take four years to build Hip-Hop.com into a premier Internet business. At that time, they hope to cash in their investment via sale of the business or portions thereof. In order to be sure that each of the Venturers "earns" his or her share of the business, they have agreed that each Venturer's stock will "vest" as follows:

   a. One-quarter of each Venturer's initial stock will vest on September 1, 2015, if the Venturer is still working for Hip-Hop.com on that date.

   b. An additional one-quarter of each Venturer's initial stock will vest on September 1, 2016, if the Venturer is still working for Hip-Hop.com on that date.

   c. An additional one-quarter of each Venturer's initial stock will vest on September 1, 2017, if the Venturer is still working for Hip-Hop.com on that date.

   d. The final one-quarter of each Venturer's initial stock will vest on September 1, 2018, if the Venturer is still working for Hip-Hop.com on that date.

If a Venturer ceases to work for Hip-Hop.com prior to September 1, 2018, for whatever reason, then any unvested stock of that Venturer will be "sold back" to the firm or "voided" at nominal or no cost to the firm.

Ignoring professional responsibility issues concerning your representation of multiple parties:

1. Prepare a Certificate/Articles of Incorporation to incorporate Hip-Hop.com in Delaware (or an MBCA jurisdiction) that meets the needs and expectations of the various Venturers and investors. (Be sure that you identify the number and types of shares to be issued.)

2. Prepare a recommendation as to how many shares should be initially issued and how those shares should be allocated among the Venturers and investors.

3. Prepare a brief memo to yourself identifying matters to be addressed in the bylaws or a separate agreement.

4. Determining Voting Rights: Using Articles and Bylaws to Change Legal Norms

Most state corporation law norms take the form of default rules—for example, that all shares have the same voting and economic rights or that centralized power resides in the board. Often, however, the default rules may not fit the needs of a particular enterprise or group of entrepreneurs. As in the case of Charlotte's venture in Problem 3-4, it may be important to provide assurances to one or more participants against centralized power and majority rule, for example, to give each participant a veto as to certain key decisions rather than being governed strictly by majority rule. A planner for the enterprise will want to understand how to change these default rules. Most (though not all) of these state-provided rules may be changed by private ordering, such as shareholders' agreements (discussed in Chapter 5). Alternatively, as explored here, the corporate law default rules can be changed by inclusion of the preferred rule in the articles of incorporation or bylaws. These two types of governance documents, which are akin to a constitution and statutes in our public government, differ as to which corporate participants enact them and how difficult it is to amend them once in place. Articles are public documents that can be changed only by action of a corporation's directors and shareholders. Bylaws often can be changed by the directors alone and are not publicly filed documents.

a. Overview of Normal Rules of Shareholder Voting for Election of Directors

MBCA §§8.04, 7.21, 7.28
Delaware G.C.L. §§141(d), 212(a), 214, 216

The default rules governing shareholders' ability to elect directors are straightforward. Directors are annually elected by plurality vote, according to votes cast on a one vote per share basis. (Majority voting, an alternative increasingly being used in public corporations, is discussed at the end of this chapter.) The number of directors is usually specified in the initial articles or bylaws. Assume, for example, a publicly traded Delaware corporation, Hypo, Inc., having 1 million common shares outstanding. The articles provide for nine directors. Under normal default rules, all nine directors will serve a one-year term. At each annual meeting, an election will be held to fill all nine positions. Each shareholder will be entitled to cast votes equal to her number of shares for each of nine candidates. The nine candidates receiving the most votes will be elected. This is called straight voting, in contrast to cumulative voting described below. The practical result is that a shareholder with 51 percent of the votes will be able to elect 100 percent of the board seats, a result that reflects the majoritarian preference of the default rules in the corporation's codes. What if an investor, as in Charlotte's venture described above, desires some assurance of a place at the boardroom table even if investing less than 51 percent, or put another way, won't any of the investors in Charlotte's problem worry that the other investors might later combine in alliance against him or her and use that majority power to exclude the investor from the board of directors? The following paragraphs describe ways that corporate planners can change the number of votes so as to respond to the needs of particular investors—for example, to ensure a board seat in particular circumstances or to provide a better chance for a particular investor to obtain a board seat.

b. Cumulative Voting

In a cumulative voting scheme, a shareholder can cast a total number of votes equal to the number of shares multiplied by the number of positions to be filled, and these votes can be spread among as many candidates as there are seats to be filled or concentrated in as few as one candidate. Thus, if a shareholder owns 100 shares in a corporation with one vote per share and three directors are being elected, he may divide 300 votes among the candidates as he chooses. If he wishes, he may cast all 300 votes for one candidate, in contrast to straight voting, which would permit him to cast only 100 votes for each of three candidates. This cumulation thus increases the likelihood that his candidate will be one of the top three vote-getters; indeed, the purpose of cumulative voting is to permit some minority shareholders to have a place on the board.

A simple example illustrates the difference between these voting schemes. Suppose Bill owns 15 of the 100 outstanding shares of Products, Inc. and wishes to see Jane elected as one of the corporation's nine directors. If Products' other shareholders do not want to see Jane elected, then they can cast votes for nine candidates other than Jane. Each of these candidates would then receive 85 votes. Under straight voting, Bill would be unable to elect Jane because he can cast only 15 votes for her. Under cumulative voting, however, Bill could cast all of his 135 votes (15 shares multiplied by nine posts) for Jane. This would ensure her election no matter how the other shareholders cast their votes. Jane would have enough votes to be in the top nine and thus be elected to the board. The other shareholders would have 765 votes (85×9), but they cannot divide them in such a way that all nine of their candidates will receive more than the 135 votes that Jane will have.

The actual mechanics of cumulative voting are much richer than that example. In any given setting your client will want to know how large a minority position must be to be guaranteed gaining a seat on the board, or how many shares an investor must have to gain a particular number of seats on the board. That requires a simple mathematical calculation, although one that will frustrate many law students who may have come to law school to avoid math. The maximum voting power of a given block of shares (i.e., how many seats on the board of directors can be controlled by a given number of shares) can be determined by the following formula. To elect X number of directors, a shareholder must have *more than* $(S \times X) \div (D + 1)$ shares, where S equals the number of shares voting and D equals the number of directors to be elected. Thus, in the example in the preceding paragraph, if Bill wished to be assured enough voting power to elect two directors, he would need to own more than $(100 \times 2) \div (9 + 1)$, or more than 20 shares.

PROBLEM 3-5

Protein, Inc. has 6 million outstanding shares. Two million of these shares are held by four institutional investors (the Cabal) who have recently agreed to vote their shares in concert in the upcoming election of Protein's nine-member board. The remaining shares are held by corporate officers, other institutional investors, and approximately 2,000 individuals. None of these shareholders owns more than 1 percent of Protein's shares, and management's holdings are infinitesimal. Assume that Protein's articles provide for cumulative voting, but that such provision has been irrelevant in the past because there have been no contested elections.

Thirty days before the annual meeting, the Cabal notifies Protein that it plans to nominate nine named individuals for election to the board, but that they will not solicit proxies in favor of these nominees. Shortly before the annual meeting, the Cabal notifies the board that the Cabal will vote its shares cumulatively.

Assume, alternatively, that Protein is incorporated in Delaware or an MBCA jurisdiction. If the Cabal votes cumulatively and intelligently, what is the maximum number of directors it can be sure of electing if:

1. All 4 million non-Cabal-owned shares submit proxies in favor of management's nominees?
2. Three million non-Cabal-owned shares submit proxies in favor of management's nominees, and the remaining 1 million shares are not voted?

c. *Class Voting, Including Dual-Class Voting Structures*

Normally, power to elect directors rests with the voting shareholders as a whole. However, a corporation may, in its articles of incorporation, divide its shares into classes and permit each class to select a specified number of directors. This traditional use of class voting serves to allocate the right to elect directors between different sets of investors.

A more controversial variation of the one share-one vote principle separates shareholders into two classes and gives one class disproportionate voting power as compared to their capital contribution to the corporation. This so-called dual-class common mechanism might be desirable, for example, for a corporation that is going public. The original founders could retain a class of voting common stock that has 10 or 100 votes per share (or some other number designated in the articles), while selling common stock to the public that has only one vote per share. This dual-class common would allow the founders to protect their control of the corporation, while giving public shareholders both significant voting power and the vast majority of the shareholders' equity. These dual-class voting schemes for companies already publicly traded have been disfavored by the SEC and curtailed by stock exchange rules but are permitted in Delaware. See Lerhman v. Cohen, 222 A.2d 800 (Del. 1966). Google adopted this structure when it went public, and highly visible media companies such as the New York Times also retain dual-class structures.

PROBLEM 3-6

Micro, Inc., a start-up high-tech venture, has 5 million outstanding shares currently held by 24 sophisticated investors and newly hired CEO Jan Stark (who owns 1,000 shares). Micro is negotiating with value investor Bill Door to obtain much-needed equity capital. Door is willing to purchase 3 million Micro shares (additional shares that are to be issued by Micro in exchange for the new funds) if he is given the ability to elect four of the nine members of the board. Stark has told the board that she favors the deal but will quit unless the board gives her one-third of the voting power in the election of the board majority. How can the board (which has the full support of the shareholders) satisfy Door and Stark, while protecting the interests of the corporation and its other shareholders?

d.   A Classified Board with Staggered Terms—Adaptability Versus Stability

MBCA §8.06
Delaware G.C.L. §141(d)

Almost all state corporation codes provide as a norm that directors shall be elected annually. However, these laws expressly allow corporations to adopt longer and staggered terms for directors (and Massachusetts requires a staggered board). For example, MBCA §8.06 allows classification of directors into two or three groups of as equal size as possible. If directors are divided into two groups, then each director serves a two-year term, and if classified into three groups, each director serves a three-year term. The terms of all directors are staggered so that the term of only one group expires each year. Staggered terms theoretically ensure that a corporation will always have experienced directors in office. Absent removal of directors (discussed below), having staggered terms means that two annual meetings would be required to replace a majority of the board of directors. Thus, shareholders—even a majority shareholder—cannot easily change corporate policies simply by electing an entirely new board. Classified boards have proven to be an effective antitakeover defense in public companies, but usage has been decreasing in recent years amid pressure from some institutional shareholders, a story explored in more detail at the end of this chapter.

In substance, staggering directors' terms operates as a constraint on the majority shareholders' ability to adapt to changed circumstances by quickly naming new directors. It does not mean that the majority will be barred forever from making such changes.

Varying statutory norms to diminish majority power requires careful planning to protect against later amendment by the majority. For example, if X Corporation adopts a provision in its bylaws providing for staggered terms for its nine-member board of directors, what is to prevent the shareholder majority from simply deleting that provision whenever it chooses, thereby declassifying the board? Corporate planners must carefully consider whether the "constitutional" provision should be placed in the corporation's articles or bylaws, as a way to prevent the majority from amending the new rule. This is discussed in the next section of this book.

PROBLEM 3-7

Revisit Charlotte's venture in Problem 3-4. How would you change your previous provisions concerning voting rights in light of the material in this subpart 4?

5. Looking Ahead: How Shareholders Act

a. The Annual Meeting and Other Forums for Shareholder Action

MBCA §§7.01-7.07, 7.21
Delaware G.C.L. §§211-213, 216, 222, 228

The corporate default rules promote adaptability to changed circumstances. If directors are managing poorly or selfishly, the shareholders can replace them at the next annual meeting or remove them prior to that time if permitted by the state law, articles, and bylaws. Alternatively, shareholders can sell their shares to a new team of managers who will use their purchased majority power to supplant the old managers. Shareholder political activity takes place against a backdrop of state statutory and judicial norms and doctrines that attempt to ensure shareholder suffrage while allowing directors to manage the corporation. On the one hand, shareholders are responsible for the election of directors and the approval of major changes in the corporation's structure or "constitution." On the other hand, directors must manage the corporation's business, a role that includes supervision of the shareholder governance process. Necessarily, directors have conflicting interests when they perceive that shareholders may seek to use their voting power either to elect a different slate of directors or to advocate policies that the directors oppose. In such circumstances, directors may be tempted to use their power to thwart shareholders' voting rights.

To minimize the risk that directors will act unfairly, corporation statutes specify in detail the substance of shareholders' voting and meeting rights, as well as the procedural rules that safeguard the shareholders' exercise of these rights. The following are some of the more important substantive and procedural statutory rules.

The annual meeting and election of directors.   The paramount shareholder function is the annual election of directors. Most corporation codes protect the exercise of this right by specifying immutably that directors shall be elected at an annually held meeting of shareholders. Although directors have some discretion as to the timing and location of the annual meeting, as part of their power to supervise corporate affairs or as a component of their ability to make or change the bylaws affecting the annual meeting, they may not entirely avoid it. Indeed, most corporation codes provide summary judicial procedures to ensure that a failure to hold a required annual meeting is quickly remedied. See MBCA §7.03(a) and Delaware G.C.L. §211(c). Thus, shareholders are usually guaranteed a chance to meet at least once per year.

Special shareholders' meetings.   All state corporation codes provide for special shareholders' meetings to address issues expressly identified in the meeting notice. Delaware's list of who can call a special meeting is short: the directors or whoever may be listed in the charter. This effectively blocks shareholder-initiated special meetings to oppose the current board. Many states follow MBCA §7.02, which authorizes the holders of 10 percent or more of a corporation's stock to call a special meeting. As with annual meetings, the board has some discretion as to the timing and location of special meetings, but may not avoid holding them if validly called as specified in the statutes, articles, or bylaws.

Action by written consent.   Corporation statutes provide a third forum by which shareholders can act—written consent in lieu of a meeting. As with the special meeting, you will want to pay particular attention as to who can initiate such action in such a forum. Recall the difference between Delaware and the MBCA as to the ability of shareholders to call a special meeting. The two statutes also differ in the degree to which they offer written consents, but they have flipped positions, with the MBCA having the more restrictive rule of permitting action by written consent only by unanimity, which effectively limits its use to small corporations with a few shareholders, while Delaware permits written consent by the vote of the number of shareholders otherwise required by corporate action—a majority in many cases. Remember, this is a default rule that can be changed by a contrary provision in the articles of incorporation: in fact, in Delaware public corporations, this is one of the more common changes to the statutory default rules.

Record date: determining shareholders entitled to vote.   The shareholders who are entitled to participate and vote at a meeting are not necessarily the shareholders who own shares on the date of the meeting. In publicly traded corporations, shares constantly change hands, making it difficult to identify and give appropriate notice to persons buying shares in the last few days before a meeting. Consequently, state corporation codes provide that the shareholders entitled to vote are those owning shares on the "record date" specified by directors. Normally, the "record date" can be set anywhere from 60 to 10 days before the meeting in question. In states like Delaware, which allow shareholder action by nonunanimous written consent, the setting of a "record date" is somewhat more complicated. See Delaware G.C.L. §228.

Despite legislative efforts to draw bright lines to protect shareholders' suffrage rights, courts are often required to rationalize conflicts between two statutory provisions, or to determine whether the directors' use of a statutorily conferred right should be enjoined or undone because inequitable. The following case illustrates the importance courts attach to fundamental shareholder voting and meeting rights when resolving such cases. However, as you read this case, be aware that following this decision, the Delaware legislature amended one of the sections in question—Delaware G.C.L. §211, authorizing nonunanimous written consent in lieu of an annual meeting only if all directorships to be filled at the annual meeting are vacant. What are the policy issues at stake in this case? Why did the legislature move so quickly in response to this decision? Does the legislative action represent an undercutting of basic shareholder rights, or an appropriate elimination of a previously unnoticed conflict between statutory provisions?

Hoschett v. TSI International Software, Ltd.

Delaware Court of Chancery, 1996
683 A.2d 43

ALLEN, CHANCELLOR.

Pending now are cross motions for summary judgment in this suit seeking an order requiring TSI International Software, Ltd. to hold an annual meeting of its stockholders as required by Section 211 of the Delaware General Corporation Law (DGCL) and, incidental to that relief, to make publicly available to shareholders a stocklist, as required by Section 219 of the corporation law statute. It is admitted that TSI has not held an annual meeting within 13 months of the filing of the complaint (or thereafter for that matter). The case presents the single issue whether stockholder written consent action, which was taken pursuant to Section 228 of DGCL after the filing of the complaint, and that purported to elect directors for TSI, satisfies the requirement to hold an annual meeting and moots the claim stated in the complaint. For the reasons briefly set forth below I conclude that the consent action, assuming that it had the effect of duly designating directors of TSI, did not satisfy the corporation's obligation to comply with Section 211 and hold an annual meeting at which the company's directors are to be elected, in conformity with the certificate of incorporation.

I.

The material facts are few and apparently not controverted. Plaintiff, Fred G. Hoschett is the registered owner of 1,200 shares of common stock of the defendant TSI International Software, Ltd., a Delaware corporation having its principal place of business in Wilton, Connecticut. Formed in 1993, TSI is a privately-held corporation having a total of 962,274 shares of common stock and 860,869 shares of convertible preferred stock issued and outstanding, which are held by less than 40 stockholders of record. Pursuant to its certificate of incorporation, holders of TSI's common and preferred stock vote together on all matters, including the election of directors, with each share of common and preferred having the right to cast one vote. TSI has never held an annual meeting for the election of directors.

On October 5, 1995, plaintiff filed this action against TSI seeking, among other things . . . an order compelling an annual meeting of stockholders for the election of directors. On February 2, 1996, after some discovery, plaintiff moved for summary judgment asserting that there are no material facts in dispute and he is entitled to judgment as a matter of law. TSI responded with a cross motion for summary judgment supported by an affidavit establishing that on November 16, 1995, the company received a written consent representing a majority of the voting power of the corporation that "elected" five individuals each "to serve as a director of [TSI] until his or her successor is duly elected and qualified." On the basis of the validity of that action, defendant asserts that it has satisfied the need to hold an annual meeting for the election of directors.

II.

Summary judgment is appropriate when the record shows that "there is no genuine issue of material fact and the moving party is entitled to judgment as a matter of law." Del. Ch. Ct. R. 56(c); Gilbert v. El Paso Co., Del. Supr., 575 A.2d 1131, 1142 (1990).

Section 211(b) of DGCL provides as follows:

> An annual meeting of stockholders shall be held for the election of directors on a date and at a time designated by or in a manner provided in the bylaws. Any other proper business may be transacted at the annual meeting.

Section 211(c) authorizes the Court of Chancery to order a corporation to hold such a meeting, but confers discretion on the Court in the exercise of such power.

Section 228(a) of DGCL provides as follows:

> Unless otherwise provided in the certificate of incorporation, any action required by this chapter to be taken at any annual or special meeting of stockholders of a corporation, or any action which may be taken at any annual or special meeting of such stockholders, may be taken without a meeting, without prior notice and without a vote, if a consent or consents in writing, setting forth the action so taken, shall be signed by the holders of outstanding stock having not less than the minimum number of votes that would be necessary to authorize or take such action at a meeting at which all shares entitled to vote thereon were present . . .

Most fundamentally, the current motion requires the court to interpret the legal meaning of these two Sections of the corporation code in a way that, to the maximum extent feasible, gives full effect to the literal terms of the language of each. For the reasons that follow, I conclude that the mandatory requirement that an annual meeting of shareholders be held is not satisfied by shareholder action pursuant to Section 228 purporting to elect a new board or to re-elect an old one.

The obligation to hold an annual meeting at which directors are to be elected, either for one year or for staggered terms, as the charter may provide, is one of the very few mandatory features of Delaware corporation law. Delaware courts have long recognized the central role of annual meetings in the scheme of corporate governance. See, e.g., Coaxial Communications, Inc. v. CNA Financial Corp., Del. Supr., 367 A.2d 994 (1976); Speiser v. Baker, Del.Ch., 525 A.2d 1001 (1987); Prickett v. American Steel and Pump Corp., Del.Ch., 251 A.2d 576 (1969). Even the shareholders' power to approve amendments to the charter does not extend so far as to permit a Delaware corporation legitimately to dispense with the annual meeting. The critical importance of shareholder voting both to the theory and to the reality of corporate governance, see Blasius Indus., Inc. v. Atlas Corp., Del. Ch., 564 A.2d 651 (1988), may be thought to justify the mandatory nature of the obligation to call and hold an annual meeting. The annual election of directors is a structured occasion that necessarily focuses attention on corporate performance. Knowing that such an occasion is necessarily to be faced annually may itself have a marginally beneficial effect on managerial attention and performance. Certainly, the annual meeting may in some instances be a bother to management, or even, though rarely, a strain, but in all events it provides a certain discipline and an occasion for interaction and participation of a kind. Whether it is welcome or resented by management, however, is in the end, irrelevant under Section 211(b) and (c) of the DGCL and similar statutes in other jurisdictions.

Plainly plaintiff has established a prima facie case for the relief he seeks. See Speiser v. Baker, Del. Ch., 525 A.2d 1001, 1005 (1987) (recognizing that plaintiff had made a prima facie case upon proving that he was a stockholder and that several years had elapsed since the last annual meeting); Saxon Industries, Inc. v. NKFW Partners, Del. Supr., 488 A.2d 1298 (1984). The question this case presents is whether a controlling shareholder or a majority group may effectively avoid the annual meeting requirement, despite the command of Section 211, by the latter-day expedient of exercising consent to designate directors under Section 228. The Delaware courts apparently have not previously addressed this precise issue. There is of course a rather strong practical argument that it is efficient to recognize such a power or effect. The argument, as I see it, would run as follows: Only a relatively small and more or less tightly bound group of shareholders comprising a voting majority could effectively exercise a Section 228 consent action without a public tender offer. Where such a small and coherent group seeks to exercise control, it is especially unlikely that the formality of notice to all shareholders and a meeting will have any practical effect whatsoever. Therefore, if the law requires an annual meeting where a small, controlling group of shareholders is willing to act by consent to designate directors, it is highly likely that the law will simply be commanding expenditure of funds in a pointless exercise.

The flaws in this position appear to be at least three. First, the principle for which this practicality argument must contend is not limited to small coherent groups of shareholders who together can exercise control. If the principle is correct, management of public companies without a small controlling group, could solicit consents (albeit in conformity with SEC proxy rules) to "re-elect" or "elect" some or all of the board without ever having an annual meeting. Admittedly, in that setting shareholders who sought to initiate some corporate change might still initiate action by their own consent solicitation contest, or could resist the effort by others to "reelect" the board by soliciting revocations of consent, but public shareholders would be at some tactical disadvantage as to timing at the least and would arguably find convincing others more difficult than if an annual meeting were held. Second, the purposes served by the annual meeting include affording to shareholders an opportunity to bring matters before the shareholder body, as provided by the corporations charter and bylaws, such as bylaw changes. These other matters of possible business are not necessarily made irrelevant by a consent designation of directors, even if such designation is effective. Finally, while the model of democratic forms should not too strictly be applied to the economic institution of a business corporation (where for instance votes are weighted by the size of the voter's investment), it is nevertheless a not unimportant feature of corporate governance that at a noticed annual meeting a form of discourse (i.e., oral reports, questions and answers and in rare instances proxy contests) among investors and between shareholders and managers is possible. The theory of the annual meeting includes the idea that a deliberative component of the meeting may occur. Shareholders' meetings are mandated and shareholders authorized by statute to transact proper business because we assume that at such meetings something said may matter. Obviously these meetings are very far from deliberative convocations, but a keen realization of the reality of the degree of deliberation that is possible, should make the preservation of residual mechanisms of corporate democracy more, not less, important.

Thus, on balance I find an argument predicated on alleged efficiency and practicality, unpersuasive. I conclude absent unanimous consent that the mandatory language of Section 211(b) places on TSI the legal obligation to convene a meeting of shareholders to elect directors pursuant to the constitutional documents of the firm.

What then is the legal meaning of the clause in Section 228 that authorizes "any action required by this chapter to be taken at an annual or special meeting" to be taken by written consent of shareholders? The established preference of our law is of course to give to such statutory language a literal reading, if that is possible. Thus "any action" must include shareholder action to remove directors from office and to designate persons as directors when there is a vacancy and the constitutional documents of the firm contemplate filling such vacancies by shareholders. See DGCL §141(k) (removal), §211(b) (e) (election). Since the term of office of each of the directors of the company had expired, they acted as holdovers even though they continued to hold office. Thus, the action to reelect them or to elect their successors logically entailed removal and filling of the resulting vacancy.

The pertinent question is, when directors are designated through a consent process that removes holdovers and designates replacements, as here, for what term do they hold office? It is this question that is raised by the intersection of Section 211 and Section 228 and whose resolution can accommodate the command of each statute. That resolution is based on an interpretation that such directors hold office only until the next annual meeting of the shareholders, at which meeting the whole body of the company's shareholders may participate, to the extent the charter and bylaws define, in the election of the board. That is, shareholders may (if the certificate of incorporation and bylaws so provide) remove holdovers and fill vacancies on the board through exercise of the consent power, but doing so does not affect the obligation under Section 211 to hold an annual meeting. . . .

Thus, in my opinion, the effort of a group constituting a majority of the voting power of the corporation to preclude an annual meeting by acting pursuant to Section 228 is of limited effect. Specifically, while it did remove directors and may well have filled vacancies, it did so only until the next annual meeting of shareholders, which continues to be a mandatory obligation of the corporation. The Court of Chancery, in all events, maintains its traditional discretionary role when administering the equitable remedies of injunction and specific performance. See DGCL §211(c) (court "may" order holding of meeting). In this instance I apprehend no reason why equity should not specifically enforce the legal obligation imposed by Section 211(b). TSI will therefore be ordered to hold an annual meeting and make available a complete list of stockholders as required by those statutory sections. . . .

b. Removal of Directors and Other Midstream Private Ordering

MBCA §§8.08-8.10
Delaware G.C.L. §§141(k), 223

Directors are elected to serve a term that normally runs from one annual meeting to the next, but under staggered terms can cover a three-year span. Under what circumstances may shareholders remove and replace one or more members prior to the expiration of their term? While the normal rule today allows shareholders to remove directors with or without cause by majority vote, that rule cannot be fully understood apart from the common law norms the rule replaces, and the statutory rules that allow variance from the new norm.

At common law, directors had a vested right to serve out their full term, and shareholders could remove directors only for good cause. This common law rule was detailed in Pilat v. Broach Systems, Inc., 260 A.2d 13, 15 (N.J. Super. 1969):

> (a) That irrespective of the existence of any provision in the certificate of incorporation or of a by-law, a corporation may remove a director during his term of office for cause arising from his acting in a manner inimical to the interests of the corporation; (b) during his term of office, a director may not be removed except for cause unless at the time of his election there existed a by-law that provided for the removal of a director without cause. If such by-law exists, then he has taken the office subject to the provisions of the by-laws; (c) a corporation may adopt a by-law providing for the removal of a director with or without cause, but such by-law, in so far as it refers to the removal of a director without cause, is of no value for the removal of a director who is in office at the time of the enactment of the by-law; (d) without a by-law which is in force prior to his election and at the time of his election, a director has a vested right to continue in his office to the end of his said term except if he is removed for cause.

All jurisdictions now have statutory default rules allowing shareholders to remove directors before the expiration of their term in office, with or without cause, by simple majority vote. Since this provision is now the norm, shareholders no longer need a provision within the corporation's bylaws or articles in order to be able to remove directors at some later date.

However, the new norms are accompanied by statutory rules that limit or eliminate shareholders' removal power when the corporation has instituted cumulative voting, staggered terms for directors, or class election of directors. The two dominant approaches are found in the MBCA and the Delaware corporation code.

Under the MBCA approach, found in §8.08, there are no restrictions on shareholders' power to remove directors if the corporation has staggered the board into staggered terms. However, if the corporation has cumulative voting, shareholders cannot remove a director if the votes cast against removal would have been sufficient to elect that director. And, if a director is elected by a particular class of shareholders, that director can be removed only by a majority vote of that class, even if the majority of the shareholders of all classes are in favor of removal. Under the MBCA approach, these statutory restrictions are immutable. However, there are provisions for judicial removal for cause under certain circumstances. See MBCA §8.09.

The Delaware approach, found in Delaware G.C.L. §141(k), differs from the MBCA in three important respects. First, it adds members of staggered boards to the list of directors protected from removal—they can only be removed for cause, a powerful insulation for the boards of such companies. Second, these Delaware protective provisions preserve the shareholders' power to remove even protected directors if done for cause, although as discussed below that is a daunting task in most settings. So, for example, the shareholders still have the power to remove a director on a classified board by majority vote if good cause is shown. Additionally, a majority retains the ability to change the default rules and thereby permit removal in any of these situations by amending the articles (if the board is agreeable to proposing such a change) to permit a without cause removal for a staggered board or to remove cumulative voting itself.

The ability to remove a director for cause, as permitted in Delaware, is not easy. Both the substantive limitation imposed by the definition of "for cause," and the procedural safeguards that must be employed, make removal for cause a weapon of last resort. Whether director conduct constitutes cause is a fact-dependent analysis. Some guidance on what constitutes sufficient cause for removal is provided by Campbell v. Loew's, Inc., 134 A.2d 852 (Del. Ch. 1957). There, a shareholder group backing Vogel, the CEO of Loew's, sought to remove two directors, Tomlinson and Meyer, who were conducting a campaign to gain control of the board. The charges against Tomlinson and Meyer, detailed in a letter from Vogel to the shareholders, were evaluated by the Chancery Court upon Tomlinson and Meyer's request for injunctive protection.

I next consider plaintiff's contention that the charges against the two directors do not constitute "cause" as a matter of law. It would take too much space to narrate in detail the contents on the president's letter. I must therefore give my summary of its charges. First of all, it charges that the two directors (Tomlinson and Meyer) failed to cooperate with Vogel in his announced program for rebuilding the company; that their purpose has been to put themselves in control; that they made baseless accusations against him and other management personnel and attempted to divert him from his normal duties as president by bombarding him with correspondence containing unfounded charges and other similar acts; that they moved into the company's building, accompanied by lawyers and accountants, and immediately proceeded upon a planned scheme of harassment. They called for many records, some going back twenty years, and were rude to the personnel. Tomlinson sent daily letters to the directors making serious charges directly and by means of innuendos and misinterpretations.

Are the foregoing charges, if proved, legally sufficient to justify the ouster of the two directors by the stockholders? I am satisfied that a charge that the directors desired to take over control of the corporation is not a reason for their ouster. Standing alone, it is a perfectly legitimate objective which is a part of the very fabric of corporate existence. Nor is a charge of lack of cooperation a legally sufficient basis for removal for cause.

The next charge is that these directors, in effect, engaged in a calculated plan of harassment to the detriment of the corporation. Certainly a director may examine books, ask questions, etc., in the discharge of his duty, but a point can be reached which his actions exceed the call of duty and become deliberately obstructive. In such a situation, if his actions constitute a real burden on the corporation then the stockholders are entitled to relief. The charges in this area made by the Vogel letter are legally sufficient to justify the stockholders in voting to remove such directors. Compare Markovitz v. Markovitz, 336 Pa. 145, 8 A.2d 46, 124 A.L.R. 359, and see 19 C.J.S. Corporations §738(4). In so concluding, I of course express no opinion as to the truth of the charges.

I therefore conclude that the charge of "a planned scheme of harassment" as detailed in the letter constitutes a justifiable legal basis for removing a director.

134 A.2d at 860-861.

As noted in Auer v. Dressel, 118 N.E.2d 590, 593 (N.Y. 1954), before directors can be removed for cause "there must be the service of specific charges, adequate notice and full opportunity of meeting the accusation." The exact procedures required are discussed in Campbell v. Loew's.

When Vogel as president caused the notice of meeting to be sent, he accompanied it with a letter requesting proxies granting authority to vote for the removal of the two named directors. It is true that the proxy form also provided a space for the stockholder to vote against such removal. However, only the Vogel accusations accompanied the request for a proxy. Thus, while the stockholder could vote for or against removal, he would be voting with only one viewpoint presented. This violates every sense of equity and fair play in a removal for cause situation.

While the directors involved or some other group could mail a letter to the stockholders and ask for a proxy which would revoke the earlier proxy, this procedure does not comport with the legal requirement that the directors in question must be afforded an opportunity to be heard before the shareholders' vote. This is not an ordinary proxy contest case and a much more stringent standard must be invoked, at least at the initial stage, where it is sought to remove a director for cause. . . .

There seems to be an absence of cases detailing the appropriate procedure for submitting a question of director removal for cause for stockholder consideration. I am satisfied, however, that to the extent the matter is to be voted upon by the use of proxies, such proxies may be solicited only after the accused directors are afforded an opportunity to present their case to the stockholders. This means, in my opinion, that an opportunity must be provided such directors to present their defense to the stockholders by a statement which must accompany or precede the initial solicitation of proxies seeking authority to vote for the removal of such director for cause. If not provided then such proxies may not be voted for removal. And the corporation has a duty to see that this opportunity is given the directors at its expense.

134 A.2d at 861-862.

Adlerstein v. Wertheimer
Delaware Court of Chancery, 2002
2002 WL 205684

LAMB, VICE CHANCELLOR.

I.

This is an action pursuant to Section 225 of the Delaware General Corporation Law ("DGCL") brought by Joseph Adlerstein, the former Chairman and CEO of SpectruMedix Corporation ("SpectruMedix" or "the Company"), a Delaware corporation. SpectruMedix is in the business of manufacturing and selling instruments to the genetics and pharmaceutical industries and is headquartered in State College, Pennsylvania. Adlerstein's complaint is against the Company and three individuals who claim to be the current directors of the Company: Steven N. Wertheimer, Judy K. Mencher, and Ilan Reich.

At issue in the Complaint are a series of actions taken on July 9, 2001, at or in conjunction with a purported meeting of the SpectruMedix board of directors held at the New York City offices of McDermott, Will & Emery ("MW & E").[1] First, a board majority (consisting of Wertheimer and Mencher) voted to issue to the I. Reich Family Limited Partnership ("Reich Partnership"), an entity affiliated with Reich, a sufficient number of shares of a new class of supervoting preferred stock to convey to the Reich Partnership a majority of the voting power of the Company's stock. Second, the same majority voted to remove Adlerstein for cause as Chief Executive Officer of the Company, to strip him of his title as Chairman of the Board, and to appoint Reich to serve as Chief Executive Officer and as Chairman of the Board. Third, immediately after the board meeting, the Reich Partnership executed and delivered to SpectruMedix a written consent in lieu of stockholders meeting purporting to remove Adlerstein as a director. When the dust settled, the board consisted of Wertheimer, Mencher, and Reich; the Reich Partnership had replaced Adlerstein as holder of majority voting control; and Reich had replaced Adlerstein as Chairman and CEO.

Adlerstein seeks a determination that the July 9 meeting was not properly convened and, therefore, all actions taken at or in conjunction with that meeting are null and void. Adlerstein also contends that, even if the meeting was duly noticed and convened, the actions taken at the meeting by Wertheimer and Mencher were the product of a breach of the fiduciary duties they owed to him in his capacity as a director and the controlling stockholder.

II.

Adlerstein is a scientist and entrepreneur. He has a Ph.D. in physics and was involved with the funding and management of a number of start-up technology companies before founding SpectruMedix (originally named Premier American Technologies Company) in 1992.

Wertheimer, an investment banker, was introduced to Adlerstein by Selbst and was elected to the board by Adlerstein on January 1, 2000. Mencher is a money manager with an expertise in high yield and distressed investments. On Wertheimer's recommendation, Adlerstein elected Mencher to the board on March 22, 2000.

In 1997, SpectruMedix completed an initial public offering of its common stock, raising net proceeds of $4.67 million, more than half of which was used to repay

---

1. Over the years Adlerstein was represented in various personal capacities by Stephen Selbst, a partner in MW & E's New York City office. Eventually Selbst also began to serve as counsel to SpectruMedix. Selbst was present at the July 9 meeting and, as counsel to SpectruMedix, schemed with Wertheimer, Mencher, and Reich to engineer Adlerstein's ouster.

existing indebtedness. SpectruMedix experienced substantial net losses over the next several years, "burning" through all of the cash raised in the IPO. . . .

In 1999, to avoid a liquidity crisis, Adlerstein loaned SpectruMedix $500,000. In exchange, SpectruMedix gave Adlerstein a note that was convertible (at Adlerstein's option) into shares of a new Series B Preferred Stock of SpectruMedix that voted with the common and carried 80,000 votes per share. In January 2000, Adlerstein converted approximately $103,000 outstanding under this loan agreement into shares of Series B Preferred Stock. As a result, although Adlerstein owned only 21.41% of the equity of SpectruMedix, he controlled 73.27% of the voting power of the Company.

Late in 1999, before joining the board, Wertheimer convinced Adlerstein to hire Manus O'Donnell, an independent management consultant, to study and report on the status of the Company's management and finances. O'Donnell conducted his study and delivered a report dated January 2, 2000, in which he concluded that, unless the Company began making sales of instruments, it had sufficient cash and cash equivalents to continue operations only until September 2001.

During September 2000, as a result of increasing concern over SpectruMedix's deteriorating financial condition, Wertheimer and Mencher convinced Adlerstein to re-hire O'Donnell. On September 15, 2000, O'Donnell updated his report, shortening the period during which sufficient cash reserves were forecasted. He stated:

> [S]ince my last forecast in December, the company burn rate has increased substantially . . . mainly due to increased headcount expense. As a result cash would last until May 2001 if grant money is received as predicted (at 115K per month from October onward). If grants are not received, then cash would be exhausted in January 2001.

As O'Donnell noted, the change in forecast was due in large part to Adlerstein's decision to increase staffing levels from 23 to 51. This headcount increase resulted in an escalation of the annual payroll by just over 100%. O'Donnell concluded by telling the board of directors that, at the then-current level of fixed expenses, SpectruMedix needed to sell and get paid for one machine per month in order to maintain an adequate cash position.

On March 28, 2001, a sexual harassment complaint was made against Adlerstein asserting that he threatened an employee's job because she objected to his inappropriate behavior toward her. An independent consultant was hired who, after an investigation, concluded that Adlerstein had been guilty of sexual harassment as defined in the Company's policy and had been less than candid in connection with the investigation. The consultant made an oral report of this conclusion to Wertheimer and Mencher on May 14, 2001. Because Adlerstein failed to pay the consultant's bill, a written report detailing the investigation was not delivered to the Company until September 2001.

On April 11, 2001, a meeting of the SpectruMedix board was held. At that meeting Adlerstein represented to the board, and the minutes of the meeting state, that three instruments had been purchased and shipped during the quarter ending March 31, 2001 and the Company was projecting sales of six to nine instruments for the quarter ending June 30, 2001. In fact, according to uncontroverted testimony, the Company sold only one instrument during the quarter ending March 31, 2001 and that sale was made on the condition that SpectruMedix would further develop the instrument to a commercially viable level of functionality.

During April 2001, Wertheimer and Mencher convinced Adlerstein to again hire O'Donnell to generate an updated report on the financial condition of the Company. The resulting report, which projected a cash balance of $66,000 for the Company as of May 31, 2001, was discussed at an April 30, 2001 meeting of the board. As reflected in the board's minutes for that meeting Adlerstein on the one hand and Wertheimer and Mencher on the other had very different reactions to the Company's financial state:

> [Adlerstein] did not regard the situation as quite as desperate as the other directors. He said that the Company had previously faced similar cash crises and had weathered them. He said that he had found money to keep the Company alive in the past, and if required to do so again, he would find the resources. Mr. Wertheimer and Ms. Mencher lauded him for his past efforts to save the Company, but said that the[y] were seeking to bring the Company to a cash neutral or profitable position as promptly as possible. The point, Ms. Mencher said, was to put the Company in a position where Dr. Adlerstein wouldn't be required to keep the Company afloat personally in the future.

This divergence in perspective continued through the July 9 meeting.

The board met again on May 25, 2001. Adlerstein reported that the Company was "low on cash" but delivered an upbeat report on the status of discussions he was having with several potential strategic partners. Wertheimer and Mencher remained concerned about the Company's deteriorating financial condition and began to question seriously the information Adlerstein was providing to them. As Mencher testified:

> [I]t became clear that we were not getting the entire picture of what was going on with the company and that the company was quickly heading . . . toward a major liquidity crisis—if it wasn't already in one—and that the company needed a crisis manager, just for somebody to get in and tell the board what was really going on and how long the company had to survive.

Thus, Wertheimer and Mencher suggested that the Company should again hire O'Donnell's firm to help the Company in reducing expenses and improving the instrument manufacturing process. Adlerstein agreed, and the entire board unanimously resolved to do so. O'Donnell and his colleague, Gordon Mason, agreed to take on such an assignment provided SpectruMedix execute a written consulting agreement.

During the month of June 2001, O'Donnell and members of his firm began to play a hands-on role at the Company's headquarters, reducing the number of employees while improving the instrument manufacturing process. Among other things, they drew up an organizational chart that defined lines of authority and responsibility in the Company, something Adlerstein had refused to do. These changes were met enthusiastically by the Company's senior employees.

Adlerstein conducted a rearguard action against O'Donnell's restructuring efforts. Most notably, he refused to sign a written contract with O'Donnell, notwithstanding the direction of the board that he do so. He also was frequently away from headquarters in State College during June but, when he did appear, acted to undo changes that had been implemented. Eventually, O'Donnell and Mason stopped working. Wertheimer and Mencher concluded that Adlerstein was intentionally impeding the progress of the consultants and resolved to investigate the situation at SpectruMedix for themselves.

Wertheimer contacted three of the four department heads at the Company and learned that these individuals were planning to quit their jobs with SpectruMedix if organizational and other changes implemented by the consultants were not kept in place. On July 2, 2001, O'Donnell forwarded a report to Wertheimer and Mencher which concluded that Adlerstein was "the central problem" at the Company, because "he is totally lacking in managerial and business competence and has demonstrated an unwillingness to accept these shortcomings." O'Donnell further opined: "For SpectruMedix to have any chance, [Adlerstein] must be removed from any operating influence within the company."

In June 2001, Wertheimer contacted Reich to discuss involving him as both an investor and manager of SpectruMedix. Wertheimer knew that Reich had the personal wealth and managerial experience to take on a restructuring of SpectruMedix.[7] As he testified at trial: "Ilan was the only guy I knew that had money and had the skills to go in and . . . pull this out of the fire. . . . No institutional investor would go anywhere near a company like this. It had to be somebody that liked to get his hands dirty, who liked to go into a company and basically try and make something out of something that was in a lot of trouble."

On June 27, 2001, Reich met with Selbst and O'Donnell to discuss the business of SpectruMedix. Adlerstein was unaware of this meeting. The next day, Reich and Adlerstein met in New York. Reich testified that he then determined that he would only be willing to invest in SpectruMedix if he, and not Adlerstein, were in charge of the Company. Reich thereafter executed a confidentiality agreement and received non-public information in due diligence.

On June 30, Reich sent an e-mail to Selbst that referred to an upcoming meeting between Selbst and Wertheimer for the purpose of discussing Adlerstein's Series B Preferred shares. Adlerstein was not copied on this e-mail and was not aware of this meeting. Also on June 30, Wertheimer had a discussion with Reich about firing Adlerstein.

On July 2, 2001, Reich participated in a conference call with Wertheimer and Mencher and later that day met with Wertheimer to discuss his potential investment. At that meeting, the option of firing Adlerstein for cause from his position as CEO due to his sexual harassment of a Company employee was discussed, as was Adlerstein's voting control over the Company. Adlerstein had no idea this meeting was taking place. But by this time Reich knew he would have an opportunity to take over SpectruMedix.

On July 3, 2001, Reich met with various department heads of the Company during a due diligence visit to the SpectruMedix headquarters. Aware of this visit, Adlerstein acted to discourage senior officials at State College from cooperating fully with Reich. As he e-mailed one of the Company's principal scientists:

> I am not willing to have you spend an inordinate amount of time satisfying [Reich's] . . . requests at the risk of exposing our innards (i.e. technologies, analysis) to someone . . . who, in the final analysis, is by no means a sure thing to invest in [SpectruMedix].

---

7. Wertheimer was aware that in the mid-1980s Reich had pleaded guilty to federal charges of trading on inside information while he was a partner in a prominent New York City law firm and served a one-year prison sentence. Nevertheless, he also knew that, from 1998 to 2000, Reich was employed as the President and CEO of Inamed Corporation, a publicly traded company, and had accomplished a significant turnaround of that company. Wertheimer knew that Reich had left Inamed in 2001 and might be interested in a new challenge.

A. SPECTRUMEDIX'S INSOLVENCY

By the beginning of July 2001, if not earlier, SpectruMedix was either insolvent or operating on the brink of insolvency. The Company had very little cash (or cash equivalents) and no material accounts receivable due. At the same time, the Company had substantial and increasing accounts payable, Adlerstein was not communicating with creditors, and key parts vendors were refusing to make deliveries unless paid in cash. Indisputably, SpectruMedix did not have sufficient cash on hand to meet its next employee payroll on July 13, 2001, and had no realistic expectation of receiving sufficient funds to do so from its operations. Moreover, the Company's auditors were unwilling to issue the opinion letter necessary for it to file an annual report with the SEC, which was due to be filed on July 10th.

B. THE JULY 9, 2001 BOARD MEETING

1. *Notice*

Wertheimer testified that, on or about July 5, 2001, he and Adlerstein spoke on the telephone about the deteriorating financial condition of the Company and matters relating to a significant arbitration involving SpectruMedix. In that proceeding, MW & E had moved to withdraw as counsel to SpectruMedix, as a result, among other things, of disputes over non-payment of fees and expenses. Wertheimer and Adlerstein may have discussed the fact that the arbitrator planned to hold a conference on the motion to withdraw on Monday, July 9, and wished to be able to speak to Adlerstein by telephone. Wertheimer testified that, during this conversation, Adlerstein agreed to convene a meeting of the board of directors at 11 a.m. on July 9, 2001, at MW & E's New York City offices. Wertheimer further testified that Adlerstein was aware that the topics to be discussed at the meeting would be (i) SpectruMedix's dire financial condition and immediate need for cash, (ii) the arbitration, including the need to retain new counsel, (iii) the formal execution of an agreement to retain O'Donnell, and (iv) the Company's certified public accountants' refusal to issue an audit opinion. Adlerstein maintains that, while he agreed to meet with Wertheimer on July 9 in MW & E's offices, the only purpose of that meeting was to be available to speak to the arbitrator about the motion to withdraw. He denies that he ever agreed to call a board meeting for that time or knew that one was to be held.

The trial record contains plainly divergent testimony on the subject of whether Adlerstein called the July 9 meeting or was given notice of it. Mencher, Reich, and Selbst all support Wertheimer's testimony, although they all learned about the meeting from Wertheimer. Thus, while their testimony is corroborative of his, it provides no independent evidence of Adlerstein's state of knowledge. Adlerstein's trial testimony was undermined by Karl Fazler, the Company's business manager, who spoke with Adlerstein on the morning of July 9, and remembered Adlerstein telling him that he was on his way to MW & E's offices in order to meet with the board of directors. At the same time, Adlerstein's testimony is buttressed, to some degree, by the fact that none of the directors received written notice of a meeting although, the evidence suggests, SpectruMedix usually circulated notice and a proposed agenda by e-mail.

2. *Adlerstein Was Kept in the Dark About the Reich Proposal*

Mencher's notes show that Reich first proposed terms for an acquisition of SpectruMedix no later than July 5. On that date, she had a teleconference with Wertheimer and Reich in which they discussed the outline of the transaction and the need to terminate Adlerstein. Her notes contain the entry "fire Joe + negotiate a settlement," followed by a summary of terms for his separation.

The documents necessary for a transaction with Reich were in draft form by July 6, 2001. Selbst sent these documents by e-mail to Wertheimer, Mencher, and Reich. He did not send them to Adlerstein, who was deliberately kept unaware that Reich had made a proposal until the July 9 meeting. At trial, Wertheimer was asked whether "[b]etween the time you got the proposal from Mr. Reich—until the time you walked in to the board meeting on July 9th, did you tell Doctor Adlerstein that you were negotiating a proposal with Ilan Reich. . . . " He responded that he had not:

> A. Because I wanted to save the company at that point. . . . So, no, I didn't tell him that this was going on, because I had no faith that he would—that he would, first of all, you know, go along with the deal; but secondly, I was also worried that he would do something to scare off the investor.

Although Adlerstein argues that the Reich proposal was finalized on Friday, July 6, the record supports the conclusion that Reich and Wertheimer were still negotiating some terms of the deal on the morning of July 9 and that final documents were not ready until that time. The deal finally negotiated provided, subject to board approval, that the Reich Partnership would invest $1 million in SpectruMedix, Reich would assume the active management of SpectruMedix, and SpectruMedix would issue shares of its Series C Preferred Stock to the Reich Partnership carrying with them voting control of the Company.

3. *The Meeting Occurs*

Adlerstein arrived late at MW & E's New York City offices to find Selbst and Wertheimer waiting for him. He inquired about the conference with the arbitrator and was told that the matter had been postponed. Mencher was hooked in by phone and, according to Wertheimer, Adlerstein called the meeting to order and "wanted to talk about lawyers and the arbitration." Wertheimer then interrupted and said that they needed to talk about finances. He then told Adlerstein that there was a proposal from Reich and handed him a term sheet showing the material elements of the deal.

After reviewing it, Adlerstein told Wertheimer and Mencher that he was not interested in the Reich proposal because it would dilute his shares in the Company and result in him losing voting control. He has since testified that his lack of interest was also because he believed the price of $1 million to be insufficient for control of SpectruMedix. He did not, however, voice this concern at the time.

In response to the objection that he did voice, Wertheimer and Mencher explained that in their judgment the Company was in immediate need of funds and the investment by Reich was needed to avoid liquidation. Wertheimer asked Adlerstein directly if he was personally in a position to provide the needed funds. Adlerstein responded that he was not.

Wertheimer and Mencher tried to engage Adlerstein in further discussion about the Reich proposal, but Adlerstein sat silent. He testified that the reason for his silence was advice given to him by Selbst in the past: "when in doubt about what to do in a situation like this, keep your mouth shut." Because he and Mencher could not get Adlerstein to engage in any dialogue regarding the proposed transaction, Wertheimer moved the transaction for a vote. Wertheimer testified:

> There was no use in talking about it, because [Adlerstein] wouldn't talk. . . . So the fact that the discussion didn't go any longer, the finger should not be pointed at us, it should be pointed at the person that cut off the discussion. That is Doctor Adlerstein.

Adlerstein has testified that when the vote on the transaction was called he did not participate. The minutes of the meeting reflect that he voted "no." Each of the others present at the meeting—Wertheimer, Mencher, and Selbst—confirms the statement in the minutes.[19]

The board then took up the question of removing Adlerstein "for cause" from his office as CEO and Chairman of SpectruMedix. The elements of "cause" assigned were mismanagement of the Company, misrepresentations to his fellow board members as to its financial situation, and sexual harassment in contravention of his employment contract. After the meeting, the Reich Partnership executed and delivered a stockholder's written consent removing Adlerstein as a director of SpectruMedix. Reich was chosen to replace him.

Some months after July 9, Adlerstein executed a written consent purporting to vote his Series B Preferred shares to remove Wertheimer and Mencher from the board. Adlerstein initiated this Section 225 action on September 11, 2001.

III.

The general purpose of Section 225 is to provide "a quick method of review of the corporate election process in order to prevent a corporation from being immobilized by controversies as to who are its proper officers and directors." Because it is summary in nature, a Section 225 proceeding is limited to those issues that must necessarily be considered in order to resolve a disputed corporate election process. A Section 225 action focuses narrowly on the corporate election at issue and is not an appropriate occasion to resolve matters ancillary or secondary to that election.

---

19. Adlerstein also testified that, when he realized Wertheimer and Mencher were prepared to act against his interests, he asked Selbst about using his voting power to prevent this from happening. According to Adlerstein, Selbst told him that he could not, due to a 10-day notice requirement for convening a meeting of shareholders. The others deny that this exchange took place. According to the minutes of the July 9 meeting, the second item of business was an amendment to the Company's bylaws, approved by a vote of 2 to 1, with Adlerstein opposed. Prior to its amendment, the bylaw purported to proscribe shareholder action by written consent. Of course, this bylaw was very likely unenforceable as a matter of Delaware law. Datapoint Corp. v. Plaza Sec. Co., 496 A.2d 1031, 1035 (Del. 1985). The importance of this bylaw and its effect on Adlerstein's right to remove Wertheimer and Mencher was not explored by the parties at trial.

Here, the question is whether the meeting held on July 9 was a meeting of the board of directors or not. If it was not, Adlerstein continues to exercise a majority of the voting power and is now the sole lawful director. If it was, I must then address a welter of arguments advanced by Adlerstein to prove that the actions taken at the July 9 meeting ought to be invalidated because Wertheimer and Mencher (and Selbst) all operated in secret to negotiate terms with Reich while keeping Adlerstein deliberately uninformed about their plan to present the Reich proposal at the July 9 meeting. The more persuasive of these arguments are predicated largely on the decisions of the Court of Chancery in VGS, Inc. v. Castiel [2000 Del. Ch. LEXIS 122 (Del. Ch. 2000)] and Koch v. Stearn [1992 Del. Ch. LEXIS 163 (Del. Ch. 1992)].

Finally, if all else fails, Adlerstein argues that Wertheimer and Mencher violated their fiduciary duties of care and loyalty to SpectruMedix in approving the Reich trans-action with inadequate information and on terms that were unfair to the Company and its stockholders. He asks for an order canceling the shares and disregarding any effort by Reich to vote them.

For the reasons next discussed, I conclude that, although the meeting of July 9 was called as a board meeting, the actions taken at it must be invalidated. Thus, it is unnecessary to reach the last issue presented by Adlerstein.

A. THE CALL OF THE MEETING

On balance, the evidence at trial indicates that Adlerstein called the July 9 meet-ing. The procedure for giving notice of a board meeting is typically set forth in a Company's certificate or bylaws. The bylaws of SpectruMedix provide that special meetings of the board "may be called by the president on two (2) days' notice to each director by mail or forty-eight (48) hours notice to each director either personally or by telegram. . . ." I credit Wertheimer's account of his July 5 telephone call with Adlerstein. There is no reason to believe that Adlerstein would not have agreed to convene a board meeting on July 9, in view of the many urgent problems confront-ing SpectruMedix at that time. Fazler's testimony that Adlerstein called him on the morning of the meeting and said that he was on his way to a board meeting provides additional support for Wertheimer on this point.

In reaching this conclusion, I have considered and reject Adlerstein's argument that the lack of any written notice or agenda for the July 9 meeting proves that it was not a board meeting. Concededly, the record supports Adlerstein's contention that, on many other occasions, someone, usually Selbst, distributed notices and agen-das for board meetings of SpectruMedix. Nevertheless, the SpectruMedix bylaws do not require either written notice or the advanced distribution of a proposed agenda. Moreover, the record shows that, on other occasions, meetings of the board of direc-tors were held without written notice or an agenda.

B. THE VALIDITY OF THE ACTIONS TAKEN AT THE JULY 9 MEETING

A more difficult issue is whether the decision of Wertheimer, Mencher, and Selbst (no doubt with the knowledge of Reich) to keep Adlerstein uninformed about their plan to present the Reich proposal for consideration at the July 9 meeting invalidates the board's approval of that proposal at the meeting.

There are several factors that weigh against a finding of invalidity. The first is the absence from SpectruMedix's bylaws of any requirement of prior notice of agenda items for meetings of the board of directors, coupled with the absence of any hard and fast legal rule that directors be given advance notice of all matters to be considered at a meeting. Second, is the good faith belief of Wertheimer and Mencher that Adlerstein should be removed from management and that, if they had told him about the Reich proposal ahead of time, he would have done something to kill the deal. Third, is the fact of SpectruMedix's insolvency and the argument that the exigencies created by that insolvency gave Wertheimer and Mencher legal warrant to "spring" the Reich proposal on Adlerstein without warning.

Ultimately, I am unable to agree that these factors, either singly or in the aggregate, provide legal justification for the conduct of the July 9 meeting. Instead, I conclude that in the context of the set of legal rights that existed within SpectruMedix at the time of the July 9 meeting, Adlerstein was entitled to know ahead of time of the plan to issue new Series C Preferred Stock with the purposeful effect of destroying his voting control over the Company. This right to advance notice derives from a basic requirement of our corporation law that boards of directors conduct their affairs in a manner that satisfies minimum standards of fairness.

Here, the decision to keep Adlerstein in the dark about the plan to introduce the Reich proposal was significant because Adlerstein possessed the contractual power to prevent the issuance of the Series C Preferred Stock by executing a written consent removing one or both of Wertheimer and Mencher from the board. He may or may not have exercised this power had he been told about the plan in advance. But he was fully entitled to the opportunity to do so and the machinations of those individuals who deprived him of this opportunity were unfair and cannot be countenanced by this court.[28]

This result is consistent with the results reached in similar cases. For example, in VGS, Inc. v. Castiel, the court struck down a merger approved by the written consent of two out of three managers of a Delaware LLC for the purpose of transferring voting control over the enterprise from one member to another. Because the disadvantaged member (who was the third manager) possessed the power to remove one of the other two managers and, thus, could have prevented the merger from happening, the court

---

28. The outcome in this case flows from the fact the Adlerstein was both a director and a controlling stockholder, not from either status individually. In the absence of some special contractual right, there is no authority to support the argument that Adlerstein's stockholder status entitled him to advance notice of actions proposed to be taken at a meeting of the board of directors. The actions may be voidable if improperly motivated. Condec v. Lunkenheimer, [230 A.2d 769] (Del. Ch. 1967). But the absence (or presence) of notice is not a critical factor. Similarly, in the absence of a bylaw or other custom or regulation requiring that directors be given advance notice of items proposed for action at board meetings, there is no reason to believe that the failure to give such notice alone would ordinarily give rise to a claim of invalidity. Dillon v. Berg, 326 F. Supp. 1214, 1221 (D. Del.), aff'd, 453 F.2d 876 (3d Cir. 1971). Nevertheless, when a director either is the controlling stockholder or represents the controlling stockholder, our law takes a different view of the matter where the decision to withhold advance notice is done for the purpose of preventing the controlling stockholder/director from exercising his or her contractual right to put a halt to the other director's schemes.

concluded that it was a breach of the duty of loyalty for the others to have acted in secret to effect the transaction. As then Vice Chancellor (now Justice) Steele wrote:

> While a majority of the board acted by written consent, as all involved surely knew, had the original member's manager received notice beforehand that his appointed manager contemplated action against his interests he would have promptly attempted to remove him. Because the two managers acted without notice to the third manager under circumstances where they knew that with notice . . . he could have acted to protect his majority interest, they breached their duty of loyalty to the original member and their fellow manager by failing to act in good faith.

Adlerstein argues that the rationale of *VGS* operates *a fortiori* in this case because the documents that governed the LLC in *VGS* allowed the LLC's managers to act by non-unanimous written consent. Thus, there was no legal necessity for them to meet with the third manager at all. Despite this unusual governance provision, the court ruled that the two managers owed a fiduciary duty to the other, in both his managerial and membership capacities, to disclose their plan to authorize the dilutive merger in order to allow him to exercise his voting control to protect his controlling position. Here, Wertheimer and Mencher could not act outside of a meeting and could not convene a meeting without notice to Adlerstein. Thus, Adlerstein argues, their obligation to give him advance notice of the Reich proposal is even clearer.

It is difficult to accept this argument fully because the absence of a meeting was itself a fundamental problem in *VGS*. If there had been a meeting, it is likely that Castiel, the controlling member, would have had some opportunity to protect himself at that time by immediately removing the third manager from office. Here, by contrast, there was a meeting, and Adlerstein had some notice of the Reich proposal before it was approved by the SpectruMedix board of directors. The question is whether he had an adequate opportunity to protect his interests.

The same question has been addressed in other cases, most notably, in Koch v. Stearn. In that case, there was a four-person board of directors and two stockholders, Stearn and Koch, each of whom had the right to appoint (and remove) two directors. Due to substantial financial pressures on the Company, three of the directors decided that Stearn should be removed from his positions as Chairman and Chief Executive Officer. They invited Stearn and his counsel to attend a meeting but did not send to either of them the draft resolutions that they had circulated among themselves calling for Stearn's removal. The board met and, over Stearn's vigorous objection, adopted the resolutions. Either then, or later in the meeting, Stearn called for his designee to quit the board but did not execute the written consent of stockholders necessary under Section 228 of the DGCL to effect the removal and replacement of that director.

The court concluded that Stearn's presence at the meeting was obtained by trickery or deceit because his fellow directors hid from him their plans for his ouster. Alternatively, the court found that, even if Stearn had waived his objection to the meeting by remaining and participating, the actions taken were, nonetheless, void, for the following reasons:

> I find that Stearn was disadvantaged by the other directors' failure to communicate their plans to him. If Stearn had seen the draft resolutions before the meeting, he could have exercised his right to remove [his designee] as a director and he could have replaced [him] with another nomi-

nee who would vote with Stearn to block Stearn's removal. Without doubt, Stearn's inability to thus protect himself constituted a disadvantage.

It is equally the case here that Adlerstein was disadvantaged "by the other directors' failure to communicate their plans to him." Had he known beforehand that Wertheimer and Mencher intended to approve the Reich proposal and to remove him from office at the July 9 meeting, he could have exercised his legal right to remove one or both of them and, thus, prevented the completion of those plans. The authority of both *Koch* and *VGS* strongly support the conclusion that Adlerstein had a right to such advance notice in order that he might have taken steps to protect his interests. . . .

IV.

For all the foregoing reasons, I have concluded that the actions taken at the July 9, 2001 meeting must be undone. Nevertheless, I recognize that the financial and business condition of SpectruMedix has changed materially since July 9, 2001. I also note plaintiff's proposal, during the trial, that I should appoint a custodian for SpectruMedix rather than reinstate Adlerstein's control. Under these circumstances, before entering a final order, the court will solicit the parties' views as to the appropriate form of relief. . . .

PROBLEM 3-8

Biotech, Inc. has 10 million common shares. As specified by its bylaws, Biotech has a nine-member board, divided into three equal classes. As specified in its articles, the corporation also has cumulative voting. Biotech's largest shareholder, Gene Robbins, owns 2 million shares. A small group of institutional investors (the Powers) collectively own 3 million shares. The remainder of the corporation's shares are widely held.

On March 10, Biotech's board fired CEO Gene Robbins in response to concerns expressed by the Powers. In late March, new CEO Helen Hall called a special board meeting to which Robbins was not invited and informed the board that she had uncovered evidence that Robbins lied to the board in several recent reports.

The board wishes to remove Robbins as a director. Assume, alternatively, that Biotech is incorporated in Delaware or in an MBCA jurisdiction. Evaluate all of the board's options for seeking Robbins's removal. What are the advantages and disadvantages of each? Are any options foreclosed?

c.   *Using Shareholder Authority to Change the Bylaws*
Delaware G.C.L. §§109, 112, 113, 141
MBCA §§2.06, 8.01, 10.20

(1)   LIMITS FROM THE CHARTER OR MANAGEMENT PLANNING

Shareholders may desire to use their power to amend bylaws in order to change statutory default rules or modifications that have been made to those rules. If such changes are sought as part of a struggle for control of the corporations, as will normally be the case, the board of director will almost certainly oppose such shareholder actions. In such case the outcome of the power struggle may depend on how corporate planners have structured the corporation.

A recurring setting for this type of battle is insurgent shareholder attempts to either eliminate or get around a staggered board provision. If the staggered board provision is contained in the certificate of incorporation and is further protected in the certificate by provisions requiring a supermajority vote to eliminate the staggered board, then shareholders likely will have no effective channel for immediate and direct action to take control.

Consider whether shareholders would have more success if they focused on changing the number of directors rather than repealing the staggered board provision. In Centaur Partners IV v. National Intergroup, Inc., 582 A.2d 923 (Del. 1990), National Intergroup's certificate of incorporation provided for a staggered board and required a vote of at least 80 percent of the shareholders to amend or repeal the charter provision or any similar provision in the bylaws. The bylaws provision implementing the staggered board provision, which had a parallel 80 percent supermajority requirement for repeal or changes, also provided that the number of directors shall be fixed by a resolution of a majority of the entire board. Centaur Partners, a 16 percent shareholder, sought to enlarge the board from nine to 15 and to elect the new directors at the next annual meeting, and wanted that action to be covered by the default rule of majority vote, not the supermajority specified for staggered board provisions. The Delaware Supreme Court first noted the strong presumption in favor of majority rule in corporate law but nevertheless rejected Centaur Partners' argument that majority rule should apply to this change.

> There exists in Delaware "a general policy against disenfranchisement." This policy is based upon the belief that "[t]he shareholder franchise is the ideological underpinning upon which the legitimacy of directorial power rests." Therefore, high vote requirements which purport to protect minority shareholders by disenfranchising the majority, must be clear and unambiguous. There must be no doubt that the shareholders intended that a supermajority would be required. When a provision which seeks to require the approval of a supermajority is unclear or ambiguous, the fundamental principle of majority rule will be held to apply.

Id. at 927 (internal citations omitted).

The Court then explained why National Intergroup's planning would be respected, despite the strong presumption in favor of majority rule.

> Corporate charters and by-laws are contracts among the shareholders of a corporation and the general rules of contract interpretation are held to apply. In the interpretation of charter and by-law provisions, "[c]ourts must give effect to the intent of the parties as revealed by the language of the certificate and the circumstances surrounding its creation and adoption." Therefore, the intent of the stockholders in enacting particular charter or by-law amendments is instructive in determining whether any ambiguity exists.
>
> In the present case, the context in which the amendments to the certificate of incorporation and accompanying by-laws were approved by the shareholders indicates that they were adopted in tandem and intended to be complementary. The relevant amendments to the certificate of incorporation and the accompanying by-law provision were adopted at the 1984 annual stockholders meeting. The changes were contained in the proxy materials which were distributed to

the stockholders prior to the 1984 annual meeting. In a section entitled "Election of Directors by Class," the proxy materials state:

> [t]he Board of Directors has unanimously adopted resolutions recommending that the stockholders amend the Corporation's Certificate of Incorporation and the Corporation's By-Laws to provide for the division of the Corporation's directors into three classes, the directors in each class to serve for a term of three years. . . . The proposed amendments also contain a provision, which if adopted, shall provide that the affirmative vote of the holders of 80% or more of the outstanding stock of the Corporation be required to amend or repeal these new provisions in the Certificate of Incorporation and the By-Laws.

This explanation illustrates the intended result of the proposed combined change in the charter and by-laws that the board be classified and that a supermajority vote of 80 percent or more be required to amend any portion of these two provisions.

The classification of the board and the 80% supermajority vote are designed to insure continuity in the board of directors and avoid hostile attempts to take over the corporation. As the proxy materials recite:

> [a] further purpose of the proposed change is to discourage unfriendly takeovers of the Corporation. The attempts to seize control of public companies through the accumulation of substantial stock positions followed by a tender offer and squeeze out merger are well known today. These transactions are often followed by a substantial restructuring of the company, a significant disposition of assets or other extraordinary corporate action.

Given the clear language of the proxy materials, the conclusion is inescapable that the stockholders, in adopting these two provisions, evidenced an intent to classify the board and impose an 80% supermajority requirement on amendments to these sections in order to thwart attempts to seize control of National.

Id. at 928 (internal citations omitted).

The following case involves a different clash between staggered voting and corporate norms. As you read this case, consider what norms the court is protecting. Has the court properly carried out its function and properly respected private ordering, or has it improperly engaged in judicial legislation? As a planner, what lessons would you take from this case?

Airgas, Inc. v. Air Products and Chemicals, Inc.
Delaware Supreme Court
8 A.3d 1182 (2010)

RIDGELY, JUSTICE:

Air Products and Chemicals, Inc. ("Air Products") and Airgas, Inc. ("Airgas") are competitors in the industrial gas business. Air Products has launched a public tender offer to acquire 100% of Airgas's shares. The Airgas board of directors has received and rejected several bids from Air Products, including its latest offer that valued Airgas at $5.5 billion, because the board determined that each offer undervalued the company. During this entire attempted takeover period, the market price of Airgas stock exceeded Air Products' offers.

To facilitate its takeover attempt, Air Products engaged in a proxy contest at the last annual meeting of Airgas stockholders. Airgas has a staggered board with nine directors, and three were up for election at that meeting. A staggered board, which

Delaware law has permitted since 1899, enhances the bargaining power of a target's board and makes it more difficult for an acquirer, like Air Products, to gain control of its target without the consent of the board.

At Airgas's last annual meeting held on September 15, 2010, Air Products nominated three directors to Airgas's board, and the Airgas shareholders elected them. Air Products also proposed a bylaw (the "January Bylaw") that would schedule Airgas's next annual meeting for January 2011, just four months after the 2010 annual meeting. The January Bylaw, which was approved by only 45.8% of the shares entitled to vote, effectively reduced the full term of the incumbent directors by eight months.

Airgas brought this action in the Court of Chancery, claiming that the January Bylaw is invalid because it is inconsistent with title 8, section 141 of the Delaware Code and the Airgas corporate charter provision that creates a staggered board. Airgas's charter requires an affirmative vote of the holders of at least 67% of the voting power of all shares to alter, amend, or repeal the staggered board provision, or to adopt any bylaw inconsistent with that provision. The Court of Chancery upheld the January Bylaw on the following basis: Airgas's charter provides that directors serve terms that expire at "the annual meeting of stockholders held in the third year following the year of their election." There is no inconsistency between Airgas's charter provision and the January Bylaw, because the January meeting would occur "in the third year after the directors' election," which (the Court of Chancery found) was all that the Airgas charter requires.

We conclude, as did the Court of Chancery, that the Airgas charter language defining the duration of directors' terms is ambiguous. We therefore look to extrinsic evidence to interpret the intent of the charter language which provides that directors' terms expire at "the annual meeting of stockholders held in the third year following the year of their election." We find that the language has been understood to mean that the Airgas directors serve three year terms. We hold that because the January Bylaw prematurely terminates the Airgas directors' terms, conferred by the charter and the statute, by eight months, the January Bylaw is invalid. Accordingly, we reverse.

FACTS AND PROCEDURAL HISTORY

THE CHARTER, THE BYLAWS, AND THE STAGGERED BOARD OF AIRGAS

Section 141(d) of the Delaware General Corporation Law ("DGCL"), which allows corporations to implement a staggered board of directors, relevantly provides:

> The directors of any corporation organized under this chapter may, by the certificate of incorporation or by an initial bylaw, or by a bylaw adopted by a vote of the stockholders, be divided into 1, 2 or 3 classes; the term of office of those of the first class to expire at the first annual meeting held after such classification becomes effective; of the second class *1 year thereafter; of the third class 2 years thereafter;* and at each annual election held after such classification becomes effective, directors shall be chosen for a full term, as the case may be, to succeed those whose terms expire. . . .

Ever since Airgas became a public corporation in 1986, it has had a three class staggered board by virtue of Article 5, Section 1 of its charter (the "Airgas Charter" or the "Charter"), which relevantly provides:

Number, Election and Term of Directors. . . . The Directors . . . shall be classified, with respect to the time for which they severally hold office, into three classes, as nearly equal in number as possible as shall be provided in the manner specified in the By-laws, one class to hold office initially for a term expiring at the annual meeting of stockholders to be held in 1987, another class to hold office initially for a term expiring at the annual meeting of stockholders to be held in 1988, and another class to hold office initially for a term expiring at the annual meeting of stockholders to be held in 1989, with the members of each class to hold office until their successors are elected and qualified. At each annual meeting of the stockholders of the Corporation, the successors to the class of Directors whose term expires at that meeting shall be elected to hold office for a term expiring at the annual meeting of stockholders held in the third year following the year of their election.

[The Court also sets out the section of the Airgas bylaws (the "Bylaws"), which implements the classified board provision of the charter and other sections of the charter that require a supermajority vote to enact a bylaw inconsistent with the staggered board or to remove a director without cause.]

Airgas has consistently held its annual meetings to enable the staggered directors to serve three year terms. Since it "went public" in 1986, Airgas has held its annual meeting no earlier than July 28 and no later than September 15 of each calendar year. Because Airgas's fiscal year ends on March 31, Airgas traditionally has held its annual meeting in late summer or early fall, to afford Airgas the necessary time to evaluate its fiscal year performance and prepare its annual report. Airgas always has held its annual meetings approximately twelve months apart. It has never held consecutive annual meetings sooner than eleven months, twenty-six days apart, or longer than twelve months, twenty-eight days since the prior annual meeting.

AIR PRODUCTS' TAKEOVER ATTEMPT

On February 11, 2010, Air Products commenced a tender offer for Airgas shares at a purchase price of $60 per share cash. On July 8, 2010, Air Products raised its offer price to $63.50 per share cash, and on September 6, 2010, Air Products again increased its bid to $65.50 per share cash. The Airgas board rejected all these bids as "grossly inadequate." The market for Airgas stock suggests that the board was correct: since Air Products launched the tender offer, Airgas shares have traded as high as $71.28. The market price closed at $69.31 on November 3, 2010, the day the parties presented their arguments to this Court.

After Airgas's board rejected Air Products' bids, Air Products could have negotiated with Airgas's board to agree on a mutually beneficial price. Instead, Air Products chose to wage a proxy contest to facilitate its tender offer. As part of its takeover strategy, Air Products nominated three persons to stand for election to Airgas's staggered board. Air Products also proposed three bylaw amendments including the January Bylaw, which relevantly provides:

The annual meeting of stockholders to be held in 2011 (the "2011 Annual Meeting") shall be held on January 18, 2011 at 10:00 a.m., and each subsequent annual meeting of stockholders shall be held in January. . . .

The January Bylaw is significant for two reasons. First, the January Bylaw substantially shortens the terms of the Airgas directors by accelerating the timing of Airgas's annual meeting. The January Bylaw would require Airgas to hold its 2011 annual meeting only four months after its 2010 meeting. That accelerated meeting date would contravene nearly two and one-half decades of Airgas practice, during which Airgas never has held its annual meeting earlier than July 28. That would also mark the first time Airgas held an annual meeting without having new fiscal year results to report to its shareholders. Additionally, if the January Bylaw is valid, Air Products need not wait a year to cause the election of another three directors to Airgas's staggered board, because the terms of the incumbent directors would be shortened by eight months.

At Airgas's annual meeting on September 15, 2010, Airgas shareholders elected the three Air Products nominees to Airgas's board and adopted Air Products' proposed bylaw amendments, including the January Bylaw. Of the 73,886,665 shares voted, a bare majority-38,321,496 shares, or 51.8%-were voted in favor of the January Bylaw. But of the 83,629,731 shares that were entitled to vote, only 45.8% were voted in favor of the January Bylaw . . .

ANALYSIS

STANDARD OF REVIEW

"Because the facts material to these claims are uncontroverted, the issues presented are all essentially questions of law that this Court reviews *de novo*." Corporate charters and bylaws are contracts among a corporation's shareholders; therefore, our rules of contract interpretation apply. If charter or bylaw provisions are unclear, we resolve any doubt in favor of the stockholders' electoral rights. "Words and phrases used in a bylaw are to be given their commonly accepted meaning unless the context clearly requires a different one or unless legal phrases having a special meaning are used." Where extrinsic evidence resolves any ambiguity, we "must give effect to the intent of the parties as revealed by the language of the certificate and the circumstances surrounding its creation and adoption."

SECTION 141(D) OF THE DGCL, THE ANNUAL MEETING TERM ALTERNATIVE, AND THE DEFINED TERM ALTERNATIVE

To implement a staggered board, as permitted by DGCL Section 141, corporations typically have used two forms of language. Many corporations provide in their charters that each class of directors serves until the "annual meeting of stockholders to be held in the third year following the year of their election." There are variations on this language, providing (for example) that each class of directors serves until the "third succeeding annual meeting following the year of their election" (collectively, the "Annual Meeting Term Alternative"). On the other hand, some corporations, such as the firm involved in *Essential Enterprises v. Automatic Steel Products, Inc.,* [159 A.2d 288 (Del. Ch. 1960)] provide in their charters that each class serves for a "term of three years." There are variations on that language as well, such as (for example) that each class of directors serves for "a three-year term" (collectively, the "Defined Term Alternative"). Unlike the Annual Meeting Term Alternative, the Defined Term

Alternative unambiguously provides in the charter itself that each class of directors serves for three years.

Article 5, Section 1 of the Airgas Charter and Article III, Section 1 of its Bylaws both employ the Annual Meeting Term Alternative. The central issue presented on this appeal is whether the Airgas Charter requires that each class of directors serves three year terms or whether it provides for a term that can expire at whatever time the annual meeting is scheduled in the third year following election. The Court of Chancery adopted the latter view without giving any weight to the uncontroverted extrinsic evidence bearing on the intended meaning of the Airgas Charter.

THE COURT OF CHANCERY'S ANALYSIS

The Court of Chancery articulated its rationale this way:

> Airgas's charter provision is not crystal clear on its face. A "full term" expires at the "annual meeting" in the "third year" following a director's year of election. The absence of a definition of annual, year, or full term leads to this puzzle. Does a "full term" contemplate a durationally defined three year period as Airgas suggests? The charter does not explicitly say so. Then, if a "full term" expires at the "annual meeting," what does "annual" mean—yearly? In turn, if "annual" means "separated by about a year," does that mean fiscal year? Calendar year? . . .
>
> The lack of a clear definition of these terms in the charter mandates my treatment of them as ambiguous terms to be viewed in the light most favorable to the stockholder franchise.
>
> Construing the ambiguous terms in that way, if the "full term" of directors does expire at the "annual meeting" in the "third year" following their year of election, I now turn to what is meant by the "annual" meeting. . . . Because this term is not otherwise defined in Airgas's charter or bylaws, I turn to the common dictionary definition, which defines "annual" as "covering the period of a year" or "occurring or happening every year or once a year." And again, construing the ambiguous terms of the charter in favor of the shareholder franchise, "annual" in this context must mean occurring once a year. . . .
>
> Airgas similarly could have defined "annual meeting" elsewhere in its charter or bylaws to require a minimum durational interval between meetings (i.e. "annual meetings must be held no less than nine months apart"). It could have said that directors shall serve "three-year terms." Had it done any of those things, then a bylaw shortening such an explicitly defined "full term" would have conflicted with its explicit provisions and thereby would have been invalid under Airgas's charter. Airgas, however, did not clearly define these terms. Airgas's charter and bylaws simply say that the successor shall take the place of any director whose term has expired "in the third year" following the year of election.
>
> As such, a January 18, 2011 annual meeting would be the "2011 annual meeting." 2011 is the third "year" after 2008. Successors to the 2008 class can be elected in the "third year following the year of their election" which is 2011. Thus, the bylaw does not violate Airgas's charter as written.

Airgas, 2010 WL 3960599, at *6-8 (citations omitted).

We agree with the Court of Chancery that the relevant Charter language is ambiguous. But as more fully discussed below, there is overwhelming extrinsic evidence that under the Annual Meeting Term Alternative adopted by Airgas, a term of three years was intended. Therefore, the January Bylaw is inconsistent with Article 5, Section 1 of the Charter because it materially shortens the directors' full three year term that the Charter language requires. It is settled Delaware law that a bylaw that is inconsistent with the corporation's charter is invalid.

ARTICLE 5, SECTION 1 OF THE CHARTER IS AMBIGUOUS

To determine whether the January Bylaw is inconsistent with the Charter, we first must address Article 5, Section 1 of the Charter. Although the Annual Meeting Term Alternative employed in that section is facially ambiguous, our precedents, and the common understanding of that language enable us to interpret that provision definitively. The "context clearly requires" the interpretation we adopt, because the relevant "legal phrase[ ] ha[s] a special meaning," and because we "must give effect to the intent of the parties as revealed by the language of the certificate and the circumstances surrounding its creation and adoption." "If there is more than one reasonable interpretation of a disputed contract term, consideration of extrinsic evidence is required to determine the meanings the parties intended." Delaware courts often look to extrinsic evidence for the common understanding of ambiguous language whether in a statute, a rule or a contractual provision.

DELAWARE PRECEDENTS

Although this Court never has been called upon to interpret the Annual Meeting Term Alternative specifically, the Delaware cases that involved similar charter language regard that language as creating a staggered board with classes of directors who serve three year terms. The Court of Chancery case law similarly reflects the understanding of the Court of Chancery-until this case-that directors of staggered boards serve a three year term. The United States District Court for the District of Delaware, applying Delaware law, has reached the same conclusion.

THE ANNUAL MEETING TERM ALTERNATIVE AND THE DEFINED
TERM ALTERNATIVE IN PRACTICE

Although practice and understanding do not control the issue before us, we agree with Airgas that "[p]ractice and understanding in the real world" are relevant. Here, we find the industry practice and understanding of similar charter language to be persuasive. Of the eighty-nine Fortune 500 Delaware corporations that have staggered boards, fifty-eight corporations use the Annual Meeting Term Alternative. More important, forty-six of those fifty-eight Delaware corporations, or 79%, expressly represent in their proxy statements that their staggered-board directors serve three year terms. Indeed, Air Products itself uses the Annual Meeting Term Alternative in its charter, and represents in its proxy statement that: "Our Board is divided into three classes for purposes of election, with *three-year terms of office* ending in successive years."

Also noteworthy is the practice and understanding of corporations that have "de-staggered" their boards. Ninety-nine of the Fortune 500 Delaware corporations have de-staggered their boards over the last decade. Of those ninety-nine corporations, sixty-four used the Annual Meeting Term Alternative, and an overwhelming majority—sixty-two, or 97%—represented in their proxy statements that their directors served three year terms. We cannot ignore this widespread corporate practice and understanding it represents. It supports a construction that the Annual Meeting Term

Alternative is intended to provide that each class of directors serves three year terms. Air Products has offered no evidence to the contrary.

MODEL FORMS AND COMMENTARY

The ABA's *Public Company Organizational Documents: Model Forms and Commentary* contains the following model charter provision for a staggered board that repeats the language that has been commonly understood for decades to provide for a three year term:

> . . . At each annual meeting of stockholders beginning with the first annual meeting of stockholders following the filing of this certificate of incorporation, *the successors of the class of directors whose terms expires at that meeting shall be elected to hold office for a term expiring at the annual meeting of stockholders to be held in the third year following the year of their election,* with each director in each such class to hold office until his or her successor is duly elected and qualified.

Notably, the accompanying commentary explains:

> The DGCL permits the certificate of incorporation to provide that the board of directors may be divided into one, two, or three classes, with the term of office of those of the first class to expire at the annual meeting next ensuing; of the second class, one year thereafter; of the third class, two years thereafter, and at each annual election held after such classification and election, *directors elected to succeed those whose terms expire shall be elected for a three-year term.* DGCL Section 141(d).

Thus, this model form commentary confirms the understanding that the Annual Meeting Term Alternative intends to provide that each class of directors is elected for a three year term.

OTHER COMMENTARY

The DGCL, from its initial enactment in 1899, has authorized Delaware corporations to stagger the terms of their boards of directors. Although the statutory language has been amended from time to time, it has remained substantially the same over the past one hundred eleven years. As early as 1917, commentators understood that the staggered board provision contemplates three year director terms. In its 1917 pamphlet entitled *Business Corporations Under the Laws of Delaware,* the Corporation Trust Company commented: "[Directors] can be divided into one, two or three classes, to serve one, two and three years, and at each annual meeting the directors are elected to serve for the term of three years, so that one class expires each year. They are elected annually by the stockholders." This historical understanding that directors are elected to serve for the term of three years is significant.

ESSENTIAL ENTERPRISES V. AUTOMATIC STEEL PRODUCTS, INC

This same understanding has long been embedded in Delaware case law addressing issues similar to those presented in this case. Fifty years ago, Chancellor Seitz considered in *Essential Enterprises* whether a bylaw that authorized the removal of directors by a majority stockholder vote was inconsistent with a charter provision that provided for staggered, three-year terms for the corporation's directors. Although the charter provided that each class of directors "shall be elected to hold office for the term of three years," Chancellor Seitz found that the charter reflected the underlying intent of DGCL Section 141(d), and explained: "While the conflict considered is between the by-law and the certificate, the empowering statute is also involved since *the certificate provision is formulated basically in the words of the statute.*" Holding that the bylaw that authorized the removal of directors by a majority stockholder vote was inconsistent with the charter provision that authorized staggered three year terms for the corporation's directors, Chancellor Seitz concluded: "Clearly the 'full term' visualized by the statute is a period of three years-not up to three years;" and the bylaw would "frustrate the plan and purpose behind the provision for staggered terms. . . ."

Air Products contends that *Essential Enterprises* and this case are distinguishable in two ways. First, Air Products argues that *Essential Enterprises* was a director "removal" case, whereas this case is an "annual meeting" case. *In form,* the January Bylaw addresses the date of Airgas's annual meeting. But *in substance,* the January Bylaw, like the bylaw in *Essential Enterprises,* has the effect of prematurely removing Airgas's directors who would otherwise serve an additional eight months on Airgas's board. In that significant respect this case is indistinguishable from *Essential Enterprises.*

Second, Air Products argues that *Essential Enterprises* is distinguishable because the charter in that case explicitly stated that each class of directors "shall be elected to hold office for the term of three years," whereas the Annual Meeting Term Alternative does not. While that is true, our preceding discussion demonstrates that the Annual Meeting Term Alternative was intended, and has been commonly understood, to provide for three year terms.

In its opinion, the Court of Chancery distinguished *Essential Enterprises* as follows:

[*Essential Enterprises* explained] that DGCL Section 141(d) "says that 'directors shall be chosen for a full term.' The certificate implements this." . . . The charter in *Essential Enterprises* explicitly called for three-year terms; Airgas's charter does not. Thus, the "full term" specified by the charter in *Essential Enterprises* was three years. The "full term" visualized by the statute based on Airgas's charter is until "the annual meeting of stockholders held in the third year following the year of their election."

Thus, the Court of Chancery heavily relied on the different wording of the Annual Meeting Term Alternative and the Defined Term Alternative to arrive at its conclusion that different wording equates to different meaning. But in doing that the Court of Chancery erred, because it failed to give proper effect to the overwhelming and uncontroverted extrinsic evidence that establishes, and persuades us, that the Annual Meeting Term Alternative and the Defined Term Alternative language mean the same thing: that each class of directors serves three year terms.

No party to this case has argued that DGCL Section 141(d) or the Airgas Charter requires that the three year terms be measured with mathematical precision. Nor is it necessary for us to define with exactitude the parameters of what deviation from 365 days (multiplied by 3) satisfies the Airgas Charter three year durational requirement. In this specific case, we may safely conclude that under any construction of "annual" within the intended meaning of the Airgas Charter or title 8, section 141(d) of the Delaware Code, four months does not qualify. In substance, the January Bylaw so extremely truncates the directors' term as to constitute a *de facto* removal that is inconsistent with the Airgas Charter. The consequence of the January Bylaw is similar to the bylaw at issue in *Essential Enterprises*. It serves to "frustrate the plan and purpose behind the provision for [Airgas's] staggered terms and [ ] it is incompatible with the pertinent language of the statute and the [Charter]." Accordingly, the January Bylaw is invalid not only because it impermissibly shortens the directors' three year staggered terms as provided by Article 5, Section 1 of the Airgas Charter, but also because it amounted to a *de facto* removal without cause of those directors without the affirmative vote of 67% of the voting power of all shares entitled to vote, as Article 5, Section 3 of the Charter required.

(2)   LIMITS ON WHAT SHAREHOLDERS CAN DO IN BYLAWS

Shareholder ability to use the bylaw to change governance is also constrained by limits on what bylaws can do. State corporation law grants primary management authority to the board of directors while reserving to the shareholders concurrent authority to make and amend bylaws. Delaware G.C.L. §141(a) provides that "[t]he business and affairs of [a] corporation . . . shall be managed by or under the direction of the board of directors, except as may be otherwise provided in this chapter or in the certificate of incorporation." Thus, looking solely at §141(a), one would conclude that the board of directors has exclusive power to manage the business and affairs of a corporation unless a provision in the certificate of incorporation limits the power and authority of the directors. Delaware G.C.L. §109(b) provides that "[t]he bylaws may contain any provision, not inconsistent with law or with the certificate of incorporation, relating to the business of the corporation, the conduct of its affairs, and its rights or powers or the rights or powers of its stockholders, directors, officers or employees." Under Delaware G.C.L. §109(a), "the power to adopt, amend or repeal bylaws shall be in the stockholders entitled to vote. . . ." Directors may be given concurrent authority to adopt, amend, or repeal bylaws by provision in the certificate of incorporation. Thus, looking only at Delaware G.C.L. §109, it would appear that the shareholders have inherent authority to take a broad array of actions "relating to the business of the corporation, the conduct of its affairs, and . . . the rights or powers of [] shareholders, directors, officers or employees."

How do we reconcile these two overlapping grants of authority? Suppose, for example, that a shareholder is proposing an amendment to a company's bylaws to require that plant closings be prohibited unless approved by a vote of the shareholders. Is there a way to reconcile the conflicting statutory provisions? Are there core common law principles that can explain away the apparent conflicting grants of authority or that require a different interpretation of the literal language of the statute? The following case gives the Delaware Supreme Court's answer. Be alert for the role that statutory interpretation and common law principles play in the court's analysis. As you read this case, keep in mind that other jurisdictions may have slightly different statutory schemes that could cause a reviewing court in those jurisdictions to find greater or lesser space for shareholder action.

CA, Inc. v. AFSCME Employees Pension Plan
Delaware Supreme Court
953 A.2d 227 (en banc 2008)

Upon Certification of Questions of Law from the United States Securities and Exchange Commission.

JACOBS, JUSTICE.

I. FACTS

CA is a Delaware corporation whose board of directors consists of twelve persons, all of whom sit for reelection each year. CA's annual meeting of stockholders is scheduled to be held on September 9, 2008. CA intends to file its definitive proxy materials with the SEC on or about July 24, 2008 in connection with that meeting.

AFSCME, a CA stockholder, is associated with the American Federation of State, County and Municipal Employees. On March 13, 2008, AFSCME submitted a proposed stockholder bylaw (the "Bylaw" or "proposed Bylaw") for inclusion in the Company's proxy materials for its 2008 annual meeting of stockholders. The Bylaw, if adopted by CA stockholders, would amend the Company's bylaws to provide as follows:

> RESOLVED, that pursuant to section 109 of the Delaware General Corporation Law and Article IX of the bylaws of CA, Inc., stockholders of CA hereby amend the bylaws to add the following Section 14 to Article II:

> The board of directors shall cause the corporation to reimburse a stockholder or group of stockholders (together, the "Nominator") for reasonable expenses ("Expenses") incurred in connection with nominating one or more candidates in a contested election of directors to the corporation's board of directors, including, without limitation, printing, mailing, legal, solicitation, travel, advertising and public relations expenses, so long as (a) the election of fewer than 50% of the directors to be elected is contested in the election, (b) one or more candidates nominated by the Nominator are elected to the corporation's board of directors, (c) stockholders are not permitted to cumulate their votes for directors, and (d) the election occurred, and the Expenses were incurred, after this bylaw's adoption. The amount paid to a Nominator under this bylaw in respect of a contested election shall not exceed the amount expended by the corporation in connection with such election.

CA's current bylaws and Certificate of Incorporation have no provision that specifically addresses the reimbursement of proxy expenses. Of more general relevance, however, is Article SEVENTH, Section (1) of CA's Certificate of Incorporation, which tracks the language of 8 *Del. C.* §141(a) and provides that:

> The management of the business and the conduct of the affairs of the corporation shall be vested in [CA's] Board of Directors.

It is undisputed that the decision whether to reimburse election expenses is presently vested in the discretion of CA's board of directors, subject to their fiduciary duties and applicable Delaware law.

On April 18, 2008, CA notified the SEC's Division of Corporation Finance (the "Division") of its intention to exclude the proposed Bylaw from its 2008 proxy materials.

The Company requested from the Division a "no-action letter" stating that the Division would not recommend any enforcement action to the SEC if CA excluded the AFSCME proposal.[2] CA's request for a no-action letter was accompanied by an opinion from its Delaware counsel, Richards Layton & Finger, P.A. ("RL&F"). The RL&F opinion concluded that the proposed Bylaw is not a proper subject for stockholder action, and that if implemented, the Bylaw would violate the Delaware General Corporation Law ("DGCL").

On May 21, 2008, AFSCME responded to CA's no-action request with a letter taking the opposite legal position. The AFSCME letter was accompanied by an opinion from AFSCME's Delaware counsel, Grant & Eisenhofer, P.A. ("G&E"). The G&E opinion concluded that the proposed Bylaw is a proper subject for shareholder action and that if adopted, would be permitted under Delaware law.

The Division was thus confronted with two conflicting legal opinions on Delaware law. Whether or not the Division would determine that CA may exclude the proposed Bylaw from its 2008 proxy materials would depend upon which of these conflicting views is legally correct. To obtain guidance, the SEC, at the Division's request, certified two questions of Delaware law to this Court. Given the short timeframe for the filing of CA's proxy materials, we concluded that "there are important and urgent reasons for an immediate determination of the questions certified," and accepted those questions for review on July 1, 2008.

II. THE CERTIFIED QUESTIONS

The two questions certified to us by the SEC are as follows:

1. Is the AFSCME Proposal a proper subject for action by shareholders as a matter of Delaware law?
2. Would the AFSCME Proposal, if adopted, cause CA to violate any Delaware law to which it is subject? . . .

III. THE FIRST QUESTION

A. PRELIMINARY COMMENTS

The first question presented is whether the Bylaw is a proper subject for shareholder action, more precisely, whether the Bylaw may be proposed and enacted by shareholders without the concurrence of the Company's board of directors. Before proceeding further, we make some preliminary comments in an effort to delineate a framework within which to begin our analysis.

First, the DGCL empowers both the board of directors and the shareholders of a Delaware corporation to adopt, amend or repeal the corporation's bylaws. 8 *Del. C.* §109(a) relevantly provides that:

---

2. Under Sections (i)(1) and (i)(2) of SEC Rule 14a-8, a company may exclude a stockholder proposal from its proxy statement if the proposal "is not a proper subject for action by the shareholders under the laws of the jurisdiction of the company's organization," or where the proposal, if implemented, "would cause the company to violate any state law to which it is subject." *See* 17 C.F.R. §240.14a-8.

> After a corporation has received any payment for any of its stock, the power to adopt, amend or repeal bylaws shall be in the stockholders entitled to vote . . . ; provided, however, any corporation may, in its certificate of incorporation, confer the power to adopt, amend or repeal bylaws upon the directors. . . . The fact that such power has been so conferred upon the directors . . . shall not divest the stockholders . . . of the power, nor limit their power to adopt, amend or repeal bylaws.

Pursuant to Section 109(a), CA's Certificate of Incorporation confers the power to adopt, amend or repeal the bylaws upon the Company's board of directors. Because the statute commands that that conferral "shall not divest the stockholders . . . of . . . nor limit" their power, both the board and the shareholders of CA, independently and concurrently, possess the power to adopt, amend and repeal the bylaws.

Second, the vesting of that concurrent power in both the board and the shareholders raises the issue of whether the stockholders' power is coextensive with that of the board, and vice versa. As a purely theoretical matter that is possible, and were that the case, then the first certified question would be easily answered. That is, under such a regime any proposal to adopt, amend or repeal a bylaw would be a proper subject for either shareholder or board action, without distinction. But the DGCL has not allocated to the board and the shareholders the identical, coextensive power to adopt, amend and repeal the bylaws. Therefore, how that power is allocated between those two decision-making bodies requires an analysis that is more complex.

Moving from the theoretical to this case, by its terms Section 109(a) vests in the shareholders a power to adopt, amend or repeal bylaws that is legally sacrosanct, *i.e.,* the power cannot be non-consensually eliminated or limited by anyone other than the legislature itself. If viewed in isolation, Section 109(a) could be read to make the board's and the shareholders' power to adopt, amend or repeal bylaws identical and coextensive, but Section 109(a) does not exist in a vacuum. It must be read together with 8 *Del. C.* §141(a), which pertinently provides that:

> The business and affairs of every corporation organized under this chapter shall be managed by or under the direction of a board of directors, except as may be otherwise provided in this chapter or in its certificate of incorporation.

No such broad management power is statutorily allocated to the shareholders. Indeed, it is well-established that stockholders of a corporation subject to the DGCL may not directly manage the business and affairs of the corporation, at least without specific authorization in either the statute or the certificate of incorporation.[6] Therefore, the shareholders' statutory power to adopt, amend or repeal bylaws is not

---

6. *See, e.g.,* McMullin v. Beran, 765 A.2d 910, 916 (Del. 2000) ("[o]ne of the fundamental principles of the Delaware General Corporation Law statute is that the business affairs of a corporation are managed by or under the direction of its board of directors."); Quickturn Design Sys., Inc. v. Shapiro, 721 A.2d 1281, 1291-92 (Del. 1998) ("One of the most basic tenets of Delaware corporate law is that the board of directors has the ultimate responsibility for managing the business and affairs of a corporation.[. . .] Section 141(a) . . . confers upon any newly elected board of directors *full* power to manage and direct the business and affairs of a Delaware corporation.") (emphasis in original) (internal citations omitted); Aronson v. Lewis, 473 A.2d 805, 811 (Del. 1984) ("[a] cardinal precept of the General Corporation Law of the State of Delaware is that directors, rather than shareholders, manage the business and affairs of the corporation.").

coextensive with the board's concurrent power and is limited by the board's management prerogatives under Section 141(a).[7]

Third, it follows that, to decide whether the Bylaw proposed by AFSCME is a proper subject for shareholder action under Delaware law, we must first determine: (1) the scope or reach of the shareholders' power to adopt, alter or repeal the bylaws of a Delaware corporation, and then (2) whether the Bylaw at issue here falls within that permissible scope. Where, as here, the proposed bylaw is one that limits director authority, that is an elusively difficult task. As one noted scholar has put it, "the efforts to distinguish by-laws that permissibly limit director authority from by-laws that impermissibly do so have failed to provide a coherent analytical structure, and the pertinent statutes provide no guidelines for distinction at all."[8] The tools that are available to this Court to answer those questions are other provisions of the DGCL and Delaware judicial decisions that can be brought to bear on this question.

B. ANALYSIS

1.

Two other provisions of the DGCL, 8 *Del. C.* §§109(b) and 102(b)(1), bear importantly on the first question and form the basis of contentions advanced by each side. Section 109(b), which deals generally with bylaws and what they must or may contain, provides that:

> The bylaws may contain any provision, not inconsistent with law or with the certificate of incorporation, relating to the business of the corporation, the conduct of its affairs, and its rights or powers or the rights or powers of its stockholders, directors, officers or employees.

And Section 102(b)(1), which is part of a broader provision that addresses what the certificate of incorporation must or may contain, relevantly states that:

---

7. Because the board's managerial authority under Section 141(a) is a cardinal precept of the DGCL, we do not construe Section 109 as an "except[ion] . . . otherwise specified in th[e] [DGCL]" to Section 141(a). Rather, the shareholders' statutory power to adopt, amend or repeal bylaws under Section 109 cannot be "inconsistent with law," including Section 141(a).

8. Lawrence A. Hamermesh, Corporate Democracy and Stockholder-Adopted By-Laws: Taking Back the Street? 73 Tul. L. Rev. 409, 444 (1998); *Id.* at 416 (noting that "neither the courts, the legislators, the SEC, nor legal scholars have clearly articulated the means of . . . determining whether a stockholder-adopted by-law provision that constrains director managerial authority is legally effective."). *See also* Randall S. Thomas & Catherine T. Dixon, Aranow & Einhorn on Proxy Contests for Corporate Control, §160.5 (3d ed. 1998) ("At some point the broad shareholder power to adopt or amend corporate by-laws must yield to the board's plenary authority to manage the business and affairs of the corporation. . . . The difficulty of pinpointing where a proposal falls on this spectrum of sometimes overlapping authority is exacerbated by the absence of state-law precedent demarcating this boundary."); John C. Coffee, Jr., The SEC and the Institutional Investor: A Half-Time Report, 15 Cardozo L. Rev. 837, 889 (1994) ("Symptomatically, persuasive Delaware authority is simply lacking that draws boundaries between the shareholder's right to amend the bylaws and the board's right to manage."); William W. Bratton & Joseph A. McCahery, Regulatory Competition, Regulatory Capture, and Corporate Self-Regulation, 73 N.C. L. Rev. 1861, 1932 n.274 (1995) ("[S]tate lawmakers have never had occasion to draw a clear line between board management authority and shareholder by-law promulgation authority. As a result, the extent to which a by-law may constrain . . . management authority is not clear.") . . .

(b) In addition to the matters required to be set forth in the certificate of incorporation by subsection (a) of this section, the certificate of incorporation may also contain any or all of the following matters:

(1) Any provision for the management of the business and for the conduct of the affairs of the corporation, and any provision creating, defining, limiting and regulating the powers of the corporation, the directors and the stockholders, or any class of the stockholders . . . ; if such provisions are not contrary to the laws of this State. Any provision which is required or permitted by any section of this chapter to be stated in the bylaws may instead be stated in the certificate of incorporation.

AFSCME relies heavily upon the language of Section 109(b), which permits the bylaws of a corporation to contain "any provision . . . relating to the . . . rights or powers of its stockholders [and] directors. . . ." The Bylaw, AFSCME argues, "relates to" the right of the stockholders meaningfully to participate in the process of electing directors, a right that necessarily "includes the right to nominate an opposing slate."

CA argues, in response, that Section 109(b) is not dispositive, because it cannot be read in isolation from, and without regard to, Section 102(b)(1). CA's argument runs as follows: the Bylaw would limit the substantive decision-making authority of CA's board to decide whether or not to expend corporate funds for a particular purpose, here, reimbursing director election expenses. Section 102(b)(1) contemplates that any provision that limits the broad statutory power of the directors must be contained in the certificate of incorporation. Therefore, the proposed Bylaw can only be in CA's Certificate of Incorporation, as distinguished from its bylaws. Accordingly, the proposed bylaw falls outside the universe of permissible bylaws authorized by Section 109(b).

Implicit in CA's argument is the premise that *any* bylaw that in *any* respect might be viewed as limiting or restricting the power of the board of directors automatically falls outside the scope of permissible bylaws. That simply cannot be. That reasoning, taken to its logical extreme, would result in eliminating altogether the shareholders' statutory right to adopt, amend or repeal bylaws. Bylaws, by their very nature, set down rules and procedures that bind a corporation's board and its shareholders. In that sense, most, if not all, bylaws could be said to limit the otherwise unlimited discretionary power of the board. Yet Section 109(a) carves out an area of shareholder power to adopt, amend or repeal bylaws that is expressly inviolate. Therefore, to argue that the Bylaw at issue here limits the board's power to manage the business and affairs of the Company only begins, but cannot end, the analysis needed to decide whether the Bylaw is a proper subject for shareholder action. The question left unanswered is what is the scope of shareholder action that Section 109(b) permits yet does not improperly intrude upon the directors' power to manage corporation's business and affairs under Section 141(a).

It is at this juncture that the statutory language becomes only marginally helpful in determining what the Delaware legislature intended to be the lawful scope of the shareholders' power to adopt, amend and repeal bylaws. To resolve that issue, the Court must resort to different tools, namely, decisions of this Court and of the Court of Chancery that bear on this question. Those tools do not enable us to articulate with doctrinal exactitude a bright line that divides those bylaws that shareholders may unilaterally adopt under Section 109(b) from those which they may not under Section 141(a). They do, however, enable us to decide the issue presented in this specific case.[14]

2.

It is well-established Delaware law that a proper function of bylaws is not to mandate how the board should decide specific substantive business decisions, but rather, to define the process and procedures by which those decisions are made. As the Court of Chancery has noted:

> Traditionally, the bylaws have been the corporate instrument used to set forth the rules by which the corporate board conducts its business. To this end, the DGCL is replete with specific provisions authorizing the bylaws to establish the procedures through which board and committee action is taken. . . . [T]here is a general consensus that bylaws that regulate the process by which the board acts are statutorily authorized.[15] . . .
> . . . I reject International's argument that that provision in the Bylaw Amendments impermissibly interferes with the board's authority under §141(a) to manage the business and affairs of the corporation. Sections 109 and 141, taken in totality, . . . make clear that bylaws may pervasively and strictly regulate the process by which boards act, subject to the constraints of equity.[16]

Examples of the procedural, process-oriented nature of bylaws are found in both the DGCL and the case law. For example, 8 *Del. C.* §141(b) authorizes bylaws that fix the number of directors on the board, the number of directors required for a quorum (with certain limitations), and the vote requirements for board action. 8 *Del. C.* §141(f) authorizes bylaws that preclude board action without a meeting. And, almost three decades ago this Court upheld a shareholder-enacted bylaw requiring unanimous board attendance and board approval for any board action, and unanimous ratification of any committee action. Such purely procedural bylaws do not improperly encroach upon the board's managerial authority under Section 141(a).

The process-creating function of bylaws provides a starting point to address the Bylaw at issue. It enables us to frame the issue in terms of whether the Bylaw is one that establishes or regulates a process for substantive director decision-making, or one that mandates the decision itself. Not surprisingly, the parties sharply divide on that question. We conclude that the Bylaw, even though infelicitously couched as a substantive-sounding mandate to expend corporate funds, has both the intent and the effect of regulating the process for electing directors of CA. Therefore, we determine that the Bylaw is a proper subject for shareholder action, and set forth our reasoning below.

Although CA concedes that "restrictive procedural bylaws (such as those requiring the presence of all directors and unanimous board consent to take action) are acceptable," it points out that even facially procedural bylaws can unduly intrude upon board

---

14. We do not attempt to delineate the location of that bright line in this Opinion. What we do hold is case specific; that is, wherever may be the location of the bright line that separates the shareholders' bylaw-making power under Section 109 from the directors' exclusive managerial authority under Section 141(a), the proposed Bylaw at issue here does not invade the territory demarcated by Section 141(a).

15. Hollinger Intern., Inc. v. Black, 844 A.2d 1022, 1078-79 (Del. Ch. 2004) (internal footnotes omitted), *aff'd*, 872 A.2d 559 (Del. 2005). . . .

16. *Id.* at 1080 n.136.

authority. The Bylaw being proposed here is unduly intrusive, CA claims, because, by mandating reimbursement of a stockholder's proxy expenses, it limits the board's broad discretionary authority to decide whether to grant reimbursement at all. CA further claims that because (in defined circumstances) the Bylaw mandates the expenditure of corporate funds, its subject matter is necessarily substantive, not process-oriented, and, therefore falls outside the scope of what Section 109(b) permits.[19]

Because the Bylaw is couched as a command to reimburse ("The board of directors shall cause the corporation to reimburse a stockholder"), it lends itself to CA's criticism. But the Bylaw's wording, although relevant, is not dispositive of whether or not it is process-related. The Bylaw could easily have been worded differently, to emphasize its process, as distinguished from its mandatory payment, component.[20] By saying this we do not mean to suggest that this Bylaw's reimbursement component can be ignored. What we do suggest is that a bylaw that requires the expenditure of corporate funds does not, for that reason alone, become automatically deprived of its process-related character. A hypothetical example illustrates the point. Suppose that the directors of a corporation live in different states and at a considerable distance from the corporation's headquarters. Suppose also that the shareholders enact a bylaw that requires all meetings of directors to take place in person at the corporation's headquarters. Such a bylaw would be clearly process-related, yet it cannot be supposed that the shareholders would lack the power to adopt the bylaw because it would require the corporation to expend its funds to reimburse the directors' travel expenses. Whether or not a bylaw is process-related must necessarily be determined in light of its context and purpose.

The context of the Bylaw at issue here is the process for electing directors—a subject in which shareholders of Delaware corporations have a legitimate and protected interest.[21] The purpose of the Bylaw is to promote the integrity of that electoral

---

19. CA actually conflates two separate arguments that, although facially similar, are analytically distinct. The first argument is that the Bylaw impermissibly intrudes upon board authority because it mandates the expenditure of corporate funds. The second is that the Bylaw impermissibly leaves no role for board discretion and would require reimbursement of the costs of a subset of CA's stockholders, even in circumstances where the board's fiduciary duties would counsel otherwise. Analytically, the first argument is relevant to the issue of whether the Bylaw is a proper subject for unilateral stockholder action, whereas the second argument more properly goes to the separate question of whether the Bylaw, if enacted, would violate Delaware law.

20. For example, the Bylaw could have been phrased more benignly, to provide that "[a] stockholder or group of stockholders (together, the 'Nominator') shall be entitled to reimbursement from the corporation for reasonable expenses ('Expenses') incurred in connection with nominating one or more candidates in a contested election of directors to the corporation's board of directors in the following circumstances. . . ." Although the substance of the Bylaw would be no different, the emphasis would be upon the shareholders' entitlement to reimbursement, rather than upon the directors' obligation to reimburse. As discussed in Part IV, *infra*, of this Opinion, in order for the Bylaw not to be "not inconsistent with law" as Section 109(b) mandates, it would also need to contain a provision that reserves the directors' full power to discharge their fiduciary duties.

21. Blasius Indus., Inc. v. Atlas Corp., 564 A.2d 651, 660 n. 2 (Del. Ch. 1988) ("Delaware courts have long exercised a most sensitive and protective regard for the free and effective exercise of voting rights."); *Id.* at 659 ("[W]hen viewed from a broad, institutional perspective, it can be seen that matters involving the integrity of the shareholder voting process involve consideration[s] not present in any other context in which directors exercise delegated power."); *See also* Unitrin, Inc. v. Am. Gen. Corp., 651 A.2d 1361, 1378 (Del. 1995); MM Cos., Inc. v. Liquid Audio, Inc., 813 A.2d 1118 (Del. 2003); and 8 *Del. C.* §211 (authorizing a shareholder to petition the Court of Chancery to order a meeting of stockholders to elect directors where such a meeting has not been held for at least 13 months).

process by facilitating the nomination of director candidates by stockholders or groups of stockholders. Generally, and under the current framework for electing directors in contested elections, only board-sponsored nominees for election are reimbursed for their election expenses. Dissident candidates are not, unless they succeed in replacing at least a majority of the entire board. The Bylaw would encourage the nomination of non-management board candidates by promising reimbursement of the nominating stockholders' proxy expenses if one or more of its candidates are elected. In that the shareholders also have a legitimate interest, because the Bylaw would facilitate the exercise of their right to participate in selecting the contestants. The Court of Chancery has so recognized:

> [T]he unadorned right to cast a ballot in a contest for [corporate] office . . . . is meaningless without the right to participate in selecting the contestants. As the nominating process circumscribes the range of choice to be made, it is a fundamental and outcome-determinative step in the election of officeholders. To allow for voting while maintaining a closed selection process thus renders the former an empty exercise.[22]

. . . The shareholders of a Delaware corporation have the right "to participate in selecting the contestants" for election to the board. The shareholders are entitled to facilitate the exercise of that right by proposing a bylaw that would encourage candidates other than board-sponsored nominees to stand for election. The Bylaw would accomplish that by committing the corporation to reimburse the election expenses of shareholders whose candidates are successfully elected. That the implementation of that proposal would require the expenditure of corporate funds will not, in and of itself, make such a bylaw an improper subject matter for shareholder action. Accordingly, we answer the first question certified to us in the affirmative.

That, however, concludes only part of the analysis. The DGCL also requires that the Bylaw be "not inconsistent with law."[23] Accordingly, we turn to the second certified question, which is whether the proposed Bylaw, if adopted, would cause CA to violate any Delaware law to which it is subject.

IV. THE SECOND QUESTION

In answering the first question, we have already determined that the Bylaw does not facially violate any provision of the DGCL or of CA's Certificate of Incorporation. The question thus becomes whether the Bylaw would violate any common law rule or precept. Were this issue being presented in the course of litigation involving the application of the Bylaw to a specific set of facts, we would start with the presumption that the Bylaw is valid and, if possible, construe it in a manner consistent with the law. The factual context in which the Bylaw was challenged would inform our analysis, and we would "exercise caution [before] invalidating corporate acts based upon hypothetical

---

22. Harrah's Entm't v. JCC Holding Co., 802 A.2d 294, 311 (Del. Ch. 2002) (quoting Durkin v. Nat'l Bank of Olyphant, 772 F.2d 55, 59 (3d Cir. 1985)).

23. 8 *Del. C.* §109(b).

injuries. . . ." The certified questions, however, request a determination of the validity of the Bylaw in the abstract. Therefore, in response to the second question, we must necessarily consider any possible circumstance under which a board of directors might be required to act. Under at least one such hypothetical, the board of directors would breach their fiduciary duties if they complied with the Bylaw. Accordingly, we conclude that the Bylaw, as drafted, would violate the prohibition, which our decisions have derived from Section 141(a), against contractual arrangements that commit the board of directors to a course of action that would preclude them from fully discharging their fiduciary duties to the corporation and its shareholders.

This Court has previously invalidated contracts that would require a board to act or not act in such a fashion that would limit the exercise of their fiduciary duties. In Paramount Communications, Inc. v. QVC Network, Inc.,[27] we invalidated a "no shop" provision of a merger agreement with a favored bidder (Viacom) that prevented the directors of the target company (Paramount) from communicating with a competing bidder (QVC) the terms of its competing bid in an effort to obtain the highest available value for shareholders. We held that:

> The No-Shop Provision could not validly define or limit the fiduciary duties of the Paramount directors. To the extent that a contract, or a provision thereof, purports to require a board to act or not act in such a fashion as to limit the exercise of fiduciary duties, it is invalid and unenforceable. [. . .][T]he Paramount directors could not contract away their fiduciary obligations. Since the No-Shop Provision was invalid, Viacom never had any vested contract rights in the provision.[28]

Similarly, in Quickturn Design Systems, Inc. v. Shapiro,[29] the directors of the target company (Quickturn) adopted a "poison pill" rights plan that contained a so-called "delayed redemption provision" as a defense against a hostile takeover bid, as part of which the bidder (Mentor Graphics) intended to wage a proxy contest to replace the target company board. The delayed redemption provision was intended to deter that effort, by preventing any newly elected board from redeeming the poison pill for six months. This Court invalidated that provision, because it would "impermissibly deprive any newly elected board of both its statutory authority to manage the corporation under 8 *Del. C.* §141(a) and its concomitant fiduciary duty pursuant to that statutory mandate." We held that:

> One of the most basic tenets of Delaware corporate law is that the board of directors has the ultimate responsibility for managing the business and affairs of a corporation. [. . .] The Quickturn certificate of incorporation contains no provision purporting to limit the authority of the board in any way. The Delayed Redemption Provision, however, would prevent a newly elected board of directors from *completely* discharging its fundamental management duties to the corporation and its stockholders for six months. While the Delayed Redemption Provision limits the board of directors' authority in only one respect, the suspension of the Rights Plan, it nonetheless restricts the board's power in an area of fundamental importance to the shareholders—negotiating a possible sale of the corporation. Therefore, we hold that the Delayed Redemption Provision is invalid

---

27. 637 A.2d 34 (Del. 1994).
28. Paramount v. QVC, 637 A.2d at 51.
29. 721 A.2d 1281 (Del. 1998).

under Section 141(a), which confers upon any newly elected board of directors *full* power to manage and direct the business and affairs of a Delaware corporation.[31]

Both *QVC* and *Quickturn* involved binding contractual arrangements that the board of directors had voluntarily imposed upon themselves. This case involves a binding bylaw that the shareholders seek to impose involuntarily on the directors in the specific area of election expense reimbursement. Although this case is distinguishable in that respect, the distinction is one without a difference. The reason is that the internal governance contract—which here takes the form of a bylaw—is one that would also prevent the directors from exercising their full managerial power in circumstances where their fiduciary duties would otherwise require them to deny reimbursement to a dissident slate. That this limitation would be imposed by a majority vote of the shareholders rather than by the directors themselves, does not, in our view, legally matter.[32]

AFSCME contends that it is improper to use the doctrine articulated in *QVC* and *Quickturn* as the measure of the validity of the Bylaw. Because the Bylaw would remove the subject of election expense reimbursement (in circumstances as defined by the Bylaw) entirely from the CA's board's discretion (AFSCME argues), it cannot fairly be claimed that the directors would be precluded from discharging their fiduciary duty. Stated differently, AFSCME argues that it is unfair to claim that the Bylaw prevents the CA board from discharging its fiduciary duty where the effect of the Bylaw is to relieve the board entirely of those duties in this specific area.

That response, in our view, is more semantical than substantive. No matter how artfully it may be phrased, the argument concedes the very proposition that renders the Bylaw, as written, invalid: the Bylaw mandates reimbursement of election expenses in circumstances that a proper application of fiduciary principles could preclude. That such circumstances could arise is not farfetched. Under Delaware law, a board may expend corporate funds to reimburse proxy expenses "[w]here the controversy is concerned with a question of policy as distinguished from personnel o[r] management."[33] But in a situation where the proxy contest is motivated by personal or petty concerns, or to promote interests that do not further, or are adverse to, those of the corporation, the board's fiduciary duty could compel that reimbursement be denied altogether.[34]

It is in this respect that the proposed Bylaw, as written, would violate Delaware law if enacted by CA's shareholders. As presently drafted, the Bylaw would afford CA's directors full discretion to determine what *amount* of reimbursement is appropriate,

---

31. [*Quickturn*, 721 A.2d] at 1291-92 (italics in original, internal footnotes omitted).

32. Only if the Bylaw provision were enacted as an amendment to CA's Certificate of Incorporation would that distinction be dispositive. *See* 8 *Del. C.* §102(b)(1) and §242.

33. Hall v. Trans-Lux Daylight Picture Screen Corp., 171 A. 226, 227 (Del. Ch. 1934); *See also* Hibbert v. Hollywood Park, Inc., 457 A.2d 339, 345 (Del. 1983) (reimbursement of "reasonable expenses" permitted where the proxy contest "was actually one involving substantive differences about corporation policy.").

34. Such a circumstance could arise, for example, if a shareholder group affiliated with a competitor of the company were to cause the election of a minority slate of candidates committed to using their director positions to obtain, and then communicate, valuable proprietary strategic or product information to the competitor.

because the directors would be obligated to grant only the "reasonable" expenses of a successful short slate. Unfortunately, that does not go far enough, because the Bylaw contains no language or provision that would reserve to CA's directors their full power to exercise their fiduciary duty to decide whether or not it would be appropriate, in a specific case, to award reimbursement at all.[35]

. . . In arriving at this conclusion, we express no view on whether the Bylaw as currently drafted, would create a better governance scheme from a policy standpoint. We decide only what is, and is not, legally permitted under the DGCL. That statute, as currently drafted, is the expression of policy as decreed by the Delaware legislature. Those who believe that CA's shareholders should be permitted to make the proposed Bylaw as drafted part of CA's governance scheme, have two alternatives. They may seek to amend the Certificate of Incorporation to include the substance of the Bylaw; *or* they may seek recourse from the Delaware General Assembly.

Accordingly, we answer the second question certified to us in the affirmative.

NOTES AND QUESTIONS

1. The two parts of the CA opinion leave ambiguity as to the reach of shareholder power to amend the bylaws. Following this case, the Delaware legislature in April 2009 addressed shareholder nominations and reimbursement for proxy expenses as a proper subject by enacting new sections 112 and 113 to the Delaware G.C.L., specifying that the bylaws can include provisions requiring the firm's proxy and proxy solicitation to include individuals nominated by shareholders (Section 112) and providing for the reimbursement by the corporation of expenses incurred in connection with the election of directors (Section 113). The statute is not mandatory for Delaware corporations but rather is an enabling statute that permits each corporation to shape the provisions to its own needs. The statute includes a list of procedures or conditions that may be included.

2. Not to be left behind, the ABA Committee on Corporate Laws proposed in June 2009 and adopted in October 2009 amendments to the MBCA §2.06 that authorized both shareholder expense reimbursement bylaws and shareholder proxy access bylaws.

3. The court in note 32 says the distinction between shareholder and director action would be dispositive if the bylaw were enacted as an amendment to the certificate of incorporation (referred to in other states as the articles of incorporation or the charter). Is such a provision likely to make its way into the certificate? Why not?

4. Although the question of shareholder power to amend the bylaws is a question of state law, note the interaction of federal law. The Delaware Supreme Court took up the case only because it was certified to it by the U.S. Securities and Exchange

---

35. *See* Malone v. Brincat, 722 A.2d 5, 10 (Del. 1998) ("Although the fiduciary duty of a Delaware director is unremitting, the exact course of conduct that must be charted to properly discharge that responsibility will change in the specific context of the action the director is taking with regard to either the corporation or its shareholders."). A decision by directors to deny reimbursement on fiduciary grounds would be judicially reviewable.

Commission. The SEC was trying to determine if a shareholder should be able to insert a proposal into management's proxy statement under SEC Rule 14a-8, a federal rule discussed below that defines the agenda space for shareholders acting via the company's proxy. One of the exceptions under which a company can exclude a shareholder proposal is if it is not a proper subject for shareholder action under state law.

PROBLEM 3-9

The directors of Bradley Corp. pass a bylaw requiring that a stockholder must hold $1,000 worth of stock for a full year to present a proposal for shareholder action at the annual meeting of shareholders. Would you expect such a bylaw to be permissible? What if the bylaw required 60 days' notice of the shareholder's intent to present a proposal? What if the bylaw only applied to nominations of candidates for director?

6.   Initial Issuance of Securities

a.   The Securities Act of 1933 and Its Requirement of Extensive Disclosure

Securities Act of 1933 §§5, 11, 12, 17

If the financing of the corporation includes the public offering of securities, the corporation and its lawyers will have to comply with federal and state securities laws. Federal regulation of the issuance of securities began with the Securities Act of 1933. Similar state laws, often referred to as "blue sky laws," were enacted even earlier in this century, beginning in Kansas in 1914.

Events of the decade preceding the enactment of the 1933 Act moved Congress to act. As one congressional report noted:

> Fully half or $25,000,000,000 worth of securities floated during this period have been proved to be worthless. . . . [T]he flotation of such a mass of essentially fraudulent securities was made possible because of the complete abandonment by many underwriters and dealers in securities of those standards of fair, honest and prudent dealing that should be basic to the encouragement of investment in any enterprise.

H.R. Rep. No. 85, 73d Cong., 1st Sess. 2 (1933).

The great losses incurred in the securities industry were probably not the only reason leading to legislation. Consumers are subject to abuse in other purchases that were not so early or completely regulated; regulation of securities purchases likely reflects the central role played by the securities market in the American capitalistic economy. Protection of investors was seen as necessary to ensure that the securities markets were efficiently allocating capital resources to produce the most productive and innovative economy.

Regulation of securities also reflects the perception that securities are different from most other commodities in a way that creates the need for special protection. Securities are intangibles, pieces of paper that have no intrinsic value in themselves;

their value comes because they represent an interest in something else. Investors cannot as easily determine the value of a security by looking at it as they might a house or an automobile. The primary mechanism used by the 1933 Act to protect investors has therefore been full and fair disclosure of material facts concerning securities, to tell the investor what stands behind the paper.

The second major aim of the 1933 Act is to deal with fraud in the sale of securities. Securities are created, not produced; they can be issued in unlimited amounts—virtually without cost—which increases the possibility of manipulation. The 1933 Act therefore provides fraud provisions tailored for these particular forms of investment.

Securities and Exchange Commission, What We Do
http://www.sec.gov/about/whatwedo.shtml (July 2013)

SECURITIES ACT OF 1933

Often referred to as the "truth in securities" law, the Securities Act of 1933 has two basic objectives:

- require that investors receive financial and other significant information concerning securities being offered for public sale; and
- prohibit deceit, misrepresentations, and other fraud in the sale of securities. . . .

PURPOSE OF REGISTRATION

A primary means of accomplishing these goals is the disclosure of financial information through the registration of securities. This information enables investors, not the government, to make informed judgments about whether to purchase a company's securities. While the SEC requires that the information provided be accurate, it does not guarantee it. Investors who purchase securities and suffer losses have important recovery rights if they can prove that there was incomplete or inaccurate disclosure of important information.

THE REGISTRATION PROCESS

In general, securities sold in the United States must be registered. The registration forms companies file provide essential facts while minimizing the burden and expense of complying with the law. In general, registration forms call for:

- a description of the company's properties and business;
- a description of the security to be offered for sale;
- information about the management of the company; and
- financial statements certified by independent accountants.

All companies, both domestic and foreign, must file their registration statements electronically. These statements and the accompanying prospectuses become public shortly after filing and investors can access them using EDGAR. Registration statements are subject to examination for compliance with disclosure requirements.

Not all offerings of securities must be registered with the Commission. Some exemptions from the registration requirement include:

- private offerings to a limited number of persons or institutions;
- offerings of limited size;
- intrastate offerings; and
- securities of municipal, state, and federal governments.

By exempting many small offerings from the regulation process, the SEC seeks to foster capital formation by lowering the cost of offering securities to the public. . . .

NOTES

1. Section 5 of the 1933 Act prohibits the offer or sale of a security unless it has been registered under the act or falls under an exemption. Registration requires extensive disclosure to the SEC and to each individual purchaser by means of a prospectus. Disclosure is required as to all significant aspects of the issuer's business, including extensive financial information and management's discussion and analysis. The SEC's instruction for the required disclosure as to management's discussion and analysis is illustrative of the disclosure obligation:

> The registrant's discussion and analysis shall be of the financial statements and of other statistical data that the registrant believes will enhance a reader's understanding of its financial condition, changes in financial condition and results of operations. . . . The purpose of the discussion and analysis shall be to provide to investors and other users information relevant to an assessment of the financial condition and results of operations of the registrant as determined by evaluating the amounts and certainty of cash flows from operations and from outside sources. . . . The discussion and analysis shall focus specifically on material events and uncertainties known to management that would cause reported financial information not to be necessarily indicative of future operating results or of future financial condition.

Regulation S-K: Standard Instructions for Filing Forms . . . 17 C.F.R. §229.303 (Instructions 1-3) (2013).

The 1933 Act and the SEC regulations emphasize some disclosures more than others. For example, there are certain risk factors that the SEC wants highlighted on the inside front cover of the prospectus, such as an absence of profitable operations in recent periods or an erratic financial history. However, the regulatory system sometimes prohibits disclosure. Prior to the filing of the registration statement with the SEC there is, in effect, a period of enforced silence as selling efforts of any kind are prohibited. After the filing date but before the registration statement has become effective, written offers can be made only by means of a prospectus (although oral offers are permitted). After SEC reforms in 2005 to the public offering process, the largest issuers, termed "Well-Known Seasoned issuers" by the SEC, were given considerably more freedom to use free-writing beyond the prospectus.

The details of registration are left to your course in securities regulation, but there is frequent tension between the silence and disclosure aspects of the federal system and the desire to sell the securities. The prospectus itself has been described as a "somewhat schizophrenic document" — on the one hand, acting as a selling document seeking to present the best possible image and, on the other, a required statutory disclosure document serving as an insurance policy against liability, which suggests a more conservative presentation. See Schneider, Manko, and Kant, Going Public — Practice, Procedure and Consequences, 27 Vill. L. Rev. 1 (1981).

2. The disclosure affirmatively required by the 1933 Act expands the more indirect disclosure required by the common law prohibitions against fraud. The common law aimed at misstatements or half-truths in statements that had been voluntarily made and seldom imposed a duty to speak absent an unusual fiduciary duty relationship. Prior to the 1920s, the tort action of deceit was the principal remedy for inadequate disclosure. The traditional elements of the cause of action required a plaintiff to show a misrepresentation (or an omission in those areas where the law imposed a duty to speak) of a material fact made by the speaker with scienter on which the plaintiff relied, causing damage as a consequence. The 1933 Act not only required affirmative disclosure beyond what existed at common law, but it also substantially reduced the elements that a plaintiff must show to recover, as compared to what would have been required at common law. If a misstatement appears in a prospectus, it is usually not necessary for the plaintiff to show reliance. Similarly, the issuer is strictly liable with no showing of intent or other scienter required. Directors and other defendants can escape liability if they show their due diligence, but that burden has been difficult for many insiders to show when a misstatement has occurred. See Escott v. Barchris Construction Corp., 283 F. Supp. 643 (S.D.N.Y. 1968). Plaintiffs also do not have to prove any causation, although defendants can seek to prove that damages occurred for some reasons other than the misrepresentation. The 1933 Act also provides a larger number of potential defendants than was available under the common law. This liability provides an impetus for accountants and underwriters to act as independent monitors of the accuracy of the prospectus.

The elements from common law fraud also provide a framework for consideration of the antifraud rules under the proxy rules and Rule 10b-5 discussed in Chapter 10, although there are some differences in the degree to which each element is required in each context.

3. Advance disclosure, as discussed in Note 1, can serve as an alternative to ex post fiduciary duty. Consider a fact situation in which promoters form a corporation and are its sole shareholders and directors. While the corporation remains in this intimate stage, the promoters sell property to the entity in exchange for stock having a par value that is three times what the promoters paid for the property and twice what the property was worth. At a time when this property was the corporation's only asset, shares were sold to outsiders at the share's par value under a regulatory regime that did not require disclosure to the purchasers of these facts. When the true facts were revealed, the corporation, now reflecting the interests of the shareholders who were fleeced in buying the shares, sues the promoters for breach of fiduciary duty based on the deception in selling the property to the corporation at the exorbitant price. This same fact situation and same legal question were the foundation for parallel cases decided by the United States Supreme Court and the Massachusetts Supreme Judicial Court.

The United States Supreme Court, in an action against one of the two promoters, held that there had been no deception of the corporation and thus no breach of fiduciary duty and no cause of action since all the shareholders at the time of the property transaction knew the facts. The Court found it immaterial in the corporation's action that outsiders subsequently subscribed for shares in ignorance of the true facts because "[o]f course, legally speaking, a corporation does not change its identity by adding a cubit to its stature." Old Dominion Copper Mining & Smelting Co. v. Lewisohn, 210 U.S. 206, 213 (1908). The Massachusetts court, in an action by the corporation against the other promoter, ruled that the promoters stand in as much a fiduciary position to the corporation when uninformed shareholders are expected to be brought in afterwards as when there are uninformed shareholders at the time of the transaction. The wrong to the corporation is immediate, even though there is no one to enforce the action until new shareholders buy into the corporations. Old Dominion Copper Mining & Smelting Co. v. Bigelow, 203 Mass. 159, 89 N.E. 193 (1909).

Since the enactment of the 1933 Act, advance disclosure has limited the number of cases for promoter liability based on fiduciary duty, but the question of how a corporation can be deceived has lingered, as set out in more detail in Parts C and D of Chapter 10.

4. The SEC does not ask if an investment is good or not, but focuses instead on disclosure, with the investor then being able to decide whether to purchase. In contrast, some states expressly regulate the substance of a transaction and exclude those that do not meet the state standards. Usually referred to as "merit" regulation, such regulation exists in a minority of states, and, though it has been declining in importance in recent decades, it remains an active approach in several states and continues to pose the question of whether disclosure alone is sufficient protection for investors. See Report on State Merit Regulation of Securities Offerings, 41 Bus. Law. 785 (1986).

5. State regulation, whether merit regulation described in Note 4 or more traditional disclosure-based regulation, has traditionally existed alongside federal rules—a dual system of regulation that added to the burden and costs of the issuance of securities. In 1996, Congress partially preempted state law. Under amended Section 18(a) of the 1933 Act stocks listed on national stock markets (the New York Stock Exchange or NASDAQ's larger market) are exempt from the registration coverage of the various states. This law replaces the overlapping structure of federal and state regulation that had been in place for 65 years with a regulatory system in which federal law regulates the registration of larger issuers.

b. What Transactions Are Covered?

Securities and Exchange Commission v. Edwards
United States Supreme Court 2004
540 U.S. 389

JUSTICE O'CONNOR delivered the opinion of the Court.

"Opportunity doesn't always knock . . . sometimes it rings." (ETS Payphones promotional brochure). And sometimes it hangs up. So it did for the 10,000 people who invested a total of $300 million in the payphone sale-and-leaseback arrangements touted by respondent under that slogan. The Securities and Exchange Commission (SEC) argues that the arrangements were investment contracts, and thus were subject to regulation under the federal securities laws. In this case, we must decide whether a moneymaking scheme is excluded from the term "investment contract" simply because the scheme offered a contractual entitlement to a fixed, rather than a variable, return.

I

Respondent Charles Edwards was the chairman, chief executive officer, and sole shareholder of ETS Payphones, Inc. (ETS). ETS, acting partly through a subsidiary also controlled by respondent, sold payphones to the public via independent distributors. The payphones were offered packaged with a site lease, a 5-year leaseback and management agreement, and a buyback agreement. All but a tiny fraction of purchasers chose this package, although other management options were offered. The purchase price for the payphone packages was approximately $7,000. Under the leaseback and management agreement, purchasers received $82 per month, a 14% annual return. Purchasers were not involved in the day-to-day operation of the payphones they owned. ETS selected the site for the phone, installed the equipment, arranged for connection and long-distance service, collected coin revenues, and maintained and repaired the phones. Under the buyback agreement, ETS promised to refund the full purchase price of the package at the end of the lease or within 180 days of a purchaser's request.

In its marketing materials and on its website, ETS trumpeted the "incomparable pay phone" as "an exciting business opportunity," in which recent deregulation had "open[ed] the door for profits for individual pay phone owners and operators." According to ETS, "[v]ery few business opportunities can offer the potential for ongoing revenue generation that is available in today's pay telephone industry." (ETS brochure); (ETS website).

The payphones did not generate enough revenue for ETS to make the payments required by the leaseback agreements, so the company depended on funds from new investors to meet its obligations. In September 2000, ETS filed for bankruptcy protection. The SEC brought this civil enforcement action the same month. It alleged that respondent and ETS had violated the registration requirements of §§5(a) and (c) of the Securities Act of 1933, the antifraud provisions of both §17(a) of the Securities Act of 1933, and §10(b) of the Securities Exchange Act of 1934, and Rule 10b-5 thereunder. The District Court concluded that the payphone sale-and-leaseback arrangement was an investment contract within the meaning of, and therefore was subject to, the federal securities laws. SEC v. ETS Payphones, Inc., 123 F.Supp.2d 1349 (N.D.Ga. 2000). The Court of Appeals reversed. 300 F.3d 1281 (C.A.11 2002) (*per curiam*). It held that respondent's scheme was not an investment contract, on two grounds. First, it read this Court's opinions to require that an investment contract offer either capital appreciation or a participation in the earnings of the enterprise, and thus to exclude schemes, such as respondent's, offering a fixed rate of return. *Id.*, at 1284-1285. Second, it held that our opinions' requirement that the return on the investment be "derived solely from the efforts of others" was not satisfied when the purchasers had a contractual entitlement to the return. *Id.,* at 1285. We conclude that it erred on both grounds.

II

"Congress' purpose in enacting the securities laws was to regulate *investments,* in whatever form they are made and by whatever name they are called." Reves v. Ernst & Young, 494 U.S. 56 (1990). To that end, it enacted a broad definition of "security," sufficient "to encompass virtually any instrument that might be sold as an investment." *Ibid.* Section 2(a)(1) of the 1933 Act, and §3(a)(10) of the 1934 Act, in slightly different formulations which we have treated as essentially identical in meaning, *Reves, supra,* at 61, n. 1, define "security" to include "any note, stock, treasury stock, security future, bond, debenture, . . . investment contract, . . . [or any] instrument commonly known as a 'security.'" "Investment contract" is not itself defined.

The test for whether a particular scheme is an investment contract was established in our decision in SEC v. W.J. Howey Co., 328 U.S. 293 (1946). We look to "whether the scheme involves an investment of money in a common enterprise with profits to come solely from the efforts of others." *Id.,* at 301. This definition "embodies a flexible rather than a static principle, one that is capable of adaptation to meet the countless and variable schemes devised by those who seek the use of the money of others on the promise of profits." *Id.,* at 299.

In reaching that result, we first observed that when Congress included "investment contract" in the definition of security, it "was using a term the meaning of which had been crystallized" by the state courts' interpretation of their "'blue sky'" laws. *Id.,* at 298. (Those laws were the precursors to federal securities regulation and were so named, it seems, because they were "aimed at promoters who 'would sell building lots in the blue sky in fee simple.'" 1 L. Loss & J. Seligman, Securities Regulation 36, 31-43 (3d ed. 1998) (quoting Mulvey, Blue Sky Law, 36 Can. L. Times 37 (1916)).) The state courts had defined an investment contract as "a contract or scheme for 'the placing of capital or laying out of money in a way intended to secure income or profit from its employment,'" and had "uniformly applied" that definition to "a variety of situations where individuals were led to invest money in a common enterprise with the expectation that they would earn a profit solely through the efforts of the promoter or [a third party]." *Howey, supra,* at 298 (quoting State v. Gopher Tire & Rubber Co., 146 Minn. 52, 56, 177 N.W. 937, 938 (1920)). Thus, when we held that "profits" must "come solely from the efforts of others," we were speaking of the profits that investors seek on their investment, not the profits of the scheme in which they invest. We used "profits" in the sense of income or return, to include, for example, dividends, other periodic payments, or the increased value of the investment.

There is no reason to distinguish between promises of fixed returns and promises of variable returns for purposes of the test, so understood. In both cases, the investing public is attracted by representations of investment income, as purchasers were in this case by ETS' invitation to "'watch the profits add up.'" Moreover, investments pitched as low-risk (such as those offering a "guaranteed" fixed return) are particularly attractive to individuals more vulnerable to investment fraud, including older and less sophisticated investors. See S. Rep. No. 102-261, Vol. 2, App., p. 326 (1992) (Staff Summary of Federal Trade Commission Activities Affecting Older Consumers). Under the reading respondent advances, unscrupulous marketers of investments could evade the securities laws by picking a rate of return to promise. We will not read into the securities laws a limitation not compelled by the language that would so undermine the laws' purposes.

Respondent protests that including investment schemes promising a fixed return among investment contracts conflicts with our precedent. We disagree. No distinction between fixed and variable returns was drawn in the blue sky law cases that the *Howey* Court used, in formulating the test, as its evidence of Congress' understanding of the term. *Howey, supra,* at 298, and n. 4. Indeed, two of those cases involved an investment contract in which a fixed return was promised. People v. White, 124 Cal. App. 548, 550-551, 12 P.2d 1078, 1079 (1932) (agreement between defendant and investors stated that investor would give defendant $5,000, and would receive $7,500 from defendant one year later); Stevens v. Liberty Packing Corp., 111 N.J. Eq. 61, 62-63, 161 A. 193, 193-194 (1932) ("ironclad contract" offered by defendant to investors entitled investors to $56 per year for 10 years on initial investment of $175, ostensibly in sale-and-leaseback of breeding rabbits).

None of our post-*Howey* decisions is to the contrary. In United Housing Foundation, Inc. v. Forman, 421 U.S. 837 (1975), we considered whether "shares" in a nonprofit housing cooperative were investment contracts under the securities laws. We identified the "touchstone" of an investment contract as "the presence of an investment in a common venture premised on a reasonable expectation of profits to be derived from the entrepreneurial or managerial efforts of others," and then laid out two examples of investor interests that we had previously found to be "profits." *Id.,* at 852. Those were "capital appreciation resulting from the development of the initial investment" and "participation in earnings resulting from the use of investors' funds." *Ibid.* We contrasted those examples, in which "the investor is 'attracted solely by the prospects of a return'" on the investment, with housing cooperative shares, regarding which the purchaser "is motivated by a desire to use or consume the item purchased." *Id.,* at 852-853 (quoting *Howey, supra,* at 300). Thus, *Forman* supports the commonsense understanding of "profits" in the *Howey* test as simply "financial returns on . . . investments." 421 U.S., at 853.

Concededly, *Forman*'s illustrative description of prior decisions on "profits" appears to have been mistaken for an exclusive list in a case considering the scope of a different term in the definition of a security, "note." See *Reves,* 494 U.S., at 68, n. 4. But that was a misreading of *Forman,* and we will not bind ourselves unnecessarily to passing dictum that would frustrate Congress' intent to regulate all of the "countless and variable schemes devised by those who seek the use of the money of others on the promise of profits." *Howey,* 328 U.S., at 299.

Given that respondent's position is supported neither by the purposes of the securities laws nor by our precedents, it is no surprise that the SEC has consistently taken the opposite position, and maintained that a promise of a fixed return does not preclude a scheme from being an investment contract. It has done so in formal adjudications, e.g., In re Abbett, Sommer & Co., 44 S.E.C. 104, 1969 WL 95359 (1969) (holding that mortgage notes, sold with a package of management services and a promise to repurchase the notes in the event of default, were investment contracts); see also In re Union Home Loans (Dec. 16, 1982), 26 S.E.C. Docket 1517, 1519 (report and order regarding settlement, stating that sale of promissory notes secured by deeds of trust, coupled with management services and providing investors "a specified percentage return on their investment," were investment contracts), and in enforcement actions, e.g., SEC v. Universal Service Assn., 106 F.2d 232, 234, 237 (C.A.7 1939) (accepting SEC's position that an investment scheme promising "assured profit of 30% per annum with no chance of risk or loss to the contributor" was a security because it satisfied the pertinent substance of the *Howey* test, "[t]he investment of money with the expectation of profit through the efforts of other persons"); see also SEC v. American Trailer Rentals Co., 379 U.S. 594, 598 (1965) (noting that "the SEC advised" the respondent that its "sale and lease-back arrangements," in which investors received "a set 2% of their investment per month for 10 years," "were investment contracts and therefore securities" under the 1933 Act).

The Eleventh Circuit's perfunctory alternative holding, that respondent's scheme falls outside the definition because purchasers had a contractual entitlement to a return, is incorrect and inconsistent with our precedent. We are considering invest-ment *contracts*. The fact that investors have bargained for a return on their investment does not mean that the return is not also expected to come solely from the efforts of others. Any other conclusion would conflict with our holding that an investment contract was offered in theory itself (service contract entitled investors to allocations of profit). We hold that an investment scheme promising a fixed rate of return can be an "investment contract" and thus a "security" subject to federal securities laws. . . .

c.   *Exemption from Registration*

Securities Act of 1933 §§3, 4
SEC Rules 147, 501-508

Securities and Exchange Commission v. Ralston Purina Co.
United States Supreme Court, 1953
346 U.S. 119

MR. JUSTICE CLARK delivered the opinion of the Court.

Section [4(2)] of the Securities Act of 1933 exempts "transactions by an issuer not involving any public offering" from the registration requirements of §5. We must decide whether Ralston Purina's offerings of treasury stock to its "key employees" are within this exemption. . . .

Ralston Purina manufactures and distributes various feed and cereal products. Its processing and distribution facilities are scattered throughout the United States and Canada, staffed by some 7,000 employees. At least since 1911 the company has had a policy of encouraging stock ownership among its employees; more particularly, since 1942 it has made authorized but unissued common shares available to some of them. Between 1947 and 1951, the period covered by the record in this case, Ralston Purina sold nearly $2,000,000 of stock to employees without registration and in so doing made use of the mails.

In each of these years, a corporate resolution authorized the sale of common stock "to employees . . . who shall, without any solicitation by the Company or its officers or employees, inquire of any of them as to how to purchase common stock of Ralston Purina Company." A memorandum sent to branch and store managers after the resolution was adopted advised that "[t]he only employees to whom this stock will be available will be those who take the initiative and are interested in buying stock at present market prices." Among those responding to these offers were employees with the duties of artist, bakeshop foreman, chow loading foreman, clerical assistant, copywriter, electrician, stock clerk, mill office clerk, order credit trainee, production trainee, stenographer, and veterinarian. The buyers lived in over fifty widely separated communities scattered from Garland, Texas, to Nashua, New Hampshire and Visalia, California. The lowest salary bracket of those purchasing was $2,700 in 1949, $2,435 in 1950 and $3,107 in 1951. The record shows that in 1947, 234 employees bought stock, 20 in 1948, 414 in 1949, 411 in 1950, and the 1951 offer, interrupted by this litigation, produced 165 applications to purchase. No records were kept of those to whom the offers were made; the estimated number in 1951 was 500.

The company bottoms its exemption claim on the classification of all offerees as "key employees" in its organization. Its position on trial was that "[a] key employee . . . is not confined to an organization chart. It would include an individual who is eligible for promotion, an individual who especially influences others or who advises others, a person whom the employees look to in some special way, an individual, of course, who carries some special responsibility, who is sympathetic to management and who is ambitious and who the management feels is likely to be promoted to a greater responsibility." That an offering to all of its employees would be public is conceded.

The Securities Act nowhere defines the scope of §[4(2)'s] private offering exemption. Nor is the legislative history of much help in staking out its boundaries. The problem was first dealt with in §4(1) of the House Bill, H.R. 5480, 73d Cong., 1st Sess., which exempted "transactions by an issuer not with or through an underwriter. . . ." The bill, as reported by the House Committee, added "and not involving any public offering." H.R. Rep. No. 85, 73d Cong., 1st Sess. 1. This was thought to be one of those transactions "where there is no practical need for . . . [the bill's] application or where the public benefits are too remote." Id., at 5. The exemption as thus delimited became law. It assumed its present shape with the deletion of "not with or through an underwriter" by §203(a) of the Securities Exchange Act of 1934, 48 Stat. 906, a change regarded as the elimination of superfluous language. H.R. Rep. No. 1838, 73d Cong., 2d Sess. 41.

Decisions under comparable exemptions in the English Companies Acts and state "blue sky" laws, the statutory antecedents of federal securities legislation have made one thing clear—to be public, an offer need not be open to the whole world. In Securities and Exchange Comm. v. Sunbeam Gold Mines Co., 9 Cir., 1938, 95 F.2d 699, 701, this point was made in dealing with an offering to the stockholders of two corporations about to be merged. Judge Denman observed that:

> In its broadest meaning the term "public" distinguishes the populace at large from groups of individual members of the public segregated because of some common interest or characteristic. Yet such a distinction is inadequate for practical purposes; manifestly an offering of securities to

all redheaded men, to all residents of Chicago or San Francisco, to all existing stockholders of the General Motors Corporation or the American Telephone & Telegraph Company, is no less "public," in every realistic sense of the word, than an unrestricted offering to the world at large. Such an offering, though not open to everyone who may choose to apply, is none the less "public" in character, for the means used to select the particular individuals to whom the offering is to be made bear no sensible relation to the purposes for which the selection is made. . . . To determine the distinction between "public" and "private" in any particular context, it is essential to examine the circumstances under which the distinction is sought to be established and to consider the purposes sought to be achieved by such distinction.

The courts below purported to apply this test. The District Court held, in the language of the *Sunbeam* decision, that "[t]he purpose of the selection bears a 'sensible relation' to the class chosen," finding that "[t]he sole purpose of the 'selection' is to keep part stock ownership of the business within the operating personnel of the business and to spread ownership throughout all departments and activities of the business." The Court of Appeals treated the case as involving "an offering, without solicitation, of common stock to a selected group of key employees of the issuer, most of whom are already stockholders when the offering is made, with the sole purpose of enabling them to secure a proprietary interest in the company or to increase the interest already held by them."

Exemption from the registration requirements of the Securities Act is the question. The design of the statute is to protect investors by promoting full disclosure of information thought necessary to informed investment decisions. The natural way to interpret the private offering exemption is in light of the statutory purpose. Since exempt transactions are those as to which "there is no practical need for . . . [the bill's] application," the applicability of §[4(2)] should turn on whether the particular class of persons affected need the protection of the Act. An offering to those who are shown to be able to fend for themselves is a transaction "not involving any public offering."

The Commission would have us go one step further and hold that "an offering to a substantial number of the public" is not exempt under §[4(2)]. We are advised that "whatever the special circumstances, the Commission has consistently interpreted the exemption as being inapplicable when a large number of offerees is involved." But the statute would seem to apply to a "public offering" whether to few or many. It may well be that offerings to a substantial number of persons would rarely be exempt. Indeed nothing prevents the commission, in enforcing the statute, from using some kind of numerical test in deciding when to investigate particular exemption claims. But there is no warrant for superimposing a quantity limit on private offerings as a matter of statutory interpretation.

The exemption, as we construe it, does not deprive corporate employees, as a class, of the safeguards of the Act. We agree that some employee offerings may come within §[4(2)], e.g., one made to executive personnel who because of their position have access to the same kind of information that the act would make available in the form of a registration statement. Absent such a showing of special circumstances, employees are just as much members of the investing "public" as any of their neighbors in the community. Although we do not rely on it, the rejection in 1934 of an amendment which would have specifically exempted employee stock offerings supports this conclusion. The House Managers, commenting on the Conference Report, said that "the participants in the employees' stock-investment plans may be in as great need of the protection afforded by availability of information concerning the issuer for which they work as are most other members of the public." H.R. Rep. No. 1838, 73d Cong., 2d Sess. 41.

Keeping in mind the broadly remedial purposes of federal securities legislation, imposition of the burden of proof on an issuer who would plead the exemption seems to us fair and reasonable. Agreeing, the court below thought the burden met primarily because of the respondent's purpose in singling out its key employees for stock offerings. But once it is seen that the exemption question turns on the knowledge of the offerees, the issuer's motives, laudable though they may be, fade into irrelevance. The focus of inquiry should be on the need of the offerees for the protections afforded by registration. The employees here were not shown to have access to the kind of information which registration would disclose. The obvious opportunities for pressure and imposition made it advisable that they be entitled to compliance with §5.

NOTE: EXEMPTIONS

Most small companies try to avoid the registration provisions because the costs will consume a significant portion of the funds to be raised. The principal costs are commissions to those who sell the securities, attorneys' fees in preparation of the material, accounting fees for the financial statements required by the material, and printing and filing fees for the disclosed documents. In addition to direct costs, there may be indirect costs such as having to restructure the corporation or having to reconstruct financial records for previous years.

Exemptions are provided for private placements, small offerings and intrastate offerings. The JOBS Act, enacted in 2012, provides a new exemption for crowdfunding; the new exemption will allow entrepreneurs and companies to raise up to $1 million from a large number of small investors, collectively constituting "a crowd."

Rule 506, promulgated by the SEC under the 1933 Act, is the most used current example of the §4(2) exemption discussed in *Ralston Purina*. Such private placements are conditioned on meeting requirements regarding disclosure, the sophistication of the purchasers, a limitation of the offerings to not more than 35 purchasers, and restrictions on selling by general solicitation. Significantly, if the issuer limits the offering only to accredited investors (e.g., banks and wealthy individuals), it can skip the requirements based on sophistication, disclosure, the ban on general solicitation, and the numerical limit on the number of purchasers. Private offerings to these accredited investors have dwarfed the usage of other exemptions and even outpaced funds raised in public offerings in some periods.

There are other exemptions permitting a local company to sell to local investors for local use (Rule 147) or issuers raising limited amounts of capital (e.g., Rule 504, up to $1 million; Rule 505, up to $5 million; Regulation A, up to $5 million; and a new exemption authorized by the JOBS Act in 2012 (referred to as "A+") that would ease regulatory burdens for offerings up to $50 million.

C.   Shareholder Investment and Governance in Publicly Held Corporations and the Impact of Federal Law

1.   How Publicly Held Corporations Are Different

The corporate law rules discussed to this point apply to all corporations, whether publicly held or owned by just a few shareholders. But a number of important differences dramatically affect the governance of publicly held corporations and influence the relative roles of law and private ordering in that setting. We will focus on four of these characteristics:

1.   The presence of a market for shares;
2.   The dominance of institutional shareholders among the census of shareholders of publicly held corporations;
3.   The practical necessity for shareholder action in public corporations to be by proxy; and
4.   Federal regulation based on a company having publicly traded shares.

a.   The Market for Shares and the Efficient Market Hypothesis

When a corporation reaches certain minimal levels of outstanding shares and net worth, its shares can be traded in a regional or national securities market. Corporations with such characteristics will generate sufficient trading volume to justify a centralized matching of buyers and sellers — the essence of a securities market. Securities markets provide three important services to publicly traded corporations and their shareholders. Two of these, liquidity and valuation, go hand in hand. The third service, the monitoring of managers, is closely related.

To understand the liquidity and valuation functions of securities markets, consider how private residences are sold. Unlike shares, private residences are unique. Bringing buyers and sellers together involves significant transaction costs. First, potential buyers must investigate a residence to see whether it fits their needs. Second, they must determine a fair price.

Securities markets reduce this type of transaction cost to near zero. As discussed at the beginning of this chapter, all publicly traded common shares have nearly identical legal characteristics, thereby eliminating the need for ordinary investors to incur legal costs to ascertain the rights attached to any particular corporation's shares. In addition, the competition between and among informed buyers and sellers means that there is a reliable market price for each share of stock, also eliminating ordinary shareholders' need to incur research costs. Thus, efficient securities markets ensure that shareholders have ongoing, free information as to the current value of their shares. Moreover, markets provide near costless liquidity, giving shareholders the ability to sell their shares at any time, for whatever purpose, without paying substantial broker's fees.

Securities markets' liquidity and valuation functions have a significant impact on corporate governance. First, the securities markets serve as a quasi-monitor of the corporation's managers. If the corporation is being poorly managed, or if its assets would have significantly greater value in some different use, a new management team may seek to acquire a majority of the corporation's shares and then replace management. This possibility of corporate takeover (see Chapters 8 and 9) motivates managers to operate the corporation efficiently and with a view to maximizing share value. As a result, shareholders can avoid the cost, or lessen their reliance on other means of monitoring or disciplining management (e.g., through litigation, voting, or direct participation in management).

(1)   PHYSICAL AND ELECTRONIC MARKETS FOR SHARES

Centralized trading of shares, once characterized by physical trading on the floor of a traditional stock exchange, now mostly occurs electronically as market makers post prices at which they will buy or sell securities. There have been two major markets for stock in the United States, the New York Stock Exchange (NYSE) and NASDAQ, with others around the world, but additional trading platforms have grown up with new technology.

A major worry of any stock trading system is the possibility of wide swings in pricing when trading is too thin or customers are panicking. To lessen price volatility, the traditional stock exchanges used specialists in each listed stock to coordinate all transactions in their assigned stocks (the NYSE still uses specialists along with electronic trading). Whenever there is a significant disparity between the number of persons wishing to buy or sell a stock, the specialist would step in and use its own funds to be the missing buyer or seller. Electronic trading offers increased possibilities for individual traders to buy and sell without intermediaries, but has also led to markets driven by high-speed trading done by computer programs and "dark pools" where traders seek to find a venues not dominated by those strategies. Technological advances have also contributed to globalization of securities trading.

(2)   THE EFFICIENT MARKET HYPOTHESIS

Clearly, national market systems are an invaluable resource for publicly traded corporations. Shareholders' confidence in these markets makes it possible for corporations to raise huge amounts of capital from investors. Think about your own willingness to invest in stock. Would you feel the need to do research on a particular NYSE-traded stock to be sure that the trading price is "fair"? And as the quoted price of a stock you own changes from day to day in the weeks and months after you purchase it, would you be concerned that you should continuously research the company whose stock you purchased? The more confidence you have that the traded stock price reflects a fair price, the more willing you will be to purchase stock, and the higher the price you will pay relative to other investments that carry higher research costs and more uncertainty as to value. Moreover, both you and lawmakers will feel less need for costly laws and regulations to ensure that prices are fair.

In the last several decades, economists have asserted that our stock exchanges and alternative trading markets provide unbiased prices. If this is so, investors can purchase or sell stocks for the prevailing quoted price without the concern that home buyers have—that the quoted price is not fair but instead represents the seller's personal biases or irrational beliefs concerning the value of her home.

Economists arrived at this belief by empirically testing stock market efficiency. The first step was to test the claim that stock prices move in a "random walk." Prices move randomly if past prices give no information as to what prices will be in the future. Consider the analogous problem of determining whether a coin will come up heads or tails based on what the last coin flip produced. You cannot systematically chart the results of past coin flips and learn from the pattern whether the next flip is more likely to be heads or tails. The next flip result is totally random. Likewise, if stock prices move randomly, then you cannot learn from studying past prices whether the next price change is more likely to be up or down.

In the 1960s, economists asserted that they had empirically proved that stock prices do move in a random walk. This debate is often presented in the form of a hypothesis, the Efficient Market Hypothesis, which can be tested. The weakest form of the EMH posits that you cannot develop a trading strategy based on the use of past prices that will enable you to beat the market return. If there were information from past prices that had not yet been incorporated into the price by the market, you could trade based on such a strategy (e.g., buy when stock has gone down for two days and back up for one), but studies over time have not revealed such winnable strategies. In essence, the current market price is unbiased in that it has already incorporated the value of information from past prices, and whatever causes the price to move tomorrow will be because of new information.

Economists then set about testing two stronger forms of the EMH. The so-called semi-strong-form hypothesis asserts that you cannot develop a trading strategy that will beat the market by using publicly available information relevant to the value of traded stocks (e.g., an announcement about earnings or a change in dividends). The market will be efficient in incorporating such information before you can effectively trade on it. The strong-form hypothesis tests an even stronger claim, that even if your trading strategy were based on nonpublic information, you would not be able to beat the market.

In simplified form, this is how trading might look if the strong-form hypothesis were true. At 9 a.m. on Tuesday, Coca-Cola stock is trading for $40 per share. At that moment, Coca-Cola issues a press release announcing the results of an interim accounting report revealing a fact previously unknown to the investing public — that Coca-Cola will earn 75 cents per share more in the third quarter of its fiscal year than previously estimated. Although you might expect that this favorable fact will immediately cause a price increase in the stock as investors rush to capitalize upon previously unknown information, in a strong-form efficient market the price of Coca-Cola stock will remain constant because the market would have already taken the information into account before it was announced. Although there is evidence that markets can be strong-form efficient in certain circumstances, there has never been widespread belief that our markets are strong-form efficient. This means that individuals who possess "inside," nonpublic information can make a profit by trading on that information. And this explains, as we will see in Chapter 12, why trading on undisclosed "inside" information is prohibited by federal securities law.

Returning to our Coca-Cola hypothetical, in a semi-strong-form efficient market, the market behaves essentially as you might expect. Assume again that at 9 a.m. on Tuesday, Coca-Cola stock is trading for $40 per share. At that moment, Coca-Cola issues a press release announcing the results of an interim accounting report revealing a fact previously unknown to the investing public — that Coca-Cola will earn 75 cents per share more in the third quarter of its fiscal year than previously estimated. By 9:05 a.m., the stock of Coca-Cola rises $2 per share, reflecting this previously unknown fact. If you buy stock at 9:05 a.m. just after learning about the new earnings report, you are buying at a price that reflects the value of Coca-Cola stock given all available public information, including the new earnings forecast.

How can markets assimilate and reflect new information so rapidly? The common explanation is the existence of a large number of sophisticated market investors who trade for their own account or for the investors they represent. These professionals track all sources of information affecting the value of stock and act instantaneously to capture the "profit" available by buying stock at the "old" fair price. In our Coca-Cola example, market professionals buy stock beginning at 9:01 a.m. for $40 per share and continue buying until the stock reaches its "new" fair value representing the new equilibrium price at which the number of willing buyers and sellers is identical.

Financial economists think about market efficiency not as an on-off switch but as degrees of efficiency. The general acceptance that our securities markets are at least semi-strong-form efficient, as illustrated in the foregoing example, has affected the laws governing corporations. The Securities and Exchange Commission has expressly relied on that belief to make major changes in its regulation of our securities markets, and the Supreme Court has relied on it as a factor in determining "reliance" in securities fraud cases. Additionally, some scholars and courts have asserted that shareholders should not be able to bring lawsuits for damages that result from mistaken decisions made by a corporation's management. Since the skill and diligence of a corporation's officers and directors are largely observable by stock analysts, its positive or negative effect on the value of a corporation's stock is presumably accurately and instantaneously reflected in the price of that stock. Since shareholders buy stock at a price reflecting the skills of the corporation's management team, they have already been compensated by a discounted share price if they buy stock in a corporation with subpar managers.

If markets meet those criteria to be considered semi-strong-form efficient, then a risk averse investor planning to invest in stocks is smart to put her money in a mutual fund that perfectly duplicates the makeup of the market in which she wishes to invest. So, if the target market is the NYSE, then she should put her money in a mutual fund that replicates the makeup of that exchange. She will then obtain the average gain or loss that the NYSE-traded stocks experience as a whole. If she tries to "beat the market" by buying only those stocks that she or her investment advisor believe will "outperform" the market, she has a 50 percent chance of guessing right and a 50 percent chance of guessing wrong. If she pays her investment advisor to help her make that guess, then she is doomed on average to have a lower net return by the amount she has paid her advisor.

Another way of putting this is to describe stock analysts as "dart throwers." By the time they can tell you about any stock that they believe is undervalued, the market will have that information and there will be no "profit" left to be made by buying the recommended stock. The Wall Street Journal tested this proposition for more than a decade with an entertaining feature.

In 1988, the Wall Street Journal began a contest. Periodically, the Journal staff would invite four professional money managers to select the stocks they thought would do best in the coming months. Then the staff would repair to a nearby tavern, pin a page from the stock quotes section to the wall, and throw darts to select their own portfolio. At the end of each contest period, the Journal would announce who had done better, the pros or the darts. In the first round, the hands-down winner of this "Investment Dartboard" contest was: the darts.

This result came as no surprise to either finance theorists or their hangers-on. After all, we had all studied from that bible of modern financial theory, Brealey and Myers' Principles of Corporate Finance. We knew that decades of scholarship had definitively proven the Efficient Capital Markets Hypothesis (ECMH), a keystone theory of modern finance that predicts that market prices are "informationally efficient" (i.e., respond to new information almost instantaneously). . . . Thus the Investment Dartboard results only confirmed what the academics already knew: you can't beat the market.

Or so it seemed from the first round. Undeterred by their initial defeat, investment managers continued to step up to the plate in subsequent Investment Dartboard contests. And as the contest continued, it soon became apparent that while the pros sometimes lost, more often they won. The Journal has now run the Investment Dartboard contest for over eight years, and over that time a clear pattern has emerged: although the darts frequently give the pros a drubbing, on average the pros are beating both the darts and the market. Indeed, as of October 1996, the pro's portfolios had produced average annual gains of 20.6% for the darts, and 11.6% for the Dow Jones Industrial Average.

Stout, How Efficient Markets Undervalue Stocks: CAPM and ECMH Under Conditions of Uncertainty and Disagreement, 19 Cardozo L. Rev. 475, 477 (1997).

What can explain this empirical phenomenon? What can explain the stock market crash of 1987, in which the market lost nearly 25 percent of its value in one day? What can explain the NASDAQ bubble and its crash in 2001, or the subsequent reflation of stock prices followed by the stunning market losses in 2008? What does it mean to say that our national stock markets are semi-strong-form efficient if overall values can vary so dramatically over a relatively short time? Do these phenomena suggest that market prices do not accurately reflect what a rational buyer or seller should be willing to pay for a particular stock, and if so, why? Do they suggest that the markets are, in fact, not as efficient as economists have asserted and courts and policy makers have believed? Even if markets are unbiased in terms of being semi-strong-form efficient (in what is called informational efficiency), that does not mean that prices will be fundamentally efficient in terms of correctly valuing an entire class of assets.

An important piece of this puzzle may lie in the growing understanding that rational traders do not always determine stock prices in the way contemplated by the EMH. Developing fields of behavioral economics and cognitive psychology provide alternative explanations to complete rational economic behavior. One example is a process by which markets could be dominated not by rational traders, but instead by so-called noise traders. Noise traders are persons who have systematic cognitive biases that prevent rational assessment of the value of available information, leading to purchase and sale decisions being made on factors—background noise—that are irrationally treated as valuable information by the trader. Noise traders force prices away from the price that available information rationally suggests is ideal, creating profit opportunities for rational traders to step in and purchase or sell until the market again comes in line with available information. However, rational traders might occasionally "ride the wave" of irrationality, hoping to get out with big profits before the market realizes that the current price is irrationally high or low. The combination of noise traders occasionally dominating the market and rational traders riding the wave could explain large one-day shifts in market prices, when no real changes in available information are apparent.

There are a number of other theories that are increasing our understanding of the conditions under which markets may, either momentarily or for long periods of time, fail to rationally reflect all available public information. However, for our purposes in this course, it is enough to understand the basic theory of efficient markets and its limits, and to know that lawmakers, regulators, and many investors sometimes base investment, regulatory policy, and judicial decisions on the belief that our markets are generally semi-strong-form efficient.

PROBLEM 3-10

Nanette is in charge of investment decisions for RRIP, a large state pension fund. RRIP has been steadily increasing its investment in Argona, Inc., a corporation that manufactures and sells Internet upgrade kits to corporate clients. Argona's shares are traded over NASDAQ and the average daily trading volume is approximately 10,000 shares. RRIP owns 60,000 Argona shares, representing 6 percent of the outstanding stock. Nanette learns from her brother, a computer scientist, that a start-up company, Surf, Inc., is beta testing a product that may well devastate Argona's market for upgrade kits. Nanette was already concerned about RRIP's investment in Argona because the market price has dropped 25 percent in the last two weeks. Assuming Nanette believes that the information is reliable, or confirms it to her satisfaction, should she sell RRIP's Argona shares immediately?

b. The Shareholder Census: The Dominance of Institutional Investors

The mix in the census of shareholders in public corporations has changed dramatically over time. For most of the twentieth century, regulators and lawmakers based their actions on the "separation of ownership from control" model thought to be representative of the shareholder population. Under this model, the controlling shareholder interests in the typical publicly traded corporation were fragmented among numerous "small stakes," geographically dispersed, passive investors who simply rubber-stamped the officers' wishes, electing those directors aligned with management. The typical shareholder's lack of interest in corporate governance was seen as a product of "rational apathy." A rational person in the shoes of a typical small stakes shareholder would not be inclined to bear the costs required to become fully informed about corporate affairs or to communicate with, and coordinate the actions of, other shareholders. She would thus tend to remain almost entirely passive, relying upon the recommendations of management when voting her shares. If a rational shareholder was dissatisfied with corporate policies or suspected that management was unfit, it was considered more rational to follow the so-called Wall Street Rule and sell her shares than to engage in shareholder-initiated corrective action. Rationally apathetic shareholder behavior resulted in a significant separation of ownership and control in publicly held American corporations throughout much of the twentieth century.

During the past 50 years, share ownership has become increasingly concentrated in the hands of large institutional investors. In 1950, institutional investors held less than 10 percent of the outstanding shares in companies traded on the NYSE. In the early twenty-first century, institutional investors held 70 percent or more of shares in our 1,000 largest corporations. The institutional investor category includes retirement vehicles such as private pension funds and public pension funds, notably those of state and local governmental retirement systems and multiemployer plans for unionized employees that are visible in corporate governance. As regulatory policy and financial theory has pushed retirement plans toward a defined contribution mode, mutual funds have become the principal vehicle for retirement plans. Mutual funds now make up the largest category of institutional investors, owning more than a quarter of all stock in public corporations. See, e.g., Marcel Kahan and Edward Rock, Embattled CEOs, 88 Tex. L. Rev. 987 (2010) Table 1. Banks and insurance companies also fit within this category but typically have not been active in corporate governance.

Each type of institutional investor has different incentives for participating or not participating in corporate governance. Professors Gilson and Gordon have noted that the dominant business plan of mutual funds leads them to compete on relative performance, making them "rationally reticent." See Ronald Gilson & Jeffrey Gordon, Agency Costs of Agency Capitalism. 113 Colum. L. Rev. 863 (2013). The census of shareholders in public corporations, however, has broadened to include not only traditional institutional investors but also other large stakes, repeat investors who affect collective behavior. "Arbitrageurs" seek out companies whose stock is in play and seek to encourage the trends that will make them money. "Value investors" are those who actively seek to influence corporate management so as to produce higher share value from underperforming companies. "Relational investors" purchase large blocks in particular companies and seek a long-term relationship with management. "Social investors" give explicit priority to social needs in guiding investment decisions. Hedge funds have become large investors since the 1990s and a subset of these funds has turned to corporate governance activism as their business plan to produce above average returns. Typically these hedge funds purchase a minority interest and agitate for changes in the firm's policies that they think will produce an increase in the value of shares, often financial changes such as cash dividends or a sale of assets. Mutual funds and other institutions are willing to align themselves with these activists in some settings. See William W. Bratton, Hedge Funds and Governance Targets, 95 Geo. L.J. 1375 (2007); Marcel Kahan and Edward B. Rock, Hedge Funds in Corporate Governance and Corporate Control, 155 U. Pa. L. Rev. 1021-1093 (2007); Alon Brav, Wei Jiang, Frank Partnoy, and Randall S. Thomas, Hedge Fund Activism, Corporate Governance, and Firm Performance, 63 J. Fin. 1729 (2008).

At the same time that hedge funds have been pursuing managers to make changes in how they operate the corporation, private equity firms have been acquiring a larger number of public corporations (albeit a trend slowed by the credit crunch after mid-2007). Martin Lipton, an iconic figure in corporate takeovers (see the discussion of poison pills in Chapter 9) observed: "Today shareholder activism is ripping through the boardrooms of public corporations and threatening the future of American business." He warned against "the demeaning effect of the parade of lawyers, accountants, consultants and auditors through board and committee meetings" as one example of how the board's role, focus, and collegiality was being destroyed. Lipton's lament led him to an interesting conclusion of embracing going-private as the solution to the problem created by "rampant, unrestrained and unregulated shareholder activism." See Martin Lipton, Keynote Address to 25th Annual Institute on Federal Securities February 7, 2007, available at http://blogs.law.harvard.edu/corpgov/files/2007/02/20070210%20Lipton%20Address.pdf.

This dramatic change in shareholder composition suggests an evolving model of shareholder governance not limited to gaining control or even exercising voting rights at formal meetings. Politically active institutional investors and allied "activist investors" can use their large shareholdings both to carry out traditional shareholder responsibilities and to engage corporate management in a sustained conversation about how corporations should be managed.

> The most significant and defining aspect of the new political process is the rise of informal, political mechanisms to supplant, and even replace, the extreme measure of the formal voting challenge. Institutional ownership concentration creates a more sophisticated and smaller audience of investors, facilitating a wide variety of less formal approaches to organizing a critical mass of shareholder support. Where a corporation is owned by a few large institutions, instead of thousands of relatively uninformed individuals, management and directors may be more readily influenced by outsiders who circulate alternative policy proposals to major investors, make informal suggestions for new director nominees, seconded by major institutions, or solicit votes for a shareholder proposal which suggests specific reforms to corporate policy or board structure. These incremental and informal means of persuasion bring the political model of governance much closer to democratic politics in the public sector, in which the informed and ongoing participation of citizens, as much or more than electoral challenges, influences policy. . . .
>
> Regular, periodic access to the corporate franchise gives shareholders, like public citizens in a democracy, a baseline of power. . . .
>
> That power, however, is not manifested merely through formal voting challenges. Instead, power can be exercised through a rich variety of means. These may include the simple communication of concerns from shareholders to management; private negotiation between shareholders, management, and directors; rallying of support for specific issues or policy changes; and the establishment of formal lobbying campaigns. Underlying each of these informal initiatives is the veiled threat of a voting challenge aimed at board representation or control. In the corporate sector, as in the public sector, it is this threat that keeps elected representatives accountable to their constituents while in office.

Pound, The Rise of the Political Model of Corporate Governance and Control, 68 N.Y.U. L. Rev. 1003, 1008-1013 (1993).

What motivates institutional and large-stakes investors to behave differently from individual shareholders? For one thing, the larger size of their holdings makes it more difficult to use the "Wall Street Rule" of selling their stock. Rapid sales of large blocks of stock might panic the market in those shares, resulting in severe price drops. Political scientist Albert Hirshman has theorized that where exit is more costly and less attractive to participants in organizations, including business firms, they might be expected to seek alternatives that give them a greater voice in management and governance. See Hirshman, Exit, Voice and Loyalty (1970). Additionally, institutions are likely to be more knowledgeable than individual investors, largely as a result of greater and less expensive access to information. Institutions will generally be repeat players and will know other repeat players in the institutional investment community, giving institutions lines of communication not available to most individual investors.

Even though institutional shareholders hold a clear majority of the shares in most publicly traded corporations, the percentage of shares held by activist institutional shareholders and allied investors is generally much less than a majority. For example, corporate pension plans are among the largest owners of publicly traded stock. The managers of these plans are often reluctant to take an active role in corporate governance or to vote counter to management's wishes for fear that such action would cost them their position as plan manager or future business from other corporations. Insurance companies and banks often are similarly disinclined to become actively involved. Less hampered than other groups by fear of retribution from angry corporate managers, public pension funds and labor organizations have been at the forefront of efforts to use shareholder voting power more aggressively.

c. *Proxy Voting*

Although institutional investors may rationally invest the time and resources necessary to attend a shareholders' meeting or be required by fiduciary duties to do so, most individual shareholders in a publicly held corporation lack sufficient incentive to do so. By executing a simple agreement appointing a "proxy" to act on his behalf, a shareholder need not be physically present to participate in a meeting. Moreover, the proxy provides a means for institutional or other significant investors to collect voting power from smaller investors or each other in advance of an actual election, and thus is a valuable tool even for the active shareholder.

The term "proxy" has multiple overlapping uses, which may cause some initial confusion. Depending on the context, "proxy" may refer to (1) the legal relationship under which one party is given the power to vote the shares of another, as in "she voted her shares by proxy"; (2) the person or entity given the power to vote, as in "she acted as his proxy"; or (3) the tangible document that evidences the relationship, as in "he mailed his proxy." A proxy designation may create an agency relationship that requires the proxy holder to follow the shareholder's instruction. Alternatively, a proxy holder may be given absolute discretion to vote as he sees fit.

We will see that shareholders exercise their principal management functions, including election of directors, at shareholders' meetings. However, the actual meeting is an extended process involving significant pre-meeting communication between and among a corporation's management and shareholders. Much of this communication centers on obtaining proxies that will determine everything from whether there is the necessary quorum present (mostly by proxy) to hold a valid meeting to who will be the corporation's directors. Both management and those who seek to oppose management on any matter to be voted on at the meeting must themselves solicit proxies from shareholders who will not attend in person. Thus, in most large corporations, the true contest in any disputed matter occurs at the proxy solicitation stage rather than at the actual shareholders' meeting. A high-visibility proxy fight is described in the excerpt from the HP/Compaq merger litigation found at the beginning of Chapter 8.

Keep in mind that the proxy process is federally regulated. We will see that the SEC plays a significant role in setting the rules for the proxy and shareholders' meeting process and in settling disputes between management and shareholders concerning the conduct of that process.

The proxy process is changing in response both to technology and to change in the shareholder census. SEC proxy rules under the 1934 Act require issuers and other soliciting persons to post their proxy materials on an Internet website and to provide shareholders with notice that the materials are available. Federal regulation requires pension plans and mutual fund holders (who now hold significant voting rights in most publicly traded corporations) to treat those voting rights like any other asset; i.e., they must vote the shares they own. In 2009, the SEC approved a rule change of the NYSE that ended the long-established practice whereby brokers and other intermediaries voted the shares in their possession in uncontested director elections, even in the absence of instructions from the beneficial owners. These changes, along with the dramatic increase in the number of issues on which shareholders vote (see, for example, the "say on pay" votes discussed in the next section) and the large number of issuers in which diversified institutions own shares, have increased the power and influence of proxy advisory firms, which publish criteria and review proposals up for shareholder vote. (See, e.g., Institutional Shareholders Services and Glass Lewis & Co.) How the main proxy advisory firms recommend that institutions vote ends up being a key part of a contested takeover battle, but concern remains over the incentives and performance of such intermediaries.

d. Federal Regulation of Publicly Held Companies

Securities Exchange Act of 1934 §§12(b), 12(g), 13(a), 14(a), 14(d)
1934 Exchange Act Rules 14a-3, 14a-4, 14a-5, 14a-9, Schedule S-K,
Forms 10-K, 10-Q, 8-K

The larger impact that publicly held corporations have on our economy has generated periodic calls for different and additional regulation of these corporations. These pleas usually are addressed to Congress and raise the policy question of the extent to which corporate governance should be a federal or state function. These issues have been debated for more than a century, particularly during the time of Theodore Roosevelt's trust-busting at the beginning of the twentieth century, during the New Deal after the Great Depression, and most recently at the beginning of the twenty-first century in the wake of the Enron and WorldCom scandals and the financial meltdown in 2007-2008. At none of these times did the federal government choose to pass a federal incorporation statute that would have federalized the rules that we have studied to this point. Beginning with the New Deal legislation, Congress did choose to supplement the existing state regulatory regime, mostly by requiring disclosure that would enhance the capacity of investors and shareholders in their dealing with corporate managers. This section introduces the disclosure paradigm. The following section brings in how recently promulgated federal rules have expanded the federal footprint and methodology, and how those changes interact with the state law and market changes we have just discussed.

At this point, federal law requires disclosure (and some ancillary regulation) in five contexts. You might think about this list as five activities that trigger federal disclosure obligations:

- *Issuing securities*—a topic that we have already discussed and that was the first place of federal regulation through the Securities Act of 1933. Disclosure and related regulation is triggered by a company decision to raise money in the public markets.
- *Periodic reporting*—required of public companies under §13 of the Securities Exchange Act of 1934. This requirement is an annual report (usually referred to by the form on which it must be filed, a 10-K), quarterly reports (10-Q), and certain immediate reports (8-K). These reports require disclosure from issuers about, for example, their business, their property, their management, and the conflicts of interest their managers might have. These filings are available to the public through the SEC's database at http://www.sec.gov. This disclosure obligation is considered in more detail in the material that immediately follows; liability is explored in more detail in Chapter 10.
- *Proxy solicitation*—the most visible focus of federal regulation in the decades after enactment of the Securities Exchange Act of 1934. It is based on section 14(a) of the Act and was intended to cure deficiencies in the shareholder voting process discussed earlier in this chapter. In that respect, the federal role is ancillary to the state role, requiring disclosure only when state law requires or permits shareholders to act. As you read the materials on this topic at the end of this chapter, be alert for the federalism issues raised in the extent to which federal rules accept or seek to go beyond the roles of shareholders and directors established by state law.
- *Tender offers*—disclosure when shareholders are asked to respond to a tender offer, a form of corporate takeover discussed in more detail in Chapter 11. As with the proxy rules, these rules are designed to allow shareholders to make an informed decision on corporate decisions in which they have a role.
- *Insider trading*—discussed in Chapter 12.

The periodic, proxy, and tender offer regulations apply to companies with a class of stock registered on a national securities exchange or over a minimum size.[1] The periodic, proxy, and disclosure regimes each draw on the SEC's Regulation S-K, which spells out what must be disclosed, for example, about the business and property of the company (Items 101-103), selected financial data (Items 301-306), and core information about managers and their conflicts of interest (Items 401-405). Since Sarbanes-Oxley, the SEC has focused particular attention on executive compensation (see, e.g., the disclosure required by Item 402 of Regulation S-K), an illustration of the agency's impact on corporate governance. The disclosure requirements seek to ensure that traders in those markets will have sufficient information as they buy or sell. Of course, those buyers and sellers are the shareholders whose position is at the center of this chapter. The periodic disclosure rules primarily are aimed at shareholders engaged in the selling (or buying) function rather than voting, but this buying and selling function can itself be a key part of corporate governance. The increase in federal disclosure

---

1. As of 2012, $10 million in assets and at least 2,000 shareholders of record or at least 500 "nonaccredited" shareholders of record (i.e., not an institution or not wealthy).

requirements connected with periodic reporting certainly acts to constrain the space within which managers operate.

While states usually determine the substantive law governing relations between a corporation and its shareholders, federal law plays the dominant role in regulating vote-related communication between and among shareholders and the corporation. Federal regulation began with the enactment of the 1934 Securities Exchange Act. Section 14(a) of that Act gave the SEC authority to regulate the proxy or consent solicitation process of the shares of a corporation required to register securities with the SEC.

The legislative history suggests that Congress was primarily concerned with preventing corporations from soliciting proxies by means of materials that did not reveal the true nature of the matter being acted upon. However, the SEC has interpreted its §14(a) mandate broadly. As the cases in the following subpart show, the rules seem designed to ensure that the proxy process allows shareholders to communicate with each other and the corporation as though all of the shareholders were gathered in a large town hall on annual meeting day. Analogizing loosely, the SEC plays the role of parliamentarian for this town meeting, laying down rules for who speaks, how long they speak, and on what topics they may speak. Consistent with this broader mission, the SEC has promulgated extensive rules to address the content and timing of proxy solicitation. The following is a thumbnail sketch of those rules.

Rule 14a-3.   Rule 14a-3 prohibits any proxy solicitation unless the person solicited is first furnished a publicly filed preliminary or final proxy statement containing the information specified in Schedule 14A of the Exchange Act rules. The required disclosure includes basic facts that informed voters would presumably possess. For example, Regulation 14A requires that the proxy statement disclose the time, date, and place of the meeting to which the solicitation relates, the revocability of the proxy, the solicitor's identity and source of funds, and the identity of and basic information about candidates for director (if the solicitation concerns election of directors). In addition, Rule 14a-3 requires that the proxy statement sent by management in connection with proxy solicitation for the annual shareholders' meeting shall be accompanied by an annual report in prescribed form.

Rule 14a-5.   Rule 14a-5 regulates the form of the proxy statement. The principal requirements relate to readability. For example, Rule 14a-5 specifies the type style (roman) and type size (normally 10 point), the manner in which material must be presented (where practicable, information should be in tabular form; all amounts should be stated in figures), and how information shall generally be presented (statements shall be divided into groups according to subject matter, and each group shall be preceded by appropriate headings).

Rule 14a-4.   Rule 14a-4 regulates the form of the proxy that solicitors ask shareholders to execute. Traditionally this proxy was often printed on a rectangular card. As a result, it has become commonplace to refer to a proxy form as a "proxy card." Increasingly, electronic communication has replaced the printed form.

Like Rule 14a-5, Rule 14a-4 imposes readability requirements. However, the overriding concern of Rule 14a-4 is to ensure that shareholders are given an opportunity to do more than grant the authority requested by the solicitor. Thus, the proxy card must provide boxes whereby a shareholder may specify whether she approves, disapproves, or abstains with respect to each matter covered by the proxy. If the matter relates to an election of directors, the proxy card must clearly provide a method whereby the solicited shareholder may withhold authority to vote for nominees favored by the solicitor.

Rule 14a-9.   Rule 14a-9 is a catch-all provision designed to supplement and reinforce the specific disclosure mandates. Rule 14a-9 prohibits the making of false or misleading statements as to any material fact, or the misleading omission of a material fact, in connection with a proxy solicitation. We will study Rule 14a-9 in Chapter 10.

Some SEC regulation seems to go beyond the parliamentarian function suggested above to regulate the substance of the governance relationship between shareholders and directors, such as shareholder nomination of directors or shareholder "say on pay." These developments and the responses they have generated are discussed in more detail at the end of the chapter.

ACME, INC.	**This Proxy Is Solicited on Behalf of the Board of Directors**
PROXY	

ACME, INC. **PROXY**   **This Proxy Is Solicited on Behalf of the Board of Directors**

55 Main St.
St, Louis, MO 63130

The undersigned appoints John Red, Mary Blue, and Lee White as Proxies, each with the power to appoint his or her substitute, and authorizes them to represent and to vote, as designated below, all the shares of common stock of Acme held on record by the undersigned on January 10, 2013 at the annual meeting of shareholders to be held on March 10, 2013 or any adjournment.

1. ELECTION OF DIRECTORS

FOR all nominees listed below (except as marked to the contrary below) ☐

WITHHOLD AUTHORITY to vote for all nominees listed below ☐

(INSTRUCTION To withhold authority to vote for any individual nominee strike a line through the nominee's name in the list below)

J. Allen, S. Brown, J. Doe, J. Green, G. Johansen, A. Jones, M. Roe, J. Smith and M. Stanton

2. PROPOSAL TO APPROVE THE APPOINTMENT OF DOLLAR AND CENTS as the independent public accountants of the corporation

☐ FOR   ☐ AGAINST   ☐ ABSTAIN

---

3. STOCKHOLDER PROPOSAL RELATING TO CUMULATIVE VOTING:

☐ FOR   ☐ AGAINST   ☐ ABSTAIN

4. In their discretion the Proxies are authorized to vote upon such other business as may properly come before the meeting.

This proxy when properly executed will be voted in the manner directed herein by the stockholder. If no direction is made, this proxy will be voted for Proposals 1 and 2 and against Proposal 3.

Please sign exactly as name appears below. When shares are held by joint tenants, both should sign. When signing as attorney, as executor, administrator, trustee or guardian, please give full title as such. If a corporation, please sign in full corporate name by President or other authorized officer. If a partnership, please sign in partnership name by authorized person.

DATED: _____ 2013   _____
                          Signature

                          _____
                          Signature if held jointly

PROBLEM 3-11

Carefully review the proxy printed on the previous page. Does it comply with Rule 14a-4?

2.   Shareholder Governance in the Public Corporation

The world described by Berle and Means in the early 1930s (discussed in Chapter 1) was one in which the largest publicly held corporations were managed without effective input or control by the shareholders. Would America allow so much of its economic wealth and power to be controlled by a small group of corporate managers—"princes of industry"—without any countervailing obligations to, or surrender of power to, shareholders or society?

The New Deal provided the federal government's answer via various methods to achieve social control over finance. New legislation reduced the role of investment bankers in underwriting and bankruptcy. A federal agency, the Securities and Exchange Commission, gained regulatory power over stock exchanges and broker-dealers. Society could and would require corporations and their managers to recognize the goals of society via federal regulation in areas such as labor law and workplace safety, later expanded to include job discrimination, pension security, environmental pollution, and foreign corrupt practices. Thus corporations would be forced to recognize the larger claims of society, and to yield power to society to enforce society's claims.

However, the New Deal did not radically change the governance relationship between managers and shareholders, nor change the balance of power in favor of shareholders. The federal government chose not to implement a federal incorporation statute and thereby prescribe internal governance rules. Substantive governance rights were largely left to state law. Rather, the federal government focused on improving the position of investors by requiring disclosure, particularly when they buy or sell securities or when they vote as shareholders, as discussed in more detail in Chapter 10.

Over the past 80 years, there have been repeated efforts by proponents of shareholder rights to use federal regulation of the proxy solicitation process to provide greater power to shareholders. Resistance to these proposals has been strong. Opponents argue that expanding shareholder rights would lead to less effective corporate decision making and that state regulation of corporations' internal affairs should be preserved. In the aftermath of Enron and the market collapses of 2001 and 2007-2008, and in a decade that saw unprecedented growth in activism and institutional shareholders, there was a perceptible shift in both federal and state law with regard to the substantive governance rights and power of shareholders. This section outlines the broader footprint of federal governance rules, and then explores the richer space for governance at the intersection of state law, federal rules, and private actors.

a.   Federal Substantive Rules as to Corporate Governance

After decades of leaving the substantive rules of corporate governance to the states, Congress has been more willing in the twenty-first century to exercise federal authority over some areas of corporate governance. For example:

- Federal law requires that boards of directors have compensation and nomination committees and that independent directors compose these committees;
- Public corporations must have internal controls, as specified in federal statutes;
- Federal law requires that public companies have claw-back provisions that recoup compensation from executives after particular financial events.

These are still limited intrusions into state authority over the substance of corporate law, and both the legality and wisdom of this federal expansion continue to be contested. For example, when the SEC banned midstream adoptions of dual-class voting, a federal appellate court found the action to be beyond the SEC's power: "With its step beyond control of voting procedure and into the distribution of voting power, the Commission would assume an authority that the Exchange Act's proponents disclaimed any intent to grant." The Business Roundtable v. Securities and Exchange Commission, 905 F.2d 406, 412 (D.C. Cir. 1990) (stating that under the SEC's interpretation of its authority, "the Commission would be able to establish a federal corporate law by using access to national capital markets as its enforcement mechanism. This would resolve a long-standing controversy over the wisdom of such a move in the face of disclaimers from Congress and with no substantive restraints on the power.")

A generation later, reviewing another SEC intrusion into state law that would have permitted individual shareholders to nominate candidates for director to be included on the proxy sent out by the company, and in the face of congressional action that seemed to resolve the earlier federalism concern by explicitly authorizing such agency action, another panel of the same court, acting on a petition of the same plaintiff, turned to different reasons to strike down the agency action. In Business Roundtable vs. SEC, 647 F.3d 1144 (D.C. Cir. 2011), the appellate court found that the SEC acted arbitrarily and capriciously (a requirement of the Administrative Procedure Act for agency action generally) for having failed to adequately assess the economic effects of the new rules, a requirement of Section 3(f) of the 1934 Act that agency rule making must "consider in addition to protection of investors, whether the action will promote efficiency, competition and capital formation." That requirement has not previously had as wide effect as the court gave it in this setting, and the case suggests a potentially large role for judicial review based on cost-benefit analysis.

In its rule making, the agency had recognized that boards may be motivated to spend significant resources in opposition to shareholder nominees and started its belief those costs may be limited by specified factors. The court found that "[b]ecause the agency failed to make tough choices about which of the competing estimates is most plausible, [or] to hazard a guess as to which is correct, we believe that it neglected its statutory obligation to assess the economic consequences of its rule." *Id.* at 1151 (internal citations and quotations omitted). The court also found that the Commission had "not sufficiently supported its conclusion that increasing the potential for election of directors nominated by shareholders would result in improved board and company performance and shareholder value." *Id.* The court also noted that "the Commission failed to respond to comments arguing that investors with a special interest, such as unions and state and local governments whose interests in jobs may well be greater than their interest in share value, can be expected to pursue self-interested objectives rather than the goal of maximizing shareholder value," and concluded that "[b]y ducking serious evaluation of the costs that could be imposed upon companies from use of the rule by shareholders representing special interests, particularly union and government pension funds, we think the Commission acted arbitrarily." *Id.* at 1152.

Sometimes the federal push for governance rules has been indirect, felt through federal pressure on self-regulatory organizations (SROs), such as the stock exchanges, ostensibly private participants in the market who are subject to federal oversight. The federal requirements for nominating and compensation committees just described are implemented through stock exchange listing requirements. Other stock exchange listing requirements ban midstream adoptions of dual-class voting (implemented by SRO rule after the SEC's rule discussed above had been struck down), and listing standards require that boards of directors of companies listed on those exchanges be composed of a majority of independent directors (something not required by state corporations statutes). There is a longer history of SRO regulation of corporate governance independent of federal rules. For example, the listing standards of the NYSE required audited financial statements before the federal government required them. Further, the NYSE requires a shareholder vote on some corporate control transactions that are not required by state law.

b. Enhancing Shareholder Power Through More High-Powered Disclosure Requirements

The importance of disclosure as required by federal law has grown dramatically over recent decades. First, there has been an increase in the amount of mandatory disclosure. The number of items in Regulation S-K, for example, now exceeds 70 and takes up 100 pages of the federal rulebook. Second, technology has made information more widely and quickly available. Third, growth in information technology has promoted more voluntary disclosure, which companies make through press releases or websites; the mandatory disclosure provides a baseline against which voluntary disclosures can be compared. Fourth, there has been a dramatic expansion of the scope of liability, both public (as illustrated in the Sarbanes-Oxley Act of 2002) and private, discussed in Chapter 10 of this book.

Sometimes disclosure is a thinly disguised effort to change the substance of an officer's or director's behavior (something that traditionally would be determined by state law). See, e.g., §406 of the Sarbanes-Oxley Act of 2002, requiring disclosure of whether a company has adopted a code of ethics for senior financial officers, and if not, the reason therefore, and §404, requiring a statement by management asserting that it is responsible for creating and assessing the effectiveness of internal controls.

c. Federal Rules Providing Shareholders Access to Persuasive Communication: Rule 14a-8

Federal law has also enhanced the shareholder governance role by expanding the matters on which shareholders may vote beyond what state law requires. So far, the federally created voting rights have been "precatory." In other words, the voting and expressive rights created by federal law are advisory only. Shareholders can only "act" for the corporation pursuant to authority granted by state corporations law. A recent example is the "say on pay" requirement enacted in 2010, which is discussed in more detail in the next section, but the federal government's interest in providing channels for shareholders to engage in persuasive but not necessarily binding communication goes back to 1942. SEC Rule 14a-8, first promulgated in 1942, permits a "qualifying shareholder" to insert a proposal into the company's proxy for the annual meeting, the most common way that voting takes place in public corporations. A shareholder can require her corporation to include a "shareholder proposal" and an accompanying supporting statement in the company's proxy materials. The proposal and supporting statement may not exceed 500 words. The rule was recast in 1993 as a series of questions and answers in an effort to more clearly communicate with investors, so that Rule 14a-8(a) (Question One) defines a "shareholder proposal" as "your recommendation or requirement that the company and/or its board of directors take action, which you intend to present at a meeting of the company's shareholders." In effect, the qualifying shareholder is making a motion at the shareholders' meeting, but is using the company's proxy material as the medium for effectively communicating her proposal to other shareholders.

To be a "qualifying shareholder" a person must at the time she submits her proposal own a minimum stake of the shares for a minimum holding period and continuously own such stock through the date of the meeting. A qualifying shareholder may use Rule 14a-8 to make only one proposal per meeting. Rule 14a-8 permits shareholders persuasive communication with the directors as to matters that are not directly within the shareholder space for decisions. It has been used by shareholders primarily interested in reform of the corporation's management practices or structures, as well as proposals from shareholders interested in broader social goals. Over the years, proponents in this latter class have used Rule 14a-8 to fight segregation and apartheid, to protect the whale and the tuna, to stop the manufacture of napalm, and to increase the number of women and minorities in the corporate workplace.

The access provided by Rule 14a-8 is subject to a number of exceptions, catalogued and explained in Rule 14a-8(i) (Question Nine). If any of these exceptions applies, then a corporation may refuse to include the submitted proposal in its proxy material.

The first Rule 14a-8(i) exception defines an essential policy choice made by the SEC—that the proxy process is intended both to permit shareholders to better carry out their voting responsibilities, such as election of directors, and to allow purely persuasive communication. As we have seen, shareholders do not have the power to directly manage the corporation. In most states they cannot initiate amendments to the Articles of Incorporation and cannot use the bylaws to interfere with state-determined limitations on shareholder power. Consistent with this state-determined limitation on shareholder power, Rule 14a-8(i)(1) allows a corporation to exclude proposals that are "not a proper subject for shareholder action under state law." (This was the basis for the certified question raised in the CA case at page 196.)

But state law has been ambiguous about shareholder power and Rule 14a-8 includes a "Note" as to how the SEC views that ambiguity: "In our experience, most proposals that are cast as recommendations or request that the board take specified action are proper under state law. Accordingly, we will assume that a proposal drafted as a recommendation or suggestion is proper unless the company demonstrates otherwise." Thus, if a shareholder casts her proposal in precatory form—as a mere request that the directors consider a particular form of action—then the proposal can be excluded only if another ground can be found in Rule 14a-8(i). In other words, the SEC and the 14a-8(i) rules recognize the importance of shareholders' ability to try to persuade the board to take actions that the shareholders do not have the power to directly mandate or carry out.

Shareholders frequently make proposals clearly designed to promote discussion of reforms that, arguably, would benefit society generally. For example, a shareholder of a power company might wish to present a proposal asking that the corporation close several of its nuclear plants; or a shareholder of a corporation with vast holdings of timber land may submit a proposal to discontinue a logging practice that allegedly threatens valuable wildlife not protected by the federal Endangered Species Act.

Directors often view these proposals as a nuisance and as a usurpation of their management responsibilities. The primary means to exclude such shareholder proposals from a company's proxy statement are the "economic irrelevance" test contained in Rule 14a-8(i)(5) and the "ordinary business" exclusion found in 14a-8(i)(7). The former allows omission of proposals that relate to operations accounting for less than 5 percent of a corporation's total assets, gross sales, and net sales if the proposal "is not otherwise significantly related" to the company's business. The latter allows exclusion of proposals relating to the "ordinary business" of the company. The difference between these sometimes overlapping provisions is often murky and can only be understood by reference to case law and SEC "no-action letter" precedents.

Where the SEC draws the line on excludability under the "ordinary business" exception is sometimes controversial. What seems socially insignificant in one era may become clearly significant in another. For example, in October 1992, the Division issued a no-action letter stating that the SEC would not bring an enforcement action against Cracker Barrel if it refused to include a shareholder proposal from a public pension fund that the company expressly prohibit discrimination on the basis of sexual orientation. See Cracker Barrel Old Country Store, Inc., SEC No-Action Letter, 1992 WL 289095 (SEC) (October 13, 1992) (the "Cracker Barrel no-action letter"). The SEC explained its action as follows:

> The Division has reconsidered the application of Rule 14a-8(c)(7) to employment related proposals in light of these concerns and the staff's experience with these proposals in recent years. As a result, the Division has determined that the fact that a shareholder proposal concerning a company's employment policies and practices for the general workforce is tied to a social issue will no longer be viewed as removing the proposal from the realm of ordinary business operations of the registrant.

In 1998, the SEC formally reversed its position, while explaining its approach to the "ordinary business" exception.

> In applying the "ordinary business" exclusion to proposals that raise social policy issues, the Division seeks to use the most well-reasoned and consistent standards possible, given the inherent

complexity of the task. From time to time, in light of experience dealing with proposals in specific subject areas, and reflecting changing societal views, the Division adjusts its view with respect to "social policy" proposals involving ordinary business. Over the years, the Division has reversed its position on the excludability of a number of types of proposals, including plant closings, the manufacture of tobacco products, executive compensation, and golden parachutes.

We believe that reversal of the Division's Cracker Barrel no-action letter . . . is warranted. Since 1992, the relative importance of certain social issues relating to employment matters has reemerged as a consistent topic of widespread public debate. In addition, as a result of the extensive policy discussions that the Cracker Barrel position engendered, and through the rulemaking notice and comment process, we have gained a better understanding of the depth of interest among shareholders in having an opportunity to express their views to company management on employment-related proposals that raise sufficiently significant social policy issues.

Reversal of the Cracker Barrel no-action position will result in a return to a case-by-case analytical approach. In making distinctions in this area, the Division and the Commission will continue to apply the applicable standard for determining when a proposal relates to "ordinary business." The standard, originally articulated in the Commission's 1976 release, provided an exception for certain proposals that raise significant social policy issues.

While we acknowledge that there is no bright-line test to determine when employment-related shareholder proposals raising social issues fall within the scope of the "ordinary business" exclusion, the staff will make reasoned distinctions in deciding whether to furnish "no-action" relief. Although a few of the distinctions made in those cases may be somewhat tenuous, we believe that on the whole the benefit to shareholders will outweigh the problematic aspects of the few decisions in the middle ground.

Amendments to Rules on Shareholder Proposals (May 21, 1998), 1998 WL 254809 (S.E.C.) at *34.

The following case explores the contours of the "socially significant" limitation on a corporation's ability to exclude shareholder proposals. Note that since this case was decided the rule has been renumbered, but that the order and the first and last digits of each rule remain the same so that what the case refers to as, e.g., Rule 14a-8(c)(5) is now Rule 14a-8(i)(5).

Lovenheim v. Iroquois Brands, Ltd.
United States District Court, District of Columbia, 1985
618 F. Supp. 554

GASCH, DISTRICT JUDGE.

I. BACKGROUND

This matter is now before the Court on plaintiff's motion for preliminary injunction.

Plaintiff Peter C. Lovenheim, owner of two hundred shares of common stock in Iroquois Brands, Ltd. (hereinafter "Iroquois/Delaware"), seeks to bar Iroquois/Delaware from excluding from the proxy materials being sent to all shareholders in preparation for an upcoming shareholder meeting information concerning a proposed resolution he intends to offer at the meeting. Mr. Lovenheim's proposed resolution relates to the procedure used to force-feed geese for production of paté de foie gras in France,[2] a type of paté imported by Iroquois/Delaware. Specifically, his resolution calls upon the Directors of Iroquois/Delaware to:

> form a committee to study the methods by which its French supplier produces paté de foie gras, and report to the shareholders its findings and opinions, based on expert consultation, on whether this production method causes undue distress, pain or suffering to the animals involved and, if so, whether further distribution of this product should be discontinued until a more humane production method is developed.

Attachment to Affidavit of Peter C. Lovenheim.

Iroquois/Delaware has refused to allow information concerning Mr. Lovenheim's proposal to be included in proxy materials being sent in connection with the next annual shareholders meeting. In doing so, Iroquois/Delaware relies on an exception to the general requirement of Rule 14a-8, Rule 14a-8(c)(5). That exception provides that an issuer of securities "may omit a proposal and any statement in support thereof" from its proxy statement and form of proxy: "if the proposal relates to operations which account for less than 5 percent of the issuer's total assets at the end of its most recent fiscal year, and for less than 5 percent of its net earnings and gross sales for its most recent fiscal year, and is not otherwise significantly related to the issuer's business." Rule 14a-8(c)(5). . . .

II. LIKELIHOOD OF PLAINTIFF PREVAILING ON MERITS . . .

C. APPLICABILITY OF RULE 14A-8(C)(5) EXCEPTION

In light of the above discussion of the service and jurisdiction issues, the likelihood of plaintiff's prevailing in this litigation turns primarily on the applicability to plaintiff's proposal of the exception to the shareholder proposal rule contained in Rule 14a-8(c)(5).

Iroquois/Delaware's reliance on the argument that this exception applies is based on the following information contained in the affidavit of its president: Iroquois/Delaware has annual revenues of $141 million with $6 million in annual profits and $78 million in assets. In contrast, its paté de foie gras sales were just $79,000 last year, representing a net loss on paté sales of $3,121. Iroquois/Delaware has only $34,000

---

2. Paté de foie gras is made from the liver of geese. According to Mr. Lovenheim's affidavit, force-feeding is frequently used in order to expand the liver and thereby produce a larger quantity of paté. Mr. Lovenheim's affidavit also contains a description of the force-feeding process:

> Force-feeding usually begins when the geese are four months old. On some farms where feeding is mechanized, the bird's body and wings are placed in a metal brace and its neck is stretched. Through a funnel inserted 10-12 inches down the throat of the goose, a machine pumps up to 400 grams of corn-based mash into its stomach. An elastic band around the goose's throat prevents regurgitation. When feeding is manual, a handler uses a funnel and stick to force the mash down. Plaintiff contends that such force-feeding is a form of cruelty to animals.

> Plaintiff has offered no evidence that force-feeding is used by Iroquois/Delaware's supplier in producing the pate imported by Iroquois/Delaware. However his proposal calls upon the committee he seeks to create to investigate this question.

in assets related to paté. Thus none of the company's net earnings and less than .05 percent of its assets are implicated by plaintiff's proposal. These levels are obviously far below the five percent threshold set forth in the first portion of the exception claimed by Iroquois/Delaware.

Plaintiff does not contest that his proposed resolution relates to a matter of little economic significance to Iroquois/Delaware. Nevertheless he contends that the Rule 14a-8(c)(5) exception is not applicable as it cannot be said that his proposal "is not otherwise significantly related to the issuer's business" as is required by the final portion of that exception. In other words, plaintiff's argument that Rule 14a-8 does not permit omission of his proposal rests on the assertion that the rule and statute on which it is based do not permit omission merely because a proposal is not economically significant where a proposal has "ethical or social significance."[8]

Iroquois/Delaware challenges plaintiff's view that ethical and social proposals cannot be excluded even if they do not meet the economic or five percent test. Instead, Iroquois/Delaware views the exception solely in economic terms as permitting omission of any proposals relating to a de minimis share of assets and profits. Iroquois/Delaware asserts that since corporations are economic entities, only an economic test is appropriate.

The Court would note that the applicability of the Rule 14a-8(c)(5) exception to Mr. Lovenheim's proposal represents a close question given the lack of clarity in the exception itself. In effect, plaintiff relies on the word "otherwise," suggesting that it indicates the drafters of the rule intended that other noneconomic tests of significance be used. Iroquois/Delaware relies on the fact that the rule examines other significance in relation to the issuer's business. Because of the apparent ambiguity of the rule, the Court considers the history of the shareholder proposal rule in determining the proper interpretation of the most recent version of that rule.

Prior to 1983, paragraph 14a-8(c)(5) excluded proposals "not significantly related to the issuer's business" but did not contain an objective economic significance test such as the five percent of sales, assets, and earnings specified in the first part of the current version.[9] Although a series of SEC decisions through 1976 allowing issuers to exclude proposals challenging compliance with the Arab economic boycott of Israel allowed exclusion if the issuer did less than one percent of their business with Arab countries or Israel, the Commission stated later in 1976 that it did "not believe that subparagraph (c)(5) should be hinged solely on the economic relativity of a proposal."

---

8. The assertion that the proposal is significant in an ethical and social sense relies on plaintiff's argument that "the very availability of a market for products that may be obtained through the inhumane force-feeding of geese cannot help but contribute to the continuation of such treatment." Plaintiff's brief characterizes the humane treatment of animals as among the foundations of western culture and cites in support of this view the Seven Laws of Noah, an animal protection statute enacted by the Massachusetts Bay Colony in 1641, numerous federal statutes enacted since 1877, and animal protection laws existing in all fifty states and the District of Columbia. An additional indication of the significance of plaintiff's proposal is the support of such leading organizations in the field of animal care as the American Society for the Prevention of Cruelty to Animals and The Humane Society of the United States for measures aimed at discontinuing use of force-feeding.

9. See Comment, The 1983 Amendments to Shareholder Proposal Rule 14a-8: A Retreat from Corporate Democracy?, 59 Tulane L. Rev. 161, 183-184 (1984) (hereinafter "Comment, 1983 Amendments").

Securities Exchange Act Release No. 12,999, 41 Fed. Reg. 52,994, 52,997 (1976). Thus the Commission required inclusion "in many situations in which the related business comprised less than one percent" of the company's revenues, profits or assets "where the proposal has raised *policy questions* important enough to be considered 'significantly related' to the issuer's business."[11]

As indicated above, the 1983 revision adopted the five percent test of economic significance in an effort to create a more objective standard. Nevertheless, in adopting this standard, the Commission stated that proposals will be includable notwithstanding their "failure to reach the specified economic thresholds if a significant relationship to the issuer's business is demonstrated on the face of the resolution or supporting statement." Securities Exchange Act Release No. 19,135, 47 Fed. Reg. 47,420, 47,428 (1982). Thus it seems clear based on the history of the rule that "the meaning of 'significantly related' is not *limited* to economic significance." Comment, 1983 Amendments (emphasis in original).

The only decision in this Circuit cited by the parties relating to the scope of §14 and the shareholder proposal rule is Medical Committee for Human Rights v. SEC, 432 F.2d 659 (D.C. Cir. 1970). That case concerned an effort by shareholders of Dow Chemical Company to advise other shareholders of their proposal directed at prohibiting Dow's production of napalm. Dow had relied on the counterpart of the 14a-8(c)(5) exemption then in effect to exclude the proposal from proxy materials and the SEC accepted Dow's position without elaborating on its basis for doing so. In remanding the matter back to the SEC for the Commission to provide the basis for its decision, id. at 682, the Court noted what it termed "substantial questions" as to whether an interpretation of the shareholder proposal rule "which permitted omission of [a] proposal as one motivated primarily by *general* political or social concerns would conflict with the congressional intent underlying §14(a) of the [Exchange] Act" 432 F.2d at 680 (emphasis in original).[15] Iroquois/Delaware attempts to distinguish *Medical Committee for Human Rights* as a case where a company sought to exclude a proposal that, unlike Mr. Lovenheim's proposal, was economically significant merely because the motivation of the proponents was political. The argument is not without appeal given the fact that the *Medical Committee* Court was confronted with a regulation that contained no reference to economic significance. Yet the *Medical Committee* decision contains language suggesting that the Court assumed napalm was not economically significant to Dow: "The management of Dow Chemical Company is repeatedly quoted in sources which include the company's own publications as proclaiming that the decision to continue manufacturing and marketing napalm was made not *because* of business considerations, but *in spite* of them; that management in essence decided to pursue a course of activity which generated little profit for the shareholders . . ." (emphasis in original).

---

11. Comment, 1983 Amendments (emphasis supplied). For example, "[p]roposals requesting the cessation of further development, planning and construction of nuclear power plants and proposals requesting shareholders be informed as to all aspects of the company's business in European communist countries have been included in this way."

15. The Court defined the purpose of §14(a) of assuring that shareholders exercise their right "to control the important decisions which affect them in their capacity as stockholders and owners of the corporation." 432 F.2d at 680-681.

This Court need not consider, as the *Medical Committee* decision implied, whether a rule allowing exclusion of all proposals not meeting specified levels of economic significance violates the scope of §14(a) of the Exchange Act. Whether or not the Securities and Exchange Commission could properly adopt such a rule, the Court cannot ignore the history of the rule which reveals no decision by the Commission to limit the determination to the economic criteria relied on by Iroquois/Delaware. The Court therefore holds that in light of the ethical and social significance of plaintiff's proposal and the fact that it implicates significant levels of sales, plaintiff has shown a likelihood of prevailing on the merits with regard to the issue of whether his proposal is "otherwise significantly related" to Iroquois/Delaware's business.[16] . . .

PROBLEM 3-12

Trylon, Inc. is a publicly traded corporation whose principal business is genetic research and sale of the resulting products. As do most American corporations, Trylon has a policy of making unrestricted charitable contributions to nonprofit organizations that its Charitable Contributions Subcommittee deems worthy causes. Such gifts never exceed 1 percent of net income annually. Included in Trylon's list of donees are a number of major medical research universities.

Trylon recently received the following shareholder proposal for inclusion in management's proxy for the upcoming annual shareholders' meeting.

> The shareholders hereby request that the corporation refrain from making charitable contribution to organizations that perform abortions.

Can management omit this proposal from its proxy materials?

PROBLEM 3-13

Publishers, Inc., a NYSE-traded corporation, recently received the following shareholder proposal for inclusion in management's proxy for the upcoming annual shareholders' meeting:

> The shareholders hereby request that the board adopt as corporate policy the following resolution to be implemented as soon as possible without violating any existing contracts or contractual obligations.
>
> *Resolved, that it is the policy of Publishers, Inc. that the company's CEO shall be compensated annually in a total amount, including bonuses and changes in value of retirement plans, deferred compensation rights, and incentive compensation rights (including vested or non-vested stock options), that is no more than 50 times the average compensation (similarly computed) of the company's full-time workforce. In other words, if in*

---

16. The result would, of course, be different if plaintiff's proposal was ethically significant in the abstract but had no meaningful relationship to the business of Iroquois/Delaware as Iroquois/Delaware was not engaged in the business of importing paté de foie gras.

a given year the average total compensation of the company's workforce is $100,000, then the maximum total compensation for the company's CEO in that year would be $5,000,000.

Can management omit this proposal from its proxy materials?

PROBLEM 3-14

Your firm has been asked to review the following shareholder proposal recently submitted by the International Sisterhood of Carpenters Pension Fund:

REINCORPORATION IN NORTH DAKOTA PROPOSAL

Resolved: That the shareholders of MacroChip ("Company") hereby request that the Board of Directors take the measures necessary to change the Company's jurisdiction of incorporation from Oregon to North Dakota.

Supporting Statement: In 2007, North Dakota enacted the North Dakota Publicly Traded Corporations Act ("NDPTCA"), which was advertised as the first shareholder-friendly incorporation law in the United States. The state's secretary of state was quoted as saying corporations "can incorporate under this new system of corporate governance that is designed to be more responsive to the shareholders, who are the owners of the company. In our state they will have a clear choice."

Under the NDPTCA, corporations formed or reincorporating in North Dakota will have a governance regime that includes the following:

- Majority voting in election of directors;
- Advisory shareholder votes on compensation reports;
- Proxy access to 5 percent shareholders who have held shares for at least two years;
- Reimbursement for successful proxy contests proportional to success; and
- Separation of the roles of board chairperson and CEO.

A complete text of the actual NDPTCA is available at http://www.legis.nd.gov/assembly/60-2007/bill-index/bi1340.html.

The MacroChip Board is actively considering reincorporating in Delaware and would like to omit the North Dakota proposal from its proxy materials. What would be the possible grounds for omitting the proposal under Rule 14a-8?

3. Strategic Combinations of Federal Rules with State Law and Market Power

Until the mid-1980s, a "truth" about Rule 14a-8 proposals was that the shareholder proponents had no chance of obtaining majority support, and little chance of obtaining even a 5 percent vote. This "truth" changed with the advent of activist shareholders, initially led by large pension funds, who began to use the shareholder proposal process to oppose management efforts to make corporations impregnable to unfriendly takeovers. By the mid-1990s, shareholder proposals to improve corporate governance structures were routinely receiving at least 30 percent of the vote, and early in the 2000s a significant number of proposals received a majority vote. These "winning" proposals have been corporate governance proposals; proposals seeking to promote broader social goals, such as the one in the *Lovenheim* case, continue to receive little support.

But all these votes are advisory. The real impact of these federal channels for persuasive communication depends on what happens next. Making a shareholder say-on-pay vote nonbinding reflects the basic notion of director centrality that is the beginning point for state law. Federal law has not been willing to overturn that core point. However, the directors' power to ignore the will of a majority of the shareholders, or the concerns expressed by a substantial number though less than a majority, has begun to give way to a new reality. To understand this new and still-evolving corporate governance landscape, one must appreciate how institutional investors have combined federal law channels and the shareholder state law rights discussed earlier in this chapter to change the directors' calculus of how to respond to nonbinding shareholder votes.

a.   Case Study: Classified Boards

One noticeable change is that many of the largest American corporations have removed provisions in their articles of incorporation requiring staggered terms for boards of directors. Shareholder activists have long argued that companies should elect all of their members annually so as to facilitate more effective monitoring and replacement of deficient managers. These pleas largely fell on deaf ears past the turn of this century. But as noted by Marcel Kahan and Edward Rock in Embattled CEOs 88 Tex. L. Rev. 987 (2010) among S&P 100 companies, "incidence of staggered boards has declined from 44% to 16% between 2003 and 2008" (although the pattern did not hold for firms outside the S&P 500).

These provisions are almost always in the firm's articles of incorporation. As a result, shareholders lack sufficient power to remove this provision without first removing the directors. Recall the default provisions of state law that require both director and shareholder approval to amend the articles; directors thus have a gatekeeper role that permits them to veto changes they don't like by simply refusing to approve the changes. Shareholders have regularly used Rule 14a-8 to submit proposals and have increasingly received a majority vote, but that alone does not effect a change in the corporation's governance rules.

Directors have shown greater willingness to implement or respond positively to the "persuasive" shareholder proposals because institutional shareholders have shown themselves more willing to use their state law power to vote directors out. If a resolution to end staggered boards achieved a majority vote of shareholders and was not implemented, the same or another activist shareholder would return the next year with a campaign to turn out the board nominees or withhold votes. The result of this one-two punch is that shareholders have waged a highly successful campaign to reshape the shareholder governance role as it relates to the election of directors.

Compare these results to efforts to change this policy by focusing only on state law rights as discussed at page 165 earlier in this chapter.

b.   Case Study: Majority Voting

The shift from plurality voting to majority voting for the election of directors represents an another significant change in public corporation governance norms.

Plurality voting for the election of directors is the norm in most states. However, for activist shareholders in publicly traded corporations, plurality voting is highly unsatisfactory. Without the ability to include nominees in the company's proxy, outside shareholders who are unwilling or unable to launch a proxy fight for their own nominees are left with only one mechanism for expressing their dissatisfaction with the current board of directors. Under Securities Exchange Act Rule 14a-4(b), companies who solicit proxies for the election of directors are required to provide not only a box where solicited shareholders may authorize the Company to vote for particular nominees, but also a box where a solicited shareholder may specifically indicate that authority is being withheld. In effect, authority withheld is a "no" vote on that nominee. Yet even if a slate of nominees receives far less than a majority of "yes" votes, and a resounding majority of "authority withheld" or "no" votes, under plurality voting the candidate is elected. Indeed, if each management-nominated candidate in an uncontested election received only one "yes" vote, and millions of "no" votes, each candidate would be elected under plurality voting.

After the SEC considered but failed to enact various shareholder access reforms in 2003-2004, shareholder governance activists began pushing for majority voting for the election of directors. Shareholder proposals were a primary tool in this effort. Although proposals took several forms, the dominant approach sought an amendment to a company's bylaw that required a director to resign if he or she did not receive a majority vote.

In 2006, both the Delaware G.C.L. and the MBCA were amended to address problems raised by the majority vote movement. The Delaware amendments permitted director resignation to be made conditional and effective upon the happening of a future event, such as failure to receive a majority vote. The Delaware amendments also expressly permitted a provision that would make such advance resignations irrevocable. The MBCA amendments authorize bylaw provisions whereby a director who fails to receive a majority vote must resign within 90 days.

Majority voting bylaws may be adopted by shareholders or the board of directors. Moreover, majority voting may be implemented by the board via policies or procedure that are not set out in the bylaws. The boards of many public companies have sought to preempt shareholder attempts to impose strict majority voting proposal by adopting their own, more board-friendly, models. The leader in this regard is Pfizer, Inc. In 2005, Pfizer amended its corporate governance principles requiring a director who did not receive a majority vote to submit his or her resignation to the Pfizer Board's Corporate Governance Committee for its consideration. As amended, the Pfizer corporate governance principles provide that:

> If an incumbent Director fails to receive the required vote for re-election, then, within 90 days following certification of the shareholder vote, the Corporate Governance Committee will act to determine whether to accept the Director's resignation and will submit such recommendation for prompt consideration by the Board, and the Board will act on the Committee's recommendation. The Corporate Governance Committee and the Board may consider any factors they deem relevant in deciding whether to accept a Director's resignation.
>
> Any Director who tenders his or her resignation pursuant to this provision shall not participate in the Corporate Governance Committee recommendation or Board action regarding whether to accept the resignation offer.

Thereafter, the board will promptly disclose its decision-making process and decision regarding whether to accept the Director's resignation offer (or the reason(s) for rejecting the resignation offer, if applicable) in a Form 8-K furnished to the Securities and Exchange Commission.

Many American public companies adopted Pfizer-style corporate governance plans. The reason the Pfizer-style plan is so attractive to companies is that the board retains full discretion to accept or reject a tendered resignation.

Not surprisingly, many shareholder governance activists continue to push for nondiscretionary majority voting plans that are embedded in bylaws that cannot be amended by the board of directors. A number of corporations, have adopted majority voting plans that are in bylaws but still leave directors with the flexibility to accept or reject a resignation tendered by a director who receives less than majority approval.

The following case occurs in the context of a shareholder effort to replace a director-adopted Pfizer-type majority-voting policy with a shareholder-adopted majority-voting bylaw. Note that the shareholder proponent is not attempting to access the company's proxy. As you read this case, consider how the matter would have been treated under the more usual Rule 14a-8(i) process.

Kistefos AS v. Trico Marine Services, Inc.

Delaware Court of Chancery 2009

2009 WL 1124477

WILLIAM B. CHANDLER III, CHANCELLOR.

Dear Counsel:

In this action for declaratory relief, plaintiff Kistefos AS ("Kistefos"), a substantial minority stockholder of Trico Marine Services, Inc. ("Trico" or the "Company"), seeks a declaration that the Company improperly rejected a proposed bylaw on grounds that the proposed bylaw, if adopted, would be inconsistent with Delaware law and the Company's certificate of incorporation. Trico recently announced that April 17, 2009 is the record date for the upcoming annual meeting, which is scheduled to take place as early as late May, but must occur no later than June 16, 2009. Plaintiff moved for expedited proceedings, and seeks a schedule that would allow the Court to grant relief before the annual meeting. On April 14, the court heard oral argument on the motion to expedite via teleconference. On the conditions set forth below, including that a stockholder vote on the proposal will be held at Trico's 2009 annual meeting, the motion to expedite is denied.

Trico is a Delaware corporation that provides marine support vessels to the global offshore oil and gas industry and operates primarily in international markets. Kistefos, a Norwegian limited company, owns approximately 22.2% of Trico's issued and outstanding common stock, and is Trico's largest stockholder. On March 14, Kistefos sent a letter to Trico's board that included several proposals to be put before Trico's stockholders for a vote at the 2009 annual meeting. Among these proposals are: (1) a proposal to amend the bylaws to change the number of directors on the board from seven to nine; (2) a proposal to amend the bylaws to change the number of directors required to constitute a quorum from a majority to seven, six of whom must be United States citizens; (3) a proposal to remove a current director from the board; and (4) if the three previous proposals are adopted, the nomination of two persons for election as directors. Also included in the March 14 letter was the proposal at issue in this case, the so-called "Proposal 8," which provides, in part, that:

> A Person shall be ineligible to serve as a director if such person fails to receive the number of votes required to elect directors at any meeting of stockholders at which such person is to be elected. . . . The term of any existing director of the Corporation who fails to receive the number of votes required to re-elect such existing director at any meeting of stockholders at which such existing director is nominated to be re-elected . . . shall immediately expire, and a vacancy in the Board of Directors shall be deemed to exist.

Trico's bylaws currently provide that directors are elected by a majority vote of stockholders. Under Trico's governing documents, however, an incumbent director who receives only a plurality of votes can continue to serve as a "holdover" director until a successor has been elected or until the director's resignation or removal. Plaintiff asserts that it submitted "Proposal 8 to give 'teeth' to the Company's otherwise illusory majority voting requirement."

In a letter dated March 25, the Company rejected Proposal 8 on the grounds that the bylaw would be invalid if adopted because it is inconsistent with, among other things, the provisions of Trico's certificate of incorporation and §§141(b) and (k) of the Delaware General Corporation Law ("DGCL"). The letter further stated that:

> For this reason, Trico's Board has unanimously resolved to reject "Proposal 8" because it is not proper business that may be transacted by the stockholders at the 2009 annual meeting. Trico will disregard this proposal if Kistefos presents it for stockholder action at the 2009 annual meeting.

Plaintiff initiated this action by filing the Verified Complaint and motion to expedite on April 8. The complaint alleges that Proposal 8 is consistent with Trico's certificate of incorporation, bylaws, and Delaware law. The motion to expedite seeks a prompt final disposition of plaintiff's claims so that Kistefos will be able to solicit stockholders to vote in favor of Proposal 8 at the annual meeting.

During a teleconference with the Court on April 14, the parties, through their attorneys, each represented their positions with respect to expedition and the status of Proposal 8 with regard to the 2009 annual meeting. Plaintiff, while arguing that the case warrants expedition, represented to the Court that such expedition would not be necessary if the stockholders were permitted to vote on Proposal 8 at the 2009 annual meeting. Trico argued that, in order to preserve its legal position that Proposal 8 was invalid because it violates Trico's certificate of incorporation and Delaware law, it must "disregard" the proposal if it is presented at the meeting. Trico offered, however, to collect and preserve the proxies submitted for and against Proposal 8, so that it could later be determined if the proposal received the required vote. Plaintiff agreed in principle with that result, but argued that it should be allowed to present Proposal 8 at the annual meeting in the same manner as other proposals. In response, Trico again took the position that it must, in order to preserve its legal position, "disregard" Proposal 8 at the meeting and prevent it from being presented to the stockholders as a valid proposal for a vote.

This remaining disagreement between the parties can be easily remedied as follows: the defendants' legal position—that Proposal 8 would be invalid if adopted because it is inconsistent with, among other things, Trico's certificate of incorporation and DGCL §§141(b) and (k) — is hereby noted and preserved. Proposal 8 will be presented for a stockholder vote at the 2009 annual meeting in the same manner as other proposals are presented to the stockholders for a vote. Because its legal position has been preserved, Trico has no reason to prevent a stockholder vote on Proposal 8. Accordingly, Kistefos will be permitted to solicit proxies and present arguments at the annual meeting regarding Proposal 8 in the same manner that it is permitted to do with respect to other proposed bylaws. In other words, the stockholders will be permitted to vote on Proposal 8 at the annual meeting in the same manner as they are permitted to vote on other proposed bylaws.

The resolution described above obviates the need for expedited proceedings. In deciding whether to expedite proceedings, the Court must determine whether "the plaintiff has articulated a sufficiently colorable claim and shown a sufficient possibility of a threatened irreparable injury," such that the additional costs of proceeding on an expedited basis are justified. In light of the now pending stockholder vote on Proposal 8, plaintiff faces no irreparable injury. The stockholders will vote on Proposal 8 at the annual meeting, and if the proposal receives the required number of votes, then the issue will be preserved and ripe for judicial review. Additionally, pending the stockholder vote on Proposal 8 at Trico's 2009 annual meeting, the issue of the legal validity of Proposal 8 is not ripe because the relevant events that must occur before the issue requires adjudication — namely, the approval of Proposal 8 by Trico's stockholders — may never occur. Absent some compelling reason to do otherwise, this Court should refrain from rendering an advisory opinion where adjudication of the issue is not needed for there to be an informed stockholder vote on the proposal.

For the foregoing reasons, and on the conditions described above, the motion to expedite is denied. If Proposal 8 is approved by the stockholders at the 2009 annual meeting, and the parties believe that there are remaining issues that require judicial intervention, then the parties should contact the Court to set a schedule.

NOTES AND QUESTIONS

1. The chancellor lets the proposals go to a shareholder vote without deciding whether such authority is within the shareholder power, leaving that issue to be determined if the proposal received the requisite number of votes. The voting results made that issue moot. The insurgent's efforts to amend the bylaws as set out in the opinion received more than 70 percent of the votes cast and more than 60 percent of the votes outstanding, but the corporation had a provision, apparently in its charter, requiring a two-thirds vote of outstanding shares in order to amend the bylaws. See Definitive Additional Proxy Soliciting Materials Filed by Non-management 921529 for Trico Marine Services, Inc. in the EDGAR database at http://www.sec.gov/Archives/edgar/data/921549/000110465909041038/a09-17352_1dfan14a.htm.

2. The Trico case involves a different context than Rule 14a-8. In the Trico-type conflict, the insurgent shareholder is willing to solicit proxies itself, as opposed to trying to get its proposal included in the company's proxy. This strategy is available only if the shareholder is able to pay, at least initially, the expense of solicitation and mailing. In order to make such a solicitation, the shareholder also would need to know who the

shareholders are and their addresses. That too has been a hotly contested subject as discussed in subpart d below.

c. Case Study: Say on Pay

The Dodd-Frank Act requires public companies to conduct shareholder votes on executive compensation, often referred to as "say on pay." Like the Rule 14a-8 votes discussed earlier in the chapter, these votes are not binding on the corporation. If a company plan fails, there is no automatic nullification of the compensation plan. Executive compensation remains in the hands of the directors, not the shareholders. Nonetheless, say on pay is now a part of the governance fabric of the public corporation, illustrating the intertwined workings of state and federal law and market forces that are the focus of this section.

In the first years of say on pay, the average shareholder vote in favor of compensation plans was about 90 percent. Slicing the data a different way, more than three-quarters of larger companies garnered at least 90 percent approval, and in only about 2 percent of companies did the company fail to get at least a majority vote for its compensation plan. Importantly, there was a clear correlation between lower-than-average returns per share and higher-than-average CEO pay on the one hand and greater shareholder opposition to compensation plans on the other.

Say on pay is an area where the presence of proxy advisory firms has been particularly important and visible. Not surprisingly, these firms have focused on and provided shareholders information about the low relative performance/high-pay dynamic just described. One study showed that a negative recommendation from ISS reduced positive say-on-pay votes by nearly 25 percent, and a Glass Lewis negative recommendation reduced the positive vote by about 13 percent. Yonca Ertimur, Fabrizio Ferri and David Oesch, Shareholder Voting and Proxy Advisors: Evidence from Say on Pay, working paper (2012) at 1, available at http://ssrn.com/abstract=2019239. Additionally, some companies receiving negative voting recommendations respond preemptively, making changes to their compensation plan to obtain a favorable recommendation, rather than submitting a disfavored plan to a possibly embarrassing shareholder vote. However, a study reporting these kinds of changes also reported a small yet statistically significant negative stock market reaction to plan changes "aligned" with ISS and Glass Lewis policies. David F. Larcker, Allan L. McCall and Gaizka Ormazabel, Outsourcing Shareholder Voting to Proxy Advisory Firms, working paper (May 10, 2013), available at http://ssrn.com/abstract=2101453.

Despite the effects outlined above, it is unclear that the level or trajectory of executive compensation has been changed by say on pay. One study concluded, "We find that the Say-on-Pay vote had no effect on the level or compensation of CEO pay." Peter Iliev and Svetla Vitanova, The Effect of Say on Pay Vote in the U.S., working paper (April 25, 2013), available at http://ssrn.com/abstract=2235064. But see Ricardo Correa and Uger Lel, Say on Pay, Executive Compensation, CEO Pay Slice and Firm Value Around the World, working paper (June 2013), available at http://ssrn.com/abnstract=2243921. See also Jesse Eisinger, In Shareholder Say-on-Pay Votes, Whispers, Not Shouts, N.Y. Times (June 27, 2013) at B5 (reporting that executive pay levels continue to rise steadily even after the implementation of say on pay).

There are some indications of a broader effect on corporate governance more generally. Poor approval ratings for say on pay have sometimes reverberated in higher rates of withheld votes for director nominees in subsequent years. For example, directors who served on the compensation committee may be at higher risk in subsequent elections. Moreover, even if a compensation plan receives majority approval (sufficient to satisfy the practices described in the prior case study), there is some evidence that falling below even 80 percent can be a reason for concern and even departure from the board. In a recent example involving Hess Oil, when shareholders cast "only" 58 percent in favor of management's say-on-pay proposal, the vote was seen as a sign of shareholder unhappiness. A hedge fund launched a proxy contest for control of the company, leading to a high-visibility proxy fight and a settlement in which the investor got several seats on the Hess board and the Hess CEO resigned as chair of the board. See Michael J. De La Merced, How Elliot and Hess Settled a Bitter Proxy Battle, N.Y. Times (May 16, 2013), available at http://dealbook.nytimes.com/2013/05/16/hess-and-elliot-settle-fight-over companys-board/html.

d. Shareholder Access to Corporate Records and Shareholder List

MBCA §§7.20, 16.01-16.04, 16.20
Delaware G.C.L. §§219, 220
1934 Securities Exchange Act Rule 14a-7

State corporation laws generally provide shareholders with access to a shareholders' list on demand not only for use in connection with proxy solicitations, but for other "proper purposes." The early state corporation codes usually continued the proper purpose requirement of the common law and sometimes conditioned a right to inspect records on holding a minimum percentage of the company's stock or stock worth a threshold amount. However, neither the common law nor early statutes regulated the types of records that need be maintained by a corporation.

The MBCA departs from the earlier codes by (1) mandating certain basic record keeping; (2) requiring that annual reports and financial statements be given to shareholders; and (3) granting shareholders an absolute right of access to minutes of shareholders' meetings, all corporate communications with shareholders in the preceding three years, a list of directors, the corporation's most recent annual report to the secretary of state, copies of its articles and bylaws, and any resolution creating shares issued. Moreover, under the MBCA, shareholder access rights are not contingent on the period of time that shares have been owned or on the percentage of stock owned.

This permissive access, however, does not extend to all records in which a dissident shareholder is likely to be interested. MBCA §16.02 gives shareholders a right to inspect corporate accounting records, the minutes or other records of board and board committee meetings, and the list of shareholders, but only when the demand is made in good faith for a proper purpose to which the records are directly related.

The statutory provisions in Delaware are set forth with less detail than the MBCA. However, Delaware compensates for lack of statutory detail with a wealth of judicial precedent. The following two cases involve shareholder efforts to access shareholder lists and other books and records. As you read these cases, consider what policy concerns underlie the court's application of the statutory standards and be alert to statutory differences as to access to shareholders' lists versus other kinds of corporate records.

Conservative Caucus v. Chevron Corp.
Delaware Court of Chancery, 1987
525 A.2d 569

HARNETT, VICE CHANCELLOR.

Plaintiff Conservative Caucus Research Analysts & Education Foundation, Inc., a nonprofit corporation, is the owner of 30 shares of stock of defendant Chevron Corporation. It seeks a stockholder list in order to communicate with other stockholders about the alleged economic risks of Chevron's business activity in Angola, and about a resolution which is proposed to be submitted in connection with the next annual meeting of Chevron. . . .

I.

It is not disputed that on January 15, 1987 plaintiff was a registered holder of 30 shares of stock of Chevron and that it made a demand under oath for a copy of Chevron's stockholder list. The demand states that a stockholder list is desired for the purpose of communicating with fellow stockholders with respect to the alleged economic risks of Chevron's business activity in Angola, the support of a resolution being proposed by James Deering Danielson, who is not a party to the present suit, which urges that the stockholders request the Board of Directors of Chevron to take certain actions relating to the government of Angola and the bringing to the attention of the stockholders that Chevron may refuse to submit the Danielson Resolution to the stockholders. The Danielson Resolution proposes that the corporation state to the Angolan government that it will terminate operations in Angola unless the government abandons the Communist system of government, initiates unconditional negotiations with certain political organizations which oppose the current government of Angola, and do other similar political acts.

The statute providing for the obtaining of a stockholder list states in part: "Any stockholder, in person or by attorney or other agent, shall, upon written demand under oath stating the purpose thereof, have the right during the usual hours for business to inspect for any proper purpose the corporation's stock ledger, a list of its stockholders, and its other books and records, and to make copies or extracts therefrom. A proper purpose shall mean a purpose reasonably related to such person's interest as a stockholder. . . ." 8 Del. C. §220(b).

A communication with other stockholders about specific matters of corporate concern, especially in connection with a pending stockholders' meeting, has consistently been held to be a proper purpose for a stockholder to obtain a stocklist.

Title 8, Del. C. §220(c) states in part: ". . . Where the stockholder seeks to inspect the corporation's stock ledger or list of stockholders and he has complied with this section respecting the form and manner of making demand for inspection of such documents, the burden of proof shall be upon the corporation to establish that the inspection he seeks is for an improper purpose. . . ."

It is clear (and not seriously disputed) that plaintiff, in stating that it seeks to communicate with the other stockholders about the economic risks of Chevron doing business in Angola, has complied with the form and manner of making a demand for a stockholder list. The burden at trial therefore was upon Chevron to establish that the inspection would be for an improper purpose.

II.

Chevron urges a number of reasons why the plaintiff's purpose is improper. None of them are meritorious.

Chevron first claims that plaintiff's purpose in seeking the stocklist is not reasonably related to plaintiff's interest as a stockholder in that it is merely to harass the corporation. Plaintiff testified at trial, however, that its primary purpose was to call to the stockholders' attention that the corporation is likely to suffer economic loss if it persists in engaging in business operations in Angola due to the likelihood of war or an unstable government. This is a purpose which is proper for discussion and consideration by a corporation. Nor are such concerns necessarily adverse to the best interests of the corporation.

A proper purpose having been stated, all others are irrelevant.

Chevron's reliance on Carpenter v. Texas Air Corp., Del. Ch., C.A. No. 7976-NC, Hartnett, V.C., (April 18, 1985), is misplaced. I denied a stockholders list in that case because of the existence of a number of factors including the fact that the demand itself was defective and the burden of persuasion therefore rested on those seeking it. I also found that the plaintiffs were sham parties fronting for a labor organization, had no real personal interest in obtaining a stockholder list, and were not stockholders of the corporation for which the list was sought. The real purpose for the obtaining of the list was found not to be to communicate with the stockholders about the forthcoming annual meeting but only to exert economic pressure in connection with a labor dispute. It was pointed out in that opinion, however, that a labor organization which is the holder of stock in a corporation can, under proper conditions, obtain a stockholder list in order to communicate with fellow stockholders.

Chevron next urges that plaintiff does not have an interest as a stockholder in obtaining the stockholder list because its interest is solely political. Chevron relies on Pillsbury v. Honeywell, Inc., Minn. Supr., 291 Minn. 322, 191 N.W.2d 406 (1971). In that case the Supreme Court of Minnesota, relying on the Delaware statute, denied a Vietnam war protestor a stockholder list because it found that he purchased his stock solely for the purpose of seeking a stockholder list and of using it to try to impose his social and political beliefs on the corporation. This motivation was not "deemed to be a proper purpose germane to his economic interest as a shareholder."

That holding is, of course, not binding on this court and it was criticized by the Delaware Supreme Court in Credit Bureau Reports, Inc. v. Credit Bureau of St. Paul, Inc. [Del. Ch., 290 A.2d 689, affd., Del. Supr. 290 A.2d 691 (1972)].

The facts are also different here. Plaintiff has testified that it seeks the stocklist to warn the stockholders about the allegedly dire economic consequences which will fall upon Chevron if it continues to do business in Angola. Some of these possible economic consequences, according to plaintiff, are: sanctions by the U.S. Government;

adverse consequences imposed by the Export-Import Bank; an embargo by the U.S. Defense Department on purchases of oil which has its source in Angola; a denial of certain federal tax credits; the risk to personnel and facilities of an unstable government; and, the risk of war in Angola. These are surely matters which might have an adverse affect on the value of the stock of Chevron. I, therefore, find that the holding in *Pillsbury* is not persuasive.

Chevron also asserts that the Danielson Resolution is not a proper subject for stockholder action because the power and duty to manage the business affairs of a Delaware corporation is vested exclusively in the board of directors. 8 Del. C. §141(a).

Chevron correctly points out that the Danielson Resolution impliedly concedes its limited effect because it states that "the stockholders request" the board of directors to establish certain policies relating to the corporation doing business in Angola.

Just because the resolution only requests the board to take certain action, however, does not make it improper nor change its purpose: to influence the board to withdraw corporate activities from an area because the continuance of business there might result in an economic loss to the corporation.

Chevron further asserts that its stockholders are entitled to privacy and should not be subject to pressure from individuals or groups whose only interest is to assert opposition or criticism to an immense range of issues, most of which have little or no impact on the primary interests of a corporation, which is to be profitable. . . .

While I agree that stockholders should be free from harassment, and that organizations which attempt to assert positions which are only marginally related to the economic interests of a corporation must be looked upon with some suspicion, here plaintiff has testified that it will only communicate by mail to the stockholders. In this present day, where all householders are constantly inundated with reams of mailed exhortations and appeals, the receipt of one more letter, no matter how useless, or bizarre, can hardly be harassment.

I therefore find that Chevron has not borne its burden of showing that plaintiff's urging Chevron to cease to do business in Angola because of the possible negative economic consequences of that activity is an improper purpose and that any other purpose is irrelevant. . . .

City of Westland Police & Fire Retirement System v. Axcelis Technologies, Inc.

Delaware Court of Chancery, 2009
2009 WL 3086537

Noble, Vice Chancellor . . .

II. Background

A. The Parties

Defendant Axcelis Technologies, Inc. ("Axcelis" or the "Company") is a Delaware corporation specializing in the manufacture of ion implantation and semiconductor equipment. Plaintiff City of Westland Police & Fire Retirement System (the "Plaintiff") is and has been the beneficial owner of shares of common stock of Axcelis since August 2007. SHI is a Japanese company that also makes and sells semiconductor equipment. In 1983, Axcelis and SHI became equal partners in a joint venture called SEN. SEN, like Axcelis and SHI, manufactures ion implantation and semiconductor equipment. SEN was an important asset to both Axcelis and SHI. . . .

The Axcelis board of directors, (the "Board") is comprised of Mary G. Puma, who currently serves as the Company's Chairwoman, Chief Executive Officer and President, as well as Stephen R. Hardis ("Hardis"), Patrick H. Nettles, H. Brian Thompson ("Thompson"), William C. Jennings, R. John Fletcher ("Fletcher"), and Geoffrey Wild.

B.   SHI'S PROPOSALS

On February 4, 2008, SHI (along with TPG Capital LLP) made an unsolicited bid to acquire Axcelis for $5.20 per share. Shares of Axcelis closed at a price of $4.18 per share that day. Three days later, Axcelis informed SHI that it would respond to its acquisition proposal after completing discussions with certain advisors. The Board rejected SHI's proposal on February 25, 2008. The Board found that the $5.20 per share price failed to compensate shareholders adequately for the synergistic value of the SEN joint venture and ignored the substantial business opportunity to take market share back from Axcelis competitors.

On March 10, 2008, SHI again proposed to acquire Axcelis, this time at a price of $6 per share. Shares of Axcelis closed at a price of $5.45 per share that day. On March 17, 2008, the Board again rejected SHI's overtures. The Board concluded that, while "a 'one company' approach combining Axcelis and SEN could yield significant operational and commercial synergies, . . . [its] view of current market conditions and of the company's prospects when market conditions do improve" led to a belief that a transaction with SHI would not be in the shareholders' best interest. The Board also noted its feeling that, in order to engage in serious, productive discussions with SHI, some exchange of confidential information would be necessary, and SHI had yet to agree to keep such information and discussions confidential.

C.   THE MAY 2008 AXCELIS SHAREHOLDERS' MEETING, DIRECTOR
ELECTION, AND THE REJECTION OF DIRECTOR RESIGNATIONS

On May 1, 2008, Axcelis held its annual shareholders' meeting. The terms of three directors were expiring, and each ran unopposed for reelection to the Board. Those directors were Hardis, Fletcher, and Thompson (the "Three Directors"). Axcelis follows the plurality voting provisions of Delaware law, and thus a director may be elected without receiving a majority of the votes cast in a given election. Each of the Three Directors received less than a majority of the votes cast in his reelection bid. The Court assumes the Plaintiff's position to be true: that the failure of the Three Directors to receive a majority of the votes cast in their reelection bids was the result of a concerted effort by at least some Axcelis shareholders to "send a message to the board, expressing their discontent with the [C]ompany's unresponsiveness to SHI" by withholding support for each of the Three Directors facing reelection at the 2008 annual meeting.[10]

The failure to receive at least a majority of the votes cast triggered one of Axcelis's corporate governance policies. Pursuant to this policy (the "Policy"),[11] directors failing to receive a majority of the stockholder vote must submit their resignations to the Board's Nominating and Corporate Governance Committee, which must then consider and recommend to the Board whether such resignations should be accepted or rejected.[12] The Board must then accept or reject any resignations submitted by its directors under the Policy. Following the May 1, 2008, vote, the Three Directors offered to resign their positions. Through a May 23, 2008, press release, the Board announced its decision not to accept those resignations.[13]

The press release stated that:

> In making their determination, the Board considered a number of factors relevant to the best interests of Axcelis. The Board noted that the three directors are experienced and knowledgeable about the Company, and that if their resignations were accepted, the Board would be left with only four remaining directors. One or more of the three directors serves on each of the key committees of the Company and Mr. Hardis serves as lead director. The Board believed that losing this experience and knowledge would harm the Company. The Board also noted that retention of these directors is particularly important if Axcelis is able to move forward on discussions with SHI following finalization of an appropriate non-disclosure agreement. The Board also expressed its intention to be responsive to the shareholder concerns that gave rise to the withhold votes. The Board is seeking to engage in confidential discussions with SHI and, prior to next year's Annual Meeting, the Board will consider recommending in favor of a declassification proposal at that meeting.

---

10. The Company attributed the results to a recommendation by Institutional Shareholder Services that stockholders withhold their votes for the reelection of the Three Directors due to the failure of the Board to support a proposed change to the Axcelis Certificate of Incorporation eliminating the classified board structure. J. Stip. Ex. O. That proposed change failed to receive the approval of the requisite 75% vote of the outstanding shares. *Id.*

11. These policies are often called "Pfizer-style" policies (because Pfizer, Inc. pioneered their use) or "plurality plus" policies. *See generally* Lisa M. Fairfax, *Making the Corporation Safe for Shareholder Democracy,* 69 Ohio St. L.J. 53, 65 (2008) (describing the Pfizer, Inc. policy). For a discussion of their use and relation to majority voting trends, see William K. Sjostrom, Jr. & Young Sang Kim, *Majority Voting for the Election of Directors,* 40 Conn. L. Rev. 459, 480 (2007).

12. The Policy provides: "At any shareholder meeting at which Directors are subject to an uncontested election, any nominee for Director who receives a greater number of votes 'withheld' from his or her election than votes 'for' such election shall submit to the Board a letter of resignation for consideration by the Nominating and Governance Committee. The Nominating and Governance Committee shall recommend to the Board the action to be taken with respect to such offer of resignation. The Board shall act promptly with respect to each such letter of resignation and shall promptly notify the Director concerned of its decision."

13. *Id.* at Ex. Q. An account of how this evolved, authored by Axcelis's General Counsel, may be found at Lynnette C. Fallon, *How One Company Got Caught in the Middle of Proxy Firm Voting Recommendations, a "Pfizer" Governance Policy, and an Unsolicited Acquisition Proposal,* 1704 PLI/Corp. 1173, (Nov. 12-14, 2008). Although the Court does not rely in any way upon this work, it may be of interest to the reader that the article's author asserts that the Board was uncertain whether the withhold vote was the result of dissatisfaction with its response to SHI's acquisition proposals or its decision not to recommend in favor of declassification.

D.   RENEWED NEGOTIATIONS WITH SHI

On June 6, 2008, less than a month after the Board's decision to retain the Three Directors, Axcelis and SHI (along with TPG Capital LLP) entered into a confidentiality agreement governing discussions between the parties. Axcelis management exchanged "a significant amount of data" in response to SHI's due diligence requests and met repeatedly with SHI during June and July 2008 to discuss such requests. Axcelis anticipated that this process would result in a revised proposal to acquire Axcelis. . . .

SHI did not submit a revised acquisition proposal to Axcelis by the extended deadline and, on September 4, 2008, SHI informed Axcelis that it was placing further discussions regarding the acquisition of Axcelis on "hold." On September 15, 2008, after Axcelis's announcement of these developments, Axcelis shares closed at a price of $1.43 per share.

E.   THE SECTION 220 DEMAND

Plaintiff delivered a Demand, dated December 9, 2008, to Axcelis by overnight mail. The Demand seeks the inspection of the following categories of books and records:

1. All minutes of agendas for meetings (including all draft minutes and agendas and exhibits to such minutes and agendas) of the Board at which the Board discussed, considered or was presented with information concerning SHI's acquisition proposals.

2. All documents reviewed, considered, or produced by the Board in connection with SHI's acquisition proposals.

3. Any and all communications between and among Axcelis directors and/or officers and SHI's directors and/or officers.

4. Any and all materials provided by SHI to the Board in connection with SHI's acquisition proposals.

5. Any and all valuation materials used to determine the Company's value in connection with SHI's acquisition proposal.

6. All minutes of agendas for meetings (including all draft minutes and exhibits to such minutes and agendas) of the Board at which the Board discussed, considered or was presented with information concerning or related to the Board's decision not to accept the resignations of Directors Stephen R. Hardis, R. John Fletcher, and H. Brian Thompson.

7. All documents reviewed, considered, or produced by the Board in connection with the Board's decision not to accept the resignations of Directors Stephen R. Hardis, R. John Fletcher, and H. Brian Thompson.

Axcelis responded by letter dated December 12, 2008, rejecting the Demand because the Company determined that it did not satisfy the demand standard set out in Section 220 and Delaware case law interpreting Section 220.

F.   FINANCIAL DIFFICULTY AND THE SALE OF SEN

In early 2009, Axcelis announced its failure to make a required payment under an indenture agreement with U.S. Bank National Association. In a move to raise needed capital, on February 26, 2009, Axcelis agreed to sell its stake in SEN to SHI for approximately $136.6 million. SHI concluded its acquisition of Axcelis's 50% stake in SEN on March 30, 2009. That day, Axcelis shares closed at a price of $0.41 per share.

G. THE ALLEGED WRONGDOING

Plaintiff alleges that there is a credible basis from which this Court can infer that the Board breached its fiduciary duties to shareholders by: (1) rebuffing the attempts by SHI to negotiate an acquisition of Axcelis for more than 18 months; (2) subsequently rejecting two above-market acquisition proposals from SHI as inadequate; (3) retaining three candidates for the Board after a majority of the shareholders refused to support them, allegedly for their failure to negotiate with SHI; and (4) selling one of Axcelis's most important assets, its stake in SEN, to SHI. . . .

III. DISCUSSION

A. APPLICABLE STANDARD

A stockholder of a Delaware corporation has a right to inspect the books and records of the corporation under 8 *Del. C.* §220. However, that right is not unlimited. The stockholder must first satisfy certain technical requirements for inspecting books and records, and then must demonstrate a proper purpose for the inspection. The statute defines a "proper purpose" as "a purpose reasonably related to such person's interest as a stockholder." Because the Plaintiff demands inspection of books and records, instead of the corporation's stock ledger or list of stockholders, it bears the burden of proving a proper purpose.

Our courts have recognized that investigation of suspected wrongdoing on the part of a corporation's management or board is a proper purpose for inspection of the corporation's books and records. Yet, a plaintiff must do more than simply state its suspicion of wrongdoing; a Section 220 demand made merely on the basis of suspicion or curiosity is insufficient. Rather, the plaintiff must present "some evidence to suggest a credible basis from which [this Court] can infer that mismanagement, waste, or wrongdoing may have occurred." This "credible basis" standard has been described as "'the lowest possible burden of proof' in Delaware jurisprudence." The plaintiff may make a credible showing that legitimate issues of wrongdoing might exist "through documents, logic, testimony or otherwise," and is not required to prove any wrongdoing actually occurred.

B. HAS THE PLAINTIFF DEMONSTRATED A PROPER PURPOSE? . . .

1. *The Board's Decision to Retain the Three Directors . . .*

The Court does not need to address the proper substantive standard of review surrounding a board's behavior under these Pfizer-type policies because the Plaintiff fails to demonstrate any credible basis from which the Court might infer the foundational assumptions upon which the Plaintiff's theory rests: that the Board's decision to retain the Three Directors was either motivated by entrenchment or was defensive in nature.

There is no support in the record of any entrenchment motive. Only the Plaintiff's bare accusations suggest such a motive, and mere accusations are insufficient. The Plaintiff has not shown why the Court should suspect that the independent,[36] outside director members of the Board were motivated to perpetuate the Three Directors in office. The Three Directors were properly reelected to the Board under Delaware corporate law's plurality voting provisions. With this fact the Plaintiffs do not, and cannot, disagree. However, because a certain number of shareholders withheld their votes, a Board-enacted governance policy was triggered requiring each of the Three Directors to submit their resignation to a Board designated committee, which would then recommend whether the Board should, it its sole discretion, accept the resignations. The Plaintiff argues that a sufficient number of shareholders withheld their votes in reliance on, and out of a desire to trigger, the Policy. If so, they were successful; these shareholders achieved their desired goal and the Policy was triggered.

The problem for the Plaintiff is that the Policy vested discretion whether to accept the resignations of the Three Directors in the Board. By refusing to accept these resignations, the Board effectuated the results of a valid shareholder election. There is no evidence that the Board identified, and then sought to thwart, the will of the shareholder franchise by refusing to accept the resignations of the Three Directors.

The Plaintiff argues that the Board's purported justifications for the retention of the Three Directors under the Policy is not logically consistent with the record, and that this inconsistency creates a credible basis from which the Court might infer wrongdoing in the form of a breach of the Board's duty of loyalty. The Plaintiff identifies this alleged inconsistency as follows: SHI claims in its public statements to have attempted to negotiate with the Axcelis Board for nearly two years, but was repeatedly rebuffed. However, the Board justifies retention of the Three Directors as essential to moving forward with any negotiations with SHI. This alleged inconsistency is not a sufficiently credible basis from which the Court might infer wrongdoing.

Moving forward with negotiations with SHI was not the sole justification for the retention of the Three Directors. The Board also credited their experience and knowledge regarding the management of Axcelis, as well as the fact that they served on a number of key Axcelis committees. The record demonstrates that, throughout the prior negotiations with SHI, the Board insisted on some form of confidentiality agreement before moving forward—a request SHI avoided. Soon after the Board's decision to retain the Three Directors was made, Axcelis and SHI entered into a confidentiality agreement and negotiations proceeded, albeit unsuccessfully. In short, the purported justifications for the retention of the Three Directors are not materially inconsistent with the record and do not demonstrate a credible basis from which to infer wrongdoing.

Nevertheless, the Plaintiff argues that the Board's exercise of discretion under the Policy warrants heightened scrutiny and a suspicion of wrongdoing. The Plaintiff's

---

36. Six of Axcelis's seven directors are outside directors not employed by the Company, and each is considered independent for purposes of the NASDAQ rules.

logic is not sufficiently credible to support such suspicion. The Plaintiff's position would require this Court to accept the theory that mere shareholder reliance upon a board-enacted governance policy could effectively rewrite the voting provisions contained in a corporation's by-laws. The Axcelis By-laws provide for director election by plurality vote, and the interposition of the Board's discretionary review required by the Policy cannot change that fact simply because the shareholders who chose to withhold their votes wish it to be so. Perhaps certain shareholders withheld their votes for the purpose of symbolically demonstrating their lack of confidence in the Board. If the purpose was the removal of the Three Directors, then those shareholders would have been better served by supporting an alternative slate of directors in the May 2008 election. A poor strategic choice cannot be the basis of a Section 220 action.

It further appears that the Plaintiff's position would require this Court to subject Axcelis to the burden of a Section 220 request merely for having adopted the Policy, and exercising its discretion under it in fidelity with Axcelis's By-laws. Unless enacting the Policy and then acting in accordance with it constitutes credible evidence of wrongdoing, the Plaintiff has failed to demonstrate the requisite credible basis to suspect wrongdoing under Delaware's Section 220 jurisprudence. If mere acting in accordance with the terms of a Pfizer-style policy is to be found credible evidence of wrongdoing, then its death knell has been rung. Reasonable people might disagree as to the utility and propriety of the Policy. However, this Court is not prepared to eliminate functionally its use at this juncture. Merely pointing out the Board's exercise of discretion under the Policy—an exercise which ultimately effectuated the shareholder franchise—is not credible evidence of wrongdoing on this record. The Three Directors took office, duly elected by a plurality of Axcelis shareholders. The ultimate result under the Policy was the result of the shareholder franchise, not an interference with it. Absent the Policy, the result of the May 2008 election would have been no different. . . .

NOTES AND QUESTIONS

1. In Compaq Computer Corp. v. Horton, 631 A.2d 1 (Del. 1993), the Delaware Supreme Court upheld a shareholder's right to inspect and copy a corporation's stock list for communicating with other shareholders to inform them of a pending shareholder's suit and for determining whether any of them would like to join in the action. The court noted that under Delaware law, the corporation seeking to avoid a shareholder's request has the burden of proving that the shareholder is not motivated by a proper purpose. The court emphasized, however, that such burden can be carried in the proper case.

> Previous cases provided valuable examples of the degree to which a stated purpose is so indefinite, doubtful, uncertain or vexatious as to warrant denial of the right of inspection. In State ex rel. Linihan v. United Brokerage Co., Del. Super., 101 A. 433, 437 (1917), the trial court held that instituting annoying or harassing litigation against the corporation was an improper purpose. In Carpenter v. Texas Air Corp., Del. Ch., C.A. No. 7976, Hartnett, V.C., slip op. at 9, 1985 WL 11548 (April 18, 1985), the court ruled improper the stockholder's plan to use a stocklist in furtherance of a scheme to bring pressure on a third corporation. In General Time Corp. v. Talley Indus., Inc.,

Del. Supr., 240 A.2d 755, 756 (1968), it was recognized that obtaining a list for purposes of selling the stockholder's names was also improper. Finally, in Insuranshares Corp. of Delaware v. Kirchner, Del. Supr., 5 A.2d 519, 521 (1939), the Court stated that neither conducting a "fishing expedition" nor satisfying idle curiosity were proper purposes to justify inspection. On the whole a fair reading of these cases leads to the conclusion that where the person making demand is acting in bad faith or for reasons wholly unrelated to his or her role as a stockholder, access to the ledger will be denied.

631 A.2d at 5.

2. Federal proxy Rule 14a-7 appears at first glance to provide an alternative means of gaining access to a shareholder list, but the benefit to shareholders ends up not being as great as it might first appear. Under Rule 14a-7, any shareholder desiring to make a proxy solicitation at an upcoming meeting may inform the corporation in writing of the planned solicitation and ask the corporation to provide "14a-7 assistance." For most solicitations, the corporation then has the choice of either mailing the proxy material for the shareholder (but at the shareholder's expense) or providing the shareholder with a list of shareholders. Not surprisingly, corporations almost always choose to mail materials for the shareholder, because this allows the corporation some control over the timing of the shareholders' mailing and eliminates concern that the shareholder will use a shareholders' list for a shareholder contest that might evolve.

3. A discussion of the breadth of inspection rights is found in Saito v. McKesson HBOC, Inc. 860 A.2d 113 (Del. 2002).

The statute, *8 Del. C. §220*, enables stockholders to investigate matters "reasonably related to [their] interest as [stockholders]" including, among other things, possible corporate wrongdoing. It does not open the door to the wide ranging discovery that would be available in support of litigation. For this statutory tool to be meaningful, however, it cannot be read narrowly to deprive a stockholder of necessary documents solely because the documents were prepared by third parties or because the documents predate the stockholder's first investment in the corporation. A stockholder who demands inspection for a proper purpose should be given access to all of the documents in the corporation's possession, custody or control, that are necessary to satisfy that proper purpose. Thus, where a *§220* claim is based on alleged corporate wrongdoing, and assuming the allegation is meritorious, the stockholder should be given enough information to effectively address the problem, either through derivative litigation or through direct contact with the corporation's directors and/or stockholders.

. . . The Court of Chancery specifically suggested that Saito and the other plaintiffs "use the 'tools at hand,' most prominently *§220* books and records actions, to obtain information necessary to sue derivatively." . . . The stated purpose of Saito's demand was:

(1) to further investigate breaches of fiduciary duties by the boards of directors of HBO & Co., Inc., McKesson, Inc., and/or McKesson HBOC, Inc. related to their oversight of their respective company's accounting procedures and financial reporting; (2) to investigate potential claims against advisors engaged by McKesson, Inc. and HBO & Co., Inc. to the acquisition of HBO & Co., Inc. by McKesson, Inc.; and (3) to gather information relating to the above in order to supplement the complaint in *Ash v. McCall, et al.,* . . . in accordance with the September 15, 2000 Opinion of the Court of Chancery.

Saito demanded access to eleven categories of documents, including those relating to Arthur Andersen's pre-merger review and verification of HBOC's financial condition; communications between or among HBOC, McKesson, and their investment bankers and accountants concerning HBOC's accounting practices; and discussions among members of the Boards of Directors of HBOC, McKesson, and/or McKesson HBOC concerning reports published in April 1997 and thereafter about HBOC's accounting practices or financial condition.

. . . Stockholders of Delaware corporations enjoy a qualified common law and statutory right to inspect the corporation's books and records. Inspection rights were recognized at common law because, "As a matter of self-protection, the stockholder was entitled to know how his agents were conducting the affairs of the corporation of which he or she was a part owner." The common law right is codified in *8 Del. C. §220*. . . .

Once a stockholder establishes a proper purpose under *§220*, the right to relief will not be defeated by the fact that the stockholder may have secondary purposes that are improper. The scope of a stockholder's inspection, however, is limited to those books and records that are necessary and essential to accomplish the stated, proper purpose.

After trial, the Court of Chancery found "credible evidence of possible wrongdoing," which satisfied Saito's burden of establishing a proper purpose for the inspection of corporate books and records. But the Court of Chancery limited Saito's access to relevant documents in three respects. First, it held that, since Saito would not have standing to bring an action challenging actions that occurred before he purchased McKesson stock, Saito could not obtain documents created before October 20, 1998. . . .

By statute, stockholders who bring derivative suits must allege that they were stockholders of the corporation "at the time of the transaction of which such stockholder complains. . . ." [8 Del. Codes §327.] . . . If a stockholder wanted to investigate alleged wrongdoing that substantially predated his or her stock ownership, there could be a question as to whether the stockholder's purpose was reasonably related to his or her interest as a stockholder, especially if the stockholder's only purpose was to institute derivative litigation. But stockholders may use information about corporate mismanagement in other ways, as well. They may seek an audience with the board to discuss proposed reforms or, failing in that, they may prepare a stockholder resolution for the next annual meeting, or mount a proxy fight to elect new directors. None of those activities would be prohibited by *§327*.

Even where a stockholder's only purpose is to gather information for a derivative suit, the date of his or her stock purchase should not be used as an automatic "cut-off" date in a *§220* action. First, the potential derivative claim may involve a continuing wrong that both predates and postdates the stockholder's purchase date. In such a case, books and records from the inception of the alleged wrongdoing could be necessary and essential to the stockholder's purpose. Second, the alleged post-purchase date wrongs may have their foundation in events that transpired earlier. In this case, for example, Saito wants to investigate McKesson's apparent failure to learn of HBOC's accounting irregularities until months after the merger was consummated. Due diligence documents generated before the merger agreement was signed may be essential to that investigation. In sum, the date on which a stockholder first acquired the corporation's stock does not control the scope of records available under *§220*. If activities that occurred before the purchase date are "reasonably related" to the stockholder's interest as a stockholder, then the stockholder should be given access to records necessary to an understanding of those activities.[10]

4. The Delaware Supreme Court affirmed the Chancery Court decision in the principal case that the shareholder failed to establish a credible basis for wrongdoing, but observed that "the relationship between the shareholder inspection right and the "plurality plus" policy adopted by the Axcelis board merits sharper focus for future guidance." City of Westland Police & Fire Retirement System v. Axcelis Technologies, Inc., 1 A.3d 281, 290-292 (Del. 2010):

---

10. As noted . . . above, a Section 220 proceeding does not open the door to wide ranging discovery. See Brehm v. Eisner, 746 A.2d 244, 266-67 (Del. 2000) (Plaintiffs "bear the burden of showing a proper purpose and [must] make specific and discrete identification, with rifled precision . . . [to] establish that each category of books and records is essential to the accomplishment of their articulated purpose . . ."); Security First Corp. v. U.S. Die Casting and Dev. Co., 687 A.2d 563, 568, 570 (Del. 1997) ("mere curiosity or desire for a fishing expedition" is insufficient.).

In this case, the Axcelis "plurality plus" policy was adopted unilaterally as a resolution of the Board, rather than as a by-law or as part of the certificate of incorporation, both of which would require shareholder approval. Here, the Axcelis Board unilaterally conferred upon the shareholders the right to elect directors by majority vote. But, the Board also conditioned that right upon the board's discretionary power to accept (or reject) the resignations of those directors who were elected by a plurality, but not a majority, shareholder vote.

There is a relationship between the shareholders' inspection right and a unilaterally adopted "plurality plus" policy whereby the directors confer upon themselves the discretion to reject resignations tendered by candidates who fail to receive a majority vote. The less-than-majority shareholder vote may be viewed as a judgment by the holders of a voting majority that those director-candidates were no longer suitable to serve (or continue to serve) as directors. Correspondingly, the Board's decision not to accept those resignations may be viewed as a contrary, overriding judgment by the Board. At stake, therefore, is the integrity of the Board decision overriding the determination by a shareholder majority. Stated differently, the question arises whether the directors, as fiduciaries, made a disinterested, informed business judgment that the best interests of the corporation require the continued service of these directors, or whether the Board had some different, ulterior motivation.

Where, as here, the board confers upon itself the power to override an exercised shareholder voting right without prior shareholder approval (as would be required in the case of a shareholder-adopted by-law or a charter provision), the board should be accountable for its exercise of that unilaterally conferred power. In this specific context, that accountability should take the form of being subject to a shareholder's Section 220 right to seek inspection of any documents and other records upon which the board relied in deciding not to accept the tendered resignations.

That is not to say that the making of a Section 220 demand, or the filing of a Section 220 action, for the purpose of investigating the suitability of directors whose tendered resignations were rejected, will automatically entitle the plaintiff shareholder to relief. It is to say that a showing that enough stockholders withheld their votes to trigger a corporation's (board-adopted) "plurality plus" policy satisfies the *Pershing Square* [L.P. v. Ceridian Corp., 923 A.2d 810, 818 (Del Ch. 2007)] requirement that "a stockholder must establish a credible basis to infer that a director is unsuitable, thereby warranting further investigation." Nevertheless, to be entitled to relief, the plaintiff must still make the additional showing articulated by the Chancellor in *Pershing Square*. That, in our view, strikes the appropriate balance between the shareholders' entitlement to information and the directors' entitlement to make decisions in the corporation's best interest free from abusive litigation.

PROBLEM 3-15

RRIP, a large state pension fund, owns 16,000 shares of Franklin Tobacco Co. (Tobacco) and wishes to make an independent proxy solicitation at Tobacco's upcoming annual shareholders' meeting in support of a proposal to phase out Tobacco's sale of tobacco products to minors in developing countries. Assuming, alternatively, that Tobacco is incorporated in Delaware or an MBCA jurisdiction, consider whether RRIP may obtain access to the following RRIP records:

- All documents relating to foreign sale of tobacco to minors;
- Financial records relating to profitability of foreign operations;
- All documents related to health consequences of tobacco use by minors; and
- All documents related to Tobacco's long-term strategies for sale of tobacco products.

4 Fiduciary Duty, Shareholder Litigation, and the Business Judgment Rule

A. Introduction to the Role of Fiduciary Duty and the Business Judgment Rule

1. Overview

MBCA §§8.01, 8.31, 8.32, 8.41, 8.42

This chapter focuses on the fiduciary duties of corporate officers and directors. In corporation law, fiduciary duty has two quite different foci. Much as described in Chapters 1 and 2 with respect to partners and ordinary agents, the fiduciary duty of loyalty operates to constrain directors and officers in their pursuit of self-interest. Thus, it is an actionable wrong for an officer or director to compete with her corporation or divert to personal use assets or opportunities belonging to her corporation. In this first aspect, fiduciary duty applies in a similar fashion to the officers and directors of both closely held and publicly traded corporations.

The long-standing second focus of corporate law fiduciary duty is directors' official conduct in directing and managing the business and affairs of the corporation. Both statutory and judge-made law assign to the directors the power, authority, and responsibility to manage the business and affairs of the corporation. In this context, fiduciary duty[1] broadens to include not only a duty of loyalty, but also a duty of care. In this second aspect, much of the case law involves publicly traded firms—and understanding fiduciary duty as it relates to the publicly traded corporation is the principal focus of this chapter.[2]

Centralized management of the corporation is a key value-enhancing attribute of corporate form, particularly for the publicly traded corporations. Correspondingly,

---

1. Note that the Model Business Corporation Act (MBCA) uses the term "standards of conduct," rather than "fiduciary duty." This omission was intended to avoid any confusion between the rules governing a director's official conduct and rules governing fiduciaries under the law of trusts (see Official Comment, MBCA §8.30). Nonetheless, the standards of conduct set forth by §8.30 do no more than restate long-standing judicial doctrine concerning fiduciary duty. As a result, courts in every state continue to identify the standards governing a director's official conduct as "fiduciary duties."

2. In Chapters 5 and 6 we will examine how lawmakers and private orderers deal with the governance problems in closely held corporations and LLCs and the role fiduciary duty plays in that setting.

it would be value reducing in the normal case to allow shareholders or judges either to make business decisions for the corporation, or to second-guess business decisions made by the directors. Thus, an essential element of the directors' authority and power is the business judgment rule—a judicial presumption that the directors have acted in accordance with their fiduciary duties of care, loyalty, and good faith. The protection provided by the business judgment rule lies in the much greater pleading and evidentiary burden that it places on plaintiffs seeking to hold directors liable for allegedly breaching their fiduciary duties while engaged in official conduct on behalf of the corporation. This greater pleading and evidentiary burden deters frivolous lawsuits. For example, any lawsuit seeking to hold directors liable for business decisions that have gone awry will be dismissed on the pleadings unless the complaining plaintiff can plead facts that, if proved, would rebut the presumptions underlying the business judgment rule. Merely alleging that a decision has turned out badly, even very badly, does not state a cause of action. In other words, with regard to directors' actions taken *as managers,* such as major business decisions or determining the corporation's long-term goals and strategies, judges interpret fiduciary duty and use the business judgment rule to provide directors with broad discretion to manage the corporation's business.

The following discussion of the business judgment rule is instructive, and you will benefit from revisiting it from time to time as you proceed through this chapter:

> The appellees-directors herein claim that they are protected by the presumption of good faith and fair dealing that arises from the business judgment rule and, therefore, they do not have the burden of proving that their decision to purchase CSC was intrinsically fair to the Browns' minority shareholders.
>
> The issue before us, then, centers on the applicability of the business judgment rule. The business judgment rule is a principle of corporate governance that has been part of the common law for at least one hundred fifty years. It has traditionally operated as a shield to protect directors from liability for their decisions. If the directors are entitled to the protection of the rule, then the courts should not interfere with or second-guess their decisions. If the directors are not entitled to the protection of the rule, then the courts scrutinize the decision as to its intrinsic fairness to the corporation and the corporation's minority shareholders. The rule is a rebuttable presumption that directors are better equipped than the courts to make business judgments and that the directors acted without self-dealing or personal interest and exercised reasonable diligence and acted with good faith. A party challenging a board of directors' decision bears the burden of rebutting the presumption that the decision was a proper exercise of the business judgment of the board.
>
> The parties have agreed that Delaware law is applicable to this dispute and they both focus on the recent case of Aronson v. Lewis (Del. 1984), 473 A.2d 805. In *Aronson,* the Delaware Supreme Court set forth the rule at 812:
>
>> . . . The business judgment rule is an acknowledgement of the managerial prerogatives of Delaware directors under Section 141(a). It is a presumption that in making a business decision the directors of a corporation acted on an informed basis, in good faith and in the honest belief that the action taken was in the best interests of the company. Absent an abuse of discretion, that judgment will be respected by the courts. The burden is on the party challenging the decision to establish facts rebutting the presumption.

Gries Sports Enter., Inc. v. Cleveland Browns Football Co., Inc., 496 N.E.2d 959, 963-964 (Ohio 1986).

In some circumstances, a director's fiduciary duty is owed directly to the shareholders. For example, directors owe shareholders a duty of disclosure when recommending that shareholders approve a merger favored by the directors. A shareholder may enforce "directly owed" fiduciary duties via an individual action against the directors, or, if class certification is appropriate, as a class action on behalf of all similarly situated shareholders. Any recovery in these "direct actions" goes to the plaintiff shareholders and not the corporation.

In most circumstances discussed in this chapter, however, a director (or officer) owes fiduciary duties to the corporation and to the shareholders collectively. A corporation may enforce fiduciary duties owed to it in two ways—an action brought by the corporation at the behest and under the direction of its directors, or a "derivative" action brought on behalf of the corporation by one or more of its shareholders. Normally, it is the directors' responsibility to institute (or choose not to institute) litigation against any officer or director who has violated his or her fiduciary duty, just as it is their responsibility to make any other business decision. The derivative suit is an exception to this normal rule. Courts will allow shareholders to maintain a derivative suit only when convinced that the managers are unable to impartially and in good faith control a particular lawsuit, as, for example, when it is obvious that a majority of the board of directors face a real danger of being found liable to the corporation for breach of fiduciary duty if the lawsuit is prosecuted. Thus, the directors' ability to control fiduciary litigation is itself protected by business judgment rule presumptions.

Until very recently, judicial doctrine and corporation codes have focused almost entirely on the management role of directors, giving little separate attention to officers. This imbalance is difficult to explain given the real-world power and importance of the CEO in the typical American publicly traded corporation.

> The governance model followed by most public corporations in the United States has historically been one of individual, rather than group, leadership. U.S. corporations have traditionally vested responsibility in the CEO as the leader of management rather than diffusing high-level responsibility among several individuals.[3]
>
> Senior management, led by the Chief Executive Officer, is responsible for running the day-to-day operations of the corporation and properly informing the board of the status of such operations. Management's responsibilities include strategic planning, risk management, and financial reporting.
>
> The board of directors has the important role of overseeing management performance on behalf of stockholders. Its primary duties are to select and oversee a well qualified and ethical CEO who, with senior management, runs the corporation on a daily basis, and to monitor management's performance and adherence to corporate standards. Effective corporate directors are diligent monitors, *but not managers,* of business operations.[4]

Corporation law's lack of separate focus on officers appears to be changing rapidly. In the post-Enron environment, both judge-made and statutory law is evolving in recognition of the critical management role played by a corporation's chief executive

---

3. The Business Roundtable, Principles of Corporate Governance, 7 (2002).
4. Id. at 1.

officer and other senior officers. As you proceed through this chapter, you will benefit by paying special attention to circumstances in which fiduciary duty rules should reflect the very different and important role played by corporate officers.

As you study the business judgment rule, consider how it affects and reflects the answer to the following policy questions. To what extent should officers or directors have discretion to take a long-term rather than short-term approach to corporate profitability, to take into account the interests of other constituencies or the larger community, or to chart a course that other, similar corporations have eschewed? To what extent may officers or directors act quickly and decisively to seize a business opportunity that might be lost without such aggressive and entrepreneurial decision making?

2.   Discretion to Determine General Business Policies

Suppose that a corporation is consistently underperforming other corporations engaged in similar business activities. Suppose, further, that the pleadings in a minority shareholder's suit suggest that the directors are carrying out their duties in good faith and with great attention, but that a plausible explanation for the corporation's underperformance is management's insistence on pursuing idiosyncratic business policies. To what extent should dissatisfied shareholders be able to obtain a trial to determine the appropriateness of the directors' business policies?

Shlensky v. Wrigley
Illinois Appellate Court, 1968
237 N.E.2d 776

SULLIVAN, JUSTICE.

This is an appeal from a dismissal of plaintiff's amended complaint on motion of the defendants. The action was a stockholders' derivative suit against the directors for negligence and mismanagement. The corporation was also made a defendant. Plaintiff sought damages and an order that defendants cause the installation of lights in Wrigley Field and the scheduling of night baseball games.

Plaintiff is a minority stockholder of defendant corporation, Chicago National League Ball Club (Inc.), a Delaware corporation with its principal place of business in Chicago, Illinois. Defendant corporation owns and operates the major league professional baseball team known as the Chicago Cubs. The corporation also engages in the operation of Wrigley Field, the Cubs' home park, the concessionaire sales during Cubs' home games, television and radio broadcasts of Cubs' home games, the leasing of the field for football games and other events and receives its share, as visiting team, of admission moneys from games played in other National League stadia. The individual defendants are directors of the Cubs and have served for varying periods of years. Defendant Philip K. Wrigley is also president of the corporation and owner of approximately 80% of the stock therein.

Plaintiff alleges that since night baseball was first played in 1935 nineteen of the twenty major league teams have scheduled night games. In 1966, out of a total of 1620 games in the major leagues, 932 were played at night. Plaintiff alleges that every member of the major leagues, other than the Cubs, scheduled substantially all of its home games in 1966 at night, exclusive of opening days, Saturdays, Sundays, holidays and days prohibited by league rules. Allegedly this has been done for the specific purpose of maximizing attendance and thereby maximizing revenue and income.

The Cubs, in the years 1961-65, sustained operating losses from its direct baseball operations. Plaintiff attributes those losses to inadequate attendance at Cubs' home games. He concludes that if the directors continue to refuse to install lights at Wrigley Field and schedule night baseball games, the Cubs will continue to sustain comparable losses and its financial condition will continue to deteriorate.

Plaintiff alleges that, except for the year 1963, attendance at Cubs' home games has been substantially below that at their road games, many of which were played at night.

Plaintiff compares attendance at Cubs' games with that of the Chicago White Sox, an American League club, whose weekday games were generally played at night. The weekend attendance figures for the two teams was similar; however, the White Sox week-night games drew many more patrons than did the Cubs' weekday games.

Plaintiff alleges that the funds for the installation of lights can be readily obtained through financing and the cost of installation would be far more than offset and recaptured by increased revenues and incomes resulting from the increased attendance.

Plaintiff further alleges that defendant Wrigley has refused to install lights, not because of interest in the welfare of the corporation but because of his personal opinions "that baseball is a 'daytime sport' and that the installation of lights and night baseball games will have a deteriorating effect upon the surrounding neighborhood." It is alleged that he has admitted that he is not interested in whether the Cubs would benefit financially from such action because of his concern for the neighborhood, and that he would be willing for the team to play night games if a new stadium were built in Chicago.

Plaintiff alleges that the other defendant directors, with full knowledge of the foregoing matters, have acquiesced in the policy laid down by Wrigley and have permitted him to dominate the board of directors in matters involving the installation of lights and scheduling of night games, even though they knew he was not motivated by a good faith concern as to the best interests of defendant corporation, but solely by his personal views set forth above. It is charged that the directors are acting for a reason or reasons contrary and wholly unrelated to the business interests of the corporation; that such arbitrary and capricious acts constitute mismanagement and waste of corporate assets, and that the directors have been negligent in failing to exercise reasonable care and prudence in the management of the corporate affairs.

The question on appeal is whether plaintiff's amended complaint states a cause of action. It is plaintiff's position that fraud, illegality and conflict of interest are not the only bases for a stockholder's derivative action against the directors. Contrariwise, defendants argue that the courts will not step in and interfere with honest business judgment of the directors unless there is a showing of fraud, illegality or conflict of interest.

The cases in this area are numerous and each differs from the others on a factual basis. However, the courts have pronounced certain ground rules which appear in all cases and which are then applied to the given factual situation. The court in Wheeler v. Pullman Iron and Steel Company, 143 Ill. 197, 207, 32 N.E. 420, 423, said:

> It is, however, fundamental in the law of corporations, that the majority of its stockholders shall control the policy of the corporation, and regulate and govern the lawful exercise of its franchise and business. . . . Every one purchasing or subscribing for stock in a corporation impliedly agrees that he will be bound by the acts and proceedings done or sanctioned by a majority of the shareholders, or by the agents of the corporation duly chosen by such majority, within the scope of the powers conferred by the charter, and courts of equity will not undertake to control the policy or business methods of a corporation, although it may be seen that a wiser policy might be adopted and the business more successful if other methods were pursued. The majority of shares of its stock, or the agents by the holders thereof lawfully chosen, must be permitted to control the business of the corporation in their discretion, when not in violation of its charter or some public law, or corruptly and fraudulently subversive of the rights and interests of the corporation or of a shareholder.

The standards set in Delaware are also clearly stated in the cases. In Davis v. Louisville Gas & Electric Co., 16 Del. Ch. 157, 142 A. 654, a minority shareholder sought to have the directors enjoined from amending the certificate of incorporation. The court said on page 659:

> We have then a conflict in view between the responsible managers of a corporation and an overwhelming majority of its stockholders on the one hand and a dissenting minority on the other—a conflict touching matters of business policy, such as has occasioned innumerable applications to courts to intervene and determine which of the two conflicting views should prevail. The response which courts make to such applications is that it is not their function to resolve for corporations questions of policy and business management. The directors are chosen to pass upon such questions and their judgment *unless shown to be tainted with fraud* is accepted as final. The judgment of the directors of corporations enjoys the benefit of a presumption that it was formed in good faith and was designed to promote the best interests of the corporation they serve. (Emphasis supplied.) . . .

Plaintiff in the instant case argues that the directors are acting for reasons unrelated to the financial interest and welfare of the Cubs. However, we are not satisfied that the motives assigned to Philip K. Wrigley, and through him to the other directors, are contrary to the best interests of the corporation and the stockholders. For example, it appears to us that the effect on the surrounding neighborhood might well be considered by a director who was considering the patrons who would or would not attend the games if the park were in a poor neighborhood. Furthermore, the long run interest of the corporation in its property value at Wrigley Field might demand all efforts to keep the neighborhood from deteriorating. By these thoughts we do not mean to say that we have decided that the decision of the directors was a correct one. That is beyond our jurisdiction and ability. We are merely saying that the decision is one properly before directors and the motives alleged in the amended complaint showed no fraud, illegality or conflict of interest in their making of that decision.

While all the courts do not insist that one or more of the three elements must be present for a stockholder's derivative action to lie, nevertheless we feel that unless the conduct of the defendants at least borders on one of the elements, the courts should not interfere. The trial court in the instant case acted properly in dismissing plaintiff's amended complaint.

We feel that plaintiff's amended complaint was also defective in failing to allege damage to the corporation. The well pleaded facts must be taken as true for the purpose of judging the sufficiency of the amended complaint. Furthermore, pleadings will be construed most strongly against the pleader prior to a verdict or judgment on the merits. New Amsterdam Casualty Co. v. Gerin, 9 Ill. App. 2d 545, 133 N.E.2d 723.

There is no allegation that the night games played by the other nineteen teams enhanced their financial position or that the profits, if any, of those teams were directly related to the number of night games scheduled. There is an allegation that the installation of lights and scheduling of night games in Wrigley field would have resulted in large amounts of additional revenues and incomes from increased attendance and related sources of income. Further, the cost of installation of lights, funds for which are allegedly readily available by financing, would be more than offset and recaptured by increased revenues. However, no allegation is made that there will be a net benefit to the corporation from such action, considering all increased costs.

Plaintiff claims that the losses of defendant corporation are due to poor attendance at home games. However, it appears from the amended complaint, taken as a whole, that factors other than attendance affect the net earnings or losses. For example, in 1962, attendance at home and road games decreased appreciably as compared with 1961, and yet the loss from direct baseball operation and of the whole corporation was considerably less.

The record shows that plaintiff did not feel he could allege that the increased revenues would be sufficient to cure the corporate deficit. The only cost plaintiff was at all concerned with was that of installation of lights. No mention was made of operation and maintenance of the lights or other possible increases in operating costs of night games and we cannot speculate as to what other factors might influence the increase or decrease of profits if the Cubs were to play night home games. . . .

Finally, we do not agree with plaintiff's contention that failure to follow the example of the other major league clubs in scheduling night games constituted negligence. Plaintiff made no allegation that these teams' night schedules were profitable or that the purpose for which night baseball had been undertaken was fulfilled. Furthermore, it cannot be said that directors, even those of corporations that are losing money, must follow the lead of the other corporations in the field. Directors are elected for their business capabilities and judgment and the courts cannot require them to forego their judgment because of the decisions of directors of other companies. Courts may not decide these questions in the absence of a clear showing of dereliction of duty on the part of the specific directors and mere failure to "follow the crowd" is not such a dereliction.

For the foregoing reasons the order of dismissal entered by the trial court is affirmed.

Affirmed.

DEMPSEY, P.J., AND SCHWARTZ, J., CONCUR.

3. Discretion to Consider Interests of Non-Shareholder Constituencies

In economic terms, a firm is made up of a number of constituencies—officers, directors, shareholders, employees, suppliers, customers. A firm's activities affect the larger community in which it does business and within which it locates its facilities. Judges have traditionally granted business judgment rule protections only when directors act in the best interests of "the corporation." But how far does that protection extend when shareholders claim that the officers and directors are impermissibly favoring the interests of non-shareholder constituents?

This question received little judicial or legislative attention until the 1980s, when "unfriendly" takeovers sparked litigation in which directors sought to justify their defensive actions as designed to protect the interests of employees, communities, or bondholders. The courts of Delaware restated the conventional view. Directors may consider the interests of other constituencies if there is "some rationally related benefit accruing to the stockholders," Revlon, Inc. v. MacAndrews & Forbes Holdings, Inc., 506 A.2d 173, 176 (Del. 1986), or if so doing "bears some reasonable relation to general shareholder interests." Mills Acquisition Co. v. Macmillan, Inc., 559 A.2d 1261, 1282 (Del. 1989).

As part of the effort by state legislatures to protect local companies and jobs (discussed in more detail in Chapter 9), more than 30 states have added "other constituency" statutes. Most of these statutes provide that in determining the best interest of the corporation, directors *may* consider the interests of suppliers, employees, customers, and affected communities. These statutes do not necessarily *require* a change in the traditional interpretation of fiduciary duty (as evidenced by their use of the permissive verb "may" rather than the mandatory "shall"). It is possible, however, that the courts will interpret these statutes so as to insulate directors from lawsuits when directors in good faith advance other constituencies' interests to the financial detriment of shareholders. While the impetus for these statutes was clearly to assist anti-takeover efforts of local firms, only a handful of other-constituency provisions are expressly limited to the takeover context. Thus, it is conceivable that these statutes will further broaden the direction entrusted to directors.

The following case is a classic example of shareholder litigation seeking to change or obtain redress for corporate policies that are intended to bestow significant benefit on non-shareholder constituencies, arguably at great cost to shareholders. Consider the extent to which the traditional justifications for the business judgment rule explain the judicial and legislative willingness to allow directors such broad discretion over corporate resources.

Dodge v. Ford Motor Co.
Michigan Supreme Court, 1919
170 N.W. 668

OSTRANDER, CHIEF JUSTICE.

[Plaintiffs, the Dodge brothers, who later left their name on a competing line of automobiles, were two of a small number of minority investors in the young Ford Motor Company; Henry Ford himself owned 58 percent of the company's stock and dominated the company. Plaintiffs challenged the company's actions in refusing to pay dividends while expanding the company's facilities and lowering the price of its cars. A lower court enjoined planned expansion of the company's facilities and ordered the company to pay a dividend in the amount of $19,275,385.96.]

To develop the points now discussed, and to a considerable extent they may be developed together as a single point, it is necessary to refer with some particularity to the facts.

When plaintiffs made their complaint and demand for further dividends, the Ford Motor Company had concluded its most prosperous year of business. The demand for its cars at the price of the preceding year continued.... It could make and could market in the year beginning August 1, 1916, more than 500,000 cars. Sales of parts and repairs would necessarily increase. The cost of materials was likely to advance, and perhaps the price of labor; but it reasonably might have expected a profit for the year of upwards of $60,000,000. It had assets of more than $132,000,000, a surplus of almost $112,000,000, and its cash on hand and municipal bonds were nearly $54,000,000. Its total liabilities, including capital stock, was a little over $20,000,000. It had declared no special dividend during the business year except the October, 1915, dividend. It had been the practice, under similar circumstances, to declare larger dividends. Considering only these facts, a refusal to declare and pay further dividends appears to be not an exercise of discretion on the part of the directors, but an arbitrary refusal to do what the circumstances required to be done. These facts and others call upon the directors to justify their action, or failure or refusal to act. In justification, the defendants have offered testimony tending to prove, and which does prove, the following facts:

It had been the policy of the corporation for a considerable time to annually reduce the selling price of cars, while keeping up, or improving, their quality. As early as in June, 1915, a general plan for the expansion of the productive capacity of the concern by a practical duplication of its plant had been talked over by the executive officers and directors and agreed upon; not all of the details having been settled, and no formal action of directors having been taken. The erection of a smelter was considered, and engineering and other data in connection therewith secured. In consequence, it was determined not to reduce the selling price of cars for the year beginning August 1, 1915, but to maintain the price and to accumulate a large surplus to pay for the proposed expansion of plant and equipment, and perhaps to build a plant for smelting ore. It is hoped, by Mr. Ford, that eventually 1,000,000 cars will be annually produced. The contemplated changes will permit the increased output.

The plan, as affecting the profits of the business for the year beginning August 1, 1916, and thereafter, calls for a reduction in the selling price of the cars. It is true that this price might be at any time increased, but the plan called for the reduction in price of $80 a car. The capacity of the plant, without the additions thereto voted to be made (without a part of them at least), would produce more than 600,000 cars annually. This number, and more, could have been sold for $440 instead of $360, a difference in the return for capital, labor, and materials employed of at least $48,000,000. In short, the plan does not call for and is not intended to produce immediately a more profitable business, but a less profitable one; not only less profitable than formerly, but less profitable than it is admitted it might be made. The apparent immediate effect will be to diminish the value of shares and the returns to shareholders.

It is the contention of plaintiffs that the apparent effect of the plan is intended to be the continued and continuing effect of it and that it is deliberately proposed, not of record and not by official corporate declaration, but nevertheless proposed, to continue the corporation henceforth as a semi-eleemosynary institution and not as a business institution. In support of this contention they point to the attitude and to the expressions of Mr. Henry Ford . . . the dominant force in the business of the Ford Motor Company. . . . A business, one of the largest in the world, and one of the most profitable, has been built up. It employs many men, at good pay.

"My ambition," said Mr. Ford, "is to employ still more men, to spread the benefits of this industrial system to the greatest possible number, to help them build up their lives and their homes. To do this we are putting the greatest share of our profits back in the business."

. . . The record, and especially the testimony of Mr. Ford, convinces that he has to some extent the attitude towards shareholders of one who has dispensed and distributed to them large gains and that they should be content to take what he chooses to give. His testimony creates the impression, also, that he thinks the Ford Motor Company has made too much money, has had too large profits, and that although large profits might be still earned, a sharing of them with the public, by reducing the price of the output of the company, ought to be undertaken. We have no doubt that certain sentiments, philanthropic and altruistic, creditable to Mr. Ford, had large influence in determining the policy to be pursued by the Ford Motor Company—the policy which has been herein referred to.

. . . These cases, after all, like all others in which the subject is treated, turn finally upon the point, the question, whether it appears that the directors were not acting for the best interests of the corporation. We do not draw in question, nor do counsel for the plaintiffs do so, the validity of the general propositions stated by counsel nor the soundness of the opinions delivered in the cases cited. The case presented here is not like any of them. The difference between an incidental humanitarian expenditure of corporate funds for the benefit of the employees, like the building of a hospital for their use and the employment of agencies for the betterment of their condition, and a general purpose and plan to benefit mankind at the expense of others, is obvious. There should be no confusion (of which there is evidence) of the duties which Mr. Ford conceives that he and the stockholders owe to the general public and the duties which in law he and his codirectors owe to protesting, minority stockholders. A business corporation is organized and carried on primarily for the profit of the stockholders. The powers of the directors are to be employed for that end. The discretion of directors is to be exercised in the choice of means to attain that end and does not extend to a change in the end itself, to the reduction of profits or to the nondistribution of profits among stockholders in order to devote them to other purposes.

There is committed to the discretion of directors, a discretion to be exercised in good faith, the infinite details of business, including the wages which shall be paid to employees, the number of hours they shall work, the conditions under which labor shall be carried on, and the prices for which products shall be offered to the public. It is said by appellants that the motives of the board members are not material and will not be inquired into by the court so long as their acts are within their lawful powers. As we have pointed out, and the proposition does not require argument to sustain it, it is not within the lawful powers of a board of directors to shape and conduct the affairs of a corporation for the merely incidental benefit of shareholders and for the primary purpose of benefiting others, and no one will contend that if the avowed purpose of the defendant directors was to sacrifice the interests of shareholders it would not be the duty of the courts to interfere.

We are not, however, persuaded that we should interfere with the proposed expansion of the business of the Ford Motor Company. In view of the fact that the selling price of products may be increased at any time, the ultimate results of the larger business cannot be certainly estimated. The judges are not business experts. It is recognized that plans must often be made for a long future, for expected competition, for a continuing as well as an immediately profitable venture. The experience of the Ford Motor Company is evidence of capable management of its affairs. It may be noticed, incidentally, that it took from the public the money required for the execution of its plan and that the very considerable salaries paid to Mr. Ford and to certain executive officers and employees were not diminished. We are not satisfied that the alleged motives of the directors, in so far as they are reflected in the conduct of the business, menace the interests of shareholders. It is enough to say, perhaps, that the court of equity is at all times open to complaining shareholders having a just grievance. . . .

Assuming the general plan and policy of expansion and the details of it to have been sufficiently, formally, approved at the October and November, 1917, meetings of directors, and assuming further that the plan and policy and the details agreed upon were for the best ultimate interest of the company and therefore of its shareholders, what does it amount to in justification of a refusal to declare and pay a special dividend or dividends? The Ford Motor Company was able to estimate with nicety its income and profit. It could sell more cars than it could make. Having ascertained what it would cost to produce a car and to sell it, the profit upon each car depended upon the selling price. That being fixed, the yearly income and profit was determinable, and, within slight variations, was certain.

There was appropriated—voted—for the smelter $11,325,000. As to the remainder voted, there is no available way for determining how much had been paid before the action of directors was taken and how much was paid thereafter; but assuming that the plans required an expenditure sooner or later of $9,895,000 for duplication of the plant, and for land and other expenditures $3,000,000, the total is $24,220,000. The company was continuing business, at a profit—a cash business. If the total cost of proposed expenditures had been immediately withdrawn in cash from the cash surplus (money and bonds) on hand August 1, 1916, there would have remained nearly $30,000,000.

Defendants say, and it is true, that a considerable cash balance must be at all times carried by such a concern. But, as has been stated, there was a large daily, weekly, monthly, receipt of cash. The output was practically continuous and was continuously, and within a few days, turned into cash. Moreover, the contemplated expenditures were not to be immediately made. The large sum appropriated for the smelter plant was payable over a considerable period of time. So that, without going further, it would appear that, accepting and approving the plan of the directors, it was their duty to distribute on or near the 1st of August, 1916, a very large sum of money to stockholders. . . .

The decree of the court below fixing and determining the specific amount to be distributed to stockholders is affirmed. In other respects, except as to the allowance of costs, the said decree is reversed.

NOTES AND QUESTIONS

1. The ABA Committee on Corporate Laws considered and soundly rejected any amendment of MBCA §8.30 to include other constituencies. In reporting its decision, the committee expressed concern about the possible implications of the new statutes:

> The proponents of other constituencies statutes correctly recognize that many groups in addition to shareholders have a continuing and important economic stake in the welfare of corporations with which they have relationships. Often the shareholder's interest in the corporation is transitory, frequently a matter of days or weeks, while that of a manager or other employee may embrace a career and that of a community far longer. Similarly, a supplier may be almost wholly dependent upon one corporate customer for its economic viability, and a corporate customer may also have a measure of dependence upon its supplier. A community and its desirability as a corporate home and a residence for its citizens may depend upon one or a handful of corporations. . . .
>
> The issue then becomes whether state corporation laws, and, in particular, a broadening of the interests that directors may consider, constitute an efficient and desirable way to provide protections for non-shareholder groups. The Committee has concluded that permitting—much less requiring—directors to consider these interests without relating such consideration in an appropriate fashion to shareholder welfare (as the Delaware courts have done) would conflict with directors' responsibility to shareholders and could undermine the effectiveness of the system that has made the corporation an efficient device for the creation of jobs and wealth.
>
> The Committee believes that the better interpretation of these statutes, and one that avoids such consequences, is that they confirm what the common law has been: directors may take into account the interests of other constituencies but only as and to the extent that the directors are acting in the best interests, long as well as short term, of the shareholders and the corporation. While the Delaware courts have related the consideration directors may give other constituencies to the interests of shareholders by stating there must be "rationally related benefits to shareholders, it may well be that other courts may choose other words with which to express the nexus.

ABA Committee on Corporate Laws, Other Constituency Statutes: Potential for Confusion, 45 Bus. Law. 2253, 2268 (1990).

2. As the twentieth century came to a close, both the hopes and fears surrounding the adoption of other constituency statutes proved unfounded. The adoption of these statutory devices had stalled, and scholarly focus by proponents or opponents had essentially disappeared. To the extent that these statutes had fanned hopes that corporate law would become a tool to encourage greater corporate social responsibility, the following commentator expressed the dominant view.

> Proponents of constituency statutes would better serve the interests they seek to advance by focusing on other measures. Constituency statutes arguably detract attention from more promising measures of change such as measures with potential to change not only whose interests may be legally considered, but who also makes corporate decisions.
>
> Constituency statutes are red herrings. As discussed above, they have been developed and invoked by corporate directors successfully as an anti-takeover mechanism. Although it is true that preventing takeovers may ultimately benefit constituency groups by forestalling plant closures, the fact that these statutes are invoked by directors casually, perhaps sometimes even cynically, does little to advance the case for consideration of constituent interests in corporate law. On some level, constituency statutes may be seen to detract attention from the need for changes in corporate law that will more effectively address the needs and rights, of employees and other constituent groups.

Jonathan D. Springer, 1999 Ann. Surv. Am. L. 85, 123 (1999).

Could the benefit corporation, discussed in the section immediately following, be seen as responsive to Springer's advice?

PROBLEM 4-1

Sportswear, Inc. is engaged in the sports clothing and shoe business. Most of its manufacturing plants are located in underdeveloped countries. For over a year, civil and human rights groups have been assailing Sportswear for taking advantage of its foreign workers. Responding to this criticism, Sportswear's board of directors investigated its overseas operations and concluded that all of its plants were operating in compliance with local laws relating to wages, health, and safety. Despite this finding, the board has decided to invest $100 million during the coming year to bring all overseas plants into compliance with American health and safety standards, and, at an annually recurring cost of approximately $200 million, to increase the wages of all overseas personnel to at least the U.S. minimum wage. During the press conference announcing these decisions, a Sportswear spokesperson stated that the board of directors expected that these expenditures, over both the short and long term, would have a significant negative impact on earnings.

A Sportswear shareholder has filed a derivative suit seeking to protect the corporation from the consequences of the board's announced plans. Is the board's action protected by the business judgment rule?

4. Benefit Corporations

Delaware General G.C.L. Subchapter XV (§§361-368)
B Labs' Model Benefit Corporation Law

The business judgment rule, as reflected in cases like Shlensky v. Wrigley and Dodge v. Ford, gives a corporation's directors and executives considerable space in determining how to allocate the firm's resources, including considerable space to operate in a socially responsible manner. For example, courts will not entertain a shareholder lawsuit seeking to change the compensation policies of Costco even if the pay and benefits package provided to its average worker is far more generous than the industry norm.[1] Likewise, Courts will not entertain a shareholder lawsuit against Google, Inc.

---

1. Costco Wholesale, the second-largest retailer in the U.S. behind Walmart, is an anomaly in an age marked by turmoil and downsizing. Despite the sagging economy and challenges to the industry, Costco pays its hourly workers an average of $20.89 an hour, not including overtime (vs. the minimum wage of $7.25 an hour). By comparison, Walmart said its average wage for full-time employees in the U.S. is $12.67 an hour, according to a letter it sent in April to activist Ralph Nader. Eighty-eight percent of Costco employees have company-sponsored health insurance; Walmart says that "more than half" of its do. Costco workers with coverage pay premiums that amount to less than 10 percent of the overall cost of their plans. It treats its employees well in the belief that a happier work environment will result in a more profitable company. "I just think people need to make a living wage with health benefits," says Jelinek. "It also puts more money back into the economy and creates a healthier country. It's really that simple." Brad Stone, Costco CEO Craig Jelinek Leads the Cheapest, Happiest Company in the World, Bloomberg Businessweek, Companies & Industry (June 6, 2013).

seeking to modify or recover damages for its charitable giving practices, even though those practices are far more generous than any other corporation.[2]

However, seemingly generous outliers like Costco and Google do not view or defend their benefits and charitable giving policies as altruistic. Rather, they justify such expenditures as being in the direct best interest of the corporation. Costco can point to the benefits of substantially higher worker productivity and morale, and much lower turnover, and show that its compensation policies are less costly than the Walmart model. Google's gifts, in substantial part, go to support the cluster of innovation that is essential to its own success.

Thus, while the business judgment rules allow a corporation to operate in what it conceives to be a socially responsible manner, both the dominant business culture and the growing influence of activist investors reinforce an environment in which the directors and corporate managers of most corporations are almost exclusively focused on maximizing shareholder value. The ideology of a century ago, as reflected in Dodge v. Ford's insistence that "a business corporation is organized and carried on primarily for the profit of the stockholders [and that the powers and discretion] of the directors are to be employed for that end" is the ideology of recent decades. So much so that it could be said in 2001, with little dissent, that the American model of corporation governance was both shareholder-centric and globally dominant.

> Despite very real differences in the corporate systems, the deeper tendency is toward convergence, as it has been since the nineteenth century. The basic law of corporate governance—indeed, most of corporate law—has achieved a high degree of uniformity across developed market jurisdictions, and continuing convergence toward a single, standard model is likely. The core legal features of the corporate form were already well established in advanced jurisdictions one hundred years ago, at the turn of the twentieth century. Although there remained considerable room for variation in governance practices and in the fine structure of corporate law throughout the twentieth century, the pressures for further convergence are now rapidly growing. Chief among these pressures is the recent dominance of a shareholder-centered ideology of corporate law among the business, government, and legal elites in key commercial jurisdictions. There is no longer any serious competitor to the view that corporate law should principally strive to increase long-term shareholder value. This emergent consensus has already profoundly affected corporate governance practices throughout the world. It is only a matter of time before its influence is felt in the reform of corporate law as well.[3]

Flying in the face of this story of shareholder-value primacy is a recently created business entity—in most adopting jurisdictions called a "benefit corporation." Benefit corporations are designed to combat the cultural, ideological, and investor pressures to use shareholder value maximization as the only legitimate metric for making or evaluating business decisions. The benefit corporation accomplishes this, in part, by requiring adopting corporations to commit to the pursuit of both profit and social benefit.

---

2. In 2012 Google, Inc. led all other American corporations in generosity, donating $144,606,000 (9.6 percent of its profits) to charity. Nader Salass, Big Businesses that Donated Most Cash: Chronicle of Philanthropy, Huffington Post (July 16, 2013).

3. Henry Hansmann and Reinier Kraakman, The End of History for Corporate Law, 89 Geo. L.J. 439, 439 (2001).

In April 2010, Maryland became the first state to adopt benefit corporation legislation. Three years later, on July 17, 2013, Governor Jack Martell signed into law House Bill 47, making Delaware the twentieth U.S jurisdiction (19 states and the District of Columbia) to authorize benefit corporations. The synopsis accompanying House Bill 47 describes Delaware's version of this new business form as follows:

> [T]his legislation . . . authorizes the creation of public benefit corporations. A public benefit corporation is a for-profit entity which is managed not only for the pecuniary interests of its stockholders but also for the benefit of other persons, entities, communities or interests. Delaware General Corporation Law Sections 362(a) and 365(a) create and impose on directors of public benefit corporations a tri-partite balancing requirement. Public benefit corporations must be managed in a manner that balances (i) the stockholders' pecuniary interests, (ii) the interests of those materially affected by the corporation's conduct, and (iii) a public benefit or public benefits identified in the corporation's certificate of incorporation.
>
> Section 362(a) requires a public benefit corporation to identify in its certificate of incorporation the specific public benefit or public benefits the corporation will promote. Section 366(b) requires public benefit corporations, at least every two years, to issue to stockholders statements that contain certain prescribed information. Section 366(c) permits the corporation in its certificate of incorporation or bylaws to impose additional specified requirements to facilitate stockholders' ability to evaluate the public benefit corporation's achievement of its purposes.
>
> Sections 362(a) and (c) require that both the certificate of incorporation and the name of the corporation clearly indicate that a corporation is a public benefit corporation. Section 364 and 366(a) require that all stock certificates and notices of meetings contain statements acknowledging that the corporation is a public benefit corporation. Section 363 requires a ninety percent vote of stockholders for an existing corporation to become a public benefit corporation and grants appraisal rights to any dissenting stockholder of a corporation that is not a public benefit corporation and becomes a public benefit corporation. . . .
>
> Section 363(c) imposes a two-thirds vote requirement for actions that would terminate the public benefit status of the corporation.
>
> Sections 365 (b) and (c) provide broad protection to directors of public benefit corporations against claims based on interests other than those of stockholders. Directors are not liable as to claims asserted on account of any claimed interest (i) in the public benefits identified in the certificate of incorporation, or (ii) of those materially affected by the corporation's conduct. . . .

Reflecting the enthusiasm that this new business form has generated in its supporters, Delaware governor Jack Martell accompanied his signing of House Bill 47 with a Huffington Post editorial describing and extolling the new business entity.

A New Kind of Corporation to Harness the Power of Private Enterprise for Public Benefit
Huffington Post, July 22, 2013
Governor Jack Martell

On July 17, I signed into law a bill enabling the formation of a new type of corporation that is hard wired to compete to be the best in America at being the best for America.

These new Delaware public benefit corporations will harness the power of private enterprise to create public benefit. In the short term, they will create high quality jobs and improve the quality of life in our communities. In the long term, as many enter the public capital markets, they will help combat the plague of short termism that we have seen over the last five years can undermine a shared and durable prosperity.

Some of the most innovative and fast growing private companies in America — like eco-home care brand Method, organic baby food business Plum Organics, fair trade company Alter Eco, and green paper supplier New Leaf Paper — will be among the first to register as Delaware public benefit corporations on August 1st when this law goes into effect.

These businesses, and over 100,000 like them, are profitable, but consider profit to be the means — not the exclusive end goal — of their business. They see profits as a means to fuel growth in social impact as well as to generate attractive returns for stockholders.

Through meetings over the last several years with my staff, the Corporation Law Council of the Delaware Bar, and the Court of Chancery, it became clear that a new Delaware corporate entity was possible that can bring together these innovative business leaders and the investors who want to back them, while maintaining the high standards that are the hallmark of Delaware corporate law.

Many of the businesses considering this new corporate structure — like waste management firm Rubicon Global, e-commerce platform Etsy, and eyewear industry disruptor Warby Parker — feel understandably constrained by existing corporate law that recognizes only one legitimate corporate purpose — to maximize value for stockholders.

Delaware public benefit corporations will function like and enjoy all the same benefits as traditional Delaware corporations and they will have three unique features that make them potential game changers. These three features concern corporate purpose, accountability, and transparency.

- **Corporate Purpose:** Delaware public benefit corporations will have a corporate purpose "to operate in a responsible and sustainable manner." In addition, to provide directors, stockholders, and ultimately the courts, some direction, they are also required to identify in their certificate of incorporation a specific public benefit purpose the corporation is obligated to pursue. The overarching language helps ensure that a public benefit corporation serves the best long term interests of society while it creates value for its stockholders. The requirement to identify a specific public benefit purpose gives managers, directors, stockholders, and the courts, important guidance to ensure accountability, while preserving flexibility for business leaders and their investors to choose the specific public benefit purpose they feel will drive the greatest total value creation.
- **Accountability:** Unlike in traditional corporations, whose directors have the sole fiduciary duty to maximize stockholder value, directors of public benefit corporations are required to meet a tri-partite balancing requirement consistent with its public benefit purpose. Directors are required to balance "the pecuniary interest of stockholders, the best interests of those materially affected by the corporation's conduct, and the identified specific public benefit purpose."
- **Transparency:** Delaware public benefit corporations are required to report on their overall social and environmental performance, giving stockholders important information that, particularly when reported against a third party

standard, can mitigate risk and reduce transaction costs. Given the trend in public equity markets toward integrated ESG (Environmental, Social and Governance) reporting and the growing private equity market for direct impact investing, this increased transparency can help investors to aggregate capital more easily as they are able to communicate more effectively the impact, and not just the return, of their investments.

The creation of Delaware public benefit corporations is a powerful, no cost, market-based solution to the systemic problem of short termism and an innovative approach to using market forces to solve our most challenging problems.

Because of Delaware's leading role in U.S. corporate law, enactment of benefit corporation legislation in my state is critical for these businesses that seek access to venture capital, private equity, and public capital markets.

Public benefit corporations are not a replacement for traditional corporations in America. But as the next generation of publicly-traded companies comes into being, benefit corporations will be among them, helping to build public trust in business, and becoming an attractive investment opportunity for the growing number of investors who increasingly want to make money and to make a difference.

And that's best for America.

NOTES AND QUESTIONS

1. Perhaps the actor most responsible for the creation and rapid growth of the benefit corporation is B Labs, a nonprofit organization founded in 2006. In addition to providing bedrock lobbying support for benefit corporation legislation, B Labs also created the program by which a corporation can become a Certified B Corp. The creation of a small, enthusiastic coterie of Certified B Corps preceded the adoption of the first benefit corporation legislation and helped fuel the adoption of the early statutes. B Labs describes the nature and purpose of certification as follows:

> B Corp certification is to sustainable business what LEED certification is to green building or Fair Trade certification is to coffee.
>
> B Corps are certified by the nonprofit B Lab to meet rigorous standards of social and environmental performance, accountability, and transparency.

More detail on B Labs and the B Corp certification process can be found at http://www.bcorporation.net

2. In advocating for benefit corporation enabling legislation, B Labs supports the adoption of Model Benefit Corporation Legislation drafted and periodically updated by Bill Clark of the law firm Drinker, Biddle & Reath LLP. To date, no state has adopted all of the key provisions advocated by B Labs. One state, Washington, has adopted a form of benefit corporation statute that departs so greatly from the B Lab model that B Lab does not count Washington in its list of states that have authorized benefit corporations. California, in contrast, adopted both benefit corporation enabling legislation and an alternative vehicle for social entrepreneurship, the so-called flexible purpose corporation. For a thorough analysis of the California experience, the key

differences between early benefit corporation statutes, and the early returns on how widely these new entities will be utilized, see Eric Talley, Corporate Form and Social Entrepreneurship, 37 Seattle U. L. Rev. ____(201_).

PROBLEM 4-2

Charlotte and Angela are former classmates at MIT. Having participated together in a recently failed venture, they are ready now to start afresh. The new venture, to be called DreamWater, Inc., will be the vehicle through which Charlotte and Angela develop and market Charlotte's patented invention: an ocean-water filtration system that could revolutionize farming in coastal regions. Charlotte and Angela plan to make a large profit through sales and licenses in the developed world and to offer the product well below cost in developing countries. Charlotte and Angela also plan to be especially generous employers. To signal to the world the priority that will be given to providing social benefit and the commitment that will be made to employees, Charlotte and Angela have hired the law firm of Bickel and Howe to incorporate their venture in Delaware as a benefit corporation. As your first assignment as a summer associate at Bickel and Howe, please carefully analyze the Delaware benefit corporation provisions and provide your supervising attorney with your recommendation of what provisions should be contained in the certificate of incorporation. As Delaware allows substantial contractual freedom, please consider to what extent you would mold DreamWater, Inc. to include the governance features recommend by B Labs.

B. The Fiduciary Duty of Loyalty

1. Introduction

We now turn to the duty of loyalty, which we examine in two classic settings: (1) circumstances in which a director personally takes an opportunity that the corporation later asserts rightfully belonged to it and (2) transactions between the corporation and the director, commonly called "conflicting interest transactions."

The core of this fiduciary duty is the requirement that a director favor the corporation's interests over her own whenever those interests conflict. As with the duty of care, there is a duty of candor aspect to the duty of loyalty. Thus, whenever a director confronts a situation that involves a conflict between her personal interests and those of the corporation, courts will carefully scrutinize not only whether she has unfairly favored her personal interest in that transaction, but also whether she has been completely candid with the corporation and its shareholders. Indeed, you will see circumstances in which failure to be completely candid is conclusive evidence of breach of the fiduciary duty of loyalty.

Both the corporate opportunity and conflicting interest transaction settings raise concerns about whether a director has fairly treated the corporation she serves. But who is to make this determination? Traditionally, that role has fallen to courts. Increasingly, however, courts and legislatures are channeling these decisions to internal corporate decision-making bodies, either disinterested directors or disinterested shareholders, with courts left to serve a lesser role. Be alert when reading the cases and statutory materials in this section to the level of judicial scrutiny. Is it the relatively restrained business judgment rule review or the more intrusive strict scrutiny evaluation of the entire fairness of the transaction?

2. The Corporate Opportunity Doctrine

a. The American Law Institute and MBCA Approaches

ALI, Principles of Corporate Governance §5.05
MBCA §8.70

Northeast Harbor Golf Club, Inc. v. Harris
Supreme Judicial Court of Maine, 1995
661 A.2d 1146

ROBERTS, JUSTICE.

Northeast Harbor Golf Club, Inc., appeals from a judgment entered in the Superior Court (Hancock County, Atwood, J.) following a nonjury trial. The Club maintains that the trial court erred in finding that Nancy Harris did not breach her fiduciary duty as president of the Club by purchasing and developing property abutting the golf course. Because we today adopt principles different from those applied by the trial court in determining that Harris's activities did not constitute a breach of the corporate opportunity doctrine, we vacate the judgment.

I. THE FACTS

Nancy Harris was the president of the Northeast Harbor Golf Club, a Maine corporation, from 1971 until she was asked to resign in 1990. The Club also had a board of directors that was responsible for making or approving significant policy decisions. The Club's only major asset was a golf course in Mount Desert. During Harris's tenure as president, the board occasionally discussed the possibility of developing some of the Club's real estate in order to raise money. Although Harris was generally in favor of tasteful development, the board always "shied away" from that type of activity.

In 1979, Robert Suminsby informed Harris that he was the listing broker for the Gilpin property, which comprised three noncontiguous parcels located among the fairways of the golf course. The property included an unused right-of-way on which the Club's parking lot and clubhouse were located. It was also encumbered by an easement in favor of the Club allowing foot traffic from the green of one hole to the next tee. Suminsby testified that he contacted Harris because she was the president of the Club and he believed that the Club would be interested in buying the property in order to prevent development.

Harris immediately agreed to purchase the Gilpin property in her own name for the asking price of $45,000. She did not disclose her plans to purchase the property to the Club's board prior to the purchase. She informed the board at its annual August meeting that she had purchased the property, that she intended to hold it in her own name, and that the Club would be "protected." The board took no action in response to the Harris purchase. She testified that at the time of the purchase she had no plans to develop the property and that no such plans took shape until 1988.

In 1984, while playing golf with the postmaster of Northeast Harbor, Harris learned that a parcel of land owned by the heirs of the Smallidge family might be available for purchase. The Smallidge parcel was surrounded on three sides by the golf course and on the fourth side by a house lot. It had no access to the road. With the ultimate goal of acquiring the property, Harris instructed her lawyer to locate the Smallidge heirs. Harris testified that she told a number of individual board members about her attempt to acquire the Smallidge parcel. At a board meeting in August 1985, Harris formally disclosed to the board that she had purchased the Smallidge property.[1] The minutes of that meeting show that she told the board she had no present plans to develop the Smallidge parcel. Harris testified that at the time of the purchase of the Smallidge property she nonetheless thought it might be nice to have some houses there. Again, the board took no formal action as a result of Harris's purchase. Harris acquired the Smallidge property from ten heirs, paying a total of $60,000. In 1990, Harris paid $275,000 for the lot and building separating the Smallidge parcel from the road in order to gain access to the otherwise land-locked parcel.

The trial court expressly found that the Club would have been unable to purchase either the Gilpin or Smallidge properties for itself, relying on testimony that the Club continually experienced financial difficulties, operated annually at a deficit, and depended on contributions from the directors to pay its bills. On the other hand, there was evidence that the Club had occasionally engaged in successful fund-raising, including a two-year period shortly after the Gilpin purchase during which the Club raised $115,000. The Club had $90,000 in a capital investment fund at the time of the Smallidge purchase.

In 1987 or 1988, Harris divided the real estate into 41 small lots, 14 on the Smallidge property and 27 on the Gilpin property. Apparently as part of her estate plan, Harris conveyed noncontiguous lots among the 41 to her children and retained others for herself. In 1991, Harris and her children exchanged deeds to reassemble the small lots into larger parcels. At the time the Club filed this suit, the property was divided into 11 lots, some owned by Harris and others by her children who are also defendants in this case. Harris estimated the value of all the real estate at the time of the trial to be $1,550,000.

In 1988, Harris, who was still president of the Club, and her children began the process of obtaining approval for a five-lot subdivision known as Bushwood on the

---

1. In fact, it appears that Harris did not take title to the property until October 26, 1985. She had only signed a purchase and sale agreement at the time of the August board meeting.

lower Gilpin property. Even when the board learned of the proposed subdivision, a majority failed to take any action. A group of directors formed a separate organization in order to oppose the subdivision on the basis that it violated the local zoning ordinance. After Harris's resignation as president, the Club also sought unsuccessfully to challenge the subdivision. See Northeast Harbor Golf Club, Inc. v. Town of Mount Desert, 618 A.2d 225 (Me. 1992). Plans of Harris and her family for development of the other parcels are unclear, but the local zoning ordinance would permit construction of up to 11 houses on the land as currently divided.

After Harris's plans to develop Bushwood became apparent, the board grew increasingly divided concerning the propriety of development near the golf course. At least two directors, Henri Agnese and Nick Ludington, testified that they trusted Harris to act in the best interests of the Club and that they had no problem with the development plans for Bushwood. Other directors disagreed.

In particular, John Schafer, a Washington, D.C., lawyer and long-time member of the board, took issue with Harris's conduct. He testified that he had relied on Harris's representations at the time she acquired the properties that she would not develop them. According to Schafer, matters came to a head in August 1990 when a number of directors concluded that Harris's development plans irreconcilably conflicted with the Club's interests. As a result, Schafer and two other directors asked Harris to resign as president. In April 1991, after a substantial change in the board's membership, the board authorized the instant lawsuit against Harris for the breach of her fiduciary duty to act in the best interests of the corporation. The board simultaneously resolved that the proposed housing development was contrary to the best interests of the corporation.

The Club filed a complaint against Harris, her sons John and Shepard, and her daughter-in-law Melissa Harris. As amended, the complaint alleged that during her term as president Harris breached her fiduciary duty by purchasing the lots without providing notice and an opportunity for the Club to purchase the property and by subdividing the lots for future development. The Club sought an injunction to prevent development and also sought to impose a constructive trust on the property in question for the benefit of the Club.

The trial court found that Harris had not usurped a corporate opportunity because the acquisition of real estate was not in the Club's line of business. Moreover, it found that the corporation lacked the financial ability to purchase the real estate at issue. Finally, the court placed great emphasis on Harris's good faith. It noted her long and dedicated history of service to the Club, her personal oversight of the Club's growth, and her frequent financial contributions to the Club. The court found that her development activities were "generally . . . compatible with the corporation's business." This appeal followed.

II. THE CORPORATE OPPORTUNITY DOCTRINE

Corporate officers and directors bear a duty of loyalty to the corporations they serve. As Justice Cardozo explained the fiduciary duty in Meinhard v. Salmon, 249 N.Y. 458, 164 N.E. 545, 546 (1928):

> A trustee is held to something stricter than the morals of the marketplace. Not honesty alone, but the punctilio of an honor the most sensitive, is then the standard of behavior. As to this there has developed a tradition that is unbending and inveterate.

Maine has embraced this "unbending and inveterate" tradition. Corporate fiduciaries in Maine must discharge their duties in good faith with a view toward furthering the interests of the corporation. They must disclose and not withhold relevant information concerning any potential conflict of interest with the corporation, and they must refrain from using their position, influence, or knowledge of the affairs of the corporation to gain personal advantage. See Rosenthal v. Rosenthal, 543 A.2d 348, 352 (Me. 1988); 13-A M.R.S.A. §716 (Supp. 1994).

Despite the general acceptance of the proposition that corporate fiduciaries owe a duty of loyalty to their corporations, there has been much confusion about the specific extent of that duty when, as here, it is contended that a fiduciary takes for herself a corporate opportunity. See, e.g., Victor Brudney & Robert C. Clark, A New Look at Corporate Opportunities, 94 Harv. L. Rev. 998, 998 (1981) ("Not only are the common formulations vague, but the courts have articulated no theory that would serve as a blueprint for constructing meaningful rules."). This case requires us for the first time to define the scope of the corporate opportunity doctrine in Maine.

Various courts have embraced different versions of the corporate opportunity doctrine. The test applied by the trial court and embraced by Harris is generally known as the "line of business" test. The seminal case applying the line of business test is Guth v. Loft, Inc., 5 A.2d 503 (Del. 1939). In *Guth*, the Delaware Supreme Court adopted an intensely factual test stated in general terms as follows:

> [I]f there is presented to a corporate officer or director a business opportunity which the corporation is financially able to undertake, is, from its nature, in the line of the corporation's business and is of practical advantage to it, is one in which the corporation has an interest or a reasonable expectancy, and, by embracing the opportunity, the self-interest of the officer or director will be brought into conflict with that of his corporation, the law will not permit him to seize the opportunity for himself.

Id. at 511.

The "real issue" under this test is whether the opportunity "was so closely associated with the existing business activities . . . as to bring the transaction within that class of cases where the acquisition of the property would throw the corporate officer purchasing it into competition with his company." Id. at 513.

The Delaware court described that inquiry as "a factual question to be decided by reasonable inferences from objective facts." Id.

The line of business test suffers from some significant weaknesses. First, the question whether a particular activity is within a corporation's line of business is conceptually difficult to answer. The facts of the instant case demonstrate that difficulty. The Club is in the business of running a golf course. It is not in the business of developing real estate. In the traditional sense, therefore, the trial court correctly observed that the opportunity in this case was not a corporate opportunity within the meaning of the *Guth* test. Nevertheless, the record would support a finding that the Club had made the policy judgment that development of surrounding real estate was detrimental to the best interests of the Club. The acquisition of land adjacent to the golf course for the purpose of preventing future development would have enhanced the ability of the Club to implement that policy. The record also shows that the Club had occasionally considered reversing that policy and expanding its operations to include the development of surrounding real estate. Harris's activities effectively foreclosed the Club from pursuing that option with respect to prime locations adjacent to the golf course.

Second, the *Guth* test includes as an element the financial ability of the corporation to take advantage of the opportunity. The court in this case relied on the Club's supposed financial incapacity as a basis for excusing Harris's conduct. Often, the injection of financial ability into the equation will unduly favor the inside director or executive who has command of the facts relating to the finances of the corporation. Reliance on financial ability will also act as a disincentive to corporate executives to solve corporate financing and other problems. In addition, the Club could have prevented development without spending $275,000 to acquire the property Harris needed to obtain access to the road.

The Massachusetts Supreme Judicial Court adopted a different test in Durfee v. Durfee & Canning, Inc., 323 Mass. 187, 80 N.E.2d 522 (1948). The *Durfee* test has since come to be known as the "fairness test." According to *Durfee*, the

> true basis of governing doctrine rests on the unfairness in the particular circumstances of a director, whose relation to the corporation is fiduciary, taking advantage of an opportunity [for her personal profit] when the interest of the corporation justly call[s] for protection. This calls for application of ethical standards of what is fair and equitable . . . in particular sets of facts.

Id. at 529 (quoting Ballantine on Corporations 204-205 (rev. ed. 1946)).

As with the *Guth* test, the *Durfee* test calls for a broad-ranging, intensely factual inquiry. The *Durfee* test suffers even more than the *Guth* test from a lack of principled content. It provides little or no practical guidance to the corporate officer or director seeking to measure her obligations.

The Minnesota Supreme Court elected "to combine the 'line of business' test with the 'fairness' test." Miller v. Miller, 301 Minn. 207, 222 N.W.2d 71, 81 (1974). It engaged in a two-step analysis, first determining whether a particular opportunity was within the corporation's line of business, then scrutinizing "the equitable considerations existing prior to, at the time of, and following the officer's acquisition." Id. The *Miller* court hoped by adopting this approach "to ameliorate the often-expressed criticism that the [corporate opportunity] doctrine is vague and subjects today's corporate management to the danger of unpredictable liability." Id. In fact, the test adopted in *Miller* merely piles the uncertainty and vagueness of the fairness test on top of the weaknesses in the line of business test.

Despite the weaknesses of each of these approaches to the corporate opportunity doctrine, they nonetheless rest on a single fundamental policy. At bottom, the corporate opportunity doctrine recognizes that a corporate fiduciary should not serve both corporate and personal interests at the same time. As we observed in Camden Land Co. v. Lewis, 101 Me. 78, 97, 63 A. 523, 531 (1905), corporate fiduciaries "owe their whole duty to the corporation, and they are not to be permitted to act when duty conflicts with interest. They cannot serve themselves and the corporation at the same time." The various formulations of the test are merely attempts to moderate the potentially harsh consequences of strict adherence to that policy. It is important to preserve some ability for corporate fiduciaries to pursue personal business interests that present no real threat to their duty of loyalty.

III.   THE AMERICAN LAW INSTITUTE APPROACH

In an attempt to protect the duty of loyalty while at the same time providing long-needed clarity and guidance for corporate decision-makers, the American Law Institute has offered the most recently developed version of the corporate opportunity doctrine. Principles of Corporate Governance §5.05 (May 13, 1992), provides as follows:

[5.05] Taking of Corporate Opportunities by Directors or Senior Executives

(a) **General Rule.** A director [§1.13] or senior executive [§1.33] may not take advantage of a corporate opportunity unless:

(1) The director or senior executive first offers the corporate opportunity to the corporation and makes disclosure concerning the conflict of interest [§1.14(a)] and the corporate opportunity [§1.14(b)];

(2) The corporate opportunity is rejected by the corporation; and

(3) Either:

(A) The rejection of the opportunity is fair to the corporation;

(B) The opportunity is rejected in advance, following such disclosure, by disinterested directors [§1.15], or, in the case of a senior executive who is not a director, by a disinterested superior, in a manner that satisfies the standards of the business judgment rule [§4.01(c)]; or

(C) The rejection is authorized in advance or ratified, following such disclosure, by disinterested shareholders [§1.16], and the rejection is not equivalent to a waste of corporate assets [§1.42].

(b) **Definition of a Corporate Opportunity.** For purposes of this Section, a corporate opportunity means:

(1) Any opportunity to engage in a business activity of which a director or senior executive becomes aware, either:

(A) In connection with the performance of functions as a director or senior executive, or under circumstances that should reasonably lead the director or senior executive to believe that the person offering the opportunity expects it to be offered to the corporation; or

(B) Through the use of corporate information or property, if the resulting opportunity is one that the director or senior executive should reasonably be expected to believe would be of interest to the corporation; or

(2) Any opportunity to engage in a business activity of which a senior executive becomes aware and knows is closely related to a business in which the corporation is engaged or expects to engage.

(c) **Burden of Proof.** A party who challenges the taking of a corporate opportunity has the burden of proof, except that if such party establishes that the requirements of Subsection (a)(3)(B) or (C) are not met, the director or the senior executive has the burden of proving that the rejection and the taking of the opportunity were fair to the corporation.

(d) **Ratification of Defective Disclosure.** A good faith but defective disclosure of the facts concerning the corporate opportunity may be cured if at any time (but no later than a reasonable time after suit is filed challenging the taking of the corporate opportunity) the original rejection of the corporate opportunity is ratified, following the required disclosure, by the board, the shareholders, or the corporate decisionmaker who initially approved the rejection of the corporate opportunity, or such decisionmaker's successor.

(e) **Special Rule Concerning Delayed Offering of Corporate Opportunities.** Relief based solely on failure to first offer an opportunity to the corporation under Subsection (a)(1) is not available if: (1) such failure resulted from a good faith belief that the business activity did not constitute a corporate opportunity, and (2) not later than a reasonable time after suit is filed challenging the taking of the corporate opportunity, the corporate opportunity is to the extent possible offered to the corporation and rejected in a manner that satisfies the standards of Subsection (a).

The central feature of the ALI test is the strict requirement of full disclosure prior to taking advantage of any corporate opportunity. Id., §5.05(a)(1). "If the opportunity is not offered to the corporation, the director or senior executive will not have satisfied §5.05(a)." Id., cmt. to §5.05(a). The corporation must then formally reject the opportunity. Id., §505(a)(2). The ALI test is discussed at length and ultimately applied by the Oregon Supreme Court in Klinicki v. Lundgren, 298 Or. 662, 695 P.2d 906 (1985). As *Klinicki* describes the test, "full disclosure to the appropriate corporate body is . . . an absolute condition precedent to the validity of any forthcoming rejection as well as to the availability to the director or principal senior executive of the defense of fairness." Id. at 920. A "good faith but defective disclosure" by the corporate officer may be ratified after the fact only by an affirmative vote of the disinterested directors or shareholders. Principles of Corporate Governance §5.05(d).

The ALI test defines "corporate opportunity" broadly. It includes opportunities "closely related to a business in which the corporation is engaged." Id., §5.05(b). It also encompasses any opportunities that accrue to the fiduciary as a result of her position within the corporation. Id. This concept is most clearly illustrated by the testimony of Suminsby, the listing broker for the Gilpin property, which, if believed by the factfinder, would support a finding that the Gilpin property was offered to Harris specifically in her capacity as president of the Club. If the factfinder reached that conclusion, then at least the opportunity to acquire the Gilpin property would be a corporate opportunity. The state of the record concerning the Smallidge purchase precludes us from intimating any opinion whether that too would be a corporate opportunity.

Under the ALI standard, once the Club shows that the opportunity is a corporate opportunity, it must show either that Harris did not offer the opportunity to the Club or that the Club did not reject it properly. If the Club shows that the board did not reject the opportunity by a vote of the disinterested directors after full disclosure, then Harris may defend her actions on the basis that the taking of the opportunity was fair to the corporation. Id., §5.05(c). If Harris failed to offer the opportunity at all, however, then she may not defend on the basis that the failure to offer the opportunity was fair. Id., cmt. to §5.05(c).

The *Klinicki* court viewed the ALI test as an opportunity to bring some clarity to a murky area of the law. *Klinicki,* 695 P.2d at 915. We agree, and today we follow the ALI test. The disclosure-oriented approach provides a clear procedure whereby a corporate officer may insulate herself through prompt and complete disclosure from the possibility of a legal challenge. The requirement of disclosure recognizes the paramount importance of the corporate fiduciary's duty of loyalty. At the same time it protects the fiduciary's ability pursuant to the proper procedure to pursue her own business ventures free from the possibility of a lawsuit. . . .

IV. CONCLUSION

The question remains how our adoption of the rule affects the result in the instant case. The trial court made a number of factual findings based on an extensive record.[3] The court made those findings, however, in the light of legal principles that are different from the principles that we today announce. Similarly, the parties did not have the opportunity to develop the record in this case with knowledge of the applicable legal standard. In these circumstances, fairness requires that we remand the case for further proceedings. Those further proceedings may include, at the trial court's discretion, the taking of further evidence.

NOTE: FAIRNESS AND THE DOCTRINE OF WASTE

Under the ALI approach, a fiduciary may take advantage of a corporate opportunity if such taking either is fair to the corporation, or is authorized in advance by disinterested directors "in a manner that satisfies the standards of the business judgment rule," or is authorized by an informed vote of disinterested shareholders, so long as the shareholders' rejection of the opportunity "is not equivalent to a waste of corporate assets." ALI Principles of Corporate Governance §5.05(a). The ALI defines "waste" as follows.

> A transaction constitutes a "waste of corporate assets" if it involves an expenditure of corporate funds or a disposition of corporate assets for which no consideration is received in exchange and for which there is no rational business purpose, or, if consideration is received in exchange, the consideration the corporation receives is so inadequate in value that no person of ordinary sound business judgment would deem it worth that which the corporation has paid.

ALI Principles of Corporate Governance §1.42.

Disinterested directors or shareholders may decide to reject a corporate opportunity even if pursuing the opportunity might be profitable to the corporation on the grounds that corporate resources may more profitably or prudently be used in other ways. Such a decision to reject a corporate opportunity would constitute a "waste of corporate assets" only if the opportunity was of such obvious importance and value to the corporation that no person of ordinary sound business judgment would have rejected the opportunity. In other words, the rejection of a corporate opportunity would constitute a waste of corporate assets only if it was akin to a "gift" of corporate assets that no person of ordinary sound business judgment would have authorized.

Shareholders may ratify corporate acts or decisions that do not constitute waste. For example, "[i]t is the law of Delaware, and general corporate law, that a validly

---

3. Harris raised the defense of *laches* and the statute of limitations but the court made no findings on those issues. We do not intimate what result the application of either doctrine would produce in this case. Similarly, it was not necessary for the court to address the issue of remedy in the first trial. The court has broad discretion to fashion an equitable remedy based on the facts and circumstances of the case. We decline to invade its province by commenting prematurely on what remedy, if any, may be appropriate.

accomplished shareholder ratification relates back to cure otherwise unauthorized acts of officers and directors. . . . It is only where a claim of gift or waste of assets, fraud or ultra vires is asserted that less than unanimous shareholder ratification is not a full defense." Michelson v. Duncan, 407 A.2d at 218-219. However, waste is treated as a void rather than voidable act.

> [I]t has long been held that shareholders may not ratify a waste except by a unanimous vote. Saxe v. Brady, Del.Ch., 184 A.2d 602, 605 (1962). The idea behind this rule is apparently that a transaction that satisfies the high standard of waste constitutes a gift of corporate property and no one should be forced against their will to make a gift of their property. In all events, informed, uncoerced, disinterested shareholder ratification of a transaction in which corporate directors have a material conflict of interest has the effect of protecting the transaction from judicial review except on the basis of waste. Lewis v. Vogelstein, 699 A.2d 327, 335 (Del.Ch. 1997).

If the rejection of a corporate opportunity constitutes a waste of corporate assets, the rejection cannot be "fair" to the corporation. Likewise, if a corporate opportunity has been rejected by the directors, a finding that such rejection is akin to waste would preclude a finding that the directors' actions are entitled to business judgment rule presumptions. A finding of waste with respect to a director-approved action necessarily constitutes a finding that the directors acted in violation of their fiduciary duties and that the corporation has been damaged by that action. Thus, the doctrine of waste serves to define the outer boundary of judicial respect for, and deference to, the directors' business judgment.

NOTES AND QUESTIONS

1. On remand, the trial court ruled that both the Gilpin and Suminsby properties were corporate opportunities and that Nancy Harris had wrongfully usurped those opportunities. The Supreme Judicial Court upheld the findings of fact, but held that the Club's claims were barred by the doctrine of *laches*. Northeast Harbor Golf Club, Inc. v. Harris, 725 A.2d 1018 (Me. 1999). With respect to the Suminsby property, the Supreme Judicial Court reasoned as follows:

> Harris contends that because she learned of the availability of the Smallidge property independent of her position as an officer of the Club, and because the purchase of that land was not closely related to the Club's business, that there was no usurpation of a corporate opportunity. In reviewing the decision of the Superior Court, we defer to the historical factual findings of the court, but the determination of whether an opportunity is a "corporate opportunity" is a question of law that we review de novo.
>
> Even if the opportunity to engage in a business activity, in which the officer or director becomes involved, is not learned of through her connection to the business of the corporation, nevertheless, such an opportunity may be considered a corporate opportunity if the officer or director knows it "is closely related to a business in which the corporation is engaged or expects to engage." Principles of Corporate Governance §5.05(b)(2). . . .
>
> In this case, the Club's normal business is maintaining and operating a golf course. That business is dependent on having sufficient land for the course itself and ensuring that the activity of golf is not hindered or affected by development of adjacent and surrounding property. The Club had frequently discussed developing some of its own land and on one occasion talked about the possibility of purchasing and developing adjacent land. The purchase of the Smallidge land,

surrounded as it is on three sides by the Club's land and adjacent to three of its golf holes, land that could be developed, is, in the circumstances of this case, sufficiently related to the Club's business to constitute a corporate opportunity.

Id. at 1021-1023.

2. The ALI approach to corporate fiduciaries' taking of corporate opportunities has been expressly adopted not only by Maine, but also by Massachusetts, see Demoulas v. Demoulas Super Markets, Inc., 677 N.E.2d 159, 181, n.36 (Mass. 1997), and, as noted in Northeast Harbour Golf Club, Inc. v. Harris, by Oregon, see Klinicki v. Lundgren, 695 P.2d 906 (Or. 1985).

3. To what extent would you describe the ALI proposal as a penalty default or information-forcing rule designed to punish managers who pursue personal interests without informing the corporation in advance of their intention? To what extent is the ALI proposal a majoritarian rule? Is it a default or immutable rule?

PROBLEM 4-3

Anna Erickson is a senior executive of Northwest Charters, Inc. (Charters), a corporation engaged in the business of providing chartered bus transportation for the intercollegiate athletic programs of northwestern colleges and universities. Charters' board has recently been considering an expansion of its business involving limited provision of chartered air transport to colleges and universities. Consider whether Erickson would be liable to Charters for breach of fiduciary duty under ALI Principles in the following circumstances.

1. Erickson recently interviewed Susan Smith for the position of vice president of marketing at Charters. In recounting her work experience, Smith told Erickson that she has spent the past year trying to promote a fast-food vegetarian restaurant chain operated by a corporation she owns called Vegan City, Inc., but that she has given up obtaining necessary financing. Intrigued, Erickson began discussing with Smith ways to make Vegan City viable. Two weeks later, without informing the Charters board of the opportunity, Erickson purchased 75 percent of the stock in Vegan City for $200,000 and became a member of its three-person board of directors. Simultaneously, Smith signed an employment contract with Vegan City agreeing to devote her full time to promoting its business. Erickson continues to work full time for Charters.

2. Erickson recently formed and became the sole shareholder of Pro Transport, Inc. Shortly thereafter, Erickson visited the National Football League's vice president for league operations, seeking advice on college expansion opportunities for Charters. After learning that the NFL was in need of extensive charter services, and without informing Charters, Erickson entered into negotiations that quickly culminated in a long-term contract between Pro Transport and the NFL for the provision of air transportation on a chartered basis for all NFL teams. How would the following facts affect your analysis?

(a) Charters is highly leveraged. When deposed, one former Charters director commented that she believed Charters would not have wanted the contract because of the financial commitments and risk involved.

(b) Prior to her first visit with the NFL, Erickson had given Charters 60 days' notice of her resignation as president to "pursue other business opportunities."

(c) The NFL initiated the discussions with Erickson at a private dinner and stipulated from the outset that they were interested only in dealing with her and her new company, and that in no event would they be willing to do business with Northwest Charters.

(d) Erickson is only a director of Charters. She is CEO of East Coast Air Transportation.

PROBLEM 4-4

Reanalyze the questions posed in Problem 4-3, assuming that the governing legal standard is MBCA §8.70.

b.   *The Delaware Approach*

Delaware G.C.L. §122(17)

Broz v. Cellular Information Systems, Inc.
Supreme Court of Delaware, 1996
673 A.2d 148

Veasey, Chief Justice.

In this appeal, we consider the application of the doctrine of corporate opportunity. The Court of Chancery decided that the defendant, a corporate director, breached his fiduciary duty by not formally presenting to the corporation an opportunity which had come to the director individually and independent of the director's relationship with the corporation. Here the opportunity was not one in which the corporation in its current mode had an interest or which it had the financial ability to acquire, but, under the unique circumstances here, that mode was subject to change by virtue of the impending acquisition of the corporation by another entity.

We conclude that, although a corporate director may be shielded from liability by offering to the corporation an opportunity which has come to the director independently and individually, the failure of the director to present the opportunity does not necessarily result in the improper usurpation of a corporate opportunity. We further conclude that, if the corporation is a target or potential target of an acquisition by another company which has an interest and ability to entertain the opportunity, the director of the target company does not have a fiduciary duty to present the opportunity to the target company. Accordingly, the judgment of the Court of Chancery is REVERSED.

I.   The Contentions of the Parties and the Decision Below

Robert F. Broz ("Broz") is the President and sole stockholder of RFB Cellular, Inc. ("RFBC"), a Delaware corporation engaged in the business of providing cellular telephone service in the Midwestern United States. At the time of the conduct at issue in this appeal, Broz was also a member of the board of directors of plaintiff below-appellee, Cellular Information Systems, Inc. ("CIS"). CIS is a publicly held Delaware corporation and a competitor of RFBC.

The conduct before the Court involves the purchase by Broz of a cellular telephone service license for the benefit of RFBC.[1] The license in question, known as the Michigan-2 Rural Service Area Cellular License ("Michigan-2"), is issued by the Federal Communications Commission ("FCC") and entitles its holder to provide cellular telephone service to a portion of northern Michigan. CIS brought an action against Broz and RFBC for equitable relief, contending that the purchase of this license by Broz constituted a usurpation of a corporate opportunity properly belonging to CIS, irrespective of whether or not CIS was interested in the Michigan-2 opportunity at the time it was offered to Broz.

II. FACTS

Broz has been the President and sole stockholder of RFBC since 1992. RFBC owns and operates an FCC license area, known as the Michigan-4 Rural Service Area Cellular License ("Michigan-4"). The license entitles RFBC to provide cellular telephone service to a portion of rural Michigan. Although Broz' efforts have been devoted primarily to the business operations of RFBC, he also served as an outside director of CIS at the time of the events at issue in this case. CIS was at all times fully aware of Broz' relationship with RFBC and the obligations incumbent upon him by virtue of that relationship.

In April of 1994, Mackinac Cellular Corp. ("Mackinac") sought to divest itself of Michigan-2, the license area immediately adjacent to Michigan-4. To this end, Mackinac contacted Daniels & Associates ("Daniels") and arranged for the brokerage firm to seek potential purchasers for Michigan-2. In compiling a list of prospects, Daniels included RFBC as a likely candidate. In May of 1994, David Rhodes, a representative of Daniels, contacted Broz and broached the subject of RFBC's possible acquisition of Michigan-2. Broz later signed a confidentiality agreement at the request of Mackinac, and received the offering materials pertaining to Michigan-2.

Michigan-2 was not, however, offered to CIS. Apparently, Daniels did not consider CIS to be a viable purchaser for Michigan-2 in light of CIS' recent financial difficulties. The record shows that, at the time Michigan-2 was offered to Broz, CIS had recently emerged from lengthy and contentious Chapter 11 proceedings. Pursuant to the Chapter 11 Plan of Reorganization, CIS entered into a loan agreement that substantially impaired the company's ability to undertake new acquisitions or to incur

---

1. The Court recognizes that the actual purchase of the Michigan-2 license was consummated by RFBC as a corporate entity, rather than by Broz acting as an individual for his own benefit. Broz is, however, the sole party in interest in RFBC and all actions taken by RFBC, including the acquisition of Michigan-2, are accomplished at the behest of Broz. Therefore, insofar as the purchase of Michigan-2 is concerned, the Court will not distinguish between the actions of Broz and those of RFBC in analyzing Broz' alleged breach of fiduciary duty. . . .

new debt. In fact, CIS would have been unable to purchase Michigan-2 without the approval of its creditors.

The CIS reorganization resulted from the failure of CIS' rather ambitious plans for expansion. From 1989 onward, CIS had embarked on a series of cellular license acquisitions. In 1992, however, CIS' financing failed, necessitating the liquidation of the company's holdings and reduction of the company's total indebtedness. During the period from early 1992 until the time of CIS' emergence from bankruptcy in 1994, CIS divested itself of some fifteen separate cellular license systems.[2] CIS contracted to sell four additional license areas on May 27, 1994,[3] leaving CIS with only five remaining license areas, all of which were outside of the Midwest.

On June 13, 1994, following a meeting of the CIS board, Broz spoke with CIS' Chief Executive Officer, Richard Treibick ("Treibick"), concerning his interest in acquiring Michigan-2. Treibick communicated to Broz that CIS was not interested in Michigan-2.[4] Treibick further stated that he had been made aware of the Michigan-2 opportunity prior to the conversation with Broz, and that any offer to acquire Michigan-2 was rejected. After the commencement of the PriCellular tender offer, in August of 1994, Broz contacted another CIS director, Peter Schiff ("Schiff"), to discuss the possible acquisition of Michigan-2 by RFBC. Schiff, like Treibick, indicated that CIS had neither the wherewithal nor the inclination to purchase Michigan-2. In late September of 1994, Broz also contacted Stanley Bloch ("Bloch"), a director and counsel for CIS, to request that Bloch represent RFBC in its dealings with Mackinac. Bloch agreed to represent RFBC, and, like Schiff and Treibick, expressed his belief that CIS was not at all interested in the transaction. Ultimately, all the CIS directors testified at trial that, had Broz inquired at that time, they each would have expressed the opinion that CIS was not interested in Michigan-2.[5]

On June 28, 1994, following various overtures from PriCellular concerning an acquisition of CIS, six CIS directors[6] entered into agreements with PriCellular to sell their shares in CIS at a price of $2.00 per share. These agreements were contingent upon, inter alia, the consummation of a PriCellular tender offer for all CIS shares at the same price. Pursuant to their agreements with PriCellular, the CIS directors also entered into a "standstill" agreement which prevented the directors from engaging in any transaction

---

2. Of these fifteen licenses, three were sold to subsidiaries of PriCellular. Specifically, the licenses held by CIS for areas in Wisconsin and Minnesota were acquired by the PriCellular subsidiaries. These transactions closed immediately upon CIS' emergence from bankruptcy.

3. These license areas, all located in Wisconsin, were to be sold to PriCellular. After completing its acquisition of CIS, however, PriCellular determined that ownership of the licenses should remain with CIS.

4. In fact, during a deposition given in March of 1995, Treibick testified that he didn't "know who frankly was hawking [the Michigan-2 license] . . . at the time . . . [W]e said forget it. It was not something we would have bought if they offered it to us for nothing."

5. We assume arguendo that informal contacts and individual opinions of board members are not a substitute for a formal process of presenting an opportunity to a board of directors. Nevertheless, in our view such a formal process was not necessary under the circumstances of this case in order for Broz to avoid liability. These contacts with individual board members do, however, tend to show that Broz was not acting surreptitiously or in bad faith.

6. All the members of the CIS board of directors except Broz and Bloch agreed to tender their shares to PriCellular.

outside the regular course of CIS' business or incurring any new liabilities until the close of the PriCellular tender offer. On August 2, 1994, PriCellular commenced a tender offer for all outstanding shares of CIS at $2.00 per share. The PriCellular tender offer mirrored the standstill agreements entered into by the CIS directors.

PriCellular's tender offer was originally scheduled to close on September 16, 1994. At the time the tender offer was launched, however, the source of the $106,000,000 in financing required to consummate the transaction was still in doubt. PriCellular originally planned to structure the transaction around bank loans. When this financing fell through, PriCellular resorted to a junk bond offering. PriCellular's financing difficulties generated a great deal of concern among the CIS insiders whether the tender offer was, in fact, viable. Financing difficulties ultimately caused PriCellular to delay the closing date of the tender offer from September 16, 1994 until October 14, 1994 and then again until November 9, 1994.

On August 6, September 6 and September 21, 1994, Broz submitted written offers to Mackinac for the purchase of Michigan-2. During this time period, PriCellular also began negotiations with Mackinac to arrange an option for the purchase of Michigan-2. PriCellular's interest in Michigan-2 was fully disclosed to CIS' chief executive, Treibick, who did not express any interest in Michigan-2, and was actually incredulous that PriCellular would want to acquire the license. Nevertheless, CIS was fully aware that PriCellular and Broz were bidding for Michigan-2 and did not interpose CIS in this bidding war.

In late September of 1994, PriCellular reached agreement with Mackinac on an option to purchase Michigan-2. The exercise price of the option agreement was set at $6.7 million, with the option remaining in force until December 15, 1994. Pursuant to the agreement, the right to exercise the option was not transferrable to any party other than a subsidiary of PriCellular. Therefore, it could not have been transferred to CIS. The agreement further provided that Mackinac was free to sell Michigan-2 to any party who was willing to exceed the exercise price of the Mackinac-PriCellular option contract by at least $500,000. On November 14, 1994, Broz agreed to pay Mackinac $7.2 million for the Michigan-2 license, thereby meeting the terms of the option agreement. An asset purchase agreement was thereafter executed by Mackinac and RFBC.

Nine days later, on November 23, 1994, PriCellular completed its financing and closed its tender offer for CIS. Prior to that point, PriCellular owned no equity interest in CIS. Subsequent to the consummation of the PriCellular tender offer for CIS, members of the CIS board of directors, including Broz, were discharged and replaced with a slate of PriCellular nominees. On March 2, 1995, this action was commenced by CIS in the Court of Chancery.

At trial in the Court of Chancery, CIS contended that the purchase of Michigan-2 by Broz constituted the impermissible usurpation of a corporate opportunity properly belonging to CIS. Thus, CIS asserted that Broz breached his fiduciary duty to CIS and its stockholders. CIS admits that, at the time the opportunity was offered to Broz, the board of CIS would not have been interested in Michigan-2, but CIS asserts that Broz usurped the opportunity nevertheless. CIS claims that Broz was required to look not just to CIS, but to the articulated business plans of PriCellular, to determine whether PriCellular would be interested in acquiring Michigan-2. Since Broz failed to do this and acquired Michigan-2 without first considering the interests of PriCellular in its capacity as a potential acquiror of CIS, CIS contends that Broz must be held to account for breach of fiduciary duty.

In assessing the contentions of the parties in light of the facts of record, the Court of Chancery concluded:

> (1) that [CIS] . . . could have legitimately required its director [Broz] to abstain from the Mackinac transaction out of deference to its own interests in extending an offer, despite the fact that it came to such director in a wholly independent way (that is, the transaction is one that falls quite close to the core transactions that the corporation was formed to engage in);
> (2) that by no later than the time by which PriCellular had extended the public tender offer, the circumstances of the company had changed so that it was quite plausibly in the corporation's interest and financially feasible for it to pursue the Mackinac transaction;
> (3) that in such circumstances as existed at the latest after October 14, 1994 (date of PriCellular's option contract on Michigan-2 RSA) it was the obligation of Mr. Broz as a director of CIS to take the transaction to the CIS board for its formal action; and
> (4) the after the fact testimony of directors to the effect that they would not have been interested in pursuing this transaction had it been brought to the board, is not helpful to defendant, in my opinion, because most of them did not know at that time of PriCellular's interest in the property and how it related to PriCellular's plan for CIS.

663 A.2d at 1186.

Based on these conclusions, the court held that:

> even though knowledge of the availability of the Michigan-2 RSA license and its associated assets came to Mr. Broz wholly independently of his role on the CIS board, that opportunity was within the core business interests of CIS at the relevant times; that at such time CIS would have had access to the financing necessary to compete for the assets that were for sale; and that the CIS board of directors were not asked to and thus did not consider whether such action would have been in the best interests of the corporation. In these circumstances I conclude that Mr. Broz as a director of CIS violated his duty of loyalty to CIS by seizing this opportunity without formally informing the CIS board fully about the opportunity and facts surrounding it and by proceeding to acquire rights for his benefit without the consent of the corporation. See Yiannatsis v. Stephanis, Del. Supr., 653 A.2d 275 (1995).

663 A.2d at 1181-1182. . . .

IV.   APPLICATION OF THE CORPORATE OPPORTUNITY DOCTRINE

The doctrine of corporate opportunity represents but one species of the broad fiduciary duties assumed by a corporate director or officer. A corporate fiduciary agrees to place the interests of the corporation before his or her own in appropriate circumstances. In light of the diverse and often competing obligations faced by directors and officers, however, the corporate opportunity doctrine arose as a means of defining the parameters of fiduciary duty in instances of potential conflict. The classic statement of the doctrine is derived from the venerable case of Guth v. Loft, Inc. In *Guth,* this Court held that:

> if there is presented to a corporate officer or director a business opportunity which the corporation is financially able to undertake, is, from its nature, in the line of the corporation's business and is of practical advantage to it, is one in which the corporation has an interest or a reasonable

expectancy, and, by embracing the opportunity, the self-interest of the officer or director will be brought into conflict with that of the corporation, the law will not permit him to seize the opportunity for himself.

Guth, 5 A.2d at 510-511.

The corporate opportunity doctrine, as delineated by *Guth* and its progeny, holds that a corporate officer or director may not take a business opportunity for his own if: (1) the corporation is financially able to exploit the opportunity; (2) the opportunity is within the corporation's line of business; (3) the corporation has an interest or expectancy in the opportunity; and (4) by taking the opportunity for his own, the corporate fiduciary will thereby be placed in a position inimicable to his duties to the corporation. The Court in *Guth* also derived a corollary which states that a director or officer may take a corporate opportunity if: (1) the opportunity is presented to the director or officer in his individual and not his corporate capacity; (2) the opportunity is not essential to the corporation; (3) the corporation holds no interest or expectancy in the opportunity; and (4) the director or officer has not wrongfully employed the resources of the corporation in pursuing or exploiting the opportunity. *Guth,* 5 A.2d at 509.

Thus, the contours of this doctrine are well established. It is important to note, however, that the tests enunciated in *Guth* and subsequent cases provide guidelines to be considered by a reviewing court in balancing the equities of an individual case. No one factor is dispositive and all factors must be taken into account insofar as they are applicable. Cases involving a claim of usurpation of a corporate opportunity range over a multitude of factual settings. Hard and fast rules are not easily crafted to deal with such an array of complex situations. As this Court noted in Johnston v. Greene, Del. Supr., 121 A.2d 919 (1956), the determination of "[w]hether or not a director has appropriated for himself something that in fairness should belong to the corporation is 'a factual question to be decided by reasonable inference from objective facts.'" Id. at 923 (quoting *Guth,* 5 A.2d at 513). In the instant case, we find that the facts do not support the conclusion that Broz misappropriated a corporate opportunity.

We note at the outset that Broz became aware of the Michigan-2 opportunity in his individual and not his corporate capacity. As the Court of Chancery found, "Broz did not misuse proprietary information that came to him in a corporate capacity nor did he otherwise use any power he might have over the governance of the corporation to advance his own interests." 663 A.2d at 1185. This fact is not the subject of serious dispute. In fact, it is clear from the record that Mackinac did not consider CIS a viable candidate for the acquisition of Michigan-2. Accordingly, Mackinac did not offer the property to CIS. In this factual posture, many of the fundamental concerns undergirding the law of corporate opportunity are not present (e.g., misappropriation of the corporation's proprietary information). The burden imposed upon Broz to show adherence to his fiduciary duties to CIS is thus lessened to some extent. See *Science Accessories Corp.,* 425 A.2d at 964 (holding that because opportunity to purchase new technology was "an 'outside' opportunity not available to SAC, defendants' failure to disclose the concept to SAC and their taking it for themselves for purposes of competing with SAC cannot be found to be in breach of any agency fiduciary duty"). Nevertheless, this fact is not dispositive. The determination of whether a particular fiduciary has usurped a corporate opportunity necessitates a careful examination of the circumstances, giving due credence to the factors enunciated in *Guth* and subsequent cases.

We turn now to an analysis of the factors relied on by the trial court. First, we find that CIS was not financially capable of exploiting the Michigan-2 opportunity. Although the Court of Chancery concluded otherwise, we hold that this finding was not supported by the evidence. *Levitt*, 287 A.2d at 673. The record shows that CIS was in a precarious financial position at the time Mackinac presented the Michigan-2 opportunity to Broz. Having recently emerged from lengthy and contentious bankruptcy proceedings, CIS was not in a position to commit capital to the acquisition of new assets. Further, the loan agreement entered into by CIS and its creditors severely limited the discretion of CIS as to the acquisition of new assets and substantially restricted the ability of CIS to incur new debt.

The Court of Chancery based its contrary finding on the fact that PriCellular had purchased an option to acquire CIS' bank debt. Thus, the court reasoned, PriCellular was in a position to exercise that option and then waive any unfavorable restrictions that would stand in the way of a CIS acquisition of Michigan-2. The trial court, however, disregarded the fact that PriCellular's own financial situation was not particularly stable. PriCellular was unable to finance the acquisition of CIS through conventional bank loans and was forced to use the more risky mechanism of a junk bond offering to raise the required capital. Thus, the court's statement that "PriCellular had other sources of financing to permit the funding of that purchase" is clearly not free from dispute. Moreover, as discussed infra, the fact that PriCellular had available sources of financing is immaterial to the analysis. At the time that Broz was required to decide whether to accept the Michigan-2 opportunity, PriCellular had not yet acquired CIS, and any plans to do so were wholly speculative. Thus, contrary to the Court of Chancery's finding, Broz was not obligated to consider the contingency of a PriCellular acquisition of CIS and the related contingency of PriCellular thereafter waiving restrictions on the CIS bank debt. Broz was required to consider the facts only as they existed at the time he determined to accept the Mackinac offer and embark on his efforts to bring the transaction to fruition. *Guth*, 5 A.2d at 513.

Second, while it may be said with some certainty that the Michigan-2 opportunity was within CIS' line of business, it is not equally clear that CIS had a cognizable interest or expectancy in the license.[7] Under the third factor laid down by this Court in *Guth*, for an opportunity to be deemed to belong to the fiduciary's corporation, the corporation must have an interest or expectancy in that opportunity. As this Court stated in

---

7. The language in the *Guth* opinion relating to "line of business" is less than clear: Where a corporation is engaged in a certain business, and an opportunity is presented to it embracing an activity as to which it has fundamental knowledge, practical experience and ability to pursue, which, logically and naturally, is adaptable to its business having regard for its financial position, and is consonant with its reasonable needs and aspirations for expansion, it may properly be said that the opportunity is within the corporation's line of business. *Guth*, 5 A.2d at 514 (emphasis supplied). This formulation of the definition of the term "line of business" suggests that the business strategy and financial well-being of the corporation are also relevant to a determination of whether the opportunity is within the corporation's line of business. Since we find that these considerations are decisive under the other factors enunciated by the Court in *Guth*, we do not reach the question of whether they are here relevant to a determination of the corporation's line of business.

Johnston, 121 A.2d at 924, "[f]or the corporation to have an actual or expectant interest in any specific property, there must be some tie between that property and the nature of the corporate business." Despite the fact that the nature of the Michigan-2 opportunity was historically close to the core operations of CIS, changes were in process. At the time the opportunity was presented, CIS was actively engaged in the process of divesting its cellular license holdings. CIS' articulated business plan did not involve any new acquisitions. Further, as indicated by the testimony of the entire CIS board, the Michigan-2 license would not have been of interest to CIS even absent CIS' financial difficulties and CIS' then current desire to liquidate its cellular license holdings.[8] Thus, CIS had no interest or expectancy in the Michigan-2 opportunity. Cf. *Guth,* 5 A.2d at 514 (holding that Loft had an interest or expectancy in the Pepsi opportunity by virtue of its need for cola syrup for use in its retail stores).

Finally, the corporate opportunity doctrine is implicated only in cases where the fiduciary's seizure of an opportunity results in a conflict between the fiduciary's duties to the corporation and the self-interest of the director as actualized by the exploitation of the opportunity. In the instant case, Broz' interest in acquiring and profiting from Michigan-2 created no duties that were inimicable to his obligations to CIS. Broz, at all times relevant to the instant appeal, was the sole party in interest in RFBC, a competitor of CIS. CIS was fully aware of Broz' potentially conflicting duties. Broz, however, comported himself in a manner that was wholly in accord with his obligations to CIS. Broz took care not to usurp any opportunity which CIS was willing and able to pursue. Broz sought only to compete with an outside entity, PriCellular, for acquisition of an opportunity which both sought to possess. Broz was not obligated to refrain from competition with PriCellular. Therefore, the totality of the circumstances indicates that Broz did not usurp an opportunity that properly belonged to CIS.

---

8. At trial, each of the members of the CIS board testified to his belief that CIS would not have been interested in the Michigan-2 opportunity at the time it was presented to Broz. The Court of Chancery chose to disregard this testimony, holding that "the after the fact testimony of directors to the effect that they would not have been interested in pursuing this transaction had it been brought to the board, is not helpful to defendant, in my opinion, because most of them did not know at that time of PriCellular's interest in the property and how it related to PriCellular's plan for CIS." 663 A.2d at 1186. We disagree with the court's assessment. First, as discussed, infra, Broz was required to consider the situation only as it existed when the opportunity was presented. Thus, the fact the CIS directors were unaware of the future plans of PriCellular does not impact adversely on the weight to be ascribed to this particular evidence. Second, testimony of the CIS board is extremely helpful to establish the propriety of Broz' actions. As discussed, infra, Broz was not required to present this opportunity to the board. He was free to evaluate the situation and determine whether the opportunity was one properly belonging to CIS. Absent such formal presentation, however, this Court must make an after-the-fact assessment of an essentially stale factual scenario. In such a setting, the testimony of the directors who controlled the business and affairs of the corporation at the time the opportunity was allegedly usurped is relevant. Such testimony gives a direct indication of the business posture and expectations of the corporation during the relevant period of time. The Court of Chancery also held that "this sort of after the fact testimony is a very thin substitute for an informed board decision made at a meeting in 'real time' (i.e., while the opportunity to act with effect continues)." Id. While it is true that contemporaneous decisionmaking or unanimous written consent is required for board action (8 Del.C. §141(f)), in our view, this testimony of the CIS board was probative and should not have been wholly discounted. See n.5, supra.

A.   PRESENTATION TO THE BOARD

In concluding that Broz had usurped a corporate opportunity, the Court of Chancery placed great emphasis on the fact that Broz had not formally presented the matter to the CIS board. The court held that "in such circumstances as existed at the latest after October 14, 1994 (date of PriCellular's option contract on Michigan-2 RSA) it was the obligation of Mr. Broz as a director of CIS to take the transaction to the CIS board for its formal action. . . ." 663 A.2d at 1185. In so holding, the trial court erroneously grafted a new requirement onto the law of corporate opportunity, viz., the requirement of formal presentation under circumstances where the corporation does not have an interest, expectancy or financial ability.

The teaching of *Guth* and its progeny is that the director or officer must analyze the situation ex ante to determine whether the opportunity is one rightfully belonging to the corporation. If the director or officer believes, based on one of the factors articulated above, that the corporation is not entitled to the opportunity, then he may take it for himself. Of course, presenting the opportunity to the board creates a kind of "safe harbor" for the director, which removes the specter of a post hoc judicial determination that the director or officer has improperly usurped a corporate opportunity. Thus, presentation avoids the possibility that an error in the fiduciary's assessment of the situation will create future liability for breach of fiduciary duty. It is not the law of Delaware that presentation to the board is a necessary prerequisite to a finding that a corporate opportunity has not been usurped.

The numerous cases decided since *Guth* are in full accord with this view of the doctrine. For instance, in Field v. Allyn, Del. Ch., 457 A.2d 1089 (1983), the Court of Chancery held that a director or officer is free to take a business opportunity for himself once the corporation has rejected it or if it can be shown that the corporation is not in a position to take the opportunity. The *Field* court held this to be true even if the fiduciary became aware of the opportunity by virtue of the fiduciary's position in the corporation. Id. at 1099. Notably, this Court affirmed the *Field* holding on the basis of the well reasoned opinion of the court below. Field v. Allyn, Del. Supr., 467 A.2d 1274 (1983). *Field* is not unique, however. The view that presentation to the board is not required where the opportunity is one that the corporation is incapable of exercising is also expressed in other cases. See, e.g., Wolfensohn v. Madison Fund, Inc., Del. Supr., 253 A.2d 72, 76 (1969).

Other cases, such as Kaplan v. Fenton, Del. Supr., 278 A.2d 834 (1971), have found no violation of the corporate opportunity doctrine where the director determined that the corporation was not interested in the opportunity, but never made formal presentation to the board. The director in *Kaplan* asked the CEO and another board member if the corporation would be interested in the opportunity and whether he should present the opportunity to the board. These questions were answered in the negative and the director then acquired the opportunity for himself. The *Kaplan* Court found no breach of the doctrine, despite the absence of formal presentation.[9]

---

9. As the parties note, *Kaplan* is distinguishable in that the Kaplan board previously rejected a similar offer to the one exploited by the defendant director. The board of CIS, however, had demonstrated a comparable lack of interest by divesting itself of holdings similar to the license at issue.

The Court of Chancery cited Yiannatsis v. Stephanis, Del. Supr., 653 A.2d 275 (1995), in support of the proposition that formal presentation to the board of directors is a necessary prerequisite to a corporate fiduciary taking an opportunity for his own. See 663 A.2d at 1182. In *Yiannatsis,* the opportunity in question was a block of stock in a closely held corporation, the holder of which was subject to a right of first refusal held by the corporation. Two of the three directors of the corporation caused the company to refuse the opportunity and, as a result, the corporation never invoked its right of first refusal. This Court held that the corporate fiduciaries had acted surreptitiously to keep the opportunity from being exercised by the corporation, when they had no reasonable ground to believe that the corporation would not be interested therein. This background of bad faith is not present in the case at bar. Here, Broz had substantial reason to believe that CIS was not interested in or able to take advantage of the Michigan-2 opportunity. Accordingly, *Yiannatsis* is not relevant to the analysis here.

Thus, we hold that Broz was not required to make formal presentation of the Michigan-2 opportunity to the CIS board prior to taking the opportunity for his own. In so holding, we necessarily conclude that the Court of Chancery erred in grafting the additional requirement of formal presentation onto Delaware's corporate opportunity jurisprudence.[10]

B. ALIGNMENT OF INTERESTS BETWEEN CIS AND PRICELLULAR

In concluding that Broz usurped an opportunity properly belonging to CIS, the Court of Chancery held that "[f]or practical business reasons CIS' interests with respect to the Mackinac transaction came to merge with those of PriCellular, even before the closing of its tender offer for CIS stock." Based on this fact, the trial court concluded that Broz was required to consider PriCellular's prospective, post-acquisition plans for CIS in determining whether to forgo the opportunity or seize it for himself. Had Broz done this, the Court of Chancery determined that he would have concluded that CIS was entitled to the opportunity by virtue of the alignment of its interests with those of PriCellular.

We disagree. Broz was under no duty to consider the interests of PriCellular when he chose to purchase Michigan-2. As stated in *Guth,* a director's right to "appropriate [an] . . . opportunity depends on the circumstances existing at the time it presented itself to him without regard to subsequent events." *Guth,* 5 A.2d at 513. At the time Broz purchased Michigan-2, PriCellular had not yet acquired CIS. Any plans to do so would still have been wholly speculative. Accordingly, Broz was not required to consider the contingent and uncertain plans of PriCellular in reaching his determination of how to proceed.

Whether or not the CIS board would, at some time, have chosen to acquire Michigan-2 in order to make CIS a more attractive acquisition target for PriCellular

---

10. Recognizing the interests the Court of Chancery sought to promote, however, we note that formal presentation to the board is often the preferred—or "safe"—approach, and we note that this litigation might have been unnecessary had this precaution been observed.

or to enhance the synergy of any combined enterprise, is speculative. The trial court found this to be a plausible scenario and therefore found that, pursuant to the factors laid down in *Guth*, CIS had a valid interest or expectancy in the license. This speculative finding cuts against the statements made by CIS' Chief Executive and the entire CIS board of directors and ignores the fact that CIS still lacked the wherewithal to acquire Michigan-2, even if one takes into account the possible availability of PriCellular's financing. Thus, the fact of PriCellular's plans to acquire CIS is immaterial and does not change the analysis.

In reaching our conclusion on this point, we note that certainty and predictability are values to be promoted in our corporation law. See Williams v. Geier, Del. Supr., 671 A.2d 1368, 1385 n. 36 (1996). Broz, as an active participant in the cellular telephone industry, was entitled to proceed in his own economic interest in the absence of any countervailing duty. The right of a director or officer to engage in business affairs outside of his or her fiduciary capacity would be illusory if these individuals were required to consider every potential, future occurrence in determining whether a particular business strategy would implicate fiduciary duty concerns. In order for a director to engage meaningfully in business unrelated to his or her corporate role, the director must be allowed to make decisions based on the situation as it exists at the time a given opportunity is presented. Absent such a rule, the corporate fiduciary would be constrained to refrain from exploiting any opportunity for fear of liability based on the occurrence of subsequent events. This state of affairs would unduly restrict officers and directors and would be antithetical to certainty in corporation law.

V.   CONCLUSION

The corporate opportunity doctrine represents a judicially crafted effort to harmonize the competing demands placed on corporate fiduciaries in a modern business environment. The doctrine seeks to reduce the possibility of conflict between a director's duties to the corporation and interests unrelated to that role. In the instant case, Broz adhered to his obligations to CIS. We hold that the Court of Chancery erred as a matter of law in concluding that Broz had a duty formally to present the Michigan-2 opportunity to the CIS board. We also hold that the trial court erred in its application of the corporate opportunity doctrine under the unusual facts of this case, where CIS had no interest or financial ability to acquire the opportunity, but the impending acquisition of CIS by PriCellular would or could have caused a change in those circumstances.

Therefore, we hold that Broz did not breach his fiduciary duties to CIS. Accordingly, we REVERSE the judgment of the Court of Chancery holding that Broz diverted a corporate opportunity properly belonging to CIS and imposing a constructive trust.

NOTES AND QUESTIONS

1. In the corporate opportunity arena, Delaware's jurisprudence has been influential, but relatively less so than in other areas of corporate governance. This may be because corporate opportunity cases often arise in a close corporation setting where

Delaware's dominance as the state of incorporation is decidedly less pronounced, and so, presumably, is its expertise in handling such cases. For a recent case that borrows from both Delaware and the ALI, while inserting a third part of its own analysis, see Ostrowski v. Avery, 703 A.2d 117, 125-128 (Conn. 1997):

> One approach, recently espoused in §5.05 of the ALI's Principles of Corporate Governance makes disclosure determinative of fiduciary liability. . . .
>
> The bright line approach taken by the Principles of Corporate Governance has appeal. It promotes efficiency because it provides clear guidance both to corporate officers and directors and to the courts that are called upon to enforce fiduciary obligations. Also, it underscores the importance of timely disclosure in order to ensure timely corporate access to all of the information that the corporation needs to determine what course of action is in the corporation's best interest. . . .
>
> Another case law approach focuses less on adequate disclosure by a corporate fiduciary and more on whether affirmative defenses, such as the corporation's financial inability to avail itself of the corporate opportunity at issue, can be proven by the corporate fiduciary. That was implicitly the position that we took in Katz Corp. v. T.H. Canty & Co., supra, 168 Conn. at 210, 362 A.2d 975. We reasoned that "there can be no expectancy in a transaction unless the corporation is financially able to undertake it." Id. Accordingly, we rejected the plaintiffs' claim for relief in part because the corporation's "cash on hand and liquid assets were insufficient to enable it to make such a substantial purchase." Id.
>
> Courts in other jurisdictions similarly afford the corporate fiduciary the opportunity to prove, as an affirmative defense, that the corporation lacked the financial ability to pursue the opportunity. Some courts permit such a defense in all cases. See, e.g., Paulman v. Kritzer, 74 Ill. App.2d 284, 292-296, 219 N.E.2d 541 (1966), aff'd, 38 Ill. 2d 101, 230 N.E.2d 262 (1967). Other courts limit the defense of financial inability to cases in which the defendant corporation can be proven to have been insolvent at the relevant time. See, e.g., Irving Trust Co. v. Deutsch, 73 F.2d 121, 124 (2d Cir.1934), cert. denied, 294 U.S. 708, 55 S.Ct. 405, 79 L.Ed. 1243 (1935); note, supra, 74 Harv. L. Rev. 773.
>
> We agree with the perception of those courts that a claim of usurpation of a corporate opportunity should be examined through a wide-angled lens that takes account of a large variety of relevant factors. Nonetheless, we are persuaded by the learned discussion in the Principles of Corporate Governance that a proper multifactor analysis must give special weight to the significance of disclosure or nondisclosure of a possible corporate opportunity to the corporation's board of directors or its shareholders. In our view, without such special weight, a multifactor analysis gives insufficient guidance to the trier of fact. . . .
>
> We adopt, for Connecticut, two major propositions of law decided by Broz. We agree with the principle that adequate disclosure of a corporate opportunity is an absolute defense to fiduciary liability for alleged usurpation of such a corporate opportunity. A corporate fiduciary who avails himself or herself of such a safe harbor should not be held accountable subsequently for opportunities embraced or forgone. The criteria for adequate disclosure are those that we have discussed earlier in this opinion. We also agree that, without prior adequate disclosure, a corporate fiduciary still may prove bona fides by clear and convincing evidence, by establishing that his or her conduct has not harmed the corporation. We add, however, that, in assessing such harm, the trier of fact must give special weight to the effect of nondisclosure on the corporation's entrepreneurial opportunities.
>
> The Delaware court's decision in Broz, moreover, does not make explicit the proper allocation of the burden of proof with regard to these affirmative defenses of corporate fiduciaries. We reiterate, therefore, that, in Connecticut, corporate fiduciaries bear the burden of proving, by clear and convincing evidence, that they have not usurped a corporate opportunity. If they wish to take advantage of a safe harbor, corporate fiduciaries must establish the adequacy of their disclosures to the corporation. In the absence of such disclosures, corporate fiduciaries like the present defendants must prove that, in light of the relevant circumstances outlined in Broz, they did not deprive the corporation of an opportunity that the corporation could have pursued. The fact of nondisclosure, although accorded special weight in this determination, is not dispositive.

2. What is the value of requiring formal presentation to the board? Consider Chancellor Allen's thoughts in Cellular Information Systems, Inc. v. Broz.

. . . [T]his sort of after the fact testimony is a very thin substitute for an informed board decision made at a meeting in "real time" (i.e., while the opportunity to act with effect continues). (Both formality and the group dynamics of board action are important in corporate law. Formality in such circumstances is not "mere formality," it is treated by courts as important because it tends to focus attention on the need for deliberation and the existence of accountability structures. With respect to group dynamics, it is an old rule that boards may act with legal effect only at duly convened meetings at which a quorum is present. Again functional reasons underlie the law's insistence on correct form.

663 A.2d 1180, 1186 (Del.Ch. 1995).

3. What is Delaware's rationale for not requiring presentation of a corporate opportunity? Consider how a Delaware lawmaker would counter the following arguments in favor of requiring presentation.

The central feature of the ALI test is the strict requirement of full disclosure prior to taking advantage of any corporate opportunity. This feature was designed to prevent individual directors and officers from substituting their own judgment for that of the corporation when determining whether it would be in the corporate interest, or whether the corporation is financially or otherwise able to take advantage of an opportunity. Doubt about the financial capacity of a corporation to pursue an opportunity may affect the incentive of a director or officer to solve corporate financing problems, and evidence regarding the corporation's financial status is often controlled by the usurping corporate director or officer. See Victor Brudney & Robert Charles Clark, "A New Look at Corporate Opportunities," 94 Harv. L. Rev. 998, 1020-22 (1981). The ALI approach recognizes the danger in allowing an individual director or officer to determine whether a corporation has the ability to take an opportunity, and accordingly disclosure to the corporation is required.

Full disclosure is likewise important to prevent individual directors and officers from using their own unfettered judgment to determine whether the business opportunity is related to the corporation's business, such that it would be in the corporate interest to take advantage of that opportunity. "The appropriate method to determine whether or not a corporate opportunity exists is to let the corporation decide at the time the opportunity is presented." Fletcher Cyc. Corp. §861.10, p. 285 (1994). This rule protects individual directors and officers because after disclosing the potential opportunity to the corporation, they can pursue their own business ventures free from the possibility of a lawsuit. If there is doubt as to whether a business opportunity is closely related to the business of the corporation, that doubt must be resolved in favor of the corporation so that the officer or director will have a strong incentive to disclose any business opportunity even remotely related to the business of the corporation.

Northeast Harbor Golf Club, Inc. v. Harris, 725 A.2d 1018, 1022 (Me. 1999).

PROBLEM 4-5

Reanalyze the questions posed in Problem 4-3, assuming that the governing legal standard is the law of Delaware. When you have completed that analysis, consider whether any of your conclusions would be changed (and if so, how and why) if Charters' Certificate of Incorporation contained the following provision:

Article 12. In the event that a director or officer of the Corporation ("the Conflicted Fiduciary") who is also a controlling shareholder or majority owner of another business entity ("the Conflicted Entity") acquires knowledge of a potential transaction or matter which may be a corporate or business opportunity for both the Corporation and the Conflicted Entity (a "Mutual Corporate Opportunity"), such Conflicted Fiduciary shall to the fullest extent permitted by law have fully satisfied and fulfilled his or her fiduciary duty with respect to such Mutual Corporate Opportunity, and the Corporation to the fullest extent permitted by law waives and renounces any claim that such Mutual Corporate Opportunity constituted a corporate opportunity that should have been presented to the Corporation, if such Conflicted Fiduciary acts in a manner consistent with the following policy: a Mutual Corporate Opportunity offered to any Conflicted Fiduciary shall at the option of the Conflicted Fiduciary belong to the Conflicted Entity, unless such Mutual Corporate Opportunity was expressly offered to the Conflicted Fiduciary in his or her capacity as a director or officer of the Corporation.

3. Conflicting Interest Transactions

a. At Common Law

In the nineteenth century, common law courts were in substantial agreement that transactions between a corporation and one or more of its directors were void or voidable simply because a conflict of interest existed. Justice Field echoed the accepted rationale for this prohibition in Wardell v. Union Pacific R.R., 103 U.S. 651, 658 (1880):

> It is among the rudiments of the law that the same person cannot act for himself and at the same time, with respect to the same matter, as the agent of another whose interests are conflicting. Thus a person cannot be a purchaser of property and at the same time the agent of the vendor. The two positions impose different obligations, and their union would at once raise a conflict between interest and duty; and, "constituted as humanity is, in the majority of cases duty would be overborne in the struggle." . . . The law, therefore, will always condemn the transactions of a party on his own behalf when, in respect of the matter concerned, he is the agent of others, and will relieve against them whenever their enforcement is seasonably resisted. Directors of corporations, and all persons who stand in a fiduciary relation to other parties, and are clothed with power to act for them, are subject to this rule; they are not permitted to occupy a position which will conflict with the interest of parties they represent and are bound to protect. They cannot, as agents or trustees, enter into contracts on behalf of those for whom they are appointed to act, and then personally participate in the benefits.

As the complexity and interconnection of American business increased, conflicting interest transactions became an accepted business reality. Judicial views evolved accordingly. By the twentieth century, most common law courts no longer viewed conflict of interest transactions as automatically void or voidable. Instead, conflicting interest transactions were voidable only if the transaction or the conduct of conflicted directors was unfair to the corporation. Thus, a conflicting interest transaction would be voided if the substantive terms of the transaction were found unfair, or, even if such terms were found fair, if the benefiting directors had in any way breached their obligation to disclose fully all relevant facts to the corporation, including, of course, the fact of their interest in the subject matter.

Globe Woolen Co. v. Utica Gas & Electric Co.
Court of Appeals of New York, 1918
224 N.Y. 483, 121 N.E. 378

CARDOZO, JUDGE.

The plaintiff, a corporation, sues to compel the specific performance of contracts to supply electric current to its mills. The defendant, also a corporation, answers that the contracts were made under the dominating influence of a common director; that their terms are unfair, and their consequences oppressive; and that hence they may not stand. A referee has sustained the defense; and the Appellate Division, with some modification, has affirmed his judgment.

The plaintiff is the owner of two mills in the city of Utica. One is for the manufacture of worsteds, and the other for that of woolens. The defendant generates and sells electricity for light and power. For many years John F. Maynard has been the plaintiff's chief stockholder, its president, and a member of its board of directors. He has also been a director of the defendant, and chairman of its executive committee. He received a single share of the defendant's stock to qualify him for office. He returned the share at once, and he has never held another. His property interest in the plaintiff is large. In the defendant he has none.

The history of the transaction may be briefly stated. At the beginning the mills were run by steam, and the plant was antiquated and inadequate. As early as 1903 one Greenidge, then the superintendent and later the general manager of the defendant's electrical department, suggested to Mr. Maynard the substitution of electric power. Nothing came of the suggestion then. Mr. Maynard was fearful that the cost of equipment would be too great unless the defendant would guarantee a saving in the cost of operation. None the less a change was felt to be important, and from time to time the subject was taken up anew. In 1904 there was an investigation of the power plant by Greenidge and a written report of its condition. For this service, though he was still in the defendant's employ, he was paid by Mr. Maynard. In 1905 the substitution of electricity was again considered, but dismissed as impracticable because of the plaintiff's continued insistence upon a guaranty of saving. In the fall of 1906 the project was renewed. It was renewed by Maynard and Greenidge, who debated it between themselves. There were other officers of the defendant who knew that the project was afoot, but they took no part in formulating it. Maynard still insisted on a guaranty of saving. The plaintiff's books were thrown open to Greenidge, who calculated for himself the cost of operation with steam and the probable cost with electricity. When the investigation was over, a contract was closed. It took the form of letters exchanged between Greenidge and Maynard. In the letter signed by Greenidge, the defendant proposed to supply the plaintiff's worsted mill with electricity at a maximum rate of $.0104 per kilowatt hour, and to guarantee that the cost for heat and light and power would show a saving each month of $300 as compared with the cost for the corresponding month in the year previous to the change. There was to be a trial period ending July 1, 1907. Then, at the plaintiff's option, the contract was to run for five years, with a privilege of renewal for a like term. In a letter signed by Maynard on October 22, 1906, the plaintiff accepted the proposal. At once the defendant made preparations to install the new equipment. Six weeks later, on December 1, 1906, Mr. Maynard laid the contract before the defendant's executive committee. He went to the meeting with Mr. Greenidge. The contract was read. Mr. Lewis, the vice president, asked Mr. Greenidge what the rate would be, and was told about $.0104 per kilowatt hour. Mr. Beardsley, another director, asked whether the contract was a profitable one for the company, and was told by Mr. Greenidge that it was. Mr. Maynard kept silent. A resolution was moved and carried that the contract be ratified. Mr. Maynard presided at the meeting, and put the resolution, but was excused from voting.

This settled the problem of power for the worsted mill. Attention was next directed to the woolen mill. Again Mr. Maynard and Mr. Greenidge put the project through unaided. In February, 1907, letters, similar in most things to the earlier ones, were exchanged. The guaranty of saving for this mill as for the other was to be $300 a month. There were, however, new provisions to the effect that the contract should apply to "current used for any purposes in any extensions or additions to the mills," and that in case of shortage of electricity the plaintiff should be preferred in service over all other customers except the city of Utica. At a meeting of the executive committee held February 11, 1907, this contract was ratified. The statement was made by Mr. Greenidge, in the presence of Mr. Maynard, that it was practically a duplicate of the first contract, except that it related to another mill. Nothing was said about the new provisions. Mr. Maynard presided and put the resolution, but did not vote.

At a cost to the plaintiff of more than $21,000 the requisite changes in the mills were made, and the new power was supplied. It quickly appeared that the defendant had made a losing contract; but only gradually did the extent of the loss, its permanence, and its causes unfold themselves. Greenidge had miscalculated the amount of steam that would be required to heat the dye houses. The expenditure for coal mounted by leaps and bounds. The plaintiff dyed more yarn and less slubbing than before. But the dyeing of yarn takes twice as much heat as that of slubbing, and thus doubles the cost of fuel. These and like changes in the output of the mills had not been foreseen by Greenidge, and Maynard had not warned of them. In 1909 the defendant became alarmed at the mounting loss. Various tests and palliatives were suggested and adopted, but there was no change in the result. Finally, in February, 1911, the defendant gave notice of rescission. At that time it had supplied the plaintiff with electricity worth $69,500.75 if paid for at the maximum rate fixed by the contract, and $60,000 if paid for at the lowest rate charged to any customer in Utica. Yet not only had it received nothing, but it owed the plaintiff under its guaranty $11,721.41. The finding is that a like loss prolonged to the end of the term would amount to $300,000.

These are the contracts which the courts below have annulled. The referee annulled them absolutely. The Appellate Division imposed the condition that the defendant reimburse the plaintiff for the cost of installation. The defendant makes no complaint of the condition. The plaintiff, appealing, stands upon its bargain.

We think the evidence supports the conclusion that the contracts are voidable at the election of the defendant. The plaintiff does not deny that this would be true if the dual director had voted for their adoption. Munson v. Syracuse, G. & C. R. R. Co., 103 N.Y. 58, 8 N.E. 355. But the argument is that by refusing to vote he shifted the responsibility to his associates, and may reap a profit from their errors. One does not divest oneself so readily of one's duties as trustee. The refusal to vote has, indeed, this importance: It gives to the transaction the form and presumption of propriety, and requires one who would invalidate it to probe beneath the surface. Davids v. Davids, 135 App. Div. 206, 209, 120 N. Y. Supp. 350. But "the great rule of law" (Andrews, J., in Munson v. Syracuse, G. & C. R. R. Co., supra, 103 N. Y. at page 73, 8 N.E. at page 358) which holds a trustee to the duty of constant and unqualified fidelity is not a thing of forms and phrases. A dominating influence may be exerted in other ways than by a vote. Adams v. Burke, 201 Ill. 395, 66 N.E. 235; Davids v. Davids, supra. A beneficiary, about to plunge into a ruinous course of dealing, may be betrayed by silence as well as by the spoken word.

The trustee is free to stand aloof, while others act, if all is equitable and fair. He cannot rid himself of the duty to warn and to denounce, if there is improvidence or oppression, either apparent on the surface, or lurking beneath the surface, but visible to his practiced eye. Davids v. Davids, supra; Crocker v. Cumberland Mining & Milling Co., 31 S.D. 137, 146, 139 N.W. 783; Fort Payne v. Hill, 174 Mass. 224, 54 N.E. 532; Wyman v. Bowman, 127 Fed. 257, 274, 62 C.C.A. 189.

There was an influence here, dominating, perhaps, and surely potent and persuasive, which was exerted by Mr. Maynard from the beginning to the end. In all the stages of preliminary treaty he dealt with a subordinate, who looked up to him as to a superior, and was alert to serve his pleasure. There was no clean-cut cleavage in those stages between his conflicting offices and agencies. Hoyle v. Plattsburgh & M. R. R. Co., 54 N.Y. 314, 328, 329, 13 Am. Rep. 595. No label identified the request of Mr. Maynard, the plaintiff's president, as something separate from the advice of Mr. Maynard, the defendant's chairman. Superior and subordinate together framed a contract, and together closed it. It came before the executive committee as an accomplished fact. The letters had been signed and delivered. Work had been begun. All that remained was a ratification, which may have been needless, and which, even if needful, took the aspect of a mere formality. There was some attempt to show that Mr. Lewis, the vice president, had seen the letters before. The testimony of Mr. Greenidge indicates the contrary. In support of the judgment, we accept his testimony as true. That the letters had been seen by others, there is not even a pretense. The members of the committee, hearing the contract for the first time, knew that it had been framed by the chairman of the meeting. They were assured in his presence that it was just and equitable. Faith in his loyalty disarmed suspicion.

There was, then, a relation of trust reposed, of influence exerted, of superior knowledge on the one side and legitimate dependence on the other. Sage v. Culver, 147 N.Y. 241, 247, 41 N.E. 513; Davids v. Davids, supra. At least, a finding that there was this relation has evidence to sustain it. A trustee may not cling to contracts thus won, unless their terms are fair and just. Crocker v. Cumberland Mining & Milling Co., supra, and cases there cited; Dongan v. MacPherson, 1902 A.C. 197, 200; Thompson on Corp. 1228, 1231. His dealings with his beneficiary are "viewed with jealousy by the courts, and may be set aside on slight grounds." Twin Lick Oil Co. v. Marbury, 91 U.S. 587, 588 (23 L. Ed. 328). He takes the risk of an enforced surrender of his bargain if it turns out to be improvident. There must be candor and equity in the transaction, and some reasonable proportion between benefits and burdens.

The contracts before us do not survive these tests. The unfairness is startling, and the consequences have been disastrous. The mischief consists in this: That the guaranty has not been limited by a statement of the conditions under which the mills are to be run. No matter how large the business, no matter how great the increase in the price of labor or of fuel, no matter what the changes in the nature or the proportion of the products, no matter even though there be extensions of the plant, the defendant has pledged its word that for ten years there will be a saving of $600 a month, $300 for each mill, $7,200 a year. As a result of that pledge it has supplied the plaintiff with electric current for nothing, and owes, if the contract stands, about $11,000 for the privilege. These elements of unfairness Mr. Maynard must have known, if indeed his knowledge be material. He may not have known how great the loss would be. He may have trusted to the superior technical skill of Mr. Greenidge to compute with approximate accuracy the comparative cost of steam and electricity. But he cannot have failed to know that he held a one-sided contract which left the defendant at his mercy. He was not blind to the likelihood that in a term of ten years there would be changes in the business. The swiftness with which some of the changes followed permits the inference that they were premeditated. There was a prompt increase in the proportion of yarns as compared with slubbing when the guaranty of saving charged the defendant with the greater cost of fuel. But, whether these and other changes were premeditated or not, at least they were recognized as possible. With that recognition, no word of warning was uttered to Greenidge or to any of the defendant's officers. There slumbered within these contracts a potency of profit which the plaintiff neither ignored in their making nor forgot in their enforcement.

It is no answer to say that this potency, if obvious to Maynard, ought also to have been obvious to other members of the committee. They did not know, as he did, the likelihood or the significance of changes in the business. There was need, too, of reflection and analysis before the dangers stood revealed. For the man who framed the contracts, there was opportunity to consider and to judge. His fellow members, hearing them for the first time, and trustful of his loyalty, would have no thought of latent peril. That they had none is sufficiently attested by the fact that the contracts were approved. There was inequality, therefore, both in knowledge and in the opportunity for knowledge. It is not important in such circumstances whether the trustee foresaw the precise evils that developed. The inference that he did might not be unsupported by the evidence. But the indefinite possibilities of hardship, the opportunity in changing circumstances to wrest unlooked-for profits and impose unlooked-for losses, these must have been foreseen. Foreseen or not, they were there, and their presence permeates the contracts with oppression and inequity.

We hold, therefore, that the refusal to vote does not nullify as of course an influence and predominance exerted without a vote. We hold that the constant duty rests on a trustee to seek no harsh advantage to the detriment of his trust, but rather to protest and renounce if through the blindness of those who treat with him he gains what is unfair. And, because there is evidence that in the making of these contracts that duty was ignored, the power of equity was fittingly exercised to bring them to an end. Judgment affirmed.

b. Transactions with a Controlling Shareholder or Director

The common law viewed all conflicting interest transactions with suspicion, but particularly those between a corporation and a person in control of the corporation. In circumstances constituting "self-dealing," transactions between the corporation and the controlling person were subject to heightened judicial scrutiny to protect the interests of the corporation and its noncontrolling shareholder.

Sinclair Oil Corp. v. Levien
Delaware Supreme Court, 1971
280 A.2d 717

WOLCOTT, CHIEF JUSTICE.

This is an appeal by the defendant, Sinclair Oil Corporation (hereafter Sinclair), from an order of the Court of Chancery, 261 A.2d 911, in a derivative action requiring Sinclair to account for damages sustained by its subsidiary, Sinclair Venezuelan Oil Company (hereafter Sinven), organized by Sinclair for the purpose of operating in Venezuela, as a result of dividends paid by Sinven, the denial to Sinven of industrial development, and a breach of contract between Sinclair's wholly-owned subsidiary, Sinclair International Oil Company, and Sinven.

Sinclair, operating primarily as a holding company, is in the business of exploring for oil and of producing and marketing crude oil and oil products. At all times relevant to this litigation, it owned about 97% of Sinven's stock. The plaintiff owns about 3000 of 120,000 publicly held shares of Sinven. Sinven, incorporated in 1922, has been engaged in petroleum operations primarily in Venezuela and since 1959 has operated exclusively in Venezuela.

Sinclair nominates all members of Sinven's board of directors. The Chancellor found as a fact that the directors were not independent of Sinclair. Almost without exception, they were officers, directors, or employees of corporations in the Sinclair complex. By reason of Sinclair's domination, it is clear that Sinclair owed Sinven a fiduciary duty. Sinclair concedes this.

The Chancellor held that because of Sinclair's fiduciary duty and its control over Sinven, its relationship with Sinven must meet the test of intrinsic fairness. The standard of intrinsic fairness involves both a high degree of fairness and a shift in the burden of proof. Under this standard the burden is on Sinclair to prove, subject to careful judicial scrutiny, that its transactions with Sinven were objectively fair.

Sinclair argues that the transactions between it and Sinven should be tested, not by the test of intrinsic fairness with the accompanying shift of the burden of proof, but by the business judgment rule under which a court will not interfere with the judgment of a board of directors unless there is a showing of gross and palpable overreaching. Meyerson v. El Paso Natural Gas Co., 246 A.2d 789 (Del. Ch. 1967). A board of directors enjoys a presumption of sound business judgment, and its decisions will not be disturbed if they can be attributed to any rational business purpose. A court under such circumstances will not substitute its own notions of what is or is not sound business judgment.

We think, however, that Sinclair's argument in this respect is misconceived. When the situation involves a parent and a subsidiary, with the parent controlling the transaction and fixing the terms, the test of intrinsic fairness, with its resulting shifting of the burden of proof, is applied. Sterling v. Mayflower Hotel Corp. [33 Del. Ch. 293, 93 A.2d 107, 38 A.L.R.2d 425 (Del. Supr. 1952)]; David J. Greene & Co. v. Dunhill International, Inc., 249 A.2d 427 (Del. Ch. 1968); Bastian v. Bourns, Inc., 256 A.2d 680 (Del. Ch. 1969) affd., Per Curiam (unreported) (Del. Supr. 1970). The basic situation for the application of the rule is the one in which the parent has received a benefit to the exclusion and at the expense of the subsidiary.

Recently, this court dealt with the question of fairness in parent-subsidiary dealings in Getty Oil Co. v. Skelly Oil Co., [267 A.2d 883 (Del. Supr. 1970)]. In that case, both parent and subsidiary were in the business of refining and marketing crude oil and crude oil products. The Oil Import Board ruled that the subsidiary, because it was controlled by the parent, was no longer entitled to a separate allocation of imported crude oil. The subsidiary then contended that it had a right to share the quota of crude oil allotted to the parent. We ruled that the business judgment standard should be applied to determine this contention. Although the subsidiary suffered a loss through the administration of the oil import quotas, the parent gained nothing. The parent's quota was derived solely from its own past use. The past use of the subsidiary did not cause an increase in the parent's quota. Nor did the parent usurp a quota of the subsidiary. Since the parent received nothing from the subsidiary to the exclusion of the minority stockholders of the subsidiary, there was no self-dealing. Therefore, the business judgment standard was properly applied.

A parent does indeed owe a fiduciary duty to its subsidiary when there are parent-subsidiary dealings. However, this alone will not evoke the intrinsic fairness standard. This standard will be applied only when the fiduciary duty is accompanied by self-dealing — the situation when a parent is on both sides of a transaction with its subsidiary. Self-dealing occurs when the parent, by virtue of its domination of the subsidiary, causes the subsidiary to act in such a way that the parent receives something from the subsidiary to the exclusion of, and detriment to, the minority stockholders of the subsidiary.

We turn now to the facts. The plaintiff argues that, from 1960 through 1966, Sinclair caused Sinven to pay out such excessive dividends that the industrial development of Sinven was effectively prevented, and it became in reality a corporation in dissolution.

From 1960 through 1966, Sinven paid out $108,000,000 in dividends ($38,000,000 in excess of Sinven's earnings during the same period). The Chancellor held that Sinclair caused these dividends to be paid during a period when it had a need for large amounts of cash. Although the dividends paid exceeded earnings, the plaintiff concedes that the payments were made in compliance with 8 Del. C. §170, authorizing payment of dividends out of surplus or net profits. However, the plaintiff attacks these dividends on the ground that they resulted from an improper motive — Sinclair's need for cash. The Chancellor, applying the intrinsic fairness standard, held that Sinclair did not sustain its burden of proving that these dividends were intrinsically fair to the minority stockholders of Sinven.

Since it is admitted that the dividends were paid in strict compliance with 8 Del. C. §170, the alleged excessiveness of the payments alone would not state a cause of action. Nevertheless, compliance with the applicable statute may not, under all circumstances, justify all dividend payments. If a plaintiff can meet his burden of proving that a dividend cannot be grounded on any reasonable business objective, then the courts can and will interfere with the board's decision to pay the dividend.

Sinclair contends that it is improper to apply the intrinsic fairness standard to dividend payments even when the board which voted for the dividends is completely dominated. In support of this contention, Sinclair relies heavily on American District Telegraph Co. (ADT) v. Grinnell Corp. (N.Y. Sup. Ct. 1969) affd., 33 A.D.2d 769, 306 N.Y.S.2d 209 (1969). Plaintiffs were minority stockholders of ADT, a subsidiary of Grinnell. The plaintiffs alleged that Grinnell, realizing that it would soon have to sell its ADT stock because of a pending anti-trust action, caused ADT to pay excessive dividends. Because the dividend payments conformed with applicable statutory law, and the plaintiffs could not prove an abuse of discretion, the court ruled that the complaint did not state a cause of action. Other decisions seem to support Sinclair's contention. In Metropolitan Casualty Ins. Co. v. First State Bank of Temple, 54 S.W.2d 358 (Tex. Civ. App. 1932), revd. on other grounds, 79 S.W.2d 835 (Sup. Ct. 1935), the court held that a majority of interested directors does not void a declaration of dividends because all directors, by necessity, are interested in and benefited by a dividend declaration.

We do not accept the argument that the intrinsic fairness test can never be applied to a dividend declaration by a dominated board, although a dividend declaration by a dominated board will not inevitably demand the application of the intrinsic fairness standard. Moskowitz v. Bantrell, 41 Del. Ch. 177, 190 A.2d 749 (Del. Supr. 1963). If such a dividend is in essence self-dealing by the parent, then the intrinsic fairness standard is the proper standard. For example, suppose a parent dominates a subsidiary and its board of directors. The subsidiary has outstanding two classes of stock, X and Y. Class X is owned by the parent and Class Y is owned by minority stockholders of the subsidiary. If the subsidiary, at the direction of the parent, declares a dividend on its Class X stock only, this might well be self-dealing by the parent. It would be receiving something from the subsidiary to the exclusion of and detrimental to its minority stockholders. This self-dealing, coupled with the parent's fiduciary duty, would make intrinsic fairness the proper standard by which to evaluate the dividend payments.

Consequently it must be determined whether the dividend payments by Sinven were, in essence, self-dealing by Sinclair. The dividends resulted in great sums of money being transferred from Sinven to Sinclair. However, a proportionate share of this money was received by the minority shareholders of Sinven. Sinclair received nothing from Sinven to the exclusion of its minority stockholders. As such, these dividends were not self-dealing. We hold therefore that the Chancellor erred in applying the intrinsic fairness test as to these dividend payments. The business judgment standard should have been applied.

We conclude that the facts demonstrate that the dividend payments complied with the business judgment standard and with 8 Del. C. §170. The motives for causing the declaration of dividends are immaterial unless the plaintiff can show that the dividend payments resulted from improper motives and amounted to waste. The plaintiff contends only that the dividend payments drained Sinven of cash to such an extent that it was prevented from expanding.

The plaintiff proved no business opportunities which came to Sinven independently and which Sinclair either took to itself or denied to Sinven. As a matter of fact, with two minor exceptions which resulted in losses, all of Sinven's operations have been conducted in Venezuela, and Sinclair had a policy of exploiting its oil properties located in different countries by subsidiaries located in the particular countries.

From 1960 to 1966 Sinclair purchased or developed oil fields in Alaska, Canada, Paraguay, and other places around the world. The plaintiff contends that these were all opportunities which could have been taken by Sinven. The Chancellor concluded that Sinclair had not proved that its denial of expansion opportunities to Sinven was intrinsically fair. He based this conclusion on the following findings of fact. Sinclair made no real effort to expand Sinven. The excessive dividends paid by Sinven resulted in so great a cash drain as to effectively deny to Sinven any ability to expand. During this same period Sinclair actively pursued a company-wide policy of developing through its subsidiaries new sources of revenue, but Sinven was not permitted to participate and was confined in its activities to Venezuela.

However, the plaintiff could point to no opportunities which came to Sinven. Therefore, Sinclair usurped no business opportunity belonging to Sinven. Since Sinclair received nothing from Sinven to the exclusion of and detriment to Sinven's minority stockholders, there was no self-dealing. Therefore, business judgment is the proper standard by which to evaluate Sinclair's expansion policies.

Since there is no proof of self-dealing on the part of Sinclair, it follows that the expansion policy of Sinclair and the methods used to achieve the desired result must, as far as Sinclair's treatment of Sinven is concerned, be tested by the standards of the business judgment rule. Accordingly, Sinclair's decision, absent fraud or gross overreaching, to achieve expansion through the medium of its subsidiaries, other than Sinven, must be upheld.

Even if Sinclair was wrong in developing these opportunities as it did, the question arises, with which subsidiaries should these opportunities have been shared? No evidence indicates a unique need or ability of Sinven to develop these opportunities. The decision of which subsidiaries would be used to implement Sinclair's expansion policy was one of business judgment with which a court will not interfere absent a showing of gross and palpable overreaching. Meyerson v. El Paso Natural Gas Co., 246 A.2d 789 (Del. Ch. 1967). No such showing has been made here.

Next, Sinclair argues that the Chancellor committed error when he held it liable to Sinven for breach of contract.

In 1961 Sinclair created Sinclair International Oil Company (hereafter International), a wholly owned subsidiary used for the purpose of coordinating all of Sinclair's foreign operations. All crude purchases by Sinclair were made thereafter through International.

On September 28, 1961, Sinclair caused Sinven to contract with International whereby Sinven agreed to sell all of its crude oil and refined products to International at specified prices. The contract provided for minimum and maximum quantities and prices. The plaintiff contends that Sinclair caused this contract to be breached in two respects. Although the contract called for payment on receipt, International's payments lagged as much as 30 days after receipt. Also, the contract required International to purchase at least a fixed minimum amount of crude and refined products from Sinven. International did not comply with this requirement.

Clearly, Sinclair's act of contracting with its dominated subsidiary was self-dealing. Under the contract Sinclair received the products produced by Sinven, and of course the minority shareholders of Sinven were not able to share in the receipt of these products. If the contract was breached, then Sinclair received these products to the detriment of Sinven's minority shareholders. We agree with the Chancellor's finding that the contract was breached by Sinclair, both as to the time of payments and the amounts purchased.

Although a parent need not bind itself by a contract with its dominated subsidiary, Sinclair chose to operate in this manner. As Sinclair has received the benefits of this contract, so must it comply with the contractual duties.

Under the intrinsic fairness standard, Sinclair must prove that its causing Sinven not to enforce the contract was intrinsically fair to the minority shareholders of Sinven. Sinclair has failed to meet this burden. Late payments were clearly breaches for which Sinven should have sought and received adequate damages. As to the quantities purchased, Sinclair argues that it purchased all the products produced by Sinven. This, however, does not satisfy the standard of intrinsic fairness. Sinclair has failed to prove that Sinven could not possibly have produced or someway have obtained the contract minimums. As such, Sinclair must account on this claim.

Finally, Sinclair argues that the Chancellor committed error in refusing to allow it a credit or setoff of all benefits provided by it to Sinven with respect to all the alleged damages. The Chancellor held that setoff should be allowed on specific transactions, e.g., benefits to Sinven under the contract with International, but denied an over all setoff against all damages claimed. We agree with the Chancellor, although the point may well be moot in view of our holding that Sinclair is not required to account for the alleged excessiveness of the dividend payments.

We will therefore reverse that part of the Chancellor's order that requires Sinclair to account to Sinven for damages sustained as a result of dividends paid between 1960 and 1966, and by reason of the denial to Sinven of expansion during that period. We will affirm the remaining portion of that order and remand the cause for further proceedings.

NOTES AND QUESTIONS

1. On remand, the Court of Chancery awarded Sinven damages in the amount of $711,095.86 to compensate for International's late payment of invoices and damages in the amount of $7,802,265.52 to compensate for International's failure to purchase the minimum contract quantities of crude oil and refined products. Levien v. Sinclair Oil Corp, 314 A.2d 216 (Del. Ch. 1973).

2. The fiduciary duty of a controlling or dominating shareholder is considered in more detail in Chapter 5 (as to close corporations) and Chapter 8 (as to fundamental corporate changes such as mergers). By statute, mergers require the approval of shareholders as well as directors.

c.   The Intersection of the Common Law and Conflicting Interest Statutes

Delaware G.C.L §144
MBCA §§8.60-8.63

As the common law moved away from the position that conflicting interest trans-actions were void, state legislatures began enacting conflicting-interest-transaction statutes.

The most influential of these early provisions was California Civ. Code §311. Eventually, the California model was copied by the Model Business Corporation Act and, in 1967, by Delaware. Subchapter F, added to the Model Act in 1991, follows a somewhat different form, as discussed below. However, most jurisdictions following the Model Act continue to base their conflict statutes on old §8.31, which is similar in form to Delaware G.C.L. §144.

In essence, Delaware G.C.L. §144 provides that no conflicting interest transaction shall be void or voidable solely by reason of the conflict if the transaction is (1) autho-rized by a majority of the disinterested directors, or (2) approved in good faith by the shareholders, or (3) fair to the corporation at the time authorized. In addition, §144 codifies the common law requirement of complete candor and fair dealing by making director or shareholder approval effective only if the interested director has disclosed all material facts.

Delaware §144 and similar statutes leave significant gaps—e.g., burden of proof, interests that constitute a conflict, standard of judicial review, and what constitutes disinterestedness—that must be filled by courts. Subchapter F, added to the Model Business Corporation Act in 1991, but not yet adopted by a majority of the states, places an emphasis on certainty and predictability rather than judicial oversight. The new approach has three features. First, MBCA §8.60 defines conflicting interest trans-actions with substantially greater precision than previous provisions. Second, MBCA §8.61(a) instructs courts that transactions falling outside of the statutory definition "may not be enjoined, set aside, or give rise to an award of damages or other sanctions . . . because a director of the corporation, or any person with whom or which he has a personal, economic, or other association, has an interest in the transaction." Put another way, transactions falling outside of the statutory definition in MBCA §8.61 do not expose an "interested" director to any special duty of candor or fair dealing, and therefore courts cannot grant relief based on an alleged violation of that duty. Finally, MBCA §§8.61(b), 8.62, and 8.63 provide that a conflicting interest transaction may not be voided as a result of such conflict if the transaction is ratified by "qualified directors," or by the vote of "qualified shares," or is fair to the corporation. These new rules define with particularity the individuals who may and may not participate in a shareholders' or directors' ratification vote.

The new MBCA conflicting interest provisions, while seeking to provide greater certainty, still leave substantial room for application of judicial doctrine and, thus, substantial room for continuing uncertainty. MBCA §8.61(b) describes the circum-stances under which a court will not grant relief solely on the grounds that a conflict of interest taints the transaction. As the official comment to §8.61 emphasizes, "if the transaction is vulnerable on some other ground, subchapter F does not make it less so for having passed through the procedures of subchapter F." Subchapter F does not tell us what those other grounds are or what role, if any, unfairness plays in a transaction ratified by disinterested shareholders or directors. However, the official comment to §8.61 provides that the section's safe harbor is "subject to a critically important predicate condition . . . that the board's action must comply with the care, best interest and good faith criteria prescribed in §8.30(a) for all directors' action."

Shapiro v. Greenfield
Court of Special Appeals of Maryland, 2000
764 A.2d 270
Reconsideration denied Jan. 31, 2001

KENNEY, JUDGE.

This appeal arises out of a derivative suit brought by minority shareholders, Marvin and Betty Greenfield (appellees), against, among others, College Park Woods, Inc. ("College Park") and its officers and directors (appellants), alleging usurpation of a corporate opportunity of College Park and seeking an accounting and dissolution of the corporation. By order dated February 23, 1998, the trial court found that the disputed transaction constituted usurpation of corporate opportunity, that there were no disinterested directors, and that the transaction was not fair and reasonable to the corporation. The trial court appointed a single receiver for College Park. Appellants filed a timely notice of appeal and presented three issues, which we have re-numbered as follows:

   I.   Whether the trial court's ruling that the Clinton Crossings Shopping Center was a corporate opportunity of College Park was clearly erroneous?
  II.   Whether the trial court erred in appointing a receiver . . . .
 III.   Whether the trial court erred in not finding that shareholder plaintiffs estopped from challenging a corporate act where shareholder plaintiffs, after being duly notified, elected not to attend the shareholders' meeting where the corporate act was voted upon?

FACTUAL BACKGROUND

Charles Shapiro was the operating officer for College Park during the relevant time period. Other officers and directors included Joan Smith, Charles' sister, and Michael Shapiro, Charles' son.[1] Appellee Marvin Greenfield is Charles Shapiro's cousin.

In 1961, College Park acquired approximately 68 acres of land in Prince George's County, on which it constructed the 72,000 square foot Clinton Plaza shopping center. By 1991, Clinton Plaza was only 50% leased and generating insufficient cash flow. It

1. Appellants include Joan Smith and Michael Shapiro.

was decided that the best use of the land was not the continuation of Clinton Plaza, but redevelopment of the property into a substantially larger shopping center. Having determined that College Park was not capable of redeveloping Clinton Plaza on its own, the directors explored suitable partnerships or joint ventures, but for some time did not find any.

Charles Shapiro, the operating officer of College Park, subsequently developed a joint venture with S. Bruce Jaffe, an occasional business partner of his with experience developing retail space. The joint venture required the creation of three entities: 1) Clinton Crossings Limited Partnership ("Clinton Crossings Partnership"), which was to own the redeveloped Clinton Plaza shopping center; 2) Clinton Crossings, Inc., which was to be a one percent owner and the general partner of Clinton Crossings Partnerships;[2] and 3) TSC/Clinton Associates Limited Partnership ("Clinton Associates"), which was to own forty-nine percent of Clinton Crossings Partnership.[3] College Park was to transfer its fee simple interest in Clinton Plaza to Clinton Crossings Partnership in exchange for a fifty percent limited partnership interest in Clinton Crossings Partnership, the owner of the redeveloped center. Clinton Associates was to contribute everything necessary for the shopping center's redevelopment with the exception of the land.

As a limited partner, College Park would have no rights to manage, direct or control the affairs of Clinton Crossings Partnership. Clinton Crossings Partnership and Clinton Associates, on the other hand, would assume the risk associated with the redevelopment, while College Park would assume none. Moreover, College Park would not be obligated to transfer its interest in Clinton Plaza until Clinton Associates had obtained a construction loan, pre-leased at least eighty percent of Phase I space, and obtained a debt coverage ratio of 1 to 1. The agreement further provided that, if Phase II of the development was not completed within five years, any unused portion of the land would revert to College Park. A capital account in Clinton Crossings Partnership was to be established for College Park, in the amount of $4.00 per square foot for land used in the redevelopment. With Phase I expected to utilize 36 acres, College Park's capital account was funded at $6,272,640.

On October 26, 1991, a special meeting of College Park's shareholders was called for the purpose of "considering and approving a resolution authorizing the corporation to enter into a limited partnership agreement with Clinton Crossings, Inc., . . . and TSC/Clinton Associates Limited Partnership. . . ." Advance notice of the meeting included documents that described the joint venture in detail. The notice also provided:

> The transaction to be considered at the Special Meeting is an interested director transaction within the meaning of Section 2-419 of the Corporations and Associations Article of the Code of Maryland because (i) Charles S. Shapiro and Michael Shapiro are each directors of the Corporation, (ii) Charles S. Shapiro is the sole shareholder of Clinton Crossings, Inc., and (iii) it is expected that Charles S. Shapiro and Michael Shapiro will each have an interest, directly or indirectly, as a limited partner in TSC/Clinton Associates Limited Partnership.

---

2. Charles Shapiro was to own all the stock of Clinton Crossings, Inc.

3. Clinton Associates was to be owned by Clinton Crossings, Inc., Charles Shapiro, S. Bruce Jaffe, and Michael Mates.

Appellees, Marvin and Betty Greenfield did not attend this special meeting. At the meeting, the shareholders present unanimously voted for the proposal. Appellees contend that following the October 26, 1991 meeting, they protested that the votes taken at the meeting were not valid as none of the directors could be considered disinterested directors and thus their votes as shareholders could not be counted. Appellees also asserted their right to inspect the corporation's books and records.

On April 2, 1992, College Park directors met to ratify actions taken by the corporation at the special meeting and other occasions. On April 3, 1993, the appellees visited the College Park offices and sought inspection of the corporate books and records. They viewed the corporation's minute book and stock ledger, in addition to a series of promissory notes executed by College Park, Charles Shapiro, and other entities which Charles Shapiro owns or controls. When they requested other documents relating to the transactions described in the April 2, 1992 minutes, they were refused. Appellees filed this suit on July 15, 1992, against College Park and its directors, Charles S. Shapiro, Michael Shapiro, and Joan Smith, requesting "damages, an accounting, the appointment of a receiver, the imposition of a constructive trust, the dissolution of the corporation, attorneys' fees, costs and other legal and equitable relief."

Between 1991 and 1994, Shapiro and Jaffe guaranteed over $2 million in bonds and expended over $1 million for marketing, advertising, and other pre-construction activities. Clinton Associates also expended over $1 million in risk capital, hiring architects, and engineers. By 1994, Jaffe had secured leases with Safeway, Caldor, Fashion Bug, Baskin Robbins, and others, had fulfilled all conditions for the construction loan commitment, and had satisfied the debt ratio and pre-leasing requirements.

Without further shareholder action, on April 20, 1994, College Park conveyed the land to Clinton Crossings Limited Partnership in exchange for a fifty percent interest in Clinton Crossings Partnership and the establishment of a capital account in the amount of $6,272,640. Charles Shapiro and Jaffe both personally guaranteed Clinton Crossings Partnership's $21.5 million construction loan with NationsBank.[6]

It was projected that, upon completion of Phase I of the redevelopment, the project would have a value of $36.5 million and immediately realize an annual positive cash flow of approximately $1 million. As a result, College Park's cash flow was expected to go from negative to approximately $500,000 annually.

On October 4, 1994, appellees amended their complaint adding CCI, Clinton Crossings Partnership, and Clinton Associates as defendants, and alleged that the Clinton Crossings redevelopment was a corporate opportunity that belonged to College Park and was usurped by the appellants. . . .

Appellants argue that the trial court erred in finding that the redevelopment plan for Clinton Crossings was a corporate opportunity that was usurped by appellants. Both parties rely on the case of Independent Distributors, Inc. v. Katz, 99 Md. App. 441, 637 A.2d 886, *cert. denied,* 335 Md. 697, 646 A.2d 363 (1994), for the proposition that officers or directors will not be held liable for usurpation of corporate opportunity if the transaction was fair and reasonable to the corporation. Several commentators, however, have criticized this Court's opinion in *Katz,* asserting that we "confus[ed]

---

6. At the time, Shapiro and Jaffe had a combined net worth of $40 million.

an interested director transaction with a corporate opportunity." Eric G. Orlinsky, Corporate Opportunity Doctrine and Interested Director Transactions: A Framework for Analysis in an Attempt to Restore Predictability, 24 Del. J. Corp. L. 451 (1999); see also James J. Hanks, Jr., Maryland Corporation Law §6.23 (1995, 1999 Supp.) ("Hanks"). Therefore, we will begin our discussion with an analysis of interested director transactions and the doctrine of usurpation of corporate opportunity.

Concepts related to corporate opportunities and interested director transactions find their genesis in a director's duty of loyalty to the corporation. The longstanding common law rule in Maryland was "that any contract between a corporation and one of its officers or directors as to a matter in which the officer or director had a substantial personal interest was void or voidable." Sullivan v. Easco Corp., 656 F. Supp. 531, 533 (D. Md. 1987) (quoting Chesapeake Const. Corp. v. Rodman, 256 Md. 531, 536, 261 A.2d 156 (1970)). In 1976, Maryland adopted Md. Code (1975, 1999 Repl. Vol.), §2-419 of the Corporations and Associations Article ("CA") and rejected the common law rule.[9] Such action recognized that "an interest conflict is not in itself a crime or a tort or necessarily injurious to others" and "in many situations, the corporation and the shareholders may secure major benefits from a transaction despite the presence of a director's conflicting interest." Dennis Block, Nancy Barton, and Stephen Radin, 1 The Business Judgment Rule: Fiduciary Duties of Corporate Directors, 266 (5th ed. 1998) (citing 2 Model Bus. Corp. Act Ann. §§8.60 to .63 Introductory Comment at 8-397 (3d ed. 1996)).

Corporations and Associations §2-419 provides that an interested director transaction is not void or voidable solely because of the conflict of interest and creates a "safe harbor" for certain transactions which satisfy the statute. Under the statute, an interested director could inform the shareholders or directors of his conflicting interests and give the board of directors or shareholders an opportunity to approve or ratify the transaction. Moreover, a nondisclosed interested director transaction may be valid, if it is found to be fair and reasonable to the corporation. CA §2-419(b)(2).

---

9. Corporations and Associations §2-419 governs Maryland interested director transactions. It provides, in part:

(a) *General rule.* — If subsection (b) of this section is complied with, a contract of other transaction between a corporation and any of its directors or between a corporation and any other corporation, firm, or other entity in which any of its directors is a director or has a material financial interest is not void or voidable solely because of any one or more of the following:

(1) The common directorship or interest;
(2) The presence of the director at the meeting of the board or a committee of the board which authorizes, approves, or ratifies the contract or transaction; or
(3) The counting of the vote of the director for the authorization, approval, or ratification of the contract or transaction.

(b) *Disclosure and ratification.* — Subsection (a) of this section applies if:

(1) The fact of the common directorship or interest is disclosed or known to:

(i) The board of directors or the committee, and the board or committee authorizes, approves, or ratifies the contract or transaction by the affirmative vote of a majority of disinterested directors, even if the disinterested directors constitute less than a quorum; or

(ii) The stockholders entitled to vote, and the contract or transaction is authorized, approved, or ratified by a majority of the votes cast by the stockholders entitled to vote other than the votes of shares owned of record or beneficially by the interested director or corporation, firm, or other entity; or

(2) The contract or transaction is fair and reasonable to the corporation.

By contrast, "[m]ost corporate opportunities do not involve transactions with the corporation; rather, they involve transactions that are taken from the corporation." Hanks, at 220.10. The principles used to determine whether a director is interested or disinterested "turn upon the involvement of the director in the contract or transaction to which the corporation is a party. A corporate opportunity typically presents the reverse factual situation: the non-involvement of the corporation in a contract or transaction in which it may have an interest." Hanks, §6.23, at 220.8, n. 328. "Simply stated, an interested director transaction statute applies where a director seeks to transact business with the corporation. Conversely, a transaction should be analyzed under the corporate opportunity doctrine where a director seeks to take an opportunity from the corporation." 24 Del. J. Corp. L. at 457. . . . Because we find that appellants' involvement in the redevelopment transaction was not a usurpation of corporate opportunity, we are not required, in this case, to reconsider *Katz*.

Essentially, appellees complain about the propriety of the transaction, with emphasis on College Park's relinquishment of College Park's fee simple interest in its property, College Park's reduced management role in the redevelopment project, and appellants' personal use of corporate assets. Although Charles Shapiro's involvement in the redevelopment project clearly demonstrates a conflict of interest, this is not a situation where appellants capitalized on an opportunity that should have been presented to the corporation, but was not. Rather, the corporation entered into a business arrangement with other entities in which certain directors had, or potentially had, a direct financial interest. Therefore, we hold that the transaction did not constitute a usurpation of corporate opportunity.

We turn now to the issue of whether the trial court properly conducted the analysis required under CA §2-419 for interested director transactions. In reviewing the Order of February 23, 1998, we note that the Order refers to previous rulings on the various transactions, the "Report of the Special Master," and to the trial court's "findings of fact and conclusions of law." We readily acknowledge the conclusions of law, or perhaps, conclusions of mixed law and fact, but the "findings of fact" upon which the trial court relied are less clear. Although there is reference to the Report of the Special Master, to which no exceptions were taken, and the trial court recognized the treatment of funds as "fungible" between College Park and the other Shapiro entities as identified by the Special Master, the trial court does not direct the findings of that Report to an interested director analysis and to the determination of whether the Clinton Crossings transaction was fair and reasonable. Thus, we are unable to review the factual underpinnings of the trial court's conclusion that the Clinton Crossings transaction was not fair and reasonable. Perhaps that conclusion was based on the loss of management rights or purely on the financial results of the transactions, but we cannot be sure. For example, the extent to which the treatment of funds, both earned and "borrowed, between the different entities affected College Park's ability to participate in the Clinton Crossings project could be part of the fair and reasonable calculus. Absent such treatment, College Park may have been able to do the project alone, achieve a better equity position, or preserve a management role. Under the circumstances, we will remand for reconsideration based on the analysis of an interested director transaction.

Part of that analysis will involve a determination of who are the interested directors. The trial court found that there were no disinterested directors. At oral argument, the parties disputed whether appellant Joan Smith was properly considered an interested director. Because the case is to be remanded to the trial court for reconsideration under CA §2-419, we will discuss Joan Smith's classification as an interested director, based on her family and financial relationship with Charles Shapiro and his financial interest in the transaction.

Both the Model Business Corporations Act ("MBCA") and the American Law Institute, Principles of Corporate Governance: Analysis and Recommendations (1994) ("ALI") expressly defined interested director. The ALI provides:

> (a) A director or officer is "interested" in a transaction or conduct if either:
>
> (1) The director or officer, or an associate of the director or officer, is a party to the transaction or conduct;
>
> (2) The director or officer has a business, financial, or familial relationship with a party to the transaction or conduct, and that relationship would reasonably be expected to affect the director's or officer's judgment with respect to the transaction or conduct in a manner adverse to the corporation;
>
> (3) The director or officer, an associate of the director or officer, or a person with whom the director or officer has a business, financial, or familial relationship, has a material pecuniary interest in the transaction or conduct (other than usual and customary director's fees and benefits) and that interest and (if present) that relationship would reasonably be expected to affect the director's or officer's judgment in a manner adverse to the corporation; or
>
> (4) The director or officer is subject to a controlling influence by a party to the transaction or conduct or person who has a material pecuniary interest in the transaction or conduct, and that controlling influence could reasonably be expected to affect the director's or officer's judgment with respect to the transaction or conduct in a manner adverse to the corporation.

ALI §1.23(1).

The MBCA defines "conflicting interest" as

> (1) "Conflicting interest" with respect to a corporation means the interest a director of the corporation has respecting a transaction effected or proposed to be effected by the corporation . . . if:
>
> > (i) whether or not the transaction is brought before the board of directors of the corporation for action, the director knows at the time of commitment that he or a related person[10] is a party to the transaction or has a beneficial financial interest in or so closely linked to the transaction and of such financial significance to the director or a related person that the interest would be reasonably expected to exert an influence on the director's judgment if he were called upon to vote on the transaction.

Model Bus. Corp. Act §8.60 (1999).

Appellants assert that Maryland rejected the MBCA and ALI definition of "interested director" and thereby rejected the concept that a director who may be related

---

10. Related person is defined as "(i) the spouse (or a parent or sibling thereof) of the director, or a child, grandchild, sibling, parent (or spouse thereof) of the director, or an individual having the same home as the director, or a trust or estate of which an individual specified in this clause (i) is a substantial beneficiary; or (ii) a trust, estate, incompetent, conservatee, or minor of which the director is a fiduciary."

to a party with a material financial interest in the transaction would also be classified as an interested party. The history of CA §2-419 suggests that that conclusion is too broad.

The Maryland statute was modeled after statutes of other jurisdictions, including Delaware, New York, and California. The Official Comment to the section provided:[11]

> Prior to 1976, the Maryland General Corporation Law, unlike most state business corporation laws, contained no provision relating to so called "interested director transactions": that is, transactions between a corporation and any corporation, firm, or other entity in which any of its directors is a director or has a material financial interest. Chapter 567, Acts of 1976, adds a new §2-419 to the Corporation Law to apply to those transactions. This section — which was modeled after similar provisions in Delaware, New York, California, and other jurisdictions — was added to ensure uniformity of treatment of those transactions in Maryland, as well as to provide clear standards to corporations and directors who engage in such transactions.

CA §2-419 (1977 Cum. Supp.). The Delaware, New York, and California statutes are all quite alike in the treatment of interested director transactions. Similar to Maryland's statute, none define the term "interested director." In New York, case law has defined a director's interest as "either self-interest in the transaction at issue or a loss of independence because a director with no direct interest in a transaction is controlled by a self-interested director." Park River Owners Corp. v. Bangser Klein Rocca & Blum, LLP, 269 A.D.2d 313, 703 N.Y.S.2d 465, 466 (2000). All of the cited approaches ultimately focus on a director's ability to exercise independent judgment and the expected influence of a particular relationship on the director. That is the appropriate subject of inquiry in determining whether a director is to be considered an interested director in a particular transaction.

The underlying purpose of the interested director statute is clear. "Directors are required to avoid only those self-interested actions which come at the expense of the [corporation] or its shareholders." Cinerama, Inc. v. Technicolor, Inc., 663 A.2d 1134, 1148 (Del. Ch. 1994), aff'd, 663 A.2d 1156 (Del. Supr. 1995). An interested director transaction may still be approved by a neutral decision making body. Oberly v. Kirby, 592 A.2d 445, 467 (Del. Sup. 1991). In other words, when a director's loyalty is questioned, courts must seek to ascertain whether the conflict "has deprived stockholders of a 'neutral decision-making body.'" Technicolor, 663 A.2d at 1170.

The definitions of the MBCA and the ALI related to interested directors and conflicting interests reflect this same consideration. When the director is actually involved in the transaction, determination is easy. When the director has no direct interests in the conflicting transaction, neither model creates a per se rule based on a familial or business relationship because a relationship between the parties does not necessarily destroy an individual's independent judgment. The pivotal provision is the second prong of the analysis, whether the relationship "would reasonably be expected to exert an influence on the director's judgment." MBCA; see also ALI ("and that relationship would reasonably be expected to affect the director's or officer's judgment with respect

_____

11. This Official Comment initially appeared in the 1977 Supplemental Code. The statute was amended in 1983 to clarify the relationship between the indemnification of corporate directors found in CA §2-418 and this statute.

to the transaction or conduct in a manner adverse to the corporation"). The adoption of a per se rule would effectively undermine the purpose of the statute. If an otherwise uninterested director were to be adjudged an interested director based solely on his relationship, familial or otherwise, to another director interested in the transaction, directors who may well retain independence and their own business judgment will be precluded from considering the transaction. On the other hand, to conclude that directors are automatically disinterested because they are not directly involved in the transaction would also undermine the goal of a neutral decision making body, as some directors, because of their familial, personal, or financial relationship, may well be influenced by those relationships to the detriment of the corporation.

Therefore, when a director does not personally benefit from the transaction but, because of that director's relationship to a party interested in the transaction, it would reasonably be expected that the director's exercise of independent judgment would be compromised, that director will be deemed an interested director within the meaning of the statute.

We are unsure whether the trial court determined Joan Smith to be an interested director simply by virtue of her status as Charles Shapiro's sister. On remand, the trial court should evaluate whether the relationship between Joan Smith and Charles Shapiro, together with their direct or indirect interests in the transaction, would reasonably be expected to influence her decision and compromise her impartiality. If it is then determined that there were no disinterested directors, the trial court should evaluate the Clinton Crossings transaction from the "fair and reasonable" perspective with findings that support the determination. . . .

Judgment Vacated. Case Remanded to the Circuit Court for Montgomery County for further Proceedings Consistent with this Opinion.

NOTES AND QUESTIONS

1. The Delaware Supreme Court has explained the effect of Delaware G.C.L. §144 as follows:

> At common law, a corporation's stockholders did have the power to nullify an interested transaction, although considerations of the transaction's fairness appear to have played some part in judicial decisions applying this rule. See, e.g., Potter v. Sanitary Co. of Am., Del. Ch., 194 A. 87 (1937); see also Marciano v. Nakash, Del. Supr., 535 A.2d 400, 403 (1987). The enactment of 8 Del. C. §144 in 1967 limited the stockholders' power in two ways. First, section 144 allows a committee of disinterested directors to approve a transaction and bring it within the scope of the business judgment rule. Second, where an independent committee is not available, the stockholders may either ratify the transaction or challenge its fairness in a judicial forum, but they lack the power automatically to nullify it. When a challenge to fairness is raised, the directors carry the burden of "establishing . . . [the transaction's] entire fairness, sufficient to pass the test of careful scrutiny by the courts." Weinberger v. UOP, Inc., Del. Supr., 457 A.2d 701, 710 (1983). If a transaction is found to be unfair to the corporation, the stockholders may then demand rescission of the transaction or, if that is impractical, the payment of rescissory damages. Id. at 714. If, however, the directors meet their burden of proving entire fairness, the transaction is protected from stockholder challenge.

Oberly v. Kirby, 592 A.2d 445, 466 (Del. 1991).

2. There is scant case law on the meaning of "good faith" in Delaware G.C.L. §144 and similar statutory provisions in other jurisdictions. Consider Chancellor Chandler's analysis of the meaning of "good faith" as it applies to ratification of a conflicting interest transaction by "independent" directors.

> Another example of how the concept of good faith may operate in a situation where ensuring director compliance with the fiduciary duties of care and loyalty (as we have traditionally defined those duties) may be insufficient to protect shareholders' interests, is found in 8 Del. C. §144(a). Under §144(a), a transaction between a corporation and its directors or officers will be deemed valid if approved by a majority of the independent directors, assuming three criteria are met: 1) the approving directors were aware of the conflict inherent in the transaction; 2) the approving directors were aware of all facts material to the transaction; and 3) the approving directors acted in good faith. In other words, the inside transaction is valid where the independent and disinterested (loyal) directors understood that the transaction would benefit a colleague (factor 1), but they considered the transaction in light of the material facts (factor 2—due care) mindful of their duty to act in the interests of the corporation, unswayed by loyalty to the interests of their colleagues or cronies (factor 3—good faith). On the other hand, where the evidence shows that a majority of the independent directors were aware of the conflict and all material facts, in satisfaction of factors 1 and 2 (as well as the duties of loyalty and care), but acted to reward a colleague rather than for the benefit of the shareholders, the Court will find that the directors failed to act in good faith and, thus, that the transaction is voidable. In such a case, the duties of care and loyalty, as traditionally defined, might be insufficient to protect the equitable interests of the shareholders, and the matter would turn on the good faith of the directors.

In re Walt Disney Company Derivative Litigation, 907 A.2d 693, 756 at fn. 464 (Del. Ch. 2005). Is good faith a fiduciary duty apart from the duties of care and loyalty? See Part C of this chapter, infra.

3. While there is little case authority, commentators assume that the requirement of a "good faith" shareholder vote in Delaware G.C.L. §144(a)(2) and similar provisions in other jurisdictions would be interpreted to preclude voting by a conflicted shareholder. See In re Cox Communications, Inc. Shareholders Litigation, 879 A.2d 604, 615 n.19 (Del. Ch. 2005). (The reference to the approval of stockholders being made in "good faith" in §144(b)(2) might be read as imposing a requirement on an interested party to the transaction that with its approving vote as a stockholder it must refrain from using its voting power to push through a transaction unfair to the corporation and correspondingly overgenerous to the interested party.) But see Williams v. Geier, 671 A.2d 1368, 1382-1383 (Del. 1996) (interested shareholder votes may be counted in the context of vote on proposed amendment to certificate of incorporation).

PROBLEM 4-6

Diversified, Inc. owns a commercial office building (the Tower) that is only 50 percent rented and is in need of significant repair. Diversified occupies one floor of the building but is scheduled to vacate as soon as suitable replacement space is located. Diversified's board consists of Baron, the company's CEO; and Nancy, Nick, and Norris, each of whom is the CEO of another corporation. Two years ago, Diversified commissioned an appraisal of the Tower that indicated an unrenovated market value of between $12 million and $15 million, and a potential for a substantially higher price if relatively inexpensive renovations were undertaken. After considering that appraisal, the board authorized Baron to attempt to find a purchaser for the Tower. Baron immediately offered the property to several sophisticated buyers and received offers ranging from $8 million to $11 million. Baron rejected these offers as insufficient and, after reporting back to the board, took no further marketing actions. Last month Baron, Nancy, Nick, and Norris formed a corporation, BNNN, Inc. BNNN then entered into a contract with Diversified to purchase the Tower for $11 million. The minutes of the Diversified board meeting at which the sale was approved state that the transaction was carried out with "a friendly corporation so that Diversified would have time to locate and move to a new headquarters." The minutes further reflected that the directors were "approving the transaction because the price of $11 million represents the highest price available determined by an attempt to sell the property to sophisticated real estate investors." Diversified did not seek shareholder approval of the transaction.

At the annual meeting of shareholders next held after the closing of sale of the Tower, Baron, Nancy, Nick, and Norris were replaced as directors by new managers favored by Diversified, Inc.'s largest institutional investors. Shortly thereafter, Diversified filed suit against the former directors and BNNN seeking rescission of the sale of the Tower, or rescissory damages. What is the likely outcome of this litigation? How would your answer change if the transaction was ratified by the shareholders after disclosure of the reasons for approving such transaction as set out in the minutes of the board meeting?

PROBLEM 4-7

John Erickson is the CEO and a director of Wood Products, Inc., which owns substantial timberlands and several pulp mills, including the Greenacre mill ("Greenacre"), located on the outskirts of Timber City. The Wood Products board recently agreed to sell Greenacre to Vision, Inc.

1. Does the planned sale of Greenacre constitute a conflicting interest transaction under either MBCA §8.60 or Delaware G.C.L. §144, assuming, alternatively, that Erickson has the following relationship with Vision:
   a. Ralph Thin, Vision's CEO and Board Chair, is the long-time boyfriend of Erickson's daughter, Jill; Ralph and Jill jointly own and occupy a home.
   b. James Thick, an outside director of Vision, recently divorced his spouse of 20 years. James is a good friend of Erickson's son, Bobby. For the past ten months James has been living with the Ericksons in a separate wing of their suburban mansion, playing golf with Bobby as often as possible. James and the Ericksons see no reason why this arrangement will not continue indefinitely.
   c. Vision's CEO is Erickson's spouse; the Ericksons are involved in an acrimonious divorce and have not lived in the same home for two years.

      d. Vision is a nonprofit corporation and plans to use Greenacre in connec-
           tion with its "Shelter for the Homeless" program; Erickson is a member of
           Vision's board of directors.
      e. Erickson owns 1,000 Vision shares.
   2. How would your analysis be affected if Erickson was the CEO, but not a direc-
      tor, of Wood Products?

d.   The Special Problem of a Director's Self-Compensation

Delaware G.C.L. §§141(h), 157
MBCA §§6.24, 8.11

Important conflicting interest problems are presented whenever the board of
directors approves the compensation of its inside directors (most commonly in the
form of salary, bonuses, and stock options) or the compensation to be paid to directors for service as a director. If directors set their own compensation without ratification by disinterested shareholders, the general rule is clear: "Like any other interested
transaction, directoral self-compensation decisions lie outside the business judgment
rule's presumptive protection, so that, where properly challenged, the receipt of
self-determined benefits is subject to an affirmative showing that the compensation
arrangements are fair to the corporation." Telxon v. Meyerson, 802 A.2d 257, 265
(Del. 2002).

One solution to this conflicting interest problem is to seek shareholder ratification. Another solution, if the compensation decision does not affect the entire board,
is to place the compensation decision in the hands of the board members who are
independent and disinterested. In cases not involving the granting of stock options,
shareholder ratification or approval by a disinterested and independent director will
remove the conflicting interest taint from the director's self-compensation decision.
Following either tack will ensure judicial deference.

Given the remarkable increase in CEO pay relative to the pay of ordinary workers
that occurred between 1980 and 2005, such judicial deference may seem misplaced.
Consider the viewpoint of the Delaware Supreme Court.

> To be sure, directors have the power, authority and wide discretion to make decisions on executive
> compensation. See 8 Del.C. §122(5). As the often-cited Court of Chancery decision by Chancellor
> Seitz in Saxe v. Brady warns, there is an outer limit to that discretion, at which point a decision of
> the directors on executive compensation is so disproportionately large as to be unconscionable and
> constitute waste. Del.Ch., 184 A.2d 602, 610 (1962); see *Grimes*, 673 A.2d at 1215 (noting that com-
> pensation decisions by an independent board are protected by the business judgment rule "unless
> the facts show that such amounts, compared with the services to be received in exchange, constitute
> waste or could not otherwise be the product of a valid exercise of business judgment") (citing *Saxe*,
> 184 A.2d at 610). See also Lori B. Marino, Comment, Executive Compensation and the Misplaced
> Emphasis on Increasing Shareholder Access to the Proxy, 147 U.Pa.L.Rev. 1205, 1235-45 (1999).

Brehm v. Eisner, 746 A.2d 244, 262-263, fn. 56 (Del. 2000).

Stock options are a contract between a corporation and the optionee, giving the optionee a right to purchase at some future date a specified amount of the

corporation's stock. The price at which the optionee may purchase stock pursuant to the option — the "strike price" — is usually determined by reference to the fair market value of the company's stock at the time the option is granted. Usually the stock option vests only after the optionee has served the company as an employee for a specified period of time and usually cannot be exercised after a set period of time — often ten years. Most publicly traded firms and many start-up companies hoping to "go public" use stock options as a key component of executive compensation packages. From the standpoint of managers, stock options cost the corporation nothing at the time of issue since no corporate assets are distributed to the optionees. However, the value of other shareholders' equity may be severely diluted by stock options that are ultimately exercised at prices far below then-prevailing market prices.

Because of these inherent risks, common law courts have traditionally subjected stock options to heightened judicial scrutiny. Chancellor Chandler summarized the elements of Delaware's special test as follows:

> [A stock option] plan must meet the requirements of a two-prong test: First, the plan must involve an identifiable benefit to the corporation. To that end, the plan must contain conditions, or the circumstances must be such that, the corporation can reasonably expect to obtain that benefit (the "Benefit Prong"). Second, the value of the options must bear a reasonable relationship to the value of the benefit passing to the corporation (the "Value Prong").

Byrne v. Lord, 1995 WL 684868, *5 (Del. Ch. 1995).

C.   The Fiduciary Duty of Care

1.   Policy Arguments for Limiting the Reach of the Duty of Care

MBCA §8.30(b)

A controversial issue in American corporate law is the role of the fiduciary duty of care in ensuring that a corporation's directors carry out their managerial responsibilities with reasonable care and diligence. Everyone agrees that a well-functioning, competent board is an essential ingredient to a corporation's long-term success, but there is substantial disagreement as to the contours of the duty of care. And, there is further disagreement as to when, if ever, the threat of fiduciary-duty-of-care-based litigation is the best mechanism for ensuring that directors carry out their duties as desired.

In some states, including Delaware, the fiduciary duty of care is defined solely by judicial doctrine. In many states, however, the common law definition is supplemented or replaced by statutory formulations. The most widely adopted definition is modeled after the pre-1998 version of MBCA §8.30(a)(2), and requires a director to carry out her duties "with the care an ordinarily prudent person in a like position would exercise under similar circumstances."

The pre-1998 version of §8.30(a)(2) borrows from the language of torts and could be interpreted as making directors liable for any harm to a corporation caused by the directors' failure to exercise ordinary care. Older judicial opinions also borrowed from the language of torts to explain why directors were liable for breach of duty of care. However, it was very rare that courts actually applied a negligence standard to the conduct of corporate directors, and equally rare that courts found directors of business corporations liable solely for breach of the duty of care. One scholar colorfully described the hunt for such cases as akin to "a search for a very small number of needles in a very large haystack."[5]

Thus, the use of tort-like phraseology by courts and corporation codes to describe directors' duty of care was misleading. In reality, liability for breach of the duty of care has always been rare, and has occurred in circumstances where the director's conduct was egregious. Courts universally recognize that directors are presumptively not liable for breach of duty of care by applying the business judgment rule. In recent years, however, scholars and corporate law practitioners have sought legislative changes that limit the risk of judicial misapplication of the fiduciary duty of care.

In 1998, the ABA Committee on Corporate Laws amended §8.30(b) to provide that "when becoming informed in connection with their decision-making function or devoting attention to their oversight function, [directors] shall discharge their duties with the care that a person in a like position would reasonably believe appropriate under the circumstances."

As the official comment to §8.30 makes clear, one important purpose of the 1998 amendments was to signal to courts in states following the MBCA that directors' duty of care should not be conceptualized or enforced under tort principles, but rather under principles developed specifically for corporations and their directors.

> In earlier versions of the Model Act the duty of care element was included in subsection (a), with the text reading: "[a] director shall discharge his duties . . . with the care an ordinarily prudent person in a like position would exercise under similar circumstances." The use of the phrase "ordinarily prudent person" in a basic guideline for director conduct, suggesting caution or circumspection vis-à-vis danger or risk, has long been problematic given the fact that risk-taking decisions are central to the directors' role. When coupled with the exercise of "care," the prior text had a familiar resonance long associated with the field of tort law. . . . The further coupling with the phrasal verb "shall discharge" added to the inference that former section 8.30(a)'s standard of conduct involved a negligence standard, with resultant confusion. In order to facilitate its understanding and analysis, independent of the other general standards of conduct for directors, the duty of care element has been set forth as a separate standard of conduct in subsection (b).

The following case and the accompanying notes provide insight into the policy reasons for limiting the reach of the duty of care.

---

5. Bishop, Sitting Ducks and Decoy Ducks: New Trends in the Indemnification of Corporate Directors and Officers, 77 Yale L.J. 1078, 1099 (1968). And see Dennis J. Block, Nancy E. Barton, and Stephen A. Radin, The Business Judgment Rule: Fiduciary Duties of Corporate Directors 72 (Prentice Hall, 4th ed. 1993) (ten modern cases finding director breach of duty of care without concurrent breach of loyalty).

Joy v. North
United States Court of Appeals, Second Circuit, 1982
692 F.2d 880

WINTER, JUDGE.

A. THE LIABILITY OF CORPORATE DIRECTORS AND OFFICERS
AND THE BUSINESS JUDGMENT RULE

While it is often stated that corporate directors and officers will be liable for negligence in carrying out their corporate duties, all seem agreed that such a statement is misleading. Whereas an automobile driver who makes a mistake in judgment as to speed or distance injuring a pedestrian will likely be called upon to respond in damages, a corporate officer who makes a mistake in judgment as to economic conditions, consumer tastes or production line efficiency will rarely, if ever, be found liable for damages suffered by the corporation. Whatever the terminology, the fact is that liability is rarely imposed upon corporate directors or officers simply for bad judgment and this reluctance to impose liability for unsuccessful business decisions has been doctrinally labelled the business judgment rule. Although the rule has suffered under academic criticism, see, e.g., Cary, Standards of Conduct Under Common Law, Present Day Statutes and the Model Act, 27 Bus. Lawyer 61 (1972), it is not without rational basis.

First, shareholders to a very real degree voluntarily undertake the risk of bad business judgment. Investors need not buy stock, for investment markets offer an array of opportunities less vulnerable to mistakes in judgment by corporate officers. Nor need investors buy stock in particular corporations. In the exercise of what is genuinely a free choice, the quality of a firm's management is often decisive and information is available from professional advisors. Since shareholders can and do select among investments partly on the basis of management, the business judgment rule merely recognizes a certain voluntariness in undertaking the risk of bad business decisions.

Second, courts recognize that after-the-fact litigation is a most imperfect device to evaluate corporate business decisions. The circumstances surrounding a corporate decision are not easily reconstructed in a courtroom years later, since business imperatives often call for quick decisions, inevitably based on less than perfect information. The entrepreneur's function is to encounter risks and to confront uncertainty, and a reasoned decision at the time made may seem a wild hunch viewed years later against a background of perfect knowledge.

Third, because potential profit often corresponds to the potential risk, it is very much in the interest of shareholders that the law not create incentives for overly cautious corporate decisions. Some opportunities offer great profits at the risk of very substantial losses, while the alternatives offer less risk of loss but also less potential profit. Shareholders can reduce the volatility[5] of risk by diversifying their holdings. In the case of the diversified shareholder, the seemingly more risky alternatives may well be the

---

5. For purposes of this opinion, "volatility" is "the degree of dispersion or variation of possible outcomes." Klein, Business Organization and Finance 147 (1980).

best choice since great losses in some stocks will over time be offset by even greater gains in others.[6] Given mutual funds and similar forms of diversified investment, courts need not bend over backwards to give special protection to shareholders who refuse to reduce the volatility of risk by not diversifying. A rule which penalizes the choice of seemingly riskier alternatives thus may not be in the interest of shareholders generally.

Whatever its merit, however, the business judgment rule extends only as far as the reasons which justify its existence. Thus, it does not apply in cases, e.g., in which the corporate decision lacks a business purpose, is tainted by a conflict of interest, is so egregious as to amount to a no-win decision, Litwin v. Allen, 25 N.Y.S.2d 667 (N.Y. Co. Sup. Ct. 1940), or results from an obvious and prolonged failure to exercise oversight or supervision. . . .

NOTES AND QUESTIONS

1. Former Delaware Chancellor Allen authored the following policy argument for limiting the reach of the duty of care:

> Corporate directors of public companies typically have a very small proportionate ownership interest in their corporations and little or no incentive compensation. Thus, they enjoy (as residual

---

6. Consider the choice between two investments in an example adapted from Klein, Business Organization and Finance 147-49 (1980):

Investment A

Estimated Probability of Outcome	Outcome Profit or Loss	Value
.4	+15	6.0
.4	+1	.4
.2	−13	−2.6
1.0		3.8

Investment B

Estimated Probability of Outcome	Outcome Profit or Loss	Value
.4	+6	2.4
.4	+2	.8
.2	+1	.2
1.0		3.4

Although A is clearly "worth" more than B, it is riskier because it is more volatile. Diversification lessens the volatility by allowing investors to invest in 20 or 200 A's which will tend to guarantee a total result near the value. Shareholders are thus better off with the various firms selecting A over B, although after the fact they will complain in each case of the 2.6 loss. If the courts did not abide by the business judgment rule, they might well penalize the choice of A in each such case and thereby unknowingly injure shareholders generally by creating incentives for management always to choose B. For purposes of this opinion, "volatility" is "the degree of dispersion or variation of possible outcomes." Klein, Business Organization and Finance 147 (1980).

owners) only a very small proportion of any "upside" gains earned by the corporation on risky investment projects. If, however, corporate directors were to be found liable for a corporate loss from a risky project on the ground that the investment was too risky (foolishly risky! stupidly risky! egregiously risky!—you supply the adverb), their liability would be joint and several for the whole loss (with I suppose a right of contribution). Given the scale of operation of modern public corporations, this stupefying disjunction between risk and reward for corporate directors threatens undesirable effects. Given this disjunction, only a very small probability of director liability based on "negligence", "inattention", "waste", etc. could induce a board to avoid authorizing risky investment projects to any extent! Obviously, it is in the shareholders' economic interest to offer sufficient protection to directors from liability for negligence, etc., to allow directors to conclude that, as a practical matter, there is no risk that, if they act in good faith and meet minimalist proceduralist standards of attention, they can face liability as a result of a business loss.

Gagliardi v. Trifoods Int'l Inc., 683 A.2d 1049, 1052 (Del. Ch. 1996).

2. Chancellor Chandler has also advanced similar policy reasons supporting a limited role for the fiduciary duty of care:

> Because this matter, by its very nature, has become something of a public spectacle—commencing as it did with the spectacular hiring of one of the entertainment industry's best-known personalities to help run one of its iconic businesses, and ending with a spectacular failure of that union, with breathtaking amounts of severance pay the consequence—it is, I think, worth noting what the role of this Court must be in evaluating decisionmakers' performance with respect to decisions gone awry, spectacularly or otherwise. It is easy, of course, to fault a decision that ends in a failure, once hindsight makes the result of that decision plain to see. But the essence of business is risk—the application of informed belief to contingencies whose outcomes can sometimes be predicted, but never known. The decisionmakers entrusted by shareholders must act out of loyalty to those shareholders. They must in good faith act to make informed decisions on behalf of the shareholders, untainted by self-interest. Where they fail to do so, this Court stands ready to remedy breaches of fiduciary duty. Even where decision-makers act as faithful servants, however, their ability and the wisdom of their judgments will vary. The redress for failures that arise from faithful management must come from the markets, through the action of shareholders and the free flow of capital, and not from this Court. Should the Court apportion liability based on the ultimate outcome of decisions taken in good faith by faithful directors or officers, those decisionmakers would necessarily take decisions that minimize risk, not maximize value. The entire advantage of the risk-taking, innovative, wealth-creating engine that is the Delaware corporation would cease to exist, with disastrous results for shareholders and society alike. That is why, under our corporate law, corporate decision makers are held strictly to their fiduciary duties, but within the boundaries of those duties are free to act as their judgment and abilities dictate, free of post hoc penalties from a reviewing court using perfect hindsight.

In re Walt Disney Shareholder Litigation, 2005 WL 2056651, *2 (Del. Ch.).

2. Duty of Care in the Decisional Setting

MBCA §§8.30, 8.31

In the decisional setting, directors consider whether to authorize a particular course of action, activity, or transaction. When so acting, directors face a constant tension created by the different perspectives and access to information of "inside" and "outside" directors. On the one hand, the board's "inside directors"—key management employees who also serve as directors—are an invaluable source of information about the corporation's business. On the other hand, the corporation's inside directors may have blind spots concerning their own business policies, and may not always be totally objective or candid in their observations and opinions about the corporation's best interests.

In publicly traded corporations, outside directors play an important and difficult duty of care role. Two examples suffice. First, much of the detailed information necessary to determine an appropriate course of action may be possessed by directors or other management personnel who are clearly committed to a particular course of action. To what extent may the outside directors rely on the recommendations of these individuals? Second, the directors are usually extremely competent business executives or are otherwise familiar with the dynamics of the type of transaction being contemplated by the corporation. Moreover, in carrying out their general monitoring and supervisory responsibilities, they have become fully informed about the corporation's business. Given this preexisting expertise and knowledge, exactly what types of additional information and expertise should the directors seek?

Smith v. Van Gorkom, below, illustrates the uncertain contours of directors' duty of care when considering whether to approve an extraordinarily important transaction or course of action. *Van Gorkom* involves a proposed merger of Trans Union Corporation with another corporation by which the Trans Union shareholders would receive cash for their shares. Unlike most corporate transactions, mergers require action by both directors and shareholders. If the merger is approved, a dissenting shareholder has an option not available in connection with most corporate transactions. She may elect to reject the consideration promised in the merger and instead receive in cash the fair value of stock as determined by a judicial appraisal. A detailed treatment of mergers is contained in Chapter 8, and this case should be reconsidered with that material. However, a detailed understanding of the mechanics and legal issues surrounding mergers is not essential at this point. The duty of care issue raised in this case goes to the directors' obligation in submitting the merger to shareholders.

As you read this case, be sure that you understand exactly how the directors' duty of care relates to the business judgment rule. Also consider carefully the court's discussion of the corollary duty of candor that applies whenever directors ask shareholders to ratify or approve directors' actions or recommendations.

Smith v. Van Gorkom
Delaware Supreme Court, 1985
488 A.2d 858

HORSEY, JUSTICE (for the majority):

This appeal from the Court of Chancery involves a class action brought by shareholders of the defendant Trans Union Corporation ("Trans Union" or "the Company"), originally seeking rescission of a cash-out merger of Trans Union into the defendant New T Company ("New T"), a wholly-owned subsidiary of the defendant, Marmon Group, Inc. ("Marmon"). Alternate relief in the form of damages is sought against the defendant members of the Board of Directors of Trans Union, New T, and Jay A. Pritzker and Robert A. Pritzker, owners of Marmon.

Following trial, the former Chancellor granted judgment for the defendant directors by unreported letter opinion dated July 6, 1982. . . .

I.

The nature of this case requires a detailed factual statement. The following facts are essentially uncontradicted:

A

Trans Union was a publicly-traded, diversified holding company, the principal earnings of which were generated by its railcar leasing business. During the period here involved, the Company had a cash flow of hundreds of millions of dollars annually. However, the Company had difficulty in generating sufficient taxable income to offset increasingly large investment tax credits (ITCs). Accelerated depreciation deductions had decreased available taxable income against which to offset accumulating ITCs. The Company took these deductions, despite their effect on usable ITCs, because the rental price in the railcar leasing market had already impounded the purported tax savings.

In the late 1970's, together with other capital-intensive firms, Trans Union lobbied in Congress to have ITCs refundable in cash to firms which could not fully utilize the credit. During the summer of 1980, defendant Jerome W. Van Gorkom, Trans Union's Chairman and Chief Executive Officer, testified and lobbied in Congress for refundability of ITCs and against further accelerated depreciation. By the end of August, Van Gorkom was convinced that Congress would neither accept the refundability concept nor curtail further accelerated depreciation.

Beginning in the late 1960's, and continuing through the 1970's, Trans Union pursued a program of acquiring small companies in order to increase available taxable income. In July 1980, Trans Union Management prepared the annual revision of the Company's Five Year Forecast. This report was presented to the Board of Directors at its July, 1980 meeting. The report projected an annual income growth of about 20%. The report also concluded that Trans Union would have about $195 million in spare cash between 1980 and 1985, "with the surplus growing rapidly from 1982 onward." . . .

B

On August 27, 1980, Van Gorkom met with Senior Management of Trans Union. Van Gorkom reported on his lobbying efforts in Washington and his desire to find a solution to the tax credit problem more permanent than a continued program of acquisitions. Various alternatives were suggested and discussed preliminarily, including the sale of Trans Union to a company with a large amount of taxable income.

Donald Romans, Chief financial Officer of Trans Union, stated that his department had done a "very brief bit of work on the possibility of a leveraged buy-out." This work had been prompted by a media article which Romans had seen regarding a leveraged buy-out by management. The work consisted of a "preliminary study" of the cash which could be generated by the Company if it participated in a leveraged buy-out. As Romans stated, this analysis "was very first and rough cut at seeing whether a cash flow would support what might be considered a high price for this type of transaction."

On September 5, at another Senior Management meeting which Van Gorkom attended, Romans again brought up the idea of a leveraged buy-out as a "possible strategic alternative" to the Company's acquisition program. Romans and Bruce S. Chelberg, President and Chief Operating Officer of Trans Union, had been working on the matter in preparation for the meeting. According to Romans: They did not "come up" with a price for the Company. They merely "ran the numbers" at $50 a share and at $60 a share with the "rough form" of their cash figures at the time. Their "figures indicated that $50 would be very easy to do but $60 would be very difficult to do under those figures." This work did not purport to establish a fair price for either the Company or 100% of the stock. It was intended to determine the cash flow needed to service the debt that would "probably" be incurred in a leveraged buy-out, based on "rough calculations" without "any benefit of experts to identify what the limits were to that, and so forth." These computations were not considered extensive and no conclusion was reached.

At this meeting, Van Gorkom stated that he would be willing to take $55 per share for his own 75,000 shares. He vetoed the suggestion of a leveraged buy-out by Management, however, as involving a potential conflict of interest for Management. Van Gorkom, a certified public accountant and lawyer, had been an officer of Trans Union for 24 years, its Chief Executive Officer for more than 17 years, and Chairman of its Board for 2 years. It is noteworthy in this connection that he was then approaching 65 years of age and mandatory retirement.

For several days following the September 5 meeting, Van Gorkom pondered the idea of a sale. He had participated in many acquisitions as a manager and director of Trans Union and as a director of other companies. He was familiar with acquisition procedures, valuation methods, and negotiations; and he privately considered the pros and cons of whether Trans Union should seek a privately- or publicly-held purchaser.

Van Gorkom decided to meet with Jay A. Pritzker, a well-known corporate take-over specialist and a social acquaintance. However, rather than approaching Pritzker simply to determine his interest in acquiring Trans Union, Van Gorkom assembled a proposed per share price for sale of the Company and a financing structure by which to accomplish the sale. Van Gorkom did so without consulting either his Board or any members of Senior Management except one: Carl Peterson, Trans Union's Controller. Telling Peterson that he wanted no other person on his staff to know what he was doing, but without telling him why, Van Gorkom directed Peterson to calculate the feasibility of a leveraged buy-out at an assumed price per share of $55. Apart from the Company's historic stock market price,[5] and Van Gorkom's long association with Trans Union, the record is devoid of any competent evidence that $55 represented the per share intrinsic value of the Company.

---

5. The common stock of Trans Union was traded on the New York Stock Exchange. Over the five year period from 1975 through 1979, Trans Union's stock had traded within a range of a high of $39½ and a low of $24¼. Its high and low range for 1980 through September 19 (the last trading day before announcement of the merger) was $38¼-$29½.

Having thus chosen the $55 figure, based solely on the availability of a leveraged buy-out, Van Gorkom multiplied the price per share by the number of shares outstanding to reach a total value of the Company of $690 million. Van Gorkom told Peterson to use this $690 million figure and to assume a $200 million equity contribution by the buyer. Based on these assumptions, Van Gorkom directed Peterson to determine whether the debt portion of the purchase price could be paid off in five years or less if financed by Trans Union's cash flow as projected in the Five Year Forecast, and by the sale of certain weaker divisions identified in a study done for Trans Union by the Boston Consulting Group ("BCG study"). Peterson reported that, of the purchase price, approximately $50-80 million would remain outstanding after five years. Van Gorkom was disappointed, but decided to meet with Pritzker nevertheless.

Van Gorkom arranged a meeting with Pritzker at the latter's home on Saturday, September 13, 1980. Van Gorkom prefaced his presentation by stating to Pritzker: "Now as far as you are concerned, I can, I think, show how you can pay a substantial premium over the present stock price and pay off most of the loan in the first five years. . . . If you could pay $55 for this Company, here is a way in which I think it can be financed."

Van Gorkom then reviewed with Pritzker his calculations based upon his proposed price of $55 per share. Although Pritzker mentioned $50 as a more attractive figure, no other price was mentioned. However, Van Gorkom stated that to be sure that $55 was the best price obtainable, Trans Union should be free to accept any better offer. Pritzker demurred, stating that his organization would serve as a "stalking horse" for an "auction contest" only if Trans Union would permit Pritzker to buy 1,750,000 shares of Trans Union stock at market price which Pritzker could then sell to any higher bidder. After further discussion on this point, Pritzker told Van Gorkom that he would give him a more definite reaction soon.

On Monday, September 15, Pritzker advised Van Gorkom that he was interested in the $55 cash-out merger proposal and requested more information on Trans Union. Van Gorkom agreed to meet privately with Pritzker, accompanied by Peterson, Chelberg, and Michael Carpenter, Trans Union's consultant from the Boston Consulting Group. The meetings took place on September 16 and 17. Van Gorkom was "astounded that events were moving with such amazing rapidity."

On Thursday, September 18, Van Gorkom met again with Pritzker. At that time, Van Gorkom knew that Pritzker intended to make a cash-out merger offer at Van Gorkom's proposed $55 per share. Pritzker instructed his attorney, a merger and acquisition specialist, to begin drafting merger documents. There was no further discussion of the $55 price. However, the number of shares of Trans Union's treasury stock to be offered to Pritzker was negotiated down to one million shares; the price was set at $38—75 cents above the per share price at the close of the market on September 19. At this point, Pritzker insisted that the Trans Union Board act on his merger proposal within the next three days, stating to Van Gorkom: "We have to have a decision by no later than Sunday [evening, September 21] before the opening of the English stock exchange on Monday morning." Pritzker's lawyer was then instructed to draft the merger documents, to be reviewed by Van Gorkom's lawyer, "sometimes with discussion and sometimes not, in the haste to get it finished."

On Friday, September 19, Van Gorkom, Chelberg, and Pritzker consulted with Trans Union's lead bank regarding the financing of Pritzker's purchase of Trans Union. The bank indicated that it could form a syndicate of banks that would finance the transaction. On the same day, Van Gorkom retained James Brennan, Esquire, to advise Trans Union on the legal aspects of the merger. Van Gorkom did not consult with William Browder, a Vice-President and director of Trans Union and former head of its legal department, or with William Moore, then the head of Trans Union's legal staff.

On Friday, September 19, Van Gorkom called a special meeting of the Trans Union Board for noon the following day. He also called a meeting of the Company's Senior Management to convene at 11:00 A.M., prior to the meeting of the Board. No one, except Chelberg and Peterson, was told the purpose of the meetings. Van Gorkom did not invite Trans Union's investment banker, Salomon Brothers or its Chicago-based partner, to attend.

Of those present at the Senior Management meeting on September 20, only Chelberg and Peterson had prior knowledge of Pritzker's offer. Van Gorkom disclosed the offer and described its terms, but he furnished no copies of the proposed Merger Agreement. Romans announced that his department had done a second study which showed that, for a leveraged buy-out, the price range for Trans Union stock was between $55 and $65 per share. Van Gorkom neither saw the study nor asked Romans to make it available for the Board meeting.

Senior Management's reaction to the Pritzker proposal was completely negative. No member of Management, except Chelberg and Peterson, supported the proposal. Romans objected to the price as being too low;[6] he was critical of the timing and suggested that consideration should be given to the adverse tax consequences of an all-cash deal for low-basis shareholders; and he took the position that the agreement to sell Pritzker one million newly-issued shares at market price would inhibit other offers, as would the prohibitions against soliciting bids and furnishing inside information to other bidders. Romans argued that the Pritzker proposal was a "lock up" and amounted to "an agreed merger as opposed to an offer." Nevertheless, Van Gorkom proceeded to the Board meeting as scheduled without further delay.

Ten directors served on the Trans Union Board, five inside (defendants Bonser, O'Boyle, Browder, Chelberg, and Van Gorkom) and five outside (defendants Wallis, Johnson, Lanterman, Morgan and Reneker). All directors were present at the meeting, except O'Boyle who was ill. Of the outside directors, four were corporate chief executive officers and one was the former Dean of the University of Chicago Business School. None was an investment banker or trained financial analyst. All members of the Board were well informed about the Company and its operations as a going concern. They were familiar with the current financial condition of the Company, as well as operating and earnings projections reported in the recent Five Year forecast. The

---

6. Van Gorkom asked Romans to express his opinions as to the $55 price. Romans stated that he "thought the price was too low in relation to what he could derive for the company in a cash sale, particularly one which enabled us to realize the values of certain subsidiaries and independent entities."

Board generally received regular and detailed reports and was kept abreast of the accumulated investment tax credit and accelerated depreciation problem.

Van Gorkom began the Special Meeting of the Board with a twenty-minute oral presentation. Copies of the proposed Merger Agreement were delivered too late for study before or during the meeting.[7] He reviewed the Company's ITC and depreciation problems and the efforts theretofore made to solve them. He discussed his initial meeting with Pritzker and his motivation in arranging that meeting. Van Gorkom did not disclose to the Board, however, the methodology by which he alone had arrived at the $55 figure, or the fact that he first proposed the $55 price in his negotiations with Pritzker.

Van Gorkom outlined the terms of the Pritzker offer as follows: Pritzker would pay $55 in cash for all outstanding shares of Trans Union stock upon completion of which Trans Union would be merged into New T Company, a subsidiary wholly-owned by Pritzker and formed to implement the merger; for a period of 90 days, Trans Union could receive, but could not actively solicit, competing offers; the offer had to be acted on by the next evening, Sunday, September 21; Trans Union could only furnish to competing bidders published information, and not proprietary information; the offer was subject to Pritzker obtaining the necessary financing by October 10, 1980; if the financing contingency were met or waived by Pritzker, Trans Union was required to sell to Pritzker one million newly-issued shares of Trans Union at $38 per share.

Van Gorkom took the position that putting Trans Union "up for auction" through a 90-day market test would validate a decision by the Board that $55 was a fair price. He told the Board that the "free market will have an opportunity to judge whether $55 is a fair price." Van Gorkom framed the decision before the Board not as whether $55 per share was the highest price that could be obtained, but as whether the $55 price was a fair price that the stockholders should be given the opportunity to accept or reject.[8]

Attorney Brennan advised the members of the Board that they might be sued if they failed to accept the offer and that a fairness opinion was not required as a matter of law.

Romans attended the meeting as chief financial officer of the Company. He told the Board that he had not been involved in the negotiations with Pritzker and knew nothing about the merger proposal until the morning of the meeting; that his studies did not indicate either a fair price for the stock or a valuation of the Company; that he did not see his role as directly addressing the fairness issue; and that he and his people "were trying to search for ways to justify a price in connection with such a [leveraged buy-out] transaction, rather than to say what the shares are worth." Romans testified: "I told the Board that the study ran the numbers at 50 and 60, and then the subsequent study at 55 and 65, and that was not the same thing as saying that I have a valuation

---

7. The record is not clear as to the terms of the Merger Agreement. The Agreement, as originally presented to the Board on September 20, was never produced by defendants despite demands by the plaintiffs. Nor is it clear that the directors were given an opportunity to study the Merger Agreement before voting on it. All that can be said is that Brennan had the Agreement before him during the meeting.

8. In Van Gorkom's words: The "real decision" is whether to "let the stockholders decide it" which is "all you are being asked to decide today."

of the company at X dollars. But it was a way—a first step towards reaching that conclusion." Romans told the Board that, in his opinion, $55 was "in the range of a fair price," but "at the beginning of the range."

Chelberg, Trans Union's President, supported Van Gorkom's presentation and representations. He testified that he "participated to make sure that the Board members collectively were clear on the details of the agreement or offer from Pritzker"; that he "participated in the discussion with Mr. Brennan, inquiring of him about the necessity for valuation opinions in spite of the way in which this particular offer was couched"; and that he was otherwise actively involved in supporting the positions being taken by Van Gorkom before the Board about "the necessity to act immediately on this offer," and about "the adequacy of the $55 and the question of how that would be tested."

The Board meeting of September 20 lasted about two hours. Based solely upon Van Gorkom's oral presentation, Chelberg's supporting representations, Romans' oral statement, Brennan's legal advice, and their knowledge of the market history of the Company's stock,[9] the directors approved the proposed Merger Agreement. However, the Board later claimed to have attached two conditions to its acceptance: (1) that Trans Union reserved the right to accept any better offer that was made during the market test period; and (2) that Trans Union could share its proprietary information with any other potential bidders. While the Board now claims to have reserved the right to accept any better offer received after the announcement of the Pritzker agreement (even though the minutes of the meeting do not reflect this), it is undisputed that the Board did not reserve the right to actively solicit alternate offers.

The Merger Agreement was executed by Van Gorkom during the evening of September 20 at a formal social event that he hosted for the opening of the Chicago Lyric Opera. Neither he nor any other director read the agreement prior to its signing and delivery to Pritzker. . . .

On February 10, the stockholders of Trans Union approved the Pritzker merger proposal. Of the outstanding shares, 69.9% were voted in favor of the merger; 7.25% were voted against the merger; and 22.85% were not voted.

II.

We turn to the issue of the application of the business judgment rule to the September 20 meeting of the Board.

The Court of Chancery concluded from the evidence that the Board of Directors' approval of the Pritzker merger proposal fell within the protection of the business judgment rule. . . .

---

9. The Trial Court stated the premium relationship of the $55 price to the market history of the Company's stock as follows: ". . . the merger price offered to the stockholders of Trans Union represented a premium of 62% over the average of the high and low prices at which Trans Union stock had traded in 1980, a premium of 48% over the last closing price, and a premium of 39% over the highest price at which the stock of Trans Union had traded any time during the prior six years."

The defendants deny that the Trial Court committed legal error in relying upon post-September 20, 1980 events and the directors' later acquired knowledge. The defendants further submit that their decision to accept $55 per share was informed because: (1) they were "highly qualified"; (2) they were "well-informed"; and (3) they deliberated over the "proposal" not once but three times. On essentially this evidence and under our standard of review, the defendants assert that affirmance is required. We must disagree.

Under Delaware law, the business judgment rule is the offspring of the fundamental principle, codified in 8 Del. C. §141(a), that the business and affairs of a Delaware corporation are managed by or under its board of directors. In carrying out their managerial roles, directors are charged with an unyielding fiduciary duty to the corporation and its shareholders. The business judgment rule exists to protect and promote the full and free exercise of the managerial power granted to Delaware directors. The rule itself "is a presumption that in making a business decision, the directors of a corporation acted on an informed basis, in good faith and in the honest belief that the action taken was in the best interests of the company." [Aronson v. Lewis, Del. Supr., 473 A.2d 805, 812 (1984).] Thus, the party attacking a board decision as uninformed must rebut the presumption that its business judgment was an informed one.

The determination of whether a business judgment is an informed one turns on whether the directors have informed themselves "prior to making a business decision, of all material information reasonably available to them." Id.

Under the business judgment rule there is no protection for directors who have made "an unintelligent or unadvised judgment." [Mitchell v. Highland-Western Glass, Del. Ch., 167 A. 831, 833 (1933).] A director's duty to inform himself in preparation for a decision derives from the fiduciary capacity in which he serves the corporation and its stockholders. Since a director is vested with the responsibility for the management of the affairs of the corporation, he must execute that duty with the recognition that he acts on behalf of others. Such obligation does not tolerate faithlessness or self-dealing. But fulfillment of the fiduciary function requires more than the mere absence of bad faith or fraud. Representation of the financial interests of others imposes on a director an affirmative duty to protect those interests and to proceed with a critical eye in assessing information of the type and under the circumstances present here.

Thus, a director's duty to exercise an informed business judgment is in the nature of a duty of care, as distinguished from a duty of loyalty. Here, there were no allegations of fraud, bad faith, or self-dealing, or proof thereof. Hence, it is presumed that the directors reached their business judgment in good faith, and considerations of motive are irrelevant to the issue before us.

The standard of care applicable to a director's duty of care has also been recently restated by this Court. In *Aronson*, supra, we stated: "While the Delaware cases use a variety of terms to describe the applicable standard of care, our analysis satisfies us that under the business judgment rule director liability is predicated upon concepts of gross negligence." 473 A.2d at 812.

We again confirm that view. We think the concept of gross negligence is also the proper standard for determining whether a business judgment reached by a board of directors was an informed one.

In the specific context of a proposed merger of domestic corporations, a director has a duty under 8 Del. C. §251(b), along with his fellow directors, to act in an informed and deliberate manner in determining whether to approve an agreement of merger before submitting the proposal to the stockholders. Certainly in the merger context, a director may not abdicate that duty by leaving to the shareholders alone the decision to approve or disapprove the agreement.

It is against those standards that the conduct of the directors of Trans Union must be tested, as a matter of law and as a matter of fact, regarding their exercise of an informed business judgment in voting to approve the Pritzker merger proposal.

III.

. . . . The issue of whether the directors reached an informed decision to "sell" the Company on September 20, 1980 must be determined only upon the basis of the information then reasonably available to the directors and relevant to their decision to accept the Pritzker merger proposal. This is not to say that the directors were precluded from altering their original plan of action, had they done so in an informed manner. What we do say is that the question of whether the directors reached an informed business judgment in agreeing to sell the Company, pursuant to the terms of the September 20 Agreement presents, in reality, two questions: (A) whether the directors reached an informed business judgment on September 20, 1980; and (B) if they did not, whether the directors' actions taken subsequent to September 20 were adequate to cure any infirmity in their action taken on September 20. We first consider the directors' September 20 action in terms of their reaching an informed business judgment.

A

On the record before us, we must conclude that the Board of Directors did not reach an informed business judgment on September 20, 1980 in voting to "sell" the Company for $55 per share pursuant to the Pritzker cash-out merger proposal. Our reasons, in summary, are as follows:

The directors (1) did not adequately inform themselves as to Van Gorkom's role in forcing the "sale" of the Company and in establishing the per share purchase price; (2) were uninformed as to the intrinsic value of the Company; and (3) given these circumstances, at a minimum, were grossly negligent in approving the "sale" of the Company upon two hours' consideration, without prior notice, and without the exigency of a crisis or emergency.

As has been noted, the Board based its September 20 decision to approve the cash-out merger primarily on Van Gorkom's representations. None of the directors, other than Van Gorkom and Chelberg, had any prior knowledge that the purpose of the meeting was to propose a cash-out merger of Trans Union. No members of Senior Management were present, other than Chelberg, Romans and Peterson; and the latter two had only learned of the proposed sale an hour earlier. Both general counsel Moore and former general counsel Browder attended the meeting, but were equally uninformed as to the purpose of the meeting and the documents to be acted upon.

Without any documents before them concerning the proposed transaction, the members of the Board were required to rely entirely upon Van Gorkom's 20-minute oral presentation of the proposal. No written summary of the terms of the merger was presented; the directors were given no documentation to support the adequacy of $55 price per share for sale of the Company; and the Board had before it nothing more than Van Gorkom's statement of his understanding of the substance of an agreement which he admittedly had never read, nor which any member of the Board had ever seen.

Under 8 Del. C. §141(e),[15] "directors are fully protected in relying in good faith on reports made by officers." The term "report" has been liberally construed to include reports of informal personal investigations by corporate officers. However, there is no evidence that any "report," as defined under §141(e), concerning the Pritzker proposal, was presented to the Board on September 20. Van Gorkom's oral presentation of his understanding of the terms of the proposed Merger Agreement, which he had not seen, and Romans' brief oral statement of his preliminary study regarding the feasibility of a leveraged buy-out of Trans Union do not qualify as §141(e) "reports" for these reasons: The former lacked substance because Van Gorkom was basically uninformed as to the essential provisions of the very document about which he was talking. Romans' statement was irrelevant to the issues before the Board since it did not purport to be a valuation study. At a minimum for a report to enjoy the status conferred by §141(e), it must be pertinent to the subject matter upon which a board is called to act, and otherwise be entitled to good faith, not blind, reliance. Considering all of the surrounding circumstances—hastily calling the meeting without prior notice of its subject matter, the proposed sale of the Company without any prior consideration of the issue or necessity therefor, the urgent time constraints imposed by Pritzker, and the total absence of any documentation whatsoever—the directors were duty bound to make reasonable inquiry of Van Gorkom and Romans, and if they had done so, the inadequacy of that upon which they now claim to have relied would have been apparent.

The defendants rely on the following factors to sustain the Trial Court's finding that the Board's decision was an informed one: (1) the magnitude of the premium or spread between the $55 Pritzker offering price and Trans Union's current market price of $38 per share; (2) the amendment of the Agreement as submitted on September 20 to permit the Board to accept any better offer during the "market test" period; (3) the collective experience and expertise of the Board's "inside" and "outside" directors; and (4) their reliance on Brennan's legal advice that the directors might be sued if they rejected the Pritzker proposal. We discuss each of these grounds seriatim:

---

15. Section 141(e) provides in pertinent part:

A member of the board of directors . . . shall, in the performance of his duties, be fully protected in relying in good faith upon the books of accounts or reports made to the corporation by any of its officers, or by an independent certified accountant, or by an appraiser selected with reasonable care by the board of directors . . . , or in relying in good faith upon the records of the corporation.

(1)

A substantial premium may provide one reason to recommend a merger, but in the absence of other sound valuation information, the fact of a premium alone does not provide an adequate basis upon which to assess the fairness of an offering price. Here, the judgment reached as to the adequacy of the premium was based on a comparison between the historically depressed Trans Union market price and the amount of the Pritzker offer. Using market price as a basis for concluding that the premium adequately reflected the true value of the Company was a clearly faulty, indeed fallacious, premise, as the defendants' own evidence demonstrates.

The record is clear that before September 20, Van Gorkom and other members of Trans Union's Board knew that the market had consistently undervalued the worth of Trans Union's stock, despite steady increases in the Company's operating income in the seven years preceding the merger. The Board related this occurrence in large part to Trans Union's inability to use its ITCs as previously noted. Van Gorkom testified that he did not believe the market price accurately reflected Trans Union's true worth; and several of the directors testified that, as a general rule, most chief executives think that the market undervalues their companies' stock. Yet, on September 20, Trans Union's Board apparently believed that the market stock price accurately reflected the value of the Company for the purpose of determining the adequacy of the premium for its sale. . . .

The parties do not dispute that a publicly-traded stock price is solely a measure of the value of a minority position and, thus, market price represents only the value of a single share. Nevertheless, on September 20, the Board assessed the adequacy of the premium over market, offered by Pritzker, solely by comparing it with Trans Union's current and historical stock price.

Indeed, as of September 20, the Board had no other information on which to base a determination of the intrinsic value of Trans Union as a going concern. As of September 20, the Board had made no evaluation of the Company designed to value the entire enterprise, nor had the Board ever previously considered selling the Company or consenting to a buy-out merger. Thus, the adequacy of a premium is indeterminate unless it is assessed in terms of other competent and sound valuation information that reflects the value of the particular business.

Despite the foregoing facts and circumstances, there was no call by the Board, either on September 20 or thereafter, for any valuation study or documentation of the $55 price per share as a measure of the fair value of the Company in a cash-out context. It is undisputed that the major asset of Trans Union was its cash flow. Yet, at no time did the Board call for a valuation study taking into account that highly significant element of the Company's assets.

We do not imply that an outside valuation study is essential to support an informed business judgment; nor do we state that fairness opinions by independent investment bankers are required as a matter of law. Often insiders familiar with the business of a going concern are in a better position than are outsiders to gather relevant information; and under appropriate circumstances, such directors may be fully protected in relying in good faith upon the valuation reports of their management. See 8 Del. C. §141(e).

Here, the record establishes that the Board did not request its Chief Financial Officer, Romans, to make any valuation study or review of the proposal to determine the adequacy of $55 per share for sale of the Company. On the record before us: The Board rested on Romans' elicited response that the $55 figure was within a "fair price range" within the context of a leveraged buy-out. No director sought any further information from Romans. No director asked him why he put $55 at the bottom of his range. No director asked Romans for any details as to his study, the reason why it had been undertaken or its depth. No director asked to see the study; and no director asked Romans whether Trans Union's finance department could do a fairness study within the remaining 36-hour period available under the Pritzker offer.

Had the Board, or any member, made an inquiry of Romans, he presumably would have responded as he testified: that his calculations were rough and preliminary; and, that the study was not designed to determine the fair value of the Company, but rather to assess the feasibility of a leveraged buy-out financed by the Company's projected cash flow, making certain assumptions as to the purchaser's borrowing needs. Romans would have presumably also informed the Board of his view, and the widespread view of Senior Management, that the timing of the offer was wrong and the offer inadequate.

The record also establishes that the Board accepted without scrutiny Van Gorkom's representation as to the fairness of the $55 price per share for sale of the Company—a subject that the Board had never previously considered. The Board thereby failed to discover that Van Gorkom had suggested the $55 price to Pritzker and, most crucially, that Van Gorkom had arrived at the $55 figure based on calculations designed solely to determine the feasibility of a leveraged buy-out.[19] No questions were raised either as to the tax implications of a cash-out merger or how the price for the one million share option granted Pritzker was calculated.

We do not say that the Board of Directors was not entitled to give some credence to Van Gorkom's representation that $55 was an adequate or fair price. Under §141(e), the directors were entitled to rely upon their chairman's opinion of value and adequacy, provided that such opinion was reached on a sound basis. Here, the issue is whether the directors informed themselves as to all information that was reasonably available to them. Had they done so, they would have learned of the source and derivation of the $55 price and could not reasonably have relied thereupon in good faith.

None of the directors, Management or outside, were investment bankers or financial analysts. Yet the Board did not consider recessing the meeting until a later hour that day (or requesting an extension of Pritzker's Sunday evening deadline) to give it time to elicit more information as to the sufficiency of the offer, either from inside

---

19. As of September 20 the directors did not know: that Van Gorkom had arrived at the $55 figure alone, and subjectively, as the figure to be used by Controller Peterson in creating a feasible structure for a leveraged buy-out by a prospective purchaser; that Van Gorkom had not sought advice, information or assistance from either inside or outside Trans Union directors as to the value of the Company as an entity or the fair price per share for 100% of its stock; that Van Gorkom had not consulted with the Company's investment bankers or other financial analysts; that Van Gorkom had not consulted with or confided in any officer or director of the Company except Chelberg; and that Van Gorkom had deliberately chosen to ignore the advice and opinion of the members of his Senior Management group regarding the adequacy of the $55 price.

Management (in particular Romans) or from Trans Union's own investment banker, Salomon Brothers, whose Chicago specialist in merger and acquisitions was known to the Board and familiar with Trans Union's affairs.

Thus, the record compels the conclusion that on September 20 the Board lacked valuation information adequate to reach an informed business judgment as to the fairness of $55 per share for sale of the Company.

(2)

This brings us to the post-September 20 "market test" upon which the defendants ultimately rely to confirm the reasonableness of their September 20 decision to accept the Pritzker proposal. In this connection, the directors present a two-part argument: (a) that by making a "market test" of Pritzker's $55 per share offer a condition of their September 20 decision to accept his offer, they cannot be found to have acted impulsively or in an uninformed manner on September 20; and (b) that the adequacy of the $17 premium for sale of the Company was conclusively established over the following 90 to 120 days by the most reliable evidence available—the marketplace. Thus, the defendants impliedly contend that the "market test" eliminated the need for the Board to perform any other form of fairness test either on September 20, or thereafter.

Again, the facts of record do not support the defendants' argument. There is no evidence: (a) that the Merger Agreement was effectively amended to give the Board freedom to put Trans Union up for auction sale to the highest bidder; or (b) that a public auction was in fact permitted to occur. . . .

(3)

The directors' unfounded reliance on both the premium and the market test as the basis for accepting the Pritzker proposal undermines the defendants' remaining contention that the Board's collective experience and sophistication was a sufficient basis for finding that it reached its September 20 decision with informed, reasonable deliberation. Compare Gimbel v. Signal Companies, Inc., Del. Ch., 316 A.2d 599 (1974), affd. per curiam, Del. Supr., 316 A.2d 619 (1974). There, the Court of Chancery preliminary enjoined a board's sale of stock of its wholly-owned subsidiary for an alleged grossly inadequate price. It did so based on a finding that the business judgment rule had been pierced for failure of management to give its board "the opportunity to make a reasonable and reasoned decision." 316 A.2d at 615. The Court there reached this result notwithstanding the board's sophistication and experience; the company's need of immediate cash; and the board's need to act promptly due to the impact of an energy crisis on the value of the underlying assets being sold—all of its subsidiary's oil and gas interests. The Court found those factors denoting competence to be outweighed by evidence of gross negligence; that management in effect sprang the deal on the board by negotiating the asset sale without informing the board; that the buyer intended to "force a quick decision" by the board; that the board meeting was called on only one-and-a-half days' notice; that its outside directors were not notified of the meeting's purpose; that during a meeting spanning "a couple of hours" a sale of assets worth $480 million was approved; and that the Board failed to obtain a current appraisal of its oil and gas interests. The analogy of *Signal* to the case at bar is significant.

(4)

Part of the defense is based on a claim that the directors relied on legal advice rendered at the September 20 meeting by James Brennan, Esquire, who was present at Van Gorkom's request. Unfortunately, Brennan did not appear and testify at trial even though his firm participated in the defense of this action. There is no contemporaneous evidence of the advice given by Brennan on September 20, only the later deposition and trial testimony of certain directors as to their recollections or understanding of what was said at the meeting. Since counsel did not testify, and the advice attributed to Brennan is hearsay received by the Trial Court over the plaintiffs' objections, we consider it only in the context of the directors' present claims. In fairness to counsel, we make no findings that the advice attributed to him was in fact given. We focus solely on the efficacy of the defendants' claims, made months and years later, in an effort to extricate themselves from liability.

Several defendants testified that Brennan advised them that Delaware law did not require a fairness opinion or an outside valuation of the Company before the Board could act on the Pritzker proposal. If given, the advice was correct. However, that did not end the matter. Unless the directors had before them adequate information regarding the intrinsic value of the Company, upon which a proper exercise of business judgment could be made, mere advice of this type is meaningless; and, given this record of the defendants' failures, it constitutes no defense here.

We conclude that Trans Union's Board was grossly negligent in that it failed to act with informed reasonable deliberation in agreeing to the Pritzker merger proposal on September 20; and we further conclude that the Trial Court erred as a matter of law in failing to address that question before determining whether the directors' later conduct was sufficient to cure its initial error. . . .

[The court further concluded that the board's later conduct did not cure its initial error.]

IV.

Whether the directors of Trans Union should be treated as one or individually in terms of invoking the protection of the business judgment rule and the applicability of 8 Del. C. §141(c) are questions which were not originally addressed by the parties in their briefing of this case. This resulted in a supplemental briefing and a second rehearing en banc on two basic questions: (a) whether one or more of the directors were deprived of the protection of the business judgment rule by evidence of an absence of good faith; and (b) whether one or more of the outside directors were entitled to invoke the protection of 8 Del. C. §141(e) by evidence of a reasonable, good faith reliance on "reports," including legal advice, rendered the Board by certain inside directors and the Board's special counsel, Brennan.

The parties' response, including reargument, has led the majority of the Court to conclude: (1) that since all of the defendant directors, outside as well as inside, take a unified position, we are required to treat all of the directors as one as to whether they are entitled to the protection of the business judgment rule; and (2) that considerations of good faith, including the presumption that the directors acted in good faith, are irrelevant in determining the threshold issue of whether the directors as a Board exercised an informed business judgment. For the same reason, we must reject defense counsel's ad hominem argument for affirmance: that reversal may result in a multi-million dollar class award against the defendants for having made an allegedly uninformed business judgment in a transaction not involving any personal gain, self-dealing or claim of bad faith. . . .

V.

The defendants ultimately rely on the stockholder vote of February 10 for exoneration. The defendants contend that the stockholders' "overwhelming" vote approving the Pritzker Merger Agreement had the legal effect of curing any failure of the Board to reach an informed business judgment in its approval of the merger.

The parties tacitly agree that a discovered failure of the Board to reach an informed business judgment in approving the merger constitutes a voidable, rather than a void, act. Hence, the merger can be sustained, notwithstanding the infirmity of the Board's action, if its approval by majority vote of the shareholders is found to have been based on an informed electorate. . . .

The settled rule in Delaware is that "where a majority of fully informed stockholders ratify action of even interested directors, an attack on the ratified transaction normally must fail." Gerlach v. Gillam, Del. Ch., 139 A.2d 591, 593 (1958). The question of whether shareholders have been fully informed such that their vote can be said to ratify director action, "turns on the fairness and completeness of the proxy materials submitted by the management to the . . . shareholders." Michelson v. Duncan, supra at 220. As this Court stated in Gottlieb v. Heyden Chemical Corp., Del. Supr., 91 A.2d 57, 59 (1952):

> [T]he entire atmosphere is freshened and a new set of rules invoked where a formal approval has been given by a majority of independent, fully informed stockholders. . . .

In Lynch v. Vickers Energy Corp., supra, this Court held that corporate directors owe to their stockholders a fiduciary duty to disclose all facts germane to the transaction at issue in an atmosphere of complete candor. We defined "germane" in the tender offer context as all "information such as a reasonable stockholder would consider important in deciding whether to sell or retain stock." Id. at 281. Accord Weinberger v. UOP, Inc., supra; Michelson v. Duncan, supra; Schreiber v. Pennzoil Corp., Del. Ch., 419 A.2d 952 (1980). In reality, "germane" means material facts.

Applying this standard to the record before us, we find that Trans Union's stockholders were not fully informed of all facts material to their vote on the Pritzker Merger and that the Trial Court's ruling to the contrary is clearly erroneous. We list the material deficiencies in the proxy materials:

(1) The fact that the Board had no reasonably adequate information indicative of the intrinsic value of the Company, other than a concededly depressed market price,

was without question material to the shareholders voting on the merger. See *Weinberger,* supra at 709 (insiders' report that cash-out merger price up to $24 was good investment held material); *Michelson,* supra at 224 (alleged terms and intent of stock option plan held not germane); *Schreiber,* supra at 959 (management fee of $650,000 held germane).

Accordingly, the Board's lack of valuation information should have been disclosed. Instead, the directors cloaked the absence of such information in both the Proxy Statement and the Supplemental Proxy Statement. Through artful drafting, noticeably absent at the September 20 meeting, both documents create the impression that the Board knew the intrinsic worth of the Company. In particular, the Original Proxy Statement contained the following:

> [a]lthough the Board of Directors regards the intrinsic value of the Company's assets to be significantly greater than their book value . . . , systematic liquidation of such a large and complex entity as Trans Union is simply not regarded as a feasible method of realizing its inherent value. Therefore, a business combination such as the merger would seem to be the only practicable way in which the stockholders could realize the value of the Company.

The Proxy stated further that "[i]n the view of the Board of Directors . . . , the prices at which the Company's common stock has traded in recent years have not reflected the inherent value of the Company." What the Board failed to disclose to its stockholders was that the Board had not made any study of the intrinsic or inherent worth of the Company; nor had the Board even discussed the inherent value of the Company prior to approving the merger on September 20, or at either of the subsequent meetings on October 8 or January 26. Neither in its Original Proxy Statement nor in its Supplemental Proxy did the Board disclose that it had no information before it, beyond the premium-over-market and the price/earnings ratio, on which to determine the fair value of the Company as a whole.

(2) We find false and misleading the Board's characterization of the Romans report in the Supplemental Proxy Statement. The Supplemental Proxy stated:

> At the September 20, 1980 meeting of the Board of Directors of Trans Union, Mr. Romans indicated that while he could not say that $55.00 per share was an unfair price, he had prepared a preliminary report which reflected that the value of the Company was in the range of $55.00 to $65.00 per share.

Nowhere does the Board disclose that Romans stated to the Board that his calculations were made in a "search for ways to justify a price in connection with" a leveraged buy-out transaction, "rather than to say what the shares are worth," and that he stated to the Board that his conclusion thus arrived at "was not the same thing as saying that I have a valuation of the Company at X dollars." Such information would have been material to a reasonable shareholder because it tended to invalidate the fairness of the merger price of $55. Furthermore, defendants again failed to disclose the absence of valuation information, but still made repeated reference to the "substantial premium."

(3) We find misleading the Board's references to the "substantial" premium offered. The Board gave as their primary reason in support of the merger the "substantial premium" shareholders would receive. But the Board did not disclose its failure to

assess the premium offered in terms of other relevant valuation techniques, thereby rendering questionable its determination as to the substantiality of the premium over an admittedly depressed stock market price. . . .

The burden must fall on defendants who claim ratification based on shareholder vote to establish that the shareholder approval resulted from a fully informed electorate. On the record before us, it is clear that the Board failed to meet that burden. Weinberger v. UOP, Inc., supra at 703; Michelson v. Duncan, supra. . . .

For the foregoing reasons, we conclude that the director defendants breached their fiduciary duty of candor by their failure to make true and correct disclosures of all information they had, or should have had, material to the transaction submitted for stockholder approval.

VI.

To summarize: we hold that the directors of Trans Union breached their fiduciary duty to their stockholders: (1) by their failure to inform themselves of all information reasonably available to them and relevant to their decision to recommend the Pritzker merger; and (2) by their failure to disclose all material information such as a reasonable stockholder would consider important in deciding whether to approve the Pritzker offer.

We hold, therefore, that the Trial Court committed reversible error in applying the business judgment rule in favor of the director defendants in this case.

On remand, the Court of Chancery shall conduct an evidentiary hearing to determine the fair value of the shares represented by the plaintiffs' class, based on the intrinsic value of Trans Union on September 20, 1980. Thereafter, an award of damages may be entered to the extent that the fair value of Trans Union exceeds $55 per share.

Reversed and remanded for proceedings consistent herewith.

McNEILLY, JUSTICE, dissenting (joined by CHRISTIE, C.J.):

The majority opinion reads like an advocate's closing address to a hostile jury. And I say that not lightly. Throughout the opinion great emphasis is directed only to the negative, with nothing more than lip service granted the positive aspects of this case. In my opinion Chancellor Marvel (retired) should have been affirmed. The Chancellor's opinion was the product of well reasoned conclusions, based upon a sound deductive process, clearly supported by the evidence and entitled to deference in this appeal. Because of my diametrical opposition to all evidentiary conclusions of the majority, I respectfully dissent.

It would serve no useful purpose, particularly at this late date, for me to dissent at great length. I restrain myself from doing so, but feel compelled to at least point out what I consider to be the most glaring deficiencies in the majority opinion. The majority has spoken and has effectively said that Trans Union's Directors have been the victims of a "fast shuffle" by Van Gorkom and Pritzker. That is the beginning of the majority's comedy of errors. The first and most important error made is the majority's assessment of the directors' knowledge of the affairs of Trans Union and their combined ability to act in this situation under the protection of the business judgment rule.

Trans Union's Board of Directors consisted of ten men, five of whom were "inside" directors and five of whom were "outside" directors. The "inside" directors were Van Gorkom, Chelberg, Bonser, William B. Browder, Senior Vice-President-Law, and Thomas P. O'Boyle, Senior Vice-President-Administration. At the time the merger was proposed the inside five directors had collectively been employed by the Company for 116 years and had 68 years of combined experience as directors. The "outside" directors were A.W. Wallis, William B. Johnson, Joseph B. Lanterman, Graham J. Morgan and Robert W. Reneker. With the exception of Wallis, these were all chief executive officers of Chicago based corporations that were at least as large as Trans Union. The five "outside" directors had 78 years of combined experience as chief executive officers, and 53 years cumulative service as Trans Union directors.

The inside directors wear their badge of expertise in the corporate affairs of Trans Union on their sleeves. But what about the outsiders? Dr. Wallis is or was an economist and math statistician, a professor of economics at Yale University, dean of the graduate school of business at the University of Chicago, and Chancellor of the University of Rochester. Dr. Wallis had been on the Board of Trans Union since 1962. He also was on the Board of Bausch & Lomb, Kodak, Metropolitan Life Insurance Company, Standard Oil and others.

William B. Johnson is a University of Pennsylvania law graduate, President of Railway Express until 1966, Chairman and Chief Executive of I.C. Industries Holding Company, and member of Trans Union's Board since 1968.

Joseph Lanterman, a Certified Public Accountant, is or was President and Chief Executive of American Steel, on the Board of International Harvester, Peoples Energy, Illinois Bell Telephone, Harris Bank and Trust Company, Kemper Insurance Company and a director of Trans Union for four years.

Graham Morgan is a chemist, was Chairman and Chief Executive Officer of U.S. Gypsum, and in the 17 and 18 years prior to the Trans Union transaction had been involved in 31 or 32 corporate takeovers.

Robert Reneker attended University of Chicago and Harvard Business Schools. He was President and Chief Executive of Swift and Company, director of Trans Union since 1971, and member of the Boards of seven other corporations including U.S. Gypsum and the Chicago Tribune.

Directors of this caliber are not ordinarily taken in by a "fast shuffle." I submit they were not taken into this multi-million dollar corporate transaction without being fully informed and aware of the state of the art as it pertained to the entire corporate panoroma of Trans Union. True, even directors such as these, with their business acumen, interest and expertise, can go astray. I do not believe that to be the case here. These men knew Trans Union like the back of their hands and were more than well qualified to make on the spot informed business judgments concerning the affairs of Trans Union including a 100 percent sale of the corporation. Lest we forget, the corporate world of then and now operates on what is so aptly referred to as "the fast track." These men were at the time an integral part of that world, all professional business men, not intellectual figureheads. . . .

NOTES AND QUESTIONS

1. The directors of Trans Union faced potentially draconian liability. For example, if on remand the Chancery Court found Trans Union's intrinsic value to be $65 per share, then the directors' liability would be $133,577,580. Given this risk, the directors reportedly settled the case by agreeing to pay $23,500,000 to plaintiffs. Of this settlement, most was paid by the corporation's insurers (see Part E of this chapter) and by the Pritzker group. Manning, Reflections and Practical Tips on Life in the Boardroom After *Van Gorkom*, 41 Bus. Law. 1 (1985). Unofficial sources report that the directors also were reimbursed for their presumably substantial litigation costs.

2. Delaware G.C.L. Section 141(e) was amended in the wake of Smith v. Van Gorkom to provide that directors could rely on opinions by a corporation's officers, even if not expressed in the form of a "report."

3. Former Delaware Supreme Court Chief Justice Norman Veasey explained the relationship between reliance on section 141(e) and business judgment rule protection, as follows:

> The Complaint, fairly construed, admits that the directors were advised by Crystal as an expert and that they relied on his expertise. Accordingly, the question here is whether the directors are to be "fully protected" (i.e., not held liable) on the basis that they relied in good faith on a qualified expert under Section 141(e) of the Delaware General Corporation Law. The Old Board is entitled to the presumption that it exercised proper business judgment, including proper reliance on the expert. . . .
>
> To survive a Rule 23.1 motion to dismiss in a due care case where an expert has advised the board in its decisionmaking process, the complaint must . . . show, for example, that: (a) the directors did not in fact rely on the expert; (b) their reliance was not in good faith; (c) they did not reasonably believe that the expert's advice was within the expert's professional competence; (d) the expert was not selected with reasonable care by or on behalf of the corporation, and the faulty selection process was attributable to the directors; (e) the subject matter (in this case the cost calculation) that was material and reasonably available was so obvious that the board's failure to consider it was grossly negligent regardless of the expert's advice or lack of advice; or (f) that the decision of the board was so unconscionable as to constitute waste or fraud. This Complaint includes no particular allegations of this nature, and therefore it was subject to dismissal as drafted.

Brehm v. Eisner, 746 A.2d 244, 261-262 (Del. 2000).

4. Note that *Van Gorkom* was a 3-2 decision. What result in *Van Gorkom* if decided by a hypothetical three-justice panel composed of former Chief Justice Veasey (Note 3, above), and current and former Delaware Chancery Court Chancellors Allen and Chandler (see Notes after Joy v. North)?

5. For thoughtful analysis of *Van Gorkom*, both pro and con, see the following articles which appeared in the Northwestern University Law Review, Winter 2002 Symposium, *Van Gorkom* and the Corporate Board: Problem, Solution, or Placebo? 96 Nw. U. L. Rev. 447 (2002): William T. Allen, Jack B. Jacobs, and Leo E. Strine, Jr., Realigning the Standard of Review of Director Due Care with Delaware Public Policy: A Critique of *Van Gorkom* and Its Progeny as a Standard of Review Problem, 96 Nw. U. L. Rev. 449; Charles M. Elson and Robert B. Thompson, *Van Gorkom's* Legacy: The Limits of Judicially Enforced Constraints and the Promise of Proprietary Incentives, 96 Nw. U. L. Rev. 579; Lawrence A. Hamermesh, A Kinder, Gentler Critique of *Van Gorkom* and Its Less Celebrated Legacies, 96 Nw. U. L. Rev. 595; Jonathan R. Macey, *Smith v. Van Gorkom:*

Insights About C.E.O.s, Corporate Law Rules, and the Jurisdictional Competition for Corporate Charters, 96 Nw. U. L. Rev. 607; Fred S. McChesney, A Bird in the Hand and Liability in the Bush: Why *Van Gorkom* Still Rankles, Probably, 96 Nw. U. L. Rev. 631; Lynn A. Stout, In Praise of Procedure: An Economic and Behavioral Defense of *Smith v. Van Gorkom* and the Business Judgment Rule 96 Nw. U. L. Rev. 675.

6. Under Delaware jurisprudence, if the plaintiff carries his burden of proving that the directors acted without requisite care in approving a merger or other major decision, the defendants then have the burden of proving that the transaction or decision was intrinsically or entirely fair to the corporation.

> In *Van Gorkom,* we held that although there was no breach of the duty of loyalty, the failure of the members of the board to adequately inform themselves represented a breach of the duty of care, which of itself was sufficient to rebut the presumption of the business judgment rule. *Van Gorkom,* 488 A.2d 858. A breach of either the duty of loyalty or the duty of care rebuts the presumption that the directors have acted in the best interests of the shareholders, and requires the directors to prove that the transaction was entirely fair.

Cede & Co. v. Technicolor, Inc., 634 A.2d 345, 371 (Del. 1993).

7. What must directors prove to establish the entire fairness of a transaction or decision if business judgment rule presumptions are lost? Most jurisdictions look to the standard enunciated in Weinberger v. UOP, Inc., 457 A.2d 701, 711 (1983):

> The concept of fairness has two basic aspects: fair dealing and fair price. The former embraces questions of when the transaction was timed, how it was initiated, structured, negotiated, disclosed to the directors, and how the approvals of the directors and the stockholders were obtained. The latter aspect of fairness relates to the economic and financial considerations of the proposed merger, including all relevant factors: assets, market value, earnings, future prospects, and any other elements that affect the intrinsic or inherent value of a company's stock. Moore, The "Interested" Director or Officer Transaction, 4 Del. J. Corp. L. 674, 676 (1979); Nathan & Shapiro, Legal Standard of Fairness of Merger Terms Under Delaware Law, 2 Del. J. Corp. L. 44, 46-47 (1977). See Tri-Continental Corp. v. Battye, Del. Supr., 74 A.2d 71, 72 (1950); Del. G.C.L. §262(h). However, the test for fairness is not a bifurcated one as between fair dealing and price. All aspects of the issue must be examined as a whole since the question is one of entire fairness. However, in a nonfraudulent transaction we recognize that price may be the preponderant consideration outweighing other features of the merger.

8. Since the plaintiffs carried their burden of piercing business judgment rule presumptions, why did the court in Smith v. Van Gorkom remand to the trial court with instructions to conduct a hearing on damages, rather than with instructions to first hold a hearing to determine whether the defendants could carry their burden of proving the transaction's entire fairness? Consider this *post hoc* explanation.

> In *Van Gorkom,* this Court concluded that the board of directors' failure to inform itself before recommending a merger to the stockholders constituted a breach of the fiduciary duty of care and rebutted the presumptive protection of the business judgment rule. Smith v. Van Gorkom, 488 A.2d at 893. In *Van Gorkom,* this Court also concluded that the directors had violated the duty of disclosure. This Court then held that the directors were liable for damages, since the record after trial reflected that the compound breaches of the duties of care and disclosure could not withstand an entire fairness analysis. Id.; accord In re Tri-Star Pictures, Inc. Litig., Del. Supr. 634 A.2d 319 (1993). Consequently, because this Court had decided the substantive entire fairness issue adversely to the

board in *Van Gorkom,* the only issue to remand was the amount of damages the Court of Chancery should assess in accordance with *Weinberger.*

Cinerama, Inc. v. Technicolor, Inc., 663 A.2d 1156, 1166 (Del. 1995).

9. Justice Horsey's opinion in Smith v. Van Gorkom indicates that an informed shareholder vote to approve the merger would have ratified and cured any breach of duty by the directors in failing to make an informed business judgment. This aspect of Smith v. Van Gorkom is no longer good law, as reflected in the following discussion in Gantler v. Stephens, 965 A.2d 695, 713 (Del. 2009):

> To restore coherence and clarity to this area of our law, we hold that the scope of the shareholder ratification doctrine must be limited to its so-called "classic" form; that is, to circumstances where a fully informed shareholder vote approves director action that does *not* legally require shareholder approval in order to become legally effective. Moreover, the only director action or conduct that can be ratified is that which the shareholders are specifically asked to approve. With one exception, the "cleansing" effect of such a ratifying shareholder vote is to subject the challenged director action to business judgment review, as opposed to "extinguishing" the claim altogether (*i.e.,* obviating all judicial review of the challenged action).

In a footnote to that discussion (id. at fn. 54) the *Gantler* court had this to say about *Van Gorkom:*

> To the extent that Smith v. Van Gorkom holds otherwise, it is overruled. 488 A.2d 858, 889-90 (Del.1985). The only species of claim that shareholder ratification can validly extinguish is a claim that the directors lacked the authority to take action that was later ratified. Nothing herein should be read as altering the well-established principle that void acts such as fraud, gift, waste and ultra vires acts cannot be ratified by a less than unanimous shareholder vote. See Michelson v. Duncan, 407 A.2d 211, 219 (Del.1979) ("[W]here a claim of gift or waste of assets, fraud or [u]ltra vires is asserted . . . a less than unanimous shareholder ratification is not a full defense."); see also Harbor Fin. Partners v. Huizenga, 751 A.2d 879, 896 (Del.Ch.1999) (explaining that ultra vires, fraud, and gift or waste of corporate assets are "void" acts that cannot be ratified by less than unanimous shareholder consent) accord Solomon v. Armstrong, 747 A.2d at 1115. "Voidable" acts are those beyond management's powers, but where they are performed in the best interests of the corporation they may be ratified by a majority vote of disinterested shareholders. See Michelson, 407 A.2d at 219.

PROBLEM 4-8

Vern Jonson is the founder and owns 30 percent of the stock of Hollywood Studios, Inc., which until its recent near bankruptcy was one of the world's leading producers of motion pictures. The other four board members are Martha Manson, who is Hollywood's executive vice president; Harvey Goldschmidt and Douglas Dancer, both former film stars now living in retirement in Hawaii; and Stuart Smith, the chief executive officer of a major industrial corporation. Since 2010, the Hollywood board has met six times a year via telephone conference, with an in-person annual meeting usually held in August as a part of a week-long golf outing in Hawaii.

In January 2014, Jonson and Manson developed a plan to radically change Hollywood's business strategy. Hollywood had for many years followed current industry practice in bidding for talent on a project-by-project basis. They envisioned a return to the 1930s-style studio, in which star actors, directors, and writers were under exclusive long-term contracts with Hollywood. Without informing the Hollywood board, Jonson and Manson engaged in intensive negotiations with targeted directors, actors, and writers. They soon realized that their strategy would succeed only if Hollywood were able to pay substantial bonuses to the stars. Accordingly, they began to secretly shop Hollywood's principal asset, its library of films, to a number of potential buyers. By the end of March, they had negotiated contracts with a number of leading actors, directors, and writers ("the salaried stars") and had reached agreement to sell Hollywood's film library in five separate transactions.

On March 31, 2014, Jonson called a special directors' meeting for 9 a.m. on April 1. The three outside directors attended by phone. Jonson outlined the plan to develop a 1930s-style studio, and described the negotiations with the salaried stars. He then outlined the contract terms, stressing that board approval must be given by 6 p.m. that day, or the contracts would lapse. Jonson accurately described the up-front financial commitment for bonus payments as $2.5 billion, stressed that "these payments must also be made by 6 p.m. today," and stated that in his opinion the "bonuses are a risk worth taking." He then outlined the terms of the five sales of Hollywood's film library for the total purchase price of $2.5 billion, and reported that "these sales will be closed at noon, assuming you guys approve all of this." He stated that "who knows what those films might appraise for? Maybe we could have gotten more, but I believe this is a great result given the time we had."

After a brief discussion, the board unanimously approved the contracts with the salaried stars, and the sales of the film library. The board was not provided with copies of any of the contracts involved. The board did not question the sums being paid out as bonuses, or the sums being received for the films. The meeting was adjourned at 10 p.m. By 6 p.m. on April 1, the film sales had been completed and all bonus payments made to the salaried stars.

Jonson and Manson planned a series of events to announce their "coup" and their vision of creating the industry's most powerful film studio. On April 3, 2014, Hollywood hosted a gala press conference in Los Angeles for the American media. The salaried stars then boarded a chartered plane to attend a second gala event scheduled for the following day in Paris. Unfortunately, the plane crashed en route, killing the salaried stars.

Because Hollywood had not obtained insurance on the lives of the salaried stars, this catastrophe left Hollywood essentially bankrupt. A shareholders' derivative suit has been filed against Jonson, Manson, and the three outside directors seeking to recover damages for breach of duty of care.

Will the Hollywood directors be liable for breach of the fiduciary duty of care? If so, to what relief would they be entitled?

3. Statutory Exculpation Provisions

MBCA §2.02(b)(4)
Delaware G.C.L. §102(b)(7)

Potential purchasers of corporate stock will be more likely to invest if they can be assured that directors will be reasonably diligent, skillful, and loyal in carrying out their duties. Rigorous judicial enforcement of directors' duty of care and loyalty may provide such assurance. As illustrated earlier in this chapter, the business judgment rule lessens the risk of unnecessary judicial interference with, or second-guessing of, directors' judgments. However, the decision in Smith v. Van Gorkom makes it clear that directors may incur substantial liability even when acting in good faith. Directors lacking protection against such risks could be expected to respond in either of two ways: (1) become overly cautious in carrying out their duties or (2) refuse to serve at all. Neither response would be in the shareholders' best interest, particularly if as a result corporations were unable to attract qualified "outside" directors.

Beginning with Delaware in 1986, approximately 40 states have now enacted legislation allowing corporations to limit or eliminate directors' liability for breach of fiduciary duty.

The following case illustrates how an exculpation clause works to lessen directors' exposure to the threat posed by the decision in Smith v. Van Gorkom.

Malpiede v. Townson
Supreme Court of Delaware, 2001
780 A.2d. 1075

Before VEASEY, CHIEF JUSTICE, WALSH, HOLLAND, BERGER, and STEELE, JUSTICES, constituting the Court en Banc.

VEASEY, CHIEF JUSTICE.

In this appeal, we affirm the holding of the Court of Chancery . . . granting . . . a motion to dismiss the plaintiffs' due care claim on the ground that the exculpatory provision in the charter of the target corporation authorized by 8 Del. C. §102(b)(7), bars any claim for money damages against the director defendants based solely on the board's alleged breach of its duty of care. . . .

FACTS

Frederick's of Hollywood ("Frederick's") is a retailer of women's lingerie and apparel with its headquarters in Los Angeles, California. This case centers on the merger of Frederick's into Knightsbridge Capital Corporation ("Knightsbridge") under circumstances where it became a target in a bidding contest. . . .

On June 14, 1996, the Frederick's board announced its decision to retain an investment bank, Janney Montgomery Scott, Inc. ("JMS"), to advise the board in its search for a suitable buyer for the company. In January 1997, JMS initiated talks with Knightsbridge. . . .

On June 13, 1997, the Frederick's board approved an offer from Knightsbridge to purchase all of Frederick's outstanding Class A and Class B shares for $6.14 per share in cash in a two-step merger transaction. The terms of the merger agreement signed by the Frederick's board prohibited the board from soliciting additional bids from third parties, but the agreement permitted the board to negotiate with third party bidders when the board's fiduciary duties required it to do so.[6] The Frederick's board then sent to stockholders a Consent Solicitation Statement recommending that they approve the transaction, which was scheduled to close on August 27, 1997.

On August 21, 1997, Frederick's received a fully financed, unsolicited cash offer of $7.00 per share from a third party bidder, Milton Partners ("Milton"). . . .

On August 27, 1997, the Frederick's board received a fully financed, unsolicited $7.75 cash offer from Veritas Capital Fund ("Veritas"). In light of these developments, the board postponed the Knightsbridge merger in order to arrange a meeting with the two new bidders. On September 2, 1997, the board sent a memorandum to Milton and Veritas outlining the conditions for participation in the bidding process. The memorandum required that the bidders each deposit $2.5 million in an escrow account and submit, before September 4, 1997, a marked-up merger agreement with the same basic terms as the Knightsbridge merger agreement. Veritas submitted a merger agreement and the $2.5 million escrow payment in accordance with these conditions. Milton did not.

On September 3, 1997, the Frederick's board met with representatives of Veritas to discuss the terms of the Veritas offer. According to the plaintiffs, the board asserts that, at this meeting, it orally informed Veritas that it was required to produce its "final, best offer" by September 4, 1997. The plaintiffs further allege that that board did not, in fact, inform Veritas of this requirement. . . .

On September 4, 1997, Knightsbridge . . . informed the board [that it now owned 41% of Frederick's common stock] and repeated its intention to vote the shares against any competing third party bids. . . .

On September 6, 1997, Knightsbridge increased its bid to match the $7.75 Veritas offer, but on the condition that the board accept a variety of terms designed to restrict its ability to pursue superior offers.[10] On the same day, the Frederick's board approved this agreement and effectively ended the bidding process. Two days later, Knightsbridge purchased additional Frederick's Class A shares on the open market, at an average price of $8.21 per share, thereby acquiring a majority of both classes of Frederick's shares.

On September 11, 1997, Veritas increased its cash offer to $9.00 per share. Relying on (1) the "no-talk" provision in the merger agreement, (2) Knightsbridge's stated intention to vote its shares against third party bids, and (3) Veritas' request for an option to dilute Knightsbridge's interest, the board rejected the revised Veritas bid. . . .

---

6. In the event that the Frederick's board terminated the merger agreement in order to accept a superior proposal by a third party bidder, the agreement entitled Knightsbridge to liquidated damages of $1.8 million.

10. The terms included: a provision prohibiting any Frederick's representative from speaking to third party bidders concerning the acquisition of the company (the "no-talk" provision); a termination fee of $4.5 million (about 7% of the value of the transaction); the appointment of a non-voting Knightsbridge observer at Frederick's board meetings; and an obligation to grant Knightsbridge any stock option that Frederick's granted to a competing bidder. The revised merger agreement did not expressly permit the Frederick's board to pursue negotiations with third parties where its fiduciary duties required it to do so.

Before the merger closed, the plaintiffs filed in the Court of Chancery the purported class action complaint that is the predecessor of the amended complaint before us. . . .

The Court of Chancery granted the directors' motion to dismiss the amended complaint under Chancery Rule 12(b)(6), concluding that . . . the exculpatory provision in the Frederick's charter precluded money damages against the directors for any breach of the board's duty of care. . . .

THE DUE CARE CLAIM

Having concluded that the complaint was properly dismissed under Chancery Rule 12(b)(6) for failure to state a claim on which relief may be granted on other fiduciary duty claims, we now turn to the due care claim. The primary due care issue is whether the board was grossly negligent, and therefore breached its duty of due care, in failing to implement a routine defensive strategy that could enable the board to negotiate for a higher bid or otherwise create a tactical advantage to enhance stockholder value.

In this case, that routine strategy would have been for the directors to use a poison pill to ward off Knightsbridge's advances and thus to prevent Knightsbridge from stopping the auction process. Had they done so, plaintiffs seem to allege that the directors could have preserved the appropriate options for an auction process designed to achieve the best value for the stockholders.

Construing the amended complaint most favorably to the plaintiffs, it can be read to allege that the board was grossly negligent in immediately accepting the Knightsbridge offer and agreeing to various restrictions on further negotiations without first determining whether Veritas would issue a counteroffer. Although the board had conducted a search for a buyer over one year, plaintiffs seem to contend that the board was imprudently hasty in agreeing to a restrictive merger agreement on the day it was proposed — particularly where other bidders had recently expressed interest. Although the board's haste, in itself, might not constitute a breach of the board's duty of care because the board had already conducted a lengthy sale process, the plaintiffs argue that the board's decision to accept allegedly extreme contractual restrictions impacted its ability to obtain a higher sale price. Recognizing that, at the end of the day, plaintiffs would have an uphill battle in overcoming the presumption of the business judgment rule, we must give plaintiffs the benefit of the doubt at this pleading stage to determine if they have stated a due care claim. Because of our ultimate decision, however, we need not finally decide this question in this case.

We assume, therefore, without deciding, that a claim for relief based on gross negligence during the board's auction process is stated by the inferences most favorable to plaintiffs that flow from these allegations. The issue then becomes whether the amended complaint may be dismissed upon a Rule 12(b)(6) motion by reason of the existence and the legal effect of the exculpatory provision of Article TWELFTH of Frederick's certificate of incorporation, adopted pursuant to 8 Del. C. §102(b)(7). That provision would exempt directors from personal liability in damages with certain exceptions (e.g., breach of the duty of loyalty) that are not applicable here. . . .[45]

B. APPLICATION OF EMERALD PARTNERS

We now address plaintiffs' argument that the trial court committed error, based on certain language in *Emerald Partners*,[57] by barring their due care claims. Plaintiffs' arguments on this point are based on an erroneous premise, and our decision here is not inconsistent with *Emerald Partners*.

In *Emerald Partners*, we made two important points about the raising of Section 102(b)(7) charter provisions. First we said: "[T]he shield from liability provided by a certificate of incorporation provision adopted pursuant to 8 Del. C. §102(b)(7) is in the nature of an affirmative defense."[58] Second, we said:

> [W]here the factual basis for a claim solely implicates a violation of the duty of care, this court has indicated that the protections of such a charter provision may properly be invoked and applied. Arnold v. Society for Savings Bancorp., Del.Supr., 650 A.2d 1270, 1288 (1994); Zirn v. VLI Corp., Del.Supr., 681 A.2d 1050, 1061 (1996).[59]

Based on this language in *Emerald Partners*, plaintiffs make two arguments. First, they argue that the Court of Chancery in this case should not have dismissed their due care claims because these claims are intertwined with, and thus indistinguishable from, the duty of loyalty and bad faith claims. Second, plaintiffs contend that the Court of Chancery incorrectly assigned to them the burden of going forward with proof.

1. The Court of Chancery Properly Dismissed Claims Based Solely on the Duty of Care

Plaintiffs here, while not conceding that the Section 102(b)(7) charter provision may be considered on this Rule 12(b)(6) motion nevertheless, in effect, conceded in oral argument in the Court of Chancery and similarly in oral argument in this Court that if a complaint unambiguously and solely asserted only a due care claim, the complaint is dismissible once the corporation's Section 102(b)(7) provision is invoked. This concession is in line with our holding in *Emerald Partners* quoted above.

---

45. Article TWELFTH provides:

TWELFTH. A director of this Corporation shall not be personally liable to the Corporation or its shareholders for monetary damages for breach of fiduciary duty as a director, except for liability (i) for any breach of the director's duty of loyalty to the Corporation or its shareholders, (ii) for acts or omissions not in good faith or which involve intentional misconduct or a knowing violation of law (iii) under Section 174 of the Delaware General Corporation Law, or (iv) for any transaction for which the director derived an improper personal benefit.

57. 726 A.2d at 1223-24.
58. Id. at 1223.
59. Id. at 1224.

Plaintiffs contended vigorously, however, that the Section 102(b)(7) charter provision does not apply to bar their claims in this case because the amended complaint alleges breaches of the duty of loyalty and other claims that are not barred by the charter provision. As a result, plaintiffs maintain, this case cannot be boiled down solely to a due care case. They argue, in effect, that their complaint is sufficiently well-pleaded that — *as a matter of law* — the due care claims are so inextricably intertwined with loyalty and bad faith claims that Section 102(b)(7) is not a bar to recovery of damages against the directors.

We disagree. It is the plaintiffs who have a burden to set forth "a short and plain statement of the claim showing that the pleader is entitled to relief." The plaintiffs are entitled to all reasonable inferences flowing from their pleadings, but if those inferences do not support a valid legal claim, the complaint should be dismissed without the need for the defendants to file an answer and without proceeding with discovery. Here we have assumed, without deciding, that the amended complaint on its face states a due care claim. Because we have determined that the complaint fails properly to invoke loyalty and bad faith claims, we are left with only a due care claim. Defendants had the obligation to raise the bar of Section 102(b)(7) as a defense, and they did. As plaintiffs conceded in oral argument before this Court, if there is only an unambiguous, residual due care claim and nothing else — *as a matter of law* — then Section 102(b)(7) would bar the claim. Accordingly, the Court of Chancery did not err in dismissing the plaintiffs' due care claim in this case.

2. The Court of Chancery Correctly Applied the Parties' Respective Burdens of Proof

Plaintiffs also assert that the trial court in the case before us incorrectly placed on plaintiffs a pleading burden to negate the elements of the 102(b)(7) charter provision. . . .

But we have held that the amended complaint here does not allege a loyalty violation or other violation falling within the exceptions to the Section 102(b)(7) exculpation provision. Likewise, we have held that, even if the plaintiffs had stated a claim for gross negligence, such a well-pleaded claim is unavailing because defendants have brought forth the Section 102(b)(7) charter provision that bars such claims. This is the end of the case.

And rightly so, as a matter of the public policy of this State. Section 102(b)(7) was adopted by the Delaware General Assembly in 1986 following a directors and officers insurance liability crisis and the 1985 Delaware Supreme Court decision in Smith v. Van Gorkom. The purpose of this statute was to permit stockholders to adopt a provision in the certificate of incorporation to free directors of personal liability in damages for due care violations, but not duty of loyalty violations, bad faith claims and certain other conduct. Such a charter provision, when adopted, would not affect injunctive proceedings based on gross negligence.[60] Once the statute was adopted, stockholders

---

60. See R. Franklin Balotti & Jesse A. Finkelstein, Delaware Law of Corporations & Business Organizations, 1-11, 1-12 (3d ed. 1998) (setting forth the Comment that accompanied the legislation explaining its purposes and effect); see also E. Norman Veasey, Jesse A. Finkelstein and C. Stephen

usually approved charter amendments containing these provisions because it freed up directors to take business risks without worrying about negligence lawsuits.

Our jurisprudence since the adoption of the statute has consistently stood for the proposition that a Section 102(b)(7) charter provision bars a claim that is found to state only a due care violation. Because we have assumed that the amended complaint here does state a due care claim, the exculpation afforded by the statute must affirmatively be raised by the defendant directors.[71] The directors have done so in this case, and the Court of Chancery properly applied the Frederick's charter provision to dismiss the plaintiffs' due care claim.

NOTES AND QUESTIONS

1. To what extent should fiduciary duty be considered an immutable rule? If it is simply a gap-filling device, should not parties be able to contract for specific rules? Or is it simply irrational to bargain away in advance the protections of fiduciary duty? Is there a difference between contracting for specific rules and simply eliminating liability for breach of fiduciary duty? Are exculpation provisions that eliminate money damages for certain breaches less troublesome than provisions that allow or directly eliminate fiduciary duty? Should lawmakers be especially protective of shareholders in publicly held corporations who might apathetically or ignorantly approve an exculpation provision?

2. For an argument that fiduciary duty cannot be contractually reduced below an immutable obligation to act in good faith, see Coffee, The Mandatory/Enabling Balance in Corporate Law: An Essay on the Judicial Role, 89 Colum. L. Rev. 1618 (1989). For thorough discussion of the contractual model of the corporation and the

---

Bigler, "Delaware Supports Directors with a Three-Legged Stool of Limited Liability, Indemnification and Insurance," 42 Bus. Law, 399-404 (1987):

> While courts have traditionally expressed deference to the judgment of directors, the directors' views and actions have not uniformly been outcome-determinative. Flaws in the directors' decision-making processes have often resulted in their decisions blowing up in their faces. . . .
>
> No doubt every director of a public company is painfully aware of the celebrated damage case of Smith v. Van Gorkom, where directors were found personally liable in damages for gross negligence in hastily approving a merger transaction. . . .
>
> Delaware has adopted new legislation modifying indemnification rights and allowing a certificate of incorporation to contain a provision limiting or eliminating the personal monetary liability of directors in certain circumstances. . . .
>
> Section 102(b)(7) is not, and was not intended to be, a panacea for directors. In addition, new section 102(b)(7) does not eliminate the duty of care that is properly imposed upon directors. . . .
>
> While section 102(b)(7) may not be a panacea, it provides a layer of protection for directors by allowing stockholders to dramatically reduce the type of situations in which a director's personal wealth is put "on the line. . . ."

71. Although an exculpatory charter provision is "in the nature of an affirmative defense" under *Emerald Partners*, the board is not required to disprove claims based on alleged breaches of the duty of loyalty to gain the protection of the provision with respect to due care claims. Rather, proving the existence of a valid exculpatory provision in the corporate charter entitles directors to dismissal of any claims for money damages against them that are based solely on alleged breaches of the board's duty of care. . . .

extent to which lawmakers should protect shareholders from themselves by making fiduciary duty or other constraints on management immutable, see Bebchuk, The Debate on Contractual Freedom in Corporate Law, 89 Colum. L. Rev. 1395 (1985); Bebchuk, Limiting Contractual Freedom in Corporate Law: The Desirable Constraints on Charter Amendments, 102 Harv. L. Rev. 1820 (1989); Butler and Ribstein, Opting Out of Fiduciary Duties: A Response to the Anti-Contractarians, 65 Wash. L. Rev. 1 (1990); Coffee, No Exit?: Opting Out, the Contractual Theory of the Corporation, and the Special Case of Remedies, 53 Brooklyn L. Rev. 919 (1988); Thompson, The Law's Limits on Contracts in a Corporation, 15 J. Corp. L. 377 (1990).

3. For detailed analysis of the directors' exculpation provisions, see Hanks, Evaluating Recent State Legislation on Director and Officer Liability Limitation and Indemnification, 43 Bus. Law. 1207 (1988); Oesterle, The Effect of Statutes Limiting Directors' Due Care Liability on Hostile Takeover Defenses, 24 Wake Forest L. Rev. 31 (1989).

4. As we saw in Smith v. Van Gorkom, directors have a duty of candor when asking shareholders to take action. Can a corporation exculpate directors for personal liability for breach of the duty of candor? In Delaware, the answer depends on whether the candor violation occurs as a result of a good faith action which nonetheless breaches the duty of care, or instead, arises either from bad faith or disloyal conduct.

> [T]he VLI directors are shielded from liability by Delaware G.C.L. §102(b)(7) and the amendment to VLI's Certificate of Incorporation giving effect to that statutory provision. The record reveals that any misstatements or omissions that occurred were made in good faith. The VLI directors lacked any pecuniary motive to mislead the VLI stockholders intentionally and no other plausible motive for deceiving the stockholders has been advanced. A good faith erroneous judgment as to the proper scope or content of required disclosure implicates the duty of care rather than the duty of loyalty. Arnold v. Society for Savings Bancorp., Inc., 650 A.2d at 1287-1288 & n. 36. Thus, the disclosure violations at issue here fall within the ambit of the protection of section 102(b)(7).

Zirn v. VLI Corp., 681 A.2d 1050, 1061-1062 (Del. 1996).

5. When a corporation agrees to exculpate its directors, it is understood that the shareholders are contracting away any right shareholders might otherwise have to hold the directors liable for damages caused solely by the directors' breach of the duty of care. However, should creditors be held to have contracted away their rights to pursue damage claims when the directors' lack of care allegedly has caused the corporation to go bankrupt? Consider the following analysis by Vice Chancellor Strine.

> One of the primary purposes of §102(b)(7) is to encourage directors to undertake risky, but potentially value-maximizing, business strategies, so long as they do so in good faith. To expose directors to liability for breach of the duty of care for derivative claims of mismanagement asserted by creditors guts this purpose by denying directors the protection of §102(b)(7) when they arguably need it most. That is, when, despite the directors' good intentions, the business plan of the firm did not generate financial success and the firm has become insolvent, the possibility of hindsight bias about the directors' prior ability to foresee that their business plans would not pan out is at its zenith and when the exculpatory charter provision is most useful.
>
> Furthermore, it is odd to think that creditors would be afforded greater leeway to press derivative claims than stockholders. Creditors are typically better positioned than stockholders to protect themselves by the simple tool of contracting. And a body of statutory law called the law of fraudulent conveyance exists specifically to protect creditors. The reality that creditors become the

residual claimants of a corporation when the equity of the corporation has no value does not justify expanding the types of claims that the corporation itself has against its directors. It simply justifies enabling creditors to exercise standing to ensure that any valuable claims the corporation possesses against its directors are prosecuted.

Production Resources Group, L.L.C. v. NCT Group, Inc., 863 A.2d 772, 777 (Del. Ch. 2004).

4. The Intersection of the Fiduciary Duties of Care and Loyalty (Including the Duty of Good Faith)

a. Introduction

For a short time, the Delaware Supreme Court's opinion in Smith v. Van Gorkom appeared to significantly expand the universe of potentially viable fiduciary duty claims against directors. As discussed in Malpiede v. Townson, Delaware G.C.L. §102(b)(7) and similar exculpation statutes adopted in other states soon after the decision in *Van Gorkom* allowed corporations and their shareholders to slam the door on damage claims based solely on claimed breaches of the duty of care. However, this still left an expanded role for the duty of care with respect to injunctive claims and lawsuits involving more than the duty of care alone.

The language of Delaware G.C.L. §102(b)(7) also created a new battleground for testing the contours of the business judgment rule. Under §102(b)(7), a corporation may not provide exculpation for breaches of the duty of loyalty, or "for acts or omissions not in good faith. . . ." This phraseology caused litigants and judges to focus on the so-called duty of good faith and its relationship to the duties of care and loyalty. Evidencing this new focus on good faith, the Delaware Supreme Court in 1993 began to refer to directors' fiduciary duty as having three components—care, loyalty, and good faith. Cede v Technicolor, Inc., 634 A.2d 345, 361 (Del. 1993). More than a decade later, the court decided that good faith was actually a subpart of the duty of loyalty.

[A]lthough good faith may be described colloquially as part of a "triad" of fiduciary duties that includes the duties of care and loyalty, the obligation to act in good faith does not establish an independent fiduciary duty that stands on the same footing as the duties of care and loyalty. . . . [T]he fiduciary duty of loyalty is not limited to cases involving a financial or other cognizable fiduciary conflict of interest. It also encompasses cases where the fiduciary fails to act in good faith.

Stone v. Ritter, 911 A.2d 362, 370 (Del. 2006).

As you read the cases in this section, be acutely aware of the interplay involved. Plaintiffs' counsel are looking for ways in which to expand the role of the duty of care in circumstances where exculpation has not foreclosed the viability of care-based claims. Additionally, plaintiffs' counsel are exploring the possibility that care-based claims barred by exculpation may be repackaged as non-exculpable claims based on directors' "acts or omissions not in good faith." Defendants' counsel are responding to the ever shifting strategies of plaintiffs' counsel with doctrinal and policy arguments that point to lesser governance role for fiduciary litigation, however packaged.

Judges, of course, determine the ultimate answers to the doctrinal and policy questions posed by litigants. However, judges are not neutral bystanders. Instead, judges, some more than others, play a central role in the development of new doctrinal understandings. Sometimes, judges seem to be advocating for new doctrinal understandings as keenly as litigants' counsel. In the aftermath of Smith v. Van Gorkom, this judicial advocacy has been particularly present in cases dealing with the nature of the duties of care and good faith. Be alert as you read the cases in this section to the advocacy role being played not only by litigants, but by the court.

b. Care, Good Faith, and Directors' Oversight Responsibilities

MBCA §§8.30, 8.42

It has long been "black letter" law that "the business and affairs of the corporation shall be managed by or under the direction of, and *subject to the oversight of,* its board of directors." MBCA §8.01(b) (emphasis supplied).

However, until the last century's end, there was almost no case law explicating the directors' oversight duties. That situation began to change in 1996 with Chancellor Allen's opinion in the principal case below, which kindled debate about directors' oversight duties. Importantly, the opinion also served as a centerpiece of the post-Smith v. Van Gorkom debate over the proper role of the duty of care, and the post-exculpation-statute-enactment debate about the nature and role of the duty of good faith.

In re Caremark International, Inc. Derivative Litigation
Delaware Court of Chancery, 1996
698 A.2d 959

OPINION

ALLEN, CHANCELLOR.

Pending is a motion pursuant to Chancery Rule 23.1 to approve as fair and reasonable a proposed settlement of a consolidated derivative action on behalf of Caremark International, Inc. ("Caremark").

I. BACKGROUND

For these purposes I regard the following facts, suggested by the discovery record, as material. Caremark, a Delaware corporation with its headquarters in Northbrook, Illinois, was created in November 1992 when it was spun-off from Baxter International, Inc. ("Baxter") and became a publicly held company listed on the New York Stock Exchange.[1] The business practices that created the problem pre-dated the spin-off.

---

1. Thirteen of the Directors have been members of the Board since November 30, 1992. Nancy Brinker joined the Board in October 1993. [Eds. note—This footnote appears at a different location in the unedited, official version of this opinion.]

During the relevant period Caremark was involved in two main health care business segments, providing patient care and managed care services. As part of its patient care business, which accounted for the majority of Caremark's revenues, Caremark provided alternative site health care services, including infusion therapy, growth hormone therapy, HIV/AIDS-related treatments and hemophilia therapy. Caremark's managed care services included prescription drug programs and the operation of multi-specialty group practices.

A.   EVENTS PRIOR TO THE GOVERNMENT INVESTIGATION

A substantial part of the revenues generated by Caremark's businesses is derived from third party payments, insurers, and Medicare and Medicaid reimbursement programs. The latter source of payments are subject to the terms of the Anti-Referral Payments Law ("ARPL") which prohibits health care providers from paying any form of remuneration to induce the referral of Medicare or Medicaid patients. From its inception, Caremark entered into a variety of agreements with hospitals, physicians, and health care providers for advice and services, as well as distribution agreements with drug manufacturers, as had its predecessor prior to 1992. Specifically, Caremark did have a practice of entering into contracts for services (e.g., consultation agreements and research grants) with physicians at least some of whom prescribed or recommended services or products that Caremark provided to Medicare recipients and other patients. Such contracts were not prohibited by the ARPL but they obviously raised a possibility of unlawful "kickbacks."

As early as 1989, Caremark's predecessor issued an internal "Guide to Contractual Relationships" ("Guide") to govern its employees in entering into contracts with physicians and hospitals. The Guide tended to be reviewed annually by lawyers and updated. Each version of the Guide stated as Caremark's and its predecessor's policy that no payments would be made in exchange for or to induce patient referrals. But what one might deem a prohibited *quid pro quo* was not always clear. Due to a scarcity of court decisions interpreting the ARPL, however, Caremark repeatedly publicly stated that there was uncertainty concerning Caremark's interpretation of the law.

To clarify the scope of the ARPL, the United States Department of Health and Human Services ("HHS") issued "safe harbor" regulations in July 1991 stating conditions under which financial relationships between health care service providers and patient referral sources, such as physicians, would not violate the ARPL. Caremark contends that the narrowly drawn regulations gave limited guidance as to the legality of many of the agreements used by Caremark that did not fall within the safe-harbor. Caremark's predecessor, however, amended many of its standard forms of agreement with health care providers and revised the Guide in an apparent attempt to comply with the new regulations.

B.   GOVERNMENT INVESTIGATION AND RELATED LITIGATION

In August 1991, the HHS Office of the Inspector General ("OIG") initiated an investigation of Caremark's predecessor. Caremark's predecessor was served with a subpoena requiring the production of documents, including contracts between Caremark's predecessor and physicians (Quality Service Agreements ("QSAs")). Under the QSAs, Caremark's predecessor appears to have paid physicians fees for monitoring patients under Caremark's predecessor's care, including Medicare and Medicaid recipients. Sometimes apparently those monitoring patients were referring physicians, which raised ARPL concerns.

In March 1992, the Department of Justice ("DOJ") joined the OIG investigation and separate investigations were commenced by several additional federal and state agencies.[2]

C. CAREMARK'S RESPONSE TO THE INVESTIGATION

During the relevant period, Caremark had approximately 7,000 employees and ninety branch operations. It had a decentralized management structure. By May 1991, however, Caremark asserts that it had begun making attempts to centralize its management structure in order to increase supervision over its branch operations.

The first action taken by management, as a result of the initiation of the OIG investigation, was an announcement that as of October 1, 1991, Caremark's predecessor would no longer pay management fees to physicians for services to Medicare and Medicaid patients. Despite this decision, Caremark asserts that its management, pursuant to advice, did not believe that such payments were illegal under the existing laws and regulations.

During this period, Caremark's Board took several additional steps consistent with an effort to assure compliance with company policies concerning the ARPL and the contractual forms in the Guide. In April 1992, Caremark published a fourth revised version of its Guide apparently designed to assure that its agreements either complied with the ARPL and regulations or excluded Medicare and Medicaid patients altogether. In addition, in September 1992, Caremark instituted a policy requiring its regional officers, Zone Presidents, to approve each contractual relationship entered into by Caremark with a physician.

Although there is evidence that inside and outside counsel had advised Caremark's directors that their contracts were in accord with the law, Caremark recognized that some uncertainty respecting the correct interpretation of the law existed. In its 1992 annual report, Caremark disclosed the ongoing government investigations, acknowledged that if penalties were imposed on the company they could have a material adverse effect on Caremark's business, and stated that no assurance could be given that its interpretation of the ARPL would prevail if challenged.

Throughout the period of the government investigations, Caremark had an internal audit plan designed to assure compliance with business and ethics policies. In

---

2. In addition to investigating whether Caremark's financial relationships with health care providers were intended to induce patient referrals, inquiries were made concerning Caremark's billing practices, activities which might lead to excessive and medically unnecessary treatments for patients, potentially improper waivers of patient co-payment obligations, and the adequacy of records kept at Caremark pharmacies.

addition, Caremark employed Price Waterhouse as its outside auditor. On February 8, 1993, the Ethics Committee of Caremark's Board received and reviewed an outside auditor's report by Price Waterhouse which concluded that there were no material weaknesses in Caremark's control structure.[3] Despite the positive findings of Price Waterhouse, however, on April 20, 1993, the Audit & Ethics Committee adopted a new internal audit charter requiring a comprehensive review of compliance policies and the compilation of an employee ethics handbook concerning such policies.[4]

The Board appears to have been informed about this project and other efforts to assure compliance with the law. For example, Caremark's management reported to the Board that Caremark's sales force was receiving an ongoing education regarding the ARPL and the proper use of Caremark's form contracts which had been approved by in-house counsel. On July 27, 1993, the new ethics manual, expressly prohibiting payments in exchange for referrals and requiring employees to report all illegal conduct to a toll free confidential ethics hotline, was approved and allegedly disseminated.[5] The record suggests that Caremark continued these policies in subsequent years, causing employees to be given revised versions of the ethics manual and requiring them to participate in training sessions concerning compliance with the law.

During 1993, Caremark took several additional steps which appear to have been aimed at increasing management supervision. These steps included new policies requiring local branch managers to secure home office approval for all disbursements under agreements with health care providers and to certify compliance with the ethics program. In addition, the chief financial officer was appointed to serve as Caremark's compliance officer. In 1994, a fifth revised Guide was published.

D. FEDERAL INDICTMENTS AGAINST CAREMARK
AND OFFICERS

On August 4, 1994, a federal grand jury in Minnesota issued a 47 page indictment charging Caremark, two of its officers (not the firm's chief officer), an individual who had been a sales employee of Genentech, Inc., and David R. Brown, a physician practicing in Minneapolis, with violating the ARPL over a lengthy period. According to the indictment, over $1.1 million had been paid to Brown to induce him to distribute Protropin, a human growth hormone drug marketed by Caremark.[6] The substantial

---

3. At that time, Price Waterhouse viewed the outcome of the OIG Investigation as uncertain. After further audits, however, on February 7, 1995, Price Waterhouse informed the Audit & Ethics Committee that it had not become aware of any irregularities or illegal acts in relation to the OIG investigation.

4. Price Waterhouse worked in conjunction with the Internal Audit Department.

5. Prior to the distribution of the new ethics manual, on March 12, 1993, Caremark's president had sent a letter to all senior, district, and branch managers restating Caremark's policies that no physician be paid for referrals, that the standard contract forms in the Guide were not to be modified, and that deviation from such policies would result in the immediate termination of employment.

6. In addition to prescribing Protropin, Dr. Brown had been receiving research grants from Caremark as well as payments for services under a consulting agreement for several years before and after the investigation. According to an undated document from an unknown source, Dr. Brown and six other researchers had been providing patient referrals to Caremark valued at $6.55 for each $1 of research money they received.

payments involved started, according to the allegations of the indictment, in 1986 and continued through 1993. Some payments were "in the guise of research grants," and others were "consulting agreements." The indictment charged, for example, that Dr. Brown performed virtually none of the consulting functions described in his 1991 agreement with Caremark, but was nevertheless neither required to return the money he had received nor precluded from receiving future funding from Caremark. In addition the indictment charged that Brown received from Caremark payments of staff and office expenses, including telephone answering services and fax rental expenses.

In reaction to the Minnesota Indictment and the subsequent filing of this and other derivative actions in 1994, the Board met and was informed by management that the investigation had resulted in an indictment; Caremark denied any wrongdoing relating to the indictment and believed that the OIG investigation would have a favorable outcome. Management reiterated the grounds for its view that the contracts were in compliance with law.

Subsequently, five stockholder derivative actions were filed in this court and consolidated into this action. The original complaint, dated August 5, 1994, alleged, in relevant part, that Caremark's directors breached their duty of care by failing adequately to supervise the conduct of Caremark employees, or institute corrective measures, thereby exposing Caremark to fines and liability.[7]

On September 21, 1994, a federal grand jury in Columbus, Ohio issued another indictment alleging that an Ohio physician had defrauded the Medicare program by requesting and receiving $134,600 in exchange for referrals of patients whose medical costs were in part reimbursed by Medicare in violation of the ARPL. Although unidentified at that time, Caremark was the health care provider who allegedly made such payments. The indictment also charged that the physician, Elliot Neufeld, D.O., was provided with the services of a registered nurse to work in his office at the expense of the infusion company, in addition to free office equipment. . . .*

The third, and final, amended complaint was filed on April 11, 1995, adding allegations that the federal indictments had caused Caremark to incur significant legal fees and forced it to sell its home infusion business at a loss. . . .[8]

E. SETTLEMENT NEGOTIATIONS

In September, following the announcement of the Ohio indictment, Caremark publicly announced that as of January 1, 1995, it would terminate all remaining financial relationships with physicians in its home infusion, hemophilia, and growth

---

7. Caremark moved to dismiss this complaint on September 14, 1994. Prior to that motion, another stockholder derivative action had been filed in the United States District Court for the Northern District of Illinois, complaining of similar misconduct on the part of Caremark, its Directors, and three employees, as well as several other claims including RICO violations. Brumberg v. Mieszala, No. 94 C 4798 (N.D. Ill.). The federal court entered a stay of all proceedings pending resolution of this case.

* [Eds. note—The complaint was twice thereafter amended to include new allegations of fraud.]

8. On January 29, 1995, Caremark entered into a definitive agreement to sell its home infusion business to Coram Health Care Company for approximately $310 million. Baxter purchased the home infusion business in 1987 for $586 million.

hormone lines of business.[9] In addition, Caremark asserts that it extended its restrictive policies to all of its contractual relationships with physicians, rather than just those involving Medicare and Medicaid patients, and terminated its research grant program which had always involved some recipients who referred patients to Caremark.

Caremark began settlement negotiations with federal and state government entities in May 1995. In return for a guilty plea to a single count of mail fraud by the corporation, the payment of a criminal fine, the payment of substantial civil damages, and cooperation with further federal investigations on matters relating to the OIG investigation, the government entities agreed to negotiate a settlement that would permit Caremark to continue participating in Medicare and Medicaid programs. On June 15, 1995, the Board approved a settlement ("Government Settlement Agreement") with the DOJ, OIG, U.S. Veterans Administration, U.S. Federal Employee Health Benefits Program, Federal Civilian Health and Medical Program of the Uniformed Services, and related state agencies in all fifty states and the District of Columbia.[10] No senior officers or directors were charged with wrongdoing in the Government Settlement Agreement or in any of the prior indictments. In fact, as part of the sentencing in the Ohio action on June 19, 1995, the United States stipulated that *no senior executive of Caremark participated in, condoned, or was willfully ignorant of wrongdoing in connection with the home infusion business practices.*

The federal settlement included certain provisions in a "Corporate Integrity Agreement" designed to enhance future compliance with law. The parties have not discussed this agreement, except to say that the negotiated provisions of the settlement of this claim are not redundant of those in that agreement.

Settlement negotiations between the parties in this action commenced in May 1995 as well, based upon a letter proposal of the plaintiffs, dated May 16, 1995. These negotiations resulted in a memorandum of understanding ("MOU"), dated June 7, 1995, and the execution of the Stipulation and Agreement of Compromise and Settlement on June 28, 1995, which is the subject of this action.[13] The MOU, approved by the Board on June 15, 1995, required the Board to adopt several resolutions, discussed below, and to create a new compliance committee. The Compliance and Ethics Committee has been reporting to the Board in accord with its newly specified duties.

After negotiating these settlements, Caremark learned in December 1995 that several private insurance company payors ("Private Payors") believed that Caremark was liable for damages to them for allegedly improper business practices related to those at issue in the OIG investigation. As a result of intensive negotiations with the

---

9. On June 1, 1993, Caremark had stopped entering into new contractual agreements in those business segments.

10. The agreement, covering allegations since 1986, required a Caremark subsidiary to enter a guilty plea to two counts of mail fraud, and required Caremark to pay $29 million in criminal fines, $129.9 million relating to civil claims concerning payment practices, $3.5 million for alleged violations of the Controlled Substances Act, and $2 million, in the form of a donation, to a grant program set up by the Ryan White Comprehensive AIDS Resources Emergency Act. Caremark also agreed to enter into a compliance agreement with the HHS.

13. Plaintiffs' initial proposal had both a monetary component, requiring Caremark's director-officers to relinquish stock options, and a remedial component, requiring management to adopt and implement several compliance related measures. The monetary component was subsequently eliminated.

Private Payors and the Board's extensive consideration of the alternatives for dealing with such claims, the Board approved a $98.5 million settlement agreement with the Private Payors on March 18, 1996. In its public disclosure statement, Caremark asserted that the settlement did not involve current business practices and contained an express denial of any wrongdoing by Caremark. After further discovery in this action, the plaintiffs decided to continue seeking approval of the proposed settlement agreement.

F. THE PROPOSED SETTLEMENT OF THIS LITIGATION

In relevant part the terms upon which these claims asserted are proposed to be settled are as follows:

1. That Caremark, undertakes that it and its employees, and agents not pay any form of compensation to a third party in exchange for the referral of a patient to a Caremark facility or service or the prescription of drugs marketed or distributed by Caremark for which reimbursement may be sought from Medicare, Medicaid, or a similar state reimbursement program;

2. That Caremark, undertakes for itself and its employees, and agents not to pay to or split fees with physicians, joint ventures, any business combination in which Caremark maintains a direct financial interest, or other health care providers with whom Caremark has a financial relationship or interest, in exchange for the referral of a patient to a Caremark facility or service or the prescription of drugs marketed or distributed by Caremark for which reimbursement may be sought from Medicare, Medicaid, or a similar state reimbursement program;

3. That the full Board shall discuss all relevant material changes in government health care regulations and their effect on relationships with health care providers on a semi-annual basis;

4. That Caremark's officers will remove all personnel from health care facilities or hospitals who have been placed in such facility for the purpose of providing remuneration in exchange for a patient referral for which reimbursement may be sought from Medicare, Medicaid, or a similar state reimbursement program;

5. That every patient will receive written disclosure of any financial relationship between Caremark and the health care professional or provider who made the referral;

6. That the Board will establish a Compliance and Ethics Committee of four directors, two of which will be non-management directors, to meet at least four times a year to effectuate these policies and monitor business segment compliance with the ARPL, and to report to the Board semi-annually concerning compliance by each business segment; and

7. That corporate officers responsible for business segments shall serve as compliance officers who must report semi-annually to the Compliance and Ethics Committee and, with the assistance of outside counsel, review existing contracts and get advanced approval of any new contract forms.

II.   LEGAL PRINCIPLES . . .

B.   DIRECTORS' DUTIES TO MONITOR CORPORATE OPERATIONS

The complaint charges the director defendants with breach of their duty of attention or care in connection with the on-going operation of the corporation's business. The claim is that the directors allowed a situation to develop and continue which exposed the corporation to enormous legal liability and that in so doing they violated a duty to be active monitors of corporate performance. The complaint thus does not charge either director self-dealing or the more difficult loyalty-type problems arising from cases of suspect director motivation, such as entrenchment or sale of control contexts. The theory here advanced is possibly the most difficult theory in corporation law upon which a plaintiff might hope to win a judgment. The good policy reasons why it is so difficult to charge directors with responsibility for corporate losses for an alleged breach of care, where there is no conflict of interest or no facts suggesting suspect motivation involved, were recently described in Gagliardi v. Trifoods Int'l, Inc., Del. Ch., 683 A.2d 1049, 1051 (1996).

1.   Potential liability for directoral decisions

Director liability for a breach of the duty to exercise appropriate attention may, in theory, arise in two distinct contexts. First, such liability may be said to follow *from a board decision* that results in a loss because that decision was ill advised or "negligent." Second, liability to the corporation for a loss may be said to arise from an *unconsidered failure of the board to act* in circumstances in which due attention would, arguably, have prevented the loss. The first class of cases will typically be subject to review under the director-protective business judgment rule, assuming the decision made was the product of *a process* that was *either* deliberately considered in good faith or was otherwise rational. See Aronson v. Lewis, 473 A.2d 805 (1984); Gagliardi v. Trifoods Int'l, Inc., 683 A.2d 1049 (Del.Ch. 1996). What should be understood, but may not widely be understood by courts or commentators who are not often required to face such questions,[15] is that compliance with a director's duty of care can never appropriately be judicially determined by reference to *the content of the board decision* that leads to a corporate loss, apart from consideration of the good faith or rationality of the process employed. That is, whether a judge or jury considering the matter after the fact, believes a decision substantively wrong, or degrees of wrong extending through "stupid" to "egregious" or "irrational," provides no ground for director liability, so long as the court determines that the process employed was either rational or employed in a *good faith* effort to advance corporate interests. To employ a different rule—one that permitted an "objective" evaluation of the decision—would expose directors to substantive second guessing by ill-equipped judges or juries, which would, in the long-run, be injurious to investor interests.[16] Thus, the business judgment rule is process oriented and informed by a deep respect for all *good faith* board decisions.

---

15. *See* American Law Institute, Principles of Corporate Governance §4.01(c) (to qualify for business judgment treatment a director must "rationally" believe that the decision is in the best interests of the corporation).

16. The vocabulary of negligence while often employed, e.g., Aronson v. Lewis, 473 A.2d 805 (Del. 1984), is not well-suited to judicial review of board attentiveness, see, e.g., Joy v. North, 692 F.2d 880, 885-6 (2d Cir. 1982), especially if one attempts to look to the substance of the decision as any evidence of possible "negligence." Where review of board functioning is involved, courts leave behind as a relevant point of reference the decisions of the hypothetical "reasonable person," who typically supplies the test for negligence liability. It is doubtful that we want business men and women to be encouraged to make decisions as hypothetical persons of ordinary judgment and prudence might. The corporate form gets its utility in large part from its ability to allow diversified investors to accept greater investment risk. If those in charge of the corporation are to be adjudged personally liable for losses on the basis of a substantive judgment based upon what any persons of ordinary or average judgment and average risk assessment talent regard as "prudent" "sensible" or even "rational," such persons will have a strong incentive at the margin to authorize less risky investment projects.

Indeed, one wonders on what moral basis might shareholders attack a *good faith* business decision of a director as "unreasonable" or "irrational." Where a director *in fact exercises a good faith effort to be informed and to exercise appropriate judgment,* he or she should be deemed to satisfy fully the duty of attention. If the shareholders thought themselves entitled to some other quality of judgment than such a director produces in the good faith exercise of the powers of office, then the shareholders should have elected other directors. Judge Learned Hand made the point rather better than can I. In speaking of the passive director defendant Mr. Andrews in Barnes v. Andrews, Judge Hand said:

> True, he was not very suited by experience for the job he had undertaken, but I cannot hold him on that account. After all it is the same corporation that chose him that now seeks to charge him. . . . Directors are not specialists like lawyers or doctors. . . . They are the general advisors of the business and if they faithfully give such ability as they have to their charge, it would not be lawful to hold them liable. Must a director guarantee that his judgment is good? Can a shareholder call him to account for deficiencies that their votes assured him did not disqualify him for his office? While he may not have been the Cromwell for that Civil War, Andrews did not engage to play any such role.[17]

In this formulation Learned Hand correctly identifies, in my opinion, the core element of any corporate law duty of care inquiry: whether there was good faith effort to be informed and exercise judgment.

2.   *Liability for failure to monitor*

The second class of cases in which director liability for inattention is theoretically possible entail circumstances in which a loss eventuates not from a decision, but from unconsidered inaction. Most of the decisions that a corporation, acting through its human agents, makes are, of course, not the subject of director attention. Legally, the board itself will be required only to authorize the most significant corporate acts or transactions: mergers, changes in capital structure, fundamental changes in business, appointment and compensation of the CEO, etc. As the facts of this case graphically demonstrate, ordinary business decisions that are made by officers and employees deeper in the interior of the organization can, however, vitally affect the welfare of the corporation and its ability to achieve its various strategic and financial goals. If this case did not prove the point itself, recent business history would. Recall for example the displacement of senior management and much of the board of Salomon, Inc.; the replacement of senior management of Kidder, Peabody following the discovery of large trading losses resulting from phantom trades by a highly compensated trader; or the extensive financial loss and reputational injury suffered by Prudential Insurance as a result its junior officers misrepresentations in connection with the distribution of limited partnership interests. Financial and organizational disasters such as these raise the question, what is the board's responsibility with respect to the organization and monitoring of the enterprise to assure that the corporation functions within the law to achieve its purposes?

---

17. 298 F. 614, 618 (S.D.N.Y. 1924).

Modernly this question has been given special importance by an increasing tendency, especially under federal law, to employ the criminal law to assure corporate compliance with external legal requirements, including environmental, financial, employee and product safety as well as assorted other health and safety regulations. In 1991, pursuant to the Sentencing Reform Act of 1984, the United States Sentencing Commission adopted Organizational Sentencing Guidelines which impact importantly on the prospective effect these criminal sanctions might have on business corporations. The Guidelines set forth a uniform sentencing structure for organizations to be sentenced for violation of federal criminal statutes and provide for penalties that equal or often massively exceed those previously imposed on corporations.[21] The Guidelines offer powerful incentives for corporations today to have in place compliance programs to detect violations of law, promptly to report violations to appropriate public officials when discovered, and to take prompt, voluntary remedial efforts.

In 1963, the Delaware Supreme Court in Graham v. Allis-Chalmers Mfg. Co.,[23] addressed the question of potential liability of board members for losses experienced by the corporation as a result of the corporation having violated the anti-trust laws of the United States. There was no claim in that case that the directors knew about the behavior of subordinate employees of the corporation that had resulted in the liability. Rather, as in this case, the claim asserted was that the directors *ought to have known* of it and if they had known they would have been under a duty to bring the corporation into compliance with the law and thus save the corporation from the loss. The Delaware Supreme Court concluded that, under the facts as they appeared, there was no basis to find that the directors had breached a duty to be informed of the ongoing operations of the firm. In notably colorful terms, the court stated that "absent cause for suspicion there is no duty upon the directors to install and operate a corporate system of espionage to ferret out wrongdoing which they have no reason to suspect exists."[24] The Court found that there were no grounds for suspicion in that case and, thus, concluded that the directors were blamelessly unaware of the conduct leading to the corporate liability.[25]

How does one generalize this holding today? Can it be said today that, absent some ground giving rise to suspicion of violation of law, that corporate directors have no duty to assure that a corporate information gathering and reporting systems exists which represents a good faith attempt to provide senior management and the Board with information respecting material acts, events or conditions within the corporation, including compliance with applicable statutes and regulations? I certainly do not believe so. I doubt that such a broad generalization of the *Graham* holding would have been accepted by the Supreme Court in 1963. The case can be more narrowly interpreted as standing for the proposition that, absent grounds to suspect deception, neither corporate boards nor senior officers can be charged with wrongdoing simply for assuming the integrity of employees and the honesty of their dealings on the company's behalf. See 188 A.2d at 130-31.

---

21. See Sentencing Reform Act of 1984, Pub.L. 98-473, Title II, §212(a)(2) (1984); 18 U.S.C.A. §§3551-3656.

23. 188 A.2d 125 (Del. 1963).

24. Id. 188 A.2d at 130.

25. Recently, the Graham standard was applied by the Delaware Chancery in a case involving Baxter. In re Baxter International, Inc. Shareholders Litig., 654 A.2d 1268, 1270 (Del. Ch., 1995).

A broader interpretation of Graham v. Allis-Chalmers—that it means that a corporate board has no responsibility to assure that appropriate information and reporting systems are established by management—would not, in any event, be accepted by the Delaware Supreme Court in 1996, in my opinion. In stating the basis for this view, I start with the recognition that in recent years the Delaware Supreme Court has made it clear—especially in its jurisprudence concerning takeovers, from Smith v. Van Gorkom through Paramount Communications v. QVC[26]—the seriousness with which the corporation law views the role of the corporate board. Secondly, I note the elementary fact that relevant and timely information is an essential predicate for satisfaction of the board's supervisory and monitoring role under Section 141 of the Delaware General Corporation Law. Thirdly, I note the potential impact of the federal organizational sentencing guidelines on any business organization. Any rational person attempting in good faith to meet an organizational governance responsibility would be bound to take into account this development and the enhanced penalties and the opportunities for reduced sanctions that it offers.

In light of these developments, it would, in my opinion, be a mistake to conclude that our Supreme Court's statement in *Graham* concerning "espionage" means that corporate boards may satisfy their obligation to be reasonably informed concerning the corporation, without assuring themselves that information and reporting systems exist in the organization that are reasonably designed to provide to senior management and to the board itself timely, accurate information sufficient to allow management and the board, each within its scope, to reach informed judgments concerning both the corporation's compliance with law and its business performance.

Obviously the level of detail that is appropriate for such an information system is a question of business judgment. And obviously too, no rationally designed information and reporting system will remove the possibility that the corporation will violate laws or regulations, or that senior officers or directors may nevertheless sometimes be misled or otherwise fail reasonably to detect acts material to the corporation's compliance with the law. But it is important that the board exercise a good faith judgment that the corporation's information and reporting system is in concept and design adequate to assure the board that appropriate information will come to its attention in a timely manner as a matter of ordinary operations, so that it may satisfy its responsibility.

Thus, I am of the view that a director's obligation includes a duty to attempt in good faith to assure that a corporate information and reporting system, which the board concludes is adequate, exists, and that failure to do so under some circumstances may, in theory at least, render a director liable for losses caused by non-compliance with applicable legal standards.[27] I now turn to an analysis of the claims asserted

---

26. E.g., Smith v. Van Gorkom, 488 A.2d 858 (Del. 1985); Paramount Communications v. QVC Network, 637 A.2d 34 (Del. 1994).

27. Any action seeking recovery for losses would logically entail a judicial determination of proximate cause, since, for reasons that I take to be obvious, it could never be assumed that an adequate information system would be a system that would prevent all losses. I need not touch upon the burden allocation with respect to a proximate cause issue in such a suit. Moreover, questions of waiver of liability under certificate provisions authorized by 8 Del. C. §102(b)(7) may also be faced.

with this concept of the director's duty of care, as a duty satisfied in part by assurance of adequate information flows to the board, in mind.

III. ANALYSIS OF THIRD AMENDED COMPLAINT AND SETTLEMENT

A. THE CLAIMS

On balance, after reviewing an extensive record in this case, including numerous documents and three depositions, I conclude that this settlement is fair and reasonable. In light of the fact that the Caremark Board already has a functioning committee charged with overseeing corporate compliance, the changes in corporate practice that are presented as consideration for the settlement do not impress one as very significant. Nonetheless, that consideration appears fully adequate to support dismissal of the derivative claims of director fault asserted, because those claims find no substantial evidentiary support in the record and quite likely were susceptible to a motion to dismiss in all events.[28]

In order to show that the Caremark directors breached their duty of care by failing adequately to control Caremark's employees, plaintiffs would have to show either (1) that the directors knew or (2) should have known that violations of law were occurring and, in either event, (3) that the directors took no steps in a good faith effort to prevent or remedy that situation, and (4) that such failure proximately resulted in the losses complained of, although under Cede & Co. v. Technicolor, Inc., 636 A.2d 956 (Del. 1994) this last element may be thought to constitute an affirmative defense.

1. *Knowing violation of statute*

Concerning the possibility that the Caremark directors knew of violations of law, none of the documents submitted for review, nor any of the deposition transcripts appear to provide evidence of it. Certainly the Board understood that the company had entered into a variety of contracts with physicians, researchers, and health care providers and it was understood that some of these contracts were with persons who had prescribed treatments that Caremark participated in providing. The board was informed that the company's reimbursement for patient care was frequently from government funded sources and that such services were subject to the ARPL. But the Board appears to have been informed by experts that the company's practices while contestable, were lawful. There is no evidence that reliance on such reports was not reasonable. Thus, this case presents no occasion to apply a principle to the effect that knowingly causing the corporation to violate a criminal statute constitutes a breach of a director's fiduciary duty. See Roth v. Robertson, N.Y. Sup. Ct., 118 N.Y.S. 351 (1909); Miller v. American Tel. & Tel. Co., 507 F.2d 759 (3rd Cir. 1974). It is not clear that

---

28. See In re Baxter International, Inc. Shareholders Litig., 654 A.2d 1268, 1270 (Del. Ch., 1995). A claim in some respects similar to that here made was dismissed. The court relied, in part, on the fact that the Baxter certificate of incorporation contained a provision as authorized by Section 102(b)(7) of the Delaware General Corporation Law, waiving director liability for due care violations. Id. at 1270. That fact was thought to require pre-suit demand on the board in that case.

the Board knew the detail found, for example, in the indictments arising from the Company's payments. But, of course, the duty to act in good faith to be informed cannot be thought to require directors to possess detailed information about all aspects of the operation of the enterprise. Such a requirement would simple be inconsistent with the scale and scope of efficient organization size in this technological age.

2.   *Failure to monitor*

Since it does appears that the Board was to some extent unaware of the activities that led to liability, I turn to a consideration of the other potential avenue to director liability that the pleadings take: director inattention or "negligence." Generally where a claim of directorial liability for corporate loss is predicated upon ignorance of liability creating activities within the corporation, as in *Graham* or in this case, in my opinion only a sustained or systematic failure of the board to exercise oversight—such as an utter failure to attempt to assure a reasonable information and reporting system exists—will establish the lack of good faith that is a necessary condition to liability. Such a test of liability—lack of good faith as evidenced by sustained or systematic failure of a director to exercise reasonable oversight—is quite high. But, a demanding test of liability in the oversight context is probably beneficial to corporate shareholders as a class, as it is in the board decision context, since it makes board service by qualified persons more likely, while continuing to act as a stimulus to *good faith performance of duty* by such directors.

Here the record supplies essentially no evidence that the director defendants were guilty of a sustained failure to exercise their oversight function. To the contrary, insofar as I am able to tell on this record, the corporation's information systems appear to have represented a good faith attempt to be informed of relevant facts. If the directors did not know the specifics of the activities that lead to the indictments, they cannot be faulted.

The liability that eventuated in this instance was huge. But the fact that it resulted from a violation of criminal law alone does not create a breach of fiduciary duty by directors. The record at this stage does not support the conclusion that the defendants either lacked good faith in the exercise of their monitoring responsibilities or conscientiously permitted a known violation of law by the corporation to occur. The claims asserted against them must be viewed at this stage as extremely weak.

B.   THE CONSIDERATION FOR RELEASE OF CLAIM

The proposed settlement provides very modest benefits. . . . Nonetheless, given the weakness of the plaintiffs' claims the proposed settlement appears to be an adequate, reasonable, and beneficial outcome for all of the parties. Thus, the proposed settlement will be approved.

NOTES AND QUESTIONS

1. In Stone v. Ritter, 911 A.2d 362 (Del. 2006), the Delaware Supreme Court expressly approved the so-called *Caremark* doctrine.

[T]he *Caremark* standard for so-called "oversight" liability draws heavily upon the concept of director failure to act in good faith. That is consistent with the definition(s) of bad faith recently approved by this Court in its recent *Disney* decision [In re Walt Disney Co. Deriv. Litig., 906 A.2d 27 (Del. 2006)], where we held that a failure to act in good faith requires conduct that is qualitatively different from, and more culpable than, the conduct giving rise to a violation of the fiduciary duty of care (i.e., gross negligence). Id. at 66. In *Disney,* we identified the following examples of conduct that would establish a failure to act in good faith:

> A failure to act in good faith may be shown, for instance, where the fiduciary intentionally acts with a purpose other than that of advancing the best interests of the corporation, where the fiduciary acts with the intent to violate applicable positive law, or where the fiduciary intentionally fails to act in the face of a known duty to act, demonstrating a conscious disregard for his duties. There may be other examples of bad faith yet to be proven or alleged, but these three are the most salient.

Id. at 67.

The third of these examples describes, and is fully consistent with, the lack of good faith conduct that the *Caremark* court held was a "necessary condition" for director oversight liability, i.e., "a sustained or systematic failure of the board to exercise oversight—such as an utter failure to attempt to assure a reasonable information and reporting system exists. . . ." In re Caremark Int'l Inc. Deriv. Litig., 698 A.2d 959, 971 (Del. Ch. 1996). Indeed, our opinion in *Disney* cited *Caremark* with approval for that proposition. In re Walt Disney Co. Deriv. Litig., 906 A.2d at 67 n.111. . . .

We hold that *Caremark* articulates the necessary conditions predicate for director oversight liability: (a) the directors utterly failed to implement any reporting or information system or controls; *or* (b) having implemented such a system or controls, consciously failed to monitor or oversee its operations thus disabling themselves from being informed of risks or problems requiring their attention. In either case, imposition of liability requires a showing that the directors knew that they were not discharging their fiduciary obligations. Guttman v. Huang, 823 A.2d 492, 506 (Del. Ch. 2003). Where directors fail to act in the face of a known duty to act, thereby demonstrating a conscious disregard for their responsibilities [In re Walt Disney Co. Deriv. Litig., 906 A.2d 27, 67 (Del. 2006)], they breach their duty of loyalty by failing to discharge that fiduciary obligation in good faith. See Guttman v. Huang, 823 A.2d at 506.

2. Board approved and monitored law compliance programs became a standard part of the corporate governance landscape in the early 1990s in response to the federal sentencing guidelines for organizations, adopted in 1991, a development cogently described by Professor John S. Baker.

> Corporate self-policing or compliance plans have become pervasive since the 1991 adoption of the guidelines for sentencing of organizations. The Sentencing Guidelines have spawned a "compliance" industry of lawyers, accountants, consultants, and corporate vice presidents, who draft codes of corporate conduct and provide employee training in both the codes and appropriate practices—which, in turn, they audit for compliance. When violations occur, theoretically the system of compliance should detect them and the corporation should "voluntarily" disclose the wrongdoing to federal law enforcement. Although the Sentencing Guidelines do not offer much guidance, the voluntarily adopted codes of conduct are supposed to be "effective program[s]," which seems to imply that their operation will result in voluntary disclosure of wrongdoing.
>
> According to the Sentencing Commission, the Guidelines adopt a "carrot and stick" approach. The "carrot" of a potentially lesser sentence upon future conviction is supposedly the incentive for a corporation to adopt a code of conduct and voluntarily disclose wrongdoing. If a

convicted corporation has not pursued these incentives, the "stick" will be the imposition of higher penalties.

John S. Baker, Jr., Reforming Corporations Through Threats of Federal Prosecution, 89 Cornell L. Rev. 310, 316-317 (2005).

3. Does it "pay off" for corporations to develop sophisticated and effective law compliance programs? There are doubters.

> The so-called "carrot and stick" approach never had much carrot to it, however. If a company adopted a compliance program and self-reported violations, it received no guarantee of leniency. On the other hand, the failure to pursue the carrot "voluntarily" virtually guaranteed being hit with the stick in the event of a corporate conviction. As the Senior Attorney at what was then Bell Atlantic put it:
>
> > We've all heard the sentencing guidelines described as using the carrot and stick. The idea is to reward good acts and to punish the bad. But, in fact, we may be somewhat off the mark. Companies today that take aggressive ethics and compliance steps run high risks of being beaten with their own acts, beaten with the carrots that were supposed to lure them to do good things. Moreover, what is offered as a reward may not really be a carrot. Instead of offering real incentives, for the most part we are only shortening the stick that will be used against companies.

John S. Baker, Jr., Reforming Corporations Through Threats of Federal Prosecution, 89 Cornell L. Rev. 310, 317 (2005).

4. While the board's heightened role in ensuring law compliance is of relatively recent origin, the board's need to ensure adequate financial accounting and reporting systems is longstanding. Consistent with that core board responsibility, audit committees have been a standard part of the governance structure of most publicly held corporations since at least the 1970s. In 1977 the New York Stock Exchange adopted new standards requiring all listed companies to have an audit committee charged with responsibility for assisting the board of directors in its oversight of the company's financial accounting and reports of the results of operations filed with the SEC or otherwise publicized. It was estimated that 90 percent of America's largest public corporations had audit committees as a standard part of their governance structure prior to the 1977 rule change. Joel Seligman, A Modest Revolution in Corporate Governance, 80 Notre Dame L. Rev. 1159, 1167 (2005).

5. The importance of the *Caremark* doctrine was magnified manyfold after the spectacular accounting scandals, corporate insider misconduct, and shareholder losses that occurred in 2001 and 2002. One of the most infamous scandals involved the Enron Corporation, and commentators often refer to corporation development occurring since 2001 as "post-*Enron*."

6. Post-*Enron*, federal law has imposed enhanced oversight duties on both officers and directors, some of which intrude into the traditional province of state corporation law. The Securities and Exchange Commission, and the listing agencies—principally the NYSE and NASDAQ—have also imposed more stringent oversight requirements on listed corporations and their officers and directors. Concomitantly, state and federal courts have begun to apply the *Caremark* doctrine in shareholder litigation claiming that directors have breached their *Caremark* oversight duties. For example, see

McCall v. Scott, 250 F.3d 997 (6th Cir. 2001); Saito v. McCall, 2004 WL 3029876 (Del. Ch.); Miller v. U.S. Foodservice, Inc., 361 F. Supp. 2d 470 (D. Md. 2005); Cohn v. Nelson, 375 F. Supp. 2d 844 (E.D. Mo. 2005).

7. Post-*Enron*, lawmakers and commentators viewed the audit committee as a weak link in the governance system of many publicly traded corporations. Therefore, strengthening audit committees became a major focus of the Sarbanes-Oxley Act of 2002 and related changes in NYSE and NASDAQ listing standards. These changes focused primarily on increasing (1) the independence and expertise of audit committee members; (2) the audit committee's control over the financial audit process, including selection of the outside auditor; (3) communication between the audit committee and the board; and (4) internal communications between the audit committee, the CEO, the CFO, and individuals charged with carrying out the internal auditing function. For a summary and critique of these and other post-*Enron* corporate governance changes, see Joel Seligman, A Modest Revolution in Corporate Governance, 80 Notre Dame L. Rev. 1159, 1167 (2005).

8. Under what circumstances might directors be liable for damages the corporation has suffered as a result of massive accounting fraud, on the grounds that the directors have failed to ensure that the corporation had in place an adequate system of financial controls or "ought to have known" that accounting fraud was occurring? An opinion by Vice Chancellor Strine dismissing such a claim sheds light both on what type of director conduct might be troublesome and what type of conduct would be exemplary.

> In this case, the plaintiffs have not come close to pleading a *Caremark* claim. Their conclusory complaint is empty of the kind of fact pleading that is critical to a *Caremark* claim, such as contentions that the company lacked an audit committee, that the company had an audit committee that met only sporadically and devoted patently inadequate time to its work, or that the audit committee had clear notice of serious accounting irregularities and simply chose to ignore them or, even worse, to encourage their continuation. From the complaint, it is impossible to tell anything about the financial compliance systems in place at NVIDIA during the Contested Period. . . . For all I know, the NVIDIA audit committee met six times a year for half-day sessions, was comprised entirely of independent directors, had retained a qualified and independent audit firm that performed no other services for the company, was given no notice of the alleged irregularities by either management or the audit firm, had paid its audit firm to perform professionally credible random tests of management's integrity in recording revenue and other important financial data, and could not have been expected to discover the accounting irregularities, even when exercising a good faith effort, because discovery required disclosure by management or uncovering by the auditors of conduct deep below the surface of the financial statements.

Guttman v. Huang, 823 A.2d 492, 507 (Del. Ch. 2003).

PROBLEM 4-9

Tyron, Inc., a major supplier of medical products, agreed to provide products at preferred prices to the Veterans Administration (VA). Beginning in 2002, Tyron employees embarked on a scheme to overcharge the VA on most transactions by providing fraudulent price lists. As a result of this scheme, Tyron received its regular price on merchandise sold to the VA, resulting in overcharges that ultimately totaled $60 million. In

2010, the VA inspector general's office informed Tyron that it was investigating allegations that Tyron sales representatives were providing false information to VA purchasing agents. The Tyron board, composed of two "inside" directors and ten "outside" directors, met to discuss these charges. Tyron's CEO and board chair, Snar Hartley, reported to the board that she suspected that there had been "isolated incidents" of fraud, but that the problems were not widespread. The board directed Hartley to write all key management personnel directing them to take all reasonable steps to detect and prevent any such fraudulent practices and to inform the VA that corrective actions had been taken. Hartley did as directed. In 2013, the VA inspector general discovered that the fraudulent practices were continuing and turned the matter over to the Justice Department, which indicted Tyron and several of its agents. At his trial for mail fraud, Al Hawkins, a regional sales manager, testified, "Yeah, I got Hartley's letter, but didn't take it seriously. They couldn't possibly expect us to meet our profit targets unless we played with the invoices." Tyron ultimately settled the cases against it, agreeing to pay fines and reimbursements in the total amount of $400 million.

A shareholder derivative suit has been filed claiming that the Tyron directors breached their fiduciary duty of care. After the discovery phase, it appears uncontroverted that the directors had no actual knowledge of the fraudulent conduct prior to the VA's 2010 investigation, and had no actual knowledge that the fraudulent conduct had not ceased after Hartley's letter to key management personnel. There is, however, deposition testimony that supports a reasonable inference that the directors were aware as early as 2006 that similar fraudulent schemes were rampant at other firms dealing with the VA, and that Pro-Med, a competitor in the medical supply business, had been suspended from dealings with the VA in the summer of 2009 for wide-scale submission of false price lists and invoices.

Assess the directors' risk of liability for breach of the duty of care.

c.   The Role and Nature of Substantive Review

The business judgment rule admonishes judges to avoid second-guessing the substantive decisions made by independent, disinterested directors except in extreme cases. However, there have always been fail-safe mechanisms by which courts could intervene if a challenged substantive decision was sufficiently beyond the pale. Waste has long been a doctrinal vehicle for entertaining such challenges. Essentially, the waste doctrine allows courts to find directors liable where direct proof of lack of care or loyalty is lacking, but the substantive decision seems explainable only as a product of the directors' failure to carry out their fiduciary responsibilities.

Saxe v. Brady, 184 A.2d 602 (Del. Ch. 1962), contains a classic statement of the doctrine of waste and the role of substantive review. There, shareholders challenged the reasonableness of investment advisory fees approved by the board of a Delaware corporation registered as an open-end investment company under the provisions of the Investment Company Act of 1940. The shareholders claimed that the fees were so unreasonable as to constitute waste. Chancellor Seitz framed the standard of review for testing waste claims as follows:

> Where waste of corporate assets is alleged, the court, notwithstanding independent stockholder ratification, must examine the facts of the situation. Its examination, however, is limited

solely to discovering whether what the corporation has received is so inadequate in value that no person of ordinary, sound business judgment would deem it worth what the corporation has paid. If it can be said that ordinary businessmen might differ on the sufficiency of the terms, then the court must validate the transaction.

Id. at 610.

Twenty-five years later, the Delaware Supreme Court cited with approval Chancellor Seitz's formulation of the waste doctrine, albeit linked more directly to the duty of care. Justice Horsey's opinion bifurcated the duty of care into two components—procedural due care and substantive due care.

> Having concluded that plaintiffs have failed to plead a claim of financial interest or entrenchment sufficient to excuse presuit demand, we examine the complaints as amended to determine whether they raise a reasonable doubt that the directors exercised proper business judgment in the transaction. By proper business judgment we mean both substantive due care (purchase terms), see Saxe v. Brady, Del.Ch., 184 A.2d 602, 610 (1962), and procedural due care (an informed decision), see Smith v. Van Gorkom, Del. Supr., 488 A.2d 858, 872-73 (1985). . . .
>
> [As to the first claim, plaintiffs] allege, at most, a claim of waste based on the assertion that GM's Board paid such a premium for the Perot holdings as to shock the conscience of the ordinary person.
>
> Thus, the issue becomes whether the complaints state a claim of waste of assets, i.e., whether "what the corporation has received is so inadequate in value that no person of ordinary, sound business judgment would deem it worth that which the corporation has paid." *Saxe,* 184 A.2d at 610. By way of reinforcing their claim of waste, plaintiffs seize upon the hush-mail feature of the repurchase as being the motivating reason for the "giant premium" approved by the GM Board. Plaintiffs then argue that buying the silence of a dissident within management constitutes an invalid business purpose. Ergo, plaintiffs argue that a claim of waste of corporate assets evidencing lack of director due care has been well pleaded.

Grobow v. Perot, 539 A.2d 180, 189 (Del. 1988).

Justice Horsey's opinion appears to locate the doctrine of waste within the duty of care. If that characterization holds, then a waste claim, standing alone, could become nothing more than an allegation that the directors breached their duty of care; thus, the directors' conduct is exculpable and a waste claim should be dismissed at the pleading stage.

Chancellor Allen's opinion in *Caremark* does not mention the waste doctrine or the substantive due process doctrine. However, Chancellor Allen does strongly assert that substantive review has no place in the analysis of the duty of care. As Allen puts it, "[A] director's duty of care can never be determined by reference to *the content of the board decision* that leads to a corporate loss, apart from a consideration of the good faith or rationality of the process employed." 698 A.2d at 967. Chancellor Allen's suggestion that the duty of good faith provides space for judicial review of director action is a point to which subsequent Delaware judicial decisions have devoted substantial attention. However, at this point, the reach of the good-faith-based claims seems reserved for instances of egregious conduct.

Still, Allen's challenge to the nature of the duty of care and the role of substantive review has subtle, but potentially important, implications. If substantive review has no place in the duty of care, does that mean that the doctrine of waste is a branch of the duty of loyalty? If substantive review has implications for review of directors' good faith, what are the contours of that review? The Delaware Supreme Court began to clarify the role of substantive review, the definition of waste, and the nature of the duty of care in the principal case, below.

Brehm v. Eisner
Delaware Supreme Court, 2000
746 A.2d 244

Before VEASEY, C.J., WALSH, HOLLAND, HARTNETT and BERGER, JJ., constituting the Court en Banc.

VEASEY, CHIEF JUSTICE:

In this appeal from the Court of Chancery, we agree with the holding of the Court of Chancery that the stockholder derivative Complaint was subject to dismissal. . . .

The claims before us are that: (a) the board of directors of The Walt Disney Company ("Disney") as it was constituted in 1995 (the "Old Board") breached its fiduciary duty in approving an extravagant and wasteful Employment Agreement of Michael S. Ovitz as president of Disney; (b) the Disney board of directors as it was constituted in 1996 (the "New Board") breached its fiduciary duty in agreeing to a "non-fault" termination of the Ovitz Employment Agreement, a decision that was extravagant and wasteful; and (c) the directors were not disinterested and independent.

This is potentially a very troubling case on the merits. On the one hand, it appears from the Complaint that: (a) the compensation and termination payouts for Ovitz were exceedingly lucrative, if not luxurious, compared to Ovitz' value to the Company; and (b) the processes of the boards of directors in dealing with the approval and termination of the Ovitz Employment Agreement were casual, if not sloppy and perfunctory. On the other hand, the Complaint is so inartfully drafted that it was properly dismissed under our pleading standards for derivative suits. From what we can ferret out of this deficient pleading, the processes of the Old Board and the New Board were hardly paradigms of good corporate governance practices. Moreover, the sheer size of the payout to Ovitz, as alleged, pushes the envelope of judicial respect for the business judgment of directors in making compensation decisions. Therefore, both as to the processes of the two Boards and the waste test, this is a close case. . . .

FACTS

This statement of facts is taken from the Complaint. We have attempted to summarize here the essence of Plaintiffs' factual allegations on the key issues before us, disregarding the many conclusions that are not supported by factual allegations.

A.   THE 1995 OVITZ EMPLOYMENT AGREEMENT

By an agreement dated October 1, 1995, Disney hired Ovitz as its president. He was a long-time friend of Disney Chairman and CEO Michael Eisner. At the time, Ovitz was an important talent broker in Hollywood. Although he lacked experience managing a diversified public company, other companies with entertainment operations had been interested in hiring him for high-level executive positions. The Employment Agreement was unilaterally negotiated by Eisner and approved by the Old Board. Their judgment was that Ovitz was a valuable person to hire as president of Disney, and they agreed ultimately with Eisner's recommendation in awarding him an extraordinarily lucrative contract.

Ovitz' Employment Agreement had an initial term of five years and required that Ovitz "devote his full time and best efforts exclusively to the Company," with exceptions for volunteer work, service on the board of another company, and managing his passive investments.[5] In return, Disney agreed to give Ovitz a base salary of $1 million per year, a discretionary bonus, and two sets of stock options (the "A" options and the "B" options) that collectively would enable Ovitz to purchase 5 million shares of Disney common stock.

The "A" options were scheduled to vest in three annual increments of 1 million shares each, beginning on September 30, 1998 (i.e., at the end of the third full year of employment) and continuing for the following two years (through September 2000). The agreement specifically provided that the "A" options would vest immediately if Disney granted Ovitz a non-fault termination of the Employment Agreement. The "B" options, consisting of 2 million shares, differed in two important respects. Although scheduled to vest annually starting in September 2001 (i.e., the year after the last "A" option would vest), the "B" options were conditioned on Ovitz and Disney first having agreed to extend his employment beyond the five-year term of the Employment Agreement. Furthermore, Ovitz would forfeit the right to qualify for the "B" options if his initial employment term of five years ended prematurely for any reason, even if from a non-fault termination.

The Employment Agreement provided for three ways by which Ovitz' employment might end. He might serve his five years and Disney might decide against offering him a new contract. If so, Disney would owe Ovitz a $10 million termination payment.[6] Before the end of the initial term, Disney could terminate Ovitz for "good cause" only if Ovitz committed gross negligence or malfeasance, or if Ovitz resigned voluntarily. Disney would owe Ovitz no additional compensation if it terminated him for "good cause." Termination without cause (non-fault termination) would entitle Ovitz to the present value of his remaining salary payments through September 30, 2000, a $10 million severance payment, an additional $7.5 million for each fiscal year remaining under the agreement, and the immediate vesting of the first 3 million stock options (the "A" Options).

Plaintiffs allege that the Old Board knew that Disney needed a strong second-in-command. Disney had recently made several acquisitions, and questions lingered about Eisner's health due to major heart surgery. The Complaint further alleges that "Eisner had demonstrated little or no capacity to work with important or well-known subordinate executives who wanted to position themselves to succeed him," citing the departures of Disney executives Jeffrey Katzenberg, Richard Frank, and Stephen Bollenbach as examples. Thus, the Board knew that, to increase the chance for long-term success, it had to take extra care in reviewing a decision to hire Disney's new president.

---

5. The agreement implicitly emphasized the importance of having Disney receive Ovitz' full attention by mentioning, in a section stating the unique nature of Ovitz' services, that the Company would specifically be entitled to equitable relief if Ovitz failed to provide it with "the exclusivity of his services."

6. All the "A" options would have vested, but he would not receive the "B" options.

But Eisner's decision that Disney should hire Ovitz as its president was not entirely well-received. When Eisner told three members of the Old Board in mid-August 1995 that he had decided to hire Ovitz, all three "denounced the decision." Although not entirely clear from the Complaint, the vote of the Old Board approving the Ovitz Employment Agreement two months later appears to have been unanimous. Aside from a conclusory attack that the Old Board followed Eisner's bidding, the Complaint fails to allege any particularized facts that the three directors changed their initial reactions through anything other than the typical process of further discussion and individual contemplation.

The Complaint then alleges that the Old Board failed properly to inform itself about the total costs and incentives of the Ovitz Employment Agreement, especially the severance package. This is the key allegation related to this issue on appeal. Specifically, plaintiffs allege that the Board failed to realize that the contract gave Ovitz an incentive to find a way to exit the Company via a non-fault termination as soon as possible because doing so would permit him to earn more than he could by fulfilling his contract. The Complaint alleges, however, that the Old Board had been advised by a corporate compensation expert, Graef Crystal, in connection with its decision to approve the Ovitz Employment Agreement. Two public statements by Crystal form the basis of the allegation that the Old Board failed to consider the incentives and the total cost of the severance provisions, but these statements by Crystal were not made until after Ovitz left Disney in December 1996, approximately 14½ months after being hired.

The first statement, published in a December 23, 1996 article in the web-based magazine *Slate,* quoted Crystal as saying, in part, "Of course, the overall costs of the package would go up sharply in the event of Ovitz's termination (*and I wish now that I'd made a spreadsheet showing just what the deal would total if Ovitz had been fired at any time*)." The second published statement appeared in an article about three weeks later in the January 13, 1997 edition of *California Law Business.* The article appears first to paraphrase Crystal: "With no one expecting failure, the sleeper clauses in Ovitz's contract seemed innocuous, Crystal says, explaining that no one added up the total cost of the severance package." The article then quotes Crystal as saying that the amount of Ovitz' severance was "shocking" and that "*[n]obody quantified this and I wish we had.*" One of the charging paragraphs of the Complaint concludes:

> 57. As has been conceded by Graef Crystal, the executive compensation consultant who advised the Old Board with respect to the Ovitz Employment Agreement, the Old Board *never* considered the costs that would be incurred by Disney in the event Ovitz was terminated from the Company for a reason other than cause prior to the natural expiration of the Ovitz Employment Agreement.

Although repeated in various forms in the Complaint, these quoted admissions by Crystal constitute the extent of the factual support for the allegation that the Old Board failed properly to consider the severance elements of the agreement. This Court, however, must juxtapose these allegations with the legal presumption that the Old Board's conduct was a proper exercise of business judgment. That presumption includes the statutory protection for a board that relies in good faith on an expert advising the Board.[9] We must decide whether plaintiffs' factual allegations, if proven, would rebut that presumption.

---

9. *See* 8 Del. C. §141(e)....

Soon after Ovitz began work, problems surfaced and the situation continued to deteriorate during the first year of his employment. To support this allegation, the plaintiffs cite various media reports detailing internal complaints and providing external examples of alleged business mistakes. The Complaint uses these reports to suggest that the New Board had reason to believe that Ovitz' performance and lack of commitment met the gross negligence or malfeasance standards of the termination-for-cause provisions of the contract.

The deteriorating situation, according to the Complaint, led Ovitz to begin seeking alternative employment and to send Eisner a letter in September 1996 that the Complaint paraphrases as stating his dissatisfaction with his role and expressing his desire to leave the Company.[10] The Complaint also admits that Ovitz would not actually resign before negotiating a non-fault severance agreement because he did not want to jeopardize his rights to a lucrative severance in the form of a "non-fault termination" under the terms of the 1995 Employment Agreement.

On December 11, 1996, Eisner and Ovitz agreed to arrange for Ovitz to leave Disney on the non-fault basis provided for in the 1995 Employment Agreement. Eisner then "caused" the New Board[11] "to rubber-stamp his decision (by 'mutual consent')." This decision was implemented by a December 27, 1996 letter to Ovitz from defendant Sanford M. Litvack, an officer and director of Disney. That letter stated:

This will confirm the terms of your agreement with the Company as follows:

1. The Term of your employment under your existing Employment Agreement with The Walt Disney Company will end at the close of business today. Consequently, your signature confirms the end of your service as an officer, and your resignation as a director, of the Company and its affiliates.

2. This letter will for all purposes of the Employment Agreement be treated as a "Non-Fault Termination." By our mutual agreement, the total amount payable to you under your Employment Agreement, including the amount payable under Section 11(c) in the event of a "Non-Fault Termination," is $38,888,230.77, net of withholding required by law or authorized by you. By your signature on this letter, you acknowledge receipt of all but $1,000,000 of such amount. Pursuant to our mutual agreement, this will confirm that payment of the $1,000,000 balance has been deferred until February 5, 1997, pending final settlement of accounts.

3. This letter will further confirm that the option to purchase 3,000,000 shares of the Company's Common Stock granted to you pursuant to Option A described in your Employment Agreement will vest as of today and will expire in accordance with its terms on September 30, 2002.

---

10. The plaintiffs allegedly have never seen the actual letter.

11. The composition of the New Board differed slightly from the composition of the Old Board. The Old Board and the New Board both included Michael D. Eisner, Roy E. Disney, Stanley P. Gold, Sanford M. Litvack, Richard A. Nunis, Sidney Poitier, Irwin E. Russell, Robert A.M. Stern, E. Cardon Walker, Raymond L. Watson, Gary L. Wilson, Reveta F. Bowers, Ignacio E. Lozano Jr. and George J. Mitchell. The Old Board included Stephen F. Bollenbach, who was not on the New Board. The New Board included Leo J. O'Donovan and Thomas S. Murphy, neither of whom was on the Old Board. Although the Complaint included Ovitz as a member of the New Board, his resignation appeared to have occurred before the New Board approved the non-fault termination. *See* In re The Walt Disney Co. Derivative Litig., 731 A.2d at 351 n. 3.

Although the non-fault termination left Ovitz with what essentially was a very lucrative severance agreement, it is important to note that Ovitz and Disney had negotiated for that severance payment at the time they initially contracted in 1995, and in the end the payout to Ovitz did not exceed the 1995 contractual benefits. Consequently, Ovitz received the $10 million termination payment, $7.5 million for part of the fiscal year remaining under the agreement and the immediate vesting of the 3 million stock options (the "A" options). As a result of his termination Ovitz would not receive the 2 million "B" options that he would have been entitled to if he had completed the full term of the Employment Agreement and if his contract were renewed.[12]

The Complaint charges the New Board with waste, computing the value of the severance package agreed to by the Board at over $140 million, consisting of cash payments of about $39 million and the value of the immediately vesting "A" options of over $101 million. The Complaint quotes Crystal, the Old Board's expert, as saying in January 1997 that Ovitz' severance package was a "shocking amount of severance."

The allegation of waste is based on the inference most favorable to plaintiffs that Disney owed Ovitz nothing, either because he had resigned (*de facto*) or because he was unarguably subject to firing for cause. These allegations must be juxtaposed with the presumption that the New Board exercised its business judgment in deciding how to resolve the potentially litigable issues of whether Ovitz had actually resigned or had definitely breached his contract. We must decide whether plaintiffs' factual allegations, if proven, would rebut that presumption. . . .

PLAINTIFFS' CONTENTION THAT THE OLD BOARD VIOLATED THE PROCESS DUTY OF CARE IN APPROVING THE OVITZ EMPLOYMENT AGREEMENT

Certainly in this case the economic exposure of the corporation to the payout scenarios of the Ovitz contract was material,[49] particularly given its large size, for purposes of the directors' decisionmaking process. And those dollar exposure numbers were

---

12. Under the 1995 Employment Agreement, Ovitz' "B" options to purchase 2,000,000 shares were scheduled to vest "in increments of 1,000,000 shares on each of September 30, 2001 and September 30, 2002." But they would not vest if Ovitz' employment "shall have terminated for any reason whatsoever more than three months prior to such scheduling date." If Ovitz' employment should terminate before October 1, 2000 (the expiration of the 1995 agreement), the "B" options "shall thereupon irrevocably terminate."

49. The term "material" is used in this context to mean relevant and of a magnitude to be important to directors in carrying out their fiduciary duty of care in decisionmaking. . . . One must also keep in mind that the size of executive compensation for a large public company in the current environment often involves huge numbers. This is particularly true in the entertainment industry where the enormous revenues from one "hit" movie or enormous losses from a "flop" place in perspective the compensation of executives whose genius or misjudgment, as the case may be, may have contributed substantially to the "hit" or "flop." See Lori B. Marino, Comment, Executive Compensation and the Misplaced Emphasis on Increasing Shareholder Access to the Proxy, 147 U. Pa. L. Rev. 1205, 1235 (1999) ("Executive compensation makes up such a small percentage of a firm's assets that even excessive pay packages will likely not cause a blip in a firm's stock value."); *cf. id.* (contrasting executive compensation with decisions by a company's board regarding takeovers, which have a great effect on a company's stock price).

reasonably available because the logical inference from plaintiffs' allegations is that Crystal or the New Board could have calculated the numbers. Thus, the objective tests of reasonable availability and materiality were satisfied by this Complaint. But that is not the end of the inquiry for liability purposes.

The Court of Chancery interpreted the Complaint to allege that only Crystal (the Board's expert)—and *not the Board itself*—failed to bring to bear all the necessary information because he (Crystal) did not quantify for the Board the maximum payout to Ovitz under the non-fault termination scenario. Alternatively, the Court of Chancery reasoned that even if the Old Board failed to make the calculation, that fact does not raise a reasonable doubt of due care because *Crystal* did not consider it critical to ascertain the potential costs of Ovitz' severance package. The Court's language is as follows:

> With regard to the alleged breach of the duty of care, Plaintiffs claim that the directors were not properly informed before they adopted the Employment Agreement because they did not know the value of the compensation package offered to Ovitz. To that end, Plaintiffs offer several statements made by Graef Crystal, the financial expert who advised the Board on the Employment Agreement, including his admission that "[n]obody quantified the total cost of the severance package and I wish we had."
>
> The fact that *Crystal* did not quantify the potential severance benefits to Ovitz for terminating early without cause (under the terms of the Employment Agreement) does not create a reasonable inference that *the Board* failed to consider the potential cost to Disney in the event that they decided to terminate Ovitz without cause. But, even if the Board did fail to calculate the potential cost to Disney, I nevertheless think that this allegation fails to create a reasonable doubt that the former Board exercised due care. Disney's expert did not consider an inquiry into the potential cost of Ovitz's severance benefits to be critical or relevant to the Board's consideration of the Employment Agreement. Merely because Crystal *now* regrets not having calculated the package is not reason enough to overturn the judgment of the Board *then*. It is the essence of the business judgment rule that a court will not apply 20/20 hindsight to second guess a board's decision, except "in rare cases [where] a transaction may be so egregious on its face that the board approval cannot meet the test of business judgment." Because the Board's reliance on Crystal and his decision not to fully calculate the amount of severance lack "egregiousness," this is not that rare case. I think it a correct statement of law that the duty of care is still fulfilled even if a Board does not know the exact amount of a severance payout but nonetheless is fully informed about the manner in which such a payout would be calculated. A board is not required to be informed of every fact, but rather is required to be reasonably informed. Here the Plaintiffs have failed to plead facts giving rise to a reasonable doubt that the Board, as a matter of law, was reasonably informed on this issue.

We believe, however, that the Complaint, fairly read, charges that Crystal admitted that "nobody"—not Crystal *and* not the directors—made that calculation, although all the necessary information presumably was at hand to do so. Thus the reading given by the Court of Chancery to this aspect of the amended complaint was too restrictive because the Court's reading fails to appreciate the breadth of the allegation—*i.e.*, that neither Crystal nor the Old Board made the calculations that Crystal—the expert—*now* believes he should have made. Moreover, the Court's alternative analysis that "Disney's expert did not consider an inquiry into the potential costs . . . to be critical or relevant to the board's consideration" is inappropriately simplistic at the pleading stage to state a comprehensive analysis of the issue.

We regard the Court's language as harmless error, however, for the following reason. The Complaint, fairly construed, admits that the directors were advised by Crystal as an expert and that they relied on his expertise. Accordingly, the question here is whether the directors are to be "fully protected" (*i.e.*, not held liable) on the basis that they relied in good faith on a qualified expert under Section 141(e) of the Delaware General Corporation Law.[51] The Old Board is entitled to the presumption that it exercised proper business judgment, including proper reliance on the expert. . . . Plaintiffs will be provided an opportunity to replead on this issue.

PLAINTIFFS' CONTENTION THAT THE OLD BOARD VIOLATED "SUBSTANTIVE DUE CARE" REQUIREMENTS AND COMMITTED WASTE AB INITIO WITH OVITZ' EMPLOYMENT AGREEMENT

Plaintiffs allege not only that the Old Board committed a procedural due care violation in the process of approving the Ovitz 1995 Employment Agreement but also that the Board committed a "substantive due care" violation constituting waste. They contend that the Court of Chancery erred in holding that the Complaint failed to set forth particularized facts creating a reasonable doubt that the directors' decision to enter into the Ovitz Employment Agreement was a product of the proper exercise of business judgment.

Plaintiffs' principal theory is that the 1995 Ovitz Employment Agreement was a "wasteful transaction for Disney *ab initio*" because it was structured to "incentivize" Ovitz to seek an early non-fault termination. The Court of Chancery correctly dismissed this theory as failing to meet the stringent requirements of the waste test, i.e., "'an exchange that is so one sided that no business person of ordinary, sound judgment could conclude that the corporation has received adequate consideration.'" Moreover, the Court concluded that a board's decision on executive compensation is entitled to great deference. It is the essence of business judgment for a board to determine if "a 'particular individual warrant[s] large amounts of money, whether in the form of current salary or severance provisions.'"

Specifically, the Court of Chancery inferred from a reading of the Complaint that the Board determined it had to offer an expensive compensation package to attract Ovitz and that they determined he would be valuable to the Company. The Court also concluded that the vesting schedule of the options actually was a disincentive for Ovitz to leave Disney. When he did leave pursuant to the non-fault termination, the Court noted that he left 2 million options (the "B" options) "on the table."[61] Although we agree with

---

51. . . . This protection, however, is not without limitation, as in a case of corporate waste.

61. Id. at 363. This statement, however, is somewhat misleading in that the "B" options would not have come into being unless the employment were extended beyond the original five years. It is correct, however, that this non-fault termination cut off the possibility of Ovitz receiving those options and that those options had been a potentially valuable incentive for Ovitz to remain in Disney's employ, an incentive that Ovitz relinquished.

the conclusion of the Court of Chancery that this particular Complaint is deficient, we do not foreclose the possibility that a properly framed complaint could pass muster.

Plaintiffs' disagreement on appeal with the decision of the Court of Chancery is basically a quarrel with the Old Board's judgment in evaluating Ovitz' worth vis-à-vis the lavish payout to him. We agree with the analysis of the Court of Chancery that the size and structure of executive compensation are inherently matters of judgment. As former Chancellor Allen stated in *Vogelstein*:

> The judicial standard for determination of corporate waste is well developed. Roughly, a waste entails an exchange of corporate assets for consideration so disproportionately small as to lie beyond the range at which any reasonable person might be willing to trade. Most often the claim is associated with a transfer of corporate assets that serves no corporate purpose; or for which no consideration at all is received. Such a transfer is in effect a gift. If, however, there is *any substantial* consideration received by the corporation, and if there is a *good faith judgment* that in the circumstances the transaction is worthwhile, there should be no finding of waste, even if the fact finder would conclude *ex post* that the transaction was unreasonably risky. Any other rule would deter corporate boards from the optimal rational acceptance of risk, for reasons explained elsewhere. Courts are ill-fitted to attempt to weigh the "adequacy" of consideration under the waste standard or, *ex post,* to judge appropriate degrees of business risk.[63]

To be sure, there are outer limits, but they are confined to unconscionable cases where directors irrationally squander or give away corporate assets. Here, however, we find no error in the decision of the Court of Chancery on the waste test.

As for the plaintiffs' contention that the directors failed to exercise "substantive due care," we should note that such a concept is foreign to the business judgment rule. Courts do not measure, weigh or quantify directors' judgments. We do not even decide if they are reasonable in this context. Due care in the decision making context is *process* due care only. Irrationality is the outer limit of the business judgment rule. Irrationality may be the functional equivalent of the waste test or it may tend to show that the decision is not made in good faith, which is a key ingredient of the business judgment rule.

PLAINTIFFS' CONTENTION THAT THE NEW BOARD COMMITTED WASTE IN ITS DECISION THAT OVITZ' CONTRACT SHOULD BE TERMINATED ON A "NON-FAULT" BASIS . . .

The Complaint alleges that it was waste for the Board to pay Ovitz essentially the full amount he was due on the non-fault termination basis because he should have been fired for cause. Ovitz' contract provided that he could be fired for cause only if he was grossly negligent or committed acts of malfeasance. Plaintiffs contend that ample grounds existed to fire Ovitz for cause under these terms. The Court of Chancery correctly concluded:

> The terms of the Employment Agreement limit "good cause" for terminating Ovitz's employment to gross negligence or malfeasance, or a voluntary resignation without the consent of the Company.

---

63. *Vogelstein*, 699 A.2d at 336 (emphasis in original) (citations omitted); accord *Grimes*, 673 A.2d at 1214.

I have reviewed the amended complaint and listened to the parties' arguments at the hearing in connection with Defendants' motion to dismiss. Still, I am unable to conclude that any of the facts alleged by Plaintiffs, even accepted as true, demonstrate that Ovitz's conduct was either grossly negligent or malfeasant during his tenure at Disney, or that Ovitz resigned voluntarily. For example, Plaintiffs allege that Ovitz sought alternative employment while he was the president of Disney. But Plaintiffs fail to explain how looking for another job constitutes gross negligence or malfeasance. The same holds true for Plaintiffs' allegation that Ovitz failed to follow Eisner's directive to meet with Director Defendant Stephen F. Bollenbach, who was then the senior executive vice president and chief financial officer of Disney. This allegation may demonstrate that Ovitz failed to become familiar with Disney's finances or that he bucked authority at Disney. However, it does not demonstrate, without more, that Ovitz was grossly negligent or committed malfeasance. None of Plaintiffs' allegations rise to the level of gross negligence or malfeasance.[68]

Construed most favorably to plaintiffs, the facts in the Complaint (disregarding conclusory allegations) show that Ovitz' performance as president was disappointing at best, that Eisner admitted it had been a mistake to hire him, that Ovitz lacked commitment to the Company, that he performed services for his old company, and that he negotiated for other jobs (some very lucrative) while being required under the contract to devote his full time and energy to Disney.

All this shows is that the Board had *arguable* grounds to fire Ovitz for cause. But what is alleged is only an *argument*—perhaps a good one—that Ovitz' conduct constituted gross negligence or malfeasance. First, given the facts as alleged, Disney would have had to persuade a trier of fact and law of this argument in any litigated dispute with Ovitz. Second, that process of persuasion could involve expensive litigation, distraction of executive time and company resources, lost opportunity costs, more bad publicity and an outcome that was uncertain at best and, at worst, could have resulted in damages against the Company.

The Complaint, in sum, contends that the Board committed waste by agreeing to the very lucrative payout to Ovitz under the non-fault termination provision because it had no obligation to him, thus taking the Board's decision outside the protection of the business judgment rule. Construed most favorably to plaintiffs, the Complaint contends that, by reason of the New Board's available arguments of resignation and good cause, it had the leverage to negotiate Ovitz down to a more reasonable payout than that guaranteed by his Employment Agreement. But the Complaint fails on its face to meet the waste test because it does not allege with particularity facts tending to show that no reasonable business person would have made the decision that the New Board made under these circumstances.

We agree with the conclusion of the Court of Chancery:

The Board made a business decision to grant Ovitz a Non-Fault Termination. Plaintiffs may disagree with the Board's judgment as to how this matter should have been handled. But where, as here, there is no reasonable doubt as to the disinterest of or absence of fraud by the Board, mere disagreement cannot serve as grounds for imposing liability based on alleged breaches of fiduciary duty and waste. There is no allegation that the Board did not consider the pertinent issues surrounding Ovitz's termination. Plaintiffs' sole argument appears to be that they do not agree with the course of action taken by the Board regarding Ovitz's separation from Disney. This will not suffice to

68. In re The Walt Disney Co. Derivative Litig., 731 A.2d at 363-364.

create a reasonable doubt that the Board's decision to grant Ovitz a Non-Fault Termination was the product of an exercise of business judgment. As demand is not excused as to Plaintiffs' claims in connection with the current Board's decision to grant Ovitz's Non-Fault Termination, these claims must be dismissed.[69]

To rule otherwise would invite courts to become super-directors, measuring matters of degree in business decisionmaking and executive compensation. Such a rule would run counter to the foundation of our jurisprudence.

Nevertheless, plaintiffs will have another opportunity—if they are able to do so consistent with Chancery Rule 11[70]—to file a short and plain statement alleging particularized facts creating a reasonable doubt that the New Board's decision regarding the Ovitz non-fault termination was protected by the business judgment rule.

d. Directors' Duty of Good Faith Explicated

The Delaware Supreme Court's opinion in Brehm v. Eisner opened the door to a new litigation strategy—repackaging process due care claims as bad faith claims. Indeed, after a book and records demand, the plaintiffs in *Brehm* filed an amended derivative complaint claiming that the Disney boards violated both their duties of care and good faith. Chancellor Chandler found the amended complaint sufficient to survive defendants' motions to dismiss.

> I conclude that plaintiffs' new complaint sufficiently pleads a breach of fiduciary duty by the Old and the New Disney Board of Directors so as to withstand a motion to dismiss under Chancery Rules 23.1 and 12(b)(6). Stated briefly, plaintiffs' new allegations give rise to a cognizable question whether the defendant directors of the Walt Disney Company should be held personally liable to the corporation for a knowing or intentional lack of due care in the directors' decision-making process regarding Ovitz's employment and termination. It is rare when a court imposes liability on directors of a corporation for breach of the duty of care, and this Court is hesitant to second-guess the business judgment of a disinterested and independent board of directors. But the facts alleged in the new complaint do not implicate merely negligent or grossly negligent decision making by corporate directors. Quite the contrary; plaintiffs' new complaint suggests that the Disney directors failed to exercise *any* business judgment and failed to make *any* good faith attempt to fulfill their fiduciary duties to Disney and its stockholders. Allegations that Disney's directors abdicated all responsibility to consider appropriately an action of material importance to the corporation puts directly in question whether the board's decision-making processes were employed in a good faith effort to advance corporate interests. In short, the new complaint alleges facts implying that the Disney directors failed to "act in good faith and meet minimal proceduralist standards of attention." Based on the facts asserted in the new complaint, therefore, I believe plaintiffs have stated cognizable claims for which demand is excused and on which a more complete factual record is necessary.

In re Walt Disney Company Derivative Litigation, 825 A.2d 275, 277 (Del. Ch. 2003).

---

69. In re The Walt Disney Co. Derivative Litig., 731 A.2d at 364 (footnote omitted).

70. Rule 11(b) provides, in part, that subject to sanctions for violating the rule, an attorney "[b]y presenting to the Court . . . a [signed] pleading . . . is certifying that to the best of the [attorney's] knowledge, information and belief, formed after an inquiry reasonable under the circumstances . . . the allegations and other factual contentions have evidentiary support or, if specifically so identified, are likely to have evidentiary support after a reasonable opportunity for further investigation or discovery."

After a full trial that "consumed thirty-seven days . . . and generated 9,360 pages of transcript from twenty-four witnesses . . . ," Chancellor Chandler concluded that the director defendants had not breached their fiduciary duties. However, in the course of his opinion, Chancellor Chandler commented on a central aspect of the duty of good faith.

> Upon long and careful consideration, I am of the opinion that the concept of *intentional der-eliction of duty,* a *conscious disregard for one's responsibilities,* is an appropriate (although not the only) standard for determining whether fiduciaries have acted in good faith. Deliberate indifference and inaction *in the face of a duty to act* is, in my mind, conduct that is clearly disloyal to the corporation.

In re Walt Disney Company Derivative Litigation, 907 A.2d. 693, 755 (Del. Ch. 2005).

In the principal case below, the Delaware Supreme Court affirmed the Chancellor's findings and used the occasion to provide additional guidance as to the nature of the obligation of good faith.

In re Walt Disney Company Derivative Litigation
Delaware Supreme Court, 2006
906 A.2d 27

JACOBS, JUSTICE

Although the appellants have balkanized their due care claim into several frag-mented parts, the overall thrust of that claim is that the compensation committee approved the OEA [Ovitz Employment Agreement] with NFT [Non-Fault Termination] provisions that could potentially result in an enormous payout, without informing themselves of what the full magnitude of that payout could be. . . .

In our view, a helpful approach is to compare what actually happened here to what would have occurred had the committee followed a "best practices" (or "best case") scenario, from a process standpoint. In a "best case" scenario, all committee members would have received, before or at the committee's first meeting on September 26, 1995, a spreadsheet or similar document prepared by (or with the assistance of) a com-pensation expert (in this case, Graef Crystal). Making different, alternative assump-tions, the spreadsheet would disclose the amounts that Ovitz could receive under the OEA in each circumstance that might foreseeably arise. One variable in that matrix of possibilities would be the cost to Disney of a non-fault termination for each of the five years of the initial term of the OEA. The contents of the spreadsheet would be explained to the committee members, either by the expert who prepared it or by a fel-low committee member similarly knowledgeable about the subject. That spreadsheet, which ultimately would become an exhibit to the minutes of the compensation com-mittee meeting, would form the basis of the committee's deliberations and decision.

Had that scenario been followed, there would be no dispute (and no basis for litigation) over what information was furnished to the committee members or when it was furnished. Regrettably, the committee's informational and decision-making pro-cess used here was not so tidy. . . . There is no exhibit to the minutes that discloses, in a single document, the estimated value of the accelerated options in the event of an NFT termination after one year. The information imparted to the committee members on that subject is, however, supported by other evidence, most notably the trial testimony of various witnesses about spreadsheets that were prepared for the compensation committee meetings.

The compensation committee members derived their information about the potential magnitude of an NFT payout from two sources. The first was the value of the "benchmark" options previously granted to Eisner and Wells[6] and the valuations by Watson[7] of the proposed Ovitz options. Ovitz's options were set at 75% of parity with the options previously granted to Eisner and to Frank Wells. Because the compensation committee had established those earlier benchmark option grants to Eisner and Wells and were aware of their value, a simple mathematical calculation would have informed them of the potential value range of Ovitz's options. Also, in August and September 1995, Watson and Russell[8] met with Graef Crystal to determine (among other things) the value of the potential Ovitz options, assuming different scenarios. Crystal valued the options under the Black-Scholes method, while Watson used a different valuation metric. Watson recorded his calculations and the resulting values on a set of spreadsheets that reflected what option profits Ovitz might receive, based upon a range of different assumptions about stock market price increases. Those spreadsheets were shared with, and explained to, the committee members at the September meeting.

The committee's second source of information was the amount of "downside protection" that Ovitz was demanding. Ovitz required financial protection from the risk of leaving a very lucrative and secure position at CAA [Creative Artists Agency], of which he was a controlling partner, to join a publicly held corporation to which Ovitz was a stranger, and that had a very different culture and an environment which prevented him from completely controlling his destiny. The committee members knew that by leaving CAA and coming to Disney, Ovitz would be sacrificing "booked" CAA commissions of $150 to $200 million — an amount that Ovitz demanded as protection against the risk that his employment relationship with Disney might not work out. Ovitz wanted at least $50 million of that compensation to take the form of an "up-front" signing bonus. Had the $50 million bonus been paid, the size of the option grant would have been lower. Because it was contrary to Disney policy, the compensation committee rejected the up-front signing bonus demand, and elected instead to compensate Ovitz at the "back end," by awarding him options that would be phased in over the five-year term of the OEA.

It is on this record that the Chancellor found that the compensation committee was informed of the material facts relating to an NFT payout. If measured in terms of the documentation that would have been generated if "best practices" had been followed, that record leaves much to be desired. The Chancellor acknowledged that, and so do we. But, the Chancellor also found that despite its imperfections, the evidentiary

---

6. [Eds. note — Frank Wells was a former president and chief operation officer at Disney; he died in a helicopter crash in 1994.]

7. [Eds. note — Raymond Watson was a member of Disney's compensation committee and a past Disney board chairman who had helped structure Wells's and Eisner's compensation packages.]

8. [Eds. note — Irwin Russell was a Disney director, chairman of the compensation committee, and Eisner's personal lawyer. Russell played a lead role in negotiating the Ovitz employment contract.]

record was sufficient to support the conclusion that the compensation committee had adequately informed itself of the potential magnitude of the entire severance package, including the options, that Ovitz would receive in the event of an early NFT. . . .

The appellants essentially concede that their proof of bad faith is insufficient to satisfy the standard articulated by the Court of Chancery. That is why they ask this Court to treat a failure to exercise due care as a failure to act in good faith. Unfortunately for appellants, that "rule," even if it were accepted, would not help their case. If we were to conflate these two duties and declare that a breach of the duty to be properly informed violates the duty to act in good faith, the outcome would be no different, because, as the Chancellor and we now have held, the appellants failed to establish any breach of the duty of care. To say it differently, even if the Chancellor's definition of bad faith were erroneous, the error would not be reversible because the appellants cannot satisfy the very test they urge us to adopt.

For that reason, our analysis of the appellants' bad faith claim could end at this point. In other circumstances it would. This case, however, is one in which the duty to act in good faith has played a prominent role, yet to date is not a well-developed area of our corporate fiduciary law. Although the good faith concept has recently been the subject of considerable scholarly writing, which includes articles focused on this specific case, the duty to act in good faith is, up to this point, relatively uncharted. Because of the increased recognition of the importance of good faith, some conceptual guidance to the corporate community may be helpful. For that reason we proceed to address the merits of the appellants' second argument.

The precise question is whether the Chancellor's articulated standard for bad faith corporate fiduciary conduct—intentional dereliction of duty, a conscious disregard for one's responsibilities—is legally correct. In approaching that question, we note that the Chancellor characterized that definition as "*an* appropriate (*although not the only*) standard for determining whether fiduciaries have acted in good faith." That observation is accurate and helpful, because as a matter of simple logic, at least three different categories of fiduciary behavior are candidates for the "bad faith" pejorative label.

The first category involves so-called "subjective bad faith," that is, fiduciary conduct motivated by an actual intent to do harm. That such conduct constitutes classic, quintessential bad faith is a proposition so well accepted in the liturgy of fiduciary law that it borders on axiomatic.[102] We need not dwell further on this category, because no such conduct is claimed to have occurred, or did occur, in this case.

The second category of conduct, which is at the opposite end of the spectrum, involves lack of due care—that is, fiduciary action taken solely by reason of gross negligence and without any malevolent intent. In this case, appellants assert claims of gross negligence to establish breaches not only of director due care but also of the

---

102. The Chancellor so recognized. ("[A]n action taken with the intent to harm the corporation is a disloyal act in bad faith.") See McGowan v. Ferro, 859 A.2d 1012, 1036 (Del. Ch. 2004) ("Bad faith is 'not simply bad judgment or negligence,' but rather 'implies the conscious doing of a wrong because of dishonest purpose or moral obliquity . . . it contemplates a state of mind affirmatively operating with furtive design or ill will.'") (quoting Desert Equities, Inc. v. Morgan Stanley Leveraged Equity Fund, II, L.P., 624 A.2d 1199, 1208, n. 16 (Del. 1993)).

directors' duty to act in good faith. Although the Chancellor found, and we agree, that the appellants failed to establish gross negligence, to afford guidance we address the issue of whether gross negligence (including a failure to inform one's self of available material facts), without more, can also constitute bad faith. The answer is clearly no.

From a broad philosophical standpoint, that question is more complex than would appear, if only because (as the Chancellor and others have observed) "issues of good faith are (to a certain degree) inseparably and necessarily intertwined with the duties of care and loyalty. . . ." But, in the pragmatic, conduct-regulating legal realm which calls for more precise conceptual line drawing, the answer is that grossly negligent conduct, without more, does not and cannot constitute a breach of the fiduciary duty to act in good faith. The conduct that is the subject of due care may overlap with the conduct that comes within the rubric of good faith in a psychological sense,[104] but from a legal standpoint those duties are and must remain quite distinct. Both our legislative history and our common law jurisprudence distinguish sharply between the duties to exercise due care and to act in good faith, and highly significant consequences flow from that distinction.

The Delaware General Assembly has addressed the distinction between bad faith and a failure to exercise due care (*i.e.,* gross negligence) in two separate contexts. The first is Section 102(b)(7) of the DGCL, which authorizes Delaware corporations, by a provision in the certificate of incorporation, to exculpate their directors from monetary damage liability for a breach of the duty of care. That exculpatory provision affords significant protection to directors of Delaware corporations. The statute carves out several exceptions, however, including most relevantly, "for acts or omissions not in good faith. . . ." Thus, a corporation can exculpate its directors from monetary liability for a breach of the duty of care, but not for conduct that is not in good faith. To adopt a definition of bad faith that would cause a violation of the duty of care automatically to become an act or omission "not in good faith," would eviscerate the protections accorded to directors by the General Assembly's adoption of Section 102(b)(7).

A second legislative recognition of the distinction between fiduciary conduct that is grossly negligent and conduct that is not in good faith, is Delaware's indemnification statute, found at 8 *Del. C.* §145. To oversimplify, subsections (a) and (b) of that statute permit a corporation to indemnify (*inter alia*) any person who is or was a director, officer, employee or agent of the corporation against expenses (including attorneys' fees), judgments, fines and amounts paid in settlement of specified actions, suits or proceedings, where (among other things): (i) that person is, was, or is threatened to be made a party to that action, suit or proceeding, and (ii) that person "acted in good

---

104. An example of such overlap might be the hypothetical case where a director, because of subjective hostility to the corporation on whose board he serves, fails to inform himself of, or to devote sufficient attention to, the matters on which he is making decisions as a fiduciary. In such a case, two states of mind coexist in the same person: subjective bad intent (which would lead to a finding of bad faith) and gross negligence (which would lead to a finding of a breach of the duty of care). Although the coexistence of both states of mind may make them indistinguishable from a psychological standpoint, the fiduciary duties that they cause the director to violate—care and good faith—are legally separate and distinct.

faith and in a manner the person reasonably believed to be in or not opposed to the best interests of the corporation. . . ."[107] Thus, under Delaware statutory law a director or officer of a corporation can be indemnified for liability (and litigation expenses) incurred by reason of a violation of the duty of care, but not for a violation of the duty to act in good faith.

Section 145, like Section 102(b)(7), evidences the intent of the Delaware General Assembly to afford significant protections to directors (and, in the case of Section 145, other fiduciaries) of Delaware corporations. To adopt a definition that conflates the duty of care with the duty to act in good faith by making a violation of the former an automatic violation of the latter, would nullify those legislative protections and defeat the General Assembly's intent. There is no basis in policy, precedent or common sense that would justify dismantling the distinction between gross negligence and bad faith.[109]

That leaves the third category of fiduciary conduct, which falls in between the first two categories of (1) conduct motivated by subjective bad intent and (2) conduct resulting from gross negligence. This third category is what the Chancellor's definition of bad faith — intentional dereliction of duty, a conscious disregard for one's responsibilities — is intended to capture. The question is whether such misconduct is properly treated as a non-exculpable, non-indemnifiable violation of the fiduciary duty to act in good faith. In our view it must be, for at least two reasons.

First, the universe of fiduciary misconduct is not limited to either disloyalty in the classic sense (i.e., preferring the adverse self-interest of the fiduciary or of a related person to the interest of the corporation) or gross negligence. Cases have arisen where corporate directors have no conflicting self-interest in a decision, yet engage in misconduct that is more culpable than simple inattention or failure to be informed of all facts material to the decision. To protect the interests of the corporation and its shareholders, fiduciary conduct of this kind, which does not involve disloyalty (as traditionally defined) but is qualitatively more culpable than gross negligence, should be proscribed. A vehicle is needed to address such violations doctrinally, and that doctrinal vehicle is the duty to act in good faith. The Chancellor implicitly so recognized in his Opinion, where he identified different examples of bad faith as follows:

> The good faith required of a corporate fiduciary includes not simply the duties of care and loyalty, in the narrow sense that I have discussed them above, but all actions required by a true faithfulness and devotion to the interests of the corporation and its shareholders. A failure to act in good faith may be shown, for instance, where the fiduciary intentionally acts with a purpose other than that of advancing the best interests of the corporation, where the fiduciary acts with the intent to violate applicable positive law, or where the fiduciary intentionally fails to act in the face of a known duty to

---

107. 8 *Del. C.* §§145(a) & (b).

109. Basic to the common law of torts is the distinction between conduct that is negligent (or grossly negligent) and conduct that is intentional. And in the narrower area of corporation law, our jurisprudence has recognized the distinction between the fiduciary duties to act with due care, with loyalty, and in good faith, as well as the consequences that flow from that distinction. Recent Delaware case law precludes a recovery of rescissory (as distinguished from out-of-pocket) damages for a breach of the duty of care, but permits such a recovery for a breach of the duty of loyalty. See Cinerama, Inc. v. Technicolor, Inc., 663 A.2d 1134, 1147-1150 (Del. Ch. 1994), aff'd, 663 A.2d 1156 (Del. 1995).

act, demonstrating a conscious disregard for his duties. There may be other examples of bad faith yet to be proven or alleged, but these three are the most salient.[110]

Those articulated examples of bad faith are not new to our jurisprudence. Indeed, they echo pronouncements our courts have made throughout the decades.[111]

Second, the legislature has also recognized this intermediate category of fiduciary misconduct, which ranks between conduct involving subjective bad faith and gross negligence. Section 102(b)(7)(ii) of the DGCL expressly denies money damage exculpation for "acts or omissions not in good faith or which involve intentional misconduct or a knowing violation of law." By its very terms that provision distinguishes between "intentional misconduct" and a "knowing violation of law" (both examples of subjective bad faith) on the one hand, and "acts . . . not in good faith," on the other. Because the statute exculpates directors only for conduct amounting to gross negligence, the statutory denial of exculpation for "acts . . . not in good faith" must encompass the intermediate category of misconduct captured by the Chancellor's definition of bad faith.

For these reasons, we uphold the Court of Chancery's definition as a legally appropriate, although not the exclusive, definition of fiduciary bad faith. We need go no further. To engage in an effort to craft (in the Court's words) "a definitive and categorical definition of the universe of acts that would constitute bad faith" would be unwise and is unnecessary to dispose of the issues presented on this appeal.

NOTES AND QUESTIONS

1. In the principal case above, Justice Jacobs noted that directors do not violate their duty of care or good faith simply because they fail to follow best corporate practices. In retrospect, Smith v. Van Gorkom could be described as a case in which the directors failed to follow best corporate practices in approving a sale of the company. Did the conduct in *Van Gorkom* depart from best practices sufficiently to constitute a breach of the directors' duty of care?

2. In Lyondell Chemical Company v. Ryan, 970 A.2d 235 (Del. 2009), a class action factually reminiscent of Smith v. Van Gorkom, the plaintiff claimed that the directors

---

110. In re Walt Disney Co. Derivative Litigation, 907 A.2d 693, 755-756 (Del. Ch. 2005).

111. *See, e.g.,* Allaun v. Consol. Oil Co., 147 A. 257, 261 (Del. Ch. 1929) (further judicial scrutiny is warranted if the transaction results from the directors' "reckless indifference to or a deliberate disregard of the interests of the whole body of stockholders"); Gimbel v. Signal Cos., Inc., 316 A.2d 599, 604 (Del. Ch. 1974), *aff'd,* 316 A.2d 619 (Del. 1974) (injunction denied because, *inter alia,* there was "[n]othing in the record [that] would justify a finding . . . that the directors acted for any personal advantage or out of improper motive or intentional disregard of shareholder interests"); In re Caremark Int'l Derivative Litig., 698 A.2d 959, 971 (Del. Ch. 1996) ("only a sustained or systematic failure of the board to exercise oversight—such as an utter failure to attempt to assure a reasonable information and reporting system exists—will establish the lack of good faith that is a necessary condition to liability."); Nagy v. Bistricer, 770 A.2d 43, 48, n. 2 (Del. Ch. 2000) (observing that the utility of the duty of good faith "may rest in its constant reminder . . . that, regardless of his motive, a director who consciously disregards his duties to the corporation and its stockholders may suffer a personal judgment for monetary damages for any harm he causes," even if for a reason "other than personal pecuniary interest").

of Lyondell breached their *Revlon* duty by selling the company for less than the best price possible. Ryan also asserted that the directors' misconduct, which looked remarkably like the directors' conduct in *Van Gorkom,* rose to the level of bad faith. Framing the claim as more than a breach of the duty of care was essential, because Lyondell's certificate of incorporation exculpated directors from money damages based solely on a violation of the duty of care. The Court of Chancery denied the defendant's motion for summary judgment. The Delaware Supreme Court reversed, providing insight into the extreme hurdle that must be overcome to successfully plead a bad faith claim against independent, disinterested directors in a transactional setting.

There is only one *Revlon* duty—to "[get] the best price for the stockholders at a sale of the company." No court can tell directors exactly how to accomplish that goal, because they will be facing a unique combination of circumstances, many of which will be outside their control. As we noted in Barkan v. Amsted Industries, Inc., "there is no single blueprint that a board must follow to fulfill its duties. . . ."

The Lyondell directors did not conduct an auction or a market check, and they did not satisfy the trial court that they had the "impeccable" market knowledge that the court believed was necessary to excuse their failure to pursue one of the first two alternatives. As a result, the Court of Chancery was unable to conclude that the directors had met their burden under *Revlon*. In evaluating the totality of the circumstances, even on this limited record, we would be inclined to hold otherwise. But we would not question the trial court's decision to seek additional evidence if the issue were whether the directors had exercised due care. Where, as here, the issue is whether the directors failed to act in good faith, the analysis is very different, and the existing record mandates the entry of judgment in favor of the directors.

As discussed above, bad faith will be found if a "fiduciary intentionally fails to act in the face of a known duty to act, demonstrating a conscious disregard for his duties." The trial court decided that the *Revlon* sale process must follow one of three courses, and that the Lyondell directors did not discharge that "known set of [*Revlon*]'duties.'" But, as noted, there are no legally prescribed steps that directors must follow to satisfy their *Revlon* duties. Thus, the directors' failure to take any specific steps during the sale process could not have demonstrated a conscious disregard of their duties. More importantly, there is a vast difference between an inadequate or flawed effort to carry out fiduciary duties and a conscious disregard for those duties.

Directors' decisions must be reasonable, not perfect. "In the transactional context, [an] extreme set of facts [is] required to sustain a disloyalty claim premised on the notion that disinterested directors were intentionally disregarding their duties." The trial court denied summary judgment because the Lyondell directors' "unexplained inaction" prevented the court from determining that they had acted in good faith. But, if the directors failed to do all that they should have under the circumstances, they breached their duty of care. Only if they knowingly and completely failed to undertake their responsibilities would they breach their duty of loyalty. The trial court approached the record from the wrong perspective. Instead of questioning whether disinterested, independent directors did everything that they (arguably) should have done to obtain the best sale price, the inquiry should have been whether those directors utterly failed to attempt to obtain the best sale price.

Lyondell Chemical Company v. Ryan, 970 A.2d 235, 242-244.

PROBLEM 4-10

Reconsider Problem 4-8. Have one or more of the Hollywood directors breached the fiduciary duty of good faith? What difference does it make whether the court views the action as a breach of the duty of care claim or as bad faith claim?

e.   *Officers' Oversight and Reporting Duties*

MBCA §§8.42

Until recently the subject of officers' fiduciary duties has received little separate attention. For officers who are also directors, the focus has been primarily on the fiduciary duties that flow from their status as directors. For officers who are not also directors, the assumption has been that officers, as agents of the corporation, are subject to the fiduciary duties imposed by the common law of agency.[11]

Under the Sarbanes-Oxley Act, the CEO and the CFO are central to the integrity of a corporation's financial reporting system, yet under state law it is still the board of directors' responsibility to ensure that the corporation has adequate internal financial controls and systems in place. What recourse do the board of directors and the corporation have when, in their view, it is the misconduct of the CEO or the CFO (who often is not a director) that has caused the corporation to make false financial reports? If officers are sued by the corporation for their role in financial reporting misconduct, are their actions, as officers, protected by business judgment rule presumptions? What is the risk that officers will be made scapegoats for the shortcomings of the directors or the misconduct of employees and lesser officers more directly involved in the financial reporting process?

Miller v. U.S. Foodservice, Inc.
United States District Court, District of Maryland, 2005
361 F. Supp. 2d 470

MEMORANDUM

BLAKE, DISTRICT JUDGE.

James L. Miller, former President, Chief Executive Officer, and Chairman to United States Foodservice, Inc. ("USF"), and director to its parent company, Koninklijke Ahold N.V. ("Royal Ahold"), sued his former employers, including three individual officers of Royal Ahold and the wholly-owned subsidiary Ahold U.S.A., Inc., for failing to provide him with the post-termination benefits he claims he is entitled to under his employment agreement. . . . Royal Ahold and USF ("the companies") countersued, claiming, among other causes of action, that Miller violated the fiduciary duties of due care, good faith, and loyalty, and therefore they are not obligated to provide him with the benefits conferred by the contract. . . .

BACKGROUND

James Miller joined USF, a Delaware corporation engaged in the food distribution business and headquartered in Columbia, Maryland, in 1983 and rose to the position

---

11. For a comprehensive evaluation of the common law rules applicable to non-director officers, see A. Gilchrist Sparks, III & Lawrence A. Hamermesh, Common Law Duties of Non-Director Corporate Officers, 48 Bus. Law. 215 (1992).

of CEO in 1994. Miller also served as USF's Chairman of the Board of Directors, President, and CEO since 1997. After Royal Ahold, an international food provider based in the Netherlands, acquired USF in 2000, Miller became a member of Royal Ahold's Executive Board (also known as its Managing Board or "RVB") on or about September 1, 2001. He served in this dual capacity as officer and director for USF and director for Royal Ahold until May 13, 2003, the day he resigned from his positions.

Miller's resignation was precipitated by an accounting scandal involving USF's income from promotional allowances, which are payments made by vendors to the company to promote their goods. In 2003, internal investigations revealed that USF "accounting irregularities" had resulted in an overstatement of USF's income by nearly $900 million for fiscal years 2000 and 2001, and during fiscal year 2002. Consequently, Royal Ahold restated its earnings in October 2003 in the 2002 Form 20-F Filed with the SEC. The 2002 Form 20-F reported that Royal Ahold "determined that certain senior officers and other USF employees had violated generally accepted accounting principles by improperly and prematurely recognizing promotional allowances" and that "material weaknesses in USF's accounting procedures and internal controls had permitted this improper revenue recognition over the preceding three years." Miller avers that he had "absolutely no involvement in the purported wrongful conduct" and that the companies have treated him as a "scapegoat" for the problem. The companies contend that as President, CEO, and Chairman of USF during the relevant years, Miller had "supervisory, managerial, and oversight responsibilit[y]" for USF's operations and accounting practices, that he knew by July 2000 of material weaknesses in USF's internal controls, and that he failed to oversee correction of the known accounting deficiencies for almost three years. The counterclaimants assert that Miller was alerted to the internal control problems by a July 24, 2000 letter from Deloitte & Touche, the company's external auditor, which stated that "deficiencies in the design and operation of [USF's] internal controls . . . could adversely affect the Company's ability to record, process, summarize, and report financial data consistent with the assertions of management in the financial statements." In addition, the companies assert that Miller intentionally misrepresented that corrective measures were being implemented several times during USF Audit Committee meetings in 2000 through 2002. (See Countercl. PP 17-21, referring to meetings on November 29, 2000, April 5, 2001, October 29, 2001, April 8, 2002, and in October and November 2002.) The companies contend they later learned that, contrary to Miller's positive assertions, "no significant progress had been made on implementing the necessary changes." (Countercl. P 19.)

At the request of senior Royal Ahold executives, Miller resigned from his USF and Royal Ahold positions on May 13, 2003. . . .

ANALYSIS . . .

IV. CORPORATE CLAIMS

A. *Duties of care and good faith*

Miller argues that Royal Ahold and USF's corporate claims fail because as an officer and director of USF (and director of Royal Ahold), his actions are protected by the business judgment rule. . . .

Under Delaware law, corporate officers and directors owe their corporation the fiduciary duties of due care, good faith, and loyalty. Malone v. Brincat, 722 A.2d 5, 10 (Del. 1998). See also 3 *Fletcher Cyclopedia Corp.* §846 ("An officer's duties appear coextensive with those of directors.") . . .

[The court then discussed *Caremark* and its progeny.]

In McCall v. Scott, 239 F.3d 808, 818-19 (6th Cir. 2001), the shareholder plaintiffs claimed that Columbia/HCA's senior management, with board knowledge, devised schemes to improperly increase revenue and profits and cultivated a philosophy that encouraged employees to falsify financial records. In the context of assessing the pleadings to determine demand futility, the court found that the plaintiffs' allegations that directors intentionally or recklessly failed to act and disregarded red flags over an almost three year period were sufficient to state a claim. Id. at 824. The red flags included the failure to act in the face of questionable audit practices, aggressive acquisition practices, a qui tam action, federal investigations and a New York Times investigation. Id. at 820-24.

The allegations in this case do not include red flags as significant as in *McCall*. Here, the companies allege that Miller knew in July 2000 of internal control problems, and that despite his awareness of the pressing nature of the problem he failed over a period of almost three years to implement corrective measures. The counterclaimants assert that this failure was particularly egregious because Mark Kaiser, the officer responsible for promotional allowance tracking and internal auditing, reported directly to Miller. The companies allege further that Miller breached his duty of good faith by intentionally misrepresenting during several USF Audit Committee meetings that stronger controls were being implemented, though later these assurances proved false. They claim that Miller knew ineffective tracking of promotional allowances "had the potential to cause USF to overstate its income and thus to show phantom profits" and that "Miller's incentive-based compensation depended on the net profitability of USF, and Miller in fact received incentive-based bonus compensation equal to or exceeding his annual salary." The companies claim that the gravity of Miller's offense is compounded by his dual role as President and CEO for USF and director for Royal Ahold.

While the companies' allegations do not directly suggest that Miller should have suspected wrongdoing, as the *Graham* decision requires, the *Caremark* court made it clear that the *Graham* decision should not be interpreted so broadly as to supplant the requirement that corporate directors and officers ensure an adequate information and reporting system exists. 698 A.2d at 969. The companies allege that despite early warnings, such as the July 2000 letter from Deloitte & Touche, that USF's information and reporting system was significantly deficient, Miller failed to implement measures to correct the problem. The *Caremark* court considered it an "elementary fact that [the provision of] relevant and timely information is an essential predicate for satisfaction of the board's supervisory and monitoring role." Id. at 970. In other words, first and foremost, directors and officers must assure that a reporting system exists which is "in concept and design adequate" to provide appropriate and timely information to them so that they may satisfy their monitoring responsibility. Id. Therefore, questions as to whether a director had grounds to suspect wrongdoing by other officers or directors presume the existence of an adequate reporting system. Id. at 970 (observing that even with adequate reporting systems, "senior officers or directors may nevertheless sometimes be misled or otherwise fail reasonably to detect acts material to the corporation's compliance with the law.").

Perhaps the most critical support for the companies' claims that Miller breached fiduciary duties of care and good faith, however, is the allegation that Miller, for a period of almost three years, intentionally misrepresented to the USF Audit Committee (and consequently to the parent company, Royal Ahold) that the internal controls were being corrected. The counterclaim details representations made by Miller at several USF Audit Committee meetings during 2000 through 2002 that indicated corrective measures were being implemented and that strengthening the company's internal controls was a top priority. The companies describe a scenario where Miller repeatedly misled the USF Audit Committee and the parent company, Royal Ahold. For example, according to the counterclaimants, at an April 8, 2002 Audit Committee meeting,

> Miller "stated that USF was abandoning its prior plans to use a particular type of tracking system because it 'was not as robust as first anticipated.' In fact, this tracking system had never been implemented at all." If these allegations are true, they may constitute persuasive evidence that Miller acted in bad faith, thereby violating duties of both care and good faith. Additionally, Miller's dual role as director and officer (President, Chairman, and CEO of USF, director to Royal Ahold) magnifies the importance of the duties he owed and allegedly violated. Construing the allegations in the light most favorable to the counterclaimants, I find that the companies have stated claims against Miller for breach of the fiduciary duties of care and good faith. . . .

NOTES AND QUESTIONS

1. Does it make sense to extend business judgment rule protection to the actions of a non-director officer?

2. The Delaware Supreme Court has now expressly held that officers owe the same fiduciary duties as directors.

> The Court of Chancery has held, and the parties do not dispute, that corporate officers owe fiduciary duties that are identical to those owed by corporate directors. That issue—whether or not officers owe fiduciary duties identical to those of directors—has been characterized as a matter of first impression for this Court. In the past, we have implied that officers of Delaware corporations, like directors, owe fiduciary duties of care and loyalty, and that the fiduciary duties of officers are the same as those of directors. We now explicitly so hold.

Gantler v. Stephens, 965 A.2d. 695, 708-709 (Del. 2009). However, a bevy of questions remain unanswered. How does the fiduciary duty owed by a corporate officer differ from the fiduciary duty that would otherwise result under agency law principles? How do we determine whether a particular corporate official is an "officer" for purposes of corporate law fiduciary duty analysis? Is an officer entitled to the protections of the business judgment rule? Should corporation law statutes allow corporations to exculpate officers to the same extent as directors?

3. Under sections 302 and 904 of the Sarbanes-Oxley Act of 2002, the corporation's chief executive officer and chief financial officer must certify in each quarterly and annual filings with the SEC, among other things, that based on their knowledge the reports are not misleading and fairly present the company's financial situation,

and that they have disclosed to the auditors and audit committee any material deficiencies in the design or operation of the company's financial controls. Knowingly making a false certification exposes the CEO or CFO to criminal penalties including up to 20 years in prison, if the false certification is also made willfully. Should a CEO or CFO face liability for breach of fiduciary duty, as in the *Miller* case, if their conduct did not violate Sarbanes-Oxley?

D.   *Special Aspects of Derivative and Direct Litigation*

1.   Derivative Litigation and the Demand Requirement

> **MBCA §§7.42, 7.44**
> **ALI, Principles of Corporate Governance §7.03**

Almost everything that directors do in managing and overseeing the operation of a corporation's business and affairs implicates fiduciary duties that the directors owe to the corporation. This presents a policy dilemma. Directors are responsible for managing the corporation, and this responsibility normally includes determining when litigation is in the corporation's best interest. However, deciding whether or not to institute a lawsuit against one or more directors for alleged breach of fiduciary duty presents the directors with a very different calculus than deciding whether to commence other types of commercial litigation—the parties who would be sued will generally include one or more of the corporation's current directors. In such cases, each director might consciously or unconsciously factor in the costs that the director herself might have to bear, or that might have to be borne by other directors or officers for whom the director cares deeply or whom the director does not want to offend. As a result, directors might in some cases decide not to pursue fiduciary duty claims, when, objectively viewed, it would be in the corporation's best interest to litigate.

Rather than entrust the litigation of all such claims to the directors, there developed in courts of equity an unusual device, the shareholder derivative suit, whereby shareholders could commence and manage fiduciary litigation on the corporation's behalf. The device and its shortcomings were succinctly described by Judge Ralph Winter:

> The derivative action is the common law's inventive solution to the problem of actions to protect shareholder interests. In its classic form, a derivative suit involves two actions brought by an individual shareholder: (i) an action against the corporation for failing to bring a specified suit and (ii) an action on behalf of the corporation for harm to it identical to the one which the corporation failed to bring. See Ross v. Bernhard, 396 U.S. 531, 90 S. Ct. 733, 24 L. Ed. 2d 729 (1970). The technical structure of the derivative suit is thus quite unusual. Moreover, the shareholder plaintiffs are quite often little more than a formality for purposes of the caption rather than parties with a real interest in the outcome. Since any judgment runs to the corporation, shareholder plaintiffs at best realize an appreciation in the value of their shares. The real incentive to bring derivative actions is usually not the hope of return to the corporation but the hope of handsome fees to be recovered by plaintiffs' counsel. As two leading commentators state:
>
>> [T]he derivative action constitutes a major bulwark against managerial self-dealing. As a practical matter this means that the rules governing plaintiffs' legal fees are critical to the operation of the corporate system: Since very few shareholders would pay an attorney's fee

out of their own pocket to finance a suit that is brought on the corporation's behalf and normally holds only a slight and indirect benefit for the plaintiff, very few derivative actions would be brought if the law did not allow the plaintiff's attorney to be compensated by a contingent fee payable out of the corporate recovery.

However, there is a danger in authorizing lawyers to bring actions on behalf of unconsulted groups. Derivative suits may be brought for their nuisance value, the threat of protracted discovery and litigation forcing settlement and payment of fees even where the underlying suit has modest merit. Such suits may be harmful to shareholders because the costs offset the recovery. Thus, a continuing debate surrounding derivative actions has been over restricting their use to situations where the corporation has a reasonable chance for benefit.

Joy v. North, 692 F.2d 880, 887 (2d. Cir. 1982).

In addition to the concerns expressed by Judge Winter, the shareholder derivative suit is troublesome simply because it involves a usurpation of the directors' normal power to manage the corporation. Given the policy reasons for the business judgment rule, why should a shareholder be able to institute a derivative action on behalf of the corporation if, in fact, the directors are able and willing to make decisions concerning such legal action in the best interests of the corporation? That, of course, is the rub. How can we know when to allow shareholders to maintain a derivative suit and when, instead, to leave directors in control of the litigation? What rules and procedures governing the derivative suit will produce the optimal benefit for corporations, directors, shareholders, and society? Courts and legislators continue to struggle with this problem. All that is certain is that any answer will of necessity involve both some dilution in the protection that the business judgment rule would normally afford directors and some restrictions on shareholders' ability to pursue a derivative suit that would not be imposed on a lawsuit brought directly by the corporation at the behest of its directors.

The compromise reached in most jurisdictions revolves around the demand requirement. Delaware and many other jurisdictions require a shareholder to make pre-suit demand on the board, explaining the claims that he wishes investigated and remedied. It is then up to the board to consider how to deal with the matters brought to their attention in the demand letter. If the board reaches a decision not to pursue the claim via litigation, the shareholder may challenge the directors' decision as a breach of fiduciary duty, but has no right to directly pursue the original claim that was the subject of his demand, unless the directors' action in refusing to institute litigation is found not to be protected by the business judgment rule.

Delaware and some other jurisdictions excuse shareholders from making pre-suit demand in circumstances where demand would be futile, for example, when the directors lack the independence to impartially consider a demand. In these jurisdictions, the demand futility exception becomes the initial battleground in derivative litigation. Defendants quickly move for dismissal on the grounds that the shareholder-plaintiff wrongfully failed to make demand.

In recent years the MBCA, the ALI Principles, and several states have adopted a universal demand requirement, which, as the name implies, requires shareholders to make pre-suit demand in virtually every circumstance. The universal demand requirement is premised in significant part on the belief that allowing exceptions to pre-suit demand imposes excessive additional litigation costs. If directors refuse to commence litigation after demand is made, then shareholders may challenge that refusal.

This moves the legal focus away from the standards governing when demand must be made (discussed in the Delaware case below) to the process (see, e.g., MBCA §7.44) by which a court will grant a corporation's motion to dismiss a derivative suit.

Aronson v. Lewis
Delaware Supreme Court, 1984
473 A.2d 805

MOORE, JUSTICE:

. . . [W]hen is a stockholder's demand upon a board of directors, to redress an alleged wrong to the corporation, excused as futile prior to the filing of a derivative suit? We granted this interlocutory appeal to the defendants, Meyers Parking System, Inc. (Meyers), a Delaware corporation, and its directors, to review the Court of Chancery's denial of their motion to dismiss this action, pursuant to Chancery Rule 23.1, for the plaintiff's failure to make such a demand or otherwise demonstrate its futility. The Vice Chancellor ruled that plaintiff's allegations raised a "reasonable inference" that the directors' action was unprotected by the business judgment rule. Thus, the board could not have impartially considered and acted upon the demand.

We cannot agree with this formulation of the concept of demand futility. In our view demand can only be excused where facts are alleged with particularity which create a reasonable doubt that the directors' action was entitled to the protections of the business judgment rule. Because the plaintiff failed to make a demand, and to allege facts with particularity indicating that such demand would be futile, we reverse the Court of Chancery and remand with instructions that plaintiff be granted leave to amend the complaint.

I.

The issues of demand futility rest upon the allegations of the complaint. The plaintiff, Harry Lewis, is a stockholder of Meyers. The defendants are Meyers and its ten directors, some of whom are also company officers.

In 1979, Prudential Building Maintenance Corp. (Prudential) spun off its shares of Meyers to Prudential's stockholders. Prior thereto Meyers was a wholly owned subsidiary of Prudential. Meyers provides parking lot facilities and related services throughout the country. Its stock is actively traded over-the-counter.

This suit challenges certain transactions between Meyers and one of its directors, Leo Fink, who owns 47% of its outstanding stock. Plaintiff claims that these transactions were approved only because Fink personally selected each director and officer of Meyers.[2]

---

2. The Court of Chancery stated that Fink had been chief executive officer of Prudential prior to the spin-off and thereafter became chairman of Meyers' board. This was not alleged in the complaint.

Prior to January 1, 1981, Fink had an employment agreement with Prudential which provided that upon retirement he was to become a consultant to that company for ten years. This provision became operable when Fink retired in April 1980. Thereafter, Meyers agreed with Prudential to share Fink's consulting services and reimburse Prudential for 25% of the fees paid Fink. Under this arrangement Meyers paid Prudential $48,332 in 1980 and $45,832 in 1981.

On January 1, 1981, the defendants approved an employment agreement between Meyers and Fink for a five year term with provision for automatic renewal each year thereafter, indefinitely. Meyers agreed to pay Fink $150,000 per year, plus a bonus of 5% of its pre-tax profits over $2,400,000. Fink could terminate the contract at any time, but Meyers could do so only upon six months' notice. At termination, Fink was to become a consultant to Meyers and be paid $150,000 per year for the first three years, $125,000 for the next three years, and $100,000 thereafter for life. Death benefits were also included. Fink agreed to devote his best efforts and substantially his entire business time to advancing Meyers' interests. The agreement also provided that Fink's compensation was not to be affected by any inability to perform services on Meyers' behalf. Fink was 75 years old when his employment agreement with Meyers was approved by the directors. There is no claim that he was, or is, in poor health.

Additionally, the Meyers board approved and made interest-free loans to Fink totalling $225,000. These loans were unpaid and outstanding as of August 1982 when the complaint was filed. At oral argument defendants' counsel represented that these loans had been repaid in full.

The complaint charges that these transactions had "no valid business purpose," and were a "waste of corporate assets" because the amounts to be paid are "grossly excessive," that Fink performs "no or little services," and because of his "advanced age" cannot be "expected to perform any such services." The plaintiff also charges that the existence of the Prudential consulting agreement with Fink prevents him from providing his "best efforts" on Meyers' behalf. Finally, it is alleged that the loans to Fink were in reality "additional compensation" without any "consideration" or "benefit" to Meyers.

The complaint alleged that no demand had been made on the Meyers board because:

13. . . . such attempt would be futile for the following reasons:
    (a) All of the directors in office are named as defendants herein and they have participated in, expressly approved and/or acquiesced in, and are personally liable for, the wrongs complained of herein.
    (b) Defendant Fink, having selected each director, controls and dominates every member of the Board and every officer of Meyers.
    (c) Institution of this action by present directors would require the defendant-directors to sue themselves, thereby placing the conduct of this action in hostile hands and preventing its effective prosecution.

The relief sought included the cancellation of the Meyers-Fink employment contract and an accounting by the directors, including Fink, for all damage sustained by Meyers and for all profits derived by the directors and Fink. . . .

IV.

A

A cardinal precept of the G.C.L. of the State of Delaware is that directors, rather than shareholders, manage the business and affairs of the corporation. 8 Del. C. §141(a). Section 141(a) states in pertinent part: "The *business and affairs* of a corporation organized under this chapter *shall be managed by or under the direction* of a board of directors except as may be otherwise provided in this chapter or in its certificate of incorporation." 8 Del. C. §141(a) (Emphasis added). The existence and exercise of this power carries with it certain fundamental fiduciary obligations to the corporation and its shareholders. Moreover, a stockholder is not powerless to challenge director action which results in harm to the corporation. The machinery of corporate democracy and the derivative suit are potent tools to redress the conduct of a torpid or unfaithful management. The derivative action developed in equity to enable shareholders to sue in the corporation's name where those in control of the company refused to assert a claim belonging to it. The nature of the action is two-fold. First, it is the equivalent of a suit by the shareholders to compel the corporation to sue. Second, it is a suit by the corporation, asserted by the shareholders on its behalf, against those liable to it.

By its very nature the derivative action impinges on the managerial freedom of directors. Hence, the demand requirement of Chancery Rule 23.1 exists at the threshold, first to insure that a stockholder exhausts his intracorporate remedies, and then to provide a safeguard against strike suits. Thus, by promoting this form of alternate dispute resolution, rather than immediate recourse to litigation, the demand requirement is a recognition of the fundamental precept that directors manage the business and affairs of corporations.

In our view the entire question of demand futility is inextricably bound to issues of business judgment and the standards of that doctrine's applicability. The business judgment rule is an acknowledgment of the managerial prerogatives of Delaware directors under §141(a). It is a presumption that in making a business decision the directors of a corporation acted on an informed basis, in good faith and in the honest belief that the action taken was in the best interests of the company. Absent an abuse of discretion, that judgment will be respected by the courts. The burden is on the party challenging the decision to establish facts rebutting the presumption.

The function of the business judgment rule is of paramount significance in the context of a derivative action. It comes into play in several ways—in addressing a demand, in the determination of demand futility, in efforts by independent disinterested directors to dismiss the action as inimical to the corporation's best interests, and generally, as a defense to the merits of the suit. However, in each of these circumstances there are certain common principles governing the application and operation of the rule.

First, its protections can only be claimed by disinterested directors whose conduct otherwise meets the tests of business judgment. From the standpoint of interest, this means that directors can neither appear on both sides of a transaction nor expect to derive any personal financial benefit from it in the sense of self-dealing, as opposed to a benefit which devolves upon the corporation or all stockholders generally. See also 8 Del. C. §144. Thus, if such director interest is present, and the transaction is not approved by a majority consisting of the disinterested directors, then the business judgment rule has no application whatever in determining demand futility. See 8 Del. C. §144(a)(1).

Second, to invoke the rule's protection directors have a duty to inform themselves, prior to making a business decision, of all material information reasonably available to them. Having become so informed, they must then act with requisite care in the discharge of their duties. While the Delaware cases use a variety of terms to describe the applicable standard of care, our analysis satisfies us that under the business judgment rule director liability is predicated upon concepts of gross negligence.

However, it should be noted that the business judgment rule operates only in the context of director action. Technically speaking, it has no role where directors have either abdicated their functions, or absent a conscious decision, failed to act. But it also follows that under applicable principles, a conscious decision to refrain from acting may nonetheless be a valid exercise of business judgment and enjoy the protections of the rule. . . .

Delaware courts have addressed the issue of demand futility on several earlier occasions. The rule emerging from these decisions is that where officers and directors are under an influence which sterilizes their discretion, they cannot be considered proper persons to conduct litigation on behalf of the corporation. Thus, demand would be futile. See, e.g., McKee v. Rogers, Del. Ch., 156 A. 191, 192 (1931) (holding that where a defendant controlled the board of directors, "[i]t is manifest then that there can be no expectation that the corporation would sue him, and if it did, it can hardly be said that the prosecution of the suit would be entrusted to proper hands"). . . .

However, those cases cannot be taken to mean that any board approval of a challenged transaction automatically connotes "hostile interest" and "guilty participation" by directors, or some other form of sterilizing influence upon them. Were that so, the demand requirements of our law would be meaningless, leaving the clear mandate of Chancery Rule 23.1 devoid of its purpose and substance.

The trial court correctly recognized that demand futility is inextricably bound to issues of business judgment, but stated the test to be based on allegations of fact, which, if true, "show that there is a reasonable inference" the business judgment rule is not applicable for purposes of a pre-suit demand.

The problem with this formulation is the concept of reasonable inferences to be drawn against a board of directors based on allegations in a complaint. As is clear from this case, and the conclusory allegations upon which the Vice Chancellor relied, demand futility becomes virtually automatic under such a test. Bearing in mind the presumptions with which director action is cloaked, we believe that the matter must be approached in a more balanced way.

Our view is that in determining demand futility the Court of Chancery in the proper exercise of its discretion must decide whether, under the particularized facts alleged, a reasonable doubt is created that: (1) the directors are disinterested and independent and (2) the challenged transaction was otherwise the product of a valid exercise of business judgment. Hence, the Court of Chancery must make two inquiries, one into the independence and disinterestedness of the directors and the other into the substantive nature of the challenged transaction and the board's approval thereof.

As to the latter inquiry the court does not assume that the transaction is a wrong to the corporation requiring corrective steps by the board. Rather, the alleged wrong is substantively reviewed against the factual background alleged in the complaint. As to the former inquiry, directorial independence and disinterestedness, the court reviews the factual allegations to decide whether they raise a reasonable doubt, as a threshold matter, that the protections of the business judgment rule are available to the board. Certainly, if this is an "interested" director transaction, such that the business judgment rule is inapplicable to the board majority approving the transaction, then the inquiry ceases. In that event futility of demand has been established by any objective or subjective standard.[8]

However, the mere threat of personal liability for approving a questioned transaction, standing alone, is insufficient to challenge either the independence or disinterestedness of directors, although in rare cases a transaction may be so egregious on its face that board approval cannot meet the test of business judgment, and a substantial likelihood of director liability therefore exists. In sum the entire review is factual in nature. The Court of Chancery in the exercise of its sound discretion must be satisfied that a plaintiff has alleged facts with particularity which, taken as true, support a reasonable doubt that the challenged transaction was the product of a valid exercise of business judgment. Only in that context is demand excused.

B

Having outlined the legal framework within which these issues are to be determined, we consider plaintiff's claims of futility here: Fink's domination and control of the directors, board approval of the Fink-Meyers employment agreement, and board hostility to the plaintiff's derivative action due to the directors' status as defendants.

Plaintiff's claim that Fink dominates and controls the Meyers' board is based on: (1) Fink's 47% ownership of Meyers' outstanding stock, and (2) that he "personally selected" each Meyers director. Plaintiff also alleges that mere approval of the employment agreement illustrates Fink's domination and control of the board. In addition, plaintiff argued on appeal that 47% stock ownership, though less than a majority, constituted control given the large number of shares outstanding, 1,245,745.

Such contentions do not support any claim under Delaware law that these directors lack independence. In Kaplan v. Centex Corp., Del. Ch., 284 A.2d 119 (1971), the Court of Chancery stated that "[s]tock ownership alone, at least when it amounts to less than a majority, is not sufficient proof of domination or control." Moreover, in the demand context even proof of majority ownership of a company does not strip the

---

8. We recognize that drawing the line at a majority of the board may be an arguably arbitrary dividing point. Critics will charge that we are ignoring the structural bias common to corporate boards throughout America, as well as the other unseen socialization processes cutting against independent discussion and decisionmaking in the boardroom. The difficulty with structural bias in a demand futile case is simply one of establishing it in the complaint for purposes of Rule 23.1. We are satisfied that discretionary review by the Court of Chancery of complaints alleging specific facts pointing to bias on a particular board will be sufficient for determining demand futility.

directors of the presumptions of independence, and that their acts have been taken in good faith and in the best interests of the corporation. There must be coupled with the allegation of control such facts as would demonstrate that through personal or other relationships the directors are beholden to the controlling person. To date the principal decisions dealing with the issue of control or domination arose only after a full trial on the merits. Thus, they are distinguishable in the demand context unless similar particularized facts are alleged to meet the test of Chancery Rule 23.1.

The requirement of director independence inheres in the conception and rationale of the business judgment rule. The presumption of propriety that flows from an exercise of business judgment is based in part on this unyielding precept. Independence means that a director's decision is based on the corporate merits of the subject before the board rather than extraneous considerations or influences. While directors may confer, debate, and resolve their differences through compromise, or by reasonable reliance upon the expertise of their colleagues and other qualified persons, the end result, nonetheless, must be that each director has brought his or her own informed business judgment to bear with specificity upon the corporate merits of the issues without regard for or succumbing to influences which convert an otherwise valid business decision into a faithless act.

Thus, it is not enough to charge that a director was nominated by or elected at the behest of those controlling the outcome of a corporate election. That is the usual way a person becomes a corporate director. It is the care, attention and sense of individual responsibility to the performance of one's duties, not the method of election, that generally touches on independence.

We conclude that in the demand-futile context a plaintiff charging domination and control of one or more directors must allege particularized facts manifesting "a direction of corporate conduct in such a way as to comport with the wishes or interests of the corporation (or persons) doing the controlling." *Kaplan*, 284 A.2d at 123. The shorthand shibboleth of "dominated and controlled directors" is insufficient. In recognizing that *Kaplan* was decided after trial and full discovery, we stress that the plaintiff need only allege specific facts; he need not plead evidence. Otherwise, he would be forced to make allegations which may not comport with his duties under Chancery Rule 11.[9]

Here, plaintiff has not alleged any facts sufficient to support a claim of control. The personal-selection-of-directors allegation stands alone, unsupported. At best it is

---

9. Chancery Rule 11 provides

   Every pleading of a party represented by an attorney shall be signed by at least 1 attorney of record in his individual name, whose address shall be stated. A party who is not represented by an attorney shall sign his pleading and state his address. Except when otherwise specifically provided by statute or rule, pleadings need not be verified or accompanied by affidavit. The signature of an attorney constitutes a certificate by him that he has read the pleading; that to the best of his knowledge, information, and belief there is good ground to support it; and that it is not interposed for delay. If a pleading is not signed or is signed with intent to defeat the purpose of this rule, it may be stricken as sham and false and the action may proceed as though the pleading had not been served. For a willful violation of this rule an attorney may be subjected to appropriate disciplinary action. Similar action may be taken if scandalous or indecent matter is inserted.

a conclusion devoid of factual support. The causal link between Fink's control and approval of the employment agreement is alluded to, but nowhere specified. The director's approval, alone, does not establish control, even in the face of Fink's 47 percent stock ownership. The claim that Fink is unlikely to perform any services under the agreement, because of his age, and his conflicting consultant work with Prudential, adds nothing to the control claim. Therefore, we cannot conclude that the complaint factually particularizes any circumstances of control and domination to overcome the presumption of board independence, and thus render the demand futile.

C

Turning to the board's approval of the Meyers-Fink employment agreement, plaintiff's argument is simple: all of the Meyers directors are named defendants, because they approved the wasteful agreement; if plaintiff prevails on the merits all the directors will be jointly and severally liable; therefore, the directors' interest in avoiding personal liability automatically and absolutely disqualifies them from passing on a shareholder's demand.

Such allegations are conclusory at best. In Delaware mere directorial approval of a transaction, absent particularized facts supporting a breach of fiduciary duty claim, or otherwise establishing the lack of independence or disinterestedness of a majority of the directors, is insufficient to excuse demand. Here, plaintiff's suit is premised on the notion that the Meyers-Fink employment agreement was a waste of corporate assets. So, the argument goes, by approving such waste the directors now face potential personal liability, thereby rendering futile any demand on them to bring suit. Unfortunately, plaintiff's claim fails in its initial premise. The complaint does not allege particularized facts indicating that the agreement is a waste of corporate assets. Indeed, the complaint as now drafted may not even state a cause of action, given the directors' broad corporate power to fix the compensation of officers.

In essence, the plaintiff alleged a lack of consideration flowing from Fink to Meyers, since the employment agreement provided that compensation was not contingent on Fink's ability to perform any services. The bare assertion that Fink performed "little or no services" was plaintiff's conclusion based solely on Fink's age and the existence of the Fink-Prudential employment agreement. As for Meyers' loans to Fink, beyond the bare allegation that they were made, the complaint does not allege facts indicating the wastefulness of such arrangements. Again, the mere existence of such loans, given the broad corporate powers conferred by Delaware law, does not even state a claim.

In sustaining plaintiff's claim of demand futility the trial court relied on Fidanque v. American Maracaibo Co., Del. Ch., 92 A.2d 311, 321 (1952), which held that a contract providing for payment of consulting fees to a retired president/director was a waste of corporate assets. In *Fidanque*, the court found after trial that the contract and payments were in reality compensation for past services. This was based upon facts not present here: the former president/director was a 70 year old stroke victim, neither the agreement nor the record spelled out his consulting duties at all, the consulting salary equalled the individual's salary when he was president and general manager of the corporation, and the contract was silent as to continued employment in the event that the retired president/director again became incapacitated and unable to perform his duties. Contrasting the facts of *Fidanque* with the complaint here, it is apparent that plaintiff has not alleged facts sufficient to render demand futile on a charge of corporate waste, and thus create a reasonable doubt that the board's action is protected by the business judgment rule.

D

Plaintiff's final argument is the incantation that demand is excused because the directors otherwise would have to sue themselves, thereby placing the conduct of the litigation in hostile hands and preventing its effective prosecution. This bootstrap argument has been made to and dismissed by other courts. Its acceptance would effectively abrogate Rule 23.1 and weaken the managerial power of directors. Unless facts are alleged with particularity to overcome the presumptions of independence and a proper exercise of business judgment, in which case the directors could not be expected to sue themselves, a bare claim of this sort raises no legally cognizable issue under Delaware corporate law.

V.

In sum, we conclude that the plaintiff has failed to allege facts with particularity indicating that the Meyers directors were tainted by interest, lacked independence, or took action contrary to Meyers' best interests in order to create a reasonable doubt as to the applicability of the business judgment rule. Only in the presence of such a reasonable doubt may a demand be deemed futile. Hence, we reverse the Court of Chancery's denial of the motion to dismiss, and remand with instructions that plaintiff be granted leave to amend his complaint to bring it into compliance with Rule 23.1 based on the principles we have announced today.

Reversed and remanded.

NOTES AND QUESTIONS

1. What distinguishes a derivative suit from a direct suit? Many jurisdictions, including Delaware, have held that a suit is derivative unless the complaining shareholders have suffered a "special injury" that is separate and distinct from that suffered by other shareholders or is based on a contractual right. Delaware recently reconsidered and rejected the "special injury" doctrine in Tooley v. Donaldson, Lufkin & Jenrette, Inc., 845 A.2d 1031 (Del. 2004). The new test is explained by Chancellor Chandler, upon whose analysis the Supreme Court based its decision in *Tooley*. See *Tooley*, 845 A.2d at 1036.

> The Supreme Court's *Tooley* decision simplified the analysis required to distinguish between direct and derivative actions, discarding the old "special injury" test. The analysis now focuses on the following questions: "Who suffered the alleged harm—the corporation or the suing stockholder individually—and who would receive the benefit of the recovery or other remedy?" This inquiry requires the Court to look: "at the body of the complaint and considering the nature of the

wrong alleged and the relief requested, has the plaintiff demonstrated that he or she can prevail without showing an injury to the corporation?" *Tooley,* 845 A.2d at 1035.

Thus, the relevant inquiry is "the nature of the wrong alleged, not merely . . . the form of words used in the complaint." "As this court recently said, 'even after *Tooley,* a claim is not "direct" simply because it is pleaded that way. . . . Instead, the court must look to all the facts of the complaint and determine for itself whether a direct claim exists.'"

Gatz v. Ponsoldt, 2004 WL 3029868, *7 (Del. Ch.).

2. Consider the efficacy of Chancery Court Rule 11 in preventing strike suits. In that regard, how does it compare to the version of Rule 11 cited in *Aronson*, supra, at footnote 9?

RULE 11. SIGNING OF PLEADINGS, MOTIONS, AND OTHER PAPERS; REPRESENTATIONS TO COURT; SANCTIONS . . .

(b) Representations to Court. By presenting to the Court (whether by signing, filing, submitting, or later advocating) a pleading, written motion, or other paper, an attorney or unrepresented party is certifying that to the best of the person's knowledge, information, and belief, formed after an inquiry reasonable under the circumstances:

(1) it is not being presented for any improper purpose, such as to harass or to cause unnecessary delay or needless increase in the cost of litigation;

(2) the claims, defenses, and other legal contentions therein are warranted by existing law or by a nonfrivolous argument for the extension, modification, or reversal of existing law or the establishment of new law;

(3) the allegations and other factual contentions have evidentiary support or, if specifically so identified, are likely to have evidentiary support after a reasonable opportunity for further investigation or discovery; and

(4) the denials of factual contentions are warranted on the evidence or, if specifically so identified, are reasonably based on a lack of information or belief.

(c) Sanctions. If, after notice and a reasonable opportunity to respond, the Court determines that subdivision (b) has been violated, the Court may, subject to the conditions stated below, impose an appropriate sanction upon the attorneys, law firms, or parties that have violated subdivision (b) or are responsible for the violation.

3. What does the phrase "reasonable doubt," a term commonly used in criminal law, mean in the context of the *Aronson* demand futility doctrine? Consider this explanation.

Aronson introduced the term "reasonable doubt" into corporate derivative jurisprudence. Some courts and commentators have questioned why a concept normally present in criminal prosecution would find its way into derivative litigation. Yet the term is apt and achieves the proper balance. Reasonable doubt can be said to mean that there is a reason to doubt. This concept is sufficiently flexible and workable to provide the stockholder with "the keys to the courthouse" in an appropriate case where the claim is not based on mere suspicions or stated solely in conclusory terms.

Grimes v. Donald, 673 A.2d 1207, 1217 (Del. 1996). Further, the court explained:

Stated obversely, the concept of reasonable doubt is akin to the concept that the stockholder has a "reasonable belief" that the board lacks independence or that the transaction was not protected by the business judgment rule. The concept of reasonable belief is an objective test and is found in various corporate contexts.

Id. at fn. 16.

4. Delaware jurisprudence warns against the practice of filing law suits that are wordy, conclusory, and based on scant investigation.

> The Complaint, consisting of 88 pages and 285 paragraphs, is a pastiche of prolix invective. It is permeated with conclusory allegations of the pleader and quotations from the media, mostly of an editorial nature (even including a cartoon). A pleader may rely on factual statements in the media as some of the "tools at hand" from which the pleader intends to derive the particularized facts necessary to comply with Chancery Rule 11(b)(3) and Chancery Rule 23.1. But many of the quotations from the media in the Complaint simply echo plaintiffs' conclusory allegations. Accordingly, they serve no purpose other than to complicate the work of reviewing courts.
>
> This is potentially a very troubling case on the merits . . . [but] the Complaint is so inartfully drafted that it was properly dismissed under our pleading standards for derivative suits.

Brehm v. Eisner, 746 A.2d 244, 249 (Del. 2000).

5. Obviously the pleading requirements under Chancery Rule 23.1 are more stringent than mere notice pleading. The exact nature of the required pleading defies easy explanation.

> Pleadings in derivative suits are governed by Chancery Rule 23.1, just as pleadings alleging fraud are governed by Chancery Rule 9(b). Those pleadings must comply with stringent requirements of factual particularity that differ substantially from the permissive notice pleadings governed solely by Chancery Rule 8(a). Rule 23.1 is not satisfied by conclusory statements or mere notice pleading. On the other hand, the pleader is not required to plead evidence. What the pleader must set forth are particularized factual statements that are essential to the claim. Such facts are sometimes referred to as "ultimate facts," "principal facts" or "elemental facts." Nevertheless, the particularized factual statements that are required to comply with the Rule 23.1 pleading rules must also comply with the mandate of Chancery Rule 8(e) that they be "simple, concise and direct." A prolix complaint larded with conclusory language, like the Complaint here, does not comply with these fundamental pleading mandates.

Brehm v. Eisner, 746 A.2d 244, 254 (Del. 2000).

6. Derivative plaintiffs face a substantial dilemma in attempting to satisfy the pleading requirements of Delaware Chancery Rule 23.1 without violating Rule 11(b)(3) (see Note 2, above). Once the defendant files a motion to dismiss for failure to make demand, certain to occur quickly after the derivative complaint is filed, the court will normally stay discovery until a decision on that motion. How can the plaintiff discover the necessary particularized facts without being able to conduct discovery? The Delaware courts have expressed consistent lack of sympathy for that concern.

> Plaintiffs complain, in effect, that the system of requiring a stockholder to plead particularized facts in a derivative suit is basically unfair because the Court will not permit discovery under Chancery Rules 26-37 to marshal the facts necessary to establish that pre-suit demand is excused. This is a common complaint, one that is echoed in the amicus brief of the Council of Institutional Investors on this appeal. But this argument has been answered by this Court on several occasions.
>
> Plaintiffs may well have the "tools at hand" to develop the necessary facts for pleading purposes. For example, plaintiffs may seek relevant books and records of the corporation under Section 220 of the Delaware General Corporation Law, if they can ultimately bear the burden of showing a proper purpose and make specific and discrete identification, with rifled precision, of the documents sought. Further, they must establish that each category of books and records is essential to the accomplishment of their articulated purpose for the inspection.

Brehm v. Eisner, 746 A.2d 244, 266 (Del. 2000).

7. If a shareholder makes pre-suit demand, what course of action may the shareholder pursue if the directors either refuse the demand, or simply take no action?

> Demand has been excused in many cases in Delaware under the *Aronson* test. The law regarding wrongful refusal is not as well developed, however. Although Delaware law does not require demand in every case because Delaware does have the mechanism of demand excusal, it is important that the demand process be meaningful. Therefore, a stockholder who makes a demand is entitled to know promptly what action the board has taken in response to the demand. A stockholder who makes a serious demand and receives only a peremptory refusal has the right to use the "tools at hand" to obtain the relevant corporate records, such as reports or minutes, reflecting the corporate action and related information in order to determine whether or not there is a basis to assert that demand was wrongfully refused. In no event may a corporation assume a position of neutrality and take no position in response to the demand. Kaplan v. Peat, Marwick, Mitchell & Co., Del.Supr., 540 A.2d 726 (1988).
>
> If a demand is made, the stockholder has spent one—but only one—"arrow" in the "quiver." The spent "arrow" is the right to claim that demand is excused. The stockholder does not, by making demand, waive the right to claim that demand has been wrongfully refused.
>
> Simply because the composition of the board provides no basis *ex ante* for the stockholder to claim with particularity and consistently with Rule 11 that it is reasonable to doubt that a majority of the board is either interested or not independent, it does not necessarily follow *ex post* that the board in fact **acted** independently, disinterestedly or with due care in response to the demand. A board or a committee of the board may **appear** to be independent, but may not always **act** independently. If a demand is made and rejected, the board rejecting the demand is entitled to the presumption of the business judgment rule unless the stockholder can allege facts with particularity creating a reasonable doubt that the board is entitled to the benefit of the presumption. If there is reason to doubt that the board acted independently or with due care in responding to the demand, the stockholder may have the basis *ex post* to claim wrongful refusal. The stockholder then has the right to bring the underlying action with the same standing which the stockholder would have had, *ex ante*, if demand had been excused as futile.

Grimes v. Donald, 673 A.2d 1207, 1217-1218 (Del. 1996).

Under the Model Business Corporation Act, with its requirement for universal demand (see §7.42), the litigation energy will be focused on judicial review of a likely motion to dismiss the derivative suit made by the corporation after the board or a committee has concluded that the derivative suit is not in the best interest of the corporation. MBCA §7.44 provides an elaborate structure that varies the burden of proof with the independence of the board or committee that responded to the demand. How will the judicial evaluation differ from that described in Grimes v. Donald above? Would you rather be a plaintiff in Delaware or in an MBCA jurisdiction?

8. Should the appellate court's review of a trial court's ruling on a motion to dismiss for failure to make demand be deferential or *de novo*? Consider the views of the Delaware Supreme Court.

> Our view is that in determining demand futility the Court of Chancery *in the proper exercise of its discretion* must decide whether, under the particularized facts alleged, a reasonable doubt is created that: (1) the directors are disinterested and independent [or] (2) the challenged transaction was otherwise the product of a valid exercise of business judgment.
>
> By implication, therefore, [this] dicta would suggest that our review is deferential, limited to a determination of whether the Court of Chancery abused its discretion. Indeed, all parties to this appeal agree that our review is for abuse of discretion.

The view we express today, however, is designed to make clear that our review of decisions of the Court of Chancery applying Rule 23.1 is *de novo* and plenary. We apply the law to the allegations of the Complaint as does the Court of Chancery. Our review is not a deferential review that requires us to find an abuse of discretion. We see no reason to perpetuate the concept of discretion in this context. The nature of our analysis of a complaint in a derivative suit is the same as that applied by the Court of Chancery in making its decision in the first instance.

Brehm v. Eisner, 746 A.2d 244, 253 (Del. 2000).

9. The *Aronson* test does not apply to every demand futility motion.

Consistent with the context and rationale of the *Aronson* decision, a court should not apply the *Aronson* test for demand futility where the board that would be considering the demand did not make a business decision which is being challenged in the derivative suit. This situation would arise in three principal scenarios: (1) where a business decision was made by the board of a company, but a majority of the directors making the decision have been replaced; (2) where the subject of the derivative suit is not a business decision of the board; and (3) where, as here, the decision being challenged was made by the board of a different corporation.

Instead, it is appropriate in these situations to examine whether the board that would be addressing the demand can impartially consider its merits without being influenced by improper considerations. Thus, a court must determine whether or not the particularized factual allegations of a derivative stockholder complaint create a reasonable doubt that, as of the time the complaint is filed, the board of directors could have properly exercised its independent and disinterested business judgment in responding to a demand. If the derivative plaintiff satisfies this burden, then demand will be excused as futile.

Rales v. Blasband, 634 A.2d 927, 934 (Del. 1993).

2.   Fiduciary Duty and *Aronson*'s First Prong

In re The Limited, Inc. Shareholders Litigation
Delaware Chancery Court, 2002
2002 WL 537692

NOBLE, VICE CHANCELLOR.

Dear Counsel:

Pending is a motion to dismiss the First Amended Consolidated Derivative Complaint ("Complaint") in a shareholder derivative suit brought on behalf of The Limited, Inc. ("The Limited" or the "Company"). The defendants are The Limited, the nominal defendant, and each of the twelve members of the Company's Board of Directors (the "Board"). The plaintiffs allege that the Company's directors committed corporate waste and breached their fiduciary duties of loyalty and due care by rescinding a Contingent Stock Redemption Agreement (the "Redemption Agreement") and funding in part with monies made available as the result of the rescission of the Redemption Agreement a self-tender offer that they also assert resulted in no consideration to the Company.

Defendants have moved to dismiss the Complaint on the basis that plaintiffs failed to meet the pre-suit demand requirements of Court of Chancery Rule 23.1. They also seek dismissal of the Complaint under Court of Chancery Rule 12(b)(6) for failure to state an actionable claim for corporate waste or breach of fiduciary duty.

I. Background

A. THE PARTIES

Common stockholder plaintiffs Rochelle Phillips, Miriam Shapiro and Peter Sullivan bring this derivative action on behalf of The Limited, against the Company and each of its directors. The plaintiffs' allegations stem from The Limited's authorization of a self-tender offer for up to 15 million shares of its stock and the rescission of an agreement that included a call option to purchase 18.75 million shares of common stock from a trust set up for the benefit of Leslie H. Wexner's ("Mr. Wexner") children. Mr. Wexner is The Limited's founder as well as its President, Chief Executive Officer, and Chairman.

The Limited, a Delaware corporation based in Columbus, Ohio, is a specialty retailer operating more than 3,000 stores nationwide.[3] In addition to being the Company's top executive, Mr. Wexner, one of the individual defendant-directors, is also its largest shareholder, owning or controlling approximately twenty-five percent of The Limited's outstanding stock at the time of the challenged transactions.[4] Also named as a defendant in the Complaint is Abigail S. Wexner ("Mrs. Wexner"), Mr. Wexner's wife, who has served on the Board since 1997.

The remaining ten members of The Limited's Board named as defendants are Raymond Zimmerman ("Zimmerman"), Allan R. Tessler ("Tessler"), Claudine B. Malone ("Malone"), Eugene M. Freedman ("Freedman"), Martin Trust ("Trust"), Kenneth B. Gilman ("Gilman"), David T. Kollat ("Kollat"), E. Gordon Gee ("Gee"), Donald B. Shackelford ("Shackelford"), and Leonard A. Schlesinger ("Schlesinger").

B. THE SELF-TENDER

On May 3, 1999, The Limited announced that the Board had authorized the repurchase of up to 15 million shares of the Company's outstanding common stock[5] through a Dutch auction tender offer.[6] Under the terms of the tender offer, the Company agreed to repurchase those shares at a premium over their pre-announcement

---

3. Compl. ¶21. The Company operates under the names: "Lerner New York," "Express," "Lane Bryant," "The Limited," "The Limited Too," "Henri Bendel," "Structure," and "Galyan's Trading Co." The Company also owns approximately 84% of Intimate Brands, Inc., which operates "Victoria's Secret" and "Bath & Body Works" stores. Id.

4. Mr. Wexner owned or controlled more than 58 million shares of The Limited. Id. ¶7.

5. Id. ¶30. These shares represented approximately six percent of The Limited's 228,165,712 shares then outstanding. Id.

6. "A Dutch auction is a form of tender offer in which the selling stockholders, rather than the buyer, determine the price to be paid for the shares purchased. The corporation establishes a price range within which individual stockholders may designate the price at which they are willing to sell their shares. The corporation then determines the lowest price at which it can purchase the number of shares it needs, and buys at that price. Any shares tendered above that price are excluded." Frank v. Arnelle, Del. Supr., No. 424, 1998 (Jan. 22, 1999) (order) (quoting Cottle v. Standard Brands Paint Co., Del. Ch., C.A. No. 9342, mem. op. at 3, Berger, V.C. (Mar. 22, 1990)).

closing price.[7] Mr. Wexner agreed that neither he nor any of his affiliates would participate in the tender.

This decision, according to the Company, was based in large part on the purportedly large amount of excess cash and cash equivalents generated by the Company's operations, an amount more than $660 million. The Board concluded that the stock repurchase was the most attractive method for utilizing the Company's excess cash and would demonstrate to the stockholders how much confidence it had in The Limited's business. Shortly after the expiration of the self-tender, The Limited announced that it had acquired 15,000,000 shares at a total cost to the Company of $750 million, $90 million more than the $660 million of cash and cash equivalents it had on hand.

C. THE CONTINGENT STOCK REDEMPTION AGREEMENT

When it made public its decision to conduct a self-tender offer, The Limited also announced that it had agreed to rescind the Redemption Agreement, an agreement it had entered into in 1996 with Mr. Wexner in both his individual capacity and as trustee of The Wexner Children's Trust (the "Children's Trust"). . . .

Under the Redemption Agreement, the Children's Trust acquired the right, through January 30, 2006, to require the Company to redeem all or a portion of the 18.75 million shares of common stock it held at $18.75 per share, a put option. The Redemption Agreement also provided the Company with a six-month window, commencing on July 31, 2006, to redeem all or part of the remaining shares still held by the Children's Trust at $25.07 per share, a call option.

During the term of the Redemption Agreement, The Limited was required to retain $350 million in a restricted cash account in order to satisfy its obligations under the agreement should either of the options be triggered. In other words, the $350 million was to remain in this restricted account until the year 2006 to cover The Limited's potential obligations under the Redemption Agreement.

II. CONTENTIONS

The Complaint asserts claims of corporate waste and breaches of the fiduciary duties of loyalty and due care in connection with the challenged transactions described above.

Plaintiffs' due care and corporate waste claims rest on the relationship between the rescission of the Redemption Agreement and the self-tender. Plaintiffs allege that the only reason for structuring the transactions in this manner was to enable Mr. Wexner to avoid the terms of the Redemption Agreement which, they assert, had become

---

7. The self-tender price was between $50 and $55 per share. Compl. ¶2. This, plaintiffs indicate, represented a significant premium over the $43.75 pre-announcement closing price. Id.

particularly unfavorable to him.[12] Plaintiffs argue that these transactions lacked any legitimate business purpose other than to benefit Mr. Wexner at the Company's expense and came without a corresponding benefit to the Company. Plaintiffs also allege a breach of the fiduciary duty of loyalty on the basis that at least half of the Board had a disqualifying self-interest in the transactions or lacked independence in approving the challenged transactions due to their personal or professional relationships with Mr. Wexner. . . .

III. ANALYSIS

A. DEMAND FUTILITY

Court of Chancery Rule 23.1 provides that where a plaintiff initiates a shareholder derivative action without first making a demand on the company's board, the complaint must allege with particularity the reasons justifying the plaintiff's failure to do so. . . .

> To meet the first prong of the *Aronson* test and adequately show the futility of a pre-suit demand, a plaintiff must plead particularized facts sufficiently demonstrating that the defendant directors had a financial interest in the challenged transaction, that they were motivated by a desire to retain their positions on the board or within the company (an entrenchment motive), or that they were dominated or controlled by a person interested in the transaction.[18]

In conducting this analysis, *Aronson* and its progeny limit the scope of my inquiry under Rule 23.1 to the allegations of the Complaint.[19] For the reasons discussed below, I find that the plaintiffs have alleged sufficient particularized facts to raise a reasonable doubt as to the disinterestedness or independence of at least six of The Limited's twelve directors.

1. *Director Disinterestedness*

The Complaint alleges that the challenged transactions were approved by the Board for the sole or primary reason of enabling Mr. Wexner to negotiate a rescission of the Redemption Agreement affecting the Trust which he controlled. "Directorial interest exists whenever divided loyalties are present, or a director either has received, or is entitled to receive, a personal financial benefit from the challenged transaction

---

12. By May 1999, the month in which The Limited announced the two challenged transactions, the price of the Company's stock was trading at more than $40 per share, significantly higher than the call price that the Company could have paid during the six-month window to exercise its option in 2006. Had the Company been empowered in May 1999 to force the Trust to sell it its shares, the Company could have purchased the Trust's 18.75 million shares for approximately $25 per share, thus realizing a savings of more than $15 per share from its then over $40 trading price. This equates to roughly $280,000,000.

18. Kahn v. Roberts, Del. Ch., C.A. No. 12324, mem. op. at 12, Hartnett, V.C. (Feb. 28, 1994), aff'd, Kahn v. Roberts, 679 A.2d 460 (Del. 1996); see also Aronson v. Lewis, 473 A.2d at 812-16.

19. Aronson v. Lewis, 473 A.2d at 808. . . .

which is not equally shared by the stockholders."[21] Because Mr. Wexner, in his individual capacity and as trustee for the Trust, negotiated the Redemption Agreement at its creation, an agreement that was for the benefit of his children, the Complaint has alleged sufficiently particularized facts creating a reasonable doubt as to his disinterestedness in connection with the Company's rescission of that agreement. Mrs. Wexner similarly stood to benefit from the rescission of the Redemption Agreement, thereby creating a reasonable doubt as to her disinterestedness as a director in the approval of the rescission.[22]

With respect to the remaining ten directors, however, the Complaint is devoid of any allegations suggesting the presence of any financial interest in the challenged transactions that would suffice for purposes of the first prong of *Aronson*.[23] At issue with these directors are the plaintiffs' allegations challenging their independence (*i.e.*, whether they were so beholden to Mr. Wexner as to create a reasonable doubt about their independence). The independence of these directors will be discussed next.

2. *Director Independence*

Independence, the *Aronson* Court held, means that a director's decision is based on the corporate merits of the subject matter before the board rather than extraneous considerations or influences. To establish lack of independence, a plaintiff meets his burden by showing that the directors are either beholden to the controlling shareholder or so under its influence that their discretion is sterilized.[24]

The Court in ascertaining the sufficiency of a complaint challenging a director's loyalty does not apply an objective "reasonable director standard"; instead, the Court must apply a "subjective 'actual person' test to determine whether a *particular* director[] . . . lacks independence because he is controlled by another."[25]

The plaintiffs do not seriously contest the independence of four of The Limited's directors. The only allegations in the Complaint with respect to Zimmerman, Tessler, Malone, and Freedman are that each had been a director of The Limited for a number of years predating the challenged transactions. Allegations as to one's position as a director and the receipt of director's fees, without more, however, are not enough for

---

21. Pogostin v. Rice, 480 A.2d 619, 624 (Del. 1984), *overruled on other grounds* Brehm v. Eisner, 746 A.2d 244 (Del. 2000).

22. I understand that Mr. Wexner, for himself and Mrs. Wexner, disclaimed any right to participate in the self-tender. That begs the question of whether they can be deemed interested in the self-tender. The answer, at least at this stage of these proceedings, is that the Redemption Agreement and the self-tender appear so interdependent that, for these purposes, they cannot be segregated.

23. These directors received no material benefit (nor risked any material detriment) that was not available to the shareholders generally. See Orman v. Cullman, Del. Ch., C.A. No. 18039, mem. op. at 19-21, Chandler, C. (Mar. 1, 2002).

24. In re Western Nat'l Corp. S'holders Litig., Del. Ch., C.A. No. 15927, mem. op. at 28, Chandler, C. (May 22, 2000) (citations omitted); see also In re Paxson Communication Corp., S'holders Litig., Del. Ch., C.A. No. 17568, mem. op. at 23, Chandler, C. (July 10, 2001) ("Even where the *potential* for domination or control by a controlling shareholder exists, the complaint must allege particularized allegations that would support an inference of domination or control.") (emphasis in original).

25. Orman v. Cullman, mem. op. at 21 (emphasis in original) (footnote omitted).

purposes of pleading demand futility.[27] As such, I find that the plaintiffs have not met their burden of raising, through allegations of particularized facts, a reasonable doubt as to the independence of Zimmerman, Tessler, Malone, or Freedman.

The Complaint states that Shackelford, a director of The Limited since 1975, was also a director of Intimate Brands, Inc., The Limited's 84% owned subsidiary, which is allegedly dependent upon The Limited for significant revenues. Shackelford's compensation from his role as a director of The Limited, alone, does not create a reasonable doubt as to that director's independence. Similarly, the receipt of director's fees from a subsidiary does not, in the absence of other facts suggesting a lack of independence, demonstrate a reasonable doubt as to that director's loyalty. Accordingly, I find that plaintiffs have failed to rebut the presumption as to Shackelford's independence as well.

The Complaint alleges that Kollat, a director of The Limited since 1976, is a principal of Audio Environments ("Audio"), a company supplying in-store music to The Limited's stores, from which Audio receives $400,000 annually in revenue. This Court has previously considered the potential impact on a director's independence from a business relationship between the director's employer (in which the director may have an interest) and the company on whose board the directors sits. "Although it has been held that a director whose small law firm received $1,000,000 in legal fees from the corporation was potentially beholden to the CEO, [a] plaintiff [who has failed to] allege[] particular facts indicating that [the money] allegedly paid to [the director] or his firm was so material as to taint [the director's] judgment . . . [fails] to create a reasonable doubt about his independence."[30] The Complaint is devoid of any allegations asserting (or from which an inference can reasonably be drawn, for that matter) that the $400,000 annual revenue that Audio receives from its dealings with The Limited and its affiliates was material to Audio's business. Moreover, the Complaint does not allege how Kollat, as "a principal," may have benefitted from any portion of those revenues. Accordingly, the plaintiffs have also failed to plead particularized facts raising a reasonable doubt as to Kollat's independence.

Gilman has served as a director since 1990. Since 1997, his principal employment has been as vice chairman and chief administrative officer of The Limited for which, during the years 1996-1998, he averaged $1.8 million in salary and bonuses. It is reasonable to infer that compensation of this magnitude is material to him. Moreover, as a general matter, compensation from one's principal employment is "typically of great consequence" to the employee. Because of Mr. Wexner's holdings of The Limited and his position, as chairman, chief executive officer, and director, these allegations of particularized facts raise a reasonable doubt as to Gilman's independence from Mr. Wexner's will.

Trust's status is similar to that of Gilman. Trust is a long-time (since 1978) director of the The Limited. His principal employment is as president and chief executive

---

27. See Grobow v. Perot, 539 A.2d 180, 188 (Del. 1988), *overruled on other grounds* Brehm v. Eisner, 746 A.2d 244 (Del. 2000) (stating that "such allegations, without more, do not establish any financial interest"); Orman v. Cullman, mem. op. at 24-26, 29 n. 62 (observing that "[the] Court's view of the disqualifying effect of [director's] fees might be different if the fees were shown to exceed materially what is commonly understood and accepted to be a usual and customary director's fee").

30. White v. Panic, Del. Ch., C.A. No. 16800, mem. op. at 18, Lamb, V.C. (Jan. 19, 2000), aff'd, 783 A.2d 543 (Del. 2001) (citing Steiner v. Meyerson, Del. Ch., C.A. No. 13139, mem. op. at 24-25, Allen C. (July 18, 1995)).

officer of a wholly-owned subsidiary of The Limited. His average compensation from that position, which can reasonably be inferred to be material to him, over the four-year period preceding the filing of the Complaint, was approximately $1.8 million. Again, these particularized facts generate a reasonable doubt as to whether Trust is able to make decisions about Mr. Wexner's interests that are independent from his control.

Schlesinger became a director of The Limited in 1996. He provided consulting services to The Limited and one of its wholly-owned subsidiaries for which, during the years 1996-1998, he received average annual compensation of $150,000. His principal occupation was as a senior administrative officer of Brown University. Thus, I must determine whether, on these particularized facts, it is appropriate to conclude that average annual consulting fees of $150,000 would be material to Schlesinger and that he was "beholden" to Mr. Wexner because of a desire to continue with those consulting services. I am satisfied that it is reasonable to infer from these allegations that continued annual compensation in excess of $150,000 would be material to Schlesinger, a senior university official, and that Schlesinger was beholden to Wexner for the continuation of the consulting services. Accordingly, plaintiffs have met their pleading burden for raising a reasonable doubt as to Schlesinger's independence.[36]

Gee, who has been a director since 1991, was president of The Ohio State University, Mr. Wexner's alma mater, from 1990 to 1997. He subsequently became president of Brown University, a position he left before the Complaint was filed. Gee, as the result of nominations by Mr. Wexner, serves on the boards of both The Limited and a subsidiary of The Limited. These facts, whether viewed singly or cumulatively, do not support any inference questioning Gee's independence. Gee, however, while president of Ohio State, successfully solicited from Wexner a $25 million grant to establish The Wexner Center for the Arts. Furthermore, Gee, while president of Brown, is alleged to have continued to solicit Mr. Wexner for donations.

Thus, the question as to Gee becomes: if a director is the head of a charitable or educational institution, under what circumstances may his independence be called into question by the charitable giving of the allegedly dominating person, in this instance, Mr. Wexner?

This Court has considered this question previously. In Lewis v. Fuqua,[37] the independence of Governor Terry Sanford was evaluated. He served with J.B. Fuqua, the allegedly controlling person, on both the board of Fuqua Industries, Inc. and the Board of Trustees of Duke University of which Governor Sanford was then the president. Governor Sanford and Fuqua had a lengthy history of political, social and business relationships. Fuqua was a generous benefactor to Duke.[38] The Court concluded that all of these facts, taken together, supported the conclusion that there was reasonable doubt of Governor Sanford's independence from the domination of Fuqua.

---

36. Orman v. Cullman, mem. op. at 32 (noting that "it is reasonable to infer that $75,000 [annually] would be material to [the director at issue]"); cf. White v. Panic, 783 A.2d at 551 n. 24. Plaintiffs note that Schlesinger took a full-time position with The Limited after the filing of this action. Plaintiffs' Brief in Opposition to Defendants' Motion to Dismiss at 17-18. I must, however, confine my consideration of whether demand would have been futile to the allegations of the Complaint. . . .

37. 502 A.2d 962 (Del. Ch. 1985).

38. He had donated $10 million to Duke University. Id. at 967.

This conclusion may be contrasted with the determination in *Disney* that the independence of Father O'Donovan had not been sufficiently called into question. Father O'Donovan was the president of Georgetown University and served as a director of The Walt Disney Company. The allegedly dominating person, Mr. Eisner, the chairman of Disney, had given $1 million to Georgetown University, which was the alma mater of one of his children. The Court in *Disney* focused on two critical distinctions from the analysis in Lewis v. Fuqua: (i) Governor Sanford had "numerous political and financial dealings" with Fuqua; no such relationship was alleged between Father O'Donovan and Mr. Eisner; and (ii) both Fuqua and Governor Sanford served together as directors (or trustees) of both Duke and Fuqua Industries. Mr. Eisner, in comparison, had no formal relationship with Georgetown University.[39]

Thus, unlike the relationship between Governor Sanford and Fuqua, Gee and Mr. Wexner are not alleged to have had lengthy political and financial dealings and they do not serve together on multiple boards. Furthermore, while Gee, as president of Brown University, may have solicited Mr. Wexner for donations, the Complaint does not allege that he was successful. Moreover, Gee left his position at Brown and the Complaint does not suggest any continuing need or desire to solicit Mr. Wexner for charitable donations.

However, the determination of whether a particular director is "beholden" to an allegedly controlling person is not limited to the power to affect the director in the future. One may feel "beholden" to someone for past acts as well. It may reasonably be inferred that Mr. Wexner's gift of $25 million to Ohio State was, even for a school of that size, a significant gift. While the gift was not to Gee personally, it was a positive reflection on him and his fundraising efforts as university president to have successfully solicited such a gift. In this context, even though there can be no "bright line" test, a gift of that magnitude can reasonably be considered as instilling in Gee a sense of "owingness" to Mr. Wexner. For that reason, I conclude that the plaintiffs have successfully alleged a reasonable doubt as to Gee's independence from Mr. Wexner's domination.

Thus, six of the twelve directors of The Limited are either interested (Mr. Wexner and Mrs. Wexner) in the challenged transactions or subject to a reasonable doubt about their independence (Gilman, Trust, Schlesinger and Gee) from Mr. Wexner's domination. Although that, of course, is not a majority of the directors, where the challenged actions are those of a board consisting of an even number of directors, plaintiffs meet their burden of demonstrating the futility of making demand on the board by showing that half of the board was either interested or not independent. Accordingly, defendants' motion under Court of Chancery Rule 23.1 is denied.

B. DUTY OF LOYALTY

With the determination that demand is excused, I now turn to consideration of defendants' application under Court of Chancery Rule 12(b)(6)'s more lenient pleading standards.

---

39. In re Walt Disney Co. Deriv. Litig., 731 A.2d at 359.

For the reasons set forth above, I am satisfied that the Complaint states a claim for breach of the duty of loyalty. The challenged transactions were approved by a unanimous board of twelve; six of those directors were either interested or subject to disqualifying doubts about their independence. As set forth below, the challenged transactions, while perhaps not constituting corporate waste, appear unfair to the stockholders.[45] Thus, because the challenged transactions were not approved by a majority of independent and disinterested directors, the Complaint states a loyalty claim that survives a challenge under Court of Chancery Rule 12(b)(6).

C.   CORPORATE WASTE

Although the challenged transactions may be questioned because of doubts about the loyalty of the directors approving them, it does not necessarily follow that they constitute corporate waste.

For plaintiffs' waste claim to survive, the Complaint, under the liberal pleading standards of Court of Chancery Rule 12(b)(6), must show that the transactions were "effected on terms 'that no person of ordinary, sound business judgment could conclude represent a fair exchange.'"[46] Plaintiffs' burden has also been described as requiring a showing that "the [transactions] in question either served no corporate purpose or [were] so completely bereft of consideration that [they] effectively constituted a gift."[47]

I will first analyze the corporate waste claim for the two transactions separately, followed by a consideration of the two transactions taken together.

1.   Rescission of the Redemption Agreement

By its terms, the Redemption Agreement required The Limited to maintain, untouched, a cash account of $350 million until 2006 to cover its potential obligations under the agreement. Because the price of the stock had risen appreciably since the creation of the Redemption Agreement, the plaintiffs allege that the rescission "destroyed a valuable option worth hundreds of millions of dollars to the Company . . . without a corresponding benefit to the Company, . . . the only benefit accruing to [Mr.] Wexner and the [Children's] Trust, which no longer faced the prospect of being forced to sell shares below market value."[48]

It is true that had the terms of the Redemption Agreement empowered the Company to trigger its call on May 3, 1999, the date of the Company's announcement, then Mr. Wexner, as trustee, would have been obligated to sell the Trust's 18,750,000

---

45. See In re The Student Loan Corp. Deriv. Litig., let. op. at 9 n. 4. Thus, I need not consider whether my conclusion as to Kollat's independence would change under the less stringent pleading requirements of Court of Chancery Rule 12(b)(6).

46. Id. at 10 (quoting Steiner v. Meyerson, mem. op. at 2); see also Harbor Finance Partners v. Huizenga, 751 A.2d 879, 892 (Del. Ch. 1999).

47. Ash v. McCall, Del. Ch., C.A. No. 17132, mem. op. at 19-20, Chandler, C. (Sept. 15, 2000), quoting Benerofe v. Cha, Del. Ch., C.A. No. 14614, mem. op. at 19, Chandler, V.C. (Sept. 12, 1996), quoting Grobow v. Perot, 539 A.2d at 189.

48. Compl. ¶37.

shares at approximately $15 below the shares' trading price at that time. The Company's call option, however, could not have been exercised until 2006, almost seven years after the date of The Limited's announcement. By that time, it is anyone's guess as to whether The Limited's stock would have continued to climb in value, whether it would have fallen below its May 1999 trading levels, or whether it would have fallen below either the put option price or the call option price. Any future benefit that the Company might have enjoyed had rescission not been effectuated, therefore, is speculation and conjecture.

The Company argues that rescinding the Redemption Agreement freed up $350 million in cash reserves that it was required to maintain. Freeing up such a substantial amount of otherwise stagnant and untouchable capital, in light of the stock market's volatility and unpredictability, it argues, is well within the realm of reason. That the plaintiffs assess the intrinsic value of the Redemption Agreement to have been between $350 and $550 million based on the Black-Scholes model is not dispositive.[49] If the stock price had fallen below $18.75 at any time prior to 2006, the Company would have been open to the risk that Mr. Wexner would exercise the Children's Trust's put rights (which he would have arguably been under a duty to do), thereby requiring the Company to expend substantial monies from its reserve to purchase the stock at a premium to market. It is well-settled that "'[c]ourts are ill-fitted to attempt to weigh the 'adequacy' of consideration under the waste standard or, *ex post*, to judge appropriate degrees of business risk.'"[50] Thus, the plaintiffs have failed to allege facts supporting a claim that rescission of the Redemption Agreement "served no corporate purpose or was so completely bereft of consideration that it effectively constituted a gift."[51]

2. The Self-Tender Offer

The Board's purported justification for the self-tender was that "'a significant share repurchase would be the most desirable use for [the Company's] excess cash' and 'it would demonstrate to the Company stockholders the Company's confidence in its business.'"[52] Plaintiffs assert that the Board's stated goals for this transaction could have been achieved by alternative means less costly to the Company. Specifically, the Complaint alleges that the Company could have avoided paying a premium of more than 15% for its shares by effectuating "an open market purchase at the prevailing market price given the large daily volume of trading in the Company's stock."[53] This, plaintiffs aver, "would have saved the Company well over $90 million."[54] The Limited could also have used its "significant excess cash to pay a dividend to shareholders . . . [meaning that] the Company could have shared the benefits of its excess cash with

---

49. See In re 3 Com Corp. S'holders Litig., Del. Ch., C.A. No. 16721, mem. op. at 12 n. 17, Steele, V.C. (Oct. 25, 1999). For a more detailed discussion of the Black-Scholes valuation model, see Lewis v. Vogelstein, 699 A.2d 327, 331-33 (Del. Ch. 1997).

50. Brehm v. Eisner, 746 A.2d at 263 (quoting Lewis v. Vogelstein, 699 A.2d at 336).

51. Ash v. McCall, mem. op. at 19-20.

52. Compl. ¶32 (quoting The Limited's May 4, 1999 Offer of Purchase) (alteration in original).

53. Id. ¶33.

54. Id.

all of its shareholders . . . [as opposed to only a relatively small number of individuals benefiting from] a self tender."[55]

"Directors are guilty of corporate waste, only when they authorize an exchange that is so one sided that no business person of ordinary, sound judgment could conclude that the corporation has received adequate consideration."[56] That the Complaint identifies viable alternatives to the Board's decision here is not enough—it is precisely this kind of judicial after-the-fact evaluation that the business judgment rule seeks to prevent.[57] Even the plaintiffs cannot dispute that the vehicle of a self-tender offer is a well-accepted option for corporate boards wanting to manage mounting cash reserves.[58] Thus, because "reasonable, informed minds might disagree on the question, . . . a reviewing court will not attempt to itself evaluate the wisdom of the bargain or the adequacy of the consideration."[59] Accordingly, I find that the plaintiffs have failed to allege that the Self-Tender is the basis for a viable corporate waste claim.

3. The Rescission and the Self-Tender Offer Together

It is the plaintiffs' position that "the two transactions *taken together* served no business purpose other than to benefit [Mr.] Wexner." At the time that these two transactions were announced, The Limited had more than $660 million in cash and cash equivalents on hand. The Complaint alleges that "[t]he only reason for a $750 million—as opposed to $500 million or $600 million—Self Tender, was to create an artificial 'need' to rescind the Redemption Agreement, and, thereby, allow [Mr.] Wexner to escape from the Redemption Agreement at the Company's expense."

The plaintiffs have failed to demonstrate that the Company received no benefit in exchange from these two transactions or that these transactions, taken together, served no corporate purpose. For one, Mr. Wexner promised not to participate in the Company's self-tender. Having done this, Mr. Wexner forfeited his ability to partake in the more than 15% premium offered by the Company for its shares. Moreover, rescinding the Redemption Agreement allowed the Company to manage the otherwise untouchable $350 million that would have been locked up by the terms of that agreement for another six to seven years. While the plaintiffs point out that The Limited only needed an additional $90 million in cash to cover its self-tender offer, nothing changes the fact that $260 million in liquid funds is a valuable asset for any company. As discussed in more detail above, the rescission of the Redemption Agreement protected the Company from a potentially costly liability that might have befallen it had the shares declined in value in the future. Considering that these transactions

---

55. Id.

56. Glazer v. Zapata Corp., 658 A.2d 176, 183 (Del. Ch. 1993).

57. For example, the plaintiffs' identification of a dividend distribution as an alternative means for managing The Limited's excess cash arguably ignores the preferential tax consequences for the capital gains that would result from the tender.

58. See Weiss v. Samsonite Corp., 741 A.2d 366, 371 (Del. Ch. 1999), aff'd, 746 A.2d 277 (Del. 1999).

59. Glazer v. Zapata Corp., 658 A.2d at 183.

conferred upon all of The Limited's shareholders, excluding Mr. Wexner and his affiliates, an opportunity to reap the benefits of a more than 15% premium for their shares, while at the same time demonstrating to the market and those individuals declining to tender their shares the Board's confidence in the Company's stock, I am unwilling to find that the two transactions, viewed together, "served no corporate purpose."[63] As such, even after accepting all of the plaintiffs' well-pled factual allegations and according them the benefit of all reasonable inferences, I find that the Complaint does not state a claim for corporate waste.

D. DUTY OF CARE

Plaintiffs, without much enthusiasm, also allege that the challenged transactions are the product of the directors' breach of their duty of care. The Complaint does not allege gross negligence or the insufficiency of the information upon which the Board based its decision. Thus, the duty of care claim will be dismissed.[65]

IV. CONCLUSION

For the foregoing reasons, defendants' motion to dismiss under Chancery Court Rule 23.1 is denied; defendants' motion under Chancery Court Rule 12(b)(6) to dismiss plaintiffs' duty of care claim and corporate waste claim is granted.[66] Otherwise, defendants' motion to dismiss is denied.

PROBLEM 4-11

Reconsider the facts of Brehm v. Eisner, supra at page 379. Assume that the defendant's motion to dismiss had been denied by the Chancery Court on the grounds that a majority of the Disney board was not disinterested and independent with respect to the challenged actions. What would be the likely outcome of a subsequently filed motion to dismiss for failure to state a cause of action?

---

63. Ash v. McCall, mem. op. at 19-20.

65. Defendants (other than Mr. Wexner and Mrs. Wexner) have also sought to invoke the exculpatory charter provision adopted under the authority of 8 Del. C. §102(b)(7). To the extent that a duty of loyalty claim is implicated, that provision, of course, is inapplicable. Malpiede v. Townson, 780 A.2d 1075, 1094-95 (Del. 2001). In addition, as to those defendants about whom there is no question as to their disinterestedness and independence, I am reluctant to evaluate the §102(b)(7) defense at this stage. First, this defense has not been asserted by the defendants on a director-by-director basis. Second, whether an independent director can obtain dismissal of the claims against him at this stage of the proceedings is an open question. See In re The Student Loan Corp. Deriv. Litig., let. op. at 11 n. 8. In any event, this has not been addressed by the parties.

66. Because Court of Chancery Rule 15(aaa) was not in effect when plaintiffs filed their answering brief in opposition to the motion to dismiss, this dismissal is without prejudice.

3.   Demand Futility Under *Aronson*'s Second Prong
      or Under the *Rales* Test

Ryan v. Gifford
Delaware Court of Chancery, 2007
918 A.2d 341

CHANDLER, CHANCELLOR.

On March 18, 2006, *The Wall Street Journal* sparked controversy throughout the investment community by publishing a one-page article, based on an academic's statistical analysis of option grants, which revealed an arguably questionable compensation practice. Commonly known as backdating, this practice involves a company issuing stock options to an executive on one date while providing fraudulent documentation asserting that the options were actually issued earlier. These options may provide a windfall for executives because the falsely dated stock option grants often coincide with market lows. Such timing reduces the strike prices and inflates the value of stock options, thereby increasing management compensation. This practice allegedly violates any stock option plan that requires strike prices to be no less than the fair market value on the date on which the option is granted by the board. Further, this practice runs afoul of many state and federal common and statutory laws that prohibit dissemination of false and misleading information. . . .

I.   FACTS

Maxim Integrated Products, Inc. is a technology leader in design, development, and manufacture of linear and mixed-signal integrated circuits used in microprocessor-based electronic equipment. From 1998 to mid-2002 Maxim's board of directors and compensation committee granted stock options for the purchase of millions of shares of Maxim's common stock to John F. Gifford, founder, chairman of the board, and chief executive officer, pursuant to shareholder-approved stock option plans filed with the Securities and Exchange Commission. Under the terms of these plans, Maxim contracted and represented that the exercise price of all stock options granted would be no less than the fair market value of the company's common stock, measured by the publicly traded closing price for Maxim stock on the date of the grant. Additionally, the plan identified the board or a committee designated by the board as administrators of its terms.

Ryan is a shareholder of Maxim and has continuously held shares since his Dallas Semiconductor Incorporated shares were converted to Maxim shares upon Maxim's acquisition of Dallas Semiconductor on April 11, 2001. He filed this derivative action on June 2, 2006, against Gifford; James Bergman, B. Kipling Hagopian, and A.R. Frank Wazzan, members of the board and compensation committee at all relevant times; Eric Karros, member of the board from 2000 to 2002, and M.D. Sampels, member of the board from 2001-2002. Ryan alleges that nine specific grants were backdated between 1998 and 2002, as these grants seem too fortuitously timed to be explained as simple coincidence. All nine grants were dated on unusually low (if not the lowest) trading days of the years in question, or on days immediately before sharp increases in the market price of the company.

A. GENESIS OF THESE CLAIMS

As practices surrounding the timing of options grants for public companies began facing increased scrutiny in early 2006, Merrill Lynch conducted an analysis of the timing of stock option grants from 1997 to 2002 for the semiconductor and semiconductor equipment companies that comprise the Philadelphia Semiconductor Index. Merrill Lynch measured the aggressiveness of timing of option grants by examining the extent to which stock price performance subsequent to options pricing events diverges from stock price performance over a longer period of time. "Specifically, it looked at annualized stock price returns for the twenty day period subsequent to options pricing in comparison to stock price returns for the calendar year in which the options were granted." In theory, companies should not generate systematic excess return in comparison to other investors as a result of the timing of options pricing events. "[I]f the timing of options grants is an arm's length process, and companies have [not] systematically taken advantage of their ability to backdate options within the [twenty] day windows that the law provided prior to the implementation of Sarbanes Oxley in 2002, there shouldn't be any difference between the two measures." Merrill Lynch failed to take a position on whether Maxim actually backdated; however, it noted that if backdating did not occur, management of Maxim was remarkably effective at timing options pricing events.

With regard to Maxim, Merrill Lynch found that the twenty-day return on option grants to management averaged 14% over the five-year period, an annualized return of 243%, or almost ten times higher than the 29% annualized market returns in the same period. . . .

II. CONTENTIONS

Plaintiff contends that all defendants breached their fiduciary duties to Maxim and its shareholders. The shareholder-approved 1983 Stock Option Plan and 1999 Stock Incentive Plan bound the board of directors to set the exercise price according to the terms of the plans. The 1999 plan allowed the board to designate a committee to approve the plans. The designated compensation committee, consisting of Bergman, Hagopian, and Wazzan, approved option grants after 1999. Plaintiff alleges that from 1998 to 2002, the board actively allowed Maxim to backdate at least nine option grants issued to Gifford, in violation of shareholder-approved plans, and to purposefully mislead shareholders regarding its actions. As a result of the active violations of the plan and the active deceit, plaintiff contends that Maxim received lower payments upon exercise of the options than would have been received had they not been backdated. Further, Maxim suffers adverse effects from tax and accounting rules. The options priced below the stock's fair market value on the date of the grant allegedly bring the recipient an instant paper gain. At the time, such compensation had to be treated as a cost to the company, thereby reducing reported earnings and resulting in overstated profits. This likely necessitates revision of the company's financial statements and tax reporting. Moreover, Gifford, the recipient of the backdated options, is allegedly unjustly enriched due to receipt of compensation in clear violation of the shareholder-approved plans. . . .

IV. MOTION TO DISMISS

A. FUTILITY OF DEMAND UNDER RULE 23.1 . . .

Delaware law recognizes two instances where a plaintiff is excused from making demand. Failure to make demand may be excused if a plaintiff can raise a reason to doubt that: (1) a majority of the board is disinterested or independent or (2) the challenged acts were the product of the board's valid exercise of business judgment.[23]

The analysis differs, however, where the challenged decision is not a decision of the board in place at the time the complaint is filed. In Rales v. Blasband, the Supreme Court of Delaware held that "[w]here there is no conscious decision by the corporate board of directors to act or refrain from acting, the business judgment rule has no application."[24] Stated differently, "the absence of board action . . . makes it impossible to perform the essential inquiry contemplated by Aronson." Accordingly, where the challenged transaction was not a decision of the board upon which plaintiff must seek demand, plaintiff must "create a reasonable doubt that, as of the time the complaint is filed, the board of directors could have properly exercised its independent and disinterested business judgment in responding to a demand."

Here, the compensation committee, not the board, approved the challenged option grants. . . . At first glance, it appears that because this decision was not a board decision, plaintiff must comply with Rales, alleging facts that raise a reason to doubt that the board members could have properly exercised their independent and disinterested business judgment in responding to a demand. The unique facts here, however, present a different situation. Maxim's board consisted of six members at all relevant times. The compensation committee, at all relevant times, consisted solely of three members, Bergman, Wazzan, and Hagopian. Thus, one half of the current board members approved each challenged transaction. Where at least one half or more of the board in place at the time the complaint was filed approved the underlying challenged transactions, which approval may be imputed to the entire board for purposes of proving demand futility, the Aronson test applies.

The spirit of Rales, if not the letter, supports this conclusion. In Rales, the current board was not the same board that originally made the decision on which the action was based. Consequently, the Supreme Court of Delaware held that the usual test for determining a derivative plaintiff's compliance with the demand obligation did not apply. Because the current board did not make the underlying challenged decision, it became impossible to test whether the current directors acted in conformity with the

---

23. Aronson v. Lewis, 473 A.2d 805, 812 (Del. 1984). . . .
24. 634 A.2d 927, 933 (Del. 1993).

business judgment rule in approving the challenged transaction. That impossibility is not present here.[29]

1.   *Demand Is Futile Under the Second Prong of* Aronson

Because the compensation committee attacked by plaintiff constitutes a majority of the board, the business judgment analysis under the second prong of *Aronson* may be readily applied. Plaintiffs may prove demand futility by raising a reason to doubt whether the challenged transactions were a valid exercise of business judgment.

Plaintiff alleges that the challenged transactions raise a reason to doubt whether the option grants were a valid exercise of business judgment. Specifically, plaintiff states that the terms of the stock option plans *required* that "[t]he exercise price of each option shall be not less than one hundred percent (100%) of the fair market value of the stock subject to the option on the date the option is granted." The board had no discretion to contravene the terms of the stock option plans. Altering the actual date of the grant so as to affect the exercise price contravenes the plan. Thus, knowing and intentional violations of the stock option plans, according to the plaintiff, cannot be an exercise of business judgment. I conclude that the unusual facts alleged raise a reason to doubt that the challenged transactions resulted from a valid exercise of business judgment.

In Sanders v. Wang,[31] then-Vice Chancellor Steele addressed the demand futility issue in a similar factual context. There, shareholders filed a derivative suit alleging that directors granted stock in excess of the number *authorized* by the employee stock ownership plan. Then-Vice Chancellor Steele held that "the plaintiffs have sufficiently alleged facts which, taken as true, show that the CA board violated an express KESOP provision limiting the number of shares they were authorized to award. . . . Thus, the facts raise doubt that the board's actions resulted from a valid exercise of business judgment." A board's knowing and intentional decision to exceed the shareholders' grant of express (but limited) authority raises doubt regarding whether such decision is a valid exercise of business judgment and is sufficient to excuse a failure to make demand.

The situation here closely mirrors that in Sanders v. Wang. Plaintiff supports his claim that backdating occurred by pointing to nine option grants over a six-year period where each option was granted during a low point. That is, every challenged option grant occurred during the lowest market price of the month or year in which it was granted. In addition to pointing specifically to highly suspicious timing, plaintiff

---

29. *Rales*, 634 A.2d at 932-35. The Supreme Court identified three scenarios in which it would be inappropriate to challenge the business judgment of a current board of directors for purposes of demand under Rule 23.1: (1) where a business decision was made by the board of a company, but a majority of the directors making the decision have been replaced; (2) where the subject of the derivative suit is not a business decision of the board; (3) and where the decision being challenged was made by the board of a different corporation. *Id.* at 934. The Supreme Court included the second scenario out of a concern that demand upon a board should not be excused when a board did not have the opportunity to consider a corporate action. Demand "permits the board to have the opportunity to take action where it has not previously considered doing so." *Id.* at 934 n. 9. . . .

31. 1999 WL 1044880 (Del. Ch., Nov. 10, 1999).

further supports his allegations with empirical evidence suggesting that backdating occurred. The Merrill Lynch analysis measured the extent to which stock price performance subsequent to options pricing events diverged from stock price performance over a longer period of time to measure the aggressiveness of the timing of option grants and found that Maxim's average annualized return of 243% on option grants to management was almost ten times higher than the 29% annualized market returns in the same period. This timing, by my judgment and by support of empirical data, seems too fortuitous to be mere coincidence. The appearance of impropriety grows even more when one considers the fact that the board granted options, not at set or designated times, but by a sporadic method.[34]

Plaintiff supports his breach of fiduciary duty claim and his assertion that demand is futile by pointing to the board's decision to ignore limitations set out in the company's stock options plans. The plans do not grant the board discretion to alter the exercise price by falsifying the date on which options were granted. Thus, the alleged facts suggest that the director defendants violated an express provision of two option plans and exceeded the shareholders' grant of express authority.

Plaintiff here points to specific grants, specific language in option plans, specific public disclosures, and supporting empirical analysis to allege knowing and purposeful violations of shareholder plans and intentionally fraudulent public disclosures. Such facts, in my opinion, provide sufficient particularity in the pleading to survive a motion to dismiss for failure to make demand pursuant to Rule 23.1.[35]

2. *Demand Is Futile Under* Rales

Even if the decision by the compensation committee was not imputable to the entire board, thereby implicating *Aronson,* demand would remain futile under the *Rales* test. Where the board has not yet made a decision, demand is excused when the complaint contains particularized facts creating a reason to doubt that a majority of the directors would have been independent and disinterested when considering the demand. Directors who are sued have a disabling interest for pre-suit demand purposes when "the potential for liability is not a mere threat but instead may rise to a substantial likelihood."

---

34. Defendants argue repeatedly that plaintiff's allegations ultimately rest upon nothing more than statistical abstractions. Nevertheless, this Court is required to draw reasonable inferences and need not be blind to probability. True, the Merrill Lynch report does not state conclusively that Gifford's options were *actually* backdated. Rather, it emphatically suggests that either defendant directors knowingly manipulated the dates on which options were granted, or their timing was extraordinarily lucky. Given the choice between improbable good fortune and knowing manipulation of option grants, the Court may reasonably infer the latter, even when applying the heightened pleading standards of Rule 23.1.

35. Defendants also object that plaintiff's allegations are not particularized for purposes of Rule 23.1 because they do not directly allege knowledge on behalf of the directors. Yet, it is difficult to understand how a plaintiff can allege that directors backdated options *without* simultaneously alleging that such directors *knew* that the options were being backdated. After all, any grant of options had to have been approved by the committee, and that committee can be reasonably expected to know the date of the options as well as the date on which they actually approve a grant. Nor is it any defense to say that directors might not have had knowledge that backdating violated their duty of loyalty. Directors of Delaware corporations should not be surprised to find that lying to shareholders is inconsistent with loyalty, which necessarily requires good faith. *See, e.g.,* Malone v. Brincat, 722 A.2d 5, 11-12 (Del. 1998).

A director who approves the backdating of options faces at the very *least* a substantial likelihood of liability, if only because it is difficult to conceive of a context in which a director may simultaneously lie to his shareholders (regarding his violations of a shareholder-approved plan, no less) and yet satisfy his duty of loyalty. Backdating options qualifies as one of those "rare cases [in which] a transaction may be so egregious on its face that board approval cannot meet the test of business judgment, and a substantial likelihood of director liability therefore exists." Plaintiff alleges that three members of a board *approved* backdated options, and another board member accepted them. These are sufficient allegations to raise a reason to doubt the disinterestedness of the current board and to suggest that they are incapable of impartially considering demand. . . .

4.   Demand Futility in the Contest of *Caremark* Claims

Stone v. Ritter
Delaware Supreme Court, 2006
911 A.2d 362

HOLLAND, JUSTICE . . .

This is an appeal from a final judgment of the Court of Chancery dismissing a derivative complaint against fifteen present and former directors of AmSouth Bancorporation ("AmSouth"), a Delaware corporation. . . . The Court of Chancery characterized the allegations in the derivative complaint as a "classic *Caremark* claim," a claim that derives its name from *In re Caremark Int'l Deriv. Litig.*[1] . . .

FACTS

This derivative action is brought on AmSouth's behalf by William and Sandra Stone, who allege that they owned AmSouth common stock "at all relevant times." The nominal defendant, AmSouth, is a Delaware corporation with its principal executive offices in Birmingham, Alabama. During the relevant period, AmSouth's wholly-owned subsidiary, AmSouth Bank, operated about 600 commercial banking branches in six states throughout the southeastern United States and employed more than 11,600 people.

In 2004, AmSouth and AmSouth Bank paid $40 million in fines and $10 million in civil penalties to resolve government and regulatory investigations pertaining principally to the failure by bank employees to file "Suspicious Activity Reports" ("SARs"), as required by the federal Bank Secrecy Act ("BSA")[4] and various anti-money-laundering ("AML") regulations. . . .

---

1. *In re Caremark Int'l Inc. Deriv. Litig.,* 698 A.2d 959 (Del. Ch. 1996).

4. 31 U.S.C. §5318 (2006) *et seq.* The Bank Secrecy Act and the regulations promulgated thereunder require banks to file with the Financial Crimes Enforcement Network, a bureau of the U.S. Department of the Treasury known as "FinCEN," a written "Suspicious Activity Report" (known as a "SAR") whenever, *inter alia,* a banking transaction involves at least $5,000 "and the bank knows, suspects, or has reason to suspect" that, among other possibilities, the "transaction involves funds derived from illegal activities or is intended or conducted in order to hide or disguise funds or assets derived from illegal activities. . . ." 31 U.S.C. §5318(g) (2006); 31 C.F.R. §103.18(a)(2) (2006).

The government investigations arose originally from an unlawful "Ponzi" scheme operated by Louis D. Hamric, II and Victor G. Nance. In August 2000, Hamric, then a licensed attorney, and Nance, then a registered investment advisor with Mutual of New York, contacted an AmSouth branch bank in Tennessee to arrange for custodial trust accounts to be created for "investors" in a "business venture." That venture (Hamric and Nance represented) involved the construction of medical clinics overseas. In reality, Nance had convinced more than forty of his clients to invest in promissory notes bearing high rates of return, by misrepresenting the nature and the risk of that investment. Relying on similar misrepresentations by Hamric and Nance, the AmSouth branch employees in Tennessee agreed to provide custodial accounts for the investors and to distribute monthly interest payments to each account upon receipt of a check from Hamric and instructions from Nance.

The Hamric-Nance scheme was discovered in March 2002, when the investors did not receive their monthly interest payments. . . .

The authorities examined AmSouth's compliance with its reporting and other obligations under the BSA. . . . On October 12, 2004, AmSouth and the USAO entered into a Deferred Prosecution Agreement ("DPA") in which AmSouth agreed: first, to the filing by USAO of a one-count Information in the United States District Court for the Southern District of Mississippi, charging AmSouth with failing to file SARs; and second, to pay a $40 million fine. . . .

On October 12, 2004, the Federal Reserve and the Alabama Banking Department concurrently issued a Cease and Desist Order against AmSouth, requiring it, for the first time, to improve its BSA/AML program. That Cease and Desist Order required AmSouth to (among other things) engage an independent consultant "to conduct a comprehensive review of the Bank's AML Compliance program and make recommendations, as appropriate, for new policies and procedures to be implemented by the Bank." KPMG Forensic Services ("KPMG") performed the role of independent consultant and issued its report on December 10, 2004 (the "KPMG Report").

Also on October 12, 2004, FinCEN and the Federal Reserve jointly assessed a $10 million civil penalty against AmSouth for operating an inadequate anti-money-laundering program and for failing to file SARs. . . . FinCEN found that "AmSouth violated the suspicious activity reporting requirements of the Bank Secrecy Act," and that "[s]ince April 24, 2002, AmSouth has been in violation of the anti-money-laundering program requirements of the Bank Secrecy Act." Among FinCEN's specific determinations were its conclusions that "AmSouth's [AML compliance] program lacked adequate board and management oversight," and that "reporting to management for the purposes of monitoring and oversight of compliance activities was materially deficient." AmSouth neither admitted nor denied FinCEN's determinations in this or any other forum.

DEMAND FUTILITY AND DIRECTOR INDEPENDENCE . . .

In this appeal, the plaintiffs concede that "[t]he standards for determining demand futility in the absence of a business decision" are set forth in Rales v. Blasband.[10] To

---

10. Rales v. Blasband, 634 A.2d 927 (Del. 1993).

excuse demand under *Rales,* "a court must determine whether or not the particularized factual allegations of a derivative stockholder complaint create a reasonable doubt that, as of the time the complaint is filed, the board of directors could have properly exercised its independent and disinterested business judgment in responding to a demand. . . ."

Critical to this demand excused argument is the fact that the directors' potential personal liability depends upon whether or not their conduct can be exculpated by the section 102(b)(7) provision contained in the AmSouth certificate of incorporation. Such a provision can exculpate directors from monetary liability for a breach of the duty of care, but not for conduct that is not in good faith or a breach of the duty of loyalty. . . .

Chancery Court Decision

The plaintiffs contend that demand is excused under Rule 23.1 because AmSouth's directors breached their oversight duty and, as a result, face a "substantial likelihood of liability" as a result of their "utter failure" to act in good faith to put into place policies and procedures to ensure compliance with BSA and AML obligations. The Court of Chancery found that the plaintiffs did not plead the existence of "red flags" — "facts showing that the board ever was aware that AmSouth's internal controls were inadequate, that these inadequacies would result in illegal activity, and that the board chose to do nothing about problems it allegedly knew existed." In dismissing the derivative complaint in this action, the Court of Chancery concluded:

> This case is not about a board's failure to carefully consider a material corporate decision that was presented to the board. This is a case where information was not reaching the board because of ineffective internal controls. . . . With the benefit of hindsight, it is beyond question that AmSouth's internal controls with respect to the Bank Secrecy Act and anti-money laundering regulations compliance were inadequate. Neither party disputes that the lack of internal controls resulted in a huge fine — $50 million, alleged to be the largest ever of its kind. The fact of those losses, however, is not alone enough for a court to conclude that a majority of the corporation's board of directors is disqualified from considering demand that AmSouth bring suit against those responsible.[36]

This Court reviews *de novo* a Court of Chancery's decision to dismiss a derivative suit under Rule 23.1.

Reasonable Reporting System Existed

The KPMG Report evaluated the various components of AmSouth's longstanding BSA/AML compliance program. The KPMG Report reflects that AmSouth's Board dedicated considerable resources to the BSA/AML compliance program and put into place numerous procedures and systems to attempt to ensure compliance. According

---

36. Stone v. Ritter, C.A. No. 1570-N, 2006 WL 302558, at *2 (Del. Ch. 2006) (Letter Opinion).

to KPMG, the program's various components exhibited between a low and high degree of compliance with applicable laws and regulations.

The KPMG Report describes the numerous AmSouth employees, departments and committees established by the Board to oversee AmSouth's compliance with the BSA and to report violations to management and the Board. . . . The KPMG Report reflects that the directors not only discharged their oversight responsibility to establish an information and reporting system, but also proved that the system was designed to permit the directors to periodically monitor AmSouth's compliance with BSA and AML regulations. For example, as KPMG noted in 2004, AmSouth's designated BSA Officer "has made annual high-level presentations to the Board of Directors in each of the last five years." Further, the Board's Audit and Community Responsibility Committee (the "Audit Committee") oversaw AmSouth's BSA/AML compliance program on a quarterly basis. The KPMG Report states that "the BSA Officer presents BSA/AML training to the Board of Directors annually," and the "Corporate Security training is also presented to the Board of Directors."

The KPMG Report shows that AmSouth's Board at various times enacted written policies and procedures designed to ensure compliance with the BSA and AML regulations. For example, the Board adopted an amended bank-wide "BSA/AML Policy" on July 17, 2003—four months before AmSouth became aware that it was the target of a government investigation. That policy was produced to plaintiffs in response to their demand to inspect AmSouth's books and records pursuant to section 220 and is included in plaintiffs' appendix. Among other things, the July 17, 2003, BSA/AML Policy directs all AmSouth employees to immediately report suspicious transactions or activity to the BSA/AML Compliance Department or Corporate Security.

COMPLAINT PROPERLY DISMISSED

In this case, the adequacy of the plaintiffs' assertion that demand is excused depends on whether the complaint alleges facts sufficient to show that the defendant *directors* are potentially personally liable for the failure of non-director bank *employees* to file SARs. Delaware courts have recognized that "[m]ost of the decisions that a corporation, acting through its human agents, makes are, of course, not the subject of director attention."[39] Consequently, a claim that directors are subject to personal liability for employee failures is "possibly the most difficult theory in corporation law upon which a plaintiff might hope to win a judgment."

For the plaintiffs' derivative complaint to withstand a motion to dismiss, "only a sustained or systematic failure of the board to exercise oversight—such as an utter failure to attempt to assure a reasonable information and reporting system exists—will establish the lack of good faith that is a necessary condition to liability." . . .

The KPMG Report—which the plaintiffs explicitly incorporated by reference into their derivative complaint—refutes the assertion that the directors "never took the necessary steps . . . to ensure that a reasonable BSA compliance and reporting system

---

39. *In re Caremark Int'l Inc. Deriv. Litig.*, 698 A.2d at 968.

existed." KPMG's findings reflect that the Board received and approved relevant policies and procedures, delegated to certain employees and departments the responsibility for filing SARs and monitoring compliance, and exercised oversight by relying on periodic reports from them. Although there ultimately may have been failures by employees to report deficiencies to the Board, there is no basis for an oversight claim seeking to hold the directors personally liable for such failures by the employees.

With the benefit of hindsight, the plaintiffs' complaint seeks to equate a bad outcome with bad faith. The lacuna in the plaintiffs' argument is a failure to recognize that the directors' good faith exercise of oversight responsibility may not invariably prevent employees from violating criminal laws, or from causing the corporation to incur significant financial liability, or both, as occurred in *Graham, Caremark* and this very case. In the absence of red flags, good faith in the context of oversight must be measured by the directors' actions "to assure a reasonable information and reporting system exists" and not by second-guessing after the occurrence of employee conduct that results in an unintended adverse outcome. Accordingly, we hold that the Court of Chancery properly applied *Caremark* and dismissed the plaintiffs' derivative complaint for failure to excuse demand by alleging particularized facts that created reason to doubt whether the directors had acted in good faith in exercising their oversight responsibilities.

5. Dismissal of Derivative Litigation at the Request of an Independent Litigation Committee of the Board

MBCA §7.44

Beginning in the late 1970s, lawyers for corporate defendants developed a new tack for responding to derivative suits for which demand was excused and therefore the protective business judgment review was not available. A corporation appointed a committee made up of directors who were not involved in the first suit and asserted for this committee the right to claim the board's power to control derivative litigation. Early case law produced three views. In Auerbach v. Bennett, 47 N.Y.2d 619, 393 N.E.2d 994, 419 N.Y.S.2d 920 (1979), the Court of Appeals of New York ruled that an interested board retains power to delegate its authority to a special litigation committee composed of disinterested directors whose recommendation that derivative litigation be dismissed would be entitled to normal business judgment rule presumptions. Thus, under the approach taken in Auerbach v. Bennett, a court would inquire into the committee members' disinterestedness, into the reasonableness of the procedures used in their deliberations, and into their good faith. However, a court following the Auerbach v. Bennett approach will not inquire into the substance of the special litigation committee's decision.

In Miller v. Register and Tribune Syndicate, Inc., 336 N.W.2d 709 (Iowa 1983), the Supreme Court of Iowa sharply disagreed with the Auerbach v. Bennett approach. The court concluded that a conflicted board has power to appoint a special litigation committee to investigate and advise the corporation concerning derivative litigation, but that such special litigation committee has no power to control derivative litigation on behalf of the corporation. Put another way, the recommendations of a special litigation committee that derivative litigation be dismissed would be entitled to no more business judgment deference than would a recommendation made directly by the interested board. The Iowa Supreme Court based its decision largely on concern that "structural bias" would prevent the special litigation committee members from exercising impartial business judgment.

In Zapata Corp. v. Maldonado, below, the Delaware Supreme Court steered a middle ground between Auerbach v. Bennett and Miller v. Register and Tribune Syndicate, Inc. As you read the following case, consider how the Delaware approach to review of special litigation committee recommendations differs not only from the New York and Iowa approaches, but also from the approaches suggested in MBCA §7.44 and ALI Principles of Corporate Governance §7.08.

Zapata Corp. v. Maldonado
Delaware Supreme Court, 1981
430 A.2d 779

QUILLEN, JUSTICE.

This is an interlocutory appeal from an order entered on April 9, 1980, by the Court of Chancery denying appellant-defendant Zapata Corporation's (Zapata) alternative motions to dismiss the complaint or for summary judgment. The issue to be addressed has reached this Court by way of a rather convoluted path.

In June, 1975, William Maldonado, a stockholder of Zapata, instituted a derivative action in the Court of Chancery on behalf of Zapata against ten officers and/or directors of Zapata, alleging, essentially, breaches of fiduciary duty. Maldonado did not first demand that the board bring this action, stating instead such demand's futility because all directors were named as defendants and allegedly participated in the acts specified. In June, 1977, Maldonado commenced an action in the United States District Court for the Southern District of New York against the same defendants, save one, alleging federal security law violations as well as the same common law claims made previously in the Court of Chancery.

By June, 1979, four of the defendant-directors were no longer on the board, and the remaining directors appointed two new outside directors to the board. The board then created an "Independent Investigation Committee" (Committee), composed solely of the two new directors, to investigate Maldonado's actions, as well as a similar derivative action then pending in Texas, and to determine whether the corporation should continue any or all of the litigation. The Committee's determination was stated to be "final, . . . not . . . subject to review by the Board of Directors and . . . in all respects . . . binding upon the Corporation."

Following an investigation, the Committee concluded, in September, 1979, that each action should "be dismissed forthwith as their continued maintenance is inimical to the Company's best interests. . . ." Consequently, Zapata moved for dismissal or summary judgment in the three derivative actions. On January 24, 1980, the District Court for the Southern District of New York granted Zapata's motion for summary judgment, Maldonado v. Flynn, S.D.N.Y., 485 F. Supp. 274 (1980), holding, under its interpretation of Delaware law, that the Committee had the authority, under the "business judgment" rule, to require the termination of the derivative action. Maldonado appealed that decision to the Second Circuit Court of Appeals.

On March 18, 1980, the Court of Chancery, in a reported opinion, the basis for the order of April 9, 1980, denied Zapata's motions, holding that Delaware law does not sanction this means of dismissal. More specifically, it held that the "business judgment" rule is not a grant of authority to dismiss derivative actions and that a stockholder has an individual right to maintain derivative actions in certain instances. Maldonado v. Flynn, Del. Ch., 413 A.2d 1251 (1980). Pursuant to the provisions of Supreme Court Rule 42, Zapata filed an interlocutory appeal with this Court shortly thereafter. The appeal was accepted by this Court on June 5, 1980. On May 29, 1980, however, the Court of Chancery dismissed Maldonado's cause of action, its decision based on principles of res judicata, expressly conditioned upon the Second Circuit affirming the earlier New York District Court's decision. The Second Circuit appeal was ordered stayed, however, pending this Court's resolution of the appeal from the April 9th Court of Chancery order denying dismissal and summary judgment.

Thus, Zapata's observation that it sits "in a procedural gridlock" appears quite accurate, and we agree that this Court can and should attempt to resolve the particular question of Delaware law. As the Vice Chancellor noted, "it is the law of the State of incorporation which determines whether the directors have this power of dismissal." We limit our review in this interlocutory appeal to whether the Committee has the power to cause the present action to be dismissed. . . .

The question to be decided becomes: When, if at all, should an authorized board committee be permitted to cause litigation, properly initiated by a derivative stockholder in his own right, to be dismissed? As noted above, a board has the power to choose not to pursue litigation when demand is made upon it, so long as the decision is not wrongful. If the board determines that a suit would be detrimental to the company, the board's determination prevails. Even when demand is excusable, circumstances may arise when continuation of the litigation would not be in the corporation's best interests. Our inquiry is whether, under such circumstances, there is a permissible procedure under §141(a) by which a corporation can rid itself of detrimental litigation. If there is not, a single stockholder in an extreme case might control the destiny of the entire corporation. This concern was bluntly expressed by the Ninth Circuit in Lewis v. Anderson, 9th Cir., 615 F.2d 778, 783 (1979), cert. denied, 449 U.S. 869 (1980): "To allow one shareholder to incapacitate an entire board of directors merely by leveling charges against them gives too much leverage to dissident shareholders." But, when examining the means, including the committee mechanism examined in this case, potentials for abuse must be recognized. This takes us to the second and third aspects of the issue on appeal.

Before we pass to equitable considerations as to the mechanism at issue here, it must be clear that an independent committee possesses the corporate power to seek the termination of a derivative suit. Section 141(c) allows a board to delegate all of its authority to a committee. Accordingly, a committee with properly delegated authority would have the power to move for dismissal or summary judgment if the entire board did.

Even though demand was not made in this case and the initial decision of whether to litigate was not placed before the board, Zapata's board, it seems to us, retained all of its corporate power concerning litigation decisions. If Maldonado had made demand on the board in this case, it could have refused to bring suit. Maldonado could then have asserted that the decision not to sue was wrongful and, if correct, would have been allowed to maintain the suit. The board, however, never would have lost its statutory managerial authority. The demand requirement itself evidences that the managerial power is retained by the board. When a derivative plaintiff is allowed to bring suit after a wrongful refusal, the board's authority to choose whether to pursue the litigation is not challenged although its conclusion reached through the exercise of that authority is not respected since it is wrongful. Similarly, Rule 23.1, by excusing demand in certain instances, does not strip the board of its corporate power. It merely saves the plaintiff the expense and delay of making a futile demand resulting in a probable tainted exercise of that authority in a refusal by the board or in giving control of litigation to the opposing side. But the board entity remains empowered under §141(a) to make decisions regarding corporate litigation. The problem is one of member disqualification, not the absence of power in the board.

The corporate power inquiry then focuses on whether the board, tainted by the self-interest of a majority of its members, can legally delegate its authority to a committee of two disinterested directors. We find our statute clearly requires an affirmative answer to this question. As has been noted, under an express provision of the statute, §141(c), a committee can exercise all of the authority of the board to the extent provided in the resolution of the board. Moreover, at least by analogy to our statutory section on interested directors, 8 Del. C. §144, it seems clear that the Delaware statute is designed to permit disinterested directors to act for the board.

We do not think that the interest taint of the board majority is per se a legal bar to the delegation of the board's power to an independent committee composed of disinterested board members. The committee can properly act for the corporation to move to dismiss derivative litigation that is believed to be detrimental to the corporation's best interest.

Our focus now switches to the Court of Chancery which is faced with a stockholder assertion that a derivative suit, properly instituted, should continue for the benefit of the corporation and a corporate assertion, properly made by a board committee acting with board authority, that the same derivative suit should be dismissed as inimical to the best interests of the corporation.

At the risk of stating the obvious, the problem is relatively simple. If, on the one hand, corporations can consistently wrest bona fide derivative actions away from well-meaning derivative plaintiffs through the use of the committee mechanism, the derivative suit will lose much, if not all, of its generally-recognized effectiveness as an intra-corporate means of policing boards of directors. . . . If, on the other hand, corporations are unable to rid themselves of meritless or harmful litigation and strike suits, the derivative action, created to benefit the corporation, will produce the opposite, unintended result. It thus appears desirable to us to find a balancing point where bona fide stockholder power to bring corporate causes of action cannot be unfairly trampled on by the board of directors, but the corporation can rid itself of detrimental litigation.

As we noted, the question has been treated by other courts as one of the "business judgment" of the board committee. If a "committee, composed of independent and disinterested directors, conducted a proper review of the matters before it, considered a variety of factors and reached, in good faith, a business judgment that [the] action was not in the best interest of [the corporation]," the action must be dismissed. See, e.g., Maldonado v. Flynn, supra, 485 F. Supp. at 282, 286. The issues become solely independence, good faith, and reasonable investigation. The ultimate conclusion of the committee, under that view, is not subject to judicial review.

We are not satisfied, however, that acceptance of the "business judgment" rationale at this stage of derivative litigation is a proper balancing point. While we admit an analogy with a normal case respecting board judgment, it seems to us that there is sufficient risk in the realities of a situation like the one presented in this case to justify caution beyond adherence to the theory of business judgment.

The context here is a suit against directors where demand on the board is excused. We think some tribute must be paid to the fact that the lawsuit was properly initiated. It is not a board refusal case. Moreover, this complaint was filed in June of 1975 and, while the parties undoubtedly would take differing views on the degree of litigation activity, we have to be concerned about the creation of an "Independent Investigation Committee" four years later, after the election of two new outside directors. Situations could develop where such motions could be filed after years of vigorous litigation for reasons unconnected with the merits of the lawsuit.

Moreover, notwithstanding our conviction that Delaware law entrusts the corporate power to a properly authorized committee, we must be mindful that directors are passing judgment on fellow directors in the same corporation and fellow directors, in this instance, who designated them to serve both as directors and committee members. The question naturally arises whether a "there but for the grace of God go I" empathy might not play a role. And the further question arises whether inquiry as to independence, good faith and reasonable investigation is sufficient safeguard against abuse, perhaps subconscious abuse. . . .

Whether the Court of Chancery will be persuaded by the exercise of a committee power resulting in a summary motion for dismissal of a derivative action, where a demand has not been initially made, should rest, in our judgment, in the independent discretion of the Court of Chancery. We thus steer a middle course between those cases which yield to the independent business judgment of a board committee and this case as determined below which would yield to unbridled plaintiff stockholder control. In pursuit of the course, we recognize that "[t]he final substantive judgment whether a particular lawsuit should be maintained requires a balance of many factors ethical, commercial, promotional, public relations, employee relations, fiscal as well as legal." Maldonado v. Flynn, supra, 485 F. Supp. at 285. But we are content that such factors are not "beyond the judicial reach" of the Court of Chancery which regularly and competently deals with fiduciary relationships, disposition of trust property, approval of settlements and scores of similar problems. We recognize the danger of judicial overreaching but the alternatives seem to us to be outweighed by the fresh view of a judicial outsider. Moreover, if we failed to balance all the interests involved, we would in the name of practicality and judicial economy foreclose a judicial decision on the merits. At this point, we are not convinced that is necessary or desirable.

After an objective and thorough investigation of a derivative suit, an independent committee may cause its corporation to file a pretrial motion to dismiss in the Court of Chancery. The basis of the motion is the best interests of the corporation, as determined by the committee. The motion should include a thorough written record of the investigation and its findings and recommendations. Under appropriate Court supervision, akin to proceedings on summary judgment, each side should have an opportunity to make a record on the motion. As to the limited issues presented by the motion noted below, the moving party should be prepared to meet the normal burden under Rule 56 that there is no genuine issue as to any material fact and that the moving party is entitled to dismiss as a matter of law. The Court should apply a two-step test to the motion.

First, the Court should inquire into the independence and good faith of the committee and the bases supporting its conclusions. Limited discovery may be ordered to facilitate such inquiries. The corporation should have the burden of proving independence, good faith and a reasonable investigation, rather than presuming independence, good faith and reasonableness. If the Court determines either that the committee is not independent or has not shown reasonable bases for its conclusions, or, if the Court is not satisfied for other reasons relating to the process, including but not limited to the good faith of the committee, the Court shall deny the corporation's motion. If, however, the Court is satisfied under Rule 56 standards that the committee was independent and showed reasonable bases for good faith findings and recommendations, the Court *may* proceed, *in its discretion*, to the next step (emphasis supplied).

The second step provides, we believe, the essential key in striking the balance between legitimate corporate claims as expressed in a derivative stockholder suit and a corporation's best interests as expressed by an independent investigating committee. The Court should determine, applying its own independent business judgment, whether the motion should be granted. This means, of course, that instances could arise where a committee can establish its independence and sound bases for its good faith decisions and still have the corporation's motion denied. The second step is intended to thwart instances where corporate actions meet the criteria of step one, but the result does not appear to satisfy its spirit, or where corporate actions would simply prematurely terminate a stockholder grievance deserving of further consideration in the corporation's interest. The Court of Chancery of course must carefully consider and weigh how compelling the corporate interest in dismissal is when faced with a non-frivolous lawsuit. The Court of Chancery should, when appropriate, give special consideration to matters of law and public policy in addition to the corporation's best interests.

If the Court's independent business judgment is satisfied, the Court may proceed to grant the motion, subject, of course, to any equitable terms or conditions the Court finds necessary or desirable. . . .

NOTES AND QUESTIONS

1. Whatever the theoretical merits of the two-step test adopted in Zapata Corp. v. Maldonado, it is not without substantial costs. Consider the remarks of Chancellor Brown in Kaplan v. Wyatt, 484 A.2d 501, 511-512 (Del. Ch. 1984):

In short, the new *Zapata* procedure, while perhaps laudatory in legal concept, has the pragmatic effect of setting up a form of litigation within litigation. (At this point in this case, we are some three years after the amended complaint was filed, we have had three full-scale, briefed arguments, we have had all of the investigation and activity previously mentioned, and as yet we have not reached the point of any of the normal discovery and motion practice permitted by the Court Rules.) The *Zapata* procedure adds, in effect, a new party to derivative litigation — the Special Litigation Committee — and a new battery of lawyers — counsel for the Committee — with the attendant expense to the corporation. It sidetracks derivative litigation as we have heretofore known it for approximately two years at a minimum while the Committee goes through its functions and while the plaintiff passively awaits his chance to resist them. And in the process the *Zapata* procedure has imposed substantial additional burdens at the trial court level in each such derivative suit in which it has been employed.

2. Given the limited cost savings available from using an independent litigation committee as a device for dismissing derivative litigation against directors (see Kaplan v. Wyatt), and the possibility that a court will not agree with the committee's recommendation in any event, does exculpation serve a legitimate corporate need by eliminating costly litigation costs for counterproductive litigation? Do the MBCA derivative suit rules seem calculated to reduce the expense of the special litigation committee device?

3. One federal district court interpreted the second step of *Zapata* this way: "The second step of the *Zapata* procedure, then, serves as a judicial back-stop to prevent [special litigation committees (SLCs)] from manipulating their procedural advantages to terminate meritorious derivative claims. It can be, to use plaintiff's phrase, an imprecise 'smell test' allowing the court to search between the lines of the SLC's report for the scent of a meritorious claim enclosed within a record that has not been opened by truly adversarial proceedings." Johnson v. Hui, 811 F. Supp. 479, 489 (N.D. Cal. 1991) (refusing to apply second step when record shows a history of good business judgment by directors).

4. The difference between a motion to dismiss for failure to make demand and a motion to dismiss based on the recommendation on a special litigation committee ("SLC") has been carefully articulated in Delaware.

An SLC is a unique creature that was introduced into Delaware law by Zapata v. Maldonado in 1981. The SLC procedure is a method sometimes employed where presuit demand has already been excused and the SLC is vested with the full power of the board to conduct an extensive investigation into the merits of the corporate claim with a view toward determining whether — in the SLC's business judgment — the corporate claim should be pursued. Unlike the demand-excusal context, where the board is presumed to be independent, the SLC has the burden of establishing its own independence by a yardstick that must be "like Caesar's wife" — "above reproach." Moreover, unlike the presuit demand context, the SLC analysis contemplates not only a shift in the burden of persuasion but also the availability of discovery into various issues, including independence.

We need not decide whether the substantive standard of independence in an SLC case differs from that in a presuit demand case. As a practical matter, the procedural distinction relating to the diametrically-opposed burdens and the availability of discovery into independence may be outcome-determinative on the issue of independence. Moreover, because the members of an SLC are vested with enormous power to seek dismissal of a derivative suit brought against their director-colleagues in a setting where presuit demand is already excused, the Court of Chancery must exercise careful oversight of the bona fides of the SLC and its process.

Beam v. Stewart, 845 A.2d 1040, 1055 (Del. 2005).

PROBLEM 4-12

Reconsider Problem 4-6. Assume the following additional or changed facts: that the derivative suit survives a motion to dismiss for lack of demand; shortly thereafter Diversified replaces Nick and Nancy as directors with two new directors; the board then creates a Special Litigation Committee whose members are the two new directors; the Special Litigation Committee finds that the derivative litigation will cost Diversified $2 million in legal fees and substantial lost reputation, and that these losses far outweigh the possible benefits of maintaining the derivative action; and finally, the Special Litigation Committee files a motion seeking dismissal of the derivative action as not in Diversified's best interests.

What is the likely outcome of this motion?

E. *Indemnification and Insurance*

> **MBCA §§8.50-8.59**
> **Delaware G.C.L. §§102(b)(1), 145**

In the past 25 years, lawmakers and corporate planners have developed a number of innovations designed to ensure that directors will not face unreasonable risk of liability in shareholder-initiated litigation. These innovations include exculpation statutes, the evolution of increasingly sophisticated demand rules, and the recognition and utilization of the disinterested litigation subcommittee. Still, these devices leave directors potentially liable for significant attorneys' fees incurred before a frivolous suit is dismissed. Additionally, directors may still face substantial litigation costs, as well as civil damages or criminal fines in shareholder litigation or separate proceedings that are more meritorious, including actions alleging self-dealing or other breach of the duty of loyalty.

Traditionally, corporations provided protection to directors from some of these additional costs by indemnifying them against possible liability for serving the corporation. Beginning in the 1950s, concerns about the reliability of indemnification led corporations to seek, and insurance companies to provide, insurance for many of these possible litigation-related costs. Insurance and indemnification continue to be mainstays in the arsenal of devices that limit directors' risk of bearing personal financial losses as a result of serving on a board.

Under general agency law principles, a principal is required to indemnify an agent either (1) pursuant to the terms of their indemnity agreement, if any, or (2) whenever the agent suffers a loss that, because of the relation, should fairly be borne by the principal. See Restatement (Third) of Agency §8.14. It might seem logical that, in the absence of corporate law provisions on the subject, indemnification of directors would be governed by general agency law. Indeed, two early cases did so. See Du Puy v. Crucible Steel Co., 288 F. 583 (W.D. Pa. 1923), and Hoch v. Duluth, 173 Minn. 374, 217 N.W. 503 (1928), both denying indemnity because the director's actions were not a direct and natural consequence of the execution of his agency.

However, in New York Dock Co. v. McCollum, 16 N.Y.S.2d 844, 847 (N.Y. Sup. 1939), the New York Supreme Court refused to apply agency law indemnification principles because "a director of a corporation is not an agent either of the corporation or of its stockholders.... [Rather] his office is a creature of the law." Furthermore, the court held that directors are not automatically entitled to indemnification if they successfully defend against a derivative suit. This case created a furor in corporate law circles and led to the first statutory indemnification provisions.

Directors' and officers' indemnification rights are generally determined by provisions in either indemnification contracts or corporate by-laws. These contractual indemnification arrangements exist against the backdrop of common law and statutory rules governing a corporation's indemnification power and responsibility. The Delaware General Corporation Law and the Model Business Corporation Act not only authorize indemnification but also place significant statutory limits on corporate power to indemnify officers and directors.

While most indemnification is a matter of contract, in certain circumstances directors and officers may have a common law or statutory right to indemnification. Some states, including Delaware (see Delaware G.C.L. §145(c)), require a corporation to indemnify its officers and directors if they are "successful on the merits or otherwise in defense of any action, suit or proceeding" related in any way to their service as an officer or director. States following the MBCA formulation make indemnification mandatory only if the defendants are *wholly* successful on the merits or otherwise. See MBCA §8.52. The MBCA version does not require indemnification where a defendant has been partially successful, as, for example, by avoiding conviction on one of four counts in a criminal case. The Delaware version has been held to require indemnification for partial success. See Merrit-Chapman & Scott Corp. v. Wolfson, 321 A.2d 138 (Del. Super. Ct. 1974).

The first insurance policies designed to protect directors and officers from unwarranted apprehension of liability initially were written on a policy form having two parts. Part One was called "Corporate Reimbursement Liability" and covered a corporation's liability to indemnify its employees, whether such liability arose from contract or was imposed by law. Part Two was termed "Director and Officer Liability" and insured named officers and directors against insurable acts for which the corporation did not provide indemnification. Specifically excluded from the contract were uninsurable acts such as willful misconduct, dishonest acts, or actions involving receipt of improper personal benefit.

Currently available insurance is similar in content to the original policy, but insurance companies have developed a variety of forms that deviate from the original two-part structure. Nonetheless, the coverage originally afforded by Part Two is still colloquially referred to as "D&O insurance," regardless of the actual terminology of a particular policy.

Owens Corning v. National Union Fire Insurance Co.

United States Court of Appeals, Sixth Circuit, 2001
257 F.3d 484

Before: Boggs and Gilman, Circuit Judges; and Beckwith, District Judge.

OPINION

BOGGS, CIRCUIT JUDGE.

In this diversity action seeking declaratory judgment, Owens Corning, a corporation organized under the laws of Delaware, seeks to recover on its insurance contract with National Union Insurance ("National Union"), which has denied payment to compensate Owens Corning for indemnifying its directors and officers, who paid a substantial amount to settle a 1991 shareholder class action. Ohio law governs the contract, although we look to the corporate law of Delaware for the standards governing indemnification. . . .

Appellant National Union issued a directors and officers ("D & O") insurance policy to Owens Corning for the policy period from March 8, 1991 through March 8, 1992. The second part of the policy, Coverage B ("the Policy"), which is the subject of this dispute, insured Owens Corning for expenses incurred when Owens Corning indemnified its directors and officers against certain liabilities. Subject to a $2.5 million deductible, Coverage B states:

> This policy shall reimburse the Company for Loss from any claim or claims which are first made against the Directors or Officers and reported to the Insurer during the Policy Period . . . for any alleged Wrongful Act in their respective capacities as Directors or Officers . . . but only when and to the extent that the Company has indemnified the Directors or Officers for such Loss pursuant to law, common or statutory, or contract, or the Charter or By-laws of the Company. . . .

On October 25, 1991, Owens Corning and six of its directors and officers were named as defendants in a class-action lawsuit brought by several Owens Corning shareholders. The lawsuit, captioned Gaetana Lavalle v. Owens Corning Fiberglass Corp. (N.D. Ohio 1991) ("*Lavalle*"), was filed immediately after a transitory decrease in Owens Corning's stock price. The *Lavalle* complaint alleged that Owens Corning's 1988 to 1991 filings with the Securities and Exchange Commission ("SEC") had misrepresented the company's future financial exposure to asbestos claims, that the defendants had failed to disclose the danger that Owens Corning's products liability insurance coverage would eventually be exhausted, and that the defendants had misled investors concerning the impact that asbestos claims would have on the company's future financial condition and prospects. . . .

Owens Corning settled the Lavalle class-action suit in 1995 for $9,975,000; National Union was kept fully apprised of the ongoing negotiations, but did not participate in the defense or settlement of the action. After indemnifying its directors and officers for their defense and settlement costs, Owens Corning requested reimbursement from National Union. National Union again denied coverage on the same grounds that it had earlier asserted. On December 1, 1995, Owens Corning filed this diversity action against National Union for breach of the Policy. Owens Corning sought a declaratory judgment that National Union was obligated to pay under the Policy all sums that Owens Corning incurred in the defense and settlement of the Lavalle lawsuit, less the $2.5 million deductible. . . .

B. PROPRIETY OF INDEMNIFICATION

The ability of a Delaware corporation to indemnify its directors for the consequences of their acts is constrained by Delaware's General Corporation Law §145. This section defines a basic structure that can be modified, within limits, by the adoption of by-laws. Del. G.C.L. §145(f). The basic structure has two types of indemnification, mandatory and permissive. Mandatory indemnification for defense expenses occurs when the director is "successful on the merits or otherwise" in defense of the action brought against him. §145(c). Permissive indemnification may occur, if the corporation so chooses, for the costs imposed on directors who have been determined to have acted in good faith. §§145(a),(b). It is common for corporations to adopt through their by-laws a requirement that they must (as opposed to may) reimburse directors for their costs. Owens Corning has done this. The requirement of good faith on the part of the directors indemnified under §§145(a),(b) however, is statutory, and cannot be waived by attempting to extend indemnification even further. See Vonfeldt v. Stifel Fin. Corp., 1999 WL 413393 at *2 (Del. Ch.); Cochran v. Stifel Fin. Corp., 2000 WL 286722 at *19 (Del. Ch.). See also Waltuch v. Conticommodity Serv. Inc., 88 F.3d 87, 95 (2d Cir. 1996) (discussing why Delaware law requires good faith in such circumstances).

A default method for the determination of good faith by the corporation is described by §145(d). It is National Union's contention that Owens Corning failed to comply with this, and therefore the indemnification was not "pursuant to law" as the Policy requires. Consequently, National Union claims it owes its policyholder nothing for the Lavalle settlement. This argument was attempted by the appellant (and rejected) in the Ninth Circuit. Safeway Stores, Inc. v. Nat'l Union Fire Ins. Co., 64 F.3d 1282, 1290 (9th Cir. 1995) (interpreting Maryland corporation law, however).

Owens Corning claims that its by-laws provide an independent basis for indemnification without reference to good faith,[21] or in the alternative, that its indemnification was mandatory under §145(c) and that the settlement constituted "success on the merits or otherwise." Although we find the indemnification did not violate Delaware law, we reject both of Owens Corning's arguments for that conclusion. First, Owens Corning cannot avoid the good-faith requirement through provision of an alternative basis for indemnification; the ability to provide indemnification is constrained by its corporate form as governed by the law of Delaware. As discussed earlier, the

---

21. National Union, by contrast, has also asserted that Owens Corning violated its own contractual agreements with its directors. (Nat'l Union Reply Br. at 7). This is unpersuasive for two reasons. First, this agreement and the Owens by-laws establish a "Reviewing Party" that can make a negative determination that stops indemnification that would otherwise occur (indemnification proceeds so long as the Reviewing Party "shall not have determined . . . that Indemnitee would not be permitted to be indemnified under applicable law"). To argue that this imposes a requirement that there "must be . . . a determination by the 'Reviewing Party' that the director should . . . be permitted to be indemnified under Delaware law," (Nat'l Union Reply Br. at 8), is, to put it charitably, an error of elementary logic. Second, the agreement explicitly provides that any rights to indemnification in the agreement are in addition to rights under the By-laws or under Delaware law, and thus cannot be asserted to limit the indemnification rights of the directors. Notably, the By-laws specifically provide that the failure to make a determination shall not create a presumption that the director has not met the requisite standard of conduct required for indemnification.

Delaware chancery courts have generally required good faith to be present for permissive indemnification, an interpretation also followed by the well-reasoned opinion of the Second Circuit in *Waltuch*.

With regard to Owens Corning's second argument, it is also extremely dubious that a payout of almost ten million dollars would be deemed "success" by the courts of Delaware. Both of the main cases on the issue, *Vonfeldt* and *Waltuch*, have declined to define the term precisely, but a reading of them suggests they would have rejected labeling Lavalle as a "success" appropriate for §145(c). See *Waltuch*, 88 F.3d at 96 & n. 12 (stating "[e]scape from . . . detriment, for whatever reason, is determinative" but also "we need not decide whether a defendant's settlement payment automatically renders that defendant 'unsuccessful' under §145(c)"); *Vonfeldt*, 1999 WL 413393 at *4 (not reaching question of whether "room might exist" for viewing "nominal consideration" as consistent with success) (emphasis added). By contrast, the Ninth Circuit's interpretation of Maryland law in *Safeway* appears willing to extend the meaning of "success" to payment of a substantial monetary settlement, so long as the defendant has not conceded liability. See 64 F.3d at 1290 n. 24. This definition arguably creates the potential for moral hazard and collusion, because it allows directors to structure settlement terms that shift costs on to their insurer. Moreover, since indemnification arising from such a "success" could presumably be challenged under Delaware law for lack of directorial good faith, equating compromise with success would create considerable tension with the mandatory nature of §145(c) indemnification.[22]

Whatever may be the merits of the Ninth Circuit's view as a general matter, an inspection of the Delaware statute shows that the provisions in sections 145(a) and 145(b) are much more clearly designed for situations where settlements are paid out. Both sections (a) and (b) explicitly mention "settlement," whereas §145(c) does not, limiting itself to costs and attorney's fees. This provides a strong indication that section (c), unlike (a) and (b), is not intended to be ordinarily applicable to settlements. Therefore, we hold that Owens Corning's indemnification arising from the *Lavalle* settlement could not have proceeded under §145(c).

However, corporations do have significant flexibility regarding their procedures, as long as they remain consistent with public policy and the controlling corporate law. See Hibbert v. Hollywood Park, Inc., 457 A.2d 339, 344 (Del. 1983); *Waltuch*, 88 F.3d at 92-93. It is not impermissible for a Delaware corporation to accord a director seeking indemnification a rebuttable presumption of good faith. See *Vonfeldt*, 1999 WL 413393, at *3. Therefore, where a corporation has extended indemnification to the maximum permissible extent, as Owens Corning has done, such a presumption may

---

22. Like the *Waltuch* court, we express no opinion on whether a payment in any amount must be considered a failure. A suit does have a "nuisance" value, based on the prospective litigation costs required to effect a dismissal of the action. If a defendant could show that the amount paid in settlement was lower than the prospective attorney's fees and other costs it would have incurred save for the settlement, there is a good argument for a label of "success" despite payment. See *Vonfeldt*, 1999 WL 413393 at *4. It would seem needlessly burdensome to create an absolute rule that would compel litigants to seek a Pyrrhic victory in court. No such showing has been attempted by Owens Corning here, however; instead it relies on the insufficient ground that there was not an "adverse judgment or finding of wrongdoing" (Owens Br. at 29)—something which is generally true of any pre-trial settlement.

be applied. This accords with learned commentary on Delaware law, which describes the powers of the corporation to include provision of "accelerated procedures for the 'determination' required by Section 145(d) . . . [or] procedures under which a favorable determination will be deemed to have been made under circumstances where the board fails or refused to act[.]" 1 R. Franklin Balotti & Jesse A. Finkelstein, Delaware Law of Corporations and Business Organizations, §4.16; *Waltuch*, 88 F.3d at 95 n. 10 (citing this treatise section). Thus, the specific provisions of §145(d) are not mandatory in these circumstances with regard to indemnification under §§145(a),(b). Our reading of these rules is that good faith may be presumed under the expansive by-laws of Owens Corning, even if the relevant determination is not specifically made. National Union could still challenge, under Delaware law, whether Owens Corning's directors were in fact acting in good faith back in 1989 and thereafter, when the factual predicate of the *Lavalle* action arose. See supra n. 4. However, National Union does not seem to have offered specific allegations on this issue in its appeal.[23]

It is not precisely clear on what grounds the district court determined that the indemnification here comported with Delaware law. The court's opinion appears to rely primarily on the claim that there was a "success" by the directors, resulting in mandatory indemnification under §145(c). Although for the reasons discussed we cannot support this interpretation, we may affirm on any grounds supported by the record. City Management Corp. v. U.S. Chem. Co., Inc., 43 F.3d 244, 251 (6th Cir. 1994). We conclude that the indemnification occurred in relation to a settlement under §145(a),[24] in which good faith was required. But we further conclude that good faith was made subject to a presumption through the corporate by-laws, and that this presumption was allowable under the corporate flexibility we believe a Delaware court would find conferred by §145(f). Given that this presumption of good faith stands unrebutted by the party ultimately made responsible, the indemnification proceeded "according to law," and was not made in breach of the Policy.

NOTES AND QUESTIONS

1. As the principal case above discusses, there are different views on what constitutes "success" in mandatory indemnification provisions.

In Green v. Westcap Corp., 492 A.2d 260 (Del. Super. 1985), Green, the vice president of Westcap, sought indemnification for expenses incurred in defending against charges that he had criminally defrauded Westcap. Green was acquitted and then claimed entitlement to indemnification under Delaware G.C.L. §145(c). Westcap argued that acquittal was not enough to satisfy §145(c)'s underlying objective of ensuring the honesty and integrity of directors.

---

23. National Union originally seems to have considered applying exclusions based on personal malfeasance by the directors but has not brought them forward in the litigation.

24. The district court cites to §145(b), which relates to suits brought on behalf of the corporation or derivative actions. Lavalle was a third party action by shareholders for their own loss and thus falls under §145(a).

In upholding Green's right to indemnification under §145(c), the court observed the following:

> In contrast to subsections (a) and (b), subsection (c) predicates recovery on indemnitee's success "on the merits or otherwise in defense of the proceeding." The distinction is understandable. Subsections (a) and (b) do not require a prior judicial determination of the validity of the indemnitee's position as to the proceeding for which indemnification is sought. Hence, in the absence of success on the merits of the defense, there is a requirement that specific factual prerequisites be established as a condition for indemnification. Subsection (c) applies only where there has been a prior proceeding in which the lack of merit of the attack upon the indemnitee has been established. In such case the director, officer, or employee is entitled to be indemnified for expenses incurred in resisting the criminal charge against him if the prior proceeding arose by reason of the fact that he is or was a director, officer, or employee of the corporation.

2. Under what circumstances and to what extent may statutory indemnification rules be supplemented, varied, or avoided by ex ante contract or ex post action by the board of directors? Statutory answers range from restrictive to permissive. Typical of the most restrictive approach is MBCA §8.59:

> A corporation may provide indemnification or advance expenses to a director or an officer only as permitted by this subchapter.

At first glance this provision might seem to make statutory procedures the only means for providing indemnification. However, the official comment to MBCA §8.59 states that this section "does not preclude provisions in articles of incorporation, bylaws, resolutions, or contracts designed to provide procedural machinery in addition to (but not inconsistent with) that provided by this subchapter."

3. At the opposite linguistic extreme from MBCA §8.59 is Delaware G.C.L. §145(f):

> The indemnification and advancement of expenses provided by, or granted pursuant to, the other subsections of this section shall not be deemed exclusive of any other rights to which those seeking indemnification or advancement of expenses may be entitled under any by-law, agreement, vote of stockholders or disinterested directors or otherwise, both as to action in his official capacity and as to action in another capacity while holding such office.

This section appears to sanction any form of indemnification and essentially to vitiate the Delaware procedural and substantive restrictions on permissive indemnification (provisions that are similar to the MBCA). Yet such a reading would be too broad as the previous principal case discusses.

4. A middle ground between the MBCA and Delaware linguistic extremes is reached in New York Bus. Corp. Law §721:

> The indemnification and advancement of expenses granted pursuant to, or provided by, this article shall not be deemed exclusive of any other rights to which a director or officer seeking indemnification or advancement of expenses may be entitled, whether contained in the certificate of incorporation or the by-laws or, when authorized by such certificate of incorporation or by-laws, (i) a resolution of shareholders, (ii) a resolution of directors, or (iii) an agreement providing for such indemnification, provided that no indemnification may be made to or on behalf of any director or officer if a judgment or other final adjudication adverse to the director or officer establishes that

his acts were committed in bad faith or were the result of active and deliberate dishonesty and were material to the cause of action so adjudicated, or that he personally gained in fact a financial profit or other advantage to which he was not legally entitled. Nothing contained in this article shall affect any rights to indemnification to which corporate personnel other than directors and officers may be entitled by contract or otherwise under law.

PROBLEM 4-13

Assume a case factually similar to Smith v. Van Gorkom in which Trans Union and its directors are sued for damages resulting from the assertedly unfair merger. Assume further that Trans Union has a long-standing bylaw providing that "the corporation shall indemnify and hold harmless each of its incumbent or former directors or officers against any loss, cost, expense, judgment, or settlement amount to the maximum extent allowed by law."

Before pre-trial discovery, a settlement agreement is reached under which the corporation's directors are obligated to pay $25 million to plaintiffs. The directors seek indemnification from New T Company (the corporation into which Trans Union merged, and which is bound to honor Trans Union's contractual obligation as a matter of law). Independent counsel appointed by the New T board investigates and concludes that the Trans Union outside directors violated their duty of care, and that the inside directors violated their duty of loyalty by obtaining lucrative employment contracts with New T, and by failing to disclose this information to Trans Union's outside directors during the deliberations concerning the merger. Based on the Independent Counsel's report, how should the New T board respond to the former Trans Union directors' demand for indemnification? In answering this question, assume alternatively that (1) the MBCA governs, or (2) the provisions of Delaware law govern.

PROBLEM 4-14

Xavia is the CFO of Astro, Inc. but does not sit on the Astro Board. Several years ago, Xavia was elected to the board of StarShoot; Astro owns 55 percent of StarShoot's voting common stock. In 2001 Xavia was indicted for mail fraud in connection with widespread securities fraud committed by StarShoot employees and was also a defendant in a derivative suit prosecuted by StarShoot minority shareholders in which it was claimed that Xavia and the other directors breached their fiduciary duties of care and loyalty in connection with the securities fraud. Xavia subsequently was acquitted in the criminal case and participated in a settlement of the derivative suit. Both Astro and StarShoot have bylaws committing the corporations to indemnify officers and directors to the maximum extent allowed by Delaware law. Xavia is seeking indemnification of her costs and expenses, including legal fees and her monetary contribution to the settlement of the derivative suit. What are Astro's and StarShoot's obligations to Xavia?

PROBLEM 4-15

Reconsider Problem 4-13. Suppose that Trans Union and its successor, New T, are covered by an executive liability policy ("the D&O policy"), which has a policy limit of $20 million per year and a $1 million deductible. Provision One of the D&O policy, which insures Trans Union for described losses for which Trans Union has indemnified its directors, reads as follows:

> Insurer shall reimburse to, or pay on behalf of, Trans Union all loss for which Trans Union lawfully grants indemnification to a director which such person became legally obligated to pay on account of any claim made against her for any wrongful act committed, attempted, or allegedly committed or attempted while this policy is in force.

For purpose of this provision, "wrongful act" is defined to mean

> any error, misstatement, misleading statement, act, omission, neglect, or breach of duty committed, attempted, or allegedly committed or attempted, by any director acting or claimed to be acted in her capacity as a director.

To what insurance payments will New T be entitled if it agrees to reimburse the former Trans Union directors for their settlement payments? How would your answer be affected if the lawsuit were maintained as a derivative suit?

5 Protecting Participants' Expectations in Closely Held Corporations

A. Introduction

Closely held businesses are fundamentally different from those that are publicly held in ways that are more dependent on the business environment than they are on law. First, closely held businesses are more intimate enterprises, lacking the separation of function that the corporate form permits with its distinct roles for shareholders, officers, and directors. Usually, a small number of participants are actively involved in the business with no rigid division between those contributing money capital and those putting in human capital. The business relationships often overlap family or other close personal ties, adding another layer of expectations and creating various means of interactions beyond those provided by the structures of entity law. Second, no market exists for the ownership interests of these enterprises. Thus there is no liquidity for one's investments and also no check on those in control that markets sometimes provide in a publicly held corporation. Most participants in a closely held business expect eventually to sell their ownership interest back to the entity or to fellow investors, or expect to pass their interest on to a son or daughter, who perhaps is, or will become, a participant in the operation and management of the firm.

The close corporation has long been a principal legal vehicle for closely held businesses; in recent years, the limited liability company (LLC), to be discussed in Chapter 6, has become the more frequently used form for non-publicly traded firms. Both are widely used to meet the needs of participants in a closely held firm that is a more intimate relationship without a market in which to sell ownership interests. Both require the participants and their lawyers to modify legal forms as provided by statute. For close corporations, the challenge is to change the corporate law norms we have previously studied in Chapters 3 and 4 so they fit the closely held firm. For LLCs, the challenge is more likely to be to supply rules for a statutory form that has fewer statutorily provided rules and is very deferential to the parties' contracts.

Corporate law norms are well suited for a publicly traded corporation. They are less well suited to the needs of participants in the intimate, illiquid setting of close corporations. Separation of ownership as found in the corporate form supports specialized investment of human and money capital. The anticipated result of this separation norm is that (1) shareholders are able to provide money capital while investing human capital elsewhere; (2) officers are able to specialize in day-to-day management without making money capital investments in the firm; and (3) the board of directors serves as a check on officers' diligence and loyalty and as a buffer against shareholders' inefficient interference in management.

Corporate norms meet the needs of publicly traded firms both by promoting the corporation's adaptability to changed circumstances and by protecting the corporation from opportunism by minority shareholders. First, shareholders and directors normally make decisions by majority rule. This ensures that action can be taken even if there is an honest disagreement as to the best course of action, and it prevents opportunistic vetoes or threats of vetoes by minority interests. Second, the officers and directors may be discharged at will, which enables a corporation to replace key personnel in the face of changed circumstances and serves as a deterrent against opportunistic conduct by any officer or director. Third, the apparent permanence of the corporation—particularly the absence of any right of a minority shareholder to dissolve the corporation at will or otherwise require the corporation to return her capital—permits the corporate managers to plan without worry about a sudden loss of capital. Finally, the statutory norm that directors manage the corporation's business affairs combines with the business judgment rule to permit directors to carry out their management responsibilities without undue interference from disgruntled minority shareholders or from judges.

In contrast to the long list of corporate law norms supporting the corporation's adaptability and freedom from minority shareholder opportunism, only one corporate law norm—free transferability of shares—enables minority shareholders to adapt individually to changed circumstances and to protect themselves unilaterally from possible majority opportunism. Even this norm is effective in protecting minority shareholders' interests only to the extent there is a developed securities market. Such an imbalance does not reflect a legal preference for majority shareholders over minority shareholders as much as it shows that the protections provided by the market can be a significant counterbalance to majority power that the law does not need to replicate. As discussed in Chapter 3, our efficient national securities markets assure minority shareholders in publicly traded firms that they will be able to sell their shares at any time, almost instantaneously, at very little cost and at a price reflecting current available information. Thus minority shareholders can effectively withdraw their capital at will, whether motivated by personal needs or dissatisfaction with management. This right to exit, in turn, makes a prospective minority shareholder contemplating investing in a publicly held corporation less troubled by the corporation's centralization of power in the board elected by the majority shareholders.

In a close corporation, the statutory norms of centralized control and majority rule, when combined with the lack of a public market for shares, leave a minority shareholder vulnerable in a way that is distinct from risks faced by investors in public corporations. After a falling out among participants in a close corporation, a minority investor might face an indefinite period with no return on capital or the prospect of being squeezed out by the majority shareholders.

The following example illustrates the problem corporate norms pose for closely held firms. Carol, Monica, and Patricia, attracted principally by the prospect of limited liability, form a closely held corporation to make customized widgets. Each contributes $50,000 and receives one-third of the corporation's shares. At the outset, Carol,

Monica, and Patricia make no use of separation of function; instead, they serve as the corporation's officers, directors, and key employees. Each receives an equal salary, but no dividends are paid. Profits in excess of salaries are reinvested in the corporation's business.

Initially, Carol, Monica, and Patricia make no use of majority rule; instead, they work together in harmony, usually making business decisions by consensus. At some later date, however, the initial harmony may end and corporate norms may come into play. For example, Carol and Patricia might decide, opportunistically or for legitimate business reasons, to use their majority power to terminate Monica's employment and salary. Or Monica might retire or decide to form a competitor firm. After Monica's human capital has been withdrawn or expelled from the firm, she will certainly wish to realize a return on her money capital investment. However, if Monica holds on to her shares, Carol and Patricia, either opportunistically or for good business reasons, may use their majority power to continue the corporation's previous policy of reinvesting all corporate profits instead of paying dividends to shareholders. Alternatively, Monica may try to realize the value of her money capital investment by selling her shares, either to the corporation or to a third party. Again, Carol and Patricia (and the corporation they control) may refuse to repurchase her shares for legitimate business reasons or may opportunistically seek to obtain Monica's shares at an unfairly low price. Monica will also have difficulty selling her shares to a third party without substantial transaction costs. And any purchaser other than Carol and Patricia (or the corporation) will surely insist on a purchase price that reflects the risks and lack of liquidity inherent in Monica's minority status.

The potential for majority opportunism inherent in corporate form can be described as a function of majority rule, separation of function, lack of guaranteed employment and dividend rights for shareholders, and denial of unilateral dissolution rights to minority shareholders. In other words, the norms that both ensure the firm's adaptability and protect the firm from minority opportunism create the risk of majority opportunism.

Of course, the degree of opportunistic risk depends in substantial part on the efficacy of judicial remedies available to minority shareholders. However, for most of this century the statutory and judicial approach to providing equitable remedies for minority shareholders has reinforced majority shareholders' discretion.

The risk of majority opportunism presented by traditional norms and judicial doctrines has undergone sustained analysis over the past 40 years, and many rules have been changed in response to the perceived shortcomings of traditional doctrine. Nonetheless, the central governance problem—how to provide an optimal amount of adaptability and protection from opportunism to both majority and minority interests—remains a persistent puzzle for lawyers and commentators. The problem is especially difficult because any reduction in the risk of majority opportunism often is accompanied by an increased risk of minority opportunism, and vice versa.

Once we spot the core corporate governance problem in a close corporation and how it differs from a publicly held firm, we must also determine the relative effectiveness of ex ante contracting or ex post judging in responding to this challenge. Contract-based solutions provide free rein to parties to determine what works best for them. Such an approach seems particularly attractive given that close corporations, more so than public corporations, show real differences in shareholders' and managers' expectations from one corporation to another. As a result, a "one size fits all" approach may be uneconomical. Giving a role for judges, based on concepts like fiduciary duty or "oppression" statutes discussed in this chapter, recognizes that advance planning may be difficult in a closely held corporation because of bounded rationality, bounded funds, or the psychological dynamics of entrepreneurs entering into ventures with others.

The remainder of this chapter examines the still evolving rules for closely held enterprises and how the law has adapted over time. Part B examines the changing judicial and legislative attitudes toward shareholders' agreements designed to protect minority shares from future majority opportunism in the corporate form. Part C examines judicially provided governance rules for close corporations, including enhanced fiduciary duties and the so-called partnership analogy. This part also addresses "oppression" statutes under which courts have provided liquidity to investors in close corporations. Part D then returns to examine the intersection between contract remedies and judicial interpretations in the context of shareholders' repurchase agreements.

B. Contracting as a Device to Limit the Majority's Discretion

1. As to Director Decisions

> **MBCA §§7.32, 8.01, 8.24(c)**
> **Delaware G.C.L. §§141(a) and (b), 350-354**

As discussed in Chapter 1, jointly owned firms (as well as long-term contractual relationships) arise when individuals making a mutual team-specific investment prefer to place constraints on the opportunistic risks inherent in remaining totally autonomous from one another. In other words, creating a jointly owned firm (like entering into a long-term contract) involves a specification of each owner's rights and duties (or, in contractual terms, an allocation of risks). State corporation law, then, can be viewed as a contract, containing standard form internal governance rules, that is provided to prospective investors by the state.

Viewing corporations as a standard form contract, one should expect that actual users of corporate form will seek to tailor the corporate "contract" to meet their particular governance needs. Thus, if prospective investors in a closely held corporation find the majoritarian-directorial bias of corporate law (and the attendant risk of majority opportunism) undesirable, it may be value-enhancing for them to "contract around" such bias. However, early corporation codes were hostile to such contracting and cast core governance rules in immutable form.

Typical of the early statutory provisions dealing with directorial power is New York Gen. Corp. Law (1929), chapter 23, §27: "the affairs of every corporation *shall* be managed by its board of directors . . ." (emphasis supplied). Similar is the early Delaware provision found in 36 Delaware Laws (1927), chapter 85, §5: "[t]he business of every corporation . . . *shall* be managed by a board of directors, except as hereinafter provided . . ." (emphasis supplied). These sections contained no "except as otherwise agreed" language or other indications that shareholders could opt out of the statutory norms by private agreement.

Not all early corporation codes contained provisions explicitly stating that directors' decisions were made by majority rule. Nonetheless, this was both the long-established common law rule and implicit in the structure of the various state codes. However, statutes that did explicitly state the decisional rule took an immutable form.

Despite the formal immutability of these rules, it remained for courts to determine the extent to which shareholders could contractually specify their wishes as to salary, dividends, or corporate policies, or otherwise limit or "sterilize" the directors' discretion to decide such matters by majority vote. The dominant judicial response, typified by three New York cases, did not allow shareholders to eliminate contractually the directors' future ability to protect the corporation's then best interests.

In McQuade v. Stoneham, 263 N.Y. 323, 189 N.E. 234 (1934), Charles Stoneham sold minority stock interests in a corporation he controlled to John McGraw and Francis McQuade. (The corporation's business was the New York Giants baseball team. McGraw was the team's manager.) McQuade paid $50,338.10 for his shares. As part of this transaction, Stoneham, McGraw, and McQuade executed a shareholders' agreement (not joined in by the corporation's other shareholders) in which Stoneham promised to use his majority power to appoint and retain McQuade and McGraw as officers and directors of the corporation at specified salaries. Nine years later, the board of directors, controlled by Stoneham, discharged McQuade from the corporation's employ. At the next shareholders' meeting, McQuade was not reelected as a director. The trial court awarded damages to McQuade for Stoneham's breach of the shareholders' agreement. The court of appeals reversed:

> The cause for dropping McQuade was due to the falling out of friends. McQuade and Stoneham had disagreed. The trial court has found in substance that their numerous quarrels and disputes did not affect the orderly and efficient administration of the business of the corporation; that plaintiff was removed because he had antagonized the dominant Stoneham by persisting in challenging his power over the corporate treasury and for no misconduct on his part. The court also finds that plaintiff was removed by Stoneham for protecting the corporation and its minority stockholders. We will assume that Stoneham put him out when he might have retained him, merely in order to get rid of him.
>
> Defendants say that the contract in suit was void because the directors held their offices charged with the duty to act for the corporation according to their best judgment and that any contract which compels a director to vote to keep any particular person in office and at stated salary is illegal. Directors are the exclusive executive representatives of the corporation, charged with administration of its internal affairs and the management and use of its assets. They manage the business of the corporation. (G.C.L., Consol. Laws, c.23, §27.) "An agreement to continue a man as president is dependent upon his continued loyalty to the interests of the corporation." Fells v. Katz, 526 N.Y. 67, 72, 175 N.E. 516, 517. So much is undisputed.
>
> Plaintiff contends that the converse of this proposition is true and that an agreement among directors to continue a man as an officer of a corporation is not to be broken so long as such officer is loyal to the interests of the corporation and that, as plaintiff has been found loyal to the corporation, the agreement of defendants is enforceable.
>
> Although it has been held that an agreement among stockholders whereby it is attempted to divest the directors of their power to discharge an unfaithful employee of the corporation is illegal as against public policy (Fells v. Katz, supra), it must be equally true that the stockholders may not, by agreement among themselves, control the directors in the exercise of the judgment vested in them by virtue of their office to elect officers and fix salaries. Their motives may not be questioned

so long as their acts are legal. The bad faith or the improper motives of the parties does not change the rule. Directors may not by agreement entered into as stockholders abrogate their independent judgment.

Stockholders may, of course, combine to elect directors. That rule is well settled. . . . The power to unite is, however, limited to the election of directors and is not extended to contracts whereby limitations are placed on the power of directors to manage the business of the corporation by the selection of agents at defined salaries.

The minority shareholders whose interests McQuade says he has been punished for protecting, are not, aside from himself, complaining about his discharge. He is not acting for the corporation or for them in this action. It is impossible to see how the corporation has been injured by the substitution of Bondy as treasurer in place of McQuade. As McQuade represents himself in this action and seeks redress for his own wrongs, "we prefer to listen to [the corporation and the minority stockholders] before any decision as to their wrongs." Faulds v. Yates, 57 Ill. 416, 417, 11 Am. Rep. 24.

263 N.Y. at 327-329, 189 N.E. at 236.

McQuade was "clarified" shortly thereafter in Clark v. Dodge, 269 N.Y. 410, 199 N.E. 641 (1936). Clark, who owned 25 percent of a corporation, sought specific enforcement of an agreement with Dodge, the owner of the remaining 75 percent. Dodge had agreed that (1) Clark would be retained as a director and as general manager (in the latter position so long as he was "faithful, efficient and competent"); (2) Clark would receive one-fourth of the corporation's net income either by way of salary or dividends; and (3) no unreasonable salary would be paid to others to reduce the net income so as to affect materially Clark's profit. In return, Clark agreed to continue to manage the business, to disclose to Dodge's son a secret formula necessary for the business, and to bequeath his stock to Dodge's wife and children if Clark himself had no children surviving him. When the two shareholders had a later falling-out, Clark sought to enforce the agreement so as to protect his position against Dodge's majority power. The court stated as follows:

"The business of a corporation shall be managed by its board of directors." (General Corporation Law [Consol. Laws, chapter 23], §27.) That is the statutory norm. Are we committed by the *McQuade* case to the doctrine that there may be no variation, however slight or innocuous, from that norm, where salaries or policies or the retention of individuals in office are concerned? . . . If the enforcement of a particular contract damages nobody—not even, in any perceptible degree, the public—one sees no reason to hold it illegal even if it impinges slightly upon the broad provisions of §27. . . . Where the directors are the sole stockholders, there seems to be no objection to enforcing an agreement between them to vote for certain people as officers. . . .

Except for the broad dicta in the *McQuade* opinion, we think there can be no doubt that the agreement here in question was legal and that the complaint states a cause of action. There was no attempt to sterilize the board of directors as in the *Manson* [Manson v. Curtis, 223 N.Y. 313, 119 N.E. 559 (1918)] and *McQuade* cases. The only restrictions on Dodge were (a) that as a stockholder he should vote for Clark as a director—a perfectly legal contract; (b) that as director he should continue Clark as general manager, so long as he proved faithful, efficient and competent—an agreement which could harm nobody; (c) that Clark should always receive as salary or dividends one-fourth of the "net income." For the purposes of this motion, it is only just to construe that phrase as meaning whatever was left for distribution after the directors had in good faith set aside whatever they deemed wise; (d) that no salaries to other officers should be paid, unreasonable in amount or incommensurate with services rendered—a beneficial and not a harmful agreement.

If there was any invasion of the powers of the directorate under that agreement, it is so slight as to be negligible; and certainly there is no damage suffered by or threatened to anybody. The broad statements in the *McQuade* opinion, applicable to the facts there, should be confined to those facts.

269 N.Y. at 414-417, 199 N.E. at 642-643.

In effect, Clark v. Dodge allowed shareholders to fix contractually their respective rights and to agree that such rights could be abrogated by the directors only when required by the corporation's best interests. However, Clark v. Dodge did not significantly alter corporation law's paternalistic approach to shareholders' agreements.

The immutability of majority rule by directors was again reaffirmed in Benintendi v. Kenton Hotel, Inc., 294 N.Y. 112, 60 N.E.2d 829 (1945). In *Benintendi,* the shareholders unanimously adopted a bylaw providing that all shareholders' and directors' actions required unanimous agreement. When the majority shareholder subsequently repudiated this bylaw, the minority shareholders filed suit seeking a declaration of the bylaw's validity and an injunction against its violation. The trial court held the agreement invalid, and the court of appeals affirmed:

> The by-law numbered 3 in our list above makes it impossible for the directors to act on any matter except by unanimous vote of all of them. Such a by-law, like the others already discussed herein, is, almost as a matter of law, unworkable and unenforceable for the reason given by the Court of King's Bench in Dr. Hascard v. Dr. Somany, 1 Freeman 503, in 1693: "prima facie in all acts done by a corporation, the major number must bind the lesser, or else differences could never be determined." The directors of a corporation are a select body, chosen by the stockholders. By §27 of the G.C.L., the board as such, is given the power of management of the corporation. At common law only a majority thereof were needed for a quorum and a majority of that quorum could transact business. Section 27 modifies that common-law rule only to the extent of permitting a corporation to enact a by-law fixing "the number of directors necessary to constitute a quorum at a number less than a majority of the board, but not less than one-third of its number." Every corporation is thus given the privilege of enacting a by-law fixing its own quorum requirement at any fraction not less than one-third, nor more than a majority, of its directors. But the very idea of a "quorum" is that, when that required number of persons goes into session as a body, the votes of a majority thereof are sufficient for binding action. Thus, while by-law No. 3 is not in explicit terms forbidden by §27 (supra) it seems to flout the plain purpose of the Legislature in passing that statute.

294 N.Y. at 119, 60 N.E.2d at 831-832.

The immutability of majority rule by directors now has no statutory support. Instead, statutory provisions granting management power to directors are now cast as default rules in almost every state, specifically permitting shareholders to restrict or eliminate the directors' discretion. Delaware G.C.L. §141(a) is typical. It provides that "the business and affairs of every corporation organized under this chapter shall be managed by or under the direction of the board of directors, *except as may be otherwise provided* in this chapter or *in its certificate of incorporation*" (emphasis supplied). See also MBCA §8.01. Most state statutes also specifically permit a corporation to provide in its articles of incorporation that an action taken by shareholders or directors requires more than a simple majority vote. Courts have interpreted these requirements as authorizing even unanimity requirements.

More recent statutes extend this contractual freedom in two additional ways. Most states now have statutes like MBCA §7.32 that permit shareholders to vary norms not only by provisions in the articles of incorporation (and sometimes the bylaws), but also in separate shareholders' agreements. These statutes also contain more affirmative and broader authorization than the simple default rules of §141(a). For example, §7.32 specifically authorizes agreements that establish who will be the officers or directors and even permits elimination of the board or transfer of corporate power to one or more shareholders. These statutes also authorize agreements as to distributions or requiring dissolution that in the past may have seemed unenforceable. Pay attention to the statutory limits on such agreement as to unanimity and duration.

In a few states, the additional contractual freedom is offered only to statutory close corporations—those enterprises that meet a statutory definition (such as, no more than 30 shareholders and shares not publicly traded) and have designated the corporation as coming within special provisions. For example, Delaware, subchapter XIV (§§341-356) entitled "Close Corporations; Special Provisions," specifically sanctions "sterilizing" shareholders' agreements (see §351) and agreements permitting shareholders to avoid majority rules by directors (§354) so long as the corporation has included a provision in its certificate that it is an electing close corporation.

The modern statutes substantially increase shareholders' "freedom of contract." Thus, the agreements in McQuade v. Stoneham and Benintendi v. Kenton Hotel, Inc. are no longer substantively inconsistent with legislative policy in many states. Nonetheless, problems and uncertainties remain when shareholders do not use the sterilizing mechanism dictated by statute. For example, if the corporation code provides that directors must act by majority vote or such greater percentage as is required by the articles of incorporation, what is the effect if, as in *Benintendi*, the shareholders include a supermajority rule in the bylaws or in a separate shareholders' agreement? Likewise, what would the result be in McQuade v. Stoneham under a corporation code that provides that the directors shall manage the corporation except as otherwise provided in the articles of incorporation, but that contains no generally applicable section sanctioning sterilization by a separate shareholders' agreement? And what result if the shareholders unanimously approve a provision in the articles of incorporation limiting the directors' discretion, and the majority later seeks to eliminate that provision by a majority-approved amendment to the articles?

Zion v. Kurtz

New York Court of Appeals, 1980
50 N.Y.2d 92, 405 N.E.2d 681, 428 N.Y.S.2d 199

MEYER, JUDGE.

[Zion and Kurtz were the only shareholders of Lombard-Wall Group, Inc. (Group). As part of the transactions surrounding Zion's purchase of a minority interest in Group, Zion and Kurtz entered into a shareholders' agreement providing that Group would not engage in any business or activities without Zion's consent. Despite this agreement, Kurtz caused the corporation to take certain actions without Zion's consent. Zion then sought declaratory and injunctive relief.]

. . . The stockholders' agreement expressly provided that it should be "governed by and construed and enforced in accordance with the laws of the State of Delaware as to matters governed by the G.C.L. of that State," and that is the generally accepted choice-of-law rule with respect to such "internal affairs" as the relationship between shareholders and directors. Subdivision (a) of §141 of the G.C.L. of Delaware provides that the business and affairs of a corporation organized under that law "shall be managed by a board of directors, except as may be otherwise provided in this chapter or in its certificate of incorporation." Included in the chapter referred to are provisions relating to close corporations, which explicitly state that a written agreement between the holders of a majority of such a corporation's stock "is not invalid, as between the parties to the agreement, on the ground that it so relates to the conduct of the business and affairs of the corporation as to restrict or interfere with the discretion or powers of the board of directors" (§350) or "on the ground that it is an attempt by the parties to the agreement or by the stockholders of the corporation to treat the corporation as if it were a partnership" (§354), and further provides that "[t]he certificate of incorporation of a close corporation may provide that the business of the corporation shall be managed by the stockholders of the corporation rather than the board of directors" and that such a provision may be inserted in the certificate by amendment if "all holders of record of all of the outstanding stock" so authorize (§351).

Clear from those provisions is the fact that the public policy of Delaware does not proscribe a provision such as that contained in the shareholders' agreement here in issue even though it takes all management functions away from the directors. Folk, in his work on the Delaware Corporation Law, states concerning §350 that "[a]lthough some decisions outside Delaware have sustained 'reasonable' restrictions upon director discretion contained in stockholder agreements, the theory of §350 is to declare unequivocally, as a matter of public policy, that stockholder agreements of this character are not invalid," that §351 "recognizes a special subclass of close corporations which operate by direct stockholder management," and with respect to §354 that it "should be liberally construed to authorize all sorts of internal agreements and arrangements which are not affirmatively improper or, more particularly, injurious to third parties."

Defendants argue, however, that Group was not incorporated as a close corporation and the stockholders' agreement provision was never incorporated in its certificate. The answer is that any Delaware corporation can elect to become a close corporation by filing an appropriate certificate of amendment (Del. G.C.L., §344) and by such amendment approved by the holders of all of its outstanding stock may include in its certificate provisions restricting directors' authority (ibid., §351). Here, not only did defendant Kurtz agree in paragraph 8.05(b) of the stockholders' agreement to "without further consideration, do, execute and deliver, or cause to be done, executed and delivered, all such further acts, things and instruments as may be reasonably required more effectively to evidence and give effect to the provisions and the intent and purposes of this Agreement," but also as part of the transaction by which . . . Zion became a Group stockholder, defendant Kurtz, while he was still the sole stockholder and sole director of Group, executed a consent to the various parts of the transaction under which he was "authorized and empowered to execute and deliver, or cause to be executed and delivered, all such other and further instruments and documents and take, or cause to be taken, all such other and further action as he may deem necessary, appropriate or desirable to implement and give effect to the Stockholders Agreement and the transactions provided for therein." Since there are no intervening rights of third persons, the agreement requires nothing that is not permitted by statute, and all of the stockholders of the corporation assented to it, the certificate of incorporation may be ordered reformed, by requiring Kurtz to file the appropriate amendments, or more directly he may be held estopped to rely upon the absence of those amendments from the corporate charter.[3]

The result thus reached accords with the weight of authority which textwriter F. Hodge O'Neal tells us sustains agreements made by all shareholders dealing with matters normally within the province of the directors, even though the shareholders could have, but had not, provided similarly by charter or by-law provision sanctioned by statute. Moreover, though we have not yet had occasion to construe subdivision (b) of §620 of the Business Corporation Law,[4] which did not become effective until September 1, 1963, it is worthy of note that in adopting that provision the Legislature had before it the Revisers' Comment that: "Paragraph (b) expands the ruling in Clark v. Dodge, 269 N.Y. 410, 199 N.E. 637 (641) (1936), and, to the extent therein provided, overrules McQuade v. Stoneham, 263 N.Y. 323, 189 N.E. 234 (1934)." Thus it is clear that no New York public policy stands in the way of our application of the Delaware statute and decisional law above referred to. . . .

GABRIELLI, JUDGE. . . .

It is beyond dispute that shareholder agreements such as the one relied upon by plaintiff in this case are, as a general rule, void as against public policy. Section 3.01 of the agreement, as interpreted both by plaintiff and by a majority of this court, would have precluded the board of directors of Group from taking any action on behalf of the corporation without first obtaining plaintiff's consent. This contractual provision, if enforced, would effectively shift the authority to manage every aspect of corporate affairs from the board to plaintiff, a minority shareholder who has no fiduciary obligations with respect to either the corporation or its other shareholders. As such, the provision represents a blatant effort to "sterilize" the board of directors in contravention of the statutory and decisional law of both Delaware and New York.

Under the statutes of Delaware, the State in which Group was incorporated, the authority to manage the affairs of a corporation is vested solely in its board of directors (Del. G.C.L., §141, subd. (a)). The same is true under the applicable New York statutes (Business Corporation Law, §701). Significantly, in both States, the courts have

---

3. The fallacy of the dissent is that it converts a shield into a sword. The notice devices on which the concept of the dissent turns are wholly unnecessary to protect the original parties, who may be presumed to have known what they agreed to. To protect an original party who has not been hurt (indeed, has expressly agreed to the limitation he is being protected against and affirmatively covenanted to see to it that all necessary steps to validate the agreement were taken) because a third party without notice could have been hurt had he been involved can only be characterized as a perversion of the liberal legislative purpose demonstrated by the Delaware statutes quoted in the text above.

4. That provision reads: "(b) A provision in the certificate of incorporation otherwise prohibited by law because it improperly restricts the board in its management of the business of the corporation, or improperly transfers to one or more shareholders or to one or more persons or corporations to be selected by him or them, all or any part of such management otherwise within the authority of the board under this chapter, shall nevertheless be valid: (1) If all the incorporators or holders of record of all outstanding shares, whether or not having voting power, have authorized such provision in the certificate of incorporation or an amendment thereof; and (2) If, subsequent to the adoption of such provision, shares are transferred or issued only to persons who had knowledge or notice thereof or consented in writing to such provision."

declined to give effect to agreements which purport to vary the statutory rule by transferring effective control of the corporation to a third party other than the board of directors. The common-law rule in Delaware was aptly stated in Abercrombie v. Davies, 35 Del. Ch. at p.611, 123 A.2d at p.899: "So long as the corporate form is used as presently provided by our statutes this Court cannot give legal sanction to agreements which have the effect of removing from directors in a very substantial way their duty to use their own best judgment on management matters."

True, the common-law rule has been modified somewhat in recent years to account for the business needs of the so-called "close corporation." The courts of our State, for example, have been willing to enforce shareholder agreements where the incursion on the board's authority was insubstantial (Clark v. Dodge, 269 N.Y. 410, 199 N.E. 641) or where the illegal provisions were severable from the otherwise legal provisions which the shareholder sought to enforce. Neither the courts of our State nor the courts of Delaware, however, have gone so far as to hold that an agreement among shareholders such as the agreement in this case, which purported to "sterilize" the board of directors by completely depriving it of its discretionary authority, can be regarded as legal and enforceable. To the contrary, the common-law rule applicable to both closely and publicly held corporations continues to treat agreements to deprive the board of directors of substantial authority as contrary to public policy.

Indeed, there heretofore has been little need for the courts to modify the general common-law rule against "sterilizing" boards of directors to accommodate the needs of closely held corporations. This is because the Legislatures of many States, including New York and Delaware, have enacted laws which enable the shareholders of closely held corporations to restrict the powers of the board of directors if they comply with certain statutory prerequisites (Del. G.C.L., §§350, 351; Business Corporation Law, §620, subd. (b)). The majority apparently construes these statutes as indications that the public policies of the enacting States no longer proscribe the type of agreement at issue here in cases involving closely held corporations. Hence, the majority concludes that there is no bar to the enforcement of the shareholder agreement in this case, even though the statutory requirements for close corporations were not fulfilled. I cannot agree.

Under Delaware law, as the majority notes, the shareholders of a close corporation are free to enter into private, binding agreements among themselves to restrict the powers of their board of directors (Del. G.C.L., §350). The same appears to be true under the present New York statutes (Business Corporation Law, §620, subd. (b)). Both the Delaware and the New York statutory schemes, however, contemplate that such variations from the corporate norm will be recorded on the face of the certificate of incorporation (Del. G.C.L., §351; Business Corporation Law, §620, subd. (b)). New York additionally requires that the existence of a substantial restriction on the powers of the board "shall be noted conspicuously on the face or back of every certificate for shares issued by (the) corporation" (Business Corporation Law, §620, subd. (g)). Significantly, in both Delaware and New York, a provision in the certificate of incorporation restricting the discretion of the board has the effect of shifting liability for any mismanagement from the directors to the managing shareholders (Del. G.C.L., §351, subds. (2)-(3); Business Corporation Law, §620, subd. (f)).

In my view, these statutory provisions are not merely directory, but rather are evidence of a clear legislative intention to permit deviations from the statutory norms for corporations only under controlled conditions. In enacting these statutes, which are tailored for "close corporations," the Legislatures of Delaware and New York were apparently attempting to accommodate the needs of those who wished to take advantage of the limited liability inherent in the corporate format, but who also wished to retain the internal management structure of a partnership. At the same time, however, the Legislatures were obviously mindful of the danger to the public that exists whenever shareholders privately agree among themselves to shift control of corporate management from independent directors to the shareholders, who are not necessarily bound by the fiduciary obligations imposed upon the board. In order to protect potential purchasers of shares and perhaps even potential creditors of the corporation, the Legislatures of Delaware and New York imposed specific strictures upon incorporated businesses managed by shareholders, the most significant of which is the requirement that restrictions on the statutory powers of the board of directors be evidenced in the certificate of incorporation. This requirement is an essential component of the statutory scheme because it ensures that potential purchasers of an interest in the corporation will have at least record notice that the corporation is being managed in an unorthodox fashion. Absent an appropriate notice provision in the certificate, there can be no assurance that an unsuspecting purchaser, not privy to the private shareholder agreement, will not be drawn into an investment that he might otherwise choose to avoid. . . .

By its holding today, the majority has, in effect, rendered inoperative both the language and the underlying purpose of the relevant Delaware and New York statutes governing "close corporations." According to the majority's reasoning, the only requirements for upholding an otherwise unlawful shareholder agreement which concededly deprives the directors of all discretionary authority are that all of the shareholders concur in the agreement and that no "intervening rights of third persons" exist at the time enforcement of the agreement is sought. The statutes in question also recognize these factors as conditions precedent to the enforcement of shareholder agreements to "sterilize" a corporate board of directors (Del. G.C.L., §351; Business Corporation Law, §620, subd. (b), pars. (1)-(2); subd. (g)). But the laws of both jurisdictions go further, requiring in each case that the "close corporation" give notice of its unorthodox management structure through its filed certificate of incorporation. The obvious purpose of such a requirement is to prevent harm to the public before it occurs. If, as the majority's holding suggests, this requirement of notice to the public through the certificate of incorporation is without legal effect unless and until a third party's interests have actually been impaired, then the prophylactic purposes of the statutes governing "close corporations" would effectively be defeated. It is this aspect of the majority's ruling that I find most difficult to accept. . . .

JASEN, JONES and FUCHSBERG, JJ., concur with MEYER, J.

GABRIELLI, J., dissents in part and votes to modify in a separate opinion in which COOKE, C.J., and WACHTLER, J., concur. . . .

NOTES AND QUESTIONS

1. Freedom of contract now underlies much of close corporation law and is a key foundation of LLC law, as you will see in the next chapter. Official support for greater "freedom of contract" can be traced back to the Uniform Business Corporation Act (UBCA), adopted by the National Conference of Commissioners on Uniform State Laws in 1928. The UBCA's preface describes greater contractual freedom as one of the drafters' principal goals:

> The attempt has been made to avoid unalterable statutory regulation of matters of intra-corporate management and to give to the incorporated group as much freedom in this regard as seems consistent with sound policy. To this end, the Act prescribes certain rules which shall apply in the absence of contrary provisions in the articles of incorporation or in the by-laws.

UBCA §31 provided as a norm that corporations shall be managed by a board of directors who shall act by majority rule. However, §31 specified that the corporation could prescribe the powers and duties of the directors or a different voting rule by provision in the articles or bylaws.

2. By 1950 a substantial number of state corporation codes still cast majority rule by directors in immutable form. Over the next 20 years, most states amended their codes to make such norm a default rule. Not surprisingly, given its case law, New York was one of the last states to make this transition, via legislation enacted in 1961 that became effective April 1, 1963. (See New York Bus. Corp. Law §§620 and 701.)

3. The court in Zion v. Kurtz discusses Delaware G.C.L. §141(a) and the close corporation supplementary provisions of that code (including §§350 and 354). On which section does the court base its decision? Could the parties' goals have been accomplished as easily under Delaware G.C.L. §141(a) as under Delaware G.C.L. §§350 and 354? Could the same result be accomplished under New York Bus. Corp. Law §620(b)?

4. New York Bus. Corp. Law §616(b) states that a supermajority provision in a certificate of incorporation may be amended by a two-thirds vote unless the certificate "specifically" provides otherwise. In a case arising out of a two-person corporation, the certificate provided that "the unanimous vote [of all shareholders] shall be necessary for the transaction of any business . . . of the corporation, including amendments to the certificate of incorporation." The New York Court of Appeals held the article to have sufficient specifics and brushed aside petitioner's argument that majority shareholders will be unable to conduct the business of the corporation in the face of opposition from the minority. "[T]here is nothing inherently unfair or improper about a voluntary organization's consensual decision to assure protection for minority shareholders, and shareholders are not without remedies where deadlocks do arise (see generally Business Corporation Law §1104)." Sutton v. Sutton, 84 N.Y.2d 37, 43, 673 N.E.2d 260, 263 (1994).

5. States differ as to whether unanimity is required for shareholders' agreements changing statutory norms. MBCA §7.32 sanctions only unanimous shareholders' agreements. In contrast, Delaware G.C.L. §350 provides that an agreement

made by the owners of at least a majority of the corporation's stock is "not invalid as between the parties to the agreement" on the ground that the agreement sterilizes directors.

6. In *Wilson v. McClenny,* 262 N.C. 121, 136 S.E.2d 569 (1964), plaintiff Wilson sought damages for breach of a shareholders' agreement between Wilson and three other shareholders of Gateway Life Insurance Company. The agreement provided that the parties, who collectively owned a minority of the corporation's shares, would use their influence and stock votes to maintain one another as officers and directors at specified salaries. Two years after executing the shareholders' agreement, the defendants actively sought to have Wilson discharged from his salaried position. Despite the objection of three directors, the defendants joined with a majority of the corporation's other directors to discharge Wilson from his salaried position. The Supreme Court of North Carolina upheld the contract:

> There is no evidence here that the contract between the plaintiff and defendants was not made in good faith or that, at the time it was made, it was not in the best interest of the corporation. . . . Since the organization of the corporation, the defendants have not owned a majority of its stock. Therefore, they could not have forced their will upon either the stockholders or the other eight directors. To remove plaintiff from the board of directors and the presidency of the corporation they ultimately required the proxies and votes of other stockholders.

262 N.C. at 129, 136 S.E.2d at 575.

PROBLEM 5-1

Joseph Jaeger, Ralph Jacqua, Sandra Jennings, and Betsy Ballester formed a corporation, Pro Ball, Inc., for the purpose of owning and operating a professional basketball franchise. Each contributed $5 million and received one-fourth of the corporation's shares. The four shareholders were also the corporation's initial directors. Jaeger, Jacqua, and Jennings were chief executive officers of publicly traded corporations, none of whom had previous experience in managing a basketball franchise. Ballester was a highly successful college basketball coach. Jaeger, Jacqua, and Jennings did not initially serve as corporate employees. However, as planned, Ballester was appointed by the directors to serve as the corporation's chief executive officer and as coach of the basketball team.

Consider whether, and under what conditions, the following shareholders' agreements are enforceable. In forming your conclusions assume, alternatively, that Pro Ball, Inc. is incorporated in a jurisdiction whose corporation statute is identical to (1) the MBCA or (2) the Delaware G.C.L. Further assume that if the agreement's validity is tested in court, this will be a case of first impression.

(a) As a part of the original deal, the four shareholders executed a written agreement promising to continue Ballester as chief executive officer and head basketball coach for ten years at a salary of $500,000.

(b) What result in (a) if the agreement was oral?

(c) What result in (a) if Jaeger was not a party to the agreement?

(d) What result in (a) if only Ballester and Jennings were parties to the agreement?

2.   Voting Agreements as to Shareholder Decisions

MBCA §§7.22, 7.30, 7.31
Delaware G.C.L. §§212, 218(a) and (c)

The legal issues in the preceding section usually arose when there was an identifiable majority and minority shareholder. The protection the minority shareholder sought usually required limiting the power of the directors. Ensuring a minority shareholder's compensation through a salary or guaranteeing dividends, for example, are decisions left to directors under corporate law norms. Courts were being asked to determine the degree to which limiting the directors' discretion was consistent with these norms and public policy.

As indicated in McQuade v. Stoneham, the common law distinguished presumptively invalid shareholder's agreements designed to control the contracting parties' future discretion to act as *directors* from presumptively valid vote-pooling agreements whereby shareholders simply agreed in advance as to how they would exercise their rights as *shareholders,* such as voting for directors. Corporate codes provide and regulate several mechanisms by which shareholders enter into agreements to affect their actions as shareholders. These include voting trusts (see MBCA §7.30, Delaware G.C.L. §218(a)), irrevocable proxies (MBCA §7.22, Delaware G.C.L. §212), and shareholder pooling agreements (MBCA §7.31, Delaware G.C.L. §218(c)).

In earlier times these agreements were indirect ways of controlling directors' discretion by controlling who would be elected directors. Agreements that went further and addressed actual director action were vulnerable to judicial invalidation for impermissibly interfering with director discretion. Now that statutes like MBCA §7.32 provide broad freedom for shareholders' agreements, what reason remains for these types of agreements, and should there be any limits? These shareholder agreements remain useful when the agreement is made by fewer than all of the corporation's shareholders or when shareholders desire to agree with creditors as to who will be the corporation's directors during the term of an outstanding loan.

Consider, for example, a corporation in which the shareholders who together own a majority of the shares wish to have decisions made within their majority group (in effect, by a majority of the majority) and to exclude any possible future realignment with those outside the group. A classic example of this type of transaction involved the corporation that owned the Ringling circus. Discord arose after the deaths of the brothers who had owned and run the circus. Two shareholders, each owning about 30 percent (one the widow of one brother and the other a daughter-in-law of a second brother), entered into a vote-pooling agreement to oust the remaining shareholder (the son of the Ringling sister) from control of the corporation. The agreement provided that the two shareholders would act jointly in exercising their voting rights and that if the parties failed to agree they would submit the disagreement to arbitration by a party named in the agreement.

The majority stockholders shared control of the corporation harmoniously until a dramatic and fatal circus fire under the big top led to criminal charges against the husband of one of the parties to the vote-pooling agreement. The criminal defendant's wife subsequently refused to vote her shares in accordance with the agreement, apparently because of the other contracting party's perceived lack of sympathy for the plight of her husband. A suit to enforce the agreement, and the defendants' assertion that the agreement was illegal and against public policy, led the court to discuss why the law would want to limit what shareholders can agree to in actions taken as shareholders:

> The only serious question presented under this point arises from the defendants' contention that the arbitration provision has the effect of providing for an irrevocable separation of voting power from stock ownership and that such a provision is contrary to the public policy of this state. Perhaps in no field of the law are the precedents more varied and irreconcilable than those dealing with this phase of the case.
>
> By adhering to strict literalism, it can be said that the present Agreement does not separate voting rights from ownership because the arbitrator only directs the parties as to how they shall vote in case of disagreement. However, recognizing substance rather than form, it is apparent that the arbitrator has voting control of the shares in the instances when he directs the parties as to how they shall vote since, if the Agreement is to be binding, they are also bound by his direction. When so considered, it is perhaps at variance with many, but not all of the precedents in other jurisdictions dealing with agreements of this general nature. . . .
>
> Directing attention to the present Agreement, what vice exists in having an arbitrator agreed upon by the parties decide how their stock shall be voted in the event they are unable to agree? The parties obviously decided to contract with respect to this very situation and to appoint as arbitrator one in whom both had confidence. The cases which strike down agreements on the ground that some public policy prohibits the severance of ownership and voting control argue that there is something very wrong about a person "who has no beneficial interest or title in or to the stock" directing how it shall be voted. Such a person, according to these cases, has "no interest in the general prosperity of the corporation" and moreover, the stockholder himself has a duty to vote. Such reasons ignore the realities because obviously the person designated to determine how the shares shall be voted has the confidence of such shareholders. Quite naturally they would not want to place such power over their investment in the hands of one whom they felt would not be concerned with the welfare of the corporation. The objection based on the so-called duty of the stockholders to vote, presumably in person, is ludicrous when considered in the light of present day corporate practice.

Ringling v. Ringling Bros.-Barnum & Bailey Combined Shows, Inc., 29 Del. Ch. 318, 49 A.2d 603 (1946), affd., 29 Del. Ch. 610, 53 A.2d 441 (1947).

Ramos v. Estrada

California Court of Appeal, 1992
8 Cal. App. 4th 1070, 10 Cal. Rptr. 2d 833

GILBERT, JUDGE.

Defendants Tila and Angel Estrada appeal a judgment which states they breached a written corporate shareholder voting agreement. We hold that a corporate shareholders' voting agreement may be valid even though the corporation is not technically a close corporation. We affirm.

FACTS

Plaintiffs Leopoldo Ramos et al. formed Broadcast Corporation for the purpose of obtaining a Federal Communications Commission (FCC) construction permit to build a Spanish language television station in Ventura County.

Ramos and his wife held 50 percent of Broadcast Corp. stock. The remaining 50 percent was issued in equal amounts to five other couples. The Estradas were one of the couples who purchased a 10 percent interest in Broadcast Corp. Tila Estrada became president of Broadcast Corp., sometimes known as the "Broadcast Group."

In 1986, Broadcast Corp. merged with a competing applicant group, Ventura 41 Television Associates (Ventura 41), to form Costa del Oro Television, Inc. (Television Inc.). The merger agreement authorized the issuance of 10,002 shares of Television Inc. voting stock.

Initially, Television Inc. was to issue 5,000 shares to Broadcast Corp. and 5,000 to Ventura 41. Each group would have the right to elect half of an eight-member board of directors. The two remaining outstanding shares were to be issued to Broadcast Corp. after the television station had operated at full power for six months. Television Inc.'s board would then increase to nine members, five of whom would be elected by Broadcast Corp.

The merger agreement contained restrictions on the transfer of stock and required each group to adopt internal shareholder agreements to carry out the merger agreement. With FCC approval, Broadcast Corp. and Ventura 41 modified their agreement to permit stock in Television Inc. to be issued directly to the respective owners of the merged entities instead of to the entities themselves. Ventura 41 sought this change so that Television Inc. would be treated as a Subchapter S corporation for tax purposes. In part, Broadcast Group agreed to this change in exchange for approval by Ventura 41 of the agreement at issue here, which is known as the June Broadcast Agreement. Among other things, the June Broadcast Agreement provides for block voting for directors by the Broadcast Group shareholders according to their ownership. . . .

[Upon the closing of the transaction, the subscribers] elected Leopoldo Ramos president, and Tila Estrada as one of the directors.

At a special directors' meeting held on October 8, 1988, Tila Estrada voted with the Ventura 41 group block to remove Ramos as president and to replace him with Walter Ulloa, a member of Ventura 41. She also joined Ventura 41 in voting to remove Romualdo Ochoa, a Broadcast Group member, as secretary and to replace him with herself.

Under the June Broadcast Agreement and the Merger Agreement, each of the groups were required to vote for the directors upon whom a majority of each respective group had agreed. The terms of that agreement expressly state that failure to adhere to the agreement constitutes an election by the shareholder to sell his or her shares pursuant to buy/sell provisions of the agreement. The agreement also calls for specific enforcement of such buy/sell provisions.

On October 15, 1988, the Broadcast Group noticed another meeting to decide how its members would vote their shares for directors at the annual meeting. All members attended except the Estradas. The group agreed to nominate *another* slate of directors which did not include either of the Estradas.

The Estradas unilaterally declared the June Broadcast Agreement null and void as of October 15, 1988, in a letter dictated for them by Paul Zevnik, the attorney for Ventura 41. Tila Estrada refused to recognize the October 15 vote of the majority of the Broadcast Group to replace her as a director of Television Inc. Ramos et al. sued the Estradas for breach of the June Broadcast Agreement, among other things.

The court ruled that the Estradas materially breached the valid June Broadcast Agreement, and it ordered their shares sold in accordance with the specific enforcement provisions of the June Broadcast Agreement. The court restrained the Estradas from voting their shares other than as provided in the June Broadcast Agreement.

DISCUSSION

The Estradas contend that the June Broadcast Agreement is void because it constitutes an expired proxy which the Estradas validly revoked. . . .

Corporations Code section 178 defines a proxy to be "a written authorization signed . . . by a shareholder . . . *giving another person or persons* power to vote with respect to the shares of such shareholder." (Emphasis added.)

Section 7.1 of the June Broadcast Agreement details the voting arrangement among the shareholders. It states, in pertinent part: "The Stockholders agree that they shall consult with each other prior *to voting their shares* in the Company. They shall attempt in good faith to reach a consensus as to the outcome of any such vote. In the case of a vote for directors, they agree that no director shall be selected who is not acceptable to at least one member (i.e., spousal unit) of each of Group A and Group B. (See ¶1.2(b)(1) above [which states that: 'The Stockholders shall be divided into two groups, Group "A" being composed of Leopoldo Ramos and Cecilia Morris, and Group "B" being composed of all the other Stockholders.'].) In the case of all *votes of Stockholders* they agree that, following consultation and compliance with the other provisions of this paragraph, *they will all vote their stock in the manner voted by a majority* of the Stockholders." (Second emphasis in original.)

No proxies are created by this agreement. The agreement has the characteristics of a shareholders' voting agreement expressly authorized by section 706, subdivision (a) for close corporations. (See also [legislative committee comment,] West's Ann. Corp. Code §186 (1990) p. 52 regarding proxies.) Although the articles of incorporation do not contain the talismanic statement that "[t]his corporation is a close corporation," the arrangements of this corporation, and in particular this voting agreement, are strikingly similar to ones authorized by the code for close corporations.

Section 706, subdivision (a) states, in pertinent part: "an agreement between two or more shareholders of a close corporation, if in writing and signed by the parties thereto, may provide that in exercising any voting rights the shares held by them shall be voted as provided by the agreement, or as the parties may agree or as determined in accordance with a procedure agreed upon by them. . . . "

Here, the members of this corporation executed a written agreement providing that they shall try to reach a consensus on all votes and that they shall consult with one another and vote their own stock in accordance with the majority of the stockholders. They entered into this agreement because they "mutually desire[d]" to limit the transferability of their stock to ensure "the Company does not pass into the control of persons whose interests might be incompatible with the interests of the Company and of the Stockholders, establishing their mutual rights and obligations in the event of death, and establishing a mechanism for determining how the Stockholders' voting rights in the Company shall be exercised. . . ."

Even though this corporation does not qualify as a close corporation, this agreement is valid and binding on the Estradas. Section 706, subdivision (d) states: "This section shall not invalidate any voting or other agreement among shareholders . . . which agreement . . . is not otherwise illegal."

The Legislative Committee comment regarding section 706, subdivision (d) states that "[t]his subdivision is intended to preserve any agreements which would be upheld under court decisions *even though they do not comply with one or more of the requirements of this section, including voting agreements of corporations other than close corporations.*" (West's Ann. Corp. Code, §706 (1990) p. 330, emphasis added.)

The California Practice Guide indicates that such "pooling" agreements are valid not only for close corporations, but also "among any number of shareholders of other corporations as well." (Friedman, Cal. Practice Guide: Corporations (The Rutter Group 1992) ¶3:159.2, pp. 3-31.)

The Estradas cite Dulin v. Pacific Wood and Coal Co. (1894), 103 Cal. 357 [37 P. 207], and Smith v. S.F. & N.P. Ry. Co. (1897), 115 Cal. 584 [47 P. 582], as support for their argument that the agreement is an expired proxy which they revoked. Their reliance on these cases is misplaced. . . .

In *Smith,* supra, three individuals purchased a majority share of stock in a corporation. To keep control of the corporation, they entered into a written agreement to pool their votes so as to vote in a block for a five-year period. Although two of the three agreed on a slate for an election, the third attempted to repudiate the agreement. The two presented the vote of all the stock held by the trio in accordance with their agreement; the third attempted to vote his own stock in the manner he desired.

The court held that the express, written agreement validly called for the trio to vote their shares as a block. (Smith v. S.F. & N.P. Ry. Co., supra, 115 Cal. at p. 598.) The court viewed the agreement as a power (to vote) coupled with an interest (in purchasing stock) which was supported by consideration. (Id., at p. 600.) The court construed the agreement as an agency; a proxy which could not be repudiated. (Id., at pp. 598-599.)

There is dicta in *Smith* suggesting that the agreement in that case constituted an irrevocable proxy. Said the court: "It is not in violation of any rule or principle of law for stockholders, who own a majority of the stock in a corporation, to cause its affairs to be managed in such way as they may think best calculated to further the ends of the corporation, and, for this purpose, *to appoint one or more proxies who shall vote in such a way as will carry out their plan. Nor is it against public policy for two or more stockholders to agree . . . upon the officers whom they will elect, and they may do this either by themselves, or through their proxies. . . .*" (Smith v. S.F. & N.P. Ry. Co., supra, 115 Cal. at pp. 600-601, emphasis added.)

The *Smith* court also held that "[a]ny plan of procedure they [stockholders] may agree upon implies a previous comparison of views, and there is nothing illegal in an agreement to be bound by the will of the majority as to the means by which the result shall be reached. If they are in accord as to the ultimate purpose, it is but reasonable that the will of the majority should prevail as to the mode by which it may be accomplished." (Smith v. S.F. & N.P. Ry. Co., supra, 115 Cal. at p. 601.)

In the instant case, the only difference from *Smith* is that the shareholders here chose to vote their stocks *themselves,* and not by proxy. What the *Smith* court held, however, is that voting agreements, like the one here, are valid. If the shareholders are unable to reach a consensus, then each shareholder must vote his or her shares according to the will of the majority.

The instant agreement is valid, enforceable and supported by consideration. It states, in pertinent part, that the stockholders entered into the agreement for the purposes of "limiting the transferability of . . . stock in the Company, ensuring that the Company does not pass into the control of persons whose interests might be incompatible with the interests of the Company and of the Stockholders, establishing their mutual rights and obligations in the event of death, and establishing a mechanism for determining how the Stockholders' voting rights . . . shall be exercised. . . ."

Section 7.2 of the agreement states that "[t]he Stockholders understand and acknowledge that the purpose of the foregoing arrangement is to preserve their relative voting power in the Company. . . . Accordingly, in the event that a Stockholder fails to abide by this arrangement for whatever reason, that failure shall constitute on [sic] irrevocable election by the Stockholder to sell his stock in the Company, triggering the same rights of purchase provided in Article IV above." . . .

The Estradas breached the agreement by their written repudiation of it. Their breach constituted an election to sell their Television Inc. shares in accordance with the terms of the buy/sell provisions in the agreement. This election does not constitute a forfeiture — they violated the agreement voluntarily, aware of the consequences of their acts and they are provided full compensation, per their agreement. The judgment is affirmed. Costs to Ramos.

NOTES AND QUESTIONS

1. In both *Ringling* and *Ramos*, the voting agreements were used to create and preserve a majority. In other situations, voting agreements can be used to ensure participation of shareholders on boards of directors, as with venture capitalists providing funds to high-tech start-up companies. The venture capitalists do not necessarily want control, but they want to make sure that they are in a position to monitor what is going on and to protect their investment if the venture does not work out. Cumulative voting may be used to create such arrangements (see Chapter 3), as may class voting. See also Lehrman v. Cohen, 43 Del. Ch. 222, 222 A.2d 800 (1966).

2. California's authorization of shareholders' voting agreements applies specifically to statutory close corporations, defined to include corporations that have a provision in their articles limiting the number of shareholders to 35 and specifically identifying the corporation as a close corporation. What would be the outcome of *Ramos* in Delaware?

C. Fiduciary Duty and Threat of Dissolution as a Check on Opportunistic Majority Action

1. Traditional Judicial Deference to Majority's Discretion

It will often be uneconomic for shareholders in closely held corporations to specify their rights and duties via express written agreement. Instead, they may choose to rely on the strength of their personal relations, supplemented by each minority shareholder's right to seek equitable relief in the event the majority acts opportunistically. Corporation law provides two principal avenues for minority shareholders' suits—a petition for involuntary dissolution and a direct or derivative suit for breach of fiduciary duty. For most of this century courts and statutes have applied the same equitable doctrines for closely held and publicly held corporations. Such interpretations have the effect of granting majority shareholders substantial discretion to take actions that displease minority shareholders.

Corporation statutes and the common law have long recognized that courts may dissolve a corporation if such action would be equitable. However, until the last third of the twentieth century, corporate norms treated involuntary dissolution as a drastic remedy, to be granted only if the complaining shareholder proved both wrongful conduct by those in control and that dissolution was the only way to prevent irreparable harm to the corporation.

As we discovered in Chapter 4, directors normally owe fiduciary duties of care and loyalty to the corporation but not to individual shareholders. Thus, under traditional norms a complaining minority shareholder must pursue most fiduciary litigation via a derivative suit, with the attendant possibility that the majority may be able to take control of the litigation. In any event, the minority shareholder is generally interested in remedying the harm done not to the corporation but to herself, a goal that is more easily accomplished through direct enforcement of shareholders' rights.

An alternative to an involuntary dissolution petition or derivative litigation is a suit to compel the payment of dividends or to protect other rights belonging directly to shareholders. It has long been recognized that shareholders may sue in their own right to challenge unfair dividend policies, to protect voting or contractual rights, and to protect other rights owed directly to them by the corporation. However, as Zidell v. Zidell below illustrates, business judgment presumptions and the majoritarian-directorial bias of the traditional norms still leave the majority with substantial discretion.

Zidell v. Zidell

Oregon Supreme Court, 1977
277 Or. 413, 560 P.2d 1086

HOWELL, JUSTICE.

These four suits were filed by Arnold Zidell, a minority shareholder of four related, closely-held corporations, seeking to compel the directors of those corporations to declare dividends. . . . Plaintiff's complaints alleged that defendants "arbitrarily, unreasonably and in bad faith" refused to declare more than a modest dividend in 1973. The trial court ordered each of the defendant corporations to declare additional dividends out of its earnings for 1973 and 1974. . . .

Defendants have appealed, contending that the court was not justified in ordering the declaration of any additional dividends. Plaintiff cross appeals, contending that both the dividends and the attorney fees should have been larger. We review de novo. The following is a summary of our review of the transcript and the exhibits.

The individual defendants are directors of the defendant corporations. The corporate defendants (Zidell, Inc., Zidell Dismantling, Inc., Zidell Explorations, Inc., and

Tube Forgings of America, Inc.) are affiliated corporations engaged in the business of scrapping shipping vessels, building and selling barges, buying and selling scrap metal, and marketing industrial valves. All are operated as divisions of the Zidell family business.

The family business began as a partnership and was later incorporated. During World War II, Sam Zidell, father of plaintiff Arnold Zidell and defendant Emery Zidell, bought out his original partner and took in Jack Rosenfeld as a 25 per cent partner. He also transferred one-half of his 75 per cent interest to his wife, Rose. Later, both Emery Zidell and Arnold Zidell came into the business. Emery has been active in the business since shortly after World War II. Arnold, who is much younger, devoted his full time to the business from 1960 until his resignation in 1973. Gradually, Emery and Arnold acquired equal shares in the business from Sam and Rose Zidell. By 1966 Sam Zidell had retired, and the partnership consisted of Emery Zidell (37 1/2%), Arnold Zidell (37 1/2%), and Jack Rosenfeld (25%).

In the meantime, three of the defendant corporations had been organized to carry on separate aspects of the family business. Their stock was held by the three partners in proportion to their partnership interests. The partners also served as directors, and Emery acted as chief executive officer. In 1968, the fourth of the defendant corporations, Zidell, Inc., was organized and the remaining partnership assets were transferred to it. The stock in Zidell, Inc., like that of the other three corporations, was held in the same proportions as the previous partnership interests.

In May, 1972, Jack Rosenfeld sold all of his stock in Tube Forgings of America, Inc., and a portion of his stock in the other three defendant corporations to Jay Zidell, Emery Zidell's son.[2] This transaction effectively gave Emery and his son Jay a majority interest in each of the family corporations. Arnold did not learn of the sale until after it was consummated.

There had previously been some animosity between Emery and Arnold, and this friction apparently increased after Jay's purchase of the Rosenfeld stock. There is evidence that some of the ill-feeling centered around the fact that Jay Zidell's salary had been increased, while Emery refused to approve a similar increase in Arnold's salary. There was other evidence that Emery was displeased with Arnold's lifestyle. Finally, in May of 1973, at a special meeting of the board of directors, Arnold demanded that his salary be raised from $30,000 to $50,000 a year, saying that if his request was not granted he would resign. His request was refused, and Arnold thereupon resigned his employment in the business. He did not resign his directorships in the defendant corporations, but when his terms expired he was not reelected.

Prior to Arnold's resignation, the customary practice had been to retain all earnings in the business rather than to distribute profits as dividends. Arnold had agreed with this policy, since all significant stockholders were active in the business and received salaries adequate for their needs. Following his resignation, however, Arnold demanded that the corporations begin declaring reasonable dividends. Thereafter, a dividend was declared and paid on the 1973 earnings of each corporation.

---

2. Jay was designated as purchaser, but his parents provided the down payment and guaranteed the payment of his installment obligations.

Arnold contends that these dividends are unreasonably small and were not set in good faith. He notes that at about the same time, corporate salaries and bonuses were increased substantially. Arnold does not contend that these salaries are excessive in his briefs on appeal. He does argue, however, that the change in compensation policy, coinciding as it did with his departure from active involvement in the business, is evidence of a concerted effort by the other shareholders to wrongfully deprive him of his right to a fair proportion of the profits of the business. He points out that each corporation had substantial retained earnings at the end of 1973, and he argues that he was entitled to a larger return on his equity.

The trial court specifically declined to rule that defendants acted in bad faith but held that larger dividends should have been declared in order to allow plaintiff a reasonable return. The court then ordered the declaration of a much larger dividend than that which had been set by the board of directors in each case.

We have recognized that those in control of corporate affairs have fiduciary duties of good faith and fair dealing toward the minority shareholders. Insofar as dividend policy is concerned, however, that duty is discharged if the decision is made in good faith and reflects legitimate business purposes rather than the private interests of those in control. See, e.g., Gottfried v. Gottfried, 73 N.Y.S.2d 692, 695 (Sup. Ct. 1947): "The essential test of bad faith is to determine whether the policy of the directors is dictated by their personal interests rather than the corporate welfare. . . ."

A similar situation was recently reviewed by the Supreme Court of Maine in Gay v. Gay's Super Markets, Inc., 343 A.2d 577 (Me. 1975). That court analyzed both the duties of corporate directors and the proper role of the courts in overseeing corporate dividend policies in the following terms:

> To justify judicial intervention in cases of this nature, it must, as a general proposition, be shown that the decision not to declare a dividend amounted to fraud, bad faith or an abuse of discretion on the part of the corporate officials authorized to make the determination.
>
> . . .
>
> The burden of demonstrating bad faith, fraud, breach of fiduciary duty or abuse of discretion on the part of the directors of a corporation rests on the party seeking judicial mandatory relief respecting the declaration of dividends. . . .
>
> Furthermore, judicial review of corporate management decisions must be viewed in the light of this other rule that "it is not the province of the court to act as general manager of a private corporation or to assume the regulation of its internal affairs. . . ." Bates Street Shirt Company v. Waite, 130 Me. 352, 359, 156 A. 293, 298 (1931).
>
> *If there are plausible business reasons supportive of the decision of the board of directors, and such reasons can be given credence, a Court will not interfere with a corporate board's right to make that decision. It is not our function to referee every corporate squabble or disagreement.* It is our duty to redress wrongs, not to settle competitive business interests. Absent any bad faith, fraud, breach of fiduciary duty or abuse of discretion, no wrong cognizable by or correctable in the Courts has occurred. (Id. at 580.) (Emphasis added.)

We agree with these authorities, and we have found no cases to the contrary.

Plaintiff had the burden of proving bad faith on the part of the directors in determining the amount of corporate dividends. In the present case, plaintiff has shown that the corporations could afford to pay additional dividends, that he has left the corporate payroll, that those stockholders who are working for the corporations are receiving generous salaries and bonuses, and that there is hostility between him and the other major stockholders. We agree with plaintiff that these factors are often present in cases of oppression or attempted squeeze-out by majority shareholders. They are not, however, invariably signs of improper behavior by the majority. See Gottfried v. Gottfried, supra at 695:

> There are no infallible distinguishing earmarks of bad faith. The following facts are relevant to the issue of bad faith and are admissible in evidence: Intense hostility of the controlling faction against the minority; exclusion of the minority from employment by the corporation; high salaries, or bonuses or corporate loans made to the officers in control; the fact that the majority group may be subject to high personal income taxes if substantial dividends are paid; the existence of a desire by the controlling directors to acquire the minority stock interests as cheaply as possible. *But if they are not motivating causes they do not constitute "bad faith" as a matter of law.* (Emphasis added.)

Defendants introduced a considerable amount of credible evidence to explain their conservative dividend policy. There was testimony that the directors took into consideration a future need for expensive physical improvements, and possibly even the relocation of a major plant; the need for cash to pay for large inventory orders; the need for renovation of a nearly obsolescent dock; and the need for continued short-term financing through bank loans which could be "called" if the corporations' financial position became insecure. There was also evidence that earnings for 1973 and 1974 were abnormally high because of unusual economic conditions that could not be expected to continue.

In rebuttal, plaintiff contends that the directors did not really make their decisions on the basis of these factors, pointing to testimony that they did not rely on any documented financial analysis to support their dividend declarations. This is a matter for consideration, but it is certainly not determinative. All of the directors of these corporations were active in the business on a day-to-day basis and had intimate first-hand knowledge of financial conditions and present and projected business needs. In order to substantiate their testimony that the above factors were taken into consideration, it was not necessary that they provide documentary evidence or show that formal studies were conducted. Their testimony is believable, and the burden of proof on this issue is on the plaintiff, not the defendants.

Nor are we convinced by plaintiff's arguments that we should approve the forced declaration of additional dividends in order to prevent a deliberate squeeze-out. Plaintiff left his corporate employment voluntarily. He was not forced out. Although the dividends he has since received are modest when viewed as a rate of return on his investment, they are not unreasonable in light of the corporations' projected financial needs. Moreover, having considered the evidence presented by both sides, we are not persuaded that the directors are employing starvation tactics to force the sale of plaintiff's stock at an unreasonably low price.

Since we have determined that plaintiff has not carried his burden of proving a lack of good faith, we must conclude that the trial court erred in decreeing the distribution of additional dividends. . . .

NOTES AND QUESTIONS

1. Under traditional analysis, the complaining shareholder has the burden of proving that the directors' failure to issue a dividend is not the product of a good faith,

informed business decision. Merely proving that there is bad blood between the parties is insufficient to establish that the directors were in fact improperly motivated. A critical factor in dividend-related cases is the corporation's accumulation of an unreasonably large cash reserve—a reserve that can only be explained by the controlling majority's bad faith. See Dodge v. Ford Motor Co., 204 Mich. 459, 509, 170 N.W. 668, 685 (1919) (in suit by minority shareholder in what was then a closely held corporation controlled by Henry Ford, court ordered that a $19 million dividend be paid; "[i]f the total cost of proposed expenditures had been immediately withdrawn in cash from the cash surplus (money and bonds) on hand August 1, 1916, there would have remained nearly $30,000,000"); Miller v. Magline, Inc., 76 Mich. App. 284, 306, 256 N.W.2d 761, 771 (1977) (in suit by recently retired minority shareholders in closely held corporation, court ordered dividend where defendant majority shareholders were paying themselves substantial bonuses and corporation had "a plethora of working capital, an overabundance of working capital").

2. Would Arnold Zidell likely prevail in his dividend suit if, instead of "voluntarily" resigning, the corporation had discharged him? For a negative answer, see Gay v. Gay's Super Markets, Inc., 343 A.2d 577, 430 N.W.2d 447 (Me. 1975).

3. Under traditional doctrine, complaining minority shareholders face the same difficulty in challenging a closely held corporation's salary policies as do complaining shareholders in a publicly held corporation. For example, in Miller v. Magline, Inc., 76 Mich. App. 284, 256 N.W.2d 761 (1977), the court placed the burden of proof on the challenging shareholders because each defendant had abstained from voting on his own compensation. In explaining why the plaintiffs had failed to carry that burden, the court of appeals quoted with approval the trial court's analysis, emphasizing both the value of the defendants' services and the fact that compensation was tied to the firm's success:

> We were impressed by the capabilities of the Magline management group and we are satisfied that the success of the corporation is attributable in no small part to their efforts and attention to their duties. . . .
>
> Magline's compensation plan for its officer-directors was primarily that of a contingent fee. . . . This results in the probability that if the corporation is a success, the return to the officers will be at the high end. On the other hand, this is balanced by the consideration that bad times bring low returns. In view of the participation by the plaintiffs in this same type of plan, prior to their severance of employment connections with the corporation, we are satisfied that the payments to these officers are within the outer limits of reasonable compensation.

76 Mich. App. at 298-299, 256 N.W.2d at 767.

4. Under traditional analysis, complaining minority shareholders in a successful corporation often face an uphill fight even when the burden of proving fairness is placed on the controlling shareholders. For example, in Cookies Food Products, Inc. v. Lakes Warehouse Distributing, Inc., 430 N.W.2d 447 (Iowa 1988), passive minority shareholders complained that compensation and other conflicting interest transactions between the corporation and the majority shareholder were unfair to the corporation. Since these contracts were not ratified by disinterested shareholders' or directors' votes, the burden of proving fairness was on the defendant. In upholding the trial court's conclusion that defendant Herrig's compensation was not exorbitant or unreasonable, the Iowa Supreme Court cited with approval the trial court's reasoning:

The reality here is that the Cookies company is profitable. In a time of economic disaster to many businesses and individuals in Iowa, this company is a shining example of success. The shareholders' investments have multiplied more than fourfold, jobs have been created in Wall Lake, more cash flows in and out of that community annually, and the consumers of Iowa are provided a good product at a fair price. For this Court to tinker with such a successful venture, and especially to "punish" Herrig for this success, would be . . . inequitable.

430 N.W.2d at 456.

2.   The Partnership Analogy as a Basis for Enhancing Minority Shareholders' Rights

The so-called partnership analogy is an early and recurring theme in judicial and academic analysis of the close corporation puzzle. Partnership norms grant each partner an equal share in profits, a right to full information about the partnership, and a right to participate in all management and policy decisions. These rights can be changed only by unanimous agreement of the partners. Moreover, partners owe each other fiduciary duties that can be enforced in a direct, rather than derivative, cause of action. And partnership norms allow any partner to dissolve the partnership at will, thereby forcing a sale of the firm's assets and a return of the partner's capital. Analysis based on the partnership analogy asserts that the expectations and internal governance needs of shareholders in typical closely held corporations are similar to those of partners in a typical partnership. Accordingly, the partnership analogy suggests that close corporation law should be based on, or draw heavily from, partnership law.

However, the utility of the partnership analogy is disputed. Shareholders now have freedom to contract around the majoritarian bias of traditional corporate norms. Why, then, should lawmakers apply partnership rules to resolve intracorporate disputes when the shareholders themselves can provide such rules? How can we be sure that partnership rules are value-maximizing for some or most close corporations, and why can lawmakers do a better job of identifying the close corporations that would benefit from such rules than can the actual users of the corporate form? As you consider the material in this section, consider what assumptions the judges or commentators are making about the contractual problems presented by mutual team-specific investment in a closely held corporation.

Donahue v. Rodd Electrotype Co.
Massachusetts Supreme Judicial Court, 1975
367 Mass. 578, 328 N.E.2d 505

TAURO, CHIEF JUSTICE.

The plaintiff, Euphemia Donahue, a minority stockholder in the Rodd Electrotype Company of New England, Inc. (Rodd Electrotype), a Massachusetts corporation, brings this suit against the directors of Rodd Electrotype, Charles H. Rodd, Frederick I. Rodd and Mr. Harold E. Magnuson, against Harry C. Rodd, a former director, officer, and controlling stockholder of Rodd Electrotype and against Rodd Electrotype (hereinafter called defendants). The plaintiff seeks to rescind Rodd Electrotype's purchase of Harry Rodd's shares in Rodd Electrotype and to compel Harry Rodd "to repay to the corporation the purchase price of said shares, $36,000, together with interest from the date of purchase." The plaintiff alleges that the defendants caused the corporation to purchase the shares in violation of their fiduciary duty to her, a minority stockholder of Rodd Electrotype.

The trial judge, after hearing oral testimony, dismissed the plaintiff's bill on the merits. He found that the purchase was without prejudice to the plaintiff and implicitly found that the transaction had been carried out in good faith and with inherent fairness. The Appeals Court affirmed with costs. . . .

The evidence may be summarized as follows: In 1935, the defendant, Harry C. Rodd, began his employment with Rodd Electrotype, then styled the Royal Electrotype Company of New England, Inc. (Royal of New England). At that time, the company was a wholly-owned subsidiary of a Pennsylvania corporation, the Royal Electrotype Company (Royal Electrotype). Mr. Rodd's advancement within the company was rapid. The following year he was elected a director, and, in 1946, he succeeded to the position of general manager and treasurer.

In 1936, the plaintiff's husband, Joseph Donahue (now deceased), was hired by Royal of New England as a "finisher" of electrotype plates. His duties were confined to operational matters within the plant. Although he ultimately achieved the positions of plant superintendent (1946) and corporate vice president (1955), Donahue never participated in the "management" aspect of the business.

In the years preceding 1955, the parent company, Royal Electrotype, made available to Harry Rodd and Joseph Donahue shares of the common stock in its subsidiary, Royal of New England. Harry Rodd took advantage of the opportunities offered to him and acquired 200 shares for $20 a share. Joseph Donahue, at the suggestion of Harry Rodd, who hoped to interest Donahue in the business, eventually obtained fifty shares in two twenty-five share lots priced at $20 a share. The parent company at all times retained 725 of the 1,000 outstanding shares. One Lawrence W. Kelley owned the remaining twenty-five shares.

In June of 1955, Royal of New England purchased all 725 of its shares owned by its parent company. The total price amounted to $135,000. Royal of New England remitted $75,000 of this total in cash and executed five promissory notes of $12,000 each, due in each of the succeeding five years. Lawrence W. Kelley's twenty-five shares were also purchased at this time for $1,000. A substantial portion of Royal of New England's cash expenditures was loaned to the company by Harry Rodd, who mortgaged his house to obtain some of the necessary funds.

The stock purchases left Harry Rodd in control of Royal of New England. Early in 1955, before the purchases, he had assumed the presidency of the company. His 200 shares gave him a dominant eighty per cent interest. Joseph Donahue, at this time, was the only minority stockholder.

Subsequent events reflected Harry Rodd's dominant influence. In June, 1960, more than a year after the last obligation to Royal Electrotype had been discharged, the company was renamed the Rodd Electrotype Company of New England, Inc. In 1962, Charles H. Rodd, Harry Rodd's son (a defendant here), who had long been a company employee working in the plant, became corporate vice president. In 1963, he joined his father on the board of directors. In 1964, another son, Frederick I. Rodd (also a defendant), replaced Joseph Donahue as plant superintendent. By 1965, Harry Rodd had evidently decided to reduce his participation in corporate management. That year Charles Rodd succeeded him as president and general manager of Rodd Electrotype.

From 1959 to 1967, Harry Rodd pursued what may fairly be termed a gift program by which he distributed the majority of his shares equally among his two sons and his daughter, Phyllis E. Mason. Each child received thirty-nine shares. Two shares were returned to the corporate treasury in 1966.

We come now to the events of 1970 which form the grounds for the plaintiff's complaint. In May of 1970, Harry Rodd was seventy-seven years old. The record indicates that for some time he had not enjoyed the best of health and that he had undergone a number of operations. His sons wished him to retire. Mr. Rodd was not averse to this suggestion. However, he insisted that some financial arrangements be made with respect to his remaining eighty-one shares of stock. A number of conferences ensued. Harry Rodd and Charles Rodd (representing the company) negotiated terms of purchase for forty-five shares which, Charles Rodd testified, would reflect the book value and liquidating value of the shares.

A special board meeting convened on July 13, 1970. As the first order of business, Harry Rodd resigned his directorship of Rodd Electrotype. The remaining incumbent directors, Charles Rodd and Mr. Harold E. Magnuson (clerk of the company and a defendant and defense attorney in the instant suit), elected Frederick Rodd to replace his father. The three directors then authorized Rodd Electrotype's president (Charles Rodd) to execute an agreement between Harry Rodd and the company in which the company would purchase forty-five shares for $800 a share ($36,000).

The stock purchase agreement was formalized between the parties on July 13, 1970. Two days later, a sale pursuant to the July 13 agreement was consummated. At approximately the same time, Harry Rodd resigned his last corporate office, that of treasurer.

Harry Rodd completed divestiture of his Rodd Electrotype stock in the following year. As was true of his previous gifts, his later divestments gave equal representation to his children. Two shares were sold to each child on July 15, 1970, for $800 a share. Each was given ten shares in March, 1971. Thus, in March, 1971, the shareholdings in Rodd Electrotype were apportioned as follows: Charles Rodd, Frederick Rodd and Phyllis Mason each held fifty-one shares; the Donahues held fifty shares.

A special meeting of the stockholders of the company was held on March 30, 1971. At the meeting, Charles Rodd, company president and general manager, reported the tentative results of an audit conducted by the company auditors and reported generally on the company events of the year. For the first time, the Donahues learned that the corporation had purchased Harry Rodd's shares. According to the minutes of the meeting, following Charles Rodd's report, the Donahues raised questions about the purchase. They then voted against a resolution, ultimately adopted by the remaining stockholders, to approve Charles Rodd's report. Although the minutes of the meeting show that the stockholders unanimously voted to accept a second resolution ratifying all acts of the company president (he executed the stock purchase agreement) in the preceding year, the trial judge found, and there was evidence to support his finding, that the Donahues did not ratify the purchase of Harry Rodd's shares.

A few weeks after the meeting, the Donahues, acting through their attorney, offered their shares to the corporation on the same terms given to Harry Rodd. Mr. Harold E. Magnuson replied by letter that the corporation would not purchase the shares and was not in a financial position to do so.[10] This suit followed.

In her argument before this court, the plaintiff has characterized the corporate purchase of Harry Rodd's shares as an unlawful distribution of corporate assets to controlling stockholders. She urges that the distribution constitutes a breach of the fiduciary duty owed by the Rodds, as controlling stockholders, to her, a minority stockholder in the enterprise, because the Rodds failed to accord her an equal opportunity to sell her shares to the corporation. The defendants reply that the stock purchase was within the powers of the corporation and met the requirements of good faith and inherent fairness imposed on a fiduciary in his dealings with the corporation. They assert that there is no right to equal opportunity in corporate stock purchases for the corporate treasury. For the reasons hereinafter noted, we agree with the plaintiff and reverse the decree of the Superior Court. However, we limit the applicability of our holding to "close corporations," as hereinafter defined. Whether the holding should apply to other corporations is left for decision in another case, on a proper record.

A. CLOSE CORPORATIONS

In previous opinions, we have alluded to the distinctive nature of the close corporation. . . . We deem a close corporation to be typified by: (1) a small number of stockholders; (2) no ready market for the corporate stock; and (3) substantial majority stockholder participation in the management, direction and operations of the corporation.

As thus defined, the close corporation bears striking resemblance to a partnership. Commentators and courts have noted that the close corporation is often little more than an "incorporated" or "chartered" partnership. The stockholders "clothe" their partnership "with the benefits peculiar to a corporation, limited liability, perpetuity and the like." . . .

Although the corporate form provides the above-mentioned advantages for the stockholders (limited liability, perpetuity, and so forth), it also supplies an opportunity for the majority stockholders to oppress or disadvantage minority stockholders. The minority is vulnerable to a variety of oppressive devices, termed "freeze-outs," which the majority may employ. . . .

The minority can, of course, initiate suit against the majority and their directors. Self-serving conduct by directors is proscribed by the director's fiduciary obligation to the corporation. However, in practice, the plaintiff will find difficulty in challenging dividend or employment policies. . . .

Thus, when these types of "freeze-outs" are attempted by the majority stockholders, the minority stockholders, cut off from all corporation-related revenues, must either

---

10. Between 1965 and 1969, the company offered to purchase the Donahue shares for amounts between $2,000 and $10,000 ($40 to $200 a share). The Donahues rejected these offers.

suffer their losses or seek a buyer for their shares. Many minority stockholders will be unwilling or unable to wait for an alteration in majority policy. Typically, the minority stockholder in a close corporation has a substantial percentage of his personal assets invested in the corporation. The stockholder may have anticipated that his salary from his position with the corporation would be his livelihood. Thus, he cannot afford to wait passively. He must liquidate his investment in the close corporation in order to reinvest the funds in income-producing enterprises.

At this point, the true plight of the minority stockholder in a close corporation becomes manifest. He cannot easily reclaim his capital. In a large public corporation, the oppressed or dissident minority stockholder could sell his stock in order to extricate some of his invested capital. By definition, this market is not available for shares in the close corporation. In a partnership, a partner who feels abused by his fellow partners may cause dissolution by his "express will . . . at any time" (G.L. c.108A, §31[1][b] and [2]) and recover his share of partnership assets and accumulated profits. If dissolution results in a breach of the partnership articles, the culpable partner will be liable in damages. By contrast, the stockholder in the close corporation or "incorporated partnership" may achieve dissolution and recovery of his share of the enterprise assets only by compliance with the rigorous terms of the applicable chapter of the General Laws. . . .

Thus, in a close corporation, the minority stockholders may be trapped in a disadvantageous situation. No outsider would knowingly assume the position of the disadvantaged minority. The outsider would have the same difficulties. To cut losses, the minority stockholder may be compelled to deal with the majority. This is the capstone of the majority plan. When the minority stockholder agrees to sell out at less than fair value, the majority has won.

Because of the fundamental resemblance of the close corporation to the partnership, the trust and confidence which are essential to this scale and manner of enterprise, and the inherent danger to minority interests in the close corporation, we hold that stockholders in the close corporation owe one another substantially the same fiduciary duty in the operation of the enterprise that partners owe to one another. In our previous decisions, we have defined the standard of duty owed by partners to one another as the "utmost good faith and loyalty." Stockholders in close corporations must discharge their management and stockholder responsibilities in conformity with this strict good faith standard. They may not act out of avarice, expediency or self-interest in derogation of their duty of loyalty to the other stockholders and to the corporation.

We contrast this strict good faith standard with the somewhat less stringent standard of fiduciary duty to which directors and stockholders of all corporations must adhere in the discharge of their corporate responsibilities. . . .

The more rigorous duty of partners and participants in a joint adventure, here extended to stockholders in a close corporation, was described by then Chief Judge Cardozo of the New York Court of Appeals in Meinhard v. Salmon, 249 N.Y. 458, 164 N.E. 545 (1928): "Joint adventurers, like copartners, owe to one another, while the enterprise continues, the duty of the finest loyalty. Many forms of conduct permissible in a workaday world for those acting at arm's length, are forbidden to those bound by fiduciary ties. . . . Not honesty alone, but the punctilio of an honor the most sensitive, is then the standard of behavior." Id. at 463-464, 164 N.E. at 546. . . .

B. EQUAL OPPORTUNITY IN A CLOSE CORPORATION

Under settled Massachusetts law, a domestic corporation, unless forbidden by statute, has the power to purchase its own shares. . . . When the corporation reacquiring its own stock is a close corporation, the purchase is subject to the additional requirement, in the light of our holding in this opinion, that the stockholders, who, as directors or controlling stockholders, caused the corporation to enter into the stock purchase agreement, must have acted with the utmost good faith and loyalty to the other stockholders.

To meet this test, if the stockholder whose shares were purchased was a member of the controlling group, the controlling stockholders must cause the corporation to offer each stockholder an equal opportunity to sell a ratable number of his shares to the corporation at an identical price. Purchase by the corporation confers substantial benefits on the members of the controlling group whose shares were purchased. These benefits are not available to the minority stockholders if the corporation does not also offer them an opportunity to sell their shares. The controlling group may not, consistent with its strict duty to the minority, utilize its control of the corporation to obtain special advantages and disproportionate benefit from its share ownership. . . .

C. APPLICATION OF THE LAW TO THIS CASE

We turn now to the application of the learning set forth above to the facts of the instant case. The strict standard of duty is plainly applicable to the stockholders in Rodd Electrotype. . . .

On its face, then, the purchase of Harry Rodd's shares by the corporation is a breach of the duty which the controlling stockholders, the Rodds, owed to the minority stockholders, the plaintiff and her son. The purchase distributed a portion of the corporate assets to Harry Rodd, a member of the controlling group, in exchange for his shares. The plaintiff and her son were not offered an equal opportunity to sell their shares to the corporation. In fact, their efforts to obtain an equal opportunity were rebuffed by the corporate representative. As the trial judge found, they did not, in any manner, ratify the transaction with Harry Rodd.

Because of the foregoing, we hold that the plaintiff is entitled to relief. Two forms of suitable relief are set out hereinafter. The judge below is to enter an appropriate judgment. The judgment may require Harry Rodd to remit $36,000 with interest at the legal rate from July 15, 1970, to Rodd Electrotype in exchange for forty-five shares of Rodd Electrotype treasury stock. This, in substance, is the specific relief requested in the plaintiff's bill of complaint. Interest is manifestly appropriate. . . . In the alternative, the judgment may require Rodd Electrotype to purchase all of the plaintiff's shares for $36,000 without interest. In the circumstances of this case, we view this as the equal opportunity which the plaintiff should have received. Harry Rodd's retention of thirty-six shares, which were to be sold and given to his children within a year of the Rodd Electrotype purchase, cannot disguise the fact that the corporation acquired one hundred per cent of that portion of his holdings (forty-five shares) which he did not intend his children to own. The plaintiff is entitled to have one hundred per cent of her forty-five shares similarly purchased. . . .

Wilkes v. Springside Nursing Home, Inc.
Massachusetts Supreme Judicial Court, 1976
370 Mass. 842, 353 N.E.2d 657

HENNESSEY, CHIEF JUSTICE.

On August 5, 1971, the plaintiff (Wilkes) filed a bill in equity for declaratory judgment. . . . Wilkes alleged that he, Quinn, Riche and Pipkin entered into a partnership agreement in 1951, prior to the incorporation of Springside, which agreement was breached in 1967 when Wilkes's salary was terminated and he was voted out as an officer and director of the corporation. Wilkes sought, among other forms of relief, damages in the amount of the salary he would have received had he continued as a director and officer of Springside subsequent to March, 1967.

A judge of the Probate Court referred the suit to a master, who, after a lengthy hearing, issued his final report in late 1973. . . . A judgment was entered dismissing Wilkes's action on the merits. We granted direct appellate review. . . .

A summary of the pertinent facts as found by the master is set out in the following pages. . . .

In 1951 Wilkes acquired an option to purchase a building and lot located on the corner of Springside Avenue and North Street in Pittsfield, Massachusetts, the building having previously housed the Hillcrest Hospital. Though Wilkes was principally engaged in the roofing and siding business, he had gained a reputation locally for profitable dealings in real estate. Riche, an acquaintance of Wilkes, learned of the option, and interested Quinn (who was known to Wilkes through membership on the draft board in Pittsfield) and Pipkin (an acquaintance of both Wilkes and Riche) in joining Wilkes in his investment. The four men met and decided to participate jointly in the purchase of the building and lot as a real estate investment which, they believed, had good profit potential on resale or rental.

The parties later determined that the property would have its greatest potential for profit if it were operated by them as a nursing home. Wilkes consulted his attorney, who advised him that if the four men were to operate the contemplated nursing home as planned, they would be partners and would be liable for any debts incurred by the partnership and by each other. On the attorney's suggestion, and after consultation among themselves, ownership of the property was vested in Springside, a corporation organized under Massachusetts law.

Each of the four men invested $1,000 and subscribed to ten shares of $100 par value stock in Springside. At the time of incorporation it was understood by all of the parties that each would be a director of Springside and each would participate actively in the management and decision making involved in operating the corporation.[7] It was, further, the understanding and intention of all the parties that, corporate resources

---

7. Wilkes testified before the master that, when the corporate officers were elected, all four men "were . . . guaranteed directorships." Riche's understanding of the parties' intentions was that they all wanted to play a part in the management of the corporation and wanted to have some "say" in the risks involved; that, to this end, they all would be directors; and that "unless you (were) a director and officer you could not participate in the decisions of (the) enterprise."

permitting, each would receive money from the corporation in equal amounts as long as each assumed an active and ongoing responsibility for carrying a portion of the burdens necessary to operate the business.

The work involved in establishing and operating a nursing home was roughly apportioned, and each of the four men undertook his respective tasks.[8] Initially, Riche was elected president of Springside, Wilkes was elected treasurer, and Quinn was elected clerk. Each of the four was listed in the articles of organization as a director of the corporation.

At some time in 1952, it became apparent that the operational income and cash flow from the business were sufficient to permit the four stockholders to draw money from the corporation on a regular basis. Each of the four original parties initially received $35 a week from the corporation. As time went on the weekly return to each was increased until, in 1955, it totaled $100.

In 1959, after a long illness, Pipkin sold his shares in the corporation to Connor, who was known to Wilkes, Riche and Quinn through past transactions with Springside in his capacity as president of the First Agricultural National Bank of Berkshire County. Connor received a weekly stipend from the corporation equal to that received by Wilkes, Riche and Quinn. He was elected a director of the corporation but never held any other office. He was assigned no specific area of responsibility in the operation of the nursing home but did participate in business discussions and decisions as a director and served additionally as financial adviser to the corporation.

In 1965 the stockholders decided to sell a portion of the corporate property to Quinn who, in addition to being a stockholder in Springside, possessed an interest in another corporation which desired to operate a rest home on the property. Wilkes was successful in prevailing on the other stockholders of Springside to procure a higher sale price for the property than Quinn apparently anticipated paying or desired to pay. After the sale was consummated, the relationship between Quinn and Wilkes began to deteriorate.

The bad blood between Quinn and Wilkes affected the attitudes of both Riche and Connor. As a consequence of the strained relations among the parties, Wilkes, in January of 1967, gave notice of his intention to sell his shares for an amount based on an appraisal of their value. In February of 1967 a directors' meeting was held and the board exercised its right to establish the salaries of its officers and employees. A schedule of payments was established whereby Quinn was to receive a substantial weekly increase and Riche and Connor were to continue receiving $100 a week. Wilkes, however, was left off the list of those to whom a salary was to be paid. The directors also set the annual meeting of the stockholders for March, 1967.

---

8. Wilkes took charge of the repair, upkeep and maintenance of the physical plant and grounds; Riche assumed supervision over the kitchen facilities and dietary and food aspects of the home; Pipkin was to make himself available if and when medical problems arose; and Quinn dealt with the personnel and administrative aspects of the nursing home, serving informally as a managing director. Quinn further coordinated the activities of the other parties and served as a communication link among them when matters had to be discussed and decisions had to be made without a formal meeting.

At the annual meeting in March, Wilkes was not reelected as a director, nor was he reelected as an officer of the corporation. He was further informed that neither his services nor his presence at the nursing home was wanted by his associates.

The meetings of the directors and stockholders in early 1967, the master found, were used as a vehicle to force Wilkes out of active participation in the management and operation of the corporation and to cut off all corporate payments to him. Though the board of directors had the power to dismiss any officers or employees for misconduct or neglect of duties, there was no indication in the minutes of the board of directors' meeting of February, 1967, that the failure to establish a salary for Wilkes was based on either ground. The severance of Wilkes from the payroll resulted not from misconduct or neglect of duties, but because of the personal desire of Quinn, Riche and Connor to prevent him from continuing to receive money from the corporation. Despite a continuing deterioration in his personal relationship with his associates, Wilkes had consistently endeavored to carry on his responsibilities to the corporation in the same satisfactory manner and with the same degree of competence he had previously shown. Wilkes was at all times willing to carry on his responsibilities and participation if permitted so to do and provided that he receive his weekly stipend.

We turn to Wilkes's claim for damages based on a breach of the fiduciary duty owed to him by the other participants in this venture. In light of the theory underlying this claim, we do not consider it vital to our approach to this case whether the claim is governed by partnership law or the law applicable to business corporations. This is so because, as all the parties agree, Springside was, at all times relevant to this action, a close corporation as we have recently defined such an entity in Donahue v. Rodd Electrotype Co. of New England, Inc., 328 N.E.2d 505 (1975). . . .

The *Donahue* decision acknowledged, as a "natural outgrowth" of the case law of this Commonwealth, a strict obligation on the part of majority stockholders in a close corporation to deal with the minority with the utmost good faith and loyalty. On its face, this strict standard is applicable in the instant case. The distinction between the majority action in *Donahue* and the majority action in this case is more one of form than of substance. Nevertheless, we are concerned that untempered application of the strict good faith standard enunciated in *Donahue* to cases such as the one before us will result in the imposition of limitations on legitimate action by the controlling group in a close corporation which will unduly hamper its effectiveness in managing the corporation in the best interests of all concerned. The majority, concededly, have certain rights to what has been termed "selfish ownership" in the corporation which should be balanced against the concept of their fiduciary obligation to the minority.

Therefore, when minority stockholders in a close corporation bring suit against the majority alleging a breach of the strict good faith duty owed to them by the majority, we must carefully analyze the action taken by the controlling stockholders in the individual case. It must be asked whether the controlling group can demonstrate a legitimate business purpose for its action. In asking this question, we acknowledge the fact that the controlling group in a close corporation must have some room to maneuver in establishing the business policy of the corporation. It must have a large measure of discretion, for example, in declaring or withholding dividends, deciding whether to merge or consolidate, establishing the salaries of corporate officers, dismissing directors with or without cause, and hiring and firing corporate employees.

When an asserted business purpose for their action is advanced by the majority, however, we think it is open to minority stockholders to demonstrate that the same legitimate objective could have been achieved through an alternative course of action less harmful to the minority's interest. If called on to settle a dispute, our courts must weigh the legitimate business purpose, if any, against the practicability of a less harmful alternative.

Applying this approach to the instant case it is apparent that the majority stockholders in Springside have not shown a legitimate business purpose for severing Wilkes from the payroll of the corporation or for refusing to reelect him as a salaried officer and director. The master's subsidiary findings relating to the purpose of the meetings of the directors and stockholders in February and March, 1967, are supported by the evidence. There was no showing of misconduct on Wilkes's part as a director, officer or employee of the corporation which would lead us to approve the majority action as a legitimate response to the disruptive nature of an undesirable individual bent on injuring or destroying the corporation. On the contrary, it appears that Wilkes had always accomplished his assigned share of the duties competently, and that he had never indicated an unwillingness to continue to do so.

It is an inescapable conclusion from all the evidence that the action of the majority stockholders here was a designed "freeze out" for which no legitimate business purpose has been suggested. Furthermore, we may infer that a design to pressure Wilkes into selling his shares to the corporation at a price below their value well may have been at the heart of the majority's plan.[14]

In the context of this case, several factors bear directly on the duty owed to Wilkes by his associates. At a minimum, the duty of utmost good faith and loyalty would demand that the majority consider that their action was in disregard of a long-standing policy of the stockholders that each would be a director of the corporation and that employment with the corporation would go hand in hand with stock ownership; that Wilkes was one of the four originators of the nursing home venture; and that Wilkes, like the others, had invested his capital and time for more than fifteen years with the expectation that he would continue to participate in corporate decisions. Most important is the plain fact that the cutting off of Wilkes's salary, together with the fact that the corporation never declared a dividend, assured that Wilkes would receive no return at all from the corporation. . . .

[A] judgment shall be entered declaring that Quinn, Riche and Connor breached their fiduciary duty to Wilkes as a minority stockholder in Springside, and awarding money damages therefor. Wilkes shall be allowed to recover from Riche, the estate of T. Edward Quinn and the estate of Lawrence R. Connor, ratably, according to the inequitable enrichment of each, the salary he would have received had he remained an officer and director of Springside. In considering the issue of damages the judge on remand shall take into account the extent to which any remaining corporate funds of Springside may be diverted to satisfy Wilkes's claim. . . .

---

14. This inference arises from the fact that Connor, acting on behalf of the three controlling stockholders, offered to purchase Wilkes's shares for a price Connor admittedly would not have accepted for his own shares.

Hetherington and Dooley, Illiquidity and Exploitation: A Proposed Statutory Solution to the Remaining Close Corporation Problem
63 Va. L. Rev. 1-4, 6, 50-52 (1977)

For a number of years, many commentators and lawmakers believed the principal legal problem concerning closely held corporations to be the organizational strictures imposed by general corporate law. They argued that close corporation shareholders could best satisfy their needs by private contractual arrangement, free of statutory constraints more appropriate for the publicly held firm. That proposition is now generally accepted, and many state statutes contain provisions permitting the substitution of what amounts to a partnership arrangement for the standard corporate management structure. In the absence of special statutory provisions, permissive judicial decisions . . . appear to provide all the flexibility needed to create arrangements tailored to the individual needs and expectations of the parties.

The emphasis on contractual arrangements reveals a fundamental misunderstanding of the nature of close corporations. Whether the parties adopt special contractual arrangements is much less important than their ability to sustain a close, harmonious relationship over time. The continuance of such a relationship is crucial because it reflects what is perhaps the fundamental assumption made by those who decide to invest in a close corporation: they expect that during the life of the firm the shareholders will be in substantial agreement as to its operation. . . .

Our thesis is that the problem of exploitation is uniquely related to illiquidity and, for that reason, it is resistant to solution by ex ante contractual arrangements or by ex post judicial relief for breach of fiduciary duty. The existing law appears to take account of the inadequacy of these approaches by offering two types of remedies specifically designed to deal with the problems of illiquidity and exploitation. The first is the familiar action for involuntary dissolution. More recently, some states have adopted a second group of remedies, including provisional directors, custodians, and direct judicial supervision, as alternatives to dissolution. We conclude that both involuntary dissolution and its alternatives are costly and ineffectual and that considerations of equity and efficiency justify permitting the minority to withdraw its investment for any reason. Accordingly, we offer a model statutory provision requiring the majority to repurchase the minority's interest at the request of the latter and subject to appropriate safeguards. . . .

The buyout right can be implemented by relatively simple statutory procedures. Under the proposed statute, a minority or fifty percent shareholder would be entitled to demand that the corporation purchase all of his shares. The shareholder, however, would be required to offer his entire equity interest. The statutory right is intended to protect the shareholder who wants to withdraw completely from the firm. It is not intended to enable a shareholder to effect a partial liquidation of his interest. This is analogous to a partner's dissolution right. In both instances, of course, the party can use the threat of withdrawal to bargain for a partial liquidation of capital, but, in that event, the remaining shareholders or partners have the choice of acquiescing or refusing, thereby forcing the demanding shareholder or partner either to stay in or to retire completely. . . .

[I]f the corporation or the remaining shareholders have not agreed to purchase all of the shares by the end of [a 90 day] period, the court is required to enter a decree dissolving the corporation. . . .

The corporation and the remaining shareholders are protected against sudden cash drains by a provision authorizing the court, upon a showing of good cause, to provide for installment payments of the purchase price for a period of time not exceeding five years. Similarly, the statute imposes a two-year holding period for newly acquired shares, during which time the shareholder may not exercise his right to be bought out. This latter limitation is intended primarily to protect new businesses where a withdrawal in the formative stages might be particularly disruptive. More broadly, it is designed to encourage prudent investment decisions by requiring shareholders to bear the initial investment risks of their decision to purchase. . . .

Another device available to protect corporate stability is a voluntary waiver of the buyout right. Use of this waiver, however, can be troublesome. On the one hand, shareholders may have legitimate reasons for agreeing to waive the buyout right. Creditors might insist on such a waiver as a condition of extending credit, for example, or the parties might want to guarantee a period of stability in order to facilitate long-range planning. On the other hand, permitting shareholders to "draft out" the right completely could lead to the use of blanket waivers at the time of incorporation and easy evasion of the remedial goals of the statute. The proposed statute effects a compromise by permitting waivers, but for no longer than two years at a time. This should ensure that minority shareholders will not waive their statutory rights casually and also should prevent majority shareholders from taking undue advantage of the minority during the limited period the waiver is in effect. . . .

Easterbrook and Fischel, Close Corporations and Agency Costs
38 Stan. L. Rev. 271, 297-300 (1986)

D. THE PARTNERSHIP ANALOGY

That closely held corporations are really "incorporated partnerships" is a common refrain. The participants in the venture view each other as partners; therefore, the argument runs, they should be governed by the law of partnerships. Equal sharing rules, automatic buy-out rights, and strict fiduciary duties are fundamental principles of partnership law and thus, proponents of the partnership analogy contend, should also be fundamental principles of the law of closely held corporations.

There is something to the analogy. We have conjectured elsewhere, and there is now some evidence, that participants in smaller firms who are unable to reduce risk by diversifying their investments are more likely to contract for equal sharing rules and to opt for other principles that constrain managers' discretion. Still, there are problems with pushing the analogy to partnerships too far. First, at least with respect to automatic buy-out rights, the analogy is based on a misstatement of partnership law. Although partnership law allows any partner (unless all agree otherwise in advance) to disinvest at any time and dissolve the firm, the withdrawing partner may be liable in damages for "wrongful" termination and may be able to disinvest only on disadvantageous terms. Thus the Hetherington and Dooley proposal for automatic buy-out rights in closely held corporations, although supposedly based on partnership law, actually goes well beyond existing doctrine.

Second, the assumption that participants in closely held corporations want to be governed by partnership law is itself questionable. The participants incorporated for a reason. Perhaps the reason was only limited liability or favorable tax treatment, and in all other respects they wanted to be treated like partners. But this is not the only possibility. Corporate law is different from partnership law in many ways, and the venturers may desire to preserve these differences. Partners, for example, are entitled to share equally in the profits and management of the partnership, are mutual agents for each other, have the right to veto any decisions made by the majority on matters outside the ordinary course of business, and have the right to dissolve the partnership at any time if they are willing to bear the consequences. Corporate law treats each of these differently. Proponents of the partnership analogy assume that participants in closely held corporations are knowledgeable enough to incorporate to obtain the benefits of favorable tax treatment or limited liability but ignorant of all other differences between corporate and partnership law. There is no support for this assumption once you realize that people have to jump through a lot of formal hoops (assisted by counsel) to incorporate but could become partners by accident.

The right inquiry is always what the parties would have contracted for had transactions costs been zero, not whether closely held corporations are more similar to partnerships than to publicly held corporations. The failure to recognize the limited role of analogical reasoning can have significant consequences. The court that decided *Donahue* was apparently so concerned about establishing the similarities between closely held corporations and partnerships that it never considered the possibility that its rule of equal opportunity might be inconsistent with the observed behavior of participants in both partnerships and closely held corporations. Both types of firms must provide some mechanism for dealing with retirements or terminations in situations where the firm will continue to exist. Most firms could not survive if the purchase of the interest of a retiring member required that everyone else be given the opportunity to sell out at the same price. Because the court never asked what the parties would have intended, it missed the boat.

Participants in business ventures are free to reflect their wishes explicitly in a written contract. Both partnership and corporate law enforce private decisions. When the parties do not or cannot contract explicitly, it will often be difficult to discern what they would have done if contracting were costless. This subtle inquiry is not made any simpler by asking whether closely held corporations are really partnerships. This latter focus simply puts everyone off the scent; indeed, it may be perverse because it directs attention away from the questions of why people formed the corporation and why, having done so, they did not adopt partnership-like rules by contract. Even if the parties did not consciously decide to opt out of the partnership rule, all this means is that they were asleep. What reason have we to think that if they were awake they would have selected the partnership rule?

NOTES AND QUESTIONS

1. As noted by Easterbrook and Fischel, a general partnership can be dissolved nonwrongfully only if the partnership is not for a term or specified undertaking. If a court decides to apply partnership law to a close corporation, how is it to decide whether to treat the "partnership" for a term or for a specified undertaking? Does the selection of corporate form indicate that the parties preferred a nonterminable-at-will relationship? Would that inference be appropriate at least in cases where the shareholders made significant team-specific investments and, therefore, from an ex ante perspective, might rationally have preferred the protection from opportunistic withdrawal provided by a nonterminable-at-will relationship? Consider, for example, the court's analysis in 68th Street Apts., Inc. v. Lauricella, 142 N.J. Super. 546, 561, 362 A.2d 78, 87 (App. Div. 1976):

> Whether the relationship is at will or for a fixed term or until the accomplishment of a particular undertaking is a question of fact. Here the nature of the project was such that substantial investments of money, time and energy would be required from which no return would be forthcoming unless and until the building was completed. The only common sense view is . . . that the principals intended their relationship not to be one from which either could withdraw at will before completion of the project, but one rather to which each committed himself until the building was completed.

Is this analysis sound from a contract interpretation point of view?

2. Under partnership law norms, the expulsion of a partner is not a wrongful dissolution if the expulsion takes place pursuant to a power conferred in the partnership agreement. See UPA §31(d). What result in Wilkes v. Springside Nursing Home, Inc. if partnership law rules are strictly applied?

3. Is the substantive result in Donahue v. Rodd Electrotype Co. correct? Consider Easterbrook and Fischel's criticism:

> Grave reflections on the plight of minority investors in closely held corporations and stirring proclamations of the fiduciary duty of the majority fill the opinion. Completely overlooked in all of this rhetoric was any consideration of the basic question — which interpretation of fiduciary duties would the parties have selected had they contracted in anticipation of this contingency? . . .
>
> The terms of the purchase in Donahue were not extraordinary. The trial court found them fair. The purpose appears to have been nothing more than an attempt to facilitate the retirement of a manager who, by virtue of advancing age and poor health, could no longer contribute. The firm doubtless was the better for his retirement.

38 Stan. L. Rev. 271, 294-295 (1986).

4. Is Hetherington and Dooley's argument internally consistent? If the most important need of shareholders in a closely held corporation is the "ability to sustain a close relationship over time," how will giving minority shareholders the right to demand a repurchase of their shares satisfy that need? Given this dominant need, would it make more sense to penalize minority shareholders for failing to choose their associates more carefully? If so, is it essential that close corporation law norms grant some leeway to the majority in making decisions adversely affecting minority shareholders' interests? From the standpoint of reinforcing the shareholders' relations, is the rule

crafted in Wilkes v. Springside Nursing Home, Inc. preferable to the rule proposed by Hetherington and Dooley?

5. Why do Hetherington and Dooley suggest that waivers of the proposed mandatory repurchase right be effective for no more than two years? Is this an unnecessary interference with contractual freedom? If Hetherington and Dooley's proposal were amended to allow permanent waivers, would the mandatory repurchase provision become an effective penalty default rule, forcing the majority either to risk minority shareholder withdrawal at will or to reveal at the outset important information about their future opportunistic intentions? Or would the waivers likely be routinely obtained? For the seminal discussion of penalty default rules, see Ayres and Gertner, Filling Gaps in Incomplete Contracts: An Economic Theory of Default Rules, 99 Yale L.J. 87 (1989).

NOTE: DIRECT VERSUS DERIVATIVE SUIT

Litigation in close corporations sometimes turns on whether the claim is a direct or a derivative suit. If it is a derivative suit in the name of the corporation, a variety of legal rules apply, including the requirement of demand on the board of directors as a precondition to suit (discussed in Chapter 4) and other rules governing settlements or bonds to secure the costs of defendants.

In a close corporation, determining whether an action must be brought as a direct or derivative suit can be difficult. In corporate litigation generally, courts commonly classify as derivative those actions that harm shareholders only indirectly by reducing the value of their proportional shares of corporate ownership. Direct actions are those that harm the complaining shareholder in a way that is separate and distinct from injury to the corporation, such as a claim based on shareholder voting rights, preemptive rights, or a right to inspect books. A minority shareholder's complaint that majority shareholders used their control to direct corporate assets to the majority while excluding the minority from some or all of these benefits could be considered derivative since the entity's assets were dissipated. In Richards v. Bryan, 879 P.2d 638 (Kan. Ct. App. 1994), a Kansas court describes why many courts are moving away from this distinction:

> In a close corporation, the corporation is generally composed of a majority share-holder or group and a minority shareholder or group. Because of the difficulty in determining if a suit must be brought as a direct or a derivative action, an increasing number of courts are abandoning the distinction between a derivative and a direct action because the only interested parties are the two sets of shareholders. Furthermore, some courts have recognized that it is often difficult and futile to bring a derivative action against a closely held corporation. As explained by one authority, "[e]ven if a minority shareholder overcomes procedural hurdles in a derivative action, a strong disadvantage is that any recovery accrues to the corporation and hence remains under the control of the very parties who may have been defendants in the litigation." 2 O'Neal and Thompson, O'Neal's Close Corporations §8.11, p. 122 (3d ed. 1992). For this reason, some courts permit oppressed minority shareholders to bring direct suits for breaches of duties by the majority, even though the minority shareholders' grievance is primarily based on damage to the corporation. 2 O'Neal and Thompson, O'Neal's Close Corporations §8.11, p. 122. Some courts allow such suits under an exception to the standing to sue doctrine, while other courts recognize a new cause of action for close corporation freeze-outs. See generally Bagdon v. Bridgestone/Firestone, Inc., 916 F.2d 379 (Ohio law allows minority shareholders in close corporations to sue individually for oppressive majority conduct

under an exception to the standing doctrine); Balvik v. Sylvester, 411 N.W.2d 383 (N.D. 1987) (oppressed minority shareholders may bring an independent action against majority shareholders under a freeze-out theory, when their reasonable expectations are thwarted by majority conduct); Steelman v. Mallory, 110 Idaho 510, 513, 716 P.2d 1282 (1986) (there is no need to file a derivative action when a corporate "squeeze-out" harms a minority shareholder in a close corporation).

In its Principles of Corporate Governance: Analysis and Recommendations §7.01(d), p. 731 (Tentative Draft No. 11, 1991), the American Law Institute recommends allowing an independent cause of action for freeze-outs in the close corporate setting under certain circumstances:

> If a corporation is closely held . . . , the court in its discretion may treat an action raising derivative claims as a direct action, exempt it from those restrictions and defenses applicable only to derivative actions, and order in individual recovery, if it finds that to do so will not (i) unfairly expose the corporation . . . to a multiplicity of actions, (ii) materially prejudice the interests of creditors in the corporation, or (iii) interfere with a fair distribution of the recovery among all interested persons.

See Schumacher v. Schumacher, 469 N.W.2d 793, 798-99 (N.D. 1991).

The creation of this cause of action and its endorsement by the American Law Institute has met with strong criticism from conservative jurists and scholars. In *Bagdon,* for example, Judge Easterbrook wrote:

> Ohio, like a few other states, has expanded the "special jury" doctrine into a general exception for closely held corporations, treating them as if they were partnerships. . . . The American Law Institute recommends that other states do the same. [Citation omitted.] The premise of this extension may be questioned. Corporations are *not* partnerships. Whether to incorporate entails a choice of many formalities. Commercial rules should be predictable; this objective is best served by treating corporations as what they are, allowing the investors and other participants to vary the rules by contract if they think deviations are warranted. So it is understandable that not all states have joined the parade.

916 F.2d at 383-384.

The Supreme Court of Kansas has never expressly ruled on the issue of whether an oppressed minority shareholder in a close corporation can bring a direct action alleging a breach of fiduciary duties when all of the alleged harm was suffered by the corporation itself. However, in Sampson v. Hunt, 233 Kan. 572, 584-85, 665 P.2d 743 (1983), the court held that "directors have the power to control and direct the affairs of the corporation, and in the *absence of fraud,* courts will generally not interfere on behalf of a dissatisfied stockholder with the discretion of the directors on questions of corporate management, policy or business." (Emphasis added.)

Because the underlying complaint in a minority shareholder freeze-out is the failure of the close corporation to fulfill the shareholder's reasonable expectations, such actions necessarily involve at least one claim of fraud. The present case is no exception. Although the statute of limitations for fraud had expired, Richards presented substantial evidence of fraudulent inducement on the part of [the majority shareholder].

In *Sampson,* the Kansas Supreme Court expressed its intent to intervene on behalf of dissatisfied shareholders if corporate directors behave fraudulently. It follows that the Supreme Court would recognize an exception to the requirement that a minority shareholder bring a derivative action when frozen out of the management of a close corporation through oppressive majority conduct.

Therefore, we conclude that if a corporation is closely held, a court, in its discretion, may treat an action raising derivative claims as a direct action if it finds to do so will not (1) unfairly expose the corporation to a multiplicity of actions; (2) materially prejudice the interests of creditors in the corporation; or (3) interfere with a fair distribution of the recovery among all interested persons.

In the present case, allowing Richards to bring a direct action for his derivative claims will not expose [the corporation] to a multiplicity of actions or interfere with a fair distribution of recovery because Richards and his wife are the only minority shareholders in the corporation. Furthermore, this is to a debtor-creditor action, and there is no indication that a resolution of Richards' claims will prejudice any creditors' interests. Therefore, Richards should be allowed to pursue his breach of fiduciary duty claim, provided that he presents sufficient evidence in the district court to defeat the defendants' motion for summary judgment.

879 P.2d at 647-648.

PROBLEM 5-2

Reconsider Zidell v. Zidell. What results in that case:
(a) If general partnership law rules applied?
(b) Under the reasoning in Wilkes v. Springside Nursing Home, Inc.?
(c) Under Hetherington and Dooley's proposed mandatory buyout rule?

Nixon v. Blackwell
Delaware Supreme Court, 1993
626 A.2d 1366

VEASEY, CHIEF JUSTICE:

In this action we review a decision of the Court of Chancery holding that the defendant directors of a closely-held corporation breached their fiduciary duties to the plaintiffs by maintaining a discriminatory policy that unfairly favors employee stockholders over plaintiffs. The Vice Chancellor found that the directors treated the plaintiffs unfairly by establishing an employee stock ownership plan ("ESOP") and by purchasing key man life insurance policies to provide liquidity for defendants and other corporate employees to enable them to sell their stock while providing no comparable liquidity for minority stockholders. We conclude that the Court of Chancery applied erroneous legal standards and made findings of fact which were not the product of an orderly and logical deductive reasoning process. Accordingly, we reverse and remand to the Court of Chancery for proceedings not inconsistent with this opinion.

I.   FACTS . . .

A.   THE PARTIES

Plaintiffs are 14 minority stockholders of Class B, non-voting, stock of E.C. Barton & Co. (the "Corporation"). The individual defendants are the members of the board of directors (the "Board" or the "directors"). The Corporation is also a defendant. Plaintiffs collectively own only Class B stock, and own no Class A stock. Their total holdings comprise approximately 25 percent of all the common stock outstanding as of the end of fiscal year 1989.

At all relevant times, the Board consisted of ten individuals who either are currently employed, or were once employed, by the Corporation. At the time this suit was filed, these directors collectively owned approximately 47.5 percent of all the outstanding Class A shares. The remaining Class A shares were held by certain other present and former employees of the Corporation.

B. MR. BARTON'S TESTAMENTARY PLAN

The Corporation is a non-public, closely-held Delaware corporation headquartered in Arkansas. It is engaged in the business of selling wholesale and retail lumber in the Mississippi Delta. The Corporation was formed in 1928 by E.C. Barton ("Mr. Barton") and has two classes of common stock: Class A voting stock and Class B non-voting stock. Substantially all of the Corporation's stock was held by Mr. Barton at the time of his death in 1967. . . . Pursuant to Mr. Barton's testamentary plan, 49 percent of the Class A voting stock was bequeathed outright to eight of his loyal employees. The remaining 51 percent, along with 14 percent of the Class B non-voting stock, was placed into an independently managed 15-year trust for the same eight people. Sixty-one percent of the Class B non-voting stock was bequeathed outright to [his second wife, who survived him]. Mr. Barton's daughter and granddaughter [from his first marriage] received 21 percent of the Class B stock in trust. The non-voting Class B shares Mr. Barton bequeathed to his family represented 75 percent of the Corporation's total equity.

. . . In 1973 the Corporation purchased all of the Class B stock held in trust for Mr. Barton's daughter and granddaughter at a price of $45 per share. Mrs. Barton [who had given a portion of her stock to her three children] sold the remainder of her Class B shares to the Corporation in January 1975 at a price of $45 per share. These transactions left Mrs. Barton's three children collectively with 30 percent of the outstanding Class B non-voting stock. The children have no voting rights despite their substantial equity interest in the Corporation. The children are also the only non-employee Class B stockholders.

There is no public market for, or trading in, either class of the Corporation's stock. This creates problems for stockholders, particularly the Class B minority stockholders, who wish to sell or otherwise realize the value of their shares. The corporation purported to address this problem in several ways over the years.

C. THE SELF-TENDERS

The Corporation occasionally offered to purchase the Class B stock of the non-employee stockholders through a series of self-tender offers. During the late 1970s the Corporation attempted to purchase the outstanding Class B shares held by Guy C. Blackwell, Owen G. Blackwell and Martha G. Hestand [Mrs. Barton's children], the Corporation's only non-employee stockholders. The Corporation first offered to repurchase the children's stock at $45 per share shortly after they acquired it from Mrs. Barton. The children rejected the offer and the stock subsequently split 25-for-1 in 1976. A second unsuccessful repurchase offer was made in 1977. At that time, the Corporation offered the children $8.22 per share. In light of the stock split, this price appears to be approximately four times the amount the Corporation paid for Mrs. Barton's Class B shares three years earlier. In 1979 the Corporation again approached the children and offered to repurchase their stock at a price of $15 per share. Martha Hestand accepted the offer and tendered her shares to the Corporation. Guy and Owen Blackwell, however, refused to sell their shares at that price. The Corporation made no further repurchase offers until May 1985, when the ESOP undertook a tender offer to repurchase 48,000 shares of Class B stock, concurrently with a tender offer by the Corporation for 39,000 Class A and 100,000 Class B shares at a price of $25 per share. The book value of the Class A stock and the Class B stock at that time was $38.39 and $26.35, respectively. The remaining children and the other plaintiffs in the present action refused to sell.

D.   THE EMPLOYEE STOCK OWNERSHIP PLAN (ESOP)

In November 1975 the Corporation established an ESOP designed to hold Class B non-voting stock for the benefit of eligible employees of the Corporation. The ESOP is a tax-qualified profit-sharing plan whereby employees of the Corporation are allocated a share of the assets held by the plan in proportion to their annual compensation, subject to certain vesting requirements. The ESOP is funded by annual cash contributions from the Corporation. Under the plan, terminating and retiring employees are entitled to receive their interest in the ESOP by taking Class B stock or cash in lieu of stock. It appears from the record that most terminating employees and retirees elect to receive cash in lieu of stock. The Corporation commissions an annual appraisal of the Corporation to determine the value of its stock for ESOP purposes. Thus, the ESOP provides employee Class B stockholders with a substantial measure of liquidity not available to non-employee stockholders. The Corporation had the option of repurchasing Class A stock from the employees upon their retirement or death. The estates of the employee stockholders did not have a corresponding right to put the stock to the Corporation.

E.   THE KEY MAN INSURANCE POLICIES

The Corporation also purchased certain key man life insurance policies with death benefits payable to the Corporation. Several early policies insuring the lives of key executives and directors were purchased during Mr. Barton's lifetime with death benefits payable to the Corporation. In 1982 the Corporation purchased additional key man policies in connection with agreements entered into between the Corporation and nine key officers and directors. Each executive executed an agreement giving the Corporation a call option to substitute Class B non-voting stock for their Class A voting stock upon the occurrence of certain events, including death and termination of employment, so that the voting shares could be reissued to new key personnel. In return, the Board adopted a resolution creating a non-binding recommendation that . . . [40%] of the key man life insurance proceeds be used to repurchase the exchanged Class B stock from the executives' estates at a price at least equal to 80 percent of their ESOP value . . . 35% for the purchase of shares of E.C. Barton & Company stock from the remaining controlling Class "A" stockholders on a prorata basis; 25% retained by the Employee Stock Ownership Trust for liquidity. . . .

In 1985 the Corporation purchased eight $300,000 key man life insurance policies. . . . The intended use for the proceeds of the key man life insurance policies was to fund the retirement of any unpaid principal and interest on promissory notes issued in payment for Class A stock acquired in one of the [company's] self-tenders . . . and the balance of said proceeds prorated and applied to the unpaid principal and/or interest of such Promissory Notes held by the survivors of the aforementioned insured key men.

In the five-year period, 1985 to 1989, the Corporation paid approximately $450,000 in net key man premiums. The premiums exceeded the Corporation's declared dividends in 1986 and 1989, even after the earnings on the policies were deducted (1986—premiums, $146,614, dividends, $93,133; 1989—premiums, $144,704, dividends, $143,374). . . .

F. DIVIDEND POLICY AND COMPENSATION

The Board from time to time paid modest dividends. Because the earnings were solid in many years and dividends relatively low, the retained earnings of the Corporation continued to increase at a relatively high level. Plaintiffs challenged these corporate decisions as unfair to the minority. There was also a challenge at trial by plaintiffs to the compensation level of the defendants. In view of the ruling of the Vice Chancellor in defendants' favor on the dividend policy and against the plaintiffs on the claim of excessive compensation, from which rulings no appeal was taken by plaintiffs, there is no need to detail the facts relating to those issues, except to the extent, hereinafter discussed, that the trial court referred to the dividend policy in connection with other issues or fairness generally. . . .

III.   RATIONALE OF THE VICE CHANCELLOR'S DECISION . . .

The only issue before this Court is the ruling by the trial court as implemented in its judgment and final order that the defendants breached their fiduciary duties by failing to provide a parity of liquidity. The theory of the trial court on this issue is based upon the fact that, as directors, defendants approved the ESOP and the key man life insurance program, both of which had the effect of benefiting them as employees, with no corresponding benefit to plaintiffs. Thus, the trial court reasoned, defendants are on both sides of the transaction and the business judgment rule does not apply. Therefore, defendants have the burden of showing the entire fairness of their actions on these issues, which burden the Vice Chancellor held they had not carried.

The following portions of the opinion of the trial court are crucial to the determination of the issues on appeal:

> The inquiry does not end, however, with a finding that defendants have not been overcompensated. They have paid low dividends over the years and have attempted to justify high levels of retained earnings in part as a means of promoting the company's growth. If defendants' focus is on appreciation in the value of the company's stock as opposed to the payment of more than minimal dividends, it would be logical to assume that defendants had or were developing a plan that would enable the company's stockholders to realize the increased value of their shares. No such general plan has been adopted, however, and the few steps defendants have taken demonstrate the validity of plaintiffs' claim of unfair treatment.

All Barton stockholders face the same liquidity problem. If they are to sell their shares, they must persuade defendants to authorize a repurchase by the company. The stockholders have no bargaining power and must accept whatever terms are dictated by defendants or retain their stock. If the stockholder is pressed for cash to pay estate taxes, for example, as has happened more than once, the stockholder is entirely at defendants' mercy. Defendants recognized their employee stockholders' liquidity needs when they established the ESOP. As noted previously, employees have the option of taking cash in lieu of the shares allocated to their accounts. Moreover, the disparity in bargaining position is eliminated for employee stockholders because the cash payment is determined on the basis of an annual valuation made by an independent party. *No similar plan or arrangement has been put into place with respect to the Class B stockholders. There is no point in time at which they can be assured of receiving cash for all or any portion of their holdings at a price determined by an independent appraiser.*

Defendants have gone one step farther in addressing their own liquidity problems. Their ESOP allocation may be handled in the same manner as other employees. However, defendants are substantial stockholders independent of their ESOP holdings. *In order to solve defendants' own liquidity problem, the company has been purchasing key man life insurance since at least 1982. The proceeds will help assure that Barton is in a position to purchase all of defendants' stock at the time of death.* In 1989, the premium cost for the key man insurance was slightly higher than the total amount paid in dividends for the year.

While the purchase of key man life insurance may be a relatively small corporate expenditure, it is concrete evidence that defendants have favored their own interests as stockholders over plaintiffs'. It also makes one wonder whether the decisions to accumulate large amounts of cash and pay low dividends were not also at least partially motivated by self-interest. The law is settled that fiduciaries may not benefit themselves at the expense of the corporation, Guth v. Loft, Inc., 23 Del. Ch. 255, 5 A.2d 503, 510 (1939), and that, when directors make self-interested decisions, they must establish the entire fairness of those decisions. Weinberger v. UOP, Inc., Del. Supr., 457 A.2d 701, 710 (1983).

I find it inherently unfair for defendants to be purchasing key man life insurance in order to provide liquidity for themselves while providing no method by which plaintiffs may liquidate their stock at fair value. By this ruling, I am not suggesting that there is some generalized duty to purchase illiquid stock at any particular price. However, the needs of all stockholders must be considered and addressed when decisions are made to provide some form of liquidity. Both the ESOP and the key man insurance provide some measure of liquidity, but only for a select group of stockholders. Accordingly, I find that relief is warranted.

Blackwell v. Nixon, Del. Ch., C.A. No. 9041, Berger, V.C. (Sept. 26, 1991) at pp. 10-13 (footnotes omitted; emphasis supplied). . . .

V. APPLICABLE PRINCIPLES OF SUBSTANTIVE LAW

Defendants contend that the trial court erred in not applying the business judgment rule. Since the defendants benefited from the ESOP and could have benefited from the key man life insurance beyond that which benefited other stockholders generally, the defendants are on both sides of the transaction. For that reason, we agree with the trial court that the entire fairness test applies to this aspect of the case. Accordingly, defendants have the burden of showing the entire fairness of those transactions. Sinclair Oil Corp. v. Levien, Del. Supr., 280 A.2d 717 (1971) (*"Levien"*); Weinberger v. UOP, Inc., Del. Supr., 457 A.2d 701 (1983) (*"Weinberger"*). . . .

Weinberger explains further the two aspects of entire fairness, fair price and fair dealing: . . . The case before us involves only the issue of fair dealing. . . .

The trial court in this case, however, appears to have adopted the novel legal principle that Class B stockholders had a right to "liquidity" equal to that which the court found to be available to the defendants. It is well established in our jurisprudence that stockholders need not always be treated equally for all purposes. See Unocal Corp. v. Mesa Petroleum Co., Del. Supr., 493 A.2d 946, 957 (1985) (discriminatory exchange offer held valid); and Cheff v. Mathes, 41 Del. Ch. 494, 199 A.2d 548, 554-56 (1964) (selective stock repurchase held valid). To hold that fairness necessarily requires precise equality is to beg the question:

> Many scholars, though few courts, conclude that one aspect of fiduciary duty is the equal treatment of investors. Their argument takes the following form: Fiduciary principles require fair conduct; equal treatment is fair conduct; hence, Fiduciary principles require equal treatment. The conclusion does not follow. The argument depends on an equivalence between *equal* and *fair* treatment. To say that fiduciary principles require equal treatment is to beg the question whether investors would contract for equal or even equivalent treatment.

Frank H. Easterbrook and Daniel R. Fischel, The Economic Structure of Corporate Law 110 (1991) (emphasis in original). This holding of the trial court overlooks the significant facts that the minority stockholders were not: (a) employees of the Corporation; (b) entitled to share in an ESOP; (c) qualified for key man insurance; or (d) protected by specific provisions in the certificate of incorporation, by-laws, or a stockholders' agreement.

There is support in this record for the fact that the ESOP is a corporate benefit and was established, at least in part, to benefit the Corporation. Generally speaking, the creation of ESOPs is a normal corporate practice and is generally thought to benefit the corporation. The same is true generally with respect to key man insurance programs. If such corporate practices were necessarily to require equal treatment for non-employee stockholders, that would be a matter for legislative determination in Delaware. There is no such legislation to that effect. If we were to adopt such a rule, our decision would border on judicial legislation. See Providence & Worcester Co. v. Baker, Del. Supr., 378 A.2d 121, 124 (1977).

Accordingly, we hold that the Vice Chancellor erred as a matter of law in concluding that the liquidity afforded to the employee stockholders by the ESOP and the key man insurance required substantially equal treatment for the non-employee stockholders. Moreover, the Vice Chancellor failed to evaluate and articulate, for example, whether or not and to what extent (a) corporate benefits flowed from the ESOP and the key man insurance; (b) the ESOP and key man insurance plans are novel, extraordinary, or relatively routine business practices; (c) the dividend policy was even relevant; (d) Mr. Barton's plan for employee management and benefits should be honored; and (e) the self-tenders showed defendants' willingness to provide an exit opportunity for the plaintiffs.

. . . The decision of the trial court did not plainly delineate and articulate findings of fact and conclusions of law so that this Court, as the reviewing court, could fathom without undue difficulty the bases for the trial court's decision. The court's decision should not be the product solely of subjective, reflexive impressions based primarily on suspicion[16] or what has sometimes been called the "smell test."[17]

We hold on this record that defendants have met their burden of establishing the entire fairness of their dealings with the non-employee Class B stockholders, and are entitled to judgment. The record is sufficient to conclude that plaintiffs' claim that the defendant directors have maintained a discriminatory policy of favoring Class A employee stockholders over Class B non-employee stockholders is without merit. The directors have followed a consistent policy originally established by Mr. Barton, the founder of the Corporation, whose intent from the formation of the Corporation was to use the Class A stock as the vehicle for the Corporation's continuity through employee management and ownership.

Mr. Barton established the Corporation in 1928 by creating two classes of stock, not one, and by holding 100 percent of the Class A stock and 82 percent of the Class B stock. Mr. Barton himself established the practice of purchasing key man life insurance with funds of the Corporation to retain in the employ of the Corporation valuable employees by assuring them that, following their retirement or death, the Corporation will have liquid assets which could be used to repurchase the shares acquired by the employee, which shares may otherwise constitute an illiquid and unsalable asset of his or her estate. Another rational purpose is to prevent the stock from passing out of the control of the employees of the Corporation into the hands of family or descendants of the employee.

The directors' actions following Mr. Barton's death are consistent with Mr. Barton's plan. An ESOP, for example, is normally established for employees. Accordingly, there is no inequity in limiting ESOP benefits to the employee stockholders. Indeed, it makes no sense to include non-employees in ESOP benefits. The fact that the Class B stock represented 75 percent of the Corporation's total equity is irrelevant to the issue of fair dealing. The Class B stock was given no voting rights because those stockholders

---

16. We note that the Vice Chancellor, as the trier of fact, expressed what can best be described as "suspicions" about the motivation for the key man insurance. This Court respects and gives deference to findings of fact by trial courts when supported by the record, and when they are the product of an orderly and logical deductive reasoning process, especially when those findings are based in part on testimony of live witnesses whose demeanor and credibility the trial judge has had the opportunity to evaluate. Footnote 3 at page 12 of the Vice Chancellor's opinion is a demonstration of credibility issues properly left to the trial court, but otherwise the crucial findings in the Vice Chancellor's opinion are somewhat vague and the opinion does not crisply and clearly set forth findings of fact in a form which we believe is entitled to such deference. Thus, we hold that these findings are not the product of an orderly and logical deductive reasoning process.

17. We are mindful of the elasticity inherent in equity jurisprudence and the traditional desirability in certain equity cases of measuring conduct by the "conscience of the court" and disapproving conduct which offends or shocks that conscience. Yet one must be wary of equity jurisprudence which takes on a random or ad hoc quality.

> Equity is a rougish [*sic*] thing. For law we have to measure, know what to trust to; Equity is according to the conscience of him that is Chancellor, and as that is larger or narrower, so it Equity. 'Tis all one as if they should make the standard for the measure we call a "foot" a Chancellor's foot; what an uncertain measure would this be. One Chancellor has a long foot, another a short foot, a third an indifferent foot. 'Tis the same thing in the Chancellor's conscience.

John Selden, 1584-1654. "Equity," Table-Talk, 1689. The Quotable Lawyer 97 (David S. Shrager and Elizabeth Frost eds., 1986).

were not intended to have a direct voice in the management and operation of the Corporation. They were simply passive investors—entitled to be treated fairly but not necessarily to be treated equally. The fortunes of the Corporation rested with the Class A employee stockholders and the Class B stockholders benefited from the multiple increases in value of their Class B stock. Moreover, the Board made continuing efforts to buy back the Class B stock. . . .

VI.   NO SPECIAL RULES FOR A CLOSELY HELD CORPORATION NOT QUALIFIED AS A CLOSE CORPORATION UNDER SUBCHAPTER XIV OF THE DELAWARE GENERAL CORPORATION LAW

We wish to address one further matter which was raised at oral argument before this Court: Whether there should be any special, judicially-created rules to "protect" minority stockholders of closely-held Delaware corporations.[18]

The case at bar points up the basic dilemma of minority stockholders in receiving fair value for their stock as to which there is no market and no market valuation. It is not difficult to be sympathetic, in the abstract, to a stockholder who finds himself or herself in that position. A stockholder who bargains for stock in a closely-held corporation and who pays for those shares (unlike the plaintiffs in this case who acquired their stock through gift) can make a business judgment whether to buy into such a minority position, and if so on what terms. One could bargain for definitive provisions of self-ordering permitted to a Delaware corporation through the certificate of incorporation or by-laws by reason of the provisions in 8 Del. C. §§102, 109, and 141(a). Moreover, in addition to such mechanisms, a stockholder intending to buy into a minority position in a Delaware corporation may enter into definitive stockholder agreements, and such agreements may provide for elaborate earnings tests, buy-out provisions, voting trusts, or other voting agreements. See, e.g., 8 Del. C. §218; Sonitrol Holding Co. v. Marceau Investissements, Del. Supr., 607 A.2d 1177 (1992).

The tools of good corporate practice are designed to give a purchasing minority stockholder the opportunity to bargain for protection before parting with consideration. It would do violence to normal corporate practice and our corporation law to fashion an ad hoc ruling which would result in a court-imposed stockholder buy-out for which the parties had not contracted.

In 1967, when the Delaware General Corporation Law was significantly revised, a new Subchapter XIV entitled "Close Corporations; Special Provisions," became a part of that law for the first time. . . . Subchapter XIV is a narrowly constructed statute which applies only to a corporation which is designated as a "close corporation" in its certificate of incorporation, and which fulfills other requirements, including a

---

18. Compare Robert B. Thompson, The Shareholder's Cause of Action for Oppression, 48 Bus. Law. 699 (1993) and F. Hodge O'Neal and Robert B. Thompson, O'Neal's Close Corporations: Law and Practice, §§8.07-8.09 (3d ed. 1987) (favoring court formulation of a special rule protecting the minority from oppression) with Frank H. Easterbrook and Daniel R. Fischel, The Economic Structure of Corporate Law 228-52 (1991) (noting that "courts have found the equal opportunity rule . . . impossible to administer," id. at 247).

limitation to 30 on the number of stockholders, that all classes of stock have to have at least one restriction on transfer, and that there be no "public offering." 8 Del. C. §342. . . . "Unless a corporation elects to become a close corporation under this subchapter in the manner prescribed in this subchapter, it shall be subject in all respects to this chapter, except this subchapter." 8 Del. C. §341. The corporation before the Court in this matter, is not a "close corporation." Therefore it is not governed by the provisions of Subchapter XIV.

One cannot read into the situation presented in the case at bar any special relief for the minority stockholders in this closely-held, but not statutory "close corporation" because the provisions of Subchapter XIV relating to close corporations and other statutory schemes preempt the field in their respective areas. It would run counter to the spirit of the doctrine of independent legal significance,[21] and would be inappropriate judicial legislation for this Court to fashion a special judicially-created rule for minority investors when the entity does not fall within those statutes, or when there are no negotiated special provisions in the certificate of incorporation, by-laws, or stockholder agreements. The entire fairness test, correctly applied and articulated, is the proper judicial approach. . . .

NOTES AND QUESTIONS

1. The Delaware Supreme Court's statement in Nixon v. Blackwell is a forceful endorsement of ex ante contracting as a response to minority shareholder concerns and a very limited role for ex post judging in resolving close corporation disputes. Delaware's dominance in corporate law derives from its being home to more than half of the country's largest companies. Do you think that orientation will influence how Delaware responds to law in the close corporation context? Ian Ayres has suggested that legislators "might want either to force close corporations to abide by public-corporation law to feed a larger (and more valuable) precedent pool, or to force close corporations to clearly opt for separate legal treatment to avoid the application of confusing (and therefore less valuable) close corporation precedent to publicly held incorporations." See Ayres, Judging Close Corporations in the Age of Statutes, 70 Wash. U. L.Q. 365, 395 (1992).

2. As Professor Charles O'Kelley notes, "[T]here are at least three possible reasons why investors . . . would not contract for the perfect governance structure. First, contracting is not costless, and the costs of contracting might exceed the predicted benefits. Second, actual investors may not be fully rational, resulting in mistaken failure to contract. Third, rational investors might predict that courts will exercise their

---

21. . . . The principle holds that the validity of a transaction accomplished pursuant to a specified section or sections of the statute will be tested by the standards applicable to those sections and not by those of other provisions, even though the ultimate economic results could have been achieved through use of procedures authorized by such other provisions and even though use of such other procedures might have created different rights among those affected by the transaction. [Eds. note—The doctrine of independent legal significance is discussed in Chapter 9 of this text.]

equitable gap-filling powers to provide optimal governance rule to the parties ex post, thereby making ex ante contracting unnecessary." See O'Kelley, Filling Gaps in the Close Corporation Contract: A Transaction Cost Analysis, 87 Nw. U. L. Rev. 216, 247 (1992). Awareness of this third reason, investor's ex ante reliance on expected ex post judging, should make efficiency-minded judges hesitate before engaging in ex post judicial contracting. "[I]f courts contract for the parties this will create disincentives for the parties themselves to identify via contract the mix between opportunism and adaptability that they prefer. A court should create this disincentive only if it is likely that the court will be able to determine ex post better that the parties themselves could ex ante which governance structure is 'ideal.'" Id.

Is this analysis helpful in the actual facts of Nixon v. Blackwell?

3. How should the recent and rapid adoption of various alternative business forms to closely held corporations affect a court's decision to apply partnership norms in resolving disputes in close corporations or other closely held businesses? The limited liability company, limited liability partnership, and other forms discussed in Chapters 2 and 6 grant participants limited liability and pass-through tax treatment while providing some or all of the internal governance rules from partnership law. The mere availability of these alternative forms would seem to bolster the court's view in Nixon v. Blackwell that participants should look out for themselves and can expect very little relief from the courts in the form of ex post fiduciary duty.

The use of these new forms does not appear to be free of ambiguity. Limited liability companies were originally driven by an effort to achieve limited liability and pass-through tax treatment for entities that because of regulatory or ethical burdens were unable to achieve that combination. Governance rules approached partnership norms only to the extent necessary to persuade the Internal Revenue Service to provide the favorable (noncorporate) tax treatment. Since 1996, when the Internal Revenue Service abandoned the use of partnership governance norms as the basis for pass-through tax treatment, many LLC statutes have been amended to decrease or eliminate the ability of members to exit. This will raise squeeze-out problems that have long been a focus of close corporation law. LLC law is likely to move closer to close corporation law and pose similar questions as to the relative attraction of ex ante contracting and ex post judging. Ex ante contracting may still be preferred over ex post judging, but the contribution of the choice of business form remains ambiguous.

3. The Modern Approach to Involuntary Dissolution

MBCA §§14.30, 14.34

At about the same time that courts began to grant relief based on the partnership analogy, courts also began to broaden the scope of equitable relief available via a minority shareholder's petition for involuntary dissolution. Some states have enacted liberal involuntary dissolution provisions that instruct courts to take into account shareholders' reasonable expectations or interests in fashioning relief. Under the evolving doctrine, courts view dissolution as a viable remedy for truly egregious conduct and are increasingly willing to order corporations to repurchase the complaining minority's shares in order to protect shareholders' reasonable expectations or to remedy oppression.

In 1990, the ABA Committee on Corporate Laws added new §14.34 to the MBCA. Section 14.34, modeled after New York Bus. Corp. Law §1118, grants the defendant corporation the right to avoid a court-ordered involuntary dissolution by electing to repurchase the complaining minority's shares for fair value. Section 14.34 is grounded in Hetherington and Dooley's thesis that illiquidity is the central problem of the close corporation. However, §14.34 gives the majority rather than the minority the right to determine whether buyout will occur.

Thompson, The Shareholder's Cause of Action for Oppression

48 Bus. Law. 699-700, 705-709, 715-719 (1993)

Corporate statutes and judicial decisions reflect norms designed for publicly held corporations and do not always meet the needs of closely held enterprises. The statutory norms of centralized control and majority rule, when combined with the lack of a public market for shares in a close corporation, leave a minority shareholder vulnerable in a way that is distinct from the risk faced by investors in public corporations. After a falling out among participants in a closely held corporation, a minority investor may face an indefinite period with no return on his or her investment in the enterprise, or perhaps a squeeze out by the majority shareholder in contravention of the investor's initial expectations.

. . . [L]egislatures and courts have responded to this dilemma [in two ways]. First, legislatures have broadened the grounds for judicial dissolution of a corporation at the request of a minority shareholder and have provided additional remedies as alternatives to involuntary dissolution. Courts, in turn, are more likely today than in the past to interpret the statutory grounds for dissolution in a way that provides relief for minority shareholders, particularly by focusing on the reasonable expectations of shareholders. Judges are more inclined to use buyouts or other alternative remedies, even in the absence of specific statutory authorization. Second, courts have expanded significantly the ability of shareholders in a close corporation to bring a direct, individual cause of action based on a majority shareholder's breach of fiduciary duty. Courts have enhanced the duty owed to minority shareholders in a close corporation and have allowed them to bring direct suit rather than just a derivative suit brought in the name of the corporation.

These two developments have not always been directly connected, but both reflect the same legal principles and illustrate the modern legal response to the awkwardness arising when close corporations are placed in a structure designed for much larger enterprises. The standards used by some courts to determine a breach of fiduciary duty leading to a direct cause of action for the shareholder are substantially the same as the standards used by other courts to define oppression as a ground for involuntary dissolution. In some states, the enhanced fiduciary duty has evolved in the absence of an oppression statute. In other states, the statutory remedy has been the dominant legal response. The two doctrines overlap but are not completely interchangeable;

there are times when one is preferred to the other. Their purposes and effects, however, are so sufficiently similar that it makes sense to think of them as two manifestations of minority shareholder's cause of action for oppression. . . .

These developments have moved close corporation law more in the direction of partnership law, where dissolution has been relatively easier, but short of the proposal of Professors Hetherington and Dooley to permit minority shareholders to force a buy out with even fewer restrictions than in partnership law. Withdrawal of an investor's capital comes at a cost to the remaining participants—they may have to reduce the size of their business, take out a potentially costly loan, or seek a new shareholder. Limitations on withdrawal rights in both partnership and close corporation law to some extent reflect these costs.

Frank Easterbrook and Dan Fischel . . . argue against pushing the partnership analogy too far. They warn against treating a decision to incorporate as a desire for other than the traditional corporate norms and, in particular, suggest that courts should not readily infer a right of a minority shareholder to withdraw capital. [Recent] statutes and decisions . . . reflect a somewhat different view, recognizing that the potential permanent disenfranchisement of a minority investor who has fallen out of favor with his or her co-venturers is not an appropriate norm for close corporations. Permitting a minority shareholder to petition for involuntary dissolution permits some judicial intervention in appropriate circumstances. This reliance on judicial decision-making permits courts to block relief where the minority shareholder's action makes it inappropriate to impose on the remaining shareholders the costs of providing immediate liquidity. Even with this role for courts to provide relief for oppression, the corporate form gives more discretion to the majority shareholders and costs less than alternative forms of doing business. . . .

Most American jurisdictions now permit a shareholder to petition for dissolution on a variety of grounds. Illegality, fraud, misapplication of assets, and waste are listed as grounds for dissolution in most state statutes, although these terms standing alone have not been cited often as grounds for dissolution by courts. Oppressive conduct by the majority or controlling shareholder now is listed widely in most state dissolution statutes, and has become the principal vehicle used by legislatures, courts, and litigants to address the particular needs of close corporations. Many states have broadened further their dissolution statutes to authorize relief if necessary to protect the rights or interests of complaining shareholders or if a close corporation participant's reasonable expectations have been frustrated. Indeed, it is fair to say that the remedy has outgrown its dissolution origins and now is better described as a general remedy for shareholder dissension within a close corporation that only rarely results in the dissolution of a corporation. Even when dissolution was the only relief granted by courts, the parties in most cases usually agreed upon an alternative that permitted one or more parties to continue operating the business. As the legislative and judicial remedies have broadened, dissolution is even less likely to be ordered. Thus, it makes more sense to view oppression not as a ground for dissolution, but as a remedy for shareholder dissension. . . .

The increased use of reasonable expectations to construe *oppression* and similar statutory terms has become an easily accessible label to identify the special nature of close corporations, underlying the legislative purpose in enacting involuntary dissolution statutes and statutes providing other remedies. . . .

Consideration of the broadened use of the oppression action is incomplete without also focusing on the remedy provided if oppression is found. The most dramatic change in legislative and judicial thinking on solutions to minority shareholder problems is reflected in the increased popularity of a buyout as a remedy for deadlock or dissension. Legislative or judicial support for this remedy now exists in half of the states, although the criteria for its use are not uniform. In some states, a statute permits the corporation or majority shareholders to buy the shares of a minority shareholder seeking involuntary dissolution. In other states, a statute authorizes courts to order buyouts as one of several possible remedies in dissolution proceedings or other litigation among shareholders. Courts also may order buyouts pursuant to their general equitable authority. . . .

In re Kemp & Beatley, Inc.

New York Court of Appeals, 1984

64 N.Y.2d 63, 473 N.E.2d 1173, 484 N.Y.S.2d 799

COOKE, CHIEF JUDGE. . . .

I.

The business concern of Kemp & Beatley, incorporated under the laws of New York, designs and manufactures table linens and sundry tabletop items. The company's stock consists of 1,500 outstanding shares held by eight shareholders. Petitioner Dissin had been employed by the company for 42 years when, in June 1979, he resigned. Prior to resignation, Dissin served as vice-president and a director of Kemp & Beatley. Over the course of his employment, Dissin had acquired stock in the company and currently owns 200 shares.

Petitioner Gardstein, like Dissin, had been a long-time employee of the company. Hired in 1944, Gardstein was for the next 35 years involved in various aspects of the business including material procurement, product design, and plant management. His employment was terminated by the company in December 1980. He currently owns 105 shares of Kemp & Beatley stock.

Apparent unhappiness surrounded petitioners' leaving the employ of the company. Of particular concern was that they no longer received any distribution of the company's earnings. Petitioners considered themselves to be "frozen out" of the company; whereas it had been their experience when with the company to receive a distribution of the company's earnings according to their stockholdings, in the form of either dividends or extra compensation, that distribution was no longer forthcoming.

Gardstein and Dissin, together holding 20.33% of the company's outstanding stock, commenced the instant proceeding in June 1981, seeking dissolution of Kemp & Beatley pursuant to §1104-a of the Business Corporation Law. Their petition alleged "fraudulent and oppressive" conduct by the company's board of directors such as to render petitioners' stock "a virtually worthless asset." Supreme Court referred the matter for a hearing, which was held in March 1982.

Upon considering the testimony of petitioners and the principals of Kemp & Beatley, the referee concluded that "the corporate management has by its policies effectively rendered petitioners' shares worthless, and . . . the only way petitioners can expect any return is by dissolution." Petitioners were found to have invested capital in the company expecting, among other things, to receive dividends or "bonuses" based upon their stock holdings. Also found was the company's "established buy-out policy" by which it would purchase the stock of employee shareholders upon their leaving its employ. . . .

Supreme Court confirmed the referee's report. It, too, concluded that due to the corporation's new dividend policy petitioners had been prevented from receiving any return on their investments. . . . The Appellate Division affirmed, without opinion.

At issue in this appeal is the scope of §1104-a of the Business Corporation Law. Specifically, this court must determine whether the provision for involuntary dissolution when the "directors or those in control of the corporation have been guilty of . . . oppressive actions toward the complaining shareholders" was properly applied in the circumstances of this case. We hold that it was, and therefore affirm.

II.

. . . [T]he Legislature has shown a special solicitude toward the rights of minority shareholders of closely held corporations by enacting §1104-a of the Business Corporation Law. That statute provides a mechanism for the holders of at least 20% of the outstanding shares of a corporation whose stock is not traded on a securities market to petition for its dissolution "under special circumstances." . . .

Section 1104-a (subd. (a), par. (1)) describes three types of proscribed activity: "illegal," "fraudulent," and "oppressive" conduct. The first two terms are familiar words that are commonly understood at law. The last, however, does not enjoy the same certainty gained through long usage. As no definition is provided by the statute, it falls upon the courts to provide guidance.

The statutory concept of "oppressive actions" can, perhaps, best be understood by examining the characteristics of close corporations and the Legislature's general purpose in creating this involuntary-dissolution statute. It is widely understood that, in addition to supplying capital to a contemplated or ongoing enterprise and expecting a fair and equal return, parties comprising the ownership of a close corporation may expect to be actively involved in its management and operation.

As a leading commentator in the field has observed: "Unlike the typical shareholder in a publicly held corporation, who may be simply an investor or a speculator and cares nothing for the responsibilities of management, the shareholder in a close corporation is a co-owner of the business and wants the privileges and powers that go with ownership. His participation in that particular corporation is often his principal or sole source of income. As a matter of fact, providing employment for himself may have been the principal reason why he participated in organizing the corporation. He may or may not anticipate an ultimate profit from the sale of his interest, but he normally draws very little from the corporation as dividends. In his capacity as an officer or employee of the corporation, he looks to his salary for the principal return on his capital investment, because earnings of a close corporation, as is well known, are distributed in major part in salaries, bonuses and retirement benefits." (O'Neal, Close Corporations [2d ed.], §1.07, at pp. 21-22.) . . .

As the stock of closely held corporations generally is not readily salable, a minority shareholder at odds with management policies may be without either a voice in protecting his or her interests or any reasonable means of withdrawing his or her investment. This predicament may fairly be considered the legislative concern underlying the provision at issue in this case; inclusion of the criteria that the corporation's stock not be traded on securities markets and that the complaining shareholder be subject to oppressive actions supports this conclusion.

Defining oppressive conduct as distinct from illegality in the present context has been considered in other forums. The question has been resolved by considering oppressive actions to refer to conduct that substantially defeats the "reasonable expectations" held by minority shareholders in committing their capital to the particular enterprise. This concept is consistent with the apparent purpose underlying the provision under review. A shareholder who reasonably expected that ownership in the corporation would entitle him or her to a job, a share of corporate earnings, a place in corporate management, or some other form of security, would be oppressed in a very real sense when others in the corporation seek to defeat those expectations and there exists no effective means of salvaging the investment.

Given the nature of close corporations and the remedial purpose of the statute, this court holds that utilizing a complaining shareholder's "reasonable expectations" as a means of identifying and measuring conduct alleged to be oppressive is appropriate. A court considering a petition alleging oppressive conduct must investigate what the majority shareholders knew, or should have known, to be the petitioner's expectations in entering the particular enterprise. Majority conduct should not be deemed oppressive simply because the petitioner's subjective hopes and desires in joining the venture are not fulfilled. Disappointment alone should not necessarily be equated with oppression.

Rather, oppression should be deemed to arise only when the majority conduct substantially defeats expectations that, objectively viewed, were both reasonable under the circumstances and were central to the petitioner's decision to join the venture. It would be inappropriate, however, for us in this case to delineate the contours of the courts' consideration in determining whether directors have been guilty of oppressive conduct. As in other areas of the law, much will depend on the circumstances in the individual case.

The appropriateness of an order of dissolution is in every case vested in the sound discretion of the court considering the application. Under the terms of this statute, courts are instructed to consider both whether "liquidation of the corporation is the only feasible means" to protect the complaining shareholder's expectation of a fair return on his or her investment and whether dissolution "is reasonably necessary" to protect "the rights or interests of any substantial number of shareholders" not limited to those complaining. Implicit in this direction is that once oppressive conduct is found, consideration must be given to the totality of circumstances surrounding the current state of corporate affairs and relations to determine whether some remedy short of or other than dissolution constitutes a feasible means of satisfying both the petitioner's expectations and the rights and interests of any other substantial group of shareholders.

By invoking the statute, a petitioner has manifested his or her belief that dissolution may be the only appropriate remedy. Assuming the petitioner has set forth a prima facie case of oppressive conduct, it should be incumbent upon the parties seeking to forestall dissolution to demonstrate to the court the existence of an adequate, alternative remedy. A court has broad latitude in fashioning alternative relief, but when fulfillment of the oppressed petitioner's expectations by these means is doubtful, such as when there has been a complete deterioration of relations between the parties, a court should not hesitate to order dissolution. Every order of dissolution, however, must be conditioned upon permitting any shareholder of the corporation to elect to purchase the complaining shareholder's stock at fair value (see Business Corporation Law, §1118).

One further observation is in order. The purpose of this involuntary dissolution statute is to provide protection to the minority shareholder whose reasonable expectations in undertaking the venture have been frustrated and who has no adequate means of recovering his or her investment. It would be contrary to this remedial purpose to permit its use by minority shareholders as merely a coercive tool. Therefore, the minority shareholder whose own acts, made in bad faith and undertaken with a view toward forcing an involuntary dissolution, give rise to the complained-of oppression should be given no quarter in the statutory protection.

III.

There was sufficient evidence presented at the hearing to support the conclusion that Kemp & Beatley had a long-standing policy of awarding de facto dividends based on stock ownership in the form of "extra compensation bonuses." Petitioners, both of whom had extensive experience in the management of the company, testified to this effect. Moreover, both related that receipt of this compensation, whether as true dividends or disguised as "extra compensation," was a known incident to ownership of the company's stock understood by all of the company's principals. Finally, there was uncontroverted proof that this policy was changed either shortly before or shortly after petitioners' employment ended. Extra compensation was still awarded by the company. The only difference was that stock ownership was no longer a basis for the payments; it was asserted that the basis became services rendered to the corporation. It was not unreasonable for the fact finder to have determined that this change in policy amounted to nothing less than an attempt to exclude petitioners from gaining any return on their investment through the mere recharacterization of distributions of corporate income. Under the circumstances of this case, there was no error in determining that this conduct constituted oppressive action within the meaning of §1104-a of the Business Corporation Law.

Nor may it be said that the Supreme Court abused its discretion in ordering Kemp & Beatley's dissolution, subject to an opportunity for a buy-out of petitioners' shares. After the referee had found that the controlling faction of the company was, in effect, attempting to "squeeze-out" petitioners by offering them no return on their investment and increasing other executive compensation, respondents, in opposing the report's confirmation, attempted only to controvert the factual basis of the report. They suggested no feasible, alternative remedy to the forced dissolution. In light of an apparent deterioration in relations between petitioners and the governing share-holders of Kemp & Beatley, it was not unreasonable for the court to have determined that a forced buy-out of petitioners' shares or liquidation of the corporation's assets was the only means by which petitioners could be guaranteed a fair return on their investments. . . .

Gimpel v. Bolstein

New York Supreme Court, 1984
125 Misc. 2d 45, 477 N.Y.S.2d 1014

ARTHUR W. LONSCHEIN, JUSTICE.

Gimpel is a shareholder in Gimpel Farms, Inc. Believing himself oppressed by the conduct of his fellow shareholders, he has brought a petition to dissolve the corporation pursuant to §1104-a of the Business Corporation Law and a derivative action pursuant to §626 of the Business Corporation Law. . . .

The essential facts may be simply stated:

Gimpel Farms is a family corporation engaged in the dairy business. It was founded in 1931 by Louis Gimpel, and control has now passed through his heirs of the second generation (his son and Robert's father, David Gimpel, and his son-in-law, Moe Bolstein) to his heirs of the third generation (Robert, his brother George, and his cousin Diane Bolstein Kaufman). David Gimpel died in 1980, leaving his voting stock to Robert and George and his non-voting stock to his wife Shirley. Moe Bolstein is still alive, but has sold all of his shares to his daughter Diane.

The family members have always participated actively in the management and daily operations of the company and have taken their recompense in the form of salary and perquisites. Moe Bolstein continues to be employed by the corporation as an officer and executive, and draws a substantial salary, although the amount of work he actually does is in dispute. Diane Kaufman's husband, Charles, and George Gimpel also are employed by the corporation in executive capacities and draw substantial salaries. It appears that no dividends have ever been paid.

Robert owns his stock by gift and bequest from his father. He was employed by the company in an important and sensitive managerial position until 1974, when he was discharged due to allegations that he had embezzled some $85,000. The defendants put forth substantial evidence to support these allegations. Robert rebuts them with a form of artful evasion properly characterized as a "non-denial denial," that is, he never actually states that he did not embezzle the funds. He says, instead, that he was never prosecuted for any crime and that the statute of limitations for such a prosecution has passed. Further, as he delicately phrases it, his father "adjusted any disputed financial transaction." This is insufficient to controvert the point, and for the purposes of this motion the court deems it established that in 1975 Robert was, in fact, a thief, that he stole from the family company, and was discharged from all company employment when his theft became known.

Since that time, Robert has received no benefits from his ownership position with this obviously profitable company. The company has continued to adhere to its policy of not paying dividends and, while the other shareholders have received substantial sums as salary, benefits and perquisites, Robert has received not a penny. Not surprisingly, he has also been excluded from all managerial decisions (there have been no formal shareholders' meetings) and has received the barest minimum of information concerning company affairs. The only opportunity Robert has had to gain from his interest came in 1980, when, after his father's death, the other shareholders offered to buy out his shares at a figure which he rejected as inadequate.

THE PETITION FOR DISSOLUTION

The court has the power to order the dissolution of a corporation where "the directors or those in control of the corporation have been guilty of illegal, fraudulent or oppressive actions toward the complaining shareholders" (BCL, §1104-a(a)(1)) or where "the property or assets of the corporation are being looted, wasted or diverted for non-corporate purposes by its directors, officers or those in control." (BCL, §1104-a(a)(2).) Dissolution under this section is discretionary. It is a "drastic" remedy, and before ordering it the court must consider whether it is the only means by which the complaining shareholders can reasonably expect to receive a fair return on their investment or whether it is reasonably necessary to protect their rights and interests. (BCL, §1104-a(b).) The corporation or any of its shareholders may avoid the proceeding by electing to purchase the petitioner's shares at their fair value. (BCL, §1118.)

Here, Robert has alleged both "oppressive" actions under §1104-a(a)(1) of the Business Corporation Law and waste and diversion of corporate assets under §1104-a(a)(2) of the Business Corporation Law. None of the respondents has elected to purchase his shares although the time in which they may do so as a matter of right has expired[4] (BCL, §1118(a)) and so the court must determine whether the statutory standards for dissolution have been met.

Robert alleges numerous acts by the majority which he claims constitute "oppressive" conduct. Stripped of the legal interpretations and conclusory language with which they are presented, the allegations fall into three categories:

(1) He has been excluded from "corporate participation";

(2) The profits of the corporation are distributed to the majority interests in the form of salaries, benefits and perquisites, with no dividends being declared; whereby Robert derives no benefit whatsoever from his ownership interest; and

---

4. Respondents in an 1104-a proceeding may frequently be reluctant to commit themselves to purchase a petitioner's shares without knowing the price in advance, and so may be tempted to delay electing to do so, in the hope that the court will rule in their favor on the necessity for dissolution. By adopting this strategy, they take the risk that the court will exercise its discretion to deny them the right to make the election after it has ordered the dissolution. In the usual case, since the petitioner is entitled to recover only the fair value of his shares through dissolution, the sound exercise of discretion would seem to dictate that the respondents be allowed to purchase his shares for that same fair value at any stage of the proceeding before dissolution has actually begun. This may not always be the case, however, and so the strategy is not without risk.

(3) He has been excluded from examination of the corporate books and records which he is entitled to examine, completing his "freeze-out" from the corporation. Robert expressly disclaims, as well he should, any claim that his dismissal in 1975 constituted "oppression" in any sense. Clearly, it was proper to dismiss a thief. Yet, he claims that his *continued* exclusion from "corporate participation" does constitute oppression.

The first question presented is whether the conduct of the majority can be said to be "oppressive" within the meaning of §1104-a of the Business Corporation Law. The term is not defined within the statute. Two definitions have gained currency in New York and in the numerous reported decisions across the country construing similar statutes.

The most prominent of these stems from the writings of F. Hodge O'Neal, and defines "oppression" as a violation by the majority of the "reasonable expectations" of the minority. This definition has been accepted by the leading New York cases dealing with "oppression."

The second definition is derived from British law, and describes "oppressive conduct" as burdensome, harsh and wrongful conduct; a lack of probity and fair dealing in the affairs of a company to the prejudice of some of its members; or a visible departure from the standards of fair dealing, and a violation of fair play on which every shareholder who entrusts his money to a company is entitled to rely.

This definition, too, has found support in New York cases.

These two approaches are, of course, not mutually exclusive, and will frequently be found to be equivalent. Often, however, it will be found that one or the other lends itself more nearly to the facts of the case as an appropriate analytical framework.

Here, the "reasonable expectations" test seems to be inappropriate, given the corporation's advanced stage of existence and the plaintiff's place and record. It is frequently said that the relationship between the founders of a close corporation approximates that between partners, and the "reasonable expectations" test is indeed an examination into the spoken and unspoken understanding upon which the founders relied when entering into the venture. Here, however, we have a corporation in its fifty-third year of existence. The sole founder, Louis, transferred ownership and control to his son and son-in-law (David and Moe) many years ago, and they ran the business as essentially equal partners until the death of David in 1980. To the extent that Louis adopted the corporate form in cooperation with David and Moe in order to facilitate their takeover of the business, the "reasonable expectations" test could be said to apply to the relationship between them. However, David is dead, and his sons now own his voting shares. Moe's shares, voting and non-voting, have all been sold to his daughter.

Thus, all present holders of the voting shares of the corporation are two generations removed from the adoption of the corporate form. While the manner of their dealing with each other may in some respects resemble that of partners, it cannot fairly be said that they entered into the business with the same "reasonable expectations" as partners do. Since they all acquired their shares by bequest or gift from other parties, they in no sense chose each other as business associates. The original participants in a close corporation enter into their agreement on the basis of the assessments of each other's talents, assets, intentions and characters and their agreement must, therefore, be regarded as personal in nature. Unless there is an unmistakable expression of their intent to the contrary, the agreement will not "run with the shares."[6] Hence, the present shareholders are not bound by whatever unwritten agreements may have existed between Louis, David and Moe, and did not form any agreement among themselves which could inure to Robert's benefit.

Also, it must be recognized that "reasonable expectations" do not run only one way. To the extent that Robert may have entertained "reasonable expectations" of profit in 1975, the other shareholders also entertained "reasonable expectations" of fidelity and honesty from him. All such expectations were shattered when Robert stole from the corporation. His own acts broke all bargains. Since then, the only expectations he could reasonably entertain were those of a discovered thief: ostracism and prosecution. To the extent that the majority has refrained from prosecuting him, they have dealt with him more kindly than he had reason to expect, not less.

Even though Robert may not lay claim to the reasonable expectation of any specific benefits, it does not necessarily follow that the majority shareholders may treat him as shabbily as they please. Where the question of oppressiveness cannot be resolved by comparing the conduct of the majority to the "reasonable expectations" of the parties, the court must look to the alternative test described above, and consider whether that conduct was inherently oppressive. Although a minority shareholder may be in the position of a stranger to them, the majority must still act with "probity and fair dealing," and if their conduct becomes "burdensome, harsh and wrongful," they may be found to have been guilty of oppression and the corporation may be subject to dissolution.

Under this test, Robert's discharge, as well as his subsequent exclusion from corporate management, were not oppressive. It was clearly not wrongful for the corporate victim of a theft to exclude the thief from the councils of power. . . . Thus, the only forms of participation which may fairly be said to be open to Robert are those open to a shareholder in the position of a stranger: possible entitlement to dividends, voting at shareholders' meetings, and access to corporate records.

Turning first to the failure to declare dividends, it seems that from the beginning of the corporation until Robert's fall from favor in 1975, the corporation had declared no dividends, apparently by consent of all shareholders, but in any event without objection from anyone. All concerned received all income from the corporation in the form of salary for their corporate positions. This policy was basic to the financial structure of the business. This can be seen by the fact that a second class of stock was created to facilitate estate planning by the major stockholders, Robert's father David, and Uncle Moe. This Class B stock had no voting rights but was equivalent to Class A stock in all other respects. It was intended that upon the death of David or Moe the bulk of this Class B stock would be inherited by their wives, and the corporation would begin to buy these shares back to pay for funeral and estate expenses and taxes, and to provide funds to the widows. The corporation has, in fact, already repurchased

---

6. Even if an original participant had had a reasonable expectation of personal employment, after his death the surviving shareholders would not be bound to employ any dolt who happened to inherit his stock.

about half of the Class B stock inherited by Robert's mother Shirley. Clearly, if the corporation were to begin to pay dividends now, the owner of the remaining shares would receive a disproportionate share of income. This was clearly against the original intent of the shareholders, and demonstrates their reliance upon a no-dividend policy. The policy was firmly established when the present majority came into control of the corporation.

Robert's claim that it was wrongful for them to continue that policy after his discharge amounts to an assertion that they were bound to change the basic structure of the business for his sole benefit and to their detriment. This assertion cannot stand.

As to his other allegations of oppression, the failures to hold shareholders' meetings, to issue proper stock certificates reflecting his actual interest in the corporation, or to allow him access to stock ledgers may all have been improper, but do not, individually or collectively, constitute oppressive conduct such as would justify dissolution.

Robert also asks for dissolution under §1104-a(a)(2) of the Business Corporation Law which allows such relief when "the property or assets of the corporation are being looted, wasted, or diverted for non-corporate purposes by its directors, officers or those in control of the corporation." The major allegation in support of this charge is that the salaries of the majority shareholders, in particular that of Moe Bolstein, who is now a former shareholder, have been excessive. It is also alleged that the corporate books have been "manipulated" so as to "affect the net income" of the corporation. In the particular circumstances of this case, these allegations, even if true, would not justify dissolution of the corporation. Robert's derivative action, wherein these same allegations are made, provides a sufficient remedy for any wrong that may have been done by these acts, as discussed below. Therefore, since dissolution is not "reasonably necessary for the protection of the rights and interests of any substantial number of shareholders or of the petitioners" (BCL, §1104-a(b)(2)), it will not be ordered on these grounds, either.

Having considered and rejected dissolution of the corporation, the court is nonetheless constrained to recognize that Robert cannot be forever compelled to remain an outcast. Even Cain was granted protection from the perpetual vengefulness of his fellow man. (Genesis 4:12-15.) While his past misdeeds provided sufficient justification for the majority's acts to date, there is a limit to what he can be forced to bear, and that limit has been reached. The other shareholders need not allow him to return to employment with the corporation, but they must by some means allow him to share in the profits.

The court is not without jurisdiction to fashion a remedy here. While the statute itself makes explicit mention of only one remedy, that being liquidation, the court is also charged to consider whether that is the only means available to protect the rights of the petitioning shareholder. (BCL, §1104-a(2)(a).) Clearly, this gives the court discretion in a proper case, to fashion an appropriate remedy. This discretion was recognized in Muller v. Silverstein, 92 A.D.2d 455, 458 N.Y.S.2d 597, where the Appellate Division reversed an order of dissolution on procedural grounds, but also observed that, since the alleged oppressive conduct consisted of failure to declare dividends, the trial court could have ordered the corporation to declare a dividend. A number of states have recognized a panoply of alternative remedies, to which a court may turn where relief is warranted, short of dissolution.

To begin with, the corporation must immediately allow Robert full access to corporate records. . . . If the administration of David Gimpel's estate has progressed to the point where stock certificates may properly be issued to Robert under David's will, this must be done promptly.

Most importantly, the majority must make an election: they must either alter the corporate financial structure so as to commence payment of dividends, or else make a reasonable offer to buy out Robert's interest. The election must be made within six months of the order to be entered hereon, and must be made known at a shareholders' meeting within that time.

If the corporation chooses to commence payment of dividends, the dividends must be substantial (consistent with sound business judgment) and not a sham. To the extent that the salaries paid to majority shareholders have been fixed so as to include amounts in lieu of dividends, the salaries must be adjusted downward. As to the relative rights of the different classes of stock, the Amended Certificate of Incorporation expressly states that they are to share equally in any dividends. The court neither directs nor prohibits any change in the structure of the classes of stock, but if any changes are made, they must be made in good faith, for a legitimate business purpose, and not for the purpose of weakening Robert's position.

If the election is made to buy out Robert's shares, the offer again must be substantial and made in good faith. The court does not now render any opinion on the method to be used in determining the reasonableness of the offer either as to whether or not the existence of the Class B shares is to be taken into account or as to the proper method for arriving at a per-share valuation. The court's order herein will be phrased as a mandatory injunction, with dissolution being one of the remedies for contempt. . . .

NOTES AND QUESTIONS

1. In connection with their 1977 article, Professors Hetherington and Dooley surveyed the results of the 54 involuntary dissolution cases reported during 1960-1976. The disposition of those cases was (1) no relief granted in 27 cases, (2) involuntary dissolution ordered in 16 cases, (3) buyout of the complaining minority's shares ordered in three cases, and (4) other relief in eight cases. See 63 Va. L. Rev. 1, 63-75 (1977).

2. In connection with a 1987 article, Professor Haynsworth undertook a similar survey of involuntary dissolution cases reported during 1984-1985. The disposition of the 37 cases decided on the merits was (1) no substantial relief granted in 4 cases, (2) involuntary dissolution ordered in 10 cases, (3) buyout of the complaining minority's shares ordered in 20 cases, and (4) other relief in 3 cases. Professor Haynsworth also found that in 11 of the buyout cases additional relief was granted, including "compensatory damages, punitive damages, an accounting, cancellation of issued stock, partial liquidation and other innovative orders." Finally, the survey disclosed that 18 of the 37 involuntary dissolution cases occurred in one jurisdiction—New York. Haynsworth, The Effectiveness of Involuntary Dissolution Suits as a Remedy for Close Corporation Dissension, 35 Clev. St. L. Rev. 25, 50-53 (1987).

3. Comparing the results of the 1960-1976 and 1984-1985 involuntary dissolution cases, two conclusions can be drawn. First, courts are now much more willing to grant significant relief to minority shareholders. Second, rather than simply granting or denying dissolution as was the norm in 1960-1976, courts are significantly more willing to tailor relief to fit the circumstances. In this regard, it should be noted that MBCA §14.34 will increase the resolution of these disputes via buyouts rather than tailored relief because the defendant's election to repurchase the complaining minority's shares for fair value will block a court's ability to use its equitable discretion.

4. The buyout remedy sounds deceptively simple. However, since there is no efficient market in which the shares of closely held corporations trade, there is no costless and impartial mechanism available to set the buyout price. Instead, courts determine fair value based on the testimony of experts. The difficulty faced by a court is illustrated by Taines v. Gene Barry One Hour Photo Process, Inc., 123 Misc. 2d 529, 531, 474 N.Y.S.2d 362, 365 (Sup. Ct. 1983); the court struggled to value the minority's shares in a corporation engaged in a one-hour photo-finishing business that utilized a revolutionary process:

> As it turns out, I find both experts' reasoning fallacious and their conclusions preposterous, and I give no weight whatsoever to either of their ultimate conclusions as to the value of the business. The petitioner's expert valued the business, as of August 27, 1981, at $20,700,000. The respondent's expert valued the same business, as of the same day, at $71,000 — a difference of nearly thirty thousand percent!

Given the uncertainties in court-determined valuation, would dissolution often be more likely to produce a fair price? Under what circumstances would dissolution be less likely to produce a fair price?

5. Reasonable expectations analysis supposedly differs from an attempt to determine what parties would have agreed to had they bargained over the matter in question. For example, Minnesota Stat. §302A.751 (1991) provides that "the court shall take into consideration the duty which all shareholders in a closely-held corporation owe one another to act in an honest, fair, and reasonable manner in the operation of the corporation and the reasonable expectations of the shareholders as they exist at the inception and develop during the course of the shareholders' relationship with the corporation and with each other." Thus, relief is to be fashioned based on the actual expectations of particular shareholders, not the hypothetical expectations of similarly situated shareholders. Still unclear is exactly how different the hypothetical bargaining and reasonable expectations approaches are in practice. Since the shareholders did not make a written or oral contract (else its terms would govern the dispute), how is the court to determine the complaining shareholders' reasonable expectations? Need they have been communicated to the other shareholders? And what kinds of expectations count?

6. What are the reasonable expectations of individuals who inherit their shares? Consider In re Smith, 154 A.D.2d 537, 546 N.Y.S.2d 382 (1989), in which Smith sought the involuntary dissolution of two corporations. He alleged oppressive conduct by the majority in refusing to, among other things, appoint him a director of both corporations. Sam Koslowitz was the corporations' only shareholder until his death in 1981. At that time, Smith, Koslowitz's wife, and Koslowitz's daughter each inherited one-third

of the two corporations' shares. From 1981 until 1986, Smith took no interest in the corporations, which were operated by the other two shareholders. In 1986 he suddenly demanded to be elected director and to have the corporations begin paying dividends. The trial court ordered dissolution, and the appellate division, citing In re Kemp & Beatley, reversed:

> While we are of the opinion, contrary to the appellants' contention, that the "reasonable expectation" standard can be applied to a case in which a stock interest is inherited, the petitioner's conduct did not evidence a reasonable expectation of being an active participant in the management of the corporations. The fact that the petitioner's attempt to become a member of the board of directors was frustrated cannot by itself amount to "oppressive actions" toward him. A stockholder has no vested right to become a director. His acquiescence in the majority shareholders' exercise of control over the day-to-day management of the corporations supports a finding that the petitioner's sudden demand to join the board was nothing more than his subjective hope and desire. His disappointment in not succeeding to be voted onto the board should not be equated with oppression.

154 A.D.2d at 539, 546 N.Y.S.2d at 384.

7. How should a court respond to a suit filed by the executor of a deceased passive shareholder, seeking a declaratory judgment that the majority shareholders' fiduciary duties obligated them to repurchase, or cause the corporation to repurchase, the deceased's shares? In Goode v. Ryan, 489 N.E.2d 1001, 1005 (Mass. 1986), the Supreme Judicial Court held that a corporation's simple refusal to repurchase the deceased passive shareholder's shares was not oppressive or a breach of fiduciary duty:

> While the plaintiff's predicament in not being able to dispose of the Gloucester stock to facilitate prompt settlement of the Marr estate is unfortunate, the situation was not caused by the defendant but is merely one of the risks of ownership of stock in a close corporation. . . . It is not the proper function of this court to reallocate the risks inherent in the ownership of corporate stock in the absence of corporate or majority shareholder misconduct.

8. For analysis of the substantive content of the phrase "reasonable expectations," see Clifford, Close Corporation Shareholder Reasonable Expectations: The Larger Context, 22 Wake Forest L. Rev. 41 (1987); Hillman, The Dissatisfied Participant in the Solvent Business Venture: A Consideration of the Relative Permanence of Partnerships and Close Corporations, 67 Minn. L. Rev. 1, 75-87 (1982); Thompson, Corporate Dissolution and Shareholders' Reasonable Expectations, 66 Wash. U. L.Q. 193, 216-228 (1988).

PROBLEM 5-3

Gaines, Harris, and Rift formed, and became equal shareholders and the directors of, Video, Inc. Their intent was to exploit a revolutionary video copying process through the development and operation of a chain of one-hour home video copying stores. Rift invested his life savings, left his former home and job, and became the president and chief operating officer of Video, Inc. at a salary well below that of his prior position. After a year, Rift's employment with the firm ended. Since that time the firm has become extremely profitable and continues to open new stores. It has paid handsome salaries to Gaines and Harris, but has reinvested profits rather than pay dividends.

Assume, alternatively, that Video, Inc. is incorporated in a jurisdiction that has the following statutory provisions: (1) MBCA §14.30 only, (2) MBCA §§14.30 and 14.34, or (3) Hetherington and Dooley's mandatory buyout provision.

What relief should Rift seek and how should the court analyze his request, assuming, alternatively, the following circumstances:

(a) Rift was fired by the board (via the votes of Gaines and Harris) after allegations of sexual harassment were made against him by several Video employees.

(b) Rift was fired by the board after he failed to support Gaines's daughter, who was running for the school board.

(c) Rift resigned in order to accept a much higher-paying job at a competitor firm.

(d) Rift terminated his employment by mutual agreement with Gaines and Harris. Since that time Rift's wife has become seriously ill, and he wishes to "cash in" his investment in Video, Inc. to provide needed medical care for her.

PROBLEM 5-4

Arch Enterprises, Inc. is a closely held business whose articles of incorporation require unanimity for all shareholders' and directors' actions. Dunlap, Packard, and Manke each own one-third of the shares and serve as an officer and one of the three directors. A board resolution provides that each of the three will receive compensation equal to one-third of the corporation's net profits. During the last two years, Dunlap has been chronically absent from work and numerous customers have complained about both her bad temper and the quality of her work. Packard and Manke asked her to resign and offered to purchase her shares. Dunlap refused and instead offered to buy out the other shareholders at a lower price.

(a) What result if Packard and Manke seek involuntary dissolution in a jurisdiction having §14.30 but not §14.34?

(b) What result in (a) in a jurisdiction having both MBCA §§14.30 and 14.34?

(c) What result if Packard and Manke sue Dunlap for breach of her fiduciary duty to the corporation?

D.   Share Repurchase Agreements

As Parts B and C reveal, close corporation disputes often involve a disagreement between minority and majority shareholders as to whether, or on what terms, the corporation shall repurchase the minority's shares. And, as Parts B and C also reveal, disputes often arise because the minority and majority shareholders no longer share an identity of interests. This may occur because the minority shareholder has retired, or because the minority shareholder has inherited the shares of a formerly active participant, or because the majority discharged the minority shareholder from the corporation's employ. A common response to the possibility of such disputes is a share repurchase agreement that specifies in advance the conditions on which the corporation (or perhaps the continuing shareholders) will repurchase the shares of a noncontinuing shareholder.

Share repurchase agreements are usually treated as fully contingent contracts. That is, courts will generally enforce the terms of a share repurchase agreement, even if events subsequent to execution make the purchase price substantially less than the then fair value of the to-be-acquired shares, unless there is some compelling equitable reason not to enforce the agreement. Still uncertain, as suggested by the cases below, is the extent to which courts will use fiduciary duty or other equitable concepts to protect minority shareholders from oppressive majority conduct in connection with a share repurchase. Also uncertain is the extent to which an agreement to have one's shares repurchased upon termination of employment converts shareholders into mere at-will employees of the corporation.

In any event, share repurchase agreements present a dilemma for investors in closely held corporations. Investors (with advice of counsel) must determine what mechanism will best serve their need for future investment liquidity and prevention of post-harmony disputes: (1) share repurchase agreements or (2) ex post negotiations, with good faith being assured by the availability of equitable relief or dissolution. On the one hand, a well-conceived repurchase agreement may prevent a deterioration in shareholder relationships and the attendant need for costly litigation. On the other hand, contracts are costly, human rationality is limited, and a poorly conceived contract may present possibilities for oppression that otherwise would not exist.

Concord Auto Auction, Inc. v. Rustin
United States District Court, Massachusetts, 1986
627 F. Supp. 1526

YOUNG, DISTRICT JUDGE.

Close corporations Concord Auto Auction, Inc. ("Concord") and E.L. Cox Associates, Inc. ("Associates") brought this action for the specific performance of a stock purchase and restriction agreement (the "Agreement"). Concord and Associates allege that Lawrence H. Rustin ("Rustin") as the administrator of E.L. Cox's estate ("Cox") failed to effect the repurchase of Cox's stock holdings as provided by the Agreement. . . .

I. BACKGROUND

Both Concord and Associates are Massachusetts Corporations. Concord operates a used car auction for car dealers, fleet operators, and manufacturers. Associates operates as an adjunct to Concord's auction business by guaranteeing checks and automobile titles. Both are close corporations with the same shareholders, all siblings: Cox (now his estate), Powell, and Thomas. At all times relevant to this action, each sibling owned one-third of the issued and outstanding stock in both Concord and Associates.

To protect "their best interests" and the best interests of the two corporations, the three shareholders entered into a stock purchase and restriction agreement on February 1, 1983. The Agreement provides that all shares owned by a shareholder at the time of his or her death be acquired by the two corporations, respectively, through life insurance policies specifically established to fund this transaction. This procedure contemplates the "orderly transfer of the stock owned by each deceased Shareholder." At issue in the instant action are the prerequisites for and effect of the repurchase requirements as set forth in the Agreement.

This dispute arises because Rustin failed to tender Cox's shares as required by Paragraph 2, Death of Shareholder. Rustin admits this but alleges a condition precedent: that Powell, specifically, and Thomas failed to effect both the annual meeting and the annual review of the stock price set in the Agreement as required by Paragraph 6, Purchase Price: "Each price shall be reviewed at least annually no later than the annual meeting of the stockholders . . . (commencing with the annual meetings for the year 1984) . . . ," here February 21, 1984. Rustin implies that, had the required meeting been held, revaluation would or should have occurred and that, after Cox's accidental death in a fire on March 14, 1984, Powell in particular as well as Thomas were obligated to revalue the stock prior to tendering the repurchase price.

There is no dispute that the By-Laws call for an annual meeting on the third Tuesday of February, here February 21, 1984. There is no dispute that none took place or that, when Cox died, the stocks of each corporation had not been formally revalued. No one disputes that Paragraph 6 of the Agreement provides for a price of $672.00 per share of Concord and a price of $744.00 per share for Associates. This totals $374,976 which is covered by insurance on Cox's life of $375,000. There is no substantial dispute that the stock is worth a great deal more, perhaps even twice as much. No one seriously disputes that Paragraph 6 further provides that: ". . . all parties may, as a result of such review, agree to a new price by a written instrument executed by all the parties and appended to an original of this instrument, and that any such new price shall thereupon become the basis for determining the purchase price for all purposes hereof unless subsequently superceded pursuant to the same procedure. The purchase price shall remain in full force and effect and until so changed."

Rustin asserts that the explicit requirement of a yearly price review "clashes" with the provision that the price shall remain in effect until changed. He argues a trial is required to determine the intent of the parties: "The question then arises, presenting this Court with a material issue of fact not susceptible to determination on a motion for summary judgment: Did the parties intend, either to reset, or at least to monitor, yearly, the correspondence between the Paragraph 6 price and the current value of the companies? If so, who, if anyone, was principally responsible for effecting the yearly review required by the Agreement, and for insuring an informed review?"

In answering these questions the Court first outlines its proper role in the interpretation of this contract.

II.   DISCUSSION

A Court sitting in diversity will apply the substantive law of the forum state, here Massachusetts. In Massachusetts as elsewhere, absent ambiguity, contracts must be interpreted and enforced exactly as written. Where the language is unambiguous, the interpretation of a contract is a question of law for the court. Further, contracts must be construed in accordance with their ordinary and usual sense.

Contrary to Rustin's assertion, the Court in applying these standards holds that there is no ambiguity and certainly no "clash" between the dual requirements of Paragraph 6 that there be an annual review of share price and that, absent such review, the existing price prevails. When, as here, the Court searches for the meaning of a document containing two unconditional provisions, one immediately following the other, the Court favors a reading that reconciles them. The Court rules that the Agreement covers precisely the situation before it: no revaluation occurred, therefore the price remains as set forth in the Agreement. This conclusion is reasonable, for the Agreement is not a casual memorialization but a formal contract carefully drafted by attorneys and signed by all parties.

Moreover, the Court interprets Paragraph 2 to provide, in unambiguous terms: "In the event of the death of any Shareholder subject to this agreement, his respective . . . administrator . . . *shall*, within sixty (60) days after the date of death . . . give written notice thereof to each Company which notice *shall* specify a purchase date not later than sixty (60) days thereafter, *offering to each Company for purchase* as hereinafter provided, and *at the purchase price set forth in Paragraph 6,* all of the Shares owned on said date by said deceased Shareholder. . . ." (Emphasis by the Court.) Rustin, therefore, was unambiguously obligated as administrator of Cox's estate to tender Cox's shares for repurchase by Concord and Associates. His failure to do so is inexcusable unless he raises cognizable defenses.

All of Rustin's defenses turn on two allegations: that his performance is excused because the surviving parties failed to review and to adjust upward the $374,976 purchase price. Rustin contends that the parties meant to review the price per share on an annual basis. No affidavit supports this assertion, nor does any exhibit. In fact, absent any evidence for this proposition, Rustin's assertion is no more than speculation and conjecture. While Rustin contends that the failure to review and revalue constitutes "unclean hands" and a breach of fiduciary duty which excuses his nonperformance, he places before the Court only argument not facts.

It simply does not follow that because a meeting was not held and the prices were not reviewed that a trial of the parties' intentions is required. The Agreement is the best evidence of the parties' intent. Although the text of the Agreement provides that share price "shall" be reviewed "at least annually," the Agreement also states that "The purchase price shall remain in full force and effect unless and until so changed." . . .

Even if competent evidence adduced at trial would support Rustin's allegations, his proposition would of necessity require judicial intervention, a course this Court does not favor. Rustin produces not a shred of evidence that the parties intended that a court should intercede to set the share price in the event the parties failed to do so themselves. Every first year law student learns that although the courts can lead an opera singer to the concert hall, they cannot make her sing. Lumley v. Guy, 118 Eng. Rep. 749 (1853). While this Court will specifically enforce a consensual bargain, memorialized in an unambiguous written document, it will not order the revision of the share price. Such intrusion into the private ordering of commercial affairs offends both good judgment and good jurisprudence. Moreover, the record before the Court indicates that the parties fully intended what their competent counsel drafted and they signed.

Moreover, the nucleus of Rustin's premise is that somehow Powell should have guaranteed the review and revision of the share prices. On the contrary, nothing in the record indicates that a reasonable trier of fact could find that Powell's duties and responsibilities included such omnipotence. More to the point, the By-Laws suggest that several individuals shared the responsibility for calling the required annual meeting: "In case the annual meeting for any year shall not be duly called or held, the Board of Directors or the President shall cuase (sic) a special meeting to be held. . . ." Pursuant to the By-Laws, Cox himself had the power, right, and authority to call a meeting of the stockholders of both companies, in order to review the price per share—or for any other purpose for that matter.

Furthermore, nothing in the record indicates that somehow Powell, Thomas, Concord, or Associates was charged with the duty of raising the share price. In fact, this is discretionary and consensual: "all parties *may*, as a result of such review, *agree to* a new price by a written instrument *executed by all parties*. . . ." Nowhere can the Court find any affirmative duty to guarantee either an annual meeting or a share price revision. To fault Powell for not doing by fiat what must be done by consensus credits Powell with powers she simply does not have. The mere fact that, as a shareholder of Concord and Associates, Powell benefits from the enforcement of the Agreement at the $374,976 purchase price does not, as matter of law, create an obligation on her part to effect a review or revision of the purchase price. One cannot breach a duty where no duty exists, and Rustin cannot manufacture by allegation a duty where neither the Agreement nor the By-Laws lends any support.

Applying the above analysis, the Court discounts three of Rustin's defenses as meritless: that specific performance is not warranted because Concord and Associates breached the Agreement they seek to enforce; that they have unclean hands because they failed to effect a review and revaluation of the shares; and that specific performance is conditional upon an annual review of share value to be held no later than the third Tuesday of February. The record demonstrates no evidence that share transfer is conditional, rather it appears absolute and automatic. Absent a duty to "guarantee" the occurrence of the annual meeting or the "review," the Court cannot find that Powell's failure, if any, to upgrade the share price constitutes a fiduciary breach.

Of Rustin's fourth defense, that the value of the stock increased so substantially that specific enforcement would be unfair and unjust to Cox's estate, little need be said. This defense as well as Rustin's counterclaims rest on the allegation that Powell, in particular, and Thomas "knew" that a revaluation would result in a higher price and "failed to effect an annual review." Of Powell, Rustin argues that she had a "special responsibility" to effect a review of the purchase price because her siblings looked to her for financial expertise and to call a meeting. Nowhere is this "special responsibility" supported by the Agreement or the By-Laws. Rustin also implies that the sisters "knew" that failure to revalue would inure to their benefit. This presumes they knew that Cox would die in an accidental fire three weeks after the deadline for the annual meeting. To call this preposterous understates it, for nothing immunized the sisters from an equally unforeseeable accident. Rustin's argument withers in the light of objectivity to a heap of conclusory straws.

Rustin goes on to argue that the sisters had a fiduciary duty to revalue the shares *after Cox's death* and *before tender.* Nowhere in the Agreement is there the slightest indication they were so obligated. Nowhere is there evidence of willfulness, intent to deceive, or knowing manipulation. . . .

Agreements, such as those before the Court, "among shareholders of closely held corporations are common and the purposes of such contracts are clear." . . . The validity of such agreements will be upheld absent any fraud, overreaching, undue influence, duress, or mistake at the time the deceased entered into the agreement, these conditions rendering the agreement void. . . .

Moreover, specific performance of an agreement to convey will not be refused merely because the price is inadequate or excessive. New England Trust Co. v. Abbott, 162 Mass. at 155, 38 N.E. 432; see Lee v. Kirby, 104 Mass. 420, 430 (1870); Allen v. Biltmore Tissue Corp., 2 N.Y.2d 534, 543, 161 N.Y.S.2d 418, 141 N.E.2d 812 (1957) ("The validity of the restriction on transfer does not rest on any abstract notion of intrinsic fairness of price. To be invalid, more than mere disparity between option price and current value of the stock must be shown"); Renberg v. Zarrow, 667 P.2d at 470 ("In the absence of fraud, overreaching, or bad faith, an agreement between the stockholders that upon the death of any of them, the stock may be acquired by the corporation is binding. Even great disparity between the price specified in a buy-sell agreement and the actual value of the stock is not sufficient to invalidate the agreement."). The fact that surviving shareholders were allowed to purchase Cox's shares on stated terms and conditions which resulted in the purchase for less than actual value of the stock does not subject the agreement to attack as a breach of the relation of trust and confidence, there being no breach of fiduciary duty.

Rather than evidence of any impropriety, the Court rules that the purchase prices were carefully set, fair when established, evidenced by an Agreement binding all parties equally to the same terms without any indication that any one sibling would reap a windfall. The courts may not rewrite a shareholder's agreement under the guise of relieving one of the parties from the hardship of an improvident bargain. The Court cannot protect the parties from a bad bargain and it will not protect them from bad luck. Cox, the party whose estate is aggrieved, had while alive every opportunity to call the annual meeting and persuade his sisters to revalue their stock. Sad though the situation be, sadness is not the touchstone of contract interpretation. . . .

. . . The Agreement shall be specifically enforced. . . .

Gallagher v. Lambert
New York Court of Appeals, 1989
74 N.Y.2d 562, 549 N.E.2d 136, 549 N.Y.S.2d 945

BELLACOSA, JUDGE.

Plaintiff Gallagher purchased stock in the defendant close corporation with which he was employed. The purchase of his 8.5% interest was subject to a mandatory buyback provision: if the employment ended for any reason before January 31, 1985, the stock would return to the corporation for book value. The corporation fired plaintiff prior to the fulcrum date, after which the buy-back price would have been higher. . . .

Gallagher was employed by defendant Eastdil Realty as a mortgage broker from 1968 to 1973. Three years later, in 1976, he returned to the company as a broker, officer and director, serving additionally as president and chief executive officer of defendant's wholly owned subsidiary, Eastdil Advisors, Inc. Gallagher was at all times an employee at will. Still later, in 1981, Eastdil offered all its executive employees an opportunity to purchase stock subject to a mandatory buy-back provision, which provided that upon "voluntary resignation or other termination" prior to January 31, 1985, an employee would be required to return the stock for book value. After that date, the formula for the buy-back price was keyed to the company's earnings. Plaintiff accepted the offer and its terms.

On January 10, 1985, Gallagher was fired by Eastdil Realty. He did not and does not now contest the firing. But he demanded payment for his shares calculated on the post-January 31, 1985 buy-back formula. Eastdil refused and Gallagher sued, asserting eight causes of action. Only three claims, based on an alleged breach of fiduciary duty of good faith and fair dealing, are before us. . . .

The parties negotiated a written contract containing a common and plain buy-back provision. Plaintiff got what he bargained for — book value for his minority shares if his employment in the corporation ended before January 31, 1985. There being no basis presented for the courts to interfere with the operation and consequences of this agreement between the parties, the order of the Appellate Division granting summary judgment to defendants, dismissing the first three causes of action, should be affirmed. . . .

Earlier this year, in Ingle v. Glamore Motor Sales, 73 N.Y.2d 183, 538 N.Y.S.2d 771, 535 N.E.2d 1311, we expressly refrained from deciding the precise issue presented by this case. There, the challenge was directed to the at-will discharge from employment and was predicated on a claimed fiduciary obligation flowing from the shareholder relationship. . . . [W]e held that "[a] minority shareholder in a close corporation, by that status alone, who contractually agrees to the repurchase of his shares upon termination of his employment for any reason, *acquires no right from the corporation or majority shareholders against at-will discharge.*" (Ingle v. Glamore Motor Sales, 73 N.Y.2d supra [emphasis added].) However, we cautioned that "[i]t is necessary . . . to appreciate and keep distinct the duty a corporation owes to a minority shareholder *as a shareholder* from any duty it might owe him as an *employee.*"

The causes before us on this appeal are based on an alleged departure from a fiduciary duty of fair dealing existing independently of the employment and arising from the plaintiff's simultaneous relationship as a minority shareholder in the corporation. Plaintiff claims entitlement to the higher price based on a breach flowing from Eastdil's premature "bad faith" termination of his at-will employment because, he asserts, the sole purpose of the firing at that time was to acquire the stock at a contractually and temporally measured lower buy-back price formula.

The claim seeking a higher price for the shares cannot be neatly divorced, as the dissent urges, from the employment because the buy-back provision links them together as to timing and consequences. Plaintiff not only agreed to the particular buy-back formula, he helped write it and he reviewed it with his attorney during the negotiation process, before signing the agreement and purchasing the minority interest. These provisions, which require an employee shareholder to sell back stock upon severance from corporate employment, are designed to ensure that ownership of all of the stock, especially of a close corporation, stays within the control of the remaining corporate owners-employees; that is, those who will continue to contribute to its successes or failures. These agreements define the scope of the relevant fiduciary duty and supply certainty of obligation to each side. They should not be undone simply upon an allegation of unfairness. This would destroy their very purpose, which is to provide a certain formula by which to value stock in the future. Indeed, the dissenters in *Ingle* itself acknowledged that employee shareholders would be precluded from complaining about the terms of an otherwise enforceable buy-back provision (Ingle v. Glamore Motor Sales, 73 N.Y.2d, supra, at 192, n.1, 538 N.Y.S.2d 771, 535 N.E.2d 1311).

Gallagher accepted the offer to become a minority stockholder, but only for the period during which he remained an employee. The buy-back price formula was designed for the benefit of both parties precisely so that they could know their respective rights on certain dates and avoid costly and lengthy litigation on the "fair value" issue. Permitting these causes to survive would open the door to litigation on both the value of the stock and the date of termination, and hinder the employer from fulfilling its contractual rights under the agreement. This would frustrate the agreement and would be disruptive of the settled principles governing like agreements where parties contract between themselves in advance so that there may be reliance, predictability and definitiveness between themselves on such matters. There being no dispute that the employer had the unfettered discretion to fire plaintiff at any time, we should not redefine the precise measuring device and scope of the agreement. Defendant agreed to abide by these terms and thus fulfilled its fiduciary duty in that respect.

The dissenting opinion uses a number of rhetorical characterizations about the defendant and about what we are deciding or avoiding to decide, none of which, we believe, require response, because our holding and rationale rest on the application of fundamental contractual principles to the plain terms in the parties' own stock repurchase agreement.

Accordingly, the order of the Appellate Division should be affirmed. . . .

KAYE, JUDGE (dissenting).

By proceeding, as if inexorably, from [Sabetay v. Sterling Drug, 69 N.Y.2d 329, 514 N.Y.S.2d 209, 506 N.E.2d 919] to *Ingle* to *Gallagher,* the court avoids confronting plaintiff's true claims and unnecessarily weakens traditional protections afforded minority shareholders in close corporations. I therefore respectfully dissent.

I.

To begin at a point of agreement, this case is significantly different from Ingle v. Glamore Motor Sales, 73 N.Y.2d 183, 538 N.Y.S.2d 771, 535 N.E.2d 1311. As the majority acknowledges, this case presents "an alleged departure from a fiduciary duty of fair dealing existing independently of the employment" that was not present in *Ingle* (majority opn., at 566, at 946 of 549 N.Y.S.2d, at 137 of 549 N.E.2d).

In *Ingle* we reached only the corporation's duty to plaintiff as *an employee,* carving out and reserving for another day any question of the duty a corporation might owe an employee as *a shareholder*, which was not in issue. The court was careful to note that Mr. Ingle had already accepted full payment for his shares without reservation; while his complaint referred to a fiduciary duty owed him as a shareholder, the only interest he asserted in the litigation was in his job. In its succinct opinion the court took pains to emphasize at least six separate times that its concern was only with Mr. Ingle's employment, not in any sense with the duty a corporation owes to a minority shareholder, or with undervaluation of shares (73 N.Y.2d, at 187, 188, 189, 538 N.Y.S.2d 771, 535 N.E.2d 1311).

Here, plaintiff *does* question the duty the corporation owes him as a shareholder. He does contend that the corporation undervalued his shares and that it did not offer a fair price for his equity interest. Indeed, that is the only question he raises; he does not challenge defendant's absolute right to terminate his employment. Yet despite careful identification and recognition in *Ingle* of the different considerations such a question would present, now that the question is before us the court finds that the very same answer and the very same rationale are wholly dispositive, with no analysis of the fiduciary obligation owed plaintiff.

The court's insistence that the rationale of *Ingle* and the other at-will employment cases must be carried over — lock, stock and barrel — even to the fiduciary obligations owed minority shareholders in close corporations, plainly represents an extension of the law to a different jural relationship. I believe this is wholly unwarranted. . . .

Pedro v. Pedro
Minnesota Court of Appeals, 1992
489 N.W.2d 798

NORTON, JUDGE.

After a request for dissolution of The Pedro Companies by respondent, Alfred Pedro, appellants, Carl and Eugene Pedro and The Pedro Companies, moved that the action proceed as a buyout pursuant to Minn. Stat. §302A.751 (1990).

After a jury awarded damages, this court determined the jury's verdict was merely advisory and remanded the case to the trial court to make findings. Pedro v. Pedro, 463 N.W.2d 285 (Minn. App. 1990) (*Pedro 1*), pet. for rev. denied (Minn. Jan. 24, 1991). On remand, the trial court awarded damages for breach of fiduciary duty and for wrongful termination of lifetime employment. In addition to other issues, appellants challenge the propriety of the trial court's rulings on these matters.

FACTS

Alfred, Carl, and Eugene Pedro are brothers who each owned a one-third interest in The Pedro Companies ("TPC"), a closely held Minnesota corporation, which manufactures and sells luggage and leather products. All three brothers worked in the business for all or most of their adult lives. TPC has annual sales of approximately $6 million. Carl has worked for TPC since 1940 and he is currently employed by the company. Eugene has worked for TPC since 1939 and is also currently employed by the company. Alfred worked for TPC for 45 years and was fired in 1987 at the age of 62. Each brother, as an equal shareholder, received the same benefit and compensation as the others. Each shareholder had an equal vote in the management of the company.

In 1968, all of the company's shareholders (the three brothers and their father) entered into a stock retirement agreement ("SRA") which was designated to facilitate the purchase of the shareholder's stock upon death, or when a living shareholder wished to sell his stock. In 1975, the father died and the company purchased his stock from his estate, pursuant to the terms of the SRA.

In 1979, the remaining shareholders (the three brothers) modified and re-executed the SRA, reducing the purchase price of the shares. The agreement provided in part:

> Until and unless changed the value of each share of stock shall be as follows: 75% of net book value at the end of the preceding calendar year. It is the intent of the parties that the value of a Stockholder's interest as herein determined does include good will.

The relationship between respondent and the other two shareholders deteriorated through 1987 and 1988, after Alfred discovered an apparent discrepancy of almost $330,000 between the internal accounting records and the TPC checking account. Approximately $40,000 was discovered in an emergency investigation, yet about $270,000 of the discrepancy remained unexplained.

Alfred was very concerned and insisted that an independent accountant be retained to locate the source of the discrepancy. In May 1987, Carl and Eugene agreed to retain an accountant to investigate the cash shortage. After a month with no results, TPC dismissed the accountant. Alfred testified that soon afterwards, the corporate accountant admitted in a meeting with all three brothers that there was a $140,000 to $147,000 discrepancy which was unexplainable.

Alfred testified that during this time, Eugene would interfere with his area of responsibility in the TPC plant and undermine his management authority. Alfred testified that he was told to cooperate, resign or be fired. He was told if he did not forget about the apparent discrepancy, his brothers would fire him. Alfred again repeated his demand that the corporation hire an independent accountant to investigate the situation.

In October 1987, a second independent accountant was hired to investigate the shortage. After concluding his investigation, the accountant issued a report identifying a $140,000 discrepancy which could not be reconciled. He testified that throughout his investigation, he was refused access to numerous documents. He also stated there were over 20 leads never followed up before he ended his investigation.

Alfred was placed on a mandatory leave of absence from TPC on October 27, 1987. In December 1987, Alfred received a written notice that he was fired and all of his pay and benefits were discontinued. Employees were informed that Alfred had a nervous breakdown.

Alfred commenced this action in February 1988. Upon remand from this court on the earlier appeal, the trial court made the following findings of fact and conclusions of law. The court awarded Alfred $766,582.33 as damages for his one-third ownership in TPC which was determined by the terms of the SRA. Alfred was awarded $58,260.69 for prejudgment interest on this award.

The trial court also awarded Alfred $563,417.67 based on its finding that the individual defendants had breached their fiduciary duties to Alfred. The award represented the difference between the fair market value of Alfred Pedro's stock as determined by the trial court and the value provided by the SRA. In addition, the trial court awarded $68,690.05 for prejudgment interest on this award.

The trial court further found that Alfred had a contract of lifetime employment with TPC. The court found wrongful termination and awarded him $256,740 as compensation for lost wages. Because the contract was for lifetime employment, the award represented lost wages until he reached the age of 72. The court reduced this award by payments made to Alfred since December 1989. Moreover, the court awarded prejudgment interest in the sum of $31,750.37 on this award.

The trial court also awarded Alfred $200,000 for attorney fees and expenses incurred by him. This award was based on the trial court's finding that appellants had acted in a manner which was "arbitrary, vexatious and otherwise not in good faith . . . prior to and during this action." The court awarded Alfred an additional $6,063 for attorney fees for having to respond to appellants' motion to recuse the trial judge and for the preparation of Findings of Fact, Conclusions of Law and Order for Judgment. . . .

ANALYSIS

I . . .

The relationship among shareholders in closely held corporations is analogous to that of partners. See Westland Capitol Corp. v. Lucht Eng'g Inc., 308 N.W.2d 709, 712 (Minn. 1981) (close corporation has been described as partnership in corporate guise). Shareholders in closely held corporations owe one another a fiduciary duty. Evans v. Blesi, 345 N.W.2d 775, 779 (Minn. App. 1984). In a fiduciary relationship "the law imposes upon them highest standards of integrity and good faith in their dealings with each other." Prince v. Sonnesyn, 222 Minn. 528, 535, 25 N.W.2d 468, 472 (1946) (citation omitted). Owing a fiduciary duty includes dealing "openly, honestly and fairly with other shareholders." Evans, 345 N.W.2d at 779.

The court's findings of fact contain many examples where appellants did not act openly, honestly, and fairly with respondent Alfred Pedro. The trial court found that at no time since the action was commenced, did appellants ever implement payments admittedly due under the SRA. Appellants interfered with respondent's responsibilities in TPC and hired a private investigator to follow him when he was not in the office. The court found appellants fabricated accusations of neglect and malfeasance which were not substantiated during the trial.

Moreover, an employee testified that after respondent was terminated, employees were informed that he had a nervous breakdown. Also, respondent testified he was told if he did not forget about the discrepancies in the financial records, his brothers would fire him. Finally, appellants admitted in their motion requesting a buyout, that they were acting "in a manner unfairly prejudicial" toward respondent pursuant to Minn. Stat. §302A.751, subd. 1(b)(2) (1990). This admission supports a finding of breach of fiduciary duty.

Appellants claim no breach of fiduciary duty can exist because there has been no diminution in the value of the corporation or the stock value of respondent's shares. In support of this assertion, appellants cite several cases where actions by an officer or director did reduce the value of the corporation, constituting a breach of fiduciary duty. See e.g., Jordan v. Duff and Phelps, Inc., 815 F.2d 429 (7th Cir. 1987); Coleman v. Taub, 638 F.2d 628 (3rd Cir. 1981); Harris v. Mardan Business Sys., Inc., 421 N.W.2d 350 (Minn. App. 1988).

However, an action depleting a corporation's value is not the exclusive method of breaching one's fiduciary duties. See *Evans,* 345 N.W.2d at 779-80 (majority shareholders breached fiduciary duty to minority shareholder by forcing his resignation). Moreover, loss in value of a shareholder's stock is not the only measure of damages. See Pavlidis v. New England Patriots Football Club, Inc., 675 F. Supp. 701, 703 (D. Mass. 1987) (damages for corporate director's breach of fiduciary duty was either profits made by director or value of property at time of breach plus interest).

Moreover, the measure of damages for the buyout was proper. In *Pedro 1,* this court stated:

> If the fair value of the shares is greater than the purchase price for the buyout as calculated from the formula in the SRA, the difference is the measure of respondent's damage resulting from having been forced to sell his shares in the company.

Pedro, 463 N.W.2d at 288. Here there was evidence in the record that the fair market value of respondent's shares equalled $1,330,000. After subtracting the undisputed purchase price set forth under the SRA of $766,582.33, the trial court properly awarded damages for breach of fiduciary duty of $563,417.67.

II

Appellants claim the evidence was insufficient for the court to find a contract for lifetime employment. They also assert damages for lost wages following the buyout were improper. Again, we are unable to set aside findings of fact unless they are clearly erroneous. Minn. R. Civ. P. 52.01. Based upon the unique facts in this case, we affirm the trial court's award of damages for lost wages.

Trial courts have broad equitable powers in fashioning relief for the buyout of shareholders in a closely held corporation. Minn. Stat. §302A.751, subd. 3a provides:

> In determining whether to order equitable relief, dissolution, or a buy-out, the court shall take into consideration the duty which all shareholders in a closely held corporation owe one another to act in an honest, fair and reasonable manner in the operation of the corporation and the reasonable expectations of the shareholders as they exist at the inception and develop during the course of the shareholders' relationship with the corporation and with each other.

This section allows courts to look to respondent's reasonable expectations when awarding damages. In addition to an ownership interest,

> [t]he reasonable expectations of such a shareholder are a job, salary, a significant place in management, and economic security for his family.

Joseph E. Olson, A Statutory Elixir for the Oppression Malady, 36 Mercer L. Rev. 627, 629 (1985) (footnote omitted).

In Pine River State Bank v. Mettille, 333 N.W.2d 622 (Minn. 1983), the supreme court explained that the court must ascertain the intent of the parties to the employment contract. Id. at 628. When ascertaining the intent, trial courts must consider the written and oral negotiations of the parties as well as the parties' situation, the type of employment and the particular circumstances of the case. Eklund v. Vincent Brass and Aluminum Co., 351 N.W.2d 371, 376 (Minn. App. 1984), pet. for rev. denied (Minn. Nov. 1, 1984).

> In a closely held corporation the nature of the employment of a shareholder may create a reasonable expectation by the employee-owner that his employment is not terminable at will.

Pedro, 463 N.W.2d at 289.

The unique facts in the record support the trial court's finding of an agreement to provide lifetime employment to respondent. Carl Pedro, Sr. worked at the corporation until his death. Eugene Pedro, who worked for over 50 years at TPC, testified that he intended to always work for the company. Carl Pedro, Jr. worked at TPC for over 34 years. Alfred Pedro testified of his expectation of a lifetime job like his father. He had already been employed by TPC for 45 years. Even the corporate accountant testified regarding Carl's and Eugene's expectations that they would work for the corporation as long as they wanted. Based upon this evidence it was reasonable for the trial court to determine that the parties did in fact have a contract that was not terminable at will.

Appellants claim a grant of damages for both lost wages and breach of fiduciary duty under §302A.751, subd. 3a allows respondent a double recovery. In support of this assertion, appellants misquote *Pedro 1* in their brief by connecting, within one block quotation, sentences from entirely different sections of the opinion. In any event, section 302A.751, subd. 3a allows the trial court to consider respondent's reasonable expectations. Even appellants concede respondent has two separate interests, as owner and employee. Thus, allowing recovery for each interest is appropriate and will not be considered a double recovery.

Finally, appellants dispute the trial court's award of damages for lost wages following the buyout. They claim once respondent's ownership interest is severed, he has no right to damages for lost wages. We believe the trial court's award of future damages for lost wages is wholly consistent with the court's broad equitable powers found in §302A.751, subd. 3a and is warranted based upon its finding of a contract for lifetime employment. . . .

NOTES AND QUESTIONS

1. It is standard legal practice to place an appropriate notice or legend on each share certificate as constructive notification to third parties that the underlying shares are subject to share transfer restrictions. Indeed, a majority of state corporation codes specifically require such constructive notification as a condition to enforcement of share transfer restrictions. Delaware G.C.L. §202(a) contains a representative provision:

> Unless noted conspicuously on the certificate representing the security or, in the case of uncertificated shares, contained in the notice [required by Delaware G.C.L. §151(f)], a restriction, even though permitted by this Section, is ineffective except against a person with actual knowledge of the restriction.

Under the common law, courts viewed with suspicion all restraints on the alienation of property, including share transfer restrictions. The modern view is the reverse. Indeed, most corporation codes now specifically sanction share transfer restrictions for any reasonable purpose. See, e.g., MBCA §6.27. Clearly reasonable purposes include making effective a share repurchase agreement, preventing transfers that would destroy a tax or securities law exemption, or preventing transfers that would destroy a corporation's ability to continue as an electing close corporation under special close corporation supplements.

2. Courts appear especially reluctant, as in Concord Auto Auction, Inc. v. Rustin, to interfere with a repurchase agreement triggered by a shareholder's death simply on the grounds of price disparity. What is the reason for this? Consider the comments in Evangelista v. Holland, 27 Mass. App. Ct. 244, 248-249, 537 N.E.2d 589, 592-593 (1989):

> Questions of good faith and loyalty do not arise when all the stockholders in advance enter into an agreement for the purchase of stock of a withdrawing or deceased stockholder. . . . That the price established by a stockholders' agreement may be less than the appraised or market value is unremarkable. Such agreements may have as their purpose: the payment of a price for a decedent's stock which will benefit the corporation or surviving stockholders by not unduly burdening them; the payment of a price tied to life insurance; or fixing a price which assures the beneficiaries of the deceased stockholder of a predetermined price for stock which might have little market value. . . . When the agreement was entered into in 1984, the order and time of death of stockholders was unknown. There was a "mutuality of risk."

In King v. Driscoll, 638 N.E.2d 488 (Mass. 1994), however, the Massachusetts Supreme Judicial Court limited the reach of that quotation in a case involving a repurchase agreement entered into by shareholders in a close corporation. The repurchase agreement was triggered when one of the shareholders, King, was discharged from his corporate position as vice-president and head of the manufacturing division. The trial court found that King's termination was in retaliation for participating in a derivative suit challenging the varying way the corporation had handled previous stock buybacks. The judge also found that company president Driscoll's course of conduct during that time exhibited a purpose to undermine King's ability to manage successfully the manufacturing division. The defendants cited Evangelista, seeking to reverse the trial court's conclusion that Driscoll and Marchant, another director, breached the duty of utmost good faith and loyalty to King when they terminated King's employment. The court distinguished the terms of the repurchase agreement from the defendant's conduct triggering the repurchase.

> Evangelista does not stand for the proposition that the existence of a buy back agreement completely relieves shareholders of the high duty owed to one another in all dealings among them.
>
> In this case, contrary to the facts of [Donahue v. Rodd Electrotype Co., 367 Mass. 578, 328 N.E.2d 505 (1975)] and Evangelista, the allegations of breach of the duty of utmost good faith and loyalty arose from the conduct of fellow shareholders Driscoll and Marchant during the whole series of events leading up to and including the termination of the plaintiff. The plaintiff did not

aver that the terms of the repurchase constituted a breach of the duty, but in essence argued that the conduct of the defendants which caused him to be terminated and, as a result, caused his stock to be repurchased constituted a breach of that duty. The judge agreed.

638 N.E.2d at 494.

For cases refusing to interfere with death-triggered share repurchases at then unfair prices, see Renberg v. Zarrow, 667 P.2d 465 (Okla. 1983); Kanawha-Roane Lands, Inc. v. Burford, 359 S.E.2d 618 (W. Va. App. 1987).

PROBLEM 5-5

A, B, and C joined together to purchase a wholesale lumber company. There was an understanding among the three that each would have input into the affairs of the company and that there would be constant communication among the shareholders. It was also understood that all three would be employed full time and that each intended to rely on employment with the corporation as the principal source of income. It was a key concern of the three that they retain ownership of the corporation. Four years later, the parties entered into a shareholders' cross-purchase agreement. Paragraph 7 of the agreement restricted the sale of stock to the terms of the agreement. It stated that upon the death or disability of a shareholder or if a shareholder retires or ceases to be employed for any reason, the corporation or the remaining shareholders shall buy the stock according to the agreement. Paragraph 8 provided that the purchase price of a buyback of the stock would be book value.

Seven years later, A and B became dissatisfied with C and caused the corporation to terminate his employment. In accordance with the agreement, the corporation gave C notice that it would purchase the stock owned by C. C feels this termination was an effort to secure the stock at an unfair price and to deprive C of salary, bonus, and participation in the business. Would C be successful in a suit for breach of fiduciary duty?

6 *The Limited Liability Company*

A. *Introduction*

A limited liability company (LLC) is formed by filing a chartering document, usually termed "articles of formation" or "articles of organization," with the state. Normally, these articles are barebones affairs. A separately adopted and nonpublic agreement, commonly termed an "operating agreement," specifies in detail the ownership rights, duties, and obligations of those who will own and manage the LLC.

To understand the nature of the LLC, it is instructive to consider how the LLC allocates among joint owners the ownership and management functions that are united in one person in a sole proprietorship. These functions are threefold: (1) serving as the firm's residual claimant and ultimate risk bearer, (2) overseeing business affairs and determining business policies, and (3) managing day-to-day affairs. In the sole proprietorship, the firm's entrepreneur, the sole proprietor, performs all three functions. The general partnership default rules divide all three functions equally among the general partners. Corporation law norms assign the sole proprietor's first function to shareholders,[1] the second function to the board of directors, and the third function to officers. The LLC permits planners to choose either a partnership-like or corporation-like allocation of functions.

Members. The LLC allocates the residual claimant status to the firm's "members." Thus, members, like shareholders in a corporation or general partners in a general partnership, share ratably in the profits of the firm, but only after all other claimants and needs of the firm have been satisfied. Most LLC statutes permit an LLC to be member managed or manager managed, usually providing member management as the default rule if the operating agreement does not provide otherwise.

Member-managed LLC. Under LLC statutory norms, members in a member-managed LLC function similarly to general partners in a general partnership. Not only are members the firm's residual claimants, but they also, collectively, have authority to manage the LLC's business and affairs. Further, each member owes fiduciary and contractual duties to the LLC in the carrying out of this management role.

---

1. The corporation does not shift ultimate risk bearing to shareholders. Instead, those who deal with the corporation bear the risk of nonpayment of their claims.

531

Managers and manager-managed LLC. LLC statutes provide that the sole proprietor's ownership functions may be allocated to one or more "managers," who may but need not be members of the LLC. In order to take advantage of this specialization of management function, the LLC is organized as a *manager-managed LLC.* In a manager-managed LLC, the members, as members, have no management authority or fiduciary responsibilities. Instead, the persons designated as managers are responsible for managing the business and affairs of the LLC.

Limited liability. In one very important respect, however, the LLC (like the corporation) fails to provide an analogue to the sole proprietor. Neither members nor managers are personally liable for the LLC's obligations. Thus, no one in the LLC is assigned the function of ultimate risk bearer; no one's personal wealth is put at risk to fulfill claims that the LLC would be unable to satisfy in case of business failure.[2]

To understand the LLC it is also important to comprehend how and why it emerged as a major business form, what needs it serves, and what ideological underpinnings constrain and shape its treatment by judges and legislators. It is important to understand and evaluate how the interplay of federal tax policy and the governance needs of entrepreneurs, investors, and business firms have interacted over time to change the nature of the LLC.

In the United States, the LLC is a relatively new and remarkably successful business form. Prior to 1990, only two states—Wyoming and Florida—had adopted LLC statutes. Between 1990 and 1994, the remaining 48 states adopted LLC acts.

The rise of the LLC occurred in the shadow of a perceived crisis—the substantial increase in malpractice litigation in the 1980s aimed at accountants, lawyers, and other professionals. These professionals were predominantly organized as general partnerships. As such, each partner was exposed to joint and several liability for the partnership's obligations, including losses resulting from another partner's or employee's negligence or misconduct. While corporate form offered potentially greater protection from vicarious liability, a switch to corporate form would impose significant tax costs for larger firms; partnership income was taxed only at the owner level, but corporate income was taxed twice, first at the entity level and again, to the extent distributed as a dividend, at the owner level.

Thus, professional firms and their advisors saw the LLC, with its limited liability for members and managers, as a far better alternative than the corporation, *if*—and it was a big *if*—the Internal Revenue Service would agree that this new business form qualified for partnership-like treatment as a pass-through entity. Under then-prevailing rules, the IRS denied an unincorporated business association partnership tax status if the association looked more like a corporation than a partnership. Four factors were assessed: (1) limited liability for owners, (2) centralized management, (3) free transferability of ownership interests, and (4) entity permanence. If an unincorporated business association had more than two of these characteristics, it would be classified and taxed as a corporation.

---

2. With no assigned residual risk bearer in the LLC, that risk necessarily falls on those with whom the LLC deals, raising concerns discussed in Chapter 7.

Since the LLC necessarily had one corporate characteristic—limited liability—Wyoming and Florida wrote their statutes to avoid the other three corporate characteristics. As a result, these first versions of the LLC had partnership-like decentralized management, dissolution at will (thereby avoiding entity permanence), and did not allow free transferability of membership interests. In 1988, the IRS ruled that a Wyoming-style LLC would be treated as a partnership for tax purposes.

The IRS's 1988 ruling opened the door for the rapid adoption of LLC legislation nationwide, but it also ensured that the first-generation LLC statutes would contain default rules (and sometimes mandatory or bullet-proof rules) similar to general partnership law.

Not surprisingly, the actual users of the LLC were predominantly very small firms who saw the LLC as an easier way to obtain limited liability and partnership tax treatment than operating in corporate form. The owner-managers of these very small firms in many cases lacked the sophistication and legal advice that often make judicial oversight and fiduciary duty regimes less necessary. However, this widespread use of the LLC by unsophisticated investors initially did not present the risk that minority investors would be subject to oppression by majority investors, because, unlike archetypal closely held corporations, the first-generation LLC provided dissolution at will, and thus exit at will, a rule derived from general partnership law.

In 1996, the IRS adopted a game-changing approach to the new entity. Effective January 1, 1997, the IRS would no longer apply the four-factor test to determine whether an unincorporated business association would be taxed as a partnership or corporation. Instead, an unincorporated firm, regardless of its attributes, would be allowed to elect whichever tax treatment it preferred without fear of second-guessing by the IRS. This new "check the box" policy had profound implications for the evolution of the LLC. Not only did the new policy provide tax-planning certainty to organizers of LLCs, but it also freed LLC planners from the need to worry about achieving a tax-driven mix of governance attributes. It also meant that LLC statutes no longer needed to provide default rules that made the LLC look more like a partnership than a corporation. Thereafter, as lobbyists and representatives of larger and more sophisticated investors continued to drive the evolution of the LLC, many states amended their LLC statutes to provide, or facilitate the adoption of, more corporation-like governance rules. These changes included lessening or eliminating a minority member's exit rights, making entity permanence the statutory norm, and allowing LLCs to have only one member. These changes made the LLC an even more desirable business form for larger professional firms, a potentially viable entity for publicly traded firms, and the most commonly used vehicle for closely held firms. At the same time, these changes made the LLC an entity certain to encounter in the closely held setting the same "oppression of minority owners" concerns that have traditionally plagued closely held corporations.

A key attribute of the LLC, both at the outset and currently, is its status as a contractual entity. While modern corporation statutes are primarily enabling, with statutes such as the Delaware Limited Liability Company Act regularly permitting planners to write an agreement changing the statutory default rules, there remain some mandatory rules, most notably the fiduciary duty of loyalty. Coming into being at a time when contractarian analysis of the corporation dominated legal thinking, the LLC was seen as a business entity intended for investors and business firms that preferred to design governance systems for themselves, rather than using the default rules in the corporate statute and one or more of the mandatory rules that went along with the corporate form. Debate continues as to whether there is or should be a mandatory core of fiduciary duty in the LLC.

As you work though the cases in this chapter, you should ask yourself what default or mandatory rules were the planners trying to avoid? Two threads stand out. First, the LLC statutes provide a series of choices such that parties will want or need a specific agreement to tailor the rules of their relationship (and for sophisticated deals will be willing to pay for such help). Second, some participants will want to use this contractual freedom to fence out judicial meddling in the parties' relationship. These participants may find it attractive to lessen the reach of fiduciary duty or judicial dissolution and may prefer nonjudicial resolution of any disputes that would be litigable.

The shift away from an IRS-rules-driven LLC opened the door for statutory innovation and state competition for the LLC-chartering business. The cases in this chapter reveal Delaware's success in the LLC field. In part this reflects an advantage seen in the prior discussion of public corporations. Delaware has developed a sophisticated judiciary in business matters and their workload makes them a repeat player in the evolving and difficult questions of business law. In contrast, LLC law in other states remains somewhat chaotic and unformed. As you will see in this chapter, Delaware LLC law not only provides a coherent and comprehensive set of rules, but also imposes fewer restrictions on planners. The resulting combination of flexibility, predictability, and certainty is attractive to planners and is decidedly less present in any other LLC jurisdiction. In this chapter, you will see repeated examples of sophisticated investors willing to plan beyond statutory default rules (and willing to pay for the planning). Note specifically Delaware's greater willingness than other states in an LLC context to permit members to contract around the fiduciary duty of loyalty and waive their right to petition a court for dissolution. Ask yourself for what set of ventures does such a public policy make sense, and keep in mind that the LLC form continues to be used for another subset of entities more like those seen in the cases in Chapter 5, entities for which planners and legislators may want very different rules.

Elf Atochem North America, Inc. v. Jaffari
Delaware Supreme Court, 1999
727 A.2d 286

VEASEY, CHIEF JUSTICE:

This is a case of first impression before this Court involving the Delaware Limited Liability Company Act (the "Act"). The limited liability company ("LLC") is a relatively new entity that has emerged in recent years as an attractive vehicle to facilitate business relationships and transactions. The wording and architecture of the Act is somewhat complicated, but it is designed to achieve what is seemingly a simple concept—to permit persons or entities ("members") to join together in an environment of private ordering to form and operate the enterprise under an LLC agreement with tax benefits akin to a partnership and limited liability akin to the corporate form.

This is a purported derivative suit brought on behalf of a Delaware LLC calling into question whether: (1) the LLC, which did not itself execute the LLC agreement in this case ("the Agreement") defining its governance and operation, is nevertheless bound by the Agreement; and (2) contractual provisions directing that all disputes be resolved exclusively by arbitration or court proceedings in California are valid under the Act. Resolution of these issues requires us to examine the applicability and scope of certain provisions of the Act in light of the Agreement.

We hold that: (1) the Agreement is binding on the LLC as well as the members; and (2) since the Act does not prohibit the members of an LLC from vesting exclusive subject matter jurisdiction in arbitration proceedings (or court enforcement of arbitration) in California to resolve disputes, the contractual forum selection provisions must govern.

Accordingly, we affirm the judgment of the Court of Chancery dismissing the action brought in that court on the ground that the Agreement validly predetermined the fora in which disputes would be resolved, thus stripping the Court of Chancery of subject matter jurisdiction.

FACTS

Plaintiff below-appellant Elf Atochem North America, Inc., a Pennsylvania Corporation ("Elf"), manufactures and distributes solvent-based maskants to the aerospace and aviation industries throughout the world. Defendant below-appellee Cyrus A. Jaffari is the president of Malek, Inc., a California Corporation. Jaffari had developed an innovative, environmentally-friendly alternative to the solvent-based maskants that presently dominate the market.

For decades, the aerospace and aviation industries have used solvent-based maskants in the chemical milling process. Recently, however, the Environmental Protection Agency ("EPA") classified solvent-based maskants as hazardous chemicals and air contaminants. To avoid conflict with EPA regulations, Elf considered developing or distributing a maskant less harmful to the environment.

In the mid-nineties, Elf approached Jaffari and proposed investing in his product and assisting in its marketing. Jaffari found the proposal attractive since his company, Malek, Inc., possessed limited resources and little international sales expertise. Elf and Jaffari agreed to undertake a joint venture that was to be carried out using a limited liability company as the vehicle.

On October 29, 1996, Malek, Inc. caused to be filed a Certificate of Formation with the Delaware Secretary of State, thus forming Malek LLC, a Delaware limited liability company under the Act. The certificate of formation is a relatively brief and formal document that is the first statutory step in creating the LLC as a separate legal entity. The certificate does not contain a comprehensive agreement among the parties, and the statute contemplates that the certificate of formation is to be complemented by the terms of the Agreement.

Next, Elf, Jaffari and Malek, Inc. entered into a series of agreements providing for the governance and operation of the joint venture. Of particular importance to this litigation, Elf, Malek, Inc., and

Jaffari entered into the Agreement, a comprehensive and integrated document of 38 single-spaced pages setting forth detailed provisions for the governance of Malek LLC, which is not itself a signatory to the Agreement. . . .

ELF'S SUIT IN THE COURT OF CHANCERY

On April 27, 1998, Elf sued Jaffari and Malek LLC, individually and derivatively on behalf of Malek LLC, in the Delaware Court of Chancery, seeking equitable remedies. Among other claims, Elf alleged that Jaffari breached his fiduciary duty to Malek LLC, pushed Malek LLC to the brink of insolvency by withdrawing funds for personal use, interfered with business opportunities, failed to make disclosures to Elf, and threatened to make poor quality maskant and to violate environmental regulations. Elf also alleged breach of contract, tortious interference with prospective business relations, and (solely as to Jaffari) fraud.

The Court of Chancery granted defendants' motion to dismiss based on lack of subject matter jurisdiction. The court held that Elf's claims arose under the Agreement, or the transactions contemplated by the agreement, and were directly related to Jaffari's actions as manager of Malek LLC. Therefore, the court found that the Agreement governed the question of jurisdiction and that only a court of law or arbitrator in California is empowered to decide these claims. Elf now appeals the order of the Court of Chancery dismissing the complaint.

GENERAL SUMMARY OF BACKGROUND OF THE ACT

The phenomenon of business arrangements using "alternative entities" has been developing rapidly over the past several years. Long gone are the days when business planners were confined to corporate or partnership structures. . . .

Limited partnerships date back to the 19th Century. They became an important and popular vehicle with the adoption of the Uniform Limited Partnership Act in 1916. Sixty years later, in 1976, the National Conference of Commissioners on Uniform State Laws approved and recommended to the states a Revised Uniform Limited Partnership Act ("RULPA"), many provisions of which were modeled after the innovative 1973 Delaware Limited Partnership (LP) Act. Difficulties with the workability of the 1976 RULPA prompted the Commissioners to amend RULPA in 1985. To date, 48 states and the District of Columbia have adopted the RULPA in either its 1976 or 1985 form. Delaware adopted the RULPA with innovations designed to improve upon the Commissioners' product. Since 1983, the General Assembly has amended the LP Act eleven times, with a view to continuing Delaware's status as an innovative leader in the field of limited partnerships.

The Delaware [Limited Liability Company] Act was adopted in October 1992. The Act is codified in Chapter 18 of Title 6 of the Delaware Code. To date, the Act has been amended six times with a view to modernization. The LLC is an attractive form of business entity because it combines corporate-type limited liability with partnership-type flexibility and tax advantages. The Act can be characterized as a "flexible statute" because it generally permits members to engage in private ordering with substantial freedom of contract to govern their relationship, provided they do not contravene any mandatory provisions of the Act. Indeed, the LLC has been characterized as the "best of both worlds."

The Delaware Act has been modeled on the popular Delaware LP Act. In fact, its architecture and much of its wording is almost identical to that of the Delaware LP Act. Under the Act, a member of an LLC is treated much like a limited partner under the LP Act. The policy of freedom of contract underlies both the Act and the LP Act.

In August 1994, nearly two years after the enactment of the Delaware LLC Act, the Uniform Law Commissioners promulgated the Uniform Limited Liability Company Act (ULLCA). To coordinate with later developments in federal tax guidelines regarding manager-managed LLCS, the Commissioners adopted minor changes in 1995. The Commissioners further amended the ULLCA in 1996. Despite its purpose to promote uniformity and consistency, the ULLCA has not been widely popular. In fact, only seven jurisdictions have adopted the ULLCA since its creation in 1994. A notable commentator on LLCs has argued that legislatures should look to either the Delaware Act or the Prototype Act created by the ABA when drafting state statutes.

POLICY OF THE DELAWARE ACT

The basic approach of the Delaware Act is to provide members with broad discretion in drafting the Agreement and to furnish default provisions when the members' agreement is silent. The Act is replete with fundamental provisions made subject to modification in the Agreement (*e.g.* "unless otherwise provided in a limited liability company agreement. . . .").

Although business planners may find comfort in working with the Act in structuring transactions and relationships, it is a somewhat awkward document for this Court to construe and apply in this case. To understand the overall structure and thrust of the Act, one must wade through provisions that are prolix, sometimes oddly organized, and do not always flow evenly. Be that as it may as a problem in mastering the Act as a whole, one returns to the narrow and discrete issues presented in this case.

FREEDOM OF CONTRACT

Section 18-1101(b) of the Act, like the essentially identical Section 17-1101(c) of the LP Act, provides that "[i]t is the policy of [the Act] to give the maximum effect to the principle of freedom of contract and to the enforceability of limited liability company agreements." Accordingly, the following observation relating to limited partnerships applies as well to limited liability companies:

> The Act's basic approach is to permit partners to have the broadest possible discretion in drafting their partnership agreements and to furnish answers only in situations where the partners have not expressly made provisions in their partnership agreement. Truly, the partnership agreement is the cornerstone of a Delaware limited partnership, and effectively constitutes the entire agreement among the partners with respect to the admission of partners to, and the creation, operation and termination of, the limited partnership. Once partners exercise their contractual freedom in their

partnership agreement, the partners have a great deal of certainty that their partnership agreement will be enforced in accordance with its terms.

In general, the commentators observe that only where the agreement is inconsistent with mandatory statutory provisions will the members' agreement be invalidated. Such statutory provisions are likely to be those intended to protect third parties, not necessarily the contracting members. As a framework for decision, we apply that principle to the issues before us, without expressing any views more broadly.

THE ARBITRATION AND FORUM SELECTION CLAUSES IN THE AGREEMENT ARE A BAR TO JURISDICTION IN THE COURT OF CHANCERY

In vesting the Court of Chancery with jurisdiction, the Act accomplished at least three purposes: (1) it assured that the Court of Chancery has jurisdiction it might not otherwise have because it is a court of limited jurisdiction that requires traditional equitable relief or specific legislation to act; (2) it established the Court of Chancery as the default forum in the event the members did not provide another choice of forum or dispute resolution mechanism; and (3) it tends to center interpretive litigation in Delaware courts with the expectation of uniformity. Nevertheless, the arbitration provision of the Agreement in this case fosters the Delaware policy favoring alternate dispute resolution mechanisms, including arbitration. Such mechanisms are an important goal of Delaware legislation, court rules, and jurisprudence.

MALEK LLC'S FAILURE TO SIGN THE AGREEMENT DOES NOT AFFECT THE MEMBERS' AGREEMENT GOVERNING DISPUTE RESOLUTION . . .

Notwithstanding Malek LLC's failure to sign the Agreement, Elf's claims are subject to the arbitration and forum selection clauses of the Agreement. The Act is a statute designed to permit members maximum flexibility in entering into an agreement to govern their relationship. It is the members who are the real parties in interest. The LLC is simply their joint business vehicle. This is the contemplation of the statute in prescribing the outlines of a limited liability company agreement.

CLASSIFICATION BY ELF OF ITS CLAIMS AS DERIVATIVE IS IRRELEVANT . . .

Although Elf correctly points out that Delaware law allows for derivative suits against management of an LLC, Elf contracted away its right to bring such an action in Delaware and agreed instead to dispute resolution in California. That is, Section 13.8 of the Agreement specifically provides that the parties (*i.e.,* Elf) agree to institute "[n]o action at law or in equity based upon *any* claim arising out of or related to this Agreement" except an action to compel arbitration or to enforce an arbitration award. Furthermore, under Section 13.7 of the Agreement, each member (*i.e.,* Elf) "consent[ed] to the exclusive jurisdiction of the state and federal courts sitting in

California in any action on a claim arising out of, under or in connection with this Agreement or the transactions contemplated by this Agreement. . . ."

THE ARGUMENT THAT CHANCERY HAS SPECIAL JURISDICTION FOR DERIVATIVE CLAIMS MUST FAIL

Elf claims that 6 Del. C. §§18-110(a), 18-111 and 18-1001 vest the Court of Chancery with subject matter jurisdiction over this dispute. According to Elf, the Act grants the Court of Chancery subject matter jurisdiction over its claims for breach of fiduciary duty and removal of Jaffari, even though the parties contracted to arbitrate all such claims in California. In effect, Elf argues that the Act affords the Court of Chancery "special" jurisdiction to adjudicate its claims, notwithstanding a clear contractual agreement to the contrary.

Again, we are not persuaded by Elf's argument. Elf is correct that 6 Del. C. §§18-110(a) and 18-111 vest jurisdiction with the Court of Chancery in actions involving removal of managers and interpreting, applying or enforcing LLC agreements respectively. As noted above, Section 18-1001 provides that a party may bring derivative actions in the Court of Chancery. Such a grant of jurisdiction may have been constitutionally necessary if the claims do not fall within the traditional equity jurisdiction. Nevertheless, for the purpose of designating a more convenient forum, we find no reason why the members cannot alter the default jurisdictional provisions of the statute and contract away their right to file suit in Delaware.

For example, Elf argues that Section 18-110(a), which grants the Court of Chancery jurisdiction to hear claims involving the election or removal of a manager of an LLC, applies to the case at bar because Elf is seeking removal of Jaffari. While Elf is correct on the substance of Section 18-110(a), Elf is unable to convince this Court that the parties may not contract to avoid the applicability of Section 18-110(a). We hold that, because the policy of the Act is to give the maximum effect to the principle of freedom of contract and to the enforceability of LLC agreements, the parties may contract to avoid the applicability of Sections 18-110(a), 18-111, and 18-1001. Here, the parties contracted as clearly as practicable when they relegated to California in Section 13.7 "any" dispute "arising out of, under or in connection with [the] Agreement or the transactions contemplated by [the] Agreement. . . ." Likewise, in Section 13.8: *"[n]o action at law or in equity based upon any claim arising out of or related to"* the Agreement may be brought, except in California, and then only to enforce arbitration in California.

Our conclusion is bolstered by the fact that Delaware recognizes a strong public policy in favor of arbitration. Normally, doubts on the issue of whether a particular issue is arbitrable will be resolved in favor of arbitration. In the case at bar, we do not believe there is any doubt of the parties' intention to agree to arbitrate *all* disputed matters in California. If we were to hold otherwise, arbitration clauses in existing LLC agreements could be rendered meaningless. By resorting to the alleged "special" jurisdiction of the Court of Chancery, future plaintiffs could avoid their own arbitration agreements simply by couching their claims as derivative. Such a result could adversely affect many arbitration agreements already in existence in Delaware.

VALIDITY OF SECTION 13.7 OF THE AGREEMENT UNDER 6 DEL. C. §18-109(D)

Elf argues that Section 13.7 of the Agreement, which provides that each member of Malek LLC "consents to the exclusive jurisdiction of the state and federal courts sitting in California in any action on a claim arising out of, under or in connection with this Agreement or the transactions contemplated by this Agreement..." is invalid under Delaware law. Elf argues that Section 13.7 is invalid because it violates 6 Del. C. §18-109(d).

Subsection 18-109(d) is part of Section 18-109 relating to "Service of process on managers and liquidating trustee." It provides:

> In a written limited liability company agreement or other writing, a manager or member *may* consent to be subject to the nonexclusive jurisdiction of the courts of, or arbitration in, a specified jurisdiction, or the exclusive jurisdiction of the courts of the State of Delaware, or the exclusivity of arbitration in a specified jurisdiction or the State of Delaware....

Section 18-109(d) does not expressly state that the parties are prohibited from agreeing to the *exclusive* subject matter jurisdiction of the courts or arbitration fora of a foreign jurisdiction. Thus, Elf contends that Section 18-109(d) prohibits vesting exclusive jurisdiction in a court outside of Delaware, which the parties have done in Section 13.7.

We decline to adopt such a strict reading of the statute. Assuming, without deciding, that Section 109(d) relates to subject matter jurisdiction and not merely *in personam* jurisdiction, it is permissive in that it provides that the parties "may" agree to the non-exclusive jurisdiction of the courts of a foreign jurisdiction or to submit to the exclusive jurisdiction of Delaware. In general, the legislature's use of "may" connotes the voluntary, not mandatory or exclusive, set of options. The permissive nature of Section 18-109(d) complements the overall policy of the Act to give maximum effect to the parties' freedom of contract. Although Section 18-109(d) fails to mention that the parties may agree to the *exclusive* jurisdiction of a foreign jurisdiction, the Act clearly does not state that the parties must agree to either one of the delineated options for subject matter jurisdiction. Had the General Assembly intended to prohibit the parties from vesting exclusive jurisdiction in arbitration or court proceedings in another state, it could have proscribed such an option. The Court of Chancery did not err in declining to strike down the validity of Section 13.7 or Section 13.8 of the Agreement.

NOTES AND QUESTIONS

1. As noted by Chief Justice Veasey in *Elf Atochem,* the Uniform Limited Liability Company Act adopted by the National Conference of Commissioners on Uniform State Laws (NCCUSL) in 1996 was an unsuccessful "uniform" act. It was premised on the need to have the LLC look as much like a partnership as possible. Delaware, instead, based its initial LLC statutes on the limited partnership, making the first-generation Delaware LLC look much more like a corporation. Events proved the Delaware approach more reflective of how LLC statutes would evolve. In 2006, the National Conference of Commissioners on Uniform State Laws adopted the Revised

Uniform Limited Liability Company Act (RULLCA). While the RULLCA reflects the strong trend toward entity permanence and corporation-like dissolution rules, it also contains provisions that are more likely to be attractive to closely held entities than to firms with more need to adapt to changed circumstances. Time will tell whether the RULLCA will gain widespread acceptance. As you proceed through this chapter, a comparison of these two competing statutory approaches will enrich your understanding of the LLC.

2. Chief Justice Veasey's enthusiasm for freedom of contract turned out to exceed the bounds of the Delaware legislature's enthusiasm with respect to LLC provisions whereby parties could agree to make a state other than Delaware the exclusive venue for litigating disputes between participants. Shortly after the decision in *Elf Atochem*, the Delaware legislature amended Section 18-109(d) to read as follows:

> In a written limited liability company agreement or other writing, a manager or member may consent to be subject to the nonexclusive jurisdiction of the courts of, or arbitration in, a specified jurisdiction, or the exclusive jurisdiction of the courts of the State of Delaware, or the exclusivity of arbitration in a specified jurisdiction or the State of Delaware, and to be served with legal process in the manner prescribed in such limited liability company agreement or other writing. Except by agreeing to arbitrate any arbitrable matter in a specified jurisdiction or in the State of Delaware, a member who is not a manager may not waive its right to maintain a legal action or proceeding in the courts of the State of Delaware with respect to matters relating to the organization or internal affairs of a limited liability company.

Why do you think the Delaware legislature responded in this fashion to the Supreme Court's decision in *Elf Atochem*?

B. *Planning for the Limited Liability Company*

Delaware LLCA §§101, 304, 306, 401-403, 503, 504, 505(c), 601-604
ULLCA §§110, 404, 407, 601

As Chief Justice Veasey noted in *Elf Atochem*, the Operating Agreement or Limited Liability Company Agreement is the cornerstone of an LLC. While LLC statutes provide default ownership-allocation rules, the LLC is an attractive business form for sophisticated investors who both need and want to tailor their own governance structures. At a minimum, the Operating Agreement should specify the basic economic and management arrangements that will govern the firm. Additionally, the Operating Agreement should specify the rules or processes that will determine how major changes in the relationships between and among members and managers will take place and what rights exist to exit from the relationship and withdraw invested capital.

As with all contracts covering continuing relations, venturers must weigh and determine the appropriate balance between certainty and adaptability. Should profit shares be fixed or set in a manner more responsive to contributions actually made? When should profits be distributed? Should all members participate in management? How should managers be selected and under what circumstances should they be subject to removal? Under what circumstances should a manager be able to voluntarily retire? Under what circumstances should members be able or be required to withdraw from the firm? To what economic payments should a withdrawing partner be entitled? If the Operating Agreement is silent on a key issue, then statutory default rules will govern. These rules may produce results that seem quite harsh ex post. But so too may the terms actually negotiated.

The following case illustrates the complexity that can be involved in negotiating an Operating Agreement. As you read through the case, consider what statutory default rules have been varied, and why.

Olson v. Halvorsen[1]
Delaware Court of Chancery, 2009
2009 WL 1317148

Lamb, Vice Chancellor.

A founder of a successful hedge fund brings this action against his two co-founders and entities created to run the fund, claiming that they failed to pay him for his equity interest in the enterprise after he was let go. At trial, the co-founders proved that there was an oral agreement reached, before any operations began, that all earnings would be paid out annually, with no deferral of compensation, and that a departing member would receive only his accrued compensation and the balance of his capital account. Following trial, the court concludes that agreement was never superceded by any other agreement relating to deferred compensation or post-termination rights. Thus, the departing founder is not entitled to any further payment.

A.   The Parties

The plaintiff in this action is Brian T. Olson, one of the founders of Viking Global, an investment management firm and hedge fund. The defendants are the two other co-founders of Viking, O. Andreas Halvorsen and David C. Ott, and the various entities through which Viking conducted its business: Viking Global Investors LP, a Delaware limited partnership ("Investors"); Viking Global Partners LLC, a Delaware limited liability company ("Partners"); Viking Global Performance LLC, a Delaware limited liability company ("Performance"); and Viking Global Founders LLC, a Delaware limited liability company ("Founders"). . . .

B.   The Facts

Halvorsen, Olson, and Ott worked together at Tiger Management, which was, at the time, one of the world's largest hedge funds. Halvorsen joined Tiger in early 1992. By 1996, Halvorsen had risen to be director of equity investments, the number two person on the investment side of Tiger and second only to the hedge fund's founder,

---

1. Judgment affirmed, Olson v. Halvorsen, 986 A.2d 1150 (Del. 2009).

Julian Robertson. Halvorsen was involved in Tiger's hiring of both Ott and Olson. In early 1999, frustrated with Robertson's management, Halvorsen decided to leave Tiger to form his own hedge fund, Viking. Dissatisfied with his compensation, Olson also resigned from Tiger at the end of 1998, but stayed at the fund for a few months to help find his replacement. Halvorsen considered Olson a brilliant analyst and contacted him to discuss the possibility of Olson joining Viking after he finished with his responsibilities at Tiger. Halvorsen also contacted Ott, who was still at Tiger, about joining Viking.

1.   THE FEBRUARY 1999 MEETING: VIKING'S CORE PRINCIPLES

After a few initial conversations, Halvorsen, Olson, and Ott met at Halvorsen's home in late February 1999 for a more in-depth discussion regarding the new Viking enterprise. At this February meeting, the three founders discussed the governance, investment strategy, compensation, and logistics related to the formation of Viking.

Halvorsen, Olson, and Ott agreed that Viking would be governed by an operating committee made up of the three of them and decisions would require a two of three vote, subject to a Halvorsen veto. The three founders agreed to allow Halvorsen a veto because he had the most experience among them and would contribute about $50 million to the fund, while Olson and Ott would each contribute somewhere between $2 million and $4 million.

The three founders also agreed that the fund would be a long/short equity fund and each would manage a portfolio within their area of expertise. Olson would manage a telecommunications, media, and technology ("TMT") portfolio. Ott would manage a consumer portfolio, and Halvorsen would manage a financial services portfolio. In addition, initially, Halvorsen would be the Chief Investment Officer (the "CIO") and would manage a CIO portfolio not tied to a specific industry, but rather focused on the most attractive investments from the sector-based portfolios.

As a function of Tiger's deferred compensation system, each of Halvorsen, Olson, and Ott forfeited large sums of money upon resigning. Wanting to avoid at Viking the perceived unfairness of the Tiger compensation system, they decided, at the February 1999 meeting, that all the profits at Viking would be paid out annually. Each year, after all other employees were paid, Halvorsen would receive 55% and Olson and Ott would each receive 22.5% of the profits.[3] In the event of a sale of Viking, the three founders discussed splitting the equity proceeds 66% to Halvorsen, 20% to Olson, and 14% to Ott. Ott wanted to think about this equity split, and later agreed to the percentages. Shortly thereafter, Ott explained to the other two that these "equity" percentages were useless and ridiculous, because if they paid out all of the profits each year, there would be no equity to split. Halvorsen agreed with Ott's logic. The three founders later changed the equity percentages to 55% to Halvorsen and 22.5% to each of Olson and Ott, to match

---

3. Months later, the three founders divided their annual compensation into two separate percentages: a job percentage (also called the work percentage) and a residual percentage (also called equity, management, or non-work percentage). The job percentage represented the three founders' contributions to Viking through their investment-related activities and was essentially a proxy for their replacement cost. The residual percentage represented the three founders' compensation for all of the other services they performed for the firm.

their profit-sharing percentages. Halvorsen, Olson, and Ott each testified that at the February meeting they all agreed that if any one of them left Viking he would only be entitled to his earned compensation and his capital account (the "cap and comp" agreement). Halvorsen testified that the three founders reached this decision based on their shared belief that one should be compensated fully for what one contributes (not a partial amount due to deferred compensation) and that, as a quid pro quo, one should not continue to take a paycheck after one leaves the firm and stops contributing.

As to logistics, the three founders decided that Halvorsen would be primarily responsible for raising capital and hiring employees, Olson would deal with the lawyers regarding formation of the necessary entities, and Ott, who was still employed at Tiger and had less time, would locate office space.

Also in early 1999, although he could not remember exactly when or for what purpose, Olson created a document summarizing the terms by which Viking would be operated. Olson shared this document with Halvorsen and Ott. The terms largely track the discussions the three founders had at the February meeting, and Olson admitted that, at the time he drafted the term sheet, the three founders had agreed that each would only be entitled to his accrued compensation and capital account balance upon leaving Viking.

2. THE VIKING ENTITIES ARE FORMED

A few months after the February meeting, the three founders, with the advice of counsel, decided to create three Delaware entities to carry on the Viking business: (1) Performance, a limited liability company, to collect Viking's performance fees of 17.5% to 20% of the annual gains of the hedge fund per year; (2) Investors, a limited partnership, to pay Viking's expenses, employ Viking's staff, enter into operational contracts on Viking's behalf, and collect a management fee of 1.5% of the hedge fund's assets under management each year; and (3) Partners, a limited liability company, to serve as the general partner of Investors. The certificates of formation for these three entities were executed on April 8, 1999 and filed with the Secretary of State of Delaware the following day.

3. THE LONG-FORM OPERATING AGREEMENTS FOR THE VIKING ENTITIES

Olson directed counsel to draft operating agreements for the Viking entities. On April 8, 1999, Viking's counsel sent Olson a first draft of the operating agreement for Partners. Counsel later provided drafts of the operating agreements for Performance and Investors. These drafts reflected the oral agreements reached by the three founders at the February meeting and the core principles listed in Olson's term sheet.[4] Each of these drafts were over 10 pages in length and came to be known during the course of this litigation as the long-form agreements.

---

4. Section 3.03 describes an "Executive Committee" (later called the "Operating Committee") with the power to act on a two of three vote, subject to Halvorsen's veto. Section 3.01(e) vests the Executive Committee with the power to require members to retire from Viking. Sections 5.03, 5.05, and 5.06 provide that a departing member is only entitled to accrued compensation and his capital account balance.

4. THE SHORT-FORM OPERATING AGREEMENTS FOR THE VIKING ENTITIES

In April 1999, the long-form agreements were not yet in final form and the Viking entities needed operating agreements to facilitate the entering of a real estate lease and the opening of bank accounts. Thus, Olson asked Viking's counsel to draft short-form operating agreements for Investors and Partners. After a few changes requested by Olson, all three founders signed short-form agreements for Investors and Partners on May 10, 1999. On September 8, 1999, the three founders also executed a short-form agreement for Performance. The short-form agreements are skeletal (each only three or four pages in length) and do not contain all of the terms agreed upon by the founders at the February meeting. The short-form agreements do, however, appear to be drafted in line with the core principles. Each short-form agreement provides that a member will be entitled to receive his accrued compensation and capital account balance upon departure.

5. THE LONG-FORM DRAFTING PROCESS CONTINUES

After the short-form agreements were executed, Olson continued to work with the attorneys to refine the long-form agreements for the Viking entities. Between April 1999 and the launch of Viking on October 1, 1999, over a dozen drafts of the long-form agreements were produced. During this period, Olson maintained responsibility for interacting with Viking's outside counsel.[6] By late 2000, the drafting process had come to a halt even though none of the three founders had signed any of the draft long-form agreements for Investors or Partners. As a result of a potential dispute with an employee, the three founding members agreed to supersede the short-form agreement for Performance by signing the Limited Liability Company Agreement of Viking Global Performance LLC dated September 28, 1999. That agreement was amended on January 11, 2002 (the "Performance Long-Form Agreement"). The Performance Long-Form Agreement provided that the Operating Committee could remove members with or without cause. Also, the Performance Long-Form Agreement reflected the three founders' original oral agreement at the February meeting that a member would receive only his accrued compensation and his capital account balance upon departure. In light of the executed Performance Long-Form Agreement, Olson admits that he is not entitled to any interest in Performance beyond his accrued compensation and capital account balance.

6. THE FOUNDERS EARNOUT AND THE FOUNDERS ENTITY

In mid-1999, Olson raised a new compensation concept with Halvorsen and Ott. Olson proposed that upon departure from Viking a founding member (or his estate)

---

6. Following Viking's launch, Brian Smith (Viking's Chief Financial Officer) and Carl Casler (then Viking's Treasurer) assumed some of the responsibility for working with the lawyers on the long-form drafts.

would be paid an earnout, through a new entity to be called Founders. Halvorsen and Ott considered the idea interesting, but Olson did not detail how the earnout would work at their first meeting, and the three founders left the issue open for discussion.

On July 14, 1999, Olson sent a memorandum to outside counsel stating that Viking would "probably" create another entity called Founders which would "embody some equity-like features relating to [the three founders'] ownership of the management company." Olson testified that, a month or two later, the three founders held a second meeting to discuss the earnout concept. Also, Olson testified that he distributed a term sheet to facilitate discussion about the earnout. Halvorsen and Ott, however, both testified that they had not seen this term sheet before the litigation.

Olson instructed the attorneys to begin work on an operating agreement for Founders in line with the terms he set forth in the term sheet. The document the attorneys prepared provided that, upon retirement or death, each founder would receive a declining percentage of his interest in Viking for six years following his departure. Olson and the outside attorneys went through nine drafts of the Founders operating agreement, dating as late as December 2000.

The drafting of the Founders operating agreement took place over about a year and a half, and at no point during that process did Olson discuss with his partners the changes he was making to what he now claims was their "agreement." . . .

Olson also added a requirement to the draft Founders operating agreement that Halvorsen keep over 89% of his capital in the fund or forfeit his veto. This concept was entirely absent from the term sheet. On April 23, 2001, CFO Brian Smith sent Halvorsen the draft Founders agreement and noted that Halvorsen had a question about the clause requiring him to maintain over 89% of his capital in the fund or lose his veto right. Halvorsen testified that he had never agreed to place any contingencies on his veto rights, was shocked to see such a clause in the draft Founders agreement, and had asked Smith about the clause. Both changes discussed above substantially track Olson's handwritten notes to the outside attorneys and were admittedly never discussed with Halvorsen or Ott.

From 1999 until 2001, Halvorsen and Ott received various drafts of the Founders agreement, but never discussed them or the earnout concept in general with Olson after the two brief meetings in the summer of 1999. None of the three founders ever signed a Founders operating agreement and both Halvorsen and Ott convincingly testified at trial that at no time did they agree to or make promises to Olson regarding the Founders earnout.

At Olson's direction, outside counsel filed a certificate of formation for Founders on September 28, 1999. Thereafter, also at Olson's direction, Founders was made a member of Performance. Founders was never made a partner of Investors, as contemplated in the draft Founders operating agreement, and Olson did not voice concern over this fact while at Viking.[11] From 2000 to 2005, at Olson's direction, Smith ran certain amounts of the three founders' residual income through the Founders

---

11. Olson did, however, ask Smith to make Founders a partner of Investors in June of 2000. Olson did not request resolutions be drawn to this effect, did not request a vote of the Operating Committee (as required), or follow up on this request.

entity. These amounts ranged from approximately $3.9 million in 2004 to $84.9 million in 2001 and totaled almost $200 million. At trial, Smith stated that he ran money through Founders for bookkeeping purposes because Olson directed him to do so. Smith described Founders as mere vestige.

7. OLSON THREATENS TO LEAVE VIKING IN 2001, RENEGOTIATES PERCENTAGES, BUT FOUNDERS IS NOT MENTIONED

Olson's TMT portfolio performed extremely well in the early days of Viking, and by the end 2001 Olson was dissatisfied with his compensation.[13] Olson demanded that no one at Viking be paid more than he.[14] When Halvorsen refused to agree to Olson's demand, Olson announced that he was leaving Viking.

Cahill, the head trader at Viking who later became Viking's president, convinced Olson and Halvorsen to address their differences and negotiate a mutually acceptable solution, which they did over a period of two or three weeks. It was unclear from the record whether Olson actually left the Viking offices during the period of dispute. As part of the negotiations, Halvorsen, Olson, and Ott agreed to reallocate their compensation percentages so that Halvorsen's share decreased and Olson's share increased.

Olson admitted that the three founders did not discuss the impact of these changes in percentages on the earnout he claims already existed or on their purported entitlement to the fair value of the Founders entity. It was clear at trial that Halvorsen and Ott thought that by readjusting these percentages only annual compensation would be affected, not retirement benefits. Both Halvorsen and Ott testified that they agreed to increase Olson's compensation because of the value he was adding to the fund, but would have never agreed to increase his retirement benefits without, at the very least, requiring him to stay at Viking for a substantial period of time. If, as Olson argues, the three were actually readjusting future compensation and retirement payouts, Olson could have left the day after the renegotiation and walked away with a massive sum of additional money, without conveying *any* additional benefit to Viking. Halvorsen testified, "I'm just trying to understand how I could possibly, if it was an issue that we had a retirement plan, I would possibly agree to someone who had just walked out the door . . . [to] double his retirement benefits and he can walk out the door that minute." Ott testified to the same effect, stating:

I would think if anyone had the thought that [the job and residual percentage renegotiations] created a long-term obligation, that we would have had further discussion and, at a minimum, at least say, "Well, you need to commit to stick around for this period of time . . ." because otherwise [Olson] could have left the next day and all you have done is given [him], per his analysis, tens of millions of dollars.

The three founders did not discuss the effect of the renegotiation on departure payouts nor did they discuss entering into an agreement with Olson obligating him to

---

13. Olson was paid over $28 million in 2000 and over $42 million in 2001.

14. Halvorsen was paid over $55 million in 2000 and over $78 million in 2001.

stay at Viking for any period of time. From this, it is logical to conclude that the three founders believed the "cap and comp" agreement was still in place.

8. FOUNDERS RESURFACES

Founders was largely off the radar screen from 2001 until 2004. In the summer of 2004, it reappeared. Cahill, who became Viking's president in 2003, testified that as he dug into Viking's various entities and operating agreements he uncovered the draft Founders agreement. Cahill testified at trial that he was alarmed by the earnout concept because he had been "told just the opposite on several occasions, that you only get paid if you work at Viking." Cahill testified that Olson told him personally on multiple occasions that the three founders' "equity" would be retired for no consideration if they left Viking.[19] After reviewing the draft Founders agreement, Cahill met with Halvorsen, Olson, Ott, and Smith to inquire about the earnout concept. Cahill was informed by each of the three founders that no agreement had ever been reached regarding an earnout. At trial, Smith testified that he believed that the three founders never agreed upon the proposed earnout and that the draft Founders operating agreement had never been finalized.

In an effort to resolve open questions about Founders, Cahill listed Founders on the management committee agendas from July 2004 until November 2004. Olson received the management committee agendas and attended the majority of the management committee meetings, but never asked why Founders was on the agenda and never insisted that the Founders operating agreement had already been agreed to. Despite appearing on the management committee agenda for months, Olson testified that Founders was not discussed at the actual meetings. Smith testified that in December 2004, before departing on paternity leave, he reminded Halvorsen, Olson, and Ott that the issues surrounding Founders had not been addressed. Both Cahill and Smith came away from the discussions in the second half of 2004 believing that there had been no resolution on the draft Founders agreement or the earnout concept. . . .

10. OLSON'S SABBATICAL

While Olson achieved remarkable returns in 2000 and 2001, the returns on his portfolio decreased substantially over the next few years. Olson communicated his disappointment in both his returns and his role at Viking at a management committee

---

19. Cahill testified that Olson told him the founders were only entitled to "cap and comp" upon departure in 1999 when Viking was attempting to lure Cahill away from Bear Stearns to become their head trader. Cahill was given a 5% "equity" interest in the firm, which, like the founders, would affect his annual compensation, but not his retirement payment. Additionally, in 2003 Viking's top analysts were clamoring for additional compensation and asked Cahill to make sure that the founders' "equity" would be available for distribution when the founders left the firm, or scaled back involvement. Cahill testified that he confirmed with Olson that the "cap and comp" agreement was in place and reported back to the analysts. Purcell also testified that on numerous occasions Olson told him that the founders would take only their "cap and comp" when they left Viking.

meeting at the end of 2004.[23] On March 6, 2005, Olson sent an email to Halvorsen, Ott, and Cahill announcing that he had decided to step away from managing the TMT portfolio and take a six-month sabbatical. During that time, Olson stated that he would work on some personal goals that he had developed before starting at Viking and that he would think about how he could transition into another role at Viking when he returned. One of the different roles Olson suggested in his email was running a separately managed fund, even though he realized that opening a separate fund would present a number of challenges for Viking. Before he left, Olson told Cahill that he could not be 100% sure that he would return to Viking.

Another reason for Olson's sabbatical appears to have been his dissatisfaction with the proposal, made immediately before his leave, to make Ott co-CIO with Halvorsen. Ott and Halvorsen later did become co-CIOs and the management committee changed the compensation formula for the CIO role while Olson was on sabbatical.[24] Ott, Halvorsen, and Smith testified that the change was not expected to have a material effect on Halvorsen's and Ott's compensation; nevertheless, Olson was not pleased.

During his sabbatical, Olson received periodic updates about the business decisions taking place at Viking, but did not regularly receive agendas or participate in management committee meetings.

11. ALTERNATIVES FOR OLSON ARE DISCUSSED

Viking failed to find a replacement to run Olson's TMT portfolio, shut the portfolio down, and managed those funds in the CIO portfolio. In June 2005, Halvorsen asked Cahill, with the assistance of Viking management, to study what role Olson could play should he return. Cahill analyzed the possibility of starting a second fund, as suggested in Olson's departing email, but came to the conclusion, along with other members of Viking's management, that a separate fund would not be in the best interest of Viking and its investors. During his attempt to find a new role for Olson, Cahill came to believe that, by and large, Viking operated more efficiently without Olson and that a number of employees resented Olson's overbearing management style.

12. OLSON IS TERMINATED

After discussing Cahill's findings, Halvorsen and the other management committee members unanimously determined that there was no longer a place at Viking for Olson. On August 23, 2005, Halvorsen sent Olson an email to schedule a meeting to discuss observations related to Olson's future role at Viking. The three founders agreed to meet on August 29, 2005 at the Viking offices. During that meeting, Halvorsen informed Olson that he would not be permitted to return to Viking at the

---

23. Olson's profit or loss as an analyst was roughly $216.7 million in 2000, $316.1 million in 2001, $41.2 million in 2002, $94.0 million in 2003, $38.7 million in 2004, and $–1.2 million in 2005. At trial, Purcell questioned whether all the profit listed should have been attributed to Olson, as opposed to other analysts.

24. The primary driver of Halvorsen's and Ott's compensation was changed from the profits of their individual portfolios to the profits of the firm as a whole.

end of his six-month sabbatical. Also at this meeting, Olson, for the first time in years, asked about Founders. Halvorsen said they had not given Founders any thought.

On October 17, 2005, the Operating Committee removed Founders as a member of Performance by written resolution. Also by written resolution of the Operating Committee, dated as of December 1, 2005, Olson was retired as a member of Performance, Investors, and Founders, effective 30 days later. Viking paid Olson his compensation for all of 2005 and the full balance of his capital accounts in each Viking entity....

At trial and in his papers, Olson focused on his alleged entitlement to fair value for his ownership interest in Founders, Investors, and Partners. The defendants proved (and Olson admitted) that the three founders orally agreed that a departing member or partner would only be entitled to his accrued compensation and his capital account balance. Olson did not prove the existence of any superceding agreement that conflicted with that understanding. Accordingly, Olson is not entitled to fair value for his ownership interest in any of the Viking entities.

A.   THE FAIR VALUE STATUTES

The Delaware Revised Uniform Limited Partnership Act ("DRULPA") states that a withdrawing partner is entitled to the fair value of his partnership interest "if not otherwise provided in a partnership agreement."[27] Section 18-604 of the Delaware Limited Liability Company Act, tracks this language and states that a resigning member is entitled to the fair value of his membership interest "if not otherwise provided in a limited liability company agreement."

B.   OPERATING AGREEMENTS GOVERN IN CONFLICT WITH FAIR VALUE STATUTES

As set forth in the language of both statutes and in a number of Delaware cases, Delaware law generally defers to the demonstrated agreement of the parties in the limited partnership and limited liability company context. Both DRULPA and the Limited Liability Company Act expressly provide that it is the policy of the act "to give the maximum effect to the principle of freedom of contract and to the enforceability of [limited liability company/partnership] agreements."[29] Accordingly, if a valid and enforceable agreement of the parties conflicts with the fair value statute, the agreement of the parties will govern.

C.   THE CAP AND COMP AGREEMENT FOR ALL VIKING ENTITIES

All the founders, including Olson, testified that they reached an oral agreement on the core principles of Viking. These core principles, Olson admitted, included that

27. 6 Del. C. §17-604.
29. 6 Del. C. §17-1101(c); 6 Del. C. §18-1101(b).

a departing member would take only his accrued compensation and capital account balance when he left Viking—an agreement that conflicts with the fair value statutes.[30] The oral agreement as to Viking's core principles was reached before any of the Viking entities were formed and was intended to apply to Viking as a whole. Thus, the original agreement governing the operation of each Viking entity, including Founders, was the oral agreement regarding the company's core principles.[31] This oral agreement was refined by subsequent signed written agreements for Investors, Partners, and Performance—all of which were in line with the "cap and comp" agreement.

D. NO DEPARTURE FROM THE "CAP AND COMP" AGREEMENT

The evidence does not suggest that Halvorsen and Ott agreed to depart from the "cap and comp" agreement when they formed Founders, but rather confirms that the "cap and comp" agreement held strong through the formation of Founders and continued past Olson's termination. . . .

The evidence overwhelmingly shows that Halvorsen, Olson, and Ott agreed that they would each take only their accrued compensation and capital account balance when they left Viking and that they never agreed to an alternative operating agreement for Founders. Moreover, Investors and Partners were both governed by signed short-form agreements that stated that a partner or member was entitled only to his accrued compensation and capital upon departure. Thus, Olson was only entitled to his accrued compensation and the balance of his capital account. . . .

NOTES AND QUESTIONS

1. Drafting for withdrawal rights has taken on greater significance as the LLC statutes have evolved. Many first-generation statutes hewed to the general partnership model so that a member had the right to withdraw from the firm at will, and the resulting dissociation triggered either (1) a buyout at "fair value" or (2) a dissolution of the firm. The trend is strongly away from this general partnership approach. The RULLCA allows a member to dissociate at will, but such dissociation neither dissolves the firm, nor provides a fair-value buyout. As a result, if the Operating Agreement does not vary the LLC statutory default rule, minority members may find the value of their membership interest "locked in" with no ready market to provide liquidity.

2. The statutory evolution in Delaware is similar to the larger trend. Under Delaware LLCA §604, unless the LLC Agreement otherwise provides, "upon resignation any resigning member . . . is entitled to receive, within a reasonable time after resignation,

---

30. Olson testified: "[W]e agreed that a departing member would receive, probably most simply stated, their capital back, their invested capital plus their accrued compensation." . . .

31. These oral agreements are examples of enforceable oral limited liability company and limited partnership agreements under Delaware law that the court alluded to in its summary judgment opinion in this case. The "cap and comp" agreement is enforceable because it is possible that it could be completed in the span of one year. . . .

the fair value of such member's limited liability company interest. . . ." Further, under the version of Delaware LLCA §603 in effect from 1992 until July 31, 2006, unless otherwise provided, a member had the right to resign upon giving six months prior written notice. However, effective August 1, 2006, the default rule in Delaware LLCA §603 has been flipped; §603 now provides that "[a] member may resign from a limited liability company only at the time or upon the happening of events specified in a limited liability company agreement and in accordance with the limited liability company agreement." Why do you think LLC statutes have evolved in this way?

3. It is not uncommon for start-up ventures to begin operation before all of the key agreements are completed. Does the failure to complete an Operating Agreement before commencing operation of an LLC present any greater or lesser risk than commencing operation as a general partnership or corporation before the partnership agreement or shareholders' agreement is finalized? How does the flipping of the default rule in Note 2 affect who bears this risk?

PROBLEM 6-1

Reconsider the facts of Problem 3-4 (pages 160-162). Assume, at least tentatively, that you and the Venturers have decided that an LLC would be preferable to a corporation as the initial business form for the venture. Prepare an Operating Agreement that meets the needs and expectations of the various Venturers and investors. In doing so, you will need to choose a state in which to form the LLC. Confine your choices to either Delaware or a jurisdiction that has adopted RULLCA, and be prepared to defend your choice. Be sure that your Operating Agreement is fully consistent with the provisions of the governing limited liability company act. As your understanding of statutory and judicial norms will increase as you proceed through this chapter, please return to this task as a part of your preparation for subsequent class sessions concerning the LLC, and update your Operating Agreement to reflect later acquired knowledge and insights.

C.   Fiduciary and Contractual Duties

1.   In General

Delaware LLCA §1101 (c)-(e), 1104
RULLCA §§110(c), 110(d)-(g), 409

LLC statutes vary in the extent to which they allow contractual variation of the common law fiduciary duties of care and loyalty. At one extreme is Delaware, which permits elimination of all duties other than the contractual duty of good faith and fair dealing. Most other states do not allow elimination of the duty of loyalty, or allow curtailment of the duty of loyalty to a lesser extent than Delaware. See, e.g., Ala. Code §10-12-21 (articles or operating agreement may modify statutory duties but may not provide for specified exceptions, including eliminating the duty of loyalty); Fla. Code §608.403 (agreement may not eliminate loyalty among other things). RULLCA does not allow elimination of the duties of care and loyalty, but does permit detailed specifications of how those duties can be satisfied that allow a careful drafter to sharply curtail those duties.

Jurisdictional differences also exist in the treatment of member-managed and manager-managed LLCs. Many jurisdictions appear to closely follow a general partnership analogy with respect to member-managed firms. This approach is reflected in RULLCA §409(a), which provides that a member in a member-managed firm "owes to the company and . . . the other members the fiduciary duties of loyalty and care. . . ." From a default rule perspective, manager-managed LLCs are functionally closer to the corporation than to the general partnership: the management function and the ownership function are separated, giving members in a manager-managed LLC a passive governance role akin to that played by shareholders in a corporation. Thus, it might seem likely that the fiduciary duties owed by managers to the LLC and its members would be analogous to the fiduciary duties owed by directors to a corporation and its shareholders.

However, assessing the nature of fiduciary duty in manager-managed LLCs is much less clear-cut than the analogy to corporation law would suggest. On the corporation law side, the corporation code in every American state allows deviations from the standard governance regime, but in practice most corporations operate with shareholders, a board of directors, and a slate of officers as set out in the statute. Additionally, corporation law allows only limited contractual reduction or variance in the directors' fiduciary duties of care and loyalty, and variance is usually accomplished in a uniform way by adoption of statutorily proscribed exculpation provisions in the corporate charter.

LLC statutes allow greater deviations from the standard governance structure, and courts and commentators have interpreted the contractual nature of the LLC so as to emphasize freedom of contract. As a result, unlike the uniformity of governance structures that characterizes usage of corporate form, the governance structures used by manager-managed LLCs often diverge from the simple member-manager dichotomy. Likewise, users of manager-managed LLCs commonly craft specialized fiduciary duty regimes, but there is no corporation-law-like uniformity in the contractual devices used to accomplish this tailoring.

The following case explores the nature of the contractual and fiduciary duties owed by managers in a manager-managed LLC. As you read the case, consider the extent to which the outcome and analysis is dictated by the LLC statute, by the parties' private ordering, or by underlying policy precepts.

Bay Center Apartments Owner, LLC v. Emery Bay PKI, LLC
Delaware Court of Chancery, 2009
2009 WL 1124451

STRINE, VICE CHANCELLOR.

I. INTRODUCTION

This action arises out of a failed condominium development project based in Emeryville, California (the "Project"). The Project was a venture of two entities, plaintiff Bay Center LLC, and defendant Emery Bay PKI, LLC ("PKI"). PKI is owned and managed by defendant Alfred E. Nevis. In November 2005, Bay Center and PKI formed defendant Emery Bay Member, LLC ("Emery Bay") and designated PKI as the managing member.

The Emery Bay "LLC Agreement" gave PKI considerable power and authority to manage the affairs of Emery Bay. The LLC Agreement also contemplated that PKI would be responsible for managing the Project, but the parties defined those responsibilities through a separate agreement, the "Development Management Agreement." PKI was not required to sign the Development Management Agreement; instead, PKI designated one of its affiliates, defendant Emery Bay ETI, LLC ("ETI"), to be the entity bound by the terms of the Development Management Agreement. ETI's only counterparty in the Development Management Agreement was a wholly owned subsidiary of Emery Bay.

Soon after the Project began, it encountered problems stemming from mismanagement and poor financial performance. Emery Bay defaulted on a construction loan it had obtained from a third-party bank (the "A&D Loan") and which Nevis had personally guaranteed (the "Personal Guarantee"). Bay Center alleges that the defendants secretly renegotiated this Loan on several occasions, resulting in the diversion of cash flow from the Project that was earmarked to repay an unsecured note from Emery Bay held by Bay Center (the "Bay Center Note"). By renegotiating the Loan in this way, Nevis avoided triggering his Personal Guarantee, and PKI avoided capital calls.

The Project experienced a host of other problems, all supposedly resulting from mismanagement of the Project by PKI's affiliates, including budget overruns in excess of $10 million, vendor complaints, poor sales, and squatters and vandalism. The Project eventually failed under the weight of these troubles, and entered into receivership in December 2007.

In its Verified Amended Complaint (the "Complaint"), Bay Center seeks monetary damages from Nevis and the entities he controlled: PKI, ETI, and Emery Bay. Bay Center's most direct route to recovery is through a breach of contract claim under the LLC Agreement. But, this approach is limited because, among other things, PKI is the only defendant who was a party to that Agreement. Bay Center therefore seeks to expand its remedial options by bringing claims for breach of the contractually implied covenant of good faith and fair dealing, breach of fiduciary duty, common law fraud, and aiding and abetting.

The defendants move to dismiss all of Bay Center's claims except those based on breach of contract. In this opinion, I deny the defendants' motion in its entirety. . . .

III. LEGAL ANALYSIS . . .

A. THE IMPLIED COVENANT OF GOOD FAITH AND FAIR DEALING

Bay Center's claim [in Count III] under the implied covenant of good faith and fair dealing is part of Bay Center's efforts to, in essence, hold PKI secondarily liable for the alleged breaches of the Development Management Agreement and Bay Center Note (collectively, the "Supporting Agreements") despite the fact that PKI was not a signatory to either of the Supporting Agreements. Bay Center's primary argument is contained in Count I, which the defendants have not moved to dismiss, and rests on the theory that PKI agreed in the LLC Agreement to ensure that the Supporting Agreements would be performed. Bay Center brings Count III in the alternative in case the court does not share Bay Center's interpretation of the LLC Agreement.

Bay Center's claim in Count I is helpful in understanding the argument Bay Center makes under Count III. In Count I, Bay Center argues that PKI was required to cause ETI to perform its obligations competently under the Development Management Agreement and to cause Emery Bay to perform its obligations under the Bay Center Note. In making this argument, Bay Center relies on the detailed terms of Article 5 of the LLC Agreement, entitled "Powers, Rights and Duties of Members." Under this article, PKI had broad authority to run Emery Bay: "[PKI] *shall manage* and conduct the operations and affairs of [Emery Bay] and make all decisions regarding [Emery Bay] and its business and assets." The LLC Agreement, "without limiting the generality" of this provision, also granted PKI the express "power and authority" to undertake a number of actions. This included the "power and authority" to: 1) "[c]ause the Development Manager to perform its obligations under the Development Management Agreement . . . or, if the Development Manager fails to perform such obligations, performing or causing such services to be performed, at no additional cost"; 2) "[p]erform, or cause to be performed, all of [Emery Bay's] obligations under any agreement to which [Emery Bay] is a party; and relatedly 3) "take all proper and necessary actions *reasonably required* to cause [Emery Bay] . . . to perform and comply with the provisions . . . of any loan commitment . . . or other contract, instrument or agreement to which [Emery Bay] is a party."

Bay Center's argument in Count I is that the fact that PKI unambiguously had the power and authority to cause performance of the Supporting Agreements meant PKI also had the obligation to do so. This argument is supported by the language surrounding the grant of express authority to perform the Supporting Agreements, such as the statement that PKI "shall manage" the affairs of Emery Bay, which can reasonably [be] read to mean that PKI had the obligation to exercise its authority on behalf of all the members, and the language cited above regarding Emery Bay's loan commitments, which tempers the efforts required to those "reasonably required" to meet the loan obligation. Likewise, the language stating that if the Development Manager fails to perform its obligations, PKI has the power and authority to "perform[ ] or caus[e] such services to be performed, *at no additional cost,* for [Emery Bay]'s benefit" supports such a reading. In other words, Bay Center reads the items listed in §5.1(a) as spelling out the core functions that PKI had to perform as part of its obligation to manage Emery Bay and attempt to make the Project a success. PKI takes a different view of the purpose of §5.1(a)'s enumeration of PKI's express powers, arguing that §5.1(a) did "not require PKI to do anything with respect to the Development Management Agreement, it simply empower[ed] it to do so if it so decide[d]."

These arguments are, of course, not before the court at this time because the defendants have not moved to dismiss Count I, but they illustrate the ambiguity that exists in the LLC Agreement as to who was responsible for the bulk of the conduct alleged in Bay Center's Complaint. The pertinent question at this stage is, if this ambiguity regarding PKI's express obligation or lack thereof to cause performance of the Supporting Agreements is resolved against Bay Center, as I assume it would be for purposes of this alternatively pled count, whether that obligation can be implied in the LLC Agreement.

This is a close question. Delaware courts rightly employ the implied covenant sparingly when parties have crafted detailed, complex agreements, lest parties be stuck by judicial error with duties they never voluntarily accepted. Nevertheless, Delaware courts have "recognized the occasional necessity of implying contract terms to ensure the parties' reasonable expectations are fulfilled." In the context of corporate entities, "[t]he implied covenant functions to protect stockholders' expectations that the company and its board will properly perform the contractual obligations they have under the operative organizational agreements." Part of corporate managers' proper performance of their contractual obligations is to use the discretion granted to them in the company's organizational documents in good faith.

Here, PKI had the obligation to manage Emery Bay and the discretion to cause the Supporting Agreements to be performed. PKI was required to carry out these functions in good faith, meaning PKI could not engage in "arbitrary or unreasonable conduct" that had the effect of preventing Bay Center from "receiving the fruits of the bargain." This bargain was, essentially, that in exchange for contributing the real estate to be developed, Bay Center would reap the rewards of PKI's project management skills and efforts. PKI's conduct allegedly frustrated the parties' intent to develop a profitable condominium complex because PKI in bad faith failed to force the entities that were contractually obligated to perform tasks that were crucial to the Project's success to fulfill their obligations, even though PKI had the express authority to do so. And Bay Center has pled facts from which it can reasonably be inferred that PKI's decision not to cause performance of the Supporting Agreements was not in good faith. For starters, Emery Bay's alleged breaches of the Bay Center Note benefited PKI by diverting cash that Emery Bay was supposed to use to repay the Note to fund the depleted A&D Loan reserves, which PKI would have otherwise had to fund through capital calls. And, the decision not to pursue claims against ETI under the Development Management Agreement was a conflicted one because Nevis, as the controller of both Emery Bay and ETI, stood on both sides of it.

Thus, Bay Center has sufficiently pled that PKI had an implied duty to cause performance of the Supporting Agreements and that Bay Center breached this duty, and I deny the defendants' motion to dismiss Count III.

B. BREACH OF FIDUCIARY DUTY

1. The LLC Agreement's Treatment of Fiduciary Duties

As a threshold matter, I address the disagreement between the parties as to what fiduciary duties existed under the LLC Agreement. The Delaware LLC Act gives members of an LLC wide latitude to order their relationships, including the flexibility to limit or eliminate fiduciary duties.[32] But, in the absence of a contrary provision in the

---

32. 6 Del. C. §18-1101(e); *see also* Elf Atochem N. Am., Inc. v. Jaffari, 727 A.2d 286, 291 (Del. 1999) ("The basic approach of the Delaware Act is to provide members with broad discretion in drafting the Agreement.").

LLC agreement, the manager of an LLC owes the traditional fiduciary duties of loyalty and care to the members of the LLC.[33]

The defendants claim that the parties took full advantage of this flexibility by eliminating all fiduciary duties in the LLC Agreement. Bay Center, in contrast, claims that the LLC Agreement specifically preserves the traditional fiduciary duties. To support these starkly opposite positions, the parties point to two separate and seemingly contradictory provisions of the LLC Agreement:

> Section 6.1 *Relationship of Members.* Each Member agrees that, to the fullest extent permitted by the Delaware Act and except as otherwise expressly provided in this Agreement or any other agreement to which the Member is a party: . . . (b) *The Members shall have the same duties and obligations to each other that members of a limited liability company formed under the Delaware Act have to each other.*

> Section 6.2 *Liability of Members.* . . . *Except for any duties imposed by this Agreement . . . each Member shall owe no duty of any kind* towards the Company or the other Members in performing its duties and exercising its rights hereunder or otherwise.

Thus, the LLC Agreement states, on a single page, that the members of Emery Bay both owe each other the default fiduciary duties that exist between members of an LLC absent alteration in an LLC agreement, and at the same time owe each other no duty of any kind not imposed by the LLC Agreement itself.

In resolving this apparent paradox for purposes of this motion, I look to the pleading standards under Rule 12(b)(6). On a motion to dismiss, the court cannot choose between reasonable interpretations of ambiguous contract provisions. Instead, defendants are only entitled to dismissal if "the interpretation of the contract on which their theory of the case rests is the '*only* reasonable construction as a matter of law.'" The determinative question is therefore whether the defendants' position that the LLC Agreement eliminates their fiduciary duties is the only reasonable one. I find that it is not.

The defendants argue that under §6.2, a duty must be expressly imposed by the LLC Agreement in order for PKI to be bound to it. According to the defendants, no fiduciary duty is expressly imposed on PKI in the LLC Agreement. But, it is reasonable to read §6.1(b) as doing precisely that. Section 6.1(b) expressly imposes the default fiduciary duties on PKI, so the default fiduciary duties are carved out of §6.2's elimination of duties by the "except for any duties imposed by this Agreement" language in that provision. The duties eliminated by §6.2 are those that are not traditional fiduciary duties or are otherwise not expressly contemplated in the LLC Agreement.

Because the existence of fiduciary duties under §6.1(b) can be reconciled with §6.2's apparent elimination of them in this way, Bay Center's reading of the LLC Agreement is more reasonable than the defendants' reading. It is a maxim of contract interpretation that, "given ambiguity between potentially conflicting terms, a contract should be read so as not to render any term meaningless." The defendants have not

---

33. The Delaware LLC Act is silent on what fiduciary duties members of an LLC owe each other, leaving the matter to be developed by the common law. The LLC cases have generally, in the absence of provisions in the LLC agreement explicitly disclaiming the applicability of default principles of fiduciary duty, treated LLC members as owing each other the traditional fiduciary duties that directors owe a corporation. . . .

offered a coherent argument for how the LLC Agreement can be read to eliminate fiduciary duties without rendering §6.1(b) meaningless. And, the interpretive scales also tip in favor of preserving fiduciary duties under the rule that the drafters of chartering documents must make their intent to eliminate fiduciary duties plain and unambiguous. As a result, the defendants' interpretation of the fiduciary duty provisions of the LLC Agreement is not the most reasonable interpretation, let alone the only reasonable interpretation. Thus, I construe the LLC Agreement in favor of Bay Center and assume, for the purposes of this motion to dismiss, that the LLC Agreement requires Emery Bay's members to act in accordance with traditional fiduciary duties.

2. Breach of Fiduciary Duty by PKI and Nevis

In Count IV, Bay Center alleges that PKI and Nevis breached their fiduciary duties to Bay Center by, among other things, improperly diverting rental income from the Project to avoid capital calls, modifying the A&D Loan without Bay Center's consent, and allowing construction employees to occupy units on the Property for free.

The defendants' only challenge to this Count with regard to PKI is the argument discussed above that the LLC Agreement eliminates fiduciary duties. Because I must assume at this stage that the LLC Agreement does impose fiduciary obligations on PKI, and because Bay Center has alleged a number of facts from which it can be inferred that PKI breached its duties, I deny the motion to dismiss Count IV as to PKI.

The analysis regarding Nevis is less straightforward. Nevis himself is not a member or officer of Emery Bay, and is thus beyond the normal scope of those who owe fiduciary duties in the corporate context. Bay Center's theory of liability rests on a line of cases, beginning with In re USACafes, L.P. Litigation, 600 A.2d 43 (Del. Ch. 1991), holding that "those affiliates of a general partner who exercise control over the partnership's property may find themselves owing fiduciary duties to both the partnership and its limited partners." Importantly, the defendants do not challenge the general applicability of this doctrine in the LLC context. . . .

In practice, the cases applying *USACafes* have not ventured beyond the clear application stated in *USACafes:* "the duty not to use control over the partnership's property to advantage the corporate director at the expense of the partnership." Limiting the application of *USACafes* to this duty provides, in my view, a rational and disciplined way of protecting investors in alternative entities with managing members who are themselves entities, while not subjecting all the individuals who work for managing members to wide-ranging causes of action. Bay Center must therefore plead that Nevis benefited himself at the expense of Emery Bay in order to withstand this motion to dismiss.

Bay Center has met this pleading burden in at least one important respect. Bay Center alleges that Nevis caused Emery Bay to make cash sweeps to satisfy the renegotiated A&D Loan, which avoided a default on the Loan, and in turn, the triggering of Nevis' substantial Personal Guarantee. Stated differently, Nevis used his control over Emery Bay's assets to stave off personal liability. . . . [A]t this stage Bay Center has created a reasonable inference that Nevis used his control over Emery Bay's property to shield himself from monetary liability at the expense of Bay Center. Under *USACafes* and its progeny, that suffices to state a claim. Thus, I deny the defendants' motion to dismiss Count IV as to Nevis.

NOTES AND QUESTIONS

1. In *Gatz Properties, LLC v. Auriga Capital Corp.*, 59 A.3d 1206 (Del. 2012) (hereinafter *Gatz*), the Delaware Supreme Court challenged the Court of Chancery's view that "default fiduciary duties" exist under the Delaware Limited Liability Company Act. In a per curiam opinion, the Court asserted that "the merits of the issue whether the LLC statute does—or does not—impose default fiduciary duties is one about which reasonable minds could differ. . . ." Id. at 1219. Rather than assume that the Delaware Supreme Court would follow the lead of the Court of Chancery, the opinion suggested that proponents of the Court of Chancery's interpretation "may be well advised to consider urging the General Assembly to resolve any statutory ambiguity on this issue." Id. The Delaware Bar quickly took this suggestion to heart, and the General Assembly equally quickly resolved the issue raised by the Supreme Court in favor of the Court of Chancery position by amending Delaware LLCA section 1104, effective August 1, 2013, to read, and include the highlighted language, as follows: "In any case not provided for in this chapter, the rules of law and equity, including *the rules of law and equity relating to fiduciary duties and* the law merchant, shall govern."

2. Writing in the shadow of the Supreme Court's *Gatz* opinion, Vice Chancellor Laster offered a compelling explanation of the important role fiduciary duty plays in protecting the reasonable expectations of investors in firms falling at the less sophisticated or less well-planned end of the spectrum of LLCs.

> One particular statutory feature of the LLC Act elevates the importance of the [fiduciary duty's] gap-filling role. Section 101(7) of the LLC Act defines a limited liability company agreement as "any agreement (whether referred to as a limited liability company agreement, operating agreement or otherwise), written, *oral* or implied, of the member or members as to the affairs of a limited liability company and the conduct of its business." 6 Del. C. §18–101(7) (emphasis added). By authorizing oral LLC agreements, and by further authorizing "any agreement . . . as to the affairs of a limited liability company and the conduct of its business" to be deemed an LLC agreement, the LLC Act creates myriad opportunities for LLC agreements that range from the minimalistic to the ill-formed to the simply incomplete. In authorizing this level of informality, the LLC Act resembles its partnership forebears, where agreements likewise can be formed orally or by implication and where fiduciary duties are an important part of the entity landscape. See, e.g., 6 Del. C. §15–101(12); 6 Del. C. §17–101(12). For the LLC Act to take the same approach suggests that the General Assembly assumed that a similar backdrop of default fiduciary duties would be available to fill the potentially considerable gaps in the parties' agreement.

Feeley v. NHAOCG, LLC, 62 A.3d 649, 663 (2012).

3. As noted by Chancellor Strine, part of the need for a default fiduciary duty regime is the limited role that the contractual duty of good faith and fair dealing can, or should, play in resolving disputes.

> The common law fiduciary duties that were developed to address those who manage business entities were, as the implied covenant [of good faith and fair dealing], an equitable gap-filler. If, rather than well thought out fiduciary duty principles, the implied covenant is to be used as the sole default principle of equity, then the risk is that the certainty of contract law itself will be undermined. The implied covenant has rightly been narrowly interpreted by our Supreme Court to apply only "when the express terms of the contract indicate that the parties would have agreed to the obligation had they negotiated the issue." The implied covenant is to be used "cautious[ly]" and does not apply to

situations that could be anticipated, which is a real problem in the business context, because fiduciary duty review typically addresses actions that are anticipated and permissible under the express terms of the contract, but where there is a potential for managerial abuse. For these reasons, the implied covenant is not a tool that is designed to provide a framework to govern the discretionary actions of business managers acting under a broad enabling framework like a barebones LLC agreement. In fact, if the implied covenant were used in that manner, the room for subjective judicial oversight could be expanded in an inefficient way. The default principles that apply in the fiduciary duty context of business entities are carefully tailored to avoid judicial second-guessing. A generalized "fairness" inquiry under the guise of an "implied covenant" review is an invitation to, at best, reinvent what already exists in another less candid guise, or worse, to inject unpredictability into both entity and contract law, by untethering judicial review from the well-understood frameworks that traditionally apply in those domains.

Auriga Capital Corp. v. Gatz Properties, LLC, 40 A.3d 849, 853-4 (Del. Ch. 2012).

4. As the Court of Chancery has noted in the parallel context of limited partnerships, there will undoubtedly be circumstances where investors have unwittingly or ill-advisedly committed funds for membership interests in LLCs that have effectively struck all of the default fiduciary duties. Assuming that the trial judges continue to strictly apply implied covenant of good faith and fair dealing, then for minority investors "the protection provided by Delaware law is scant." *Gerber v. Enterprise Products Holdings, LLC*, 2012 WL 34442 (Del. Ch.). Time will tell how investors and business planners will react and adjust to this reality.

2. Mimicking Corporate Form

Delaware LLCA §1101(c)-(e)
RULLCA §§110, 409

Operating as an LLC may offer substantial advantages for business associations that anticipate frequent related party transactions, believe the advantages of such transactions outweigh the risks, and want such transactions to be insulated from judicial review to the maximum extent possible. One method of increasing certainty is to mimic corporate form—specifically adopt corporation law default rules—and then tailor and modify those rules to fit the needs of a particular venture. The following case exemplifies the advantages and continuing drafting pitfalls of such approach.

Kahn v. Portnoy
Delaware Court of Chancery, 2008
2008 WL 5197164

CHANDLER, CHANCELLOR.

Limited liability companies are primarily creatures of contact, and the parties have broad discretion to design the company as they see fit in an LLC agreement. With this discretion, however, comes the risk—for both the parties and this Court—that the resulting LLC agreement will be incomplete, unclear, or even incoherent.

In this case, plaintiff alleges that the director defendants breached their fiduciary duties to the company by approving a transaction that was allegedly designed to benefit a director at the expense of the company. As the company in this case is an LLC, the fiduciary duties of the directors are defined in the LLC agreement. This agreement, however, explicitly imports and modifies the familiar and well defined fiduciary duties from Delaware corporate law. The result is a company whose directors are governed by a modified version of the fiduciary duties of directors of Delaware corporations. Unfortunately, the agreement in this case fails to clearly articulate the contours of these contractual fiduciary duties. The result is an LLC agreement that provides an ambiguous definition of fiduciary duties and is open to more than one reasonable interpretation.

Since I am faced with a motion to dismiss for failure to state a claim, I am not allowed to choose between reasonable interpretations of ambiguous provisions of a contract. Accordingly, and for the reasons stated below, I must deny the motion to dismiss.

I. BACKGROUND . . .

B. THE PARTIES AND THE FACTS

Nominal defendant TravelCenters of America, LLC ("TA" or the "Company") is a publicly traded Delaware LLC with its principal executive offices in Westlake, Ohio. TA is one of the largest operators of truck stops in the United States. Plaintiff Alan R. Kahn is a TA shareholder.

Defendant Hospitality Properties Trust ("HPT") is a publicly traded real estate investment trust ("REIT"). HPT owns real property, some of which it leases to TA. Reit Management & Research LLC ("RMR") is a privately owned company held by defendant Barry M. Portnoy ("Portnoy") and his son, Adam D. Portnoy, with Portnoy as the majority beneficial owner. RMR provides management services to companies that own and operate real estate, including TA and HPT.

The individual defendants are the directors of TA. Defendant Portnoy is a director of TA and HPT. Portnoy is also the founder and a director of: HRPT Properties Trust ("HRPT"), a publicly traded REIT that primarily owns office buildings; Senior Housing Properties Trust ("SNH"), a publicly traded REIT that primarily owns assisted living facilities and nursing homes; and Five Star Quality Care Inc. ("FVE"), a publicly traded company that operates senior living facilities leased from SNH. Portnoy was a partner at the law firm of Sullivan & Worcester LLP from 1978 to 1997 and was chairman of that firm from 1994 to 1997. Portnoy's wife is the founder of Immigrant Learning Center, Inc. (the "ILC"), a not-for-profit adult learning center based in Malden, Massachusetts. Plaintiff alleges that the individual director defendants, RMR, and Sullivan & Worcester LLP make regular financial contributions to the ILC.

[Defendant directors O'Brien, Koumantzelis, Gilmore, and Donelan have many relationships with Portnoy, Portnoy's companies, and the ILC, discussed below.]

2. *The Petro Transaction*

On May 30, 2007, HPT agreed to acquire Petro Stopping Holdings, L.P. for $630 million plus $25 million in transactions costs, and TA agreed to acquire Petro Stopping Centers, L.P. ("Petro Centers"), a truck stop operator with operations throughout the United States (collectively the "Petro Transaction"). The transaction was organized so that HPT acquired the real estate of 40 Petro Centers truck stops. HPT then leased those facilities to TA (the "Petro Lease Transaction") pursuant to a May 30, 2007 lease agreement (the "Petro Lease Agreement").

Plaintiff alleges that the terms of the Petro Lease Agreement are more favorable to HPT than to TA and require TA to pay HPT above-market rent. In support of this allegation, plaintiff alleges that a typical REIT capitalization rate of 7.5 percent is appropriate for non-distressed properties and would imply an annual rent of $49 million. Plaintiff alleges that the Petro Lease Agreement obligates TA to pay an annual rent of $62 million, representing a 9.5 percent capitalization rate.

Plaintiff alleges that TA's directors breached their fiduciary duties to TA by approving the Petro Lease Transaction, a transaction plaintiff alleges was designed to benefit HPT, RMR, and Portnoy at the expense of TA. Plaintiff contends that the terms of the Petro Lease Agreement benefit HPT because it is able to collect above-market rents and benefit RMR (and therefore Portnoy) because RMR collects as a fee a percentage of the gross rent collected by HPT. By contrast, the fees that RMR collects from TA are allegedly not affected by the above market rent because those fees are based on a percentage of TA's "gross fuel gross margin (the difference between wholesale and retail price)" and non-fuel revenues.

II. ANALYSIS

A. ENFORCEMENT OF THE LLC AGREEMENT

The well settled policy of the Delaware Limited Liability Company Act is to give maximum effect to the principle of freedom of contract. LLC agreements are contracts that are enforced according to their terms, and all fiduciary duties, except for the implied contractual covenant of good faith and fair dealing, can be waived in an LLC agreement. Accordingly, I will look to the terms of the LLC Agreement to determine the fiduciary duties the directors owe the Company and whether the directors can be personally liable if they breach those duties.

B. RULE 12(B)(6) . . .

1. *The LLC Agreement and the Pleading Requirements*

TA is governed by the terms of the Amended and Restated Limited Liability Company Agreement of TravelCenters (the "LLC Agreement"). The LLC Agreement provides that the "authority, powers, functions and duties (including fiduciary duties)" of the board of directors will be identical to those of a board of directors of a business corporation organized under the Delaware General Corporation Law ("DGCL"), unless otherwise specifically provided for in the LLC Agreement. Section 7.5(a)[17] of the LLC Agreement makes several modifications to the duties owed by the directors of a Delaware corporation.

Defendants argue that the second sentence of §7.5(a) alters the pleading standard by creating a presumption that the board of directors acted in accordance with their duties, notwithstanding that the board's decision may have been interested. According to defendants, the presumption can only be overcome by clear and convincing evidence; therefore, plaintiffs must demonstrate through clear and convincing evidence that they have rebutted this presumption and are entitled to relief. Defendants' interpretation of §7.5(a), however, is not the only reasonable interpretation of that provision. Since the Court is deciding a motion to dismiss, I must adopt the reasonable interpretation that is most favorable to plaintiff, the nonmoving party.

The clause on which defendants rely—the second of two sentences in §7.5(a)—must be read in its context. When read in light of its location in the LLC Agreement, the second sentence in §7.5(a) could reasonably be interpreted to apply only to board decisions that involve a conflict between a shareholder and the board or a shareholder and the Company.

The first sentence of §7.5(a) specifies that certain courses of action by the board of directors are deemed approved by shareholders if the course of action is "(i) approved by a Share Plurality . . . or (ii) on terms no less favorable to the Company than those generally being provided to or available from unrelated third parties or (iii) fair and reasonable to the Company. . . ." Such approval is deemed to exist notwithstanding certain conflicts of interest. The second sentence of §7.5(a)—the clause on which defendants rely—follows the sentence that deems approval of certain interested transactions. It provides:

> It shall be presumed that, in making its decision and notwithstanding that such decision may be interested, the Board of Directors acted properly and in accordance with its duties (including fiduciary duties), and in any proceeding brought by or on behalf of any Shareholder or the Company challenging such approval, the Person bringing or prosecuting such proceeding shall have the burden of overcoming such presumption by clear and convincing evidence.

---

17. Section 7.5(a) provides, in full, as follows:

Unless otherwise expressly provided in this Agreement or required by the Delaware LLC Act, whenever a potential conflict of interest exists or arises between any Shareholder or an Affiliate thereof, and/or one or more Directors or their respective Affiliates and/or the Company, any resolution or course of action by the Board of Directors in respect of such conflict of interest shall be permitted and deemed approved by all Shareholders, and shall not constitute a breach of this Agreement, of any agreement contemplated herein, or of any duty stated or implied by law or equity, including any fiduciary duty, if the resolution or course of action in respect of such conflict of interest is (i) approved by a Share Plurality (with interested Shareholders not counted for any purpose), or (ii) on terms no less favorable to the Company than those generally being provided to or available from unrelated third parties or (iii) fair and reasonable to the Company, taking into account the totality of the relationships between the parties involved (including other transactions that may be particularly favorable or advantageous to the Company). It shall be presumed that, in making its decision and notwithstanding that such decision may be interested, the Board of Directors acted properly and in accordance with its duties (including fiduciary duties), and in any proceeding brought by or on behalf of any Shareholder or the Company challenging such approval, the Person bringing or prosecuting such proceeding shall have the burden of overcoming such presumption by clear and convincing evidence.

This sentence directly follows the first sentence in the section and is contained in the same paragraph. While it creates a presumption that certain board decisions are proper notwithstanding certain conflicts of interest, under at least one reasonable interpretation, the sentence does not create a presumption for all decisions of the board. The presumption applies to the board in making "its decision." Read in the context of the preceding sentence, it would be reasonable to interpret "its decision" to refer only to the conflicted board decisions dealt with in the first sentence of §7.5(a). The first sentence applies to decisions of the board of directors that pose a conflict between "any Shareholder or an Affiliate thereof, and/or one or more Directors or their respective Affiliates and/or the Company." One reasonable way to read this clause is that it only includes conflicts (1) between a shareholder and the board or (2) between a shareholder and the Company, or (3) both. Under this reading, the clause would not apply to director decisions where there is a conflict between the directors and the Company. Thus, the second sentence of §7.5(a) would only create a presumption for transactions in which there is a conflict between a shareholder and the board or a shareholder and the Company, but not where there is a conflict between a director and the company.

Under this reasonable interpretation, §7.5(a) would not apply to the decision of the board to approve the challenged Petro Lease Transaction because the conflicts of interest were not between a shareholder and a director or a shareholder and the company. The Petro Lease Transaction involved a board decision in the face of a conflict between a single director (Portnoy) and the Company. Plaintiff alleges that Portnoy stood on both sides of the Petro Lease Transaction and stood to benefit personally from the transaction. The other directors allegedly acted in the best interest of Portnoy at the expense of the Company. As I have shown, under one reasonable interpretation, §7.5(a) would not apply to the decision to approve the Petro Lease Transaction. Because the application of §7.5(a) is ambiguous, I must adopt the reasonable interpretation that favors the nonmoving party. Under that interpretation, §7.5(a) would not apply to the board decision that is challenged in this case.

Even assuming, *arguendo,* that §7.5(a) applies to the decision of the board to approve the Petro Lease Transaction, the "clear and convincing" language in §7.5(a) does not necessarily alter the pleading standard. The Court does not apply a standard of proof at the motion to dismiss stage of the proceedings; rather, I must only determine whether plaintiff would be entitled to relief under any reasonable interpretation of the facts alleged. While it is true that the complaint must be dismissed if plaintiff would not succeed even if all his well pleaded allegations were proven true, plaintiff need not meet a heightened evidentiary standard at the pleading stage.

2. *Fiduciary Duties Under the LLC Agreement*

The LLC Agreement specifies that the Company will be managed by a board of directors that, subject to exceptions elsewhere in the LLC Agreement, has the same powers and duties (including fiduciary duties) as a board of directors of a corporation organized under the DGCL. The directors of a Delaware corporation owe the corporation dual duties of due care and loyalty. Implicated in this case is the duty of loyalty which requires that directors act in the best interest of the company and prohibits them from using their positions as directors to further their own self-interest. The business judgment rule is a presumption that the Court will not second guess decisions made by directors unless "the directors are interested or lack independence relative to the decision, do not act in good faith, act in a manner that cannot be attributed to a rational business purpose or reach their decision by a grossly negligent process. . . ."

After expressly importing corporate fiduciary duty concepts, the LLC Agreement modifies the duties owed by the TA directors. Specifically, §7.5(a) of the LLC Agreement modifies the duties of the directors with respect to certain transactions; however, as explained above, under at least one reasonable interpretation, §7.5(a) does not modify the directors' fiduciary duties because the challenged Petro Lease Transaction involves conflicts of interest between TA directors and the Company. Under this interpretation, the duties of the director defendants are defined by the duties owed by the directors of a Delaware corporation. Whether the defendants can be personally liable for violating their duties, however, is governed by the exculpatory provisions in §10.2 of the LLC Agreement.

3. The Exculpatory Provisions

The LLC Agreement contains two provisions that exculpate TA directors from personal liability for monetary damages. Both of these provisions contain exceptions for certain conduct that is not exculpated, and the two provisions define these exceptions differently. [Section 10.2(a) does not exculpate director "acts or omissions not in good faith" and §10.2(b) does not exculpate directors who "acted in bad faith."] . . .

It is well settled that good faith does not constitute an independent fiduciary duty; it is encompassed within the fiduciary duty of loyalty. The duty of loyalty, however, is not limited to cases in which there is a conflict of interest between a fiduciary and the company. A director does not act in good faith, even if there is not a direct conflict of interest as to that director, unless the director "acts in the good faith belief that her actions are in the corporation's best interest." Thus, a director does not act in good faith if the director acts with a subjective belief that her actions are not in the best interest of the corporation, such as when she is acting for the benefit of a related person at the expense of the company. This is "classic, quintessential bad faith. . . ."

The complaint sets forth sufficient factual allegations to show, at this preliminary stage, that Portnoy's loyalties to the company were divided with respect to the Petro Lease Transaction. As I have explained, the duty of good faith requires that Portnoy act with a good faith belief that his actions are in the best interest of TA. Portnoy, as a director of HPT and TA, is therefore bound to act in the best interest of both companies. Thus, when Portnoy acted on behalf of TA in approving the transaction, his loyalties as an HPT director raise at least a reasonable doubt as to whether he was acting in the best interest of TA.[36] Additionally, Portnoy's interest in RMR means that Portnoy stands to benefit personally from the transaction if TA is bound to pay above market rents to HPT. As explained above, plaintiff has alleged that payments to HPT filter through to RMR (and Portnoy) through agreements between RMR and HPT.

---

36. Defendants argue that the second sentence of §7.5(a) requires the Court to ignore director conflicts of interest, however, I have concluded that there is ambiguity regarding whether §7.5(a) applies to the Petro Lease Transaction.

Intentionally acting to benefit oneself at the expense of the Company is a quintessential example of failing to act in good faith, which requires a director to act with the good faith belief that his actions are in the best interest of the company. Plaintiff's well pleaded factual allegations, which support the allegation that Portnoy used the Petro Lease Transaction to benefit himself at the expense of the Company, are sufficient allegations of bad faith to survive a motion to dismiss.

Making the same presumptions in plaintiff's favor, I am unable to conclude with reasonable certainty that the other directors acted in good faith when they approved the Petro Lease Transaction. Plaintiff alleges that the members of the TA board were beholden to Portnoy and approved the Petro Lease Transaction to benefit Portnoy at the expense of TA. Plaintiff supports this allegation with specific factual allegations regarding the board members' relationships to Portnoy and Portnoy-related entities. For example, O'Brien is a director of TA, its President and Chief Executive Officer, a Senior Vice President of RMR, and President and a director of RMR Advisors. Accordingly, O'Brien owes a duty of loyalty to TA and RMR, entities that, according to the complaint, have diverging interests with respect to the Petro Lease Transaction. Additionally, the allegations in the complaint are sufficient to support, at least at the motion to dismiss stage, the claim that O'Brien was beholden to Portnoy and acted to benefit him at the expense of TA. O'Brien has extensive relationships with many Portnoy-related entities and receives compensation for his services. In addition to his positions with TA and RMR, O'Brien is also President of five of the seven RMR Funds and a trustee of each of the RMR funds. These factual allegations support plaintiff's claim that O'Brien was beholden to Portnoy and that he acted to benefit RMR and Portnoy at the expense of TA.

Plaintiff's allegations with respect to the other three directors are sufficient for similar reasons. Koumantzelis, Gilmore, and Donelan all serve as directors of other Portnoy related entities and are compensated for their service. Koumantzelis, for example, is a director of TA and FVE, a trustee for each of the RMR Funds, and was a trustee of HPT from its founding in 1995 until 2007. For 2007, he received $94,480 in fees as a director of TA, $74,440 in fees as a director of FVE, and $43,750 in fees as trustee for the RMR Funds. As detailed above, Portnoy has extensive relationships with each of these entities. Portnoy is the founder and a director of FVE. Portnoy is also a portfolio manager at each of the RMR funds, and his son, Adam D. Portnoy, is the President of each of the RMR funds. Koumantzelis is also the Chairman of the Board of Trustees of the ILC, a not-for-profit organization founded by Portnoy's wife. Koumantzelis, like the other director defendants, makes regular financial contributions to the ILC.

The complaint alleges similar facts with respect to Gilmore and Donelan. Gilmore is a director of TA and FVE. For 2007, she was paid $89,480 in fees as a director of TA and $70,940 in fees as a director of FVE, compensation the complaint alleges is material to Gilmore because it exceeds the compensation from her position as a clerk in the United States Bankruptcy Court. Gilmore also worked at Sullivan & Worcester LLP from 1993 to 2000, during part of which time Portnoy was a partner and chairman of the firm. Donelan is a director of TA and a trustee of HRPT and the ILC. In 2007, Donelan was paid $88,980 in fees as a director of TA and $73,600 in fees as a trustee of HRPT.

These allegations support plaintiff's contention that the directors were beholden to Portnoy and acted to benefit RMR and Portnoy at the expense of the Company. Additionally, there is not a single director on TA's board that is free of the influence of being otherwise involved in the web of Portnoy-related entities that could question whether the board was acting to benefit the Company and not Portnoy individually. The allegation that the directors intentionally acted to benefit RMR and a director at the expense of the Company, as supported by the well pleaded factual allegations in the complaint, is sufficient to survive the motion to dismiss. In light of the favorable inferences I must draw in plaintiff's favor, I am unable to conclude with reasonable certainty that there is no set of facts that can be inferred from these allegations upon which plaintiff could show that the directors acted in bad faith. Accordingly, plaintiff has met the notice pleading burden of Rule 12(b)(6). . . .

NOTES AND QUESTIONS

1. How would you redraft §7.5(a) of the TA Limited Liability Company Agreement to avoid the ambiguity found by Chancellor Chandler? How do you think the public investors would have responded if the section had been drafted to avoid the ambiguity?

2. Planners have greater ability in Delaware to limit the scope of fiduciary duty in an LLC than in a corporation. The extent of this difference is illustrated in Sutherland v. Sutherland, 2009 WL 857468 (Del. Ch.). In *Sutherland*, two minority shareholders filed a derivative complaint on behalf of two related corporations alleging that the controlling shareholders had engaged in numerous self-dealing transactions to the detriment of the corporations. The controlling shareholders asserted that the transactions were insulated from judicial review by exculpatory and other clauses in the corporations' certificates of incorporation providing that interested directors were to be treated as disinterested for purposes of approving conflicting interest transactions. Vice Chancellor Lamb did not agree with this interpretation, but reasoned that if so interpreted, the provisions would be void as against public policy.

> However, if, *arguendo*, the meaning of the provision is as the defendants suggest, interested directors would be treated as disinterested for the purposes of approving corporate transactions. Because approval by a majority of disinterested directors affords a transaction the presumptions of the business judgment rule, all interested transactions would be immunized from entire fairness analysis under this scheme. Thus, the only basis that would remain to attack a self-dealing transaction would be waste.
>
> The question that remains then is whether such a far-reaching provision would be enforceable under Delaware law. It would not. If the meaning of the above provision were as the defendants suggest, it would effectively eviscerate the duty of loyalty for corporate directors as it is generally understood under Delaware law. While such a provision is permissible under the Delaware Limited Liability Company Act and the Delaware Revised Uniform Limited Partnership Act, where freedom of contract is the guiding and overriding principle, it is expressly forbidden by the DGCL. Section 102(b)(7) of the DGCL provides that a corporate charter may contain a provision eliminating or limiting personal liability of a director for money damages in a suit for breach of fiduciary duty, so long as such provision does not affect director liability for "any breach of the director's duty of loyalty to the corporation or its stockholders. . . ."
>
> The effect of the provision at issue would be to do exactly what is forbidden. It would render any breach of the duty of loyalty relating to a self-dealing transaction beyond the reach of a court

to remedy by way of damages. The exculpatory charter provision, if construed in the manner suggested by the defendants, would therefore be void as "contrary to the laws of this State" and against public policy. As such, it could not form the basis for a dismissal of claims of self-dealing.

3. There are, as yet, a small number of publicly traded LLCs. Can you see how the wider contractual freedom in a Delaware LLC would be attractive to the management of a publicly held entity? As in Kahn v. Portnoy, it is not uncommon for these publicly traded LLCs to adopt the guise of a corporation for governance purposes. This can be done easily by providing in the Operating Agreement that the LLC will be managed by a board of directors, using the term "shareholder" rather than "member" and "shares" instead of "member's interest." The Operating Agreement could further provide that the authority, powers, functions, and duties (including fiduciary duties) of the board of directors will be identical to those of a board of directors organized under the Delaware General Corporation Law to modify or eliminate a manager's fiduciary duties in ways that would not be permitted for an actual corporation.

4. In Wood v. Baum, 953 A.2d 136 (Del. 2007), the Operating Agreement of Municipal Mortgage & Equity, LLC (MME) generally adopted for MME the guise and norms of corporate form but contained the following exculpatory provision: "No director or officer of the Company shall be liable, responsible, or accountable in damages or otherwise to the Company or any Shareholders for act or omission performed or omitted by him or her, or for any decision, except in the case of fraudulent or illegal conduct of such person." The complaint alleged that the ten current members of MME's board of directors and one past director had breached the fiduciary duties owed to MME in connection with related party transactions and other misuse of MME's assets. The Court affirmed the Court of Chancery's dismissal of the complaint based on the exculpation provision. Would this exculpation provision be permitted if the LLC were actually organized as a corporation?

D. *Judicial Dissolution*

1. Legal Standard

Delaware LLCA §802
RULLCA §701

Most first-generation LLC statutes provided some form of easy exit for disgruntled members. Some statutes imported dissolution at will from the general partnership, while others provided a withdrawing member with a right to be paid the fair value of the membership interest. After the IRS promulgated the check-the-box rule, the tax-driven pressure to make the LLC look like a partnership disappeared, and LLC statutes moved away not only from either form of easy exit but from any exit at all. Thus, in cases of deadlock or perceived oppression, the only recourse for a disgruntled member may be a petition for judicial dissolution. The following case examines the grounds on which courts in many states are permitted to grant such a petition. About one-fourth of the states follow the close corporation pattern of conditioning a member's right to dissolution on a finding of oppression or unfairly prejudicial conduct. Most of the remaining states, including Delaware, use a statute asking whether it is reasonably practicable to carry on the business in conformity with the operating agreement.

Fisk Ventures, LLC v. Segal

Delaware Court of Chancery, 2009
2009 WL 73957

CHANDLER, CHANCELLOR. . . .

This case presents the narrow question of whether it is "reasonably practicable," under 6 Del. C. §18-802, for a Delaware limited liability company to continue to operate. . . .

I.   BACKGROUND

Genitrix, LLC ("Genitrix" or the "Company"), originally a Maryland limited liability company, was formed by Dr. Andrew Segal in 1996 to commercialize his biotechnology concepts of directing the human immune system to attack cancer and infectious diseases. Although initially promising, the Company's financial condition has deteriorated to the point where currently Genitrix is in critical financial straits.

The LLC Agreement provides that Genitrix's business purpose is:

> (a) to engage in research and development, and /or generate through the manufacture and sale and licensing of biomedical technology, including that related to the use of opsonin molecules, in combination with other organic molecules, to produce immunizing and therapeutic drugs for human and animal diseases, and (b) to engage in all action necessary, convenient or incidental to the foregoing. Without the express approval of the Board, the Company shall not engage in any other business activity.

As this Court stated in a previous opinion, "[t]he Company has no office, no capital funds, no grant funds, and generates no revenue."[2] Genitrix, as it currently stands, is unable to operate in furtherance of its business purposes.

In forming Genitrix, Segal obtained a patent rights license from the Whitehead Institute of Biomedical Research ("Whitehead") concerning the Company's core technology. In 1997, Genitrix entered into a Patent License Agreement (the "Whitehead Agreement") with Whitehead and Massachusetts Institute of Technology.

The Whitehead Agreement was entered into among Genitrix, Whitehead, and M.I.T. It provides for the exclusive license to Genitrix of certain patent rights, owned by Whitehead. Genitrix paid for the prosecution and issuance of the patents owned by Whitehead. As set forth in Article 2 of the Whitehead Agreement, the license gives Genitrix the worldwide right to develop, sell and commercialize Licensed Products and Licensed Services derived from the patent rights. Article 11 of the Whitehead Agreement provides that the license is not assignable, except in limited circumstances

---

2. Fisk Ventures v. Segal, C.A. No. 3017-CC, 2008 WL 1961156, at *6 (Del. Ch. July 3, 2008).

including "in connection with the sale or transfer of all or substantially all of Genitrix's equity and assets."

In September 1997, H. Fisk Johnson, head of Fisk Ventures, LLC, became an investor in Genitrix. As a condition to Johnson's investment, Genitrix was redomiciled in Delaware. In the initial investment round, Johnson contributed $842,000 in cash in exchange for Class B interests in Genitrix. Investments by other Class C investors brought the total cash investment in Genitrix to $1.1 million. Segal received a $500,000 Class A investment credit in exchange for his contribution of patent rights that he obtained from Whitehead. To continue operating, Genitrix has relied on equity and debt investments and grants from institutions to provide capital. In recent years, both Segal and Fisk Ventures have paid for certain Company expenses.

As a Class B member of Genitrix, Fisk Ventures negotiated a "Put Right" with respect to the Class B membership interests, found in §11.5 of the LLC Agreement. Section 11.5(a) allows "the holders of the Class B Interests . . . to sell any or all of such Member's Class B Interests to the Company on such terms as are set forth herein," at any time after "the fourth anniversary of the date of this Agreement." After exercising the Put Right, the LLC Agreement requires an adjustment of the book value of all Company assets based upon an independent valuation of Genitrix conducted by "a nationally recognized, reputable investment banker."

Under §11.5(c), the put price for the Class B interests is deemed to "equal the amount of such Class B Interest holder's Capital Account balance after such balance has been adjusted as required by Section 11.5(b)." If that put price "exceeds 50% of the tangible assets of the Company," Genitrix must issue notes to the pertinent Class B holders that are payable one-third within thirty days of receipt of the valuation; one-third on the first anniversary of the exercise date of the Put Right; and the balance on the second anniversary of such exercise. In the event of a default by the Company, the Class B Interest holders may replace one of Segal's representatives with an additional Class B representative.

Fisk Ventures has been free to exercise the Put Right ever since September 11, 2001 — the fourth anniversary date of the LLC Agreement. The Put Right permits Fisk Ventures, at their sole discretion, to exit their investment in Genitrix — for fair market value — for any reason or for no reason.

Soon after formation, a four-person Board was organized to manage the affairs of Genitrix, with Segal and Johnson each appointing two representatives. The Genitrix Board now consists of five representatives. Under §7.5 of the LLC Agreement, the Genitrix Board can only act pursuant to approval of 75% of its members, whether by vote or by written consent.

Segal was originally appointed as both President and Chief Executive Officer of Genitrix. Segal ceased to be CEO of the Company in March 2006, but continues to serve as President.

Only a handful of Board meetings have been held over the entire course of Genitrix's existence. Segal maintains that §7.5 of the LLC Agreement contemplates that Genitrix's Board can operate by written consent without a meeting, provided that the requisite 75% of the representatives approve such action. Segal and his appointees declined to attend Board meetings from about September 2006 until July 2008, requesting instead that the Board conduct business by e-mail. Segal and the Class B representatives held a two-hour board meeting by telephone on August 5, 2008.

II. ANALYSIS . . .

2.   Freedom of Contract and Limited Liability Companies

"Limited Liability Companies are creatures of contract, 'designed to afford the maximum amount of freedom of contract, private ordering and flexibility to the parties involved.'" Delaware's LLC Act thus allows LLC members to "'arrange a manager/investor governance relationship;' the LLC Act provides defaults that can be modified by contract" as deemed appropriate by the LLC's managing members. The LLC Act explicitly states that "[i]t is the policy of this chapter to give the maximum effect to the principle of freedom of contract and to the enforceability of limited liability company agreements."

Genitrix's LLC Agreement provides that the Company "shall be dissolved and its affairs wound up only on the first to occur of the following: (a) the written consent of Members holding at least 75% of the Membership Interests, voting as provided in §3.5; and (b) the entry of a decree of judicial dissolution of the Company under Section 18-802 of the Act." Segal, as the controlling member of Genitrix's Class A membership interest, opposes dissolution. Since the managing members are hopelessly deadlocked to the extent that 75% of the membership interest in Genitrix will not be voted in favor of dissolution, the only other opportunity for members seeking dissolution would be through a decree of judicial dissolution in accordance with the LLC agreement.

3.   Standard for Dissolution of a Limited Liability Company

The Court of Chancery may decree judicial dissolution of a Delaware limited liability company "whenever it is not reasonably practicable to carry on the business in conformity with a limited liability company agreement."[13] Section 18-802 has the "obvious purpose of providing an avenue of relief when an LLC cannot continue to function in accordance with its chartering agreement."[14]

In interpreting §18-802, this Court has by analogy often looked to the dissolution statute for limited partnerships, 6 Del. C. §17-802. In so doing, the Court has found that "the test of §17-802 is whether it is 'reasonably practicable' to carry on the business of a limited partnership, and not whether it is impossible." To decide whether to dissolve a partnership pursuant to §17-802, the courts have historically looked to the "business of the partnership and the general partner's ability to achieve that purpose in conformity with the partnership agreement." For example, in *PC Tower,* this Court found that the relevant partnership agreement stated that the partnership's business purpose was to acquire land in the hope of making a future profit. The Court held that the partnership was unable to carry on its business in a reasonably practicable manner

---

13. 6 Del. C. §18-802.
14. Haley v. Talcott, 864 A.2d 86, 94 (Del. Ch. 2004).

because there was (1) a depressed real estate market, (2) property debt was in excess of value, and (3) uncontradicted evidence of a heavily leveraged property where the rent payments were supposed to be forthcoming from a declared insolvent entity. Thus, because it was no longer reasonably practicable to use the partnership's property "for profit and for an investment," the Court ordered dissolution of the partnership.[19]

Applying the same logic in the limited liability company context, there is no need to show that the purpose of the limited liability company has been "completely frustrated." The standard is whether it is reasonably practicable for Genitrix to continue to operate its business in conformity with its LLC Agreement.

The text of §18-802 does not specify what a court must consider in evaluating the "reasonably practicable" standard, but several convincing factual circumstances have pervaded the case law: (1) the members' vote is deadlocked at the Board level; (2) the operating agreement gives no means of navigating around the deadlock; and (3) due to the financial condition of the company, there is effectively no business to operate.

These factual circumstances are not individually dispositive; nor must they all exist for a court to find it no longer reasonably practicable for a business to continue operating. In fact, the Court in *Haley v. Talcott* found that although the limited liability company was "technically functioning" and "financially stable," meaning that it received rent checks and paid a mortgage, it should be dissolved because the company's activity was "purely a residual, inertial status quo that just happens to exclusively benefit one of the 50% members."[22] If a board deadlock prevents the limited liability company from operating or from furthering its stated business purpose, it is not reasonably practicable for the company to carry on its business.

4.   *Judicial Dissolution of a Limited Liability Company*

More than sufficient undisputed evidence exists in this case to demonstrate the futility of Genitrix's deadlocked board, the LLC Agreement's failure to prescribe a solution to a potentially deadlocked board, and Genitrix's dire financial straits. For these reasons, and as explained further below, I conclude that it is not reasonably practicable to carry on the business operations of Genitrix in conformity with the LLC Agreement.

a.   *Genitrix's Board Is Deadlocked*

Under the LLC Agreement, Genitrix's Board has the exclusive power to manage the business and affairs of the company. The Board is unable to act unless both the Class B and the Class A shareholders agree on a course of action. The LLC Agreement imposes a 75% voting requirement for business issues: "Approval of at least 75% of the Representatives shall be required to authorize any of the actions . . . specified in this Agreement as requiring the authorization of the Board." The LLC Agreement requires the cooperation of the Board's managing members in order to accomplish or overcome any issue facing Genitrix. This type of charter provision, unless a "tie-breaking"

---

19. PC Tower Ctr., Inc. v. Tower Ctr. Dev. Assoc. Ltd. P'ship, C.A. No. 10788, 1989 WL 63901, at *6 (Del. Ch. June 8, 1989).
22. Haley v. Talcott, 864 A.2d at 91, 96 (Del. Ch. 2004).

clause exists, is almost always a recipe for disaster. In this case, unfortunately, the parties are behaving true to form.

Although Genitrix's Board is charged to run the Company, the Board is unable to act and is hopelessly deadlocked. Fisk Ventures and Segal have a long history of disagreement and discord over a wide range of issues concerning the direction and operation of Genitrix. On one of the most important issues facing the Company, the raising and use of operating capital, the Board is unable to negotiate acceptable terms to all involved parties. Additionally, the Board has even been considerably deadlocked over whether to have Board meetings. The parties have a history of discord and disagreement on almost every issue facing the Company. There exists almost a five-year track record of perpetual deadlock. Indeed, concerning the current issue, dissolution, the Board is equally deadlocked.

Given the Board's history of discord and disagreement, I do not believe that these parties will ever be able to harmoniously resolve their differences. Consequently, I conclude that Genitrix's Board is deadlocked and unable to resolve any issue, including the current issue of dissolution, facing Genitrix.

b. Navigating the Deadlock in the LLC Agreement

In examining the four corners of Genitrix's LLC Agreement I conclude that no provision exists that would allow the Board to circumvent the deadlocked stalemate. The document was negotiated by sophisticated parties engaged in an arm's length negotiation. The product of that negotiation, the LLC Agreement, was carefully drafted in such a way that solved one problem but led directly to the deadlock now gripping the Company. The provision requiring a 75% vote for Board action was agreed upon by the parties to specifically prohibit board domination by one party over another. The provision has certainly accomplished its intended purpose. Unfortunately, it has also led to a stalemate, and the LLC Agreement on its face provides no means of remedying the situation.

Segal argues that since Fisk Ventures owns a Put Right, provided for in §11.5 of the LLC Agreement, which allows Fisk Ventures to exit its investment by forcing Genitrix to buy out Fisk Ventures for the fair value of its investment, the LLC Agreement contains a provision that will resolve the Board's deadlock. Segal points to Fisk Ventures' Put Right as a proper "exit mechanism" and as an alternative to judicial dissolution. Under §11.5, the amount to be paid to the Class B investors is to be determined by an independent valuation. If the price exceeds 50% of the value of Genitrix's tangible assets, they will gain creditor status, giving their holder greater security and a higher priority than they currently have as purely equity members.

Segal ignores the fact, however, that the Put Right contemplated in the LLC Agreement grants its owner an option, to be freely exercised at the will and pleasure of its holder.[26] Nowhere in §11.5 or in the entire LLC Agreement does the Company have the right to force a buyout if it considers one of its members belligerent or uncooperative. Fisk Ventures holds the option, not Genitrix. Fisk Ventures negotiated for

---

26. Nor does Segal explain how Genitrix would be able to pay Fisk Ventures if it were to exercise its Put Right.

and obtained the Put Right as consideration for its original investment in Genitrix and it would be inequitable for this Court to force a party to exercise its option when that party deems it in its best interests not to do so. I am not permitted to second guess a party's business decision in choosing whether or not to exercise its previously negotiated option rights.

c.   Not Reasonably Practicable to Carry on the Business

As noted previously, Genitrix is in dire financial condition. "The Company has no office, no capital funds, no grant funds, and generates no revenue." Genitrix has survived up to this point on equity and debt investments, and on grants from institutions such as the National Institute of Health. The Company does not have any further source of funding, and no realistic expectation of additional grants or infusions of capital.

Segal argues that one of the major sources of Board contention and deadlock has been Fisk Ventures' unwillingness to allow further capital infusion without significant anti-dilution protections. For this reason alone, Segal argues, Genitrix has been unable to raise additional funds. Segal further contends that if Fisk Ventures is forced to exercise its Put Right then Genitrix will be free to raise funds to effect the buy-back. But again, Segal fails to realize that Fisk Ventures has the right to protect itself against what it perceives as Company actions that would diminish the value of its stake in Genitrix. This Court will not substitute its business judgment for that of Fisk Ventures simply because Segal believes that will be in his best interest.

Additionally, Segal believes that dissolution should be denied because it would destroy any value the Company has preserved in its Whitehead Patent License. As stated above, the Whitehead Agreement is the legal vehicle for the grant of significant patent rights now licensed to Genitrix. Under Article 11 of the Whitehead Agreement, the license is not assignable except "in connection with the sale or transfer of all or substantially all of Genitrix's equity and assets." Segal argues that the Company's members will then lose all of the considerable value of that asset, and Genitrix's own patents, which are subordinate to Whitehead's patent, because a purchaser will not be free to operate without a license from Whitehead. This argument is unconvincing.

First, it appears equally likely that a purchaser could enter into a separate licensing agreement with Whitehead for use of its patent. Alternatively, the terms of the Whitehead Agreement could be renegotiated or altered in the sale negotiations. Second, it is ultimately futile to enter into an operating agreement that on its face is doomed to conflict and deadlock, to become mired in a deadlock for years on issues of financing and operations, and then to demand that the Court force the opposing party in the deadlock to capitulate in order to preserve a fleeting hope that additional financing might become available to help preserve some future potential value in a licensing agreement. That argument leads to the same deadlock that now exists on every issue of this company. The value of the Whitehead Agreement is hotly contested and I am unconvinced that any potential value it theoretically might have could not be accessed through a fair and proper sale of the asset. One thing is certain, however. These parties will never be able to reach agreement on how to dispose of this asset, whatever its potential value.

Finally, Segal's argument that Fisk Ventures cannot seek judicial dissolution because it comes to the Court with unclean hands is without merit. The LLC Agreement is a negotiated contract and Fisk Ventures has the right to attempt to maximize its position in accordance with the LLC Agreement's terms. If Fisk Ventures chooses to exercise its leverage under the LLC Agreement to benefit itself, it is perfectly within its right to do so. Additionally, Segal offers no facts to support his contentions that Fisk Ventures seeks dissolution simply to buy Genitrix's assets at fire sale prices. A party cannot simply allege a conclusory inequitable action as a last ditch effort to persuade the Court to deny a motion for judgment on the pleadings and to allow that party an opportunity to take discovery.

Ultimately, even if the financial progress of Genitrix is impeded by the deadlock in the boardroom, if that deadlock cannot be remedied through a legal mechanism set forth within the four corners of the operating agreement, dissolution becomes the only remedy available as a matter of law. The Court is in no position to redraft the LLC Agreement for these sophisticated and well-represented parties. . . .

NOTES AND QUESTIONS

1. In jurisdictions with LLC statutes that follow the close corporation approach of permitting judicial dissolution if the conduct of those in control is unfairly prejudicial, or oppressive, courts have been more willing to look at the expectations of the investors, in an analysis that echoes some of the cases in Chapter 5. For example, in Kirksey v. Grohmann, 754 N.W.2d 825 (S.D. 2008), four sisters inherited a ranch and formed an LLC, with each sister receiving a 25 percent membership interest. One sister, who had been living and working on the ranch for many years, was appointed manager of the LLC; another sister leased a portion of the ranch from the LLC as grazing land. The remaining sisters ("the absentee sisters") lived a great distance from the ranch. The arrangement proved unsatisfactory to the absentee sisters, who could not get any information about the operation of the LLC and came to believe that the LLC was not being operated fairly. Despite the fact that the LLC was operating profitably, the South Dakota Supreme Court reversed the lower court's denial of the absentee sisters' petition for judicial dissolution.

> The sisters created their company with the understanding that they would have relatively equal say in its overall management and operation. Although each sister has an equal vote, there no longer exists equality in the decision making. Grohmann and Randell have all the power with no reason to change the terms of a lease extremely favorable to them. Leaving two sisters, half the owners, with all the power in the operation of the company cannot be a reasonable and practicable operation of a business. Moreover, their deadlock certainly impedes the continued function of the business in conformity with its operating agreement. No procedure exists in the company's documentation to break a tie vote and protect the company in the event of changed conditions. As long as the company remains in control of, and favorable only to, half its members, it cannot be said to be reasonably practicable for it to continue in accord with its operating agreement. . . .
>
> Here, we have two members of an LLC that hold all the power, with the other two having no power to influence the company's direction. We recognize that forced dissolution is a drastic remedy and may produce financial repercussions for the sisters, but how can one reasonably conclude that the economic purpose of this company is not reasonably frustrated? The members cannot

communicate regarding the LLC except through legal counsel. The company remains static, serving the interests of only half its owners. They neither trust nor cooperate with each other. The sisters formed their company contemplating equal ownership and management, yet only an impenetrable deadlock prevails.

We conclude that the economic purpose of the Kirksey Family Ranch, LLC is being unreasonably frustrated, and it is not reasonably practicable to carry on the LLC's business in conformity with its articles of organization and operating agreement. The circuit court erred when it granted Grohmann and Randell summary judgment. We remand for an order of judicial dissolution and winding up of the company's business . . . .

Id. at 831.

2. Contexts that would not lead to judicial relief in a corporate dissolution setting are not likely to fare better in an LLC context. For example, consider Horning v. Horning Construction, LLC, 816 N.Y.S.2d 877, 881, 884, 885 (N.Y. Sup. 2006).

> Petitioner has asked for an order directing dissolution of the LLC pursuant to LLCL §§702, 703, and 704. Section 702 allows for a judicial decree of dissolution, "whenever it is not reasonably practicable to carry on the business in conformity with the articles of organization or operating agreement. . . ." Dissolution in the absence of an operating agreement can only be had upon satisfaction of the standard of §702, i.e., "whenever it is not reasonably practicable to carry on the business." . . .
>
> One certainly can sympathize with petitioner's plight. In 2001, he had a thriving corporation and wished to reduce his work schedule. Whether for estate and gift tax reasons, or otherwise, he brought in two trusted men and gave them each one third ownership of a new venture set up as a LLC. But he did this without prior or contemporaneous execution of an operating agreement giving him fair exit rights in the event of future disharmony. Moreover, during the next few years, despite having failed to secure an operating agreement to protect him, he transferred the business of his corporation to the LLC (something he did not have to do if he was dissatisfied with the parties' arrangements), and the LLC grew substantially even in relation to the corporation's previous level of business. Despite petitioner's stated frustration with the failure of the members to reach terms on an operating agreement, he was happy to keep doing business through the LLC until he unsuccessfully proposed a buyout to respondents in 2005, the company's most successful year. Only then did he seek dissolution. The company continues to thrive in the ups and downs of the construction business.
>
> Even in the corporate context, with the more liberal involuntary dissolution standards designed to protect minority interests, courts have rejected dissolution petitions in similar circumstances (or even worse scenarios from petitioner's perspective). Matter of Fazio Realty Corp., 10 A.D.3d 363, 365, 781 N.Y.S.2d 118 (2d Dept. 2004) ("While it cannot be disputed that there exists considerable and apparently increasing internal corporate conflict, under the circumstances, the petitioners failed to demonstrate that the dissension between them and the appellant resulted in a deadlock precluding the successful and profitable conduct of the corporation's affairs."). . . .
>
> A fortiori, petitioner's showing under the more stringent standard of LLCL §702 is insufficient here. Summary determination is appropriate on this record.

2. Waiver

Delaware LLCA §802
RULLCA §§110(c)(7)

There has been substantial debate as to the advisability of allowing LLC participants to contract away the fiduciary duties of care and loyalty. There has been less attention to the advisability of allowing LLC members to completely waive the fail-safe exit rights provided by judicial dissolution. As you read the following case, consider whether freedom of contract is too extensive with regard to waiver of the right to seek judicial dissolution of a limited liability company.

R&R Capital, LLC v. Buck & Doe Run Valley Farms, LLC
Delaware Court of Chancery, 2008
2008 WL 3846318

CHANDLER, CHANCELLOR.

For Shakespeare, it may have been the play, but for a Delaware limited liability company, *the contract's the thing.*[1] Ultimately, it is the contract that compels the Court's decision in this case because it is the contract that "defines the scope, structure, and personality of limited liability companies." On June 2, 2008, two New York LLCs filed a petition with this Court seeking dissolution of nine separate Delaware LLCs. The respondent Delaware LLCs, some of which have had their certificates of formation canceled by the state pursuant to 6 Del. C. §18-1108 for failure to pay their annual taxes, have moved to dismiss the petition. That motion is based primarily on two arguments. First, with respect to two of the respondent entities, the petitioners lack standing to seek dissolution because they are neither members nor managers. For reasons explained more fully below, I conclude that this argument is meritorious, but incomplete. Consequently, I grant respondent's motion to dismiss the claims against Pandora Farms, LLC and Pandora Racing, LLC pursuant to 6 Del C. §§18-802 and 18-803, but cannot dismiss the claim pursuant to 6 Del. C.§18-805. Second, with respect to the other respondent entities, of which the petitioners are members, the respondents argue that petitioners have waived their right to seek dissolution in the respective LLC Agreements. Again, for reasons explained at length below, I conclude that this argument is meritorious and that Delaware's strong policy in favor of freedom of contract in the LLC Agreements requires such a result.

I. BACKGROUND

The factual background of this dispute is somewhat predictable; the procedural background, however, is a veritable nightmare. Generally, the respondent entities were formed years ago with capital contributions from the Russet brothers (presumably the Rs in R&R Capital) and Linda Merritt. The bulk of the capital (over $9.7 million) was provided by the petitioners, but Merritt had the sole and exclusive power to manage the entities. These respondent entities own land and race horses. Unfortunately, the relationship between the financiers, the Russets, and their appointed manager,

---

1. *Compare* William Shakespeare, Hamlet act 1, sc. 2, ln. 604 ("the play's the thing"), *with* Travel-Centers of Am., LLC v. Brog, C.A. No. 3516-CC, 2008 WL 1746987, at *1 (Del. Ch. Apr. 3, 2008) ("Limited Liability Companies are creatures of contract").

Merritt, has deteriorated, and, perhaps predictably, the parties have turned to the courts. . . .

The June 2 petition for dissolution seeks, in the alternative, the winding up and dissolution of the respondent entities or the appointment of a receiver. The petitioners allege that most of the respondent entities have had their certificates of formation canceled for failing to designate a registered agent, for failing to pay annual taxes, or for both. They further allege that Merritt's attempts to revive the cancelled certificates are ineffective as a matter of law, that Merritt has refused to provide an accounting of the canceled entities, and that Merritt—along with her "longtime boyfriend" Leonard Pelullo—has defrauded the entities and orchestrated self-dealing transactions. Neither Merritt nor Pelullo, however, is a party to this action. . . .

II. Analysis . . .

A. THE PANDORA ENTITIES

Before the Court need look to any contractual language, however, it must consider the argument of Pandora Racing, LLC and Pandora Farms, LLC (collectively, the "Pandora Entities"), which contend that the claims against them must be dismissed on account of standing. Specifically, the Pandora Entities dispute petitioners' ability to seek dissolution or winding up under 6 Del. C. §§18-802 or 18-803. Under section 18-802, "[o]n application *by or for a member or manager,* the Court of Chancery may decree dissolution of a limited liability company whenever it is not reasonably practicable to carry on the business in conformity with a limited liability company agreement." Similarly, under section 18-803, only managers or members have standing to wind up a limited liability company's affairs.

The petitioners, however, are neither members nor managers of the Pandora Entities. The sole member of the two Pandora Entities is PDF Properties, LLC. There is no authority for the proposition that a member of an LLC which is itself a member of another LLC can seek dissolution or the winding up of the latter LLC. Under the plain language of the LLC Act, the petition to dissolve or wind up the affairs of the Pandora Entities must be dismissed.

The petition, however, also seeks the appointment of a receiver for the Pandora Entities pursuant to 6 Del. C. §18-805. Section 18-805 permits any "creditor, member or manager of the Limited liability company, or any other person who shows good cause" to present an application for the appointment of a receiver. The Pandora Entities do not challenge petitioners' ability to seek relief pursuant to section 18-805 and, therefore, that claim survives this motion.

B. THE WAIVER ENTITIES

Petitioners are members of the other seven respondent entities, and there is no question, therefore, that they have statutory standing to seek relief under sections 18-802, 18-803, and 18-805. Nevertheless, Buck & Doe Run Valley Farms, LLC, Grays

Ferry Properties, LLC, Hope Land, LLC, Merritt Land, LLC, Unionville Land, LLC, Moore Street, LLC, and PDF Properties, LLC (collectively, the "Waiver Entities") contend that the petitioners cannot pursue this action because they have waived their rights to seek dissolution or the appointment of a liquidator. Specifically, the Waiver Entities point to provisions of their respective LLC Agreements in which the members purported to waive these rights. The petitioners concede that the contractual language purports to effect such a waiver, but nonetheless argue that the waiver is invalid as a matter of law. Because neither Delaware's LLC Act nor its policy precludes such a waiver, and because the waiver of such rights would not leave an LLC member inequitably remediless, this Court concludes that petitioners have indeed waived these rights and grants the Waiver Entities' motion to dismiss.

1. The LLC Agreements

The seven Waiver Entities have identical LLC Agreements and each one addresses dissolution explicitly. Specifically, their Agreements limit the events that shall cause dissolution to five events:

> (i) an Event of Withdrawal of a Member . . . ; (ii) the affirmative vote of all Members; (iii) upon the sale of all or substantially all of the Company's assets; (iv) the conversion of the Company into a corporation or other Person; or (v) upon the entry of a decree of judicial dissolution under Section 18-802 of the Act.

The Agreements, however, further provide that the Members have waived the right to seek dissolution under section 18-802. The seven LLC Agreements contain the following provision:

> *Waiver of Dissolution Rights.* The Members agree that irreparable damage would occur if any member should bring an action for judicial dissolution of the Company. Accordingly each member accepts the provisions under this Agreement as such Member's sole entitlement on Dissolution of the Company and waives and renounces such Member's right to seek a court decree of dissolution or to seek the appointment by a court of a liquidator for the Company.

Although not addressed by the parties, the Court notes that there is an apparent tension between these two provisions. Section 10.1 provides that one means by which dissolution of the limited liability company will occur is the "entry of a decree of judicial dissolution under Section 18-802 of the Act." Section 13.1, however, appears to prohibit members from seeking the entry of such a decree. If these provisions actually conflicted, the Waiver Entities' argument would be rendered unpersuasive by virtue of ambiguity in the Agreement. This Court is constrained, however, by rules of interpretation that require it to attempt to "harmoniz[e] seemingly conflicting contract provisions," and these provisions can in fact be harmonized. A "decree of judicial dissolution" may be entered by the Court under section 18-802 upon an "application by *or for* a member or manager." Although the members and managers of the Waiver Entities have apparently waived *their* rights to make an application under section 18-802, the members and managers cannot waive the rights of others to make such applications *for* them. Consequently, under the interpretive principle requiring harmonization, sections 10.1 and 13.1 do not conflict because it is possible both that a court could enter a "decree of judicial dissolution under Section 18-802 of the Act" and that the members could nonetheless have waived *their* right to seek such a decree.

2.   *Freedom of Contract and Limited Liability Companies*

As this Court has noted, "Limited Liability Companies are creatures of contract, 'designed to afford the maximum amount of freedom of contract, private ordering and flexibility to the parties involved.'" Delaware's LLC Act leaves to the members of a limited liability company the task of "arrang[ing] a manager/investor governance relationship;" the Act generally provides defaults that can be modified by contract. Indeed, the Act itself explicitly provides that "[i]t is the policy of this chapter to give the maximum effect to the principle of freedom of contract and to the enforceability of limited liability company agreements." It is this flexibility that gives "uncorporate" entities like limited liability companies their allure; "a principle attraction of the LLC form of entity is the statutory freedom granted to members to shape, by contract, their own approach to common business 'relationship' problems."

The members of the Waiver Entities obviously availed themselves of this flexibility. Their respective LLC Agreements outline—often in great detail—the governance structure the members agreed would best serve the companies. Moreover, as noted above, the LLC Agreements also provide for the dissolution of the entities. In those Agreements, the members agreed that the initiation of a dissolution action would cause "irreparable damage," and they therefore agreed to waive their rights to seek dissolution or the appointment of a liquidator. To the extent this waiver is enforceable under the statute and public policy, petitioners' suit against the Waiver Entities under sections 18-802, 18-803, and 18-805 is barred by contract and must be dismissed.

3.   *The LLC Act Does Not Prohibit Waiver of These Rights*

Petitioners make two distinct but ultimately unavailing arguments as to why the LLC Act prohibits waiver of a member's right to seek dissolution. First, petitioners point to 6 Del. C. §18-109(d) for the proposition that non-managing members may not waive their rights to maintain legal actions in Delaware courts absent an agreement to arbitrate. Because the petitioners are not managing members and because there is no agreement to arbitrate in place, petitioners argue that the section 13.1 waiver violates this statutory provision and is therefore void. Section 18-109, however, is captioned "Service of process on managers and liquidating trustees," and is at most a venue provision. . . .

Petitioner's second statutory argument is based on the principle that certain provisions of the LLC Act are mandatory and non-waivable. As the Supreme Court has explained, "[t]he Act can be characterized as a 'flexible statute' because it generally permits members to engage in private ordering with substantial freedom of contract to govern their relationship, provided they do not contravene any mandatory provisions of the Act." Generally, the mandatory provisions of the Act are "those intended to protect third parties, not necessarily the contracting members." Finally, "[i]n general, the legislature's use of 'may' connotes the voluntary, not mandatory or exclusive, set of options."

Petitioners proffer a far broader rule and argue that "[s]tatutory provisions that do not contain the qualification 'unless otherwise provided in a limited liability company agreement' (or a variation thereof) are mandatory and may not be waived." Petitioners, however, offer no authority for this assertion and, in fact, authorities they cite directly contradict it. In Elf Atochem North America, Inc. v. Jaffari, for example, a case on which petitioners heavily rely, the Supreme Court held that a provision of the LLC Act not containing petitioners' magical phrase was nonetheless permissive and subject to modification. Indeed, in *Elf*, the Supreme Court explicitly noted that the "unless otherwise provided" phrase was merely one example of the means by which a court could ascertain the intent of the General Assembly. Indeed, in other provisions, the General Assembly explicitly forbids waiver. For example, the Act overtly bars members from "eliminat[ing] the implied contractual covenant of good faith and fair dealing."

Sections 18-802, 18-803, and 18-805 are not mandatory provisions of the LLC Act that cannot be modified by contract. First, the Act does not expressly say that these provisions cannot be supplanted by agreement, and, in fact, section 18-803 does include the "unless otherwise provided" phrase. Second, the provisions employ permissive rather than mandatory language. Section 18-802 states that the "Court of Chancery *may* decree dissolution" and section 18-805 states that "the Court of Chancery . . . *may* either appoint" a trustee or receiver. Finally, and most importantly, none of the rights conferred by these provisions that are waived in the LLC Agreement is designed to protect third parties. This Court has recognized that third parties have no interest in dissolution under section 18-802, and section 18-805 specifically permits creditors to petition the Court for the appointment of a receiver for a canceled limited liability company. The rights of third-party creditors under section 18-805 are not affected by the LLC Agreement. In sum, the LLC Act "expressly encourages 'made-to-order' structuring of limited liability companies" and "offers explicit assurance that contractual arrangements will be given effect to the fullest permissible extent." Because the waiver of a member's right to petition for dissolution or the appointment of a receiver does not violate the LLC Act and does not interfere with the rights of third parties, the waiver is valid and enforceable under the statute.

4.   *Public Policy Does Not Prohibit Waiver of These Rights*

Finally, petitioners argue that the Court should refuse to enforce their knowing, voluntary waiver of their right to seek dissolution or the appointment of a receiver because such waivers violate the public policy of Delaware and offend notions of equity. This argument too must fail. First, as discussed throughout this Opinion and others, in treatises, and in the LLC Act itself, the public policy of Delaware with respect to limited liability companies is freedom of contract. Second, there are legitimate business reasons why a firm would want to set up its governance structure so that its members could not petition the Court for dissolution. Finally, the LLC Act provides protections that cannot be waived; this Court need not exercise its equitable discretion and disregard a negotiated agreement among sophisticated parties to allow this action to proceed.

The hunt for legislative intent with respect to Delaware's LLC Act is rather simple, because the General Assembly explicitly stated that the "policy" of the Act is "to give the maximum effect to the principle of freedom of contract and to the enforceability of limited liability company agreements." The LLC Act provides members with "the broadest possible discretion in drafting their [LLC] agreements" and assures that "once [members] exercise their contractual freedom in their [LLC] agreement, the [members] have a great deal of certainty that their [LLC] agreement will be enforced in accordance with its terms." One treatise concludes that "[f]lexibility lies at the core of the DLLC Act. Rather than imposing a host of immutable rules, the statute generally allows parties to order their affairs, contractually, as they deem appropriate."

Chief Justice Steele has powerfully argued that the freedom of contract principle must be assiduously guarded lest the courts erode the primary attraction of limited liability companies. In his remarks on fiduciary duties and alternative entities, the Chief Justice rhetorically asks, "why should courts seek to incorporate uncertainty, inconsistency, and unpredictability into the world of negotiated agreements?" Similarly, Professor Larry Ribstein, whose scholarship on limited liability companies has been frequently cited by both this Court and the Supreme Court, emphasizes that it is the rigor with which Delaware courts apply the contractual language of LLC Agreements that makes limited liability companies successful. Indeed, "Delaware is a freedom of contract state, with a policy of enforcing the voluntary agreements of sophisticated parties in commerce." Here, the LLC Agreement is a contract between sophisticated parties. The business relationships between the individuals behind the petitioners and Lynda Merritt is extensive; clearly these were parties who knew how to make use of the law of alternative entities. The mere fact that the business relationship has now soured cannot justify the petitioners' attempt to disregard the agreement they made. Therefore, contrary to petitioners' argument that Delaware's public policy will not countenance their unambiguous contractual waiver, the state's policy mandates that this Court respect and enforce the parties' agreement.

In addition to Delaware's general policy promoting the freedom of contract, there are legitimate business reasons why members of a limited liability company may wish to waive their right to seek dissolution or the appointment of a receiver. For example, it is common for lenders to deem in loan agreements with limited liability companies that the filing of a petition for judicial dissolution will constitute a noncurable event of default. In such instances, it is necessary for all members to prospectively agree to waive their rights to judicial dissolution to protect the limited liability company. Otherwise, a disgruntled member could push the limited liability company into default on all of its outstanding loans simply by filing a petition with this Court. In fact, one of the petitioners here, R&R Capital, LLC, has acted as a lender to some of the Waiver Entities and included such a provision in its loan agreement with respondent Unionville Land, LLC.[47]

Finally, petitioners' plea to this Court's sense of equity is misplaced. The LLC Act does not abandon petitioners with no recourse as they "sit idly by while Merritt (the manager) seeks to continue operating seven entities that have had their certificates of formation canceled and two entities whose narrow purposes have been fulfilled." Instead, the LLC Act preserves the implied covenant of good faith and fair dealing. The petition filed is replete with allegations about the unbecoming conduct of Merritt, and

---

47. This information, of course, is not included in the petition and the Court does not rely on it in reaching its decision. . . .

petitioners' brief opposing the motion to dismiss likewise criticizes her. Petitioners, however, have not named Merritt as a party in this action. Although, fairly construed, the petition may allege a breach of the implied covenant, the petitioners unambiguously have failed to state a claim upon which relief can be granted because they have not named the alleged bad-faith actor in their petition. It is the unwaivable protection of the implied covenant that allows the vast majority of the remainder of the LLC Act to be so flexible. There is no threat to equity in allowing members to waive their right to seek dissolution, because there is no chance that some members will be trapped in a limited liability company at the mercy of others acting unfairly and in bad faith.

III. CONCLUSION

When parties wish to launch a new enterprise, the form of the limited liability company offers a highly customizable vehicle in which to do so. The flexibility of such an entity springs from its roots in contract; the parties have "the broadest possible discretion" to set the structure of the limited liability company. Indeed, "LLC members' rights begin with and typically end with the Operating Agreement." The allure of the limited liability company, however, would be eviscerated if the parties could simply petition this court to renegotiate their agreements when relationships sour. Here, the sophisticated members of the seven Waiver Entities knowingly, voluntarily, and unambiguously waived their rights to petition this Court for dissolution or the appointment of a receiver under the LLC Act. This waiver is permissible and enforceable because it contravenes neither the Act itself nor the public policy of the state. Moreover, with respect to the two other respondent entities—the Pandora Entities—the petitioners lack statutory standing to seek dissolution or the winding up of the entities. They may, however, petition for the appointment of a receiver.

These parties have cases pending in both state and federal courts in Delaware, Pennsylvania, and New York. These parties, however, originally came together and negotiated a series of agreements that led to the nine entities presently before the Court; perhaps the most prudent resolution to their problems is once again negotiation—a negotiated settlement. With Shakespeare this Opinion began, and with Shakespeare it too shall end:

> Recall—lest another court these parties try—
> "Our remedies oft in ourselves do lie."[55]

NOTES AND QUESTIONS

1. RULLCA §110(c)(7) prohibits modification or waiver of a court's right to decree dissolution on the grounds specified in RULLCA §701(a)(4) and (5). In a number of states where there is no express statutory prohibition, courts have interpreted the common law as prohibiting such waivers. Sivsa Entertainment v. World Intern. Network,

---

55. William Shakespeare, All's Well That Ends Well act 1, sc. 1, ln. 231.

Cal. App. 2 Dist., 2004 WL 1895080 (appears that right to dissolution may not be waived by agreement); Darwin Limes, LLC v. Limes, 2007 WL 1378357 (Oh. App. 2007) (this reading is consistent with the tenet of many LLC statutes that the right to petition for judicial dissolution may not be subject to contrary agreement); Zulawaski v. Taylor, 2005 WL 3823584 (N.Y. Sup. 2005) (operating agreement cannot trump statutory right to seek dissolution). What are the policy reasons for allowing or prohibiting waiver of the right to seek judicial dissolution?

2. Do freedom of contract and the ability to generate a deadlock (as in *Fisk*) suggest an overarching reason for making the dissolution remedy non-waivable?

E. Balancing Equitable Discretion and Respect for Private Ordering in Other Contexts

VGS, Inc. v. Castiel

Court of Chancery of Delaware, 2000

2000 WL 1277372

aff'd, 781 A.2d 696 (Del. 2001)

STEELE, VICE CHANCELLOR.

One entity controlled by a single individual forms a one "member" limited liability company. Shortly thereafter, two other entities, one of which is controlled by the owner of the original member, become members of the LLC. The LLC Agreement creates a three-member Board of Managers with sweeping authority to govern the LLC. The individual owning the original member has the authority to name and remove two of the three managers. He also acts as CEO. The unaffiliated third member becomes disenchanted with the original member's leadership. Ultimately the third member's owner, also the third manager, convinces the original member's owner's appointed manager to join him in a clandestine strategic move to merge the LLC into a Delaware corporation. The appointed manager and the disaffected third member do not give the original member's owner, still a member of the LLC's board of managers, notice of their strategic move. After the merger, the original member finds himself relegated to a minority position in the surviving corporation. While a majority of the board acted by written consent, as all involved surely knew, had the original member's manager received notice beforehand that his appointed manager contemplated action against his interests he would have promptly attempted to remove him. Because the two managers acted without notice to the third manager under circumstances where they knew that with notice that he could have acted to protect his majority interest, they breached their duty of loyalty to the original member and their fellow manager by failing to act in good faith. The purported merger must therefore be declared invalid. . . .

I. FACTS

David Castiel formed Virtual Geosatellite LLC (the "LLC") on January 6, 1999 in order to pursue a Federal Communications Commission ("FCC") license to build and operate a satellite system which its proponents claim could dramatically increase the "real estate" in outer space capable of transmitting high speed internet traffic and other communications. When originally formed, it had only one Member–Virtual Geosatellite Holdings, Inc. ("Holdings"). On January 8, 1999, Ellipso, Inc. ("Ellipso") joined the LLC as its second Member. Several weeks later, on January 29, 1999, Sahagen Satellite Technology Group LLC ("Sahagen Satellite") became the third Member of the LLC.

David Castiel controls both Holdings and Ellipso. Peter Sahagen, an aggressive and apparently successful venture capitalist, controls Sahagen Satellite.

Pursuant to the LLC Agreement, Holdings received 660 units (representing 63.46% of the total equity in the LLC), Sahagen Satellite received 260 units (representing 25%), and Ellipso received 120 units (representing 11.54%). The founders vested management of the LLC in a Board of Managers. As the majority unitholder, Castiel had the power to appoint, remove, and replace two of the three members of the Board of Managers. Castiel, therefore, had the power to prevent any Board decision with which he disagreed. Castiel named himself and Tom Quinn to the Board of Managers. Sahagen named himself as the third member of the Board.

Not long after the formation of the LLC, Castiel and Sahagen were at odds. Castiel contends that Sahagen wanted to control the LLC ever since he became involved, and that Sahagen repeatedly offered, unsuccessfully, to buy control of the LLC. Sahagen maintains that Castiel ran the LLC so poorly that its mission had become untracked, additional necessary capital could not be raised, and competent managers could not be attracted to join the enterprise. Further, Sahagen claims that Castiel directed LLC assets to Ellipso in order to prop up a failing, cash-strapped Ellipso. At trial, these issues and other similar accusations from both sides were explored in great detail. For our purposes here, all that need be concluded is the unarguable fact that Castiel and Sahagen had very different ideas about how the LLC should be managed and operated.

Sahagen ultimately convinced Quinn that Castiel must be ousted from leadership in order for the LLC to prosper. As a result, Quinn (Castiel's nominee) covertly "defected" to Sahagen's camp, and he and Sahagen decided to wrest control of the LLC from Castiel. Many LLC employees and even some of Castiel's lieutenants testified that they believed it to be in the LLC's best interest to take control from Castiel.

On April 14, 2000, without notice to Castiel, Quinn and Sahagen acted by written consent to merge the LLC under Delaware law into VGS, Inc. ("VGS"), a Delaware corporation. Accordingly, the LLC ceased to exist, its assets and liabilities passed to VGS, and VGS became the LLC's legal successor-in-interest. VGS's Board of Directors is comprised of Sahagen, Quinn, and Neel Howard. Of course, the incorporators did not name Castiel to VGS's Board.

On the day of the merger, Sahagen executed a promissory note to VGS in the amount of $10 million plus interest. In return, he received two million shares of VGS Series A Preferred Stock. VGS also issued 1,269,200 shares of common stock to Holdings, 230,800 shares of common stock to Ellipso, and 500,000 shares of common stock to Sahagen Satellite. Once one does the math, it is apparent that Holdings and Ellipso went from having a 75% controlling combined ownership interest in the LLC to having only a 37.5% interest in VGS. On the other hand, Sahagen and Sahagen Satellite went from owning 25% of the LLC to owning 62.5% of VGS.

There can be no doubt why Sahagen and Quinn, acting as a majority of the LLC's board of managers, did not notify Castiel of the merger plan. Notice to Castiel would have immediately resulted in Quinn's removal from the board and a newly constituted majority which would thwart the effort to strip Castiel of control. Had he known in advance, Castiel surely would have attempted to replace Quinn with someone loyal to Castiel who would agree with his views. Clandestine machinations were, therefore, essential to the success of Quinn and Sahagen's plan.

II. Analysis

A. The Board of Managers Did Have Authority
to Act by Majority Vote

The LLC Agreement does not expressly state whether the Board of Managers must act unanimously or by majority vote. Sahagen and Quinn contend that because a number of provisions would be rendered meaningless if a unanimous vote was required, a majority vote is implied. Castiel, however, maintains that a unanimous vote must be implied when the majority owner has blocking power.

Section 8.01(b)(i) of the LLC Agreement states that, "[t]he Board of Managers shall initially be composed of three (3) Managers." Sahagen Satellite has the right to designate one member of the initial board, and if the Board of Managers increased in number, Sahagen Satellite could "designate a number of representatives on the Board of Managers that is less than Sahagen's then current Percentage Interest." If unanimity were required, the number of managers would be irrelevant-Sahagen, and his minority interest, would have veto power in any event. The existence of language in the LLC Agreement discussing expansion of the Board is therefore quite telling.

Also persuasive is the fact that Section 8.01(c) of the LLC Agreement, entitled "Matters Requiring Consent of Sahagen," provides that Sahagen's approval is needed for a merger, consolidation, or reorganization of the LLC. If a unanimity requirement indeed existed, there would have been no need to expressly list matters on which Sahagen's minority interest had veto power.

Section 12.01(a)(i) of the LLC Agreement also supports Sahagen's argument. This section provides that the LLC may be dissolved by written consent by either the Board of Managers or by Members holding two-thirds of the Common Units. The effect of this Section is to allow any combination of Holdings and Sahagen Satellite, or Holdings and Ellipso, as Members, to dissolve the LLC. It seems unlikely that the Members designed the LLC Agreement to permit Members holding two-thirds of the Common Units to dissolve the LLC but denied their appointed Managers the power to reach the same result unless the minority manager agreed.

Castiel takes the position that while the Members can act by majority vote, the Board of Managers can act only by unanimous vote. He maintains that if the Board fails to agree unanimously on an issue the issue should be put to an LLC Members' vote with the majority controlling. The practical effect of Castiel's interpretation would be that whenever Castiel and Sahagen disagreed, Castiel would prevail because the issue would be submitted to the Members where Castiel's controlling interest would carry the vote. If that were the case, both Sahagen's Board position and Quinn's Board position would be superfluous. I am confident that the parties never intended that result, or if they had so intended, that they would have included plain and simple language in the agreement spelling it out clearly.

B. BY FAILING TO GIVE NOTICE OF THEIR PROPOSED ACTION, SAHAGEN AND QUINN FAILED TO DISCHARGE THEIR DUTY OF LOYALTY TO CASTIEL IN GOOD FAITH

Section 18-404(d) of the LLC Act states in pertinent part:

Unless otherwise provided in a limited liability company agreement, on any matter that is to be voted on by managers, the managers may take such action without a meeting, *without prior notice* and without a vote if a consent or consents in writing, setting forth the action so taken, shall be signed by the managers having not less than the minimum number of votes that would be necessary to authorize such action at a meeting (emphasis added).

Therefore, the LLC Act, read literally, does not require notice to Castiel before Sahagen and Quinn could act by written consent. The LLC Agreement does not purport to modify the statute in this regard.

Those observations cannot complete the analysis of Sahagen and Quinn's actions, however. Sahagen and Quinn knew what would happen if they notified Castiel of their intention to act by written consent to merge the LLC into VGS, Inc. Castiel would have attempted to remove Quinn, and block the planned action. Regardless of his motivation in doing so, removal of Quinn in that circumstance would have been within Castiel's rights as the LLC's controlling owner under the Agreement.

Section 18-404(d) has yet to be interpreted by this Court or the Supreme Court. Nonetheless, it seems clear that the purpose of permitting action by written consent without notice is to enable LLC managers to take quick, efficient action in situations where a minority of managers could not block or adversely affect the course set by the majority even if they were notified of the proposed action and objected to it. The General Assembly never intended, I am quite confident, to enable two managers to deprive, clandestinely and surreptitiously, a third manager representing the majority interest in the LLC of an opportunity to protect that interest by taking an action that the third manager's member would surely have opposed if he had knowledge of it. My reading of Section 18-404(d) is grounded in a classic maxim of equity—"Equity looks to the intent rather than to the form." In this hopefully unique situation, this application of the maxim requires construction of the statute to allow action without notice only by *a constant or fixed majority*. It cannot apply to an illusory, will-of-the wisp majority which would implode should notice be given. Nothing in the statute suggests that this court of equity should blind its eyes to a shallow, too clever by half, manipulative attempt to restructure an enterprise through an action taken by a "majority" that existed only so long as it could act in secrecy.

Sahagen and Quinn each owed a duty of loyalty to the LLC, its investors and Castiel, their fellow manager. Castiel or his entities owned a majority interest in the LLC and he sat as a member of the board representing entities and interests empowered by the

Agreement to control the majority membership of the board. The majority investor protected his equity interest in the LLC through the mechanism of appointment to the board rather than by the statutorily sanctioned mechanism of approval by members owning a majority of the LLC's equity interests. It may seem somewhat incongruous, but this Agreement allows the action to merge, dissolve or change to corporate status to be taken by a simple majority vote of the board of managers rather than rely upon the default position of the statute which requires a majority vote of the equity interest. Instead the drafters made the critical assumption, known to all the players here, that the holder of the majority equity interest has the right to appoint and remove two managers, ostensibly guaranteeing control over a three-member board. When Sahagen and Quinn, fully recognizing that this was Castiel's protection against actions adverse to his majority interest, acted in secret, without notice, they failed to discharge their duty of loyalty to him in good faith. They owed Castiel a duty to give him prior notice even if he would have interfered with a plan that they conscientiously believed to be in the best interest of the LLC. Instead, they launched a preemptive strike that furtively converted Castiel's controlling interest in the LLC to a minority interest in VGS without affording Castiel a level playing field on which to defend his interest. "[Another] traditional maxim of equity holds that equity regards and treats that as done which in good conscience ought to be done." In good conscience, under these circumstances, Sahagen and Quinn should have given Castiel prior notice.

Many hours were spent at trial focusing on contentions that Castiel has proved to be an ineffective leader in whom employees and investors have lost confidence. I listened to testimony regarding delayed FCC licensing, a suggested new management team for the LLC, and the alleged unlocked value of the LLC. A substantial record exists fully flushing out the rancorous relationships of the members and their wildly disparate views on the existing state of affairs as well as the LLC's prospects for the future. But the issue of who is best suited to run the LLC should not be resolved here but in board meetings where all managers are present and all members appropriately represented, and/or in future litigation, if it unfortunately becomes necessary.

Likewise, the parties spent much time and effort arguing over the standard to be applied to the actions taken by Sahagen and Quinn. Specifically, the parties debated whether the standard should be entire fairness or the business judgment rule. It should be clear that the actions of Sahagen and Quinn, in their capacity as managers constituted a breach of their duty of loyalty and that those actions do not, therefore, entitle them to the benefit or protection of the business judgment rule. They intentionally used a flawed process to merge the LLC into VGS, Inc., in an attempt to prevent the member with majority equity interest in the LLC from protecting his interests in the manner contemplated by the very LLC Agreement under which they purported to act. Analysis beyond a look at the process is clearly unnecessary. Perhaps, had notice been given and an attempt then made to block Castiel's anticipated action to replace Quinn, the allegedly disinterested and independent member that Castiel himself had appointed, the analysis might be different. However, this, as all cases must be reviewed as it is presented, not as it might have been.

III.   CONCLUSION

For the reasons stated above, I find that a majority vote of the LLC's Board of Managers could properly effect a merger. But, I also find that Sahagen and Quinn failed to discharge their duty of loyalty to Castiel in good faith by failing to give him advance notice of their merger plans under the unique circumstances of this case and the structure of this LLC Agreement. Accordingly, I declare that the acts taken to merge the LLC into VGS, Inc., to be invalid and the merger is ordered rescinded. An order consistent with this opinion, resolving the current claims of the parties is attached. . . .

7 The Corporation as a Device to Allocate Risk

A. Introduction

Creditors and other outsiders who provide resources to a corporation or another business association expect to be paid in the future from the assets purchased by those resources and the value created by the operation of the business. But what if there is a downturn in the economy, the assets are not used wisely, the resources are invested in assets that cannot be easily liquidated, or the business inflicts tortious harms on outsiders? If any of those possibilities occurs, the corporation may not be able to pay its obligations. The law's recognition of the corporation as an entity separate from its participants and the extension of limited liability to those participants means that the introduction of a corporation or other limited liability entity into a transaction shifts some or all of those risks away from the shareholders to those whom the corporation owes money.

If "no asset" or minimally capitalized entities are likely to shift too much risk away from corporate participants and onto third parties, the same possible responses that we have seen in earlier chapters are also available here: private ordering and state-provided rules. Creditors often require personal guaranties from individuals before extending credit to a no-asset corporation, insist on contractual protection preserving the shareholder equity capital already contributed, or raise their price for taking additional risk. But not all creditors request, or have the economic bargaining power to require, such protection, and a typical tort victim will not have the opportunity to choose a high-asset tortfeasor.

The state-provided legal responses could include shareholders' unlimited liability for the obligations of the enterprise or regulating the amount of the shareholders' contributions to the corporation's capital. Unlimited liability, while common in the early part of the nineteenth century, has disappeared as a legal requirement in corporations statutes. Indeed, the number of alternative limited liability entities proliferated in the closing years of the twentieth century with the recognition of limited liability companies (LLCs) and limited liability partnerships (LLPs). Similarly, state regulation of investor contribution has also withered. Since shareholders (or members in a LLC) are the residual claimants to the entity's assets and come after creditors in priority of payment, the amount of shareholder contribution, if it remains in the corporation, provides creditors a cushion against the possible dissipation described above. Delaware and some other states still have language that suggests that shareholders must provide some sort of permanent capital, but the number has been decreasing and LLC statutes have not made use of such a requirement.

Part B of this chapter explores the statutory rules designed to regulate the amount of capital placed at risk by shareholders or other residual owners in exchange for limited liability. As the impact of those statutes has decreased, greater emphasis has been put on judicial monitoring though the use of "piercing the veil," a broad equitable doctrine discussed in Part C by which courts impose personal liability on investors and managers in a limited liability business enterprise, either a corporation or an LLC. Part D examines the rules determining when an individual's actions will contractually bind the corporation or, instead, result in personal liability for the actor.

B. Corporate Law Rules Specifying an "Equity Cushion"

1. Historical Overview

In the early years of the nineteenth century, limited liability was not a strongly established corporate law norm. In some parts of the country incorporation statutes routinely provided that shareholders would be personally liable for their corporation's debts. Moreover, courts in some jurisdictions required shareholders to contribute funds necessary to pay corporate debts. This judicial liability rule assumed that corporations have inherent power to assess shareholders for funds needed by the corporation, and that it would be inequitable for a corporation not to use that power to raise funds needed to pay its debts. On the other hand, many state legislatures did not routinely include provisions mandating personal liability in incorporation acts. And, absent such provisions, the majority of court decisions treated shareholders' limited liability as a legally unavoidable by-product of recognizing a corporation's separate legal identity.

The judicial recognition of limited liability did not leave creditors without a substitute source of wealth from which to seek payment of corporate debts. The purchase price paid by shareholders for their shares was to become the permanent capital of the corporation. Shareholders were, in theory, entitled to profits made by the corporation but were not entitled to a return of the permanent capital until all creditors' claims had been satisfied in full. Thus, the permanent capital—sometimes called "capital stock," "legal capital," "stated capital," or, simply, "capital"—served as an "equity cushion" reducing the riskiness of extending credit to corporations.

Justice Story's opinion in Wood v. Dummer, a case involving a creditor's suit to hold shareholders responsible for unpaid debts of an incorporated bank, contains the classic statement of this theory:

> It appears to me very clear upon general principles, as well as the legislative intention, that the capital stock of banks is to be deemed a pledge or trust fund for the payment of the debts contracted by the bank. The public, as well as the legislature, have always supposed this to be a fund appropriated

for this purpose. The individual stockholders are not liable for the debts of the bank in their private capacities. The charter relieves them from personal responsibility, and substitutes the capital stock in its stead. Credit is universally given to this fund by the public, as the only means of repayment. During the existence of the corporation it is the sole property of the corporation, and can be applied only according to its charter, that is, as a fund for payment of its debts, upon the security of which it may discount and circulate notes. Why, otherwise, is any capital stock required by our charters? If the stock may, the next day after it is paid in, be withdrawn by the stockholders without payment of the debts of the corporation, why is the amount so studiously provided for, and its payment by the stockholders so diligently required? To me this point appears so plain upon principles of law, as well as common sense, that I cannot be brought into any doubt, that the charters of our banks make the capital stock a trust fund for the payment of all the debts of the corporation. The bill-holders and other creditors have the first claims upon it; and the stockholders have no rights, until all the other creditors are satisfied. They have the full benefit of all the profits made by the establishment, and cannot take any portion of the fund, until all the other claims on it are extinguished. Their rights are not to the capital stock, but to the residuum after all demands on it are paid.

30 F. Cas. 435, 436 (C.C.D. Me. 1824) (No. 17,944).

By the end of the nineteenth century general corporation laws had replaced special chartering. These early general corporation laws almost uniformly limited shareholders' liability to the amount paid or agreed to be paid for shares. In addition, these early general corporation laws contained so-called legal capital rules that codified the common law's "equity cushion" or permanent capital requirements.

The heart of the early legal capital statutes was the concept of "par value." Prior to the enactment of legal capital rules, it became customary for corporations to identify a "par value" at which its shares were to be sold. This par value would be stated in the corporation's charter and specified on each stock certificate. Both potential investors and creditors assumed that par value was the price at which stock would be sold by the corporation. Thus, creditors would also assume that a corporation's permanent capital could be easily calculated by multiplying the number of outstanding shares by their par value. In other words, if a corporation's shares had a stated par value of $100, and if the corporation had issued 100,000 shares, then a creditor could reasonably assume that the corporation had at its disposal a permanent capitalization in the amount of $10 million.

The early corporation codes built on this existing custom. The typical code required each corporation to specify (in its articles of incorporation) a par value for its stock, and defined a corporation's legal capital as an amount equal to the product obtained by multiplying the number of outstanding shares times the par value of such shares. The typical statute permitted corporations to make periodic distributions to shareholders out of profits or surplus, but prohibited distributions to shareholders out of a corporation's permanent or legal capital.

The legal capital restrictions based on par value continued to be a near-universal feature of general corporation codes until 1980, when the ABA Committee on Corporate Laws deleted such provisions from the Model Business Corporation Act (MBCA). Delaware is among the minority of states that continues to have legal capital rules in its corporation codes. The remaining states, many of which follow the MBCA, restrict distributions to shareholders but do not use the legal capital concept.

2.   Statutory Rules Governing the Equity Cushion

a.   Minimum Initial Capitalization Requirements

MBCA §6.21
Delaware G.C.L. §§153, 154

As long as corporation law required all shares to have a par value, and custom required that shares be issued for an equivalent price, a corporation's initial issuance of shares would automatically produce an equity cushion that creditors could easily calculate. Mirroring the assumption that par value and purchase price were connected, and that creditors would rely on par value as an indicator of the corporation's equity cushion, most codes required that shares be sold for no less than par value.

In the twentieth century, however, both law and custom changed. Investors came to accept that there was no necessary connection between par value and issue price. Thus, it became common for corporations to offer shares to the public at a price far in excess of the par value selected for such shares. For example, a corporation could without market resistance create shares having a low par value — say, $0.01 per share — and then sell these shares to the public for $100 per share. In recognition of this change in custom and practice, corporation codes soon permitted corporations to create and issue shares having no par value at all.

Despite the disconnection of par value and issue price, it would be relatively simple for corporation codes to require an equity cushion. Indeed, for much of the twentieth century, a number of state corporation codes specified a minimum total amount of capital that each corporation must possess before starting business. However, the required minimum capital was invariably insignificant (typically between $500 and $1,000), and such rules have been abandoned.

Instead, corporation codes that retain legal capital restrictions now define the required "equity cushion" in a way that allows corporations to choose to avoid having such a cushion. Typical is Delaware G.C.L. §154. Under the Delaware scheme, a corporation's permanent capital is termed simply "capital." Section 154 permits a corporation's directors to specify by resolution what amount of the consideration paid for shares shall constitute capital. The only limit on such authority is that capital cannot be less than an amount equal to the aggregate par value of issued shares having a par value. Thus, if a corporation issues 100,000 shares having a par value of $0.01 per share, the directors may elect to treat as little as $1,000 as capital, even if the corporation actually receives total consideration in the amount of $10,000,000.

The 1980 amendments to the Model Business Corporation Act, continued in the current MBCA, simply take one further step. Although the MBCA allows corporations to create shares with par value (see MBCA §2.02(b)(2)(iv)), doing so has no legal significance. The MBCA contains no provision that prohibits issuance of shares at a price below par value. (In contrast, Delaware G.C.L. §153 requires that shares with par value be sold for at least that amount.) In addition, the MBCA contains no concept such as "capital" or "legal capital" that is used to restrict distributions to shareholders. Thus, the MBCA not only makes no attempt to ensure that corporations will provide a significant equity cushion but also provides no standard form mechanism by which corporations may do so.

b. Quality and Valuation of Consideration Paid for Shares

MBCA §6.21
Delaware G.C.L. §152

A central concern of traditional legal capital statutes is the quality of consideration paid by shareholders. In order for creditors to assume that the aggregate par value of issued shares represents an equity cushion, or perhaps a trust fund on which they may later draw, they must be convinced that the consideration paid by shareholders was worth par value. In the nineteenth century, investor confidence might well have been shaken by cases in which shareholders "paid" for their shares either by promising to render future services or by executing a note promising to pay an agreed sum in the future. Accordingly, many of the early corporation codes explicitly prohibited the issuance of shares for promissory notes or future services.

Some corporation codes continue to prohibit expressly the issuance of shares in exchange for promissory notes or future services. Statutes that were silent were sometimes interpreted to prohibit the use of promissory notes. See, e.g., Cahall v. Lofland, 12 Del. Ch. 299, 114 A.224 (1921); Sohland v. Baker, 15 Del. Ch. 431, 141 A.277 (1927). The MBCA and Delaware now leave to the discretion of each corporation's board of directors the determination of what type of consideration is acceptable.

Regardless of whether corporation codes limit the types of consideration that may be paid for shares, directors and shareholders face potential liability if shares are sold for insufficient consideration. All corporation codes authorize the directors to determine an appropriate issue price, and provide that shareholders are liable to pay the amount for which their shares were issued. These rules will create potential liability only if the directors set an unfairly low price or set a fair price but accept consideration that has insufficient value.

Directors will be liable for setting an unfairly low price, or accepting consideration having insufficient value, only if their actions constitute a breach of fiduciary duty. Absent fraud on their part, shareholders face no liability for purchasing stock at a bargain price. On the other hand, if shareholders pay less than all of the agreed purchase price, then they remain liable for the remainder. However, if shareholders tender property that the directors evaluate and agree to accept in full payment of the issue price, then the shareholders will not be liable to make up any shortfall if it is later discovered that the property was not worth the agreed purchase price.

c. Limits on Distributions to Shareholders

MBCA §6.40
Delaware G.C.L. §§154, 170, 244

From their inception, general corporation codes have placed restrictions on corporations' power to distribute money or property to shareholders with respect to their shares. The most common forms of distribution subject to such restrictions are dividends and payments for share repurchases. Payments to shareholders for services, rent, and so on are not distributions with respect to shares and have never been subject to statutory restrictions. Currently, state codes are split into two main camps—those that restrict distributions solely by reference to insolvency tests and those that restrict distributions by reference to legal capital rules (alone or in combination with insolvency tests).

The post-1980 MBCA adopts an approach now followed by most states. Such statutes restrict corporations' power solely by reference to two insolvency rules—commonly referred to as the equity and bankruptcy insolvency tests. Under these tests, a corporation is permitted to distribute assets to shareholders so long as after such distribution the corporation (1) will be able to pay its debts in the ordinary course of business—that is, will be solvent in the equitable sense; and (2) will still have assets equal to or in excess of its liabilities (and the dissolution preference of its senior equity securities)—that is, will be solvent in the balance sheet or bankruptcy sense.

Delaware and a small number of other states purport to impose greater restrictions on distributions. Generally, these statutes authorize distributions to shareholders only out of "surplus." This would appear to be a more stingy standard because surplus is usually defined as net assets of the corporation in excess of capital. The crucial connection, which will not be obvious from reading the statute, is that if distributions are authorized only out of surplus, that means one cannot touch capital. Defined slightly differently in the various states that still use the legal capital terminology, capital includes at least the aggregate par value of a corporation's outstanding shares and, in some cases, the entirety of the consideration paid by the shareholders for their shares. By any definition, capital provides an additional amount by which assets must exceed liabilities before a distribution can be made (as compared to the MBCA standard, which requires essentially that assets exceed liabilities). The bigger this equity cushion, the less risk there is for a creditor. In many cases, however, the amount of capital (and thus the cushion) is very small.

Some of the statutes distinguish between "earned surplus"—a corporation's net undistributed profits, sometimes called retained earnings—and "capital surplus"—the consideration paid for the shares that is not designated as capital. States making this distinction (based on the pre-1980 MBCA) usually place more restrictions on distributions out of capital surplus than out of earned surplus. In addition, some of these states restrict distributions for share repurchases more stringently than ordinary dividends. Delaware, which does not distinguish between capital surplus and earned surplus, allows dividends and share repurchases to be made out of surplus whatever its source.

Most state corporation codes specify the conditions under which directors will be held liable for authorizing distributions to shareholders in violation of legal capital or insolvency restrictions. Statutes commonly provide that the directors, if held liable, can recover from shareholders the amount that the shareholder received with knowledge that the distribution violated law. Moreover, corporate distributions that make a corporation insolvent may be voided under state fraudulent transfer statutes. See In re Kettle Fried Chicken of America, Inc., 513 F.2d 807 (6th Cir. 1975).

Statutory restrictions do not result in substantial litigation for a variety of reasons, but primarily because it is possible for most solvent corporations to make distributions that clearly do not violate statutory rules. The hard cases raise questions about the ability of insiders to adjust various balance sheet categories and thereby increase the amount of distributions that can be authorized under the statute.

Klang v. Smith's Food & Drug Centers, Inc.
Delaware Supreme Court, 1997
702 A.2d 150

Before VEASEY, CHIEF JUSTICE, and WALSH, HOLLAND, HARTNETT and BERGER, JUSTICES, constituting the Court en Banc.

VEASEY, CHIEF JUSTICE:

This appeal calls into question the actions of a corporate board in carrying out a merger and self-tender offer. Plaintiff in this purported class action alleges that a corporation's repurchase of shares violated the statutory prohibition against the impairment of capital. Plaintiff also claims that the directors violated their fiduciary duty of candor by failing to disclose material facts prior to seeking stockholder approval of the transactions in question.

No corporation may repurchase or redeem its own shares except out of "surplus," as statutorily defined, or except as expressly authorized by provisions of the statute not relevant here. Balance sheets are not, however, conclusive indicators of surplus or a lack thereof. Corporations may revalue assets to show surplus, but perfection in that process is not required. Directors have reasonable latitude to depart from the balance sheet to calculate surplus, so long as they evaluate assets and liabilities in good faith, on the basis of acceptable data, by methods that they reasonably believe reflect present values, and arrive at a determination of the surplus that is not so far off the mark as to constitute actual or constructive fraud.

We hold that, on this record the Court of Chancery was correct in finding that there was no impairment of capital and there were no disclosure violations. Accordingly, we affirm.

FACTS

Smith's Food & Drug Centers, Inc. (SFD) is a Delaware corporation that owns and operates a chain of supermarkets in the Southwestern United States. Slightly more than three years ago, Jeffrey P. Smith, SFD's Chief Executive Officer, began to entertain suitors with an interest in acquiring SFD. At the time, and until the transactions at issue, Mr. Smith and his family held common and preferred stock constituting 62.1% voting control of SFD. Plaintiff and the class he purports to represent are holders of common stock in SFD.

On January 29, 1996, SFD entered into an agreement with The Yucaipa Companies (Yucaipa), a California partnership also active in the supermarket industry. Under the agreement, the following would take place:

(1) Smitty's Supermarkets, Inc. (Smitty's), a wholly-owned subsidiary of Yucaipa that operated a supermarket chain in Arizona, was to merge into Cactus Acquisition, Inc. (Cactus), a subsidiary of SFD, in exchange for which SFD would deliver to Yucaipa slightly over 3 million newly-issued shares of SFD common stock;

(2) SFD was to undertake a recapitalization, in the course of which SFD would assume a sizable amount of new debt, retire old debt, and offer to repurchase up to

fifty percent of its outstanding shares (other than those issued to Yucaipa) for $36 per share; and

(3) SFD was to repurchase 3 million shares of preferred stock from Jeffrey Smith and his family.

SFD hired the investment firm of Houlihan Lokey Howard & Zukin (Houlihan) to examine the transactions and render a solvency opinion. Houlihan eventually issued a report to the SFD Board replete with assurances that the transactions would not endanger SFD's solvency, and would not impair SFD's capital in violation of 8 Del. C. §160. On May 17, 1996, in reliance on the Houlihan opinion, SFD's Board determined that there existed sufficient surplus to consummate the transactions, and enacted a resolution proclaiming as much. On May 23, 1996, SFD's stockholders voted to approve the transactions, which closed on that day. The self-tender offer was over-subscribed, so SFD repurchased fully fifty percent of its shares at the offering price of $36 per share. . . .

PLAINTIFF'S CAPITAL-IMPAIRMENT CLAIM

A corporation may not repurchase its shares if, in so doing, it would cause an impairment of capital, unless expressly authorized by Section 160. A repurchase impairs capital if the funds used in the repurchase exceed the amount of the corporation's "surplus," defined by 8 Del. C. §154 to mean the excess of net assets over the par value of the corporation's issued stock.[5]

Plaintiff asked the Court of Chancery to rescind the transactions in question as violative of Section 160. As we understand it, plaintiff's position breaks down into two analytically distinct arguments. First, he contends that SFD's balance sheets constitute conclusive evidence of capital impairment. He argues that the negative net worth that appeared on SFD's books following the repurchase compels us to find a violation of Section 160. Second, he suggests that even allowing the Board to "go behind the balance sheet" to calculate surplus does not save the transactions from violating Section 160. In connection with this claim, he attacks the SFD Board's off-balance-sheet method of calculating surplus on the theory that it does not adequately take into account all of SFD's assets and liabilities. Moreover, he argues that the May 17, 1996 resolution of the SFD Board conclusively refutes the Board's claim that revaluing the corporation's assets gives rise to the required surplus. We hold that each of these claims is without merit.

SFD's BALANCE SHEETS DO NOT ESTABLISH A VIOLATION OF 8 DEL. C. §160

In an April 25, 1996 proxy statement, the SFD Board released a pro forma balance sheet showing that the merger and self-tender offer would result in a deficit to

---

5. Section 154 provides, "Any corporation may, by resolution of its board of directors, determine that only a part of the consideration . . . received by the corporation for . . . its capital stock . . . shall be capital. . . . The excess . . . of the net assets of the corporation over the amount so determined to be capital shall be surplus. Net assets means the amount by which total assets exceed total liabilities. Capital and surplus are not liabilities for this purpose."

surplus on SFD's books of more than $100 million. A balance sheet the SFD Board issued shortly after the transactions confirmed this result. Plaintiff asks us to adopt an interpretation of 8 Del. C. §160 whereby balance-sheet net worth is controlling for purposes of determining compliance with the statute. Defendants do not dispute that SFD's books showed a negative net worth in the wake of its transactions with Yucaipa, but argue that corporations should have the presumptive right to revalue assets and liabilities to comply with Section 160.

Plaintiff advances an erroneous interpretation of Section 160. We understand that the books of a corporation do not necessarily reflect the current values of its assets and liabilities. Among other factors, unrealized appreciation or depreciation can render book numbers inaccurate. It is unrealistic to hold that a corporation is bound by its balance sheets for purposes of determining compliance with Section 160. Accordingly, we adhere to the principles of Morris v. Standard Gas & Electric Co. [63 A.2d 577 (1949)] allowing corporations to revalue properly its assets and liabilities to show a surplus and thus conform to the statute.

It is helpful to recall the purpose behind Section 160. The General Assembly enacted the statute to prevent boards from draining corporations of assets to the detriment of creditors and the long-term health of the corporation. That a corporation has not yet realized or reflected on its balance sheet the appreciation of assets is irrelevant to this concern. Regardless of what a balance sheet that has not been updated may show, an actual, though unrealized, appreciation reflects real economic value that the corporation may borrow against or that creditors may claim or levy upon. Allowing corporations to revalue assets and liabilities to reflect current realities complies with the statute and serves well the policies behind this statute.

THE SFD BOARD APPROPRIATELY REVALUED CORPORATE ASSETS TO COMPLY WITH 8 DEL. C. §160

Plaintiff contends that SFD's repurchase of shares violated Section 160 even without regard to the corporation's balance sheets. Plaintiff claims that the SFD Board was not entitled to rely on the solvency opinion of Houlihan, which showed that the transactions would not impair SFD's capital given a revaluation of corporate assets. The argument is that the methods that underlay the solvency opinion were inappropriate as a matter of law because they failed to take into account all of SFD's assets and liabilities. In addition, plaintiff suggests that the SFD Board's resolution of May 17, 1996 itself shows that the transactions impaired SFD's capital, and that therefore we must find a violation of 8 Del. C. §160. We disagree, and hold that the SFD Board revalued the corporate assets under appropriate methods. Therefore the self-tender offer complied with Section 160, notwithstanding errors that took place in the drafting of the resolution.

On May 17, 1996, Houlihan released its solvency opinion to the SFD Board, expressing its judgment that the merger and self-tender offer would not impair SFD's capital. Houlihan reached this conclusion by comparing SFD's "Total Invested Capital" of $1.8 billion—a figure Houlihan arrived at by valuing SFD's assets under the "market multiple" approach—with SFD's long-term debt of $1.46 billion. This comparison yielded an approximation of SFD's "concluded equity value" equal to $346 million, a figure clearly in excess of the outstanding par value of SFD's stock. Thus, Houlihan concluded, the transactions would not violate 8 Del. C. §160.

Plaintiff contends that Houlihan's analysis relied on inappropriate methods to mask a violation of Section 160. Noting that 8 Del. C. §154 defines "net assets" as "the amount by which total assets exceeds total liabilities," plaintiff argues that Houlihan's analysis is erroneous as a matter of law because of its failure to calculate "total assets" and "total liabilities" as separate variables. In a related argument, plaintiff claims that the analysis failed to take into account all of SFD's liabilities, i.e., that Houlihan neglected to consider current liabilities in its comparison of SFD's "Total Invested Capital" and long-term debt. Plaintiff contends that the SFD Board's resolution proves that adding current liabilities into the mix shows a violation of Section 160. The resolution declared the value of SFD's assets to be $1.8 billion, and stated that its "total liabilities" would not exceed $1.46 billion after the transactions with Yucaipa. As noted, the $1.46 billion figure described only the value of SFD's long-term debt. Adding in SFD's $372 million in current liabilities, plaintiff argues, shows that the transactions impaired SFD's capital.

We believe that plaintiff reads too much into Section 154. The statute simply defines "net assets" in the course of defining "surplus." It does not mandate a "facts and figures balancing of assets and liabilities" to determine by what amount, if any, total assets exceeds total liabilities. The statute is merely definitional. It does not require any particular method of calculating surplus, but simply prescribes factors that any such calculation must include. Although courts may not determine compliance with Section 160 except by methods that fully take into account the assets and liabilities of the corporation, Houlihan's methods were not erroneous as a matter of law simply because they used Total Invested Capital and long-term debt as analytical categories rather than "total assets" and "total liabilities."

We are satisfied that the Houlihan opinion adequately took into account all of SFD's assets and liabilities. Plaintiff points out that the $1.46 billion figure that approximated SFD's long-term debt failed to include $372 million in current liabilities, and argues that including the latter in the calculations dissipates the surplus. In fact, plaintiff has misunderstood Houlihan's methods. The record shows that Houlihan's calculation of SFD's Total Invested Capital is already net of current liabilities. Thus, subtracting long-term debt from Total Invested Capital does, in fact, yield an accurate measure of a corporation's net assets.

The record contains, in the form of the Houlihan opinion, substantial evidence that the transactions complied with Section 160. Plaintiff has provided no reason to distrust Houlihan's analysis. In cases alleging impairment of capital under Section 160, the trial court may defer to the board's measurement of surplus unless a plaintiff can show that the directors "failed to fulfill their duty to evaluate the assets on the basis of acceptable data and by standards which they are entitled to believe reasonably reflect present values." In the absence of bad faith or fraud on the part of the board, courts will not "substitute [our] concepts of wisdom for that of the directors." Here, plaintiff does not argue that the SFD Board acted in bad faith. Nor has he met his burden of showing that the methods and data that underlay the board's analysis are unreliable or that its determination of surplus is so far off the mark as to constitute actual or constructive fraud.[12] Therefore, we defer to the board's determination of surplus, and hold that SFD's self-tender offer did not violate 8 Del. C. §160.

On a final note, we hold that the SFD Board's resolution of May 17, 1996 has no bearing on whether the transactions conformed to Section 160. The record shows that the SFD Board committed a serious error in drafting the resolution: the resolution states that, following the transactions, SFD's "total liabilities" would be no more than $1.46 billion. In fact, that figure reflects only the value of SFD's long-term debt. Although the SFD Board was guilty of sloppy work, and did not follow good corporate practices, it does not follow that Section 160 was violated. The statute requires only that there exist a surplus after a repurchase, not that the board memorialize the surplus in a resolution. The statute carves out a class of transactions that directors have no authority to execute, but does not, in fact, require any affirmative act on the part of the board. The SFD repurchase would be valid in the absence of any board resolution. A mistake in documenting the surplus will not negate the substance of the action, which complies with the statutory scheme. . . .

[The Court also affirmed the Chancery Court's dismissal of the disclosure claims in which the court observed that equity valuations derived by Houlihan in the course of rendering its solvency opinion are an "accounting rather than a legal or economic 'concept' and would not have been material to shareholders."] In Barkan [v. Armsted Indus, Inc. 567 A.2d 1279,1289] and again in Citron v. Fairchild Camera & Instrument [569 A.2d 53 (1989)], we expressed our reluctance to force disclosure of data generated solely for accounting purposes. In *Barkan,* we held that an estimate of a corporation's "liquidation value" prepared as part of a capital-impairment test was not material. Similarly, in *Citron* we held that valuation estimates "prepared primarily for accounting purposes rather than for establishing the fair market value of [the corporation's] share" were immaterial. The holding in both cases was premised upon the sentiment that figures generated for purely accounting purposes are useless predictors of market value, and are at least as likely to mislead stockholders as to enlighten them. In light of *Barkan* and *Citron,* we defer to the finding of the Court of Chancery that Houlihan's equity valuations would not alter the "total mix" of information available to SFD's stockholders. . . .

NOTES AND QUESTIONS

1. To apply either of the state regimes limiting distributions, you will need some basic understanding of a *balance sheet,* one of the core financial statements in accounting. The accounting system provides a way of presenting a business's financial position for use by creditors, investors, regulators, and managers. The balance sheet presents

---

12. We interpret 8 Del. C. §172 to entitle boards to rely on experts such as Houlihan to determine compliance with 8 Del. C. §160. Plaintiff has not alleged that the SFD Board failed to exercise reasonable care in selecting Houlihan, nor that rendering a solvency opinion is outside Houlihan's realm of competence. Compare 8 Del. C. §141(e) (providing that directors may rely in good faith on records, reports, experts, etc.).

the company's assets, liabilities, and owners' equity at a particular point in time. The *income statement,* in contrast, is a financial statement that seeks to show the net effects of a company's operations over a period of time, for example the last year. There is another financial statement you may encounter, a *statement of changes in financial position,* that reconciles the changes during a particular period.

To use a balance sheet, you must understand the fundamental accounting equation on which it is based:

Assets = Liabilities + Equity

Balance sheets are often presented in the same form as the one in Problem 7-1, with assets on the left side and liabilities and equity on the right side. This defines the basic structure accountants have devised to present financial information in this context: the left side (the assets of the corporation) will always balance the right side (claims on the corporation's assets either by creditors or shareholders). Double-entry bookkeeping is also part of the structure; it is the means by which the effect of ongoing transactions of the corporation can be presented. For balance sheet purposes, if an increase is made to the left side (e.g., cash received from a loan), a corresponding change must be made to the right side (e.g., an increase in short-term liabilities).

Using simple algebra, you can rearrange the basic equation so that:

Equity = Assets − Liabilities

This reflects a basic point first presented in Chapter 3, that shareholders have the residual claim to the corporation's assets, whatever is left after all prior claims have been paid. If assets go up while liabilities remain the same, shareholder equity will necessarily go up. If liabilities increase more than assets, shareholder equity necessarily goes down.

The distribution statutes seek to protect creditors against excessive corporate funds being diverted to shareholders. In using a balance sheet for that purpose, legal regimes to some extent are relying on the discipline or monitoring function that traditionally has been one of the functions of accounting systems. For example, accountants traditionally have used historical cost as the basis for entries on a balance sheet, and there is a reluctance to change those historical numbers until there is a reliable event, for example, a sale to a third party in a market transaction. This illustrates what sometimes has been labeled accounting conservatism, an attitude that "pushes accountants toward the pessimistic side, to offset the natural optimism, if not exuberance, of business owners or managers in reporting the results of operations." Herwitz and Barrett, Accounting for Lawyers (2d ed. 1998 at 62).

In inflationary times or where there are rapid changes in the value of assets, the traditional balance sheet with figures based on historical cost may not reflect actual value. For accountants, there is often a trade-off between the reliability of figures, particularly if that is to be measured by third-party transactions and not management's own figures, and relevance, for investors and others want to know current value, not some historical figures. As the principal case illustrates, distribution statutes do not necessarily incorporate accounting rules, but in departing from usual accounting principles, the question remains "whether permitting dividends from the unrealized appreciation in fixed assets fulfilled the legislature's desire to proscribe dividends which impaired capital, so as to protect creditors." Cox, Financial Information, Accounting and the Law at 257-258.

2. Revaluing assets to market value is not the only way to increase the amount available for shareholder distributions under the statutory tests. In those states that permit distributions out of surplus, it is possible to create surplus not just from new earnings or an increase in assets but also by reducing the amount of capital. Since capital is determined from par value, this would require a decrease in par value. Note how this is accomplished. It requires amending the corporation's articles of incorporation, which necessitates action by shareholders (who are to receive the anticipated dividend) but not creditors.

3. A corporation with a history of losses may have a negative surplus account even though it is currently profitable. For example, in a high-tech start-up company liabilities may exceed assets, thus eating into the owner's equity originally contributed to the business, but the corporation during the last year has turned a profit. Under many statutes that permit distributions only out of surplus, the corporation would be unable to pay dividends or repurchase shares until the original capital is restored (i.e., earnings must be used to restore the cushion before they are used to pay shareholders). Delaware and a small number of other states relax the distribution restrictions by allowing distributions, sometimes termed *nimble dividends,* not only out of surplus, but also out of the corporation's profits for the year of distributions and/or the preceding fiscal year.

4. In light of the different ways that managers can avoid dividend restrictions, including those described in the previous notes, the ABA Committee on Corporate Laws concluded that par value and legal capital rules were ineffective and might cause creditors to expect protections that did not exist. Consequently, the Committee deleted par value and legal capital from the Model Act. See Changes in the Model Business Corporation Act—Amendments to Financial Provisions, 34 Bus. Law. 1867, 1867-1868 (1979). Is this sufficient justification for the changes? Consider the alternatives discussed in the next two notes. Is the relaxation of statutory rules requiring an equity cushion the result of a competition among the states for incorporation business? If so, is it the result of a race to the top or the bottom?

5. Notably, California has bucked the trend toward less restrictive statutory rules. In 1975, California enacted a new general corporation code that deleted preexisting legal capital rules. The legislative comment to new §500 states that the old rules "do not provide adequate protection to creditors, particularly trade creditors" and are being replaced "[f]or the purpose of establishing meaningful protection for creditors and shareholders and to rationalize restrictions upon the payment of dividends and repurchase of shares. . . ." Section 500 permits distributions to shareholders under two alternative circumstances. First, distributions are permitted to the extent of a corporation's retained earnings. Second, distributions are authorized to the extent that immediately afterwards (1) the sum of the corporation's assets is equal to at least 125 percent of its liabilities, and (2) the sum of the corporation's current assets (cash and other assets readily convertible into cash) is equal to at least 125 percent of its current liabilities. Section 501 continues the traditional rule that in no event may distributions be made that would render a corporation unable to meet its obligations as they mature.

6. While American state legislatures have done little to ensure that corporations maintain an equity cushion, the European Union (EU) and its member states have insisted on such cushions. Council Directive 77/91/EEC, 20 O.J. Eur. Comm. No. 126, 1 (1976), commonly referred to as the Second Company Law Directive, requires member states to establish minimum capital requirements and restrictions on distributions to shareholders. The key elements of this directive are Articles 6, 7, and 15.

Article 6 instructs member states to prohibit any corporation from commencing business until it has received capital from its shareholders worth at least 25,000 European Currency Units. Some member states require substantially greater capital as a precondition to starting business, and some require greater capital for publicly held corporations than for closely held. Under Article 7, capital may be provided in the form of money or other property capable of economic assessment. However, an undertaking to provide services or supplies is an impermissible form of consideration. Article 15 prohibits distributions to shareholders out of the required minimum capital. For a detailed look at the EU rules, see Keustermans, Countertrends in Financial Provisions for the Protection of Corporate Creditors: The Model Business Corporation Act and the E.E.C. Corporate Directives, 14 Denver J. Intl. L. & Poly. 275 (1986).

7. Disputes sometimes arise when a shareholder is retiring or otherwise withdrawing from the business and sells shares back to the corporation. As may be common in many close corporations that do not have excessive amounts of cash on hand even if they have a positive net worth, the corporation may give a long-term note in exchange for the shares. If the corporation later gets in financial trouble, creditors who now worry about getting full payment may see the "shareholder turned creditor" as jumping up in the line of payment. The Model Act specifies measurement rules that permit such two-step transactions. The Commentary acknowledges the possibility that some transactions might be challenged as fraudulent conveyances.

8. For a thorough treatment of the legal capital systems, see Manning and Hanks, Legal Capital (3d ed. 1990). For a detailed analysis of modern American statutes, see Kummert, State Statutory Restrictions on Financial Distribution by Corporations to Shareholders, Part II, 59 Wash. L. Rev. 187 (1984). For a look at the nineteenth-century view of limited liability and the requirement of permanent capital, see Dodd, American Business Corporations Until 1860, at 74-79 (1954).

PROBLEM 7-1

Stage Performances Corporation has been in the business of promoting rock concerts for several years. It has generally been profitable but has suffered small operating losses each of the last two years. Stage Performances has 80,000 outstanding shares, each having a par value of $1.00. Jack Sanders is the corporation's chief executive officer and the owner of 40,000 shares. Molly Maguire, Margaret Mahoney, and Michael Martin own the remaining 40,000 shares. Sanders, Maguire, Mahoney, and Martin are also the corporation's directors. Stage Performances' balance sheet as of December 31, 2005, is set out below. The book and market value of the corporation's assets and liabilities are identical.

Assets		Liabilities	
Cash (from advance ticket sales)	$1,000,000	Current liability	$540,000
		Long-term debt	400,000
Fixed assets	40,000		
		Equity	
		Capital	$80,000
		Surplus	20,000
	$1,040,000		$1,040,000

In answering the following questions assume, alternatively, that Stage Performances Corporation is incorporated in Delaware or in a jurisdiction following the MBCA.

(a) On December 31, 2013, Stage Performances issued a $100,000 dividend to its shareholders. Eighteen months later the corporation declared bankruptcy. What result if the trustee sues the directors to recover portions of the December 31, 2013, dividend allegedly distributed in violation of the governing corporation code?

(b) How would your answer to (a) change if Stage Performances did not go bankrupt until five years after declaring the dividend?

(c) How would the above balance sheet and your answer to (a) change if the following occurred shortly before the December 31, 2013, dividend?

(1) Jack Sanders purchased an additional 1,000 Stage Performance shares, giving as consideration his unsecured promissory note in the amount of $100,000.

(2) Jack Sanders purchased an additional 1,000 Stage Performance shares, paying with shares of another closely held corporation owned by Sanders. The directors valued the shares at $100,000. The shares later proved worthless.

(3) The board of directors by amendment to the articles of incorporation changed the par value of the corporation's shares to $0.01.

(d) How would your answer to (a) change if the corporation had a net profit in 2012, already reflected in the above balance sheet, in the amount of $90,000?

(e) How would your answer to (a) change if the above balance sheet reflects only historical values and if, before approving the December 31, 2013, dividend, the board of directors concluded, based on Jack Sanders's statements, that the corporation's fixed assets had a fair market value of $140,000?

PROBLEM 7-2

Harvey, the owner of 1,000 of the 1,800 shares of HD, Inc. desires to withdraw from the business and enjoy retirement. As of December 31, 2013, the corporation's balance sheet showed its assets exceeded its liabilities by $140,000. On January 1, 2014, the corporation purchased Harvey's shares, but since cash was tight, it gave him a note for the entire purchase amount, with a ten-year term. During the first seven years of the note, interest only would be owed in monthly payments; thereafter there would be 36 equal monthly installments of principal and interest. The note was secured by (1) the equipment, tools, inventory, and personal property of the corporation; (2) a pledge of the certificate evidencing ownership of the 1,000 shares; and (3) a life insurance policy in the principal sum of $100,000 covering the life of Harvey. Ten months later, the corporation missed two payments on the note, and news reached Harvey that the corporation was in serious financial difficulty. Harvey foreclosed on the security, and nothing was left for other creditors of the corporation. Can the creditors recover anything from Harvey?

C. Piercing the Veil

1. Introduction

During the nineteenth century, most state legislatures enacted general corporation statutes providing limited liability to shareholders. As discussed in Part B, these statutes also sought to provide protection for creditors by specifying the type and amount of consideration that must be paid into the corporation by shareholders in return for their shares and restricting the money that could be taken out of the corporation (before creditors' claims were paid) via distributions to shareholders. But, perhaps because these statutory rules were not always effective, courts remained willing to entertain suits by creditors seeking to impose personal liability on shareholders, a process usually described as "piercing the corporate veil."

The "black letter" law of veil piercing is usually stated in broad generalities. Most courts would probably agree with the following restatement: "The separateness of the corporate entity is normally to be respected. However, a corporation's veil will be pierced whenever corporate form is employed to evade an existing obligation, circumvent a statute, perpetrate fraud, commit a crime, or work an injustice." Such black letter formulations, however, give judges or practitioners little structure with which to approach the analysis of particular cases. Frederick J. Powell suggested a three-part test in a 1931 treatise on parent and subsidiary corporations that continues to be cited in modern cases, not just those involving parents and subsidiaries. To pierce the veil, Powell required that (1) the parent completely control and dominate the subsidiary, (2) the parent's conduct in using the subsidiary was unjust, fraudulent, or wrongful toward the plaintiff, and (3) plaintiff actually suffered some harm as a result. F.J. Powell, Parent and Subsidiary Corporations: Liability of a Parent Corporation for the Obligations of Its Subsidiary 4-6 (1931). Powell used much of his treatise to compile a list of factors that satisfy the alter ego or instrumentality requirement of the first prong of the test or the injustice part of the second prong of the test. Subsequent judicial and academic writers have expanded and rearranged those lists, and most court opinions are structured so as to give the appearance that the court has actually applied the test and weighted the factors. Judge Frank Easterbrook, writing for the Seventh Circuit, made the following observation: "Such an approach, requiring courts to balance many imponderables, all important, but none dispositive and frequently lacking a common metric to boot, is quite difficult to apply because it avoids formulating a real rule of decision. This keeps people in the dark about the legal consequences of their acts. . . ." Secon Service Systems, Inc. v. St. Joseph Bank & Trust Co., 855 F.2d 406, 414 (7th Cir. 1988).

Benjamin Cardozo described aspects of veil piercing as "enveloped in the mists of metaphor,"[1] a description amplified in a leading modern commentary:

> This is jurisprudence by metaphor or epithet. . . . The metaphors are no more than conclusory terms, affording little understanding of the court's action and little help in predicting results in future cases. . . . As a result we are faced with hundreds of decisions that are irreconcilable, and not entirely comprehensible.

P. Blumberg, The Law of Corporate Groups: Procedural Problems in the Law of Parent and Subsidiary Corporations 8 (1983).

This exasperation at veil-piercing cases is no different than the long-expressed dissatisfaction with judicial opinions applying fiduciary duty. However, as is true with respect to fiduciary duty, commentators and courts in recent years have begun to shed light on the dynamics of veil piercing.

Scholars have identified three central dimensions or factors that may affect the likelihood that veil piercing will occur. The first is the distinction between plaintiffs suing to enforce contract claims and those suing to enforce tort claims. Because contract claimants have an opportunity to bargain with the corporation, it has been asserted that courts should be more reluctant to pierce the corporate veil in contract cases than in tort cases, where the injured party has not consented to tortious conduct. The second factor is the identity of the person behind the veil. Many commentators argue that courts should be more willing to pierce the corporate veil to reach other corporations than to reach a real person. The final factor is the distinction between closely held and publicly held corporations. Because most publicly held corporations are not effectively controlled by their shareholders, it seems unlikely that courts would find it equitable or efficient to hold such shareholders personally liable for a corporation's debts. So doing would defeat one of the central expectations underlying the stability of our national securities market system. By contrast, there are no market consequences of holding shareholders in closely held corporations personally liable.

Professor Robert Thompson's empirical study surveyed all cases involving veil piercing that appear in the Westlaw system through 1985.[2] Thompson's study sheds a somewhat different light on the factors affecting veil piercing. As all commentators would have predicted, Thompson found no cases in which courts pierced the corporate veil to impose liability on shareholders in a publicly held corporation. However, the study produced surprising results as to the frequency with which courts pierced the corporate veil in contract cases as opposed to tort cases, and in cases seeking to impose liability on real persons as opposed to incorporated shareholders.

Thompson found that courts pierced the corporate veil in approximately 40 percent of all surveyed cases. Table 1, below, shows how the frequency of veil piercing is affected by the number and identity of the persons whom plaintiffs seek to reach by piercing the corporate veil. Table 2, below, shows how the frequency of veil piercing is

---

1. Berkey v. Third Ave. Ry., 244 N.Y. 84, 94, 155 N.E. 58, 61 (1926).
2. Piercing the Corporate Veil: An Empirical Study, 76 Cornell L. Rev. 1036 (1991). Copyright © 1991 by Cornell University. All rights reserved.

affected by the substantive context of the suit—that is, by whether the plaintiff has a tort or contract claim.

Section 2, below, presents cases organized by context—contract or tort—and involving real persons as defendants. Section 3 then introduces cases in which plaintiffs seek to pierce the corporate veil to reach incorporated shareholders. As you read the following materials, consider how the different contexts explain the result. Based on these cases, does veil piercing appear to be a random event, or can its application be predicted with reasonable certainty?

TABLE 1

Identity of Shareholders	Total Number of Cases	Pierce	No Pierce	% Piercing
Individuals:				
—One	276	137	139	49.64
—Two or Three	238	110	128	46.22
—Close but More than Three	263	92	171	34.98
—Public Shareholders	9	0	9	0.00
Total Individuals	786	339	447	43.13
Corporate:				
—Parent	386	142	244	36.79
—Subsidiary	68	19	49	27.94
—Sibling	183	76	107	41.53
Total Corporate	637	237	400	37.21

TABLE 2

Context	Total Cases	Pierce	No Pierce	% Piercing
Contract	779	327	452	41.98
Tort	226	70	156	30.97

With the advent of LLCs and LLPs in providing limited liability to their members or partners, veil piercing now arises in these newer entities. Some LLC statutes explicitly incorporate corporate veil-piercing principles. Most LLC statutes explicitly state that the liability shield does not protect a person from liability for his or her own tortious acts. There is no indication that the liability protection of these new entities will be markedly different from the protection provided by corporate form, and piercing the veil should follow parallel paths in each form of business association.

A number of recent empirical studies address the question of piercing in cases subsequent to the Thompson study and/or adding additional factors. See Christina L. Boyd and David Hoffman, Disputing Limited Liability, 104 Nw. U. L. Rev. 853 (2010) (examining 690 complaints from dockets in federal courts during 2000-2005); John H. Matheson, The Modern Law of Corporate Groups: An Empirical Study of Piercing the

Corporate Veil in the Parent-Subsidiary Context, 87 N.C. L. Rev. 1091 (2009) (examining 360 parent-subsidiary cases from January 1, 1990, to March 1, 2008); T. Richmond McPherson III & Nader S. Raja, Corporate Justice: An Empirical Study of Piercing Rates and Factors Courts Consider When Piercing the Corporate Veil, 45 Wake Forest L. Rev. 931 (2010) (examining 236 cases, a sample of reported decisions during 1996-2005); Peter B. Oh, Veil-Piercing, 89 Tex. L. Rev. 81 (2010) (examining almost 3,000 reported cases through 2006).

Boyd and Hoffman are able to use dockets as opposed to decided cases and test factors like judge ideology, race, and gender (finding no statistically significant difference as to the last two and a significant difference but in the opposite direction than predicted for ideology). Oh studies reported cases through 2006 and emphasizes the importance of fraud. Omitting fraud cases, he finds the piercing rate in tort cases slightly above the rate in contracts (without reporting any tests for statistical significance), disagreeing with the most surprising result of the initial Thompson study. In contrast, the Matheson study and the McPherson and Raja study, which track cases in the time after the original Thompson study, find a lower overall piercing rate than Thompson's period but confirm higher rates in contract than in tort, as showed up in Thompson's initial data.

2. Piercing the Corporate Veil to Reach Real Persons

a. Contract Cases

The separate existence of the corporation serves to insulate the individual participants from the obligations of the enterprise. Officers who sign contracts on behalf of the corporation are not personally liable if the corporation does not pay. Such officers can also be shareholders of the corporation without necessarily being exposed to personal liability. The fundamental premise is that those who deal with the corporation can adjust their price and terms according to the degree of security that the corporation provides. Piercing the corporate veil in contract cases becomes a search for the factors that lead courts not to trust the bargaining relationship. Fraud or conduct approaching fraud is clearly a reason to pierce. As you read the following cases, consider the extent to which factors like undercapitalization and lack of corporate formalities should be a basis for a court to disregard the corporate entity in a bargain setting.

Consumer's Co-op v. Olsen
Wisconsin Supreme Court, 1988
142 Wis. 2d 465, 419 N.W.2d 211

Ceci, Justice.

. . . The trial court entered judgment in favor of Consumer's Co-op for the sum of $38,851.42, having found the case at bar to be an "appropriate case to pierce the corporate veil. . . ." We disagree and, therefore, reverse.

ECO was incorporated by Chris Olsen on January 14, 1980. There were 2,200 shares of common stock authorized; 1,125 shares were issued to Chris Olsen for $3,589.00 on the day of the corporation's inception, and the remaining 1,075 shares authorized were issued to Jack and Nancy Olsen. The total initial capitalization was $7,018.25. When ECO commenced operations, Chris Olsen remained employed elsewhere on a full-time basis, with his work at ECO constituting only a part-time endeavor. ECO initially serviced only one customer and employed only one individual on a part-time basis for this purpose. In July of 1980, Chris Olsen commenced full-time employment with ECO.

The corporate officers were elected at one of the two formal board of directors meetings and consisted of Chris Olsen, Jack Olsen, and Nancy Olsen. The majority stockholder, Chris Olsen, was at all times relevant to this action the president and general manager of ECO. Jack Olsen, the father of Chris Olsen, was the treasurer and accountant, and Nancy Olsen, the mother of Chris Olsen, was the secretary. While Chris and Jack Olsen testified that the board of directors met and conferred about four or five times each week, there exists formal record only of the first meeting at which the corporate officers were elected and the meeting authorizing a reorganization under Chapter 11 of the United States Bankruptcy Code.

In 1977, Chris Olsen had opened a personal charge account with Consumer's Co-op. Shortly after the incorporation of ECO in January of 1980, this personal charge account was changed to a corporate charge account. Chris Olsen testified that no personal charges were made on the corporate account, and all billings were thereafter to ECO. Additionally, there was testimony that abundant measures were taken to assure that all corporate business was done in the corporation's name: the corporate name was either affixed to, or printed on, virtually all of the property and equipment associated with the day-to-day operation of the corporation.

By the end of 1981, ECO's difficulties were manifested by a negative shareholder equity of $2,723.02. The situation worsened: at the end of 1982, ECO had a negative shareholder equity of $62,815.60; at the end of 1983, a negative shareholder equity of $148,927.92; and, finally, a negative shareholder equity of $189,362.26 at the end of 1984. No dividends were paid at any time.

Throughout the relevant period of ECO's corporate existence, Consumer's Co-op had extended credit to ECO on an open account primarily for the purchase of bulk fuel. Commencing in June or July of 1983, ECO failed to remain current in the monthly payments on its account with Consumer's Co-op. However, Consumer's Co-op continued to extend credit to ECO until March 21, 1984, notwithstanding its policy to terminate credit after sixty days and the fact that after charges become more than thirty days old, the monthly statements of account explicitly stated that "additional credit cannot be extended until your account is brought current."

Finally, there was no evidence to indicate that corporate funds were used to pay personal expenses. There was, however, ample evidence that substantial personal assets were used to subsidize the operation of the corporation in the form of unprofitable leasing agreements and foregone salaries and rent.

I.

. . . [T]he trial court articulated as significant to its decision to disregard the corporate existence of ECO its factual finding of "control" of ECO by Chris Olsen and its finding that the corporation was "undercapitalized." The court expressly found no fraud to have been involved in the transaction at bar. . . .

Our analysis of the questions before us today commences with an examination of extant Wisconsin case law. In Milwaukee Toy Co. v. Industrial Commission of Wisconsin, 203 Wis. 493, 495, 234 N.W. 748 (1931), this court articulated the following fundamental premise implicated with respect to the imposition of personal liability on shareholders for corporate debts: "By legal fiction the corporation is a separate entity and is treated as such under all ordinary circumstances." . . .

Notwithstanding the unwavering adherence to the general principle of shareholder nonliability, there exist exceptions justifying, metaphorically, the "piercing of the corporate veil" or, stated otherwise, "disregarding the corporate fiction." The circumstances in which exceptions to the general rule of limited shareholder liability were described in *Milwaukee Toy* to be present where "applying the corporate fiction would accomplish some fraudulent purpose, operate as a constructive fraud, or defeat some strong equitable claim. . . ." However, the court in *Milwaukee Toy* cautioned with the well-heeded admonition: "the fiction of corporate entity is not to be lightly regarded." . . .

The concept of a minimally adequate level of capitalization was expressly addressed in Gelatt v. DeDakis (In re Mader's), 77 Wis. 2d 578, 254 N.W.2d 171 (1977). . . .

Our holding and rationale in support thereof in In re Mader's is consistent with the following commentary:

> The attempt to do corporate business without providing any sufficient basis of financial responsibilities to creditors is an abuse of the separate entity and will be ineffectual to exempt the stockholders from corporate debts. It is coming to be recognized as the policy of the law that stockholders should in good faith put at the risk of the business unencumbered capital reasonably adequate for its prospective liabilities. If the capital is illusory or trifling compared with the business to be done and the risks of loss, this is ground for denying the separate entity privilege. It has been stated that a corporation's capitalization is a major consideration of courts in deciding whether a legitimate separate corporate entity was maintained. (1 W. Fletcher, Cyclopedia Corporations, §44.1 at 528 (rev. ed. 1983).) . . .

[Appellant argues] that because of the volitional nature of a contractual relationship and the opportunity to investigate the capital structure or obtain a personal guarantee prior to extending credit, inadequate capitalization is not relevant to a determination of whether to disregard the separate legal entity of a corporation. A similar argument was rejected in Labadie Coal Co. v. Black, 672 F.2d 92, 100 (D.C. Cir. 1982), upon the following well-stated grounds:

> We recognize the position of some commentators that undercapitalization should not play an important part in contract cases, principally because a person dealing with a corporation in a contract setting is expected to have had the opportunity to investigate the corporation with which it deals, and essentially to have assumed the risk that the corporation may prove unable to meet its financial obligations. This position has not been adopted by most of the courts who have considered the problem, however. Furthermore, as another commentator has noted, "If the prior opportunity to investigate is a consideration, then the plaintiffs' lack of sophistication is equally tenable against the presumption that they knowingly assumed the risk of the corporation's undercapitalization." [Barber, Piercing the Corporate Veil, 17 Willamette L. Rev. 371, 386 (1981).]
> This [undercapitalization] is only a single example of how the "unfairness" prong of the piercing test may be satisfied. . . . The "errant" party need not have willfully wronged the other party, nor

need he have engaged in anything amounting to fraud in their relationship. The essence of the fairness test is simply that an individual businessman cannot hide from the normal consequences of *carefree* entrepreneuring by doing so through a corporate shell. (Emphasis in original.) (Footnotes omitted.)

We agree that inadequate capitalization may be a factor relevant to whether an injustice is present sufficient to justify piercing the corporate veil in a contract case. The volitional nature of a contractual relationship presents a cognizable distinction between contract and tort cases; however, this distinction is more appropriately recognized as one which may justify the application of the doctrines of estoppel and waiver than as to preclude the invocation of the equitable remedy of piercing the corporate veil in a contract case. Stated otherwise, whether a contractual relationship is truly one in which a creditor had the opportunity to investigate the capital structure of a debtor and knowingly failed to exercise the right to investigate before extending credit, such that the creditor should be precluded from piercing the corporate veil, should be decided with respect to the particular facts of each case rather than by the denial to all contract creditors of resort to this equitable remedy by a presumption of an "assumption of risk."

While significant, undercapitalization is not an independently sufficient ground to pierce the corporate veil. In order for the corporate veil to be pierced, in addition to undercapitalization, additional evidence of failure to follow corporate formalities or other evidence of pervasive control must be shown.

Consequently, we hold today, as we have previously, that both inadequate capitalization and disregard of corporate formalities are significant to a determination of whether the corporation has a separate existence such that shareholders can claim the accoutrement of incorporation: nonliability for corporate debts. That neither factor will independently justify piercing the corporate veil may perhaps be most visibly demonstrated by a delineation of those elements comprising that which is ordinarily deemed the "alter ego" theory or "instrumentality" rule. . . . The "instrumentality" or "alter ego" doctrine requires proof of the following elements:

> (1) Control, not mere majority or complete stock control, but complete domination, not only of finances but of policy and business practice in respect to the transaction attacked so that the corporate entity as to this transaction had at the time no separate mind, will or existence of its own; and
> (2) Such control must have been used by the defendant to commit fraud or wrong, to perpetrate the violation of a statutory or other positive legal duty, or dishonest and unjust act in contravention of plaintiff's legal rights; and
> (3) The aforesaid control and breach of duty must proximately cause the injury or unjust loss complained of. [Fletcher, supra §43.10 at 490]

Application of the above framework indicates that failure to follow corporate formalities is a factor relevant to the first element, whereas inadequate capitalization is primarily significant with respect to whether control has been exercised in such a manner as to result in injustice. Stated otherwise, it is apparent that just as control, absent a showing of injustice, would not justify exception to the general rule of corporate nonliability, injustice, absent the establishment of control, would not constitute adequate grounds to pierce the corporate veil. Hence, "The absence of any one of these elements prevents 'piercing the corporate veil.'" Fletcher, §43.10 at 490. However, in determining those factors which will satisfy the elements fundamental to piercing the corporate veil, we agree that because of the equitable nature of this remedy, flexibility must be maintained:

> It is not the presence or absence of any particular factor that is determinative. Rather, it is a combination of factors which, when taken together with an element of injustice or abuse of corporate privilege, suggest that the corporate entity attacked had "no separate mind, will or existence of its own" and was therefore the "mere instrumentality or tool" of the [shareholder]. (Glenn v. Wagner, 313 N.C. 450, 458, 329 S.E.2d 326, 332 (1985).)

II.

While holding in both tort and contract cases that inadequate capitalization is a factor significant to piercing the corporate veil, we reject the respondent's contention that there is a continuing requirement to maintain an adequate level of capitalization. Such an approach was implicitly rejected by this court in In re Mader's, in which the court indicated that "the shareholders have assumed an appropriate proprietary risk . . . where a corporation is once provided with a reasonably adequate fund of stated capital. . . ." 77 Wis. 2d at 608-09, 254 N.W.2d 171. Thus, we agree that "the adequacy of capital is to be measured as of the time of formation of the corporation. A corporation that was adequately capitalized when formed but which subsequently suffers financial reverses is not undercapitalized." Fletcher, §44.1 at 529. . . . Hence, while a court's examination of the adequacy of capitalization may inquire beyond the capitalization at the inception of the corporation, such inquiry may be made only in those circumstances where, as in In re Mader's, the corporation distinctly changes the nature or magnitude of its business. . . . Finally, with regard to that amount of capital which constitutes sufficient capitalization, we restate the following standard which emphasizes economic viability rather than an inflexible computation of minimal capitalization: a corporation is undercapitalized when there is an "obvious inadequacy of capital, 'measured by the nature and magnitude of the corporate undertaking.'" Ruppa [v. American States Insurance Co. (1979)], 91 Wis. 2d at 645, 284 N.W.2d 318 (quoting Anderson [v. Abbott], 321 U.S. at 362).

III.

With respect to the facts at issue herein, the respondent has failed to convince us that corporate formalities were so egregiously ignored, or that control so pervasively exercised, such as to constitute a situation where recognition of "the corporate fiction would accomplish some fraudulent purpose, operate as a constructive fraud, or defeat some strong equitable claim. . . ." *Milwaukee Toy*, 203 Wis. at 496, 234 N.W. 748. In the case at bar, stock was issued, officers were elected, meetings of the board of directors were frequently held, and all business was undertaken in the corporate name. Moreover, there was no indication of improper commingling of personal and corporate assets. Those financial transactions between Chris Olsen and the corporation were approved, though informally, by the board of directors and were undertaken for the purpose of infusing, rather than improperly withdrawing, capital. We do not find the fact that the meetings of the board of directors were informal to be of particular significance. This is particularly true in light of the passage of our close corporation law, §180.995, Stats.

The Wisconsin close corporation law provides generally for greater flexibility with respect to corporate form and expressly provides: "The failure of a statutory close corporation to observe usual corporate formalities or requirements relating to the exercise of its corporate powers or the management of its business and affairs is not grounds for imposing personal liability on the shareholders for obligations of the corporation." Section 180.995(20), Stats. The close corporation law was designed to accommodate the "special needs" of closely held corporations. . . . It would appear . . . that the purpose of the legislature in adopting §180.995 was precisely to avoid the strict application advocated by the respondent herein. . . .

As we have explained above, a gross inadequacy in capitalization may constitute an "injustice" such as to justify the piercing of a corporate veil under an instrumentality analysis, where, in addition, "control" and "causation" are established. While the trial court stated in its findings of fact that the corporation was "undercapitalized," there is no indication of whether this finding was based upon the court's finding with respect to initial capitalization or its capitalization at some later point. We find that the initial capitalization of over $7,000.00 was not, and could not be reasonably viewed as, an obvious inadequacy of capital as measured by the slight size of the initial undertaking. Furthermore, we need not reach the question of whether the increase in the size of ECO's undertaking was of such a nature and magnitude that additional capital would be required. To the extent that it could be argued that the business expansion required additional capital, the right to assert this position was waived in the most unmistakable manner. . . .

While not binding upon this court, we note that the issue of waiver and estoppel in the context of precluding the operation of the equitable remedy of piercing the corporate veil was recently addressed by the federal district court for the western district of Wisconsin in Bostwick-Braun Co. v. Szews, 645 F. Supp. 221 (W.D. Wis. 1986). At issue in *Bostwick-Braun* was a creditor's attempt to pierce the corporate veil for a contract claim on the basis of undercapitalization. While the court opined that undercapitalization would be relevant under Wisconsin law to a determination of the propriety of piercing the corporate veil in a contract claim, the court nevertheless refused to impose this equitable remedy on the basis of its finding that the right to assert undercapitalization as a basis to pierce the corporate veil had been waived or, alternatively, that the creditor was estopped from asserting such a claim. Specifically, the court found:

> Estoppel would appear to be established here by virtue of plaintiff's unexercised right to ascertain the capital structure of the BENNS Corporation coupled with the defendants' continued purchases of merchandise from plaintiff in the corporation's name. Defendants had the right to rely on plaintiff's failure to exercise its right. Even stronger is the waiver argument. Absent allegations of fraud, it is impossible to square plaintiff's conduct during the six years it did business with the corporation with anything but an intentional relinquishment of its right to challenge the corporation's adequacy of capital. Plaintiff continued to advance the corporation credit while it had the right

In the present case, the circumstances indicative of waiver are substantially stronger. Specifically, there was evidence indicating that commencing in June or July of 1983, ECO failed to remain current in its monthly payments on its open account. Nevertheless, Consumer's Co-op continued to extend credit. By December 31, 1983, the statement of account indicated that $20,386.14 was owed to the Consumer's Co-op, and $10,780.06 was past due. The statement expressly indicated: "additional credit cannot be extended until your account is brought current." Despite the obvious depreciation of ECO's financial status and the indication on the statement that additional credit would not be extended, credit was continued through March 21, 1984. In sum, Consumer's Co-op continued to permit ECO to become further indebted from the $20,386.14 due on the account as of December 31, 1983, to $40,661.44 owed for credit extended through March 21, 1984. Credit remained available notwithstanding the fact that the account and the statements were in the name of ECO. No personal guarantee was requested initially, or as a condition to the continued receipt of credit.

As the above-stated facts indicate, Consumer's Co-op not only had an opportunity to investigate the capital foundation of ECO, but knew, given the delinquency in the payments on ECO's account, that ECO's business was failing. By continuing to extend credit and increase ECO's indebtedness, notwithstanding and in contravention of its own policy to terminate credit after sixty days, Consumer's Co-op waived the right to claim inadequacy of capitalization as a basis to pierce the corporate veil. Likewise, a similarly strong basis would exist to deny Consumer's Co-op's claim on the ground of estoppel: Consumer's Co-op failed to terminate credit despite the unequivocal indication of the financial difficulties of ECO and, thus, caused ECO to substantially increase its indebtedness in reasonable reliance upon Consumer Co-op's relinquishment of its right to examine its capital structure before continuing to extend credit or to demand a personal guarantee as a condition to the continued availability of credit. . . .

For these reasons, we find that application of the exception to the general rule of limited shareholder liability is, as such, not necessary to prevent an inequitable result and would, in fact, create an inequity. At its inception, ECO commenced operations as a separate legal entity. There is inadequate evidence indicating such a degree of "control" as to constitute the absence of a separate corporate existence under the first prong of the instrumentality test. Although the board of directors failed to regularly record minutes of meetings, they met frequently, thus fulfilling, in substance, the purpose attendant with this requirement. Likewise, great measures were taken to promote and distinguish the corporate name, and all business was undertaken in the name of ECO. Further, contrary to there being any indication of an improper draining or siphoning of corporate funds, there was substantial evidence of the shareholders' commitment of their personal assets to the corporation.

Additionally, in view of the fact that ECO commenced business as a part-time operation, the initial stated capital was not "obviously insufficient." Thus, to the extent that "control" may have been exercised under the first prong of an instrumentality analysis, because no "injustice" was created by an inadequacy of initial capitalization, the corporate veil must not be pierced.

Finally, we need not reach the issue of whether the change in the size and nature of the corporation was of such significance as to require an increase in capitalization; Consumer's Co-op is precluded from asserting any claim as to subsequent undercapitalization as a factor constituting an "injustice" justifying disregard of the separate legal entity of the corporation on both the grounds of waiver and estoppel. . . .

K.C. Roofing Center v. On Top Roofing, Inc.
Missouri Court of Appeals, 1991
807 S.W.2d 545

KENNEDY, JUDGE.

This is an action by creditors to "pierce the corporate veil" and establish personal liability of individuals for corporate debt.

Plaintiffs Kansas City Roofing Center (KCRC) and Lumberman's Mutual Wholesale Company (Lumberman's) filed suit against On Top Roofing, Inc. (On Top) and Russell and Carol Nugent to recover damages for unpaid roofing supplies delivered to On Top. KCRC and Lumberman's sought to pierce the corporate veil of On Top and hold Russell and Carol Nugent personally liable for the debts incurred by On Top. . . . After a bench trial, the trial court found in favor of the plaintiffs and pierced the corporate veil and held Russell Nugent personally liable for those debts. . . .

Most of the facts are derived from the testimony of Russell Nugent, who was called as an adverse witness by the plaintiffs and who also testified as part of the defendants' case. He testified that he had been involved in the roofing business in the greater Kansas City area for more than 25 years. Russell Nugent roofing, Inc. was incorporated on March 24, 1977. Russell and his wife Carol Nugent were the sole shareholders, officers and directors of the corporation. The corporation's name was changed to On Top Roofing, Inc. on December 7, 1985. Russell and Carol Nugent remained the sole shareholders, officers and directors of On Top. The Nugents continued to do business as On Top until August 27, 1987, when On Top ceased doing business and RNR, Inc. was incorporated. Russell and Carol Nugent were the sole shareholders, officers and directors of RNR, Inc. RNR, Inc. went out of business sometime in 1988 and RLN Construction, Inc. was incorporated. Russell and Carol Nugent were the sole shareholders, officers and directors of RLN Construction, Inc. Nugent testified that he is currently doing business as Russell Nugent, Inc. and it was incorporated in late 1988 or early 1989, at which time RLN Construction, Inc. went out of business.

Nugent testified that none of his roofing corporations were actively doing business at the same time as any of his other roofing corporations. When one roofing company was incorporated, the prior roofing company ceased doing business. All of Nugent's roofing companies, from Russell Nugent Roofing, Inc. in 1977 to the present Russell Nugent, Inc., have been located at the same business address at 614 Main in Grandview, Missouri, and have utilized the same business telephone number.

The articles of incorporation for Russell Nugent Roofing, Inc. and its successor On Top Roofing, Inc. required the corporation to maintain a board of directors consisting of three members. The court found that the corporation elected a board of three members in the first few years of its existence, but for several years prior to 1987

Russell and Carol Nugent were the only directors. Russell Nugent, Inc. presently has only one director, Russell Nugent. The articles have never been amended to provide for less than three directors. Nugent's corporation did not hold an annual meeting in 1988 or 1989, or, if annual meetings were held, no minutes were kept.

From April through August 17, 1987, KCRC advanced approximately $45,000 in roofing supplies to On Top. When On Top failed to pay for the supplies, KCRC filed suit and sought to pierce the corporate veil and have Russell and Carol Nugent personally satisfy the debt.

Nugent or one of his employees ordered 1,360 rolls of Genstar shakeliner felt from Lumberman's on November 25, 1987, at a cost of $7,367.77. A default judgment in that amount, plus costs and interest, was taken in favor of Lumberman's against On Top on August 24, 1988. The current amount due and owing on the judgment, with interest as of January 2, 1990, was $8,287.77. Lumberman's was unable to collect the judgment against On Top and filed suit to pierce the corporate veil and hold Russell and Carol Nugent personally liable for the debt. Nugent testified that he allowed Lumberman's to take the default judgment against On Top because On Top was no longer in business when the felt was ordered and delivered to On Top and Lumberman's had actually sold the felt to RNR, Inc., the successor corporation to On Top. Nugent testified that the default judgment was against the wrong corporation and he believed he did not have to contest the lawsuit.

Nugent testified that in March of 1987, On Top could not pay its trade debts as they accrued. Nugent testified that he stopped buying materials from suppliers when the suppliers refused to advance any more material on credit. He admitted in his testimony that in the early part of 1987 he made a decision to only pay secured creditors; the only creditors he paid were those creditors "who had secured my personal guarantee or had loans against my house. . . ." Numerous roofing suppliers, in addition to Lumberman's, have taken default judgments against On Top or its successors.

J & S Tool Fastener, Inc. got a default judgment against On Top in 1986. Nugent testified that he did not recall whether On Top had any money in 1986 and had "no idea" why J & S Tool Fastener was not paid. On Top's corporate income tax return for 1986 shows that Nugent paid himself and his wife over $100,000 in salaries in 1986.

Russell and Carol Nugent owned the property at 614 Main and charged the corporation rent. Nugent testified that the rent he charged the corporation varied; he paid or did not pay rent to himself based upon how well the corporation was doing. The corporate tax return for 1986 reflects that the corporation paid $99,290 in rent in 1986. Nugent did not know why the rent paid in 1985 was less than the rent paid in 1986. He was unable to explain what the corporation paid rent for, although he testified that the corporation paid rent other than for just the property at 614 Main.

The trial court found that On Top purchased "substantial amounts of roofing supplies from Plaintiffs knowing it owed between $75,000.00 and $100,000.00 to previous suppliers which it was unable to pay." Mid-Am Building Supply, Inc. filed a petition against On Top on April 22, 1987, to recover $72,119.68 for roofing supplies delivered to On Top. Wood Castle Forest Products, Inc. got a judgment in the amount of $37,380 against On Top for supplies that On Top ordered on March 17, 1987, and May 2, 1987.

Nugent was questioned at trial about his succession of roofing companies:

Q. Has it been your position to change to a new corporation when the debts are built up?
A. No. I changed every time I needed a fresh start. It's a very competitive business.

The questioning continued:

Q. So, are you agreeing then that you've had five different corporate names in the last five years?
A. I've had more than that, haven't I?
Q. And why is it again, sir, that you continue to change from one corporate name to another?
A. To get a fresh start. It's a very competitive business.

On October 1, 1987, Nugent sold the assets of On Top (excluding accounts receivable) to Nuco Leasing, Inc. Nugent and his wife are the sole shareholders, officers and directors of Nuco Leasing. Included within the sale of On Top's assets was a license agreement for Nuco Leasing to use the name and logo of On Top Roofing. Nugent testified that he did not believe that RNR, Inc., RLN Construction, Inc. or Russell Nugent, Inc. had any license agreements to use the On Top Roofing name.

Nugent testified that once On Top went out of business in August of 1987, he did not use the trade name or fictitious name On Top Roofing. He testified that he used the fictitious name Tops N Roofing when he was doing business as RNR, Inc. and RLN Construction, Inc., and he used the name Top Roofing when he was doing business as Russell Nugent, Inc. Nugent admitted in his testimony that Russell Nugent, Inc., his most recent roofing corporation, was not listed in the telephone book, but in the 1989-1990 telephone book there was a listing for On Top Roofing at 614 Main. He testified that at some point the name on the sign on the building at 614 Main was changed from On Top Roofing to Top Roofing, although Top Roofing was not a registered fictitious name. Photographs taken in February of 1989 were admitted into evidence which depicted the premises at 614 Main with the On Top Roofing name on the building. Photographs taken in July of 1989 were admitted into evidence which showed Nugent's business trucks with the On Top Roofing name painted on the sides. Nugent was still using estimate sheet forms with On Top Roofing Co. at the top as late as November of 1989. At the time of trial Nugent was mailing out to prospective clients flyers with the name On Top Roofing at the top with RNR, Inc. d.b.a. in small letters above the On Top name.

In its findings of fact, the trial court found that Russell Nugent exercised total control of the business activities of On Top. The court found that Carol Nugent "did not control the activities of the corporation, and was not active in making the business decisions leading to the events triggering Plaintiffs' claims." In its conclusions of law, the court stated that there was no evidence that Carol Nugent was an active participant in the wrongful and unjust conduct and it would therefore not be proper to pierce the corporate veil to reach her assets. As to Russell Nugent, the court concluded that plaintiffs had sustained their burden and entered judgment against him for the full amount of plaintiffs' claims. . . .

The law with respect to piercing the corporate veil in Missouri is set forth in Collet v. American Natl. Stores, Inc., 708 S.W.2d 273 (Mo. App. 1986). Courts will pierce the corporate veil or disregard the corporate entity once a plaintiff shows: "(1) Control, not mere majority or complete stock control, but complete domination, not only of finances, but of policy and business practice in respect to the transaction attacked so that the corporate entity as to this transaction had at the time no separate mind, will or existence of its own; and (2) Such control must have been used by the defendant to commit fraud or wrong, to perpetrate the violation of a statutory or other positive legal duty, or dishonest and unjust act in contravention of plaintiff's legal rights; and (3) The aforesaid control and breach of duty must proximately cause the injury or unjust loss complained of." Id. at 284. "Where a corporation is used for an improper purpose and to perpetrate injustice by which it avoids its legal obligations, 'equity will step in, pierce the corporate veil and grant appropriate relief.'" Irwin v. Bertelsmeyer, 730 S.W.2d 302, 304 (Mo. App. 1987) (quoting Pasta House Co. v. Miller, 691 S.W.2d 460, 462 (Mo. App. 1985)).

There was substantial evidence to support the trial court's finding that the three-part test for piercing the corporate veil was satisfied in this case. Russell Nugent was clearly in control of On Top Roofing, Inc. He and his wife were the sole shareholders of the corporation and he was the president and chief operating officer and clearly made all the decisions.

There also was substantial evidence to support the second and third prongs of the test. A court may pierce the corporate veil or disregard the separate legal entity of the corporation and the individual where the separateness is used as a subterfuge to defraud a creditor. But actual fraud is not necessarily a predicate for piercing the corporate veil; it may also be pierced to prevent injustice or inequitable consequences. From the evidence it appears that Russell Nugent was operating an intricate corporate shell game in which he would cease doing business as one corporate entity when he was unable to pay the corporation's creditors and he then would form another corporation in place of the prior one in order to get a "fresh start." After On Top supposedly went out of business in the summer of 1987, for at least two years Nugent continued to run an On Top Roofing Yellow Pages ad, kept the On Top Roofing name on the sign on the building at 614 Main, kept the On Top Roofing name on the side of his roofing trucks, continued to use bid estimate sheets with the On Top Roofing name on them, and continued to represent to callers over the telephone that he was still operating as On Top Roofing. Although Nugent was only paying secured creditors of On Top, he went ahead and ordered the supplies from the plaintiffs—both of which were unsecured—at a time when On Top was insolvent and had outstanding debt of approximately $100,000 to other roofing suppliers.

Through his domination and control over On Top, Russell Nugent was using it for the unfair or inequitable purpose of avoiding their debts to plaintiffs. Nugent continued to hold On Top out to the public as though it was still operating after it supposedly went out of business, yet he refused to honor On Top's obligations to its creditors. The actions of Nugent worked at least an injustice if not to defraud the plaintiffs. It would be unfair, unjust or inequitable to allow Nugent to hide behind the corporate shield and avoid his legal obligations to plaintiffs. We hold that the trial court did not err in piercing the corporate veil and holding Russell Nugent personally liable for the debts owed plaintiffs.

Nugent also alleges that the trial court erred in admitting evidence of his involvement with corporate entities other than On Top "because said evidence was irrelevant and immaterial to the issues raised by the pleadings. . . ." Nugent argues that evidence addressing the conduct of his subsequent corporations is "completely irrelevant" to the issue of whether the corporate veil of On Top should be pierced.

Evidence is relevant if it tends to prove or disprove a fact in issue, or to corroborate evidence which is relevant and which bears on the principal issue. The evidence in question helped shed light on the issue of whether Nugent should be held personally liable to prevent injustice or prevent a wrong. The evidence demonstrates a pattern of activity or scheme or plan which is corroborative of plaintiffs' position, and it is admissible even though subsequent to plaintiffs' dealings with defendants. . . . The trial court did not abuse its discretion in allowing the testimony of Nugent's involvement with corporate entities other than On Top Roofing, Inc.

Judgment affirmed. . . .

NOTES AND QUESTIONS

1. Easterbrook and Fischel argue that courts should pierce the corporate veil in contract cases principally to remedy fraud or misrepresentation:

> Employees, consumers, trade creditors, and lenders are voluntary creditors. The compensation they demand will be a function of the risk they face. One risk is the possibility of nonpayment because of limited liability. Another is the prospect, common to all debtor-creditor relations, that after the terms of the transaction are set the debtor will take increased risk, to the detriment of the lender.
>
> So long as these risks are known, the firm pays for the freedom to engage in risky activities. Any creditor can get the risk-free rate by investing in T-bills or some low-risk substitute. The firm must offer a better risk-return combination to attract investment. If it cannot make credible promises to refrain from taking excessive risks, it must pay higher interest rates (or, when the creditors are employees and trade creditors, higher prices for the work or goods delivered on credit). There is no "externality." Voluntary creditors receive compensation in advance for the risk that the firm will be unable to meet its obligations. . . .
>
> For the costs of excessive risk taking to be fully internalized, creditors must be able to assess the risk of default accurately. If the creditor is misled into believing that the risk of default is lower than it actually is, the creditor will not demand adequate compensation. This will lead to an excessive amount of risk taking by firms, because some of the costs are now shifted to creditors.

Easterbrook and Fischel, Limited Liability and the Corporation, 52 U. Chi. L. Rev. 89, 104-105, 112 (1985).

2. Thompson's study, discussed supra at page 607, supports Easterbrook and Fischel's argument as to the importance of misrepresentation or fraud. When courts identified an element of misrepresentation in the facts of a case, they pierced in 98 of 107 contract cases, or 91.6 percent of the time. Conversely, if the court explicitly noted the absence of misrepresentation, piercing occurred in only 7.7 percent of the cases. This result is consistent with the view that parties should be able to allocate risks as they choose and that absent fraud or other bargaining defects, courts should not interfere with the parties' allocation. However, the incompleteness of this factor is emphasized by the large number of contract cases in which misrepresentation was not

cited as either present or absent. Courts pierced in 220 of 672 of these cases, or 32.7 percent of the time.

3. The importance of undercapitalization remains a controversial factor in piercing analysis. Note that the quotation in Consumer's Co-op v. Olsen, supra page 611 — "It is coming to be recognized as the policy of the law that stockholders should in good faith put at the risk of the business unencumbered capital reasonably adequate for its prospective liabilities" — is actually a quote from page 303 of Professor Henry Ballantine's treatise, Ballantine on Corporations (1946). What was coming to be recognized in 1946 has not progressed very far in the succeeding years. In a Seventh Circuit case, Judge Easterbrook noted that "we are unaware of any decision relying on undercapitalization alone as a grounds for disregarding the corporate entity in a contract case." Secon Service Systems, Inc. v. St. Joseph Bank & Trust Co., 855 F.2d 406, 416 (7th Cir. 1988). But cf. Slottow v. American Casualty Co., 1 F.3d 912, 917 (9th Cir. 1993) ("Under California law inadequate capitalization of a subsidiary may alone be a basis for holding the parent corporation liable for acts of the subsidiary," citing Minton v. Cavaney, 56 Cal. 2d 576, 15 Cal. Rptr. 641, 364 P.2d 473 (1961)).

Thompson's study suggests that undercapitalization is not a dominant factor in piercing cases, as it occurs in less than 20 percent of all contract cases. In the cases in which it is present, courts pierce about 70 percent of the time. 76 Cornell L. Rev. 1036, 1066 (1991). What is the connection between undercapitalization and misrepresentation? Can undercapitalization itself be a form of misrepresentation? Should a court ever pierce on the basis of undercapitalization if the complaining creditor knew about the undercapitalization before extending credit? For a negative answer, see Bartle v. Home Owners Cooperative, 309 N.Y. 103, 127 N.E.2d 832 (1955) (court refused to pierce veil of bankrupt corporation organized to construct homes for veterans at a cost; corporation was capitalized and operated so that at best it would break even, but creditors were not misled).

4. When undercapitalization is considered, analysis is usually limited, as it was in Consumer's Co-op v. Olsen, to the time of incorporation. Why is undercapitalization less of a concern if it occurs later in a corporation's life but still before a creditor's harm? Should it make a difference, as in Consumer's Co-op v. Olsen, that the corporation's capital was dissipated without the shareholder's withdrawing large sums as compensation for services?

In evaluating the importance of the lack of withdrawals in Consumer's Co-op v. Olsen, consider the withdrawals via salary and rent that occurred in K.C. Roofing Center v. On Top Roofing, Inc. What result in that case if all other facts remained unchanged but Nugent never withdrew any money from On Top via salary or rent?

5. Do statutory provisions, such as MBCA §6.20(b), that allow promissory notes and future services to count as consideration undercut the significance of undercapitalization as a piercing factor? Suppose, for example, that the shareholders of a close corporation exchanged nothing for their shares but the promise of future services. Suppose further that it is impossible to tell what value the corporation placed on these services, or on anything else, because the corporation kept no minutes of meetings. Should the veil be pierced in favor of trade creditors? For a negative answer, see Henry J. Mills Co. v. Crawfish Capitol Seafood, Inc., 569 So. 2d 1108 (La. Ct. App. 1990). Is such a result defensible? What result on these facts under Consumer's Co-op v.

Olsen? What should be the effect of Wisconsin's close corporation statute providing that informality shall not be the basis for piercing the corporate veil?

6. How important are formalities in cases like K.C. Roofing Center v. On Top Roofing, Inc.? If Nugent had scrupulously avoided any subsequent representations by signs, letterheads, or otherwise that had led creditors to believe that On Top was still in business, could he have achieved his "fresh start"?

7. In a portion of the opinion that is omitted here, the court in Consumer's Co-op v. Olsen refers to the doctrine of equitable subordination. This doctrine comes into play when creditors and shareholders assert competing claims to corporate assets. For example, the corporation may have assets worth $100. Carl, a supplier, has an unsecured claim against the corporation for unpaid bills in the amount of $100. Joanne, the corporation's principal shareholder, seeks to foreclose on the corporation's assets pursuant to a note and mortgage that she claims gives her priority over Carl. When equitable, courts will subordinate Joanne's claim to that of Carl. Equitable subordination is a less drastic remedy than piercing the corporate veil, because shareholders lose only what they have voluntarily placed at risk. Courts often cite undercapitalization as a reason to subordinate a shareholder's claim to that of creditors. But the reasons for subordinating are often stated simply in terms of the insider's fiduciary and equitable responsibilities.

8. The classic equitable subordination case is Pepper v. Litton, 308 U.S. 295 (1939). Pepper was owed substantial royalties by Dixie Splint Coal Company, which was controlled by Litton. Instead of paying Pepper, who had commenced suit, Litton caused Dixie Splint to confess a judgment in Litton's favor for previously accrued but unpaid salary. Litton then enforced his judgment, levying against the assets of Dixie Splint and leaving the corporation with no assets to satisfy Pepper's claim. Pepper sought to have Litton's foreclosure sale overturned and to have Litton's salary claims subordinated to Pepper's royalty claims. Justice Douglas spoke for the Supreme Court, which upheld the district court's decision in Pepper's favor:

> [E]ven though we assume that the alleged salary claim on which the Litton judgment was based was not fictitious but actually existed, we are of the opinion that the District Court properly disallowed or subordinated it. . . .
>
>   Though disallowance of such claims will be ordered where they are fictitious or a sham these cases do not turn on the existence or non-existence of the debt. Rather they involve simply the question of order of payment. At times equity has ordered disallowance or subordination by disregarding the corporate entity. That is to say, it has treated the debtor-corporation simply as a part of the stockholder's own enterprise, consistently with the course of conduct of the stockholder. But in that situation as well as in the others to which we have referred, a sufficient consideration may be simply the violation of rules of fair play and good conscience by the claimant; a breach of the fiduciary standards of conduct which he owes the corporation, its stockholders and creditors.

308 U.S. at 303, 310-311.

9. Section 510(c) of the Bankruptcy Act of 1978 provides that "the court may . . . under principles of equitable subordination, subordinate for purposes of distribution all or part of one allowed claim to all or part of another allowed claim. . . ." H.R. Rep. 595, 95th Cong., 1st Sess. 359 (1977), states that "this section [was] intended to codify case law, such as Pepper v. Litton." Equitable subordination is sometimes referred to as the "Deep Rock" doctrine, since an important application of the

doctrine involved the Deep Rock Oil Company. See Taylor v. Standard Gas & Electric Co., 306 U.S. 307 (1939).

PROBLEM 7-3

When National Shoe Company moved much of its operations offshore, it was left with excess manufacturing capacity, including a building ("the Shoe Works Building") on which National was obligated to make ground lease payments to local development authority for another 15 years. Thereafter, National was contacted by Abe Lincoln, who was interested in leasing the Shoe Works Building to be used by a manufacturing business that he was attempting to establish. During the course of negotiations with National, Lincoln formed two Delaware corporations—Honest Abe, Inc., to conduct the planned manufacturing venture, and Realty Co. Lincoln, which was the sole shareholder of each corporation. Subsequently, National agreed to lease the Shoe Works Building to Realty; Lincoln signed the lease on Realty's behalf. Realty had no paid-in capital, no officers or directors were ever elected, and no corporate formalities were observed. Realty's only income was from its sublease of the Shoe Works Building to Honest Abe, Inc., which is now in bankruptcy. Realty has now defaulted on payment due to National under the lease. Can National recover from Abe Lincoln?

b. Tort Cases

Tort cases are different in part because the corporate entity has never provided insulation for an individual committing a tortious act even if the individual purported to be acting as an officer or otherwise in the name of a corporation. Thus, the same individual who signs a contract on behalf of the corporation and is insulated from liability if the corporation does not perform on the contract would incur personal liability if acting in the same capacity for the same corporation taking actions that were deemed tortious. See Restatement (Second) of Agency §343. Piercing the corporate veil is not necessary to reach such individuals; they are liable as a result of agency law. There has been an increase of statutory provisions, such as those in the environmental or pensions area, imposing similar direct liability for an individual's own wrongful acts even if purportedly taken in a corporate capacity.

If the shareholder/officers/directors do not directly participate in the tort committed by someone else in the corporation, when should individuals lose the insulating protection of the separate corporate entity? Since the use of the corporate form is a choice only of the insiders, and those who are victimized by the entity with insufficient assets have no opportunity to choose the entity who would harm them, the use of corporate form in this setting offers an increased likelihood that the business enterprise will externalize part of the costs of its business.

This approach, based on direct or vicarious liability, emphasizes the participation of those who act as officers or directors, although piercing is usually described as reaching shareholders. In the close corporation context, where most piercing occurs, this distinction has little practical importance since the same people are shareholders, directors, and officers. As you read the following cases, consider whether it is important that the defendants are both active participants in running the business as officers and are receiving the financial benefit of the business as shareholders. Would the result be different if they were filling only one of those functions?

Western Rock Co. v. Davis
Texas Court of Civil Appeals, 1968
432 S.W.2d 555

LANGDON, JUSTICE.

. . . [Plaintiffs] sued Western Rock Company, a corporation, G.L. Stroud, L.C. Fuller, and other parties, in Jack County, Texas, seeking damages sustained to their respective homes and business properties because of alleged negligent blasting operations conducted in a rock quarry near Jacksboro, Texas, during the period August, 1965, through April, 1966. . . .

It is contended that the court erred in overruling the pleas of G.L. Stroud, President of Western Rock Company, and of L.C. Fuller who was merely a director of such corporation and took no part in the operation of the quarry or the blasting complained of and thus was not responsible for torts or negligence of said corporation or its president; that there was no testimony or insufficient testimony showing blasting operations of Western Rock Company resulted in damages to plaintiffs' buildings or to connect such damage with the alleged blasting or to show negligence on the part of any of the appellants which was a proximate cause of such claimed damage and that each plea of privilege should therefore have been sustained rather than overruled.

We affirm.

It is argued that since Fuller was merely a director of Western Rock Company, a part of the time during the period August, 1965, to May of 1966, and nothing more, he cannot be held responsible for the torts of the corporation.

Many of the authorities cited and relied upon by appellants are also relied upon by the appellees. Thus, the chief dispute is whether or not the record in this case reveals that appellees' cause of action against appellant Fuller is based upon more than the fact that he was a director of Western Rock Company.

The evidence deemed pertinent is summarized as follows:

At all times relevant to this cause it is undisputed that Fuller, Stroud and the latter's wife were on the Board of Directors of Western Rock Company, and that the latter company engaged in blasting activities commencing in August, 1965, and continuing through April, 1966. Stroud, his wife, and Mrs. Fuller (wife of appellant Fuller) were the officers of Western Rock. Fifty percent of the latter company was owned by Stroud and wife. Fuller testified he was owner of the other half interest and again testified it was owned by Machinery Investment Corporation which is wholly owned by him and his immediate family.

The physical assets used by Western Rock Company in the conduct of its business and operations were leased from Fuller and Fuller's family corporation. Under this arrangement Fuller was in a position to profit if Western Rock Company profited. He was also in a position to withdraw all assets from Western Rock in the event Western Rock became insolvent.

Fuller described his relationship with Western Rock Company, during the period of time in question, as follows: "Well, you might say I was their father-confessor. Everything they did, every damn piece of equipment they had, every bank loan they had and everything else, I was the man behind it. So I done it all from that standpoint. I furnished them the money."

Fuller attended the meetings of the Board of Directors of Western Rock and visited the job site in Jacksboro, Texas, on at least three occasions.

During the Jacksboro job, Fuller testified that he was in touch with Stroud, who was personally supervising the Jacksboro operation, "At least five times a week, every day in the week."

Fuller was familiar with the operation and knew that blasting activities were being carried on during this period of time although at one point he refused to admit such knowledge.

During the early fall of 1965, during the time Fuller and Stroud were in daily contact, Stroud began to learn of complaints of damages being sustained by the people in Jacksboro by reason of the blasting activity being carried on, under his supervision, by Western Rock Company.

After complaints had been referred to Stroud, he set about making tests to measure the disturbance of the various blasts. During this period Western Rock Company began to run into financial difficulties.

A suit for damages and injunctive relief was filed against Western Rock on November 12, 1965. A letter from Mr. Hendricks Brown dated November 27, 1965, was received by Stroud advising that there was a serious question as to whether insurance coverage would be available to protect the company from a recovery of damages.

Although from the record such delay is inconceivable, it was not before January of 1966, according to Stroud, that he informed Fuller that Western Rock Company, whose financial condition had been steadily deteriorating, had received complaints — that tests had been performed to determine the violence of the blast — that a petition seeking damages and injunctive relief against the activities of Western Rock had been filed and served on Western Rock — that the attorney representing the insurance company had informed Western Rock that in all probability there was no insurance coverage available.

After learning in January of 1966 of the impending lawsuit for damages and injunctive relief and the fact that the company very likely had no insurance protection, it was decided by Fuller and Stroud to continue with such blasting activities — which they did. Stroud further testified that if Fuller had told him to cease all blasting activities, he would have complied. Fuller did not tell Stroud to cease blasting. He and Stroud knowingly continued to engage in blasting activities for another four months.

On May 27, 1966, the claim filed against Western Rock Company was submitted to a jury. L.C. Fuller, on or about May 27, 1966, personally stepped in and assumed full control of the Western Rock Company operation. He personally took over the assets of the corporation and continued to operate in the name of Western Rock Company. When the trial was concluded and the verdict was rendered against Western Rock Company, all assets of Western Rock Company were assigned to and repossessed by Fuller's family corporation. Stroud, who had been personally supervising and directing the operations of Western Rock, took over as superintendent of the operation for Fuller when the latter assumed personal control of the operation. Stroud, although "unemployed" at the time of the Plea of Privilege hearing, was last employed by another of the Fuller family corporations.

Fuller's personal attorney was sent to Jacksboro sometime before the trial of the lawsuit against Western Rock. Either Fuller, personally, or his personal attorney gave instructions to cease blasting.

It appears obvious from the record that appellees' cause of action against Fuller is based upon ample proof that he was the dominating force behind Western Rock, a shell corporation, which had no assets and was in financial difficulty. That the corporation served as a device through which Fuller and Stroud could carry on destructive blasting activities at the expense of the property owners of Jacksboro, and at the same time be personally insulated from legal and financial responsibility against wrongs which were knowingly permitted, directed and controlled by them through the corporation device. . . .

We are of the opinion and hold that the evidence was adequate to support the judgment of the court that L.C. Fuller and G.L. Stroud were legally responsible, individually and jointly, for negligent conduct which was a proximate cause of damages sustained in Jack County and upon which this suit is based. Further that such evidence supported a finding of a causal relationship between the blasting operations carried on by Western Rock and the damages sustained by the appellees.

Baatz v. Arrow Bar
South Dakota Supreme Court, 1990
452 N.W.2d 138

SABERS, JUSTICE.

Kenny and Peggy Baatz (Baatz), appeal from summary judgment dismissing Edmond, LaVella, and Jacquette Neuroth, as individual defendants in this action.

FACTS

Kenny and Peggy were seriously injured in 1982 when Roland McBride crossed the center line of a Sioux Falls street with his automobile and struck them while they were riding on a motorcycle. McBride was uninsured at the time of the accident and apparently is judgment proof.

Baatz alleges that Arrow Bar served alcoholic beverages to McBride prior to the accident while he was already intoxicated. Baatz commenced this action in 1984, claiming that Arrow Bar's negligence in serving alcoholic beverages to McBride contributed to the injuries they sustained in the accident. Baatz supports his claim against Arrow Bar with the affidavit of Jimmy Larson. Larson says he knew McBride and observed him being served alcoholic beverages in the Arrow Bar during the afternoon prior to the accident, while McBride was intoxicated. See Baatz v. Arrow Bar, 426 N.W.2d 298 (S.D. 1988), for a more complete statement of the facts.

Edmond and LaVella Neuroth formed the Arrow Bar, Inc. in May 1980. During the next two years they contributed $50,000 to the corporation pursuant to a stock subscription agreement. The corporation purchased the Arrow Bar business in June 1980 for $155,000 with a $5,000 down payment. Edmond and LaVella executed a promissory note personally guaranteeing payment of the $150,000 balance. In 1983 the corporation obtained bank financing in the amount of $145,000 to pay off the purchase agreement. Edmond and LaVella again personally guaranteed payment of the corporate debt. Edmond is the president of the corporation, and Jacquette Neuroth serves as the manager of the business. Based on the enactment of SDCL 35-4-78 and 35-11-1 and advice of counsel, the corporation did not maintain dram shop liability insurance at the time of the injuries to Kenny and Peggy.

In 1987 the trial court entered summary judgment in favor of Arrow Bar and the individual defendants. Baatz appealed that judgment and we reversed and remanded to the trial court for trial. *Baatz,* supra. Shortly before the trial date, Edmond, LaVella, and Jacquette moved for and obtained summary judgment dismissing them as individual defendants. Baatz appeals. We affirm. . . .

1. INDIVIDUAL LIABILITY AS EMPLOYEES

SDCL 35-4-78 protects persons from the risk of injury or death resulting from intoxication enhanced by the particular sale of alcoholic beverages. Accordingly, the statute "established a standard of care or conduct, a breach of which is negligence as a matter of law." That standard of care may be breached either by the liquor licensee or an employee of the licensee. Selchert v. Lien, 371 N.W.2d 791 (S.D. 1985).

Neuroths claim there is no evidence that they individually violated the standard of care created by SDCL 35-4-78. They claim the licensee is the corporation, Arrow Bar, Inc., leaving them liable only if one of them, as an employee, served alcoholic beverages to McBride while he was intoxicated. They claim the record is void of any evidence indicating that any one of them served McBride on the day of the accident.

Baatz argues that this court's decision in *Selchert,* supra, allowed a cause of action against both the liquor licensee and the licensee's employees. Baatz claims that each of the Neuroths admitted in deposition to being an employee of the corporation. Consequently, under his reasoning, a cause of action may be brought against the Neuroths in their individual capacities. However, Baatz reads the decision in *Selchert* too broadly. . . . While a cause of action may be brought against a licensee's employee, it must be established that that employee violated the standard of care established by the statute. Employee status alone is insufficient to sustain a cause of action. Baatz failed to offer evidence that any of the Neuroths personally served McBride on the day of the accident.

Baatz also argues that Jacquette Neuroth, as manager of the bar, is liable under the doctrine of respondeat superior. Under this doctrine, an employer may be liable for the conduct of an employee. However, in this case, Jacquette Neuroth is not the employer. The employer of the individuals who may have served McBride is the corporation, Arrow Bar, Inc. Therefore, Baatz' argument misapplies the doctrine of respondeat superior.

2. INDIVIDUAL LIABILITY BY PIERCING THE CORPORATE VEIL

Baatz claims that even if Arrow Bar, Inc. is the licensee, the corporate veil should be pierced, leaving the Neuroths, as the shareholders of the corporation, individually liable. . . . Factors that indicate injustices and inequitable consequences and allow a court to pierce the corporate veil are:

1. fraudulent representation by corporation directors;
2. undercapitalization;
3. failure to observe corporate formalities;
4. absence of corporate records;
5. payment by the corporation of individual obligations; or
6. use of the corporation to promote fraud, injustice, or illegalities. . . .

Baatz advances several arguments to support his claim that the corporate veil of Arrow Bar, Inc. should be pierced, but fails to support them with facts, or misconstrues the facts.

First, Baatz claims that since Edmond and LaVella personally guaranteed corporate obligations, they should also be personally liable to Baatz. However, the personal guarantee of a loan is a contractual agreement and cannot be enlarged to impose tort liability. Moreover, the personal guarantee creates individual liability for a corporate obligation, the opposite of factor (5), above. As such, it supports, rather than detracts from, recognition of the corporate entity.

Baatz also argues that the corporation is simply the alter ego of the Neuroths, and, in accord with Loving Saviour Church v. United States, 556 F. Supp. 688 (D.S.D. 1983), affd., 728 F.2d 1085 (8th Cir. 1984), the corporate veil should be pierced. Baatz' discussion of the law is adequate, but he fails to present evidence that would support a decision in his favor in accordance with that law. When an individual treats a corporation "as an instrumentality through which he is conducting his personal business," a court may disregard the corporate entity. Baatz fails to demonstrate how the Neuroths were transacting personal business through the corporation. In fact, the evidence indicates the Neuroths treated the corporation separately from their individual affairs.

Baatz next argues that the corporation is undercapitalized. Shareholders must equip a corporation with a reasonable amount of capital for the nature of the business involved. Baatz claims the corporation was started with only $5,000 in borrowed capital, but does not explain how that amount failed to equip the corporation with a reasonable amount of capital. In addition, Baatz fails to consider the personal guarantees to pay off the purchase contract in the amount of $150,000, and the $50,000 stock subscription agreement. There simply is no evidence that the corporation's capital in whatever amount was inadequate for the operation of the business. . . .

Finally, Baatz argues that Arrow Bar, Inc. failed to observe corporate formalities because none of the business' signs or advertising indicated that the business was a corporation. Baatz cites SDCL 47-2-36 as requiring the name of any corporation to contain the word corporation, company, incorporated, or limited, or an abbreviation for such a word. In spite of Baatz' contentions, the corporation is in compliance with the statute because its corporate name—Arrow Bar, Inc.—includes the abbreviation of the word incorporated. Furthermore, the "mere failure upon occasion to follow all the forms prescribed by law for the conduct of corporate activities will not justify" disregarding the corporate entity. [Larson v. Western Underwriters, Inc., 77 S.D. 157, 87 N.W.2d 883 (1958).] Even if the corporation is improperly using its name, that alone is not a sufficient reason to pierce the corporate veil. This is especially so where, as here, there is no relationship between the claimed defect and the resulting harm. . . .

In summary, Baatz fails to present specific facts that would allow the trial court to find the existence of a genuine issue of material fact. There is no indication that any of the Neuroths personally served an alcoholic beverage to McBride on the day of the accident. Nor is there any evidence indicating that the Neuroths treated the corporation in any way that would produce the injustices and inequitable consequences necessary to justify piercing the corporate veil. In fact, the only evidence offered is otherwise. Therefore, we affirm summary judgment dismissing the Neuroths as individual defendants.

WUEST, C.J., and MORGAN and MILLER, JJ., concur.

HENDERSON, JUSTICE (dissenting).

This corporation has no separate existence. It is the instrumentality of three shareholders, officers, and employees. Here, the corporate fiction should be disregarded. . . .

A corporate shield was here created to escape the holding of this Court relating to an individual's liability in a dram shop action. Thus, our holdings in Baatz v. Arrow Bar, 426 N.W.2d 298 (S.D. 1988), Selchert v. Lien, 371 N.W.2d 791 (S.D. 1985) and Walz v. City of Hudson, 327 N.W.2d 120 (S.D. 1982) have been totally circumvented.

As a result of this holding, the message is now clear: Incorporate, mortgage the assets of a liquor corporation to your friendly banker, and proceed with carefree entrepreneuring. . . .

Baatzes had their case thrown out of court when many facts were in dispute. I am reminded of the old lawyer, before a jury, who expressed his woe of corporations. He cried out to the jury: "A corporation haveth no soul and its hind end you can kicketh not."

FACTS JUSTIFYING JURY TRIAL

Peggy Baatz, a young mother, lost her left leg; she wears an artificial limb; Kenny Baatz, a young father, has had most of his left foot amputated; he has been unable to work since this tragic accident. Peggy uses a cane. Kenny uses crutches. Years have gone by since they were injured and their lives have been torn asunder.

Uninsured motorist was drunk, and had a reputation of being a habitual drunkard; Arrow Bar had a reputation of serving intoxicated persons. (Supported by depositions on file.) An eyewitness saw uninsured motorist in an extremely intoxicated condition, shortly before the accident, being served by Arrow Bar. . . . A police officer testified, by deposition, that uninsured motorist was in a drunken stupor while at the Arrow Bar.

Are the Neuroths subject to personal liability? It is undisputed, by the record, that the dismissed defendants (Neuroths) are immediate family members and stockholders of Arrow Bar. By pleadings, at settled record 197, it is expressed that the dismissed defendants are employees of Arrow Bar. Seller of the Arrow Bar would not accept Arrow Bar, Inc., as buyer. Seller insisted that the individual incorporators, in their individual capacity be equally responsible for the selling price. Thus, the individuals are the real party in interest and the corporate entity, Arrow Bar, Inc., is being used to justify any wrongs perpetrated by the incorporators in their individual capacity. Conclusion: Fraud is perpetrated upon the public. At a deposition of Edmond Neuroth (filed in this record), this "President" of "the corporation" was asked why the Neuroth family incorporated. His answer: "Upon advice of counsel, as a shield against individual liability." The corporation was undercapitalized (Neuroths borrowed $5,000 in capital). . . .

Clearly, it appears a question arises as to whether there is a fiction established to escape our previous holdings and the intent of our State Legislature. Truly, there are fact questions for a jury to determine: (1) negligence or no negligence of the defendants and (2) did the Neuroth family falsely establish a corporation to shield themselves from individual liability, i.e., do facts in this scenario exist to pierce the corporate veil? . . .

Therefore, I respectfully dissent.

NOTES AND QUESTIONS

1. Easterbrook and Fischel argue that courts should be alert to the need to pierce the corporate veil to prevent corporate managers from engaging in excessively risky activities. However, they also argue that in many cases the corporation will purchase insurance, resulting in allocation of risks to a more efficient risk bearer—the insurance company:

> When corporations must pay for the right to engage in risky activities, they will tend to undertake projects only where social benefits equal social costs at the margin. Where high transaction costs prohibit those affected by risky activities from charging an appropriate risk premium, however, the probability that firms with limited liability will undertake projects with an inefficiently high level of risk increase. Firms capture the benefits from such activities while bearing only some of the costs; other costs are shifted to involuntary creditors. This is a real cost of limited liability, but its magnitude is reduced by corporations' incentives to insure. . . .
>
> Managers who have firm-specific investments of human capital cannot diversify the risk of business failure. . . . The possibility of bankruptcy also represents a real cost to those with firm-specific investments of human capital, and firms must compensate those who bear this risk. The purchase of insurance in amounts greater than the amount of the firm's capital is one method of reducing the amount that the firm must pay. . . . The insurance company now bears the risk of business failure caused by tortious conduct. Thus the purchase of insurance might be thought to reduce the managers' incentives to take care, incentives already too low because of the existence of limited liability. The purchase of insurance has the effect, however, of creating a contract creditor where none may have existed before. The insured corporation must pay (through higher premiums) for engaging in risky activities. Because the firm will now bear the costs of engaging in risky projects, it will tend to equate social benefits and costs when making investment decisions.

Easterbrook and Fischel, Limited Liability and the Corporation, 52 U. Chi. L. Rev. 89, 107-108 (1985).

2. Should courts pierce the corporate veil whenever close corporations have intentionally elected to undertake a risky course of action without adequate insurance? Legislatures set minimum insurance requirements for certain risky activities, such as driving an automobile. In Walkovszky v. Carlton, 18 N.Y.2d 414, 223 N.E.2d 6, 276 N.Y.S.2d 585 (1966), a plaintiff had been injured by a New York City taxicab owned by a corporation having no assets that could be reached for the benefit of the plaintiff. It further appeared that an individual had organized a series of corporations, each with no assets, and had regularly drained the corporations of any available assets. The corporation did maintain the minimum insurance as required by New York legislation. The New York Court of Appeals refused to hold the individual shareholder liable for the obligations of the corporations: "if the insurance coverage required by the statute is inadequate for the protection of the public, the remedy lies not with the courts, but with the legislature." A strong dissent by Judge Keating noted that "[f]rom their inception these corporations were intentionally undercapitalized for the purpose of avoiding responsibility for acts which were bound to arise as a result of the operation of a large taxi fleet having cars out on the street 24 hours a day and engaged in public transportation. And during the course of these corporations' existence all income was continually drained out of the corporation for the same purpose." He argued that the legislature in enacting the minimum insurance "could not have intended to shield those individuals who organized corporations, with the specific intent of avoiding responsibility to the public, where the operation of the corporate enterprise yielded profits sufficient to purchase additional insurance."

3. To the extent that limited liability permits an owner to escape the full tort costs of the bar business in Baatz v. Arrow Bar or the taxicab business in Walkovszky v. Carlton, it can encourage overinvestment in hazardous activity and causes a portion of the costs of these businesses to be borne by accident victims. Imposing liability on individuals would encourage them to internalize the costs of accidents, although it may well result in fewer investors in cabs or bars and higher tariffs. Is there a reason why society might want to permit such use of a corporation? Stephen Presser argues for a democratic justification, a desire to encourage individual investment by those of moderate means as opposed to firms owned only by the wealthy. See S. Presser, Piercing the Corporate Veil 1-12 (1991).

Professors Henry Hansmann and Reinier Kraakman have taken tort concerns further and argued for unlimited liability of all shareholders for tort claims of either closely held firms or publicly held firms. Hansmann and Kraakman, Toward Unlimited Shareholder Liability for Corporate Torts, 100 Yale L.J. 1879 (1991). See also Leebron, Limited Liability, Tort Victims and Creditors, 91 Colum. L. Rev. 1569 (1991). In part, their proposal is based on a concern that potentially massive tort claims could exceed the net assets of even the largest corporations. Their proposal has been challenged on the administrative feasibility of its collection regime and the distributional consequences. See Grundfest, The Limited Future of Unlimited Liability: A Capital Markets Perspective, 102 Yale L.J. 387 (1992) (markets will find ways to provide legal liability even if legal rules seek to decree otherwise); Alexander, Unlimited Shareholder Liability Through a Procedural Lens, 106 Harv. L. Rev. 387 (1992) (discussing jurisdictional complications that would restrict liability recovery in an extended liability regime); Thompson, Unpacking Limited Liability: Direct and Vicarious Liability of Corporate Participants for Torts of the Enterprise, 47 Vand. L. Rev. 1, 5 (1994) ("Neither ability to control nor distributive concerns of tort law support liability for passive shareholders").

4. Could it be argued that piercing the corporate veil in tort cases is, or should be, equivalent to allowing involuntary creditors to sue the corporation's officers and directors for breach of fiduciary duty? For example, suppose that in both Baatz v. Arrow Bar and Western Rock Co. v. Davis the plaintiffs obtained a sizeable judgment against the corporation, and that the corporation then went bankrupt. What result in each of those cases if the trustee in bankruptcy then sued the corporation's principal officers and directors for breach of fiduciary duty to the corporation? See Slottow v. American Casualty Co., 1 F.3d 912, 916 (9th Cir. 1993) (under California law, a corporation's employees owe no independent fiduciary duty to a third party with whom they deal on behalf of their employer). Do other-constituencies statutes have a role to play in such litigation? Is there any objection to deciding whether to pierce on behalf of involuntary creditors by analogy to fiduciary duty? Does such an analogy unfairly relegate involuntary creditors to the same status as those who have bargained with the corporation? If involuntary creditors bargained for a piercing rule behind a veil of ignorance, what rule would they select?

PROBLEM 7-4

Members of the Pierson family incorporated Pierson, Inc. to enter the home construction business. The family contributed $1,000 in initial equity and lent the corporation an additional $140,000 over a two-year period. The corporation employed three family members full time and made a profit of $9,000 the first year; on the advice of counsel, corporate formalities have been scrupulously followed. When the housing industry went into a recession and costs rose, the corporation used inferior and cheaper material in one project that later failed. This caused damage that rendered the corporation insolvent. Can the tort creditors recover against the financially solvent shareholders?

3. Piercing the Corporate Veil to Reach Incorporated Shareholders

When the shareholder behind the corporation is another corporation instead of an individual, the piercing analysis becomes more complicated. The tort rule that holds individuals liable for their tortious acts taken in the name of the corporation will not often cover corporate shareholders since as intangible entities they do not physically act for the subsidiary, but rather appoint real people to serve as officers and directors. Even the contract claims become more difficult to the extent that the various corporate entities create confusion that may mislead those who deal with the subsidiary. As you read the following cases, look for the difference between derivative liability usually addressed under piercing the veil and direct liability for one's own tortious or statutorily prohibited acts which, as discussed in the last section, can lead to liability without the necessity to pierce the veil. Consider how that distinction can be drawn when the investor or manager is itself an artificial entity. Does it advance the discussion to distinguish between the actions of the parent that are those of a mere shareholder versus the more active involvement of a parent in the management of the business that would be comparable to that of an officer or director?

Craig v. Lake Asbestos
United States Court of Appeals, Third Circuit, 1988
843 F.2d 145

SLOVITER, CIRCUIT JUDGE. . . .

II. PROCEDURAL AND FACTUAL BACKGROUND

[The original plaintiffs, Clarence and Duveen Craig, New Jersey residents, brought suit to recover damages for personal injuries stemming from Clarence's exposure to asbestos fibers while employed at the Owens-Corning plant in Berlin, New Jersey. The defendants included all of the corporations that had manufactured, sold, or supplied asbestos to Owens-Corning. One of those defendants, North American Asbestos Corporation (NAAC), was dismissed from the Craigs' suit because NAAC had been dissolved in 1978. The remaining defendants settled with the plaintiffs. However, one of those defendants, Lake Asbestos of Quebec, Ltd. (LAQ), settled conditionally, so as to maintain its right to receive contribution from Cape Industries (Cape), which had owned all of the stock of NAAC, and from Charter Consolidated, P.L.C. (Charter), which owned a majority of Cape's shares. The parties stipulated that Cape was the alter ego of its former subsidiary, NAAC.]

The following relevant facts are not disputed: Charter is a publicly held investment holding and finance company; Cape also is a publicly owned holding company. Both are incorporated under the laws of the United Kingdom and have their principal places of business in England. Through its subsidiaries, Cape engaged until 1979 in the mining of asbestos in South Africa and the distribution of that product to the industrial market. Between 1953 and 1978, Cape's wholly-owned subsidiary NAAC sold asbestos fiber in the United States.

Charter, through a subsidiary, acquired a 16% interest in Cape in 1965, which it expanded by gradual purchases and a 1969 tender offer until, by 1978, it held 67.3% of Cape's outstanding shares. From 1965 to 1969 Charter placed two of its own executives on Cape's Board of Directors. In 1969, after Charter acquired a majority of Cape's shares, Charter nominated a third director onto that Board, and has since that time, except for a brief period, maintained three directors on Cape's Board. During these years, Cape's Board consisted of between ten and fourteen directors. The majority were Cape employees, but there were two and sometimes three outside directors connected with neither Cape nor Charter. The managing director of Cape, originally R.H. Dent and later G.A. Higham, sat on the Board of Charter.

In 1973, Cape and its wholly-owned subsidiary NAAC were named as defendants in two asbestos injury suits filed in Texas. Cape unsuccessfully challenged jurisdiction.

Ultimately, these cases were settled for $20 million, with Cape and NAAC responsible for $5.2 million. Thereafter, Cape declined to defend other asbestos litigation in the United States, permitting default judgments totaling $78 million to be entered against it.

[Cape had no American assets to attach. When plaintiffs attempted to enforce these judgments, the English courts required new trials. Further, English product liability law made it almost impossible to establish liability.]

NAAC was dissolved in 1978; in its place was formed the Continental Products Corporation (CPC), which ostensibly had no ties to Cape. However, Charles G. Morgan, NAAC's former president, was the president and sole shareholder of CPC, which had received its start-up funds through Cape's payment of "termination compensation" to Morgan. CPC, which received its shipments of asbestos from Cape through a newly formed corporation in Liechtenstein, distributed asbestos to the former customers of NAAC in the United States for several years until terminating business in 1981. In 1979, Cape sold all of its asbestos mining and marketing subsidiaries to Transvaal Consolidated Land and Exploration Company Limited (TCL) with the agreement that Cape would indemnify TCL for asbestos-injury judgments in U.S. cases instituted within three years after the date of the sale only on condition that TCL continue Cape's policy of defaulting on judgments in the United States. As a result of these actions, Cape has apparently been able to avoid paying anything toward the injury claims of asbestos victims.

III.   The District Court Decision

The district court, after determining that New Jersey law should be used, applied a three-part test to determine whether the corporate veil of Charter should be pierced: the "plaintiff must demonstrate (1) control by one corporation of another, which is (2) used in a way that results in fraud or injustice; and which (3) is the proximate cause of plaintiff's alleged injury." The court concluded that under New Jersey law, actual fraud is not required and that it is sufficient if "the privilege inherent in incorporation is abused and a subsidiary used to perpetrate injustice." The court then found that Cape's purposeful scheme to insulate itself from liability in the asbestos litigation by liquidating NAAC and at the same time continuing to take advantage of the United States market by distributing asbestos in this country through CPC "unquestionably" established the "fraud" or "injustice" factor. The court also found that Cape's strategy of not appearing in the asbestos litigation was the proximate cause of the injury to either the plaintiffs Craig or the co-defendant LAQ.

The district court then addressed what it considered "the most difficult issue in this case," the issue of Charter's control over Cape. As the district court correctly noted, under New Jersey law the corporate veil of a parent corporation may not be pierced unless "the parent so dominated the subsidiary that it had no separate existence but was merely a conduit for the parent." State Dept. of Environ. Protection v. Ventron Corp., 94 N.J. 473, 501, 468 A.2d 150, 164 (1983). Based on its findings of the facts regarding Charter's relationship with Cape, which we will discuss in depth below, the district court concluded that Charter's control of Cape was "actual, participatory and pervasive," and that "Cape functioned as an operational division of Charter and exercised no independent will of its own." The district court therefore found Charter to be the alter ego of Cape and entered judgment holding Charter liable for Cape's tort obligation in the stipulated amount of $40,000. Charter appeals. . . .

V. DISCUSSION

A federal court sitting in diversity must apply the state substantive law as pronounced by the state's highest court or, if there has been no such decision, must predict how the state's highest court would decide were it confronted with the problem. Fortunately for us in this case, we need not engage in the difficult problem of divining that which has not yet been spoken because the New Jersey Supreme Court has recently clearly and definitively set forth New Jersey law on piercing the corporate veil. See State Dept. of Environ. Protection v. Ventron Corp., 94 N.J. at 499-501, 468 A.2d at 164-65 (1983).

Ventron presented a situation comparable to that here because New Jersey's Department of Environmental Protection sought to impose liability on a parent corporation for the dumping of toxic wastes by its wholly-owned subsidiary. The New Jersey trial court, affirmed on this issue by the Appellate Division, had pierced the parent's corporate veil and held the parent liable for the pollution caused by the subsidiary. The New Jersey Supreme Court expressly disagreed with the reasoning of those courts. The court stated: "We begin with the fundamental propositions that a corporation is a separate entity from its shareholders and that a primary reason for incorporation is the insulation of shareholders from the liabilities of the corporate enterprise." *Ventron,* 94 N.J. at 500, 468 A.2d at 164. It continued, "even in the case of a parent corporation and its wholly-owned subsidiary, limited liability normally will not be abrogated. Mueller v. Seaboard Commercial Corp., 5 N.J. 28, 34 [73 A.2d 905] (1950)." It explained that the corporate veil may be pierced only where (1) "the parent so dominated the subsidiary that it had no separate existence but was merely a conduit for the parent" and (2) "the parent has abused the privilege of incorporation by using the subsidiary to perpetrate a fraud or injustice, or otherwise to circumvent the law." New Jersey is thus in line with the approach taken generally on this issue.

We accept for purposes of this appeal the district court's findings and conclusion that Cape's scheme to avoid asbestos-injury liability in the United States constituted the type of "fraud or injustice" that would satisfy that element of the standard for piercing the corporate veil. Although we therefore do not reach the legal issue of the type of fraud required, we appreciate the district court's sensitivity to the asbestos victim's lack of redress under a scenario whereby the seller of the injurious material (NAAC) is dissolved, its parent (Cape) suffers default judgments that may be uncollectible, and nevertheless the product from the same source continues to be sold and distributed in the United States. We comment merely that evasion of tort liability has never, in itself, been sufficient basis to disregard corporate separateness.

We turn instead to consider whether the evidence produced of record shows the type of control necessary to constitute Cape the alter ego of Charter. We reject at the outset LAQ's suggestion that the control test can be "diluted," and that "all that is

required here is the injustice . . . from the legal fiction of corporate separateness."
Ventron makes clear that piercing the corporate veil "depends on" a finding of dominance. Only after there has been such a finding does one reach the fraud or injustice
issue.

The control which a parent must exercise over a subsidiary so as to warrant piercing the veil between them is more than "mere majority or complete stock control" ;
instead it is "complete domination, not only of finances but of policy and business
practice in respect to the transaction attacked so that the corporate entity as to this
transaction had at the time no separate mind, will or existence of its own." [1 W.
Fletcher, Cyclopedia of the Law of Private Corporations §43, at 490 (rev. perm. ed.
1983).] In another context, this court has listed some of the factors that must be considered to determine if the corporate veil should be pierced. These include:

> gross undercapitalization . . . "failure to observe corporate formalities, non-payment of dividends,
> the insolvency of the debtor corporation at the time, siphoning of funds of the corporation by the
> dominant stockholder, non-functioning of other officers or directors, absence of corporate records,
> and the fact that the corporation is merely a facade for the operations of the dominant stockholder
> or stockholders."

It is assumed to be the norm that a parent will have "not only the potential to exercise control over the subsidiary, but to exercise it to a substantial degree." P. Blumberg,
The Law of Corporate Groups: Tort, Contract, and Other Common Law Problems in
the Substantive Law of Parent and Subsidiary Corporations §10.02, at 187 (1987). It is
patently clear since *Ventron* that in New Jersey even the exercise of significant control
by the parent over the subsidiary will not suffice to pierce the corporate veil. The relationship between the parent and subsidiary in *Ventron* was that Velsicol owned 100%
of the Wood Ridge stock, all directors of Wood Ridge were officers of Velsicol, and
the Wood Ridge board of directors met monthly in the Velsicol offices in Chicago.
"At the meetings, the board not only reviewed financial statements, products development, and public relations, but also the details of the daily operations of Wood Ridge.
For example, the Wood Ridge board considered in detail personnel practices, sales
efforts, and production. Velsicol arranged for insurance coverage, accounting, and
credit approvals for Wood Ridge." 94 N.J. at 484, 468 A.2d at 155.

Based on these facts, the New Jersey Supreme Court found that the record supported the lower court's conclusion that the "Velsicol [the parent corporation] personnel, directors and officers were constantly involved in the day-to-day operations of
the business of Wood Ridge [the subsidiary]." Id. Nonetheless, the Supreme Court
held "those conclusions are not sufficient to support the further conclusion that the
intrusion of Velsicol into Wood Ridge's affairs reached the point of dominance." Id.
at 501, 468 A.2d at 165. Because of both the lack of the requisite "dominance" and
because the *Ventron* court thought that the subsidiary had not been incorporated for
an "unlawful purpose," the Court decided that the common-law doctrine of piercing
the corporate veil was not applicable.

It is against the standard established in the *Ventron* decision that we must examine
the conclusion of the district court that sufficient control was exercised by Charter
over Cape to pierce the corporate veil under New Jersey law. The district court based
its conclusion on findings of fact regarding Charter's publicly announced intentions

in connection with its tender offer to "control" Cape and use it to expand Charter's industrial activities; on Charter's involvement in Cape's financial and management affairs; on the presence of three Charter nominees on Cape's Board; and on Charter's ownership of a majority of Cape's stock and its ability to exercise control through that ownership if it so wished.

It is to be expected that a corporation seeking to acquire majority ownership of another will seek to achieve control. Thus, Charter's statements upon which the district court relied, including particularly the statement that Charter "takes direct management responsibility for mining operations, both in the U.K. and overseas," when viewed in the context of a takeover bid, do not add to the inquiry of how it exercised the control it eventually achieved. Indeed, R.H. Dent, the Chairman of Cape who had opposed the takeover, remained in that position for 10 years following the acquisition.

The district court also relied on its finding of "much evidence of Charter's widespread involvement in Cape's financial and management decisions." The court looked to the evidence that Charter had promised to give Cape "strong financial backing," Cape "routinely consulted Charter on 'financial decisions of a major character,'" Charter arranged financing for various Cape projects, and Cape agreed to discuss its dividend recommendations with Charter before they were presented to Cape's Board. In addition, a Charter statement revealed its plan to "maintain . . . close scrutiny of new capital expenditure projects"; a letter from the Chairman of Cape to the head of Charter confirmed a meeting at Charter, subsequently held, to discuss the "future executive structure of Cape"; Charter on at least one occasion expressed displeasure to the Cape Board when the Cape Board decided to make an acquisition without consulting Charter; Cape subsequently agreed that it would consider "Charter's policy towards the size of its shareholding in Cape" when making future acquisition decisions; the Chairman of Cape, R.H. Dent, who also sat on Charter's Board, regularly reported to Charter on Cape's financial results; and Dent sought to discuss with Charter his remaining as Chairman of Cape beyond the age of 60.

The involvement in Cape's financial and managerial affairs fails to rise to the high standard of domination necessary to pierce the corporate veil set out in *Ventron*. There, although the parent was "*constantly* involved in the day-to-day business" of its subsidiary, the Court held that the control over the subsidiary had not reached the required "point of dominance." 94 N.J. at 501, 468 A.2d at 165 (emphasis added). In this case, there is no evidence that Charter's intrusion into Cape's affairs is even "constant" or day-to-day. Moreover, and significantly, the district court found that "the two corporate groups each maintained separate books, records, bank accounts, offices and staff; each consulted their own financial advisors, accountants and stockbrokers." See Hargrave v. Fibreboard Corp., 710 F.2d 1154, 1162 (5th Cir. 1983) (court refuses to pierce corporate veil when presented with "nothing more nefarious than the interest and involvement that properly may be demonstrated by an active parent corporation").

The district court concluded that Charter's majority share of stock ownership gave it an "omnipresence in the minds of the Cape Board members" such that Cape was nothing more than an "operating division" of Charter. However, potential control is not enough. See Scalise v. Beech Aircraft Corp., 276 F. Supp. 58, 62 (E.D. Pa. 1967) ("although stock ownership and identity of officers and directors naturally subject the subsidiary to a measure of control, the issue . . . is how such control is exercised"). Moreover, if the actual control exercised in *Ventron* was insufficient, the mere power to control cannot be determinative. . . .

VI. CONCLUSION

For the reasons set forth above, the judgment of the district court will be reversed, and the case remanded to the district court for entry of judgment in favor of Charter.

United States v. Bestfoods
United States Supreme Court, 1998
524 U.S. 51

JUSTICE SOUTER delivered the opinion of the Court.

The United States brought this action for the costs of cleaning up industrial waste generated by a chemical plant. The issue before us, under the Comprehensive Environmental Response, Compensation, and Liability Act of 1980 (CERCLA), 42 U.S.C. §9601 et seq., is whether a parent corporation that actively participated in, and exercised control over, the operations of a subsidiary may, without more, be held liable as an operator of a polluting facility owned or operated by the subsidiary. We answer no, unless the corporate veil may be pierced. But a corporate parent that actively participated in, and exercised control over, the operations of the facility itself may be held directly liable in its own right as an operator of the facility.

In 1980, CERCLA was enacted in response to the serious environmental and health risks posed by industrial pollution. "As its name implies, CERCLA is a comprehensive statute that grants the President broad power to command government agencies and private parties to clean up hazardous waste sites." Key Tronic Corp. v. United States, 511 U.S. 809, 814 (1994). If it satisfies certain statutory conditions, the United States may, for instance, use the "Hazardous Substance Superfund" to finance cleanup efforts which it may then replenish by suits brought under §107 of the Act against, among others, "any person who at the time of disposal of any hazardous substance owned or operated any facility." So, those actually "responsible for any damage, environmental harm, or injury from chemical poisons [may be tagged with] the cost of their actions," S. Rep. No. 96-848, p. 13 (1980). The term "person" is defined in CERCLA to include corporations and other business organizations, and the term "facility" enjoys a broad and detailed definition as well.[2] The phrase "owner or operator" is defined only by tautology, however, as "any person owning or operating" a facility, §9601(20)(A)(ii), and

---

2. "The term 'facility' [§9601(9)] means (A) any building, structure, installation, equipment, pipe or pipeline (including any pipe into a sewer or publicly owned treatment works), well, pit, pond, lagoon, impoundment, ditch, landfill, storage container, motor vehicle, rolling stock, or aircraft, or (B) any site or area where a hazardous substance has been deposited, stored, disposed of, or placed, or otherwise come to be located; but does not include any consumer product in consumer use or any vessel."

it is this bit of circularity that prompts our review. Cf. Exxon Corp. v. Hunt, [475 U.S. 355], at 363 (CERCLA, "unfortunately, is not a model of legislative draftsmanship").

In 1957, Ott Chemical Co. (Ott I) began manufacturing chemicals at a plant near Muskegon, Michigan, and its intentional and unintentional dumping of hazardous substances significantly polluted the soil and ground water at the site. In 1965, respondent CPC International, Inc. [which has since changed its name to Bestfoods] incorporated a wholly owned subsidiary to buy Ott I's assets in exchange for CPC stock. The new company, also dubbed Ott Chemical Co. (Ott II), continued chemical manufacturing at the site, and continued to pollute its surroundings. CPC kept the managers of Ott I, including its founder, president, and principal shareholder, Arnold Ott, on board as officers of Ott II. Arnold Ott and several other Ott II officers and directors were also given positions at CPC, and they performed duties for both corporations.

In 1972, CPC sold Ott II to Story Chemical Company, which operated the Muskegon plant until its bankruptcy in 1977. Shortly thereafter, when respondent Michigan Department of Natural Resources (MDNR) examined the site for environmental damage, it found the land littered with thousands of leaking and even exploding drums of waste, and the soil and water saturated with noxious chemicals. MDNR sought a buyer for the property who would be willing to contribute toward its cleanup, and after extensive negotiations, respondent Aerojet-General Corp. arranged for transfer of the site from the Story bankruptcy trustee in 1977. Aerojet created a wholly owned California subsidiary, Cordova Chemical Company (Cordova/California), to purchase the property, and Cordova/California in turn created a wholly owned Michigan subsidiary, Cordova Chemical Company of Michigan (Cordova/Michigan), which manufactured chemicals at the site until 1986.

By 1981, the federal Environmental Protection Agency had undertaken to see the site cleaned up, and its long-term remedial plan called for expenditures well into the tens of millions of dollars. To recover some of that money, the United States filed this action under §107 in 1989, naming five defendants as responsible parties: CPC, Aerojet, Cordova/California, Cordova/Michigan, and Arnold Ott. (By that time, Ott I and Ott II were defunct.) After the parties (and MDNR) had launched a flurry of contribution claims, counterclaims, and cross-claims, the District Court consolidated the cases for trial in three phases: liability, remedy, and insurance coverage. So far, only the first phase has been completed; in 1991, the District Court held a 15-day bench trial on the issue of liability. Because the parties stipulated that the Muskegon plant was a "facility," that hazardous substances had been released at the facility, and that the United States had incurred reimbursable response costs to clean up the site, the trial focused on the issues of whether CPC and Aerojet, as the parent corporations of Ott II and the Cordova companies, had "owned or operated" the facility within the meaning of §107(a)(2).

[The district court held both CPC and Aerojet directly liable as an operator (as opposed to indirect liability under veil piercing) using an "actual control" test focusing on if the parent "exerted power or influence over the subsidiary's business during a period of disposal of hazardous waste." The Sixth Circuit (en banc and divided 7-6) limited operator liability based on parental control of the subsidiary to situations where state law-piercing requirements are met. The appellate court seemed to leave a little room for broader liability if the parent operated the facility instead of or as a sort of joint venture alongside its subsidiary.]

It is a general principle of corporate law deeply "ingrained in our economic and legal systems" that a parent corporation (so-called because of control through owner-ship of another corporation's stock) is not liable for the acts of its subsidiaries. Douglas & Shanks, Insulation from Liability Through Subsidiary Corporations, 39 Yale L. J. 193 (1929) (hereinafter Douglas) . . . Thus, it is hornbook law that "the exercise of the 'control' which stock ownership gives to the stockholders . . . will not create liability beyond the assets of the subsidiary. That 'control' includes the election of directors, the making of by-laws . . . and the doing of all other acts incident to the legal status of stockholders. Nor will a duplication of some or all of the directors or executive officers be fatal." Douglas 196 (footnotes omitted). Although this respect for corporate distinc-tions when the subsidiary is a polluter has been severely criticized in the literature, see, e.g., Note, Liability of Parent Corporations for Hazardous Waste Cleanup and Damages, 99 Harv. L. Rev. 986 (1986), nothing in CERCLA purports to reject this bed-rock principle, and against this venerable common-law backdrop, the congressional silence is audible. The Government has indeed made no claim that a corporate parent is liable as an owner or an operator under §107 simply because its subsidiary is subject to liability for owning or operating a polluting facility.

But there is an equally fundamental principle of corporate law, applicable to the parent-subsidiary relationship as well as generally, that the corporate veil may be pierced and the shareholder held liable for the corporation's conduct when, inter alia, the corporate form would otherwise be misused to accomplish certain wrongful purposes, most notably fraud, on the shareholder's behalf. [Anderson v. Abbott, 321 U.S. 349 (1944).] Nothing in CERCLA purports to rewrite this well-settled rule, either. CERCLA is thus like many another congressional enactments in giving no indication "that the entire corpus of state corporation law is to be replaced simply because a plaintiff's cause of action is based upon a federal statute," Burks v. Lasker, 441 U.S. 471, 478 (1979), and the failure of the statute to speak to a matter as fundamental as the liability implications of corporate ownership demands application of the rule that "in order to abrogate a common-law principle, the statute must speak directly to the ques-tion addressed by the common law," United States v. Texas, 507 U.S. 529, 534 (1993) (internal quotation marks omitted). The Court of Appeals was accordingly correct in holding that when (but only when) the corporate veil may be pierced,[9] may a parent corporation be charged with derivative CERCLA liability for its subsidiary's actions.[10]

If the act rested liability entirely on ownership of a polluting facility, this opinion might end here; but CERCLA liability may turn on operation as well as ownership,

9. There is significant disagreement among courts and commentators over whether, in enforcing CERCLA's indirect liability, courts should borrow state law, or instead apply a federal common law of veil piercing. . . . Since none of the parties challenges the Sixth Circuit's holding that CPC and Aerojet incurred no derivative liability, the question is not presented in this case, and we do not address it further.

10. Some courts and commentators have suggested that this indirect, veil-piercing approach can subject a parent corporation to liability only as an owner, and not as an operator. See, e.g., Lansford-Coaldale Joint Water Auth. v. Tonolli Corp., 4 F.2d 1209, at 1220; Oswald, Bifurcation of the Owner and Operator Analysis under CERCLA, 72 Wash. U. L. Q. 223, 281-282 (1994) (hereinafter Oswald). We think it is otherwise, however. If a subsidiary that operates, but does not own, a facility is so pervasively con-trolled by its parent for a sufficiently improper purpose to warrant veil piercing, the parent may be held derivatively liable for the subsidiary's acts as an operator.

and nothing in the statute's terms bars a parent corporation from direct liability for its own actions in operating a facility owned by its subsidiary. As Justice (then-Professor) Douglas noted almost 70 years ago, derivative liability cases are to be distinguished from those in which "the alleged wrong can seemingly be traced to the parent through the conduit of its own personnel and management" and "the parent is directly a participant in the wrong complained of." Douglas 207, 208. In such instances, the parent is directly liable for its own actions. The fact that a corporate subsidiary happens to own a polluting facility operated by its parent does nothing, then, to displace the rule that the parent "corporation is [itself] responsible for the wrongs committed by its agents in the course of its business," Mine Workers v. Coronado Coal Co., 259 U.S. 344, 395, 66 L. Ed. 975, 42 S. Ct. 570 (1922), and whereas the rules of veil-piercing limit derivative liability for the actions of another corporation, CERCLA's "operator" provision is concerned primarily with direct liability for one's own actions. It is this direct liability that is properly seen as being at issue here.

Under the plain language of the statute, any person who operates a polluting facility is directly liable for the costs of cleaning up the pollution. This is so regardless of whether that person is the facility's owner, the owner's parent corporation or business partner, or even a saboteur who sneaks into the facility at night to discharge its poisons out of malice. If any such act of operating a corporate subsidiary's facility is done on behalf of a parent corporation, the existence of the parent- subsidiary relationship under state corporate law is simply irrelevant to the issue of direct liability. See Riverside Market Dev. Corp. v. International Bldg. Prods., Inc., 931 F.2d 327, 330 (CA5) ("CERCLA prevents individuals from hiding behind the corporate shield when, as 'operators,' they themselves actually participate in the wrongful conduct prohibited by the Act"), cert. denied, 502 U.S. 1004 (1991); United States v. Kayser-Roth Corp., 910 F.2d 24, 26 (CA1 1990) ("a person who is an operator of a facility is not protected from liability by the legal structure of ownership").[12]

This much is easy to say; the difficulty comes in defining actions sufficient to constitute direct parental "operation." Here of course we may again rue the uselessness of CERCLA's definition of a facility's "operator" as "any person . . . . operating" the facility, which leaves us to do the best we can to give the term its "ordinary or natural meaning." In a mechanical sense, to "operate" ordinarily means "to control the functioning of; run: operate a sewing machine." American Heritage Dictionary 1268 (3d ed. 1992); see also Webster's New International Dictionary 1707 (2d ed. 1958) ("to work; as, to operate a machine"). And in the organizational sense more obviously intended by CERCLA, the word ordinarily means "to conduct the affairs of; manage: operate a business." American Heritage Dictionary, supra, at 1268; see also Webster's New International Dictionary, supra, at 1707 ("to manage"). So, under CERCLA, an

---

12. See Oswald 257 ("There are . . . instances . . . in which the parent has not sufficiently overstepped the bounds of corporate separateness to warrant piercing, yet is involved enough in the facility's activities that it should be held liable as an operator. Imagine, for example, a parent who strictly observed corporate formalities, avoided interwining officers and directors, and adequately capitalized its subsidiary, yet provided active, daily supervision and control over hazardous waste disposal activities of the subsidiary. Such a parent should not escape liability just because its activities do not justify a piercing of the subsidiary's veil").

operator is simply someone who directs the workings of, manages, or conducts the affairs of a facility. To sharpen the definition for purposes of CERCLA's concern with environmental contamination, an operator must manage, direct, or conduct operations specifically related to pollution, that is, operations having to do with the leakage or disposal of hazardous waste, or decisions about compliance with environmental regulations.

B

With this understanding, we are satisfied that the Court of Appeals correctly rejected the District Court's analysis of direct liability. But we also think that the appeals court erred in limiting direct liability under the statute to a parent's sole or joint venture operation, so as to eliminate any possible finding that CPC is liable as an operator on the facts of this case.

1

By emphasizing that "CPC is directly liable under section 107(a)(2) as an operator because CPC actively participated in and exerted significant control over Ott II's business and decision-making," the District Court applied the "actual control" test of whether the parent "actually operated the business of its subsidiary," as several Circuits have employed it.

The well-taken objection to the actual control test, however, is its fusion of direct and indirect liability; the test is administered by asking a question about the relationship between the two corporations (an issue going to indirect liability) instead of a question about the parent's interaction with the subsidiary's facility (the source of any direct liability). If, however, direct liability for the parent's operation of the facility is to be kept distinct from derivative liability for the subsidiary's own operation, the focus of the enquiry must necessarily be different under the two tests. "The question is not whether the parent operates the subsidiary, but rather whether it operates the facility, and that operation is evidenced by participation in the activities of the facility, not the subsidiary. Control of the subsidiary, if extensive enough, gives rise to indirect liability under piercing doctrine, not direct liability under the statutory language." Oswald 269. The District Court was therefore mistaken to rest its analysis on CPC's relationship with Ott II, premising liability on little more than "CPC's 100-percent ownership of Ott II" and "CPC's active participation in, and at times majority control over, Ott II's board of directors." The analysis should instead have rested on the relationship between CPC and the muskegon facility itself.

In addition to (and perhaps as a reflection of) the erroneous focus on the relationship between CPC and Ott II, even those findings of the District Court that might be taken to speak to the extent of CPC's activity at the facility itself are flawed, for the District Court wrongly assumed that the actions of the joint officers and directors are necessarily attributable to CPC. The District Court emphasized the facts that CPC placed its own high-level officials on Ott II's board of directors and in key management positions at Ott II, and that those individuals made major policy decisions and conducted day-to-day operations at the facility: "Although Ott II corporate officers set the day-to-day operating policies for the company without any need to obtain formal approval from CPC, CPC actively participated in this decision-making because high-ranking CPC officers served in Ott II management positions." [777 F. Supp. 549] at 559; see also id., at 575 (relying on "CPC's involvement in major decision-making and day-to-day operations through CPC officials who served within Ott II management, including the positions of president and chief executive officer," and on "the conduct of CPC officials with respect to Ott II affairs, particularly Arnold Ott"); id., at 558 ("CPC actively participated in, and at times controlled, the policy-making decisions of its subsidiary through its representation on the Ott II board of directors"); id., at 559 ("CPC also actively participated in and exercised control over day-to-day decision-making at Ott II through representation in the highest levels of the subsidiary's management").

In imposing direct liability on these grounds, the District Court failed to recognize that "it is entirely appropriate for directors of a parent corporation to serve as directors of its subsidiary, and that fact alone may not serve to expose the parent corporation to liability for its subsidiary's acts." American Protein Corp. v. AB Volvo, 844 F.2d 56, 57 (CA2), cert. denied, 488 U.S. 852; see also Kingston Dry Dock Co. v. Lake Champlain Transp. Co., 31 F.2d 265, 267 (CA2 1929) (L. Hand, J.) ("Control through the ownership of shares does not fuse the corporations, even when the directors are common to each"); Henn & Alexander [Laws of Corporations 3d ed. 1983 at 355] (noting that it is "normal" for a parent and subsidiary to "have identical directors and officers").

This recognition that the corporate personalities remain distinct has its corollary in the "well established principle [of corporate law] that directors and officers holding positions with a parent and its subsidiary can and do 'change hats' to represent the two corporations separately, despite their common ownership." Lusk v. Foxmeyer Health Corp., 129 F.3d 773, 779 (CA5 1997); see also Fisser v. International Bank, 282 F.2d 231, 238 (CA2 1960). Since courts generally presume "that the directors are wearing their 'subsidiary hats' and not their 'parent hats' when acting for the subsidiary," P. Blumberg, Law of Corporate Groups: Procedural Problems in the Law of Parent and Subsidiary Corporations §1.02.1, at 12 (1983); see, e.g., United States v. Jon-T Chemicals, Inc., 768 F.2d 686, 691 (CA5 1985), cert. denied, 475 U.S. 1014 (1986), it cannot be enough to establish liability here that dual officers and directors made policy decisions and supervised activities at the facility. The Government would have to show that, despite the general presumption to the contrary, the officers and directors were acting in their capacities as CPC officers and directors, and not as Ott II officers and directors, when they committed those acts.[13] The District Court made no such enquiry here, however, disregarding entirely this time-honored common law rule.

---

13. We do not attempt to recite the ways in which the Government could show that dual officers or directors were in fact acting on behalf of the parent. Here, it is prudent to say only that the presumption that an act is taken on behalf of the corporation for whom the officer claims to act is strongest when the act is perfectly consistent with the norms of corporate behavior, but wanes as the distance from those accepted norms approaches the point of action by a dual officer plainly contrary to the interests of the subsidiary yet nonetheless advantageous to the parent.

In sum, the District Court's focus on the relationship between parent and subsidiary (rather than parent and facility), combined with its automatic attribution of the actions of dual officers and directors to the corporate parent, erroneously, even if unintentionally, treated CERCLA as though it displaced or fundamentally altered common law standards of limited liability. Indeed, if the evidence of common corporate personnel acting at management and directorial levels were enough to support a finding of a parent corporation's direct operator liability under CERCLA, then the possibility of resort to veil piercing to establish indirect, derivative liability for the subsidiary's violations would be academic. There would in essence be a relaxed, CERCLA-specific rule of derivative liability that would banish traditional standards and expectations from the law of CERCLA liability. But, as we have said, such a rule does not arise from congressional silence, and CERCLA's silence is dispositive.

2

We accordingly agree with the Court of Appeals that a participation-and-control test looking to the parent's supervision over the subsidiary, especially one that assumes that dual officers always act on behalf of the parent, cannot be used to identify operation of a facility resulting in direct parental liability. Nonetheless, a return to the ordinary meaning of the word "operate" in the organizational sense will indicate why we think that the Sixth Circuit stopped short when it confined its examples of direct parental operation to exclusive or joint ventures, and declined to find at least the possibility of direct operation by CPC in this case.

In our enquiry into the meaning Congress presumably had in mind when it used the verb "to operate," we recognized that the statute obviously meant something more than mere mechanical activation of pumps and valves, and must be read to contemplate "operation" as including the exercise of direction over the facility's activities. The Court of Appeals recognized this by indicating that a parent can be held directly liable when the parent operates the facility in the stead of its subsidiary or alongside the subsidiary in some sort of a joint venture. We anticipated a further possibility above, however, when we observed that a dual officer or director might depart so far from the norms of parental influence exercised through dual officeholding as to serve the parent, even when ostensibly acting on behalf of the subsidiary in operating the facility. See n. 13, supra. Yet another possibility, suggested by the facts of this case, is that an agent of the parent with no hat to wear but the parent's hat might manage or direct activities at the facility.

Identifying such an occurrence calls for line drawing yet again, since the acts of direct operation that give rise to parental liability must necessarily be distinguished from the interference that stems from the normal relationship between parent and subsidiary. Again, norms of corporate behavior (undisturbed by any CERCLA provision) are crucial reference points. Just as we may look to such norms in identifying the limits of the presumption that a dual officeholder acts in his ostensible capacity, so here we may refer to them in distinguishing a parental officer's oversight of a subsidiary from such an officer's control over the operation of the subsidiary's facility. "Activities that involve the facility but which are consistent with the parent's investor status, such as monitoring of the subsidiary's performance, supervision of the subsidiary's finance and capital budget decisions, and articulation of general policies and procedures, should not give rise to direct liability." Oswald 282. The critical question is whether, in degree and detail, actions directed to the facility by an agent of the parent alone are eccentric under accepted norms of parental oversight of a subsidiary's facility.

There is, in fact, some evidence that CPC engaged in just this type and degree of activity at the Muskegon plant. The District Court's opinion speaks of an agent of CPC alone who played a conspicuous part in dealing with the toxic risks emanating from the operation of the plant. G.R.D. Williams worked only for CPC; he was not an employee, officer, or director of Ott II, see Tr. of Oral Arg. 7, and thus, his actions were of necessity taken only on behalf of CPC. The District Court found that "CPC became directly involved in environmental and regulatory matters through the work of . . . Williams, CPC's governmental and environmental affairs director. Williams . . . became heavily involved in environmental issues at Ott II." 777 F. Supp. at 561. He "actively participated in and exerted control over a variety of Ott II environmental matters," ibid., and he "issued directives regarding Ott II's responses to regulatory inquiries," id., at 575.

We think that these findings are enough to raise an issue of CPC's operation of the facility through Williams's actions, though we would draw no ultimate conclusion from these findings at this point. Not only would we be deciding in the first instance an issue on which the trial and appellate courts did not focus, but the very fact that the District Court did not see the case as we do suggests that there may be still more to be known about Williams's activities. Indeed, even as the factual findings stand, the trial court offered little in the way of concrete detail for its conclusions about Williams's role in Ott II's environmental affairs, and the parties vigorously dispute the extent of Williams's involvement. Prudence thus counsels us to remand, on the theory of direct operation set out here, for reevaluation of Williams's role, and of the role of any other CPC agent who might be said to have had a part in operating the Muskegon facility.[14]

NOTES AND QUESTIONS

1. In exactly what way is Charter's conduct in Craig v. Lake Asbestos less reprehensible than the conduct of the defendants in K.C. Roofing Center v. On Top Roofing,

---

14. There are some passages in the District Court's opinion that might suggest that, without reference to Williams, some of Ott II's actions in operating the facility were in fact dictated by, and thus taken on behalf of CPC. See, e.g., 777 F. Supp. at 561 ("CPC officials engaged in . . . missions to Ott II in which Ott II officials received instructions on how to improve and change"); id., at 559 ("CPC executives who were not Ott II board members also occasionally attended Ott II board meetings"). But nothing in the District Court's findings of fact, as written, even comes close to overcoming the presumption that Ott II officials made their decisions and performed their acts as agents of Ott II. Indeed, the finding that "Ott II corporate officers set the day-to-day operating policies for the company without any need to obtain formal approval from CPC," ibid., indicates just the opposite. Still, the Government is, of course, free on remand to point to any additional evidence, not cited by the District Court, that would tend to establish that Ott II's decisionmakers acted on specific orders from CPC.

Inc., or the defendant in Western Rock Co. v. Davis? Consider the following defense of Charter's actions:

> In recent years, individuals and companies have purchased asbestos companies, hoping to salvage them despite the problems with asbestos lawsuits. There never has been any thought that these people have exposed their personal assets to liability for company's judgments.
>
> The wrongdoing Charter is accused of is not operating through Cape. The wrongdoing is allowing Cape to fold its subsidiary so that Cape would have no remaining U.S. assets once Cape and NAAC started facing liability verdicts. Although this may be distasteful, it is not a misuse of Cape's corporate structure. It does not generate liability on the part of Charter for Cape's activities which would not otherwise exist. . . .
>
> The piercing of the corporate veil is not necessary to prevent fraud, illegality or injustice, since the corporate structure was established for traditional reasons, not to avoid impending judgment. It is not injustice merely to take advantage of corporate protections set up early in the investment. It is precisely this kind of protections that corporations are designed to give shareholders. This protection has encouraged investment and has been the backbone of our country's economy. This should not be forgotten in any zeal to protect individuals, even if they have been injured. The cure may be worse than the disease.

Nazarewych v. Bell Asbestos Mines, Ltd., 19 Phila. 429, 1989 Phila. City. Rptr. (LEXIS, States library, Pa. file).

2. In Walkovszky v. Carlton, discussed at supra page 631, the New York Court of Appeals distinguished an effort to reach the shareholder behind all the corporations from an effort to reach the larger corporate entity.

> It is one thing to assert that a corporation is a fragment of a larger corporate combine which actually conducts the business. (See Berle, The Theory of Enterprise Entity, 47 [Colum.] L. Rev. 343, 348-350.) It is quite another to claim that the corporation is a "dummy" for its individual stockholders who are in reality carrying on the business in their personal capacities for purely personal rather than corporate ends. Either circumstance would justify treating the corporation as an agent and piercing the corporate veil to reach the principal but a different result would follow in each case. In the first, only a larger corporate entity would be held financially responsible . . . while, in the other, the stockholder would be personally liable. . . . Either the stockholder is conducting the business in his individual capacity or he is not. If he is, he will be liable; if he is not, then it does not matter — insofar as his personal liability is concerned — that the enterprise is actually being carried on by a larger "enterprise entity." (See Berle, The Theory of Enterprise Entity, 47 [Colum.] L. Rev. 343.)

18 N.Y.2d 414, 421, 223 N.E.2d 6, 10, 276 N.Y.S.2d 585, 591 (1966).

The motion before the court in *Walkovszky* went to the shareholder's personal liability, so the court did not have to consider the question of enterprise liability; the court did, however, say this in dicta: "If it is not fraudulent for the owner-operator of a single cab corporation to take out only the minimum required liability insurance, the enterprise does not become either illicit or fraudulent merely because it consists of many such corporations. . . . [W]hatever rights he may be able to assert against parties other than the registered owner of the vehicle come into being not because he has been defrauded but because, under the principle of respondeat superior, he is entitled to hold the whole enterprise responsible for the acts of its agents."

3. The discussion in Note 2 involves corporate siblings—corporations owned by the same shareholder. Is there any reason to have less concern for sibling corporations, or for an incorporated controlling shareholder (usually called a parent corporation), than for an individual controlling shareholder? Thompson's study, discussed earlier in this chapter, found that courts actually pierce the veil less often when the target is a parent or sibling shareholder than when the target is a real person. See Table 2, supra page 608. What could explain this lesser frequency? Is there any reason why courts should be more protective of incorporated shareholders than real persons?

The reluctance to hold corporations liable within groups is more curious in the tort setting considered in Section B. Recall that in Thompson's study, Table 2 showed that courts were more reluctant to pierce in tort settings than in contract settings. The great majority (152 of 226, or 67 percent) of the tort cases occurred in corporate groups, so the reluctance to pierce in torts seems tied to a reluctance to pierce in corporate groups.

> The continuing puzzle is why courts remain so willing to provide limited liability to parent corporations in tort cases. The various arguments for limited liability do not have much impact in the parent-subsidiary situation. There do not appear to be large transaction costs to reach the parent corporation. There is no impact on the public market for shares of the subsidiary. No adverse diversification effects appear that would lead to overdeterrence or excessive monitoring. Yet externalization of some of the costs of the business clearly does occur. Even if piercing would be harsh to a passive parent corporation that did not participate in the wrongful action, it would seem to be outweighed by the harshness to those injured. It may be that these risks are viewed as remote, so that no extra preventive actions would be taken if liability were imposed, or that other methods of covering the injury are more efficient, combined with a desire to defer to the legislature to make such decisions. To the extent that a parent corporation does not exercise dominance in the manner used traditionally to support piercing, a greater likelihood exists that the parent-subsidiary structure remains responsive to the usual credit markets so that a sufficient amount of preventive care is taken and no additional corrective liability would be beneficial.

Thompson, Unpacking Limited Liability: Direct and Vicarious Liability of Corporate Participants for Torts of the Enterprise, 47 Vand. L. Rev. 1, 40 (1994).

4. Consider the following explanation of why courts should be alert to the greater danger posed by multiple corporations:

> Creditors of a constituent corporation may be exposed to greater risks than creditors of a single corporation. First, the availability of funds from other corporations reduces the practical importance of adequate initial capitalization; constituent corporations can attract investments from related corporations more easily than new capital could be raised from groups of stockholders. Second, the danger of commingling assets and properties is greater between corporations themselves, than between corporations and shareholders. Third, there is a greater chance that, because its economic viability is tied to that of other corporations, the constituent corporation will be unable to develop the kind of independent profit-making activities that might be expected of single corporate units. In the final analysis, the subsidiary will be responsive to the dictates of the owners of the enterprise, who will be most interested in the overall return on their investment.

Landers, A Unified Approach to Parent, Subsidiary, and Affiliate Questions in Bankruptcy, 42 U. Chi. L. Rev. 589, 596-597 (1975).

5. Consider the following partial rebuttal of Landers's argument:

It has been argued that the case for limited liability is weaker for corporate than for personal shareholders because affiliated corporations, even if engaged in totally unrelated lines of business, will be managed differently from independent firms, since the owners will seek to maximize the profits of the enterprise as a whole rather than the profits of any individual corporation. Normally, however, the profits of the group will be maximized by maximizing the profits of each constituent corporation. Indeed, if the corporations are engaged in truly unrelated lines of business, the profits of each will be completely independent. . . .

The important difference between a group of affiliates engaged in related businesses and one engaged in a number of unrelated businesses is not that the conduct of corporations in the first group will differ from that of nonaffiliated corporations in the same businesses, but that the creditor dealing with a group of affiliates in related businesses is more likely to be misled into thinking that he is dealing with a single corporation. The misrepresentation principle seems adequate to deal with these cases.

R. Posner, Economic Analysis of Law 299-300 (2d ed. 1977).

  6. And consider the analysis of Easterbrook and Fischel:

Allowing creditors to reach the assets of parent corporations does not create unlimited liability for any people. Thus the benefits of diversification, liquidity, and monitoring by the capital market are unaffected. Moreover, the moral-hazard problem is probably greater in parent-subsidiary situations because subsidiaries have less incentive to insure. In publicly held corporations, the inability of managers to diversify their firm-specific investments in human capital creates incentives to insure. The same is not true for managers of subsidiaries if, as often will be the case, these people are also managers of the parent. Bankruptcy of the subsidiary will not cause them to lose their positions in the parent or suffer any other loss of firm-specific human capital (though it might impose a reputational loss on them). If limited liability is absolute, a parent can form a subsidiary with minimal capitalization for the purpose of engaging in risky activities. If things go well, the parent captures the benefits. If things go poorly, the subsidiary declares bankruptcy, and the parent creates another with the same managers to engage in the same activities. This asymmetry between benefits and costs, if limited liability were absolute, would create incentives to engage in a socially excessive amount of risky activities.

Easterbrook and Fischel, Limited Liability and the Corporation, 52 U. Chi. L. Rev. 89, 111 (1985).

  7. Does Easterbrook and Fischel's analysis in Note 6 cut in favor of or against liability for Charter in Craig v. Lake Asbestos?

  8. Piercing the veil has traditionally been a product of state common law. Federal legislative provisions, such as those regulating the environmental and pension areas, have raised the possibility that federal law might set an easier standard for piercing than state law in order to provide more money to clean up natural resources or to protect the retirement income of workers. The Supreme Court in footnote 9 of *Bestfoods* left unresolved whether state or federal law would resolve this question. Some cases suggest a conflict between limited liability and federal policy, but even where courts have said that they are going to apply federal common law, the results seem to track traditional state law. See Oswald and Schipani, CERCLA and the Erosion of Traditional Corporate Law Doctrine, 86 Nw. L. Rev. 259 (1992). Can the same thing be said for the Supreme Court's analysis of CERCLA liability in *Bestfoods*?

  9. Corporate shareholders differ from individual shareholders in that an individual who controls a corporation is likely to name herself as a director and an officer. The corporation, as an artificial person, cannot do that so it likely will select its

employees to be directors and officers of the subsidiary. While overlap of directors and officers has been a factor sometimes cited by courts in piercing the veil, notice how the Supreme Court restricts the use of such a theory for operator liability under CERCLA. The Court first declares such overlap as normal and appropriate. It then applies a presumption that such overlap directors are wearing their subsidiary "hat" and not their parent "hat" when acting for the subsidiary. While such an interpretation purports to be of a federal statute, it is likely to affect common law piercing cases generally.

10. In Janus Capital Group, Inc. v. First Derivative Traders, 131 S. Ct. 2296 (U.S. 2011), plaintiffs sought to hold a mutual fund adviser liable for misstatements in the prospectus of a mutual fund. The adviser formed the mutual fund, and all officers of the fund were officers of the adviser, but the two entities maintained separateness and only one member of the board of trustees of the fund was associated with the adviser (greater independence than is required by the applicable federal securities statute, which permits up to 60 percent of the board of a mutual fund to be composed of interested persons). The Court, evidencing a formalistic approach to corporate separateness, declined to disregard the corporate form where the corporate formalities were observed: "[A]ny reapportionment of liability in the securities industry in light of the close relationship between investment advisers and mutual funds is properly the responsibility of Congress and not the courts."

PROBLEM 7-5

Konrad, while riding a motorcycle, was struck by a truck owned by Contrux, Inc., a company engaged in transporting goods. Konrad seeks to recover from Telecom, Inc., the parent of Contrux, because he fears that Contrux has insufficient assets to pay his claim. Contrux is a wholly owned subsidiary of Telecom. It was organized as a nonunion subsidiary to take advantage of a lower wage and benefit package that such status would permit. Telecom contributed $25,000 in initial capital and periodically advanced money to Contrux for operating expenses in the form of debt (totaling $750,000 by the time of trial). Telecom had a security interest in Contrux's tangible assets — the trucks and other vehicles used in Contrux's business. Contrux had a negative net worth and net operating losses each of the four years it was actively in business. Contrux had separate officers and followed corporate formalities. Its lack of net worth and lack of unencumbered assets meant that Contrux officers often involved Telecom in most important business decisions. Contrux purchased $1 million in liability insurance and an additional $10 million in excess coverage, purchased from separate insurance companies, at premiums of $17,000 and $4,000, respectively. It is undisputed that this amount of insurance exceeded requirements of federal trucking regulations. The insurance was purchased through an agency that itself was a wholly owned subsidiary of Telecom. The insurance company providing the excess insurance coverage has turned out to be insolvent. Konrad asserts that the excess insurance carrier was never strong enough to receive even a minimum insurance rating in the Best Insurance Guide, a private reporting service that monitors insurance companies. Should Konrad be able to recover from Telecom?

4.   Piercing in LLCs

Kaycee Land and Livestock v. Flahive
Wyoming Supreme Court, 2002
46 P.3d 323 2002

KITE, JUSTICE.

This matter comes before this court as a question certified to us by the district court for resolution under W.R.A.P. 11. The certified question seeks resolution of whether, in the absence of fraud, the entity veil of a limited liability company (LLC) can be pierced in the same manner as that of a corporation. We answer the certified question in the affirmative.

CERTIFIED QUESTION

The question we have agreed to answer is phrased as follows:

In the absence of fraud, is a claim to pierce the Limited Liability entity veil or disregard the Limited Liability Company entity in the same manner as a court would pierce a corporate veil or disregard a corporate shield, an available remedy against a Wyoming Limited Liability Company under Wyoming's Limited Liability Company Act, Wyo. Stat. §[§]17-15-101 through 17-15-144 (2000) . . . ?

FACTS

In a W.R.A.P. 11 certification of a question of law, we rely entirely upon the factual determinations made in the trial court. The district court submitted the following statement of facts in its order certifying the question of law:

1.   Flahive Oil & Gas is a Wyoming Limited Liability Company with no assets at this time.
2.   [Kaycee Land and Livestock] entered into a contract with Flahive Oil & Gas LLC allowing Flahive Oil & Gas to use the surface of its real property.
3.   Roger Flahive is and was the managing member of Flahive Oil & Gas at all relevant times.
4.   [Kaycee Land and Livestock] alleges that Flahive Oil & Gas caused environmental contamination to its real property located in Johnson County, Wyoming.
5.   [Kaycee Land and Livestock] seeks to pierce the LLC veil and disregard the LLC entity of Flahive Oil & Gas Limited Liability Company and hold Roger Flahive individually liable for the contamination.
6.   There is no allegation of fraud.

DISCUSSION

The question presented is limited to whether, in the absence of fraud, the remedy of piercing the veil is available against a company formed under the Wyoming Limited

Liability Company Act (Wyo. Stat. Ann. §§17-15-101 to -144 (LexisNexis 2001)). To answer this question, we must first examine the development of the doctrine within Wyoming's corporate context. As a general rule, a corporation is a separate entity distinct from the individuals comprising it. Opal Mercantile v. Tamblyn, 616 P.2d 776, 778 (Wyo. 1980). Wyoming statutes governing corporations do not address the circumstances under which the veil can be pierced. However, since 1932, this court has espoused the concept that a corporation's legal entity will be disregarded whenever the recognition thereof in a particular case will lead to injustice. See Caldwell v. Roach, 44 Wyo. 319, 12 P.2d 376, 380 (1932). In Miles v. CEC Homes, Inc., 753 P.2d 1021, 1023 (Wyo. 1988) (quoting Amfac Mechanical Supply Co. v. Federer, 645 P.2d 73, 77 (Wyo. 1982)), this court summarized the circumstances under which the corporate veil would be pierced pursuant to Wyoming law:

> "Before a corporation's acts and obligations can be legally recognized as those of a particular person, and vice versa, it must be made to appear that the corporation is not only influenced and governed by that person, but that there is such a unity of interest and ownership that the individuality, or separateness, of such person and corporation has ceased, and that the facts are such that an adherence to the fiction of the separate existence of the corporation would, under the particular circumstances, sanction a fraud or promote injustice. Quoting Arnold v. Browne, 27 Cal. App. 3d 386, 103 Cal. Rptr. 775 (1972) (overruled on other grounds)."

We provided the following factors to be considered in determining whether a corporate entity may be disregarded:

> "Among the possible factors pertinent to the trial court's determination are: commingling of funds and other assets, failure to segregate funds of the separate entities, and the unauthorized diversion of corporate funds or assets to other than corporate uses; the treatment by an individual of the assets of the corporation as his own; the failure to obtain authority to issue or subscribe to stock; the holding out by an individual that he is personally liable for the debts of the corporation; the failure to maintain minutes or adequate corporate records and the confusion of the records of the separate entities; the identical equitable ownership in the two entities; the identification of the equitable owners thereof with the domination and control of the two entities; identification of the directors and officers of the two entities in the responsible supervision and management; the failure to adequately capitalize a corporation; the absence of corporate assets, and undercapitalization; the use of a corporation as a mere shell, instrumentality or conduit for a single venture or the business of an individual or another corporation; the concealment and misrepresentation of the identity of the responsible ownership, management and financial interest or concealment of personal business activities; the disregard of legal formalities and the failure to maintain arm's length relationships among related entities; the use of the corporate entity to procure labor, services or merchandise for another person or entity; the diversion of assets from a corporation by or to a stockholder or other person or entity, to the detriment of creditors, or the manipulation of assets and liabilities between entities so as to concentrate the assets in one and the liabilities in another; the contracting with another with intent to avoid performance by use of a corporation as a subterfuge of illegal transactions; and the formation and use of a corporation to transfer to it the existing liability of another person or entity [citation]." 645 P.2d at 77-78 (quoting Arnold v. Browne, supra, 103 Cal. Rptr. at 781-82). Miles, 753 P.2d at 1023-24.

Wyoming courts, as well as courts across the country, have typically utilized a fact driven inquiry to determine whether circumstances justify a decision to pierce a corporate veil. Opal Mercantile, 616 P.2d at 778. This case comes to us as a certified question in the abstract with little factual context, and we are asked to broadly pronounce that there are no circumstances under which this court will look through a failed attempt to create a separate LLC entity and prevent injustice. We simply cannot reach that conclusion and believe it is improvident for this court to prohibit this remedy from applying to any unforeseen circumstance that may exist in the future.

We have long recognized that piercing the corporate veil is an equitable doctrine. State ex rel. Christensen v. Nugget Coal Co., 60 Wyo. 51, 144 P.2d 944, 952 (1944). The concept of piercing the corporate veil is a judicially created remedy for situations where corporations have not been operated as separate entities as contemplated by statute and, therefore, are not entitled to be treated as such. The determination of whether the doctrine applies centers on whether there is an element of injustice, fundamental unfairness, or inequity. The concept developed through common law and is absent from the statutes governing corporate organization. See Wyo. Stat. Ann. §§17-16-101 to -1803. Appellee Roger Flahive suggests that, by the adoption of §17-16-622(b)—a provision from the revised Model Business Corporation Act—the Wyoming legislature intended to explicitly authorize piercing in the corporate context and, by inference, prevent its application in the LLC context. A careful review of the statutory language and legislative history leads to a different conclusion. Section 17-16-622(b) reads: "Unless otherwise provided in the articles of incorporation, a shareholder of a corporation is not personally liable for the acts or debts of the corporation except that he may become personally liable by reason of his own acts or conduct." Mr. Flahive contrasts that language with the LLC statute which simply states the underlying principle of limited liability for individual members and managers. Wyo. Stat. Ann. §17-15-113. Section 17-15-113 provides:

> Neither the members of a limited liability company nor the managers of a limited liability company managed by a manager or managers are liable under a judgment, decree or order of a court, or in any other manner, for a debt, obligation or liability of the limited liability company.

However, we agree with Commentator Gelb that: "It is difficult to read statutory §17-15-113 as intended to preclude courts from deciding to disregard the veil of an improperly used LLC." Harvey Gelb, Liabilities of Members and Managers of Wyoming Limited Liability Companies, 31 Land & Water L. Rev. 133 at 142 (1996).

Section 17-16-622—the statute relied upon by Mr. Flahive as indicating legislative intent to allow piercing of the corporate veil—when considered in the context of its legislative history, provides no support for the conclusion that the legislature intended in any way to limit application of the common-law doctrine to LLCs. As previously explained, §17-16-622 was adopted from the revised Model Business Corporation Act, and the comments therein clarify that subsection (b) "sets forth the basic rule of nonliability of shareholders for corporate acts or debts that underlies modern corporation law" and "recognizes that such liability may be assumed voluntarily or by other conduct." 1 Model Bus. Corp. Act Ann. §6.22 at 6-94 to 6-95 (Supp. 1997). This provision was added in 1984 and was not intended to "treat exhaustively the statutory bases for imposing liability on shareholders." Id. at 6-96, 144 P.2d 944. The official comments in the revised Model Business Corporation Act specifically recognize the separate existence of the common law by stating: "Shareholders may also become liable for corporate obligations by their voluntary actions or by other conduct under the common law doctrine of 'piercing the corporate veil.'" Id.

We note that Wyoming was the first state to enact LLC statutes. Many years passed before the Internal Revenue Service's approval of taxation of LLCs as partnerships led to other states adopting LLC legislation and the broad usage of this form for business organizations. Wyoming's statute is very short and establishes only minimal requirements for creating and operating LLCs. It seems highly unlikely that the Wyoming legislature gave any consideration to whether the common-law doctrine of piercing the veil should apply to the liability limitation granted by that fledgling statute. It is true that some other states have adopted specific legislation extending the doctrine to LLCs while Wyoming has not. However, that situation seems more attributable to the fact that Wyoming was a pioneer in the LLC arena and states which adopted LLC statutes much later had the benefit of years of practical experience during which this issue was likely raised.

Mr. Flahive insists that, if the legislature intended for liability to be asserted against the members of an LLC, it could have added similar language to the LLC chapter at the same time it adopted provisions of the revised Model Business Corporation Act. However, adoption of those amendments in 1989, twelve years after the enactment of the LLC statutes, while remaining silent on the issue of piercing the veil in the LLC statutes, is far too attenuated to indicate a clear legislative intent to restrict application of the common law to LLCs. It stands to reason that, because it is an equitable doctrine, "[t]he paucity of statutory authority for LCC piercing should not be considered a barrier to its application." Lack of explicit statutory language should not be considered an indication of the legislature's desire to make LLC members impermeable. Moreover,

> "It is not to be presumed that the legislature intended to abrogate or modify a rule of the common law by the enactment of a statute upon the same subject; it is rather to be presumed that no change in the common law was intended unless the language employed clearly indicates such an intention. . . . The rules of common law are not to be changed by doubtful implication, nor overturned except by clear and unambiguous language." McKinney v. McKinney, [59 Wyo. 204,] 135 P.2d [940,] 942 [(1943)], quoting from 25 R.C.L. 1054, §280.

Allstate Insurance Company v. Wyoming Insurance Department, 672 P.2d 810, 824 (Wyo. 1983).

With the dearth of legislative consideration on this issue in Wyoming, we are left to determine whether applying the well established common law to LLCs somehow runs counter to what the legislature would have intended had it considered the issue. In that regard, it is instructive that: "Every state that has enacted LLC piercing legislation has chosen to follow corporate law standards and not develop a separate LLC standard." Philip P. Whynott, The Limited Liability Company §11:140 at 11-5 (3d ed. 1999). Statutes which create corporations and LLCs have the same basic purpose—to limit the liability of individual investors with a corresponding benefit to economic development. Eric Fox, Piercing the Veil of Limited Liability Companies, 62 Geo. Wash. L. Rev. 1143, 1145-46 (1994). Statutes created the legal fiction of the corporation being a completely separate entity which could act independently from individual persons. If the corporation were created and operated in conformance with the statutory requirements, the law would treat it as a separate entity and shelter the individual shareholders from any liability caused by corporate action, thereby encouraging investment.

However, courts throughout the country have consistently recognized certain unjust circumstances can arise if immunity from liability shelters those who have failed to operate a corporation as a separate entity. Consequently, when corporations fail to follow the statutorily mandated formalities, co-mingle funds, or ignore the restrictions in their articles of incorporation regarding separate treatment of corporate property, the courts deem it appropriate to disregard the separate identity and do not permit shareholders to be sheltered from liability to third parties for damages caused by the corporations' acts.

We can discern no reason, in either law or policy, to treat LLCs differently than we treat corporations. If the members and officers of an LLC fail to treat it as a separate entity as contemplated by statute, they should not enjoy immunity from individual liability for the LLC's acts that cause damage to third parties. Most, if not all, of the expert LLC commentators have concluded the doctrine of piercing the veil should apply to LLCs. It also appears that most courts faced with a similar situation—LLC statutes which are silent and facts which suggest the LLC veil should be pierced—have had little trouble concluding the common law should be applied and the factors weighed accordingly. See, e.g., Hollowell v. Orleans Regional Hospital, No. Civ. A. 95-4029, 1998 WL 283298 (E.D. La. May 29, 1998); Ditty v. CheckRite, Ltd., Inc., 973 F. Supp. 1320 (D. Utah 1997); Tom Thumb Food Markets, Inc. v. TLH Properties, LLC, No. C9-98-1277, 1999 WL 31168 (Minn. Ct. App. Jan. 26, 1999).

Certainly, the various factors which would justify piercing an LLC veil would not be identical to the corporate situation for the obvious reason that many of the organizational formalities applicable to corporations do not apply to LLCs. The LLC's operation is intended to be much more flexible than a corporation's. Factors relevant to determining when to pierce the corporate veil have developed over time in a multitude of cases. It would be inadvisable in this case, which lacks a complete factual context, to attempt to articulate all the possible factors to be applied to LLCs in Wyoming in the future. . . .

The certified question presents an interesting internal inconsistency. It begins, "In the absence of fraud," thereby presenting the assumption that a court may pierce an LLC's veil in a case of fraud. Thus, the certified question assumes that, when fraud is found, the courts are able to disregard the LLC entity despite the statutory framework which supposedly precludes such a result. Either the courts continue to possess the equitable power to take such action or they do not. Certainly, nothing in the statutes suggests the legislature gave such careful consideration and delineated the specific circumstances under which the courts can act in this arena. If the assumption is correct, individual LLC members can be held personally liable for damages to innocent third parties when the LLC has committed fraud. Yet, when the LLC has caused damage and has inadequate capitalization, co-mingled funds, diverted assets, or used the LLC as a mere shell, individual members are immune from liability. Legislative silence cannot be stretched to condone such an illogical result.

In *Amfac Mechanical Supply Co.,* this court clarified that a showing of fraud or an intent to defraud is not necessary to disregard a corporate entity. 645 P.2d at 79. We clearly stated: "Fraud is, of course, a matter of concern in suits to disregard corporate fictions, but it is not a prerequisite to such a result." Id. Other courts have echoed this view: "Liability on the basis of fraud, however, does not encompass the entire spectrum of cases in which the veil was pierced in the interest of equity." Fox, supra at 1169. Thus, even absent fraud, courts have the power to impose liability on corporate shareholders. Id. at 1170. This same logic should naturally be extended to the LLC context. We have made clear that: "Each case involving the disregard of the separate entity doctrine must be governed by the special facts of that case." *Opal Mercantile*, 616 P.2d at 778. Determinations of fact are within the trier of fact's province. Id. The district court must complete a fact intensive inquiry and exercise its equitable powers to determine whether piercing the veil is appropriate under the circumstances presented in this case.

CONCLUSION

No reason exists in law or equity for treating an LLC differently than a corporation is treated when considering whether to disregard the legal entity. We conclude the equitable remedy of piercing the veil is an available remedy under the Wyoming Limited Liability Company Act.

NOTES AND QUESTIONS

1. LLC statutes uniformly include a provision protecting members and managers from liability, but these provisions are not uniform across jurisdictions. Some (but only in a relatively small number of states) make a specific analogy to corporate principles. A few states identify specific parts of the common law of piercing that are not to be followed: for example, failure to follow entity formalities is not a reason to pierce the veil. Some of the statutes codify for LLCs a principle we saw in subpart 2 of Part C: the limited liability shield does not block participant liability for one's own tortious acts. Still other statutes provide limited liability with no limitation, which could provide participants even broader protection than the corporate shield. Despite these statutory differences, there is no discernible difference in the corporate and the LLC piercing cases. Indeed, not only do courts apply traditional common law corporate veil-piercing principles to LLCs, but they also often write opinions as if the LLC were in fact a corporation, oblivious to the separate status of the LLC.

2. LLP statutes add another wrinkle to piercing the limited liability shield. Almost all of the LLP statutes contain a specific reference to the partner's liability for his or her own negligence, a principle consistent with the professional context of many of these entities and consistent with the cases in subpart 2 above, where participants are held liable for their own wrongful acts. In addition, many of these statutes extend this direct liability beyond one's own actions to include negligent actions of another under the partner's direct supervision and control. This opens up the possibility of vicarious individual liability that is possible under agency and tort principles but that has not been made explicit in corporate decisions or statutes. As yet there are no indications that this broader statutory language will result in vicarious liability. More generally there was some suggestion that possible holes in the liability shield of Arthur Andersen's LLP affected the firm's decision in 2002 in the wake of the Enron scandal not to try to continue as a going concern.

5. **Relationship of Corporate Separateness Principles
    and Equitable Principles Holding Human Controllers
    of Entity Fiduciaries Liable**

Feeley v. NHAOCG, LLC
Delaware Court of Chancery, 2012
62 A.3d 649

LASTER, Vice Chancellor.

[Two groups of investors formed Oculus Capital Group, LLC, sharing ownership 50/50. Each of the two ownership groups was in turn an LLC. The managing member of Oculus, AK-Feel, LLC, was made up of Christopher J. Feeley and Andrea Akel, who had worked together at another company and wanted to strike out on their own. Feeley was the managing member of this LLC and in that capacity controlled the activities of both AK-Feel and Oculus. In addition, Feeley was president and CEO of Oculus. The nonmanaging member of Oculus was composed of entities affiliated with: George Akel, Andrea's father, to whom she had turned after other sources of finance proved unavailable; David Newman, who in the past had invested with George Akel; and David Hughes, who in the past had invested with Newman (collectively "NHA"). NHA alleged that "Feeley failed miserably" in his managerial roles at Oculus and that his supposed acumen as a financier proved illusory; the NHA parties were particularly angry about the only project he arguably found, the "Gatherings," which they said ended in disaster due to Feeley's gross negligence. The control dispute that sparked litigation was resolved, so that what remained of the litigation was NHA's counterclaim seeking to recover damages from AK-Feel and Feeley for the failed Gatherings transactions and certain related claims.]

2. THE CLAIM AGAINST FEELEY AS CONTROLLER OF AK-FEEL

Feeley contends that NHA cannot sue him for breach of fiduciary duty as the managing member of AK-Feel, because to do so would disregard the separate existence of AK-Feel. Feeley equates this result to piercing AK-Feel's corporate veil, and he contends that NHA has not carried the heavy burden Delaware law imposes on a party seeking to pierce. Feeley's argument improperly seeks to apply principles of corporate separateness that govern claims brought by third parties to the fiduciary relationships that exist within a business venture. But although Feeley can be sued by NHA for breach of fiduciary duty in his capacity as the party who controls AK-Feel, he cannot be sued in that capacity for breach of the duty of care.

As Feeley correctly observes, the separate legal existence of juridical entities is fundamental to Delaware law. Delaware law likewise respects the correlative principle of limited liability, which generally enables those who form entities to limit their risk to the amount of their investment in the entity. . . .

Numerous legal rules and doctrines circumvent the general principles of corporate separateness and legal liability. A government may choose to impose liability directly on owners or managers for certain types of activities. *See* Thompson, [The Limits of Liability in the New Limited Liability Entities, 32 Wake Forest L. Rev. 1,] 12 & n. 59. The doctrine of piercing the corporate veil allows courts to permit contractual creditors to reach the assets of the owners of the entity based on a multi-factor test. *See id.* at 9-10. Courts also may use piercing to benefit tort claimants, who additionally can recover from the individuals who committed the tort. *See id.* at 12; *see also* Robert B. Thompson, Piercing the Corporate Veil: An Empirical Study, 76 Cornell L. Rev. 1036, 1058 (1991) (reviewing statistical occurrence of piercing cases based on an underlying tort).

The doctrine of piercing the corporate veil traditionally has not been applied to address internal claims of mismanagement or self-dealing brought by investors against the entity's decision-makers. In the corporate context, historically the predominant limited liability vehicle, it has been unnecessary. The authority and concomitant duty to manage a Delaware corporation rests with the board of directors. *See* 8 *Del. C.* §141(a). The members of a board of directors of a Delaware corporation must be natural persons. *See* 8 *Del. C.* §141(d). Those individuals owe fiduciary duties of loyalty and care to the corporation. *See* Mills Acq. Co. v. Macmillan, Inc., 559 A.2d 1261, 1280 (Del. 1989). Those duties require that the directors exercise their managerial authority on an informed basis in the good faith pursuit of maximizing the value of the corporation for the benefit of its residual claimants, *viz.*, the stockholders. *See* eBay Domestic Hldgs., Inc. v. Newmark, 16 A.3d 1, 35 (Del. Ch. 2010). When stockholders contend that the board members breached their duties, a right of action exists (directly or derivatively) against natural persons.

Breach of fiduciary duty is an equitable claim, and it is a maxim of equity that "equity regards substance rather than form." Monroe Park v. Metro. Life Ins. Co., 457 A.2d 734, 737 (Del. 1983); *accord* Gatz v. Ponsoldt, 925 A.2d 1265, 1280 (Del. 2007) ("It is the very nature of equity to look beyond form to the substance of an arrangement."). Courts applying equitable principles therefore had little trouble extending liability for breach of fiduciary duty beyond the natural persons who served as directors to outsiders like majority stockholders who effectively controlled the corporation. *See, e.g.,* S. Pac. Co. v. Bogert, 250 U.S. 483, 488, 39 S. Ct. 533, 63 L. Ed. 1099 (1919); Sterling v. Mayflower Hotel Corp., 33 Del. Ch. 293, 298, 93 A.2d 107, 110 (Del. 1952). And because the application of equitable principles depended on the substance of control rather than the form, it did not matter whether the control was exercised directly or indirectly through subsidiaries. The United States Supreme Court's rejection of the corporate separateness argument in *Southern Pacific* is illustrative:

> The Southern Pacific contends that the doctrine under which majority stockholders exercising control are deemed trustees for the minority should not be applied here, because it did not itself own directly any stock in the old Houston Company; its control being exerted through a subsidiary, Morgan's Louisiana & Texas Railroad & Steamship Company, which was the majority stockholder in the old Houston Company. But the doctrine by which the holders of a majority of the stock of a corporation who dominate its affairs are held to act as trustee for the minority does not rest upon such technical distinctions. It is the fact of control of the common property held and exercised, not the particular means by which or manner in which the control is exercised, that creates the fiduciary obligation.

250 U.S. at 491-92, 39 S. Ct. 533. Delaware corporate decisions consistently have looked to who wields control in substance and have imposed the risk of fiduciary liability on the actual controllers.[3]

The Delaware alternative entity statutes highlight the tension between corporate separateness and the outcomes achieved in equity by imposing fiduciary duties on those actually in control. Delaware's original alternative entity statute, the LP Act, does not restrict service as a general partner to natural persons, opening the door to corporations serving in that role. [See 6 Del. C. §17–101(5).] At the same time, the LP Act declares as public policy the goal of granting the broadest freedom of contract possible. [See 6 Del. C. §17–101(5).] Other Delaware alternative entity statutes, including the LLC Act and the Delaware Statutory Trusts Act, are modeled on the LP Act, permit entities to serve in managerial roles, and adopt the same policy of maximizing freedom of contract. [See 6 Del. C. 18–1101(b).]

This Court soon confronted the question of what to do with the human controllers of an entity fiduciary. In In re USACafes, L.P. Litigation, 600 A.2d 43 (Del. Ch. 1991), Chancellor Allen considered whether limited partners of USACafes, L.P., could sue the directors of USACafes General Partner, Inc., its corporate general partner, for breach of fiduciary duty. Defendants Sam and Charles Wyly comprised two of the six directors on the board of the corporate general partner, owned 100% the stock of the corporate general partner, and held 47% of the limited partnership units. In the challenged transaction, USACafes sold its assets to Metsa Acquisition Corp., a third party acquirer, for $72.6 million, representing $10.25 per partnership unit. Metsa paid an additional $15 to $17 million to the Wylys and the other directors of the corporate general partner in the form of consideration for covenants not to compete, releases of claims, forgiveness of loans, and payments under employment agreements. See id. at 47-48. The defendants conceded that the general partner owed fiduciary duties to the limited partners, but they argued that the members of the board of the corporate general partner only owed fiduciary duties to its stockholders, not to the limited partners. Id.

Chancellor Allen rejected the defendants' argument. Finding no precedent on point, Chancellor Allen started from the general principle that "one who controls property of another may not, without express or implied agreement, intentionally use that property in a way that benefits the holder of the control to the detriment of the property or its beneficial owner." Id. at 48. He then noted the equitable tradition of looking to the substance of where control lay, observing that "[w]hen control over corporate property was recognized to be in the hands of the shareholders who controlled the enterprise, the fiduciary duty was found to extend to such persons as well." Id. Analogizing the corporate general partner to a corporate trustee, a structure where there was a longer tradition of an entity acting as fiduciary, Chancellor Allen noted that courts held the individuals who controlled or made decisions on behalf of the corporate trustee liable for breaches of trust. See id. at 48-49 (citing 4 A. Scott & W. Fratcher, The Law of Trusts §326.03, at 304-06 (4th ed.1989)). He concluded that

---

3. See Kahn v. Lynch Commc'n Sys. Inc., 638 A.2d 110, 11-14 (Del. 1994) (holding that 43% stockholder that exercised actual control over subsidiary could be liable for breach of fiduciary duty) . . .

"[t]he theory underlying fiduciary duties is consistent with recognition that a director of a corporate general partner bears such a duty towards the limited partnership." *Id.* at 49.

> Consider, for example, a classic self-dealing transaction: assume that a majority of the board of the corporate general partner formed a new entity and then caused the general partner to sell partnership assets to the new entity at an unfairly small price, injuring the partnership and its limited partners. Can it be imagined that such persons have not breached a duty to the partnership itself? And does it not make perfect sense to say that the gist of the offense is a breach of the equitable duty of loyalty that is placed upon a fiduciary?

Id. Chancellor Allen recognized that the resulting fiduciary duty "may well not be so broad as the duty of the director of a corporate trustee." *Id.* He left to future cases the task of delineating the full scope of the duty, holding only that "it surely entails the duty not to use control over the partnership's property to advantage the corporate director at the expense of the partnership." *Id.*

In subsequent decisions involving limited partnerships, this Court has followed *USACafes* consistently, holding that the individuals and entities who control the general partner owe to the limited partners at a minimum the duty of loyalty identified in *USACafes*. This Court's decisions also have extended the doctrine to other alternative entities, such as LLCs and statutory trusts. In doing so, this Court has noted the tension between corporate separateness and the application of fiduciary principles, but has nevertheless adhered to *USACafes. See* Gelfman [v. Weedon Investors, L.P. 792 A.2d 977 (applying *USACafes* to directors and officers of corporate general partner)]; *Gotham P'rs, L.P.,* 795 A.2d at 34 (Del. Ch. 2001).

The Delaware Supreme Court indisputably has the authority to revisit this Court's approach and address the tensions created by *USACafes.* The high court might hold, contrary to *USACafes,* that when parties bargain for an entity to serve as the fiduciary, that entity is the fiduciary, and the parties cannot later circumvent their agreement by invoking concepts of control or aiding and abetting. Or the high court might distinguish between cases involving default fiduciary duties, in which traditional equitable principles of control and aiding and abetting could be permitted to extend liability beyond the entity fiduciary, and cases involving purely contractual duties, in which parties would be limited to contractual remedies against their contractual counterparties. Doubtless many other approaches could be envisioned. But in this Court, and for purposes of this decision, *USACafes* and its progeny are *stare decisis.*

Feeley therefore can be reached and potentially held liable for breach of fiduciary duty in his capacity as the controller of AK-Feel. In Count IV, however, NHA seeks to hold Feeley liable only for a breach of the duty of care. Chancellor Allen noted in *USACafes* that while the parties in control of a corporate general partner are fiduciaries, the duties they owe "may well not be so broad as the duty of the director of a corporate trustee." 600 A.2d at 49; *see also id.* at n. 3 (declining to determine if corporate opportunity theory or waste theories could be pursued against a controlling general partner). *USACafes* has not been extended beyond duty of loyalty claims. *See Bay Ctr.,* 2009 WL 1124451, at *10 ("In practice, the cases applying *USACafes* have not ventured beyond the clear application stated in *USACafes:* the duty not to use control over the partnership's property to advantage the corporate director at the expense of the partnership." (internal quotation marks omitted)). Because Count IV only asserts claims against Feeley for gross negligence, it is dismissed.

D. Ambiguous or Legally Defective Allocation of the Risk of Loss

1. Introduction

Parts B and C examined the protection provided voluntary and involuntary creditors by statutory rules governing a corporation's capital structure and by judicial willingness to pierce the entity's veil. The central concern of those parts was an inquiry into what investors must do, in general, to be entitled to limited liability.

Part D turns to the problem of how courts should resolve disputes between insiders and outsiders where there has been actual bargaining, but bargaining that has resulted in an ambiguous or legally defective allocation of the risk of loss. This is a traditional contract law problem, but it is complicated in the corporate area by limited liability and the artificiality of the corporate entity. Concerns arise as to three particular problems. The first, considered in subpart 2, is who shall bear the loss from contracts intended to bind a corporation that does not exist at the time of contract formation, either because it has not yet been formed or because it has been dissolved. The second problem, introduced in subpart 3, is who shall bear the loss from unauthorized actions by corporate agents who purport to act for their corporation. The final problem, also examined in subpart 3, is who shall bear the loss on contracts that commit the corporation to do something beyond its power.

2. Contracts on Behalf of Nonexistent Entities

a. Introduction

MBCA §§2.03, 14.20

A corporation is an artificial entity. It is created upon the filing of articles of incorporation with the secretary of state. See MBCA §2.03. And it continues to exist until dissolved, whether by (1) voluntary action of directors and shareholders (see MBCA §§14.01-14.05), (2) involuntary dissolution by administrative decree (see MBCA §14.20), or (3) involuntary dissolution by judicial decree (see §14.30).

The existence or nonexistence of a corporation is significant in a contract setting for two reasons. First, if the corporation does not exist, then it cannot have any agents. In other words, individuals cannot act for a corporation before it is formed or after it is dissolved, because there is no corporation to act as the principal. Second, if the corporation does not exist, then actions taken by individuals to benefit the nonexistent principal will not be protected by the general agency law rule (so long as she does not exceed her authority, an agent is not a party to, or personally liable with respect to, contracts she makes as agent for her principal).

Contracts to benefit a nonexistent corporation occur in two settings—before incorporation occurs, and during periods when a corporation has been dissolved by the state for failure to pay taxes, make required annual reports, maintain a registered agent or office, or other similar reasons. And, during those periods, contracts may be entered into, purportedly for the benefit of nonexistent corporations, with creditors who have full knowledge that the corporation is then nonexistent or with creditors who have no actual or constructive knowledge that the corporation does not then exist.

Both creditors and those who act for a nonexistent corporation may face unexpected difficulties in enforcing their contractual expectations. When a creditor's expectations with respect to a contract executed on behalf of a then nonexistent corporation are not fulfilled, then the creditor may seek to enforce his rights by judicial action. If the corporation on whose behalf the contract was executed now exists, and if that corporation has a deep pocket, the creditor may sue the corporation. However, the corporation may be able to defend successfully, particularly if the contract is executory. The corporation will correctly assert that since it did not exist when the contract was made, it did not become a party to the contract as a result of the actions of those persons who did act. Moreover, the corporation will argue, it has not subsequently expressly or impliedly adopted the contract.

The deep pocket may belong not to the corporation but to the corporation's officers, directors, shareholders, or promoters. Undoubtedly, these corporate insiders expected, reasonably or not, that they would not be personally liable on contracts entered into for the then nonexistent corporation's benefit. The remainder of this section examines corporate law rules determining whether those insiders' expectations of limited liability will be fulfilled. The examination focuses on two settings—first, situations in which insiders acting for a nonexistent corporation attempted to contract around the personal liability that would normally result from contracting as an unincorporated principal or co-principal, and, second, situations in which insiders acting for a nonexistent corporation made no attempt to contract around personal liability.

As you read these materials, consider what is required to contract around the default rule of unlimited personal liability. In what circumstances should a court shield insiders from personal liability even if they have ambiguously or defectively contracted around personal liability? To what extent should courts seek to ascertain the parties' true intent?

b. Ambiguous Attempts to Contract Around Personal Liability

RKO-Stanley Warner Theatres, Inc. v. Graziano
Pennsylvania Supreme Court, 1976
467 Pa. 220, 355 A.2d 830

EAGEN, JUSTICE.

On April 30, 1970, RKO-Stanley Warner Theatres, Inc., (RKO), as seller, entered into an agreement of sale with Jack Jenofsky and Ralph Graziano, as purchasers. This agreement contemplated the sale of the Kent Theatre, a parcel of improved commercial real estate located at Cumberland and Kensington Avenues in Philadelphia, for a total purchase price of $70,000.[1] Settlement was originally scheduled for September 30, 1970, and, at the request of Jenofsky and Graziano, continued twice, first to October 16, 1970 and then to October 21, 1970. However, Jenofsky and Graziano failed to complete settlement on the last scheduled date.

Subsequently, on November 13, 1970, RKO filed a complaint in equity seeking judicial enforcement of the agreement of sale. Although Jenofsky, in his answer to the complaint,[3] denied personal liability for the performance of the agreement, the chancellor, after a hearing, entered a decree nisi granting the requested relief sought by RKO. . . . This appeal ensued.

At the time of the execution of this agreement, Jenofsky and Graziano were engaged in promoting the formation of a corporation to be known as Kent Enterprises, Inc. Reflecting these efforts, Paragraph 19 of the agreement, added by counsel for Jenofsky and Graziano, recited:

> It is understood by the parties hereto that it is the intention of the Purchaser to incorporate. Upon condition that such incorporation be completed by closing, all agreements, covenants, and warranties contained herein shall be construed to have been made between Seller and the resultant corporation and all documents shall reflect same.

In fact, Jenofsky and Graziano did file Articles of Incorporation for Kent Enterprises, Inc., with the State Corporation Bureau on October 9, 1970; twelve days prior to the scheduled settlement date. Jenofsky now contends the inclusion of Paragraph 19 in the agreement and the subsequent filing of incorporation papers, released him from any personal liability resulting from the non-performance of the agreement.

The legal relationship of Jenofsky to Kent Enterprises, Inc., at the date of the execution of the agreement of sale was that of promoter. As such, he is subject to the general rule that a promoter, although he may assume to act on behalf of a projected corporation and not for himself, will be held personally liable on contracts made by him for the benefit of a corporation he intends to organize. This personal liability will continue even after the contemplated corporation is formed and has received the benefits of the contract, unless there is a novation or other agreement to release liability.

The imposition of personal liability upon a promoter where that promoter has contracted on behalf of a corporation is based upon the principle that one who assumes to act for a nonexistent principal is himself liable on the contract in the absence of an agreement to the contrary. As stated in Comment (a) under §326 of the Restatement of Agency, Second: "there is an inference that a person intends to make a present contract with an existing person. If, therefore, the other party knows that there is no

---

1. The purchase price of $70,000 was to be payable as follows: (1) $2,500 at or prior to the execution of the agreement; (2) $22,500 in cash or certified check upon delivery of the deed; and (3) the execution and delivery by Jenofsky and Graziano to RKO of a purchase money mortgage in the principal sum of $45,000, with interest thereon at 8%.

3. The chancellor ordered Jenofsky and Graziano to pay $22,500 to RKO and to execute and deliver to RKO their note and purchase money mortgage in the principal sum of $45,000 in accordance with the terms of the agreement.

principal capable of entering into such a contract, there is a rebuttable inference that, although the contract is nominally in the name of the nonexistent person, the parties intend that the person signing as agent should be a party, unless there is some indication to the contrary."

However, even though a contract is executed by a promoter on behalf of a proposed corporation, where the person with whom the contract is made agrees to look to the corporation alone for responsibility, the promoter incurs no personal liability with respect to the contract.

In O'Rorke v. Geary, 207 Pa. 240, 56 A. 541 (1903), wherein this Court affirmed on the basis of the opinion of the court below, there is set forth the three possible understandings that parties may have when an agreement is executed by a promoter on behalf of a proposed corporation. It is stated therein:

> When a party is acting for a proposed corporation, he cannot, of course, bind it by anything he does, at the time, but he may (1) take on its behalf an offer from the other which, being accepted after the formation of the company, becomes a contract; (2) make a contract at the time binding himself, with the stipulation or understanding, that if a company is formed it will take his place and that then he shall be relieved of responsibility; or (3) bind himself personally without more and look to the proposed company, when formed, for indemnity. (Id. at 242, 56 A. at 542.)

Both RKO and Jenofsky concede the applicability of alternative No. 2 to the instant case. That is, they both recognize that Jenofsky (and Graziano) was to be initially personally responsible with this personal responsibility subsequently being released. Jenofsky contends the parties, by their inclusion of Paragraph 19 in the agreement, manifested an intention to release him from personal responsibility upon the mere formation of the proposed corporation, provided the incorporation was consummated prior to the scheduled closing date. However, while Paragraph 19 does make provision for recognition of the resultant corporation as to the closing documents, it makes no mention of any release of personal liability. Indeed, the entire agreement is silent as to the effect the formation of the projected corporation would have upon the personal liability of Jenofsky and Graziano. Because the agreement fails to provide expressly for the release of personal liability, it is, therefore, subject to more than one possible construction.

In Consolidated Tile and Slate Co. v. Fox, 410 Pa. 336, 339, 189 A.2d 228, 229 (1963), we stated that where an agreement is ambiguous and reasonably susceptible of two interpretations, "it must be construed most strongly against those who drew it." We further stated, "if the language of the contract is ambiguous and susceptible of two interpretations, one of which makes it fair, customary and such as prudent men would naturally execute, while the other makes it inequitable, unusual, or such as reasonable men would not likely enter into, the construction which makes it rational and probable must be preferred." Instantly, the chancellor determined that the intent of the parties to the agreement was to hold Jenofsky personally responsible until such time as a corporate entity was formed and until such time as that corporate entity adopted the agreement. We believe this construction represents the only rational and prudent interpretation of the parties' intent.

As found by the court below, this agreement was entered into on the financial strength of Jenofsky and Graziano, alone as individuals. Therefore, it would have been illogical for RKO to have consented to the release of their personal liability upon the mere formation of a resultant corporation prior to closing, for it is a well-settled rule that a contract made by a promoter, even though made for and in the name of a proposed corporation, in the absence of a subsequent adoption (either expressly or impliedly) by the corporation, will not be binding upon the corporation. If, as Jenofsky contends, the intent was to release personal responsibility upon the mere incorporation prior to closing, the effect of the agreement would have been to create the possibility that RKO, in the event of non-performance, would be able to hold no party accountable; there being no guarantee that the resultant corporation would ratify the agreement.[5] Without express language in the agreement indicating that such was the intention of the parties, we may not attribute this intention to them.

Therefore, we hold that the intent of the parties in entering into this agreement was to have Jenofsky and Graziano personally liable until such time as the intended corporation was formed and ratified the agreement.[6]

Decree affirmed. . . .

MANDERINO, JUSTICE (dissenting).

I dissent. Contrary to the majority's finding that the agreement was ambiguous because of its failure to provide expressly for the release of appellant Jenofsky from personal liability, I find clear on the face of paragraph 19 of the agreement an intention to release Jenofsky from personal liability upon the mere formation of the proposed corporation, provided the incorporation was completed prior to the scheduled closing date. According to paragraph 19, once the incorporation was completed, "all agreements . . . [would] be construed to have been made between the seller and the resultant corporation. . . ."

It is inconceivable to me how the majority can agree with the Chancellor's finding that Jenofsky was to be personally responsible until the new corporation in some way adopted the agreement. There is no language anywhere in the agreement to suggest such a far-fetched interpretation. Paragraph 19 clearly states that Jenofsky was to be released from personal liability as soon as the corporation was formed.

Nor is it our duty to decide the logic, or lack of logic, of the parties in entering into this agreement. This was not a contract of adhesion, and, just because we might not have entered into the same contract, we nevertheless cannot read beyond its clearly intended meaning. I would therefore reverse the decision of the court en banc.

---

5. In this regard, we note that there is no allegation by Jenofsky that Kent Enterprises, Inc., either expressly adopted or attempted to ratify the agreement entered into with RKO.

6. We are buttressed in this conclusion by reference to alternative No. 2, set forth in O'Rorke v. Geary, supra, and conceded by both parties to represent their intentions herein. This alternative clearly envisions some affirmative action by the projected corporation before the release of the promoter's personal liability will be effected, i.e., "if a company is formed *it will take his place.*" (Emphasis supplied.) Similarly, Comment (b) under §326 of the Restatement of Agency, Second, provides that parties "may agree to a present contract by which the promoter is bound, but with an agreement that his liability terminates if the corporation is formed *and manifests its willingness to become a party.*" (Emphasis supplied.)

*c.   Allocating Losses When Insiders Make No Attempt
to Contract Around Personal Liability*

MBCA §2.04

Timberline Equipment Co. v. Davenport
Oregon Supreme Court, 1973
267 Or. 64, 514 P.2d 1109

DENECKE, JUSTICE.

Plaintiff brought this action for equipment rentals against the defendant Dr. Bennett and two others. In addition to making a general denial, Dr. Bennett alleged as a defense that the rentals were to a de facto corporation, Aero-Fabb Corp., of which Dr. Bennett was an incorporator, director and shareholder. He also alleged plaintiff was estopped from denying the corporate character of the organization to whom plaintiff rented the equipment. The trial court held for plaintiff. Dr. Bennett, only, appeals.

On January 22, 1970, Dr. Bennett signed articles of incorporation for Aero-Fabb Co. The original articles were not in accord with the statutes and, therefore, no certificate of incorporation was issued for the corporation until June 12, 1970, after new articles were filed. The leases were entered into and rentals earned during the period between January 22nd and June 12th.

Prior to 1953 Oregon had adopted the common-law doctrine that prohibited a collateral attack on the legality of a defectively organized corporation which had achieved the status of a de facto corporation.

In 1953 the legislature adopted the Oregon Business Corporation Act. The Model Business Corporation Act was used as a working model for the Oregon Act.

ORS 57.321 of the Oregon Business Corporation Act provides:

> Upon the issuance of the certificate of incorporation, the corporate existence shall begin, and such certificate of incorporation shall be conclusive evidence that all conditions precedent required to be performed by the incorporators have been complied with and that the corporation has been incorporated under the Oregon Business Corporation Act, except as against this state in a proceeding to cancel or revoke the certificate of incorporation or for involuntary dissolution of the corporation.

This section is virtually identical to §56 of the [pre-1984] Model Act. The Comment to the Model, prepared as a research project by the American Bar Foundation and edited by the American Bar Association Committee on Corporate Laws, states:

> Under the Model Act, de jure incorporation is complete upon the issuance of the certificate of incorporation, except as against the state in certain proceedings challenging the corporate existence. In this respect, the Model Act provisions are the same as those in many states, although in a number of them some further action is required before the corporation has legal existence, such as local filing or recording or publication.

Under the unequivocal provisions of the Model Act, any steps short of securing a certificate of incorporation would not constitute apparent compliance. Therefore a de facto corporation cannot exist under the Model Act.

Like provisions are made throughout the Model Act in respect of the conclusiveness of the issuance by the secretary of state of the appropriate certificate in connection with filings made in his office. . . .

In some states, however, issuance of the certificate of incorporation and compliance with any additional requirements for filing, recording or publication is not conclusive evidence of incorporation. In those states, such action is stated to be only prima facie evidence of incorporation, and in others the effect is merely one of estoppel preventing any question of due incorporation being raised in legal actions by or against the corporation. (Model Business Corporation Act Annotated §56, p. 205 (2d ed. 1971)).

ORS 57.793 provides:

> All persons who assume to act as a corporation without the authority of a certificate of incorporation issued by the Corporation Commissioner, shall be jointly and severally liable for all debts and liabilities incurred or arising as a result thereof.

This is merely an elaboration of §146 of the [pre-1984] Model Act. The Comment states:

> This section is designed to prohibit the application of any theory of de facto incorporation. The only authority to act as a corporation under the Model Act arises from completion of the procedures prescribed in §§53 to 55 inclusive. The consequences of those procedures are specified in §56 as being the creation of a corporation. No other means being authorized, the effect of §146 is to negate the possibility of a de facto corporation.
>
> Abolition of the concept of de facto incorporation, which at best was fuzzy, is a sound result. No reason exists for its continuance under general corporate laws, where the process of acquiring de jure incorporation is both simple and clear. The vestigial appendage should be removed. (2 Model Business Corporation Act Annotated §146, pp. 908-909 (2d ed. 1971)). . . .

We hold the principle of de facto corporation no longer exists in Oregon.

The defendant also contends that the plaintiff is estopped to deny that it contracted with a corporation.

The doctrine of "corporation by estoppel" has been recognized by this court but never fully dissected. Corporation by estoppel is a difficult concept to grasp and courts and writers have "gone all over the lot" in attempting to define and apply the doctrine. One of the better explanations of the problem and the varied solutions is contained in Ballantine, Manual of Corporation Law and Practice §§28-30 (1930):

> The so-called estoppel that arises to deny corporate capacity does not depend on the presence of the technical elements of equitable estoppel, viz., misrepresentations and change of position in reliance thereon, but on the nature of the relations contemplated, that one who has recognized the organization as a corporation in business dealings should not be allowed to quibble or raise immaterial issues on matters which do not concern him in the slightest degree or affect his substantial rights. (Ballantine, supra, at 92.)

As several writers have pointed out, in order to apply the doctrine correctly, the cases must be classified according to who is being charged with estoppel. Ballantine, supra, at 91; 1 Hornstein, Corporation Law and Practice §30, p. 31, n.6 (1959).

When a defendant seeks to escape liability to a corporation plaintiff by contending that the plaintiff is not a lawful corporate entity, courts readily apply the doctrine of corporation by estoppel. Thompson Optical Institute v. Thompson, (119 Or. 252, 237 P. 965), well illustrates the equity of the doctrine in this class of cases. R.A. Thompson carried on an optical business for years. He then organized a corporation to buy his optical business and subscribed to most of the stock in this corporation. He chaired the first meeting at which the Board resolved to purchase the business from him. The corporation and Thompson entered into a contract for the sale of the business which included a covenant by Thompson not to compete. Thereafter, Thompson sold all of his stock to another individual. Some years later Thompson re-entered the optical business in violation of the covenant not to compete. The corporation brought suit to restrain Thompson from competing. Thompson defended upon the ground that the corporation had not been legally organized. We held, "The defendant cannot be heard to challenge the validity of the contract or the proper organization of the corporation." 119 Or. at 260, 237 P. at 968.

The fairness of estopping a defendant such as Thompson from denying the corporate existence of his creation is apparent.

On the other hand, when individuals such as the defendants in this case seek to escape liability by contending that the debtor is a corporation, Aero-Fabb Co., rather than the individual who purported to act as a corporation, the courts are more reluctant to estop the plaintiff from attacking the legality of the alleged debtor corporation.

The most appealing explanation of why the plaintiff may be estopped is based upon the intention of the parties. The creditor-plaintiff contracted believing it could look for payment only to the corporate entity. The associates, whatever their relationship to the supposed corporate entity, believed their only potential liability was the loss of their investment in the supposed corporate entity and that they were not personally liable.

From the plaintiff-creditor's viewpoint, such reasoning is somewhat tenuous. The creditor did nothing to create the appearance that the debtor was a legal corporate entity. The creditor formed its intention to contract with a debtor corporate entity because someone associated with the debtor represented, expressly or impliedly, that the debtor was a legal corporate entity.

We need not decide whether the doctrine of corporation by estoppel would apply in such a case as this. The trial court found that if this doctrine was still available under the Business Corporation Act defendants did not prove all the elements necessary for its application, and, moreover, it would be inequitable to apply the doctrine.

Under the explanation stated above for the application of the doctrine of estoppel in this kind of case, it is necessary that the plaintiff believe that it was contracting with a corporate entity. The evidence on this point is contradictory and the trial court apparently found against defendants.

The trial court found, and its findings are supported by the evidence, that all the defendants were partners prior to January 1970 and did business under the name "Aero-Fabb Co." Not until June 1970 were the interests in this partnership assigned to the corporation "Aero-Fabb Co." and about the same time the assumed business name "Aero-Fabb Co." was cancelled.

The trial court found, and the evidence supported the finding, that two of the leases entered into by plaintiff were with "Kenneth L. Davenport, dba Aero-Fabb Co." The other was with "Kenneth L. Davenport, dba Aero-Fabb Corp." "Aero-Fabb Corp."

was never the corporate name; the name of the corporation for which a certificate was finally issued was "Aero-Fabb Co." The correspondence and records of plaintiff sometimes referred to the debtor as "Aero-Fabb Co." and others as "Aero-Fabb Corp."

Plaintiff's bookkeeper testified that she thought it was a corporation because, "This was the way the information was given to me." It is uncertain whether the information was given to her by someone employed by plaintiff or by a company with whom she made a credit check. In any event, plaintiff's salesman said Mr. Davenport, speaking for the organization, stated several times that he was in a partnership with Drs. Gorman and Bennett. The salesman was dubious and checked the title to the land on which the debtors' operation was being conducted and found it was in the name of the three defendants as individuals.

A final question remains: Can the plaintiff recover against Dr. Bennett individually?

In the first third of this century the liability of persons associated with defectively organized corporations was a controversial and well-documented legal issue. The orthodox view was that if an organization had not achieved de facto status and the plaintiff was not estopped to attack the validity of the corporate status of the corporation, all shareholders were liable as partners. This court, however, rejected the orthodox rule. In Rutherford v. Hill, 22 Or. 218, 29 P. 546, 29 Am. St. R. 596, 17 L.R.A. 549 (1892), we held that a person could not be held liable as a partner merely because he signed the articles of incorporation though the corporation was so defectively formed as to fall short of de facto status. The court stated that under this rule a mere passive stockholder would not be held liable as a partner. We went on to observe, however, that if the party actively participated in the business he might be held liable as a partner.

This controversy subsided 30 or 40 years ago probably because the procedure to achieve de jure corporate status was made simpler; so the problem did not arise.

The Model Act and the Oregon Business Corporation Act, ORS 57.793, solve the problem as follows:

> All persons who assume to act as a corporation without the authority of a certificate of incorporation issued by the Corporation Commissioner, shall be jointly and severally liable for all debts and liabilities incurred or arising as a result thereof.

We have found no decisions, comments to the Model Act, or literature attempting to explain the intent of this section.

We find the language ambiguous. . . .

We conclude that the category of "persons who assume to act as a corporation" does not include those whose only connection with the organization is as an investor. On the other hand, the restriction of liability to those who personally incurred the obligation sued upon cannot be based upon logic or the realities of business practice. When several people carry on the activities of a defectively organized corporation, chance frequently will dictate which of the several active principals directly incurs a certain obligation or whether an employee, rather than an active principal, personally incurs the obligation.

We are of the opinion that the phrase, "persons who assume to act as a corporation" should be interpreted to include those persons who have an investment in the organization and who actively participate in the policy and operational decisions of the organization. Liability should not necessarily be restricted to the person who personally incurred the obligation.

The trial court found that Dr. Bennett "acted in the business venture which was subsequently incorporated on June 12, 1970."

The proposed business of the corporation which was to be formed was to sell airplanes, recondition airplanes and give flying lessons. Land was leased for this purpose. Equipment was rented from plaintiff to level and clear for access and for other construction.

There is evidence from which the trial court could have found that while Drs. Bennett and Gorman, another defendant, entrusted the details of management to Davenport, they endeavored to and did retain some control over his management. All checks required one of their signatures. Dr. Bennett frequently visited the site and observed the activity and the presence of the equipment rented by plaintiff. He met with the organization's employees to discuss the operation of the business. Shortly after the equipment was rented and before most of the rent had accrued, Dr. Bennett was informed of the rentals and given an opinion that they were unnecessary and ill-advised. Drs. Bennett and Gorman thought they had Davenport and his management "under control."

This evidence all supports the finding that Dr. Bennett was a person who assumed to act for the organization and the conclusion of the trial court that Dr. Bennett is personally liable.

Affirmed.

NOTES AND QUESTIONS

1. What contractual language would be required to shield Jenofsky and Graziano from personal liability? Should a promoter escape liability if he executes a contract using the following language: "By: Edwin A. Boss, agent for a Minnesota corporation to be formed who will be the obligor"? Such language was held ambiguous, and liability imposed on the promoter, in Stanley J. How & Assocs., Inc. v. Boss, 222 F. Supp. 936 (S.D. Iowa 1963).

2. Why do courts impose such a heavy burden on parties explicitly attempting to contract around liability? Is such burden appropriate given the possibility that courts often use the doctrine of corporation by estoppel to protect parties who have not even attempted to contract around liability? Is it important that in both *Graziano* and *Stanley J. How* the corporation formed to take the place of the promoter had insufficient assets to perform the contract? Could the strict interpretation of provisions designed to contract around personal liability be a proxy for piercing the corporate veil on the grounds of fraudulent undercapitalization? If so, what does that indicate as to the language that will be required to contract around personal liability?

3. The court in Timberline Equipment Co. v. Davenport notes the old common law rule that persons who act as a corporation without authority are treated as general partners and, thus, as jointly and severally liable for debts incurred. At first glance, an analogy to general partnership law is appealing. Under UPA §6, a partnership is an association of two or more persons to carry on as co-owners a business for profit.

Persons who intend to own jointly a business as a corporation, but fail to incorporate, seem to fall squarely within this definition. However, as to passive investors, the better analogy is to limited partnership law. Limited partnership statutes provide a procedure whereby individuals who erroneously and in good faith believe themselves to be limited partners can escape future liability. Under RULPA §304(a) such persons may prevent further exposure to liability either by filing the necessary certificate to create a limited partnership or by filing a certificate notifying the public of withdrawal from the firm. As to liability to creditors who extend credit before such curative step is taken, RULPA §304(b) provides that such liability exists "only if the third party actually believed in good faith that the person was a general partner at the time of the transaction."

4. Section 2.04 of the MBCA, unlike its predecessor, §146 of the pre-1984 MBCA, does not use language that could be interpreted to impose absolute personal liability on those who transact business while the corporation is nonexistent. Why would an absolute liability rule be inappropriate? Some commentators argue that an absolute liability rule would result in windfall recoveries for creditors who all along thought they were dealing with corporations, and would be inconsistent with the parties' reasonable expectations. See Ribstein, Limited Liability and Theories of the Corporation, 50 Md. L. Rev. 80, 121-124 (1991).

5. In many circumstances courts promote efficiency by attempting to provide litigants with the result they would have bargained for absent transaction costs. However, in some circumstances it may be more efficient to provide a penalty default rule — that is, a rule the parties probably did not intend. Consider the following explanation of one role played by penalty defaults:

> If it is costly for the courts to determine what the parties would have wanted, it may be efficient to choose a default rule that induces the parties to contract explicitly. In other words, penalty defaults are appropriate when it is cheaper for the parties to negotiate a term ex ante than for the courts to estimate ex post what the parties would have wanted. Courts, which are publicly subsidized, should give parties incentives to negotiate ex ante by penalizing them for inefficient gaps.

Ayres and Gertner, Filling Gaps in Incomplete Contracts: An Economic Theory of Default Rules, 99 Yale L.J. 87, 93 (1989).

There are no significant transaction cost barriers to making sure that a corporation has been formed, or has not been dissolved, before transacting business. Could an absolute liability rule be justified on the grounds that society subsidizes litigation, and that it is more efficient to grant creditors an occasional windfall than to impose on society the costs involved in sorting out, ex post, whether limited liability should be available for individuals who both failed to incorporate and to contract around limited liability?

6. What is the relationship between the doctrine of corporation by estoppel enunciated in Timberline Equipment Co. v. Davenport and piercing the corporate veil? For an opinion holding that it would be inequitable to apply the doctrine of corporation by estoppel in circumstances where the creditor would be entitled to pierce the corporate veil, see Quality Interiors, Inc. v. American Management & Development Corp., 1990 WL 199248 (Ohio Ct. App.).

7. Ambiguous or legally defective allocations of the risk of loss also occur in an LLC setting with results similar to corporate law. See Water Waste & Land, Inc. v. Lanham,

955 P.2d 1001 (Col. 1998) (LLC statute that having LLC articles on file is notice that the entity is an LLC does not displace the common law of agency that an agent is liable on a contract entered on behalf of a principal if the principal is not fully disclosed).

3. Allocating the Risk of Loss from Unauthorized Actions

a. *Agent's Unauthorized Actions*

We have considered the problem presented by an agent's unauthorized actions on two earlier occasions, once in connection with the relationship between sole proprietor and agent (see Chapter 1 at pages 39-49) and once in connection with the agency relationship between partners (see Chapter 2 at pages 135-141). The problem presented by corporate agents involves the same general agency law concepts as apply in the proprietorship and partnership settings—actual authority, apparent authority, inherent authority, and related notions of estoppel and economic efficiency. A black letter definition of those agency concepts appears in the discussions cited above.

This section considers how courts deal with agency problems in the corporate setting. The loss from an unauthorized transaction will be borne either by the corporation (and, thus, by its residual claimants, the shareholders) or the creditor (unless the unauthorized agent is able to satisfy the claim). As you read the cases below, consider how such losses should be allocated. Does or should it make a difference whether the principal is a closely held or publicly held corporation?

General Overseas Films, Ltd. v. Robin International, Inc.
United States District Court, S.D. New York, 1982
542 F. Supp. 684

SOFAER, DISTRICT JUDGE:

In this action, plaintiff General Overseas Films, Ltd. ("GOF") seeks to collect on a loan guarantee that it alleges was provided on behalf of The Anaconda Company ("Anaconda") by Charles H. Kraft, Anaconda's Vice President and Treasurer. Plaintiff GOF claims that Anaconda promised through Kraft to guarantee the repayment of loans made by GOF to Robin International, Inc. ("Robin"). Plaintiff also claims that Anaconda, acting through Kraft, guaranteed Robin's obligations and liabilities in connection with certain related transactions.

In 1976, Nicholas Reisini approached Robert Haggiag, whom he had known since 1955, for a loan of $500,000 to Robin, a company that Reisini owned and controlled. Haggiag, an international film producer, was and is "solely empowered and responsible for the operations and transactions of GOF." Reisini told Haggiag that Robin was building the Soviet Union's United Nations Mission in Riverdale, New York. . . . Reisini told Haggiag that there were claims of approximately $1,000,000 against the project, but that he believed the claims could be settled for about one-half that amount.

Haggiag agreed on behalf of GOF to lend Robin and Reisini $500,000 for the purpose of settling the claims against Robin. . . .

In November 1976, Haggiag asked Reisini about payment on the note. Reisini assured Haggiag that the money due him would be paid, but that presently he was short of cash. Thereafter, Reisini asked Haggiag to consider whether he would extend the January 15 due date if Reisini could provide a guarantee from a large public company. Reisini mentioned the name Anaconda and said that the company had some involvement in constructing the mission in Riverdale.

Reisini introduced Haggiag to Charles Kraft, who was then Vice-President and Treasurer of Anaconda. Kraft told Haggiag that Anaconda would guarantee Robin's debt to GOF for up to $1,000,000. Reisini agreed to give GOF a $1,000,000 note, and Kraft agreed to provide Anaconda's guarantee for the same amount. . . . Haggiag met with Kraft and Reisini on December 13, 1976 and received the note and guarantee, which specified September 13, 1977 as the due date.

Shortly before September 13, 1977, Reisini again told Haggiag that he did not have the cash to pay the note. He assured Haggiag that the money would be forthcoming and asked Haggiag to extend the due date. Haggiag agreed, and also exchanged the $1,000,000 note for an $800,000 note. . . . In addition, Haggiag received a letter from Kraft purporting to confirm the continuation of Anaconda's guarantee, but only to the extent of $800,000.

Just before December 15, 1977, the due date of the $800,000 note, Reisini asked Haggiag for yet another extension. Haggiag agreed to return the $800,000 note in exchange for two notes, one in the amount of $500,000, payable January 31, 1978, and the other for $300,000, payable March 13, 1978.

Reisini paid Haggiag $500,000, satisfying the first note. Before the $300,000 note became due, however, Reisini once again asked for Haggiag's forbearance. Haggiag agreed to accept a $300,000 demand note in exchange for the $300,000 note due March 13. Soon after, Haggiag learned that Reisini and Kraft had been implicated in a number of fraudulent transactions.[1] Haggiag demanded payment, but Reisini and Robin have not paid. Robin apparently has no defense, but is insolvent. GOF is therefore seeking to recover from Anaconda on the basis of the guarantee extended by Kraft in Anaconda's name. . . .

Anaconda asserts as its primary defense to the action that the guarantee extended by Kraft does not bind Anaconda, since Kraft lacked actual or apparent authority to engage in the transaction. Plaintiff concedes that Kraft had no actual authority to bind Anaconda to this undertaking; it relies solely on Kraft's apparent authority to do so. Since on this record it is clear that Kraft lacked apparent authority to engage in the transactions considered, Anaconda's other defenses need not be addressed.

The general rule in New York is that "(o)ne who deals with an agent does so at his peril, and must make the necessary effort to discover the actual scope of authority." Ford v. Unity Hospital, 32 N.Y.2d 464, 472, 346 N.Y.S.2d 238, 244, 299 N.E.2d 659, 664

---

1. During pre-trial proceedings in the present case, two related cases were pending before this Court. Anaconda Co. v. Bank of New York, 78 Civ. 5583, Anaconda Co. v. Bankers Trust Co., 78 Civ. 5560, and one was pending before the Northern District of California, Anaconda Co. v. Wells Fargo Bank, C790055 (N.D. Calif.). Each of these cases was settled. In addition, Reisini and Kraft were both convicted in criminal cases brought by the United States Attorney for the Southern District of New York.

(1973). The doctrine of apparent authority delineates the grounds for imposing on the principal losses caused by its agent's unauthorized acts. The law recognizes that an agent, such as Kraft, may engage in a fraudulent transaction entirely without his principal's approval but nevertheless under circumstances that warrant holding his principal accountable. As the Court of Appeals for this Circuit explained:

> Apparent authority is based on the principle of estoppel. It arises when a principal places an agent in a position where it appears that the agent has certain powers which he may or may not possess. If a third person holds the reasonable belief that the agent was acting within the scope of his authority and changes his position in reliance on the agent's act, the principal is estopped to deny that the agent's act was not authorized. (Masuda v. Kawasaki Dockyard Co., 328 F.2d 662, 665 (2d Cir. 1964).

The doctrine rests not upon the agent's acts or statements but upon the acts or omissions of the principal. It is invoked when the principal's own misleading conduct is responsible for the agent's ability to mislead. As defined in the Restatement a principal causes his agent to have apparent authority

> by written or spoken words or any other conduct of the principal which, reasonably interpreted, causes the third person to believe that the principal consents to have the act done on his behalf. . . . (Restatement, Agency 2d §27 (1958).)

Therefore, to determine whether Kraft had apparent authority to guarantee the loan on behalf of Anaconda requires a "factual inquiry (focusing upon) the principal's (Anaconda's) manifestations to the third person (Haggiag). . . ." Hawaiian Paradise Park Corp. v. Friendly Broadcasting Co., 414 F.2d 750, 756 (9th Cir. 1969). The Ninth Circuit has stated:

> The principal's manifestations giving rise to apparent authority may consist of direct statements to the third person, directions to the agent to tell something to the third person, or the granting of permission to the agent to perform acts and conduct negotiations under circumstances which create in him a reputation of authority in the area in which the agent acts and negotiates. (Id. (citing Seavey, Law of Agency, §8, at 13).)

The initial question, therefore, is whether Anaconda's conduct permitted Haggiag actually and reasonably to believe that Kraft was authorized to execute this guarantee. Under the law of New York, the circumstances of the transaction known to the plaintiff must also be scrutinized to determine whether it fulfilled its primary "duty of inquiry."

GOF relies on several aspects of Anaconda's conduct in arguing that Anaconda conferred apparent authority on Kraft for the transactions in which he engaged with GOF. Anaconda placed Kraft in a high and visible corporate position, with broad powers over financial affairs. It gave Kraft Anaconda stationery displaying his corporate titles, an office in the company's executive suite, business cards, access to the corporate seal, and put his picture in its annual report. Anaconda officers and publications announced to the financial community that Kraft was the individual at Anaconda with whom to discuss the company's "financial needs." Plaintiff argues that "Anaconda held Kraft out as having the full range of authority and responsibility for Anaconda's financial matters," and characterizes Kraft as Anaconda's "emissary to the financial community." Specifically, Anaconda adopted and made available to Kraft Article 9 of Anaconda's bylaws, conferring upon Kraft, as Treasurer, authority "to sign checks, notes, drafts, bills of exchange and other evidences of indebtedness. . . ." Kraft showed this bylaw, as well as his picture in Anaconda's annual report, to Haggiag at their initial meeting. By these actions, plaintiff contends, Anaconda gave such convincing evidence of Kraft's authority to sign guarantees that several sophisticated banks extended some $34 million in credit to Reisini's companies, at Kraft's request, through transactions similar to GOF's with Robin. GOF argues:

> That six sophisticated banks had agreed to all of Kraft's proposals over a six-year period is vivid testimony to the widespread recognition among professionals of the authority inherent in the position of a corporate Treasurer.

Those transactions, moreover, constitute in plaintiff's view strong evidence of the reasonableness of GOF's conduct: "six sophisticated financial institutions and Kraft's own superiors did not question for more than six years the fact that Kraft's actions on behalf of Anaconda were proper, legitimate and fully authorized." Further, GOF cites as evidence of the reasonableness of its belief in Kraft's apparent authority the fact that Haggiag asked a distinguished member of the bar whether the papers Kraft presented Haggiag were in good order; the attorney allegedly told Haggiag that the papers appeared to be in proper form. Haggiag also inquired as to Anaconda's interest, and was told that the company had supplied or produced the walls of the Russian mission that Robin had built. Finally, GOF contends that, had Haggiag inquired further into Kraft's authority, he would not have discovered anything to cast doubt upon the transactions' propriety, since Kraft was the person at Anaconda authorized to produce evidence as to both the authority to transact business on behalf of Anaconda and any changes in that authority.

GOF's arguments would have force in a situation that fell within the range of transactions in which companies like Anaconda normally engage. But the transaction involved in this case is extraordinary, and should have alerted Haggiag to the danger of fraud. Because the circumstances surrounding the transaction were such as to put Haggiag on notice of the need to inquire further into Kraft's power and good faith, Anaconda cannot be bound.

A corporate treasurer, it is true, must be regarded as having broad authority to commit his or her company in financial dealings. Large companies such as Anaconda generally establish ongoing relations with several banks. The banks are kept informed of the financial status of these companies through regular reports. They are also advised of exactly whom to deal with at such companies in all financial matters, and are provided with evidence of the individual officer's authority. In this case, Anaconda designated Kraft as its authorized contact in financial affairs, and it widely published Article 9 of its bylaws as evidencing the scope of Kraft's authority. Anaconda thereby placed Kraft in a position that enabled him to commit the company, when he was acting within the scope of Article 9, to any transaction that appeared reasonably related to Anaconda's business. See Restatement 2d, Agency, §39 ("Unless otherwise agreed, authority to act as agent includes only authority to act for the benefit of the principal"). Anaconda and companies like Anaconda often need on-the-spot, informal commitments from banks, and they operate in a manner that enables them to obtain such commitments. Banks, on the other hand, need and compete for customers such as

Anaconda, and they reasonably attempt to meet the needs of such customers by dealing as swiftly and informally with authorized officers as the circumstances of a particular transaction reasonably permit.

The existence of apparent authority depends in part upon "who the contracting third party is." Lee v. Jenkins Bros., 268 F.2d at 370. GOF is not a bank, or otherwise the type of company with whom Anaconda needed to deal swiftly and regularly in its financial affairs. It had no relationship with Anaconda before the transaction concerning Robin. It had neither the need nor the capacity to seek or compete for Anaconda's financial business by extending services or courtesies without the investigation normally made. GOF maintained no file on Anaconda; it had no idea of the company's financial condition beyond glancing at Anaconda's latest annual report. A bank with whom Anaconda (and Kraft) regularly dealt might more reasonably rely on Kraft's position as evidence of broad authority in most types of financial matters. But given GOF's lack of experience and knowledge in banking, GOF's lack of a prior relationship with Anaconda, and GOF's lack of any interest in creating an ongoing relationship with Anaconda, it cannot claim to have the same reasonable basis for such reliance. The messages Anaconda implicitly may have conveyed in its dealings with banks could not have been intended for a company in GOF's situation nor reasonably available to such a company as a basis for its reliance.

More important, the nature of the specific transaction—a guarantee by Anaconda of the debt of an unrelated corporation—was extraordinary and thus sufficient to require inquiry by GOF before it relied on Kraft's purported authority. Article 9 of Anaconda's bylaws is properly cited by plaintiff as conduct of the principal which could give rise to apparent authority. But GOF has no basis for arguing that Article 9 of Anaconda's bylaws conferred or reasonably appeared to confer authority on Kraft to sign a guarantee, let alone one to a third, unrelated company. The bylaw implicitly but clearly refutes the notion that Kraft had authority to sign guarantees. The language conferring power on him to sign evidences of indebtedness occurs in a context that pertains entirely to Anaconda's direct borrowing activities. It reads:

> The Treasurer or Assistant Treasurer shall have the custody of all the funds and securities of the Company, and shall have power on behalf of the Company to sign checks, notes, drafts, bills of exchange and other evidences of indebtedness, to borrow money for the current needs of the business of the Company and assign and deliver for money so borrowed stocks and securities and warehouse receipts or other documents representing metals in store or transit and to make short-term investments of surplus funds of the Company and shall perform such other duties as may be assigned to him from time to time by the Board of Directors, the Chairman of the Board, the Vice Chairman of the Board or the President.

[The court held that a guarantee is not an "evidence of indebtedness."] . . .

Plaintiff contends that, regardless of whether a guarantee is an evidence of indebtedness, the language of Article 9, when reasonably interpreted, gives the appearance of such authority. This argument proceeds on the theory that Kraft's actual "authority in other transactions gave him apparent authority in this transaction." But the nature of a guarantee is such that "[h]owever general the character of the agency may be, a contract of guaranty or suretyship is not normally to be inferred from such an agency." 2 S. Williston, A Treatise on the Law of Contracts, §277A, at 230 (3d ed. 1959).

The guarantee of Robin's debt to GOF, standing alone, had no apparent connection with the financial interests of Anaconda. Unlike a loan or other debt undertaken by Anaconda for its own benefit, a guarantee results in a loan by the creditor of funds to a third party, or, as in this case, in the creditor's agreement to defer collecting on a loan previously extended to a third party. Unless the transaction has other elements connecting it to the guarantor, it is not the sort of arrangement in which the guarantor company's treasurer or other financial officer normally should be expected to engage:

> [S]uch a contract is unusual and extraordinary and so not normally within the powers accruing to an agent by implication, however general the character of the agency; ordinarily the power exists only if expressly given. Consequently a manager, superintendent, or the like, of business or property cannot ordinarily bind his principal as surety for third persons. (2A C.J.S., Agency §181, at 849 (1979).)

. . . Where an agent purports to bind his principal to such a commitment the third party is put on notice that the transaction is of questionable validity:

> If [the third person] knows that the agent is acting for the benefit of himself or a third person, the transaction is suspicious upon its face, and the principal is not bound unless the agent is authorized. Thus, where the agent signs the principal's name as an accommodation endorser . . . the other party obtains no rights against the principal because of such transaction, unless authorized. (Restatement 2d, Agency, §165, comment c, at 390.)

Thus, "[g]enerally, contracts of guaranty and suretyship not in the regular line of corporate business cannot be made by corporate officers without express authority; ordinarily there is no apparent authority in an officer to make such a contract." National Surety Corp. v. Inland Properties, Inc., 286 F. Supp. at 181.

Had Kraft purported to borrow money for Anaconda, or in a credible manner for Anaconda's benefit, he could have bound Anaconda even if he in fact intended and managed to steal the money involved. Had Anaconda itself done anything to suggest it had an interest in Robin or in the transactions at issue, a stronger case for apparent authority would be presented. But in this case, Anaconda was neither directly nor indirectly involved in the transaction between GOF and Robin, and GOF has not pointed to any actions by Anaconda suggesting involvement. The only connection between Anaconda and Robin suggested to Haggiag was a vague statement by Reisini that Anaconda had provided "curtain walls" in the Russian mission. These remarks are of minimal significance since they can in no way be attributed to Anaconda, and therefore cannot give rise to apparent authority. Moreover, Haggiag admits that the words curtain walls "sounded strange," and that he had no real interest in the subject. Kraft made no representation about any connection between Robin and Anaconda, and even if he had, he could not thereby have supplied any more of a basis for apparent authority than he did by his assertions to Haggiag that he had the power to execute the guarantee. The situations in which courts have bound principals on guarantees issued by their agents are those in which authority to do so is express, or clearly implied from functions assigned to and performed by the agent involved. Otherwise, such a guaranty has no apparent relationship to the principal's business, and one who receives what appears to be a guarantee is put on notice that he must inquire further before relying on it. Under these circumstances, Kraft's authority to bind Anaconda to this transaction was far from apparent.

Plaintiff relies heavily on the fact that six banks were also taken in by Kraft and Reisini in various ways. It argues that the banks' similar conduct shows that GOF's belief in Kraft's authority, and its reliance on him, was commercially reasonable; GOF also argues that Haggiag properly relied on the existence of parallel transactions as evidence of Kraft's authority. But the banks in fact treated Article 9 of Anaconda's bylaws as evidence that Kraft lacked authority to sign guarantees. Not one of them accepted a simple guarantee arrangement. Instead they designed alternative arrangements that they felt provided them security but at the same time avoided a guarantee as such. . . .

In any event, GOF cannot safely rely upon the conduct of the banks with whom Anaconda dealt as establishing Kraft's apparent authority or as reflecting reasonable reliance upon Kraft's position or representations. . . . They doubted Kraft's authority to sign guarantees, and structured the transactions to avoid the limitation implicit in Article 9, through the use of letters-of-credit that differed markedly from those normally used by corporations in their regular commercial dealings. Nor did those banks which had explanations for Anaconda's interest in the loan behave entirely in accordance with customary practice; for example, one bank paid the funds Robin had borrowed directly to Robin, even though the funds were allegedly intended for the purchase of copper from Anaconda. The record in those cases, including the five week trial in Anaconda Co. v. Bankers Trust Co., 78 Civ. 5560, establishes that those settlements were affected by the strong case of negligence made by the banks against Anaconda's parent company. That case of negligence, however, was based on events and conduct that have no pertinence to GOF's claim.[4]

Plaintiff's argument that Haggiag's knowledge of some of these transactions made his belief in Kraft's authority more reasonable is entirely misplaced. . . . In fact, the only transaction involving Kraft and Reisini of which Haggiag had any detailed knowledge should have alerted him to the importance of requiring a board of directors resolution demonstrating express authority for a corporate officer to execute a guarantee of an unrelated third party's debt. . . .

A plaintiff "claiming reliance on (an) agent's apparent authority must not fail to heed warning or inconsistent circumstances." S. Williston, supra, §277A, at 227. "The duty of diligence in ascertaining whether an agent is exceeding his authority devolves on those who deal with him, not on his principal." Strip Clean Floor Refinishing v. New York District Council No. 9, 333 F. Supp. at 396. Moreover, the course of conduct pursued, with Haggiag's knowledge, by the Swiss Bank shows the weakness of plaintiff's assertion that further inquiry would have been futile because Kraft purportedly was the officer entrusted by Anaconda with producing evidence of its agents' authority.

---

4. Plaintiff's Reply Memorandum argues that Anaconda should have discovered the frauds of Kraft prior to the GOF transactions. The argument is in the nature of a negligence claim, and was effectively pursued by some of the banks with whom Kraft dealt. But it is unavailable to GOF, since all the events that could arguably prove negligence occurred long after the loan agreement between GOF and Robin was extended in December 1976, pursuant to Kraft's promise to provide a guarantee. . . .

The documentation requested by the Swiss Bank required authorization Kraft could not easily provide. By requiring it, that bank avoided the fate that befell GOF.

Thus, the circumstances presented by the record not only demonstrate an absence of apparent authority, they also show that GOF failed to satisfy its obligation under New York law of making a reasonable attempt to discover the actual scope of Kraft's authority. . . . Haggiag made no investigation of the circumstances of Anaconda's guarantee. He did not engage counsel. His purported "consultation" with an attorney consisted of showing the papers for a few moments to a lawyer he neither knew well nor retained. He regarded the assurances of his brother and friends as sufficient. In his deposition, Haggiag explains, "I just said what business do you have with Anaconda, not because I want to find out, and he [Reisini] said they make curtain walls. . . . That's the only thing I remember." Haggiag's failure to discharge his duty to inquire about the scope of Kraft's authority is demonstrated by his vague knowledge of Anaconda's ostensible motive for executing the guarantee. The novelty of this transaction—a corporation's guarantee of an unrelated third party's debt to a film company not in the business of lending—warranted scrutiny of its circumstances, including Anaconda's motive for guaranteeing the loan and the security Anaconda obtained for the guarantee.

The evidence in the record fails to establish that Anaconda through its conduct misled plaintiff so as to warrant a finding that Kraft had "apparent authority" to bind Anaconda to the guarantee. Indeed, Haggiag's negligence, not Anaconda's, precipitated the loss. Accordingly, judgment shall be entered for the defendant Anaconda, with costs. . . .

A & M Farm Center, Inc. v. AGCO Finance, LLC
Court of Appeals of Indiana, 2010
Transfer Denied June 24, 2010
921 N.E.2d 54 (Table) Unpublished Disposition

BARNES, Judge.

FACTS

AGCO is a Delaware limited liability company with its principal office in Johnston, Iowa. AGCO is a financier of various equipment and machinery for customers throughout the United States. A & M is an agricultural equipment dealer located in Valparaiso, Indiana. Louis Abbett is the president of A & M. Dennis Leek was the manager of A & M, and in 1994, he became a shareholder and vice-president. Leek was responsible for the day-to-day operations of A & M.

Most of A & M's business involves selling and leasing John Deere equipment. Approximately ten percent of A & M's business is leasing equipment. Many of A & M's customers financed their purchases through AGCO . . . .

In October 1994, A & M provided AGCO with a Corporate Dealer's Resolution Certificate, which provided that Leek, Abbett, and Janice Sampson were:

authorized to execute on behalf of and in the name of [A & M] any and all agreements, assignments, transfers, endorsements, security documents, negotiable instruments or other documents necessary to the conduct of the affairs of [A & M] and any and all other documents to which [AGCO] is a party or in respect to or concerned with the wholesale and retail finance or lease plans of [AGCO]. The powers vested in the said named persons shall continue in full force and effect until written notice of rescission or modification thereof has been received by [AGCO] and [A & M] shall save harmless [AGCO] for any loss suffered or liability incurred by it in reliance on this resolution after revocation or termination by operation of law or otherwise, in the absence of such notice.

Id. at 74. AGCO and A & M transacted business for several years with Leek signing all of the contracts and agreements on behalf of A & M. Leek signed over one hundred Variable Rate Loan Contracts and Security Agreements or related financing documents with AGCO on behalf of A & M.

At some point, while still employed by A & M, Leek began another business, Cable Tech, Inc. In late 2000, Cable Tech entered into three leases with A & M for equipment and financed the leases through AGCO. The leases were signed by Leek on behalf of A & M and Phil Norman, president of Cable Tech. Each of the leases also contained a letter, which provided:

> This letter is to certify that I am engaged in a bona fide agricultural and/or industrial operation, and the equipment covered by the attached Lease Agreement is for my personal use in the operation.
> Please accept this Lease Agreement with full recourse, notwithstanding any provision of our Retail Financing Agreement Recourse Supplement.

Id. at 219, 228, 236. The letters were signed by Leek on behalf of A & M. While processing the lease finance applications, AGCO received credit reports that erroneously indicated Leek was a former employee of A & M. Leek was, in fact, still employed at A & M.

On May 1, 2001, and May 2, 2001, Cable Tech converted the leases into three Variable Rate Loan Contract and Security Agreements with AGCO for the equipment in the amounts of $217,718.12, $50,294.36, and $144,791.37. The agreements were signed by Leek and Norman as borrowers. Additionally, the agreements contained letters signed by Leek on behalf of A & M, which provided:

> This letter is to certify that I am engaged in a bona fide agricultural and/or other industrial operation, and the equipment covered by the attached Retail Contract is for my personal use in the operation.
> * * * * *
> Please accept this Retail Contract with full recourse, notwithstanding any provision of our Retail Financing Agreement Recourse Supplement.

Id. at 87, 92.

Abbett was unaware of Cable Tech's agreements and full recourse agreements with AGCO until 2002. Cable Tech defaulted on the agreements in mid–2002, and AGCO declared all amounts immediately due and payable. Cable Tech was indebted to AGCO for principal and interest in the amount of $276,123. AGCO demanded that A & M accept the reassignment of the Cable Tech agreements under the full recourse agreements, which A & M failed or refused to do. On January 31, 2003, Leek resigned his positions as director, officer, shareholder, and employee of A & M.

In 2004, AGCO filed a complaint against A & M, Abbett, and Cable Tech. A default judgment was entered against Cable Tech. AGCO filed a motion for summary judgment against A & M and Abbett, arguing that A & M was liable to AGCO under the recourse agreements, that Leek had actual, apparent, or inherent authority to enter into the Cable Tech contracts, and that Abbett was liable pursuant to a personal guarantee. A & M argued that there were genuine issues of material fact regarding whether AGCO's belief in Leek's authority to enter into the agreements was reasonable. A & M contended that Leek was acting adversely to A & M when he entered into the agreements. Additionally, Abbett argued that his signature had been forged on the personal guarantee. The trial court granted AGCO's motion for summary judgment against A & M, but denied the motion for summary judgment against Abbett. The trial court ordered A & M to pay $276,123 plus attorney fees of $51,432.47. The trial court later entered a nunc pro tunc order finding that there was "no just reason for delay." *Id.* at 32.

ANALYSIS

The issue is whether the trial court properly granted AGCO's motion for summary judgment against A & M. Summary judgment is appropriate only where there is no genuine issue of material fact and the moving party is entitled to judgment as a matter of law. Ind. Trial Rule 56(C); Mangold v. Ind. Dep't of Natural Res., 756 N.E.2d 970, 973 (Ind. 2001). All facts and reasonable inferences drawn from those facts are construed in favor of the nonmovant. *Mangold,* 756 N.E.2d at 973. Our review of a summary judgment motion is limited to those materials designated to the trial court. *Id.* We must carefully review a decision on summary judgment to ensure that a party was not improperly denied its day in court. *Id.* at 974.

"In general, a principal will be bound by a contract entered into by the principal's agent on his behalf only if the agent had authority to bind him." Heritage Dev. of Indiana, Inc. v. Opportunity Options, Inc., 773 N.E.2d 881, 888 (Ind. Ct. App. 2002). An agent's authority to enter into a contract on his principal's behalf will typically be actual, apparent, or inherent. Gallant Ins. Co. v. Isaac, 751 N.E.2d 672, 675 (Ind. 2001). The question of whether an agency relationship exists and of the agent's authority is generally a question of fact. *Heritage Dev.,* 773 N.E.2d at 888. A & M contends that genuine issues of material fact exist regarding whether Leek had actual, apparent, or inherent authority to enter into the Cable Tech agreements with AGCO.

A. ACTUAL AUTHORITY

Actual authority is created by written or spoken words or other conduct of the principal which, reasonably interpreted, causes the agent to believe that the principal desires him so to act on the principal's account." Menard, Inc. v. Dage–MTI, Inc., 726 N.E.2d 1206, 1210 (Ind. 2000) (quoting Scott v. Randle, 697 N.E.2d 60, 66 (Ind. Ct. App. 1998), *trans. denied*). The focus of actual authority is the belief of the agent. *Scott,* 697 N.E.2d at 66.

A & M argues that it did not give Leek actual authority to enter into the Cable Tech agreements or full recourse agreements. A & M points out that Abbett had previously financed personal equipment through AGCO, that Abbett did not sign the documents on behalf of A & M, and that A & M did not sign a full recourse agreement regarding the transaction. AGCO counters that Leek had actual authority as a result of A & M's 1994 Corporate Dealer's Resolution Certificate, which gave Leek the authority to enter into "any and all agreements, assignments, transfers, endorsements, security documents, negotiable instruments or other documents necessary to the conduct of the affairs of [A & M]" and "any and all other documents to which [AGCO] is a party or in respect to or concerned with the wholesale and retail finance or lease plans of [AGCO]." Appellant's App. p. 74. Leek, in fact, signed hundreds of AGCO documents on A & M's behalf.

We conclude that genuine issues of material fact exist regarding whether Leek had actual authority to enter into the Cable Tech agreements. The focus here is whether Leek himself believed that he had actual authority to enter into the agreements based upon A & M's conduct. *See Scott*, 697 N.E.2d at 66. Leek testified in his deposition that he thought he had authority to enter into the contracts. Although A & M had given Leek authority to sign agreements on its behalf with AGCO, there is no indication that A & M gave Leek actual authority to enter into contracts that were adverse to A & M but beneficial to Leek. On a previous occasion, Abbett had entered into financing agreements with AGCO to purchase equipment for one of his other businesses. Abbett did not sign those agreements on behalf of A & M and did not have A & M enter into full recourse provisions on those agreements. Prior to the Cable Tech agreements, A & M had not previously entered into a financing agreement with a full recourse provision. Despite the unusual nature of the Cable Tech agreements, Leek did not inform Abbett of the agreements. Under these circumstances, we conclude that genuine issues of material fact exist regarding Leek's actual authority.

B.   APPARENT AUTHORITY

Apparent authority refers to a third party's reasonable belief that the principal has authorized the acts of its agent; it arises from the principal's indirect or direct manifestations to a third party and not from the representations or acts of the agent. *Gallant*, 751 N.E.2d at 675. "The necessary manifestation is one made by the principal to a third party, who in turn is instilled with a reasonable belief that another individual is an agent of the principal." *Id.* at 676. "[B]ecause an agent's apparent authority emanates not from the agency itself but from the principal's indirect and direct manifestations, . . . a third party is required under the rule of law to 'use reasonable diligence and prudence to ascertain' the extent of any limitations of which he or she has become aware." *Id.* at 1216 n. 10 (quoting 3 Am. Jur. 2D Agency §83 (1986)). "[I]t is critical to the application of the doctrine that the party dealing with the agent reasonably believes that the agent is acting with authority. Where he knows, or should know, the agent is exceeding his authority, the principal will not be bound." *Grosam v. Laborers' Int'l. Union of North America, Local 41*, 489 N.E.2d 656, 658 (Ind. Ct. App. 1986), *trans. denied.*

A & M argues that AGCO's belief that Leek had authority to enter into the Cable Tech agreements with their full recourse provisions was unreasonable. AGCO was aware that Leek was both a vice-president of A & M and a principal of Cable Tech. Further, A & M had not previously entered into full recourse provisions. The Cable Tech agreements contained letters signed by Leek on behalf of A & M, which provided:

> This letter is to certify that I am engaged in a bona fide agricultural and/or other industrial operation, and the equipment covered by the attached Retail Contract is for my personal use in the operation.
> * * * * *
> Please accept this Retail Contract with full recourse, notwithstanding any provision of our Retail Financing Agreement Recourse Supplement.

Id. at 87, 92. Thus, Leek was modifying the prior limited recourse agreement entered into by Abbett on behalf of A & M. Leek was, in effect, having A & M guarantee the debt of his other company. Moreover, when Leek entered into the Cable Tech leases, a credit check performed by AGCO indicated, although incorrectly, that Leek was no longer employed at AGCO.

Under the totality of the circumstances, genuine issues of material fact exist regarding whether AGCO knew or should have known that Leek was exceeding his authority.[3] We conclude that genuine issues of material fact exist as to whether Leek had apparent authority to enter into the Cable Tech agreements on A & M's behalf.

C. INHERENT AUTHORITY

Inherent authority refers to acts done on the principal's account that accompany or are incidental to transactions the agent is authorized to conduct if, although they are forbidden by the principal, the third party reasonably believes that the agent is authorized to do them and has no notice that the agent is not so authorized. *Menard,* 726 N.E.2d at 1212. "Inherent agency power is a term used . . . to indicate the power of an agent which is derived not from authority, apparent authority or estoppel, but solely from the agency relation and exists for the protection of persons harmed by or dealing with a servant or other agent." *Id.* at 1211 (quoting Koval v. Simon Telelect, Inc., 693 N.E.2d 1299, 1304 (Ind. 1998)). In *Menard,* our supreme court observed, based upon the Restatement (Second) of Agency §161, comment a, that "if one appoints an agent to conduct a series of transactions over a period of time, it is fair that he should bear losses which are incurred when such an agent, although without authority to do so, does something which is usually done in connection with the transactions he is employed to conduct." *Id.* at 1212.

---

3. AGCO relies upon AutoXchange.com, Inc. v. Dreyer & Reinbold, Inc., 816 N.E.2d 40, 48-49 (Ind. Ct. App. 2004), for the proposition that Leek had apparent authority. However, *AutoXchange* is distinguishable because there was no evidence in *AutoXchange* that the agent was engaging in self-dealing or that the third party was aware of such self-dealing.

Leek had inherent authority here if: (1) first, Leek acted within the usual and ordinary scope of his authority as vice-president and manager of A & M; (2) second, AGCO reasonably believed that Leek was authorized to enter into the Cable Tech agreements; and (3) third, AGCO had no notice that Leek was not authorized to enter into the Cable Tech agreements with their full recourse provisions without Abbett's approval. *See id.* at 1212-13. Again, we conclude that genuine issues of material fact exist regarding whether Leek had inherent authority to enter into the Cable Tech agreements with their full recourse provisions.

Although Leek was authorized to sign AGCO agreements on behalf of A & M, A & M had not previously entered into a full recourse provision. Further, Leek was a principal of Cable Tech and the vice-president/manager of A & M. AGCO was aware that Leek was participating on both sides of the transaction, and the full recourse provision was clearly adverse to A & M's interests.[4] Under these circumstances and those discussed above, we conclude that genuine issues of material fact exist regarding whether Leek had inherent authority.

CONCLUSION

We acknowledge that our supreme court has held: "if one of two innocent parties must suffer due to a betrayal of trust—either the principal or the third party—the loss should fall on the party who is most at fault. Because the principal puts the agent in a position of trust, the principal should bear the loss." *Menard,* 726 N.E .2d at 1216 (quoting *Koval,* 693 N.E.2d at 1304). A jury may very well determine that A & M is the most at fault and should suffer the loss here. However, a jury may alternatively determine that, despite the fact that Leek was, no doubt, processing AGCO agreements in his capacity as vice-president and manager of A & M, several key differences exist in the personal transactions he conducted with AGCO, which we highlighted and discussed. Because genuine issues of material fact exist regarding whether Leek had actual, apparent, or inherent authority to enter into the Cable Tech agreements with their full recourse provisions on behalf of A & M, we conclude that the trial court erred by granting summary judgment to AGCO. We reverse and remand.

NOTES AND QUESTIONS

1. As to routine transactions, consumers and creditors reasonably assume that they need make no inquiry as to an agent's authority to act for her corporation. Courts protect such expectations by, in effect, cloaking all corporate agents with inherent authority as to routine matters, thereby allocating the risk of loss to corporations. However, courts do not extend creditors blanket protection as to extraordinary transactions. As

---

4. Again, AGCO relies upon *AutoXchange,* 816 N.E.2d at 49, for the proposition that Leek had inherent authority. However, *AutoXchange* is distinguishable because there was no evidence in *AutoXchange* that the agent was engaging in self-dealing or that the third party was aware of such self-dealing.

General Overseas Films v. Robin International illustrates, when an agent's unauthorized actions are sufficiently egregious, courts will use agency rules to allocate resulting loss to creditors.

2. The two principal cases parallel Blackburn v. Witter in Chapter 1. Where an agent has disregarded instructions or overstepped actual authority a court must decide who should bear this risk—the principal who put the agent in a position where the wrongdoing might occur, or the third party who dealt with the agent and perhaps should been on notice of the agent's lack of authority. The Restatement (Second) of Agency includes two concepts that could create liability for the principal: apparent authority and inherent agency power. Apparent authority traditionally applied to those situations in which the principal manifested the existence of authority to the third party. Inherent agency power permitted application of similar responsibility to the principal where words are not directed at a third party. See Restatement (Second) of Agency §8A, Comment b. The Restatement (Third) of Agency uses a broader definition of "manifestation" to eliminate the traditional distinction between apparent authority and inherent agency power. "In this Restatement conduct may constitute a manifestation sufficient to create apparent authority even though it does not use the word 'authority' and even though it does not consist of words targeted specifically to a third party." Restatement (Third) of Agency (2006) §1.03 Reporter's Notes.

3. The difference in terminology should not mask the underlying policy question. When a principal names an agent as president, for example, to what extent does such status as an officer create apparent authority? *General Overseas Films* suggests such authority cannot extend to extraordinary transactions, where the principal is not benefiting.

4. If you are an attorney for a corporation whose board is worried about the possibility of a runaway officer, what might you suggest to the board as a way to protect itself against the possible renegade actions of the officer?

5. Should courts apply agency rules to give more, less, or the same protection to closely held and publicly held corporations? Presumably courts will seek to provide the level of protection that will produce net societal gains. Thus, courts should weigh the cost to particular corporations of bearing the expected loss from unauthorized agent action against the transaction costs that will be imposed as a result of such level of protection. If courts strictly protect corporations by insisting that creditors prove that the corporation has manifested consent, then creditors will henceforth demand greater transaction-specific contractual assurances from corporations. If courts loosely protect corporations, then fraud may increase, but the transaction costs of assuring creditors of agents' authority will presumably go down. The efficient rule produces the lowest total costs. Can close corporations more easily bear the potential losses from unauthorized agents' actions than they can bear the transaction costs of assuring creditors? Is that a valid assumption?

b. *Ultra Vires*
MBCA §3.04
Delaware G.C.L. §124

An ultra vires act is simply one that a corporation is unauthorized to do by its articles or by the statutes that regulate it. Before the advent of general incorporation laws, courts construed corporate purposes clauses narrowly, consistent with the presumed intent of the legislature. The classic example of the strict rule is an English case, The Ashbury Railway Carriage & Iron Co. v. Riche, 33 Law T. Rep. N.S. 450 (1875). The railway corporation's charter, granted by Parliament, expressly empowered the corporation to sell or lend railway plant or carry on the business of mechanical engineering or general contracting. The corporation entered into a contract with Riche to raise the capital needed by Riche to construct and operate a railway line in Belgium. The corporation later sought to repudiate the partially performed contract because the activities that it had contracted to perform were unauthorized by its charter. Thus, the corporation was without power to act. The House of Lords agreed that the contract was ultra vires and unenforceable against the corporation. Lord Chancellor Cairns explained:

> The question is not the illegality of the contract, but the competency and power of the company to make the contract. I am of opinion that this contract was, as I have said, entirely beyond the powers of the company to make the contract. If so it is not a question whether the contract ever was ratified or not ratified. If it was a contract void at its beginning it was void for this reason—because the company could not make the contract. If every shareholder of the company had been in this room, and every shareholder of the company had said, "That is a contract which we desire to make, which we authorize the directors to make, to which we sanction the placing of the seal of the company," the case would not have stood in any different position to that in which it stands now. The company would thereby by unanimous assent have been attempting to do the very thing which by the Act they were prohibited from doing.

33 Law T. Rep. N.S. at 452.

With the inception of general incorporation statutes, corporate purposes clauses became a function not of legislative will but of the incorporators' desires. As a result, courts were freed to rethink the ultra vires doctrine. Since many cases in which corporations asserted the ultra vires doctrine involved opportunistic attempts to renege on a deal made but now regretted, courts did not hesitate to find exceptions to the literal dictates of the ultra vires doctrine. Herbert Hovenkamp describes and explains the changed view as follows:

> Classical corporate theory both narrowed and privatized ultra vires. When one thinks of the corporation as an entity composed of private persons but created by the state for a public purpose, strict scrutiny of corporate powers and activities seems appropriate. On the other hand, when the corporation is simply an alternative form of business organization, it should be able to do the same things as any other business firm. By the 1880s and 1890s courts had retreated from the view that a corporation's powers were defined by a strict construction of its charter. They became much more willing to imply authority from other explicit powers. Even the Supreme Court, which usually construed corporate powers narrowly, held in 1896 that the express power granted to a corporation to run a railroad implied the power to operate a hotel, at least if the hotel was for the convenience of railroad passengers and employees. In 1894, William W. Cook, a prominent corporations treatise writer, noted that the traditional ultra vires doctrine was disappearing rapidly. By 1898, he proclaimed it dead, at least in state courts.

Hovenkamp, The Classical Corporation in American Legal Thought, 76 Geo. L.J. 1593, 1663-1664 (1988).

The demise of the strict ultra vires doctrine was followed in the twentieth century by statutory provisions designed to confirm the limited role of the ultra vires doctrine. The impetus for these statutes was the work of the drafters of the Uniform Business Corporation Act. In its final form, the uniform act distinguished between corporate capacity and corporate authority. A corporation had the capacity or power to act possessed by a natural person. However, it had authority to act only in furtherance of its charter and in accordance with corporate law rules. This clarification was followed in a number of states.

In more recent years, the Model Business Corporation Act and the statutes of many states have gone a step further and specifically provided that the validity of a corporate action may not be challenged on the grounds that it exceeds the corporation's power except in two principal circumstances: (1) a suit by the shareholders to enjoin the corporation from performing the ultra vires act, and (2) a derivative or direct suit against the persons who took the ultra vires action on behalf of the corporation.

These changes have lessened but not eliminated the importance of the ultra vires concept. Notice that litigants often "throw in" an ultra vires claim in order not to overlook any possible avenue for convincing a court of their position. Occasionally, however, the allocation of loss between insiders and outsiders will turn on the court's understanding and application of the ultra vires doctrine.

The distinction between the defense of ultra vires and the defense of lack of agent's authority is often misunderstood. The ultra vires statutes merely confirm that a corporation has the capacity of a real person. The corporation's authority may be limited by provisions in its articles or by common law rules. For example, common law doctrines establish that the act of directors in conveying corporate property for no consideration, or for woefully inadequate consideration, may not be ratified by less than unanimous shareholder action. Many courts describe such gifts or wasteful acts as ultra vires. No such act can be in furtherance of corporate purposes, unless ratified by all shareholders, and, thus, such act is beyond the corporation's power. However, for a case holding both that a guaranty issued without authority is ultra vires and that the corporation cannot assert either an ultra vires defense or a lack of officer authority defense, see Inter-Continental Corp. v. Moody, 411 S.W.2d 578 (Tex. Civ. App. 1966).

PROBLEM 7-6

C Corp. secured a contract with the state to perform certain work on a highway construction project. C desired to subcontract a portion of the work relating to drainage grates and entered into a subcontract with B, Inc. C later discovered that the price quoted for the grates in the contract actually reflected material costs rather than labor costs and that they were so high in comparison to prevailing labor costs that B should have known they were incorrect. In preparing to defend the suit, C learned that at the time of the contract B's corporate status had been suspended by the secretary of state for failure to file its annual report and nonpayment of fees. Can C make an ultra vires claim to avoid the contract with B? Would the result be different if the disadvantage of the bargain were in the opposite direction and one of B's shareholders sued to enjoin the contract's performance?

8

Mergers and Other "Friendly"
Control Transactions

A. *Introduction*

This chapter introduces mergers and other "friendly" transactions whereby control over a corporation or. its assets is transferred to another corporation or a new controlling shareholder. We use the term "friendly" to connote transactions that are supported by the directors of the corporation experiencing the change in control. In contrast, Chapter 9 will introduce "unfriendly" takeovers, where outsiders threaten to buy a controlling amount of a corporation's stock over the objection of that corporation's directors. Friendly control transactions account for almost all of the transactions referred to as "mergers and acquisitions," colloquially known as "M & A activity."

Friendly transactions occur, or are considered, for a variety of reasons, including the following:

- Combining the assets of two formerly separate corporations under one management team may produce economies of scale or other synergistic gains that will make the combined corporations worth more than the sum of their parts.[1]
- The current CEO may be nearing retirement (recall Smith v. Van Gorkom in Chapter 4).

---

1. Two firms may consummate a merger because they expect that the assets of the two firms can be used more efficiently in combination than separately. This might be achieved if merging allows them to lower their costs, improve their products, or expand their operations more effectively than they could as separate entities.

In some cases, these efficiencies can be realized through cost savings arising from the increased size of the merged entity, often referred to as economies of scale or scope. This may result from consolidating and spreading certain fixed overhead costs across the combined operations. For instance . . . [w]hen two supermarket chains merge, distribution centers made redundant by the merger can be eliminated, and the costs of the remaining distribution centers can be spread over a larger number of supermarkets. [In mergers involving a joining of firms that compete in the same market] efficiencies might also come from combining the best elements of each firm's operations.

President's Council of Economic Advisers, Economic Organization and Competition Policy, 19 Yale J. Reg. 541, 551 (2002).

- The management team of the acquiring corporation may be objectively better able to manage the acquired assets than can the acquired corporation's current management.
- The management team of the acquired corporation may anticipate receiving personal benefits from the control transfer (e.g., lucrative employment contracts or significant stock ownership in the acquiring corporation).
- The transaction may reduce taxes, in which case gains will come at the expense of other taxpayers.

Our focus in this chapter is the principal legal form used to carry out these friendly transactions — the statutory merger. We focus on the statutory merger not only because of its dominance in the transactional world but also because the legal norms that surround the statutory merger establish a baseline against which we can measure and understand competing control-transfer forms.

Subpart 1 of Part B examines the special governance rules that apply to statutory mergers — the most important being the requirement that a merger be approved by both the board and the shareholders of the participant corporations. Subpart 2 introduces "dissenter's rights" — a protective device that gives shareholders who vote against a merger the right to have their shares purchased for cash at "fair value" as determined in a judicially supervised appraisal process. These voting and dissenter's rights protections reflect lawmakers' awareness that mergers pose special risks for shareholders — that managers might negligently or disloyally effectuate a transfer of the corporation's assets at an unfair price. Together, voting and dissenter's rights stand as significant checks on managerial misconduct in connection with these transactions.

Subpart 1 of Part C introduces transactional alternatives to the merger — forms that may provide less shareholder protection. The availability of these alternatives creates opportunities for creative corporate planners to "contract around" voting or appraisal rights. Subpart 2 examines judicial doctrines that impede or facilitate private ordering that lessens shareholders' voting or appraisal rights.

Part D explores the intersection between fiduciary duty and appraisal rights, particularly in a cash-out merger by a controlling shareholder. In form, appraisal rights reflect concerns with providing liquidity and individual adaptability to shareholders even if no breach of fiduciary duty is involved. However, as illustrated in the cases in Part D, appraisal rights increasingly play a role in addressing concern about opportunistic behavior by directors or controlling shareholders. To what extent do fiduciary duty suits and appraisal rights reinforce each other? To what extent are they exclusive remedies?

Building on Part D, Part E explores the differences and relationships between the remedies provided by appraisal and the entire fairness review common in controlling shareholder-dominated mergers. Exactly what is the "fair value" to which dissenting shareholders are entitled? How is the recovery in a fiduciary duty suit likely to differ? Part E also explores judicial responses to transactional forms and possible cleansing devices developed by lawyers to reduce the intensity of judicial review in the controlled shareholder setting.

Finally, we look at situations in which directors might forgo a corporate transaction such as a merger and instead individually sell their shares to a new group. A negotiated share exchange can change control as effectively as a merger (if the insiders own enough shares). Moreover, such transactions avoid collective shareholder participation and dissenter's rights. Part F examines efforts to use fiduciary duty to challenge this use of majority power.

B.   *The Statutory Template*

1.   **Mergers**

> **MBCA §§11.01, 11.02, 11.04, 11.05, 11.07**
> **Delaware G.C.L. §§251, 253, 259-261**

A statutory merger is a transaction whereby two or more corporations are combined into one of the corporations, usually referred to as the surviving corporation. When the merger is effected, the legal existence of all constituent corporations, other than the surviving corporation, ceases. By operation of law (e.g., Del. G.C.L. §259), the assets and liabilities of all constituent corporations pass to the surviving corporation, and the outstanding shares of stock in the disappearing corporations are canceled. In a consolidation, the surviving entity is not one of the constituent corporations but, rather, a newly created consolidated corporation.

The statutory template for a merger (found in §251 in the Delaware G.C.L. and chapter 11 of the Model Business Corporation Act) establishes the core requirements for a merger:

- There must be a plan or an agreement of a merger between the constituent corporations (see, e.g., Del. G.C.L. §251(a) with requirements that the plan specify such things as which corporation will be the surviving corporation and the consideration to be provided in the merger; see also MBCA §11.02(c)). In the archetypical merger, shareholders of the disappearing company receive shares of the surviving corporation in exchange for their disappearing shares; however, the consideration may be cash or other securities as specified by the planners in the merger agreement, flexibility that leads to cash-out transactions, discussed in Part D of the chapter.
- The directors of each constituent corporation must adopt that plan (see Delaware G.C.L. §251(b) and MBCA §11.04(a)).
- The shareholders must approve the merger (subject to various exceptions) (Delaware G.C.L. §251(c) and MBCA §11.04(e)).
- The approved plan of merger must be filed with a state official such as the corporations commissioner for the merger to become effective as set forth in the merger plan (Delaware G.C.L. §251(c) and MBCA §11.06).
- Delaware G.C.L. §262 and MBCA chapter 13 sometimes provide shareholders a right to judicial appraisal (valuation) in lieu of amount provided in the merger agreement as discussed in the next subsection.

Note first how the statutory requirements for this corporate action differ from authorization for other kinds of corporate action found in Delaware G.C.L. §141 and

MBCA §8.01. A merger is one of the few corporate actions that the directors cannot do by themselves. In addition, shareholders normally do not have the right to get cash from the corporation in exchange for their shares. In this sense mergers are atypical transactions, and you should anticipate what it is about these transactions that requires a departure from the usual governance rules.

Early corporation codes required unanimous shareholder approval for mergers, a requirement that was later dropped to a supermajority (often two-thirds) of the shareholders of each corporation taking part in the merger. Most states now require approval by only a majority of shareholders, although it usually must be an absolute majority of all shares entitled to vote, not just a majority of votes cast at a particular meeting.

The above-described governance model, which in most cases requires that a merger be approved by the shareholders of both parties to a merger, is built on certain key assumptions. First, lawmakers presumably believe that shareholders can make an informed decision to approve or reject the merger, and that in the normal case the participation of shareholders in the decision-making process adds value for corporations and shareholders. This first assumption relies on another key precept: management will be able to provide the shareholders with sufficient, digestible, and unbiased information about the pros and cons of the planned merger. Further, lawmakers must believe that it will not be unduly burdensome for corporations to await the decision of their shareholders before beginning the critically important and costly process of integrating their assets and personnel. As you read the following case, consider whether these assumptions hold true for mergers involving a complex integration of previously separate businesses, and whether the participation of shareholders in the approval process is worth the cost and expense, including delay and possible litigation, that it entails.

Hewlett v. Hewlett-Packard Co.
Delaware Court of Chancery, 2002
2002 WL 818091

CHANDLER, CHANCELLOR.

This lawsuit challenges the shareholder vote in connection with the proposed merger of defendant Hewlett-Packard Company ("HP") and Compaq Computer Corporation ("Compaq"). HP is a publicly traded Delaware corporation with its principal place of business in Palo Alto, California. Compaq is a publicly traded Delaware corporation with its principal place of business in Houston, Texas. Both companies are global providers of computers and computer-related products and services. Plaintiff Walter B. Hewlett ("Hewlett") has been a director of HP for approximately 15 years. He is the son of the late William R. Hewlett, one of HP's founders. Hewlett and plaintiff Edwin E. van Bronkhorst serve as co-trustees of the William R. Hewlett Revocable Trust (together with Hewlett and van Bronkhorst, the "Hewlett Parties").

After a hotly contested proxy battle between Hewlett and HP, HP's shareholders approved the issuance of shares in connection with the merger at a special meeting on March 19, 2002, by a very slim margin. On March 28, the Hewlett Parties filed this action pursuant to 8 Del. C. §225(b) challenging the validity of that vote. . . .

II. FACTUAL BACKGROUND

. . . In the spring of 2001, HP began to consider seriously the prospect of acquiring and merging with Compaq. The . . . HP board met thirteen times to discuss the proposed merger before it finally voted unanimously in favor of the merger on September 3, 2001.

In connection with the proposed merger, HP engaged McKinsey & Company ("McKinsey") to assess its strategic alternatives. At a board meeting on July 17, 2001, McKinsey made a presentation to HP's board. One portion of this presentation addressed the long-term strategic options available to HP, a subject on which the board conducted a "pretty rich dialogue." Another portion of the presentation addressed the projected effects of a merger with Compaq and identified five main areas of synergy and risk that would aggregate to create the overall financial impact of the merger. HP decided to focus specifically on two of these five items, hard cost synergy and revenue risk, in its external models.[4] The other three items, all of which would have positive financial effects, were purposely omitted from external models in order to allow HP to "under-promise and over-deliver" on its targets.[5]

HP management, including CEO and Chairwoman Carleton S. Fiorina, CFO Robert Wayman, and others, believed that the integration of the two companies would be vital to the ultimate success of the merger. Accordingly, HP began planning the integration process very early on. . . .

On September 3, 2001, HP and Compaq entered into a merger agreement, effective September 4, 2001. The merger was announced publicly on September 4. In connection with this announcement, HP made its first public statements about the financial effects of the merger, emphasizing the projected cost synergies of $2.5 billion and noting a projected revenue loss of less than 5%. HP and Compaq also announced on September 4 that the two co-leads of the integration effort would be Jeff Clarke, CFO of Compaq, and Webb McKinney, a senior executive of HP.

The integration effort headed by Clarke and McKinney was overseen by an Integration Steering Committee consisting of Fiorina, Wayman, Michael Capellas (Compaq's CEO), Clarke, McKinney, Bob Napier (the Chief Information Officer of the new company), and Susan Bowick (the Human Resources Vice President of the new company). The Steering Committee met weekly throughout the process to review the status of integration. At these meetings, the Steering Committee reviewed a standard status chart that consisted of updated status reports from each of 23 different integration teams . . . (including the "value capture" team, an important group for purposes of this litigation). Top executives of both companies also obtained information about integration through conversations with the managers in charge of specific integration functions.

---

4. These two items reappear later as the $2.5 billion cost synergy and 4.9% revenue loss numbers that were repeated by HP throughout the proxy campaign. . . .

5. The factors that HP identified but decided not to include in external communications were hard revenue synergies, such as printer pull-through generated by bundling HP printers with Compaq computers in place of the Lexmark printers currently used by Compaq; revenue aspirations, such as improved product momentum; and cost synergy upsides, or cost synergies not yet supported by firm data. . . .

Throughout the process, integration planning focused on four main pillars: product roadmaps, go-to-market, financial accountability, and launch. From a logistical standpoint, integration initially was to be conducted by a "clean team," a select group of HP and Compaq employees who had access to sensitive, nonpublic information from both companies in a "clean room." The clean team, through its access to this information, was able to start immediately identifying and estimating specific cost synergies (such as those related to procurement), determining what products and services the new company would offer, and working on plans to market those products and services, among other things. As integration progressed, the clean team grew from several hundred employees to well over a thousand, and ultimately integration planning expanded to include "unclean" members of the company's business units.

Shortly after the merger was announced, Fiorina and Wayman attended a meeting in New York with several people from Deutsche Bank, including George Elling, a senior research analyst at Deutsche Bank who was an early and enthusiastic supporter of the merger. At the meeting, HP and Deutsche Bank discussed the merger and their commercial relationship. Deutsche Bank had a prior business relationship with HP, and since August 2001 Deutsche Bank's investment bankers had been working to expand that relationship. . . .

On September 19, 2001, Deutsche Bank sent a letter to Wayman urging HP to engage Deutsche Bank as an advisor in support of the merger. . . . Then, on November 6, 2001, Hewlett publicly announced his opposition to the merger. Wayman testified that "it wasn't really until the proxy battle was announced" that he decided to consider Deutsche Bank's offer. . . . On February 22, 2002, after negotiations about the fee and the scope of the engagement, the parties entered into an engagement letter according to which HP paid Deutsche Bank $1 million, with an additional $1 million to be paid in the event the merger was consummated.[14] . . .

Meanwhile, on November 8, 2001, two days after Walter Hewlett's announcement that he would vote against the merger, HP management received the first of several value capture updates ("VCUs," and each individually a "VCU") from the value capture team, one of many groups involved in the integration process. The value capture team's mandate is to "drive [the] overall top-down corporate planning process to achieve full value of the merger by 2004." The November 8 VCU was generated primarily from clean team reports, with some management oversight, and it analyzed whether the numbers established earlier in the process by management and its consultants were attainable. Although overall revenue estimates were lower than they had been in September due to economic changes affecting the combined entity as well as the standalone prospects for HP and Compaq, the November 8 VCU indicated that the projected effects of the merger remained accurate and were, in fact, conservative. The projected revenue loss arising from the merger remained at or below 4.9%, and the estimated synergy target increased. . . . HP management viewed this report as a

---

14. DTX 305 (engagement letter dated February 22, 2002). Pursuant to this agreement, Deutsche Bank performed a variety of services for HP, including tracking information about the views of significant shareholders, analyzing possible divestitures for the combined business, monitoring arbitrage activity, and informing HP about Wall Street's view of the merger.

validation of the assumptions it had made and the targets it had created with McKinsey in the summer of 2001.

On December 19, 2001, HP filed with the SEC, pursuant to Rule 425, the contents of a presentation to HP stockholders (the "December 19 425 Filing"). This document contained the same information about cost synergies and revenue loss that HP consistently presented since its first public announcement in September 2001. It also contained examples of the effects of these numbers based on management's September 2001 forecasts for fiscal year 2003, as well as analysis based on the then-current Wall Street estimates for that same period. Fiorina and Wayman testified at trial that pages 25 to 28 were always covered in HP management's presentations to shareholders. . . . [O]n page 25, the document applies all of the merger-related numbers—$2.5 billion in cost synergies and a 5% revenue loss with a 12% contribution margin—to the then-current Wall Street estimates of the standalone EPS for HP in fiscal year 2003. This calculation shows the merger to be 13% accretive to HP shareholders, with a stand-alone EPS of $1.28 and a post-merger EPS of $1.44. The footnotes to page 25 indicate expected fiscal year 2003 revenues, based on Bank of America research dated October 11, 2001, of $78.5 billion.

On January 17, 2002, HP announced that it had established January 28, 2002, as the record date for a special meeting of its shareholders to consider and vote upon the issuance of shares required for the proposed merger. The meeting date was set for March 19, 2002, and management's final joint proxy statement/prospectus (the "S-4") was mailed to shareholders on or about February 6, 2002. The final version of the S-4 included the same relevant financial information that appeared in the public announcement of the merger on September 4 and also in the December 19 425 Filing. Specifically, in the section entitled "Financial Benefits of the Merger," HP management disclosed exactly the same cost synergy, revenue loss, and operating profit loss numbers—$2.5 billion, $4.1 billion (representing 4.9% of estimated revenue for fiscal year 2003), and $500 million (applying a 12% contribution margin to the expected revenue loss), respectively—that it had disclosed in the December 19 425 Filing and indeed in nearly every public statement since the announcement of the merger. HP also indicated that it expected the merger to result in EPS accretion of approximately 13% in fiscal 2003, based on consensus Wall Street projections. Once again, as in the December 19 425 Filing, these numbers are clearly described as "assumptions" based on "estimated" results and "anticipate[d]" savings.

While HP was making these presentations and engaging in the proxy contest with Hewlett, the integration process was continuing. The integration process consisted of three separate phases, with the launch date for the new combined company set for May 7, 2002. Sometime in mid-January, HP entered into Phase III of its integration planning. This meant that management and the clean team had completed substantial detailed plans and, for the first time, "unclean" members of the business units were to be involved in the integration process. HP reached this point in the integration process at least two weeks earlier than it originally expected. In addition to being ahead of schedule, the integration teams continued to provide positive reports to HP management, especially with respect to cost synergies and revenue loss goals. According to a VCU dated January 30, the integration teams had identified $X billion in cost synergies, well in excess of HP's public target of $2.5 billion. Moreover, the supply chain value capture team had identified significant additional procurement synergies. HP had also exceeded its revenue targets. It had expected immediate revenue loss due to uncertainty surrounding future product lines, especially in areas in which one of the two companies was significantly stronger than the other, but these immediate revenue losses had not occurred. Fiorina testified that by February 4:

> our revenue loss assumptions were validated, that they were conservative and that we were doing better than those revenue loss assumptions in the market currently, during a period of great uncertainty. I knew, as well, we had revenue synergies, revenue upsides, that were real, that were achievable, that were not part of the financial model we had delivered to the street at all.

Accordingly, at a Goldman Sachs Technology Conference on February 4, Fiorina stated that HP had "now entered the third and final phase of our integration planning. We are at the point where detailed business plans are being drawn up for the new company. We are over-achieving on both our cost-reduction and revenue targets."

The January 30 VCU was the first of several VCUs to include "bottom-up" numbers generated by the business units instead of focusing solely on the "top-down" numbers from management as previous VCUs had done.[29] At this point in the process, the goal from HP management's perspective was to identify the relevant gaps between top-down and bottom-up numbers so that those gaps could be closed. To that end, the January 30 VCU identified specific actions, on a group-by-group basis, that could be used to bridge the gaps between those two sets of numbers. . . .

The next several VCUs—dated February 14, February 28, and March 14—all reflected growing gaps between the top-down and bottom-up numbers. Each VCU was worse than the previous one, and by March 14 the bottom-up numbers were significantly below the numbers implied in the S-4. The Hewlett Parties contend that this is because the underlying facts about the progress of the integration effort did not support the positive statements about the merger being made by HP management. HP responds, to the contrary, that lower numbers from the bottom-up roll-ups are to be expected, for three main reasons. First, the bottom-up plans are generated with imperfect information because the business units do not have complete access to all of the clean room information generated by the 23 integration teams. Second, the bottom-up plans are generated by people who are contemplating the newly combined business units for the first time and are essentially unfamiliar with half of their new

---

29. The value capture team and management establish top-down or "stretch" targets. Tr. 714:18-715:9 (Clarke). The business units develop plans to meet those targets and provide them to the value capture team. The value capture team works with the business groups to assist them in implementing the top-down targets. Clarke made this point at trial when he testified:

> Financial planning is also important but a different part of the process. It is a process that every company goes through on a regular basis. We build financial plans. We look at them. We revise them. Very frequently you need to keep working on them to get to the right level of what can be. I think one of the greatest jobs of senior management is to determine how high to set the bar. If you set it too low, people underachieve. If you set it too high, they give up because they don't know how to get there. So the challenge is to make them be better than they think they can be but make it reachable.

businesses. Third, because the business units are accountable for the numbers they report, the numbers will naturally be conservative.[35]

HP's explanation of the gaps between the bottom-up and top-down numbers is compelling. Clarke, who is one of the heads of the value capture team (in addition to being one of the heads of the entire integration process) and who has access to clean room information, testified credibly that he believed all along, and continues to believe, that the merger-related targets are attainable. Wayman and Fiorina, who have a broad understanding of the progress made by the 23 integration teams through their positions on the Integration Steering Committee, reached similar conclusions. Fiorina explained in her testimony why the bottom-up plans are inherently based on imperfect information and indicated that this was, in fact, by design. Clarke testified that if there were not sufficient gaps between the two sets of numbers at this point then he would make new numbers to *create* gaps. Finally, all three of them testified, to use Wayman's phrase, that "closure comes towards the end," meaning that all budgeting and planning processes typically have similar gaps that are rapidly eliminated as the processes reach their conclusions.

This testimony is corroborated by evidence in the record. For example, although the February 14 VCU indicates that the bottom-up group plans would yield an EPS for fiscal year 2003 of $1.30, or 21% less than the number implied by the estimates contained in the S-4, there are several limiting factors affecting the validity of the group plans. . . . The minutes of a February 14, 2002, meeting of the new company's Executive Council (the "EC") reflect that the EC was not overly concerned by the gaps because the group numbers were incomplete and based on faulty assumptions. The minutes indicate that procurement savings (which appear to be substantial) were "still not factored in" and that "[i]n some cases it looks like we are assuming way too much share loss."

The February 28 and March 14 VCUs appear to be similarly limited. Management was aware of additional cost and revenue synergies that the business teams were not including, partially for the reasons described above and partially by design. The EC, in its March 14 meeting, reiterated the stance it had taken one month earlier, rejecting several of the pessimistic assumptions behind the bottom-up plans. Management identified specific problems with the group reports; for example, every group assumed that it would lose market share, an assumption not shared by management, and the group plans still did not include cost synergies from two key functional integration teams,

---

35. Clarke, Wayman, and Fiorina all testified about the business units producing conservative numbers because they were committing to targets for which they would be held accountable. Fiorina described this aspect of the process as follows:

What happens in February that is different is all of a sudden, but as planned, when we entered Phase III, you bring new people into the planning process, people who haven't been spending months in the clean room, people who in many cases have literally just been named. We don't, for example—we didn't name the CFOs of the new businesses until late February or early March. And so what you had going on is new people being introduced who are grappling for the first time with their new businesses, for which they will be held accountable, and not only have they not had as much time, not only are they not fully familiar with all that has gone into this, but as well, as is the human dynamic in this, they want to come up with a set of numbers that they think they can knock out of the park, because they know ultimately they will be held accountable.

information technology and facilities. Moreover, management also believed that the current negative state of the economy was affecting the bottom-up numbers.

Top HP management was receiving negative financial information at this time from other sources as well. First, on March 10, 2002, Ken Wach, who had been "named on a future basis when the company is combined to be the chief financial person for the enterprise systems group," sent Wayman and others an e-mail indicating that the report he attached to the e-mail was "a frightening reality check on the clean room and value capture revenue work." Then, two days later, Clarke sent virtually identical e-mails to Wayman and Capellas, attaching "the latest roll-up from the value capture" and indicating that "[i]t is ugly—both companies are deteriorating." The Hewlett Parties again contend that these e-mails, like the February and March VCUs, show that the integration process was not going as well as HP management was stating publicly. HP again responds, as with the VCUs, by attempting to explain away the discrepancies between the data in the e-mails and the top-down plans.

HP asserts that Wach's study is bounded by the same limitations as the VCUs and that, in fact, the numbers generated by Wach are identical to those contained in the March 14 VCU. Specifically, Wayman explained at trial that Wach was new to the value capture process and was in a position of having to learn about half of his new business at the same time that he was learning how to work with a new boss (formerly from Compaq). . . . With respect to Clarke's e-mail, Clarke testified as follows:

> I was frustrated. I was sending a note to Michael. I also sent a note to Bob Wayman that evening. I was frustrated that the work that we had done in the executive committee was not and the targets we had set were not being accepted by the business groups. I had a visibility to substantial opportunities around procurement, around upside revenue, around other areas, and the business groups were not addressing those. They were not working on those.

In early March, as management was receiving these e-mails and the controversial VCUs, Hewlett and HP were actively engaged in the proxy contest and each was trying to secure as many votes as possible. In this regard, it was widely known that Institutional Shareholder Services, Inc. ("ISS") played a critical role, because several institutions usually follow ISS recommendations and in this case Barclays Global Investors had committed to voting its approximately 60 million shares of HP stock in accordance with the ISS recommendation. On March 5, 2002, ISS issued a report to its subscribers recommending that HP shareholders vote in favor of the merger. The ISS report notes that both sides had made various claims about the financial benefits of the merger. ISS did not try to resolve this debate, reasoning that "the financial and strategic prospects of an HP-Compaq combination are a matter on which reasonable people can (and do) disagree. The accretive or dilutive impact of the merger, and the corresponding appreciation or depreciation of HP's stock value, is highly sensitive to a number of assumptions about which there is no clear agreement among expert observers."[54] Accordingly, ISS focused instead on the integration process and how that

---

54. The author of the ISS report on the merger testified:

> We assumed that the numbers we were receiving from each side were accurate. I think we understood, of course, that each side has a perspective and took the numbers with a grain of salt.

process would affect long-term value. With respect to integration, ISS concluded in its report that it would be "hard to remain unimpressed in the face of such enthusiastic attention paid to the integration effort," and that "management has done everything it can to maximize the chance that integration will be a success." The plaintiffs contend that HP obtained ISS's endorsement by misrepresenting the financial benefits of the merger and the progress of the integration efforts.

The plaintiffs also allege that HP improperly enticed or coerced Deutsche Bank to vote in favor of the merger by using the "carrot" of potential future business. Deutsche Bank is a global banking company comprised of three separate groups: Corporate and Investment Bank ("CIB"), Corporate Investments ("CI"), and Private Clients and Asset Management ("PCAM"). Deutsche Bank Asset Management ("DBAM"), which is part of PCAM, is a very large asset fund manager that operates a number of funds that invest money on behalf of individuals and institutions worldwide. . . .

Voting decisions for shares held by DBAM are made by a five-member committee known as the Proxy Working Group (the "PWG"). For much of the proxy contest, both HP management and Spencer Fleischer, one of Hewlett's advisors, believed that DBAM would follow its common practice and vote its shares in accordance with ISS's recommendation. Thornton and Griswold, the Deutsche Bank commercial bankers advising HP, were told by Margaret Preston of DBAM that this was the case, and they informed Wayman accordingly. . . .

The PWG first met to discuss the merger on March 11, 2002. At that point, the PWG had not met with representatives for either side;[66] the PWG members had merely reviewed the ISS report and certain public information about the merger. The PWG made no decision on the merger at this meeting, but instead arranged another meeting on Friday, March 15, in order to allow additional time for research and deliberation. At the March 15 meeting, the PWG decided to vote its Compaq shares in favor of the merger, but its HP shares against the merger. Dean Barr, Global Chief Investment Officer of PCAM, informed Fleischer later that day of this result and of the similar independent determination by Deutsche Bank's European Proxy Committee. . . .

[Almost immediately HP representatives began hearing rumors that DBAM was voting against the merger. HP, through Wayman, expressed its concerns to Deutsche Bank commercial bankers Griswold and Thornton, who arranged for a special telephone meeting of the PWG to be held on the morning of the proxy vote. Hewlett and Fleischer learned of the meeting only a short time before it began, and made a brief presentation to the PWG, which began at 6:30 a.m. Fiorina and Waymans began their presentation to the PWG at approximately 7:00 a.m., and upon its completion left the telephonic meeting to conduct the HP shareholders' meeting.]

After Fiorina and Wayman left the call, the PWG deliberated about the merits of the merger and revoted, this time deciding to vote DBAM's HP shares in favor of the merger. . . .

While the PWG was debating about the merger, Fiorina was beginning to conduct the special meeting of HP shareholders. The meeting, which was scheduled to begin

---

66. Mr. Hewlett's advisors had been requesting a meeting with the PWG since at least February 2002. Mr. Barr had consistently told Mr. Hewlett's advisors and others that he would only schedule a meeting if both sides wanted, and had, the opportunity to present their respective positions to the PWG.

at 8:00 a.m., actually began around 8:30 a.m. because of long lines and heightened security. Fiorina conducted the meeting, closing the polls "when I ascertained that we had no more lines, the cards had been collected and I could see no further hands in the audience indicating they had cards that they wanted to be collected," and ending the meeting shortly after 10:00 a.m.[82] Following the special meeting, HP management publicly claimed that the HP shareholders had approved the proposed merger by a "slim but sufficient" margin, which currently appears to be approximately 45.2 million votes (subject to successful challenges to individual votes in the "snake pit" process) out of 1,644,781,070 shares present at the special meeting. This lawsuit was then filed on March 28, 2002.

III. THE DISCLOSURE CLAIM

This Court stated in its opinion denying HP's motion to dismiss that the burden on the plaintiffs with respect to the disclosure claim would be as follows: "At trial, the plaintiffs have the burden of proving, through analysis of reports of the integration team," that "HP management knowingly misrepresented material facts about integration in an effort to persuade ISS and possibly others to approve of the merger." The question before me, therefore, is whether HP management knowingly and intentionally made material misrepresentations about the progress of the integration process.

To support their claim that it did, the Hewlett Parties rely on the VCUs generated in February and March and on the early March e-mails sent by Wach and Clarke. The plaintiffs contend that these documents all demonstrate that the integration process was going poorly, contrary to public statements by HP management, and that the combined company would not meet the revenue projections implied in the S-4. The plaintiffs also question the accuracy of Fiorina's statements at the Goldman Sachs Technology Conference on February 4, 2002. Ultimately, the plaintiffs' allegations boil down to two arguments: that HP management overstated the progress that was being made on the integration process, and that HP management was overly optimistic about the substantive results that the integration process would create. In connection with the second of these claims, the plaintiffs contend that HP should have made corrective disclosures about its financial projections after receiving the VCUs and the March e-mails.

I find both of these contentions to be without merit. The public statements made by HP management about the progress of the integration process, specifically Fiorina's February 4 statements, were supported by the facts when they were made and were neither false nor misleading. HP had entered Phase III of its integration planning by February 4, and detailed business plans were being created. Information available to management also indicated that the company was overachieving on both its cost-reduction and its revenue targets. Specifically, the January 30 VCU identified $X billion in cost synergies, or more than $X over HP's external target of $2.5 billion in

---

82. Tr. 214:11-215:20 (Fiorina). Fiorina also testified that she first learned that Deutsche Bank had switched its vote after the meeting had ended. Tr. 189:1-5 (Fiorina).

synergies, and expected revenue losses following the announcement of the merger had not materialized. Moreover, HP management continued to be aware of revenue synergies and other cost upsides that were not included in the external projections.

The evidence before me also supports ISS's conclusion that "management has done everything it can to maximize the chance that integration will be a success." As indicated by the McKinsey report presented to HP's board on July 30 and by the naming of the integration team heads on the same day as the first public announcement of the merger, HP management focused on integration even before the merger was announced. HP's board believed from the beginning that successful integration of the two companies would be critical to the success of the merger. HP acted accordingly by planning its integration efforts carefully and thoroughly. It selected hundreds of its "best" and "brightest" managers for the integration teams. It also involved key senior executives in the process through the Integration Steering Committee, which was actively involved through, among other things, weekly meetings about integration. Nothing in the record indicates that HP lied to or deliberately misled ISS or the HP shareholders about its integration efforts.

The crux of the Hewlett Parties' second argument is that HP learned in February and March that the top-line revenue projections implied in the S-4 and used illustratively in the December 19 425 Filing were unattainable. This argument proceeds from two faulty premises: first, that the revenue numbers generated in the value capture process and contained in the VCUs represent realistic projections of expected future results; and second, that the estimated revenue, profit, and EPS numbers found in the S-4 and the December 19 425 Filing represented firm commitments by HP management. I am persuaded by HP's arguments that several factors limit the accuracy of the VCUs. Consequently, I find that it is reasonable for HP to believe that it will achieve better results than those contained in the VCUs. Additionally, I am unable to conclude that HP committed to the financial numbers implied in the S-4. The projections in the S-4 were clearly labeled as forward-looking estimates, and the December 19 425 Filing clearly indicates that those projections were made on September 4. More importantly, however, the numbers relied upon by the plaintiffs are purely illustrative and indeed are only one set of several presented by HP. The important numbers discussed repeatedly by HP management are the merger-related numbers of $2.5 billion in cost synergies and not more than 4.9% revenue loss. No evidence in the record before me contradicts the reasoned views of HP management about the limitations of the VCUs or suggests that HP will be unable to meet its merger-related targets. To the extent that the plaintiffs need to prove a subjective element for this claim to succeed, they fail completely to do so. Failing to prove that HP affirmatively and knowingly misrepresented facts about integration, the plaintiffs fall back on the argument that HP should have disclosed the negative information contained in the VCUs and the early March e-mails because that information would have been material to shareholders. It is well-settled that omitted facts are material if there is a "substantial likelihood that the disclosure of the omitted fact would have been viewed by the reasonable investor as having significantly altered the 'total mix' of information made available." I cannot agree with the plaintiffs that the VCUs and the e-mails from Wach and Clarke were material. While this information clearly would be material if presented in final reports or projections, that is simply not the case here. . . .

The plaintiffs have been unable to prove that HP misrepresented or omitted material facts about integration in the proxy contest. Instead, the evidence demonstrates that HP's statements concerning the merger were true, complete, and made in good faith. During the trial, members of HP's senior management testified credibly, in accordance with the evidence and without exception, that throughout the proxy contest they believed that the cost synergy and revenue loss targets were realistic and, in fact, would be exceeded. Finally, there is no legal requirement that companies disclose all documents generated in a budgeting process. I therefore find in favor of HP on the disclosure claim.

IV.   THE VOTE-BUYING CLAIM[92]

The Hewlett Parties' vote-buying claim centers on the March 19, 2002 telephone conference at which members of Deutsche Bank's PWG entertained competing presentations on the merits of the proposed merger from Walter Hewlett and HP management. The plaintiffs contend that during the telephone conference, Deutsche Bank was coerced by threats, either implied or explicit, from HP management that Deutsche Bank's future business relationship with HP would suffer if the shares of HP held by Deutsche Bank were voted against the merger. Accordingly, they ask this Court to set aside the resulting vote of a portion of the HP shares held by Deutsche Bank in favor of the merger.

As stated in the opinion denying HP's motion to dismiss, the Hewlett Parties bear the following burden with respect to the vote-buying claim:

> At trial, the plaintiffs will have the significant burden of presenting sufficient evidence for me to find that Deutsche Bank was coerced by HP management during their March 19, 2002 telephone conference into voting 17 million shares in favor of the proposed merger and that the switch of those votes was not made by Deutsche Bank for independent business reasons.[93]

Therefore, the plaintiffs must prove that HP management used the business relationship between HP and Deutsche Bank as a weapon to coerce Deutsche Bank into voting for the merger. That is, they must establish that it was HP management's improper influence that caused Deutsche Bank to switch some of the proxies it had voted against the merger on March 15 to favor the merger on March 19.

The vote-buying claim turns entirely on circumstantial evidence. . . .

---

92. I note initially, although the matter is disputed, that it appears at this point that the number of votes switched by Deutsche Bank likely will not be enough to change the ultimate outcome in this case. . . . The plaintiffs, however, relying on record evidence, contend that the number of shares voted by Deutsche Bank (as a whole, apparently, and not just by the participants in the March 19 call) may be as high as 24 million. If this number is in fact correct, and if all of these shares were initially voted against the merger and then later voted in favor of the merger as a result of improper influence by HP management, then the resulting swing—48 million votes—would appear to be outcome-determinative.

93. . . . My statement in the opinion on the motion to dismiss was not intended to imply that, in its role as a fiduciary to the beneficial owners of HP shares held by Deutsche Bank, it would be proper for Deutsche Bank to advance its own business interests rather than the best interests of the beneficial HP owners. The plaintiffs' argument that Deutsche Bank, as a shareholder, can vote HP shares in any way it chooses is incorrect to the extent that it implies that Deutsche Bank could make that determination based on considerations other than the best interests of the beneficial owners of the HP shares.

The plaintiffs first rely upon a voicemail message left by Fiorina for Wayman on March 17 after HP management became aware that Deutsche Bank might have voted against the merger. In that message, Fiorina told Wayman:

> Talking to Alan Miller again today. He remains very nervous about Deutsche. . . . And so the suggestion is that you call the guy at Deutsche again first thing Monday morning. And if you don't get the right answer from him, then you and I need to demand a conference call, an audience, etc. to make sure that we get them in the right place. . . . So if you take Deutsche . . . get on the phone and see what we can get, but we may have to do something extraordinary for those two to bring 'em over the line here.

The plaintiffs contend that Fiorina's comment that HP "demand a conference call" and her reference to "do[ing] something extraordinary" support their allegation that HP management was willing to, and did, improperly pressure Deutsche Bank to switch its vote.

The plaintiffs next question the motive behind the scheduling of the March 19, 2002, conference call. The parties acknowledge that Deutsche Bank had existing commercial relationships with HP. Deutsche Bank was also providing services to HP in connection with the merger. It is undisputed that Deutsche Bank desired to continue and expand its business relationships with HP. Because of this desire, the plaintiffs contend, Deutsche Bank was susceptible to the threat that business opportunities would be withheld if Deutsche Bank voted against the merger.

Based on these statements and inferences, the plaintiffs allege that HP management coerced Deutsche Bank by using the threat of lost future business opportunities to compel the CIB group, through Griswold and Thornton, in turn to force PCAM, of which the PWG was a part, to reconsider its vote against the merger. In the face of this threat, the plaintiffs insist, the PWG ignored its fiduciary duty to the beneficial owners of HP shares controlled by PCAM and voted in favor of the merger so that Deutsche Bank's CIB group might avoid the loss of some unspecified future business. Based on the evidence before me, however, I cannot agree that these circumstances are sufficient to demonstrate a vote-buying scheme.

First, I do not believe that Fiorina's voicemail evidences an intent to employ improper means to persuade Deutsche Bank to vote in favor of the merger. Fiorina testified credibly at trial that by "do[ing] something extraordinary," she meant that HP management needed to take the steps necessary to gain an audience at Deutsche Bank for HP's presentation in favor of the merger. These steps included flying to New York for a personal presentation to Deutsche Bank, making independent HP board members available to speak to Deutsche Bank, or having someone from Compaq speak to Deutsche Bank. Under the circumstances, with the hotly contested shareholder vote less than 48 hours away, such actions would be somewhat extraordinary. In light of the proximity of the shareholder vote and the perceived narrow margin separating votes for or against the merger, I believe the contents of Fiorina's message are not sufficient to support an inference that HP management intended to coerce Deutsche Bank. Rather, Fiorina's message reflects reasonable actions taken by an executive faced with unexpected adverse information.

Second, although members of Deutsche Bank's CIB group were contacted by HP management and attempted to arrange a meeting with the PWG, the evidence does not show that the intervention of the commercial bankers resulted from a threat by HP to withdraw future business from Deutsche Bank. Other than introducing the participants in the March 19 conference call, the CIB individuals (Griswold and Thornton) neither contributed to the substantive discussions of the proposed merger nor offered any input during the PWG's consideration of how to vote the HP shares controlled by Deutsche Bank. Moreover, it appears that Griswold and Thornton helped arrange the hastily convened conference call because they were distressed that they had misled their client, HP, about the process DBAM would follow in voting shares on the merger. Both Griswold and Thornton testified, without exception, that they had erroneously advised HP that shares held by DBAM as index, or passive, shares would be voted according to the ISS recommendation. Feeling "stupid," "shocked," and "embarrassed" about having misstated the facts regarding the voting process, both Griswold and Thornton believed that it was only appropriate to create an opportunity, albeit at the last minute and with no assurance as to its outcome, for the proxy contestants (and particularly their client) to present their positions on the merits of the merger to the PWG. . . .

The circumstances surrounding the March 19 conference call give rise to reasonably conflicting inferences, not all of which are benevolent. It is troubling, for example, that the March 19 telephone conference was initiated at the urging of individuals from the CIB group of Deutsche Bank and that those individuals also attended the telephone conference. This fact raises clear questions about the integrity of the internal ethical wall that purportedly separates Deutsche Bank's asset management division from its commercial division. Nevertheless, no evidence credibly demonstrates that Griswold and Thornton arranged the conference call in response to a threat from HP management to withhold future business.

Ultimately, the recording of the March 19 conference call, as well as the testimonies of Fiorina, Wayman, and the individuals at Deutsche Bank participating in the call, fail to support the plaintiffs' vote-buying contention. . . .

Following HP management's presentation on the merits, the PWG debated about the merger without reference to how its decision would affect business between HP and Deutsche Bank. The PWG focused instead on the harm the companies and their shareholders would suffer if the merger was not approved, as well as other substantive issues relating to the merits of the merger, such as the revenue synergy from printer pull-through. After this substantive discussion, the PWG voted 4-1, by secret ballot, in favor of the merger.

The committee then spoke to Klaus Kaldermorgen, Deutsche Bank's European Proxy Committee representative, about how he would vote the shares he controlled. Again, the discussion concerned the substantive merits of the merger and no mention was made of any threat to Deutsche Bank from a business relationship standpoint. . . .

The final circumstance offered by the plaintiffs to prove that the PWG's vote was the result of improper influence from HP management is Fiorina's closing remarks during the conference call. Fiorina ended her presentation by stating:

> Gentlemen, we appreciate your time. I need to go try and get ready for a shareowner meeting. We very, very much appreciate your willingness to listen to us this morning. This is obviously of great importance to us as a company. *It is of great importance to our ongoing relationship.* We very much would like to have your support here. We think this is a crucially important decision for this company.

This is the only statement from HP management that plaintiffs point to as evidence that Deutsche Bank was coerced during the March 19, 2002, telephone conference. That statement does not, in my opinion, demonstrate that Fiorina was attempting to coerce Deutsche Bank. Fiorina testified that the statement was the typical way she ended similar calls after making HP's standard presentation to investors. For thirty minutes prior to that closing statement, Fiorina and Wayman presented management's case for the merger and responded to concerns specifically raised by members of the PWG. The plaintiffs can point to nothing in those exchanges that indicates a threat from management that future business would be withheld by HP from Deutsche Bank and there is no indication that the PWG believed its discretion had been limited because of such a threat. Instead, the record establishes that all of the questions posed by the proxy committee — some of which were prompted by concerns raised just minutes before by Walter Hewlett's presentation in opposition to the merger — went to the merits of the transaction. Accordingly, I must find in favor of HP on the vote-buying claim. . . .

2.   Dissenter's Rights

MBCA §§13.01(4), 13.02, 13.24
Delaware G.C.L. §262

If a shareholder dissents when asked to approve a merger or other covered transaction, and if the transaction nonetheless obtains the requisite shareholder approval, the dissenting shareholder may demand that his shares be repurchased by the corporation for fair value. If the dissenting shareholder and corporation cannot agree to a price within the time frame and procedures outlined by the appraisal statute, then fair value will be determined in a judicial proceeding. These rights — commonly called "dissenter's rights" or "appraisal rights" — are historically tied to the relaxation of shareholders' ability to limit a corporation's adaptability.

In the nineteenth century, while directors were permitted to control the enterprise, unanimous shareholder approval was required for business combinations. This permitted each shareholder to avoid being forced to continue in an enterprise dramatically different from the one in which that shareholder had invested. However, it also gave each shareholder a veto that could be used strategically to limit the corporation's flexibility to adapt to changed circumstances. Over time, all American jurisdictions moved from a unanimous vote to a supermajority vote or a majority vote. During this same time, appraisal was provided to those shareholders who dissented from these corporate actions. The conventional view is that appraisal rights were a trade-off for the loss of the veto, providing shareholders with an "out" when the managers and the majority shareholders dramatically changed the enterprise.

Before a shareholder elects to pursue appraisal, he must weigh the costs and benefits of the proceeding. What is the likelihood that the court will find a "fair value" significantly higher than the corporation's offer? What will be the consequence if the court finds a lower value than the corporation offers? How long will the shareholder be without his money? Who will pay the costs of the proceeding?

Traditional statutes like Delaware G.C.L. §262 offer little comfort to a risk-averse shareholder considering appraisal in lieu of the terms offered in the merger approved by the corporation. The shareholder will receive judicially determined fair value, plus interest, even if that amount is less than what the corporation offered to shareholders as part of the terms of the merger. Moreover, the court is empowered to assess the corporation's expenses against the dissenting shares if equitable.

The Model Business Corporation Act (MBCA) is much more sympathetic to risk-averse dissenters. Section 13.25 requires the corporation to make payment to the dissenter as soon as the corporate action is consummated. This payment must represent the corporation's good faith judgment as to the fair value of the dissenter's shares. If the court finds a higher fair value in the appraisal proceeding, the dissenting shareholder will receive the difference. The MBCA also exposes dissenters to less potential liability for costs and expenses. The corporation usually will be required to pay the costs of the appraisal, including the expense of the appraiser. The dissenter may be charged for some or all of the costs or expenses only if the dissenter acted arbitrarily, vexatiously, or not in good faith in demanding payment or exercising his appraisal rights. The court apportions attorneys' fees as it finds equitable.

When should appraisal rights be available? From a policy standpoint, coverage should include transactions satisfying two criteria. First, the proposed transaction either will require the shareholder to invest in a fundamentally different enterprise or will constitute a cash-out and final settling-up of the shareholder's investment. Second, other protective devices (such as the market or fiduciary litigation) are likely to be ineffective or more costly in protecting the shareholder's investment expectations.

With respect to mergers, most statutes provide that appraisal rights exist only when voting rights exist. There is one important exception. The shareholders of a corporation merged out of existence via a short-form merger still receive appraisal rights. With respect to other transactional forms, as we will see in Part C, there are widely different approaches between jurisdictions as to when dissenter's rights are available.

One final difference with respect to mergers is the so-called market-out exception. Delaware denies appraisal rights for most publicly traded shares, if the merger consideration received in exchange is also publicly traded stock. The MBCA eliminated a market-out in 1978, but readopted that exception, in different form, in 1999. See MBCA §13.02(b). Under that section, the market-out exception does not apply to a corporate transaction that is an interested transaction as defined in §13.01 (5.1), a subset of transactions that will be important in the cases to follow in this chapter. Delaware's "exception to the exception" in §262(b), (b)(1), and (b)(2) is more convoluted and difficult to follow. A key result is that shareholders retain access to appraisal rights in cash-out mergers, a recurring example of interested transactions in a merger setting.

As you become more familiar with the statutory rules governing mergers and dissenter's rights, consider what policies are reflected by each rule and exception. Consider also to what extent the underlying policies would be better served by different provisions or by other devices, including fiduciary-duty-based litigation.

NOTES AND QUESTIONS

1. There are exceptions to the norm that shareholders must approve a merger. The most common are the "de minimis change" exception and the "short-form merger" exception. The de minimis change exception denies voting rights to shareholders of the surviving corporation in a merger having terms that will not significantly affect the pre-merger shareholders' voting or equity rights, nor require a change in the corporation's articles of incorporation. Under MBCA §11.04(g) (and §6.21(f)) a merger has a "de minimis effect" on voting and equity rights if the merger increases the number of outstanding common shares of the surviving corporation by not more than 20 percent. For example, if the surviving corporation had 100,000 common shares immediately before the merger, no more than 20,000 additional shares may be issued in the merger.

2. The short-form merger is a procedure that allows a corporation that owns most of the shares of another corporation (the "subsidiary") to merge with that subsidiary by director action alone. Short-form mergers are not based solely on the futility of a shareholder vote because the qualifying ownership percentage is not tied to the number of votes required to approve the merger. Indeed, in every jurisdiction the threshold ownership percentage is much higher than the number of votes needed.

PROBLEM 8-1

The boards of directors of Delta Corp. and Sigma Corp. have agreed to a corporate combination. For each fact pattern below, identify the voting and dissenter's rights that must be provided to the shareholders of Delta Corp. and Sigma Corp. In so doing, assume first that both corporations are incorporated in Delaware, and then that both corporations are governed by the MBCA.

(a) Delta Corp. will merge into Sigma Corp. Prior to the merger, Delta Corp. has 30 shareholders and Sigma Corp. has 40 shareholders. Each corporation has 1,000 common shares issued and outstanding. The merger agreement provides that upon consummation of the merger each outstanding common share of Delta Corporation will be converted into a common share of Sigma Corp. (In other words, the merger share-exchange ratio is 1 for 1.) After the merger (assuming that no shareholder of either corporation exercises appraisal rights): Sigma Corp. will have 2,000 common shares outstanding; the pre-merger Sigma shareholders will continue to hold, collectively, 1,000 Sigma shares; the pre-merger Delta shareholder will now hold, collectively, 1,000 newly issued Sigma shares.

(b) Delta Corp. will merge into Sigma Corp. Prior to the merger, Delta Corp. has 30 shareholders and Sigma Corp. has 40 shareholders. Each corporation has 1,000 common shares issued and outstanding. The merger agreement provides that upon consummation of the merger each outstanding common share of Delta Corporation will be exchanged for $1,000 in cash. After the merger (assuming that no shareholder of either corporation exercises appraisal rights): Sigma Corp. will have 1,000 common shares outstanding; the pre-merger Sigma shareholders will continue to hold, collectively, 1,000 Sigma shares; the pre-merger Delta shareholders will have cash, but no Sigma shares.

(c) Delta Corp. will sell all of its assets to Sigma Corp. Prior to the asset sale, Delta Corp. has 30 shareholders and Sigma Corp. has 40 shareholders. Each corporation has 1,000 common shares issued and outstanding. The asset purchase agreement provides that Delta Corporation will exchange its assets for 1,000 Sigma common shares; Sigma Corp. will also assume all of Delta Corp.'s liabilities. Immediately after this exchange is effected, Delta Corporation will be dissolved and its only asset—the 1,000 Sigma common shares—will be distributed pro rata to the Delta shareholders. After the asset sale and liquidation of Delta Corp. (assuming that no shareholder of either corporation exercises appraisal rights): Sigma Corp. will have 2,000 common shares outstanding; the pre-merger Sigma shareholders will continue to hold, collectively, 1,000 Sigma shares; the pre-merger Delta shareholders will now hold, collectively, 1,000 newly issued Sigma shares.

(d) Delta Corp. will merge into Sigma Corp. Prior to the merger, Delta Corp. has 10 million shares outstanding and 2,500 shareholders. The largest Delta shareholder owns 3 percent of the outstanding stock, and Delta senior executives and directors, collectively, own 700,000 shares. Sigma Corp., before the merger, has 10 million shares outstanding, and its shares are traded on the New York Stock Exchange. No one person owns more than 2 percent of Sigma stock. Sigma senior executives and directors, collectively, own 300,000 Sigma shares. The merger agreement provides that upon consummation of the merger, each outstanding common share of Delta will be converted into one-half of a common share of Sigma. (In other words, the merger exchange rate is 2 for 1.) After the merger (assuming no shareholder of either corporation exercises appraisal rights), Sigma Corp. will have 15 million common shares outstanding; the pre-merger Sigma shareholders will continue to hold, collectively, 10 million Sigma shares; and the pre-merger Delta shareholders will now hold, collectively, 5 million newly issued Sigma shares.

(e) How does your analysis in transaction (d) change if the currency for the merger is cash for the Delta shareholders in exchange for their Delta shares?

(f) How would your analysis of the fact pattern in (d) be affected if prior to the merger Sigma owned 51 percent of Delta Corp.'s outstanding stock?

C. Contracting Around Appraisal and Voting Rights

1. Use of Alternative Transactional Forms

a. Introductory Note

There are a number of transactional alternatives to the statutory merger. The most prominent are the asset sale, the sale of a control block of stock, and the so-called "triangular" merger. There are significant tax, accounting, and liability reasons to consider in choosing between the traditional merger form and one of these alternative forms. To a great extent, participants in a friendly controlled transaction can "contract around" the normal default rules provided by mergers by choosing different transactional forms, and the voting and appraisal rules that attach to such forms. This is particularly true as affecting the shareholders of the acquiring company; it is much less true for shareholders of the "target" or disappearing corporation in the transaction. As you proceed through this section, consider how much contractual freedom planners have for each participant corporation.

b. Sale of Assets

MBCA §§12.01, 12.02
Delaware G.C.L. §271

An alternative method of transferring ownership and control of corporate assets from one corporation to another is to convey title by one or more bills of sale. Asset sales differ from mergers in several respects. First, the corporation selling assets does not automatically go out of existence upon consummation of the sale, although it can by following the asset sale with a dissolution. Second, the selling corporation need not transfer all of its assets, as will occur in a merger. Third, the liabilities of the selling corporation will not necessarily pass to the purchasing corporation by operation of law.

Despite these legal differences between the two mechanisms, an asset sale can usually be structured to achieve the same substantive result that would occur via the merger: a corporation sells all of its assets to another corporation; the purchasing corporation assumes all liabilities of the selling corporation; and the selling corporation dissolves simultaneously with the consummation of the sale, with the disappearing corporation distributing to its shareholders the shares or other consideration received in the asset sale. Our focus in this part of the chapter is on whether corporate planners can control who gets voting rights or appraisal rights by structuring a transaction as a merger, a sale of assets, or some other way.

If the directors of a corporation wish to sell substantially all of the corporation's assets other than in the ordinary course of business, they must submit the proposal to their shareholders for approval, normally by majority vote. In Delaware, these shareholders get a vote but are not provided appraisal rights as they would have been in a merger. Unlike the statutory merger, the shareholders of the *acquiring* company, in both Delaware and the MBCA jurisdictions, do not have a right to approve or disapprove the transaction. This denial of voting rights might make sense in an archetypal sale of assets, where the purchasing corporation is so much larger than the selling corporation that the transaction is of no real significance to the purchasing corporation's shareholders. However, denial of voting rights to shareholders of the acquiring corporation is not limited to such situations.

If less than all of a corporation's assets are to be sold, corporate planners must determine whether the transaction is qualitatively and quantitatively significant enough to require approval by the selling corporation's shareholders. Existing precedent suggests that this determination is subject to significant risk of judicial second-guessing. For example, in Katz v. Bregman, 431 A.2d 1274 (Del. Ch. 1981), a sale of 51 percent of a corporation's total assets was held to be "substantially all" of the corporation's assets. The court emphasized that the assets sold constituted the corporation's long-time principal business, and that the corporation planned to undertake a radically different business post-sale. The test for substantiality was stated in Oberly v. Kirby, 592 A.2d 445, 464 (1991), as follows:

[T]he rule announced in Gimbel v. Signal Cos., Del. Ch., 316 A.2d 599, aff'd, Del. Supr., 316 A.2d 619 (1974), makes it clear that the need for shareholder . . . approval is to be measured not by the size of a sale alone, but also by its qualitative effect upon the corporation. Thus, it is relevant to ask whether a transaction "is out of the ordinary and substantially affects the existence and purpose of the corporation." [*Gimbel,* 316 A.2d] at 606.

c. *Triangular Mergers*

Many corporate combinations are structured as "triangular mergers." Imagine an ordinary merger as a straight line running between the acquired and acquiring corporation. In a triangular merger, the transactions look like a triangle. One point on the triangle is the corporation financing and masterminding the acquisition (the acquiring parent), which transfers the merger consideration to a wholly owned subsidiary corporation—the second point on the triangle. The merger then takes place between the acquired corporation—the third point on the triangle—and the acquiring company's subsidiary. The consideration flowing to the acquired corporation's shareholders is the same as if the transaction were structured as a straight merger, usually cash or securities of the acquiring parent.

There are two basic forms of triangular mergers—a *forward triangular merger* and a *reverse triangular merger,* although there are often variations on these two basic forms that involve subsidiaries of subsidiaries. In a forward triangular merger, the acquired corporation merges into the *acquiring* subsidiary. In a reverse triangular merger, the acquiring subsidiary merges into the *acquired* corporation; in form the acquired corporation is the surviving corporation, but the acquiring corporation ends up with all, or at least a controlling amount of, the acquired corporation's stock.

There are a variety of tax, accounting, and liability reasons for using a triangular merger form. However, from a corporate governance perspective, the principal reason is to eliminate the voting and appraisal rights that the shareholders of the acquiring parent would otherwise have. In most states, the only shareholders entitled to voting and dissenter's rights are the shareholders of the actual parties to the merger. Thus, the acquiring parent receives the voting and appraisal rights belonging to the acquiring subsidiary, which are then exercised by the acquiring parent's board, which obviously will not dissent from the transaction. The shareholders of the parent corporation—who would have received voting rights if the transaction were cast as a straight merger—are shut out of the decision-making process and receive no dissenter's rights protection.

d. *Compulsory Share Exchanges*
MBCA §§11.03, 11.04

A compulsory share exchange is a relatively less-used statutory proceeding that, like a reverse triangular merger, permits one corporation to acquire *all* the shares of another while leaving the acquired corporation in existence. This transfer can be accomplished by a simple majority vote of shareholders of the acquired corporation, but only needs board approval of the acquiring corporation. Nonconsenting shareholders of the acquired corporation are forced to give up their shares subject to their appraisal rights. Shareholders of the acquiring corporation do not receive appraisal rights.

2.   De Facto Mergers

As the preceding discussion in this chapter makes clear, when two corporations agree to a corporate combination, shareholders' voting and appraisal rights will differ depending on the transactional form chosen. Naturally, the corporate parties to a combination, with the advice of their attorneys and other planners, will choose a transactional structure intended to achieve the optimal balance of costs and advantages (including consequences not discussed here of financial accounting, tax, securities, and stock exchange rules and regulations). Often the parties will elect a transaction form that denies shareholders voting and appraisal rights that would have been available had the parties chosen to structure the transaction as an ordinary merger. Shareholders denied voting or appraisal rights may ask courts to intervene and recharacterize the transaction as a merger under the de facto merger doctrine. The defendants will argue that the court should respect the legislature's action in creating overlapping statutory provisions, and should not interfere with the defendants' choice of which statutorily authorized tools to use in structuring the challenged corporate combination.

A classic "de facto merger" case is Farris v. Glen Alden Corp., 143 A.2d 25 (Pa. 1958). Glen Alden "acquired" the assets of List Corp. in exchange for Glen Alden common stock and Glen Alden's assumption of List's liabilities. Immediately thereafter List Corp. dissolved and distributed the Glen Alden shares pro rata to the List shareholders. As a result, former List shareholders owned 72.5% of the outstanding shares of Glen Alden, Glen Alden was renamed List Alden, and former List directors assumed control of the List Alden board of directors.

The Pennsylvania statute then in effect granted appraisal rights to shareholders of both the acquiring and acquired corporations in a merger, but only to the shareholders of the selling corporation in a transfer of substantially all of a corporation's assets. Honoring the form of the transaction in *Farris*—List's sale of substantially all of its assets to Glen Alden—would deny appraisal rights to the Glen Alden shareholders. Instead, the Pennsylvania Supreme Court affirmed the trial court's determination that Glen Alden shareholders should be given appraisal rights as if the transaction had taken place via a merger.

> The rationale of Lauman v. Lebanon Valley R. R. Co., 30 Pa. 42 (Pa. 1858), and of the present section of the Business Corporation Law based thereon, is that when a corporation combines with another so as to lose its essential nature and alter the original fundamental relationships of the shareholders among themselves and to the corporation, a shareholder who does not wish to continue his membership therein may treat his membership in the original corporation as terminated and have the value of his shares paid to him.
>
> Does the combination outlined in the present "reorganization" agreement so fundamentally change the corporate character of Glen Alden and the interest of the plaintiff as a shareholder therein, that to refuse him the rights and remedies of a dissenting shareholder would in reality force him to give up his stock in one corporation and against his will accept shares in another? If so, the combination is a merger within the meaning of section 908, subd. A of the corporation law.

. . . So, as in the present case, when as part of a transaction between two corporations, one corporation dissolves, its liabilities are assumed by the survivor, its executives and directors take over the management and control of the survivor, and, as consideration for the transfer, its stockholders acquire a majority of the shares of stock of the survivor, then the transaction is no longer simply a purchase of assets or acquisition of property . . . but a merger governed by section 908, subd. A of the corporation. To divest shareholders of their right of dissent under such circumstances would require express language which is absent from the 1957 amendments.

Even were we to assume that the combination provided for in the reorganization agreement is a "sale of assets" to which section 908, subd. A does not apply, it would avail the defendants nothing; we will not blind our eyes to the realities of the transaction. Despite the designation of the parties and the form employed, Glen Alden does not in fact acquire List, rather, List acquires Glen Alden, and under section 311, subd. D, the right of dissent would remain with the shareholders of Glen Alden.

Farris v. Glen Alden Corp., 143 A.2d 25, 29-31 (Pa. 1958).

The de facto merger, or "substance over form" doctrine, has intuitive appeal as a means to ensure that shareholders are fairly treated. Nonetheless, the Delaware courts have long supported a competing doctrine—that each provision of the corporation code has independent legal significance and is entitled to equal judicial respect. As you read the following two cases, consider the underlying judicial policy choices being made. What shareholder and corporate interests and expectations are at stake? Is a statutory merger the dominant paradigm against which alternative transactional strategies should be measured? If so, should a court be willing to second-guess only egregious "misuse" of such statutory overlaps, or should the court seek to ensure that shareholders receive appraisal rights anytime that the transaction looks more like a traditional merger than an alternative type of transaction? Or, instead, should the court simply defer to the legislature to amend the statute if it sees fit?

Applestein v. United Board & Carton Corp.
New Jersey Superior Court, Chancery Division, 1960
159 A.2d 146

KILKENNY, J.S.C.

The parties herein, by written stipulation, have submitted for determination, as upon motions and cross-motions for partial summary judgment, a single limited issue. That issue is whether the agreement of July 7, 1959 among United Board and Carton Corporation, hereinafter referred to as "United," Interstate Container Corporation, hereinafter referred to as "Interstate," and Saul L. Epstein, hereinafter referred to as "Epstein," and the transaction set forth in the proxy solicitation statement, hereinafter called "proxy statement," dated September 22, 1959, amount to a merger, entitling dissenting stockholders of United to an appraisal of their stock, and is therefore invalid. . . .

United is an active corporation of New Jersey, organized in 1912. Its business consists in the manufacture and sale of paperboard, folding boxes, corrugated containers and laminated board, in that relative order of importance. Its present authorized capital stock consists of 400,000 shares, of which 240,000 have already been issued and are held by a great number of stockholders, no one of whom holds in excess of 10%

of the outstanding shares. There are 160,000 shares not yet issued. The United stock is publicly held, there being 1,086 shareholders of record as of September 22, 1959, and the stock is traded on the New York Stock Exchange. . . . Its business is managed by the usual staff of officers and a board of directors consisting of seven directors.

Interstate was incorporated under the laws of New York in 1939. It owns several operating subsidiaries located in various parts of the northeastern section of the United States. It is engaged primarily in the manufacture and sale of corrugated shipping containers, and also containers which have the dual use of carriers and point of purchase displays. The major portion of its business is corrugated containers. Its corrugated board, other than that consumed by its own container operations, is used by outside plants for the manufacture of corrugated containers and, in some instances, for display items. Interstate has issued and outstanding 1,250 shares, all of which are owned and controlled by a single stockholder, Epstein, who thereby owns and controls Interstate. . . .

United entered into a written agreement with Interstate and Epstein on July 7, 1959. In its language, it is not designated or referred to as a merger agreement, *eo nomine*. In fact, the word "merger" nowhere appears in that agreement. On the contrary, the agreement recites that it is an "exchange of Interstate stock for United Stock." Epstein agrees to assign and deliver to United his 1,250 shares of the common stock of Interstate solely in exchange for 160,000 as yet unissued shares of voting common stock (par value $10) of United. Thus, by this so-called "exchange of stock" United would wholly own Interstate and its subsidiaries, and Epstein would thereupon own a 40% stock interest in United. . . .

The agreement of July 7, 1959 does not contemplate the continued future operation of Interstate, as a subsidiary corporation of United. Rather, it provides that United will take over all the outstanding stock of Interstate, that all of Interstate's "assets and liabilities will be recorded on the books of the Company (United)," and that Interstate will be dissolved. At the time of closing, Epstein has agreed to deliver the resignations of the officers and directors of Interstate and of its subsidiary corporations, so that, in effect, Interstate would have no officers, directors, or stockholders, other than United's. The agreement further stipulates that the by-laws of United shall be amended to increase the number of directors from 7 to 11. It provides for the filling of the additional directorships, it pre-ordains who will be the officers and new directors of United in the combined enterprise, and even governs the salaries to be paid. Epstein would become the president and a director of United and, admittedly, would be in "effective control" of United. As stated in the proxy statement, "The transaction will be accounted for as a 'pooling of interests' of the two corporations." . . .

In notifying its stockholders of a meeting to be held on October 15, 1959, in its proxy statement United advised the stockholders that "the proposal to approve the issuance of the common stock of the company is being submitted to the vote of the stockholders solely because of the requirements of the New York Stock Exchange; and accordingly stockholders who vote against or who do not vote in favor of the proposal will not, in the opinion of Luttinger & Passannante, general counsel for the company, be entitled to any rights of appraisal of their stock." They were also advised that adoption of the proposal would require the affirmative vote of the holders of only a *majority* of the shares present at the meeting in person or by proxy, provided a majority of all shares outstanding and entitled to vote thereon was present at the meeting. . . .

The legal contention of Epstein and Interstate, and the four intervening United stockholders—Conway, Terry, McKenney, and Corsuti—is that the transaction constitutes a valid purchase by United of Epstein's shares in Interstate, and thereby the property of Interstate, . . . to be followed by a merger of United, as the parent corporation, with its wholly-owned corporation, Interstate, pursuant to N.J.S.A. 14:12-10. Thus, it is claimed that United's dissenting stockholders have no appraisal rights . . . since N.J.S.A. 14:12-10 expressly provides that . . . appraisal rights . . . shall not apply to a merger under N.J.S.A. 14:12-10.

When a corporation *sells or exchanges* all, or substantially all of its property and assets, including its good will, as permitted by R.S. 14:3-5, the stockholders of the *selling* corporation must approve by a two-thirds vote, and objecting stockholders of the *selling* corporation are given appraisal rights, as provided in N.J.S.A. 14:12-6 in the case of a merger.

But when a corporation *buys* real or personal property, or the stock of another corporation, as permitted under R.S. 14:3-9, stockholder approval is not required, and objecting shareholders of the *purchasing* corporation are given no appraisal rights in such a case. Further, the *buying* corporation may pay for such property or stock acquired by it in cash or in the capital stock of the purchasing corporation.

It is true that our present corporation law, R.S. 14:3-5, sanctions a corporate sale of all or substantially all of the property and assets of the selling corporation, with stockholder approval and appraisal rights in favor of objecting shareholders of the selling corporation. Likewise, our statute, R.S. 14:3-9, allows a corporate purchase of the property and stock of another corporation to be paid for in cash or the stock of the purchasing corporation. There is no dispute as to the existence of these present statutory devices for the sale and acquisition of corporate property and shares of stock. Hence, if the purchase by United of Interstate and its shares represented a bona fide utilization of the corporate power conferred by R.S. 14:3-9, and if the intended dissolution of Interstate represented a bona fide merger of a parent corporation with a wholly-owned corporation under N.J.S.A. 14:12-10, without more, United's dissenting shareholders would then have no right to an appraisal of their shares.

But when an authorized device, such as that provided for in a sale or purchase of assets, or a dissolution, is used to bring about a virtual consolidation or merger, minority stockholders may object on the ground that a direct method has been authorized for such a purpose. If consolidation or merger is permitted through a pretended sale of assets or dissolution, minority stockholders may be frozen out of their legal rights of appraisal. If the court is obliged to consider only the device employed, or the mere form of the transaction, a corporate merger in fact can be achieved without any compliance with the statutory requirements for a valid merger, and without any regard for the statutory rights of dissenting shareholders. It would be strange if the powers conferred by our Legislature upon corporations under R.S. 14:3-9 for a purchase of the property and shares of another corporation and, under N.J.S.A. 14:12-10, for the merger of a parent corporation with a wholly-owned corporation can effect a corporate merger de facto, with all the characteristics and consequences of a merger, without any of the legislative safeguards and rights afforded to a dissenting shareholder in a de jure merger under R.S. 14:12-1 et seq. If that were so, we obtain the anomalous result of one part of the corporation law rendering nugatory another part of the same law in accomplishing the same result.

That the proposed corporate action is more than an "exchange of Interstate stock for United stock," as it is labeled in the agreement of July 7, 1959, and more than a purchase by United of Epstein's Interstate stock and the corporate properties of Interstate, pursuant to R.S. 14:3-9, is demonstrated by the following facts. . . .

[By the exchange of stock Epstein will acquire 40 percent of United's outstanding stock; United's board will be increased from seven to eleven and two of the present seven will resign. The agreement specifies who will fill the six openings, assuring Epstein "effective" control of the board.]

Thus, every factor present in a corporate merger is found in this corporate plan, except, perhaps, a formal designation of the transaction as a "merger." There is proposed: (1) a transfer of all the shares and all the assets of Interstate to United; (2) an assumption by United of Interstate's liabilities; (3) a "pooling of interests" of the two corporations; (4) the absorption of Interstate by United, and the dissolution of Interstate; (5) a joinder of officers and directors from both corporations on an enlarged board of directors; (6) the present executive and operating personnel of Interstate will be retained in the employ of United; and (7) the shareholders of the absorbed corporation, Interstate, as represented by the sole stockholder, Epstein, will surrender his 1,250 shares in Interstate for 160,000 newly issued shares in United, the amalgamated enterprise. . . .

. . . A study of these texts and of the cases cited above, and the many cases cited by the respective parties in their briefs, satisfies this court that it is proper to disregard the *form* of a sale or purchase of assets transaction, when its characteristics are virtually identical to those of a statutory merger or consolidation for the purpose of insuring dissenting stockholders their appraisal rights. It is also clear from that study that each case must be judged on its own peculiar facts, without any slavish adherence to determinations made in other cases, where there are similarities and also degrees of difference. Where, as here, we have more than a simple purchase by United of the assets of Interstate, as noted above, the conclusion is fairly drawn that the transaction in question will cause United to alter its existing fundamental relationship with its present shareholders, and will result in shifting the working control of United to Epstein and his associates in Interstate. In substance, regardless of the form, the transaction in question would be a merger of United and Interstate, or what the court described in the *Farris* case [Farris v. Glen Alden Corp., 393 Pa. 427, 143 A.2d 25 (1958)] as a "de facto merger."

Counsel for Interstate and Epstein has contended that this doctrine of de facto merger applies only to the dissenting stockholders of the corporation being *acquired*, and not to those of the *acquiring* corporation. He argues, therefore, that even if this court holds that the corporate combination in this case is a de facto merger, the dissenting stockholders of United have no right to an appraisal of their shares because United would be acquiring Interstate. If, as this court holds, the transaction amounts to a merger in fact and in substance, there is no logical or legal reason for distinguishing between dissenting stockholders of the *acquired* corporation and those of the *acquiring* corporation. That distinction may be pertinent in a simple sale of assets transaction to determine whether it comes under R.S. 14:3-5, as a *sale*, in which the dissenting stockholders of the *selling* corporation have appraisal rights; or comes under R.S. 14:3-9, as a *purchase,* in which the dissenting stockholders of the *purchasing* corporation are given no statutory appraisal rights.

Where there is a de jure merger, formally expressed and clearly intended, the statute makes no such distinction. Under N.J.S.A. 14:12-6 and 14:12-7, the dissenting stockholders "of *any* of the corporations, merged or consolidated," are given appraisal rights as set forth therein. It matters not whether they are the stockholders of the absorbed or absorbing corporation. Whether a merger is de jure or de facto, the reason for protecting the dissenting stockholders will apply equally, whether they are stockholders of the *acquired* or *acquiring* corporation. The reason for statutory protection is that stockholders should not be forced against their will into something fundamentally different from that for which they bargained when they acquired their shares. If the argument of these defendants were sound, then by the simple device of labeling one of the corporations the *acquiring* corporation and the other the *acquired* corporation, the substantial rights of appraisal would be arbitrarily taken away.

Furthermore, in this case, if it were necessary to make the determination, it seems clear to this court that while United appears to be acquiring Interstate, the converse is more probably true in practical effect. We cannot blind ourselves to the realities of the situation in this case, as shown by the facts. Even United in its proxy statement concedes that Epstein and Interstate are taking over United, by their reference to the fact that Epstein and Interstate will be in "effective control" of United. While technically Interstate, a corporate entity, is being dissolved, and the name Interstate will disappear from this corporate combination, the control and management passes out of United and its 1,086 present shareholders to Epstein and his associates in Interstate. In substance, therefore, United is being sold to Epstein and Interstate, and the present board of directors and management of United are abdicating to Epstein and his corporate alter ego, Interstate. There is no good reason why the proposal should not have been submitted to the stockholders of United for their approval as a merger. The dissenting stockholders then would have the statutory right to object to the plan and obtain an appraisal of their respective shares. The majority, no matter however overwhelming it may turn out to be, may not trample upon the property and appraisal rights of the minority shareholders of United, no matter how few they may be in number.

. . . Accordingly, the shareholders of United are and were entitled to be notified and advised of their statutory rights of dissent and appraisal. The failure of the corporate officers of United to take these steps and to obtain stockholder approval of the agreement by the statutory two-thirds vote under R.S. 14:12-3 at a properly convened meeting of the stockholders would render the proposed corporate action invalid. . . .

Hariton v. Arco Electronics, Inc.
Delaware Supreme Court, 1963
188 A.2d 123

SOUTHERLAND, CHIEF JUSTICE.

This case involves a sale of assets under §271 of the corporation law, 8 Del. C. It presents for decision the question presented, but not decided, in Heilbrunn v. Sun Chemical Corporation, Del., 150 A.2d 755. It may be stated as follows:

A sale of assets is effected under §271 in consideration of shares of stock of the purchasing corporation. The agreement of sale embodies also a plan to dissolve the selling corporation and distribute the shares so received to the stockholders of the seller, so as to accomplish the same result as would be accomplished by a merger of the seller into the purchaser. Is the sale legal?

The facts are these:

The defendant Arco and Loral Electronics Corporation, a New York corporation, are both engaged, in somewhat different forms, in the electronic equipment business. In the summer of 1961 they negotiated for an amalgamation of the companies. As of October 27, 1961, they entered into a "Reorganization Agreement and Plan." The provisions of this Plan pertinent here are in substance as follows:

1. Arco agrees to sell all its assets to Loral in consideration (inter alia) of the issuance to it of 283,000 shares of Loral.

2. Arco agrees to call a stockholders meeting for the purpose of approving the Plan and the voluntary dissolution.

3. Arco agrees to distribute to its stockholders all the Loral shares received by it as a part of the complete liquidation of Arco.

At the Arco meeting all the stockholders voting (about 80%) approved the Plan. It was thereafter consummated.

Plaintiff, a stockholder who did not vote at the meeting, sued to enjoin the consummation of the Plan on the grounds (1) that it was illegal, and (2) that it was unfair. The second ground was abandoned. Affidavits and documentary evidence were filed, and defendant moved for summary judgment and dismissal of the complaint. The Vice Chancellor granted the motion and plaintiff appeals.

The question before us we have stated above. Plaintiff's argument that the sale is illegal runs as follows:

The several steps taken here accomplish the same result as a merger of Arco into Loral. In a "true" sale of assets, the stockholder of the seller retains the right to elect whether the selling company shall continue as a holding company. Moreover, the stockholder of the selling company is forced to accept an investment in a new enterprise without the right of appraisal granted under the merger statute. §271 cannot therefore be legally combined with a dissolution proceeding under §275 and a consequent distribution of the purchaser's stock. Such a proceeding is a misuse of the power granted under §271, and a de facto merger results.

The foregoing is a brief summary of plaintiff's contention.

Plaintiff's contention that this sale has achieved the same result as a merger is plainly correct. The same contention was made to us in Heilbrunn v. Sun Chemical Corporation, Del., 150 A.2d 755. Accepting it as correct, we noted that this result is made possible by the overlapping scope of the merger statute and §271, mentioned in Sterling v. Mayflower Hotel Corporation, 33 Del. Ch. 293, 93 A.2d 107, 38 A.L.R.2d 425. We also adverted to the increased use, in connection with corporate reorganization plans, of §271 instead of the merger statute. . . .

We now hold that the reorganization here accomplished through §271 and a mandatory plan of dissolution and distribution is legal. This is so because the sale-of-assets statute and the merger statute are independent of each other. They are, so to speak, of equal dignity, and the framers of a reorganization plan may resort to either type of corporate mechanics to achieve the desired end. This is not an anomalous result in our corporation law. As the Vice Chancellor pointed out, the elimination of accrued dividends, though forbidden under a charter amendment (Keller v. Wilson & Co., 21 Del. Ch. 391, 190 A. 115) may be accomplished by a merger. Federal United Corporation v. Havender, 24 Del. Ch. 318, 11 A.2d 331.

In Langfelder v. Universal Laboratories, D.C., 68 F. Supp. 209, Judge Leahy commented upon "the general theory of the Delaware Corporation Law that action taken pursuant to the authority of the various sections of that law constitute acts of independent legal significance and their validity is not dependent on other sections of the Act." 68 F. Supp. 211, footnote. . . .

Plaintiff concedes, as we read his brief, that if the several steps taken in this case had been taken separately they would have been legal. That is, he concedes that a sale of assets, followed by a separate proceeding to dissolve and distribute, would be legal, even though the same result would follow. This concession exposes the weakness of his contention. To attempt to make any such distinction between sales under §271 would be to create uncertainty in the law and invite litigation.

We are in accord with the Vice Chancellor's ruling, and the judgment below is affirmed.

NOTES AND QUESTIONS

1. A discernible theme in most appraisal statutes is a greater concern for dissenters whose shares are being acquired than for dissenters in the acquiring corporation. Should courts build on this theme and override private ordering when it is used to the disadvantage of shareholders of the acquired company? Professor Ronald Gilson has described the case for this approach:

> In a structural approach to corporate law, it is precisely when market constraints on managerial behavior fail that there is a role for legal constraints. The typical corporate structure reflects this in the historical distinction between the protections given the shareholders of acquiring and target companies. It is only the latter who are subject to last period problems and therefore cannot rely on their management for protection, and require, instead, the barrier of a shareholder vote as a protection against management. It is, of course, recognition of this problem that prompts the statutory and judicial concern for the situation in which the form of the transaction is cast as a minnow swallowing a whale in order to circumvent statutory protection against final period problems given target shareholders. And it is precisely the principle derived from understanding this problem — transactions which present final period problems require additional mechanisms for shareholder protection — which should govern determination of the breadth of application of the de facto merger doctrine.

R. Gilson, The Law and Finance of Corporate Acquisitions 579 (Foundation Press, 1986).

2. Delaware courts periodically reaffirm their adherence to the doctrine of independent legal significance. See, e.g., Thorpe v. Cerbco, 676 A.2d 436, 444 (Del. 1996) (Delaware G.C.L. §271 has independent legal significance from the duty of loyalty); Nixon v. Blackwell, 626 A.2d 1366, 1380 (Del. 1993) (expressly acknowledging that the principle of independent legal significance is considered an important tool by corporate planners, and refusing to create special rules for close corporations that

could have elected to be covered by the provisions of Delaware G.C.L., Subchapter XIV, because to do so "would run counter to the spirit of the doctrine of independent legal significance . . .").

3. In Irving Bank Corp. v. Bank of New York Co., 530 N.Y.S.2d 757 (Sup. Ct. 1988), the court cited with approval both *Applestein* and *Farris* in describing New York's version of the de facto merger doctrine.

> We need not discuss, at this time, extensively the requirements for a de facto merger. It is clear, however, that two factors are necessary: (1) *The actual merger must take place soon after the initial transaction,* and (2) *the seller corporation must quickly cease to exist.* [Emphasis supplied.]
>
> In Lirosi v. Elkins, 89 A.D.2d 903, 453 N.Y.S.2d 718 (2d Dep't 1982), the court held that a transfer of assets from one corporation to another, and the subsequent dissolution of the former corporation, constituted a de facto merger. In Gilbert v. Burnside, 197 N.Y.S.2d 623 (1959), rev'd 13 A.D.2d 982 (2d Dep't 1961) aff'd 11 N.Y.2d 960, 229 N.Y.S.2d 10, 183 N.E.2d 325, the court held a "reorganization agreement" to be a de facto merger where the agreement provided for the sale of all of the assets of a corporation and its subsequent dissolution. In both cases, the Court found that the dissolution of the acquired corporation was an imminently expected occurrence. [Court's discussion of *Farris* omitted.]
>
> A study of those cases in which courts have found de facto merger demonstrates that the factual situation of each case must be independently studied, without "slavish adherence to determinations made in other cases, where there are similarities and also degrees of difference." (Applestein v. United Board & Carton Corp., 60 N.J. Super. at 351, 159 A.2d at 156.)
>
> Specifically lacking in the instant case is the immediate dissolution or cessation of the business of the target corporation as well as an assumption of all debts and obligations.
>
> We note further, that [defendant] BNY is planning a purchase of the stock, not the assets of [plaintiff] IBC. Where the acquiror corporation purchases all the target's assets, leaving the target as a mere shell, the transaction bears a distinct resemblance to a merger. Here, IBC will survive as a corporate entity, with all its assets intact. Although a merger may occur in the future, the instant transaction is not a merger, but the acquisition of a subsidiary. All the above-mentioned cases which found a de facto merger involved asset sales. See also Fidanque v. American Maracaibo Co., 33 Del. Ch. 262, 92 A.2d 311 (1952) where a stock sale did not result in a de facto merger.

530 N.Y.S.2d at 760.

4. The ALI Principles of Corporate Governance §7.21 incorporates an approach pioneered in California that seeks to lessen the extent to which shareholder appraisal rights are dependent upon the form chosen for the transaction. Under the ALI approach, shareholders of the parent corporation which uses a subsidiary to effect a merger would normally receive appraisal rights as if the parent corporation had been a direct participant in the merger. And if a corporation uses its own stock to purchase a substantial portion of the assets of another corporation, its shareholders get appraisal rights (as do the shareholders of the selling corporation) if the transaction results in the acquiring corporation's pre-transaction shareholders owning less than 60 percent of the stock outstanding immediately after the acquisition is effected. It remains to be seen whether the ALI approach will become a significant standard in state corporation codes other than California.

PROBLEM 8-2

The directors of Conglomerate, Inc., a publicly traded corporation, and Carmen Carson, the sole shareholder of Fashion Wear, Inc., have reached an agreement in principle whereby Conglomerate will exchange 5 million authorized but unissued Conglomerate shares for all of Fashion Wear's assets. Conglomerate will assume Fashion Wear's liabilities and appoint Carson as Conglomerate's new CEO. It is expected that Fashion Wear will remain in existence as an empty corporate shell for an indefinite period of time. Immediately after this exchange, pre-transaction Conglomerate shareholders will own approximately 60 percent of Conglomerate's outstanding stock and Carmen Carson will own the remainder.

(a) What dissenter's rights will be available to Conglomerate shareholders in an MBCA jurisdiction, assuming that there is yet no controlling precedent preventing application of the de facto merger doctrine?

(b) What dissenter's rights will be available to Conglomerate shareholders in a jurisdiction which has adopted the standards embodied in ALI Principles of Corporate Governance §§1.38 and 7.21?

D. Cash-Out Mergers and the Intersection Between the Appraisal Remedy and Fiduciary-Duty-Based Judicial Review

1. Cash-Out Mergers and the Business Purpose Test

Traditionally, corporate law has imposed heightened "fairness" obligations on fiduciaries involved in self-dealing transactions. This concern is especially acute in connection with a mid-twentieth-century innovation — the "cash-out" merger.

Specific statutory authorization for the use of cash as consideration in a merger was uncommon prior to 1970. For example, until 1967 in Delaware and 1969 under the MBCA, cash was not authorized as consideration in a merger. When these "cash" statutes were interpreted by courts as not requiring the same consideration for all shareholders, the way was open for a controlling shareholders to expel minorities from the enterprise via a merger (or similar fundamental-change effecting transaction); to accomplish this "cash out" the merger agreement would provide that the controlling shareholder swap its majority interest in the disappearing corporation stock in the merged enterprise while the minority shareholders would be required to surrender their equity interest in the old entity in return for cash. As a result, the controlling shareholder could become the sole owner of the business, while former minority investors were forces to relinquish any continuing interest in the firm.

In the 1970s, unhappy minority shareholders increasingly sought to challenge cash-out mergers via class actions, rather than seeking the "fair value" of their shares in an appraisal. Controlling-shareholder defendants asserted that such complaints were barred by the general rule that appraisal is a dissenting shareholder's exclusive remedy, unless the transaction is "unlawful or fraudulent" (see pre-1999 MBCA §13.02(b)) and the underlying dispute amounts to something more than "a difference of opinion as to value." Stauffer v. Standard Brands, Inc., 187 A.2d 78, 80 (Del. 1962). In response to this litigation, several jurisdictions adopted business purpose tests as a means of giving closer scrutiny to cash-out mergers, and, correspondingly, creating larger exceptions to the appraisal exclusivity rule.

Delaware joined the business purpose club with its holding in Singer v. Magnavox Co., 380 A.2d 969 (Del. 1977), which involved a shareholder complaint seeking rescission or compensatory damages in connection with a controlling shareholder-dominated cash-out merger. The plaintiffs alleged that the transaction was fraudulent because it did not serve a valid corporate business purpose, but instead, was designed solely to freeze out the minority at a grossly unfair price. The defendant sought, and the trial court granted, dismissal of the complaint on the grounds that the reasons for, or purposes of, the merger were as a matter of law irrelevant and that unhappy minority shareholders' only recourse was to seek an appraisal. The Delaware Supreme Court strongly disagreed with the defendants' argument.

> At the core of defendants' contention is the premise that a shareholder's right is exclusively in the value of his investment, not its form. And, they argue, that right is protected by a §262 appraisal which, by definition, results in fair value for the shares. This argument assumes that the right to take is coextensive with the power to take and that a dissenting stockholder has no legally protected right in his shares, his certificate or his company beyond a right to be paid fair value[8] when the majority is ready to do this. Simply stated, such an argument does not square with the duty stated so eloquently and so forcefully by Chief Justice Layton in *Guth*.

380 A.2d at 977-978. The court then reversed the trial court's dismissal of plaintiff's complaint.

> We hold, therefore, that a §251 merger, made for the sole purpose of freezing out minority stockholders, is an abuse of the corporate process; and the complaint, which so alleges in this suit, states a cause of action for violation of a fiduciary duty for which the Court may grant such relief as it deems appropriate under the circumstances.
>
> This is not to say, however, that merely because the Court finds that a cash-out merger was not made for the sole purpose of freezing out minority stockholders, all relief must be denied to the minority stockholders in a §251 merger. On the contrary, the fiduciary obligation of the majority to the minority stockholders remains and proof of a purpose, other than such freeze-out, without more, will not necessarily discharge it. In such case the Court will scrutinize the circumstances for compliance with the *Sterling* rule of "entire fairness" and, if it finds a violation thereof, will grant such relief as equity may require.

380 A.2d at 980.

Singer, in effect, required controlling shareholders to prove a valid business purpose for a cash-out merger. Left unclear was the extent to which the controlling shareholder must consider the business needs of the controlled corporation or its other shareholders. In Tanzer v. International General Indus., Inc., 379 A.2d 1121, a case decided only 26 days after *Singer*, minority shareholders sought to enjoin a cash-out merger. The Chancery Court denied the injunction, finding that the controlling shareholder

---

8. That argument was rejected in Jutkowitz v. Bourns, Cal. Super. Ct. C.A. 000268 (Nov. 19, 1975), wherein the Court correctly summarized some of the values besides money which may be at stake in a "going-private" merger:

> Money may well satisfy some or most minority shareholders, but others may have differing investment goals, tax problems, a belief in the ability of . . . management to make them rich, or even a sentimental attachment to the stock which leads them to have a different judgment as to the desirability of selling out.

sought to cash-out the minority in order to facilitate its own long-term debt financing, and that this constituted "a legitimate and present and compelling business reason . . ." for the transaction. 379 A.2d at 1124. The shareholders appealed, arguing that "a freeze-out merger imposed on a subsidiary corporation by a parent, and designed solely for the purpose of benefiting the parent, is impermissible under Delaware law." Id. at 1123. The Delaware Supreme Court upheld the Chancery Court.

> Although we have stated that IGI is entitled as majority stockholder to vote its own corporate concerns, it should be clearly noted that IGI's purpose in causing the [cash-out] merger must be bona fide. As a stockholder, IGI need not sacrifice its own interest in dealing with a subsidiary; but that interest must not be suspect as a subterfuge, the real purpose of which is to rid itself of unwanted minority shareholders in the subsidiary. That would be a violation of *Singer* and any subterfuge or effort to escape its mandate must be scrutinized with care and dealt with by the Trial Court. And, of course, in any event, a bona fide purpose notwithstanding, IGI must be prepared to show that it has met its duty, imposed by *Singer* and Sterling v. Mayflower Hotel Corp., Del. Supr., 33 Del. Ch. 293, 93 A.2d 107 (1952), of "entire fairness" to the minority.

379 A.2d at 1124.

The following case illustrates another court's use of the business purpose and entire fairness doctrines. As you read it, consider how the controlling shareholder could have demonstrated a sufficient business purpose.

Coggins v. New England Patriots Football Club, Inc.
Massachusetts Supreme Judicial Court, 1986
492 N.E.2d 1112

LIACOS, JUSTICE.

On November 18, 1959, William H. Sullivan, Jr. (Sullivan), purchased an American Football League (AFL) franchise for a professional football team. The team was to be the last of the eight original teams set up to form the AFL (now the American Football Conference of the National Football League). For the franchise, Sullivan paid $25,000. Four months later, Sullivan organized a corporation, the American League Professional Football Team of Boston, Inc. Sullivan contributed his AFL franchise; nine other persons each contributed $25,000. In return, each of the ten investors received 10,000 shares of voting common stock in the corporation. Another four months later, in July, 1960, the corporation sold 120,000 shares of nonvoting common stock to the public at $5 a share.

Sullivan had effective control of the corporation from its inception until 1974. By April, 1974, Sullivan had increased his ownership of shares from 10,000 shares of voting stock to 23,718 shares, and also had acquired 5,499 shares of nonvoting stock. Nevertheless, in 1974 the other voting stockholders ousted him from the presidency and from operating control of the corporation. He then began the effort to regain control of the corporation—an effort which culminated in this and other law suits.

In November, 1975, Sullivan succeeded in obtaining ownership or control of all 100,000 of the voting shares, at a price of approximately $102 a share (adjusted cash value), of the corporation, by that time renamed the New England Patriots Football

Club, Inc. (Old Patriots). "Upon completion of the purchase, he immediately used his 100% control to vote out the hostile directors, elect a friendly board and arrange his resumption of the presidency and the complete control of the Patriots. In order to finance this coup, Sullivan borrowed approximately $5,348,000 from the Rhode Island Hospital National Bank and the [LaSalle] National Bank of Chicago. As a condition of these loans, Sullivan was to use his best efforts to reorganize the Patriots so that the income of the corporation could be devoted to the payment of these personal loans and the assets of the corporation pledged to secure them. At this point they were secured by all of the voting shares held by Sullivan. In order to accomplish in effect the assumption by the corporation of Sullivan's personal obligations, it was necessary, as a matter of corporate law, to eliminate the interest of the nonvoting shares."

On October 20, 1976, Sullivan organized a new corporation called the New Patriots Football Club, Inc. (New Patriots). The board of directors of the Old Patriots and the board of directors of the New Patriots[5] executed an agreement of merger of the two corporations providing that, after the merger, the voting stock of the Old Patriots would be extinguished, the nonvoting stock would be exchanged for cash at the rate of $15 a share, and the name of the New Patriots would be changed to the name formerly used by the Old Patriots. As part of this plan, Sullivan gave the New Patriots his 100,000 voting shares of the Old Patriots in return for 100% of the New Patriots stock.

General Laws c.156B, §78(c)(1)(iii), as amended through St. 1976, c.327, required approval of the merger agreement by a majority vote of each class of affected stock. Approval by the voting class, entirely controlled by Sullivan, was assured. The merger was approved by the class of nonvoting stockholders at a special meeting on December 8, 1976. On January 31, 1977, the merger of the New Patriots and the Old Patriots was consummated.

David A. Coggins (Coggins) was the owner of ten shares of nonvoting stock in the Old Patriots. Coggins, a fan of the Patriots from the time of their formation, was serving in Vietnam in 1967 when he purchased the shares through his brother. Over the years, he followed the fortunes of the team, taking special pride in his status as an owner.[8] When he heard of the proposed merger, Coggins was upset that he could be forced to sell. Coggins voted against the merger and commenced this suit on behalf of those stockholders, who, like himself, believed the transaction to be unfair and illegal. A judge of the Superior Court certified the class as "stockholders of New England Patriots Football Club, Inc. who have voted against the merger . . . but who have neither turned in their shares nor perfected their appraisal rights . . . [and who] desire only to void the merger."

The trial judge found in favor of the Coggins class but determined that the merger should not be undone. Instead, he ruled that the plaintiffs are entitled to rescissory damages, and he ordered that further hearings be held to determine the amount of damages. After the judge rendered his decision, motions were made to permit intervention by plaintiffs in two related cases, Pavlidis v. New England Patriots Football

---

5. The two boards were identical. Each member of the board of directors of the Old Patriots (as constituted after Sullivan had regained control) was a member of the board of directors of the New Patriots. Each of the officers of the Old Patriots held the same position with the New Patriots.

8. It was, in part, the goal of the Old Patriots, in offering stock to the public, to generate loyal fans.

Club, Inc., 737 F.2d 1227 (1st Cir. 1984), and Sarrouf v. New England Patriots Football Club, Inc., 397 Mass. 542, 492 N.E.2d 1122 (1986).[9] The trial judge allowed the motion of the *Pavlidis* plaintiffs, and allowed the motion of the *Sarrouf* plaintiffs, but only as to those plaintiffs in the *Sarrouf* action who were not granted relief in that case.

We conclude that the trial judge was correct in ruling that the merger was illegal and that the plaintiffs have been wronged. Ordinarily, rescission of the merger would be the appropriate remedy. This merger, however, is now nearly ten years old, and, because an effective and orderly rescission of the merger now is not feasible, we remand the case for proceedings to determine the appropriate monetary damages to compensate the plaintiffs. We conclude further that intervention by the *Pavlidis* plaintiffs should not have been allowed, and that no stockholders in the *Sarrouf* class should be allowed to intervene as plaintiffs in the *Coggins* case. . . .

A controlling stockholder who is also a director standing on both sides of the transaction bears the burden of showing that the transaction does not violate fiduciary obligations. "As was said in Geddes v. Anaconda Copper Mining Co., 254 U.S. 590, 599 [1921]: 'The relation of directors to corporations is of such a fiduciary nature that transactions between boards having common members are regarded as jealously by the law as are personal dealings between a director and his corporation, and where the fairness of such transactions is challenged the burden is upon those who would maintain them to show their entire fairness and where a sale is involved the full adequacy of the consideration. Especially is this true where a common director is dominating in influence or in character.' This rule is applicable even though no corruption or dishonesty is shown. . . ." Lazenby v. Henderson, 241 Mass. 177, 180 (1922). Cf. Weinberger v. UOP, Inc. (similar standard of review). Judicial inquiry into a freeze-out merger in technical compliance with the statute may be appropriate, and the dissenting stockholders are not limited to the statutory remedy of judicial appraisal where violations of fiduciary duties are found.

FACTORS IN JUDICIAL REVIEW

. . . Judicial scrutiny should begin with recognition of the basic principle that the duty of a corporate director must be to further the legitimate goals of the corporation. The result of a freeze-out merger is the elimination of public ownership in the corporation. The controlling faction increases its equity from a majority to 100%, using corporate processes and corporate assets. The corporate directors who benefit from this transfer of ownership must demonstrate how the legitimate goals of the corporation are furthered. A director of a corporation violates his fiduciary duty when he uses the corporation for his or his family's personal benefit in a manner detrimental to the corporation. Because the danger of abuse of fiduciary duty is especially great in a freeze-

---

9. The plaintiffs in *Pavlidis* "voted to accept the New Patriots' offer of $15.00 per share for their common stock in the [Old] Patriots corporation. They now claim that they were induced to accept this offer by a misleading proxy statement . . . contain[ing] various misrepresentations. . . . They seek to rescind the merger or to receive a higher price per share for the stock they sold." The plaintiffs in *Sarrouf* objected to the merger but sought the statutory remedy of appraisal.

out merger, the court must be satisfied that the freeze-out was for the advancement of a legitimate corporate purpose. If satisfied that elimination of public ownership is in furtherance of a business purpose, the court should then proceed to determine if the transaction was fair by examining the totality of the circumstances.

The plaintiffs here adequately alleged that the merger of the Old Patriots and New Patriots was a freeze-out merger undertaken for no legitimate business purpose, but merely for the personal benefit of Sullivan. While we have recognized the right to "selfish ownership" in a corporation, such a right must be balanced against the concept of the majority stockholder's fiduciary obligation to the minority stockholders. Wilkes v. Springside Nursing Home, Inc., 370 Mass. 842, 851 (1976). Consequently, the defendants bear the burden of proving, first, that the merger was for a legitimate business purpose, and, second, that, considering totality of circumstances, it was fair to the minority.

The decision of the Superior Court judge includes a finding that "the defendants have failed to demonstrate that the merger served any valid corporate objective unrelated to the personal interests of the majority shareholders. It thus appears that the sole reason for the merger was to effectuate a restructuring of the Patriots that would enable the repayment of the [personal] indebtedness incurred by Sullivan. . . ." The trial judge considered the defendants' claims that the policy of the National Football League (NFL) requiring majority ownership by a single individual or family made it necessary to eliminate public ownership. He found that "the stock ownership of the Patriots as it existed just prior to the merger fully satisfied the rationale underlying the policy as expressed by NFL Commissioner Pete Rozelle. Having acquired 100% control of the voting common stock of the Patriots, Sullivan possessed unquestionable authority to act on behalf of the franchise at League meetings and effectively foreclosed the possible recurrence of the internal management disputes that had existed in 1974. Moreover, as the proxy statement itself notes, the Old Patriots were under no legal compulsion to eliminate public ownership." Likewise, the defendants did not succeed in showing a conflict between the interests of the league owners and the Old Patriots' stockholders. We perceive no error in these findings. They are fully supported by the evidence. Under the approach we set forth above, there is no need to consider further the elements of fairness of a transaction that is not related to a valid corporate purpose.

REMEDY

The plaintiffs are entitled to relief. They argue that the appropriate relief is rescission of the merger and restoration of the parties to their positions of 1976. We agree that the normally appropriate remedy for an impermissible freeze-out merger is rescission. Because Massachusetts statutes do not bar a cash freeze-out, however, numerous third parties relied in good faith on the outcome of the merger. The trial judge concluded that the expectations of those parties should not be upset, and so chose to award damages rather than rescission.

We recognize that, because rescission is an equitable remedy, the circumstances of a particular case may not favor its employment. The goals of a remedy instituted after

a finding that a merger did not serve the corporate purpose should include furthering the interests of the corporation. Ordinarily, we would remand with instructions
for the trial judge to determine whether rescission would be in the corporation's best
interests, but such a remedy does not appear to be equitable at this time. This litigation has gone on for many years. There is yet at least another related case pending (in
the Federal District Court). Furthermore, other factors weigh against rescission. The
passage of time has made the 1976 position of the parties difficult, if not impossible, to
restore. A substantial number of former stockholders have chosen other courses and
should not be forced back into the Patriots corporation. In these circumstances the
interests of the corporation and of the plaintiffs will be furthered best by limiting the
plaintiffs' remedy to an assessment of damages.

We do not think it appropriate, however, to award damages based on a 1976
appraisal value. To do so would make this suit a nullity, leaving the plaintiffs with no
effective remedy except appraisal, a position we have already rejected. Rescissory damages must be determined based on the present value of the Patriots, that is, what the
stockholders would have if the merger were rescinded. Determination of the value of
a unique property like the Patriots requires specialized expertise, and, while the trial
judge is entitled to reach his own conclusion as to value, the credibility of testimony
on value will depend in part on the familiarity of the witness with property of this kind.
On remand, the judge is to take further evidence on the present value of the Old
Patriots on the theory that the merger had not taken place. Each share of the Coggins
class is to receive, as rescissory damages, its aliquot share of the present assets.

The trial judge dismissed the plaintiffs' claims against the individual defendants
based on waste of corporate assets. The remedy we order is intended to give the plaintiffs what they would have if the merger were undone and the corporation were put
back together again. The trial judge's finding that the sole purpose of the merger
was the personal financial benefit of William H. Sullivan, Jr., and the use of corporate
assets to accomplish this impermissible purpose, led inescapably to the conclusion
that part of what the plaintiffs otherwise would have benefitted by, was removed from
the corporation by the individual defendants. We reverse the dismissal of the claim
for waste of corporate assets and remand this question to the trial court. The present
value of the Patriots, as determined on remand, should include the amount wrongfully
removed or diverted from the corporate coffers by the individual defendants. . . .

In most cases we would turn to rescission as the appropriate remedy. In the circumstances of this case, however, rescission would be an inequitable solution. Therefore,
we remand for a determination of the present value of the nonvoting stock, as though
the merger were rescinded. The claim for waste of corporate assets brought against the
individual defendants is reinstated. Those stockholders who voted against the merger,
who did not turn in their shares, who did not perfect their appraisal rights, but who
are part of the Coggins class, are to receive damages in the amount their stock would
be worth today, plus interest at the statutory rate. . . .

NOTES AND QUESTIONS

1. The procedural history of this case illustrates several of the various possible
challenges to a cash-out merger. The *Sarrouf* plaintiffs sought appraisal and received

$80 per share, as compared to the $15 offered in the merger. In addition, the plaintiffs received 9 percent interest compounded annually from January 31, 1977, the date the merger was approved. See Sarrouf v. New England Patriots Football Club, Inc., 492 N.E.2d 1122 (Mass. 1986). The *Pavlidis* plaintiffs voted to accept the $15 merger price and later alleged they were misled by the proxy disclosures, a violation of federal law. Their federal claim failed. See Pavlidis v. New England Patriots Football Club, Inc., 675 F. Supp. 688 (D. Mass. 1986). The *Coggins* plaintiffs sued for breach of fiduciary duty and were permitted to get rescissory value, "its aliquot share of the present assets." After the Supreme Judicial Court's decision in favor of the *Coggins* plaintiffs, the parties settled. A fund of $584,000 was created from which plaintiffs' attorneys received $220,550. The remainder was distributed pro rata to the *Coggins* class members, yielding them $158.64 per share.

2. Should recovery of different dissenting shareholders in the same corporation turn on their litigation strategy? Should plaintiffs be able to bring class actions on several theories?

3. M & W, Inc. v. Pacific Guardian Life Ins. Co., 1998 WL 32685 (Haw. App. Jan. 30, 1998) opinion ordered depublished (Sept. 10, 1998), aff'd. 966 P.2d 1098 (Haw. Sept. 10, 1998) (summary affirmance), illustrates the careful scrutiny of asserted business purpose called for by the court in *Tanzer*. Meiji, the owner of 85 percent of PGL, created MML and then effectuated a cash-out merger of PGL into MML. Minority shareholders of PGL complained that the merger violated the *Singer* test, which the Hawai'i Supreme Court had adopted in 1980. Defendants Meiji and MML asserted that the merger was carried out for a proper business purpose. The trial and appellate courts both placed heavy emphasis on an internal Meiji document that detailed the controlling shareholder's reasons for the transaction as: "(1) easier 'operational expansion' in the United States; (2) 'improved investment efficiency'; (3) reduction of expenses; and (4) 'smoother operation' of PGL." Id. at *14. The document noted that wholly owned corporations were more valuable than corporations with minority shareholders, citing expected gains from "[t]he reduction of 'legal fees . . . , audit fees, stockholders administration fees and directors and officers liability insurance premiums. . . .'" Id. at *15 (internal quotation omitted). Further, the document described how Meiji, which had been plagued by shareholder litigation, expected "an 'increase of creative time' for directors and management . . . and 'easier implementation of Incentive program for C.E.O.'" Id. Based on this evidence, the trial court found that Meiji had not established a sufficient business purpose to satisfy the *Singer* test, and the appellate court held that this finding was not "clearly erroneous." Id.

4. Under what circumstance could a controlling shareholder obtain summary judgment if sued for breach of fiduciary duty in connection with a cash-out merger in a business-purpose-test jurisdiction?

PROBLEM 8-3

In 2007, local entrepreneur Janice Brown acquired 100 percent of the stock of New York City Performing Arts Center, Inc. (Center), which then owned and operated a performing arts center featuring two theatres and an opera hall. Brown borrowed heavily to finance this acquisition, pledging all of her stock and Center's assets as security for the loan. In 2010, Center sought to acquire the Upstate Shakespeare Festival. To finance this project, Center incorporated Shakespeare, Inc. (Shakespeare) and sold 40 percent of its common stock to the public to obtain the funds needed to acquire the Festival. Many of these shares were purchased by patrons delighted by the prospect of bringing the Festival to New York City. In 2013, Center discovered that the performing arts facility had significant roof and structural defects. In order to obtain financing for this project, Center needed to pledge Shakespeare's assets as security. To accomplish this, Center used its voting power and control to effectuate a merger with Shakespeare in which the minority shareholders of Shakespeare were "cashed out" at $25 per share.

Dissenting minority shareholders of Shakespeare have now filed a complaint seeking rescission of the merger on the ground that the controlling shareholder had no purpose other than to freeze out the minority at a grossly unfair price. Evaluate the prospects for this litigation under the entire fairness and business purpose doctrines of cases like *Singer, Tanzer,* and *Coggins.*

2. The *Weinberger* Approach

Between 1977 and 1983, Delaware jurisprudence encouraged dissatisfied shareholders to challenge cash-out mergers via a cost-spreading, class action suit rather than to pursue an individual appraisal action. As discussed supra at page 719, the *Singer* case and its progeny made it relatively easy for shareholders to obtain an entire fairness review. During this same period of time, two Delaware Supreme Court decisions in the Lynch v. Vickers Energy Corp. litigation further increased plaintiffs' preference for the class action. Additionally, as that litigation makes clear, plaintiffs had strong reason to avoid the valuation method then employed in appraisal actions.

The Lynch v. Vickers Energy Corp. litigation grew out of a tender offer in which Vickers Energy Corp. ("Vickers"), the controlling shareholder of Transocean, Inc., sought to acquire the remaining Transocean stock at $12 per share. More than 4 million shares were tendered to Vickers. Subsequently, Lynch filed a class action suit alleging that Vickers violated its fiduciary duty in connection with the tender offer. The trial court found that Vickers, as a controlling shareholder, had a fiduciary duty of candor, but had not breached that duty. 351 A.2d 570 (Del. Ch. 1976). In *Lynch I,* 383 A.2d 278 (Del. 1978), the Delaware Supreme Court reversed, finding that Vickers had breached its duty of candor in failing to disclose material information concerning the value of the Transocean stock, including the fact that immediately before the tender offer, Vickers had authorized its agents to purchase Transocean shares for up to $15 per share.

On remand, the trial judge concluded that although the control transaction at issue was not directly covered by Delaware's appraisal remedy, "a proceeding analogous to an appraisal hearing such as is provided in a merger case is appropriate here . . . in a situation in which active fraud has not been alleged or proved." 402 A.2d 5, 11 (Del. Ch. 1979).

The trial court then applied the Delaware block method, which requires the court to determine the corporation's asset, market, and earnings values, appropriately weight these values, and then add the weighted values together to arrive at a "fair value." Despite the fact that (1) Transocean's oil reserves gave the corporation an asset value far in excess of market value, (2) the stock market was severely depressed, and (3) Vickers had been willing to pay $15 per share in pre-tender offer purchases, the trial judge gave only a 40 percent weight to asset value. The resulting calculations were as follows:

Asset Value	$17.50 × 40% =	$ 7.00
Market Value	9.48 × 40% =	3.80
Earnings Value	5.25 × 20% =	1.05
Total		$11.85

Since the merger consideration exceeded the actual fair value of Transocean's shares, the plaintiff had not been damaged.

In *Lynch II*, 429 A.2d 497 (Del. 1981), the Delaware Supreme Court, with two of its five judges dissenting, reversed the trial court again. Perhaps exasperated with the results produced by the Delaware block method, the court majority held that basing relief on the difference between the price offered and the fair value of the stock was inappropriate. The court stressed the fact that unlike in the typical appraisal case, the corporation had breached its fiduciary duty.

> The difference is important because the appraisal approach . . . has a built-in limitation, namely, gain to the corporation resulting from a statutory merger is not a factor which is included in determining the value of shares, and it was not considered by the Chancellor. But that limitation does not apply when a fiduciary has breached a duty to those to whom it is owed. . . . [A] claim founded on breach of fiduciary duty permits a different form of relief, that is, an accounting or rescission or other remedy afforded for breach of trust by a fiduciary.

429 A.2d at 501.

The court concluded that rescission was impracticable so long after the tender offer. Instead, a fair result could be achieved "by ordering damages which are the monetary equivalent of rescission and which will, in effect, equal the increment in value that Vickers enjoyed as a result of acquiring and holding the Transocean stock in issue." Id.

The principal case below involved a merger of UOP, Inc. into its controlling shareholder, The Signal Companies, Inc. The plaintiff claimed that Signal lacked a proper business purpose, had failed to prove the transaction's entire fairness, and had breached its duty of candor, entitling the plaintiff to rescissory damages per *Lynch II*. The trial court found for the defendant on all counts, noting as to the business purpose claim that Signal had not used its controlling position, since the merger agreement with UOP provided that unless a majority of the minority shareholders approved, the merger would not be put into effect.

Faced with the Chancery Court's continuing hostility to *Singer* and *Lynch*, and the shareholder-plaintiffs-bar's continuing avoidance of the appraisal remedy, the Delaware Supreme Court used the case below to modernize the appraisal remedy and reshape the rules governing fiduciary-duty-based review of cash-out mergers. As you read this case, carefully identify how the court has changed the incentives of both controlling and dissenting shareholders.

Weinberger v. UOP, Inc.
Delaware Supreme Court, 1983
457 A.2d 701

MOORE, JUSTICE:

This post-trial appeal was reheard en banc from a decision of the Court of Chancery. It was brought by the class action plaintiff below, a former shareholder of UOP, Inc., who challenged the elimination of UOP's minority shareholders by a cash-out merger between UOP and its majority owner, The Signal Companies, Inc. . . .

In ruling for the defendants, the Chancellor re-stated his earlier conclusion that the plaintiff in a suit challenging a cash-out merger must allege specific acts of fraud, misrepresentation, or other items of misconduct to demonstrate the unfairness of the merger terms to the minority. We approve this rule and affirm it.

The Chancellor also held that even though the ultimate burden of proof is on the majority shareholder to show by a preponderance of the evidence that the transaction is fair, it is first the burden of the plaintiff attacking the merger to demonstrate some basis for invoking the fairness obligation. We agree with that principle. However, where corporate action has been approved by an informed vote of a majority of the minority shareholders, we conclude that the burden entirely shifts to the plaintiff to show that the transaction was unfair to the minority. See, e.g., Michelson v. Duncan, Del. Supr., 407 A.2d 211, 224 (1979). But in all this, the burden clearly remains on those relying on the vote to show that they completely disclosed all material facts relevant to the transaction.

Here, the record does not support a conclusion that the minority stockholder vote was an informed one. Material information, necessary to acquaint those shareholders with the bargaining positions of Signal and UOP, was withheld under circumstances amounting to a breach of fiduciary duty. We therefore conclude that this merger does not meet the test of fairness, at least as we address that concept, and no burden thus shifted to the plaintiff by reason of the minority shareholder vote. Accordingly, we reverse and remand for further proceedings consistent herewith.

In considering the nature of the remedy available under our law to minority shareholders in a cash-out merger, we believe that it is, and hereafter should be, an appraisal under 8 Del. C. §262 as hereinafter construed. We therefore overrule Lynch v. Vickers Energy Corp., Del. Supr., 429 A.2d 497 (1981) (*Lynch II*), to the extent that it purports to limit a stockholder's monetary relief to a specific damage formula. See *Lynch II*, 429 A.2d at 507-508 (McNeilly & Quillen, JJ., dissenting). But to give full effect to §262 within the framework of the General Corporation Law we adopt a more liberal, less rigid and stylized, approach to the valuation process than has heretofore been permitted by our courts. While the present state of these proceedings does not admit the plaintiff to the appraisal remedy per se, the practical effect of the remedy we do grant him will be co-extensive with the liberalized valuation and appraisal methods we herein approve for cases coming after this decision.

Our treatment of these matters has necessarily led us to a reconsideration of the business purpose rule announced in the trilogy of Singer v. Magnavox Co., Del. Supr., 380 A.2d 969 (1977); Tanzer v. International General Industries, Inc., Del. Supr., 379 A.2d 1121 (1977); and Roland International Corp. v. Najjar, Del. Supr., 407 A.2d 1032

(1979). For the reasons hereafter set forth we consider that the business purpose requirement of these cases is no longer the law of Delaware.

I ...

Signal is a diversified, technically based company operating through various subsidiaries. Its stock is publicly traded on the New York, Philadelphia and Pacific Stock Exchanges. UOP, formerly known as Universal Oil Products Company, was a diversified industrial company engaged in various lines of business, including petroleum and petro-chemical services and related products, construction, fabricated metal products, transportation equipment products, chemicals and plastics, and other products and services including land development, lumber products and waste disposal. Its stock was publicly held and listed on the New York Stock Exchange.

In 1974 Signal sold one of its wholly-owned subsidiaries for $420,000,000 in cash. See Gimbel v. Signal Companies, Inc., Del. Ch., 316 A.2d 599, affd., Del. Supr., 316 A.2d 619 (1974). While looking to invest this cash surplus, Signal became interested in UOP as a possible acquisition. Friendly negotiations ensued, and Signal proposed to acquire a controlling interest in UOP at a price of $19 per share. UOP's representatives sought $25 per share. In the arm's length bargaining that followed, [in April 1975] an understanding was reached whereby Signal agreed to purchase from UOP 1,500,000 shares of UOP's authorized but unissued stock at $21 per share [and to make a cash tender offer for 4,300,000 publicly held shares of UOP, also at a price of $21 per share. The two transactions together represented 50.5 percent of UOP's outstanding shares. Immediately before the announcement of the tender offer, UOP's common stock had been trading on the New York Stock Exchange at a fraction under $14 per share. Although the resulting tender offer was greatly oversubscribed, Signal limited its total purchase so as not to exceed its goal of becoming a 50.5 percent shareholder of UOP. Signal nominated and elected six of the thirteen UOP directors. When the president and chief executive officer of UOP retired during 1975, Signal caused him to be replaced by James V. Crawford, a longtime Signal employee. Crawford succeeded his predecessor on UOP's board of directors and also was made a director of Signal.]

By the end of 1977 Signal basically was unsuccessful in finding other suitable investment candidates for its excess cash, and by February 1978 considered that it had no other realistic acquisitions available to it on a friendly basis. Once again its attention turned to UOP.

The trial court found that at the instigation of certain Signal management personnel, including William W. Walkup, its board chairman, and Forrest N. Shumway, its president, a feasibility study was made concerning the possible acquisition of the balance of UOP's outstanding shares. This study was performed by two Signal officers, Charles S. Arledge, vice president (director of planning), and Andrew J. Chitiea, senior vice president (chief financial officer). Messrs. Walkup, Shumway, Arledge and Chitiea were all directors of UOP in addition to their membership on the Signal board.

Arledge and Chitiea concluded that it would be a good investment for Signal to acquire the remaining 49.5% of UOP shares at any price up to $24 each. Their report was discussed between Walkup and Shumway who, along with Arledge, Chitiea and

Brewster L. Arms, internal counsel for Signal, constituted Signal's senior management. In particular, they talked about the proper price to be paid if the acquisition was pursued, purportedly keeping in mind that as UOP's majority shareholder, Signal owed a fiduciary responsibility to both its own stockholders as well as to UOP's minority. It was ultimately agreed that a meeting of Signal's executive committee would be called to propose that Signal acquire the remaining outstanding stock of UOP through a cash-out merger in the range of $20 to $21 per share.

The executive committee meeting was set for February 28, 1978. As a courtesy, UOP's president, Crawford, was invited to attend, although he was not a member of Signal's executive committee. On his arrival, and prior to the meeting, Crawford was asked to meet privately with Walkup and Shumway. He was then told of Signal's plan to acquire full ownership of UOP and was asked for his reaction to the proposed price range of $20 to $21 per share. Crawford said he thought such a price would be "generous," and that it was certainly one which should be submitted to UOP's minority shareholders for their ultimate consideration. He stated, however, that Signal's 100% ownership could cause internal problems at UOP. He believed that employees would have to be given some assurance of their future place in a fully-owned Signal subsidiary. Otherwise, he feared the departure of essential personnel. Also, many of UOP's key employees had stock option incentive programs which would be wiped out by a merger. Crawford therefore urged that some adjustment would have to be made, such as providing a comparable incentive in Signal's shares, if after the merger he was to maintain his quality of personnel and efficiency at UOP.

Thus, Crawford voiced no objection to the $20 to $21 price range, nor did he suggest that Signal should consider paying more than $21 per share for the minority interests. Later, at the executive committee meeting the same factors were discussed, with Crawford repeating the position he earlier took with Walkup and Shumway. Also considered was the 1975 tender offer and the fact that it had been greatly oversubscribed at $21 per share. For many reasons, Signal's management concluded that the acquisition of UOP's minority shares provided the solution to a number of its business problems.

Thus, it was the consensus that a price of $20 to $21 per share would be fair to both Signal and the minority shareholders of UOP. Signal's executive committee authorized its management "to negotiate" with UOP "for a cash acquisition of the minority ownership in UOP, Inc., with the intention of presenting a proposal to [Signal's] board of directors . . . on March 6, 1978." . . .

Between Tuesday, February 28, 1978 and Monday, March 6, 1978, a total of four business days, Crawford spoke by telephone with all of UOP's non-Signal, i.e., outside, directors. Also during that period, Crawford retained Lehman Brothers to render a fairness opinion as to the price offered the minority for its stock. He gave two reasons for this choice. First, the time schedule between the announcement and the board meetings was short (by then only three business days) and since Lehman Brothers had been acting as UOP's investment banker for many years, Crawford felt that it would be in the best position to respond on such brief notice. Second, James W. Glanville, a long-time director of UOP and a partner in Lehman Brothers, had acted as a financial advisor to UOP for many years. Crawford believed that Glanville's familiarity with UOP, as a member of its board, would also be of assistance in enabling Lehman Brothers to render a fairness opinion within the existing time constraints.

Crawford telephoned Glanville, who gave his assurance that Lehman Brothers had no conflicts that would prevent it from accepting the task. Glanville's immediate personal reaction was that a price of $20 to $21 would certainly be fair, since it represented almost a 50% premium over UOP's market price. Glanville sought a $250,000 fee for Lehman Brothers' services, but Crawford thought this too much. After further discussions Glanville finally agreed that Lehman Brothers would render its fairness opinion for $150,000.

During this period Crawford also had several telephone contacts with Signal officials. In only one of them, however, was the price of the shares discussed. In a conversation with Walkup, Crawford advised that as a result of his communications with UOP's non-Signal directors, it was his feeling that the price would have to be the top of the proposed range, or $21 per share, if the approval of UOP's outside directors was to be obtained. But again, he did not seek any price higher than $21.

Glanville assembled a three-man Lehman Brothers team to do the work on the fairness opinion. These persons examined relevant documents and information concerning UOP, including its annual reports and its Securities and Exchange Commission filings from 1973 through 1976, as well as its audited financial statements for 1977, its interim reports to shareholders, and its recent and historical market prices and trading volumes. In addition, on Friday, March 3, 1978, two members of the Lehman Brothers team flew to UOP's headquarters in Des Plaines, Illinois, to perform a "due diligence" visit, during the course of which they interviewed Crawford as well as UOP's general counsel, its chief financial officer, and other key executives and personnel.

As a result, the Lehman Brothers team concluded that "the price of either $20 or $21 would be a fair price for the remaining shares of UOP." They telephoned this impression to Glanville, who was spending the weekend in Vermont.

On Monday morning, March 6, 1978, Glanville and the senior member of the Lehman Brothers team flew to Des Plaines to attend the scheduled UOP directors' meeting. Glanville looked over the assembled information during the flight. The two had with them the draft of a "fairness opinion letter" in which the price had been left blank. Either during or immediately prior to the directors' meeting, the two-page "fairness opinion letter" was typed in final form and the price of $21 per share was inserted.

On March 6, 1978, both the Signal and UOP boards were convened to consider the proposed merger. Telephone communications were maintained between the two meetings. Walkup, Signal's board chairman, and also a UOP director, attended UOP's meeting with Crawford in order to present Signal's position and answer any questions that UOP's non-Signal directors might have. Arledge and Chitiea, along with Signal's other designees on UOP's board, participated by conference telephone. All of UOP's outside directors attended the meeting either in person or by conference telephone.

First, Signal's board unanimously adopted a resolution authorizing Signal to propose to UOP a cash merger of $21 per share as outlined in a certain merger agreement and other supporting documents. This proposal required that the merger be approved by a majority of UOP's outstanding minority shares voting at the stockholders meeting at which the merger would be considered, and that the minority shares voting in favor of the merger, when coupled with Signal's 50.5% interest would have to comprise at least two-thirds of all UOP shares. Otherwise the proposed merger would be deemed disapproved.

UOP's board then considered the proposal. Copies of the agreement were delivered to the directors in attendance, and other copies had been forwarded earlier to the directors participating by telephone. They also had before them UOP financial data for 1974-1977, UOP's most recent financial statements, market price information, and budget projections for 1978. In addition they had Lehman Brothers' hurriedly prepared fairness opinion letter finding the price of $21 to be fair. Glanville, the Lehman Brothers partner, and UOP director, commented on the information that had gone into preparation of the letter.

Signal also suggests that the Arledge-Chitiea feasibility study, indicating that a price of up to $24 per share would be a "good investment" for Signal, was discussed at the UOP directors' meeting. The Chancellor made no such finding, and our independent review of the record . . . satisfies us by a preponderance of the evidence that there was no discussion of this document at UOP's board meeting. Furthermore, it is clear beyond peradventure that nothing in that report was ever disclosed to UOP's minority shareholders prior to their approval of the merger.

After consideration of Signal's proposal, Walkup and Crawford left the meeting to permit a free and uninhibited exchange between UOP's non-Signal directors. Upon their return a resolution to accept Signal's offer was then proposed and adopted. While Signal's men on UOP's board participated in various aspects of the meeting, they abstained from voting. However, the minutes show that each of them "if voting would have voted yes." . . .

Despite the swift board action of the two companies, the merger was not submitted to UOP's shareholders until their annual meeting on May 26, 1978. In the notice of that meeting and proxy statement sent to shareholders in May, UOP's management and board urged that the merger be approved. The proxy statement . . . also advised the shareholders that Lehman Brothers had given its opinion that the merger price of $21 per share was fair to UOP's minority. However, it did not disclose the hurried method by which this conclusion was reached.

As of the record date of UOP's annual meeting, there were 11,488,302 shares of UOP common stock outstanding, 5,688,302 of which were owned by the minority. At the meeting only 56%, or 3,208,652, of the minority shares were voted. Of these, 2,953,812, or 51.9% of the total minority, voted for the merger, and 254,840 voted against it. When Signal's stock was added to the minority shares voting in favor, a total of 76.2% of UOP's outstanding shares approved the merger while only 2.2% opposed it.

By its terms the merger became effective on May 26, 1978, and each share of UOP's stock held by the minority was automatically converted into a right to receive $21 cash.

II.

A

A primary issue mandating reversal is the preparation by two UOP directors, Arledge and Chitiea, of their feasibility study for the exclusive use and benefit of Signal.

This document was of obvious significance to both Signal and UOP. Using UOP data, it described the advantages to Signal of ousting the minority at a price range of $21-$24 per share. Mr. Arledge, one of the authors, outlined the benefits to Signal:[6]

Purpose of the Merger

    (1) Provides an outstanding investment opportunity for Signal—(Better than any recent acquisition we have seen.)

    (2) Increases Signal's earnings.

    (3) Facilitates the flow of resources between Signal and its subsidiaries—(Big factor—works both ways.)

    (4) Provides cost savings potential for Signal and UOP.

    (5) Improves the percentage of Signal's "operating earnings" as opposed to "holding company earnings."

    (6) Simplifies the understanding of Signal.

    (7) Facilitates technological exchange among Signal's subsidiaries.

    (8) Eliminates potential conflicts of interest.

Having written those words, solely for the use of Signal, it is clear from the record that neither Arledge nor Chitiea shared this report with their fellow directors of UOP. We are satisfied that no one else did either. This conduct hardly meets the fiduciary standards applicable to such a transaction. . . .

The Arledge-Chitiea report speaks for itself in supporting the Chancellor's finding that a price of up to $24 was a "good investment" for Signal. It shows that a return on the investment at $21 would be 15.7% versus 15.5% at $24 per share. This was a difference of only two-tenths of one percent, while it meant over $17,000,000 to the minority. Under such circumstances, paying UOP's minority shareholders $24 would have had relatively little long-term effect on Signal, and the Chancellor's findings concerning the benefit to Signal, even at a price of $24, were obviously correct.

Certainly, this was a matter of material significance to UOP and its shareholders. Since the study was prepared by two UOP directors, using UOP information for the exclusive benefit of Signal, and nothing whatever was done to disclose it to the outside UOP directors or the minority shareholders, a question of breach of fiduciary duty arises. This problem occurs because there were common Signal-UOP directors participating, at least to some extent, in the UOP board's decision-making processes without full disclosure of the conflicts they faced.[7]

---

6. The parentheses indicate certain handwritten comments of Mr. Arledge.

7. Although perfection is not possible, or expected, the result here could have been entirely different if UOP had appointed an independent negotiating committee of its outside directors to deal with Signal at arm's length. See, e.g., Harriman v. E.I. duPont de Nemours & Co., 411 F. Supp. 133 (D. Del. 1975). Since fairness in this context can be equated to conduct by a theoretical, wholly independent, board of directors acting upon the matter before them, it is unfortunate that this course apparently was neither considered nor pursued. Particularly in a parent-subsidiary context, a showing that the action taken was as though each of the contending parties had in fact exerted its bargaining power against the other at arm's length is strong evidence that the transaction meets the test of fairness. Getty Oil Co. v. Skelly Oil Co., Del. Supr., 267 A.2d 883, 886 (1970); Puma v. Marriott, Del. Ch., 283 A.2d 693, 696 (1971).

B

In assessing this situation, the Court of Chancery was required to:

examine what information defendants had and to measure it against what they gave to the minority stockholders, in a context in which "complete candor" is required. In other words, the limited function of the Court was to determine whether defendants had disclosed all information in their possession germane to the transaction in issue. And by "germane" we mean, for present purposes, information such as a reasonable shareholder would consider important in deciding whether to sell or retain stock. . . .

. . . Completeness, not adequacy, is both the norm and the mandate under present circumstances.

Lynch v. Vickers Energy Corp., Del. Supr., 383 A.2d 278, 281 (1977) (*Lynch I*). This is merely stating in another way the long-existing principle of Delaware law that these Signal designated directors on UOP's board still owed UOP and its shareholders an uncompromising duty of loyalty. The classic language of Guth v. Loft, Inc., Del. Supr., 5 A.2d 513, 510 (1939), requires no embellishment:

A public policy, existing through the years, and derived from a profound knowledge of human characteristics and motives, has established a rule that demands of a corporate officer or director, peremptorily and inexorably, the most scrupulous observance of his duty, not only affirmatively to protect the interests of the corporation committed to his charge, but also to refrain from doing anything that would work injury to the corporation, or to deprive it of profit or advantage which his skill and ability might properly bring to it, or to enable it to make in the reasonable and lawful exercise of its powers. The rule that requires an undivided and unselfish loyalty to the corporation demands that there shall be no conflict between duty and self-interest.

Given the absence of any attempt to structure this transaction on an arm's length basis, Signal cannot escape the effects of the conflicts it faced, particularly when its designees on UOP's board did not totally abstain from participation in the matter. There is no "safe harbor" for such divided loyalties in Delaware. When directors of a Delaware corporation are on both sides of a transaction, they are required to demonstrate their utmost good faith and the most scrupulous inherent fairness of the bargain. The requirement of fairness is unflinching in its demand that where one stands on both sides of a transaction, he has the burden of establishing its entire fairness, sufficient to pass the test of careful scrutiny by the courts. Sterling v. Mayflower Hotel Corp., Del. Supr., 93 A.2d 107, 110 (1952).

There is no dilution of this obligation where one holds dual or multiple directorships, as in a parent-subsidiary context. Levien v. Sinclair Oil Corp., Del. Ch., 261 A.2d 911, 915 (1969). Thus, individuals who act in a dual capacity as directors of two corporations, one of whom is parent and the other subsidiary, owe the same duty of good management to both corporations, and in the absence of an independent negotiating structure (see note 7, supra), or the directors' total abstention from any participation in the matter, this duty is to be exercised in light of what is best for both companies. The record demonstrates that Signal has not met this obligation.

C

The concept of fairness has two basic aspects: fair dealing and fair price. The former embraces questions of when the transaction was timed, how it was initiated, structured, negotiated, disclosed to the directors, and how the approvals of the directors and the stockholders were obtained. The latter aspect of fairness relates to the economic and financial considerations of the proposed merger, including all relevant factors: assets, market value, earnings, future prospects, and any other elements that affect the intrinsic or inherent value of a company's stock. However, the test for fairness is not a bifurcated one as between fair dealing and price. All aspects of the issue must be examined as a whole since the question is one of entire fairness. However, in a non-fraudulent transaction we recognize that price may be the preponderant consideration outweighing other features of the merger. Here, we address the two basic aspects of fairness separately because we find reversible error as to both.

D

Part of fair dealing is the obvious duty of candor required by *Lynch I,* supra. Moreover, one possessing superior knowledge may not mislead any stockholder by use of corporate information to which the latter is not privy. Delaware has long imposed this duty even upon persons who are not corporate officers or directors, but who nonetheless are privy to matters of interest or significance to their company. Brophy v. Cities Service Co., Del. Ch., 70 A.2d 5, 7 (1949). With the well-established Delaware law on the subject, and the Court of Chancery's findings of fact here, it is inevitable that the obvious conflicts posed by Arledge and Chitiea's preparation of their "feasibility study," derived from UOP information, for the sole use and benefit of Signal, cannot pass muster.

The Arledge-Chitiea report is but one aspect of the element of fair dealing. How did this merger evolve? It is clear that it was entirely initiated by Signal. The serious time constraints under which the principals acted were all set by Signal. It had not found a suitable outlet for its excess cash and considered UOP a desirable investment, particularly since it was now in a position to acquire the whole company for itself. For whatever reasons, and they were only Signal's, the entire transaction was presented to and approved by UOP's board within four business days. Standing alone, this is not necessarily indicative of any lack of fairness by a majority shareholder. It was what occurred, or more properly, what did not occur, during this brief period that makes the time constraints imposed by Signal relevant to the issue of fairness.

The structure of the transaction, again, was Signal's doing. So far as negotiations were concerned, it is clear that they were modest at best. Crawford, Signal's man at UOP, never really talked price with Signal, except to accede to its management's statements on the subject, and to convey to Signal the UOP outside directors' view that as between the $20-$21 range under consideration, it would have to be $21. The latter is not a surprising outcome, but hardly arm's length negotiations. Only the protection of benefits for UOP's key employees and the issue of Lehman Brothers' fee approached any concept of bargaining.

As we have noted, the matter of disclosure to the UOP directors was wholly flawed by the conflicts of interest raised by the Arledge-Chitiea report. All of those conflicts were resolved by Signal in its own favor without divulging any aspect of them to UOP.

This cannot but undermine a conclusion that this merger meets any reasonable test of fairness. The outside UOP directors lacked one material piece of information generated by two of their colleagues, but shared only with Signal. True, the UOP board had the Lehman Brothers' fairness opinion, but that firm has been blamed by the plaintiff for the hurried task it performed, when more properly the responsibility for this lies with Signal. There was no disclosure of the circumstances surrounding the rather cursory preparation of the Lehman Brothers' fairness opinion. Instead, the impression was given UOP's minority that a careful study had been made, when in fact speed was the hallmark, and Mr. Glanville, Lehman's partner in charge of the matter, and also a UOP director, having spent the weekend in Vermont, brought a draft of the "fairness opinion letter" to the UOP directors' meeting on March 6, 1978 with the price left blank. We can only conclude from the record that the rush imposed on Lehman Brothers by Signal's timetable contributed to the difficulties under which this investment banking firm attempted to perform its responsibilities. Yet, none of this was disclosed to UOP's minority.

Finally, the minority stockholders were denied the critical information that Signal considered a price of $24 to be a good investment. Since this would have meant over $17,000,000 more to the minority, we cannot conclude that the shareholder vote was an informed one. Under the circumstances, an approval by a majority of the minority was meaningless. *Lynch I*, 383 A.2d at 279, 281; Cahall v. Lofland, Del. Ch., 114 A. 224 (1921).

Given these particulars and the Delaware law on the subject, the record does not establish that this transaction satisfies any reasonable concept of fair dealing, and the Chancellor's findings in that regard must be reversed.

E

Turning to the matter of price, plaintiff also challenges its fairness. His evidence was that on the date the merger was approved the stock was worth at least $26 per share. In support, he offered the testimony of a chartered investment analyst who used two basic approaches to valuation: a comparative analysis of the premium paid over market in ten other tender offer-merger combinations, and a discounted cash flow analysis.

In this breach of fiduciary duty case, the Chancellor perceived that the approach to valuation was the same as that in an appraisal proceeding. Consistent with precedent, he rejected plaintiff's method of proof and accepted defendants' evidence of value as being in accord with practice under prior case law. This means that the so-called "Delaware block" or weighted average method was employed wherein the elements of value, i.e., assets, market price, earnings, etc., were assigned a particular weight and the resulting amounts added to determine the value per share. This procedure has been in use for decades. However, to the extent it excludes other generally accepted techniques used in the financial community and the courts, it is now clearly outmoded. It is time we recognize this in appraisal and other stock valuation proceedings and bring our law current on the subject.

While the Chancellor rejected plaintiff's discounted cash flow method of valuing UOP's stock, as not corresponding with "either logic or the existing law," it is significant that this was essentially the focus, i.e., earnings potential of UOP, of Messrs. Arledge and Chitiea in their evaluation of the merger. Accordingly, the standard "Delaware block" or weighted average method of valuation, formerly employed in appraisal and other stock valuation cases, shall no longer exclusively control such proceedings. We believe that a more liberal approach must include proof of value by any techniques or methods which are generally considered acceptable in the financial community and otherwise admissible in court, subject only to our interpretation of 8 Del. C. §262(h), infra. See also D.R.E. 702-05. This will obviate the very structured and mechanistic procedure that has heretofore governed such matters.

Fair price obviously requires consideration of all relevant factors involving the value of a company. This has long been the law of Delaware as stated in [Tri-Continental Corp. v. Battye, Del. Supr., 74 A.2d 71, 72 (1950)]:

> The basic concept of value under the appraisal statute is that the stockholder is entitled to be paid for that which has been taken from him, viz., his proportionate interest in a going concern. By value of the stockholder's proportionate interest in the corporate enterprise is meant the true or intrinsic value of his stock which has been taken by the merger. In determining what figure represents this true or intrinsic value, the appraiser and the courts must take into consideration all factors and elements which reasonably might enter into the fixing of value. Thus, market value, asset value, dividends, earning prospects, the nature of the enterprise and any other facts which were known or which could be ascertained as of the date of merger and which throw any light on *future prospects* of the merged corporation are not only pertinent to an inquiry as to the value of the dissenting stockholders' interest, but *must be considered* by the agency fixing the value. (Emphasis added.)

This is not only in accord with the realities of present day affairs, but it is thoroughly consonant with the purpose and intent of our statutory law. Under 8 Del. C. §262(h), the Court of Chancery:

> shall appraise the shares, determining their *fair* value exclusive of any element of value arising from the accomplishment or expectation of the merger, together with a fair rate of interest, if any, to be paid upon the amount determined to be the *fair* value. In determining such *fair* value, the Court shall take into account *all relevant factors.* . . . (Emphasis added.)

See also Bell v. Kirby Lumber Corp., Del. Supr., 413 A.2d 137, 150-151 (1980) (Quillen, J., concurring).

It is significant that §262 now mandates the determination of "fair" value based upon "all relevant factors." Only the speculative elements of value that may arise from the "accomplishment or expectation" of the merger are excluded. We take this to be a very narrow exception to the appraisal process, designed to eliminate use of pro forma data and projections of a speculative variety relating to the completion of a merger. But elements of future value, including the nature of the enterprise, which are known or susceptible of proof as of the date of the merger and not the product of speculation, may be considered. When the trial court deems it appropriate, fair value also includes any damages, resulting from the taking, which the stockholders sustain as a class. If that was not the case, then the obligation to consider "all relevant factors" in the valuation process would be eroded. We are supported in this view not only by *Tri-Continental Corp.*, 74 A.2d at 72, but also by the evolutionary amendments to §262. . . .

It was not until the 1981 amendment to §262 that the reference to "fair value" was repeatedly emphasized and the statutory mandate that the Court "take into account all relevant factors" appeared (§262(h)). Clearly, there is a legislative intent to fully compensate shareholders for whatever their loss may be, subject only to the narrow limitation that one can not take speculative effects of the merger into account.

Although the Chancellor received the plaintiff's evidence, his opinion indicates that the use of it was precluded because of past Delaware practice. While we do not suggest a monetary result one way or the other, we do think the plaintiff's evidence should be part of the factual mix and weighed as such. Until the $21 price is measured on remand by the valuation standards mandated by Delaware law, there can be no finding at the present stage of these proceedings that the price is fair. Given the lack of any candid disclosure of the material facts surrounding establishment of the $21 price, the majority of the minority vote, approving the merger, is meaningless.

The plaintiff has not sought an appraisal, but rescissory damages of the type contemplated by Lynch v. Vickers Energy Corp., Del. Supr., 429 A.2d 497, 505-06 (1981) (*Lynch II*). In view of the approach to valuation that we announce today, we see no basis in our law for *Lynch II*'s exclusive monetary formula for relief. On remand the plaintiff will be permitted to test the fairness of the $21 price by the standards we herein establish, in conformity with the principle applicable to an appraisal — that fair value be determined by taking "into account all relevant factors" [see 8 Del. C. §262(h), supra]. In our view this includes the elements of rescissory damages if the Chancellor considers them susceptible of proof and a remedy appropriate to all the issues of fairness before him. To the extent that *Lynch II* purports to limit the Chancellor's discretion to a single remedial formula for monetary damages in a cash-out merger, it is overruled.

While a plaintiff's monetary remedy ordinarily should be confined to the more liberalized appraisal proceeding herein established, we do not intend any limitation on the historic powers of the Chancellor to grant such other relief as the facts of a particular case may dictate. The appraisal remedy we approve may not be adequate in certain cases, particularly where fraud, misrepresentation, self-dealing, deliberate waste of corporate assets, or gross and palpable overreaching are involved. Under such circumstances, the Chancellor's powers are complete to fashion any form of equitable and monetary relief as may be appropriate, including rescissory damages. Since it is apparent that this long completed transaction is too involved to undo, and in view of the Chancellor's discretion, the award, if any, should be in the form of monetary damages based upon entire fairness standards, i.e., fair dealing and fair price.

Obviously, there are other litigants, like the plaintiff, who abjured an appraisal and whose rights to challenge the element of fair value must be preserved. Accordingly, the quasi-appraisal remedy we grant the plaintiff here will apply only to: (1) this case; (2) any case now pending on appeal to this Court; (3) any case now pending in the Court of Chancery which has not yet been appealed but which may be eligible for direct appeal to this Court; (4) any case challenging a cash-out merger, the effective date of which is on or before February 1, 1983; and (5) any proposed merger to be presented at a shareholders' meeting, the notification of which is mailed to the stockholders on or before February 23, 1983. Thereafter, the provisions of 8 Del. C. §262, as herein construed, respecting the scope of an appraisal and the means for perfecting the same, shall govern the financial remedy available to minority shareholders in a cash-out merger. Thus, we return to the well established principles of Stauffer v. Standard Brands, Inc., Del. Supr., 187 A.2d 78 (1962) and David J. Greene & Co. v. Schenley Industries, Inc., Del. Ch., 281 A.2d 30 (1971), mandating a stockholder's recourse to the basic remedy of an appraisal.

III

Finally, we address the matter of business purpose. The defendants contend that the purpose of this merger was not a proper subject of inquiry by the trial court. The plaintiff says that no valid purpose existed—the entire transaction was a mere subterfuge designed to eliminate the minority. The Chancellor ruled otherwise, but in so doing he clearly circumscribed the thrust and effect of *Singer.* Weinberger v. UOP, 426 A.2d at 1342-1343, 1348-1350. This has led to the thoroughly sound observation that the business purpose test "may be . . . virtually interpreted out of existence, as it was in *Weinberger.*"[9]

The requirement of a business purpose is new to our law of mergers and was a departure from prior case law.

In view of the fairness test which has long been applicable to parent-subsidiary mergers, Sterling v. Mayflower Hotel Corp., Del. Supr., 93 A.2d 107, 109-110 (1952), the expanded appraisal remedy now available to shareholders, and the broad discretion of the Chancellor to fashion such relief as the facts of a given case may dictate, we do not believe that any additional meaningful protection is afforded minority shareholders by the business purpose requirement of the trilogy of *Singer, Tanzer, Najjar,* and their progeny. Accordingly, such requirement shall no longer be of any force or effect. . . .

NOTES AND QUESTIONS

1. How could Signal implement the merger without disclosing the Arledge-Chitiea Report to the UOP shareholders? In a similar fact pattern, Getty Oil Company sought to cash out the minority shareholders in its controlled subsidiary, Skelly Oil Company. To avoid the structural problems pointed out in *Weinberger,* the members of Getty's negotiating team resigned from the Skelly board. The Delaware Supreme Court held that in the ensuing negotiation, Getty had satisfied its fiduciary obligations.

> On the basis of this record we are satisfied that Getty dealt fairly with Skelly throughout the transaction. Indeed, the adversarial nature of the negotiations completely supports a conclusion that they were conducted at arm's length. There is no credible evidence indicating that Getty, as the majority shareholder, dictated the terms of this merger.

Rosenblatt v. Getty Oil Co., 493 A.2d 929, 937 (Del. 1985).

---

9. Weiss, The Law of Take Out Mergers: A Historical Perspective, 56 N.Y.U. L. Rev. 624, 671 n.300 (1981).

2. Suppose that UOP's board had designated its independent directors as a Special Committee authorized to negotiate with Signal on UOP's behalf. Suppose, further, that Signal's board, relying on nonpublic information about UOP equally available to the UOP Special Committee, voted unanimously to authorize the Signal Negotiating Team to accept a deal with UOP at the best price possible, but in no event at more than $25 per share. And, suppose that the Signal Board's reserve price — the highest price it was willing to pay — was not disclosed to the UOP Special Committee, or, later, to the UOP minority shareholders. Does Signal's failure to disclose its reserve price constitute lack of fair dealing and a breach of the fiduciary duty owed to UOP's minority shareholders? Consider Vice Chancellor Strine's analysis.

> The plaintiffs' next argument has some of the flavor of a "gotcha" claim. In [the disclosure documents], the Pure stockholders are told that the Unocal board authorized the Offer at the specific exchange ratio ultimately used in the Offer. That statement is false because the Unocal board actually gave its management authority to make an offer at a greater exchange ratio than was eventually offered.
>
> The plaintiffs argue that this false statement is materially misleading. Moreover, they submit that the specific figure authorized by the Unocal board should have been shared with the Pure board by Ling, since he heard it and yet reinjected himself into the negotiations regarding the Special Committee's powers.
>
> In general, I disagree with the plaintiffs that a controlling stockholder must reveal its reserve price in these circumstances. Our law contemplates the possibility of a price negotiation in negotiated mergers involving a controlling stockholder, a practical impossibility if the reserve price of the controlling stockholder must be revealed. The same is true in the tender offer context.
>
> Furthermore, I do not believe that the mere fact that Ling re-entered the Pure board process when the Special Committee sought authority adverse to Unocal's interest means that he had a duty to expose everything he knew about Unocal's negotiating posture. Significant to this conclusion is the absence of any persuasive evidence that the Special Committee was denied any material information from Pure that was available to Unocal in making its bid. Unocal's own subjective reserve price is not such information.

In re Pure Resources, Inc. Shareholder Litigation, 808 A.2d 421, 451 (2002).

3. How much information should Signal's proxy materials have provided UOP minority shareholders about the substance of the Lehman Brothers' Fairness Opinion? Would it have been sufficient to simply reveal the conclusion — "that the price of either $20 or $21 per share would be fair"? This question remains unresolved, and Delaware courts have expressed conflicting views, as discussed by Vice Chancellor Strine in *Pure Resources*.

> These conflicting impulses were manifested recently in two Supreme Court opinions. In one, Skeen v. Jo-Ann Stores, Inc., 750 A.2d 1170 (Del. 2000), the Court was inclined towards the view that a summary of the bankers' analyses and conclusions was not material to a stockholders' decision whether to seek appraisal. In the other, McMullin v. Beran, 765 A.2d 910 (Del. 2000), the Court implied that information about the analytical work of the board's banker could well be material in analogous circumstances.
>
> In my view, it is time that this ambivalence be resolved in favor of a firm statement that stockholders are entitled to a fair summary of the substantive work performed by the investment bankers upon whose advice the recommendations of their board as to how to vote on a merger or tender rely. I agree that our law should not encourage needless prolixity, but that concern cannot reasonably apply to investment bankers' analyses, which usually address the most important issue to stockholders — the sufficiency of the consideration being offered to them for their shares in a merger or tender offer.

Moreover, courts must be candid in acknowledging that the disclosure of the banker's "fairness opinion" alone and without more, provides stockholders with nothing other than a conclusion, qualified by a gauze of protective language designed to insulate the banker from liability.

The real informative value of the banker's work is not in its bottom-line conclusion, but in the valuation analysis that buttresses that result. This proposition is illustrated by the work of the judiciary itself, which closely examines the underlying analyses performed by the investment bankers when determining whether a transaction price is fair or a board reasonably relied on the banker's advice. Like a court would in making an after-the-fact fairness determination, a . . . minority stockholder engaging in the before-the-fact decision . . . would find it material to know the basic valuation exercises that First Boston and Petrie Parkman undertook, the key assumptions that they used in performing them, and the range of values that were thereby generated.

In re Pure Resources, Inc. Shareholder Litigation, 808 A.2d 421, 449 (Del. Ch. 2002).

PROBLEM 8-4

Reconsider the facts in Problem 8-3 (at page 725), under the following changed facts.

Suppose that instead of simply using its control to effectuate the cash-out merger with Shakespeare, Center structured the transaction as described in the following excerpts from the proxy material sent to Shakespeare shareholders:

> 7. The merger agreement was negotiated by Janice Brown, on behalf of Center, and, on behalf of Shakespeare, by a committee (the Special Committee) composed of the two independent members of its seven-member board of directors. . . .
>
> 9. The Special Committee commissioned a valuation study which revealed that the fair value of Shakespeare's outstanding shares was "most likely in a range between $25 and $28 per share . . . however, a favorable outcome of current television contract negotiations could result in a substantially higher value." Based on this study, the Special Committee attempted to negotiate a merger price of $26.50 per share. As a part of its negotiating efforts the Special Committee shared the valuation study with Brown, who then shared it with the full Center board. Though Brown argued for a lower price, the Center board selected a $25 per share merger price because, in its judgment, Shakespeare's shareholders were entitled to a fair price, but not the highest possible fair price. This price was then presented to the Special Committee as a take it or leave it offer.
>
> 10. The Special Committee by a two to one vote recommended the merger to the full Shakespeare board, which then approved it by a six to one vote. The lone dissenter on each vote stated that she believed that the price was unfair to the minority, especially in light of the ongoing television contract renewal negotiations.
>
> 11. State law requires that a merger be approved by a majority vote of the shares entitled to vote. Since Center will vote its shares in favor of the merger, the vote required by state law is assured. Nonetheless, the merger agreement between Shakespeare and Center provides that the merger will not be considered approved by Shakespeare's shareholders, and will not be consummated, unless approved by the vote of a majority of the outstanding Shakespeare shares not held by Center.

At a special shareholders' meeting held on September 15, 2013, more than 50 percent of the Shakespeare minority shareholders approved the proposed merger with Center. Immediately thereafter, Center pledged the Festival's assets as security for the renovation loan.

Dissenting minority shareholders of Shakespeare have now filed a complaint seeking rescission of the merger on the grounds that the merger had no business purpose, and that the price offered was grossly unfair.

(a) What are the prospects for this litigation under the doctrines of cases like *Singer, Tanzer,* and *Coggins*?

(b) In a jurisdiction that follows *Weinberger*?

(c) How are these prospects changed if the complaint is broadened to include a claim that Center violated its fiduciary duty in that the merger was not the product of fair dealing?

E.   Appraisal and Entire Fairness Review
After Weinberger

1.   Valuation Under Statutory Appraisal

MBCA §13.01(4)
Delaware G.C.L. §262(h)

Appraisal is available to shareholders in both arm's-length and controlling shareholder-dominated mergers. After *Weinberger*, however, the appraisal remedy has taken on increased significance in the latter context, both because *Weinberger* instructed trial courts to use realistic valuation methods and because *Weinberger* diminished the attractiveness of other remedies.

Our examination in Part C of when appraisal rights are available suggests that the appraisal remedy acts to balance the firm's need to adapt to changed circumstances and the dissenter's need for liquidity and protection from opportunism. In a cash-out merger, issues of liquidity disappear, leaving only concerns about opportunism.

How effective is the appraisal remedy at balancing the needs of the firm and minority shareholders? To a significant extent, the answer depends on how legislatures define what it is that shareholders are entitled to in return for their stock. Almost all statutes provide that shareholders are entitled to the fair value of their shares, but there are subtle differences in these statutes. Moreover, the generality of the term "fair value" creates uncertainty. As a result, debate continues on several issues, including (1) whether minority shareholders who are cashed out are entitled to any gains, from synergy or other sources, that may occur after the merger; and (2) whether "fair value" should reflect a discount because the appraised stock is a minority interest or is not readily marketable.

The following case illustrates the uncertainties present in the judicial appraisal of fair value.

Cede & Co. v. Technicolor, Inc.
Delaware Supreme Court, 1996
684 A.2d 289

HOLLAND, JUSTICE.

This appeal is from a final judgment of the Court of Chancery in an appraisal action. The proceeding arises from a cash-out merger of the minority shareholders of Technicolor Incorporated ("Technicolor"), a Delaware corporation. With the approval from a majority of Technicolor's shareholders, MacAndrews & Forbes Group Incorporated ("MAF") merged its wholly-owned subsidiary, Macanfor Corporation ("Macanfor"), into Technicolor. The only defendant-appellee in this appraisal action is Technicolor, the surviving corporation of the merger. The plaintiffs-appellants are Cinerama, Incorporated, the beneficial owner of 201,200 shares of Technicolor common stock, and Cede & Company, the record owner of those shares (collectively "Cinerama.")

Cinerama contends, inter alia, that the Court of Chancery erred, as a matter of law, in appraising the fair value of its Technicolor shares [at $21.60 per share]. . . .

FACTS . . .

Technicolor was a corporation with a long and prominent history in the film/audio-visual industries. By the early eighties, Technicolor's increase in market share had leveled off. The company's core business earnings had stagnated.

Technicolor engaged in a number of distinct businesses through separate operating units. Technicolor's Professional Services Group was its main source of revenue and profit. The Videocassette Duplicating Division operated one of the largest duplicating facilities in the world. The Consumer Services Group operated film processing laboratories ("Consumer Photo Processing Division" or "CPPD"), which provided film processing services to other photofinishers. CPPD also operated the Standard Manufacturing Company ("Standard"), which manufactured film splicers and associated equipment. The Government Services Group ("Government Services") provided photographic and non-photographic support and management services under contract to governmental agencies. Technicolor's Gold Key Entertainment Division ("Gold Key"), licensed motion pictures and other programs for television exhibition. The Audio Visual Division ("Audio Visual") distributed film and video equipment.

Morton Kamerman ("Kamerman"), Technicolor's Chief Executive Officer and Board Chairman, concluded that Technicolor's principal business, theatrical film processing, did not offer sufficient long-term growth for Technicolor. Kamerman proposed that Technicolor enter the field of rapid processing of consumer film by establishing a network of stores across the country offering one-hour development of film. The business, named One Hour Photo ("OHP") would require Technicolor to open approximately 1,000 stores over five years and to invest about $150 million.

In May 1981, Technicolor's Board of Directors approved Kamerman's plan. The following month, Technicolor announced its ambitious venture with considerable fanfare. On the date of its OHP announcement, Technicolor's stock had risen to a high of $22.13. . . .

[OHP quickly proved to be a disaster.] Technicolor's September 1982 financial statements, for the fiscal year ending June 1982, reported an eighty percent decline of consolidated net income—from $17,073 million in fiscal 1981 to $3,445 million in 1982. Profits had declined in Technicolor's core business, film processing. Technicolor's management also attributed the decline in profits to write-offs for losses in its Gold Key and Audio Visual divisions, which had already been targeted for sale. By September 1982, Technicolor's stock had reached a new low of $8.37 after falling by the end of June to $10.37 a share.

In the late summer of 1982, Ronald O. Perelman ("Perelman"), MAF's controlling stockholder, concluded that Technicolor would be an attractive candidate for a take-over or acquisition by MAF. [Negotiation ensued and the Technicolor board agreed to support a two-step takeover—first, a cash-tender offer, followed by a cash-out merger of all shares not tendered in the first step.] . . .

In November 1982, MAF commenced an all-cash tender offer of $23 per share to the shareholders of Technicolor. When the tender offer closed on November 30, 1982, MAF had gained control of Technicolor. By December 3, 1982, MAF had acquired 3,754,181 shares, or 82.19%, of Technicolor's shares. Thereafter, MAF and Technicolor were consolidated for tax and financial reporting purposes.

The Court of Chancery made a factual finding that, "upon acquiring control" of Technicolor, Perelman and his associates "began to dismember what they saw as a badly conceived melange of businesses." Perelman testified: "Presumably we made the evaluation of the business of Technicolor before we made the purchase, not after." That evaluation assumed the retention of the Professional and Government Services Groups and the disposition of OHP, CPPD, Gold Key, and Audio Visual.

Consequently, immediately after becoming Technicolor's controlling share-holder, MAF "started looking for buyers for several of the [Technicolor] divisions." Bear Stearns & Co. was also retained by MAF in December 1982 to assist it in dispos-ing of Technicolor assets. A target date of June 30, 1983 was set for liquidating all of Technicolor's excess assets. As of December 31, 1982, MAF was projecting that $54 mil-lion would be realized from asset sales. . . .

VALUATION OF TECHNICOLOR

PERELMAN PLAN OR KAMERMAN PLAN

The merger was accomplished on January 24, 1983. The parties agree that the appraised value of Technicolor must be fixed as of that date. See Alabama By-Products Corp. v. Neal, Del. Supr., 588 A.2d 255, 256-257 (1991). There is a fundamental dis-agreement between the litigants, however, concerning the nature of the enterprise to be appraised.

Cinerama argues that the Court of Chancery should have valued Technicolor as it existed on the date of the merger and, in particular, with due regard for the strate-gies that had been conceived and implemented following the merger agreement by MAF's controlling shareholder, Ronald O. Perelman ("Perelman Plan"). Technicolor argues that the Court of Chancery properly considered Technicolor without regard to the Perelman Plan and only as it existed on or before October 29, 1982, with the then extant strategies that had been conceived and implemented by Technicolor's Chairman, Morton Kamerman ("Kamerman Plan"). According to Cinerama:

> Reduced to its simplest form, the dispute was whether the trial court should value Perelman's
> Technicolor—a company whose business plans and strategies focused on the processing and dupli-
> cation of film and videotape and the provision of services to the United States Government and
> which planned and expected to generate $50 million in cash during 1983 from the sale of unwanted
> and/or unsuccessful businesses, namely, OHP, CPPD, Gold Key and Audio Visual; or Kamerman's

Technicolor—a company whose business plans and strategies assumed diversification away from a concentration on film processing and videotape duplication for the professional market toward consumer oriented businesses, especially OHP. . . .

The economic experts for both parties used a form of discounted cash flow methodology to value Technicolor. . . .[3]

THE PARTIES' CONTENTIONS

PERELMAN PLAN OR KAMERMAN PLAN

In the Court of Chancery, Cinerama argued that the Perelman Plan—which contemplated the sale of several businesses, focusing the company on film processing, and the new videocassette duplication business—was governing the operation of Technicolor on January 24, 1983. Consequently, Cinerama argued Perelman's Plan had to govern any expert's projection of net cash flow. For example, according to Cinerama, Technicolor's previous projections of negative cash flow from OHP's operation would be irrelevant in the appraisal valuation. In support of its position, Cinerama presented evidence that, prior to the merger date, Perelman had not only formulated, but had also implemented, a plan for how OHP and certain other Technicolor assets would be sold.

Technicolor argued to the Court of Chancery that the Perelman Plan, which it admitted called for the liquidation of OHP and a number of its other businesses, was not sufficiently defined on the date of the merger to form the factual premise for the Cinerama expert's cash flow projections from asset sales. The Court of Chancery unequivocally rejected that assertion by Technicolor. The Court of Chancery made a specific factual finding that "the record supports the conclusion that MAF intended from the outset to realize by one technique or another the capital value of One Hour Photo and to terminate that division's drain on the company's cash flow. Insofar as sale of that enterprise is involved, the 'Perelman Plan' was fixed by the merger date."

In view of that adverse factual determination, Technicolor's alternative contention was a legal argument. According to Technicolor, any value attributable to the Perelman Plan as of the merger date had to be excluded as arising from the expectation of the merger. See Delaware G.C.L. §262(h). Thus, Technicolor argued that the net cash flows which followed from the Perelman Plan should be excluded from the statutory appraisal valuation, as a matter of law.

In response, Cinerama argued to the Court of Chancery that this Court had construed the statutory phrase "exclusive of any element of value arising from the accomplishment or expectation of the merger" to exclude "[o]nly the speculative elements of value that may arise from the 'accomplishment or expectation' of the merger. . . . But elements of future value . . . which are known or susceptible of proof as of the date

---

3. Cinerama's expert opined that the statutory appraisal fair value of Technicolor on a per share basis as of January 24, 1983 was $62.75. Technicolor's expert opined that the statutory appraisal fair value of Technicolor at the time of the merger was $13.14 per share.

of the merger and not the product of speculation, may be considered." Weinberger v. UOP, Inc., Del. Supr., 457 A.2d 701, 713 (1983). Thus, Cinerama argued any nonspeculative element of future value that could be proven may be considered in a statutory appraisal proceeding, even if it is an "element of value arising from the accomplishment or expectation of the merger." See Delaware G.C.L. §262(h).

COURT OF CHANCERY'S HOLDING

MAJORITY ACQUIROR PRINCIPLE
PROXIMATE CAUSE EXCEPTION

The Court of Chancery acknowledged that, based upon the quoted language from *Weinberger,* Cinerama's legal argument appeared to be persuasive. The Court of Chancery concluded, however, "that reading [of *Weinberger*] is too difficult to square with the plain words of the statute to permit the conclusion that that is what was intended." The Court of Chancery then stated "in order to understand the quoted passage [from *Weinberger*] when read together with the statutory language, I assume an unexpressed phrase to the effect 'unless, but for the merger, such elements of future value would not exist.'" According to the Court of Chancery, the language in *Weinberger* would read: "But elements of future value, including the nature of the enterprise, which are known or susceptible of proof as of the date of the merger and not the product of speculation, may be considered [unless, but for the merger, such elements of future value would not exist]." Weinberger v. UOP, Inc., Del. Supr., 457 A.2d 701, 713 (1983).

In explaining the "but for" caveat that it had superimposed upon this Court's holding in *Weinberger,* the Court of Chancery reasoned that, as a matter of policy, the valuation process in a statutory appraisal proceeding should be the same irrespective of whether a merger is accomplished in one or two steps:

> Delaware law traditionally and today accords to a dissenting shareholder "his proportionate interest in a going concern" and that going concern is the corporation in question, with its asset deployment, business plan and management unaffected by the plans or strategies of the acquiror. When value is created by substituting new management or by redeploying assets "in connection with the accomplishment or expectation" of a merger, that value is not, in my opinion, a part of the "going concern" in which a dissenting shareholder has a legal (or equitable) right to participate.
>
> If one accepts this principle, the question arises how is it to be applied in a two-step arms'-length acquisition transaction. In such a transaction there will be a period following close [to] the first-step tender offer in which the [majority] acquiror may, as a practical matter, be in a position to influence or change the nature of the corporate business, or to freeze controversial programs until they are reviewed following the second-step merger.

Accordingly, the Court of Chancery concluded that "[f]uture value that would not exist *but for* the merger . . . even if it is capable of being proven on the date of the merger," is irrelevant in a Delaware statutory appraisal proceeding. (Emphasis added.) Consequently, the Court of Chancery held "that value added to [Technicolor] by the implementation or the expectation of the implementation of Mr. Perelman's new business plan for [Technicolor] is not value to which, in an appraisal action, [Cinerama] is entitled to a pro rata share, but is value that is excluded from consideration by the statutory exclusion for value arising from the merger or its expectation. . . ."

PERELMAN PLAN

SUSCEPTIBLE OF PROOF/NON-SPECULATIVE

The underlying assumption in an appraisal valuation is that the dissenting shareholders would be willing to maintain their investment position had the merger not occurred. Cavalier Oil Corp. v. Harnett, Del. Supr., 564 A.2d 1137, 1145 (1989). Accordingly, the Court of Chancery's task in an appraisal proceeding is to value what has been taken from the shareholder, i.e., the proportionate interest in the going concern. Id. at 1144 (citing Tri-Continental Corp. v. Battye, Del. Supr., 74 A.2d 71, 72 (1950)). To that end, this Court has held that the corporation must be valued as an operating entity. Id. We conclude that the Court of Chancery did not adhere to this principle.

The Court of Chancery determined that Perelman "had a fixed view of how [Technicolor's] assets would be sold before the merger and had begun to implement it" prior to January 24, 1983. Consequently, the Court of Chancery found that the Perelman Plan for Technicolor was the operative reality on the date of the merger. Nevertheless, the Court of Chancery held that Cinerama was not entitled to an appraisal of Technicolor as it was actually functioning on the date of the merger pursuant to the Perelman Plan.

The Court of Chancery reached that holding by applying its *majority acquiror principle* and correlative *proximate cause exception*. The Court of Chancery excluded any value that was admittedly part of Technicolor as a going concern on the date of the merger, if that value was created by substituting new management or redeploying assets during the transient period between the first and second steps of this two-step merger, i.e., Perelman's Plan. The Court of Chancery reasoned that valuing Technicolor as a going concern, under the Perelman Plan, on the date of the merger, would be tantamount to awarding Cinerama a proportionate share of a control premium, which the Court of Chancery deemed to be both economically undesirable and contrary to this Court's holding in Bell v. Kirby Lumber Corp., Del. Supr., 413 A.2d 137, 140-142 (1980). See also Rapid-American Corp. v. Harris, Del. Supr., 603 A.2d 796, 805-807 (1992). Thus, the Court of Chancery concluded "that value [added by a majority acquiror] is not . . . a part of the 'going concern' in which a dissenting shareholder has a legal (or equitable) right to participate." . . .

In a two-step merger, to the extent that value has been added following a change in majority control before cash-out, it is still value attributable to the going concern, i.e., the extant "nature of the enterprise," on the date of the merger. See Rapid-American Corp. v. Harris, 603 A.2d at 805. The dissenting shareholder's proportionate interest is determined only after the company has been valued as an operating entity on the date of the merger. Cavalier Oil Corp. v. Harnett, 564 A.2d at 1144; cf. Walter W.B. v. Elizabeth P.B., Del. Supr., 462 A.2d 414, 415 (1983). Consequently, value added to the going concern by the "majority acquiror" during the transient period of a two-step merger, accrues to the benefit of all shareholders and must be included in the appraisal process on the date of the merger. . . .

In this case, the question in the appraisal action was the fair value of Technicolor stock on the date of the merger, January 24, 1983, as Technicolor was operating pursuant to the Perelman Plan. The Court of Chancery erred, as a matter of law, by determining the fair value of Technicolor on the date of the merger "but for" the Perelman Plan; or, in other words, by valuing Technicolor as it was operating on October 29, 1982, pursuant to the Kamerman Plan. By failing to accord Cinerama the full proportionate value of its shares in the going concern on the date of the merger, the Court of Chancery imposed a penalty upon Cinerama for lack of control. . . .

The "accomplishment or expectation" of the merger exception in Section 262 is very narrow, "designed to eliminate use of pro forma data and projections of a speculative variety relating to the completion of a merger." Weinberger v. UOP, Inc., 457 A.2d at 713. That narrow exclusion does not encompass known elements of value, including those which exist on the date of the merger because of a majority acquiror's interim action in a two-step cash-out transaction. Cf. In re Shell Oil Co., 607 A.2d at 1218-1219. "[O]nly the *speculative* elements of value that may arise from the 'accomplishment or expectation' of the merger" should have been excluded from the Court of Chancery's calculation of fair value on the date of the merger. Weinberger v. UOP, Inc., 457 A.2d at 713 (emphasis added); cf. In re Shell Oil Co., 607 A.2d at 1219.

The Court of Chancery's determination not to value Technicolor as a going concern on the date of the merger under the Perelman Plan resulted in an understatement of Technicolor's fair value in the appraisal action. That result was inevitable when the Court of Chancery valued Technicolor pursuant to a discounted cash flow model with the negative factual input and assumptions from the Kamerman Plan rather than the Perelman Plan. Consequently, the Court of Chancery permitted MAF to "reap a windfall from the appraisal process by cashing out a dissenting shareholder [Cinerama]," for less than the fair value of its interest in Technicolor as a going concern on the date of the merger. Cavalier Oil Corp. v. Harnett, 564 A.2d at 1145.

Cinerama has asked this Court to make an appraisal of the fair value of its Technicolor shares on the date of the merger, rather than remand this protracted litigation to the Court of Chancery. This Court will not make an independent determination of value on appeal. Rapid-American Corp. v. Harris, 603 A.2d at 799. This appraisal action will be remanded to the Court of Chancery for a recalculation of Technicolor's fair value on the date of the merger. See id. . . .

LAW OF CASE

PERELMAN PLAN IS VALUATION ELEMENT . . .

In an effort to convey this Court's comprehensive interpretation of the statutory "all relevant information," we recognized in *Technicolor I* "that the majority [MAF] may have insight into their company's [Technicolor's] future based primarily on bits and pieces of nonmaterial information that have value as a totality." Id. at 1187 n.8. Consequently, in *Technicolor I,* we said "[i]t is this information that, if available in a *statutory appraisal proceeding, the Court of Chancery must* evaluate to determine if future earnings will affect the fair value of shares on the day of the merger." Id.[11] (emphasis added) (citing 8 Del. C. §262(h)). . . . Thus, the law of this case required the Court of Chancery to consider nonspeculative information about the Perelman Plan.

The record is replete with information about Technicolor's future that was known on the date of the merger. Cf. Rosenblatt v. Getty Oil Co., Del. Supr., 493 A.2d 929, 941-942 (1985). MAF's October 18, 1982 financing package presented to the lending banks, Chase Manhattan Bank and Bank of America, contemplated that MAF would realize $50 million in net proceeds from the sale of assets by the end of 1983. Moreover, the loan agreement between MAF and the banks specifically identified OHP, CPPD, Gold Key and Audio Visual as assets which could be sold by MAF on behalf of Technicolor. . . .

EVIDENTIARY ISSUES

Cinerama has raised several evidentiary contentions which we will address briefly because this matter will be remanded for further proceedings. Cinerama argues that the Court of Chancery's reliance upon the stock market price of Technicolor's shares in September 1982 was improper for two reasons: first, that price reflected the market's negative opinion of the Kamerman Plan; and, second, the market never had an opportunity to price Technicolor stock in the context of the Perelman Plan. This Court has recognized that the "market price of shares may not be representative of true value." Paramount Communications, Inc. v. Time Inc., Del. Supr., 571 A.2d 1140, 1150 n. 12 (1989). Moreover, in this case, we noted that "[i]nformation and insight not communicated to the market may not be reflected in stock prices." *Technicolor I,* 542 A.2d at 1187 n. 8. Nevertheless, Cinerama's objection goes to the weight, if any, to be given to the stock market price for Technicolor stock in September 1982, rather than its admissibility. See In re Delaware Racing Ass'n, Del. Supr., 213 A.2d 203, 211 (1965); cf. Rapid-American Corp. v. Harris, Del. Supr., 603 A.2d 796, 806 (1992) (rejecting "exclusive reliance upon market value in an appraisal action"). Upon remand, Cinerama can renew its argument that the September 1982 stock market price was of little significance to the issue of fair value on the date of the merger in January 1983.

NOTES AND QUESTIONS

1. In 1999, the Committee on Corporate Law adopted sweeping changes to the MBCA's appraisal provisions. Prior to these amendments, MBCA §13.01(3) defined "fair value" as "the value of the shares immediately before the effectuation of the

---

11. In *Technicolor I,* recognizing the potential for investor harm in cash-out transactions, this Court held that Cinerama was entitled to discovery in the appraisal proceeding to obtain this information. *Technicolor I,* 542 A.2d at 1187 n. 8; cf. Randall S. Thomas, Improving Shareholder Monitoring of Corporate Management by Expanding Statutory Access to Information, 38 Ariz. L. Rev. 331 (1996).

corporate action to which the dissenter objects, *excluding any appreciation or depreciation in anticipation of the corporate action unless exclusion would be inequitable.*" (Emphasis
added.) What is the operative difference between the MBCA definition of "fair value"
pre-1999, the definition contained in current MBCA §13.01(4), and the definition set
out in Delaware G.C.L. §262(h), as that section is interpreted in the principal case
above?

2. A central policy question concerning the appraisal remedy is the appropriateness of imposing so-called minority or marketability discounts. Advocates and fact
finders often misuse these terms, which were succinctly defined in Lawson, Mardon,
Wheaton, Inc. v. Smith, 716 A.2d 550, 561-562 (N.J. Super. 1998), as follows:

> In general, the concept of a marketability discount stems from the fact that marketability
> problems often affect shares of closely-held corporations, and that as a result, a discount should be
> applied to reflect the illiquidity of such shares. This illiquidity is the result of the fact that there is
> no large pool of potential buyers for these businesses when they come on the market; consequently,
> the longer it takes to sell an asset, the lower its ultimate value will be and such businesses must be
> sold at a substantial discount in order to attract buyers. See James Edward Harris, Valuation of
> Closely Held Partnerships and Corporations: Recent Developments Concerning Minority Interest
> and Lack of Marketability Discounts, 42 Ark. L. Rev. 649, 657 (1989). Thus, a discount for lack of
> marketability has been justified on the ground that the shares of a closely-held corporation cannot
> be readily sold on a public market, regardless of whether or not the shares in question represent
> a minority interest. Blake v. Blake Agency, Inc., 107 A.D.2d 139, 486 N.Y.S.2d 341, 349 (N.Y. App.
> Div.), appeal denied, 65 N.Y.2d 609, 494 N.Y.S.2d 1028, 484 N.E.2d 671 (1985); see also Harry J.
> Haynsworth, Valuation of Business Interests, 33 Mercer L. Rev. 437, 489 (1982) (an astute investor
> will pay less for an interest that cannot be freely traded, and a discount to compensate for this illi-
> quidity factor is well established). . . . However, a marketability discount is different from a minority
> discount: "Marketability discounts are applied to all the stock of a corporation that is not widely
> traded, whereas minority fair market value discounts only apply to minority shareholders." Robblee
> v. Robblee, 68 Wash. App. 69, 841 P.2d 1289, 1294 (1992). While minority discounts are downward
> adjustments to the value of dissenting shares due to their lack of voting power to control corpo-
> rate actions, marketability discounts are downward adjustments to the value of shares due to the
> limited supply of potential buyers. Paul Gordon, Comment, Submitting "Fair Value" to Final Offer
> Arbitration, 63 U. Colo. L. Rev. 751, 766-767 (1992).

3. The overwhelming trend in modern cases is to reject minority and marketability
discounts. This sentiment was reflected in the 1999 amendments to the MBCA, which
make such discounts inappropriate in most circumstances. See MBCA §13.01(4)(iii).
Also see the similar position reflected in ALI Principles of Corporate Governance
§7.22(a). The Delaware Supreme Court's explanation for this approach is widely
cited:

> The application of a discount to a minority shareholder is contrary to the requirement that
> the company be viewed as a "going concern." Cavalier's argument, that the only way Harnett would
> have received value for his 1.5% stock interest was to sell his stock, subject to market treatment of
> its minority status, misperceives the nature of the appraisal remedy.
> Where there is no objective market data available, the appraisal process is not intended to
> reconstruct a pro forma sale but to assume that the shareholder was willing to maintain his invest-
> ment position, however slight, had the merger not occurred. Discounting individual share holdings
> injects into the appraisal process speculation on the various factors which may dictate the market-
> ability of minority shareholdings. More important, to fail to accord to a minority shareholder the
> full proportionate value of his shares imposes a penalty for lack of control, and unfairly enriches

the majority shareholders who may reap a windfall from the appraisal process by cashing out a dissenting shareholder, a clearly undesirable result.

Cavalier Oil Co. v. Harnett, 564 A.2d 1137, 1145 (Del. 1989).

4. Given Delaware's strong deference to non-conflicted private ordering, should the Court of Chancery in an appraisal proceeding afford substantial or controlling weight to the share price terms negotiated in an arm's length merger? Consider the following answer.

Section 262(h) unambiguously calls upon the Court of Chancery to perform an *independent* evaluation of "fair value" at the time of a transaction. It vests the Chancellor and Vice Chancellors with significant discretion to consider "all relevant factors" and determine the going concern value of the underlying company. Requiring the Court of Chancery to defer—conclusively or presumptively—to the merger price, even in the face of a pristine, unchallenged transactional process, would contravene the unambiguous language of the statute and the reasoned holdings of our precedent. It would inappropriately shift the responsibility to determine "fair value" from the court to the private parties. Also, while it is difficult for the Chancellor and Vice Chancellors to assess wildly divergent expert opinions regarding value, inflexible rules governing appraisal provide little additional benefit in determining "fair value" because of the already high costs of appraisal actions. Appraisal is, by design, a flexible process. Therefore, we reject [the] contention that the Vice Chancellor erred by insufficiently deferring to the merger price, and we reject [the] call to establish a rule requiring the Court of Chancery to defer to the merger price in any appraisal proceeding.

Golden Telecom, Inc. v. Global GT LP, 11 A.3d 214, 217-218 (Del. 2010).

5. Following *Weinberger*'s freeing mandate, the Court of Chancery judges have become experts in the strengths, weaknesses, and best practices of valuation methodology. Consider the following summary of the current dominant approach.

Generally speaking, "it is preferable to take a more robust approach involving multiple techniques—such as a DCF analysis, a comparable transactions analysis (looking at precedent transaction comparables), and a comparable companies analysis (looking at trading comparables/multiples)—to triangulate a value range, as all three methodologies individually have their own limitations." A comparable or market-based approach endeavors to draw inferences about a company's future expected cash flows from the market's expectations about comparable companies. "[T]he utility of a market-based method depends on actually having companies that are sufficiently comparable that their trading multiples provide a relevant insight into the subject company's own growth prospects." When there are a number of corporations competing in a similar industry, these methods are most reliable. On the other hand, when the "comparables" involve companies that offer different products or services, are at a different stage in their growth cycle, or have vastly different multiples, a comparable companies or comparable transactions analysis is inappropriate. . . .

The comparable companies method of valuing a company's equity involves several steps including: (1) finding comparable, publicly traded companies that have reviewable financial information; (2) calculating the ratio between the trading price of the stocks of each of those companies and some recognized measure reflecting their income such as revenue, EBIT, or EBITDA; (3) correcting these derived ratios to account for differences, such as in capital structure, between the public companies and the target company being valued; and, finally, (4) applying the average multiple of the comparable companies to the relevant income measurement of the target company . . .

A comparable transactions analysis "involves identifying similar transactions, quantifying those transactions through financial metrics, and then applying the metrics to the company at issue to ascertain a value." As with the comparable companies analysis, "[t]he utility of the comparable transactions methodology is directly linked to the 'similarity between the company the court is valuing and the companies used for comparison. . . .'"

The basic premise underlying the DCF methodology is that the value of a company is equal to the value of its projected future cash flows, discounted to the present value at the opportunity cost of capital. Calculating a DCF involves three steps: (1) one estimates the values of future cash flows for a discrete period, where possible, based on contemporaneous management projections; (2) the value of the entity attributable to cash flows expected after the end of the discrete period must be estimated to produce a so-called terminal value, preferably using a perpetual growth model; and (3) the value of the cash flows for the discrete period and the terminal value must be discounted back using the capital asset pricing model or "CAPM."

Merion Capital LP v. 3M Cogent, Inc., 2013 WL 3793896, at *7, 9, 13 (Del. Ch., July 8, 2013).

PROBLEM 8-5

In 2010, John Pearl, CEO and sole shareholder of Woodstock, Inc., purchased 4 percent of the stock of Lion Studios Corp. After careful study, he concluded that Lion Studios would be significantly more profitable if it sold off its film distribution subsidiary and emphasized its cable TV and foreign syndication businesses. In March 2013, Pearl increased his ownership of Lion Studios to 90 percent via a cash tender offer at $45 per share, a price $15 per share more than the pre-tender offer market price. As announced at the time of the tender offer, Woodstock then cashed out the remaining Lion Studios' shareholders via a short-form merger with a newly formed Woodstock subsidiary, Lion Studios II. As Pearl predicted, Lion Studios II has prospered under Pearl's business plan and management. In September 2014, financial analysts estimated that Lion Studios has doubled in value since the takeover.

Should Lion Studios' shareholders who dissent from the short-form merger receive a portion of the post-takeover prosperity experienced by Lion Studios II?

2.   Appraisal as the Exclusive Remedy

a.   In Delaware

In *Weinberger*, the Delaware Supreme authorized a "quasi-appraisal remedy" for litigants and potential litigants whose rights, or at least expectations, vested prior to the decision. The Court then provided guidance as to the remedy available to dissatisfied minority shareholders in future cases:

> Thereafter, the provisions of 8 Del. C. §262, as herein construed . . . shall govern the financial remedy available to minority shareholders in a cash-out merger. Thus, we return to the well established principles of Stauffer v. Standard Brands, Inc., Del. Supr., 187 A.2d 78 (1962) and David J. Greene & Co. v. Schenley Industries, Inc., Del. Ch., 281 A.2d 30 (1971), mandating a stockholder's recourse to the basic remedy of an appraisal.

Weinberger v. UOP, Inc., 457 A.2d. 701, 715 (1983).

Could this passage from *Weinberger* fairly be read as making appraisal the exclusive remedy for shareholders seeking redress for an allegedly unfair cash-out merger? The

Delaware Court of Chancery initially answered this question in the affirmative, with one exception.

> In brief, the issue is not whether defendants still have a duty to treat the minority with entire fairness. They do. The issue is the nature of the remedy available for an alleged breach of that duty. Where, as here, there are no allegations of non-disclosures or misrepresentations, Weinberger mandates that plaintiffs' entire fairness claims be determined in an appraisal proceeding.

Rabkin v. Philip A. Hunt Chemical Corp., 480 A.2d 655, 660 (Del. Ch. 1984).

The Delaware Supreme Court promptly reversed.

> In conclusion we find that the trial court erred in dismissing the plaintiffs' actions for failure to state a claim upon which relief could be granted. As we read the complaints and the proposed amendments, they assert a conscious intent by Olin, as the majority shareholder of Hunt, to deprive the Hunt minority of the same bargain that Olin made with Hunt's former majority shareholder, Turner and Newall. But for Olin's allegedly unfair manipulation, the plaintiffs contend, this bargain also was due them. In short, the defendants are charged with bad faith which goes beyond issues of "mere inadequacy of price." Cole v. National Cash Credit Association, Del. Ch., 156 A. 183, 187-88 (1931). In *Weinberger* we specifically relied upon this aspect of Cole in acknowledging the imperfections of an appraisal where circumstances of this sort are present.
>
> Necessarily, this will require the Court of Chancery to closely focus upon *Weinberger*'s mandate of entire fairness based on a careful analysis of both the fair price and fair dealing aspects of a transaction. We recognize that this can present certain practical problems, since stockholders may invariably claim that the price being offered is the result of unfair dealings. However, we think that plaintiffs will be tempered in this approach by the prospect that an ultimate judgment in defendants' favor may have cost plaintiffs their unperfected appraisal rights. Moreover, our courts are not without a degree of sophistication in such matters. A balance must be struck between sustaining complaints averring faithless acts, which taken as true would constitute breaches of fiduciary duties that are reasonably related to and have a substantial impact upon the price offered, and properly dismissing those allegations questioning judgmental factors of valuation. Cole v. National Cash Credit Association, 156 A. at 187-88. Otherwise, we face the anomalous result that stockholders who are eliminated without appraisal rights can bring class actions, while in other cases a squeezed-out minority is limited to an appraisal, provided there was no deception, regardless of the degree of procedural unfairness employed to take their shares. Without that balance, Weinberger's concern for entire fairness loses all force.

Rabkin v. Philip A. Hunt Chemical Corp., 498 A.2d 1099, 1107-1108 (Del. 1985).

Rabkin opened the door for "cashed out" minority shareholders to avoid the costly appraisal mechanism in favor of a direct action (almost always on behalf of the minority shareholders as a class) seeking damages for the controlling shareholders failure to act with entire fairness. While shareholders might *elect* to pursue an appraisal, they would be *forced* to pursue an appraisal (or no action at all) only if their claim amounted simply to a disagreement about the value of the cashed out shares. Put differently, cashed out minority shareholders would be able to maintain a fiduciary-duty-based, entire fairness action against the controlling shareholder simply by alleging "specific acts of fraud, misrepresentation, or other items of misconduct to demonstrate the unfairness of the merger terms to the minority."[1]

---

1. Weinberger v. UOP, Inc., 457 A.2d. 701, 703 (1983) (supra, Casebook page 728).

Under Delaware G.C.L. section 253, a majority shareholder owning at least 90 percent of the target subsidiary's stock is permitted to merge with the target without the need for advance notice to, or the approval by, the target's minority shareholders. The principal case, below, which arose in the context of a short-form merger used to cash-out minority shareholders, reduced the availability of, and changed the nature of, fiduciary duty actions in the context of short-form, cash-out-mergers. As you read the opinion, consider the extent to which appraisal is now the exclusive remedy available to minority shareholders who believe they have been "wronged" in a short-form cash-out, and note how the Supreme Court adjusts the appraisal standard given the reduced availability of fiduciary duty.

Glassman v. Unocal Exploration Corp.
Delaware Supreme Court (en banc), 2001
777 A.2d 242

BERGER, JUSTICE.

In this appeal, we consider the fiduciary duties owed by a parent corporation to the subsidiary's minority stockholders in the context of a "short-form" merger. Specifically, we take this opportunity to reconcile a fiduciary's seemingly absolute duty to establish the entire fairness of any self-dealing transaction with the less demanding requirements of the short-form merger statute. . . .

I.   FACTUAL AND PROCEDURAL BACKGROUND

Unocal Corporation is an earth resources company primarily engaged in the exploration for and production of crude oil and natural gas. At the time of the merger at issue, Unocal owned approximately 96% of the stock of Unocal Exploration Corporation ("UXC"), an oil and gas company operating in and around the Gulf of Mexico. In 1991, low natural gas prices caused a drop in both companies' revenues and earnings. Unocal investigated areas of possible cost savings and decided that, by eliminating the UXC minority, it would reduce taxes and overhead expenses.

In December 1991 the boards of Unocal and UXC appointed special committees to consider a possible merger. The UXC committee consisted of three directors who, although also directors of Unocal, were not officers or employees of the parent company. The UXC committee retained financial and legal advisors and met four times before agreeing to a merger exchange ratio of .54 shares of Unocal stock for each share of UXC. Unocal and UXC announced the merger on February 24, 1992, and it was effected, pursuant to 8 Del. C. §253, on May 2, 1992. The Notice of Merger and Prospectus stated the terms of the merger and advised the former UXC stockholders of their appraisal rights.

Plaintiffs filed this class action, on behalf of UXC's minority stockholders, on the day the merger was announced. They asserted, among other claims, that Unocal and its directors breached their fiduciary duties of entire fairness and full disclosure. The Court of Chancery conducted a two day trial and held that: (i) the Prospectus did not contain any material misstatements or omissions; (ii) the entire fairness standard does not control in a short-form merger; and (iii) plaintiffs' exclusive remedy in this case was appraisal. The decision of the Court of Chancery is affirmed.

II.   DISCUSSION

The short-form merger statute, as enacted in 1937, authorized a parent corporation to merge with its wholly-owned subsidiary by filing and recording a certificate evidencing the parent's ownership and its merger resolution. In 1957, the statute was expanded to include parent/subsidiary mergers where the parent company owns at least 90% of the stock of the subsidiary. The 1957 amendment also made it possible, for the first time and only in a short-form merger, to pay the minority cash for their shares, thereby eliminating their ownership interest in the company. . . .

This Court first reviewed §253 in Coyne v. Park & Tilford Distillers Corporation.[1] There, minority stockholders of the merged-out subsidiary argued that the statute could not mean what it says because Delaware law "never has permitted, and does not now permit, the payment of cash for whole shares surrendered in a merger and the consequent expulsion of a stockholder from the enterprise in which he has invested." The *Coyne* court held that §253 plainly does permit such a result and that the statute is constitutional.

The next question presented to this Court was whether any equitable relief is available to minority stockholders who object to a short-form merger. In Stauffer v. Standard Brands Incorporated,[3] . . . The Court of Chancery held that appraisal was the stockholders' exclusive remedy, and dismissed the complaint. This Court affirmed, but explained that appraisal would not be the exclusive remedy in a short-form merger tainted by fraud or illegality:

[T]he exception [to appraisal's exclusivity] . . . refers generally to all mergers, and is nothing but a reaffirmation of the ever-present power of equity to deal with illegality or fraud. But it has no bearing here. No illegality or overreaching is shown. The dispute reduces to nothing but a difference of opinion as to value. Indeed it is difficult to imagine a case under the short merger statute in which there could be such actual fraud as would entitle a minority to set aside the merger. This is so because the very purpose of the statute is to provide the parent corporation with a means of eliminating the minority shareholder's interest in the enterprise. Thereafter the former stockholder has only a monetary claim.

The *Stauffer* doctrine's viability rose and fell over the next four decades. Its holding on the exclusivity of appraisal took on added significance in 1967, when the long-form merger statute — §251 — was amended to allow cash-out mergers. In David J. Greene & Co. v. Schenley Industries, Inc.,[5] the Court of Chancery applied *Stauffer* to a long-form cash-out merger. *Schenley* recognized that the corporate fiduciaries had to establish

---

1. Del. Supr., 154 A.2d 893 (1959).
3. Del. Supr., 187 A.2d 78 (1962).
5. Del. Ch., 281 A.2d 30 (1971).

entire fairness, but concluded that fair value was the plaintiff's only real concern and that appraisal was an adequate remedy. . . .

In 1977, this Court started retreating from *Stauffer* (and *Schenley*). Singer v. Magnavox Co. held that a controlling stockholder breaches its fiduciary duty if it effects a cash-out merger under §251 for the sole purpose of eliminating the minority stockholders. . . .

Singer's business purpose test was extended to short-form mergers two years later in Roland International Corporation v. Najjar.[9] The *Roland* majority wrote:

> The short form permitted by §253 does simplify the steps necessary to effect a merger, and does give a parent corporation some certainty as to result and control as to timing. But we find nothing magic about a 90% ownership of outstanding shares which would eliminate the fiduciary duty owed by the majority to the minority.

. . . After *Roland*, there was not much of *Stauffer* that safely could be considered good law. But that changed in 1983, in Weinberger v. UOP, Inc., when the Court dropped the business purpose test, made appraisal a more adequate remedy, and said that it was "return[ing] to the well established principles of *Stauffer* . . . and *Schenley* . . . mandating a stockholder's recourse to the basic remedy of an appraisal." . . .

By referencing both *Stauffer* and *Schenley,* one might have thought that the *Weinberger* court intended appraisal to be the exclusive remedy "ordinarily" in non-fraudulent mergers where "price . . . [is] the preponderant consideration outweighing other features of the merger." In Rabkin v. Philip A. Hunt Chemical Corp.,[18] however, the Court dispelled that view. The *Rabkin* plaintiffs claimed that the majority stockholder breached its fiduciary duty of fair dealing by waiting until a one year commitment to pay $25 per share had expired before effecting a cash-out merger at $20 per share. The Court of Chancery dismissed the complaint, reasoning that, under *Weinberger,* plaintiffs could obtain full relief for the alleged unfair dealing in an appraisal proceeding. This Court reversed, holding that the trial court read *Weinberger* too narrowly and that appraisal is the exclusive remedy only if stockholders' complaints are limited to "judgmental factors of valuation."

Rabkin, through its interpretation of *Weinberger,* effectively eliminated appraisal as the exclusive remedy for any claim alleging breach of the duty of entire fairness. But *Rabkin* involved a long-form merger, and the Court did not discuss, in that case or any others, how its refinement of *Weinberger* impacted short-form mergers. Two of this Court's more recent decisions that arguably touch on the subject are Bershad v. Curtiss-Wright Corp.[20] and Kahn v. Lynch Communication Systems, Inc.,[21] both long-form merger cases. In *Bershad,* the Court included §253 when it identified statutory merger provisions from which fairness issues flow.

In parent-subsidiary merger transactions the issues are those of fairness—fair price and fair dealing. These flow from the statutory provisions permitting mergers,

---

9. Del. Supr., 407 A.2d 1032 (1979).
18. Del. Supr., 498 A.2d 1099 (1985).
20. Del. Supr., 535 A.2d 840 (1987).
21. Del. Supr., 638 A.2d 1110 (1994).

8 Del. C. §§251-253 (1983), and those designed to ensure fair value by an appraisal, 8 Del. C. §262 (1983) . . . ; and in *Lynch,* the Court described entire fairness as the "exclusive" standard of review in a cash-out, parent/subsidiary merger.

Mindful of this history, we must decide whether a minority stockholder may challenge a short-form merger by seeking equitable relief through an entire fairness claim. Under settled principles, a parent corporation and its directors undertaking a short-form merger are self-dealing fiduciaries who should be required to establish entire fairness, including fair dealing and fair price. The problem is that §253 authorizes a summary procedure that is inconsistent with any reasonable notion of fair dealing. In a short-form merger, there is no agreement of merger negotiated by two companies; there is only a unilateral act—a decision by the parent company that its 90% owned subsidiary shall no longer exist as a separate entity. The minority stockholders receive no advance notice of the merger; their directors do not consider or approve it; and there is no vote. Those who object are given the right to obtain fair value for their shares through appraisal.

The equitable claim plainly conflicts with the statute. If a corporate fiduciary follows the truncated process authorized by §253, it will not be able to establish the fair dealing prong of entire fairness. If, instead, the corporate fiduciary sets up negotiating committees, hires independent financial and legal experts, etc., then it will have lost the very benefit provided by the statute—a simple, fast and inexpensive process for accomplishing a merger. We resolve this conflict by giving effect the intent of the General Assembly. In order to serve its purpose, §253 must be construed to obviate the requirement to establish entire fairness.

Thus, we again return to *Stauffer,* and hold that, absent fraud or illegality, appraisal is the exclusive remedy available to a minority stockholder who objects to a short-form merger. In doing so, we also reaffirm *Weinberger*'s statements about the scope of appraisal. The determination of fair value must be based on *all* relevant factors, including damages and elements of future value, where appropriate. So, for example, if the merger was timed to take advantage of a depressed market, or a low point in the company's cyclical earnings, or to precede an anticipated positive development, the appraised value may be adjusted to account for those factors. We recognize that these are the types of issues frequently raised in entire fairness claims, and we have held that claims for unfair dealing cannot be litigated in an appraisal.[26] But our prior holdings simply explained that equitable claims may not be engrafted onto a statutory appraisal proceeding; stockholders may not receive rescissionary relief in an appraisal. Those decisions should not be read to restrict the elements of value that properly may be considered in an appraisal.

Although fiduciaries are not required to establish entire fairness in a short-form merger, the duty of full disclosure remains, in the context of this request for stockholder action. Where the only choice for the minority stockholders is whether to accept the merger consideration or seek appraisal, they must be given all the factual information that is material to that decision. The Court of Chancery carefully considered plaintiffs' disclosure claims and applied settled law in rejecting them. We affirm this aspect of the appeal on the basis of the trial court's decision.

---

26. Alabama By-Products Corporation v. Neal, Del. Supr., 588 A.2d 255, 257 (1991).

III.   Conclusion

Based on the foregoing, we affirm the Court of Chancery and hold that plaintiffs' only remedy in connection with the short-form merger of UXC into Unocal was appraisal.

NOTES AND QUESTIONS

1. In the last paragraph of *Glassman*, Justice Berger emphasizes that controlling shareholders in short-form mergers are still subject to a fiduciary duty of full disclosure. Consider Chancellor Chandler's analysis of that obligation.

> The Delaware Supreme Court has made it clear that the fiduciary duty of disclosure applies in a short-form merger, even though there is no necessity for entire fairness. . . .
>
> Thus, all information material to the decision whether to accept the merger consideration or to seek an appraisal must be disclosed, even in a short-form merger. Indeed, in such a context, stockholders may have an even greater need for full disclosure precisely because elements of procedural fairness are missing. As recognized by this Court repeatedly, a forced seller with the exclusive options of accepting an offered price or seeking a higher price through an appraisal remedy is "if anything, . . . a more compelling case for the application of the recognized disclosure standards."

Erickson v. Centennial Beauregard Cellular, LLC, 2003 WL 1878583 at *5.

2. What consequence should flow where the fiduciary fails to observe its "duty of full disclosure"? In *Berger v. Pubco Corp.*, 976 A.2d. 132 (Del. en banc 2009), the dispute arose in a short-form merger in which

> the Court of Chancery found that except for the financial statements, the disclosures in the Notice provided no significant detail. For example, the description of the Company comprised only five sentences, one of which vaguely stated that "[t]he Company owns other income producing assets." No disclosures relating to the company's plans or prospects were made, nor was there any meaningful discussion of Pubco's actual operations or disclosure of its finances by division or line of business. Rather, the unaudited financial statements lumped all of the company's operations together. The financial statements did indicate that Pubco held a sizeable amount of cash and securities, but did not explain how those assets were, or would be, utilized. Finally, the Notice contained no disclosure of how Kanner had determined the $20 per share merger price that he unilaterally had set.

The Delaware Supreme Court analyzed four possible remedies:

1. A *"replicated appraisal" proceeding* that would duplicate the precise sequence of events and requirements of the appraisal statute. The minority shareholders would receive (in a supplemental disclosure) all information material to making an informed decision whether to elect appraisal. Shareholders who elect appraisal would then make a formal demand for appraisal and remit to the corporation their stock certificates and the entire merger consideration that they received. Thereafter, the corporation would have the opportunity, as contemplated by the appraisal statute, to attempt to reach a settlement with the appraisal claimants. If no settlement were reached, a formal appraisal action could then be commenced by the dissenting shareholders or by the corporation.

2. *An entire fairness review.* The consequence of the fiduciary's adjudicated failure to disclose material facts would be to render *Glassman* inapplicable. As a result, the remedy would be the same as in a long-form cash-out merger under 8 Del. C. §251(a) — a shareholder class action for breach of fiduciary duty, where the legality of the merger (and the liability of the controlling stockholder fiduciaries) is determined under the traditional "entire fairness" review standard.

3. *A quasi-appraisal proceeding to which shareholders would be required to opt in and place a portion of the merger consideration in escrow in case the quasi-appraisal proceeding resulted in a determination of lower value.* The shareholders would be furnished the material information of which they were deprived. The shareholders must then be afforded an opportunity to choose whether or not to participate in an action to determine the "fair value" of their shares. The shareholders who chose to participate would have to formally opt in to the proceeding and place into escrow a prescribed portion of the merger consideration that they received. The Court of Chancery identified the purpose of the escrow requirement as to "replicate a modicum of the risk that would inhere" if the proceeding were an actual appraisal.

4. *A quasi-appraisal remedy with no opt-in or escrow required.* All minority shareholders should have been treated as members of a class entitled to seek the quasi-appraisal recovery, without being burdened by any precondition or requirement that they opt in or escrow any portion of the merger proceeds paid to them.

The Delaware Supreme Court rejected the entire fairness option because it would disregard the intent of the General Assembly, as described in *Glassman* and Stauffer v. Standard Brands, Inc., that in a legally valid, non-fraudulent, short-form merger the minority shareholders' remedy should be limited to an appraisal. Moreover, validating such an approach would disserve the purpose of *Glassman*'s disclosure requirement, which is to enable the minority stockholders to make an informed decision whether or not to seek an appraisal. A remedy that sidesteps appraisal altogether would frustrate that purpose.

The replicated appraisal remedy was seen by the court as giving maximum effect to the legislative intent recognized in *Glassman*, but would effectuate that legislative intent at an unacceptable cost measured in terms of practicality of application and fairness to the minority. As to practicality, the court noted that given the substantial passage of time since the merger, it would be difficult for stockholders to secure the cooperation of the former record holders or nominees needed to perfect demand in accordance with the statute. As to fairness, the court noted the unfairness of requiring the minority stockholders to bear the risk of the corporation's creditworthiness, which would result from their having to pay back a portion of the merger proceeds to the company. The court also pointed to the unfairness to the minority shareholders, on whose behalf significant litigation expense and effort were successfully devoted, to limit their relief to requiring the fiduciary merely to fulfill the disclosure obligation it had all along.

In evaluating the two quasi-appraisal options, the court concluded that treating all shareholders as initially within the class was less burdensome to the shareholders than an opt-in requirement while no more burdensome to the corporation in terms of providing early identification of which shareholders are (and are not) members of the class. The court tested the escrow requirement against the rationale stated in Gilliland v. Motorola, Inc. 873 A.2d 305, 312 (Del. Ch. 2005): "to mimic, at least in small part, the risks of a statutory appraisal . . . to promote well-reasoned judgments by potential class members and to avoid awarding a 'windfall' to those shareholders who made an informed decision [after receiving the original notice of merger] to take the cash rather than pursue their statutory appraisal remedy." The court noted Delaware law in other contexts (e.g., Weinberger) that allows the minority to enjoy that dual benefit in the related setting of a class action challenging a long-form merger on fiduciary duty grounds. In that setting the shareholder class members may retain the merger proceeds and simultaneously pursue the class action remedy.

> Lastly, fairness requires that the corporation be held to the same strict standard of compliance with the appraisal statute as the minority shareholders. Our case law is replete with examples where dissenting minority shareholders that failed to comply strictly with certain technical requirements of the appraisal statute, were held to have lost their entitlement to an appraisal, and, consequently, lost the opportunity to recover the difference between the fair value of their shares and the merger price. In fairness, majority stockholders that deprive their minority shareholders of material information should forfeit their statutory right to retain the merger proceeds payable to shareholders who, if fully informed, would have elected appraisal.
>
> In cases where the corporation does not comply with the disclosure requirement mandated by *Glassman,* the quasi-appraisal remedy that operates in the fairest and most balanced way and that best effectuates the legislative intent underlying Section 253, is the one that does not require the minority shareholders seeking a recovery of fair value to escrow a portion of the merger proceeds they received. We hold, for these reasons, that the quasi-appraisal remedy ordered by the Court of Chancery was legally erroneous in the circumstances presented here.

Berger, 976 A.2d 132 at 144.

3. Does the decision in *Glassman* provide an incentive for controlling shareholders to act abusively toward minority shareholders in a short-form merger? For example, is there any reason why a controlling shareholder should not intentionally offer an unfair price, knowing that many minority shareholders will not seek appraisal?

4. In Montgomery Cellular Holding Co., Inc. v. Dobler, 880 A.2d 206 (Del. 2005), Price Communications Wireless, Inc. ("Price"), was the owner of more than 94 percent of the stock of Montgomery Cellular Holding Co., Inc. ("MCHC"). Price agreed to sell MCHC to Verizon for $1.7 billion and to use its best efforts to first acquire all of the shares held by minority shareholders; if Price were unable to acquire all of the outstanding shares, the $1.7 billion purchase price would be reduced proportionately. Price cashed-out the minority shareholders in MCHC via a short-form merger for $8,102.33 per share—a per share price substantially less than the proportionate reduction in purchase price that Price would otherwise have experienced pursuant to the Verizon agreement. In the appraisal proceeding, the Court of Chancery awarded the plaintiffs $19,621.74 per share, plus interest, but refused to require Price to pay the plaintiffs' attorneys' fees and expert witness fees because the defendant's conduct was not sufficiently egregious. The Supreme Court reversed the Chancery's fee-shifting decision.

> Delaware follows the "American Rule," whereby a prevailing party is generally expected to pay its own attorney's fees and costs. This Court has recognized limited equitable exceptions to that rule, including the exception for "bad faith" conduct during the litigation. . . . The bad faith exception

is applied in "extraordinary circumstances" as a tool to deter abusive litigation and to protect the integrity of the judicial process.

In this case, the Court of Chancery's factual findings . . . compel the conclusion that [Price's] conduct during the cash-out merger and during the course of the appraisal proceeding rose to the level of bad faith that both this Court and the Court of Chancery have found justifies an award of attorneys' fees. . . .

The Court of Chancery found that Price's CEO, Robert Price, set the merger price unilaterally, after ignoring repeated suggestions from Verizon that he hire an independent financial advisor. The resulting unfairly low price, which was not based on any legitimate valuation of MCHC, forced the minority shareholders to initiate an appraisal action — their only remedy in a short form merger. Although the bad faith exception does not apply to the conduct that gives rise to the substantive appraisal claim in a short form merger, evidence of a party's prelitigation conduct can be relevant to show the motive or intent driving that party's conduct during that appraisal litigation. Here, Price's failure reasonably to ascertain MCHC's fair value before setting the merger price was a motive for Price later to lie under oath and to allow the destruction of documents to obstruct the petitioners' efforts to uncover evidence of MCHC's true value — evidence that was essential to enforcing the only remedy that was available to the petitioners.

MCHC's conduct during the litigation also interfered with the Court's performance of its duty to determine the fair value of the company, and unnecessarily prolonged and increased the costs of the litigation. MCHC repeatedly refused to produce documents that had been requested in discovery . . . until the Court of Chancery ordered them to do so nine months after the initial document request. Even after that order was issued, MCHC could not produce most of the information requested because MCHC had destroyed the computers where the information was stored. MCHC admitted that it destroyed the computers *after* the Court of Chancery had ordered their production.

Additionally, the Court of Chancery found that Robert Price, the CEO of Price and MCHC, had lied under oath about the valuation method he had used to determine the merger price. . . .

Finally, MCHC introduced, and relied upon, expert valuation testimony that the Court found was "fatally flawed" in both its methodology and its data. The Court was forced to reject completely the valuation testimony of MCHC's expert, Gartrell, because the Vice Chancellor found that testimony was not credible and was designed "to deprive the minority shareholders of the existing value" in the company.

Montgomery Cellular, 808 A.2d 206 at 227-229.

When a controlling shareholder uses a short-form merger and conducts itself in the manner described, should appraisal be the exclusive remedy?

PROBLEM 8-6

Reconsider the facts in Problem 8-4. How does the *Glassman* case affect your analysis of the likely outcome of the dissenting minority shareholders' class action in a jurisdiction following *Weinberger?* In light of *Glassman,* would you expect the plaintiffs to recast their complaint? How?

b. *Exclusivity in Other Jurisdictions*

MBCA §§13.02(d), 13.40
California Corp. Code §1312
ALI, Principles of Corporate Governance §7.24

Delaware, by common law, has continued to provide for an expansive fiduciary duty alternative to appraisal in cases of self-dealing, except in the short form merger context.

In many other states, the "exclusivity" topic is specifically addressed in the statute, but in different ways. The pre-1999 version of the MBCA, still the basis for exclusivity statutes in the majority of MBCA states, relegated dissenting shareholders to the appraisal remedy unless a merger was "fraudulent" or "unlawful," leaving it to the case law to work out the parameters of those exceptions. The following case and the notes that follow it examine the meaning and applicability of such exclusivity provisions in the context of a cash-out merger by a controlling shareholder, the terms of which require the minority shareholders to surrender their shares for a cash amount the controlling shareholder knows is unfair. The 2006 versions of the MBCA provide for an exception from the exclusivity provision of §13.40 in the case of an interested transaction that has not been cleansed by disinterested director or shareholder action under §§8.62 and 8.63.

Stringer v. Car Data Systems, Inc.
Oregon Supreme Court, 1992
841 P.2d 1183

PETERSON, JUSTICE. . . .

Plaintiffs were minority shareholders in Consumer Data Systems, Inc. (CDS), an Oregon corporation. They filed this action, claiming a violation of various rights incident to a cash-out merger involving CDS and another corporation, Car Data Systems, Inc. (Car Data). . . .

Plaintiffs' complaint alleges that plaintiffs Stringer and Schubert and two other shareholders owned 43 percent of the shares of CDS. Thirty-two individuals, including the six directors of CDS, owned the remaining 57 percent of CDS. According to the complaint, "[i]n late 1988 or early 1989, the CDS Directors and the larger CDS shareholders, Donald Smith, Mark Kallenberger and Lawrence Custer . . . , decided to squeeze the Minority Shareholders out of their ownership in CDS and to offer them a nominal sum for their stock, which sum was significantly below the fair market value of the stock." The directors and larger shareholders formed a new company that subsequently became Car Data, transferred their shares in CDS to Car Data in exchange for its stock, and solicited all the remaining shareholders, except for the four minority shareholders, to participate in their plan. A total of 32 CDS shareholders transferred their stock, amounting to 57 percent of the CDS shares, to Car Data. Car Data shareholders then voted for a merger between Car Data and CDS. Pursuant to the merger proposal, each CDS shareholder would receive $0.002 per share. As owner of 57 percent of CDS, Car Data voted for the merger. The merger was approved over the objections of plaintiffs and two other minority shareholders.

Plaintiffs claimed that their shares were worth at least $0.10 per share and refused to accept the $0.002 offered them. Car Data rejected plaintiffs' demand for $0.10 per share and instituted an appraisal proceeding in the circuit court pursuant to ORS 60.591. Plaintiffs instituted this action in the circuit court against Car Data, CDS, the 32 individual former shareholders of CDS and the present shareholders of Car Data (the shareholder defendants), and the lawyers who represented both CDS and Car Data during the merger process. Plaintiffs' complaint contained three claims for relief: (1) a claim for breach of fiduciary duty against all defendants, in which they prayed for rescission of the merger and appointment of a receiver, or, alternatively, for compensatory damages and an award of punitive damages against Car Data and the shareholder defendants; (2) a claim for civil conspiracy against all defendants, in which they sought compensatory damages and punitive damages against Car Data and the shareholder defendants; and (3) a derivative claim against the former directors of CDS for failing to obtain the best price for all shareholders. . . .

Defendants moved to dismiss plaintiffs' claim on the grounds that (1) plaintiffs' sole remedy is under the appraisal procedure, and (2) even if appraisal is not the sole remedy, plaintiffs' complaint "fail[s] to state facts to support a claim for relief . . . for breach of fiduciary duty." The circuit court dismissed plaintiffs' complaint.

Plaintiffs appealed, pursuing their damages claims on theories of breach of fiduciary duty and civil conspiracy, but abandoned their derivative claim and rescission claim. The Court of Appeals affirmed. Stringer v. Car Data Systems, Inc., [108 Or. App. 523, 816 P.2d 677, modified on reconsideration, 110 Or. App. 14, 821 P.2d 418 (1991)]. . . .

We quote pertinent portions of plaintiffs' complaint:

12

Throughout 1988 and into 1989, CDS experienced continued success in selling its product. Its revenues during this period were increasing at a much faster rate than its expenses. All shareholders had a reasonable belief that the value of CDS would rise significantly over the next few years.

13

In late 1988 or early 1989, the CDS Directors and the larger CDS shareholders, Donald Smith, Mark Kallenberger and Lawrence Custer (collectively referred to herein as the "Controlling Shareholders"), decided to squeeze the Minority Shareholders out of their ownership in CDS and to offer them a nominal sum for their stock, which sum was significantly below the fair market value of the stock (the "Plan"). The principal purpose of the Plan was to deprive the Minority Shareholders of most of the present value of their stock in CDS and to deprive the Minority Shareholders of their share of the anticipated significant rise in the value of CDS stock over the next few years." . . .

24

Throughout April 1989, while all defendants were carrying forth the Plan to squeeze out the Minority Shareholders, all defendants knew the $0.002 per share to be offered the Minority Shareholders was grossly less than the present fair market value of the shares.

25

Throughout April 1989, while all defendants . . . were carrying forth the Plan to squeeze out the Minority Shareholders, all such defendants believed that the value of the CDS stock would greatly increase over the next few years, based on the increased business sales and profitability of CDS.

26

In early 1989, CDS received an offer from a third party to purchase substantially all of the corporation's assets. This offer was at a price substantially greater than $0.002 per share.

27

At a shareholders' meeting on February 6, 1989, the shareholders voted to reject this offer. All of the Majority Shareholders voted to reject this offer.

The thrust of plaintiffs' claims here is this (quoting from their brief):

> The majority shareholders owe a duty of loyalty, good faith, fair dealing, and full disclosure
> to the minority shareholders. This duty is breached when the majority transfers corporate assets to
> themselves and offers the minority a mere fraction of the true value of their shares.

As stated above, ORS 60.554(2) provides that a dissenting shareholder "may not challenge the corporate action creating the shareholder's entitlement unless the action is unlawful or fraudulent with respect to the shareholder or the corporation." The dispositive question here is whether plaintiffs have alleged facts that would establish that defendants' conduct was "unlawful or fraudulent" within the meaning of ORS 60.554(2).

We start with the observation that this court may not question the wisdom of the Legislative Assembly in enacting the Oregon Business Corporation Act. That law drew upon the Model Business Corporation Act and contains procedures for majority shareholders to "squeeze out" minority shareholders. The legislative decision involved considerations affecting both majority shareholders and dissenting shareholders.

> The accompanying proposals as a whole are designed to benefit both minority shareholders
> and controlling shareholders. Minority shareholders benefit because the assertion of their rights
> is made easier, and penalties are introduced for vexatious obstruction by corporate management.
> Controlling shareholders benefit directly and indirectly. They benefit directly by the added incentives for dissenters to settle without a judicial appraisal. They benefit indirectly because the provision of an adequate appraisal right diminishes the justification for courts to enjoin or set aside
> corporate changes because of the absence of an "adequate remedy at law," or because the corporate
> action "would operate as a fraud."

Con[ard], Amendments of Model Business Corporation Act Affecting Dissenters' Rights (Sections 73, 74, 80, and 81), 33 Bus. Law. 2587, 2593 (1978). . . .

Plaintiffs' complaint in this case alleged neither fraud nor misleading representations that were relied upon by plaintiffs. From plaintiffs' complaint, one can infer only that the amount paid by CDS was unfair and unreasonably low, in an attempt to avoid paying fair value to plaintiffs for their shares.

Cases such as this are the very kind addressed by the statutory scheme. With the exception of punitive damages, every element of damages that plaintiffs seek herein is recoverable under ORS 60.551 to 60.594. The complaint contains no allegations of fact that, if proved, would support a punitive damages award. The legislative plan expressly provides for recovery of attorney fees and expenses and of expert fees and expenses for arbitrary or vexatious action, or actions "not in good faith" in connection with the cash-out merger. See [MBCA §13.31]. This provision suggests to us that the legislature intended that, even if the corporation offers too little money to the dissenters for their shares "arbitrarily, vexatiously or not in good faith," and if the disagreement is solely as to the value of the shares, statutory appraisal is the exclusive remedy.[10]

---

10. Where the dissenting shareholders vote for the merger or surrender their shares as a result of misrepresentation or fraud, they may bring a separate action for damages. See Weinberger v. UOP, Inc., [457 A.2d 701 (Del. 1983)], and Rabkin v. Philip A. Hunt Chemical Corp., 498 A.2d 1099 (Del. 1985). No such claims are made in this case.

The last clause of ORS 60.551(4) also is significant. To the extent, if any, that plaintiffs seek damages for "any appreciation or depreciation in anticipation of the corporate action," those damages can be considered if "exclusion would be inequitable." We agree with the Delaware Supreme Court that "there is a legislative intent to fully compensate shareholders for whatever their loss may be, subject only to the narrow limitation that one cannot take speculative effects of the merger into account." Weinberger v. UOP, Inc., 457 A.2d 701, 714 (Del. 1983).

> "Thus, market value, asset value, dividends, earning prospects, the nature of the enterprise and any other facts which were known or which could be ascertained as of the date of merger and which throw any light on future prospects of the merged corporation are not only pertinent to an inquiry as to the value of the dissenting stockholders' interest, but must be considered by the agency fixing the value."
>
> This is not only in accord with the realities of present day affairs, but it is thoroughly consonant with the purpose and intent of our statutory law.

Id. at 713 (quoting Tri-Continental Corp. v. Battye, 74 A.2d 71, 72 (Del. 1950)). . . .

Plaintiffs' complaint clearly alleges a disagreement as to valuation, and we also can infer payment by Car Data of an unreasonably low price. Where the allegations show only a disagreement as to price, however, with no allegations that permit any inference of self-dealing, fraud, deliberate waste of corporate assets, misrepresentation, or other unlawful conduct, the remedy afforded by ORS 60.551 to 60.594 is exclusive. That is true even if the majority shareholders acted arbitrarily or vexatiously or not in good faith. Stepak v. Schey, 51 Ohio St. 3d 8, 553 N.E.2d 1072, 1075 (1990) (remedy for breach of fiduciary duty involving only the price that a shareholder receives is limited to appraisal statute); Schloss Associates v. C & O Ry., 73 Md. App. 727, 536 A.2d 147, 158 (1988) ("What we have then is essentially a complaint over price—the amount and how it was established—for which the statutory appraisal right is a wholly adequate remedy."); Green v. Santa Fe Industries, Inc., 70 N.Y.2d 244, 519 N.Y.S.2d 793, 800, 514 N.E.2d 105, 112 (1987) ("Here, . . . all of the actions with which defendant corporations are charged relate to price; there are no claims asserted against individual defendants based on dual representation; and it cannot be said that the defendants are charged with bad faith which goes beyond issues of 'mere inadequacy of price.'" Cole v. National Cash Register Credit Association, 18 Del. Ch. 47, 156 A.2d 187-88 [1931]).

It may be that the $0.002 offer was insulting to plaintiffs, and it may even have been motivated by bad faith. But, because the facts alleged in the complaint, if established, support no claim for damages apart from the fair value of the shares, we believe that the legislature intended that dissenting shareholders in the position of plaintiffs be limited to their remedies under the appraisal statutes.

The decision of the Court of Appeals and the judgment of the circuit court are affirmed.

NOTES AND QUESTIONS

1. To what extent may an appraisal action be used to litigate shareholder claims, provide a remedy for, or otherwise take into account claims based on breach of fiduciary

duty or wrongdoing in connection with the merger? Except as noted in *Glassman*, Delaware seemingly limits the appraisal action to issues of valuation.

> The Court of Chancery correctly denied Cinerama's [the dissenting shareholder in an arm's-length merger] motion to amend and enlarge its appraisal action to include its claim for rescissory relief for conspiracy, illegality, fraud, and breach of fiduciary duty. As previously noted, statutory appraisal is limited to "the payment of fair value of the shares . . . by the surviving or resulting corporation." 8 Del. C. §262(i). A determination of fair value does not involve an inquiry into claims of wrongdoing in the merger. In contrast, in a fraud action seeking monetary relief for unfair dealing, the focus of the suit is whether wrongdoing can be established. See *Weinberger*, 457 A.2d at 714. Hence, the necessary party defendants in a "fraud in the merger" action are the alleged wrongdoers because it is they who arguably caused the injury and should pay any damage award. To permit Cinerama to amend its statutory appraisal action to include its fraud claims would impermissibly broaden the legislative remedy. It would also fail to bring before the Court the necessary parties for the fashioning of any appropriate relief for a fraud.
>
> Finally, to judicially expand an appraisal proceeding to include unfair dealing claims would likely create unforeseeable administrative and procedural problems for litigants and the courts. In most cases only a small proportion of shareholders will have perfected appraisal rights and thus have access to the expanded appraisal remedy. If shareholders are permitted to litigate fraud claims in appraisal proceedings, shareholders not seeking appraisal would be required to litigate "entire fairness" claims identical to the claims litigated by shareholders with perfected appraisal rights but through separate actions. This would create a substantial risk of inconsistent judgments and raise issues of collateral estoppel. . . .

Cede & Co. v. Technicolor, Inc., 542 A.2d 1182, 1189-1190 (Del. 1988) (usually referred to as *Cede I*).

2. California courts take a different view of the scope of appraisal actions.

> In [Sturgeon Petroleum Ltd. v. Merchants Petroleum Co.], it was held that a shareholder may litigate his claim of misconduct in an appraisal proceeding, and to the extent he is able to prove that the value of his shares was diminished by misconduct in connection with the merger, his recovery could be adjusted in that proceeding. (147 Cal. App. 3d 134, 141, 195 Cal. Rptr. 29, [33].)
>
> We see nothing in the appraisal statutes to prevent vindication of a shareholder's claim of misconduct in an appraisal proceeding, and plaintiff does not claim to the contrary. Thus, there is merit in defendants' position that since plaintiff could have obtained full compensation by way of appraisal, he should not be able to avoid the statutorily mandated procedure by simply choosing not to invoke it.
>
> Contrary to plaintiff's assertion, appraisal is as adequate a remedy for a shareholder who bases his claim of undervaluation on breach of fiduciary duty as to one who argues that his shares were undervalued due to a good faith dispute of their worth, provided that the issue of misconduct may be litigated in an appraisal proceeding.

Steinberg v. Amplica, Inc., 729 P.2d 683, 690 (Cal. 1986).

3. In determining whether breach of fiduciary duty claims may be raised in an appraisal proceeding, courts distinguish between claims that the corporation or its officers and directors breached fiduciary obligations in connection with the merger, and claims that the corporation was damaged by breaches of fiduciary duty unrelated to a merger. Consider the Delaware Court of Chancery's explanation and discussion:

> It is settled law that a breach of fiduciary duty claim arising from the merger, such as an entire fairness claim, must be brought as a separate action directly challenging the merger. Rabkin v. Philip A. Hunt Chemical Corp., Del. Supr., 498 A.2d 1099, 1105 (1985). However, breach of

fiduciary duty claims that do not arise from the merger are corporate assets that may be included in the determination of fair value. Cavalier Oil Corp. v. Harnett, 564 A.2d at 1142-44. . . .

ITI argues that if the Court agrees to value the derivative claims, the parties will be forced to conduct a trial within a trial; petitioners will escape the requirements of Chancery Court Rule 23.1; and the validity of the claim will be decided without the alleged wrongdoers being before the Court. I understand ITI's concern. However, I anticipate that the value of the claims, if any, will be established through expert testimony in much the same manner that evidence typically is presented as to the value of other corporate assets. Since the derivative claims will not be litigated, petitioners will not be encroaching on the directors' managerial functions and the demand requirements of Rule 23.1 will not be triggered. Similarly, the fact that the alleged wrongdoers are not defendants will not be disabling as there will be no determination of liability.

Bomarko, Inc. v. International Telecharge, Inc., 1994 WL 198726, *3 (Del. Ch.)

4. The law of the various states concerning the exclusivity of the appraisal remedy remains a nonuniform mixture of statutes and case law. The following categories capture the range of variations currently employed.

- Some state statutes provide that appraisal is not exclusive in a conflict setting. The California statute, for example, has long provided that appraisal is not exclusive whenever one party to a merger or reorganization is controlled by another party. See California Corporations Code §1312(b) and (c). The 2006 version of the Model Business Corporation Act (§13.40) specifies exclusivity as a general rule and then provides an exception from the exclusivity in (b)(3) for an interested transaction (defined by a new subsection 5.1 to section 13.01) unless the interested transaction has been cleansed as set forth in §8.62 or 8.63.

- In several large commercial states where the statute is silent on exclusivity or contains an exclusivity requirement with a general exception for unlawful or fraudulent conduct, courts have ruled (in contrast to the principal case above) that appraisal is not exclusive. This includes Delaware for long-form mergers as discussed in the previous subsection, as well as Massachusetts and New Jersey and most federal courts when they have been called upon to apply state law.

- A number of states have exclusivity statutes with exceptions for unlawful or fraudulent actions, including those that have based their statute on the pre-1999 version of the MBCA. In many of these states there are decisions, such as *Stringer,* permitting alternative actions to appraisal only where there is actual fraud and not for mere breaches of fiduciary duty or self-dealing.

- In a few states the legislature has departed from the MBCA language to insert an explicit preference for pure exclusivity, eliminating even an exception for fraudulent action. For example, in Fleming v. International Pizza Supply Corp., 676 N.E.2d 1051 (Ind. 1997), the court noted that the Indiana legislature had adopted most of the provisions of the MBCA. "In contrast, when our legislature adopted [§13.02] as part of the BCL, it provided:

    A shareholder . . . who is entitled to dissent and obtain payment for the shareholder's shares under this chapter . . . may not challenge the corporate action creating . . . the shareholder's entitlement. Ind. Code §23-1-44-8(c).

676 N.E.2d at 1054-1055. The court then concluded:

[W]e think the defendants are correct in their argument that, in a merger or asset sale, the exclusive remedy available to a shareholder seeking payment for the value of the shareholder's shares is the statutory appraisal procedure. We believe the legislature clearly and unambiguously made the determination that separate actions would not lie for breach of fiduciary duty and fraud when it rejected the language of RMA §13.02(b) and used instead the language of Ind. Code §23-1-44-8(c).

676 N.E.2d at 1057.

5. Reconsider the scope of an appraisal proceeding in Delaware as outlined in the next to last paragraph of the *Glassman* opinion, supra at page 754. Justice Berger stresses two points that are essential if appraisal is to fulfill its role as an exclusive remedy for minority shareholders who are involuntarily forced out of the enterprise at a price set unilaterally by the majority. First, "if the merger was timed to take advantage of a depressed market, or a low point in the company's cyclical earnings, or to precede an anticipated positive development, the appraised value may be adjusted to account for these factors." Second, even though *Glassman* insulates parent corporations and their fiduciaries from entire fairness claims arising out of short-form mergers, the duty of full disclosure remains and minority shareholders "must be given all the factual information that is material to that decision" (to accept the merger consideration or seek appraisal). Should jurisdictions that embrace appraisal exclusivity without exception for breach of fiduciary duty also broaden the scope of the appraisal remedy to mirror the features outlined by Justice Berger in *Glassman*?

PROBLEM 8-7

Reconsider the facts in Problem 8-4. What are the prospects for the minority shareholders' cause of action in a jurisdiction that follows *Stringer*?

3. Litigating Entire Fairness Claims

The following case demonstrates the elements of an entire fairness claim and sheds particular light on how the trial court applies the entire fairness standard of review in a fully litigated case.

In re Emerging Communications, Inc.
Shareholders Litigation
Delaware Court of Chancery, 2004
2004 WL 1305745

OPINION

JACOBS, J. Sitting by designation as Vice Chancellor under Del. Const., art. IV, §13(2).

Addressed in this Opinion are the merits of consolidated statutory appraisal and class actions for breach of fiduciary duty. These actions all arise out of the two-step "going private" acquisition of the publicly owned shares of Emerging Communications, Inc. ("ECM"), by Innovative Communications Corporation, L.L.C. ("Innovative"), ECM's majority stockholder. The first step tender offer was commenced on August 18, 1998 by Innovative for 29% of ECM's outstanding shares at a price of $10.25 per share. The balance of ECM's publicly held shares were acquired in a second-step cash-out merger of ECM into an Innovative subsidiary, at the same price, on October 19, 1998.

At the time of this two-step transaction (the "Privatization"), 52% of the outstanding shares of ECM, and 100% of the outstanding shares of Innovative, were owned by Innovative Communication Company, LLC ("ICC"). ICC, in turn, was wholly owned by ECM's Chairman and Chief Executive Officer, Jeffrey J. Prosser ("Prosser"). Thus, Prosser had voting control of both of the parties to the Privatization transaction. . . .

There are two groups of defendants: (1) the "ECM defendants," which consist of ECM, ICC, and Innovative; and (2) the "Board defendants," who were ECM's directors at the time of the Privatization. In addition to Jeffrey Prosser . . . ECM's directors were Richard Goodwin[2]; John Raynor; Sir Shridath Ramphal; Salvatore Muoio; John Vondras; and Terrence Todman. Each of the board defendants served as an ECM director at Prosser's request. . . .

B. BACKGROUND LEADING TO THE FORMATION OF ECM

ECM's corporate predecessor, Atlantic TeleNetwork, Inc. ("ATN"), was a company that Prosser and a partner, Cornelius Prior, formed in 1987 to acquire the Virgin Islands Telephone Corporation ("Vitelco").

Vitelco, which was ATN's (and later ECM's) principal subsidiary, was (and still is) the exclusive provider of local wired telephone service in the [United States Virgin Islands ("USVI")], where Vitelco operates a modern, fully digital telecommunications network. . . .

By 1993, Prosser and Prior had a falling out. That led to a management deadlock. . . . Prosser and Prior decided to split ATN into two new companies (the "Split Off"). One of those companies, to be controlled by Prosser, would consist of ATN's Virgin Islands Group. That company was ECM. . . . The Split Off was approved by ATN's board of directors and shareholders, and was consummated on December 30, 1997. Although ATN had no controlling stockholder before the Split Off (Prosser and Prior owned a large but not majority position), as a result of the Split Off Prosser ended up owning 52% of ECM's 10,959,131 shares, and ECM's public shareholders were relegated to the position of minority stockholders.

On December 31, 1997, ECM began trading as a public company on the American Stock Exchange. Shortly after Prosser obtained control of ECM, he appointed his long-

---

2. [Eds. note—An omitted portion of the opinion notes the following: Richard Goodwin, a member of the Massachusetts Bar, is a noted author of books on American history, government, and politics. In 1959, Mr. Goodwin served as a law clerk to U.S. Supreme Court Justice Felix Frankfurter, and during the 1960s he served as assistant special counsel to President John F. Kennedy. During the 1980s and part of the 1990s, Mr. Goodwin also served as a consultant to the government of the USVI.]

time ATN directors, Raynor and Ramphal, to the ECM board. Prosser also appointed Messrs. Goodwin, Muoio and Vondras to the ECM board.

C. THE PROPOSED, BUT LATER ABORTED, MERGER
OF INNOVATIVE INTO ECM . . .

[B]efore the Split Off had been completed, Prosser indicated that he intended to merge Innovative into ECM, and he began exploring a combination of the two companies in January 1998. On January 20, 1998, ECM hired Prudential[3] to advise it on the fairness of a potential merger . . . (the "Proposed Merger"). During the next month, Prosser formulated the terms of the Proposed Merger, assisted by Prudential, the law firm of Cahill, Gordon and Reindel, ECM's legal advisors ("Cahill Gordon"), and director John Raynor. . . .

At the March 9, 1998 meeting of the ECM board, Prosser formally presented the Proposed Merger, whereby Innovative would merge into ATNCo (the wholly-owned ECM subsidiary that held Vitelco). . . . No privatization of ECM was contemplated as part of this transaction. At the March 9, 1998 board meeting, the ECM board also constituted a special committee, consisting of Messrs. Goodwin, Raynor, and Ramphal (the "First Special Committee"), to consider Prosser's Proposed Merger. Those persons were appointed at the suggestion of Prosser.

The law firm retained to serve as counsel to the First Special Committee was Cahill Gordon. The firm that was retained as the financial advisor to ECM and the First Special Committee in connection with the Proposed Merger was Prudential. . . .

D. PROSSER ABANDONS THE MERGER IN FAVOR
OF THE PRIVATIZATION

During the third week of May 1998, Prosser began having significant reservations about the Proposed Merger, because the low market interest in ECM's common stock had caused that stock to be undervalued.[7] On May 21, 1998, Prosser, together with Raynor, met with representatives of Prudential and Cahill Gordon to discuss the feasibility of Innovative acquiring all of the outstanding stock of ECM. By that point, Prosser had decided (in Raynor's words) to "flip the transaction." Having concluded that the market was not recognizing ECM's intrinsic value, Prosser switched from being a seller of ECM stock to becoming a buyer of that stock. Although Prosser had placed a value of $13.25 per share on ECM for purposes of the Split Off that had occurred only 5 months before, as a buyer of that same stock he was now proposing to pay only $9.125 per share.

---

3. [Eds. note—Prudential had previously advised Prosser in connection with the split-off that created ECM.]

7. On the last trading day before the public announcement of the Privatization, the reported closing price was $7.00 per share. Prosser informed the ECM board that the ECM stock price had failed to reach the desired appreciation as a result of the small public float and the fact that the stock was not followed by Wall Street analysts.

Between May 22 and May 28, Prosser, Prudential and Cahill formulated the terms of a Privatization proposal to be presented to ECM's board. . . . On May [29], Prosser delivered to the ECM board a letter withdrawing the Proposed Merger and proposing instead that Innovative acquire all the ECM shares it did not already own. The proposed Privatization was structured as a first-step cash tender offer for ECM's publicly traded shares at $9.125 per share, to be followed by a second-step cash-out merger at the same price.

Prosser's May 29th letter was the first occasion that the ECM board and the First Special Committee (other than Raynor) learned of the abandonment of the Proposed Merger in favor of the Privatization. Those directors were never told of the roles played by Prudential, Cahill and Raynor—all supposedly retained to represent the interest of the ECM minority stockholders—in formulating the terms of the newly-substituted going private transaction.

On the same day that Prosser proposed the Privatization, he told ECM's board that he (Prosser) had retained ECM's former advisors, Prudential and Cahill Gordon, to represent Innovative as the buyer in that transaction. Prudential was an especially valuable advisor to ECM, because it understood ECM's business and properties and had been ECM's only advisor during its brief life as a stand-alone company. Thus, the advisors that initially were retained to work *for* the interests of ECM and its minority stockholders would now be working to serve the interests of Innovative, the party now bargaining *against* ECM. There is no evidence that the ECM board objected either to Prosser's co-opting these valuable advisors, or to the timing of the proposed Privatization.[11]

E. THE FORMATION OF THE SECOND SPECIAL COMMITTEE AND THE NEGOTIATION OF THE TRANSACTION TERMS

At the May 29 ECM directors' meeting, the board formed another special committee (the "Second Special Committee") to review the fairness of the proposed Privatization. The directors selected to serve as members of this Second Special Committee were Messrs. Richard Goodwin, John Vondras, and Shridath Ramphal.

There were several obstacles to the ability of these three directors to operate as a fully functioning Special Committee. Located on different continents and separated by a time difference of 14 hours, the three Committee members were never able to meet in person. Instead, they had to conduct their business by telephone and fax. Even teleconferences were difficult to arrange and as a result, the Second Special Committee never met collectively—even by telephone—to consider the $10.25 final negotiated offer whose approval it ultimately recommended.

---

11. At that time (May 1998), Prosser knew that ECM's stock price was artificially depressed, because the market was not viewing ECM as a U.S. telephone company, but, rather, as a developing nation/third world phone company. That perception, Prosser knew, was unfair, because ECM had all the characteristics of a U.S. telephone company—a stable government, dollar economy, English language, American courts and legal system—and none of the characteristics of a third world company. Trial Tr. Vol. 10 (Prosser) at 1728-29, 1801-02, 1807. Rather than educate the market or afford it time to understand ECM's true characteristics, Prosser exploited the market unfairness by proposing the Privatization at a price that reflected a "premium" over ECM's then-current depressed market price level.

Because one of the Second Special Committee members lived in Indonesia and the other lived in England, practicality dictated that Goodwin would be the Committee chair. In that capacity, Goodwin was designated to—and did—take the lead role in negotiating with Prosser and in selecting the Committee's legal and financial advisors. Mr. Goodwin interviewed William Schwitter of Paul, Hastings, Janofsky & Walker LLP ("Paul Hastings"), as a potential legal advisor to the Second Special Committee, and on June 5, 1998, the Committee retained the Paul Hastings firm as its legal counsel. Later, after meeting with representatives of J.P. Morgan and Houlihan Lokey Howard & Zukin ("Houlihan") at his home in Massachusetts, Goodwin recommended that the Committee retain Houlihan as its financial advisor, and in mid-July, 1998, the Second Special Committee retained Houlihan in that capacity.

As part of its pre-financial analysis investigation of ECM, Houlihan conducted (among other things) a review of ECM's financial information. That information included financial projections for ECM, dated March 25, 1998 (the "March projections"), that had been prepared by James Heying, ECM's then-Chief Financial Officer and Executive Vice President of Acquisitions. What Houlihan was *not* provided, however, were financial projections dated June 22, 1998 (the "June projections") that Prosser had caused Heying to prepare as part of Prosser's and ICC's application to the RTFC [Rural Telephone Finance Cooperative, which provided funds at below-market interest rates] to finance the acquisition of ECM's minority shares.

The June projections forecasted substantially higher growth than did the March projections. Based on the June projections, as modified by the RFTC, the RFTC concluded in July 1998 that ECM was worth (for loan approval purposes) approximately $28 per share. Recognizing that the Privatization gave Prosser "the opportunity to retain control at a price below the true market value of the company," the RTFC approved financing that would enable Prosser to offer up to $11.40 per share. That suggests, and Prosser later confirmed, that he always planned (and gave himself sufficient elbow room) to increase his initial offer by some amount. Moreover, the $60 million RTFC loan represented the amount Prosser had asked for, not the limit of what the RTFC would have allowed him to borrow.

Although Prosser made the June projections available to his legal advisor (Cahill), his financial advisor (Prudential), and his lender (the RTFC), the June projections were never provided to the Second Special Committee, Houlihan, or the ECM board. Instead, Prosser directed Heying to send Houlihan the March projections, even though the June projections were available by that point. As a result, the Committee and its advisors believed—mistakenly—that the March projections were the most recent projections available.

On August 4, 1998, the Committee met with Houlihan to discuss Houlihan's preliminary analysis, which had been furnished to the Committee members in the form of a draft presentation booklet. After explaining in detail his firm's assumptions and methodologies, Houlihan's representative informed the Committee that it was not prepared to opine that $9.125 was a price that was fair to the minority stockholders. After further discussion, the Second Special Committee agreed that $9.125 would not provide adequate compensation to the ECM minority.

Before beginning its negotiations with Prosser, the Committee members discussed different strategies for obtaining the highest possible price for the minority shareholders. . . . They concluded, however, that the approach best calculated to achieve the highest price was not to demand a specific price from Prosser, but, rather, to negotiate with Prosser for the highest price he would pay for the shares and then determine whether that price represented fair value for the minority stockholders.[22]

Between August 5 and August 10, 1998, in a series of telephone conversations, Messrs. Goodwin and Prosser negotiated the buyout price for ECM's publicly held shares. During the first conversation, which took place on August 7, Goodwin told Prosser that his initial offer of $9.125 was inadequate. . . .

Eventually, Prosser told Goodwin that he would consider the matter and call Goodwin back. Shortly thereafter, Prosser raised his offer by one eighth of a point, to $9.25 per share. Goodwin reported that offer to the Second Special Committee, which rejected it as inadequate. Goodwin then called Prosser and told Prosser that he would have to improve his offer. In a later negotiation, Prosser raised his offer to $10 per share. Again, Goodwin reported that offer to his fellow Committee members and to Houlihan. The Committee rejected that revised offer, and thereafter, Prosser raised his offer to $10.125 per share. The Second Special Committee rejected that offer as well.

In response, Prosser raised his offer to $10.25 per share, but told Goodwin that $10.25 was his final offer. Because the price had been going up in roughly quarter point increments, Goodwin countered by asking for $10.50 per share. Prosser rejected that request, pointing out that $10.25 was already "straining the limits of [his] financing" for the transaction.[25] At that point, Goodwin made a judgment that the Committee "had reached the limits of how far we could push . . . ," and informed the other Committee members—Ramphal and Vondras—of his conclusion. Ramphal and Vondras agreed to stop the negotiations at that point. . . .[27]

The Committee having obtained what they believed was the highest available price, the question then became whether that price was fair. On August 12, 1998, Goodwin and Vondras had a telephonic meeting with Houlihan and Paul Hastings to review Prosser's $10.25 offer. Having updated its financial analysis, Houlihan concluded that the revised offer price of $10.25 was fair to ECM's public shareholders from a financial

---

22. There is evidence that sometime after the August 4th meeting, Houlihan told Goodwin that a one point increase above the original $9.125 offer, i.e., an increase to $10.125, would enable Houlihan to furnish a fairness opinion.

25. . . . The record shows that, in fact, Prosser's financing would have enabled him to increase his offer to $11.40 per share, and that the implied equity value of ECM was $305 million, or $28 per share. Goodwin testified that Prosser's representation about the limits of his financing, truthful or not, had no impact except to signal to him (Goodwin) that the negotiations had to end.

27. The plaintiffs contend that the negotiations between Prosser and Goodwin were not arm's length, and that, in fact, the Special Committee's entire process was "bankrupt." To prove that point, the plaintiffs rely heavily upon the fact that Goodwin's regular practice was to send faxes to Special Committee members (or their counsel) through Prosser's secretary, Eling Joseph, and ask her to fax it to the others. Although Goodwin told Ms. Joseph that the Committee materials were confidential, this practice did create the potential of giving Prosser access to almost every document that circulated among the Special Committee, including Houlihan's financial analysis. Goodwin did not deny having routed his communications through Ms. Joseph, and defended that practice on the basis of convenience, not necessity. The defendants respond that there is no evidence that Prosser or his advisors saw these faxes.

point of view. Goodwin and Vondras thereafter voted to recommend that the full ECM board approve the Privatization.[28]

F.   ECM'S DIRECTORS AND SHAREHOLDERS APPROVE THE PROPOSED PRIVATIZATION

A telephonic meeting of the ECM board to consider Prosser's revised offer to buy all of ECM's publicly held stock for $10.25 per share, was held on August 13, 1998, the following day. Present at that meeting were Mr. Schwitter and Houlihan representatives. Not attending were Messrs. Prosser (at the request of the Board) and Todman (due to a scheduling conflict). The Board members who had not served on the Special Committee had received copies of Houlihan's fairness analysis before the meeting.

At the meeting, the Special Committee members described the process they had employed. Houlihan then explained its financial analysis and confirmed that in its opinion, the $10.25 per share price was fair to the minority stockholders from a financial point of view. After discussion, the board determined to approve the Privatization, but only if a majority of the shares held by the minority stockholders were tendered in the first-step tender offer. The meeting was then adjourned to August 17, 1998, at which time the board was told that Prosser would agree to this non-waivable minimum tender condition. The full board, acting upon the unanimous recommendation of the Second Special Committee, then voted to approve the Privatization.

On August 18, 1998, ECM publicly announced the execution of a definitive merger agreement that provided for the Tender Offer and Merger at $10.25 per share, and that the Tender Offer was subject to the minimum tender condition. The Tender Offer commenced on August 24, 1998. At the time of the Tender Offer, there were 10,959,131 outstanding ECM shares, of which 5,606,873 shares were owned by Prosser through ICC, and the remaining 5,352,258 were held by the public. As of September 25, 1998, 3,206,844 of those shares (i.e., a majority of the minority shares) had been tendered. On October 19, 1998, a special meeting of ECM shareholders took place, at which the Merger was approved by a vote of 5,760,660 FOR, and 4,466 AGAINST, out of 10,959,131 shares entitled to vote. The Merger was consummated that same day. . . .

II.   THE PARTIES' CONTENTIONS AND THE ISSUES PRESENTED

As earlier noted, the plaintiffs have brought and litigated two separate actions—a statutory appraisal action and a class action asserting claims that the Privatization

---

Prosser testified that Ms. Joseph never disclosed any of those materials to him, including Houlihan's valuation materials. The record discloses, however, that at least on one occasion the confidentiality of the faxed Committee materials was breached. Even if that had not occurred, this practice cannot help but undermine confidence in the integrity of the bargaining process. It is manifest that Goodwin's decision to route those materials through the secretary who shared the same office as Prosser—Goodwin's bargaining adversary—rather than route them through the office of the Committee's counsel, Mr. Schwitter, created a serious risk of compromising the Committee's process and its effectiveness in negotiating the highest available value.

28. Ramphal did not attend the Committee's August 12 meeting, even by telephone. Shortly after the meeting, Goodwin contacted Ramphal and gave him a detailed account of what had occurred.

was not entirely fair to ECM's minority shareholders. In a statutory appraisal action, the Court must determine the "fair value" of the corporation whose stock is being appraised. . . . In a class action seeking to invalidate a "going private" acquisition of a corporation's minority stock by its majority stockholder, the standard under which this Court reviews the validity of the transaction and the liability of the fiduciaries charged with breach of duty, is entire fairness. . . . That standard of review has two aspects: fair dealing and fair price. . . . Because the plaintiffs' class action damages claim is identical (dollar-wise) to their statutory appraisal claim, the fiduciary "fair price," and statutory "fair value," contentions converge and are addressed in connection with the statutory appraisal claim. . . .

III.   THE FAIR PRICE AND FAIR VALUE OF ECM . . .

E.   THE FAIR VALUE OF ECM AND THE UNFAIRNESS OF THE MERGER PRICE

As a consequence of the foregoing determinations, the fair value of ECM on the merger date is found to be $416,996,000, or $38.05 per share. Under 8 Del. C. §262, Greenlight, as the single appraisal claimant, is entitled to recover that per share amount, multiplied by the 750,300 shares for which it seeks appraisal, plus interest as determined in Part III F, infra, of this Opinion.

From that fair value finding it further follows that the $10.25 per share merger price was not a "fair price" within the meaning of the Delaware fiduciary duty case law beginning with Weinberger v. UOP, Inc. Although that, without more, is dispositive, the unfairness of the merger price rests upon more than that one bit of simple deductive logic. The overwhelming weight of the credible evidence of record also compels that conclusion. . . .

IV.   WAS THE TRANSACTION THE PRODUCT OF FAIR DEALING?

A.   THRESHOLD ISSUES

1.   Is a Fair Dealing Analysis Required?

In this case, this Court's determination of ECM's "fair value" disposes of both Greenlight's appraisal action and the "fair price" aspect of the plaintiffs' fiduciary duty claim. The determination that price is not fair raises a preliminary, threshold question of whether in this case any "fair dealing" analysis need be undertaken at all. . . .

What the Supreme Court has decided is that where an interested merger is found to be unfair and the corporation's charter has a Section 102(b)(7) exculpatory provision, this Court must then proceed to "identify the breach or breaches of fiduciary duty upon which liability [for damages] will be predicated in the *ratio decidendi* of its determination that entire fairness has not been established." That is, "when entire fairness is the applicable standard of judicial review, a determination that the director defendants are exculpated from paying monetary damages can be made only *after the basis* for their liability has been decided."

That mandate, I find, is applicable here. In this case the defendants have raised a §102(b)(7) exculpatory defense. In determining that the merger price was not fair, this Court did not address whether the unfairness was the product of a breach of fiduciary duty or if so, the nature or character of that duty. Accordingly, a "fair dealing" analysis is required in this case, if only to enable the Court to determine the "basis for the [defendants'] liability" for §102(b)(7) exculpation purposes. . . .

(c) The Burden of Proof Issue

The final threshold issue is which side has the burden of proof. Both sides agree that because the Privatization is a self-dealing transaction of which the majority stockholder stands on both sides, entire fairness is the standard of review *ab initio*. The only question is whether the burden of proof, which normally falls upon the defendants, has shifted to the plaintiffs in this particular case.

The defendants argue that the burden of establishing that the merger was not entirely fair has shifted to the plaintiffs, because the merger was approved by both an informed independent committee of disinterested directors and an informed majority of minority stockholders. The short answer is that the merger was not approved by a committee of independent directors who were properly informed or independent of Prosser, nor was it approved by an informed vote of a majority of ECM's minority stockholders.

B. FAIR DEALING ANALYZED

A fair dealing analysis requires the Court to address "issues of when the transaction was timed, how it was initiated, structured, negotiated, and disclosed to the board, and how director and shareholder approval was obtained."

1. Timing, Initiation and Structure

Our courts have recognized that a freeze-out merger of the minority proposed by the majority stockholder is inherently coercive. Where, as here, the freeze-out merger is initiated by the majority stockholder, that fact, even though not dispositive, is evidence of unfair dealing.

Another circumstance that evidences the absence of fair dealing is where the transaction is timed in a manner that is financially disadvantageous to the stockholders and that enables the majority stockholder to gain correspondingly. This case is the diametric opposite of Jedwab v. MGM Grand Hotels, Inc., where this Court found that the timing of a merger was not unfair because there was no "persuasive indication . . . that from the minority's point of view this [was] a particularly poor time to liquidate their investment." Here, the evidence of unfair timing could not be more persuasive. Prosser's initial proposal was to merge Innovative into a wholly owned subsidiary of ECM. That would have benefited ECM stockholders and enabled them to remain as investors in a larger merged company. Because ECM's stock price was depressed, Prosser abandoned that proposal at the eleventh hour and "flipped" the deal for his sole personal benefit to take advantage of the temporarily and artificially depressed stock price. That stock price then became the "floor" for the equally depressed and unfair Privatization price, and benefited Prosser to the same extent that it disadvantaged the minority stockholders who were now being squeezed out of the enterprise.

In addition to, and apart from, the unfairness of its initiation and timing, the transaction was also unfairly structured, in that Prudential and Cahill, the firms that had been retained as advisors to ECM in the initially Proposed (but later abandoned) Merger, were co-opted by Prosser to serve as his advisors. That switch was unfair to ECM, because during ECM's entire existence, Prudential and Cahill had been its advisers and they possessed material nonpublic information about ECM's values, business and prospects. As such, Prudential and Cahill were in the best position to represent the interests of the ECM minority. Those same advisers were now switching sides to represent interests that were adverse to that same minority.

At a minimum, ECM's board (including Prosser) or the Special Committee should have insisted that Prudential and Cahill remain as advisors to ECM, and that Prosser retain other financial and legal advisors. Failing that, the board—or at the very least the Special Committee—should have insisted that Prudential and Cahill recuse themselves from the negotiations. By doing neither, ECM was deprived of the advantage of knowledgeable advisors. That advantage was conferred upon ECM's controlling stockholder and to-be-adversary in the transaction—Prosser. There is no evidence that either the full board or the Special Committee ever considered that issue.

2. *The Adequacy of the Minority Shareholders' Representation*

(a) *The Independence of the Board and of the Special Committee*

A critical aspect of any fair dealing analysis is the adequacy of the representation of the minority stockholders' interests. In this case, that issue is particularly critical, because a majority of the ECM board members were not independent of Prosser, making it necessary to appoint a Special Committee to negotiate on the minority stockholders' behalf. Unfortunately, a majority of the Special Committee members also lacked independence, and the one Committee member who arguably was independent did not function effectively as a champion of the minority's interests.

Besides Prosser, the ECM board had six members, all of whom Prosser had directly appointed: Raynor, Ramphal, Muoio, Goodwin, Vondras, and Todman. It is undisputed that Prosser, whose wholly-owned entity was the acquirer of ECM's minority interest, was conflicted. But, most of the remaining directors also had disabling conflicts because they were economically beholden to Prosser. Directors who "through personal or other relationships are beholden to the controlling person[]" lack independence from that person.[141]

Raynor, who was Prosser's long time lawyer, was clearly conflicted. In 1996, 1997, and 1998, virtually one hundred percent of the legal fees that Raynor generated for his law firm were attributable to work he performed for Prosser and Prosser-owned entities.... In 1998, the year of the Privatization, Raynor became "of counsel" at his firm and was put on a retainer arrangement wherein ATNCo paid compensation of $25,000 per month to Raynor, and $5,000 per month to his firm, to cover Raynor's office rental

---

141. Aronson v. Lewis, 473 A.2d 805, 815 (Del. 1984).

cost. That amount represented all of Raynor's compensation for 1998. Raynor also served as a Prosser nominee to the ATNI board, and as a director of Innovative, ECM, ATNCo and Vitelco. As a highly paid consultant to, and later full-time employee of, Prosser and his companies, Raynor was clearly beholden to Prosser and, thus, not independent.

If further evidence of non-independence were needed, in July 1998—during ECM's consideration of the Privatization proposal—Prosser agreed to pay Raynor $2.4 million over a five year period as compensation for his past services. [This arrangement was never] disclosed to the ECM board, Compensation Committee or the Special Committee, yet Raynor voted as an ECM director to approve the Privatization. That disclosure omission was highly material. Goodwin testified that the $2.4 million payment arrangement should have been disclosed to the board. For Raynor to have participated in the board's Privatization deliberations and vote as an ECM director without disclosing this contemporaneously negotiated compensation arrangement, was misleading to Raynor's fellow directors and a breach of his fiduciary duty owed to them and to ECM.

Ramphal was similarly beholden to Prosser. Ramphal was originally introduced to Prosser by his son-in-law, Sir Ronald Sanders, who had a consulting arrangement with Prosser at that time. Like Sanders, Ramphal also fell into a lucrative consultancy with Prosser. In 1993 and 1994, Ramphal was paid consulting fees of $140,000 in both years, and in 1995 he was paid $120,000. On average, those amounts represented 22.5% of Ramphal's total income for that period. Those amounts were in addition to the $30,000 directors' fee that Ramphal received annually. Moreover, in 1998, Ramphal received $115,000 for his service on the ECM Board and special committees.

Given these undisputed facts, the defendants have not shown that Ramphal was independent of, i.e., not beholden to, Prosser, and the Court affirmatively finds that he was not. . . .

Muoio was also a consultant to a Prosser entity and beholden to Prosser. As of mid-1997, Muoio was on an annual $200,000 retainer for providing banking/financial advisory services, and he viewed Prosser as a source of additional future lucrative consulting fees. In March 1998, Muoio sought up to an additional $2 million for serving as financial adviser on a potential acquisition by ECM of CoreComm Inc. That effort was unsuccessful only because the acquisition ultimately never took place.

Lastly, Goodwin, Vondras and Todman received annual directors' fees of $100,000, a generous amount given that ECM's board met only three or four times in 1998. Goodwin and Vondras each also received $50,000 and $15,000 for their service on the Special Committee. The $115,000 Vondras received in 1998 for serving on ECM's board and Special Committee represented approximately 10% of his income for that year.

Although the directors' fees received by Goodwin, Vondras and Todman would not, without more, necessarily constitute a disabling financial interest, the record shows that all three of these directors—indeed, all the board defendants—expected to continue as directors of Prosser entities and benefit from the substantial compensation which accompanied that status. In fact, all of ECM's directors except Muoio were appointed to the Innovative board after the Privatization. That expectation, coupled with the fact that his director and committee fees represented a sizeable portion of his income, was sufficient to vitiate Vondras' independence for purposes of considering objectively whether the Privatization was fair to the minority stockholders. . . .

In summary, the Court finds that a majority of the full board of ECM (Raynor, Ramphal, Vondras, and Muoio) were beholden to Prosser and, thus, were not independent of him. The Court further finds that a majority of the Special Committee (Ramphal and Vondras) were beholden to, and therefore not independent of, Prosser, leaving Goodwin as the only arguably independent Committee member and Todman as the only arguably independent non-Committee director. As previously found, Goodwin, as Committee chair, did almost all of the Committee's work himself. Unfortunately, the work that Goodwin performed in that role, including his negotiations with Prosser, were fatally compromised and, consequently, inadequate to represent the interests of ECM's minority shareholders effectively.[162]

(b)   The Committee's Ineffectiveness as the Minority's Representative

There are several reasons why Mr. Goodwin's efforts as the Special Committee's chairman, and as its sole functioning member, were doomed to failure.

The first is that Prosser withheld the June projections, and knowledge of their existence, from the Committee and its advisors, Houlihan and Paul Hastings. As a consequence, Goodwin and Houlihan were deprived of information that was essential to an informed assessment of the fair value of ECM and of the gross inadequacy of merger price Prosser was offering. Thus disabled, Goodwin was not in a position to negotiate vigorously for a substantial increase in Prosser's opening offer ($9.125 per share) or, alternatively, to make a considered judgment to shut down the negotiations, thereby preventing the Privatization from going forward at all. That nondisclosure, without more, was enough to render the Special Committee ineffective as a bargaining agent for the minority stockholders.

Second, Prosser misled Goodwin by falsely representing that $10.25 per share was already straining the limits of the financing available to him. In fact, Prosser's financing would have enabled him to increase his offer to $11.40 per share, and the record evidence indicates that the RTFC was willing to lend him more, based on its implied valuation of ECM as conservatively worth about $28 per share. There is no evidence that Goodwin knew of Prosser's financing arrangements or the RTFC's valuation (for merger financing purposes) of ECM.

Third, and finally, Goodwin was careless, if not reckless, by routing all of his communications with the other Special Committee members through Eling Joseph, Prosser's secretary. The result was to give Prosser access to the Committee's confidential deliberations and strategy. That inexplicable method of channeling communications to

---

162. As former Justice (then Vice Chancellor) Hartnett appropriately observed in Lewis v. Fuqua, 502 A.2d 962, 967 (Del. Ch. 1985), in addressing the independence of a special litigation committee appointed to review a derivative action, "[i]f a single member committee is to be used, the member should, like Caesar's wife, be above reproach." Here, as in *Fuqua,* Goodwin's "past and present associations raise a question of fact as to his independence" (502 A.2d at 967), which, given the burden of proof, would ordinarily be resolved against Goodwin's independence. The Court assumes, without deciding, however, that Goodwin was independent, but nonetheless concludes on other grounds that the Special Committee was not an effective representative of the minority stockholders' interests.

Goodwin's fellow Committee members further confirms the severe information imbalance that existed between the two "bargaining" sides. In fact, there was no effective bargaining, because Prosser held all the cards and misled Goodwin into believing that he (Goodwin) and the Committee's financial advisor (Houlihan), possessed all the information that was material to negotiating a fair price. Nothing could have been further from the truth.

3.   *The Adequacy of the Board and Shareholder Approvals*

The fourth and final aspect of fair dealing concerns the adequacy of the board and shareholder approvals of the challenged transaction. In this case, those approvals were uninformed and, accordingly, of no legal consequence.

It is undisputed that the Privatization was approved by a unanimous vote of all ECM directors, with Prosser abstaining, at a board of directors' meeting held on August 17, 1998. The board's approval was not informed, however, because the voting board members were ignorant of the existence of the June Projections and of the inadequacy of the Houlihan valuation that was based upon the March projections.

Moreover, Raynor, who was conflicted, voted in favor of the Privatization but did not disclose to the other voting board members, the $2.4 million compensation payout arrangement that he had recently negotiated with Prosser. As previously found, that nondisclosure was material.

By not disclosing these facts, Prosser and Raynor violated the fiduciary duty of disclosure they owed to their fellow directors of ECM.

The approval of the transaction by a majority of the minority shareholders was also legally ineffective, because the misdisclosures and omissions in the disclosure documents sent to shareholders in connection with the Privatization rendered that vote uninformed. Those misdisclosures and omissions also violated the fiduciary duty of disclosure owed by ECM's majority stockholder and by the ECM directors who were responsible for the accuracy of those documents. The plaintiffs claim several disclosure violations, but the Court need address only three of them.

First, the Proxy Statement omitted to disclose to the minority shareholders the existence of the June projections and the fact that those projections had been furnished to Prudential and the RTFC, but were withheld from the Special Committee and its advisors. That omission was materially misleading, not only in its own right but also because the proxy statement contained affirmative representations that the public was being provided with the same projections to which Prosser was privy. . . . Those misdisclosures were highly material because knowledge of the June projections would have enabled the shareholders to understand ECM's intrinsic worth and the extent of the market's undervaluation of their company.

Second, the disclosure documents misled minority stockholders about the Special Committee's and the board's independence from Prosser. The Schedule 14D-9, which was disseminated in connection with the first-step tender offer, disclosed the members of the Special Committee and their compensation, but not their consulting relationships or retainer agreements with other Prosser entities. Specifically, there was no disclosure of Raynor's or Ramphal's long-standing financial relationships with Prosser, including Raynor's $2.4 million payout arrangement for past services and Ramphal's significant consulting arrangements or his conflict concerning the economic and career prospects of his son-in-law. . . .

In short, the disclosure documents were crafted to reassure the minority stockholders that their interests had been effectively represented by a Special Committee of directors who were independent of Prosser and his entities on the other side of the transaction. That impression was materially false and misleading and was sufficient, without more, to render the approving vote of the stockholders uninformed.[172]

For all these reasons, the Court finds that the Privatization transaction, and the $10.25 per share merger price that has been adjudicated as unfair, were the product of unfair dealing. . . .

V. THE DEFENDANTS' FIDUCIARY DUTY BREACHES AND LIABILITY THEREFOR

Having concluded that the Privatization was not entirely fair, the Court must next determine the nature of the fiduciary duty violation—whether of care, loyalty, or good faith—that resulted in the unfair transaction. Under Emerald Partners v. Berlin,[174] that is necessary to enable the Court to adjudicate which (if any) of the director defendants is liable for money damages, because ECM's §102(b)(7) charter provision [Article Seventh] exculpates those directors found to have violated *solely* their duty of care from liability for money damages. . . .

The liability of the directors must be determined on an individual basis because the nature of their breach of duty (if any), and whether they are exculpated from liability for that breach, can vary for each director.

Prosser is liable in his capacity as a director for breach of his duty of loyalty, conduct that is not exculpated under Article Seventh. Prosser is also liable on the basis that he "derived an improper personal benefit" from the Privatization transaction—which is another exception to the exculpatory coverage of Article Seventh.

Raynor also is liable for breaching his fiduciary duty of loyalty—conduct that is excluded from the exculpatory shield of Article Seventh. Raynor did not personally and directly benefit from the unfair transaction (as did Prosser), but Raynor actively assisted Prosser in carrying out the Privatization, and he acted to further Prosser's interests in that transaction, which were antithetical to the interests of ECM's minority stockholders.

Raynor acted in concert with Prosser, who was the source of Raynor's livelihood, to "flip" the transaction from a merger of Innovative into ATNCo, to a going private merger of ECM into Innovative. Raynor also assisted Prosser and Innovative in obtaining RTFC financing for the Privatization at the time when Raynor was still serving on the First Special Committee, ostensibly to safeguard the interests of ECM's minority stockholders. After the Second Special Committee was formed, Raynor attended a

---

172. See Clements v. Rogers, 790 A.2d 1222, 1242-43 (Del. Ch. 2001) (accuracy of disclosures concerning the independence and effectiveness of a special negotiating committee are of particular importance where the transaction is with a controlling stockholder).

174. 787 A.2d 85 (Del. 2001).

meeting with Prosser and two ECM officers and the RTFC to discuss issues relating to the structuring of the revised deal. Finally, on July 20, 1998, Opus Capital Partners ("Opus") sent a letter to Goodwin, complaining that the initial $9.125 price was too low and should be around $30. This letter was somehow "leaked" to Cahill, Prudential, and Raynor, and Raynor reported the contents of the Opus letter to the RTFC. . . .

Although Raynor did not benefit directly from the transactions, his loyalties ran solely to Prosser because Raynor's economic interests were tied solely to Prosser and he acted to further those economic interests. Accordingly, Raynor is liable to Greenlight and the shareholder class for breaching his fiduciary duty of loyalty and/or good faith.

The Court also concludes, albeit with reluctance, that Muoio is similarly liable, even though Muoio's conduct was less egregious than that of Prosser and Raynor. Unlike Raynor, Muoio did nothing affirmatively to assist Prosser in breaching his fiduciary duties of loyalty and good faith. Like his fellow directors, Muoio was also not independent of Prosser.

Muoio is culpable because he voted to approve the transaction even though he knew, or at the very least had strong reasons to believe, that the $10.25 per share merger price was unfair. Muoio was in a unique position to know that. He was a principal and general partner of an investment advising firm, with significant experience in finance and the telecommunications sector. From 1995 to 1996, Muoio had been a securities analyst for, and a vice president of, Lazard Freres & Co. in the telecommunications and media sector. From 1985 to 1995, he was a securities analyst for Gabelli & Co., Inc., in the communications sector, and from 1993 to 1995, he was a portfolio manager for Gabelli Global Communications Fund, Inc.

Hence, Muoio possessed a specialized financial expertise, and an ability to understand ECM's intrinsic value, that was unique to the ECM board members (other than, perhaps, Prosser). Informed by his specialized expertise and knowledge, Muoio conceded that the $10.25 price was "at the low end of any kind of fair value you would put," and expressed to Goodwin his view that the Special Committee might be able to get up to $20 per share from Prosser. In these circumstances, it was incumbent upon Muoio, as a fiduciary, to advocate that the board reject the $10.25 price that the Special Committee was recommending. As a fiduciary knowledgeable of ECM's intrinsic value, Muoio should also have gone on record as voting against the proposed transaction at the $10.25 per share merger price. Muoio did neither. Instead he joined the other directors in voting, without objection, to approve the transaction.

ECM's directors other than Prosser and Raynor could plausibly argue that they voted for the transaction in reliance on Houlihan's opinion that the merger term price was fair. In Muoio's case, however, that argument would be implausible. Muoio's expertise in this industry was equivalent, if not superior, to that of Houlihan, the Special Committee's financial advisor. That expertise gave Muoio far less reason to defer to Houlihan's valuation. Knowing (or at least having very strong reasons to suspect) that the price was unfair, why, then, would Muoio vote to approve this deal? . . .

The credible evidence persuades the Court that Muoio's conduct is explainable in terms of only one of two possible mindsets. The first is that Muoio made a deliberate judgment that to further his personal business interests, it was of paramount importance for him to exhibit his primary loyalty to Prosser. The second was that Muoio, for whatever reason, "consciously and intentionally disregarded" his responsibility to safeguard the minority stockholders from the risk, of which he had unique knowledge, that the transaction was unfair.[189] If motivated by either of those mindsets, Muoio's conduct would have amounted to a violation of his duty of loyalty and/or good faith. Because Muoio has not established to the satisfaction of the Court, after careful scrutiny of the record, that his motivation was of a benign character, he is not exculpated from liability to Greenlight and the shareholder class.

That leaves the four remaining directors—Goodwin, Ramphal, Todman, and Vondras—whose conduct, while also highly troublesome, is far more problematic from a liability standpoint. . . .

A logical starting point in the analysis is first to consider the conduct of the members of the Second Special Committee: Goodwin, Ramphal and Vondras. Because Ramphal was located in London and Vondras in Indonesia, they never met in person with each other or with Goodwin, who became the Committee's sole working member. Put differently, all Committee initiatives and decisions were made initially by Goodwin, subject to concurrence by Ramphal and Vondras, who on all relevant issues willingly deferred to Goodwin and relied upon his recommendations, both as to the Committee's process and the transaction price.

Although Goodwin negotiated a merger price ($10.25 per share) that this Court has found to be unfair, there is no persuasive evidence that Goodwin knew or should have known that this was the case. Primarily, that is because critical information was withheld from Goodwin, from the other Committee members, from and their financial advisor, Houlihan. . . .

The plaintiffs insist, however, that Goodwin's fiduciary violations were of a character far more egregious than duty of care violations. Plaintiffs urge that: (1) Goodwin (as well as Ramphal and Vondras) were financially not independent of Prosser and were motivated to do whatever was needed to remain in Prosser's good graces, (2) Goodwin willingly acceded to retaining the Special Committee's legal and financial advisors from among candidates that had been selected by Prosser or his advisors, (3) Goodwin's "negotiations" with Prosser were nothing more than a scripted minuet wherein Goodwin, on behalf of the Committee, would bargain for a negligible price increase, (4) that bargaining, coupled with the gilt-edged credentials of all three Committee members, would create a credible record of "arm's length" negotiations sufficient to survive entire fairness review. Goodwin's decision to route his communications through Ms. Joseph was, plaintiffs argue, further dramatic evidence that his true loyalties were to serve Prosser and his interests. This conduct, plaintiffs insist, violated Prosser's (and Ramphal's and Vondras's) fiduciary duties of loyalty and/or good faith—conduct that is not exculpated under Article Seventh.

It is correct (and this Court has found) that with the possible exception of Goodwin, none of the Committee members was independent of Prosser, that viewed with perfect hindsight the magnitude of the negotiated price increase was negligible, and that Goodwin permitted his communications with Ramphal and Vondras to be

---

189. See In re Walt Disney Co. Derivative Litig., 825 A.2d 275, 289 (Del. Ch. 2003).

routed through Prosser's secretary. In quite different circumstances that might establish a violation of the duties of good faith and/or loyalty, especially since the burden of establishing exculpation falls upon the directors seeking exculpation. But here that procedural burden does not help the plaintiffs, because the evidence, viewed as a whole, fails to establish a *prima facie* case of bad faith or disloyalty that these directors would be called upon to negate or disprove.

More specifically, although Goodwin, Ramphal and Vondras, because of their relationship to Prosser, might have been motivated to aid Prosser in his scheme to force out ECM's minority at an unfair price, there is no evidence that they actually engaged in such improperly motivated conduct, or otherwise acted with disloyal intent. To be sure, Goodwin's conduct may fairly be described as having violated his duty of care. And, given the non-independence of Ramphal and Vondras, their wholesale abdications to Goodwin of their responsibility as Committee members to take an active and direct role in the process, also bespeaks a failure to observe the requisite due care.[191] But negligent or even gross negligent conduct, however misguided, does not automatically equate to disloyalty or bad faith. There is no evidence that Goodwin, Ramphal and Vondras intentionally conspired with Prosser to engage in a process that would create the illusion, but avoid the reality, of arm's length bargaining to obscure the true purpose of benefiting Prosser at the expense of the minority stockholders.

Nor, in these circumstances, did those directors' conduct amount to a breach of their fiduciary duty to act in good faith. Although the Supreme Court has yet to define the precise conduct that would actionably violate that duty, this Court has recently held that directors can be found to have violated their duty of good faith if they "*consciously and intentionally disregard[] their responsibilities,* adopting a 'we don't care about the risks' attitude concerning a material corporate decision."[192] Here, there is no evidence that Goodwin, Ramphal, or Vondras acted with conscious and intentional disregard of their responsibilities, or made decisions with knowledge that they lacked material information. Because the conduct of those director defendants was, solely and at most, a violation of their duty of care, they are exculpated from liability under Article Seventh.

The foregoing analysis and conclusion are equally applicable to the seventh director, Todman. The circumstance that differentiates Todman from Goodwin, Ramphal and Vondras is that Todman played no role in the negotiation of the merger terms, his sole involvement being to cast his vote as a director in favor of the Privatization. . . .

---

191. See Cede & Co. v. Technicolor, Inc., 634 A.2d 345, 368 (Del. 1993) ("[W]e have stated that a director's duty of care requires a director to take an active and direct role in the context of a sale of a company from beginning to end.")

192. In re Walt Disney, 825 A.2d at 289 (italics in original). Elaborating on that formulation, the Chancellor observed that directors actionably violate their duty of good faith if they "*knew* that they were making material decisions without adequate information and without adequate deliberation, and . . . they simply did not care if the decisions caused the corporations and its stockholders to suffer injury or loss." Id.

VI. CONCLUSION

For the reasons set forth above . . .

(2) In the fiduciary duty action, defendants Innovative, ICC, Prosser, Raynor and Muoio are jointly and severally liable to the plaintiff class and to Greenlight (in its capacity as holder of litigation rights assigned by former ECM shareholders) in an amount equal to $27.80 per share.[193]

NOTES AND QUESTIONS

1. It is standard fare, as in the principal case above, for disgruntled minority share-holders to assert that a majority-shareholder-dominated cash-out merger was timed by the controller to take advantage of a temporary market underpricing of the cor-poration's stock. Consider footnotes 3 and 7 on page 770 in *Emerging Communications*. Are Prosser's explanations for the undervaluation of EMC's stock credible? Are they consistent with the Efficient Market Hypothesis? Is it fair to say that Prosser is acting on the basis of nonpublicly available information? Is it not always the case that a cash-out merger is motivated by the controller's belief that the corporation's stock is worth more than the controller will be required to pay?

2. If the standard of review is entire fairness, will it ever be possible for the defendants to obtain summary judgment on that issue? Consider Justice Holland's assertion.

[A]n application of the entire fairness standard is not an implication of liability. Similarly, an appli-cation of the entire fairness standard *ab initio* does not mean that a trial is always inevitable. When the standard of review is entire fairness, *ab initio*, director defendants can move for summary judg-ment on either the issue of entire fairness or the issue of burden shifting.

Emerald Partners v. Berlin, 787 A.2d 85, 99 (Del. 2001). How likely is it that the fair price component of entire fairness can be determined at the summary judgment stage?

3. If entire fairness is the standard of review *ab initio*, would it be appropriate for the trial court to grant a summary judgment motion on exculpation grounds in favor of an independent director whose conduct clearly involves, at most, a breach of the duty of care?

[W]hen entire fairness is the applicable standard of judicial review, this Court has held that injury or damages becomes a proper focus only *after* a transaction is determined *not* to be entirely fair. *A fortiori,* the exculpatory effect of a Section 102(b)(7) provision only becomes a proper focus of judi-cial scrutiny after the directors' potential personal liability for the payment of monetary damages has been established. Accordingly, although a Section 102(b)(7) charter provision may provide exculpation for directors against the payment of monetary damages that is attributed exclusively to violating the duty of care, even in a transaction that requires the entire fairness review standard *ab initio,* it cannot eliminate an entire fairness analysis by the Court of Chancery.

Emerald Partners v. Berlin, 787 A.2d 85, 93 (Del. 2001).

---

193. $27.80 per share is equal to the difference between the fair value of ECM on the merger date ($38.05 per share) and the merger price paid to the ECM minority shareholders ($10.25 per share).

If the Court of Chancery determines that [a] transaction was entirely fair, the director defendants have no liability for monetary damages. The Court of Chancery should address the Section 102(b)(7) charter provision only if it makes a determination that the challenged transaction was not entirely fair. The director defendants' Section 102(b)(7) request for exculpation must then be examined in the context of the completed judicial analysis that resulted in a finding of unfairness. The director defendants can avoid personal liability for paying monetary damages only if they have established that their failure to withstand an entire fairness analysis is exclusively attributable to a violation of the duty of care.

Id. at 98. Was this procedure followed in *Emerging Communications*?

PROBLEM 8-8

Assume a case with facts identical to those in *Emerging Communications*, except that Prosser owns (through a wholly owned company) roughly 20 percent of ECM's stock.

(a) How, if at all, would that change in facts affect the proceedings or outcome?

(b) Assume, additionally, that the governing law is the MBCA; would appraisal now be the exclusive remedy available to disgruntled shareholders?

PROBLEM 8-9

Assume facts identical to those in Smith v. Van Gorkom, page 331, supra, except that:

1. All dates in the case are changed by adding 30 years (for example, for purposes of this problem, the special meeting of the Trans Union board at which the merger was first approved, occurs on September 20, 2010, and the stockholder vote occurs on February 10, 2011).

2. Trans Union's certificate of incorporation contains a provision exculpating its directors to the maximum extent allowed by the Delaware General Corporation Law.

3. In addition to being a social acquaintance of Jay Pritzker, Van Gorkom has been a director of Marmon (New T's parent) for 15 years.

4. On September 18, 2010, Pritzker agreed to give Van Gorkom 5 percent of the stock in New T as a finder's fee upon the successful consummation of the merger of Trans Union and New T; Van Gorkom orally disclosed his contingent interest in New T at the September 20 meeting of the Trans Union board.

5. Immediately after the consummation of the merger, two Trans Union shareholders filed a class action alleging breaches of fiduciary duty and seeking to recover rescissory damages from Van Gorkom and the directors of Trans Union.

What result if, after pretrial discovery is completed, the defendants file a motion for summary judgment based on the exculpation provision contained in Trans Union's certificate of incorporation? Assume that the case goes to trial, and the directors are unable to carry their burden of proving the entire fairness of the merger. Will the exculpation provision prevent an award of damages against the directors?

4. The Interaction of Planners and Lawmakers in the Evolution of Cash-Out Merger Law

Weinberger represented a sharp change in the judicial approach to the cash-out merger, a then relatively new phenomenon. It also represented but one move in an intricate and ongoing dance whose "partners" are some of the nation's most creative and effective lawyers and judges. In this dance, judges and lawyers take the lead in turns. Lawyers structure cash-out merger transactions with an eye to minimizing the potential for costly litigation and judicial review. In so doing, planners are alert to the "rules of the road" that judges have created in earlier opinions and to the paths left open or closed by those opinions. Subsequently, judges take the lead, as they review deals structures, and, on occasion seek to shape and change how deals will be structured in the future. Lawyers react to changes in the planning environment, occasionally with new deal innovations, and judges then respond to those innovations, and so the never-ending interactive dance continues. The material in this section provides a clear lens through which to view this dance and to develop an appreciation for the role effective lawyers and judges play in corporate transactions and the production of value-maximizing cash-out merger law. You will see that this dance involves a back and forth between lawyers and judges concerning the judicial-review-minimizing effect of: (1) traditional "cleansing devices" (such as a majority-of-the-minority-shareholders approval condition or use of independent board committees); and (2) the ramifications on judicial review of structuring cash-out deals as mergers (requiring corporate action) or, instead, as tender offers (involving direct dealing between the controlling and minority shareholders), followed by a short-form merger.

As to the effect of cleansing devices, *Weinberger* is the starting point, but it raised more questions than it answered. Prior to *Weinberger*, planners knew that a cash-out merger must meet both the business purpose and entire fairness tests. The *Weinberger* planners used a minority-shareholder-approval condition in hopes of satisfying their fiduciary duty. The *Weinberger* court did provide some incentives for use of such a structure: the business purpose test was eliminated and the use of a minority-shareholder-approval condition would thereafter give rise to a shift in the burden of persuasion on the issue of whether the cash-out merger satisfied the controlling shareholder's entire fairness obligation.

Weinberger's famous footnote 7, encouraged use of a second cleansing device—an independent negotiating committee—without clarifying the effect of such use on the level of judicial review:

> Although perfection is not possible, or expected, the result here could have been entirely different if UOP had appointed an independent negotiating committee of its outside directors to deal with Signal at arm's length. Since fairness in this context can be equated to conduct by a theoretical, wholly independent, board of directors acting upon the matter before them, it is unfortunate that this course apparently was neither considered nor pursued. Particularly in a parent-subsidiary context, a showing that the action taken was as though each of the contending parties had in fact exerted its bargaining power against the other at arm's length is strong evidence that the transaction meets the test of fairness.[2]

---

2. Weinberger v. UOP, 457 A.2d at 713 (supra, Casebook page 728) (internal citations omitted).

Thereafter some Chancery Court decisions suggested that use of an independent negotiating committee should result in a shift in the standard of review from entire fairness to the business judgment rule. But in Kahn v. Lynch, Communication, Inc., 638 A.2d 1110 (Del. 1984), the Delaware Supreme Court dashed these hopes—use of an independent negotiating committee could yield no more than a shift in the burden of persuasion. The court also adopted a clear rationale for the inviolability of the entire fairness standard of review.

> Parent subsidiary mergers, unlike stock options, are proposed by a party that controls, and will continue to control, the corporation, whether or not the minority stockholders vote to approve or reject the transaction. The controlling stockholder relationship has the potential to influence, however subtly, the vote of [ratifying] minority stockholders in a manner that is not likely to occur in a transaction with a noncontrolling party.
>
> Even where no coercion is intended, shareholders voting on a parent subsidiary merger might perceive that their disapproval could risk retaliation of some kind by the controlling stockholder. For example, the controlling stockholder might decide to stop dividend payments or to effect a subsequent cash out merger at a less favorable price, for which the remedy would be time consuming and costly litigation. At the very least, the potential for that perception, and its possible impact upon a shareholder vote, could never be fully eliminated. Consequently, in a merger between the corporation and its controlling stockholder—even one negotiated by disinterested, independent directors—no court could be certain whether the transaction terms fully approximate what truly independent parties would have achieved in an arm's length negotiation. Given that uncertainty, a court might well conclude that even minority shareholders who have ratified a . . . merger need procedural protections beyond those afforded by full disclosure of all material facts. One way to provide such protections would be to adhere to the more stringent entire fairness standard of judicial review.

Id. at 1116-1117.

In emphasizing the inviolability of the entire fairness standard of review, the *Lynch* court was unequivocal—"this Court holds that the *exclusive* standard of judicial review in examining the propriety of an interested cash-out merger transaction by a controlling or dominating shareholder is entire fairness." Id. at 1117 (emphasis added by authors). Thus, after *Lynch*, planners' options in carrying out a cash-out merger focused on how best to survive an entire fairness challenge. These options widened substantially in 2001 with the Delaware Supreme Court's *Glassman* decision, excerpted above (at page 754).

This brings us to the second contextual focus of this section—the evolution of an alternative cash-out deal structure. As you will recall, *Glassman* held that Delaware's short form merger statute exempts those mergers from Lynch's uncompromising requirements. As the *Glassman* court stated, controlling shareholders "are not required to establish entire fairness in a short-form merger," and, "absent fraud or illegality, appraisal is the exclusive remedy available to a minority stockholder who objects to a short-form merger . . ."[3] *Glassman* opened the door for planners to experiment with a new transactional structure—commonly called a *Siliconix* transaction—that combined a first step tender offer to obtain 90 percent voting control, followed by a short-form merger to cash-out remaining minority shares.

_____

3. Id.

To understand the impetus for the *Siliconix* transaction, we need to introduce you briefly to the tender offer, which we will examine in detail in Chapter 9. For now it is enough to understand the following about controlling shareholder tender offers. In essence, such tender offers involve a direct transaction between the controlling shareholder and the minority shareholders whose shares the controller seeks to acquire. The controller initiates the potential transaction by publicly offering to buy a specified number of shares from the minority shareholders on specified terms. Each minority shareholder is free to accept or reject the offer; acceptance is accomplished by tendering shares to the controlling shareholder in the manner specified in the offering.

Because a tender offer, by itself, cannot accomplish the cash-out of all minority shareholders (as would happen with a merger where approval by a majority subjects all shareholders to the merger terms), and because the tender offer does not put the controlling shareholder directly on both sides of the transaction, as would be the case in a *Lynch* transaction, it can be argued that controlling shareholder tender offers should not be subjected to the same strict fiduciary standards that apply to *Lynch* transactions. But, what if a tender offer is immediately followed by a short-form merger, accomplishing the same result as if the cash-out had taken place via a one-step *Lynch* transaction? Should not such a transaction be reviewed for entire fairness?

In the *Siliconix* case, which gives the *Siliconix* transaction form its name, Vice Chancellor Noble opined that "as a general principle, our law holds that a controlling shareholder extending an offer for minority-held shares in the controlled corporation is under no obligation, absent evidence that material information about the offer has been withheld or misrepresented or that the offer is coercive in some significant way, to offer any particular price for the minority-held stock."[4] Following inexorably from this determination, Noble further opined that "unless coercion or disclosure violations can be shown, no defendant has the duty to demonstrate the entire fairness of [a first step tender offer].[5] Because *Glassman* insulates the second step from entire fairness review, *Siliconix* transactions became an attractive alternative to *Lynch* transactions, at least from the controlling shareholder's point of view.

In the following case, Chancellor Strine examines the landscape created by *Lynch* and *Siliconix* and suggests ways in which corporation law might evolve to eliminate or lessen the seemingly unjustifiable disparities. He also provides a detailed look at how Delaware law shapes the incentives of planners and lawyers in the structuring and review of cash-out deals. As you read this opinion, be alert to the evolutionary dance between planners and lawmakers that is so central to the on-going creation of American corporation law.

---

4. In re Siliconix Inc. Shareholders Litigation, 2001 WL 716787 (Del. Ch.) at 7.
5. Id.

In re Cox Communications, Inc.
Shareholders Litigation
Delaware Court of Chancery, 2005
879 A.2d 604

OPINION

STRINE, VICE CHANCELLOR. . . .

II. FACTUAL BACKGROUND

Cox is one of the nation's largest broadband communications companies, with a particularly strong cable television franchise. Throughout its history, the eponymous Cox has been controlled by its founding family, the Coxes. At various times, the Family has found it convenient to take Cox public, in order to raise money from the public capital markets. At other times, the Family has found it preferable to run Cox as a private company.

As of the summer of 2004, Cox was a public company, whose shares were listed on the New York Stock Exchange. The Cox Family controlled 74% of Cox's voting power. By summer 2004, the Family decided that it would be in its best interest to acquire the remaining shares of Cox that it did not own—some 245.5 million shares—and to take Cox private again. This idea was broached with top management of Cox by Family representatives on the Cox board, including the Chairman James C. Kennedy. On August 1, 2004, a Cox board meeting was held at which the Family previewed its intention to offer to pay $32 per share as an initial bid in a merger transaction whereby the Family would acquire all of the public shares of Cox (the "Proposal"). In a letter that followed the meeting, the Family made clear that it expected that Cox would form a special committee of independent Cox directors (the "Special Committee") to respond to and negotiate its Proposal. Indeed, the Proposal specifically required approval by the Special Committee. The Family did not threaten to change the board in order to pursue a merger if the Special Committee did not find favor with its Proposal. But the Family did state that it would not sell its Cox shares or support a sale of Cox to a third party.

At 4:06 a.m. on the next morning, August 2, the Proposal was announced publicly before the markets opened. The Proposal set in course two separate strands of activity. One involved the formation and start of work by the Special Committee. The other involved a race to the courthouse by various plaintiffs. I describe the latter activity first because it took place largely without any consideration of what the Special Committee was planning to do. After describing the initial jockeying among the plaintiffs, I will return to discuss the key events that led to an actual transaction between the Family and Cox, and the settlement of this litigation.

A. THE PLAINTIFFS RUSH TO COURT TO CHALLENGE THE NEGOTIABLE PROPOSAL

Beginning at 8:36 a.m. on August 2, and continuing throughout the day, a flurry of hastily drafted complaints were filed with this court. The first of the complaints consisted of paragraphs cobbled together from public documents, and rested on the core premises that Cox was poised for growth, that the Family's Proposal undervalued the company, that the offer was timed to allow the Family to reap for itself Cox's expected profits from heavy capital investments made in recent years, and that the directors of Cox were acquiescing to the Family's wishes. At 9:28 a.m., the Abbey Gardy firm, which is lead counsel in this action, filed its initial complaint, the second complaint filed that morning. That complaint was even less meaty than the first filed complaint. It is exemplary of hastily-filed, first-day complaints that serve no purpose other than for a particular law firm and its client to get into the medal round of the filing speed (also formerly known as the lead counsel selection) Olympics. The complaint's allegations were entirely boilerplate, with no particular relevance to the situation facing Cox. Most notably, the complaint's strained accusations of wrongdoing reflected, but did not maturely and thoughtfully confront, the reality that the Family's Proposal was just that, a proposal, subject to the expected evaluation of a Special Committee of independent directors, which would soon be formed and have the chance to hire advisors.

By the end of the day, six complaints of this ilk were filed in this court. . . .

A food fight then ensued among the plaintiffs' firms for lead counsel status. The Prickett Jones firm filed motions to expedite and to consolidate the cases under a committee structure it would lead. The rest of the filing plaintiffs lined up behind Abbey Gardy. The fight was resolved at a hearing on August 24, and confirmed in an order dated August 30, in which the court determined that Abbey Gardy would be lead counsel. . . .

The court largely denied the motion to expedite, for the obvious reason that there was as yet no transaction to enjoin. The only thing on the table was a Proposal by the Family that was subject to ongoing examination and negotiation by the Cox board through its Special Committee. . . .

As it turns out, the denial of the motion to expedite was the last substantial activity that would occur in the litigation challenging the Proposal until the consideration of the settlement itself. All the important events were transpiring on the business front, even those that involved the plaintiffs themselves. I therefore describe the course of those events next.

B.   GETTING TO A DEAL AND A SETTLEMENT: A TALE OF TWO NEGOTIATION PATHS LEADING TO THE SAME PLACE AT THE SAME TIME

After the public announcement of the Proposal, the Cox board formed the Special Committee as anticipated in the Family's Proposal. It was comprised of three Cox directors who were not employees or officers of Cox, or otherwise affiliates of the Family, including Janet M. Clarke who was the Chairwoman. The board resolution creating the Special Committee specifically stated that the Cox board would not authorize or recommend any transaction with the Family unless the transaction was recommended to the full board by the Special Committee.

On August 5, 2004, the Special Committee selected Fried, Frank, Harris, Shriver & Jacobson LLP as its legal counsel. On August 16, the Special Committee retained

Goldman, Sachs & Co. as its financial advisor. After that, the Special Committee, with the aid of its advisors, gathered public and non-public financial information about Cox and its prospects, including non-public projections of the company's future performance. The Special Committee did so for the evident purposes of considering the attractiveness of Cox's opening bid and determining how to respond to that bid. During this stage, the Special Committee communicated with representatives of the Family to understand the basis for the Proposal and to hear their views about value. Goldman Sachs used this input and other information to develop valuation information to help its clients develop a bargaining position.

By late September, the Special Committee had worked with Goldman Sachs to develop a presentation to the Family's financial advisors. That presentation was designed to impress upon the Family the Special Committee's view that Cox had a bright future and should be valued much higher than the Proposal's $32 per share price. . . . After the meeting with the financial advisors, Fried Frank met with the Family's legal advisors and expressed the Special Committee's desire that any merger or tender offer transaction be subject to a non-waivable majority of minority approval condition or "Minority Approval Condition."

On October 4, 2004, the Special Committee initiated the beginning of real negotiations by sending a letter to the Family unanimously rejecting the $32 price as unacceptable. Various rounds of discussions were had, at which the Family's and the Special Committee's financial advisors jousted over value. On October 11, the Family raised its bid to $33.50 per share and hinted that this might be its final bid. The next day, the Special Committee communicated to the Family that if the $33.50 bid was the Family's final bid, it would be rejected, and if that bid was intended to lead to a deal at $35.00, then the Family should know that the Special Committee would reject that price as well.

By this time, the plaintiffs in this case, through their lead counsel, Arthur N. Abbey of Abbey Gardy, had been invited into the negotiation dance by the Family's litigation counsel, Kevin G. Abrams of Richards Layton & Finger, but on a separate track from the Special Committee. On October 12, the plaintiffs' counsel and their financial advisor, Richard L. Smithline, met with the financial and legal advisors for the Family. Smithline presented valuation materials designed to support the plaintiffs' position that the Family should raise its bid to at least $38 per share. The plaintiffs were not informed, apparently, that the Family had already told the Special Committee that it was prepared to raise its bid to $33.50.

This established a pattern. The Special Committee dealt with the Family in a direct manner: Clarke had direct contact with the Family's key representative, Kennedy, as well as through communications between the Special Committee's advisors and the Family's advisors. By contrast, the plaintiffs, as might be expected, dealt exclusively with litigation counsel for the Family, aside from the one meeting at which the plaintiffs' financial advisors were given the opportunity to make a presentation to the Family's financial advisors. Litigation counsel for the Family decided what, if any, information the plaintiffs would be told about the bargaining dynamic between the Special Committee and the Family.

Consistent with this pattern, on October 12, Kennedy called Clarke and told her that the Family would withdraw its $33.50 offer unless an in-person meeting between principals for the Family and the Special Committee members themselves resulted in an agreement. It was eventually agreed that this meeting would occur on October 15.

Meanwhile, on October 13, Abrams told Abbey that the Family might raise its offer to $33.50 and might agree to a majority of the minority condition. Later that day, Abbey told Abrams that the plaintiffs would accept a settlement at $37 per share with a Minority Approval Condition.

On October 15, Kennedy and one of his top subordinates for the Family's Holding Company met with the Special Committee. No advisors were present. After some discussion, Kennedy indicated that the Family might raise its offer to $34 per share. After even more talk, Kennedy signaled a willingness to offer $34.50 with the proviso that if the Special Committee did not accept that price, the Family would cease consideration of taking Cox private.

The Special Committee adjourned to caucus with their advisors. Upon their return, Clarke told Kennedy that the Special Committee would not recommend a price lower than $35.25 per share. Kennedy responded that if that was the Special Committee's position, the Family would withdraw its Proposal.

The Special Committee then caucused again with its advisors. Clarke was empowered to negotiate the best obtainable price, subject to a confirming opinion as to financial fairness by Goldman Sachs, agreement to a Minority Approval Condition, settlement of this litigation, and negotiation of a merger agreement.

Clarke met with Kennedy later that day. She said the Special Committee would accept a deal at $35 per share. Naturally, having framed the bidding this way, Clarke opened the door to Kennedy offering to split the difference between his previous $34.50 overture and her $35 price. Kennedy did so and Clarke agreed that the Special Committee would recommend that $34.75 per share price, subject to the conditions described.

After that occurred, Abrams was informed of the state of play. He called Abbey and told him that the Family's "best and final offer" was $34.75 per share and that the Family would not settle this case at any higher price. Abbey remembers being told that this was the Family's "best and absolutely final offer." I have little doubt that, without being explicitly told so, Abbey knew that this meant that the Family had likely reached the end of its bargaining process with the Special Committee. As Abrams stated in court, he told Abbey that the Family was "prepared to proceed with this transaction without you." As Abrams also noted, "[Mr. Abbey] knows that when I say best and final, that's it, and he was not going to get an additional penny from me." In other words, Abbey was told that the proverbial "train was leaving the station."

Abbey told Abrams that he would consider the offer in consultation with the plaintiffs' financial advisor but that the deal would also have to include a Minority Approval Condition. The next morning Abbey orally agreed to these terms. Abrams promptly informed the Special Committee's lawyers and the transactional counsel for the Family that the litigation was settled in principle and that a formal Memorandum of Understanding would be prepared.

As of that time, the Special Committee's financial advisors were finalizing their analysis in advance of determining whether they could deliver a fairness opinion. The Special Committee and the Family were also negotiating the terms of the actual merger agreement.

By October 18, the Special Committee and the Family reached accord on a final merger contract. The Special Committee met and received a favorable fairness presentation from Goldman Sachs. After receiving that, the Special Committee unanimously recommended the merger to the full board. At a later meeting, the full Cox board also voted to approve the deal based upon the recommendation of the Special Committee.

That same day, Abrams and Abbey reached agreement on an MOU stating that the Family acknowledged that the desirability of settling this action and the efforts of the plaintiffs' counsel in this action were causal factors that led to the Family increasing its bid to $34.75, and agreeing to the Minority Approval Condition. A similar MOU was also executed with a group of plaintiffs who had filed similar actions in Georgia. The negotiations involving those plaintiffs are not described in the record before me in any detail.

The next day, October 19, Cox and the Family signed the merger agreement.

C.   THE SETTLEMENT IS PRESENTED TO THE COURT FOR APPROVAL AND THE MERGER CLOSES

The parties moved promptly to complete confirmatory discovery and negotiate a final stipulation of settlement. Only after that was done, they swear, was there any discussion of the amount of attorneys fees the plaintiffs' counsel would seek.

In the attorneys' fee negotiations, the Family eventually agreed not to oppose a fee request of up to $4.95 million. Separately, the Family forged a deal by which it agreed not to oppose a fee request from the Georgia plaintiffs of more than $1.25 million. In both cases, the Family agreed to pay whatever fee was awarded rather than to require that any fee award be withheld from the merger consideration to be paid to the public stockholders of Cox. According to the plaintiffs' counsel Arthur Abbey, he would have sought a fee much larger than $4.95 million had the defendants refused to agree not to oppose a fee request up to that amount.

The Stipulation of Settlement was presented to the court on November 10, 2004. Notice was promptly issued to the public stockholders on November 24, 2004. By that time, the Family had already commenced their tender offer at $34.75 per share.

On December 2, 2004, the tender offer expired. Approximately 189.7 million of Cox's 245.5 million public shares were tendered, satisfying the Minority Approval Condition and giving the Family over 90% of the Cox shares. On December 8, 2004, a back end, short-form merger was executed taking Cox private.

III.   OBJECTORS TO THE PLAINTIFFS' FEE EMERGE

When the deadline to object to the proposed settlement expired, no objections to the settlement itself had been filed. But an objection was made to the plaintiffs' counsel request for an award of attorneys' fees. . . . The points that the objectors make have less to do with this case in particular, and more to do with concerns about how the common law rules that Delaware uses to govern mergers with controlling stockholders create inefficient incentives for plaintiffs' lawyers and corporate defense counsel, leading to lawsuits that exist, in [the objectors'] view, almost entirely as a vehicle for the payment of attorneys' fees and the entry of a judgment of the court providing the defendants with a broad release from any future lawsuits relating to the underlying transactions. . . .

IV.   LEGAL ANALYSIS

A.   THE DELAWARE LAW OF MERGERS WITH CONTROLLING STOCKHOLDERS . . .

In the important case of Kahn v. Lynch Communication, Inc.,[26] the Delaware Supreme Court . . . held that regardless of the procedural protections employed, a merger with a controlling stockholder would always be subject to the entire fairness standard. . . . But, in order to encourage the use of procedural devices such as special committees and Minority Approval Conditions that tended to encourage fair pricing, the Court did give transactional proponents a modest procedural benefit—the shifting of the burden of persuasion on the ultimate issue of fairness to the plaintiffs—if the transaction proponents proved, in a factually intensive way, that the procedural devices had, in fact, operated with integrity. . . .

B.   A TEMPERED DESCRIPTION OF THE OBJECTORS' CRITICISM OF THE INCENTIVE EFFECTS CREATED BY *LYNCH*

The incentive system that *Lynch* created for plaintiffs' lawyers is its most problematic feature . . . and the consequence that motivates the objectors' contentions here. After *Lynch,* there arose a pattern of which this case is simply one of the latest examples. . . .

As the objectors point out and this court has often noted in settlement hearings regarding these kind of cases in the past, the ritualistic nature of a process almost invariably resulting in the simultaneous bliss of three parties—the plaintiffs' lawyers, the special committee, and the controlling stockholders—is a jurisprudential triumph of an odd form of tantra. I say invariably because the record contains a shocking omission—the inability of the plaintiffs, despite their production of expert affidavits, to point to one instance in the precise context of a case of this kind (i.e., cases started by attacks on negotiable going-private proposals) of the plaintiffs' lawyers refusing to settle once a special committee has agreed on price with a controller.

That bears repeating. In no instance has there been a situation when the controller's lawyer told the plaintiffs' lawyer this is my best and final offer and received the answer, "sign up your deal with the special committee, and we'll meet you in the Chancellor's office for the scheduling conference on our motion to expedite." Rather, in every instance, the plaintiffs' lawyers have concluded that the price obtained by the

---

26. 638 A.2d 1110 (Del. 1994).

special committee was sufficiently attractive, that the acceptance of a settlement at that price was warranted.[39]

The objectors use this admittedly material fact to buttress another argument they make about *Lynch.* That argument, which is again something members of this court have grasped for some time, rests in the ease for the plaintiffs' lawyers of achieving "success" in this ritual. When a controlling stockholder announces a "proposal" to negotiate a going private merger, the controller is, like any bidder, very unlikely to present his full reserve price as its opening bid. Moreover, given the nature of *Lynch* and its progeny, and their emphasis on the effectiveness of the special committee as a bargaining agent, the controller knows, and special committee members will demand, that real price negotiations proceed after the opening bid, and that those negotiations will almost certainly result in any consummated deal occurring at a higher price.

For plaintiffs' lawyers, the incentives are obvious.[40] By suing on the proposal, the plaintiffs' lawyers can claim that they are responsible, in part, for price increases in a deal context in which price increases are overwhelmingly likely to occur. Added to this incentive is the fact that the plaintiffs' lawyers know that the *Lynch* standard gives them the ability, on bare satisfaction of notice pleading standards and Rule 11, to defeat a motion to dismiss addressed to any complaint challenging an actual merger agreement with a special committee, even one conditioned on Minority Approval. Because of this ability, the plaintiffs' claims always have settlement value because of the costs of discovery and time to the defendants. Add to this another important ingredient, which is that once a special committee has negotiated a material price increase with the aid of well-regarded financial and legal advisors, the plaintiffs' lawyers can contend with a straight-face that it was better to help get the price up to where it ended than to risk that the controller would abandon the deal. Abandonment of the deal, the plaintiffs' lawyers will say with accuracy, will result in the company's stock price falling back to its pre-proposal level, which is always materially lower as it does not reflect the anticipation of a premium-generating going private transaction. Having vigorously aided the special committee to get into the range of fairness and having no reason to suspect that the special committee was disloyal to its mission, the plaintiffs' lawyers can say, in plausible good faith, that it was better for the class to take this improved bid, which is now well within the range of fairness, rather than to risk abandonment of the transaction. Moreover, for those stockholders who wish to challenge the price, appraisal still remains an option.

C. *SILICONIX:* ANOTHER ROAD TO GOING PRIVATE IS PAVED

Of course, things cannot be quite that simple. And they are not. To describe why, I must add more jurisprudential context and then bring in the arguments raised by the plaintiffs' experts.

---

39. See Elliott J. Weiss & Lawrence J. White, "File Early, Then Free Ride: How Delaware Law (Mis) Shapes Shareholder Class Actions," 57 Vand. L. Rev. 1797, 1820 & n. 84, 1833-34 (2004).

40. Cf. Weiss & White, 57 Vand. L. Rev. at 1857 n. 183 (stating that the rule of *Lynch* "appears to have had the effect of encouraging plaintiffs' attorneys to settle cases challenging squeeze outs, largely without regard to whether the merger terms agreed to by an SNC [special negotiating committee] are entirely fair").

Under Delaware law, the doctrine of independent legal significance exists. That doctrine permits corporations to take, if the DGCL permits it, a variety of transactional routes to the same destination. For years, there had existed a strand of Delaware law that stated that a controlling stockholder who made a tender offer—as opposed to a merger proposal—to acquire the rest of the controlled company's shares had no duty to offer a fair price. So long as the controller did not actually coerce the minority stockholders or commit a disclosure violation, its tender offer was immune from equitable intervention for breach of fiduciary duty. [T]his basic proposition . . . was reaffirmed in *Solomon v. Pathe Communications Corp.*[45] less than two years after *Lynch* was decided. In the tender offer context, the doctrine of implicit coercion that *Lynch* is premised upon was unrecognized. . . .

The opportunity that the tender offer line of cases presented for transactional planners interested in deal certainty was tempered, however, by the unsettled nature of a related question . . . whether the short-form merger would be subject to the *Lynch* standard. In *In re Unocal Exploration Corp. Shareholders Litigation*[46] that uncertainty was resolved. . . . In that transactional context, stockholders who believed that the price was unfair had an exclusive remedy: appraisal.

After *Unocal Exploration* was decided by this court, transactional lawyers put together the *Solomon* strand of authority with that new certainty and generated a new, and less negotiation- and litigation-intensive route to going private: a front tender offer designed to get the controller 90% of the shares, coupled with a back-end short-form merger. In subsequent cases in this Court, it was held that this method of transaction—which came to be known by the first written decision addressing it—*In re Siliconix Inc. Shareholders Litigation*[47]—did not trigger entire fairness review so long as the offer was not actually coercive and there was full disclosure. In the later case of *Pure Resources*,[48] this Court held that the mere fact that the controller had taken the *Siliconix* route did not relieve it of fiduciary duties. Although those duties did not include a duty to pay a fair price, the court held that a *Siliconix* transaction could be subject to fairness review to protect the minority unless:

(i) the offer is subject to a nonwaivable majority of the minority tender condition,

(ii) the controlling shareholder commits to consummate a short-form merger promptly after increasing its holdings above ninety percent,

(iii) the controlling shareholder "has made no retributive threats," and

(iv) the independent directors are given complete discretion and sufficient time "to react to the tender offer, by (at the very least) hiring their own advisors," providing a recommendation to the non-controlling shareholders, and disclosing adequate information to allow the non-controlling shareholders an opportunity for informed decision making. . . .

Since *Siliconix* was decided, controllers have therefore had two different transactional methods to choose between in attempting to go private. One can imagine various reasons why a controller might prefer one route or the other, depending on variables like the

---

45. 672 A.2d 35, 39 (Del. 1996).

46. 793 A.2d 329 (Del. Ch. 2000), aff'd, 777 A.2d 242 (Del. 2001).

47. 2001 WL 716787 (Del. Ch. June 19, 2001).

48. 808 A.2d 421 (Del. Ch. 2002).

controller's ownership stake, the extent of the public float, the presence of big holders, the desire for certainty and closure, and which route might yield the best price for it. For example, the further a controller was from 90% to begin with, the more attractive the merger route might be, and vice versa, simply for efficiency reasons in both cases.

D.   THE PLAINTIFFS' EXPERT COUNTER ATTACK

For present purposes, however, what is relevant is the empirical evidence that the plaintiffs have submitted to counter the objectors' position. To confront the scholarly work of Weiss and White, who are of the view that litigation of this kind is of no material benefit to minority stockholders, the plaintiffs have submitted an affidavit from Professor Guhan Subramanian of the Harvard Law School.

Subramanian makes two major arguments. First, Subramanian cites to his own recent scholarly studies to support his view that the *Lynch* form of transaction results, on average, in going private transactions that pay the minority a higher premium in comparison to the pre-announcement market price than do *Siliconix* deals. Second, Subramanian attempts to show that the filing of lawsuits under *Lynch* challenging going private merger proposals by controlling stockholders are a material factor in producing these more favorable results. . . .

In recent work, Professor Subramanian studied the prices at which going-private transactions occurred since *Siliconix,* breaking them down between merger, or *Lynch,* transactions and tender offer, or *Siliconix,* transactions. Subramanian finds that the final premium paid over the pre-announcement market price was on average higher in *Lynch* deals than *Siliconix* deals, and that the difference was statistically significant.[52] Likewise, he finds that controllers, on average, increase their opening bids more when pursuing a *Lynch* merger than a *Siliconix* tender offer and that the difference is statistically significant. Subramanian, after controlling for other possible factors, concludes that these outcomes differ primarily because of the stronger bargaining hand given to the special committee in the *Lynch* context versus the *Siliconix* context. . . .

Subramanian infers that the controller can pay a lower price in the *Siliconix* context because the weaker hand of the special committee and plaintiffs, combined, will enable controllers to keep more nickels in their pockets and still close deals. For that reason, Subramanian thinks Lynch, and the role that it provides to plaintiffs as a watchdog, "polices the worst control shareholder deals, and benefits target company shareholders. . . ."[54]

E.   THE COURT'S DISTILLATION OF THE EXPERT INPUT

Where does this leave us? . . .

First, the record supports the proposition that *Lynch* deals tend to generate higher final premiums than *Siliconix* deals. One would suspect that this would be so for several

---

52. Subramanian, Post-Siliconix Freeze-Outs: Theory & Evidence, at Table 1 (Working Draft, Jan. 2005).

54. Subramanian Aff. ¶31 (quoting Robert B. Thompson & Randall S. Thomas, The New Look of Shareholder Litigation: Acquisition Oriented Class Actions, 57 Vand. L. Rev. 133, 202 (2004)).

reasons, including: 1) the greater leverage that the form of transaction gives to special committees; 2) the fact that the governing standard of review always gives the plaintiffs settlement value; 3) the reality that signing up a merger when the votes are locked up results in the greatest certainty for a controller; and 4) signing up a merger with a special committee and a settlement with plaintiffs' lawyers provides not only deal certainty, but a broad release and the most effective discouragement of appraisal claims. One cannot tell, of course, how important each of them is as a factor, but one awkward fact strongly suggests that the threat of bare knuckles litigation over fairness is not as important as the special committee's role as a negotiating force.

That awkward fact is the absence of evidence that "traditional" plaintiffs' lawyers, who attacked going private proposals by controllers, have ever refused to settle once they have received the signal that the defendants have put on the table their best and final offer—i.e., an offer that is acceptable to the special committee. There are examples of when the plaintiffs have settled at a lower price than the special committee demanded, but no examples of when the iron fist of the plaintiffs' bar demanded more than the velvet glove of the special committee. The plaintiffs' bar would say, of course, this is because they did such a good job in each case that the price concessions they helped the special committee extract were of such inarguable fairness that it would been silly to fight on.

Perhaps what can be most charitably said is that the pendency of litigation and the theoretical threat that the plaintiffs will press on provides special committee members with additional clout that they wield to get good results, and that gives lawyers for controllers leverage to get their clients to pay a higher price to ensure deal closure and the utmost reduction of litigation risk.[59]

Second, there is much that remains to be explored about the actual price differences between *Lynch* and *Siliconix* deals. . . .

Third, litigation under *Lynch* never seems to involve actual litigation conflict if the lawsuit begins with a suit attacking a negotiable proposal. These cases almost invariably settle or are dismissed voluntarily by the plaintiffs. In those instances when there is actual litigation conflict in an "attack" on a going private transaction that has occurred because the complaint actually sought to stop a real transaction—an agreed-upon merger or a tender offer that was actively being pressed.[61] In those situations, it is also much more likely that a plaintiff with a large stake who has hired a non-traditional law firm will mount a challenge. The *Pure Resources* and *Emerging Communications* transactions are good examples of these realities. Indeed, in *Emerging Communications,* the original plaintiffs pressed forward with a settlement after confirmatory discovery that would have resulted in a final price of $10.25 binding those stockholders who did not seek appraisal to the same price negotiated by the special committee. Only after

---

59. The affidavit filed by John H. Simpson (a former investment banker who represented buyers and special committees in going private transactions) on the plaintiffs' behalf makes this argument in a bit more aggressive form, stating that the pendency of litigation acts as a cop on the scene, keeping the controller and special committee honest and generating a higher deal price.

61. In an earlier hearing in this case, the Family's counsel, Kevin Abrams, noted that in a *Lynch* setting "I can't run the risk . . . of running a quasi-appraisal on behalf of a class consisting of hundreds of millions of shares when there is a litigable question over fair value." . . .

objection by a large holder represented by a very large firm that more usually represents corporate defendants than stockholders was the settlement abandoned. The ultimate result was an award of damages based on a $38.05 per share value, in a detailed opinion by Vice Chancellor (Justice) Jacobs that found glaringly obvious procedural and substantive problems with the special committee process.

Fourth, minority stockholders seem to be doing more than tolerably well under both the *Lynch* and *Siliconix* regimes. Even if premiums to market are lower in *Siliconix* transactions, the premiums paid are large in comparison to the routine, day-to-day trading prices, in which minority and liquidity discounts will be suffered. For that reason, at every settlement, the plaintiffs' lawyers say that they could not risk pushing farther, lest the controller decide not to press on and offer a deal, and the stockholders suffer the fate of continuing as owners of minority shares in a going concern. After all, events that generate liquidity for all minority stockholders at substantial premiums are usually welcomed by stockholders. . . .

V. ARE THE PLAINTIFFS ENTITLED TO AN AWARD OF ATTORNEYS' FEES AND IN WHAT AMOUNT? . . .

[Eds. note—The Court awarded attorneys' fees and expenses (though in an amount substantially less than requested) on the grounds that the attorneys' involvement likely played at least a small role in achieving the price increase negotiated by the Special Committee.]

VI. A CODA ON THE JURISPRUDENTIAL ELEPHANT IN THE CORNER

Before concluding, I feel obliged to add a coda. The present case illustrates, in my view, the need to adjust our common law of corporations to take appropriate account of the positive and negative consequences flowing from the standard of review governing going private mergers.

Lynch is a well-motivated decision that belies any contention that Delaware law blindly favors management. The incentive it creates for the use of well-functioning special committees is useful and has benefited minority stockholders. But its failure to provide any additional incentive for the use of Minority Approval Conditions—except as a settlement add-on—is less useful. Even more, by creating a standard of review that makes it impossible for a controlling stockholder to structure a going private merger in any fashion that will enable a successful attack on a complaint that alleges financial unfairness on a notice pleading basis, *Lynch* has generated perverse incentives for both defense and plaintiffs' counsel that cast doubt on the integrity of the representative litigation process. . . .

In this corner of our law, a relatively modest alteration of *Lynch* would do much to ensure . . . integrity, while continuing to provide important, and I would argue, enhanced, protections for minority stockholders. That alteration would permit the invocation of the business judgment rule for a going private merger that involved procedural protections that mirrored what is contemplated in an arms-length merger under §251—independent, disinterested director and stockholder approval. Put simply, if a controller proposed a merger, subject from inception to negotiation and approval of the merger by an independent special committee and a Minority Approval Condition, the business judgment rule should presumptively apply. In that situation, the controller and the directors of the affected company should be able to obtain dismissal of a complaint unless: 1) the plaintiffs plead particularized facts that the special committee was not independent or was not effective because of its own breach of fiduciary duty or wrongdoing by the controller (e.g., fraud on the committee); or 2) the approval of the minority stockholders was tainted by misdisclosure, or actual or structural coercion.

This alteration would promote the universal use of a transactional structure that is very favorable to minority stockholders—one that deploys an active, disinterested negotiating agent to bargain for the minority coupled with an opportunity for the minority to freely decide whether to accept or reject their agent's work product. Indeed, the plaintiffs' own expert, Professor Subramanian, supports reform of precisely this kind.[85] And *Lynch* in its current form could be retained to govern any merger in which the controller refuses to use both of these techniques from the inception of the process, allowing for the controller to proceed, get appropriate burden-shifting credit for use of special committee or a Minority Approval Condition, but remain subject to the entire fairness standard.

Importantly, this revised standard would not diminish the integrity-enforcing potential of litigation in any material way, in my view. Plaintiffs who believed that a special committee breached its fiduciary duties in agreeing to a merger would continue to have the practical ability to press a claim. . . .

This standard would also encourage the filing of claims only by plaintiffs and plaintiffs' lawyers who genuinely believed that a wrong had been committed. The chance to free ride on the expected increase in the controller's original proposal would be eliminated and therefore litigation would only be filed by those who believed that they possessed legal claims with value.[87]

Importantly, a revision along these lines would leave in place another remedial option that is viable for stockholders who believe that the ultimate price paid in a negotiated merger is unfair—appraisal. . . .

---

85. Guhan Subramanian, Fixing Freezeouts, [115 Yale L.J. 2 (2005) (Harvard Law School Olin Series Discussion Paper # 501, December 2004)] at 48 (arguing for business judgment rule treatment for controlling stockholder mergers when these conditions exist). Reform of this kind would also be consistent with the views expressed in *Pure Resources*, 808 A.2d at 444 n. 43, and *Cysive*, 836 A.2d 531 (Del. Ch. 2003), as well as by Professors Gilson and Gordon in their excellent article. Ronald J. Gilson & Jeffrey N. Gordon, Controlling Controlling Stockholders, 152 U. Pa. L. Rev. 785 (2003).

87. Weiss and White argue, with persuasive power, that stockholders with a very large stake will tend to litigate more sparingly but also more aggressively in those cases when they believe their economic interests have been injured. Weiss & White, 57 Vand. L. Rev. at 1841-45. Such stockholders have little motivation to attack mere proposals, which is why most suits attacking such proposals are brought by repeat plaintiffs with nominal stakes. Even the holdings of Abbey Gardy's client, M & R, do not reflect a very large stake, certainly not of the magnitude involved in *Emerging Communications,* a vigorously prosecuted attack on an actual merger agreement.

Of course, a revision in *Lynch* alone is arguably not complete. The plaintiffs have presented a cogent argument that the negotiating leverage wielded by special committees in mergers with controlling stockholders results in better outcomes for stockholders than does the ability of stockholders to reject a structurally non-coercive tender offer made by a controlling stockholder. The jarring doctrinal inconsistency between the equitable principles of fiduciary duty that apply to *Lynch* and *Siliconix* deals has been noted by this court before. . . .

A principled reconciliation of the two lines of authority could center on much the same solution articulated above, as Professors Gilson and Gordon have suggested in an important scholarly article.[92] In the case of a tender offer by a controlling stockholder, the controlling stockholder could be relieved of the burden of proving entire fairness if: 1) the tender offer was recommended by an independent special committee; 2) the tender offer was structurally non-coercive in the manner articulated by *Pure Resources;* and 3) there was a disclosure of all material facts. In that case, the transaction should be immune from challenge in a breach of fiduciary duty action unless the plaintiffs pled particularized facts from which it could be inferred that the special committee's recommendation was tainted by a breach of fiduciary duty or that there was a failure in disclosure. That is, an alteration on the *Lynch* line could be accompanied by a strengthening of equitable review in the *Siliconix* line. But in both cases, there would remain a strong incentive for controllers to afford stockholders the procedural protection of both a special committee with real clout and of non-coerced, fully informed approval by the minority stockholders.

As important, this incentive would enable transactional planners to know that they can structure transactions in a way that affords them the opportunity to obtain a dismissal on the complaint. In this way, the alteration brings this area of our law into harmony with the rest of Delaware corporate law that gives substantial deference to decisions made by disinterested, independent directors and approved by disinterested, non-coerced stockholders. That deference is consistent with the central notion of our law, which respects business judgments made by impartial directors and approved by unconflicted stockholders. This deference is illustrated by the landmark decision in *Aronson v. Lewis,*[94] which presumes that independent directors can impartially decide whether to cause the company to sue a controlling stockholder.

By comparison to *Aronson*, it seems a modest move to give presumptive deference to a tender offer or merger that has not only the approval of a special committee of independent directors but also the support of the disinterested stockholders themselves. And, by doing so, our common law would encourage the consistent use of the transaction structure that best protects minority stockholders while simultaneously discouraging the filing of premature lawsuits of dubious integrity and social utility.

By now, experience has proven that special committees and independent board majorities are willing to say no to controllers. Experience has also shown that disinterested stockholders, given a non-coercive choice, will reject low ball tender offers by

---

92. Ronald J. Gilson & Jeffrey N. Gordon, Controlling Controlling Stockholders, 152 U. Pa. L. Rev. 785, 827-28 (2003).

94. 473 A.2d 805 (Del. 1984) (supra, Casebook page 402).

controllers. The sociological inference of implicit coercion originated in *Citron* and accepted in *Lynch* is not one that we accept in the more difficult demand refusal setting. If both the independent directors and the disinterested stockholders are given the ability to say no and do not, ought we not presumptively assume that the transaction was fair? This is corporate law, after all, a species of commercial law involving stockholders (increasingly of the institutional investor variety) who would be well-positioned to protect themselves through diversification, the voting power that this new incentive system would invest in them, and through the potent litigation weapons that would remain in their arsenal. It is also important not to forget that they would remain shielded by the strong role that our law gives to independent directors.

The difficulty, of course, is that our courts are not presented with an opportunity to evolve the common law in this area because the incentives *Lynch* creates make a frontal challenge to the existing regime irrational for defendants. Perhaps in some modest way, the objectors have forced us to move closer to a re-examination of *Lynch*. Judicial recognition that *Lynch* suits attacking proposals to negotiate a going private merger are not meritorious when filed may embolden some controller and some special committee to ignore the filing of a prematurely filed suit, and to concentrate on negotiating a mutually acceptable and fair merger. . . .

And by recognizing that complaints attacking negotiable proposals are not meritorious and do not give rise to a presumptive claim to a fee, there is a somewhat greater possibility that some group of defendants might challenge the viability of a complaint attacking a merger negotiated by a special committee and subject to an effective Minority Approval Condition from the get-go, irrespective of *Lynch,* and ask this court to certify the standard of review question to the Supreme Court for re-examination. Easing this risk is the jurisprudential reality surfaced earlier. In *Lynch,* the argument that both special committee and an effective majority of the Minority Approval Condition should, as a tandem, justify invocation of the business judgment rule, was never presented. Therefore, it is arguable that the Supreme Court has never been asked to address the precise question that would be posed if a controller, from the inception of a transaction, made clear that its merger proposal was conditioned upon the use of both of these procedural protections, so as to most closely replicate the process by which an arms-length merger is approved under §251. . . .

NOTES AND QUESTIONS

1. At the conclusion of his "Coda on the Jurisprudential Elephant in the Corner," Chancellor Strine invites a future courageous planner to structure a *Lynch* transaction so that it is from the outset both subject to a Minority Approval Condition and in the hands of an independent negotiating committee, and, when shareholder fiduciary challenges are mounted, to assert that the appropriate standard of review is the business judgment rule. In *MFW Shareholders Litigation,* 67 A.3d 496 (2013), Chancellor Strine received the case he had invited and, not surprisingly, held that the effective use of both cleansing mechanisms results in a shift in the standard of review from entire fairness to the business judgment rule. Consider Strine's explanation for that decision.

This case thus presents, for the first time, the question of what should be the correct standard of review for mergers between a controlling stockholder and its subsidiary, when the merger is conditioned on the approval of both an independent, adequately empowered special committee that fulfills its duty of care, and the uncoerced, informed vote of a majority of the minority stockholders. . . .

A choice about our common law of corporations must therefore be made, and the court is persuaded that what is optimal for the protection of stockholders and the creation of wealth through the corporate form is adopting a form of the rule the defendants advocate. By giving controlling stockholders the opportunity to have a going private transaction reviewed under the business judgment rule, a strong incentive is created to give minority stockholders much broader access to the transactional structure that is most likely to effectively protect their interests. In fact, this incentive may make this structure the common one, which would be highly beneficial to minority stockholders. That structure, it is important to note, is critically different than a structure that uses only *one* of the procedural protections. The "or" structure does not replicate the protections of a third-party merger under the DGCL approval process, because it only requires that one, and not both, of the statutory requirements of director and stockholder approval be accomplished by impartial decisionmakers. The "both" structure, by contrast, replicates the arm's-length merger steps of the DGCL by "requir[ing] two independent approvals, which it is fair to say serve independent integrity-enforcing functions."[156]

When these two protections are established up-front, a potent tool to extract good value for the minority is established. From inception, the controlling stockholder knows that it cannot bypass the special committee's ability to say no. And, the controlling stockholder knows it cannot dangle a majority-of-the-minority vote before the special committee late in the process as a deal-closer rather than having to make a price move. From inception, the controller has had to accept that any deal agreed to by the special committee will also have to be supported by a majority of the minority stockholders. That understanding also affects the incentives of the special committee in an important way. The special committee will understand that those for whom it is bargaining will get a chance to express whether they think the special committee did a good or poor job. Although it is possible that there are independent directors who have little regard for their duties or for being perceived by their company's stockholders (and the larger network of institutional investors) as being effective at protecting public stockholders, the court thinks they are likely to be exceptional, and certainly our Supreme Court's jurisprudence does not embrace such a skeptical view. The Supreme Court has held that independent directors are presumed to be motivated to do their duty with fidelity, like most other people, and has also observed that directors have a more self-protective interest in retaining their reputations as faithful, diligent fiduciaries. The requirement that a majority of the minority approve the special committee's recommendation enhances both motivations, because most directors will want to procure a deal that their minority stockholders think is a favorable one, and virtually all will not want to suffer the reputational embarrassment of repudiation at the ballot box. That is especially so in a market where many independent directors serve on several boards, and where institutional investors and their voting advisors, such as ISS and Glass Lewis, have computer-aided memory banks available to remind them of the past record of directors when considering whether to vote for them or withhold votes at annual meetings of companies on whose boards they serve.

The premise that independent directors with the right incentives can play an effective role on behalf of minority investors is one shared by respected scholars sincerely concerned with protecting minority investors from unfair treatment by controlling stockholders. Their scholarship and empirical evidence indicates that special committees have played a valuable role in generating outcomes for minority investors in going private transactions that compare favorably with the premiums received in third-party merger transactions.

But, like these scholars, the court is aware that even impartial directors acting in good faith and with due care can sometimes come out with an outcome that minority investors themselves

---

156. *In re Cox Commc'ns, Inc. S'holders Litig.*, 879 A.2d 604, 618 (Del. Ch. 2005).

do not find favorable. Conditioning the going private transaction's consummation on a majority-of-the-minority vote deals with this problem in two important and distinct ways. The first was just described. Because a special committee in this structure knows from the get-go that its work will be subject to disapproval by the minority stockholders, the special committee has a strong incentive to get a deal that will gain their approval. And, critically, so does another key party: the controlling stockholder itself, which will want to close the deal, having sunk substantial costs into the process.

But the second is equally important. If, despite these incentives, the special committee approves a transaction that the minority investors do not like, the minority investors get to vote it down, on a full information base and without coercion. In the *Unitrin* case nearly a generation ago, our Supreme Court noted the prevalence of institutional investors in the target company's stockholder base in concluding that a proxy contest centering on the price of a takeover offer was viable, despite insiders having increased their stock ownership to 28%, stating that "[i]nstitutions are more likely than other shareholders to vote at all [and] more likely to vote against manager proposals."[163] Market developments in the score of years since have made it far easier, not harder, for stockholders to protect themselves. With the development of the internet, there is more public information than ever about various commentators', analysts', institutional investors', journalists' and others' views about the wisdom of transactions. Likewise, the internet facilitates campaigns to defeat management recommendations. Not only that, institutional investor holdings have only grown since 1994, making it easier for a blocking position of minority investors to be assembled.[164] Perhaps most important, it is difficult to look at the past generation of experience and conclude that stockholders are reluctant to express positions contrary to those espoused by company management. Stockholders have been effective in using their voting rights to adopt precatory proposals that have resulted in a sharp increase in so-called majority voting policies and a sharp decrease in structural takeover defenses. Stockholders have mounted more proxy fights, and, as important, wielded the threat of a proxy fight or a "withhold vote" campaign to secure changes in both corporate policies and the composition of corporate boards. Stockholders have voted against mergers they did not find favorable, or forced increases in price. Nor has timidity characterized stockholder behavior in companies with large blockholders or even majority stockholders; such companies still face stockholder activism in various forms, and are frequently the subject of lawsuits if stockholders suspect wrongdoing. . . . As our Supreme Court has recognized more than once, the application of fiduciary duty principles must be influenced by current corporate practices. Given the evident and growing power of modern stockholders, there seems to be little basis to doubt the fairness-assuring effectiveness of an upfront majority-of-the-minority vote condition when that condition is combined, as it was here, by a promise that the controller would not proceed with a transaction without both the approval of the special committee and the approval of a majority of the minority. Although one of the rationales identified in *Lynch* for fairness review of a going private merger with only one of the protections was that minority stockholders might be too afraid in any circumstance to vote freely, that rationale was one advanced in the context of a deal structure where the minority was expressly faced with a situation where a controller informed the special committee that it would put a lower priced offer directly to the stockholders in the intrinsically more coercive form of a tender offer. . . . The "both" structure limits coercion like this because the controller cannot end run the special committee in this way, and thus addresses the rationale advanced in *Lynch*.

2. The Chancellor's decision in *MFW Shareholders Litigation* provided planners a much stronger inducement to use the dual protective devices that the Delaware Supreme Court had previously embraced, raising uncertainty has to how his opinion

---

163. *Unitrin, Inc. v. Am. Gen. Corp.*, 651 A.2d 1361, 1382 (Del .1995) (citation and internal quotation marks omitted).

164. See . . . Matteo Tonello & Stephan Rabimov, *The 2010 Institutional Investment Report: Trends In Asset Allocation and Portfolio Composition*, Conference Bd. (2009), at 26 (showing that institutional ownership of equities in the 1,000 largest U.S. companies increased from 57% in 1994 to 69% in 2008).

would fare on appeal. The prior year, in a case where the independent negotiating committee cleansing device was found ineffective on the facts of the case, the Court had this to say about the "rewards" available for effectively using the dual cleansing devices.

The Defendants' second argument on appeal is that the Court of Chancery committed reversible error by failing to determine which party bore the burden of proof before trial. The Defendants submit that the Court of Chancery further erred by ultimately allocating the burden to the Defendants, because the Special Committee was independent, was well-functioning, and did not rely on the controlling shareholder for the information that formed the basis for its recommendation.

When a transaction involving self-dealing by a controlling shareholder is challenged, the applicable standard of judicial review is entire fairness, with the defendants having the burden of persuasion. In other words, the defendants bear the burden of proving that the transaction with the controlling stockholder was entirely fair to the minority stockholders. In the Court of Chancery and on appeal, both the Plaintiff and the Defendants agree that entire fairness is the appropriate standard of judicial review for the Merger. . . .

In *Kahn v. Lynch Communication Systems, Inc.,* this Court held that when the entire fairness standard applies, the defendants may shift the burden of persuasion by one of two means: first, they may show that the transaction was approved by a well-functioning committee of independent directors; or second, they may show that the transaction was approved by an informed vote of a majority of the minority shareholders. Nevertheless, even when an interested cash-out merger transaction receives the informed approval of a majority of minority stockholders or a well-functioning committee of independent directors, an entire fairness analysis is the only proper standard of review. Accordingly, "[r]egardless of where the burden lies, when a controlling shareholder stands on both sides of the transaction the conduct of the parties will be viewed under the more exacting standard of entire fairness as opposed to the more deferential business judgment standard."

In *Emerald Partners v. Berlin,* we noted that "[w]hen the standard of review is entire fairness, *ab initio,* director defendants can move for summary judgment on either the issue of entire fairness or the issue of burden shifting." In this case, the Defendants filed a summary judgment motion, arguing that the Special Committee process shifted the burden of persuasion under the preponderance standard to the Plaintiff. The Court of Chancery found the summary judgment record was insufficient to determine that question of burden shifting prior to trial.

Lynch and its progeny set forth what is required of an independent committee for the defendants to obtain a burden shift. In this case, the Court of Chancery recognized that, in *Kahn v. Tremont Corp.,* this Court held that "[t]o obtain the benefit of a burden shifting, the controlling shareholder must do more than establish a perfunctory special committee of outside directors." Rather, the special committee must "function in a manner which indicates that the controlling shareholder did not dictate the terms of the transaction and that the committee exercised real bargaining power 'at an arms-length.'" In this case, the Court of Chancery properly concluded that:

A close look at *Tremont* suggests that the [burden shifting] inquiry must focus on how the special committeee actually negotiated the deal—was it "well functioning"—rather than just how the committee was set up. The test, therefore, seems to contemplate a look back at the substance, and efficacy, of the special committee's negotiations, rather than just a look at the composition and mandate of the special committee.

The Court of Chancery expressed its concern about the practical implications of such a factually intensive burden shifting inquiry because it is "deeply enmeshed" in the ultimate entire fairness analysis.

Subsuming within the burden shift analysis questions of whether the special committee was substantively effective in its negotiations with the controlling stockholder—questions fraught with factual complexity—will, absent unique circumstances, guarantee that the burden shift will rarely be determinable on the basis of the pretrial record alone. If we take seriously the notion, as I do, that a standard of review is meant to serve as the framework through which the court evaluates the parties' evidence and trial testimony in reaching a decision, and, as important, the framework through which the litigants determine how best to prepare their cases for trial, it is problematic to adopt an analytical approach whereby the burden allocation can only be determined in a post-trial opinion, after all the evidence and all the arguments have been presented to the court.

We agree with these thoughtful comments. However, the general inability to decide burden shifting prior to trial is directly related to the reason why entire fairness remains the applicable standard of review even when an independent committee is utilized, *i.e.*, "because the underlying factors which raise the specter of impropriety can never be completely eradicated and still require careful judicial scrutiny."

This case is a perfect example. The Court of Chancery could not decide whether to shift the burden based upon the pretrial record. After hearing all of the evidence presented at trial, the Court of Chancery found that, although the independence of the Special Committee was not challenged, "from inception, the Special Committee fell victim to a controlled mindset and allowed Grupo Mexico to dictate the terms and structure of the merger." The Court of Chancery concluded that "although the Special Committee members were competent businessmen and may have had the best of intentions, they allowed themselves to be hemmed in by the controlling stockholder's demands."

. . . Delaware has long adhered to the principle that the controlling shareholders have the burden of proving an interested transaction was entirely fair. However, in order to encourage the use of procedural devices that foster fair pricing, such as special committees and minority stockholder approval conditions, this Court has provided transactional proponents with what has been described as a "*modest procedural benefit*—the shifting of the burden of persuasion on the ultimate issue of entire fairness to the plaintiffs—if the transaction proponents proved, in a factually intensive way, that the procedural devices had, in fact, operated with integrity." We emphasize that in *Cox*, the procedural benefit of burden shifting was characterized as "modest."

Once again, in this case, the Court of Chancery expressed uncertainty about whether "there is much, if any, practical implication of a burden shift." According to the Court of Chancery, "[t]he practical effect of the *Lynch* doctrine's burden shift is slight. One reason why this is so is that shifting the burden of persuasion under a preponderance standard is not a major move, if one assumes . . . that the outcome of very few cases hinges on what happens if . . . the evidence is in equipoise."

. . . Nevertheless, we recognize that the purpose of providing defendants with the opportunity to seek a burden shift is not only to encourage the use of special committees, but also to provide a reliable pretrial guide for the parties regarding who has the burden of persuasion. Therefore, which party bears the burden of proof must be determined, if possible, before the trial begins. The Court of Chancery has noted that, in the interest of having certainty, "it is unsurprising that few defendants have sought a pretrial hearing to determine who bears the burden of persuasion on fairness" given "the factually intense nature of the burden-shifting inquiry" and the "modest benefit" gained from the shift.

The failure to shift the burden is not outcome determinative under the entire fairness standard of review. We have concluded that, because the only "modest" effect of the burden shift is to make the plaintiff prove unfairness under a preponderance of the evidence standard, the benefits of clarity in terms of trial presentation outweigh the costs of continuing to decide either during or after trial whether the burden has shifted. Accordingly, we hold prospectively that, if the record does not permit a pretrial determination that the defendants are entitled to a burden shift, the burden of persuasion will remain with the defendants throughout the trial to demonstrate the entire fairness of the interested transaction.

The Defendants argue that if the Court of Chancery rarely determines the issue of burden shifting on the basis of a pretrial record, corporations will be dissuaded from forming special committees of independent directors and from seeking approval of an interested transaction by an informed vote of a majority of the minority shareholders. That argument underestimates the importance of either or both actions to the process component—fair dealing—of the entire fairness standard. This Court has repeatedly held that any board process is materially enhanced when the decision is attributable to independent directors. Accordingly, judicial review for entire fairness of how the transaction was structured, negotiated, disclosed to the directors, and approved by the directors will be significantly influenced by the work product of a properly functioning special committee of independent directors. Similarly, the issue of how stockholder approval was obtained will be significantly influenced by the affirmative vote of a majority of the minority stockholders.

A fair process usually results in a fair price. Therefore, the proponents of an interested transaction will continue to be incentivized to put a fair dealing process in place that promotes judicial confidence in the entire fairness of the transaction price. Accordingly, we have no doubt that the effective use of a properly functioning special committee of independent directors and the informed conditional approval of a majority of minority stockholders will continue to be integral parts of the best practices that are used to establish a fair dealing process.

Americas Mining Corp. v. Theriault, 51 A.3d. 1213, 1239-1244 (De. 2012).

Was the Delaware Supreme Court signaling how it would likely rule on the standard shifting issue decided by Chancellor Strine in his *MFW Shareholders Litigation* opinion?

F. Transfer of Control for a Premium

Part F explores the limits on the controlling shareholder's ability to transfer control for a premium. As you read these materials, consider whether the rules strike a proper balance between allowing a corporation and its controlling shareholder to adapt to changed circumstances and protecting the corporation and its minority shareholders from opportunism. Keep in mind as you evaluate these materials that an alternative to transfer of control via sale of the controlling shareholder's stock is a merger or asset sale that would provide equal benefit to both controlling and noncontrolling shareholders.

1. Fundamental Principles

a. Sale of Control Block

A control block of stock can be sold for a significant premium over the market price of noncontrol block stock. While there has been occasional scholarly support for a rule requiring controlling shareholders to share sale premiums with other shareholders (see, e.g., Andrews, The Stockholder's Right to Equal Opportunity in the Sale of Shares, 78 Harv. L. Rev. 505 (1965)), the common law norm, stated succinctly in Zeitlin v. Hanson Holdings, Inc., 397 N.E.2d 387, 388-389 (N.Y. 1979), affords wide latitude to controlling shareholders:

> Recognizing that those who invest the capital necessary to acquire a dominant position in the ownership of a corporation have the right of controlling that corporation, it has long been settled law that, absent looting of corporate assets, conversion of a corporate opportunity, fraud or other acts of bad faith, a controlling stockholder is free to sell, and a purchaser is free to buy, that controlling interest at a premium price (see Barnes v. Brown, 80 N.Y. 527; Levy v. American Beverage Corp., 265 App. Div. 208; Essex Universal Corp. v. Yates, 305 F.2d 572).
>
> Certainly, minority shareholders are entitled to protection against such abuse by controlling shareholders. They are not entitled, however, to inhibit the legitimate interests of the other

stockholders. It is for this reason that control shares usually command a premium price. The premium is the added amount an investor is willing to pay for the privilege of directly influencing the corporation's affairs.

In this action plaintiff Zetlin contends that minority stockholders are entitled to an opportunity to share equally in any premium paid for a controlling interest in the corporation. This rule would profoundly affect the manner in which controlling stock interests are now transferred. It would require, essentially, that a controlling interest be transferred only by means of an offer to all stockholders, i.e., a tender offer. This would be contrary to existing law and if so radical a change is to be effected it would best be done by the Legislature.

The following case shows the impact of the common law rule on minority shareholders whose stock is not publicly traded.

Tryon v. Smith
Oregon Supreme Court, 1951
229 P.2d 251

LATOURETTE, JUSTICE.

Actions by former minority stockholders of the First National Bank of Eugene against Richard Shore Smith, former president and director of said bank, who, together with his family and bank directors, owned approximately 70 per cent of the capital stock of said bank, to recover damages for alleged fraud in the sale of stock of said bank to Transamerica Corporation. . . .

The undisputed evidence discloses that Transamerica made an offer to Smith to purchase from Smith all of the outstanding capital stock of the bank. Smith refused the offer and told Transamerica that he would "have nothing to do with any of the stock except the controlling interest of the stock in which I am interested, including my own and that of my family." Smith also told Transamerica that if it desired to purchase stock of the minority it would have to deal directly with them, that he wanted the minority to have the privilege of selling their stock, and that they were entitled to more than book value and should have at least $220.00 per share. The evidence discloses that the book value of the stock was $200.00 per share at the time of the transactions, and that actual sales theretofore made were for $160.00 and $170.00 per share, to the knowledge of some of the minority stockholders.

Transamerica then proceeded to deal with the minority stockholders and offered them $220.00 per share for their stock, telling at least some of them that Smith and his associates were to receive for their stock more than Transamerica offered to pay to the minority stockholders for their stock. The minority stockholders thereupon signed up with Transamerica for the sale of their stock at $220.00 per share. Inquiry was never made of Smith or his associates by the minority stockholders of the price Smith and his associates were to receive from Transamerica for their stock, nor did Smith or his associates ever suggest to the minority stockholders, or any of them, that they should sell their stock; in other words, Smith and his associates had nothing whatsoever to do, directly or indirectly, with the sale of the stock of the minority stockholders. In the sale of their stock, the minority stockholders acted freely, at arm's length, and of their own volition. When the sale of the stock was consummated, Smith and his associates received from Transamerica for their stock $460.00 per share as against $220.00 per share which the plaintiffs received for their stock.

The basis for a right of recovery by plaintiffs is found in paragraphs V, VI, VII and VIII of the various complaints. . . .

VIII

That plaintiff is advised and believes that Transamerica Corporation was willing to pay the sum of Four Hundred Twelve and 00/100 ($412.00) Dollars per share for all of the capital stock of the said bank, but in consequence of the failure of the defendant to advise plaintiff of such fact and due to the advice of the defendant to plaintiff that she should sell her stock at a lower figure, plaintiff did, on or about the 5th [d]ay of December, 1945, sell to the said Transamerica Corporation her 62 shares of stock for the sum of Two Hundred Twenty And 00/100 ($220.00) Dollars per share, and plaintiff has been damaged thereby in the sum of Eleven Thousand Nine Hundred Four And 00/100 ($11,904.00) Dollars.

. . . Plaintiffs, in order to support their position, declare the law to be that majority stockholders of a corporation stand in a fiduciary relation and are under obligations of trust and confidence to the minority stockholders, and for that reason Smith was guilty of unfaithfulness in not apprising the minority stockholders of the Transamerica offer and of what he and his associates were to receive from Transamerica for their stock.

It is generally held that majority stockholders may sell their stock at any time and for any price obtainable without informing other stockholders of the price or terms of sale, provided they act in good faith. 3 Fletcher, Corporations (Perm. Ed.), §900. . . .

The rule is well laid down in Fletcher, supra, at p.306, as follows: "Ordinarily a director possesses the same right as any other stockholder to deal freely with his shares of stock and to dispose of them at such a price as he may be able to obtain, provided the director acts in good faith, since the corporation as such has no interest in its outstanding stock or in dealing in its shares among its stockholders. In other words, the mere fact that a man accepts the position of a director or an official in a corporation should not as a rule deprive him of his right to dispose of his stock as he sees fit and to make any profit that he might gain, provided in the sale of that stock he has done nothing to injure the corporation and its stockholders." . . .

There being no fiduciary relationship existing between the stockholders of the bank so far as the sale of individual stock was concerned, there was no duty upon the part of Smith to apprise minority stockholders of Transamerica's offer. The fact that Smith et al. received more for their stock than the minority is no evidence of fraud, since it is generally recognized that the stock of majority stockholders is of more value than that of the minority. . . .

We have carefully read the authorities briefed by plaintiffs and find in every instance that the cases dealt with corporate management, sales of minority stock to majority stockholders, or matters not germane to the question before us, with these two exceptions: Enyart v. Merrick, 148 Or. 321, 34 P.2d 629, and Dunnett v. Arn, 10 Cir., 71 F.2d 912. . . .

In the *Dunnett* case, the majority stockholders actively urged the minority stockholders, coupled with certain misrepresentations, to sell their stock to a third party. The minority stockholders acted upon the advice and misrepresentations of the majority stockholders—a clear case of fraud.

The facts in the above cases are a far cry from the facts in the instant case.

No case has been cited holding that a fiduciary relationship exists between majority and minority stockholders under facts comparable to the facts in this case.

Since there was no fiduciary relationship between the parties and no fraud, duress, domination or interference on the part of Smith in the sale of plaintiffs' stock to Transamerica, the judgment of the trial court is affirmed.

b. Sale of Corporate Office

A control block of stock has less value to a transferee if control over the board of directors cannot be transferred at the same time. Accordingly, it is accepted corporate practice for sellers to contractually promise that shortly after the sale, the current directors will resign seriatim and name the new controlling shareholder nominees to replace them on the board of directors.

There has been little controversy about this practice when the controlling shareholder owns a majority of the corporation's stock. However, if the controlling shareholder is transferring less than a majority block of a corporation's stock, rarely litigated factual and policy issues are posed.

Essex Universal Corp. v. Yates
United States Court of Appeals, Second Circuit, 1962
305 F.2d 572

LUMBARD, CHIEF JUDGE . . .

[Yates, the owner of 28.3 percent of the shares of Republic Pictures Corporation, contracted to sell those shares to Essex Universal Corp. and to ensure that Essex's nominees were placed in control of the Republic board as a part of the closing of the transaction. Yates sought to avoid this contract on the grounds that his own agreement to effectuate an immediate transfer in control of the Republic board violated public policy. The trial court granted summary judgment to Yates. The Second Circuit reversed and remanded, but each of the three judges wrote separately to explain their view of the standards that should govern the trial court's further proceedings.]

It is established beyond question under New York law that it is illegal to sell corporate office or management control by itself (that is, accompanied by no stock or insufficient stock to carry voting control). . . . The rationale of the rule is undisputable: persons enjoying management control hold it on behalf of the corporation's stockholders, and therefore may not regard it as their own personal property to dispose of as they wish. Any other rule would violate the most fundamental principle of corporate democracy, that management must represent and be chosen by, or at least with the consent of, those who own the corporation. . . .

The next question is whether it is legal to give and receive payment for the immediate transfer of management control to one who has achieved majority share control but would not otherwise be able to convert that share control into operating control for some time. I think that it is. . . .

The easy and immediate transfer of corporate control to new interests is ordinarily beneficial to the economy and it seems inevitable that such transactions would be discouraged if the purchaser of a majority stock interest were required to wait some period before his purchase of control could become effective. Conversely, it would greatly hamper the efforts of any existing majority group to dispose of its interest if it could not assure the purchaser of immediate control over corporation operations. I can see no reason why a purchaser of majority control should not ordinarily be permitted to make his control effective from the moment of the transfer of stock.

Thus, if Essex had been contracting to purchase a majority of the stock of Republic, it would have been entirely proper for the contract to contain the provision for immediate replacement of directors. Although in the case at bar only 28.3 percent of the stock was involved, it is commonly known that a person or group owning so large a percentage of the voting stock of a corporation which, like Republic, has at least the 1,500 shareholders normally requisite to listing on the New York Stock Exchange, is almost certain to have share control as a practical matter. If Essex was contracting to acquire what in reality would be equivalent to ownership of a majority of stock, i.e., if it would as a practical certainty have been guaranteed of the stock voting power to choose a majority of the directors of Republic in due course, there is no reason why the contract should not similarly be legal. Whether Essex was thus to acquire the equivalent of majority stock control would, if the issue is properly raised by the defendants, be a factual issue to be determined by the district court on remand.

Because 28.3 percent of the voting stock of a publicly owned corporation is usually tantamount to majority control, I would place the burden of proof on this issue on Yates as the party attacking the legality of the transaction. Thus, unless on remand Yates chooses to raise the question whether the block of stock in question carried the equivalent of majority control, it is my view that the trial court should regard the contract as legal and proceed to consider the other issues raised by the pleadings. If Yates chooses to raise the issue, it will, in my view, be necessary for him to prove the existence of circumstances which would have prevented Essex from electing a majority of the Republic board of directors in due course. It will not be enough for Yates to raise merely hypothetical possibilities of opposition by the other Republic shareholders to Essex' assumption of management control. Rather, it will be necessary for him to show that, assuming neutrality on the part of the retiring management, there was at the time some concretely foreseeable reason why Essex' wishes would not have prevailed in shareholder voting held in due course. In other words, I would require him to show that there was at the time of the contract some other organized block of stock of sufficient size to outvote the block Essex was buying, or else some circumstance making it likely that enough of the holders of the remaining Republic stock would band together to keep Essex from control.

CLARK, CIRCUIT JUDGE (concurring in the result).

Since Barnes v. Brown, 80 N.Y. 527, teaches us that not all contracts like the one before us are necessarily illegal, summary judgment seems definitely improper and the action should be remanded for trial. But particularly in view of our lack of knowledge of corporate realities and the current standards of business morality, I should prefer to avoid too precise instructions to the district court in the hope that if the action again comes before us the record will be generally more instructive on this important issue than it now is. I share all the doubts and questions stated by my brothers in their opinions and perhaps have some additional ones of my own. My concern is lest we may be announcing abstract moral principles which have little validity in daily business practice other than to excuse a defaulting vendor from performance of his contract of sale. Thus, for fear of a possible occasional contract inimical to general stockholder interest we may be condemning out of hand what are more often normal and even desirable business relationships. . . .

FRIENDLY, CIRCUIT JUDGE (concurring). . . .

I have no doubt that many contracts, drawn by competent and responsible counsel, for the purchase of blocks of stock from interests thought to "control" a corporation although owning less than a majority, have contained provisions like paragraph 6 of the contract sub judice. However, developments over the past decades seem to me to show that such a clause violates basic principles of corporate democracy. To be sure, stockholders who have allowed a set of directors to be placed in office, whether by their vote or their failure to vote, must recognize that death, incapacity or other hazard may prevent a director from serving a full term, and that they will have no voice as to his immediate successor. But the stockholders are entitled to expect that, in that event, the remaining directors will fill the vacancy in the exercise of their fiduciary responsibility. A mass seriatim resignation directed by a selling stockholder, and the filling of vacancies by his henchmen at the dictation of a purchaser and without any consideration of the character of the latter's nominees, are beyond what the stockholders contemplated or should have been expected to contemplate. This seems to me a wrong to the corporation and the other stockholders which the law ought not countenance, whether the selling stockholder has received a premium or not.

Right in this Court we have seen many cases where sudden shifts of corporate control have caused serious injury; Pettit v. Doeskin Products, Inc., 270 F.2d 95 (2d Cir., 1959), cert. denied, 362 U.S. 910, 80 S. Ct. 660, 4 L. Ed. 2d 618 (1960); United States v. Crosby, 294 F.2d 928 (2d Cir., 1961), cert. denied Mittelman v. United States, 368 U.S. 984, 82 S. Ct. 599, 7 L. Ed. 2d 523 (1962); and Kirtley v. Abrams, 299 F.2d 341 (2d Cir., 1962), are a few recent examples. To hold the seller for delinquencies of the new directors only if he knew the purchaser was an intending looter is not a sufficient sanction. . . . [Refusing to enforce such contract is] not contraindicated, as Judge Lumbard suggests, by the conceded desirability of preventing the dead hand of a former 'controlling' group from continuing to dominate the board after a sale, or of protecting a would-be purchaser from finding himself without a majority of the board after he has spent his money. A special meeting of stockholders to replace a board may always be called, and there could be no objection to making the closing of a purchase contingent on the results of such an election. I perceive some of the difficulties of mechanics such a procedure presents, but I have enough confidence in the ingenuity of the corporate bar to believe these would be surmounted.

c.   Negligent Sale of Corporate Control

What if control is sold to wrongdoers who loot or otherwise intentionally harm the purchased corporation? Will the selling shareholder be liable to the corporation and its minority shareholders for the harm suffered? Chancellor Allen's opinion in the following case summarizes the fiduciary and tort law framework that determines who bears the risk of loss from such wrongdoing.

Harris v. Carter
Delaware Court of Chancery, 1990
582 A.2d 222

ALLEN, CHANCELLOR: . . .

A

A number of cases may be cited in support of the proposition that when transferring control of a corporation to another, a controlling shareholder may, in some circumstances, have a duty to investigate the *bona fides* of the buyer—that is, in those circumstances, to take such steps as a reasonable person would take to ascertain that the buyer does not intend or is unlikely to plan any depredations of the corporation. The circumstance to which these cases refer is the existence of facts that would give rise to suspicion by a reasonably prudent person. The leading case is Insuranshares Corporation, 35 F. Supp. 22 (E.D. Pa. 1940).

In that case defendants, who comprised the entire board of directors of the corporation involved, sold their 27% stock interest in the corporation and resigned as directors. The resignations were done seriatim, in a way that permitted the designation of the buyers as successor directors. The buyers proceeded to loot the corporation.

As here, the sellers contended that they could have no liability for the wrongs that followed their sale. They merely sold their stock and resigned. These were acts that they were privileged to do, they claimed. Judge Kirkpatrick rejected this position:

> Those who control a corporation, either through majority stock ownership, ownership of large blocks of stock less than a majority, officeholding, management contracts, or otherwise, owe some duty to the corporation in respect of the transfer of the control to outsiders. The law has long ago reached the point where it is recognized that such persons may not be wholly oblivious of the interest of everyone but themselves, even in the act of parting with control, and that, under certain circumstances, they may be held liable for whatever injury to the corporation made possible by the transfer. Without attempting any general definition, and stating the duty in minimum terms as applicable to the facts of this case, it may be said that the owners of control are under a duty not to transfer it to outsiders if the circumstances surrounding the proposed transfer are such as to awaken suspicion and put a prudent man on his guard—unless a reasonably adequate investigation discloses such facts as would convince a reasonable person that no fraud is intended or likely to result. . . . If, after such investigation, the sellers are deceived by false representations, there might not be liability, but if the circumstances put the seller on notice and if no adequate investigation is made and harm follows, then liability also follows.

35 F. Supp. at 25.

This statement represents the majority view on the subject. There is a minority view. Judging from a single fifty year old case, in New York a controlling shareholder may apparently not be held liable in any sale of control setting, other than one in which he had actual knowledge of a planned depredation by his buyer. While in Gerdes v.

Reynolds, 28 N.Y.S.2d 622, 652-654 (1941) the Supreme Court, Special Term held that a seller of corporate control could be liable for wrongs of his buyer without actual knowledge of his buyer's purpose if he knew facts that should have put him on guard, in Levy v. American Beverage Corp., 265 A.D. 208, 38 N.Y.S.2d 517 (1942), the New York Supreme Court-Appellate Division held to the contrary (p. 524-526). That court concluded that a selling majority shareholder could be held to account for the looting of the corporation by his buyer only if he had knowledge of the improper purpose of his buyer.

Although there are few cases applying the principle of the *Insuranshares* case that do fix liability on a seller, it is the principle of *Insuranshares* and not the actual notice rule of *Levy* that has commanded the respect of later courts. In Swinney v. Keebler Company, 480 F.2d 573, 577 (1973), the Second Circuit Court of Appeals acknowledged *Insuranshares* as "the leading case." It aptly summarized the principle of that case:

> Liability was predicated upon breach of a duty not to transfer control since the circumstances surrounding the transfer were "such as to awaken suspicion and put a prudent man on his guard—unless a reasonably adequate investigation discloses such facts as would convince a reasonable person that no fraud is intended or likely to result." 35 F. Supp. at 25.

Swinney v. Keebler Company, 480 F.2d at 577. The appeals court went on:

> The district court properly rejected the test applied in Levy v. American Beverage Corp., 265 App. Div. 208, 38 N.Y.S.2d 517, 526 (1942), to the effect that, before the transferor can be found liable, it must have actual notice that the transferee intends to loot the corporation. We agree with the district court that "[t]o require knowledge of the intended looting on the part of the seller in order to impose liability on him places a premium on the 'head in the sand' approach to corporate sales," 329 F. Supp. at 223, and with Judge Friendly that "[t]o hold the seller for delinquencies of the new directors only if he knew the purchaser was an intending looter is not a sufficient sanction." Essex Universal Corporation v. Yates, 305 F.2d 572, 581 (2nd Cir. 1962) (concurring opinion).

Id. at n.6.

B

While Delaware law has not addressed this specific question, one is not left without guidance from our decided cases. Several principles deducible from that law are pertinent. First, is the principle that a shareholder has a right to sell his or her stock and in the ordinary case owes no duty in that connection to other shareholders when acting in good faith. Frantz Manufacturing Co. v. EAC Industries, Del. Supr., 501 A.2d 401, 408 (1985).

Equally well established is the principle that when a shareholder presumes to exercise control over a corporation, to direct its actions, that shareholder assumes a fiduciary duty of the same kind as that owed by a director to the corporation. Sterling v. Mayflower Hotel Corp., Del. Supr., 33 Del. Ch. 293, 93 A.2d 107, 109-110 (1952). A sale of controlling interest in a corporation, at least where, as is alleged here, that sale is coupled with an agreement for the sellers to resign from the board of directors in such a way as to assure that the buyer's designees assume that corporate office, does, in my opinion, involve or implicate the corporate mechanisms so as to call this principle into operation.

More generally, it does not follow from the proposition that ordinarily a shareholder has a right to sell her stock to whom and on such terms as she deems expedient, that no duty may arise from the particular circumstances to take care in the exercise of that right. It is established American legal doctrine that unless privileged, each person owes a duty to those who may foreseeably be harmed by her action to take such steps as a reasonably prudent person would take in similar circumstances to avoid such harm to others. While this principle arises from the law of torts and not the law of corporations or of fiduciary duties, that distinction is not, I think, significant unless the law of corporations or of fiduciary duties somehow privileges a selling shareholder by exempting her from the reach of this principle. The principle itself is one of great generality and, if not negated by privilege, would apply to a controlling shareholder who negligently places others foreseeably in the path of injury.

That a shareholder may sell her stock (or that a director may resign his office) is a right that, with respect to the principle involved, is no different, for example, than the right that a licensed driver has to operate a motor vehicle upon a highway. The right exists, but it is not without conditions and limitations, some established by positive regulation, some by common-law. Thus, to continue the parallel, the driver owes a duty of care to her passengers because it is foreseeable that they may be injured if, through inattention or otherwise, the driver involves the car she is operating in a collision. In the typical instance a seller of corporate stock can be expected to have no similar apprehension of risks to others from her own inattention. But, in some circumstances, the seller of a control block of stock may or should reasonably foresee danger to other shareholders; with her sale of stock will also go control over the corporation and with it the opportunity to misuse that power to the injury of such other shareholders. Thus, the reason that a duty of care is recognized in any situation is fully present in this situation. I can find no universal privilege arising from the corporate form that exempts a controlling shareholder who sells corporate control from the wholesome reach of this common-law duty.[17] Certainly I cannot read the Supreme Court's opinion in *Frantz,* supra, as intending to lay down a rule applicable to the question here posed.

Thus, I conclude that while a person who transfers corporate control to another is surely not a surety for his buyer, when the circumstances would alert a reasonably prudent person to a risk that his buyer is dishonest or in some material respect not truthful, a duty devolves upon the seller to make such inquiry as a reasonably prudent person would make, and generally to exercise care so that others who will be affected by his actions should not be injured by wrongful conduct.

---

17. A privilege arguably does exist with respect to foreseeable risk of financial injury to share values that might arise from a risky though honest future business plan that the buyer may have in mind. Such a privilege would not be involved here when the thrust of the complaint is that Mascolo engaged in—and Carter defendants should have foreseen or at least investigated—dishonest transactions.

NOTES AND QUESTIONS

1. As Zetlin v. Hanson Holdings, Inc. and other cases have recognized, courts have been willing to find controlling shareholders liable in "looting" contexts. See, e.g., DeBaun v. First Western Bank & Trust Co., 46 Cal. App. 3d 686, 120 Cal. Rptr. 354 (1975).

2. Should the size of the premium put a seller on notice of the need to investigate? How does the nature of the corporation's assets affect the seller's duty?

3. Consider the standard enunciated in Gerdes v. Reynolds, 28 N.Y.S.2d 622, 653 (N.Y.S. Ct. 1941):

> [T]he principal factors which [determine whether the seller has a duty to investigate] are the nature of the assets which are to pass into the possession and control of the purchasers by reason of the transaction, the method by which the transaction is to be consummated, and the relation of the price paid to the value of the stock.
>
> The immediate consequence of the resignation of the entire body of officers and directors of a corporation obviously is at least potentially different where the corporation's assets are land and buildings and where they are securities which to all intents and purposes are practically negotiable, and such potential difference must be taken into account, both by the officers and directors and by a court judging their conduct, in considering whether their en masse resignations would leave the assets without proper care and protection, because the risk of dissipation or speedy misapplication obviously is greater. . . . An assumption that the officers and directors of Reynolds Investing Company fully performed the fiduciary duty resting upon them thus requires an assumption that they realized that by doing what they did they were placing in the hands of those whom they elected as their successors the custody and possession of practically negotiable securities of a value of more than double the amount of the agreed purchase price, and were so placing such custody and possession at a time when a large part of the purchase price (over $600,000) still remained unpaid.

4. In Clagett v. Hutchinson, 583 F.2d 1259 (4th Cir. 1978), a controlling shareholder sold his control block for $34.75 per share when minority shares were trading at $7.50 to $10 per share, and the corporation was allegedly harmed by the purchaser. In finding that the controlling shareholder had no duty to investigate, the court reasoned as follows:

> While the price paid for Hutchison's shares was indeed a premium price, it was nevertheless a premium paid for the element of control of the corporation. McDaniel v. Painter, 418 F.2d at 548. The premium payment is further justifiable since Laurel was a commercial business subject to further development as an on-going business. Thus, the premium price paid to Hutchison cannot be said to be so unreasonable as to place him on notice of the likelihood of fraud on the corporation or the remaining stockholders. Swinney v. Keebler Co., 480 F.2d at 578-579; Insuranshares Corp. of Delaware v. Northern Fiscal Corp., 35 F. Supp. 22, 26 (E.D. Pa. 1940). Finally, as a matter of logic, it seems farfetched to pay a 400% Premium for stock simply in order to acquire control of a corporation in order to loot it. Certainly a cheaper corporate enterprise could be acquired for such malevolent purposes.

583 F.2d. at 1262.

5. In Caplan v. Yates, 246 N.Y.S.2d 913 (N.Y.A.D. 1964), a minority shareholder sued to set aside the seriatim transfer of control of Lionel Corp.'s board of directors. The transfer occurred as a part of Roy Cohn's sale of his 55,000 Lionel

shares—which block constituted only 3 percent of the corporation's outstanding stock. Cohn delivered control over the ten-member Lionel board at closing, as required by the purchase agreement, by having six directors under his control resign and replace themselves with the purchaser's nominees. The trial court vacated the election of these nominees. The Supreme Court, Appellate Division affirmed, noting that "no claim was made that the stock interest which changed hands even approximated the percentage necessary to validate the substitution." 246 N.Y.S.2d at 915. The Supreme Court also rejected the argument that the complaining shareholder lacked standing to challenge the board's election of replacement directors. Id. at 915-916.

6. The American Law Institute's Principles of Corporate Governance suggest the debate over control premiums turns on an empirical question: What is the source of control premiums?

> If the premium is paid for the opportunity to exploit minority shareholders, the sale should be discouraged by requiring the premium to be shared. If the premium reflects only what otherwise would have been the corporation's share of the efficiency gains that will result from the transfer of control, requiring the premium to be shared will not discourage the transfer of control, because even with a sharing requirement the sale will still make the controlling shareholder better off. If, alternatively, the premium reflects a differential in value between controlling and minority shares that is not the result of exploiting minority shareholders—for example, because control allows a controlling shareholder the opportunity to direct the fortunes of the corporation, rather than rely exclusively on independent management whose interests may diverge from those of shareholders—the argument is that there then is no reason to discourage beneficial transfers of control by a sharing requirement.

ALI, Principles of Corporate Governance §5.16, official comment.

PROBLEM 8-10

Francis McEwen founded, and until July 25, 2014, owned 600,000 shares of the stock of Third Mortgage, Inc. (3M), a company engaged in the business of making high-risk loans to homeowners. The remaining 80 percent of 3M's stock was publicly traded and held by approximately 2,500 shareholders. In early July 2006, Sara Brock inquired whether McEwen would be interested in selling his stock to her client for the nonnegotiable price of $100 per share, a premium of $60 per share over the then-market price. McEwen quickly assented and the purchase contract was negotiated and executed in 72 hours. During the negotiations, Brock disclosed that her client was Charles Agar, a well-known and highly respected international financier. The purchase agreement called for a closing on July 20, 2014, and was conditioned on the immediate appointment of Agar, Brock, and three other Agar nominees as the new 3M board of directors.

On July 17, 2014, at a specially called directors' meeting, McEwen reported the terms of the Agar purchase agreement, and summarized his negotiations with Brock. Brock then gave a report detailing Agar's plans to modernize 3M and increase its profitability. One outside director noted that the board's most recent valuation study had predicted that a sale of 3M would likely yield only $180 million, or $60 per share, and commented that McEwen "was getting a great price" and that "Agar must have a very good plan for increasing the company's value to pay such a high price." A short discussion ensued concerning the qualifications of the proposed nominees. In preparation for the meeting, McEwen had commissioned Dun and Bradstreet reports on each nominee. Four of the five nominees had outstanding reputations in the business community, but the directors were previously unfamiliar with Brock. Her Dun and Bradstreet report revealed that she had worked as a broker for several Wall Street investment banking firms over the past 15 years, and had recently formed a private consulting firm, Brock and Associates, the financial status of which was listed as "New Record—No negative information." The board resolved that each director-nominee, including Agar, should be requested to submit a résumé and a letter agreeing to serve as a director if elected. The board voted unanimously to support the requested transfer of control and to keep the purchase agreement confidential until closing as requested by Brock.

On July 20, the board reconvened. Brock hand-delivered the five "willingness-to-serve" letters and résumés, and the directors reviewed them briefly. The directors then resigned seriatim, replacing themselves with Agar and his nominees. Simultaneously, McEwen transferred his stock to Brock, as agent for Charles Agar, receiving in return a cashier's check in the amount of $60 million.

Sara Brock then assumed the position of 3M CEO. Over the next three weeks she liquidated all of 3M's assets in a series of sales to bona fide purchasers, purportedly in accordance with resolutions adopted by the new board of directors. The proceeds from these sales—approximately $120 million—were funneled through numerous off-shore banks and dummy corporations. When Brock disappeared on August 16, 2006, these funds could not be traced, though 3M investigators believe that $70 million was transferred to "off-shore financiers" to repay the principal and "interest" on the "loan" Brock obtained to purchase McEwen's stock. The investigators quickly discovered that Agar and the other three putative 3M directors were totally unaware of the actions that Brock claimed to be taking on their behalf, including Brock's negotiations with McEwen and her forgery of the "willingness to serve" letters. In short, the entire Agar transaction was a fraud.

3M is now in bankruptcy, and the trustee has filed civil actions against McEwen and the pre-sale 3M directors, claiming that the immediate transfer of control to Brock was illegal per se and the product of gross negligence by McEwen and the other 3M directors. Additionally, the complaint alleges that McEwen and the other 3M directors breached their fiduciary duty by not assuring that all 3M shareholders had an equal opportunity to sell their shares at a premium. As trial judge, how would you rule, assuming that this is a case of first impression in your jurisdiction?

2.   Sale of Corporate Opportunity

a.   *Premium Received in Compensation for Sale of Corporate Asset*

Perlman v. Feldmann
United States Court of Appeals, Second Circuit, 1955
219 F.2d 173

CLARK, CHIEF JUDGE.

This is a derivative action brought by minority stockholders of Newport Steel Corporation to compel accounting for, and restitution of, allegedly illegal gains which accrued to defendants as a result of the sale in August, 1950, of their controlling interest in the corporation. The principal defendant, C. Russell Feldmann, who represented and acted for the others, members of his family,[1] was at that time not only the dominant stockholder, but also the chairman of the board of directors and the president of the corporation. Newport, an Indiana corporation, operated mills for the production of steel sheets for sale to manufacturers of steel products, first at Newport, Kentucky, and later also at other places in Kentucky and Ohio. The buyers, a syndicate organized as Wilport Company, a Delaware corporation, consisted of end-users of steel who were interested in securing a source of supply in a market becoming even tighter in the Korean War. Plaintiffs contend that the consideration paid for the stock included compensation for the sale of a corporate asset, a power held in trust for the corporation by Feldmann as its fiduciary. This power was the ability to control the allocation of the corporate product in a time of short supply, through control of the board of directors; and it was effectively transferred in this sale by having Feldmann procure the resignation of his own board and the election of Wilport's nominees immediately upon consummation of the sale. . . .

Jurisdiction below was based upon the diverse citizenship of the parties. Plaintiffs argue here, as they did in the court below, that in the situation here disclosed the vendors must account to the non-participating minority stockholders for that share of their profit which is attributable to the sale of the corporate power. Judge Hincks denied the validity of the premise, holding that the rights involved in the sale were only those normally incident to the possession of a controlling block of shares, with which a dominant stockholder, in the absence of fraud or foreseeable looting, was entitled to deal according to his own best interests. Furthermore, he held that plaintiffs had failed to satisfy their burden of proving that the sales price was not a fair price for the stock per se. Plaintiffs appeal from these rulings of law which resulted in the dismissal of their complaint.

---

1. The stock was not held personally by Feldmann in his own name, but was held by the members of his family and by personal corporations. The aggregate of stock thus had amounted to 33% of the outstanding Newport stock and gave working control to the holder. The actual sale included 55,552 additional shares held by friends and associates of Feldmann, so that a total of 37% of the Newport stock was transferred.

The essential facts found by the trial judge are not in dispute. Newport was a relative newcomer in the steel industry with predominantly old installations which were in the process of being supplemented by more modern facilities. Except in times of extreme shortage Newport was not in a position to compete profitably with other steel mills for customers not in its immediate geographical area. Wilport, the purchasing syndicate, consisted of geographically remote end-users of steel who were interested in buying more steel from Newport than they had been able to obtain during recent periods of tight supply. The price of $20 per share was found by Judge Hincks to be a fair one for a control block of stock, although the over-the-counter market price had not exceeded $12 and the book value per share was $17.03. But this finding was limited by Judge Hincks' statement that "[what] value the block would have had if shorn of its appurtenant power to control distribution of the corporate product, the evidence does not show." It was also conditioned by his earlier ruling that the burden was on plaintiffs to prove a lesser value for the stock.

Both as director and as dominant stockholder, Feldmann stood in a fiduciary relationship to the corporation and to the minority stockholders as beneficiaries thereof. Pepper v. Litton, 308 U.S. 295. . . . Although there is no Indiana case directly in point, the most closely analogous one emphasizes the close scrutiny to which Indiana subjects the conduct of fiduciaries when personal benefit may stand in the way of fulfillment of trust obligations. In Schemmel v. Hill, 91 Ind. App. 373, 169 N.E. 678, McMahan, J., said: ". . . In a transaction between a director and his corporation, where he acts for himself and his principal at the same time in a matter connected with the relation between them, it is presumed, where he is thus potential[ly] on both sides of the contract, that self-interest will overcome his fidelity to his principal, to his own benefit and to his principal's hurt." And the judge added: "Absolute and most scrupulous good faith is the very essence of a director's obligation to his corporation. The first principal duty arising from his official relation is to act in all things of trust wholly for the benefit of his corporation."

In Indiana, then, as elsewhere, the responsibility of the fiduciary is not limited to a proper regard for the tangible balance sheet assets of the corporation, but includes the dedication of his uncorrupted business judgment for the sole benefit of the corporation, in any dealings which may adversely affect it. Although the Indiana case is particularly relevant to Feldmann as a director, the same rule should apply to his fiduciary duties as majority stockholder, for in that capacity he chooses and controls the directors, and thus is held to have assumed their liability. . . . This, therefore, is the standard to which Feldmann was by law required to conform in his activities here under scrutiny.

It is true, as defendants have been at pains to point out, that this is not the ordinary case of breach of fiduciary duty. We have here no fraud, no misuse of confidential information, no outright looting of a helpless corporation. But on the other hand, we do not find compliance with that high standard which we have just stated and which we and other courts have come to expect and demand of corporate fiduciaries. In the often-quoted words of Judge Cardozo: "Many forms of conduct permissible in a workaday world for those acting at arm's length, are forbidden to those bound by fiduciary ties. A trustee is held to something stricter than the morals of the market place. Not honesty alone, but the punctilio of an honor the most sensitive, is then the standard of behavior. As to this there has developed a tradition that is unbending and inveterate. Uncompromising rigidity has been the attitude of courts of equity when petitioned to undermine the rule of undivided loyalty by the 'disintegrating erosion' of particular exceptions." Meinhard v. Salmon, 249 N.Y. 458, 464, 164 N.E. 545, 546, 62 A.L.R. 1. The actions of defendants in siphoning off for personal gain corporate advantages to be derived from a favorable market situation do not betoken the necessary undivided loyalty owned by the fiduciary to his principal.

The corporate opportunities of whose misappropriation the minority stockholders complain need not have been an absolute certainty in order to support this action against Feldmann. . . .

This rationale is equally appropriate to a consideration of the benefits which Newport might have derived from the steel shortage. In the past Newport had used and profited by its market leverage by operation of what the industry had come to call the "Feldmann Plan." This consisted of securing interest-free advances from prospective purchasers of steel in return for firm commitments to them from future production. The funds thus acquired were used to finance improvements in existing plants and to acquire new installations. In the summer of 1950 Newport had been negotiating for cold-rolling facilities which it needed for a more fully integrated operation and a more marketable product, and Feldmann plan funds might well have been used toward this end.

Further, as plaintiffs alternatively suggest, Newport might have used the period of short supply to build up patronage in the geographical area in which it could compete profitably even when steel was more abundant. Either of these opportunities was Newport's, to be used to its advantage only. Only if defendants had been able to negate completely any possibility of gain by Newport could they have prevailed. It is true that a trial court finding states: "Whether or not, in August, 1950, Newport's position was such that it could have entered into 'Feldmann Plan' type transactions to procure funds and financing for the further expansion and integration of its steel facilities and whether such expansion would have been desirable for Newport, the evidence does not show." This, however, cannot avail the defendants, who—contrary to the ruling below—had the burden of proof on this issue, since fiduciaries always have the burden of proof in establishing the fairness of their dealings with trust property.

Defendants seek to categorize the corporate opportunities which might have accrued to Newport as too unethical to warrant further consideration. It is true that reputable steel producers were not participating in the gray market brought about by the Korean War and were refraining from advancing their prices, although to do so would not have been illegal. But Feldmann plan transactions were not considered within this self-imposed interdiction: the trial court found that around the time of the Feldmann sale Jones & Laughlin Steel Corporation, Republic Steel Company, and Pittsburgh Steel Corporation were all participating in such arrangements. In any event, it ill becomes the defendants to disparage as unethical the market advantages from which they themselves reaped rich benefits.

We do not mean to suggest that a majority stockholder cannot dispose of his controlling block of stock to outsiders without having to account to his corporation for profits or even never do this with impunity when the buyer is an interested customer, actual or potential, for the corporation's product. But when the sale necessarily results in a sacrifice of this element of corporate good will and consequent unusual profit to the fiduciary who has caused the sacrifice, he should account for his gains. So in a time of market shortage, where a call on a corporation's product commands an unusually large premium, in one form or another, we think it sound law that a fiduciary may not appropriate to himself the value of this premium. Such personal gain at the expense of his coventurers seems particularly reprehensible when made by the trusted president and director of his company. In this case the violation of duty seems to be all the clearer because this triple role in which Feldmann appears, though we are unwilling to say, and are not to be understood as saying, that we should accept a lesser obligation for any one of his roles alone.

Hence to the extent that the price received by Feldmann and his codefendants included such a bonus, he is accountable to the minority stockholders who sue here. Restatement, Restitution §§190, 197 (1937); Seagrave Corp. v. Mount, 6 Cir., 212 F.2d 389. And plaintiffs, as they contend, are entitled to a recovery in their own right, instead of in right of the corporation (as in the usual derivative actions), since neither Wilport nor their successors in interest should share in any judgment which may be rendered. Defendants cannot well object to this form of recovery, since the only alternative, recovery for the corporation as a whole, would subject them to a greater total liability.

The case will therefore be remanded to the district court for a determination of the question expressly left open below, namely, the value of defendants' stock without the appurtenant control over the corporation's output of steel. We reiterate that on this issue, as on all others relating to a breach of fiduciary duty, the burden of proof must rest on the defendants. Judgment should go to these plaintiffs and those whom they represent for any premium value so shown to the extent of their respective stock interests.

The judgment is therefore reversed and the action remanded for further proceedings pursuant to this opinion.

SWAN, CIRCUIT JUDGE (dissenting).

. . . My brothers say that "the consideration paid for the stock included compensation for the sale of a corporate asset," which they describe as "the ability to control the allocation of the corporate product in a time of short supply, through control of the board of directors; and it was effectively transferred in this sale by having Feldmann procure the resignation of his own board and the election of Wilport's nominees immediately upon consummation of the sale." The implications of this are not clear to me. If it means that when market conditions are such as to induce users of a corporation's product to wish to buy a controlling block of stock in order to be able to purchase part of the corporation's output at the same mill list prices as are offered to other customers, the dominant stockholder is under a fiduciary duty not to sell his stock, I cannot agree. . . .

NOTES AND QUESTIONS

1. In another case arising from this same transaction, Birnbaum v. Newport Steel Corp., 193 F.2d 461, 462 (2d Cir. 1952) (see Chapter 10 at page 998), the minority shareholders alleged these additional facts:

During this period (June-August 1950) Follansbee Steel Corporation and Newport were negotiating for a merger of the two corporations, which merger, on the terms offered by Follansbee, would have been highly profitable to all the stockholders of Newport. However, in August 1950, Feldmann, acting in his official capacity as president of Newport, rejected the Follansbee offer, and on August 31, 1950 sold his stock to the defendant Wilport Company at a price of $22 per share which was twice the then market value of the stock.

If these facts had been proven, would the plaintiffs have been entitled to broader relief?

2. The earlier district court opinion included the following finding of fact:

Since the Wilport nominees took over the management of Newport on August 31, 1950, substantial improvements have been made in Newport's property and the corporation has enjoyed continued prosperity. Although the Wilport stockholders have purchased substantial quantities of steel from Newport, no sales were made at less than Newport's quoted mill prices. There is no evidence of any sort that Newport suffered from mismanagement or inefficient management since August 31, 1950, or that it has suffered or is likely to suffer any harm whatsoever at the hands of its new management, or that its management has in any way failed to do anything which could have been done for the good of the corporation.

129 F. Supp. 162, 175-176 (D. Conn. 1952).

3. Consider the analysis by Easterbrook and Fischel in Corporate Control Transactions, 91 Yale L.J. 698, 717-718 (1982):

. . . There are several problems with [the court's analysis in Perlman v. Feldmann]. Foremost is its assumption that the gain resulting from the "Plan" was not reflected in the price of Newport's stock. Newport stock was widely traded, and the existence of the Feldmann Plan was known to investors. The going price of Newport shares prior to the transaction therefore reflected the full value of Newport, including the value of advances under the Feldmann Plan. The Wilport syndicate paid some two-thirds more than the going price and thus could not profit from the deal unless (a) the sale of control resulted in an increase in the value of Newport, or (b) Wilport's control of Newport was the equivalent of looting. To see the implications of the latter possibility, consider the following simplified representation of the transaction. Newport has only 100 shares, and Wilport pays $20 for each of 37 shares. The market price of shares is $12, and hence the premium over the market price is $8 × 37 = $296. Wilport must extract more than $296 from Newport in order to gain from the deal; the extraction comes at the expense of the other 63 shares, which must drop approximately $4.75 each, to $7.25.

Hence, the court's proposition that Wilport extracted a corporate opportunity from Newport—the functional equivalent of looting—has testable implications. Unless the price of Newport's outstanding shares plummeted, the Wilport syndicate could not be extracting enough to profit. In fact, however, the value of Newport's shares rose substantially after the transaction. Part of this increase may have been attributable to the rising market for steel companies at the time, but even holding this factor constant, Newport's shares appreciated in price.[43] The data refute the court's proposition that Wilport appropriated a corporate opportunity of Newport.

---

43. Charles Cope has computed changes in the price of Newport shares using the market model, well developed in the finance literature, under which the rate of return on a firm's shares is a function of the market rate of return, the volatility of the firm's price in the past, a constant, and a residual component that represents the consequences of unanticipated events. Increases in this residual reflect good news for the firm. Cope found a significant positive residual for Newport in the month of the sale to Wilport. See Cope, Is the Control Premium Really a Corporate Asset? (April 1981) (unpublished paper on file with Yale Law Journal).

It seems, then, that the source of the premium in Perlman is the same as the source of the gains for the shares Wilport did not buy: Wilport installed a better group of managers and, in addition, furnished Newport with a more stable market for its products. The gains from these changes must have exceeded any loss from abolition of the Feldmann Plan.

PROBLEM 8-11

In the mid-1990s, the management of North American Telcom, Inc. (NAT), then the world's fourth largest long-distance telephone service provider, developed a long-range plan to enter the local telephone service business. In early 1999, these plans were upset by a U.S. Supreme Court decision invalidating FCC regulations that required regional telephone companies to provide low-cost access to their transmission lines to any provider wishing to offer local telephone service. Congress responded with legislation providing that such access must be made available beginning in 2005. Critics charged that this delay in implementation gave the regional telephone companies an unfair advantage in building their own long-distance business. Proponents of the legislation argued that this delay gave local and regional cable TV systems a window of opportunity to enter the local telephone provider business, since their transmission lines were already in place.

In response to this setback, NAT began an intensive search for investments that would provide local telephone access. The regional telephone company for the midwestern states offered NAT access, but only at a price that was economically untenable. In June 1999, Cal Watin, NAT's CEO, visited Jon Mallon, the founder and majority shareholder of Midwestern Cable TV, Inc. (MCTV). MCTV had extensive transmission line coverage in the midwestern states, and had recently publicly announced plans to develop its own local and long distance telecommunication business during the period of transmission line shortage created by the recent Supreme Court and Congressional actions. Watin, speaking for NAT, offered to purchase Mallon's majority interest in MCTV for $80 per share, double the then market price, but only if the sale could be closed in two weeks, and only if Watin would transfer control of the board of directors at that time. Watin explained that NAT needed to use MCTV's cable lines in order to gain local telephone access immediately, and that he was unwilling to proceed in any other manner. Convinced that this was an outstanding price for his stock, Mallon accepted the offer.

After NAT's assumption of control, the new MCTV board canceled the prior board's plans to expand into the long distance and Internet provider business. Instead, the board directed MCTV to concentrate on its regional cable TV business.

In September 1999, Sig Owens, the owner of a 4 percent interest in MCTV, filed a derivative suit against Mallon and the current and former directors of MCTV. The complaint alleges that while MCTV will operate profitably under NAT's control, it will forgo the opportunity to develop into a full service phone company. In effect, charges Owens, the premium Mallon received for his stock was, in significant part, compensation for giving NAT access to local telephone transmission lines in the Midwest five years earlier than otherwise possible, and at the expense of MCTV's long-term interests.

What are the prospects for this litigation?

b.   Proper and Improper Use of Majority Power

Thorpe v. CERBCO, Inc.
Delaware Supreme Court, 1996
676 A.2d 436

WALSH, JUSTICE.

In this appeal from the Court of Chancery we address the duties owed to a corporation by controlling shareholders who are also directors. The shareholder-plaintiff in this derivative suit, Merle Thorpe ("Thorpe") alleged that the controlling shareholders of CERBCO, Inc. had usurped an opportunity which belonged to the corporation. That opportunity was the potential sale of control of one of CERBCO's subsidiaries. The Chancellor held that the defendants, George and Robert Erikson ("the Eriksons"), who were directors, officers and controlling shareholders of CERBCO, breached their duty of loyalty by failing to make complete disclosure to CERBCO of this corporate opportunity and by not removing themselves from consideration of the matter. The court concluded however that, as controlling shareholders, the Eriksons had the right under Del. G.C.L. §271 to veto any transaction which CERBCO would have entered into which constituted the sale of all or substantially all of the assets of the corporation. Thus, according to the Chancellor, the Eriksons' conduct caused no injury to CERBCO. . . .

I.

. . . CERBCO is a holding company with voting control of three subsidiaries. At the relevant time, 1990, only one of these subsidiaries, Insituform East, Inc. ("East"), was profitable. The continued profitability of East was in doubt, however, because its regional license to conduct its primary business was about to expire. This license to exploit a process used in the in-place repair of pipes was obtained from Insituform of North America, Inc. ("INA").

CERBCO's capital structure consisted of two classes of stock. Class A was entitled to one vote per share, and Class B was entitled to 10 votes per share. In addition, the Class B shares were empowered to elect 75% of the board of directors. The Erikson brothers constituted CERBCO's controlling group of shareholders, owning 247,564 or 78% of the outstanding Class B shares, and 111,000 or 7.6% of the outstanding shares of Class A. Thus, while the Eriksons owned 24.6% of CERBCO's total equity, they exercised effective voting control with approximately 56% of the total votes. The Eriksons also constituted two of the four members of CERBCO's board of directors.

East's capital structure and that of the other two subsidiaries is similar to that of CERBCO. East's certificate of incorporation provides for each of the 318,000 Class B shares to have ten votes, while the 4.3 million Class A shares have one vote each. In addition, the Class B shares elect 75% of the board of directors. CERBCO owned 1.1 million shares of Class A (26% of the outstanding Class A shares) and 93% of the Class B shares.

In the fall of 1989, INA explored the possibility of acquiring one of its sublicensees. East, because of its location and profitability, seemed a likely prospect. James

D. Krugman ("Krugman"), INA's Chairman, retained Drexel, Burnham, Lambert & Company ("Drexel") to advise him. Based on public information, Drexel performed financial analyses and devised hypothetical plans for acquisition of control of East. These financial analyses, however, incorrectly assumed that East had a single class of shares and that the market capitalization of its Class A common stock represented the market capitalization of the whole firm.

In January 1990, Krugman met with the Eriksons to discuss the possibility of INA's acquiring East. At this first meeting Krugman was unaware of CERBCO's capital structure, which conferred control on the Eriksons, and presumably approached the Eriksons in their representative capacities as officers and directors. Although the factual record is disputed as to what occurred at this meeting, the Chancellor found that the Eriksons made a counterproposal to Krugman after he expressed interest in purchasing East from CERBCO.[2] This counterproposal involved the Eriksons' selling their controlling interest in CERBCO to INA. It is unclear whether or not the Eriksons explicitly stated that they would block an attempt by INA to buy East from CERBCO. Nevertheless, the Chancellor found that Krugman was led to believe that the Eriksons would permit only the transaction involving their sale of CERBCO stock to INA.

After the first meeting with the Eriksons, Krugman believed it necessary to consider seriously the Eriksons' proposal. Thereafter, INA had Drexel perform comparative financial projections of transactions by which it could gain control of East . . . [which studies] suggested that, while a direct purchase of CERBCO's East stock had a higher initial cost than a purchase of the Eriksons' holdings, in certain respects it would be preferable since the indebtedness of Capital Copy, one of CERBCO's subsidiaries, would not be assumed in the latter transaction.

The Eriksons did not inform CERBCO's outside directors, George Davies and Robert Long, that INA had approached the Eriksons with the intention of buying East from CERBCO, but did inform them of INA's interest in buying the Eriksons' stock. Upon learning this, Davies suggested to Robert Erikson that CERBCO sell East to INA, but Robert Erikson rejected this idea.

At the February 22, 1990 CERBCO board meeting, Davies asked whether INA had ever been interested in buying East. The Eriksons denied that INA had ever made such an offer, and had INA done so, the Eriksons indicated that they would likely vote their shares to reject it. According to draft minutes of the February 22, 1990 meeting, Rogers & Wells, who regularly served as counsel to CERBCO, advised the members of the Board that, as part of a proposed letter of intent that was being negotiated between the parties, INA would be given access to CERBCO's books and records for its due diligence review prior to the execution of a final agreement. The outside directors agreed.

In addition to securing the cooperation of CERBCO officials in making CERBCO's records available in INA's due diligence examination, the Eriksons also sought board

---

2. The Chancellor noted "that Krugman, himself, repeatedly stated in his deposition that once the Eriksons knew that INA was interested in controlling East, it was the Eriksons who proposed that INA purchase their stock, rather than the East stock from CERBCO."

approval of their use of Rogers & Wells as their personal counsel in their negotiations with INA. Rogers & Wells gave CERBCO its written statement that, in its opinion, there was no conflict of interest between the Eriksons and CERBCO because the proposed transaction was a private deal by the Eriksons that did not implicate CERBCO's interests. The board thereafter consented to the representation.

On March 12, 1990, the Eriksons and INA signed a letter of intent ("LOI") for the sale of the Eriksons' controlling interest in CERBCO for $6 million. The letter of intent required the Eriksons to give INA access to CERBCO's books and records, subject to INA's agreement to keep the information confidential, and required INA to indemnify the Eriksons for any costs associated with litigation arising from the consummation of the proposed transaction. . . .

On May 11, 1990, Thorpe lodged a demand with the CERBCO board that the proposed transaction be rejected or that the Eriksons provide an accounting for the control premium associated with the sale of their Class B shares. In July, the two outside directors formed a special committee, which terminated representation by Rogers & Wells and hired Morgan, Lewis & Bockius to represent CERBCO.

While negotiations between the Eriksons and INA continued, the LOI expired and on May 30 INA paid the Eriksons $75,000 to extend the terms through August 1, 1990.

At the September 14, 1990 CERBCO board meeting, the board considered an alternative transaction involving the issuance of authorized CERBCO Class B stock to INA so that it could have a measure of control over East. The Eriksons objected to this proposal, which would destroy not only the Eriksons' control value, but that of the other CERBCO shareholders.

On September 18, 1990, the letter of intent between the Eriksons and INA expired without consummation of the sale. Evidently, the Eriksons and INA were unable to agree on such issues as indemnification for liabilities that might arise out of an SEC suit pending at the time, and the payment of litigation costs related to the transaction which the Eriksons had already incurred. . . .

III.

The August 9, 1995 opinion of the Court of Chancery, after trial, is the subject of this appeal and can be summarized as follows. The Chancellor found that the Eriksons did not act appropriately when Krugman informed them of INA's interest in gaining control of East. The Eriksons' lack of candor and negotiations with INA on their own behalf constituted a breach of the duty of loyalty which the Eriksons owed as directors to the corporation.[6]

Despite finding this breach, the Chancellor held that the plaintiffs would not be awarded damages since the defendants actions were wholly fair. Two reasons were

---

6. This finding of violation of the duty of loyalty was not cross-appealed and forms the predicate for further discussion of the damages claim.

advanced to support the denial of damages. First, no sale had occurred and therefore damages were speculative. The Chancellor found it impossible to calculate a meaningful remedy, i.e., the difference in the value of the control premium in 1990 minus the value of the control premium today.

The second reason given by the Chancellor for not awarding damages is that §271 confers upon the Eriksons the right to veto any corporate change constituting the sale of substantially all of the corporation's assets. Under the facts of this case, any alternative transaction conceivably undertaken by CERBCO would implicate the provisions of §271 and therefore be subject to disapproval by the Eriksons. Accordingly, the Chancellor held the Eriksons could not be penalized for their breach of the duty of loyalty.

IV.

As the Chancellor acknowledged at the threshold of his opinion, this "action raises issues falling within the gravitational pull of two basic precepts of corporate law: (1) that controlling shareholders have a right to sell their shares, and in doing so capture and retain a control premium; and (2) that corporate officers or directors may not usurp a corporate opportunity." Forced to reconcile these two imperatives, the trial court, in essence, concluded that the former trumped the latter. Thus, the Eriksons' right to pursue a control premium relieved them from any liability for the breach of fiduciary duty in the process.

We agree that in a particular setting these two precepts of corporate law may tend to pull in opposite directions, but the statutorily granted rights under §271 cannot be interpreted to completely vitiate the obligation of loyalty. The shareholder vote provided by §271 does not supersede the duty of loyalty owed by control persons, just as the statutory power to merge does not allow oppressive conduct in the effectuation of a merger. Rather, this statutorily conferred power must be exercised within the constraints of the duty of loyalty. Bershad v. Curtiss-Wright Corp., Del. Supr., 535 A.2d 840, 845 (1987); Ringling Bros.-Barnum & Bailey Combined Shows v. Ringling, Del. Supr., 53 A.2d 441, 447 (1947). In practice, the reconciliation of these two precepts of corporate law means that the duty of a controlling shareholder/director will vary according to the role being played by that person and the stage of the transaction at which the power is employed.

The fundamental proposition that directors may not compete with the corporation mandates the finding that the Eriksons breached the duty of loyalty. Guth v. Loft, Inc., Del. Supr., 5 A.2d 503, 510 (1939); see also Broz v. Cellular Information Systems, Inc., Del. Supr., 673 A.2d 148, 154-155 (1996). When INA's president, Krugman, approached the Eriksons, he did so to inquire about INA's purchase of CERBCO's shares in East, not the purchase of the Eriksons' shares in CERBCO. Since the Eriksons were approached in their capacities as directors, their loyalty should have been to the corporation. The Chancellor correctly found that the Eriksons had breached that duty of loyalty through self-interest in subsequent actions. The Eriksons should have informed the CERBCO board of INA's interest in gaining control of East since INA originally wanted to deal with CERBCO.[7] See Restatement (Second) of Agency §381.

Once INA had expressed an interest in acquiring East, CERBCO should have been able to negotiate with INA unhindered by the dominating hand of the Eriksons. Cf. Weinberger v. UOP, Inc., Del. Supr., 457 A.2d 701, 710-711 (1983) (director should not participate in negotiations if conflict of interest would result); *Bershad*, 535 A.2d at 845. The Eriksons were entitled to profit from their control premium and to that end compete with CERBCO but only after informing CERBCO of the opportunity. Thereafter, they should have removed themselves from the negotiations and allowed the disinterested directors to act on behalf of CERBCO.

V.

[Here the court found the Chancellor use of *Weinberger* entire fairness analysis inappropriate and, instead, applied Guth v. Loft's traditional corporate opportunity analysis.]

. . . In this case, it is clear that the opportunity was one in which the corporation had an interest. Despite this fact, CERBCO would never be able to undertake the opportunity to sell its East shares. Every economically viable CERBCO sale of stock could have been blocked by the Eriksons under §271. Since the corporation was not able to take advantage of the opportunity, the transaction was not one which, considering all of the relevant facts, fairly belonged to the corporation. See Fliegler v. Lawrence, Del. Supr., 361 A.2d 218, 220 (1976) (finding no liability since corporation was not financially or legally able to take advantage of opportunity).

B.

Generally, the corporate opportunity doctrine is applied in circumstances where the director and the corporation compete against each other to buy something, whether it be a patent, license, or an entire business. This case differs in that both the Eriksons and CERBCO wanted to sell stock, and the objects of the dispute, their respective blocks of stock to be sold, were not perfectly fungible. In order for the Eriksons and CERBCO to compete against one another, their stock must have been rough substitutes in the eyes of INA. If INA considered none of the CERBCO transactions to be an acceptable substitute to the INA-Erikson transaction, then the opportunity was never really available to CERBCO. Thus, those transactions which were not economically rational alternatives need not be considered by a court evaluating a corporate opportunity scenario.

---

7. Because of CERBCO's clear interest in the opportunity in this case, disclosure to the board of directors was required. See Restatement (Second) of Agency §381. Disclosure to and informed approval by the board may insulate a director from liability where the corporate opportunity doctrine otherwise applies. See Fliegler v. Lawrence, Del. Supr., 361 A.2d 218, 220 (1976). A director who opts not to inform the board of the opportunity acts at his peril, unless he is ultimately able to demonstrate post hoc that the corporation was not deprived of an opportunity in which it had an interest in or capability of engaging. Broz v. Cellular Information Systems, Inc., Del. Supr., 673 A.2d 148, 157 (1996).

The Chancellor thoroughly examined the evidence presented by the parties to determine that only one transaction presented a serious alternative to an Erikson-INA deal. This one viable alternative involved the sale of all of CERBCO's East stock for a price of $12.8 million. This finding was logically derived from the record below and will not be disturbed on appeal. Levitt v. Bouvier, Del. Supr., 287 A.2d 671, 673 (1972).

C.

After dispensing with unrealistic alternatives, we are left to consider a CERBCO sale of all its East stock to INA. Whether or not the Eriksons had a right to block an alternative transaction turns on whether this transaction would constitute all or substantially all of CERBCO's assets and require shareholder approval under §271. We are satisfied that the Court of Chancery correctly applied the law to the facts of this case in making the determination that, in 1990, CERBCO's investment in East constituted substantially all of CERBCO's assets. . . .

In the opinion below, the Chancellor determined that the sale of East would constitute a radical transformation of CERBCO. In addition, CERBCO's East stock accounted for 68% of CERBCO's assets in 1990 and this stock was its primary income generating asset. We therefore affirm the decision that East stock constituted "substantially all" of CERBCO's assets as consistent with Delaware law.

D.

Because the alternative transaction would have been covered by §271, the Eriksons had the statutory right as shareholders to veto this transaction. Given their power, the Eriksons would obviously never allow CERBCO to enter a transaction against their economic interests. Damages cannot be awarded on the basis of a transaction that has a zero probability of occurring due to the lawful exercise of statutory rights.

It is true that the Eriksons breached their fiduciary duties and that damages flowing from that breach are to be liberally calculated. See Milbank, Tweed, Hadley & McCloy v. Boon, 2d Cir., 13 F.3d 537, 543 (1994). Section 271 must, however, be given independent legal significance apart from the duty of loyalty. Cf. Orzeck v. Englehart, Del. Supr., 195 A.2d 375, 377 (1963) (compliance with one provision of the General Corporation Law protects actions from invalidation). While the failure of CERBCO to sell East to INA is certainly related to the Eriksons' faithlessness, that failure did not proximately result from the breach. Instead the Eriksons' §271 rights are ultimately responsible for the nonconsummation of the transaction. Even if the Eriksons had behaved faithfully to their duties to CERBCO, they still could have rightfully vetoed a sale of substantially all of CERBCO's assets under §271. Thus, the §271 rights, not the breach, were the proximate cause of the nonconsummation of the transaction. Accordingly, transactional damages are inappropriate.

While this denial of transactional damages may seem incompatible with our decision to award damages for the breach of fiduciary duty, the two holdings are reconcilable. At the time that Krugman approached the Eriksons, they had the duty to present that opportunity to CERBCO. Instead the Eriksons negotiated with INA for their own benefit and are therefore liable for value received in the course of this negotiation and expenditures made by CERBCO to aid the Eriksons in their negotiations. While the Eriksons did have a duty to present that opportunity to CERBCO, they had no responsibility to ensure that a transaction was consummated. Any INA-CERBCO transaction would have required a shareholder vote and the Eriksons were entitled to pursue their own interests in voting their shares. The failure of INA and CERBCO to reach an agreement was proximately caused by the Eriksons' ability to block the transaction, not by the Eriksons' breach of the duty of loyalty. Consequently, no liability arises from the breach for the inability of CERBCO to take advantage of the opportunity to sell its control of East to INA.

VI.

Despite the finding of breach of loyalty by the Eriksons, the Chancellor concluded that the Eriksons were not liable because the corporation had not been harmed and the Eriksons had not profited substantially. As discussed in part IV, supra, we view the record differently and determine that as a matter of law damages should have been awarded. The Eriksons profited from their dealings with INA, and CERBCO incurred certain expenses in connection with these negotiations which it would not otherwise have incurred had the Eriksons not attempted to expropriate the INA sale opportunity.

Even though the corporation may not have been able to effectuate the transaction because of the Eriksons' rights under §271, some recovery is warranted because of the breach of fiduciary duty. Delaware law dictates that the scope of recovery for a breach of the duty of loyalty is not to be determined narrowly. Although this Court in In re Tri-Star Pictures, Inc., Litig., Del. Supr., 634 A.2d 319 (1993), was addressing disclosure violations, we reasoned from a more general standard concerning the duty of loyalty:

"[T]he absence of specific damage to a beneficiary is not the sole test for determining disloyalty by one occupying a fiduciary position. It is an act of disloyalty for a fiduciary to profit personally from the use of information secured in a confidential relationship, even if such profit or advantage is not gained at the expense of the fiduciary. The result is nonetheless one of unjust enrichment which will not be countenanced by a Court of Equity." Oberly v. Kirby, Del. Supr., 592 A.2d 445, 463 (1991). The distinction we noted in Oberly explains why no Delaware court has extended the damage rule to actions for breach of the duty of loyalty. . . .

In re Tri-Star Pictures, 634 A.2d at 334 (footnote omitted); accord Milbank, 13 F.3d at 543 ("breaches of a fiduciary relationship in any context comprise a special breed of cases that often loosen normally stringent requirements of causation and damages"). The strict imposition of penalties under Delaware law are designed to discourage disloyalty.

The rule, inveterate and uncompromising in its rigidity, does not rest upon the narrow ground of injury or damage to the corporation resulting from a betrayal of confidence, but upon a broader foundation of a wise public policy that, for the purpose of removing all temptation, extinguishes all possibility of profit flowing from a breach of the confidence imposed by the fiduciary relation. Guth v. Loft, Inc., Del. Supr., 5 A.2d 503, 510 (1939).

Once disloyalty has been established, the standards evolved in Oberly v. Kirby and *Tri-Star* require that a fiduciary not profit personally from his conduct, and that the beneficiary not be harmed by such conduct. While there are no transactional damages in this case, we find the Eriksons liable for damages incidental to their breach of duty. Specifically the Eriksons are liable to CERBCO for the amount of $75,000 received from INA in connection with the letter of intent. See J. Leo Johnson, Inc. v. Carmer, Del. Supr., 156 A.2d 499, 503 (1959); see also Restatement (Second) of Agency §388 (agent must account for value received from third parties in connection with services on behalf of principal). In addition, the Eriksons must reimburse CERBCO for any expenses, including legal and due diligence costs, that the corporation incurred to accommodate the Eriksons' pursuit of their own interests prior to the deal being abandoned by the Eriksons and INA.

The opinion below is AFFIRMED IN PART and REVERSED IN PART, and this matter is REMANDED to the Court of Chancery for a further determination of damages. Once those damages are fixed, the court should proceed to examine anew any petition for counsel fees on behalf of the plaintiffs.

PROBLEM 8-12

Reconsider the facts in Problem 8-11, page 825, supra.

Suppose that Watin initially approached Mallon to suggest a merger of NAT and MCTV at a cash-out price of $60 per share, a premium of 50 percent over the then-market price of MCTV shares. Mallon insisted that he was only interested in selling his control block, and that he would veto any merger. After NAT and Mallon entered into the agreement described in Problem 8-11, Mallon called a special meeting of the MCTV board, described the purchase agreement, and asked that the board agree to facilitate the transaction by giving NAT access to MCTV books and records, and by resigning seriatim at the closing so as to give NAT immediate control of MCTV management. When asked by an outside director whether a merger between NAT and MCTV would be worth considering, Mallon replied "I fully explored that option, and it is not something that they are interested in." The board then agreed to back the transaction, which closed as scheduled.

(a) Suppose that, upon discovering this additional information, Sig Owens amends his derivative complaint to include a breach of corporate opportunity claim. What is the likely outcome of such claim?

(b) How would your analysis of the corporate opportunity claim be changed if Mallon owned only 35 percent of MCTV's stock?

9 Changes in Control: Hostile Acquisitions

A. The Market for Corporate Control

Mergers and other transactions described in Chapter 8 permit changes in control of a corporation, but only with the consent of the existing control group. Since mergers require the approval first of the board of directors and then the shareholders, the board can act as a gatekeeper, deflecting any offers that it does not think appropriate. The board may use this gatekeeping authority to promote value-increasing decisions for the firm, but if the motivation of the acquisition is to replace inefficient management, there will be concern that the current control group will exercise this gatekeeper function in an opportunistic fashion.

Direct dealings between the shareholders and potential alternative management teams are one way to counter this opportunistic behavior. A potential acquiror who seeks control without the consent of the current control group can (1) make a tender offer seeking to buy sufficient shares to gain control of the board, or (2) launch a proxy fight seeking the authority to vote sufficient shares to gain control of the board of directors. Hostile tender offers were rare until the 1960s. Proxy fights occurred regularly prior to that time, but only a small number in any given year. The surge in hostile takeovers triggered a long-running debate on the benefit of takeovers to society and the need, if any, for government regulation.

The potential relationship between an acquiring firm and shareholders of a target company raises a new set of concerns. The collective action problems found in large corporations with large numbers of dispersed, passive shareholders can reappear in a hostile acquisition context. If shareholders lack the ability or sufficient incentive to investigate and act collectively in response to an offer from an outside party, there is the possibility of shareholders accepting an inadequate offer. Studies of takeover premiums paid to target shareholders in the 1970s and 1980s show positive returns of 30 percent or more. See Jensen and Ruback, The Market for Corporate Control: The Scientific Evidence, 11 J. Fin. Econ. 5 (1983) (summarizing several studies and reporting price changes of target firms, net of marketwide price movements, of 30 percent in tender offers, 20 percent in mergers, and 8 percent in proxy fights). Of course, overall gains can mask coercive behavior in a subset of takeover transactions, and even a premium may be inadequate compensation to the shareholders who desire a larger proportion of gains derived from a takeover. In addition, even if takeovers are good for shareholders, their gains might come at the expense of some other constituency, such as employees, bondholders, or communities that lose plants and company headquarters. As one governor said upon signing a state anti-takeover law, "Pennsylvania doesn't need any more of the kind of takeovers which have destroyed communities, disrupted families, and put thousands of workers out of a job."

This chapter addresses how to balance the concern that directors may be acting opportunistically with concerns that acquiring companies posing as friends to the target shareholders might be taking advantage of them or that the bidders, with the acquiescence of the target shareholders, are taking advantage of other constituencies.

Possible responses to this situation are those discussed elsewhere in this book. Prior to 1968, the matter was left to the markets, at least as to tender offers. An acquiring firm would make an offer, via an advertisement in a national newspaper, to purchase shares of the target company. The announcement usually offered cash at a premium over the company's then current market price. If the offer were first-come, first-served for less than all of the company's stock, the stockholder's fear of losing the premium could provoke a hasty decision. Congressional concern about shareholders of the target companies being forced to make decisions to tender without complete information led to the passage of the Williams Act, which is discussed in more detail in Chapter 11.

Even prior to 1968, there was government regulation of combinations in the form of antitrust review, although that monitoring decreased significantly during the takeover boom of the 1980s. Early takeover statutes at the state level required all takeovers to receive regulatory approval of a state official, approval that could be withheld on very broad grounds. In 1982, the Supreme Court ruled that an Illinois statute with this impact was unconstitutional as impermissible state regulation of interstate commerce. See Edgar v. MITE Corp., 457 U.S. 624 (1982).

A possible response to an ill-informed shareholder decision is to mandate the supply of additional information that for whatever reason is not being provided by the markets. Since the passage of the Securities Exchange Act of 1934, the federal government has required disclosure to shareholders when their proxies are solicited to approve a merger. The Williams Act, a 1968 amendment to that law, extended required disclosure to shareholders faced with tender offers. A tender offeror must disclose its identity and background, the source and amount of funds to be used in making the purchase, and the purpose of the purchase, including any plans to liquidate the target or change its corporate structure. See §14(d)(1) of the 1934 Act.

In addition to requiring disclosure, the Williams Act provides certain procedural protections to shareholders faced with a tender offer. For example, a tender offer must remain open for 20 business days, blocking a bidder's effort to force a hasty decision by shareholders. SEC Rule 14e-1(a). If more shares are tendered than the bidder sought to purchase, the bidder must buy a pro rata portion from each shareholder. This prevents use of a first-come, first-served strategy to pressure shareholders to tender. See §14(d)(6) of the 1934 Act. Also, the bidder must pay the same price for all shares purchased, and if the offering price is increased before the end of the offer, those who have already tendered must receive the increased price. See §14(d)(7) of the 1934 Act.

Efforts to interpret the federal act to prohibit defensive tactics blocking tender offers have been rebuffed by courts, as discussed in more detail in Chapter 11.

If shareholders are being exploited and are unable to coordinate their response to a tender offer, the possibility of the board acting as an agent to coordinate shareholder response presents a familiar option. Indeed, the board acts for the entire body of shareholders in any number of corporate actions, albeit limited by fiduciary duty and other contractual or market restraints. More recently, boards have been viewed as protectors of other constituencies as well, a controversial idea that continues to be debated. Yet hostile takeovers necessarily involve a challenge to the board's continuation in office, raising the possibility of self-dealing in any actions the board takes to block tender offers. The question of the appropriate level of judicial review under the legal standards discussed in Chapters 4 and 8 takes on new significance and a different focus as discussed in this chapter.

One characteristic of takeovers is the significant premium paid to shareholders of the acquired corporation. In recent years such premiums have routinely exceeded 30 percent of the pre-tender offer share price, and often have ranged much higher. This phenomenon puzzles economists because it suggests that share prices do not measure the value of the corporation's underlying assets. For example, suppose that X Corporation has 10 million outstanding shares that trade on the NYSE at $10 per share. Traditional finance theory suggests that the asset must be worth $100 million, the stock market value of the corporation's equity. Why, then, would a purchaser be willing to pay $15 per share in a tender offer?

Reflecting on the sources and distributions of takeover premiums will inform your consideration of the appropriate judicial response to hostile takeovers. The following articles frame the discussion of gains in takeovers.

Coffee, Regulating the Market for Corporate Control: A Critical Assessment of the Tender Offer's Role in Corporate Governance
84 Colum. L. Rev. 1145, 1162-1173 (1984)

. . . Those who have sought to explain the phenomenon of the hostile takeover have usually begun with its most striking fact: bidders have been willing to pay extraordinarily high premiums (sometimes over 100%) for the stock of target corporations, even though the securities so solicited were presumably efficiently priced because they were typically traded on major stock exchanges. Why are such lucrative premiums paid? Most of the explanations can be grouped under one of the following four headings:

1. THE DISCIPLINARY HYPOTHESIS

Viewed through the lens supplied by the "market for corporate control" thesis, the role of the tender offer is to replace inefficient management. The bidder, it is argued, pays a premium over the market price because it believes that the target's assets have not been optimally utilized and that under superior management they would earn a higher return, thereby justifying the tender offer premium. In this light, the higher the premium, the greater the degree of mismanagement that the bidder must perceive. So viewed, the hostile tender offer appears a benign and socially desirable phenomenon, which benefits both the bidder and the target's stockholders, who simply divide among themselves the value that the incumbent management's inefficiency denied them. . . .

2.   THE SYNERGY HYPOTHESIS

An alternative explanation of the hostile takeover views the takeover premium as justified not by the sub-optimal performance of the target, but rather as the result of the target's having a unique value to the bidder that is in excess of its value to the market generally. Put simply, the value of the combined enterprise is expected to be greater than the sum of its separate parts as independent companies. Such "synergistic gains" may be the result of a variety of factors that are independent of the inefficient management thesis: unique product complementarity between the two companies, specialized resources possessed by the target, economies of scale, cost reductions, lowered borrowing costs, or the capital market's response to the combined enterprise. Professor Gilson and Lucian Bebchuk have separately articulated this view in a series of carefully reasoned articles. However, their thesis is subject to two important objections. First, studies of postacquisition experiences of acquiring companies have typically found that the expected synergy seldom materializes in the form of higher profits. Second, this theory gives little attention to the disciplinary or deterrent impact of hostile takeovers. These flaws do not invalidate the theory, but do suggest that it is only a partial explanation.

3.   THE EMPIRE BUILDING HYPOTHESIS

A more skeptical explanation for high takeover premiums begins from the obvious possibility that the bidder simply may have overpaid. Those who take a "behavioral" view of the modern corporation have long argued that firms tend to maximize size, not profits. Management may pursue size maximization, even when it is not in the interests of shareholders, for any of a variety of reasons: (1) greater size tends to correspond with higher compensation for management; (2) increased size implies greater security from a takeover or other control contest; (3) enhanced prestige and psychic income are associated with increased size and national visibility; (4) greater size often translates into oligopolistic market power; or, finally, (5) expansion offers opportunities for advancement to the executive staff of the bidding firm. Under this "empire building" thesis, the high premiums paid in tender offers are less an indication of the potential latent in the target's assets than of an overly optimistic assessment by the bidder of its own capabilities as a manager. From this perspective, the takeover process may result not in greater efficiency, but only in a net transfer of wealth from the bidder's shareholders to those of the target. Much empirical data suggest that these wealth transfers occur frequently, but it is considerably more difficult to argue that they predominate.[56] Nonetheless, the Empire Building Hypothesis suggests that the most important conflict of interests in corporate control contests may be on the bidder's side of the transaction—between the interests of the bidder's management and those of its own shareholders. In any case, as a model which explains takeover activity, the Empire Building Hypothesis focuses singlemindedly on only one variable (the effect on the bidder) and therefore cannot be taken as more than a partial explanation.

4.   The Exploitation Hypothesis

Gain to the bidder in a takeover can come either through the creation of new value or through the transfer of existing value from other investors. Recent commentators have suggested that such wealth transfers may result from the target shareholders being trapped in a classic "prisoner's dilemma" in which they are faced with a choice between an unsatisfactory current price offered by the bidder and a potentially even lower price in the future.[59]

Two distinct scenarios have been suggested to explain how exploitation might occur. Professor Carney has pointed to the recent appearance of the two-tier bid, in which a high premium is paid in a partial bid for 51% of the target's stock, but then a takeout merger is eventually effected at a price below the pre-tender offer market price, with the result that the average price received amounts to a net loss for the target's shareholders.[60] Actual transactions in which the bidder acquires the target at an average price below the pre-tender trading price remain exceedingly rare, however.

---

56. It is undisputed that in some cases bidder shareholders have experienced dramatic declines in stock values in response to a takeover bid. In the DuPont acquisition of Conoco, for example, DuPont paid $7.54 billion, at that time the largest acquisition in U.S. history. The value of DuPont stock fell by $789 million (a 9.9% drop), and a $641 million decline occurred on the day of the offer's announcement. Similarly, Texaco's recent offer of $9.9 billion for Getty may have been excessive in light of the stock market's capitalization of Texaco, a much larger company, at "just over $9 billion"; in effect, Texaco will be paying a higher price for Getty's reserves than the stock market appears to place on its own vastly larger reserves. . . . Similarly, a study by First Boston Corp. of recent oil industry acquisitions found that "almost without exception, the stocks of buyers of oil companies have declined following such transactions." Nonetheless, after averaging the results of several studies, one survey has found bidders to average a gain in stock price of 3.8% (after adjustment for general market movement). This average figure is open to question on a variety of methodological grounds, both because it does not include extensive postacquisition experience and because alternate methodological approaches have been developed, which call into question much of the data so averaged. Based on this different approach to the computation of the gains, [one] study found that acquirers suffer significant losses in mergers.

59. Prisoner's dilemmas arise when the affected shareholders are unable to communicate or coordinate their actions to resist a tender offer. In the case of the two-tier takeover, the inability of shareholders to coordinate their actions and resist the initial partial tender offer at an attractive premium leaves them vulnerable to the second stage merger at a price below market. Rational investors, had they been able to coordinate, might have rejected the tender offer.

60. [Carney, Shareholder Coordination Costs, Shark Repellents and Takeout Mergers: The Case Against Fiduciary Duties, 1983 A.B.F. Res. J. 341, 349, 353.] The most often cited example of a two-tier bid was U.S. Steel's successful offer for 51% of Marathon Oil in 1981 for a cash price of $125 per share: as disclosed in advance, U.S. Steel then acquired the remaining 49% of Marathon through a subsidiary pursuant to a post-tender merger for securities having a value on a per share basis of approximately $86. See Radol v. Thomas, 534 F. Supp. 1302, 1305 n.2 (S.D. Ohio 1982). Thus, the average price paid was $105.50.

Another, more popular form of the exploitation thesis argues that bidders overreach target shareholders by exploiting temporary depressions in the target's stock price in order to seize control of the target in a bargain purchase. A variation on this same theme views the recent high rate of takeover activity as the product of systematic undervaluation on the part of the stock market, which, it is asserted, capitalizes industrial corporations at levels well below their "going concern" value or, at times, even below their book value. If, as the saying goes, "the cheapest oil that can be found is on the floor of the New York Stock Exchange," the rational bidder will exploit these opportunities to make a bargain purchase, rather than pay a higher price to develop equivalent plant and production facilities. Although this view that acquisitions are really bargain purchases has been sharply questioned,[65] those favoring it tend to see the stock market as either dominated by an extreme pessimism, which results in arbitrarily low valuations, or as preoccupied with short-term trading profits because institutional investors focus largely on the prospect of short-term price changes in securities. Because corporate bidders continue to value target companies on the basis of their discounted future earnings, which method results in higher valuations, a disparity arguably arises between these two measures of value that justifies the tender offer premium. In effect, this view postulates that there are two distinct markets for corporate shares with only imperfect arbitrage between them: one market for corporate control and another for investment profit. . . .

5. An Overview

The major watershed highlighted by the foregoing survey is between those explanations that see takeovers as creating wealth and those that see takeovers as primarily transferring existing wealth. The first two theories—the Disciplinary Hypothesis and the Synergy Hypothesis—postulate that takeovers create wealth in the form of higher stock prices, and that the bidder and target shareholders share the gains. The Empire Building and Exploitation Hypotheses view the takeover less benignly and see it as a mechanism which frequently transfers wealth between different groups of

---

65. As popular as the "bargain purchase" view is, it involves a basic paradox: why does the market sell established reserves of oil companies at prices well below the costs that other oil companies incur regularly to find new reserves? As MIT Economics Professor M.A. Adelman has succinctly put it, "[e]ither you have to conclude that the whole financial community and oil industry is composed of idiots, or there is something wrong with that explanation." See Blumstein, Buying vs. Exploring for Oil, N.Y. Times, Mar. 19, 1984, at D1, col. 3. Another popular explanation is that investors have a different time horizon within which they are seeking to maximize their gains than the oil firms, which are asserted to have a longer-term perspective. This view, however, seems equally questionable. Why do corporate firms have different time horizons from the investors who own them? This view in fact suggests a failure in corporate accountability. Another explanation much heard among Wall Street analysts is that the oil firms are worth more broken up than as a single entity; in this view, "the companies' other operations drag down the price of their stock so that the market price does not reflect the full value of oil in the ground." Blumstein, supra. In essence, this thesis is a particularized statement of the "empire building" hypothesis, since it holds that these corporations have grown beyond their optimal size and have failed to divest themselves of less profitable operations.

shareholders. Under the Empire Building thesis, target shareholders profit at the expense of bidder shareholders, while under the various Exploitation Hypotheses, the reverse is true, as bidder shareholders receive gains at the expense of target shareholders. Thus, if one asks "who wins and who loses from takeovers," these different explanations give every possible answer. Yet, even though these various theories are inconsistent, it does not follow that one must be entirely valid and the others false. Rather, under a pluralistic interpretation, each theory may have a partial validity and may accurately describe the motivations underlying some (but not all) takeovers. The empirical evidence gives some support for this "disaggregated" perspective, because instances can be identified in which the gains to either class of shareholders (bidder or target) came at the expense of the other. . . . .

Black, Bidder Overpayment in Takeovers:
Manager Ignorance and the Winner's Curse
41 Stanford L. Rev. 597, 625-626 (1989)

A second source of expected overpayment, in addition to managers' optimism, is their ignorance about bidding theory. In an auction of an asset of uncertain value, bidders are vulnerable to the "winner's curse": Even if they estimate value accurately on average, they win the bidding primarily when they overestimate an asset's true value, and thus tend to overpay on average. The auction need not be explicit; it is enough that there are potential bidders waiting in the wings to make a higher offer if the first bid is too low.

If uncertainty is high, a bidder that takes the apparently conservative approach of offering a little less than its best estimate of value will still overpay, on average. Winner's curse theory dictates that bidders must offer substantially less than they think an asset is worth, and be prepared to have only a fraction of their bids succeed. Winner's curse problems apply, however, only to an asset whose value is "common" to all bidders. Thus, a bidder who has unique synergy with a target faces a winner's curse risk only to the extent of the target's value to other bidders.

I know of no evidence that the investment bankers who advise managers on takeover bids, let alone the corporate managers themselves, know anything about winner's curse theory. My personal experience as a takeover lawyer is that they do not. Also, experiments show that "avoiding the winner's curse is not easy. Even experienced subjects who are given significant learning opportunities fail to solve the buy-a-firm problem and fail to understand the need to become more conservative when the number of bidders increases."[69] Moreover, even if some managers have developed strategies that offset the winner's curse, it's a good bet that others have not. Those who haven't will be more likely to succeed in acquiring a target.

---

69. Thaler, Anomalies: The Winner's Curse, 2 J. Econ. Persp. 191, 196 (1988).

Kraakman, Taking Discounts Seriously:
The Implications of "Discounted" Share Prices as an
Acquisition Motive
88 Colum. L. Rev. 891, 897-900 (1988)

The discount claim assumes that acquisition premia reflect the existing value of target assets, a value that may be much higher than the pre-bid market value of target shares. A discount hypothesis must explain why these values differ. Apart from specialized tax claims, two broad explanations of discounts are possible: the misinvestment hypothesis and the market hypothesis.

The misinvestment hypothesis comes closest to traditional accounts of takeover gains. This account locates discrepancies between share prices and asset values in a rational mistrust of managers' future investment decisions. As such, it belongs to the broader family of agency cost theories. Unlike accounts of manager-shareholder conflict over operating slack and perquisites, however, the misinvestment hypothesis follows more recent analyses of manager-shareholder conflict over the distribution of corporate returns. In this view, managers exercise discretionary control over what Professor Jensen terms "free cash flows"—those cash flows exceeding the investment requirements of the firm's existing projects. If managers are reluctant to distribute these cash flows and are unable—or unwilling—to discover profitable new investments, shareholders must inevitably price firms at below informed appraisals of their asset values. . . .

The alternative discount hypothesis—the market hypothesis—fits less easily with standard accounts of the securities market. In this view, share prices may discount asset values for reasons endogenous to the formation of market prices. . . .

Modern objections to identifying share prices with asset values typically fall into two classes. The first class includes "valuation" challenges that question whether a single valuation model can apply across the markets for shares and firms or within the share market itself. Even if traders in both the asset and share markets value corporate assets similarly, share prices might nonetheless discount asset values simply because assets and shares differ in ways that matter to traders. For example, the share prices of firms holding liquid assets might discount asset values if traders placed an intrinsic value on the right to liquidate firms in the asset market—a right that minority shareholders in these firms would necessarily lack. Alternatively, overlapping clienteles of traders within the securities market might have heterogeneous demands for timing, magnitude, or tax attributes of shareholder distributions. In this case, shares might sell at either a discount or a premium relative to asset values.

The second and more prominent class of objections to equating share prices with asset values challenges the price setting role of informed traders. Thus, there is a growing theoretical literature on "mispricing" behavior, which argues that uninformed traders may introduce persistent biases or cumulative noise into share prices or that speculative trading might lead to positive or negative price "bubbles." Large-scale noise trading—arising from misconceived strategies, erroneous valuation assumptions, fashion and fads, or simple pleasure in trading—might distort share prices and generate discounts or premia through the sheer pressure of trading. In addition, some commentators suggest that noise trading further distorts share prices by encouraging informed traders to speculate on noise and by imposing "noise trader risk" on all traders in a noisy market.

GLOSSARY OF TAKEOVER TACTICS

Hostile takeovers have spawned a unique vocabulary both in the popular press and among participants, beginning with the names given to the parties themselves. The acquiring company is referred to as a **bidder** or, more pejoratively, as a **raider.** A bidder such as Maremont in Cheff v. Mathes, infra page 846, would be portrayed today as engaging in a **bust-up** takeover, seeking to break up the target and sell it off in pieces. Financing for many raiders during the 1980s was provided by issuing **junk bonds,** a term that refers to bonds that are higher risk and therefore bear a higher interest rate.

The company sought to be acquired is a **target.** A **white knight** is a second bidder, thought to be friendly to target management, who makes an offer to rescue the target from a hostile bidder. A friendly party who does not acquire control but acquires a large block of target stock with the acquiescence of target management is a **white squire. Arbs** or **arbitragers** are regular market participants who seek to make money by short-term purchases or sales of stock. When arbs determine that a company is "in play" as a potential target, they will purchase large blocks of the target stock hoping to sell out for the higher takeover price. Other key terms are discussed below.

Front-end loaded tender offer.   In Chapter 8 we saw several examples of controlling shareholders cashing out minority shareholders. Often, such transactions are the second step in a two-tiered tender offer. In the first step, the bidder acquires a controlling interest in the target via a tender offer, usually for cash. In the second step, the remaining shares are acquired through merger. In a front-end loaded tender offer, the consideration in the tender offer is worth more than the consideration in the second-step merger. Such tender offers are viewed as coercive because shareholders who do not tender in the first step will be forced to accept less for the untendered shares. The transaction becomes even more coercive if the consideration is junk bonds or illiquid securities.

Golden parachutes.   This phrase describes the lucrative compensation and fringe benefits given to target management to ease their descent if they are fired after a hostile takeover. Parachutes are promoted as a means of keeping needed executives when a company is "in play." Contracts extended to a larger number of lower-level employees are sometimes referred to as **tin parachutes.**

Greenmail.   This is a pejorative term for a target's repurchase of its own shares from a raider where the target pays a premium for the shares to induce the unwanted suitor to go away. As illustrated by Cheff v. Mathes, infra page 846, courts have upheld such payments against claims based on fiduciary duty. But see Heckman v. Ahmanson, 168 Cal. App. 3d 119, 214 Cal. Rptr. 177 (1985) (affirming preliminary injunction because plaintiff demonstrated a reasonable probability of success on the merits against a greenmail payment). Federal tax law imposes a tax on some repurchases, but the definition is fairly limited and often can be avoided by planning. I.R.C. §5881. Some corporations have passed charter provisions forbidding the payment of greenmail.

Lock-ups and termination fees.   Once a hostile takeover begins or seems likely, target company management may seek a deal with an acquirer of its choice. That white knight may be reluctant to bid, or to continue bidding, because of the substantial unre-imbursed expenses and opportunity costs incurred if the bid is unsuccessful. The con-tractual provisions (or **deal protection provisions**) include **termination fees** or **stock options at a bargain price** designed to compensate the white knight for serving as a **stalk-ing horse** in the auction contest. Even in a friendly transaction, the acquiring corpora-tion may seek such protection for fear that a bidding contest will occur. See, e.g., Smith v. Van Gorkom, supra page 331. At some point in an auction contest, target company management may grant a **lock-up option** to the preferred bidder. A lock-up option gives the white knight a right to purchase the corporation's most valuable assets—its **crown jewels.** Such options make other bids unlikely because many of the key assets are now promised to the white knight. Lock-up options create value if they induce a white knight to make a final bid that the knight would otherwise be unwilling to make, unless the lock-up prematurely forecloses the auction, preventing another bidder from presenting an even higher bid. A friendly agreement may also include contract clauses to protect the purchaser, such as **MAC** (material adverse changes), which permit the purchaser and out if certain conditions occur. **Reverse termination fees** also protect the purchaser.

Poison pills.   This colorful term refers to stock rights or warrants issued to a potential target's shareholders prior to a takeover. These rights lie unused and almost worthless until triggered by a hostile acquisition. At that point the rights explode in a way that makes the acquisition particularly painful for the bidder to digest. In the more popular versions of the pill, the target shareholders get the right to redeem their shares in the target company for a price well above market price or the target share-holders get the right to purchase shares of the acquiring company at a reduced price after a follow-up merger between the two companies. These rights typically are written to exclude any shares of the target owned by the acquiring company. The acquiring company finds itself with a target corporation depleted of assets or filled with new obli-gations. The legal questions raised by poison pills are discussed in more detail later in this chapter at page 860.

Recapitalizations and leveraged buyouts (LBOs) by management (MBOs).   Target management may seek to respond to the bidder's offer by providing shareholders a rearranged financial package that offers shareholders an immediate cash payment for their shares, often financed by huge additional borrowings by the corporation. This may take the form of a tender offer backed by management as an alternative to the initial tender offer by a hostile bidder. The alternative may also include lock-ups and leg-ups and raise auction duties of the target board.

Shark repellent amendments (or "porcupine provisions") to the corporation's charter and/or bylaws.   The defensive tactics discussed above usually are taken by the board of directors without participation of the shareholders. Judicial review of those actions therefore parallels review of other board actions in managing the corporation, with such adjustment as the court thinks necessary to reflect the board's possible self-interest. Some defensive tactics, however, include shareholder approval and these invoke a different kind of judicial review. These provisions include the following:

(1) Supermajority amendments. These provisions raise the vote required to effect a merger or similar transaction from the simple majority or two-thirds normally required by corporate law to a figure as high as 90 percent. This requirement applies to mergers or similar transactions with certain defined control persons and often can be waived by the target's board of directors. Most state corporation codes permit a corporation to increase the required vote by changing its articles or bylaws. But see Georgia-Pacific Corp. v. Great Northern Nekoosa Corp., 731 F. Supp. 38 (D. Me. 1990) (§707 of Maine corporation code requiring two-thirds vote for removal of directors cannot be increased pursuant to §611's general authorization to increase percentage of vote required for shareholder action).

(2) Fair price amendments. These provisions, like the supermajority provisions, focus on second-step transactions that may follow the acquisition of control by a raider. These provisions build on the supermajority concept in that they waive the supermajority vote if the second-step transaction offers a "fair price" as defined in the provision. The definition of fair price is often elaborate and can be designed so it exceeds any price offered for the stock in the first stage. This imbalance may cause some shareholders not to tender or raise the bidder's costs to the point where a tender offer will not be initiated.

(3) Staggered board amendments. If a corporation divided its board into three classes serving staggered three-year terms, the shareholder with a newly acquired majority of shares may only be able to elect one-third of the board at the next annual meeting and thus be denied control of the assets for which it has just invested a substantial sum of money. The ability of the new controlling shareholder to acquire control of the majority of the board turns on the state statutes and the corporation's charter and bylaw provisions governing the right to call special meetings and to remove directors. Note that Delaware law allows directors serving staggered terms to be removed only for cause, a provision that seems designed to make takeovers more difficult.

(4) Dual-class capitalization. Management can gain insulation beyond their actual share ownership if their shares have multiple votes per share or the public shares have fractional votes per share. Charter amendments to provide dual-class stock increased during the 1980s when the New York Stock Exchange declared a moratorium on its longstanding rule against dual-class stock in the face of competition from other exchanges without similar rules. In 1988 the SEC promulgated Rule 19c-4, which banned dual-class amendments in existing publicly traded corporations. An SEC study expressed concern over shareholder voting in situations where the reduced voting was coupled with a "sweetener," or increased dividend on the reduced voting stock. The SEC also pointed to the rational apathy and collective action problems of shareholders responding to such a proposal. A federal court of appeals held that the rule exceeded the SEC's authority, The Business Roundtable v. SEC, 905 F.2d 406 (D.C. Cir. 1990), and returned the matter to the regulation of the stock exchange. In 1994 the NYSE, the American Stock Exchange, and NASDAQ agreed to adopt rules similar to Rule 19c-4 that substantially limit listed companies' ability to depart from a one-share, one-vote capital structure.

B.   Judicial Review of Tender Offer Defenses

1.   Traditional Review

The focus in takeover litigation is usually specific actions taken by directors to fend off what the directors view as an unwanted offer, even if the offer provides terms that shareholders may find attractive. In other cases, the directors seek to fend off the possibility of an unfriendly offer, even if the prospects of such an offer are hypothetical or uncertain. Why do directors need to take such defensive actions? Recall from Chapter 3 and your first exposure to the governance rules of corporations that statutes allocate all corporate powers to directors. Shareholders in contrast have rather limited powers to vote, sell, or sue. Usually these powers pose no threat to directors. However, if an outsider seeks to employ sufficient resources to buy control of the company or win a proxy contest to displace current managers, then those shareholders' powers take on great significance. Takeover defenses essentially involve the directors' efforts to prevent shareholders from exercising their power to vote or to sell in the unfriendly takeover context—that relatively rare circumstance where shareholders' collective choices might reduce or eliminate the directors' control of the corporation. Directors and their legal advisors attempt to employ takeover defenses and tactics that will be protected by the business judgment rule; when they are successful in so doing, shareholders' ability to sue is also essentially eliminated.

As you go through the remainder of this chapter, be alert to which shareholder power is being curtailed by the defensive measure in question. Why is the particular device designed as it is? Have the courts applied the proper standard of review in deciding whether to allow the defensive measure to stand, or, instead, to provide relief to complaining shareholders?

The following case involves a historically common defense mechanism: the directors cause the corporation to purchase the outsider's stock, generally at a price above the prevailing market price of the corporation's shares. What standard of review should a court use when a shareholder complaint asserts that the directors breached their fiduciary duties in authorizing such transaction? As the following case shows, courts have traditionally accorded directors less deference than if business judgment rule presumptions were in place, but more deference than if the transaction involved traditional self-dealing.

Cheff v. Mathes
Delaware Supreme Court, 1964
199 A.2d 548

CAREY, JUSTICE.

This is an appeal from the decision of the Vice Chancellor in a derivative suit holding certain directors of Holland Furnace Company liable for loss allegedly resulting from improper use of corporate funds to purchase shares of the company. . . .

[Holland Furnace Company, a manufacturer of hot air furnaces and air conditioning equipment, maintains its main plants and principal office in Holland, Michigan.

From this central point it sells its products to consumers through some 400 branch offices and numerous smaller offices situated in 43 states. Management considers its practice of directly employing the retail salesman — unique in the furnace business — to be a vital factor in the company's success. In other words, the organization purports to operate a large, integrated business in which there are no intermediate dealers. Notwithstanding Holland's growth over the years, in the period immediately preceding the transactions complained of, its sales and earnings had decreased and its marketing methods had been made the subject of serious charges leveled against it by the Federal Trade Commission.[1]

The members of Holland's seven-member board, each a defendant in this lawsuit, are (1) P.T. Cheff, the corporation's CEO; (2) Katharine Cheff, P.T.'s wife, and the daughter of the company's founder; (3) Edgar Landwehr, Katherine's nephew; (4) Robert Trenkamp, the corporation's outside attorney; (5) John Ames, an investment banker; (6) Ralph Boalt, a corporate executive at an unrelated company; and (7) George Spatta, CEO of an unrelated corporation.

Hazelbank United Interest, Inc. (Hazelbank) owns 164,950 of Holland's 883,585 outstanding shares. Hazelbank is an investment vehicle for the Cheff/Landwehr family. Katherine Cheff owns 48 percent of Hazelbank's shares; Edgar Landwehr owns 9 percent. Landwehr also owns 24,000 Holland shares, and the Cheff's own 12,000 Holland shares. Other directors own insignificant amounts of Holland shares. Directors receive $200 per meeting. The only other compensation paid to Holland's directors was P.T. Cheff's salary as CEO, and Robert Trenkamp's fees for legal services (averaging approximately $50,000 per year).]

During the first five months of 1957, the monthly trading volume of Holland's stock on the New York Stock Exchange ranged between 10,300 shares to 24,200 shares. In the last week of June 1957, however, the trading increased to 37,800 shares, with a corresponding increase in the market price. In June of 1957, Mr. Cheff met with Mr. Arnold H. Maremont, who was President of Maremont Automotive Products, Inc. and Chairman of the boards of Motor Products Corporation and Allied Paper Corporation. Mr. Cheff testified, on deposition, that Maremont generally inquired about the feasibility of merger between Motor Products and Holland. Mr. Cheff testified that, in view of the difference in sales practices between the two companies, he informed Mr. Maremont that a merger did not seem feasible. In reply, Mr. Maremont stated that, in the light of Mr. Cheff's decision, he had no further interest in Holland nor did he wish to buy any of the stock of Holland.

None of the members of the board apparently connected the interest of Mr. Maremont with the increased activity of Holland stock. However, Mr. Trenkamp and Mr. Staal, the Treasurer of Holland, unsuccessfully made an informal investigation in order to ascertain the identity of the purchaser or purchasers. The mystery was

---

1. [Eds. note — Holland was later fined $100,000, and Cheff was sentenced to six months in jail for willful disobedience of a Federal Trade Commission cease-and-desist order that resulted from the proceedings referred to in the opinion. Those proceedings suggested that the Holland sales force sometimes falsely represented themselves as heating engineers and would dismantle a furnace after gaining entry to the house of a potential customer. After refusing to reassemble the furnace on the claim that it was defective and dangerous, the salesperson often was successful in closing the sale for a new furnace.]

resolved, however, when Maremont called Ames in July of 1957 to inform the latter that Maremont then owned 55,000 shares of Holland stock. At this juncture, no requests for change in corporate policy were made, and Maremont made no demand to be made a member of the board of Holland.

Ames reported the above information to the board at its July 30, 1957 meeting. Because of the position now occupied by Maremont, the board elected to investigate the financial and business history of Maremont and corporations controlled by him. Apart from the documentary evidence produced by this investigation, which will be considered infra, Staal testified, on deposition, that "leading bank officials" had indicated that Maremont "had been a participant, or had attempted to be, in the liquidation of a number of companies." Staal specifically mentioned only one individual giving such advice, the Vice President of the First National Bank of Chicago. Mr. Cheff testified, at trial, of Maremont's alleged participation in liquidation activities. Mr. Cheff testified that: "Throughout the whole of the Kalamazoo-Battle Creek area, and Detroit too, where I spent considerable time, he is well known and not highly regarded by any stretch." This information was communicated to the board.

On August 23, 1957, at the request of Maremont, a meeting was held between Mr. Maremont and Cheff. At this meeting, Cheff was informed that Motor Products then owned approximately 100,000 shares of Holland stock. Maremont then made a demand that he be named to the board of directors, but Cheff refused to consider it. Since considerable controversy has been generated by Maremont's alleged threat to liquidate the company or substantially alter the sales force of Holland, we believe it desirable to set forth the testimony of Cheff on this point: "Now we have 8500 men, direct employees, so the problem is entirely different. He indicated immediately that he had no interest in that type of distribution, that he didn't think it was modern, that he felt furnaces could be sold as he sold mufflers, through half a dozen salesmen in a wholesale way."

Testimony was introduced by the defendants tending to show that substantial unrest was present among the employees of Holland as a result of the threat of Maremont to seek control of Holland. Thus, Mr. Cheff testified that the field organization was considering leaving in large numbers because of a fear of the consequences of a Maremont acquisition; he further testified that approximately "25 of our key men" were lost as the result of the unrest engendered by the Maremont proposal. Staal, corroborating Cheff's version, stated that a number of branch managers approached him for reassurances that Maremont was not going to be allowed to successfully gain control. Moreover, at approximately this time, the company was furnished with a Dun and Bradstreet report, which indicated the practice of Maremont to achieve quick profits by sales or liquidations of companies acquired by him. The defendants were also supplied with an income statement of Motor Products, Inc., showing a loss of $336,121.00 for the period in 1957.

On August 30, 1957, the board was informed by Cheff of Maremont's demand to be placed upon the board and of Maremont's belief that the retail sales organization of Holland was obsolete. The board was also informed of the results of the investigation by Cheff and Staal. Predicated upon this information, the board authorized the purchase of company stock on the market with corporate funds, ostensibly for use in a stock option plan.

Subsequent to this meeting, substantial numbers of shares were purchased and, in addition, Mrs. Cheff made alternate personal purchases of Holland stock. As a result of purchases by Maremont, Holland and Mrs. Cheff, the market price rose. . . . On September 4th, Maremont proposed to sell his current holdings of Holland to the corporation for $14.00 a share. However, because of delay in responding to this offer, Maremont withdrew the offer. At this time, Mrs. Cheff was obviously quite concerned over the prospect of a Maremont acquisition, and had stated her willingness to expend her personal resources to prevent it.

On September 30, 1957, Motor Products Corporation, by letter to Mrs. Bowles, made a buy-sell offer to Hazelbank. At the Hazelbank meeting of October 3, 1957, Mrs. Bowles presented the letter to the board. The board took no action, but referred the proposal to its finance committee. Although Mrs. Bowles and Mrs. Putnam were opposed to any acquisition of Holland stock by Hazelbank, Mr. Landwehr conceded that a majority of the board were in favor of the purchase. Despite this fact, the finance committee elected to refer the offer to the Holland board on the grounds that it was the primary concern of Holland.

Thereafter, Mr. Trenkamp arranged for a meeting with Maremont, which occurred on October 14-15, 1957, in Chicago. Prior to this meeting, Trenkamp was aware of the intentions of Hazelbank and Mrs. Cheff to purchase all or portions of the stock then owned by Motor Products if Holland did not so act. As a result of the meeting, there was a tentative agreement on the part of Motor Products to sell its 155,000 shares at $14.40 per share. On October 23, 1957, at a special meeting of the Holland board, the purchase was considered. All directors, except Spatta, were present. The dangers allegedly posed by Maremont were again reviewed by the board. Trenkamp and Mrs. Cheff agree that the latter informed the board that either she or Hazelbank would purchase part or all of the block of Holland stock owned by Motor Products if the Holland board did not so act. The board was also informed that in order for the corporation to finance the purchase, substantial sums would have to be borrowed from commercial lending institutions. A resolution authorizing the purchase of 155,000 shares from Motor Products was adopted by the board. The price paid was in excess of the market price prevailing at the time. . . .

Under the provisions of 8 Del. C. §160, a corporation is granted statutory power to purchase and sell shares of its own stock. Such a right, as embodied in the statute, has long been recognized in this State. The charge here is not one of violation of statute, but the allegation is that the true motives behind such purchases were improperly centered upon perpetuation of control. . . . [I]f the actions of the board were motivated by a sincere belief that the buying out of the dissident stockholder was necessary to maintain what the board believed to be proper business practices, the board will not be held liable for such decision, even though hindsight indicates the decision was not the wisest course. See Kors v. Carey, Del. Ch., 158 A.2d 136. On the other hand, if the board has acted solely or primarily because of the desire to perpetuate themselves in office, the use of corporate funds for such purposes is improper. See Bennett v. Propp, Del., 187 A.2d 405, and Yasik v. Wachtel, 25 Del. Ch. 247, 17 A.2d 309.

Our first problem is the allocation of the burden of proof to show the presence or lack of good faith on the part of the board in authorizing the purchase of shares. Initially, the decision of the board of directors in authorizing a purchase was presumed to be in good faith and could be overturned only by a conclusive showing by plaintiffs of fraud or other misconduct. In *Kors,* cited supra, the court merely indicated that the directors are presumed to act in good faith and the burden of proof to show to the contrary falls upon the plaintiff. However, in Bennett v. Propp, supra, we stated:

> We must bear in mind the inherent danger in the purchase of shares with corporate funds to remove a threat to corporate policy when a threat to control is involved. The directors are of necessity confronted with a conflict of interest, and an objective decision is difficult. . . . Hence, in our opinion, the burden should be on the directors to justify such a purchase as one primarily in the corporate interest. (187 A.2d 405, at page 409.)

. . . To say that the burden of proof is upon the defendants is not to indicate, however, that the directors have the same "self-dealing interest" as is present, for example, when a director sells property to the corporation. The only clear pecuniary interest shown on the record was held by Mr. Cheff, as an executive of the corporation, and Trenkamp, as its attorney. The mere fact that some of the other directors were substantial shareholders does not create a personal pecuniary interest in the decisions made by the board of directors, since all shareholders would presumably share the benefit flowing to the substantial shareholder. Accordingly, these directors other than Trenkamp and Cheff, while called upon to justify their actions, will not be held to the same standard of proof required of those directors having personal and pecuniary interest in the transaction. . . .

Plaintiffs urge that the sale price was unfair in view of the fact that the price was in excess of that prevailing on the open market. However, as conceded by all parties, a substantial block of stock will normally sell at a higher price than that prevailing on the open market, the increment being attributable to a "control premium." Plaintiffs argue that it is inappropriate to require the defendant corporation to pay a control premium, since control is meaningless to an acquisition by a corporation of its own shares. However, it is elementary that a holder of a substantial number of shares would expect to receive the control premium as part of his selling price, and if the corporation desired to obtain the stock, it is unreasonable to expect that the corporation could avoid paying what any other purchaser would be required to pay for the stock. In any event, the financial expert produced by defendant at trial indicated that the price paid was fair and there was no rebuttal. Ames, the financial man on the board, was strongly of the opinion that the purchase was a good deal for the corporation. . . .

The question then presented is whether or not defendants satisfied the burden of proof of showing reasonable grounds to believe a danger to corporate policy and effectiveness existed by the presence of the Maremont stock ownership. It is important to remember that the directors satisfy their burden by showing good faith and reasonable investigation; the directors will not be penalized for an honest mistake of judgment, if the judgment appeared reasonable at the time the decision was made.

In holding that employee unrest could as well be attributed to a condition of Holland's business affairs as to the possibility of Maremont's intrusion, the Vice Chancellor must have had in mind one or both of two matters: (1) the pending proceedings before the Federal Trade Commission concerning certain sales practices of Holland; (2) the decrease in sales and profits during the preceding several years. Any other possible reason would be pure speculation. In the first place, the adverse decision of the F.T.C. was not announced until after the complained-of transaction. Secondly, the evidence clearly shows that the downward trend of sales and profits had reversed itself, presumably because of the reorganization which had then been completed. Thirdly, everyone who testified on the point said that the unrest was due to the possible threat presented by Maremont's purchases of stock. There was, in fact, no testimony whatever of any connection between the unrest and either the F.T.C. proceedings or the business picture.

The Vice Chancellor found that there was no substantial evidence of a liquidation posed by Maremont. This holding overlooks an important contention. The fear of the defendants, according to their testimony, was not limited to the possibility of liquidation; it included the alternate possibility of a material change in Holland's sales policies, which the board considered vital to its future success. The unrebutted testimony before the court indicated: (1) Maremont had deceived Cheff as to his original intentions, since his open market purchases were contemporaneous with his disclaimer of interest in Holland; (2) Maremont had given Cheff some reason to believe that he intended to eliminate the retail sales force of Holland; (3) Maremont demanded a place on the board; (4) Maremont substantially increased his purchases after having been refused a place on the board; (5) the directors had good reason to believe that unrest among key employees had been engendered by the Maremont threat; (6) the board had received advice from Dun and Bradstreet indicating the past liquidation or quick sale activities of Motor Products; (7) the board had received professional advice from the firm of Merrill Lynch, Fenner & Beane, who recommended that the purchase from Motor Products be carried out; (8) the board had received competent advice that the corporation was over-capitalized; (9) Staal and Cheff had made informal personal investigations from contacts in the business and financial community and had reported to the board of the alleged poor reputation of Maremont. The board was within its rights in relying upon that investigation, since 8 Del. C. §141(f) allows the directors to reasonably rely upon a report provided by corporate officers. See Graham v. Allis-Chalmers Manufacturing Co., Del., 188 A.2d 125.

Accordingly, we are of the opinion that the evidence presented in the court below leads inevitably to the conclusion that the board of directors, based upon direct investigation, receipt of professional advice, and personal observations of the contradictory action of Maremont and his explanation of corporate purpose, believed, with justification, that there was a reasonable threat to the continued existence of Holland, or at least existence in its present form, by the plan of Maremont to continue building up his stock holdings. We find no evidence in the record sufficient to justify a contrary conclusion. The opinion of the Vice Chancellor that employee unrest may have been engendered by other factors or that the board had no grounds to suspect Maremont is not supported in any manner by the evidence.

. . . [T]he Vice Chancellor found that the purpose of the acquisition was the improper desire to maintain control, but, at the same time, he exonerated those individual directors whom he believed to be unaware of the possibility of using non-corporate funds to accomplish this purpose. Such a decision is inconsistent with his finding that the motive was improper, within the rule enunciated in *Bennett*. If the actions were in fact improper because of a desire to maintain control, then the presence or absence of a non-corporate alternative is irrelevant, as corporate funds may not be used to advance an improper purpose even if there is no non-corporate alternative available. Conversely, if the actions were proper because of a decision by the board made in good faith that the corporate interest was served thereby, they are not rendered improper by the fact that some individual directors were willing to advance personal funds if the corporation did not. It is conceivable that the Vice Chancellor considered this feature of the case to be of significance because of his apparent belief that any excess corporate funds should have been used to finance a subsidiary corporation. That action would not have solved the problem of Holland's over-capitalization. In any event, this question was a matter of business judgment, which furnishes no justification for holding the directors personally responsible in this case.

Accordingly, the judgment of the court below is reversed and remanded with instruction to enter judgment for the defendants.

PROBLEM 9-1

Railway, Inc., a publicly traded company engaged in the truck leasing business, has a nine-member board. Three directors are independent. Four directors, including CEO Raoul Rogers, are corporate employees. Two directors are individuals with close family ties to Rogers. In January, Rogers and the other "inside" directors began investigating a possible leveraged buyout of Railway. In the contemplated transaction the inside directors would form a new corporation, which, with primarily borrowed funds, would acquire all of Railway's assets.

On February 12, Rogers learned that noted takeover artist Paul Jay had acquired 7 percent of the outstanding Railway stock. Rogers's publicly announced purpose in making this investment was to "hold for investment while seeking ways to participate with current Railway management in the development of a long-term strategy to maximize the value of Railway's outstanding stock." On February 14, Railway held a special board meeting which the outside directors attended by teleconference. Rogers reported Jay's purchase and statement and stated that "Jay is a liquidator and takeover artist. I know what he wants." Rogers then asked for and received board permission to negotiate a purchase of Jay's shares. On February 16, Railway purchased Jay's stock for a 75 percent premium over the then prevailing market price. The Railway inside directors are continuing to study the possibility of a management buyout, but have not taken their proposal to the board.

A derivative suit has now been filed, alleging that the directors violated their fiduciary duties in approving the repurchase of Jay's shares. What result under Cheff v. Mathes?

2. The Enhanced Scrutiny Framework

a. Introduction

As takeovers accelerated, the Delaware courts refined rules applicable in a takeover context and defined more particularly the role of the courts in reviewing the defensive tactics of a target board of directors. In 1985, shortly after the landmark decision in Smith v. Van Gorkom, supra page 329, the Delaware Supreme Court began to adjust the doctrinal backdrop against which hostile takeovers play out. This judicial activity coincided with the development of increasingly creative and aggressive defensive tactics that tested the competence and legitimacy of both the judiciary and the corporate governance system.

b.   The Unocal Doctrine

Unocal Corp. v. Mesa Petroleum Co.
Delaware Supreme Court, 1985
493 A.2d 946

MOORE, JUSTICE.

We confront an issue of first impression in Delaware—the validity of a corporation's self-tender for its own shares which excludes from participation a stockholder making a hostile tender offer for the company's stock.

The Court of Chancery granted a preliminary injunction to the plaintiffs, Mesa Petroleum Co., Mesa Asset Co., Mesa Partners II, and Mesa Eastern, Inc. (collectively "Mesa"),[1] enjoining an exchange offer of the defendant, Unocal Corporation (Unocal) for its own stock. The trial court concluded that a selective exchange offer, excluding Mesa, was legally impermissible. We cannot agree with such a blanket rule. . . .

I . . .

On April 8, 1985, Mesa, the owner of approximately 13% of Unocal's stock, commenced a two-tier "front loaded" cash tender offer for 64 million shares, or approximately 37%, of Unocal's outstanding stock at a price of $54 per share. The "back-end" was designed to eliminate the remaining publicly held shares by an exchange of securities purportedly worth $54 per share. However, pursuant to an order entered by the United States District Court for the Central District of California on April 26, 1985, Mesa issued a supplemental proxy statement to Unocal's stockholders disclosing that the securities offered in the second-step merger would be highly subordinated, and that Unocal's capitalization would differ significantly from its present structure. Unocal has rather aptly termed such securities "junk bonds."

Unocal's board consists of eight independent outside directors and six insiders. It met on April 13, 1985, to consider the Mesa tender offer. Thirteen directors were present, and the meeting lasted nine and one half hours. . . . Mr. Sachs [on behalf of Goldman Sachs & Co. and Dillon Read & Co.] opined that the minimum cash value that could be expected from a sale or orderly liquidation for 100% of Unocal's stock was in excess of $60 per share. . . .

Mr. Sachs also presented various defensive strategies available to the board if it concluded that Mesa's two-step tender offer was inadequate and should be opposed.

---

1. T. Boone Pickens, Jr., is President and Chairman of the Board of Mesa Petroleum and President of Mesa Asset and controls the related Mesa entities.

One of the devices outlined was a self-tender by Unocal for its own stock with a reasonable price range of $70 to $75 per share. The cost of such a proposal would cause the company to incur $6.1-6.5 billion of additional debt, and a presentation was made informing the board of Unocal's ability to handle it. The directors were told that the primary effect of this obligation would be to reduce exploratory drilling, but that the company would nonetheless remain a viable entity.

The eight outside directors, comprising a clear majority of the thirteen members present, then met separately with Unocal's financial advisors and attorneys. Thereafter, they unanimously agreed to advise the board that it should reject Mesa's tender offer as inadequate, and that Unocal should pursue a self-tender to provide the stockholders with a fairly priced alternative to the Mesa proposal. The board then reconvened and unanimously adopted a resolution rejecting as grossly inadequate Mesa's tender offer. Despite the nine and one-half hour length of the meeting, no formal decision was made on the proposed defensive self-tender.

On April 15, the board met again with four of the directors present by telephone and one member still absent. This session lasted two hours. Unocal's Vice President of Finance and its Assistant General Counsel made a detailed presentation of the proposed terms of the exchange offer. A price range between $70 and $80 per share was considered, and ultimately the directors agreed upon $72. The board was also advised about the debt securities that would be issued, and the necessity of placing restrictive covenants upon certain corporate activities until the obligations were paid. The board's decisions were made in reliance on the advice of its investment bankers, including the terms and conditions upon which the securities were to be issued. Based upon this advice, and the board's own deliberations, the directors unanimously approved the exchange offer. Their resolution provided that if Mesa acquired 64 million shares of Unocal stock through its own offer (the Mesa Purchase Condition), Unocal would buy the remaining 49% outstanding for an exchange of debt securities having an aggregate par value of $72 per share. The board resolution also stated that the offer would be subject to other conditions that had been described to the board at the meeting, or which were deemed necessary by Unocal's officers, including the exclusion of Mesa from the proposal (the Mesa exclusion). . . .

Unocal's exchange offer was commenced on April 17, 1985, and Mesa promptly challenged it by filing this suit in the Court of Chancery. On April 22, the Unocal board met again and was advised by Goldman Sachs and Dillon Read to waive the Mesa Purchase Condition as to 50 million shares. This recommendation was in response to a perceived concern of the shareholders that, if shares were tendered to Unocal, no shares would be purchased by either offeror. The directors were also advised that they should tender their own Unocal stock into the exchange offer as a mark of their confidence in it.

Another focus of the board was the Mesa exclusion. Legal counsel advised that under Delaware law Mesa could only be excluded for what the directors reasonably believed to be a valid corporate purpose. The directors' discussion centered on the objective of adequately compensating shareholders at the "back-end" of Mesa's proposal, which the latter would finance with "junk bonds." To include Mesa would defeat that goal, because under the proration aspect of the exchange offer (49%) every Mesa share accepted by Unocal would displace one held by another stockholder. Further, if

Mesa were permitted to tender to Unocal the latter would in effect be financing Mesa's own inadequate proposal. . . .

III

. . . When a board addresses a pending takeover bid it has an obligation to determine whether the offer is in the best interest of the corporation and its shareholders. In that respect a board's duty is no different from any other responsibility it shoulders, and its decisions should be no less entitled to the respect they otherwise would be accorded in the realm of business judgment. See also Johnson v. Trueblood, 629 F.2d 287, 292-293 (3d Cir. 1980). There are, however, certain caveats to a proper exercise of this function. Because of the omnipresent specter that a board may be acting primarily in its own interests, rather than those of the corporation and its shareholders, there is an enhanced duty which calls for judicial examination at the threshold before the protections of the business judgment rule may be conferred.

This Court has long recognized that: "We must bear in mind the inherent danger in the purchase of shares with corporate funds to remove a threat to corporate policy when a threat to control is involved. The directors are of necessity confronted with a conflict of interest, and an objective decision is difficult." Bennett v. Propp, Del. Supr., 187 A.2d 405, 409 (1962). In the face of this inherent conflict directors must show that they had reasonable grounds for believing that a danger to corporate policy and effectiveness existed because of another person's stock ownership. Cheff v. Mathes, 199 A.2d at 554-55. However, they satisfy that burden "by showing good faith and reasonable investigation. . . ." Id. at 555. Furthermore, such proof is materially enhanced, as here, by the approval of a board comprised of a majority of outside independent directors who have acted in accordance with the foregoing standards. See Aronson v. Lewis, 473 A.2d at 812, 815; Puma v. Marriott, Del. Ch., 283 A.2d 693, 695 (1971); Panter v. Marshall Field & Co., 646 F.2d 271, 295 (7th Cir. 1981).

IV

A

In the board's exercise of corporate power to forestall a takeover bid our analysis begins with the basic principle that corporate directors have a fiduciary duty to act in the best interests of the corporation's stockholders. Guth v. Loft, Inc., Del. Supr., 5 A.2d 503, 510 (1939). As we have noted, their duty of care extends to protecting the corporation and its owners from perceived harm whether a threat originates from third parties or other shareholders.[10] But such powers are not absolute. A corporation

---

10. It has been suggested that a board's response to a takeover threat should be a passive one. Easterbrook & Fischel [Takeover Bids, Defensive Tactics, and Shareholders' Welfare], 36 Bus. Law. at 1750. However, that clearly is not the law of Delaware, and as the proponents of this rule of passivity readily concede, it has not been adopted either by courts or state legislatures. Easterbrook & Fischel [The Proper Role of a Target's Management in Responding to a Tender Offer], 94 Harv. L. Rev. at 1194.

does not have unbridled discretion to defeat any perceived threat by any Draconian means available.

The restriction placed upon a selective stock repurchase is that the directors may not have acted solely or primarily out of a desire to perpetuate themselves in office. See Cheff v. Mathes, 199 A.2d at 556; Kors v. Carey, 158 A.2d at 140. Of course, to this is added the further caveat that inequitable action may not be taken under the guise of law. Schnell v. Chris-Craft Industries, Inc., Del. Supr., 285 A.2d 437, 439 (1971). The standard of proof established in Cheff v. Mathes and discussed supra, is designed to ensure that a defensive measure to thwart or impede a takeover is indeed motivated by a good faith concern for the welfare of the corporation and its stockholders, which in all circumstances must be free of any fraud or other misconduct. Cheff v. Mathes, 199 A.2d at 554-555. However, this does not end the inquiry.

B

A further aspect is the element of balance. If a defensive measure is to come within the ambit of the business judgment rule, it must be reasonable in relation to the threat posed. This entails an analysis by the directors of the nature of the take-over bid and its effect on the corporate enterprise. Examples of such concerns may include: inadequacy of the price offered, nature and timing of the offer, questions of illegality, the impact on "constituencies" other than shareholders (i.e., creditors, customers, employees, and perhaps even the community generally), the risk of nonconsummation, and the quality of securities being offered in the exchange. See Lipton and Brownstein, Takeover Responses and Directors' Responsibilities: An Update, p. 7, ABA National Institute on the Dynamics of Corporate Control (December 8, 1983). While not a controlling factor, it also seems to us that a board may reasonably consider the basic stockholder interests at stake, including those of short term speculators, whose actions may have fueled the coercive aspect of the offer at the expense of the long term investor. Here, the threat posed was viewed by the Unocal board as a grossly inadequate two-tier coercive tender offer coupled with the threat of greenmail.

Specifically, the Unocal directors had concluded that the value of Unocal was substantially above the $54 per share offered in cash at the front end. Furthermore, they determined that the subordinated securities to be exchanged in Mesa's announced squeeze out of the remaining shareholders in the "back-end" merger were "junk bonds" worth far less than $54. It is now well recognized that such offers are a classic coercive measure designed to stampede shareholders into tendering at the first tier, even if the price is inadequate, out of fear of what they will receive at the back end of the transaction. Wholly beyond the coercive aspect of an inadequate two-tier tender offer, the threat was posed by a corporate raider with a national reputation as a "greenmailer."

In adopting the selective exchange offer, the board stated that its objective was either to defeat the inadequate Mesa offer or, should the offer still succeed, provide the 49% of its stockholders, who would otherwise be forced to accept "junk bonds," with $72 worth of senior debt. We find that both purposes are valid.

However, such efforts would have been thwarted by Mesa's participation in the exchange offer. First, if Mesa could tender its shares, Unocal would effectively be subsidizing the former's continuing effort to buy Unocal stock at $54 per share. Second, Mesa could not, by definition, fit within the class of shareholders being protected from its own coercive and inadequate tender offer.

Thus, we are satisfied that the selective exchange offer is reasonably related to the threats posed. It is consistent with the principle that "the minority stockholder shall receive the substantial equivalent in value of what he had before." Sterling v. Mayflower Hotel Corp., Del. Supr., 93 A.2d 107, 114 (1952). See also Rosenblatt v. Getty Oil Co., 493 A.2d 929, 944 (1985). This concept of fairness, while stated in the merger context, is also relevant in the area of tender offer law. Thus, the board's decision to offer what it determined to be the fair value of the corporation to the 49% of its shareholders, who would otherwise be forced to accept highly subordinated "junk bonds," is reasonable and consistent with the directors' duty to ensure that the minority stockholders receive equal value for their shares.

V

Mesa contends that it is unlawful, and the trial court agreed, for a corporation to discriminate in this fashion against one shareholder. It argues correctly that no case has ever sanctioned a device that precludes a raider from sharing in a benefit available to all other stockholders. However, as we have noted earlier, the principle of selective stock repurchases by a Delaware corporation is neither unknown nor unauthorized. Cheff v. Mathes, 199 A.2d at 554; Bennett v. Propp, 187 A.2d at 408; Martin v. American Potash & Chemical Corporation, 92 A.2d at 302; Kaplan v. Goldsamt, 380 A.2d 568-569; Kors v. Carey, 158 A.2d at 140-141; 8 Del. C. §160. The only difference is that heretofore the approved transaction was the payment of "greenmail" to a raider or dissident posing a threat to the corporate enterprise. All other stockholders were denied such favored treatment, and given Mesa's past history of greenmail, its claims here are rather ironic.

However, our corporate law is not static. It must grow and develop in response to, indeed in anticipation of, evolving concepts and needs. Merely because the General Corporation Law is silent as to a specific matter does not mean that it is prohibited. See Providence and Worcester Co. v. Baker, Del. Supr., 378 A.2d 121, 123-124 (1977). In the days when *Cheff, Bennett, Martin* and *Kors* were decided, the tender offer, while not an unknown device, was virtually unused, and little was known of such methods as two-tier "front-end" loaded offers with their coercive effects. Then, the favored attack of a raider was stock acquisition followed by a proxy contest. . . .

More recently, as the sophistication of both raiders and targets has developed, a host of other defensive measures to counter such ever mounting threats has evolved and received judicial sanction. These include defensive charter amendments and other devices bearing some rather exotic, but apt, names: Crown Jewel, White Knight, Pac Man, and Golden Parachute. Each has highly selective features, the object of which is to deter or defeat the raider.

Thus, while the exchange offer is a form of selective treatment, given the nature of the threat posed here the response is neither unlawful nor unreasonable. If the board of directors is disinterested, has acted in good faith and with due care, its decision in the absence of an abuse of discretion will be upheld as a proper exercise of business judgment. . . .

Mesa contends that the basis of this action is punitive, and solely in response to the exercise of its rights of corporate democracy. Nothing precludes Mesa, as a stockholder, from acting in its own self-interest. However, Mesa, while pursuing its own interests, has acted in a manner which a board consisting of a majority of independent directors has reasonably determined to be contrary to the best interests of Unocal and its other shareholders. In this situation, there is no support in Delaware law for the proposition that, when responding to a perceived harm, a corporation must guarantee a benefit to a stockholder who is deliberately provoking the danger being addressed. There is no obligation of self-sacrifice by a corporation and its shareholders in the face of such a challenge. . . .

VI

In conclusion, there was directorial power to oppose the Mesa tender offer, and to undertake a selective stock exchange made in good faith and upon a reasonable investigation pursuant to a clear duty to protect the corporate enterprise. Further, the selective stock repurchase plan chosen by Unocal is reasonable in relation to the threat that the board rationally and reasonably believed was posed by Mesa's inadequate and coercive two-tier tender offer. Under those circumstances the board's action is entitled to be measured by the standards of the business judgment rule. Thus, unless it is shown by a preponderance of the evidence that the directors' decisions were primarily based on perpetuating themselves in office, or some other breach of fiduciary duty such as fraud, overreaching, lack of good faith, or being uninformed, a Court will not substitute its judgment for that of the board.

In this case that protection is not lost merely because Unocal's directors have tendered their shares in the exchange offer. Given the validity of the Mesa exclusion, they are receiving a benefit shared generally by all other stockholders except Mesa. In this circumstance the test of Aronson v. Lewis, 473 A.2d at 812, is satisfied. See also Cheff v. Mathes, 199 A.2d at 554. If the stockholders are displeased with the action of their elected representatives, the powers of corporate democracy are at their disposal to turn the board out. Aronson v. Lewis, Del. Supr., 473 A.2d 805, 811 (1984). See also 8 Del. C. §§141(k) and 211(b).

With the Court of Chancery's findings that the exchange offer was based on the board's good faith belief that the Mesa offer was inadequate, that the board's action was informed and taken with due care, that Mesa's prior activities justify a reasonable inference that its principle objective was greenmail, and implicitly, that the substance of the offer itself was reasonable and fair to the corporation and its stockholders if Mesa were included, we cannot say that the Unocal directors have acted in such a manner as to have passed an "unintelligent and unadvised judgment." Mitchell v. Highland-Western Glass Co., Del. Ch., 167 A. 831, 833 (1933). The decision of the Court of Chancery is therefore reversed, and the preliminary injunction is vacated.

NOTES AND QUESTIONS

1. While issuing a preliminary injunction against the Unocal exchange offer, the vice chancellor held that the plaintiff had not demonstrated a likelihood of success on its claim that Unocal's directors had breached their Smith v. Van Gorkom duties of care. In addition, the vice chancellor was satisfied that the directors acted in a good faith belief that the tender offer was inadequate. Nonetheless, the vice chancellor held that the business judgment rule did not apply for two reasons: (1) selective tender offers are inherently suspect, and (2) by participating in the Unocal tender offer, the directors had conflicting interests inconsistent with the business judgment rule. Since Unocal had made no attempt to prove the fairness of the exchange offer as it applied to Mesa, the plaintiff was entitled to a preliminary injunction.

2. Can you amend Unocal's plan so that it effectively protects other Unocal shareholders without discriminating against Mesa?

3. The Delaware court in Unocal Corp. v. Mesa Petroleum pointed to the coercive nature of Mesa's offer of $54 cash per share at the front end and junk bonds that in the board's view were worth far less than $54 as compensation to be forced on remaining minority shareholders in a back-end merger. Compare the possible coerciveness of Mesa's proposal to the defensive tactics taken by the Unocal board. If you were a Unocal shareholder with 100 shares of stock, what would you end up with after the Unocal exchange? When Mesa did not complete its tender offer in the face of the selective buyback, Unocal shareholders got the $72 of senior debt for 49 percent of their shares and retained their remaining shares. What would you expect the price of the remaining shares to be? Does the fact that the shares quickly dropped into the mid-$20s make the Unocal offer itself coercive?

4. The Securities and Exchange Commission reacted to *Unocal* by promulgating Rule 14d-10 under the Williams Act, which prohibited selective tender offers. The interaction of federal and state law is considered in more detail in Chapter 11, but a federal court has upheld Rule 14d-10 against an argument that it exceeds the SEC's power. See Polaroid Corp. v. Disney, 862 F.2d 987, 995 (3d Cir. 1988).

5. Several states now have statutes rejecting the heightened *Unocal* test in favor of the traditional business judgment rule. See Pennsylvania Stat. Ann. tit. 15, §1715(d) (Purdon):

> [T]here shall not be any greater obligation to justify, or higher burden of proof with respect to, any act as the board of directors, any committee of the board or any individual director relating to or affecting an acquisition or potential or proposed acquisition of control of the corporation than is applied to any other act as a board of directors, any committee of the board or any individual director.

See also Indiana Bus. Corp. Law §23-1-35-1(f); Ohio Gen. Corp. Law §1701.59(C).

PROBLEM 9-2

Reconsider Problem 9-1, page 852, supra.
(a) What result under Pennsylvania Stat. Ann., §1715?
(b) What result under Unocal v. Mesa Petroleum?

c.   Poison Pills

MBCA §§6.01, 6.02
Delaware G.C.L. §§141, 151, 157, 160

"Poison pill" is a colloquial name for various rights given to shareholders entitling them to additional securities of the company upon the happening of certain events. These plans have been adopted by a majority of America's largest corporations, making them one of the most popular defensive tactics adopted by management seeking to deter hostile takeovers. Like many popular defensive tactics, a poison pill is usually enacted by the directors, so a primary legal issue is whether the particular plan is within director authority. Challenges to the plans may be based on statutes and fiduciary duty.

New York City–based law firm Wachtell, Lipton popularized the use of poison pills in the mid-1980s. At the time, there was nothing specific in state corporation statutes about these kinds of shareholders' rights. These plans are an example of lawyers using general powers in a new way to make takeovers more difficult, time consuming, and expensive for an acquiror unless the acquiror negotiates with the target's board of directors. Poison pills come in a variety of forms and undoubtedly will continue to evolve. Description of "flip-in" and "flip-over" pills will give you an appreciation of the possible variations.

In a flip-in plan, directors cause the corporation to issue certain "rights" to all current shareholders, often issued as a dividend to these shareholders. At the time of issuance, the rights have little current value; rather, these rights flower upon a triggering event, for example, an acquiror obtaining 20 percent of the shares of the corporation or making an announcement of a tender offer. Upon the occurrence of the triggering event, each holder obtains the right to purchase additional shares of stock in the corporation, for example, to purchase $200 of stock for $100. The sting or poison of the plan is that acquirors are excluded from the right so that a successful raider will find its shares in the target diluted.

The board of directors usually can redeem these rights prior to the triggering event. Thus, there is an incentive for a raider to come to the board before crossing the threshold. Some would say that a tender offer against a poison pill can be prohibitively expensive.

A flip-over works on the same principles, but the rights given to shareholders are to purchase shares (again at a discount) in any company into which the target company is merged. A raider could thus avoid this pill by continuing to operate the target as a separate company, an option that is feasible but one that most acquirers find to be very unattractive financially.

Moran v. Household International, Inc.
Delaware Supreme Court, 1985
500 A.2d 1346

McNeilly, Justice . . .

I . . .

On August 14, 1984, the Board of Directors of Household International, Inc. adopted the Rights Plan by a fourteen to two vote. The intricacies of the Rights Plan are contained in a 48-page document entitled "Rights Agreement." Basically, the Plan provides that Household common stockholders are entitled to the issuance of one Right per common share under certain triggering conditions. There are two triggering events that can activate the Rights. The first is the announcement of a tender offer for 30 percent of Household's shares ("30% trigger") and the second is the acquisition of 20 percent of Household's shares by any single entity or group ("20% trigger").

If an announcement of a tender offer for 30 percent of Household's shares is made, the Rights are issued and are immediately exercisable to purchase 1/100 share of new preferred stock for $100 and are redeemable by the Board for $.50 per Right. If 20 percent of Household's shares are acquired by anyone, the Rights are issued and become non-redeemable and are exercisable to purchase 1/100 of a share of preferred. If a Right is not exercised for preferred, and thereafter, a merger or consolidation occurs, the Rights holder can exercise each Right to purchase $200 of the common stock of the tender offeror for $100. This "flip-over" provision of the Rights Plan is at the heart of this controversy.

Household is a diversified holding company with its principal subsidiaries engaged in financial services, transportation and merchandising. HFC, National Car Rental and Vons Grocery are three of its wholly-owned entities.

Household did not adopt its Rights Plan during a battle with a corporate raider, but as a preventive mechanism to ward off future advances. The Vice-Chancellor found that as early as February 1984, Household's management became concerned about the company's vulnerability as a takeover target and began considering amending its charter to render a takeover more difficult. After considering the matter, Household decided not to pursue a fair price amendment.

In the meantime, appellant Moran, one of Household's own Directors and also Chairman of the Dyson-Kissner-Moran Corporation, ("D-K-M") which is the largest single stockholder of Household, began discussions concerning a possible leveraged buy-out of Household by D-K-M. D-K-M's financial studies showed that Household's stock was significantly undervalued in relation to the company's break-up value. It is uncontradicted that Moran's suggestion of a leveraged buy-out never progressed beyond the discussion stage.

Concerned about Household's vulnerability to a raider in light of the current takeover climate, Household secured the services of Wachtell, Lipton, Rosen and Katz ("Wachtell, Lipton") and Goldman, Sachs & Co. ("Goldman, Sachs") to formulate a takeover policy for recommendation to the Household Board at its August 14 meeting. After a July 31 meeting with a Household Board member and a pre-meeting distribution of material on the potential takeover problem and the proposed Rights Plan, the Board met on August 14, 1984.

Representatives of Wachtell, Lipton and Goldman, Sachs attended the August 14 meeting. The minutes reflect that Mr. Lipton explained to the Board that his recommendation of the Plan was based on his understanding that the Board was concerned about the increasing frequency of "bust-up"[4] takeovers, the increasing takeover activity

---

4. "Bust-up" takeover generally refers to a situation in which one seeks to finance an acquisition by selling off pieces of the acquired company.

in the financial service industry, such as Leucadia's attempt to take over Arco, and the possible adverse effect this type of activity could have on employees and others concerned with and vital to the continuing successful operation of Household even in the absence of any actual bust-up takeover attempt. Against this factual background, the Plan was approved.

Thereafter, Moran and the company of which he is Chairman, D-K-M, filed this suit. . . . The trial was held, and the Court of Chancery ruled in favor of Household. Appellants now appeal from that ruling to this Court.

II

The primary issue here is the applicability of the business judgment rule as the standard by which the adoption of the Rights Plan should be reviewed. Much of this issue has been decided by our recent decision in Unocal Corp. v. Mesa Petroleum Co., Del. Supr., 493 A.2d 946 (1985). . . .

This case is distinguishable from the ones cited, since here we have a defensive mechanism adopted to ward off possible future advances and not a mechanism adopted in reaction to a specific threat. This distinguishing factor does not result in the Directors losing the protection of the business judgment rule. To the contrary, pre-planning for the contingency of a hostile takeover might reduce the risk that, under the pressure of a takeover bid, management will fail to exercise reasonable judgment. Therefore, in reviewing a pre-planned defensive mechanism it seems even more appropriate to apply the business judgment rule. See Warner Communications v. Murdoch, D. Del., 581 F. Supp. 1482, 1491 (1984).

Of course, the business judgment rule can only sustain corporate decision making or transactions that are within the power or authority of the Board. Therefore, before the business judgment rule can be applied it must be determined whether the Directors were authorized to adopt the Rights Plan.

III

Appellants vehemently contend that the Board of Directors was unauthorized to adopt the Rights Plan. First, appellants contend that no provision of the Delaware General Corporation Law authorizes the issuance of such Rights. Secondly, appellants, along with the SEC, contend that the Board is unauthorized to usurp stockholders' rights to receive hostile tender offers. Third, appellants and the SEC also contend that the Board is unauthorized to fundamentally restrict stockholders' rights to conduct a proxy contest. We address each of these contentions in turn.

A

While appellants contend that no provision of the Delaware General Corporation Law authorizes the Rights Plan, Household contends that the Rights Plan was issued pursuant to 8 Del.C. §§151(g) and 157. It explains that the Rights are authorized by

§157 and the issue of preferred stock underlying the Rights is authorized by §151. Appellants respond by making several attacks upon the authority to issue the Rights pursuant to §157.

Appellants begin by contending that §157 cannot authorize the Rights Plan since §157 has never served the purpose of authorizing a takeover defense. Appellants contend that §157 is a corporate financing statute, and that nothing in its legislative history suggests a purpose that has anything to do with corporate control or a takeover defense. Appellants are unable to demonstrate that the legislature, in its adoption of §157, meant to limit the applicability of §157 to only the issuance of Rights for the purposes of corporate financing. Without such affirmative evidence, we decline to impose such a limitation upon the section that the legislature has not. Compare Providence & Worchester Co. v. Baker, Del. Supr., 378 A.2d 121, 124 (1977) (refusal to read a bar to protective voting provisions into 8 Del. C. §212(a)).

As we noted in *Unocal*:

> [O]ur corporate law is not static. It must grow and develop in response to, indeed in anticipation of, evolving concepts and needs. Merely because the General Corporation Law is silent as to a specific matter does not mean that it is prohibited.

493 A.2d at 957. See also Cheff v. Mathes, Del. Supr., 199 A.2d 548 (1964).

Secondly, appellants contend that §157 does not authorize the issuance of sham rights such as the Rights Plan. They contend that the Rights were designed never to be exercised, and that the Plan has no economic value. In addition, they contend the preferred stock made subject to the Rights is also illusory, citing Telvest, Inc. v. Olson, Del. Ch., C.A. No. 5798, Brown, V.C. (March 8, 1979).

Appellants' sham contention fails in both regards. As to the Rights, they can and will be exercised upon the happening of a triggering mechanism, as we have observed during the current struggle of Sir James Goldsmith to take control of Crown Zellerbach. See Wall Street Journal, July 26, 1985, at 3, 12. As to the preferred shares, we agree with the Court of Chancery that they are distinguishable from sham securities invalidated in *Telvest*, supra. The Household preferred, issuable upon the happening of a triggering event, have superior dividend and liquidation rights.

Third, appellants contend that §157 authorizes the issuance of Rights "entitling holders thereof to purchase from the corporation any shares of *its* capital stock of any class . . ." (emphasis added). Therefore, their contention continues, the plain language of the statute does not authorize Household to issue rights to purchase another's capital stock upon a merger or consolidation.

Household contends, inter alia, that the Rights Plan is analogous to "anti-destruction" or "anti-dilution" provisions which are customary features of a wide variety of corporate securities. While appellants seem to concede that "anti-destruction" provisions are valid under Delaware corporate law, they seek to distinguish the Rights Plan as not being incidental, as are most "anti-destruction" provisions, to a corporation's statutory power to finance itself. We find no merit to such a distinction. We have already rejected appellants' similar contention that §157 could only be used for financing purposes. We also reject that distinction here.

"Anti-destruction" clauses generally ensure holders of certain securities of the protection of their right of conversion in the event of a merger by giving them the right to convert their securities into whatever securities are to replace the stock of their company. See Broad v. Rockwell International Corp., 5th Cir., 642 F.2d 929, 946, cert. denied, 454 U.S. 965 (1981); Wood v. Coastal States Gas Corp., Del. Supr., 401 A.2d 932, 937-39 (1979); B.S.F. Co. v. Philadelphia National Bank, Del. Supr., 204 A.2d 746, 750-751 (1964). The fact that the rights here have as their purpose the prevention of coercive two-tier tender offers does not invalidate them. . . .

B

Appellants contend that the Board is unauthorized to usurp stockholders' rights to receive tender offers by changing Household's fundamental structure. We conclude that the Rights Plan does not prevent stockholders from receiving tender offers, and that the change of Household's structure was less than that which results from the implementation of other defensive mechanisms upheld by various courts.

Appellants' contention that stockholders will lose their right to receive and accept tender offers seems to be premised upon an understanding of the Rights Plan which is illustrated by the SEC amicus brief which states: "The Chancery Court's decision seriously understates the impact of this plan. In fact, as we discuss below, the Rights Plan will deter not only two-tier offers, but virtually all hostile tender offers."

The fallacy of that contention is apparent when we look at the recent takeover of Crown Zellerbach, which has a similar Rights Plan, by Sir James Goldsmith. Wall Street Journal, July 26, 1985, at 3, 12. The evidence at trial also evidenced many methods around the Plan ranging from tendering with a condition that the Board redeem the Rights, tendering with a high minimum condition of shares and Rights, tendering and soliciting consents to remove the Board and redeem the Rights, to acquiring 50% of the shares and causing Household to self-tender for the Rights. One could also form a group of up to 19.9% and solicit proxies for consents to remove the Board and redeem the Rights. These are but a few of the methods by which Household can still be acquired by a hostile tender offer.

In addition, the Rights Plan is not absolute. When the Household Board of Directors is faced with a tender offer and a request to redeem the Rights, they will not be able to arbitrarily reject the offer. They will be held to the same fiduciary standards any other board of directors would be held to in deciding to adopt a defensive mechanism, the same standard as they were held to in originally approving the Rights Plan. See Unocal, 493 A.2d at 954-955, 958.

In addition, appellants contend that the deterence of tender offers will be accomplished by what they label "a fundamental transfer of power from the stockholders to the directors." They contend that this transfer of power, in itself, is unauthorized.

The Rights Plan will result in no more of a structural change than any other defensive mechanism adopted by a board of directors. The Rights Plan does not destroy the assets of the corporation. The implementation of the Plan neither results in any outflow of money from the corporation nor impairs its financial flexibility. It does not dilute earnings per share and does not have any adverse tax consequences for the corporation or its stockholders. The Plan has not adversely affected the market price of Household's stock.

Comparing the Rights Plan with other defensive mechanisms, it does less harm to the value structure of the corporation than do the other mechanisms. Other mechanisms result in increased debt of the corporation. See Whittaker Corp. v. Edgar, [N.D. Ill., 535 F. Supp. 933 (1982)] (sale of "prize asset"), Cheff v. Mathes, supra (paying greenmail to eliminate a threat), Unocal Corp. v. Mesa Petroleum Co., supra (discriminatory self-tender).

There is little change in the governance structure as a result of the adoption of the Rights Plan. The Board does not now have unfettered discretion in refusing to redeem the Rights. The Board has no more discretion in refusing to redeem the Rights than it does in enacting any defensive mechanism.

The contention that the Rights Plan alters the structure more than do other defensive mechanisms because it is so effective as to make the corporation completely safe from hostile tender offers is likewise without merit. As explained above, there are numerous methods to successfully launch a hostile tender offer.

C

Appellants' third contention is that the Board was unauthorized to fundamentally restrict stockholders' rights to conduct a proxy contest. Appellants contend that the "20% trigger" effectively prevents any stockholder from first acquiring 20% or more shares before conducting a proxy contest and further, it prevents stockholders from banding together into a group to solicit proxies if, collectively, they own 20% or more of the stock.[12] In addition, at trial, appellants contended that read literally, the Rights Agreement triggers the Rights upon the mere acquisition of the right to vote 20% or more of the shares through a proxy solicitation, and thereby precludes any proxy contest from being waged.[13]

Appellants seem to have conceded this last contention in light of Household's response that the receipt of a proxy does not make the recipient the "beneficial owner" of the shares involved which would trigger the Rights. In essence, the Rights Agreement provides that the Rights are triggered when someone becomes the "beneficial owner" of 20% or more of Household stock. Although a literal reading of the Rights Agreement definition of "beneficial owner" would seem to include those shares which one has the right to vote, it has long been recognized that the relationship between grantor and recipient of a proxy is one of agency, and the agency is revocable by the grantor at any time. Henn, Corporations §196, at 518. Therefore, the holder of a proxy is not the "beneficial owner" of the stock. As a result, the mere acquisition of the right to vote 20% of the shares does not trigger the Rights.

---

12. Appellants explain that the acquisition of 20% of the shares triggers the Rights, making them non-redeemable, and thereby would prevent even a future friendly offer for the ten-year life of the Rights.

13. The SEC still contends that the mere acquisition of the right to vote 20% of the shares through a proxy solicitation triggers the rights. We do not interpret the Rights Agreement in that manner.

The issue, then, is whether the restriction upon individuals or groups from first acquiring 20% of shares before waging a proxy contest fundamentally restricts stockholders' right to conduct a proxy contest. Regarding this issue the Court of Chancery found:

> Thus, while the Rights Plan does deter the formation of proxy efforts of a certain magnitude, it does not limit the voting power of individual shares. On the evidence presented it is highly conjectural to assume that a particular effort to assert shareholder views in the election of directors or revisions of corporate policy will be frustrated by the proxy feature of the Plan. Household's witnesses, Troubh and Higgins described recent corporate takeover battles in which insurgents holding less than 10% stock ownership were able to secure corporate control through a proxy contest or the threat of one.

Moran, 490 A.2d at 1080.

We conclude that there was sufficient evidence at trial to support the Vice-Chancellor's finding that the effect upon proxy contests will be minimal. Evidence at trial established that many proxy contests are won with an insurgent ownership of less than 20%, and that very large holdings are no guarantee of success. There was also testimony that the key variable in proxy contest success is the merit of an insurgent's issues, not the size of his holdings.

IV

Having concluded that the adoption of the Rights Plan was within the authority of the Directors, we now look to whether the Directors have met their burden under the business judgment rule.

The business judgment rule is a "presumption that in making a business decision the directors of a corporation acted on an informed basis, in good faith and in the honest belief that the action taken was in the best interests of the company." Aronson v. Lewis, Del. Supr., 473 A.2d 805, 812 (1984) (citations omitted). Notwithstanding, in *Unocal* we held that when the business judgment rule applies to adoption of a defensive mechanism, the initial burden will lie with the directors. The "directors must show that they had reasonable grounds for believing that a danger to corporate policy and effectiveness existed. . . . [T]hey satisfy that burden 'by showing good faith and reasonable investigation. . . .'" *Unocal,* 493 A.2d at 955 (citing Cheff v. Mathes, 199 A.2d at 554-55). In addition, the directors must show that the defensive mechanism was "reasonable in relation to the threat posed." *Unocal,* 493 A.2d at 955. Moreover, that proof is materially enhanced, as we noted in *Unocal,* where, as here, a majority of the board favoring the proposal consisted of outside independent directors who have acted in accordance with the foregoing standards. *Unocal,* 493 A.2d at 955; *Aronson,* 473 A.2d at 815. Then, the burden shifts back to the plaintiffs who have the ultimate burden of persuasion to show a breach of the directors' fiduciary duties. *Unocal,* 493 A.2d at 958.

There are no allegations here of any bad faith on the part of the Directors' action in the adoption of the Rights Plan. There is no allegation that the Directors' action was taken for entrenchment purposes. Household had adequately demonstrated, as explained above, that the adoption of the Rights Plan was in reaction to what it perceived to be the threat in the market place of coercive two-tier tender offers. Appellants do contend, however, that the Board did not exercise informed business judgment in its adoption of the Plan. . . .

To determine whether a business judgment reached by a board of directors was an informed one, we determine whether the directors were grossly negligent. Smith v. Van Gorkom, Del. Supr., 488 A.2d 858, 873 (1985). Upon a review of this record, we conclude the Directors were not grossly negligent. The information supplied to the Board on August 14 provided the essentials of the Plan. The Directors were given beforehand a notebook which included a three-page summary of the Plan along with articles on the current takeover environment. The extended discussion between the Board and representatives of Wachtell, Lipton and Goldman, Sachs before approval of the Plan reflected a full and candid evaluation of the Plan. Moran's expression of his views at the meeting served to place before the Board a knowledgeable critique of the Plan. The factual happenings here are clearly distinguishable from the actions of the directors of Trans Union Corporation who displayed gross negligence in approving a cash-out merger. Id.

In addition, to meet their burden, the Directors must show that the defensive mechanism was "reasonable in relation to the threat posed." The record reflects a concern on the part of the Directors over the increasing frequency in the financial services industry of "boot-strap" and "bust-up" takeovers. The Directors were also concerned that such takeovers may take the form of two-tier offers. In addition, on August 14, the Household Board was aware of Moran's overture on behalf of D-K-M. In sum, the Directors reasonably believed Household was vulnerable to coercive acquisition techniques and adopted a reasonable defensive mechanism to protect itself.

V

. . . While we conclude for present purposes that the Household Directors are protected by the business judgment rule, that does not end the matter. The ultimate response to an actual takeover bid must be judged by the Directors' actions at that time, and nothing we say here relieves them of their basic fundamental duties to the corporation and its stockholders. Unocal, 493 A.2d at 954-55, 958; Smith v. Van Gorkom, 488 A.2d at 872-873; [Aronson v. Lewis, Del. Supr., 473 A.2d 805, 812-813 (1984)]; Pogostin v. Rice, Del. Supr., 480 A.2d 619, 627 (1984). Their use of the Plan will be evaluated when and if the issue arises.

Affirmed.

NOTES AND QUESTIONS

1. A number of courts have found poison pills illegally discriminatory under statutory provisions similar to Delaware G.C.L. §151. See, e.g., Amalgamated Sugar Co. v. NL Industries, 644 F. Supp. 1229 (S.D.N.Y. 1986) (construing New Jersey Law); West Point-Pepperell, Inc. v. Farley, Inc., 711 F. Supp. 1088 (N.D. Ga. 1988) (construing Georgia law); R.D. Smith & Co. v. Preway Inc., 644 F. Supp. 868 (W.D. Wis. 1986)

(construing Wisconsin law). However, in each case in which a court has challenged the board's authority to enact a poison pill, the affected state's legislature has followed with a statute authorizing the pills. Indeed, many states have enacted statutes even if there has not been an invalidating judicial decision in that jurisdiction; more than half the states have such statutes.

2. Not all statutes authorizing poison pills give directors carte blanche powers. In Bank of New York Co. v. Irving Bank Corp., 536 N.Y.S.2d 923 (Sup. Ct. 1988), the New York Supreme Court invalidated a flip-in poison pill on the grounds that New York Bus. Corp. Law §505 prohibited discrimination among shareholders of the same class. New York's legislature then modified §505, expressly permitting corporations to void or preclude the exercise of rights or options held by "interested persons," a term defined in New York Bus. Corp. Law §912(a)(10) as the holder of 20 percent or more of the corporation's stock. As confirmed in Avon Products, Inc. v. Chartwell Associates L.P., 738 F. Supp. 686 (S.D.N.Y.), aff'd, 907 F.2d 322 (2d Cir. 1990), a poison pill discriminating against a less than 20 percent shareholder is still impermissible under New York law.

PROBLEM 9-3

La2morrow, Inc. ("LA") is a NASDAQ-traded corporation with 50 million common shares outstanding. In November 2014, LA shares traded at a peak of $185 per share. Recently LA shares have been trading in the range of $10 to $12 per share. LA has experienced substantial operating losses since its formation in 2005 and has laid off more than half of its employees since November 2012. At its June 2014 board meeting, LA's CEO, Larry Lane, reported to the board that the company was nearing profitability, and that he was gravely concerned that LA's low stock price might prompt an unfriendly takeover bid by a cash-rich company. Lane then suggested that the board authorize a poison pill to protect the company, and further suggested that in order to save money LA's general counsel should be instructed to "copy" a plan from the SEC filings of another company. Without discussion, the board so resolved. At the August 2014 board meeting, LA's general counsel, Art Liberale, presented the board with a poison pill rights plan identical to the Household Finance rights plan described in the *Moran* case. Larry Lane proposed that the plan's "20 percent trigger" be reduced to a "10 percent trigger." Art Liberale accepted this proposal as a friendly amendment. The board then unanimously approved the plan.

An LA shareholder has now filed a derivative suit seeking cancellation of the poison pill rights plan. LA has filed a motion for judgment on the pleadings. Should this motion be granted? If not, is it likely that the case can be decided via a motion for summary judgment?

d. *The* Revlon *Rule*

The effect of *Unocal* and *Moran* was initially unclear. On one hand, the language of *Unocal* supported greater judicial scrutiny of takeover defenses than the preexisting Cheff v. Mathes standard. Still, the actual decision in *Unocal* sanctioned a selective repurchase plan that discriminated against an unwanted suitor. In addition, *Moran,* applying *Unocal,* upheld the validity of poison pill rights plans, giving management a powerful tool to prevent hostile takeovers.

Was the real effect of *Unocal* simply to provide new clothing for Delaware's traditional review of directors' action to prevent a takeover? The following case established that *Unocal*'s enhanced scrutiny would be employed to curb directors' discretion.

Revlon, Inc. v. MacAndrews & Forbes Holdings, Inc.
Delaware Supreme Court, 1986
506 A.2d 173

MOORE, JUSTICE:

In this battle for corporate control of Revlon, Inc. (Revlon), the Court of Chancery enjoined certain transactions designed to thwart the efforts of Pantry Pride, Inc. (Pantry Pride) to acquire Revlon. The defendants are Revlon, its board of directors, and Forstmann Little & Co. and the latter's affiliated limited partnership (collectively, Forstmann). The injunction barred consummation of an option granted Forstmann to purchase certain Revlon assets (the lock-up option), a promise by Revlon to deal exclusively with Forstmann in the face of a takeover (the no-shop provision), and the payment of a $25 million cancellation fee to Forstmann if the transaction was aborted. The Court of Chancery found that the Revlon directors had breached their duty of care by entering into the foregoing transactions and effectively ending an active auction for the company. The trial court ruled that such arrangements are not illegal per se under Delaware law, but that their use under the circumstances here was impermissible. We agree. Thus, we granted this expedited interlocutory appeal to consider for the first time the validity of such defensive measures in the face of an active bidding contest for corporate control. Additionally, we address for the first time the extent to which a corporation may consider the impact of a takeover threat on constituencies other than shareholders.

In our view, lock-ups and related agreements are permitted under Delaware law where their adoption is untainted by director interest or other breaches of fiduciary duty. The actions taken by the Revlon directors, however, did not meet this standard. Moreover, while concern for various corporate constituencies is proper when addressing a takeover threat, that principle is limited by the requirement that there be some rationally related benefit accruing to the stockholders. We find no such benefit here. . . .

I

[In the summer of 1985, Revlon's chief executive officer, Michel C. Bergerac, rejected overtures from his counterpart at Pantry Pride, Ronald O. Perelman, concerning the possible acquisition of Revlon by Pantry Pride in the $40 to $42 per share range if friendly or $45 if the acquisition were hostile. This and all subsequent overtures were rebuffed, perhaps in part, the court noted, because of Mr. Bergerac's strong personal antipathy to Mr. Perelman.

Revlon's board met in August to consider the impending hostile bid. Of the fourteen directors, six were part of the company's senior management, two held significant blocks of stock, and four of the remaining six had had some relationship with companies doing business with Revlon. The court noted that on this record "we cannot conclude that this board is entitled to certain presumptions that generally attach to the decisions of a board whose majority consists of truly outside independent directors."

After hearing from Felix Rohatyn and William Loomis of Lazard Freres, the company's investment banker, and from its special counsel, Martin Lipton, the board adopted two defensive tactics: a poison pill plan and the company's repurchase of five million of its thirty million shares.

After Pantry Pride launched a hostile tender offer at $47.50, Revlon commenced its own tender offer, now increased to ten million shares. Eighty-seven percent of Revlon's shareholders tendered in response to this offer and the company purchased the shares pro rata from those who tendered. The consideration for the ten million shares was not cash but senior subordinated notes (and a fractional share of cumulative convertible preferred stock). Lazard Freres opined that the notes would trade at their face value on a fully distributable basis. The notes contained covenants that limited Revlon's ability to incur additional debt, sell assets, or pay dividends unless otherwise approved by the "independent" (nonmanagement) members of the board.

During the next six weeks, Pantry Pride made four additional cash bids at successively higher prices. Revlon pursued negotiations with other bidders and agreed on October 3 to a leveraged buyout by Forstmann. Under the terms of the buyout, a new company formed by Forstmann would purchase each Revlon share for $56 cash, Revlon management would purchase stock in the new company by exercising their Revlon golden parachutes, Forstmann would assume Revlon's $475 million debt incurred in the issuance of the notes, and Revlon would redeem the poison pill and waive the restrictive covenants of the notes for Forstmann or in connection with any offer superior to Forstmann's. The agreement contemplated either Revlon or an acquirer selling off various divisions of Revlon, including its cosmetics and fragrance division, to provide cash for the transaction.

The announcement of this agreement, including the waiver of the note covenants, led to a decline in the price of the notes. One director later reported a deluge of telephone calls from irate noteholders, and the Wall Street Journal reported threats of litigation by the noteholders.

Pantry Pride again raised its offer, this time to $56.25. Efforts to reach agreement failed. Pantry Pride announced that it would engage in fractional bidding and top any Forstmann offer by a slightly higher one. The court found that Forstmann, but not Pantry Pride, had been made privy to certain Revlon financial data. With this data Forstmann made a $57.25 offer subject to these conditions:

- Forstmann would receive a lock-up option to purchase two Revlon divisions for $525 million, some $100 to $175 million below the value ascribed to them by Lazard Freres;
- Revlon would agree to a no-shop provision, blocking its discussion with other suitors;

- Revlon would pay a $25 million cancellation fee to Forstmann if the deal fell through;
- Revlon's current management would not participate in the merger;
- The poison pill would be redeemed and the note covenants would be waived. Forstmann agreed to support the par value of the notes by an exchange of new notes.

Forstmann said it would withdraw its offer if it were not immediately accepted. The Revlon board unanimously approved Forstmann's proposal because (1) it was for a higher price than the Pantry Pride bid (although the court noted that the Forstmann proposal must be discounted for the time value of money because of the delay in approving the merger and consummating the transaction, so that the exact difference between the two bids remained unsettled); (2) it protected the noteholders; and (3) Forstmann's financing was firmly in place.

Pantry Pride filed suit and raised its offer to $58 conditioned upon nullification of the poison pill, waiver of the covenants, and an injunction of the Forstmann lock-up. The trial court concluded that the Revlon directors had breached their duty of loyalty by making concessions to Forstmann out of concern for directors' liability to the noteholders rather than maximizing the sales price of the company for the stockholders' benefit.]

II

[To determine the propriety of a preliminary injunction, the court looked to Pantry Pride's probability of success on the merits, addressing first the directors' responsibility for managing the business and affairs of the corporation subject to their fiduciary duties and describing the court's role as governed by the business judgment rule as set out in *Unocal*. Under these standards the court found the adoption of the poison pill to be valid and found any further challenge to the poison pill as moot since the board had agreed to redeem the pill for any cash proposal of $57.25 or more per share.]

C

The second defensive measure adopted by Revlon to thwart a Pantry Pride takeover was the company's own exchange offer for 10 million of its shares. The directors' general broad powers to manage the business and affairs of the corporation are augmented by the specific authority conferred under 8 Del. C. §160(a), permitting the company to deal in its own stock. *Unocal*, 493 A.2d at 953-954; Cheff v. Mathes, Del. Supr., 199 A.2d 548, 554 (1964); Kors v. Carey, Del. Ch., 158 A.2d 136, 140 (1960). However, when exercising that power in an effort to forestall a hostile takeover, the board's actions are strictly held to the fiduciary standards outlined in *Unocal*. These standards require the directors to determine the best interests of the corporation and its stockholders, and impose an enhanced duty to abjure any action that is motivated by considerations other than a good faith concern for such interests. *Unocal*, 493 A.2d at 954-955; see Bennett v. Propp, Del. Supr., 187 A.2d 405, 409 (1962).

The Revlon directors concluded that Pantry Pride's $47.50 offer was grossly inadequate. In that regard the board acted in good faith, and on an informed basis, with reasonable grounds to believe that there existed a harmful threat to the corporate enterprise. The adoption of a defensive measure, reasonable in relation to the threat posed, was proper and fully accorded with the powers, duties, and responsibilities conferred upon directors under our law. *Unocal,* 493 A.2d at 954; *Pogostin v. Rice,* 480 A.2d at 627.

D

However, when Pantry Pride increased its offer to $50 per share, and then to $53, it became apparent to all that the break-up of the company was inevitable. The Revlon board's authorization permitting management to negotiate a merger or buyout with a third party was a recognition that the company was for sale. The duty of the board had thus changed from the preservation of Revlon as a corporate entity to the maximization of the company's value at a sale for the stockholders' benefit. This significantly altered the board's responsibilities under the *Unocal* standards. It no longer faced threats to corporate policy and effectiveness, or to the stockholders' interests, from a grossly inadequate bid. The whole question of defensive measures became moot. The directors' role changed from defenders of the corporate bastion to auctioneers charged with getting the best price for the stockholders at a sale of the company.

III

This brings us to the lock-up with Forstmann and its emphasis on shoring up the sagging market value of the Notes in the face of threatened litigation by their holders. Such a focus was inconsistent with the changed concept of the directors' responsibilities at this stage of the developments. The impending waiver of the Notes covenants had caused the value of the Notes to fall, and the board was aware of the noteholders' ire as well as their subsequent threats of suit. The directors thus made support of the Notes an integral part of the company's dealings with Forstmann, even though their primary responsibility at this stage was to the equity owners.

The original threat posed by Pantry Pride—the break-up of the company—had become a reality which even the directors embraced. Selective dealing to fend off a hostile but determined bidder was no longer a proper objective. Instead, obtaining the highest price for the benefit of the stockholders should have been the central theme guiding director action. Thus, the Revlon board could not make the requisite showing of good faith by preferring the noteholders and ignoring its duty of loyalty to the shareholders. The rights of the former already were fixed by contract. The noteholders required no further protection, and when the Revlon board entered into an auction-ending lock-up agreement with Forstmann on the basis of impermissible considerations at the expense of the shareholders, the directors breached their primary duty of loyalty.

The Revlon board argued that it acted in good faith in protecting the noteholders because *Unocal* permits consideration of other corporate constituencies. Although such considerations may be permissible, there are fundamental limitations upon that prerogative. A board may have regard for various constituencies in discharging its responsibilities, provided there are rationally related benefits accruing to the stockholders. *Unocal*, 493 A.2d at 955. However, such concern for non-stockholder interests is inappropriate when an auction among active bidders is in progress, and the object no longer is to protect or maintain the corporate enterprise but to sell it to the highest bidder.

Revlon also contended that by Gilbert v. El Paso Co., Del. Ch., 490 A.2d 1050, 1054-1055 (1984), it had contractual and good faith obligations to consider the noteholders. However, any such duties are limited to the principle that one may not interfere with contractual relationships by improper actions. Here, the rights of the noteholders were fixed by agreement, and there is nothing of substance to suggest that any of those terms were violated. The Notes covenants specifically contemplated a waiver to permit sale of the company at a fair price. The Notes were accepted by the holders on that basis, including the risk of an adverse market effect stemming from a waiver. Thus, nothing remained for Revlon to legitimately protect, and no rationally related benefit thereby accrued to the stockholders. Under such circumstances we must conclude that the merger agreement with Forstmann was unreasonable in relation to the threat posed.

A lock-up is not per se illegal under Delaware law. Its use has been approved in an earlier case. Thompson v. Enstar Corp., Del. Ch. (1984). Such options can entice other bidders to enter a contest for control of the corporation, creating an auction for the company and maximizing shareholder profit. Current economic conditions in the takeover market are such that a "white knight" like Forstmann might only enter the bidding for the target company if it receives some form of compensation to cover the risks and costs involved. However, while those lock-ups which draw bidders into the battle benefit shareholders, similar measures which end an active auction and foreclose further bidding operate to the shareholders' detriment. . . .

The Forstmann option had a . . . destructive effect on the auction process. Forstmann had already been drawn into the contest on a preferred basis, so the result of the lock-up was not to foster bidding, but to destroy it. The board's stated reasons for approving the transaction were: (1) better financing, (2) noteholder protection, and (3) higher price. As the Court of Chancery found, and we agree, any distinctions between the rival bidders' methods of financing the proposal were nominal at best, and such a consideration has little or no significance in a cash offer for any and all shares. The principal object, contrary to the board's duty of care, appears to have been protection of the noteholders over the shareholders' interests.

While Forstmann's $57.25 offer was objectively higher than Pantry Pride's $56.25 bid, the margin of superiority is less when the Forstmann price is adjusted for the time value of money. In reality, the Revlon board ended the auction in return for very little actual improvement in the final bid. The principal benefit went to the directors, who avoided personal liability to a class of creditors to whom the board owed no further duty under the circumstances. Thus, when a board ends an intense bidding contest on an insubstantial basis, and where a significant by-product of that action is to protect the directors against a perceived threat of personal liability for consequences stemming from the adoption of previous defensive measures, the action cannot withstand the enhanced scrutiny which *Unocal* requires of director conduct.

In addition to the lock-up option, the Court of Chancery enjoined the no-shop provision as part of the attempt to foreclose further bidding by Pantry Pride. The no-shop provision, like the lock-up option, while not per se illegal, is impermissible under the *Unocal* standards when a board's primary duty becomes that of an auctioneer responsible for selling the company to the highest bidder. The agreement to negotiate only with Forstmann ended rather than intensified the board's involvement in the bidding contest.

It is ironic that the parties even considered a no-shop agreement when Revlon had dealt preferentially, and almost exclusively, with Forstmann throughout the contest. After the directors authorized management to negotiate with other parties, Forstmann was given every negotiating advantage that Pantry Pride had been denied: cooperation from management, access to financial data, and the exclusive opportunity to present merger proposals directly to the board of directors. Favoritism for a white knight to the total exclusion of a hostile bidder might be justifiable when the latter's offer adversely affects shareholder interests, but when bidders make relatively similar offers, or dissolution of the company becomes inevitable, the directors cannot fulfill their enhanced *Unocal* duties by playing favorites with the contending factions. Market forces must be allowed to operate freely to bring the target's shareholders the best price available for their equity.[16] Thus, as the trial court ruled, the shareholders' interests necessitated that the board remain free to negotiate in the fulfillment of that duty.

The court below similarly enjoined the payment of the cancellation fee, pending a resolution of the merits, because the fee was part of the overall plan to thwart Pantry Pride's efforts. We find no abuse of discretion in that ruling. . . .

V

In conclusion, the Revlon board was confronted with a situation not uncommon in the current wave of corporate takeovers. A hostile and determined bidder sought the company at a price the board was convinced was inadequate. The initial defensive tactics worked to the benefit of the shareholders, and thus the board was able to sustain its *Unocal* burdens in justifying those measures. However, in granting an asset option lock-up to Forstmann, we must conclude that under all the circumstances the directors allowed considerations other than the maximization of shareholder profit to affect their judgment, and followed a course that ended the auction for Revlon, absent court intervention, to the ultimate detriment of its shareholders. No such defensive measure can be sustained when it represents a breach of the directors' fundamental duty of care. See Smith v. Van Gorkom, Del. Supr., 488 A.2d 858, 874 (1985). In that

---

16. By this we do not embrace the "passivity" thesis rejected in *Unocal*. See 493 A.2d at 954-955, nn.8-10. The directors' role remains an active one, changed only in the respect that they are charged with the duty of selling the company at the highest price attainable for the stockholders' benefit.

context the board's action is not entitled to the deference accorded it by the business judgment rule. The measures were properly enjoined. The decision of the Court of Chancery, therefore, is affirmed.

NOTES AND QUESTIONS

1. If the auction duty is assumed to apply, how must it be conducted? In Mills Acquisition Co. v. Macmillan, Inc., 559 A.2d 1261 (Del. 1988), the Delaware Supreme Court enjoined an acquisition where target management tipped one bidder as to the other bidder's secret bid. Such rulings have led to bidding by elaborate scripts.

2. Did the Revlon directors breach their duty of care or of loyalty? Apparently, the answer is both. See Mills Acquisition Co. v. Macmillan, Inc., 559 A.2d 1261, 1284 n.4 (Del. 1988). What is the implication of this for the directors' indemnification and insurance claims?

PROBLEM 9-4

Transunited, Inc. has a nine-member board. The eight outside directors own incidental amounts of Transunited stock; six of the outside directors are CEOs of major industrial corporations, and two are partners in leading investment banking firms The ninth director, Transunited's CEO Jane Gorkom, owns 7 percent of Transunited's outstanding shares.

On January 5, 2014, the board assembled for an emergency meeting called by Jane to consider the sale of Transunited to a corporation controlled by noted takeover artist Norma Pritzker. Gorkom informed the board that Pritzker was offering a 100 percent premium to acquire all of the corporation's assets, but that her offer required an immediate acceptance and the inclusion in the merger agreement of two "deal cementing" provisions—a "no-shop provision" and a "lock-up option" giving Pritzker the right to purchase Transunited's furniture division for $150 million less than its recently appraised value. The board then heard reports by the firm's outside legal counsel and an outside valuation expert. Outside counsel opined that the merger documents (which had been provided to the directors with the meeting notice) were fair. The valuation expert opined that the price offered by Pritzker "was a high price" for the company.

A brief discussion ensued. Two directors, including one investment banker, argued that it was imprudent not to seek other bids. The other investment banker/director argued that Pritzker's offer was "higher than any price we could dream of getting in an auction." The directors then approved the merger and the merger agreement (including the "deal cementing" provisions), with two directors dissenting, subject to later shareholder approval.

A shareholder class action has been filed seeking to enjoin the lock-up option, the no-shop clause, and the holding of the scheduled shareholders' meeting. What result?

e.   *Refining* Revlon *and* Unocal

Revlon and *Unocal* established the broad contours of Delaware's hostile takeover jurisprudence. Left unanswered, however, were a number of questions. What are the exact contours of the board of directors' duty to auction? What will the Delaware Supreme Court consider to be legitimate threats to corporate policy under the *Unocal* test? When will a board of directors be required to remove its takeover defenses to allow shareholders to consider a hostile offer? What are the limits on the board's power to grant lock-up options or promise termination fees?

Interspersed among a number of Court of Chancery decisions, the following two Delaware Supreme Court cases provide substantial definition to the *Unocal/Revlon* framework.

(1)   THE *TIME* CASE

Paramount Communications, Inc. v. Time, Inc.
Delaware Supreme Court, 1990
571 A.2d 1140

HORSEY, JUSTICE:

[This suit seeks to enjoin Time Incorporated's tender offer for 51 percent of the outstanding shares of Warner Communications, Inc. The tender offer replaced a planned merger agreement between Time and Warner that had been abandoned in the face of Paramount's all-cash offer to purchase all of the outstanding shares of Time for $175 per share. Paramount and shareholders of Time filed suits alleging that the merger agreement resulted in a change of control that effectively put Time up for sale, thereby triggering *Revlon* duties, and that Time's response to the Paramount tender offer breached its duties under *Unocal*.

The boards of directors of Time and Warner agreed to a stock-for-stock merger on March 3, 1989, culminating three years of discussions between the two media companies. Time's traditional business of magazine and book publication had been expanded to include pay television programming through its Home Box Office, Inc. and Cinemax subsidiaries and cable television franchises. Warner, a long-recognized name in the movie business, possessed an international distribution system, large interests in the music and recording business, and cable television systems.

In 1987 a special committee of executives proposed that Time should expand in the areas of ownership and creation of video programming. In the spring of 1987, Time and Warner discussed the possibility of a joint venture between the two companies through the creation of a jointly owned cable company that would produce and distribute movies. Tax considerations and other issues caused this plan to be abandoned, but Time's interest in Warner continued over the next year. In July 1988 the Time board considered several companies in the entertainment industry and concluded that Warner was a superior candidate for consolidation.

Discussions between the two companies reached an impasse over certain corporate governance issues. Warner insisted on a stock swap in order to preserve the Warner shareholders' equity in the resulting corporation. Time preferred to pay cash and/or securities to acquire Warner. Time wanted to dominate the discussion of who would be CEO at the merged company in order to preserve the "Time culture." The court noted that the primary concern of Time's outside directors—the preservation of the "Time culture"—sprang from Time's recognition as a respected journalistic institution. Several of Time's outside directors feared that a merger with an entertainment company would divert Time's focus from news journalism and threaten the Time culture.

During the fall of 1988, Time held informal discussions with several companies including Paramount. Time steadfastly maintained it was not placing itself up for sale and terminated talks with Capital Cities/ABC when that company wanted to control the resulting board.

Warner and Time resumed negotiations in January 1989, leading to the merger agreement in March. The resulting company would have a 24-member board, with 12 members representing each corporation. The company would have co-CEOs for the first few years, with Time's president to be designated as sole CEO upon the retirement of Warner CEO, Steve Ross. The board would create an editorial committee with a majority of members representing Time and an entertainment committee controlled by Warner board members. The parties agreed on an exchange rate favoring Warner by which former Warner stockholders would own about 62 percent of the common stock of Time-Warner, Inc. Time's board had recognized the potential need to pay a premium in the stock ratio in exchange for dictating the governing arrangement of the new Time-Warner and to preserve the Time culture.

At its March 3 meeting, the Time board adopted several defensive tactics, including an automatic stock exchange where each company would acquire about 10 percent of the shares of the other, a no-shop clause preventing Time from considering any other consolidation proposals regardless of their merits, and agreements with various banks that the Chancellor found to be futile efforts to "dry up" money for a hostile takeover.

On June 7, 1989, after Time had sent out extensive proxy statements to its shareholders seeking approval of the merger, but before the shareholders' meeting scheduled for June 23, Paramount announced its all-cash offer. Paramount's offer was subject to several conditions, including requiring Time to terminate its merger and stock exchange agreement with Warner, and Time removing certain defensive tactics including its poison pill. In response to the Paramount offer of $175 per share, the trading price of Time stock rose from $126 to $170. Over the following eight days Time's board met three times to discuss Paramount's offer. After hearing from Time's financial advisers, who said that Time's per share value was materially higher than $175 on an auction basis, the board concluded that Paramount's $175 bid was inadequate.

The court said that the board's prevailing belief was that Paramount's bid presented a threat to Time's control of its own destiny and retention of the Time culture. The board feared that Paramount's cash premium would be a tempting prospect to institutional investors who held large quantities of Time stock. Certain Time directors expressed their concern that their stockholders would not comprehend the long-term benefits of the Warner merger. Thus, the Time-Warner merger was recast as an outright cash and securities acquisition of Warner by Time, 51 percent to be acquired in a $70 per share cash tender offer with the remaining 49 percent to be acquired later for cash and securities. To provide the funds required for the acquisition, Time would take on $7 to $10 billion of debt, thus eliminating the company's low debt status, which had been one of the principal transaction-related benefits of the original merger. The Chancellor found the initial Time-Warner transaction to have been negotiated at arm's length and the restructured Time-Warner transaction to have resulted from Paramount's offer and its expected effect on a Time shareholder vote.

On June 23 Paramount raised its all-cash offer to $200 per share. The Time board reiterated its belief that the offer was still inadequate and that the Warner transaction offered a greater long-term value to the stockholders and, unlike Paramount, was not a threat to Time's survival and its "culture."]

II

The Shareholder Plaintiffs first assert a *Revlon* claim. They contend that the March 4 Time-Warner agreement effectively put Time up for sale, triggering *Revlon* duties, requiring Time's board to enhance short-term shareholder value and to treat all other interested acquirors on an equal basis. The Shareholder Plaintiffs base this argument on two facts: (i) the ultimate Time-Warner exchange ratio of .465 favoring Warner, resulting in Warner shareholders' receipt of 62% of the combined company; and (ii) the subjective intent of Time's directors as evidenced in their statements that the market might perceive the Time-Warner merger as putting Time up "for sale" and their adoption of various defensive measures.

The Shareholder Plaintiffs further contend that Time's directors, in structuring the original merger transaction to be "takeover-proof," triggered *Revlon* duties by foreclosing their shareholders from any prospect of obtaining a control premium. In short, plaintiffs argue that Time's board's decision to merge with Warner imposed a fiduciary duty to maximize immediate share value and not erect unreasonable barriers to further bids. . . .

Paramount asserts only a *Unocal* claim in which the shareholder plaintiffs join. Paramount contends that the Chancellor, in applying the first part of the *Unocal* test, erred in finding that Time's board had reasonable grounds to believe that Paramount posed both a legally cognizable threat to Time shareholders and a danger to Time's corporate policy and effectiveness. Paramount also contests the court's finding that Time's board made a reasonable and objective investigation of Paramount's offer so as to be informed before rejecting it. Paramount further claims that the court erred in applying *Unocal*'s second part in finding Time's response to be "reasonable." Paramount points primarily to the preclusive effect of the revised agreement which denied Time shareholders the opportunity both to vote on the agreement and to respond to Paramount's tender offer. Paramount argues that the underlying motivation of Time's board in adopting these defensive measures was management's desire to perpetuate itself in office.

The Court of Chancery posed the pivotal question presented by this case to be: Under what circumstances must a board of directors abandon an in-place plan of corporate development in order to provide its shareholders with the option to elect and realize an immediate control premium? As applied to this case, the question becomes:

Did Time's board, having developed a strategic plan of global expansion to be launched through a business combination with Warner, come under a fiduciary duty to jettison its plan and put the corporation's future in the hands of its shareholders?

While we affirm the result reached by the Chancellor, we think it unwise to place undue emphasis upon long-term versus short-term corporate strategy. Two key predicates underpin our analysis. First, Delaware law imposes on a board of directors the duty to manage the business and affairs of the corporation. 8 Del. C. §141(a). This broad mandate includes a conferred authority to set a corporate course of action, including time frame, designed to enhance corporate profitability. Thus, the question of "long-term" versus "short-term" values is largely irrelevant because directors, generally, are obliged to charter a course for a corporation which is in its best interests without regard to a fixed investment horizon. Second, absent a limited set of circumstances as defined under *Revlon*, a board of directors, while always required to act in an informed manner, is not under any per se duty to maximize shareholder value in the short term, even in the context of a takeover.[12] In our view, the pivotal question presented by this case is: "Did Time, by entering into the proposed merger with Warner, put itself up for sale?" A resolution of that issue through application of *Revlon* has a significant bearing upon the resolution of the derivative *Unocal* issue.

A

We first take up plaintiffs' principal *Revlon* argument, summarized above. In rejecting this argument, the Chancellor found the original Time-Warner merger agreement not to constitute a "change of control" and concluded that the transaction did not trigger *Revlon* duties. The Chancellor's conclusion is premised on a finding that "[b]efore the merger agreement was signed, control of the corporation existed in a fluid aggregation of unaffiliated shareholders representing a voting majority—in other words, in the market." The Chancellor's findings of fact are supported by the record and his conclusion is correct as a matter of law. However, we premise our rejection of plaintiffs' *Revlon* claim on broader grounds, namely, the absence of any substantial evidence to conclude that Time's board, in negotiating with Warner, made the dissolution or break-up of the corporate entity inevitable, as was the case in *Revlon*.

Under Delaware law there are, generally speaking and without excluding other possibilities, two circumstances which may implicate *Revlon* duties. The first, and clearer one, is when a corporation initiates an active bidding process seeking to sell itself or to effect a business reorganization involving a clear break-up of the company. See, e.g., Mills Acquisition Co. v. Macmillan, Inc., Del. Supr., 559 A.2d 1261 (1988). However, *Revlon* duties may also be triggered where, in response to a bidder's offer, a target abandons its long-term strategy and seeks an alternative transaction involving the break-up of the company. Thus, in *Revlon*, when the board responded to Pantry

---

12. Thus, we endorse the Chancellor's conclusion that it is not breach of faith for directors to determine that the present stock market price of shares is not representative of true value or that there may indeed be several market values for any corporation's stock. We have so held in another context. See [Smith v. Van Gorkom], 488 A.2d at 876.

Pride's offer by contemplating a "bust-up" sale of assets in a leveraged acquisition, we imposed upon the board a duty to maximize immediate shareholder value and an obligation to auction the company fairly. If, however, the board's reaction to a hostile tender offer is found to constitute only a defensive response and not an abandonment of the corporation's continued existence, *Revlon* duties are not triggered, though *Unocal* duties attach.[14] See, e.g., Ivanhoe Partners v. Newmont Mining Corp., Del. Supr., 535 A.2d 1334, 1345 (1987).

The plaintiffs insist that even though the original Time-Warner agreement may not have worked "an objective change of control," the transaction made a "sale" of Time inevitable. Plaintiffs rely on the subjective intent of Time's board of directors and principally upon certain board members' expressions of concern that the Warner transaction *might* be viewed as effectively putting Time up for sale. Plaintiffs argue that the use of a lock-up agreement, a no-shop clause, and so-called "dry-up" agreements prevented shareholders from obtaining a control premium in the immediate future and thus violated *Revlon*.

We agree with the Chancellor that such evidence is entirely insufficient to invoke *Revlon* duties; and we decline to extend *Revlon*'s application to corporate transactions simply because they might be construed as putting a corporation either "in play" or "up for sale." The adoption of structural safety devices alone does not trigger *Revlon*. Rather, as the Chancellor stated, such devices are properly subject to a *Unocal* analysis.

Finally, we do not find in Time's recasting of its merger agreement with Warner from a share exchange to a share purchase a basis to conclude that Time had either abandoned its strategic plan or made a sale of Time inevitable. The Chancellor found that although the merged Time-Warner company would be large (with a value approaching approximately $30 billion), recent takeover cases have proven that acquisition of the combined company might nonetheless be possible. The legal consequence is that *Unocal* alone applies to determine whether the business judgment rule attaches to the revised agreement. Plaintiffs' analogy to *Macmillan* thus collapses and plaintiffs' reliance on *Macmillan* is misplaced.

B

We turn now to plaintiffs' *Unocal* claim. We begin by noting, as did the Chancellor, that our decision does not require us to pass on the wisdom of the board's decision to enter into the original Time-Warner agreement. That is not a court's task. Our task is simply to review the record to determine whether there is sufficient evidence to support the Chancellor's conclusion that the initial Time-Warner agreement was the product of a proper exercise of business judgment.

---

14. Within the auction process, any action taken by the board must be reasonably related to the threat posed or reasonable in relation to the advantage sought, see Mills Acquisition Co. v. Macmillan, Inc., Del. Supr., 559 A.2d 1261, 1288 (1988). Thus, a *Unocal* analysis may be appropriate when a corporation is in a *Revlon* situation and *Revlon* duties may be triggered by a defensive action taken in response to a hostile offer. Since *Revlon*, we have stated that differing treatment of various bidders is not actionable when such action reasonably relates to achieving the best price available for the stockholders. *Macmillan*, 559 A.2d at 1286-1287.

We have purposely detailed the evidence of the Time board's deliberative approach, beginning in 1983-84, to expand itself. Time's decision in 1988 to combine with Warner was made only after what could be fairly characterized as an exhaustive appraisal of Time's future as a corporation. After concluding in 1983-84 that the corporation must expand to survive, and beyond journalism into entertainment, the board combed the field of available entertainment companies. By 1987 Time had focused upon Warner; by late July 1988 Time's board was convinced that Warner would provide the best "fit" for Time to achieve its strategic objectives. The record attests to the zealousness of Time's executives, fully supported by their directors, in seeing to the preservation of Time's "culture," i.e., its perceived editorial integrity in journalism. We find ample evidence in the record to support the Chancellor's conclusion that the Time board's decision to expand the business of the company through its March 3 merger with Warner was entitled to the protection of the business judgment rule. See Aronson v. Lewis, Del. Supr., 473 A.2d 805, 812 (1984).

. . . The court ruled that *Unocal* applied to all director actions taken, following receipt of Paramount's hostile tender offer, that were reasonably determined to be defensive. Clearly that was a correct ruling and no party disputes that ruling.

In *Unocal*, we held that before the business judgment rule is applied to a board's adoption of a defense measure, the burden will lie with the board to prove (a) reasonable grounds for believing that a danger to corporate policy and effectiveness existed; and (b) that the defensive measure adopted was reasonable in relation to the threat posed. *Unocal*, 493 A.2d 946. Directors satisfy the first part of the *Unocal* test by demonstrating good faith and reasonable investigation. We have repeatedly stated that the refusal to entertain an offer may comport with a valid exercise of a board's business judgment. See, e.g., *Macmillan*, 559 A.2d at 1285 n.35; *Van Gorkom*, 488 A.2d at 881; Pogostin v. Rice, Del. Supr., 480 A.2d 619, 627 (1984).

Unocal involved a two-tier, highly coercive tender offer. In such a case, the threat is obvious: shareholders may be compelled to tender to avoid being treated adversely in the second stage of the transaction. In subsequent cases, the Court of Chancery has suggested that an all-cash, all-shares offer, falling within a range of values that a shareholder might reasonably prefer, cannot constitute a legally recognized "threat" to shareholder interests sufficient to withstand a *Unocal* analysis. AC Acquisitions Corp. v. Anderson, Clayton Co., Del. Ch., 519 A.2d 103 (1986); see Grand Metropolitan, PLC v. Pillsbury Co., Del. Ch., 588 A.2d 1049 (1988); City Capital Associates v. Interco, Inc., Del. Ch., 551 A.2d 787 (1988). In those cases, the Court of Chancery determined that whatever danger existed related only to the shareholders and only to price and not to the corporation.

From those decisions by our Court of Chancery, Paramount and the individual plaintiffs extrapolate a rule of law that an all-cash, all-shares offer with values reasonably in the range of acceptable price cannot pose any objective threat to a corporation or its shareholders. Thus, Paramount would have us hold that only if the value of Paramount's offer were determined to be clearly inferior to the value created by management's plan to merge with Warner could the offer be viewed—objectively—as a threat.

Implicit in the plaintiffs' argument is the view that a hostile tender offer can pose only two types of threats: the threat of coercion that results from a two-tier offer promising unequal treatment for nontendering shareholders; and the threat of inadequate value from an all-shares, all-cash offer at a price below what a target board in good faith deems to be the present value of its shares. See, e.g., *Interco*, 551 A.2d at 797; see also BNS, Inc. v. Koppers, D. Del., 683 F. Supp. 458 (1988). Since Paramount's offer was all-cash, the only conceivable "threat," plaintiffs argue, was inadequate value.[17] We disapprove of such a narrow and rigid construction of *Unocal*, for the reasons which follow.

Plaintiffs' position represents a fundamental misconception of our standard of review under *Unocal* principally because it would involve the court in substituting its judgment for what is a "better" deal for that of a corporation's board of directors. To the extent that the Court of Chancery has recently done so in certain of its opinions, we hereby reject such approach as not in keeping with a proper *Unocal* analysis. See, e.g., *Interco*, 551 A.2d 787, and its progeny; but see TW Services, Inc. v. SWT Acquisition Corp., Del. Ch., C.A. No. 1047, Allen, C. (March 2, 1989).

The usefulness of *Unocal* as an analytical tool is precisely its flexibility in the face of a variety of fact scenarios. *Unocal* is not intended as an abstract standard; neither is it a structured and mechanistic procedure of appraisal. Thus, we have said that directors may consider, when evaluating the threat posed by a takeover bid, the "inadequacy of the price offered, nature and timing of the offer, questions of illegality, the impact on "constituencies" other than shareholders, . . . the risk of non-consummation and the quality of securities being offered in the exchange." 493 A.2d at 955. The open-ended analysis mandated by *Unocal* is not intended to lead to a simple mathematical exercise: that is, of comparing the discounted value of Time-Warner's expected trading price at some future date with Paramount's offer and determining which is the higher. Indeed, in our view, precepts underlying the business judgment rule mitigate against a court's engaging in the process of attempting to appraise and evaluate the relative merits of a long-term versus a short-term investment goal for shareholders. To engage in such an exercise is a distortion of the *Unocal* process and, in particular, the application of the second part of *Unocal*'s test, discussed below.

In this case, the Time board reasonably determined that inadequate value was not the only legally cognizable threat that Paramount's all-cash, all-shares offer could present. Time's board concluded that Paramount's eleventh hour offer posed other threats. One concern was that Time shareholders might elect to tender into Paramount's cash offer in ignorance or a mistaken belief of the strategic benefit which a business combination with Warner might produce. Moreover, Time viewed the conditions attached to Paramount's offer as introducing a degree of uncertainty that skewed a comparative

---

17. Some commentators have suggested that the threats posed by hostile offers be categorized into not two but three types: "(i) *opportunity loss* . . . [where] a hostile offer might deprive target shareholders of the opportunity to select a superior alternative offered by target management [or, we would add, offered by another bidder]; (ii) *structural coercion*, . . . the risk that disparate treatment of non-tendering shareholders might distort shareholders' tender decisions; and . . . (iii) *substantive coercion*, . . . the risk that shareholders will mistakenly accept an underpriced offer because they disbelieve management's representations of intrinsic value." The recognition of substantive coercion, the authors suggest, would help guarantee that the *Unocal* standard becomes an effective intermediate standard of review. Gilson & Kraakman, Delaware's Intermediate Standard for Defensive Tactics: Is There Substance to Proportionality Review?, 44 The Business Lawyer, 247, 267 (1989).

analysis. Further, the timing of Paramount's offer to follow issuance of Time's proxy notice was viewed as arguably designed to upset, if not confuse, the Time stockholders' vote. Given this record evidence, we cannot conclude that the Time board's decision of June 6 that Paramount's offer posed a threat to corporate policy and effectiveness was lacking in good faith or dominated by motives of either entrenchment or self-interest.

Paramount also contends that the Time board had not duly investigated Paramount's offer. Therefore, Paramount argues, Time was unable to make an informed decision that the offer posed a threat to Time's corporate policy. Although the Chancellor did not address this issue directly, his findings of fact do detail Time's exploration of the available entertainment companies, including Paramount, before determining that Warner provided the best strategic "fit." In addition, the court found that Time's board rejected Paramount's offer because Paramount did not serve Time's objectives or meet Time's needs. Thus, the record does, in our judgment, demonstrate that Time's board was adequately informed of the potential benefits of a transaction with Paramount. We agree with the Chancellor that the Time board's lengthy pre-June investigation of potential merger candidates, including Paramount, mooted any obligation on Time's part to halt its merger process with Warner to reconsider Paramount. Time's board was under no obligation to negotiate with Paramount. *Unocal*, 493 A.2d at 954-955; see also *Macmillan*, 559 A.2d at 1285 n.35. Time's failure to negotiate cannot be fairly found to have been uninformed. The evidence supporting this finding is materially enhanced by the fact that twelve of Time's sixteen board members were outside independent directors. *Unocal*, 493 A.2d at 955; Moran v. Household Intern., Inc., Del. Supr., 500 A.2d 1346, 1356 (1985).

We turn to the second part of the *Unocal* analysis. The obvious requisite to determining the reasonableness of a defensive action is a clear identification of the nature of the threat. As the Chancellor correctly noted, this "requires an evaluation of the importance of the corporate objective threatened; alternative methods of protecting that objective; impacts of the 'defensive' action, and other relevant factors." It is not until both parts of the *Unocal* inquiry have been satisfied that the business judgment rule attaches to defensive actions of a board of directors. As applied to the facts of this case, the question is whether the record evidence supports the Court of Chancery's conclusion that the restructuring of the Time-Warner transaction, including the adoption of several preclusive defensive measures, was a *reasonable response* in relation to a perceived threat.

Paramount argues that, assuming its tender offer posed a threat, Time's response was unreasonable in precluding Time's shareholders from accepting the tender offer or receiving a control premium in the immediately foreseeable future. Once again, the contention stems, we believe, from a fundamental misunderstanding of where the power of corporate governance lies. Delaware law confers the management of the corporate enterprise to the stockholders' duly elected board representatives. 8 Del. C. §141(a). The fiduciary duty to manage a corporate enterprise includes the selection of a time frame for achievement of corporate goals. That duty may not be delegated to the stockholders. *Van Gorkom*, 488 A.2d at 873. Directors are not obliged to abandon a deliberately conceived corporate plan for a short-term shareholder profit unless there is clearly no basis to sustain the corporate strategy. See, e.g., *Revlon*, 506 A.2d 173.

Although the Chancellor blurred somewhat the discrete analyses required under *Unocal*, he did conclude that Time's board reasonably perceived Paramount's offer to be a significant threat to the planned Time-Warner merger and that Time's response was not "overly broad." We have found that even in light of a valid threat, management actions that are coercive in nature or force upon shareholders a management-sponsored alternative to a hostile offer may be struck down as unreasonable and nonproportionate responses. *Macmillan,* 559 A.2d 1261; *AC Acquisitions Corp.,* 519 A.2d 103.

Here, on the record facts, the Chancellor found that Time's responsive action to Paramount's tender offer was not aimed at "cramming down" on its shareholders a management-sponsored alternative, but rather had as its goal the carrying forward of a pre-existing transaction in an altered form.[19] Thus, the response was reasonably related to the threat. The Chancellor noted that the revised agreement and its accompanying safety devices did not preclude Paramount from making an offer for the combined Time-Warner company or from changing the conditions of its offer so as not to make the offer dependent upon the nullification of the Time-Warner agreement. Thus, the response was proportionate. We affirm the Chancellor's rulings as clearly supported by the record. Finally, we note that although Time was required, as a result of Paramount's hostile offer, to incur a heavy debt to finance its acquisition of Warner, that fact alone does not render the board's decision unreasonable so long as the directors could reasonably perceive the debt load not to be so injurious to the corporation as to jeopardize its well being.

C. CONCLUSION

Applying the test for grant or denial of preliminary injunctive relief, we find plaintiffs failed to establish a reasonable likelihood of ultimate success on the merits. Therefore, we affirm.

NOTES AND QUESTIONS

1. The *Time* court provides managers a broad power to define threats to shareholders, including failure by shareholders to appreciate the benefits of the board's defensive strategy. Would this reason work if Paramount's offer had not been timed to follow issuance of Time's proxy notice?

2. Time's "corporate culture" plays a prominent role in this case. Do you think that Time's journalistic tradition gives it a culture that permits its directors to more easily say no to a raider than could directors of other companies?

Consider the following advertisement from a clothing maker:

The Brooks Brothers Promise . . . Despite the troubled retail environment, Brooks Brothers is resolved to uphold the values that have kept us the leader in understated American style for 173

---

19. The Chancellor cited Shamrock Holdings, Inc. v. Polaroid Corp., Del. Ch., 559 A.2d 257 (1989), as a closely analogous case. In that case, the Court of Chancery upheld, in the face of a takeover bid, the establishment of an employee stock ownership plan that had a significant antitakeover effect. The Court of Chancery upheld the board's action largely because the ESOP had been adopted *prior* to any contest for control and was reasonably determined to increase productivity and enhance profits. The ESOP did not appear to be primarily a device to affect or secure corporate control.

years . . . The values we live by are well-defined: We originated what has become the classic American style of dress . . . Our way of doing business is grounded in honesty and reliability . . . We continually update our clothing to bring you classic style in contemporary good taste . . . BROOKS BROTHERS IS FAMILY. For generations we have nurtured a spirit of loyalty and commitment among our associates and customers, providing superior personal service. These values have long made Brooks Brothers unique in all of retailing. They constitute our promise to you that the Brooks Brothers experience has no equal . . . .

/s/ [president of Brooks Brothers]

Could the board of this company resist a takeover by a raider who seemed likely to change this culture? How different is this from Cheff v. Mathes?

3. In Moran v. Household International, Inc., supra page 860, the Delaware Supreme Court sanctioned poison pills but left open the possibility that the board "has no more discretion in refusing to redeem the Rights than it does in enacting any defensive mechanism." Subsequently, the Delaware Court of Chancery required the redemption of poison pills in two cases: City Capital Associates Ltd. Part. v. Interco, Inc., 551 A.2d 787 (Del. Ch. 1988), and Grand Metropolitan PLC v. Pillsbury Co., 558 A.2d 1049 (Del. Ch. 1988). In Paramount Communications, Inc. v. Time, Inc., supra page 876, the Supreme Court criticized these decisions for having too restricted a view of threats to which a board may respond, resulting in the court's "substituting its judgment for what is a 'better' deal for that of a corporation's board of directors."

4. Consider the comments of Chancellor Allen in TW Services, Inc. v. SWT Acquisition Corp., 1989 WL 20290 (Del. Ch. March 2, 1999):

> The so-called "poison pill" can, of course, be seen as an attempt to address the flaw (as some would see it) in the corporation law that gives a board of directors a critical role in mergers (and other extraordinary transactions) but gives it no role with respect to public tender offers—a form of extraordinary transaction that threatens equivalent impacts upon the corporation and all of its constituencies including existing shareholders. Thus, with the development of that innovation, boards of directors began taking upon themselves, unilaterally in practically all instances, the power to reject a public tender offer (or more correctly, to preclude its completion as a practical matter) by adopting the poison pill stock rights plan.
>
> In Moran v. Household International, Inc., Del. Supr., 500 A.2d 1346 (1985), our Supreme Court opined that Delaware corporations were authorized to issue securities of this type, but noted that there could be a self-serving aspect to the use of this power. It held that a board that took such power to itself would be held to a fiduciary standard when called upon to consider releasing the power (by redeeming the pill) in light of all of the circumstances of a particular tender offer. Significantly, the Supreme Court cited the Unocal case at this point in its opinion. See Moran v. Household International., Inc., supra, at 1354. This court has understood that citation to mean that a decision not to redeem a pill in the face of a hostile tender offer is a defensive step that has to be "reasonable in relation to the threat posed" by such offer.

PROBLEM 9-5

Reconsider Paramount Communications, Inc. v. Time, Inc. What result if the facts were changed as follows:

(a) Time and Warner considered, but never agreed to, a stock-for-stock merger.

(b) In June 1999 Time agreed to acquire Warner for $70 per share in cash and securities via a first-tier tender offer and a second-tier merger. Additionally, Time then put in place a variety of defensive measures to protect itself from any unfriendly take-over bid, including a poison pill, a no-shop clause preventing Time from considering any other consolidation proposals regardless of the merits.

(c) Time and Paramount had no contact prior to June 1999. After the public announcement of the Time-Warner transaction, Paramount attempted to negotiate with Time, and, when rebuffed, publicly announced its willingness to acquire Time in a $200 per share cash tender offer. Shortly thereafter Paramount filed suit seeking to enjoin the Time-Warner transaction.

(2) THE *QVC* CASE

Paramount Communications, Inc. v. QVC Network, Inc.
Delaware Supreme Court, 1994
637 A.2d 34

VEASEY, CHIEF JUSTICE.

In this appeal we review an order of the Court of Chancery dated November 24, 1993 (the "November 24 Order"), preliminarily enjoining certain defensive measures designed to facilitate a so-called strategic alliance between Viacom Inc. ("Viacom") and Paramount Communications, Inc. ("Paramount") approved by the board of directors of Paramount (the "Paramount Board" or the "Paramount directors") and to thwart an unsolicited, more valuable, tender offer by QVC Network Inc. ("QVC"). In affirming, we hold that the sale of control in this case, which is at the heart of the proposed strategic alliance, implicates enhanced judicial scrutiny of the conduct of the Paramount Board under Unocal Corp. v. Mesa Petroleum Co., Del. Supr., 493 A.2d 946 (1985), and Revlon, Inc. v. MacAndrews & Forbes Holdings, Inc., Del. Supr., 506 A.2d 173 (1986). We further hold that the conduct of the Paramount Board was not reasonable as to process or result. . . .

I. FACTS

. . . This action arises out of a proposed acquisition of Paramount by Viacom through a tender offer followed by a second-step merger (the "Paramount-Viacom transaction"), and a competing unsolicited tender offer by QVC. The Court of Chancery granted a preliminary injunction. QVC Network Inc. v. Paramount Communications Inc., Del. Ch., 635 A.2d 1245, Jacobs, V.C. (1993), (the "Court of Chancery Opinion"). We affirmed by order dated December 9, 1993. Paramount Communications Inc. v. QVC Network Inc., Del. Supr., Nos. 427 and 428, 1993, 637 A.2d 828, Veasey, C.J. (Dec. 9, 1993) (the "December 9 Order").[1] . . .

---

1. We accepted this expedited interlocutory appeal on November 29, 1993. After briefing and oral argument in this Court held on December 9, 1993, we issued our December 9 Order affirming the November 24 Order of the Court of Chancery. In our December 9 Order, we stated, "It is not feasible, because of the exigencies of time, for this Court to complete an opinion setting forth more comprehensively the rationale of the Court's decision. Unless otherwise ordered by the Court, such an opinion will follow in due course." December 9 Order at 3. This is the opinion referred to therein.

Paramount is a Delaware corporation with its principal offices in New York City. Approximately 118 million shares of Paramount's common stock are outstanding and traded on the New York Stock Exchange. The majority of Paramount's stock is publicly held by numerous unaffiliated investors. Paramount owns and operates a diverse group of entertainment businesses, including motion picture and television studios, book publishers, professional sports teams, and amusement parks.

There are 15 persons serving on the Paramount Board. Four directors are officer-employees of Paramount: Martin S. Davis ("Davis"), Paramount's Chairman and Chief Executive officer since 1983; Donald Oresman ("Oresman"), Executive Vice-President, Chief Administrative Officer, and General Counsel; Stanley R. Jaffe, President and Chief Operating Officer; and Ronald L. Nelson, Executive Vice President and Chief Financial Officer. Paramount's 11 outside directors are distinguished and experienced business persons who are present or former senior executives of public corporations or financial institutions.

Viacom is a Delaware corporation with its headquarters in Massachusetts. Viacom is controlled by Sumner M. Redstone ("Redstone"), its Chairman and Chief Executive Officer, who owns indirectly approximately 85.2 percent of Viacom's voting Class A stock and approximately 69.2 percent of Viacom's nonvoting Class B stock through National Amusements, Inc. ("NAI"), an entity 91.7 percent owned by Redstone. Viacom has a wide range of entertainment operations, including a number of well-known cable television channels such as MTV, Nickelodeon, Showtime, and The Movie Channel. Viacom's equity co-investors in the Paramount-Viacom transaction include NYNEX Corporation and Blockbuster Entertainment Corporation.

QVC is a Delaware corporation with its headquarters in West Chester, Pennsylvania. QVC has several large stockholders, including Liberty Media Corporation, Comcast Corporation, Advance Publications, Inc., and Cox Enterprises Inc. Barry Diller ("Diller"), the Chairman and Chief Executive Officer of QVC, is also a substantial stockholder. QVC sells a variety of merchandise through a televised shopping channel. QVC has several equity co-investors in its proposed combination with Paramount including BellSouth Corporation and Comcast Corporation.

Beginning in the late 1980s, Paramount investigated the possibility of acquiring or merging with other companies in the entertainment, media, or communications industry. Paramount considered such transactions to be desirable, and perhaps necessary, in order to keep pace with competitors in the rapidly evolving field of entertainment and communications. Consistent with its goal of strategic expansion, Paramount made a tender offer for Time Inc. in 1989, but was ultimately unsuccessful. See Paramount Communications, Inc. v. Time Inc., Del. Supr., 571 A.2d 1140 (1990) ("*Time-Warner*").

Although Paramount had considered a possible combination of Paramount and Viacom as early as 1990, recent efforts to explore such a transaction began at a dinner meeting between Redstone and Davis on April 20, 1993. Robert Greenhill ("Greenhill"), Chairman of Smith Barney Shearson Inc. ("Smith Barney"), attended and helped facilitate this meeting. After several more meetings between Redstone and Davis, serious negotiations began taking place in early July.

It was tentatively agreed that Davis would be the chief executive officer and Redstone would be the controlling stockholder of the combined company, but the parties could not reach agreement on the merger price and the terms of a stock option to be granted to Viacom. [Negotiations broke down, but reopened when Davis learned of QVC's potential interest in Paramount.]

On September 12, 1993, the Paramount Board met again and unanimously approved the Original Merger Agreement whereby Paramount would merge with and into Viacom. The terms of the merger provided that each share of Paramount common stock would be converted into 0.10 shares of Viacom Class A voting stock, 0.90 shares of Viacom Class B nonvoting stock, and $9.10 in cash. In addition, the Paramount Board agreed to amend its "poison pill" Rights Agreement to exempt the proposed merger with Viacom. The Original Merger Agreement also contained several provisions designed to make it more difficult for a potential competing bid to succeed. We focus, as did the Court of Chancery, on three of these defensive provisions: a "no-shop" provision (the "No-Shop Provision"), the Termination Fee, and the Stock Option Agreement.

First, under the No-Shop Provision, the Paramount Board agreed that Paramount would not solicit, encourage, discuss, negotiate, or endorse any competing transaction unless: (a) a third party "makes an unsolicited written, bona fide proposal, which is not subject to any material contingencies relating to financing"; and (b) the Paramount Board determines that discussions or negotiations with the third party are necessary for the Paramount Board to comply with its fiduciary duties.

Second, under the Termination Fee provision, Viacom would receive a $100 million termination fee if: (a) Paramount terminated the Original Merger Agreement because of a competing transaction; (b) Paramount's stockholders did not approve the merger; or (c) the Paramount Board recommended a competing transaction.

The third and most significant deterrent device was the Stock Option Agreement, which granted to Viacom an option to purchase approximately 19.9 percent (23,699,000 shares) of Paramount's outstanding common stock at $69.14 per share if any of the triggering events for the Termination Fee occurred. In addition to the customary terms that are normally associated with a stock option, the Stock Option Agreement contained two provisions that were both unusual and highly beneficial to Viacom: (a) Viacom was permitted to pay for the shares with a senior subordinated note of questionable marketability instead of cash, thereby avoiding the need to raise the $1.6 billion purchase price (the "Note Feature"); and (b) Viacom could elect to require Paramount to pay Viacom in cash a sum equal to the difference between the purchase price and the market price of Paramount's stock (the "Put Feature"). Because the Stock Option Agreement was not "capped" to limit its maximum dollar value, it had the potential to reach (and in this case did reach) unreasonable levels.

After the execution of the Original Merger Agreement and the Stock Option Agreement on September 12, 1993, Paramount and Viacom announced their proposed merger. In a number of public statements, the parties indicated that the pending transaction was a virtual certainty. Redstone described it as a "marriage" that would "never be torn asunder" and stated that only a "nuclear attack" could break the deal. Redstone also called Diller and John Malone of Tele-Communications Inc., a major stockholder of QVC, to dissuade them from making a competing bid.

Despite these attempts to discourage a competing bid, Diller sent a letter to Davis on September 20, 1993, proposing a merger in which QVC would acquire Paramount for approximately $80 per share. [Thereafter, QVC attempted to engage Paramount in meaningful merger negotiations.]

On October 21, 1993, QVC filed this action and publicly announced an $80 cash tender offer for 51 percent of Paramount's outstanding shares (the "QVC tender offer"). Each remaining share of Paramount common stock would be converted into 1.42857 shares of QVC common stock in a second-step merger. The tender offer was conditioned on, among other things, the invalidation of the Stock Option Agreement, which was worth over $200 million by that point.[5] QVC contends that it had to commence a tender offer because of the slow pace of the merger discussions and the need to begin seeking clearance under federal antitrust laws.

Confronted by QVC's hostile bid, which on its face offered over $10 per share more than the consideration provided by the Original Merger Agreement, Viacom realized that it would need to raise its bid in order to remain competitive. . . .

At a special meeting on October 24, 1993, the Paramount Board approved the Amended Merger Agreement and an amendment to the Stock Option Agreement. . . .

Although the Amended Merger Agreement offered more consideration to the Paramount stockholders and somewhat more flexibility to the Paramount Board than did the Original Merger Agreement, the defensive measures designed to make a competing bid more difficult were not removed or modified. In particular, there is no evidence in the record that Paramount sought to use its newly-acquired leverage to eliminate or modify the No-Shop Provision, the Termination Fee, or the Stock Option Agreement when the subject of amending the Original Merger Agreement was on the table.

Viacom's tender offer commenced on October 25, 1993, and QVC's tender offer was formally launched on October 27, 1993. Diller sent a letter to the Paramount Board on October 28 requesting an opportunity to negotiate with Paramount, and Oresman responded the following day by agreeing to meet. The meeting, held on November 1, was not very fruitful, however, after QVC's proposed guidelines for a "fair bidding process" were rejected by Paramount on the ground that "auction procedures" were inappropriate and contrary to Paramount's contractual obligations to Viacom.

On November 6, 1993, Viacom unilaterally raised its tender offer price to $85 per share in cash and offered a comparable increase in the value of the securities being proposed in the second-step merger. At a telephonic meeting held later that day, the Paramount Board agreed to recommend Viacom's higher bid to Paramount's stockholders.

QVC responded to Viacom's higher bid on November 12 by increasing its tender offer to $90 per share and by increasing the securities for its second-step merger by a similar amount. In response to QVC's latest offer, the Paramount Board scheduled a meeting for November 15, 1993. Prior to the meeting, Oresman sent the members of the Paramount Board a document summarizing the "conditions and uncertainties" of QVC's offer. One director testified that this document gave him a very negative impression of the QVC bid.

---

5. By November 15, 1993, the value of the Stock Option Agreement had increased to nearly $500 million based on the $90 QVC bid. See Court of Chancery Opinion, 635 A.2d 1245, 1271.

At its meeting on November 15, 1993, the Paramount Board determined that the new QVC offer was not in the best interests of the stockholders. The purported basis for this conclusion was that QVC's bid was excessively conditional. The Paramount Board did not communicate with QVC regarding the status of the conditions because it believed that the No-Shop Provision prevented such communication in the absence of firm financing. Several Paramount directors also testified that they believed the Viacom transaction would be more advantageous to Paramount's future business prospects than a QVC transaction. Although a number of materials were distributed to the Paramount Board describing the Viacom and QVC transactions, the only quantitative analysis of the consideration to be received by the stockholders under each proposal was based on then-current market prices of the securities involved, not on the anticipated value of such securities at the time when the stockholders would receive them. . . .

II. APPLICABLE PRINCIPLES OF ESTABLISHED DELAWARE LAW . . .

A. THE SIGNIFICANCE OF A SALE OR CHANGE OF CONTROL . . .

In the case before us, the public stockholders (in the aggregate) currently own a majority of Paramount's voting stock. Control of the corporation is not vested in a single person, entity, or group, but vested in the fluid aggregation of unaffiliated stockholders. In the event the Paramount-Viacom transaction is consummated, the public stockholders will receive cash and a minority equity voting position in the surviving corporation. Following such consummation, there will be a controlling stockholder who will have the voting power to: (a) elect directors; (b) cause a break-up of the corporation; (c) merge it with another company; (d) cash-out the public stockholders; (e) amend the certificate of incorporation; (f) sell all or substantially all of the corporate assets; or (g) otherwise alter materially the nature of the corporation and the public stockholders' interests. Irrespective of the present Paramount Board's vision of a long-term strategic alliance with Viacom, the proposed sale of control would provide the new controlling stockholder with the power to alter that vision.

Because of the intended sale of control, the Paramount-Viacom transaction has economic consequences of considerable significance to the Paramount stockholders. Once control has shifted, the current Paramount stockholders will have no leverage in the future to demand another control premium. As a result, the Paramount stockholders are entitled to receive, and should receive, a control premium and/or protective devices of significant value. There being no such protective provisions in the Viacom-Paramount transaction, the Paramount directors had an obligation to take the maximum advantage of the current opportunity to realize for the stockholders the best value reasonably available.

B. THE OBLIGATIONS OF DIRECTORS IN A SALE OR CHANGE
OF CONTROL TRANSACTION . . .

In the sale of control context, the directors must focus on one primary objective—to secure the transaction offering the best value reasonably available for the stockholders—and they must exercise their fiduciary duties to further that end. The decisions of this Court have consistently emphasized this goal. *Revlon,* 506 A.2d at 182 ("The duty of the board . . . [is] the maximization of the company's value at a sale for the stockholders' benefit."); [Mills Acquisition Co. v. Macmillan, Inc., Del. Supr., 559 A.2d 1261, 1288 (1988)] ("[I]n a sale of corporate control the responsibility of the directors is to get the highest value reasonably attainable for the shareholders."); [Barkan v. Amsted Industries, Inc., Del. Supr., 567 A.2d 1279, 1286 (1989)] ("[T]he board must act in a neutral manner to encourage the highest possible price for shareholders."). See also Wilmington Trust Co. v. Coulter, Del. Supr., 200 A.2d 441, 448 (1964) (in the context of the duty of a trustee, "[w]hen all is equal . . . it is plain that the Trustee is bound to obtain the best price obtainable").

In pursuing this objective, the directors must be especially diligent. See Citron v. Fairchild Camera and Instrument Corp., Del. Supr., 569 A.2d 53, 66 (1989) (discussing "a board's active and direct role in the sale process"). In particular, this Court has stressed the importance of the board being adequately informed in negotiating a sale of control: "The need for adequate information is central to the enlightened evaluation of a transaction that a board must make." *Barkan,* 567 A.2d at 1287. . . .

In determining which alternative provides the best value for the stockholders, a board of directors is not limited to considering only the amount of cash involved, and is not required to ignore totally its view of the future value of a strategic alliance. See *Macmillan,* 559 A.2d at 1282 n.29. Instead, the directors should analyze the entire situation and evaluate in a disciplined manner the consideration being offered. Where stock or other non-cash consideration is involved, the board should try to quantify its value, if feasible, to achieve an objective comparison of the alternatives. In addition, the board may assess a variety of practical considerations relating to each alternative, including:

> [an offer's] fairness and feasibility; the proposed or actual financing for the offer, and the consequences of that financing; questions of illegality; . . . the risk of non-consum[m]ation; . . . the bidder's identity, prior background and other business venture experiences; and the bidder's business plans for the corporation and their effects on stockholder interests.

Macmillan, 559 A.2d at 1282 n.29. These considerations are important because the selection of one alternative may permanently foreclose other opportunities. While the assessment of these factors may be complex, the board's goal is straightforward: Having informed themselves of all material information reasonably available, the directors must decide which alternative is most likely to offer the best value reasonably available to the stockholders.

C. ENHANCED JUDICIAL SCRUTINY OF A SALE OR CHANGE OF CONTROL TRANSACTION

Board action in the circumstances presented here is subject to enhanced scrutiny. Such scrutiny is mandated by: (a) the threatened diminution of the current stockholders' voting power; (b) the fact that an asset belonging to public stockholders (a control premium) is being sold and may never be available again; and (c) the traditional concern of Delaware courts for actions which impair or impede stockholder voting rights. . . . In *Macmillan,* this Court held:

> When *Revlon* duties devolve upon directors, this Court will continue to exact an enhanced judicial scrutiny at the threshold, as in *Unocal,* before the normal presumptions of the business judgment rule will apply.[15]

559 A.2d at 1288. The *Macmillan* decision articulates a specific two-part test for analyzing board action where competing bidders are not treated equally:[16]

> In the face of disparate treatment, the trial court must first examine whether the directors properly perceived that shareholder interests were enhanced. In any event the board's action must be reasonable in relation to the advantage sought to be achieved, or conversely, to the threat which a particular bid allegedly poses to stockholder interests.

Id. See also Roberts v. General Instrument Corp., Del. Ch., C.A. No. 11639, 1990 WL 118356, Allen, C. (Aug. 13, 1990), reprinted at 16 Del. J. Corp. L. 1540, 1554 ("This enhanced test requires a judicial judgment of reasonableness in the circumstances.").

The key features of an enhanced scrutiny test are: (a) a judicial determination regarding the adequacy of the decisionmaking process employed by the directors, including the information on which the directors based their decision; and (b) a judicial examination of the reasonableness of the directors' action in light of the circumstances then existing. The directors have the burden of proving that they were adequately informed and acted reasonably.

Although an enhanced scrutiny test involves a review of the reasonableness of the substantive merits of a board's actions,[17] a court should not ignore the complexity of the directors' task in a sale of control. There are many business and financial considerations implicated in investigating and selecting the best value reasonably available. The board of directors is the corporate decisionmaking body best equipped to make these judgments. Accordingly, a court applying enhanced judicial scrutiny should be deciding whether the directors made a *reasonable* decision, not a *perfect* decision. If a board selected one of several reasonable alternatives, a court should not second-guess that choice even though it might have decided otherwise or subsequent events may have cast doubt on the board's determination. Thus, courts will not substitute their business judgment for that of the directors, but will determine if the directors' decision was, on

---

15. Because the Paramount Board acted unreasonably as to process and result in this sale of control situation, the business judgment rule did not become operative.

16. Before this test is invoked, "the plaintiff must show, and the trial court must find, that the directors of the target company treated one or more of the respective bidders on unequal terms." *Macmillan,* 559 A.2d at 1288.

17. It is to be remembered that, in cases where the traditional business judgment rule is applicable and the board acted with due care, in good faith, and in the honest belief that they are acting in the best interests of the stockholders (which is not this case), the Court gives great deference to the substance of the directors' decision and will not invalidate the decision, will not examine its reasonableness, and "will not substitute our views for those of the board if the latter's decision can be 'attributed to any rational business purpose.' " *Unocal,* 493 A.2d at 949 (quoting Sinclair Oil Corp. v. Levien, Del. Supr., 280 A.2d 717, 720 (1971)). See [Aronson v. Lewis, Del. Supr., 473 A.2d 805, 812 (1984)].

balance, within a range of reasonableness. See *Unocal,*493 A.2d at 955-956; *Macmillan,* 559 A.2d at 1288; [Nixon v. Blackwell, Del. Supr., 626 A.2d 1366, 1378 (1993)].

D. *REVLON* AND *TIME-WARNER* DISTINGUISHED

The Paramount defendants and Viacom assert that the fiduciary obligations and the enhanced judicial scrutiny discussed above are not implicated in this case in the absence of a "break-up" of the corporation, and that the order granting the preliminary injunction should be reversed. This argument is based on their erroneous interpretation of our decisions in *Revlon* and *Time-Warner.*

In *Revlon,* we reviewed the actions of the board of directors of Revlon, Inc. ("Revlon"), which had rebuffed the overtures of Pantry Pride, Inc. and had instead entered into an agreement with Forstmann Little & Co. ("Forstmann") providing for the acquisition of 100 percent of Revlon's outstanding stock by Forstmann and the subsequent break-up of Revlon. Based on the facts and circumstances present in *Revlon,* we held that "[t]he directors' role changed from defenders of the corporate bastion to auctioneers charged with getting the best price for the stockholders at a sale of the company." 506 A.2d at 182. We further held that "when a board ends an intense bidding contest on an insubstantial basis, . . . [that] action cannot withstand the enhanced scrutiny which *Unocal* requires of director conduct." Id. at 184.

It is true that one of the circumstances bearing on these holdings was the fact that "the break-up of the company . . . had become a reality which even the directors embraced." Id. at 182. It does not follow, however, that a "break-up" must be present and "inevitable" before directors are subject to enhanced judicial scrutiny and are required to pursue a transaction that is calculated to produce the best value reasonably available to the stockholders. In fact, we stated in *Revlon* that "when bidders make relatively similar offers, or dissolution of the company becomes inevitable, the directors cannot fulfill their enhanced *Unocal* duties by playing favorites with the contending factions." Id. at 184. *Revlon* thus does not hold that an inevitable dissolution or "break-up" is necessary.

The decisions of this Court following *Revlon* reinforced the applicability of enhanced scrutiny and the directors' obligation to seek the best value reasonably available for the stockholders where there is a pending sale of control, regardless of whether or not there is to be a break-up of the corporation. In *Macmillan,* this Court held:

> We stated in *Revlon,* and again here, that *in a sale of corporate control* the responsibility of the directors is to get the highest value reasonably attainable for the shareholders.

559 A.2d at 1288 (emphasis added). In *Barkan,* we observed further:

> We believe that the general principles announced in *Revlon,* in Unocal Corp. v. Mesa Petroleum Co., Del. Supr., 493 A.2d 946 (1985), and in Moran v. Household International, Inc., Del. Supr., 500 A.2d 1346 (1985) govern this case and every case in which a *fundamental change of corporate control* occurs or is contemplated.

567 A.2d at 1286 (emphasis added).

Although *Macmillan* and *Barkan* are clear in holding that a change of control imposes on directors the obligation to obtain the best value reasonably available to the stockholders, the Paramount defendants have interpreted our decision in *Time-Warner* as requiring a corporate break-up in order for that obligation to apply. The facts in *Time-Warner,* however, were quite different from the facts of this case, and refute Paramount's position here. In *Time-Warner,* the Chancellor held that there was no change of control in the original stock-for-stock merger between Time and Warner because Time would be owned by a fluid aggregation of unaffiliated stockholders both before and after the merger:

> If the appropriate inquiry is whether a change in control is contemplated, the answer must be sought in the specific circumstances surrounding the transaction. Surely under some circumstances a stock for stock merger could reflect a transfer of corporate control. That would, for example, plainly be the case here if Warner were a private company. But where, as here, the shares of both constituent corporations are widely held, corporate control can be expected to remain unaffected by a stock for stock merger. This in my judgment was the situation with respect to the original merger agreement. When the specifics of that situation are reviewed, it is seen that, aside from legal technicalities and aside from arrangements thought to enhance the prospect for the ultimate succession of [Nicholas J. Nicholas, Jr., president of Time], neither corporation could be said to be acquiring the other. *Control of both remained in a large, fluid, changeable and changing market.*
>
> The existence of a control block of stock in the hands of a single shareholder or a group with loyalty to each other does have real consequences to the financial value of "minority" stock. The law offers some protection to such shares through the imposition of a fiduciary duty upon controlling shareholders. *But here, effectuation of the merger would not have subjected Time shareholders to the risks and consequences of holders of minority shares. This is a reflection of the fact that no control passed to anyone in the transaction contemplated.* The shareholders of Time would have "suffered" dilution, of course, but they would suffer the same type of dilution upon the public distribution of new stock.

Paramount Communications Inc. v. Time Inc., Del. Ch., No. 10866, 1989 WL 79880, Allen, C. (July 17, 1989), reprinted at 15 Del. J. Corp. L. 700, 739 (emphasis added). Moreover, the transaction actually consummated in *Time-Warner* was not a merger, as originally planned, but a sale of Warner's stock to Time.

In our affirmance of the Court of Chancery's well-reasoned decision, this Court held that "The Chancellor's findings of fact are supported by the record and *his conclusion is correct as a matter of law.*" 571 A.2d at 1150 (emphasis added). Nevertheless, the Paramount defendants here have argued that a break-up is a requirement and have focused on the following language in our *Time-Warner* decision:

> However, we premise our rejection of plaintiffs' *Revlon* claim on different grounds, namely, the absence of any substantial evidence to conclude that Time's board, in negotiating with Warner, made the dissolution or breakup of the corporate entity inevitable, as was the case in *Revlon.*
>
> Under Delaware law there are, generally speaking and *without excluding other possibilities,* two circumstances which may implicate *Revlon* duties. The first, and clearer one, is when a corporation *initiates an active bidding process seeking to sell itself* or to effect a business reorganization involving a clear breakup of the company. However, *Revlon* duties may also be triggered where, in response to a bidder's offer, a target abandons its long-term strategy and seeks an alternative transaction involving the breakup of the company.

Id. at 1150 (emphasis added) (citation and footnote omitted).

The Paramount defendants have misread the holding of *Time-Warner*. Contrary to their argument, our decision in *Time-Warner* expressly states that the two general scenarios discussed in the above-quoted paragraph are not the *only* instances where "*Revlon* duties" may be implicated. The Paramount defendants' argument totally ignores the phrase "without excluding other possibilities." Moreover, the instant case is clearly within the first general scenario set forth in *Time-Warner*. The Paramount Board, albeit unintentionally, had "initiate[d] an active bidding process seeking to sell itself" by agreeing to sell control of the corporation to Viacom in circumstances where another potential acquiror (QVC) was equally interested in being a bidder.

The Paramount defendants' position that *both* a change of control *and* a break-up are *required* must be rejected. Such a holding would unduly restrict the application of *Revlon*, is inconsistent with this Court's decisions in *Barkan* and *Macmillan*, and has no basis in policy. There are few events that have a more significant impact on the stockholders than a sale of control or a corporate break-up. Each event represents a fundamental (and perhaps irrevocable) change in the nature of the corporate enterprise from a practical standpoint. It is the significance of *each* of these events that justifies: (a) focusing on the directors' obligation to seek the best value reasonably available to the stockholders; and (b) requiring a close scrutiny of board action which could be contrary to the stockholders' interests.

Accordingly, when a corporation undertakes a transaction which will cause: (a) a change in corporate control; *or* (b) a break-up of the corporate entity, the directors' obligation is to seek the best value reasonably available to the stockholders. This obligation arises because the effect of the Viacom-Paramount transaction, if consummated, is to shift control of Paramount from the public stockholders to a controlling stockholder, Viacom. Neither *Time-Warner* nor any other decision of this Court holds that a "break-up" of the company is essential to give rise to this obligation where there is a sale of control.

III.   BREACH OF FIDUCIARY DUTIES BY PARAMOUNT BOARD

We now turn to duties of the Paramount Board under the facts of this case and our conclusions as to the breaches of those duties which warrant injunctive relief.

A.   THE SPECIFIC OBLIGATIONS OF THE PARAMOUNT BOARD

Under the facts of this case, the Paramount directors had the obligation: (a) to be diligent and vigilant in examining critically the Paramount-Viacom transaction and the QVC tender offers; (b) to act in good faith; (c) to obtain, and act with due care on, all material information reasonably available, including information necessary to compare the two offers to determine which of these transactions, or an alternative course of action, would provide the best value reasonably available to the stockholders; and (d) to negotiate actively and in good faith with both Viacom and QVC to that end.

Having decided to sell control of the corporation, the Paramount directors were required to evaluate critically whether or not all material aspects of the Paramount-Viacom transaction (separately and in the aggregate) were reasonable and in the best interests of the Paramount stockholders in light of current circumstances, including: the change of control premium, the Stock Option Agreement, the Termination Fee, the coercive nature of both the Viacom and QVC tender offers,[18] the No-Shop Provision, and the proposed disparate use of the Rights Agreement as to the Viacom and QVC tender offers, respectively.

These obligations necessarily implicated various issues, including the questions of whether or not those provisions and other aspects of the Paramount-Viacom transaction (separately and in the aggregate): (a) adversely affected the value provided to the Paramount stockholders; (b) inhibited or encouraged alternative bids; (c) were enforceable contractual obligations in light of the directors' fiduciary duties; and (d) in the end would advance or retard the Paramount directors' obligation to secure for the Paramount stockholders the best value reasonably available under the circumstances.

The Paramount defendants contend that they were precluded by certain contractual provisions, including the No-Shop Provision, from negotiating with QVC or seeking alternatives. Such provisions, whether or not they are presumptively valid in the abstract, may not validly define or limit the directors' fiduciary duties under Delaware law or prevent the Paramount directors from carrying out their fiduciary duties under Delaware law. To the extent such provisions are inconsistent with those duties, they are invalid and unenforceable. See *Revlon*, 506 A.2d at 184-185.

Since the Paramount directors had already decided to sell control, they had an obligation to continue their search for the best value reasonably available to the stockholders. This continuing obligation included the responsibility, at the October 24 board meeting and thereafter, to evaluate critically both the QVC tender offers and the Paramount-Viacom transaction. . . .

B. THE BREACHES OF FIDUCIARY DUTY BY THE PARAMOUNT BOARD . . .

When entering into the Original Merger Agreement, and thereafter, the Paramount Board clearly gave insufficient attention to the potential consequences of the defensive measures demanded by Viacom. The Stock Option Agreement had a number of unusual and potentially "draconian" provisions, including the Note Feature and the Put Feature. Furthermore, the Termination Fee, whether or not unreasonable by itself, clearly made Paramount less attractive to other bidders, when coupled with the Stock Option Agreement. Finally, the No-Shop Provision inhibited the Paramount

---

18. Both the Viacom and the QVC tender offers were for 51 percent cash and a "back-end" of various securities, the value of each of which depended on the fluctuating value of Viacom and QVC stock at any given time. Thus, both tender offers were two-tiered, front-end loaded, and coercive. Such coercive offers are inherently problematic and should be expected to receive particularly careful analysis by a target board. See *Unocal*, 493 A.2d at 956.

Board's ability to negotiate with other potential bidders, particularly QVC which had already expressed an interest in Paramount.[20]

Throughout the applicable time period, and especially from the first QVC merger proposal on September 20 through the Paramount Board meeting on November 15, QVC's interest in Paramount provided the *opportunity* for the Paramount Board to seek significantly higher value for the Paramount stockholders than that being offered by Viacom. QVC persistently demonstrated its intention to meet and exceed the Viacom offers, and frequently expressed its willingness to negotiate possible further increases.

The Paramount directors had the opportunity in the October 23-24 time frame, when the Original Merger Agreement was renegotiated, to take appropriate action to modify the improper defensive measures as well as to improve the economic terms of the Paramount-Viacom transaction. Under the circumstances existing at that time, it should have been clear to the Paramount Board that the Stock Option Agreement, coupled with the Termination Fee and the No-Shop Clause, were impeding the realization of the best value reasonably available to the Paramount stockholders. Nevertheless, the Paramount Board made no effort to eliminate or modify these counterproductive devices, and instead continued to cling to its vision of a strategic alliance with Viacom. Moreover, based on advice from the Paramount management, the Paramount directors considered the QVC offer to be "conditional" and asserted that they were precluded by the No-Shop Provision from seeking more information from, or negotiating with, QVC.

By November 12, 1993, the value of the revised QVC offer on its face exceeded that of the Viacom offer by over $1 billion at then current values. This significant disparity of value cannot be justified on the basis of the directors' vision of future strategy, primarily because the change of control would supplant the authority of the current Paramount Board to continue to hold and implement their strategic vision in any meaningful way. Moreover, their uninformed process had deprived their strategic vision of much of its credibility. See [Smith v. Van Gorkom, Del. Supr., 488 A.2d 858, 872 (1985)]; Cede v. Technicolor, [Del. Supr., 634 A.2d 345, 367 (1993)]; Hanson Trust PLC v. ML SCM Acquisition Inc., 2d Cir., 781 F.2d 264, 274 (1986).

When the Paramount directors met on November 15 to consider QVC's increased tender offer, they remained prisoners of their own misconceptions and missed opportunities to eliminate the restrictions they had imposed on themselves. Yet, it was not "too late" to reconsider negotiating with QVC. The circumstances existing on November 15 made it clear that the defensive measures, taken as a whole, were problematic: (a) the No-Shop Provision could not define or limit their fiduciary duties; (b) the

---

20. We express no opinion whether certain aspects of the No-Shop Provision here could be valid in another context. Whether or not it could validly have operated here at an early stage solely to prevent Paramount from actively "shopping" the company, it could not prevent the Paramount directors from carrying out their fiduciary duties in considering unsolicited bids or in negotiating for the best value reasonably available to the stockholders. *Macmillan*, 559 A.2d at 1287. As we said in *Barkan:* "Where a board has no reasonable basis upon which to judge the adequacy of a contemplated transaction, a no-shop restriction gives rise to the inference that the board seeks to forestall competing bids." 567 A.2d at 1288. See also *Revlon*, 506 A.2d at 184 (holding that "[t]he no-shop provision, like the lock-up option, while not per se illegal, is impermissible under the *Unocal* standards when a board's primary duty becomes that of an auctioneer responsible for selling the company to the highest bidder").

Stock Option Agreement had become "draconian"; and (c) the Termination Fee, in context with all the circumstances, was similarly deterring the realization of possibly higher bids. Nevertheless, the Paramount directors remained paralyzed by their uninformed belief that the QVC offer was "illusory." This final opportunity to negotiate on the stockholders' behalf and to fulfill their obligation to seek the best value reasonably available was thereby squandered. . . .

IV.   VIACOM'S CLAIM OF VESTED CONTRACT RIGHTS

Viacom argues that it had certain "vested" contract rights with respect to the No-Shop Provision and the Stock Option Agreement. In effect, Viacom's argument is that the Paramount directors could enter into an agreement in violation of their fiduciary duties and then render Paramount, and ultimately its stockholders, liable for failing to carry out an agreement in violation of those duties. Viacom's protestations about vested rights are without merit. This Court has found that those defensive measures were improperly designed to deter potential bidders, and that such measures do not meet the reasonableness test to which they must be subjected. They are consequently invalid and unenforceable under the facts of this case.

The No-Shop Provision could not validly define or limit the fiduciary duties of the Paramount directors. To the extent that a contract, or a provision thereof, purports to require a board to act or not act in such a fashion as to limit the exercise of fiduciary duties, it is invalid and unenforceable. Cf. Wilmington Trust v. Coulter, 200 A.2d at 452-454. Despite the arguments of Paramount and Viacom to the contrary, the Paramount directors could not contract away their fiduciary obligations. Since the No-Shop Provision was invalid, Viacom never had any vested contract rights in the provision.

As discussed previously, the Stock Option Agreement contained several "draconian" aspects, including the Note Feature and the Put Feature. While we have held that lock-up options are not per se illegal, see Revlon, 506 A.2d at 183, no options with similar features have ever been upheld by this Court. Under the circumstances of this case, the Stock Option Agreement clearly is invalid. Accordingly, Viacom never had any vested contract rights in that Agreement.

Viacom, a sophisticated party with experienced legal and financial advisors, knew of (and in fact demanded) the unreasonable features of the Stock Option Agreement. It cannot be now heard to argue that it obtained vested contract rights by negotiating and obtaining contractual provisions from a board acting in violation of its fiduciary duties. As the Nebraska Supreme Court said in rejecting a similar argument in ConAgra, Inc. v. Cargill, Inc., 222 Neb. 136, 382 N.W.2d 576, 587-588 (1986), "To so hold, it would seem, would be to get the shareholders coming and going." Likewise, we reject Viacom's arguments and hold that its fate must rise or fall, and in this instance, fall, with the determination that the actions of the Paramount Board were invalid.

V.   CONCLUSION

The realization of the best value reasonably available to the stockholders became the Paramount directors' primary obligation under these facts in light of the change of control. That obligation was not satisfied, and the Paramount Board's process was deficient. The directors' initial hope and expectation for a strategic alliance with Viacom was allowed to dominate their decisionmaking process to the point where the arsenal of defensive measures established at the outset was perpetuated (not modified or eliminated) when the situation was dramatically altered. QVC's unsolicited bid presented the opportunity for significantly greater value for the stockholders and enhanced negotiating leverage for the directors. Rather than seizing those opportunities, the Paramount directors chose to wall themselves off from material information which was reasonably available and to hide behind the defensive measures as a rationalization for refusing to negotiate with QVC or seeking other alternatives. Their view of the strategic alliance likewise became an empty rationalization as the opportunities for higher value for the stockholders continued to develop.

It is the nature of the judicial process that we decide only the case before us—a case which, on its facts, is clearly controlled by established Delaware law. Here, the proposed change of control and the implications thereof were crystal clear. In other cases they may be less clear. The holding of this case on its facts, coupled with the holdings of the principal cases discussed herein where the issue of sale of control is implicated, should provide a workable precedent against which to measure future cases.

For the reasons set forth herein, the November 24, 1993, Order of the Court of Chancery has been affirmed, and this matter has been remanded for proceedings consistent herewith, as set forth in the December 9, 1993, Order of this Court.

NOTES AND QUESTIONS

1. The *QVC* decision makes clear that the *Revlon* duty applies only to a subset of acquisition transactions. A subsequent case, Lyondell Chemical Co. v. Ryan, 970 A.2d 235 (Del. 2009), illustrates that even within the same transaction, judicial review under the *Revlon* standard applies only to board actions after the *Revlon* trigger has occurred. In that case a bidder filed a Schedule 13D disclosing its right to acquire 8.3 percent of Lyondell stock and its interest in a possible transaction. The Lyondell board met and chose to do nothing. A meeting two months or so later between the two CEOs led to negotiations that over the course of eight days produced an agreement that, the plaintiff asserted, failed to achieve the best price for shareholders. The Supreme Court noted the Court of Chancery's focus on the actions during the waiting period where the trial court noted that it

> clearly questions whether the Defendants "engaged" in the sale process. . . . This is where the 13D filing in May 2007 and the subsequent two months of (apparent) Board inactivity become critical. . . . [T]he Directors made *no apparent effort* to arm themselves with *specific knowledge* about the present value of the Company in the May through July 2007 time period, despite *admittedly knowing* that the 13D filing . . . effectively put the Company "in play," and, therefore, presumably, also knowing that an offer for the sale of the Company could occur at any time. It is these facts that raise the specter of "bad faith" in the present summary judgment record. . . .

970 A.2d 235, 242 quoting Ryan v. Lyondell Chemical Co. (Del. Ch.), 2008 WL 4174038 at *2 (emphasis by the Chancery Court).

The Supreme Court took issue with the lower court's lumping together of the entire period of director response:

> The problem with the trial court's analysis is that *Revlon* duties do not arise simply because a company is "in play." The duty to seek the best available price applies only when a company embarks on a transaction—on its own initiative or in response to an unsolicited offer—that will result in a change of control. Basell's Schedule 13D did put the Lyondell directors and the market in general, on notice that Basell was interested in acquiring Lyondell. The directors responded by promptly holding a special meeting to consider whether Lyondell should take any action. The directors decided that they would neither put the company up for sale nor institute defensive measures to fend off a possible hostile offer. Instead, they decided to take a "wait and see" approach. That decision was an entirely appropriate exercise of the directors' business judgment. The time for action under *Revlon* did not begin until July 10, 2007, when the directors began negotiating the sale of Lyondell.
>
> The Court of Chancery focused on the directors' two months of inaction, when it should have focused on the one week during which they considered Basell's offer.

970A.2d 235, 242 (Del. 2009).

2. The Delaware Supreme Court in Lyondell, discussed in the previous note, reversed the trial court's failure to give summary judgment for the directors as to their good faith in pursuing Revlon duties. The Supreme Court distinguished that claim from a claim that could be brought alleging breach of duty of care (which would be covered by exculpation discussed in Chapter 4). As to good faith in the context of a takeover, the Supreme Court said:

> There is only one *Revlon* duty—to "[get] the best price for the stockholders at a sale of the company." No court can tell directors exactly how to accomplish that goal, because they will be facing a unique combination of circumstances, many of which will be outside their control. As we noted in Barkan v. Amsted Industries, Inc. [567 A.2d 1279, 1287 (Del. 1989)], "there is no single blueprint that a board must follow to fulfill its duties." That said, our courts have highlighted both the positive and negative aspects of various boards' conduct under *Revlon*. The trial court drew several principles from those cases: directors must "engage actively in the sale process," and they must confirm that they have obtained the best available price either by conducting an auction, by conducting a market check, or by demonstrating "an impeccable knowledge of the market."
>
> The Lyondell directors did not conduct an auction or a market check, and they did not satisfy the trial court that they had the "impeccable" market knowledge that the court believed was necessary to excuse their failure to pursue one of the first two alternatives. As a result, the Court of Chancery was unable to conclude that the directors had met their burden under *Revlon*. In evaluating the totality of the circumstances, even on this limited record, we would be inclined to hold otherwise. But we would not question the trial court's decision to seek additional evidence if the issue were whether the directors had exercised due care. Where, as here, the issue is whether the directors failed to act in good faith, the analysis is very different, and the existing record mandates the entry of judgment in favor of the directors.
>
> As discussed above, bad faith will be found if a "fiduciary intentionally fails to act in the face of a known duty to act, demonstrating a conscious disregard for his duties." The trial court decided that the *Revlon* sale process must follow one of three courses, and that the Lyondell directors did not discharge that "known set of [*Revlon*] 'duties.'" But, as noted, there are no legally prescribed steps that directors must follow to satisfy their *Revlon* duties. Thus, the directors' failure to take any specific steps during the sale process could not have demonstrated a conscious disregard of their duties. More importantly, there is a vast difference between an inadequate or flawed effort to carry out fiduciary duties and a conscious disregard for those duties.

Directors' decisions must be reasonable, not perfect. "In the transactional context, [an] extreme set of facts [is] required to sustain a disloyalty claim premised on the notion that disinterested directors were intentionally disregarding their duties." The trial court denied summary judgment because the Lyondell directors' "unexplained inaction" prevented the court from determining that they had acted in good faith. But, if the directors failed to do all that they should have under the circumstances, they breached their duty of care. Only if they knowingly and completely failed to undertake their responsibilities would they breach their duty of loyalty. The trial court approached the record from the wrong perspective. Instead of questioning whether disinterested, independent directors did everything that they (arguably) should have done to obtain the best sale price, the inquiry should have been whether those directors utterly failed to attempt to obtain the best sale price.

Viewing the record in this manner leads to only one possible conclusion. The Lyondell directors met several times to consider Basell's premium offer. They were generally aware of the value of their company and they knew the chemical company market. The directors solicited and followed the advice of their financial and legal advisors. They attempted to negotiate a higher offer even though all the evidence indicates that Basell had offered a "blowout" price. Finally, they approved the merger agreement, because "it was simply too good not to pass along [to the stockholders] for their consideration." We assume, as we must on summary judgment, that the Lyondell directors did absolutely nothing to prepare for Basell's offer, and that they did not even consider conducting a market check before agreeing to the merger. Even so, this record clearly establishes that the Lyondell directors did not breach their duty of loyalty by failing to act in good faith. In concluding otherwise, the Court of Chancery reversibly erred.

970 A.2d 235, 242-243 (Del. 2009).

3. In the aftermath of Paramount Communications, Inc. v. QVC Network, Inc., stock option lock-ups became less common while termination fees remained popular in major deals. Why would termination fees persist but not stock option lock-ups? In the Court of Chancery opinion, the Vice Chancellor found the $100 million termination fee reasonable but the stock option lock-up unreasonable. Paramount appealed the enjoining of the stock option lock-up. QVC did not cross-appeal the decision not to enjoin the termination fee. The Delaware Supreme Court affirmed the Chancellor, but in its December 9 order (described in footnote 1 and accompanying text, supra page 886) strongly suggested that the employment of both stock option lock-ups and termination fees might jeopardize the enforceability of an otherwise valid termination fee:

16. The Stock Option Agreement, the termination fee, and the "no-shop" provision, taken together, were clearly designed to impede potential competing bidders for Paramount. . . .

17. Preliminary injunctive relief was appropriate, and the nature and scope of the relief ordered by the Court of Chancery in the November 24, 1993 Order was within the discretion of the Court of Chancery. It appears to this Court, however, that all of the defensive measures contained in the September 12, 1993 agreements and reincorporated in the October 24, 1993 amended agreements are inseparable. Because there is no cross-appeal from the Vice Chancellor's decision . . . it is unnecessary for purposes of this Order for this Court to determine whether the decision of the Vice Chancellor to treat the termination fee separately and differently was in error.

Paramount Communications v. QVC Network, 637 A.2d 828, 1993 WL 544314, at *4-5 (Del. 1993).

What message does the quoted portion of the December 9 order send to lawyers and investment bankers?

PROBLEM 9-6

Reconsider the facts of Paramount v. QVC. Suppose that on September 20, 1993, QVC made an unsolicited, bona fide written proposal to acquire Paramount for $85 per share. After brief negotiations, Paramount accepts QVC's offer. What rights does Viacom have under the Termination Agreement and the Stock Option Agreement?

C.   *Judicial Review of Voting Contest Defenses*

1.   Judicial Limits on Inequitable Actions

MBCA §§7.01, 7.07
Delaware G.C.L. §211

Schnell v. Chris-Craft Industries, Inc.
Delaware Supreme Court, 1971
285 A.2d 437

HERRMANN, JUSTICE (for the majority of the Court):

This is an appeal from the denial by the Court of Chancery of the petition of dissident stockholders for injunctive relief to prevent management[*] from advancing the date of the annual stockholders' meeting from January 11, 1972, as previously set by the by-laws, to December 8, 1971.

The opinion below is reported at 285 A.2d 430. This opinion is confined to the frame of reference of the opinion below for the sake of brevity and because of the strictures of time imposed by the circumstances of the case.

[The Court of Chancery reported the facts of this case as follows:

"Plaintiffs, who are stockholders of the defendant, seek a preliminary injunction against the carrying out by such corporation of a change in the date of its annual meeting of stockholders which was ostensibly accomplished by an amendment to its by-laws adopted at a directors' meeting held on October 18, 1971. As a result of such change in by-law and the fixing of a new date by the directors, such annual meeting is now scheduled to be held on December 8, 1971 instead of on the date fixed in the by-law in question before its amendment, namely the second Tuesday in January, 1972.

"Plaintiffs and other dissident stockholders, who constitute a stockholders committee on which the plaintiff Schnell serves, are dissatisfied with defendant's recent business performance, which has been poor, plaintiffs contending that defendant has sustained losses of over $6,500,000 over the past two years. Accordingly, they have embarked on a proxy contest against present management with the purpose in mind of electing new directors and installing new management at Chris-Craft.

"The stockholders committee in question has had a formal existence since September, 1971. However, certain of its members have sought to impose their views

---

[*] We use this word as meaning "managing directors."

on Chris-Craft's management since 1970, arguing that new management, achieved in one way or another, would be able to lift the defendant corporation from its slough of business losses. . . .

"Plaintiffs contend that by advancing the date of defendant's annual meeting by over a month and by the selection of an allegedly isolated town in up-state New York as the place for such meeting, defendant's board has deliberately sought to handicap the efforts of plaintiffs and other stockholders sympathetic to plaintiffs' views adequately to place their case before their fellow stockholders for decision because of the exigencies of time. Plaintiffs accordingly pray for the entry of a preliminary injunction enjoining the convening of the annual meeting of stockholders of Chris-Craft as now scheduled for December 8, 1971 on the ground that the change in defendant's by-laws made on October 18, 1971 was improperly accomplished and constitutes a manipulation of corporate machinery solely to insure that present management may be perpetuated in office to Chris-Craft's detriment. Plaintiffs further pray that the order which they seek to have entered reinstate the former annual meeting date of January 11, 1972, as provided for in the by-laws before the October 18, 1971 amendment, or that the Court fix such other date and place as the Court may deem to be fair and reasonable for such annual meeting. . . .

"On October 18, 1971, at a meeting of seven members of defendant's board of directors held in New York, notice of which, according to defendant's secretary, was given as required by the by-laws to every member of the board (minutes of which, however, were unjustifiably withheld from plaintiffs until the Court orally directed their production), Section 1 of Article 1 of Chris-Craft's by-laws was amended pursuant to the provisions of 8 Del. C. §211(b) allegedly to give more flexibility in fixing the date of the annual meeting and to permit the directors to set a convenient date within a specified period rather than having a fixed date set by the by-laws. Such by-law amendment reads in part as follows:

> 1. Annual Meeting. The annual meeting of stockholders of Chris-Craft Industries, Inc. (hereinafter called the "Corporation") shall be held for the election of the directors . . . in the two month period commencing December 1 and ending on January 31 and at such time as shall be designated by the Board. . . .

"At the same October 18 meeting, at which two directors, Linowes and Rochlis, were absent, the directors present fixed December 8, 1971, at 9:30 A.M. as the date and time for the annual meeting of the stockholders of Chris-Craft. Such meeting also named the Holiday Inn at Cortland, New York, where defendant operates a plant, as the place of such annual meeting of stockholders, and October 29, 1971, as the record date for stockholders eligible to vote at such meeting.

"As a result of such by-law amendment adopted pursuant to statutory authority and action taken thereunder, defendant's stockholders, to whom notice was mailed on November 8, will have received thirty days notice of the annual meeting as now scheduled under the terms of the applicable by-law, as amended on October 18, 1971, a change accomplished more than sixty days before the date of annual meeting fixed in the pertinent by-law before its amendment, namely January 11, 1972.

"Plaintiffs contend, however, that notwithstanding defendant's compliance with the Delaware law having to do with the fixing and noticing of annual meetings, the obvious design of defendant's management has been to impede the efforts of plaintiffs and others aligned with them to solicit votes in favor of a rival slate of directors and thus constitutes a use of corporate machinery to retain present management's control and not for a purpose beneficial to the defendant and its stockholders.

"In support of such contention, plaintiffs cite Condec Corporation v. Lunkenheimer Company, 43 Del. Ch. 353, 230 A.2d 769, a case in which the plaintiff's clear majority of Lunkenheimer stock was sought to be nullified by the simple expedient of the issuance by Lunkenheimer's management of 75,000 additional shares, thereby apparently breaking Condec's majority after it had legitimately acquired control. The Court caused such improperly issued stock, authorized, as it were, at the last minute, to be cancelled. Likewise the attempted freezing out of a minority stockholder interest by a majority is actionable, Bennett v. Breuil Petroleum Corp., 34 Del. Ch. 6, 99 A.2d 236. Compare McPhail v. L.S. Starrett Co., 257 F.2d 388 (1st Cir.).

"Defendant for its part does not concede that its management has taken advantage of a change in the Delaware Corporation Law in order to blunt the attack on it of a substantial group of dissident stockholders, arguing, in addition to its contentions about weather conditions in Cortland, New York in January, as opposed to early December, that the normal delays in delivery of notices to stockholders resulting from Christmas mails supply another reason for choosing a pre-Christmas date for the annual meeting. Finally, defendant argues that as a result of its current financial records having been put in final form in connection with the settlement of a lawsuit in New York, defendant's final financial statements through August 31, 1971 are now ready for the December meeting but would be stale by mid-January."]

It will be seen that the Chancery Court considered all of the reasons stated by management as business reasons for changing the date of the meeting; but that those reasons were rejected by the Court below in making the following findings:

> I am satisfied, however, in a situation in which present management has disingenuously resisted the production of a list of its stockholders to plaintiffs or their confederates and has otherwise turned a deaf ear to plaintiffs' demands about a change in management designed to lift defendant from its present business doldrums, management has seized on a relatively new section of the Delaware Corporation Law for the purpose of cutting down on the amount of time which would otherwise have been available to plaintiffs and others for the waging of a proxy battle. Management thus enlarged the scope of its scheduled October 18 directors' meeting to include the by-law amendment in controversy after the stockholders committee had filed with the S.E.C. its intention to wage a proxy fight on October 16.
>
> Thus plaintiffs reasonably contend that because of the tactics employed by management (which involve the hiring of two established proxy solicitors as well as a refusal to produce a list of its stockholders, coupled with its use of an amendment to the Delaware Corporation Law to limit the time for contest), they are given little chance, because of the exigencies of time, including that required to clear material at the S.E.C., to wage a successful proxy fight between now and December 8. . . .

In our view, those conclusions amount to a finding that management has attempted to utilize the corporate machinery and the Delaware Law for the purpose of perpetuating itself in office; and, to that end, for the purpose of obstructing the legitimate efforts of dissident stockholders in the exercise of their rights to undertake a proxy contest against management. These are inequitable purposes, contrary to established principles of corporate democracy. The advancement by directors of the by-law date of a stockholders' meeting, for such purposes, may not be permitted to stand. Compare Condec Corporation v. Lunkenheimer Company, Del. Ch., 230 A.2d 769 (1967).

When the by-laws of a corporation designate the date of the annual meeting of stockholders, it is to be expected that those who intend to contest the reelection of incumbent management will gear their campaign to the by-law date. It is not to be expected that management will attempt to advance that date in order to obtain an inequitable advantage in the contest.

Management contends that it has complied strictly with the provisions of the new Delaware Corporation Law in changing the by-law date. The answer to that contention, of course, is that inequitable action does not become permissible simply because it is legally possible.

Management relies upon American Hardware Corp. v. Savage Arms Corp., 37 Del. Ch. 10, 135 A.2d 725, affd. 37 Del. Ch. 59, 136 A.2d 690 (1957). That case is inapposite for two reasons: it involved an effort by stockholders, engaged in a proxy contest, to have the stockholders' meeting adjourned and the period for the proxy contest enlarged; and there was no finding there of inequitable action on the part of management. We agree with the rule of *American Hardware* that, in the absence of fraud or inequitable conduct, the date for a stockholders' meeting and notice thereof, duly established under the by-laws, will not be enlarged by judicial interference at the request of dissident stockholders solely because of the circumstance of a proxy contest. That, of course, is not the case before us.

We are unable to agree with the conclusion of the Chancery Court that the stockholders' application for injunctive relief here was tardy and came too late. The stockholders learned of the action of management unofficially on Wednesday, October 27, 1971; they filed this action on Monday, November 1, 1971. Until management changed the date of the meeting, the stockholders had no need of judicial assistance in that connection. There is no indication of any prior warning of management's intent to take such action; indeed, it appears that an attempt was made by management to conceal its action as long as possible. Moreover, stockholders may not be charged with the duty of anticipating inequitable action by management, and of seeking anticipatory injunctive relief to foreclose such action, simply because the new Delaware Corporation Law makes such inequitable action legally possible.

Accordingly, the judgment below must be reversed and the cause remanded, with instructions to nullify the December 8 date as a meeting date for stockholders; to reinstate January 11, 1972 as the sole date of the next annual meeting of the stockholders of the corporation; and to take such other proceedings and action as may be consistent herewith regarding the stock record closing date and any other related matters.

WOLCOTT, CHIEF JUSTICE (dissenting):

I do not agree with the majority of the Court in its disposition of this appeal. The plaintiff stockholders concerned in this litigation have, for a considerable period of time, sought to obtain control of the defendant corporation. These attempts took various forms.

In view of the length of time leading up to the immediate events which caused the filing of this action, I agree with the Vice Chancellor that the application for injunctive relief came too late.

I would affirm the judgment below on the basis of the Vice Chancellor's opinion.

PROBLEM 9-7

Michelle Weaver is a new stockholder of Forest Products, Inc., a Delaware corporation, and has announced that she is exploring the feasibility of seeking control of the corporation. The corporation has a 12-member board divided into three groups of four with staggered three-year terms. Weaver recently delivered a proposal to be submitted at the next annual meeting of stockholders calling for an amendment to the company's bylaws increasing the size of the board from 12 to 17 and nominating 9 individuals for the board (for the 5 new seats, plus the 4 members of the staggered board with terms expiring at the next annual meeting).

On March 19, the board fixed April 17 as the record date for determining the shareholders entitled to vote. While no date for the annual meeting was fixed, it was anticipated that the meeting would be held in May.

On March 28, Weaver made a tender offer conditioned upon the success of her proxy fight. The company's proxy solicitor informed the board that if it did not present the stockholders with an economic alternative to Weaver's offer, Weaver would prevail in the proxy fight by a significant margin. The board received an opinion from its financial adviser that Weaver's offer was inadequate and unfair to shareholders. The financial adviser said greater value could be obtained from certain alternative strategies but adequate exploration and implementation of those strategies would take 8 to 12 weeks.

(a) If the board then canceled the record date and elected to defer the annual meeting, how should a court rule on Weaver's petition that the meeting be held in May?

(b) If, in the alternative, the board amended the bylaws to increase the size of the Forest Products board by two and then filled the newly created positions (placing the new positions in the classes of directors with terms to expire the next year and the following year), could Weaver successfully challenge the action?

(c) Should the actions be tested under *Schnell*, *Unocal*, or both?

2. Enhanced Review of Good-Faith Actions

MM Companies, Inc. v. Liquid Audio, Inc.
Delaware Supreme Court, 2003
813 A.2d 1118

Before HOLLAND, BERGER and STEELE, JUSTICES.

HOLLAND, JUSTICE:

This is an expedited appeal from a final judgment entered by the Court of Chancery. That final judgment permitted an incumbent board of directors to adopt defense measures which changed the size and composition of the board's membership. The record reflects that those defensive actions were taken for the primary purpose of impeding the shareholders' right to vote effectively in an impending election for successor directors. We have concluded that the judgment of the Court of Chancery must be reversed. . . .

BACKGROUND FACTS

Liquid Audio is a publicly traded Delaware corporation, with its principal place of business in Redwood City, California. Liquid Audio's primary business consists of providing software and services for the digital transmission of music over the Internet. MM is a publicly traded Delaware corporation with its principal place of business in New York, New York. As of October 2002, MM was part of a group that collectively held slightly over 7% of Liquid Audio's common stock.

For more than a year, MM has sought to obtain control of Liquid Audio. On October 26, 2001, MM sent a letter to the Liquid Audio board of directors indicating its willingness to acquire the company at approximately $3 per share. Liquid Audio's board rejected MM's offer as inadequate, after an analysis of the offer and consultation with its investment banker, Broadview International LLC ("Broadview").

Liquid Audio's bylaws provide for a staggered board of directors that is divided into three classes. Only one class of directors is up for election in any given year. The effect is to prevent an insurgent from obtaining control of the company in under two years.

From November 2001, until August 2002, the Liquid Audio board of directors consisted of five members divided into three classes. Class I had two members (defendants Flynn and Imbler), whose terms expire in 2003; Class II had one member (defendant Winblad), whose term expires in 2004; and Class III had two members (defendants Kearby and Doig), whose terms expired in 2002. Defendants Flynn, Doig and Imbler were not elected to the Board by the stockholders of Liquid Auido. They were appointed to the Board by the directors of Liquid Audio to fill vacancies on the Board.

In October 2001, prior to the appointment of defendants Doig and Imbler to the Board, MM requested the Liquid Audio board to call a special meeting of the company's stockholders to consider filling the existing vacancies on the Board and to consider other proposals to be presented to the stockholders. On October 24, 2001, the Liquid Audio board issued a press release which stated that it had denied MM's request to call a special meeting because the Board believed that under the Liquid Audio bylaws stockholders are not permitted to call special meetings. Thereafter, the Board appointed defendants Doig and Imbler to the Liquid Audio board of directors.

MM's VARIOUS ACTIONS

On November 13, 2001, MM announced its intention to nominate its own candidates for the two seats on Liquid Audio's board of directors that were up for election at the next annual meeting. . . . [In the ensuing months, MM took various steps to obtain control of Liquid Audio, including filing a Delaware G.C.L. section 220 action seeking access to a list of Liquid Audio's stockholders.]

On June 10, 2002, MM filed proxy materials with the Securities and Exchange Commission ("SEC") and commenced soliciting proxies for a shareholder meeting Liquid Audio planned to have on July 1, 2002. In addition to proposing two nominees for the Board, MM's proxy statement included a takeover proposal to increase the size of the Board by an additional four directors and to fill those positions with its nominees. As outlined in its initial proxy materials, MM's takeover proposal sought to expand the Board from five members to nine. If MM's two directors were elected and its four proposed directors were also placed on the Board, MM would control a majority of the Board.

ALLIANCE MERGER

On June 13, 2002, Liquid Audio announced a stock-for-stock merger transaction with Alliance Entertainment Corp. ("Alliance"). This announcement came three days after MM mailed its proxy statement and other materials to the stockholders of Liquid Audio, and one day before the scheduled Court of Chancery hearing in connection with the Section 220 complaint. In addition to announcing the merger, the Liquid Audio board also announced that: the July 1, 2002 meeting would be postponed; a special meeting of stockholders of Liquid Audio would be held sometime in the future to vote upon the merger; and, if the merger received the requisite stockholder and regulatory approval, the merger would "close in the Fall of 2002." Based upon this announcement, the annual meeting was postponed indefinitely by the Liquid Audio board. . . .

After Liquid Audio announced that the annual meeting would be postponed indefinitely, MM filed an amended complaint, seeking an order of the Court of Chancery directing Liquid Audio to hold the annual meeting as soon as possible. . . .

After expedited discovery, a trial was held on July 15, 2002. The Court of Chancery ordered that the annual meeting of Liquid Audio's shareholders occur on September 26, 2002. The record date for the meeting was August 12, 2002.

BOARD ADDS TWO DIRECTORS

By the middle of August 2002, it was apparent that MM's nominees, Holtzman and Mitarotonda, would be elected at the annual meeting, to serve in place of the two incumbent nominees, as members of the Liquid Audio board. On August 23, 2002, Liquid Audio announced that the Board had amended the bylaws to increase the size of the Board to seven members from five members. The Board also announced that defendants James D. Somes and Judith N. Frank had been appointed to fill the newly created directorships. Defendant Somes was appointed to serve as a Class II member of the Board and defendant Frank was appointed to serve as a Class I member of the Board. After the Board expanded from five directors to seven, MM revised its proxy statement to note that its proposal to add four directors, if successful, would have resulted in a board with eleven directors, instead of nine.

MM CHALLENGES BOARD EXPANSION

On August 26, 2002, MM filed its initial lawsuit challenging the Board's decision to add two directors. In the initial complaint, MM alleged that the Board expansion interfered with MM's ability to solicit proxies in favor of its two nominees for election to the Liquid Audio board at the annual meeting. In support of this claim, MM alleged that "some stockholders would believe that electing two members of a seven member board, rather than two members of a five-member board, would not be worthwhile, and, thus, such stockholders simply would not vote."

At the September 26, 2002 annual meeting, the two directors proposed by MM, Holtzman and Mitarotonda, were elected to serve as directors of the Board. Liquid Audio's stockholders, however, did not approve MM's takeover proposals that would have expanded the Board and placed MM's four nominees on the Board. The stockholders' vote on both issues was consistent with the recommendation of Institutional Investor Services ("ISS"), a proxy voting advisory service, which had recommended that the stockholders vote in favor of MM's two nominees, but recommended against stockholders voting to give MM outright and immediate control of the Board.

Following the election of MM's two nominees to the Liquid Audio board of directors at the annual meeting, MM filed an amended lawsuit, challenging the Board's appointment of directors Somes and Frank. In the amended complaint, MM alleged that the expansion of the Liquid Audio board, its timing, and the Board's appointment of two new directors violated the principles of *Blasius* and *Unocal.* According to MM, that action frustrated MM's attempt to gain a "substantial presence" on the Board for at least one year and guaranteed that Liquid Audio's management will have control of, or a substantial presence on, the Board for at least two years.

BOARD'S PRIMARY PURPOSE: IMPEDE EFFECTIVE VOTE

The expedited trial was held by the Court of Chancery, as scheduled. . . .

[The testimony of each member of the Board] reflects that the Director Defendants were concerned that incumbent directors Winblad and Imbler would resign from the Liquid Audio board if MM's nominees were elected to the board at the annual meeting, which would result in MM gaining control of the Board. The record also reflects that the timing of the Director Defendants' decision to expand the Board was to accomplish its primary purpose: to minimize the impact of the election of MM's nominees to the Board. The Court of Chancery's post-trial ruling from the bench states:

> The board's concern was that given the past acrimonious relationship between MM and Liquid Audio, a relationship characterized by litigation, if MM's two nominees were elected, the possibility of continued acrimony might cause one or more of the current board members to resign. If one director resigned, that would deadlock the board two-to-two; and if two directors resigned,

then MM would gain control on a two-to-one basis. Either scenario could jeopardize the pending merger, which the incumbent board favored. That was the *primary* reason. [Emphasis added.]

After making that factual determination, the Court of Chancery recognized the effect of the Board's action in changing the size and composition of its membership immediately prior to the election of directors at the annual meeting:

> By adding two additional directors, the board foreclosed the result that it feared: The possibility of a deadlock or of MM taking control of the board. The reason is that even if MM's two nominees were elected at the 2002 annual meeting, the current directors would still constitute a majority of five. The result of the board's action was to *diminish the influence of any nominees of MM* that were elected, at least in numerical terms.

Thus, based upon the evidence presented at trial, including an assessment of the witnesses' credibility, the Court of Chancery concluded that the Director Defendants amended the bylaws to expand the Board from five to seven, appointed two additional members of the Board, and timed those actions for the *primary purpose* of diminishing the influence of MM's nominees, if they were elected at the annual meeting.

CORPORATE GOVERNANCE PRINCIPLES

The most fundamental principles of corporate governance are a function of the allocation of power within a corporation between its stockholders and its board of directors. The stockholders' power is the right to vote on specific matters, in particular, in an election of directors. The power of managing the corporate enterprise is vested in the shareholders' duly elected board representatives. Accordingly, while these "fundamental tenets of Delaware corporate law provide for a separation of control and ownership," the stockholder franchise has been characterized as the "ideological underpinning" upon which the legitimacy of the directors managerial power rests.

Maintaining a proper balance in the allocation of power between the stockholders' right to elect directors and the board of directors' right to manage the corporation is dependent upon the stockholders' unimpeded right to vote effectively in an election of directors. This Court has repeatedly stated that, if the stockholders are not satisfied with the management or actions of their elected representatives on the board of directors, the power of corporate democracy is available to the stockholders to replace the incumbent directors when they stand for re-election. Consequently, two decades ago, this Court held:

> The Courts of this State will not allow the wrongful subversion of corporate democracy by manipulation of the corporate machinery or by machinations under the cloak of Delaware law. Accordingly, careful judicial scrutiny will be given a situation in which the right to vote for the election of successor directors has been *effectively frustrated* and denied.

This Court and the Court of Chancery have remained assiduous in carefully reviewing any board actions designed to interfere with or impede the effective exercise of corporate democracy by shareholders, especially in an election of directors.

CORPORATE GOVERNANCE REVIEW STANDARDS

The "defining tension" in corporate governance today has been characterized as "the tension between deference to directors' decisions and the scope of judicial review."[12] The appropriate standard of judicial review is dispositive of which party has the burden of proof as any litigation proceeds from stage to stage until there is a substantive determination on the merits. Accordingly, identification of the correct analytical framework is essential to a proper judicial review of challenges to the decision-making process of a corporation's board of directors. . . .

In *Blasius,* Chancellor Allen set forth a cogent explanation of why judicial review under the deferential traditional business judgment rule standard is inappropriate when a board of directors acts for the *primary* purpose of impeding or interfering with the effectiveness of a shareholder vote, especially in the specific context presented in *Blasius* of a contested election for directors:

> [T]he ordinary considerations to which the business judgment rule originally responded are simply not present in the shareholder voting context. That is, a decision by the board to act for the primary purpose of preventing the effectiveness of a shareholder vote inevitably involves the question who, as between the principal and the agent, has authority with respect to a matter of internal corporate governance. That, of course, is true in a very specific way in this case which deals with the question who should constitute the board of directors of the corporation, but it will be true in every instance in which an incumbent board seeks to thwart a shareholder majority. A board's decision to act to prevent the shareholders from creating a majority of new board positions and filling them does not involve the exercise of the corporation's power over its property, or with respect to its rights or obligations; rather, it involves allocation, between shareholders as a class and the board, of effective power with respect to governance of the corporation. . . . Action designed principally to interfere with the effectiveness of a vote inevitably involves a conflict between the board and shareholder majority. Judicial review of such action involves a determination of the legal and equitable obligations of an agent towards his principal. This is not, in my opinion, a question that a court may leave to the agent finally to decide so long as he does so honestly and competently; that is, it may not be left to the agent's business judgment.[18]

In *Blasius,* the Chancellor did not adopt a rule of *per se* invalidity once a plaintiff has established that a board of directors has acted for the primary purpose of interfering with or impeding the effective exercise of a shareholder vote. Instead, the Chancellor concluded that such situations required enhanced judicial scrutiny, pursuant to which the board of directors "bears the heavy burden of demonstrating a compelling justification for such action."

In *Blasius,* the Chancellor then applied that compelling justification standard of enhanced judicial review in examining a board's action to expand its size in the context of a contested election of directors, exactly what the Liquid Audio board did in this case. In *Blasius,* notwithstanding the fact that the incumbent board of directors believed in good faith that the leveraged recapitalization proposed by the plaintiff was ill-advised and less valuable than the company's business plan, Chancellor Allen

---

12. E. Norman Veasey, The Defining Tension in Corporate Governance in America, 52 Bus. Law. 393 (1997).

18. Blasius Indus., Inc. v. Atlas Corp., 564 A.2d 651, 659-60 (Del.Ch.1988).

explained why the incumbent board of directors' good faith beliefs were not a proper basis for interfering with the stockholder franchise in a contested election for successor directors.

> The only justification that can be offered for the action taken is that the board knows better than do the shareholders what is in the corporation's best interest. While that premise is no doubt true for any number of matters, it is irrelevant (except insofar as the shareholders wish to be guided by the board's recommendation) when the question is who should comprise the board. . . . It may be that the Blasius restructuring proposal was or is unrealistic and would lead to injury to the corporation and its shareholders if pursued. . . . The board certainly viewed it in that way, and that view, held in good faith, entitled the board to take certain steps to evade the risk it perceived. It could, for example, expend corporate funds to inform shareholders and seek to bring them to a similar point of view. But there is a vast difference between expending corporate funds to inform the electorate and exercising power for the primary purpose of foreclosing effective shareholder action. A majority of shareholders, who were not dominated in any respect, could view the matter differently than did the board. If they do, or did, they are entitled to employ the mechanisms provided by the corporation law and the Atlas certificate of incorporation to advance that view.

In *Blasius,* the Chancellor set aside the board's action to expand the size of its membership for the primary purpose of impeding and interfering with the effectiveness of a shareholder vote in a contested election for directors. In this case, not only did the Liquid Audio board of directors take similar action in expanding the size of its membership and appointing two new directors to fill those positions, but it took that action for the same *primary* purpose.

COMPELLING JUSTIFICATION WITHIN UNOCAL

The *Blasius* compelling justification standard of enhanced judicial review is based upon accepted and well-established legal tenets. This Court and the Court of Chancery have recognized the substantial degree of congruence between the rationale that led to the *Blasius* "compelling justification" enhanced standard of judicial review and the logical extension of that rationale *within* the context of the *Unocal* enhanced standard of judicial review. Both standards recognize the inherent conflicts of interest that arise when a board of directors acts to prevent shareholders from effectively exercising their right to vote either contrary to the will of the incumbent board members generally or to replace the incumbent board members in a contested election.

In *Gilbert,* we held that a reviewing court must apply the *Unocal* standard of review whenever a board of directors adopts any defensive measure "in response to some threat to corporate policy and effectiveness which touches upon issues of control."[24] Later, in *Stroud,* this Court acknowledged that board action interfering with the exercise of the shareholder franchise often arises during a hostile contest for control when an acquiror launches both a proxy fight and a tender offer.[25] Accordingly, in *Stroud,* we held that "such action necessarily invoked both *Unocal* and *Blasius.*"

---

24. Gilbert v. El Paso Co., 575 A.2d 1131, 1144 (Del. 1990).
25. Stroud v. Grace, 606 A.2d at 92 n. 3.

In *Stroud,* we emphasized, however, that the *Blasius* and *Unocal* standards of enhanced judicial review ("tests") are *not* mutually exclusive. In *Stroud,* we then explained why our holding in *Gilbert* did not render *Blasius* and its progeny meaningless:

> In certain circumstances, a court must recognize the special import of protecting the share-holders' franchise within *Unocal*'s requirement that any defensive measure be proportionate and "reasonable in relation to the threat posed." A board's unilateral decision to adopt a defensive measure touching "upon issues of control" that purposefully disenfranchises its shareholders is strongly suspect under *Unocal,* and cannot be sustained without a "compelling justification."

Thus, the same circumstances must be extant before the *Blasius* compelling justification enhanced standard of judicial review is required to sustain a board's action either independently, in the absence of a hostile contest for control, or within the *Unocal* standard of review when the board's action is taken as a defensive measure. The "compelling justification" standard set forth in *Blasius* is applied independently or within the *Unocal* standard only where "the primary purpose of the board's action is to interfere with or impede exercise of the shareholder franchise and the shareholders are not given a full and fair opportunity to vote" effectively. Accordingly, this Court has noted that the non-deferential *Blasius* standard of enhanced judicial review, which imposes upon a board of directors the burden of demonstrating a compelling justification for such actions, is rarely applied either independently or within the *Unocal* standard of review.

In *Unitrin,* for example, although the board's action in adopting a repurchase program was a defensive measure that implicated the shareholders' franchise and called for an application of the *Unocal* standard of review, it did not require the board to demonstrate a compelling justification for that action.[31] In *Unitrin,* the primary purpose of the repurchase program was not to interfere with or impede the shareholders' right to vote; the shareholders' right to vote effectively remained extant; and, in particular, we noted that the shareholders retained sufficient voting power to challenge the incumbent board by electing new directors with a successful proxy contest.[32]

In this case, however, the Court of Chancery was presented with the ultimate defensive measure touching upon an issue of control. It was a defensive action taken by an incumbent board of directors for the primary purpose of interfering with and impeding the effectiveness of the shareholder franchise in electing successor directors. Accordingly, the incumbent board of directors had the burden of demonstrating a compelling justification for that action to withstand enhanced judicial scrutiny within the *Unocal* standard of reasonableness and proportionality.

---

31. Unitrin, Inc. v. American Gen. Corp., 651 A.2d 1361 (Del. 1995).

32. Id. at 1382-83. With regard to shareholder rights plans, it has been stated that: "Indeed, the Delaware courts, at the same time that they seemed to be giving license to boards to maintain the pill indefinitely and otherwise block a bid, also indicated that they would protect against managerial moves to impede voting by shareholders to remove them." Lucian Arye Bebchuk, John C. Coates, IV & Guhan Subramanian, The Powerful Antitakeover Force of Staggered Boards: Theory, Evidence, and Policy, 54 Stanford L. Rev. 887, 907 (2002).

Unocal Required Compelling Justification

This case presents a paragon of when the compelling justification standard of *Blasius* must be applied within *Unocal*'s requirement that any defensive measure be proportionate and reasonable in relation to the threat posed. The *Unocal* standard of review applies because the Liquid Audio board's action was a "defensive measure taken in response to some threat to corporate policy and effectiveness which touches upon issues of control." The compelling justification standard of *Blasius* also had to be applied *within* an application of the *Unocal* standard to that specific defensive measure because the primary purpose of the Board's action was to interfere with or impede the effective exercise of the shareholder franchise in a contested election for directors.

The Court of Chancery properly decided to examine the Board's defensive action to expand from five to seven members and to appoint two new members in accordance with the *Unocal* standard of enhanced judicial review. Initially, the Court of Chancery concluded that defensive action was not preclusive or coercive. If a defensive measure is not draconian, because it is neither coercive nor preclusive, proportionality review under *Unocal* requires the focus of enhanced judicial scrutiny to shift to the range of reasonableness.

After the Court of Chancery determined that the Board's action was not preclusive or coercive, it properly proceeded to determine whether the Board's action was reasonable and proportionate in relation to the threat posed. Under the circumstances presented in this case, however, the Court of Chancery did not "recognize the special [importance] of protecting the shareholder's franchise within Unocal's requirement that any defensive measure be proportionate and reasonable in relation to the threat posed." Since the Court of Chancery had already concluded that the *primary purpose* of the Liquid Audio board's defensive measure was to interfere with or impede an effective exercise of the shareholder's franchise in a contested election of directors, the Board had the burden of demonstrating a compelling justification for that action.

When the *primary purpose* of a board of directors' defensive measure is to interfere with or impede the effective exercise of the shareholder franchise in a contested election for directors, the board must first demonstrate a compelling justification for such action as a condition precedent to any judicial consideration of reasonableness and proportionately. As this case illustrates, such defensive actions by a board need not actually prevent the shareholders from attaining any success in seating one or more nominees in a contested election for directors and the election contest need not involve a challenge for outright control of the board of directors. To invoke the *Blasius* compelling justification standard of review *within* an application of the *Unocal* standard of review, the defensive actions of the board only need to be taken for the primary purpose of interfering with or impeding the effectiveness of the stockholder vote in a contested election for directors.

Board Expansion Invalid

The record reflects that the primary purpose of the Director Defendants' action was to interfere with and impede the effective exercise of the stockholder franchise in a contested election for directors. The Court of Chancery concluded that the Director Defendants amended the bylaws to provide for a board of seven and appointed two additional members of the Board for the primary purpose of diminishing the influence of MM's two nominees on a five-member Board by eliminating either the possibility of a deadlock on the board or of MM controlling the Board, if one or two Director Defendants resigned from the Board. That defensive action by the Director Defendants compromised the essential role of corporate democracy in maintaining the proper allocation of power between the shareholders and the Board, because that action was taken in the context of a contested election for successor directors. Since the Director Defendants did not demonstrate a compelling justification for that defensive action, the bylaw amendment that expanded the size of the Liquid Audio board, and permitted the appointment of two new members on the eve of a contested election, should have been invalidated by the Court of Chancery.

One of the most venerable precepts of Delaware's common law corporate jurisprudence is the principle that "inequitable action does not become permissible simply because it is legally possible."[40] At issue in this case is not the validity generally of either a bylaw that permits a board of directors to expand the size of its membership or a board's power to appoint successor members to fill board vacancies. In this case, however, the incumbent Board timed its utilization of these otherwise valid powers to expand the size and composition of the Liquid Audio board for the primary purpose of impeding and interfering with the efforts of the stockholders' power to effectively exercise their voting rights in a contested election for directors. As this Court held more than three decades ago, "these are inequitable purposes, contrary to established principles of corporate democracy . . . and may not be permitted to stand."[41]

NOTES AND QUESTIONS

1. May directors postpone a shareholder meeting at which a proposed noncoercive merger is certain to be defeated in the hope that further communication will convince shareholders to approve the transaction? Then–Vice Chancellor Strine approved such an action in Mercier v. Inter-Tel, Inc., 929 A.2d 786 (2007):

> I conclude that well-motivated, independent directors may reschedule an imminent special meeting at which the shareholders are to consider an all cash, all shares offer from a third-party acquiror when the directors: (1) believe that the merger is in the best interests of the stockholders; (2) know that if the meeting proceeds the stockholders will vote down the merger; (3) reasonably fear that in the wake of the merger's rejection, the acquiror will walk away from the deal and the corporation's stock price will plummet; (4) want more time to communicate with and provide information to the stockholders before the stockholders vote on the merger and risk the irrevocable loss of the pending offer; and (5) reschedule the meeting within a reasonable time period and do not preclude or coerce the stockholders from freely deciding to reject the merger.

Id. at 787-788.

---

40. Schnell v. Chris-Craft Indus., Inc., 285 A.2d 437, 439 (Del. 1971).
41. Id.

2. How can *Mercier* be squared with *Blasius* and *Liquid Audio*? Are not the directors in all three cases equally guilty of intentionally interfering with the shareholders right to exercise their voting rights, based on a belief that the shareholders are going to vote the wrong way, either out of selfishness or ignorance? For then–Vice Chancellor Strine, the key difference lies in the directors' role in the matter to be voted on.

> In dictum, *Blasius* seemed to suggest that its reasoning applied to all stockholder votes, not just those involving the election of directors. But the reasoning of *Blasius* is far less powerful when the matter up for consideration has little or no bearing on whether the directors will continue in office. Here's a news flash: directors are not supposed to be neutral with regard to matters they propose for stockholder action. As a matter of fiduciary duty, directors should not be advising stockholders to measures that are in the stockholders' best interests. And when directors believe that measures are in the stockholders' best interests, they have a fiduciary duty to pursue the implementation of those measures in an efficient fashion. That does not mean, of course, that directors can use inequitable means that dupe or dragoon stockholders into consenting. But it does mean that directors can use the legal means at their disposal in order to pursue stockholder approval, means that often include tools like the ability to set and revise meeting dates or to adjourn a convened meeting. Post-*Blasius* cases have wrestled with that reality and display understandable discomfort about using such a stringent standard of review in circumstances when a stockholder vote has no bearing on issues of corporate control.

Id. at 808.

3. Compare the judicial response in protecting shareholder opportunity to vote to that of the prior subchapter in protecting shareholder ability to decide on a takeover by selling into a tender offer. Chancellor Allen, who wrote *Blasius*, had also written in *Interco* that "there may come a time" when the board's fiduciary duty requires redemption of a poison pill so that the shareholders may decide:

> To acknowledge that directors may employ the recent innovation of "poison pills" to deprive shareholders of the ability effectively to choose to accept a noncoercive offer, after the board has had a reasonable opportunity to explore or create alternatives, or attempt to negotiate on the shareholders' behalf, would, it seems to me, be so inconsistent with widely shared notions of appropriate corporate governance as to threaten to diminish the legitimacy and authority of our corporation law.

551 A.2d 787, 799-800 (Del. Ch. 1988).

The Delaware Supreme Court did not have the opportunity to review the *Interco* decision when the case settled. A year later in the *Time* case the Supreme Court reached out to respond to *Interco,* saying: "We disapprove of such a narrow and rigid construction" that is "a fundamental misconception of our standard of review." Paramount Communications, Inc. v. Time, Inc., 571 A.2d 1140, 1153 (Del. 1990). That decision provided substantial room for boards to employ a "just say no" response when asked to redeem a poison pill.

PROBLEM 9-8

Reconsider Problem 9-7 on page 906, supra. How would *Liquid Audio* change your analysis of questions (a) and (b)?

PROBLEM 9-9

Forward, Inc. owns 11 percent of the common stock of Treadwell, Inc., a Delaware corporation, and is committed to a business plan of gaining control of Treadwell. On January 5, 2014, Forward offered to acquire all of Treadwell's outstanding stock for $40 per share. Treadwell refused to negotiate or to redeem its recently deployed poison pill. Forward then commenced a campaign to unseat three of the nine directors on Treadwell's staggered board. On June 22, 2014, the election inspector announced that all three Forward candidates had been elected. On June 23, 2014, Treadwell announced a plan to buy up to 40 percent of its stock for junk bonds having a fair market value of $60 per share. It is expected that the fair market value of nontendered shares will drop to approximately $20 per share if the repurchase is fully subscribed. Also on June 23, the Treadwell board of directors voted to expand its size from nine to ten. Treadwell's CEO, who was one of the three candidates ousted by Forward nominees, is selected to fill the new post. The three Forward directors dissent from these actions.

Advise Forward as to its rights and the most strategic way to pursue them.

D.   *Testing the Limits of Preplanned Defenses*

Courts and legislatures in many states have given boards of directors significant power to unilaterally adopt poison pills that greatly increase a board's ability to resist unwanted takeover attempts. Creative planners continue to push the limits of this discretion, devising protective devices that conceivably could make a corporation completely invulnerable to unfriendly takeover by any means. The following case explores the legality of one such device—the "dead hand" poison pill.

Carmody v. Toll Brothers, Inc.
Delaware Court of Chancery, 1998
723 A.2d 1180

JACOBS, VICE CHANCELLOR . . .

I.   FACTS

A.   BACKGROUND LEADING TO ADOPTION OF THE PLAN

The firm whose rights plan is being challenged is Toll Brothers (sometimes referred to as "the company"), a Pennsylvania-based Delaware corporation that designs, builds, and markets single family luxury homes in thirteen states and five regions in the United States. The company was founded in 1967 by brothers Bruce and Robert Toll, who are its Chief Executive and Chief Operating Officers, respectively, and who own approximately 37.5% of Toll Brothers' common stock. The company's board of directors has nine members, four of whom (including Bruce and Robert Toll) are senior executive officers. The remaining five members of the board are "outside" independent directors.

From its inception in 1967, Toll Brothers has performed very successfully, and "went public" in 1986. As of June 3, 1997, the company had issued and outstanding 34,196,473 common shares that are traded on the New York Stock Exchange. . . .

B.   THE RIGHTS PLAN

The Rights Plan was adopted on June 12, 1997, at which point Toll Brothers' stock was trading at approximately $18 per share—near the low end of its established price range of $16 3/8 to $25 3/16 per share. After considering the industry economic and financial environment and other factors, the Toll Brothers board concluded that other companies engaged in its lines of business might perceive the company as a potential target for an acquisition. The Rights Plan was adopted with that problem in mind, but not in response to any specific takeover proposal or threat. The company announced that it had done that to protect its stockholders from "coercive or unfair tactics to gain control of the Company" by placing the stockholders in a position of having to accept or reject an unsolicited offer without adequate time.

1.   The Rights Plan's Flip In and Flip Over Features

The Rights Plan would operate as follows: there would be a dividend distribution of one preferred stock purchase right (a "Right") for each outstanding share of common stock as of July 11, 1997. Initially the Rights would attach to the company's outstanding common shares, and each Right would initially entitle the holder to purchase one thousandth of a share of a newly registered series Junior A Preferred Stock for $100. The Rights would become exercisable [when an acquiror obtains, or commences a tender offer to obtain, 15% or more of Toll Brothers' stock]. . . . Once exercisable, the Rights remain exercisable until their Final Expiration Date (June 12, 2007, ten years after the adoption of the Plan), unless the Rights are earlier redeemed by the company.

The dilutive mechanism of the Rights is "triggered" by certain defined events. One such event is the acquisition of 15% or more of Toll Brothers' stock by any person or group of affiliated or associated persons. Should that occur, each Rights holder (except the acquiror and its affiliates and associates) becomes entitled to buy two shares of Toll Brothers common stock or other securities at half price. That is, the value of the stock received when the Right is exercised is equal to two times the exercise price of the Right. In that manner, this so-called "flip in" feature of the Rights Plan would massively dilute the value of the holdings of the unwanted acquiror.

The Rights also have a standard "flip over" feature, which is triggered if after the Stock Acquisition Date, the company is made a party to a merger in which Toll Brothers is not the surviving corporation, or in which it is the surviving corporation and its common stock is changed or exchanged. In either event, each Rights holder becomes entitled to purchase common stock of the acquiring company, again at half-price, thereby impairing the acquiror's capital structure and drastically diluting the interest of the acquiror's other stockholders. . . .

2. The Dead Hand Feature of the Rights Plan

In substance, the "dead hand" provision operates to prevent any directors of Toll Brothers, except those who were in office as of the date of the Rights Plan's adoption (June 12, 1997) or their designated successors, from redeeming the Rights until they expire on June 12, 2007.

According to the complaint, this "dead hand" provision has a twofold practical effect. First, it makes an unsolicited offer for the company more unlikely by eliminating a proxy contest as a useful way for a hostile acquiror to gain control, because even if the acquiror wins the contest, its newly-elected director representatives could not redeem the Rights. Second, the "dead hand" provision disenfranchises, in a proxy contest, all shareholders that wish the company to be managed by a board empowered to redeem the Rights, by depriving those shareholders of any practical choice except to vote for the incumbent directors. Given these effects, the plaintiff claims that the only purpose that the "dead hand" provision could serve is to discourage future acquisition activity by making any proxy contest to replace incumbent board members an exercise in futility.

II. OVERVIEW OF THE PROBLEM AND THE PARTIES' CONTENTIONS . . .

A. OVERVIEW

The critical issue on this motion is whether a "dead hand" provision in a "poison pill" rights plan is subject to legal challenge on the basis that it is invalid as ultra vires, or as a breach of fiduciary duty, or both. Although that issue has been the subject of scholarly comment, it has yet to be decided under Delaware law, and to date it has been addressed by only two courts applying the law of other jurisdictions.

Some history may elucidate the issue by locating its relevance within the dynamic of state corporate takeover jurisprudence. Since the 1980s, that body of law, largely judge-made, has been racing to keep abreast of the ever-evolving and novel tactical and strategic developments so characteristic of this important area of economic endeavor that is swiftly becoming a permanent part of our national (and international) economic landscape.

For our purposes, the relevant history begins in the early 1980s with the advent of the "poison pill" as an antitakeover measure. That innovation generated litigation focused upon the issue of whether any poison pill rights plan could validly be adopted under state corporation law. The seminal case, Moran v. Household International, Inc., 490 A.2d 1059, 1072 (Del. 1985). . . .

It being settled that a corporate board could permissibly adopt a poison pill, the next litigated question became: under what circumstances would the directors' fiduciary duties require the board to redeem the rights in the face of a hostile takeover proposal? That issue was litigated, in Delaware and elsewhere, during the second half of the 1980s. The lesson taught by that experience was that courts were extremely reluctant to order the redemption of poison pills on fiduciary grounds. The reason was the prudent deployment of the pill proved to be largely beneficial to shareholder issue was litigated, in Delaware and elsewhere, during the second half of the 1980s.

The lesson taught by that experience was that courts were extremely reluctant to order the redemption of poison pills on fiduciary interests: it often resulted in a bidding contest that culminated in an acquisition on terms superior to the initial hostile offer.

Once it became clear that the prospects were unlikely for obtaining judicial relief mandating a redemption of the poison pill, a different response to the pill was needed. That response . . . was the foreseeable next step in the evolution of takeover strategy: a tender offer coupled with a solicitation for shareholder proxies to remove and replace the incumbent board with the acquiror's nominees who, upon assuming office, would redeem the pill. Because that strategy, if unopposed, would enable hostile offerors to effect an "end run" around the poison pill, it again was predictable and only a matter of time that target company boards would develop counterstrategies. With one exception—the "dead hand" pill—these counterstrategies proved "successful" only in cases where the purpose was to delay the process to enable the board to develop alternatives to the hostile offer. The counterstrategies were largely unsuccessful, however, where the goal was to stop the proxy contest (and as a consequence, the hostile offer) altogether. . . .

For example, in cases where the target board's response was either to (i) amend the bylaws to delay a shareholders meeting to elect directors, or (ii) delay an annual meeting to a later date permitted under the bylaws, so that the board and management would be able to explore alternatives to the hostile offer (but not entrench themselves), those responses were upheld. On the other hand, where the target board's response to a proxy contest (coupled with a hostile offer) was (i) to move the shareholders meeting to a later date to enable the incumbent board to solicit revocations of proxies to defeat the apparently victorious dissident group, or (ii) to expand the size of the board, and then fill the newly created positions so the incumbents would retain control of the board irrespective of the outcome of the proxy contest, those responses were declared invalid.

This litigation experience taught that a target board, facing a proxy contest joined with a hostile tender offer, could, in good faith, employ non-preclusive defensive measures to give the board time to explore transactional alternatives. The target board could not, however, erect defenses that would either preclude a proxy contest altogether or improperly bend the rules to favor the board's continued incumbency.

In this environment, the only defensive measure that promised to be a "show stopper" (i.e., had the potential to deter a proxy contest altogether) was a poison pill with a "dead hand" feature. The reason is that if only the incumbent directors or their designated successors could redeem the pill, it would make little sense for shareholders or the hostile bidder to wage a proxy contest to replace the incumbent board. Doing that would eliminate from the scene the only group of persons having the power to give the hostile bidder and target company shareholders what they desired: control of the target company (in the case of the hostile bidder) and the opportunity to obtain an attractive price for their shares (in the case of the target company stockholders). It is against that backdrop that the legal issues presented here, which concern the validity of the "dead hand" feature, attain significance. . . .

III. ANALYSIS

A. THE RIPENESS AND DERIVATIVE CLAIM DEFENSES

1. The Ripeness Argument . . .

The ripeness argument runs as follows: the harm claimed to flow from the "dead hand" provision is improper interference with the shareholders' right to vote.[19] That harm cannot occur unless there is a specific hostile takeover proposal that involves a proxy contest in which the acquiror seeks to replace the incumbent board with its own nominees who, if elected, would redeem the pill. The complaint alleges no such specific hostile acquisition proposal. Moreover, because the Toll Brothers board is "staggered" into three classes, the "dead hand" provision could not cause any cognizable harm unless and until the hostile bidder (i) first makes a fair offer which it commits to keep open for more than one year, (ii) then successfully conducts two proxy fights that replace two-thirds of the incumbent board, and also (iii) commits to conduct a third proxy fight to replace the remaining minority of "Continuing" Directors, and (iv) during this entire time the Continuing Directors obdurately refuse to redeem the Rights even though the bidder's offer is fair. The defendants urge that because none of these events has occurred, the plaintiff's claims are not ripe for adjudication.

Stripped of its bells and whistles, this argument boils down to the proposition that the adoption of a facially invalid rights plan, on a "clear day" where there is no specific hostile takeover proposal, can never be the subject of a legal challenge. Not surprisingly, the defendants cite no authority which supports that proposition, nor could they, since the case law holds to the contrary. . . .

2. The Derivative Claim Defense

Also misguided is the argument that the invalidity claims are derivative and must be dismissed under Rule 23.1 for failure to make a pre-suit demand or plead facts establishing that a demand would be futile. That argument lacks merit because the plaintiff's claims are individual, not derivative, and even if the claims were derivative, the complaint satisfies the requirements for demand excusal. . . .

B. THE VALIDITY OF THE DEAD HAND PROVISION

1. The Invalidity Contentions

The plaintiff's complaint attacks the "dead hand" feature of the Toll Brothers poison pill on both statutory and fiduciary duty grounds. The statutory claim is that the "dead hand" provision unlawfully restricts the powers of future boards by creating

---

19. The basis for the "vote interference" claim is that any shareholder vote to elect a new board that would dismantle the poison pill would be an exercise in futility, because only the Continuing Directors (the incumbent board or their designees) would have the power to redeem the Rights.

different classes of directors—those who have the power to redeem the poison pill, and those who do not. Under Del. G.C.L. §§141(a) and (d), any such restrictions and director classifications must be stated in the certificate of incorporation.[27] The complaint alleges that because those restrictions are not stated in the Toll Brothers charter, the "dead hand" provision of the Rights Plan is ultra vires and, consequently, invalid on its face.[28]

The complaint also alleges that even if the Rights Plan is not ultra vires, its approval constituted a breach of the Toll Brothers board's fiduciary duty of loyalty in several respects. It is alleged that the board violated its duty of loyalty because (a) the "dead hand" provision was enacted solely or primarily for entrenchment purposes; (b) it was also a disproportionate defensive measure, since it precludes the shareholders from receiving tender offers and engaging in a proxy contest, in contravention of the principles of Unocal Corp. v. Mesa Petroleum Co. ("*Unocal*"), as elucidated in Unitrin, Inc. v. American General Corp. ("*Unitrin*"), and (c) the "dead hand" provision purposefully interferes with the shareholder voting franchise without any compelling justification, in derogation of the principles articulated in Blasius Indus. v. Atlas Corp. ("*Blasius*").

2. *The Statutory Invalidity Claims*

Having carefully considered the arguments and authorities marshaled by both sides, the Court concludes that the complaint states legally sufficient claims that the "dead hand" provision of the Toll Brothers Rights Plan violates Delaware G.C.L. §§141(a) and (d). There are three reasons.

First, it cannot be disputed that the Rights Plan confers the power to redeem the pill only upon some, but not all, of the directors. But under §141(d), the power to create voting power distinctions among directors exists only where there is a classified board, and where those voting power distinctions are expressed in the certificate of incorporation. Section 141(d) pertinently provides:

> . . . The certificate of incorporation may confer upon holders of any class or series of stock the right to elect 1 or more directors who shall serve for such term, and have such voting powers as shall be stated in the certificate of incorporation. The terms of office and voting powers of the directors elected in the manner so provided in the certificate of incorporation may be greater than or less than those of any other director or class of directors. . . .

The plain, unambiguous meaning of the quoted language is that if one category or group of directors is given distinctive voting rights not shared by the other directors,

---

27. The plaintiff also relies upon the doctrine that prohibits a board of directors from entering into contracts or other arrangements that would amount to an abdication or substantial restriction of the board's statutory power to manage the corporation. . . .

28. At oral argument the plaintiff raised, for the first time, a separate statutory invalidity argument, namely, that even if the "dead hand" provision had been expressed in the certificate of incorporation, that provision would still run afoul of the Delaware General Corporation Law. Implicit in that argument is the proposition that our corporation statute deprives the shareholders of the power to contract for that particular kind of restriction on directorial power. Because this contention was not fairly presented or addressed in the briefing, it comes too late and is not considered on this motion.

those distinctive voting rights must be set forth in the certificate of incorporation. In the case of Toll Brothers (the complaint alleges), they are not.

Second, §141(d) mandates that the "right to elect 1 or more directors who shall . . . have such [greater] voting powers" is reserved to the stockholders, not to the directors or a subset thereof. Absent express language in the charter, nothing in Delaware law suggests that some directors of a public corporation may be created less equal than other directors, and certainly not by unilateral board action. Vesting the pill redemption power exclusively in the Continuing Directors transgresses the statutorily protected shareholder right to elect the directors who would be so empowered. For that reason, and because it is claimed that the Rights Plan's allocation of voting power to redeem the Rights is nowhere found in the Toll Brothers certificate of incorporation, the complaint states a claim that the "dead hand" feature of the Rights Plan is ultra vires, and hence, statutorily invalid under Delaware law.

Third, the complaint states a claim that the "dead hand" provision would impermissibly interfere with the directors' statutory power to manage the business and affairs of the corporation. That power is conferred by Del. G.C.L. §141(a), which mandates:

> The business and affairs of every corporation organized under this chapter shall be managed by or under the direction of a board of directors, except as may be otherwise provided in this chapter or in its certificate of incorporation. . . .

The "dead hand" poison pill is intended to thwart hostile bids by vesting shareholders with preclusive rights that cannot be redeemed except by the Continuing Directors. Thus, the one action that could make it practically possible to redeem the pill—replacing the entire board—could make that pill redemption legally impossible to achieve. The "dead hand" provision would jeopardize a newly-elected future board's ability to achieve a business combination by depriving that board of the power to redeem the pill without obtaining the consent of the "Continuing Directors," who (it may be assumed) would constitute a minority of the board. In this manner, it is claimed, the "dead hand" provision would interfere with the board's power to protect fully the corporation's (and its shareholders') interests in a transaction that is one of the most fundamental and important in the life of a business enterprise. . . .

The defendants offer two arguments in response. . . .

Neither contention has merit. The first is basically an argument that the Rights Plan does not violate any fiduciary duty of the board. That is unresponsive to the statutory invalidity claim. The second argument rests upon an analogy that has no basis in fact. In adopting the Rights Plan, the board did not, nor did it purport to, create a special committee having the exclusive power to redeem the pill. The analogy also ignores fundamental structural differences between the creation of a special board committee and the operation of the "dead hand" provision of the Rights Plan. The creation of a special committee would not impose long term structural power-related distinctions between different groups of directors of the same board. The board that creates a special committee may abolish it at any time, as could any successor board. On the other hand, the Toll Brothers "dead hand" provision, if legally valid, would embed structural power-related distinctions between groups of directors that no successor board could abolish until after the Rights expire in 2007. . . .

3.   The Fiduciary Duty Invalidity Claims . . .

(a)   The Blasius Fiduciary Duty Claim

The validity of antitakeover measures is normally evaluated under the *Unocal/ Unitrin* standard. But where the defensive measures purposefully disenfranchise shareholders, the board will be required to satisfy the more exacting *Blasius* standard, which our Supreme Court has articulated as follows:

> A board's unilateral decision to adopt a defensive measure touching "upon issues of control" that purposefully disenfranchises its shareholders is strongly suspect under *Unocal,* and cannot be sustained without a "compelling justification."[39]

The complaint alleges that the "dead hand" provision purposefully disenfranchises the company's shareholders without any compelling justification. The disenfranchisement would occur because even in an election contest fought over the issue of the hostile bid, the shareholders will be powerless to elect a board that is both willing and able to accept the bid, and they "may be forced to vote for [incumbent] directors whose policies they reject because only those directors have the power to change them."

A claim that the directors have unilaterally "create[d] a structure in which shareholder voting is either impotent or self defeating" is necessarily a claim of purposeful disenfranchisement. Given the Supreme Court's rationale for upholding the validity of the poison pill in *Moran,* and the primacy of the shareholder vote in our scheme of corporate jurisprudence, any contrary view is difficult to justify. In *Moran,* the Supreme Court upheld the adoption of a poison pill, in part because its effect upon a proxy contest would be "minimal," but also because if the board refused to redeem the plan, the shareholders could exercise their prerogative to remove and replace the board. In *Unocal,* the Supreme Court reiterated that view — that the safety valve which justifies a board being allowed to resist a hostile offer a majority of shareholders might prefer, is that the shareholders always have their ultimate recourse to the ballot box. Those observations reflect the fundamental value that the shareholder vote has primacy in our system of corporate governance because it is the "ideological underpinning upon which the legitimacy of directorial power rests."[44] . . .

The defendants contend that the complaint fails to allege a valid stockholder disenfranchisement claim, because the Rights Plan does not on its face limit a dissident's ability to propose a slate or the shareholders' ability to cast a vote. The defendants also urge that even if the Plan might arguably have that effect, it could occur only in a very specific and unlikely context, namely, where (i) the hostile bidder makes a fair offer that it is willing to keep open for more than one year, (ii) the current board refuses to

---

39. *Stroud v. Grace,* 606 A.2d 75, 92 n.3 (Del. 1992).

44. *Blasius,* 564 A.2d at 659. . . .

redeem the Rights, and (iii) the offeror wages two successful proxy fights and is committed to wage a third.

This argument, in my opinion, begs the issue and is specious. It begs the issue because the complaint does not claim that the Rights Plan facially restricts the shareholders' voting rights. What the complaint alleges is that the "dead hand" provision will either preclude a hostile bidder from waging a proxy contest altogether, or, if there should be a contest, it will coerce those shareholders who desire the hostile offer to succeed to vote for those directors who oppose it—the incumbent (and "Continuing") directors. Besides missing the point, the argument is also specious, because the hypothetical case the defendants argue must exist for any disenfranchisement to occur, rests upon the unlikely assumption that the hostile bidder will keep its offer open for more than one year. Given the market risks inherent in financed hostile bids for public corporations, it is unrealistic to assume that many bidders would be willing to do that. . . .

(b) *The* Unocal/Unitrin *Fiduciary Duty Claim*

The final issue is whether the complaint states a legally cognizable claim that the inclusion of the "dead hand" provision in the Rights Plan was an unreasonable defensive measure within the meaning of *Unocal.* I conclude that it does.

As a procedural matter, it merits emphasis that a claim under *Unocal* requires enhanced judicial scrutiny. In that context, the board has the burden to satisfy the Court that the board (1) "had reasonable grounds for believing that a danger to corporate policy and effectiveness existed," and (2) that its "defensive response was reasonable in relation to the threat posed." Such scrutiny is, by its nature, fact-driven and requires a factual record. For that reason, as the Supreme Court recently observed, enhanced scrutiny "will usually not be satisfied by resting on a defense motion merely attacking the pleadings." Only "conclusory complaints without well-pleaded facts [may] be dismissed early under Chancery Rule 12."

The complaint at issue here is far from conclusory. Under *Unitrin,* a defensive measure is disproportionate (i.e., unreasonable) if it is either coercive or preclusive. The complaint alleges that the "dead hand" provision "disenfranchises shareholders by forcing them to vote for incumbent directors or their designees if shareholders want to be represented by a board entitled to exercise its full statutory prerogatives." That is sufficient to claim that the "dead hand" provision is coercive. The complaint also alleges that that provision "makes an offer for the Company much more unlikely since it eliminates use of a proxy contest as a possible means to gain control . . . [because] . . . any directors elected in such a contest would still be unable to vote to redeem the pill;" and "renders future contests for corporate control of Toll Brothers prohibitively expensive and effectively impossible." A defensive measure is preclusive if it makes bidder's ability to wage a successful proxy contest and gain control either "mathematically impossible" or "realistically unattainable." These allegations are sufficient to state a claim that the "dead hand" provision makes a proxy contest "realistically unattainable," and therefore is disproportionate and unreasonable under *Unocal.*

IV. CONCLUSION

The Court concludes that for the reasons discussed above, the complaint states claims under Delaware law upon which relief can be granted.[52] Accordingly, the defendants' motion to dismiss is denied. IT IS SO ORDERED.

NOTES AND QUESTIONS

1. For a case upholding a dead hand poison pill, see Invacare Corp. v. Healthdyne Technologies, Inc., 968 F. Supp. 1578 (N.D. Ga. 1997). The court in *Invacare* rejected the argument that the "continuing director" provisions were invalid because they constituted restrictions on the board's authority that should have been contained in the articles of incorporation, because the Georgia Corporation Code did not support such a requirement. Additionally, the court found that other features of the Georgia Corporation Code indicated that "Georgia corporate law embraces the concept of continuing directors as part of a defense against hostile takeovers." 968 F. Supp. at 1580.

2. In all of the cases we have studied in this chapter, directors erected defensive barriers unilaterally. What would be the standard of review if a board submits a take-over defense to a shareholder vote and obtains shareholder approval? In Williams v. Geier, 671 A.2d 1368 (Del. 1996), the board of Cincinnati Milacron (Milacron) recommended to its shareholders a proposed amendment to the Articles creating so-called "tenure voting." Under the proposed amendment, each Milacron share would be entitled to ten votes, but upon transfer by sale or otherwise, a share would be entitled to only one vote until held by the transferee for 36 months. Because Milacron's management controlled a significant block of Milacron stock, tenure voting would give management the ability to block any attempted unfriendly takeover if management held on to its shares while other shareholders sold. A shareholder suit was filed seeking injunctive or other relief. The Court of Chancery granted summary judgment for the defendants.

On appeal, a majority of the Supreme Court concluded that neither *Unocal* nor *Blasius* applied because the directors had not acted unilaterally, but instead, had acted only after obtaining shareholder approval. Thus, business judgment review was appropriate, and, under that standard, summary judgment for the defendants was appropriate.

The two dissenting judges strongly disagreed. Noting that for purposes of the summary judgment, the Geier family (which included Milacron's CEO) must be treated

---

52. For the sake of clarity, it must be emphasized that the "dead hand" provision at issue here is of unlimited duration; that is, it remains effective during the entire life of the poison pill. There are also "dead hand" provisions of limited duration (e.g., six months), which are sometimes referred to as "diluted" or "deferred redemption" provisions. Some commentators have urged that such limited duration "dead hand" provisions stand on a different footing and should be upheld; others have argued the contrary. In any event, this case does not involve the validity of a "dead hand" provision of limited duration, and nothing in this Opinion should be read as expressing a view or pronouncement on that subject.

as Milacron's controlling shareholder, the dissenting judges argued that the minority shareholders were powerless to prevent adoption of the tenure-vote amendment, creating a circumstance where heightened judicial review was required and summary judgment was inappropriate.

> In our opinion, the Board's decision proposing and recommending the adoption of the Recapitalization Plan should be subject to a heightened level of judicial scrutiny, under the rationale of *Unocal*, 493 A.2d 946, or *Blasius*, 564 A.2d 651, or both. When the voting rights of minority stockholders are changed without their consent, there is the omnipresent specter of inherent conflict between a board's duty to all the stockholders and the desires of the block of stockholders holding a majority of the shares. This conflict is similar to the conflict that existed in *Unocal*.

671 A.2d at 1387.

3. In Quickturn Design Systems, Inc. v. Shapiro, 721 A.2d 1281 (Del. 1998), the Delaware Supreme Court invalidated a so-called "no hands" poison pill. Quickturn was facing an unfriendly takeover bid by Mentor Graphics. Its Rights plan initially contained a "dead hand" provision similar to the "continuing director" provision at issue in Carmody v. Toll Brothers. However, shortly after the Court of Chancery decision in *Toll Brothers,* the Quickturn directors amended the company's Rights plan, replacing the "dead hand" provision with a delayed redemption or "no hands" provision. As amended, the Rights plan stipulated that "if a majority of the directors are replaced by shareholder action, the newly elected board cannot redeem the rights for six months if the purpose or effect of the redemption would be to facilitate a [merger or similar transaction between the company and an unfriendly suitor]." *Quickturn Design Systems,* 721 A.2d at 1289. The Court of Chancery invalidated the "no hands" provision because its adoption violated the directors' fiduciary duty. On appeal, the Delaware Supreme Court affirmed the invalidation of the "no hands" poison pill on different grounds.

> One of the most basic tenets of Delaware corporate law is that the board of directors has the ultimate responsibility for managing the business and affairs of a corporation. Because Section 141(a) requires that any limitation on the board's authority be set out in the certificate of incorporation. The Quickturn certificate of incorporation contains no provision purporting to limit the authority of the board in any way. The Delayed Redemption Provision, however, would prevent a newly elected board of directors from *completely* discharging its fundamental management duties to the corporation and its stockholders for six months. While the Delayed Redemption Provision limits the board of directors' authority in only one respect, the suspension of the Rights Plan, it nonetheless restricts the board's power in an area of fundamental importance to the shareholders—negotiating a possible sale of the corporation. Therefore, we hold that the Delayed Redemption Provision is invalid under Section 141(a), which confers upon any newly elected board of directors *full* power to manage and direct the business and affairs of a Delaware corporation.
>
> In discharging the statutory mandate of Section 141(a), the directors have a fiduciary duty to the corporation and its shareholders. This unremitting obligation extends equally to board conduct in a contest for corporate control. The Delayed Redemption Provision prevents a newly elected board of directors from completely discharging its fiduciary duties to protect fully the interests of Quickturn and its stockholders.
>
> This Court has recently observed that "although the fiduciary duty of a Delaware director is unremitting, the exact course of conduct that must be charted to properly discharge that responsibility will change in the specific context of the action the director is taking with regard to either the corporation or its shareholders." This Court has held "[t]o the extent that a contract, or a provision thereof, purports to require a board to act *or not act* in such a fashion as to limit the exercise of

fiduciary duties, it is invalid and unenforceable." The Delayed Redemption Provision "tends to limit in a substantial way the freedom of [newly elected] directors' decisions on matters of management policy." Therefore, "it violates the duty of each [newly elected] director to exercise his own best judgment on matters coming before the board."

PROBLEM 9-10

Jane Matlock is the CEO of Quartz, Inc., a publicly traded corporation. The Matlock family owns 55 percent of Quartz's stock. Sarah Browning, Jane's mother, owns most of the Matlock family stock and is terminally ill. Jane stands to inherit most of her mother's estate, but a significant portion of Sarah's Quartz stock will likely be sold to pay estate taxes. Matlock chairs the nine-member Quartz board of directors. The other eight directors are all "outsiders" who serve, or have served, as CEOs of publicly traded companies. The outside directors, collectively, hold insignificant amounts of Quartz stock and hold no Quartz stock options. Recently Ralph Raider approached Matlock to discuss a possible merger of Quartz and a company controlled by Raider. Matlock rebuffed Raider, telling him that Quartz was committed to going it alone. The next day, Matlock called an emergency meeting of the Quartz board. Matlock told the board about her encounter with Raider, and about the likelihood that the Matlock family's stockholdings would soon be substantially reduced. Matlock expressed her fear that Raider would take advantage of this situation to make an unfriendly, coercive, tender offer. After several hours of discussion, the board resolved to recommend that the shareholders adopt an amendment to the Quartz certificate of incorporation, thereby creating a species of "tenure voting." In pertinent part, the amendment provides as follows:

> All stockholders owning common stock on the effective date of this amendment are entitled to ten votes per share. Holders of shares acquired after the date of this amendment shall be entitled to one vote for each share which as of the record date in question has been owned for less than 36 months, and to ten votes for each share which as of the record date in question has been held for 36 months or longer.

The amendment received a yes vote from shareholders (including the Matlock family) owning 70 percent of Quartz common shares, and a no vote from shareholders owning 25 percent of Quartz common shares. A recently filed shareholders' suit asks that the amendment be declared invalid. What result?

E. *Testing the Limits of "Deal Protection Devices" in Friendly Mergers*

Omnicare, Inc. v. NCS Healthcare, Inc.
Delaware Supreme Court (en banc 2003)
818 A.2d 914

HOLLAND, JUSTICE, for the majority:

NCS Healthcare, Inc. ("NCS"), a Delaware corporation [a leading independent provider of pharmacy services to long-term-care institutions, including skilled nursing facilities, assisted living facilities, and other institutional health care facilities], was the object of competing acquisition bids, one by Genesis Health Ventures, Inc. ("Genesis"), a Pennsylvania corporation, [a leading provider of health care and support services to the elderly] and the other by Omnicare, Inc. ("Omnicare"), a Delaware corporation [in the institutional pharmacy business, with annual sales in excess of $2.1 billion during its last fiscal year]. . . . [After a period of seeking various financial solutions to what had been a difficult time in its industry, including discussion with Omnicare, the NCS board and the two shareholders who controlled a majority of its voting stock agreed to a merger with Genesis.] The merger agreement between Genesis and NCS contained a provision authorized by Section 251(c) of Delaware's corporation law [now found in Section 146]. It required that the Genesis agreement be placed before the corporation's stockholders for a vote, even if the NCS board of directors no longer recommended it. At the insistence of Genesis, the NCS board also agreed to omit any effective fiduciary [out] clause from the merger agreement. In connection with the Genesis merger agreement, two stockholders of NCS, who held a majority of the voting power, agreed unconditionally to vote all of their shares in favor of the Genesis merger. Thus, the combined terms of the voting agreements and merger agreement guaranteed, *ab initio*, that the transaction proposed by Genesis would obtain NCS stockholder's approval.

[Several months after approving the merger agreement, but before the stockholder vote was scheduled, the NCS board of directors withdrew its prior recommendation in favor of the Genesis merger in the face of an Omnicare bid offering "the NCS stockholders an amount of cash equal to more than twice the then current market value of the shares to be received in the Genesis merger."] The Court of Chancery ruled that the voting agreements, when coupled with the provision in the Genesis merger agreement requiring that it be presented to the stockholders for a vote pursuant to 8 Del. C. §251(c), constituted defensive measures within the meaning of Unocal Corp. v. Mesa Petroleum Co. After applying the *Unocal* standard of enhanced judicial scrutiny, the Court of Chancery held that those defensive measures were reasonable. We have concluded that, in the absence of an effective fiduciary out clause, those defensive measures are both preclusive and coercive. Therefore, we hold that those defensive measures are invalid and unenforceable. . . .

FACTUAL BACKGROUND

[NCS common stock consists of Class A shares and Class B shares. The Class B shares are entitled to ten votes per share and the Class A shares are entitled to one vote per share. The shares are virtually identical in every other respect. As of July 28, 2002, NCS had 18,461,599 Class A shares and 5,255,210 Class B shares outstanding. Two of the four directors own 65 percent of the stockholder voting power. Jon H. Outcalt, Chairman of the board of directors, owns 202,063 shares of NCS Class A common stock and 3,476,086 shares of Class B common stock. Kevin B. Shaw, President, CEO, and a director of NCS at the time the merger agreement executed with Genesis, owned 28,905 shares of NCS Class A common stock and 1,141,134 shares of Class B common stock.]

The NCS board has two other members, defendants Boake A. Sells and Richard L. Osborne. Sells is a graduate of the Harvard Business School. He was Chairman and CEO at Revco Drugstores in Cleveland, Ohio from 1987 to 1992, when he was replaced by new owners. Sells currently sits on the boards of both public and private companies. Osborne is a full-time professor at the Weatherhead School of Management at Case Western Reserve University. He has been at the university for over thirty years. Osborne currently sits on at least seven corporate boards other than NCS. . . .

LEGAL ANALYSIS

BUSINESS JUDGMENT OR ENHANCED SCRUTINY

The "defining tension" in corporate governance today has been characterized as "the tension between deference to directors' decisions and the scope of judicial review." [E. Norman Veasey, The Defining Tension in Corporate Governance in America, 52 Bus. Law. 393, 403 (1997).] The appropriate standard of judicial review is dispositive of which party has the burden of proof as any litigation proceeds from stage to stage until there is a substantive determination on the merits. Accordingly, identification of the correct analytical framework is essential to a proper judicial review of challenges to the decision-making process of a corporation's board of directors. . . .

DEAL PROTECTION DEVICES REQUIRE ENHANCED SCRUTINY

The dispositive issues in this appeal involve the defensive devices that protected the Genesis merger agreement. The Delaware corporation statute provides that the board's management decision to enter into and recommend a merger transaction can become final only when ownership action is taken by a vote of the stockholders. Thus, the Delaware corporation law expressly provides for a balance of power between boards and stockholders which makes merger transactions a shared enterprise and ownership decision. Consequently, a board of directors' decision to adopt defensive devices to protect a merger agreement may implicate the stockholders' right to effectively vote contrary to the initial recommendation of the board in favor of the transaction. . . .

There are inherent conflicts between a board's interest in protecting a merger transaction it has approved, the stockholders' statutory right to make the final decision to either approve or not approve a merger, and the board's continuing responsibility to effectively exercise its fiduciary duties at all times after the merger agreement is executed. These competing considerations require a threshold determination that board-approved defensive devices protecting a merger transaction are within the limitations of its statutory authority and consistent with the directors' fiduciary duties. Accordingly, in Paramount v. Time, we held that the business judgment rule applied to the Time board's original decision to merge with Warner. We further held, however, that defensive devices adopted by the board to protect the original merger transaction must withstand enhanced judicial scrutiny under the *Unocal* standard of review, even when that merger transaction does not result in a change of control.

ENHANCED SCRUTINY GENERALLY

... A board's decision to protect its decision to enter a merger agreement with defensive devices against uninvited competing transactions that may emerge is analogous to a board's decision to protect against dangers to corporate policy and effectiveness when it adopts defensive measures in a hostile takeover contest....

[I]n applying enhanced judicial scrutiny to defensive devices designed to protect a merger agreement, a court must first determine that those measures are not preclusive or coercive *before* its focus shifts to the "range of reasonableness" in making a proportionality determination.

... Defensive devices taken to protect a merger agreement executed by a board of directors are intended to give that agreement an advantage over any subsequent transactions that materialize before the merger is approved by the stockholders and consummated. This is analogous to the favored treatment that a board of directors may properly give to encourage an initial bidder when it discharges its fiduciary duties under *Revlon.*

Therefore, in the context of a merger that does not involve a change of control, when defensive devices in the executed merger agreement are challenged *vis-à-vis* their effect on a subsequent competing alternative merger transaction, this Court's analysis in *Macmillan* is didactic. In the context of a case of defensive measures taken against an existing bidder, we stated in *Macmillan*:

> In the face of disparate treatment, the trial court must first examine whether the directors properly perceived that shareholder interests were enhanced. In any event the board's action must be reasonable in relation to the advantage sought to be achieved [by the merger it approved], or conversely, to the threat which a [competing transaction] poses to stockholder interests. If on the basis of this enhanced *Unocal* scrutiny the trial court is satisfied that the test has been met, then the directors' actions necessarily are entitled to the protections of the business judgment rule.

The latitude a board will have in either maintaining or using the defensive devices it has adopted to protect the merger it approved will vary according to the degree of benefit or detriment to the stockholders' interests that is presented by the value or terms of the subsequent competing transaction....

DEAL PROTECTION DEVICES

Defensive devices, as that term is used in this opinion, is a synonym for what are frequently referred to as "deal protection devices." Both terms are used interchangeably to describe any measure or combination of measures that are intended to protect the consummation of a merger transaction. Defensive devices can be economic, structural, or both.

Deal protection devices need not all be in the merger agreement itself. In this case, for example, the Section 251(c) provision in the merger agreement was combined with the separate voting agreements to provide a structural defense for the Genesis merger agreement against any subsequent superior transaction. Genesis made the NCS board's defense of its transaction absolute by insisting on the omission of any effective fiduciary out clause in the NCS merger agreement.

Genesis argues that stockholder voting agreements cannot be construed as deal protection devices taken by a board of directors because stockholders are entitled to vote in their own interest. Genesis cites Williams v. Geier[57] and Stroud v. Grace[58] for the proposition that voting agreements are not subject to the Unocal standard of review. Neither of those cases, however, holds that the operative effect of a voting agreement must be disregarded per se when a *Unocal* analysis is applied to a comprehensive and combined merger defense plan.

In this case, the stockholder voting agreements were inextricably intertwined with the defensive aspects of the Genesis merger agreement. In fact, the voting agreements with Shaw and Outcalt were the linchpin of Genesis' proposed tripartite defense. Therefore, Genesis made the execution of those voting agreements a non-negotiable condition precedent to its execution of the merger agreement. In the case before us, the Court of Chancery held that the acts which locked up the Genesis transaction were the Section 251(c) provision and "the execution of the voting agreement by Outcalt and Shaw."

With the assurance that Outcalt and Shaw would irrevocably agree to exercise their majority voting power in favor of its transaction, Genesis insisted that the merger agreement reflect the other two aspects of its concerted defense, i.e., the inclusion of a Section 251(c) provision and the omission of any effective fiduciary out clause. Those dual aspects of the merger agreement would not have provided Genesis with a complete defense in the absence of the voting agreements with Shaw and Outcalt.

THESE DEAL PROTECTION DEVICES UNENFORCEABLE

In this case, the Court of Chancery correctly held that the NCS directors' decision to adopt defensive devices to completely "lock up" the Genesis merger mandated "special scrutiny" under the two part test set forth in *Unocal*. That conclusion is consistent with our holding in Paramount v. Time that "safety devices" adopted to protect a transaction that did not result in a change of control are subject to enhanced judicial scrutiny under a *Unocal* analysis. The record does not, however, support the Court of Chancery's conclusion that the defensive devices adopted by the NCS board to protect the Genesis merger were reasonable and proportionate to the threat that NCS perceived from the potential loss of the Genesis transaction.

Pursuant to the judicial scrutiny required under *Unocal*'s two stage analysis, the NCS directors must first demonstrate "that they had reasonable grounds for believing that a danger to corporate policy and effectiveness existed. . . ." To satisfy that burden, the NCS directors are required to show they acted in good faith after conducting a reasonable investigation. The threat identified by the NCS board was the possibility of losing the Genesis offer and being left with no comparable alternative transaction.

The second stage of the *Unocal* test requires the NCS directors to demonstrate that their defensive response was "reasonable in relation to the threat posed." This inquiry

---

57. Williams v. Geier, 671 A.2d 1368 (Del. 1996).
58. Stroud v. Grace, 606 A.2d 75 (Del. 1992).

involves a two-step analysis. The NCS directors must first establish that the merger deal protection devices adopted in response to the threat were not "coercive" or "preclusive," and then demonstrate that their response was within a "range of reasonable responses" to the threat perceived. In *Unitrin,* we stated:

- A response is "coercive" if it is aimed at forcing upon stockholders a management sponsored alternative to a hostile offer.
- A response is "preclusive" if it deprives stockholders of the right to receive all tender offers or precludes a bidder from seeking control by fundamentally restricting proxy contests or otherwise.

This aspect of the *Unocal* standard provides for a disjunctive analysis. If defensive measures are either preclusive or coercive they are draconian and impermissible. In this case, the deal protection devices of the NCS board were *both* preclusive and coercive.

This Court enunciated the standard for determining stockholder coercion in the case of Williams v. Geier. A stockholder vote may be nullified by wrongful coercion "where the board or some other party takes actions which have the effect of causing the stockholders to vote in favor of the proposed transaction for some reason other than the merits of that transaction." . . .

In this case, the Court of Chancery did not expressly address the issue of "coercion" in its Unocal analysis. It did find as a fact, however, that NCS's public stockholders (who owned 80% of NCS and overwhelmingly supported Omnicare's offer) will be forced to accept the Genesis merger because of the structural defenses approved by the NCS board. Consequently, the record reflects that any stockholder vote would have been robbed of its effectiveness by the impermissible coercion that predetermined the outcome of the merger without regard to the merits of the Genesis transaction at the time the vote was scheduled to be taken. Deal protection devices that result in such coercion cannot withstand Unocal's enhanced judicial scrutiny standard of review because they are not within the range of reasonableness.

Although the minority stockholders were not forced to vote for the Genesis merger, they were required to accept it because it was a *fait accompli.* The record reflects that the defensive devices employed by the NCS board are preclusive and coercive in the sense that they accomplished a *fait accompli.* In this case, despite the fact that the NCS board has withdrawn its recommendation for the Genesis transaction and recommended its rejection by the stockholders, the deal protection devices approved by the NCS board operated in concert to have a preclusive and coercive effect. Those tripartite defensive measures—the Section 251(c) provision, the voting agreements, and the absence of an effective fiduciary out clause—made it "mathematically impossible" and "realistically unattainable" for the Omnicare transaction or any other proposal to succeed, no matter how superior the proposal.

The deal protection devices adopted by the NCS board were designed to coerce the consummation of the Genesis merger and preclude the consideration of any superior transaction. The NCS directors' defensive devices are not within a reasonable range of responses to the perceived threat of losing the Genesis offer because they are preclusive and coercive. Accordingly, we hold that those deal protection devices are unenforceable.

EFFECTIVE FIDUCIARY OUT REQUIRED

The defensive measures that protected the merger transaction are unenforceable not only because they are preclusive and coercive but, alternatively, they are unenforceable because they are invalid as they operate in this case. Given the specifically enforceable irrevocable voting agreements, the provision in the merger agreement requiring the board to submit the transaction for a stockholder vote and the omission of a fiduciary out clause in the merger agreement completely prevented the board from discharging its fiduciary responsibilities to the minority stockholders when Omnicare presented its superior transaction. "To the extent that a [merger] contract, or a provision thereof, purports to require a board to act or not act in such a fashion as to limit the exercise of fiduciary duties, it is invalid and unenforceable."[74]

In *QVC*, this Court recognized that "[w]hen a majority of a corporation's voting shares are acquired by a single person or entity, or by *a cohesive group acting together* [as in this case], there is a significant diminution in the voting power of those who thereby become minority stockholders." Therefore, we acknowledged that "[i]n the absence of devices protecting the minority stockholders, stockholder votes are likely to become mere formalities," where a cohesive group acting together to exercise majority voting powers have already decided the outcome. Consequently, we concluded that since the minority stockholders lost the power to influence corporate direction through the ballot, "minority stockholders must rely for protection solely on the fiduciary duties owed to them by the directors."

Under the circumstances presented in this case, where a cohesive group of stockholders with majority voting power was irrevocably committed to the merger transaction, "[e]ffective representation of the financial interests of the minority shareholders imposed upon the [NCS board] an affirmative responsibility to protect those minority shareholders' interests." The NCS board could not abdicate its fiduciary duties to the minority by leaving it to the stockholders alone to approve or disapprove the merger agreement because two stockholders had already combined to establish a majority of the voting power that made the outcome of the stockholder vote a foregone conclusion.

The Court of Chancery noted that Section 251(c) of the Delaware General Corporation Law now permits boards to agree to submit a merger agreement for a stockholder vote, even if the Board later withdraws its support for that agreement and recommends that the stockholders reject it.[80] . . . .

---

74. Paramount Communications Inc. v. QVC Network Inc., 637 A.2d 34, 51 (Del. 1993) (citation omitted). *Restatement (Second) of Contracts* §193 explicitly provides that a "promise by a fiduciary to violate his fiduciary duty *or a promise that tends to induce such a violation is unenforceable on grounds of public policy.*" The comments to that section indicate that "[d]irectors and other officials of a corporation act in a fiduciary capacity and are subject to the rule stated in this Section." *Restatement (Second) of Contracts* §193 (1981) (emphasis added).

80. Section 251(c) was amended in 1998 to allow for the inclusion in a merger agreement of a term requiring that the agreement be put to a vote of stockholders whether or not their directors continue to recommend the transaction. Before this amendment, Section 251 was interpreted as precluding a stockholder vote if the board of directors, after approving the merger agreement but before the stockholder vote, decided no longer to recommend it. See Smith v. Van Gorkom, 488 A.2d 858, 887-88 (Del. 1985).

Taking action that is otherwise legally possible, however, does not ipso facto comport with the fiduciary responsibilities of directors in all circumstances. . . .

The directors of a Delaware corporation have a continuing obligation to discharge their fiduciary responsibilities, as future circumstances develop, after a merger agreement is announced. Genesis anticipated the likelihood of a superior offer after its merger agreement was announced and demanded defensive measures from the NCS board that *completely* protected its transaction. Instead of agreeing to the absolute defense of the Genesis merger from a superior offer, however, the NCS board was required to negotiate a fiduciary out clause to protect the NCS stockholders if the Genesis transaction became an inferior offer. By acceding to Genesis' ultimatum for complete protection *in futuro*, the NCS board disabled itself from exercising its own fiduciary obligations at a time when the board's own judgment is most important, i.e. receipt of a subsequent superior offer.

Any board has authority to give the proponent of a recommended merger agreement reasonable structural and economic defenses, incentives, and fair compensation if the transaction is not completed. To the extent that defensive measures are economic and reasonable, they may become an increased cost to the proponent of any subsequent transaction. Just as defensive measures cannot be draconian, however, they cannot limit or circumscribe the directors' fiduciary duties. Notwithstanding the corporation's insolvent condition, the NCS board had no authority to execute a merger agreement that subsequently prevented it from effectively discharging its ongoing fiduciary responsibilities.

The stockholders of a Delaware corporation are entitled to rely upon the board to discharge its fiduciary duties at all times. The fiduciary duties of a director are unremitting and must be effectively discharged in the specific context of the actions that are required with regard to the corporation or its stockholders as circumstances change. The stockholders with majority voting power, Shaw and Outcalt, had an absolute right to sell or exchange their shares with a third party at any price. This right was not only known to the other directors of NCS, it became an integral part of the Genesis agreement. In its answering brief, Genesis candidly states that its offer "came with a condition—Genesis would not be a stalking horse and would not agree to a transaction to which NCS's controlling shareholders were not committed."

The NCS board was required to contract for an effective fiduciary out clause to exercise its continuing fiduciary responsibilities to the minority stockholders.[88] The issues in this appeal do not involve the general validity of either stockholder voting agreements or the authority of directors to insert a Section 251(c) provision in a merger agreement. In this case, the NCS board combined those two otherwise valid actions and caused them to operate in concert as an absolute lock up, in the absence of an effective fiduciary out clause in the Genesis merger agreement.

---

88. See Paramount Communications Inc. v. QVC Network Inc., 637 A.2d at 42-43. Merger agreements involve an ownership decision and, therefore, cannot become final without stockholder approval. Other contracts do not require a fiduciary out clause because they involve business judgments that are within the exclusive province of the board of directors' power to manage the affairs of the corporation. See Grimes v. Donald, 673 A.2d 1207, 1214-15 (Del. 1996).

In the context of this preclusive and coercive lock up case, the protection of Genesis' contractual expectations must yield to the supervening responsibility of the directors to discharge their fiduciary duties on a continuing basis. The merger agreement and voting agreements, as they were combined to operate in concert in this case, are inconsistent with the NCS directors' fiduciary duties. To that extent, we hold that they are invalid and unenforceable. . . .

VEASEY, CHIEF JUSTICE, with whom STEELE, JUSTICE, joins dissenting. . . .

AN ANALYSIS OF THE PROCESS LEADING TO THE LOCK-UP REFLECTS A QUINTESSENTIAL, DISINTERESTED AND INFORMED BOARD DECISION REACHED IN GOOD FAITH

. . . Going into negotiations with Genesis, the NCS directors knew that, up until that time, NCS had found only one potential bidder, Omnicare. Omnicare had refused to buy NCS except at a fire sale price through an asset sale in bankruptcy. Omnicare's best proposal at that stage would not have paid off all creditors and would have provided nothing for stockholders. The Noteholders, represented by the Ad Hoc Committee, were willing to oblige Omnicare and force NCS into bankruptcy if Omnicare would pay in full the NCS debt. Through the NCS board's efforts, Genesis expressed interest that became increasingly attractive. Negotiations with Genesis led to an offer paying creditors off and conferring on NCS stockholders $24 million—an amount infinitely superior to the prior Omnicare proposals.

But there was, understandably, a *sine qua non*. In exchange for offering the NCS stockholders a return on their equity and creditor payment, Genesis demanded certainty that the merger would close. If the NCS board would not have acceded to the Section 251(c) provision, if Outcalt and Shaw had not agreed to the voting agreements and if NCS had insisted on a fiduciary out, there would have been no Genesis deal! Thus, the only value-enhancing transaction available would have disappeared. NCS knew that Omnicare had spoiled a Genesis acquisition in the past, and it is not disputed by the Majority that the NCS directors made a reasoned decision to accept as real the Genesis threat to walk away.

When Omnicare submitted its conditional eleventh-hour bid, the NCS board had to weigh the economic terms of the proposal against the uncertainty of completing a deal with Omnicare. . . . As a matter of business judgment, the risk of negotiating with Omnicare and losing Genesis at that point outweighed the possible benefits. . . .

A lock-up permits a target board and a bidder to "exchange certainties." Certainty itself has value. The acquirer may pay a higher price for the target if the acquirer is assured consummation of the transaction. The target company also benefits from the certainty of completing a transaction with a bidder because losing an acquirer creates the perception that a target is damaged goods, thus reducing its value. . . .

Situations will arise where business realities demand a lock up so that wealth-enhancing transactions may go forward. Accordingly, any bright-line rule prohibiting lock-ups could, in circumstances such as these, chill otherwise permissible conduct.

OUR JURISPRUDENCE DOES NOT COMPEL THIS COURT TO INVALIDATE THE JOINT ACTION OF THE BOARD AND THE CONTROLLING STOCKHOLDERS

The Majority invalidates the NCS board's action by announcing a new rule that represents an extension of our jurisprudence. That new rule can be narrowly stated as follows: A merger agreement entered into after a market search, before any prospect of a topping bid has emerged, which locks up stockholder approval and does not contain a "fiduciary out" provision, is per se invalid when a later significant topping bid emerges. As we have noted, this bright-line, per se rule would apply regardless of (1) the circumstances leading up to the agreement and (2) the fact that stockholders who control voting power had irrevocably committed themselves, *as stockholders*, to vote for the merger. Narrowly stated, this new rule is a judicially-created "third rail" that now becomes one of the given "rules of the game," to be taken into account by the negotiators and drafters of merger agreements. In our view, this new rule is an unwise extension of existing precedent.

. . . Outcalt and Shaw were fully informed stockholders. As the NCS controlling stockholders, they made an informed choice to commit their voting power to the merger. The minority stockholders were deemed to know that when controlling stockholders have 65% of the vote they can approve a merger without the need for the minority votes. Moreover, to the extent a minority stockholder may have felt "coerced" to vote for the merger, which was already a *fait accompli*, it was a meaningless coercion—or no coercion at all—because the controlling votes, those of Outcalt and Shaw, were already "cast." Although the fact that the controlling votes were committed to the merger "precluded" an overriding vote against the merger by the Class A stockholders, the pejorative "preclusive" label applicable in a *Unitrin* fact situation has no application here. Therefore, there was no meaningful minority stockholder voting decision to coerce.

In applying *Unocal* scrutiny, we believe the Majority incorrectly preempted the proportionality inquiry. In our view, the proportionality inquiry must account for the reality that the contractual measures protecting this merger agreement were necessary to obtain the Genesis deal. The Majority has not demonstrated that the director action was a disproportionate response to the threat posed. Indeed, it is clear to us that the board action to negotiate the best deal reasonably available with the only viable merger partner (Genesis) who could satisfy the creditors and benefit the stockholders, was reasonable in relation to the threat, by any practical yardstick.

AN ABSOLUTE LOCK-UP IS NOT A PER SE VIOLATION OF FIDUCIARY DUTY

. . . In this case, Genesis made it abundantly clear early on that it was willing to negotiate a deal with NCS but only on the condition that it would not be a "stalking horse." Thus, it wanted to be certain that a third party could not use its deal with NCS as a floor against which to begin a bidding war. As a result of this negotiating position, a "fiduciary out" was not acceptable to Genesis. The Majority Opinion holds that such a negotiating position, if implemented in the agreement, is invalid per se where there

938 9. Changes in Control: Hostile Acquisitions

is an absolute lock-up. We know of no authority in our jurisprudence supporting this new rule, and we believe it is unwise and unwarranted.

The Majority relies on our decision in *QVC* to assert that the board's fiduciary duties prevent the directors from negotiating a merger agreement without providing an escape provision. Reliance on *QVC* for this proposition, however, confuses our statement of a board's responsibilities when the directors confront a superior transaction and turn away from it to lock up a less valuable deal with the very different situation here, where the board committed itself to the *only* value-enhancing transaction available. The decision in *QVC* is an extension of prior decisions in *Revlon* and *Mills* that prevent a board from ignoring a bidder who is willing to match and exceed the favored bidder's offer. The Majority's application of "continuing fiduciary duties" here is a further extension of this concept and thus permits, wrongly in our view, a court to second-guess the risk and return analysis the board must make to weigh the value of the only viable transaction against the prospect of an offer that has not materialized.

The Majority also mistakenly relies on our decision in *QVC* to support the notion that the NCS board should have retained a fiduciary out to save the minority stockholder from Shaw's and Outcalt's voting agreements. Our reasoning in *QVC*, which recognizes that minority stockholders must rely for protection on the fiduciary duties owed to them by directors, does not create a *special* duty to protect the minority stockholders from the consequences of a controlling stockholder's ultimate decision unless the controlling stockholder stands on both sides of the transaction, which is certainly not the case here. Indeed, the discussion of a minority stockholders' lack of voting power in QVC notes the importance of enhanced scrutiny in change of control transactions precisely because the minority stockholders' interest in the newly merged entity thereafter will hinge on the course set by the controlling stockholder. In *QVC*, Sumner Redstone owned 85% of the voting stock of Viacom, the surviving corporation. Unlike the stockholders who are confronted with a transaction that will relegate them to a minority status in the corporation, the Class A stockholders of NCS purchased stock knowing that the Charter provided Class B stockholders voting control.

PROBLEM 9-11

Ciaran Archer founded SpaceCom, Inc. in 1977. He and members of his immediate family own 53 percent of SpaceCom's common stock, which is traded over-the-counter. SpaceCom has five directors: Ciaran Archer, who serves as Chair, Monica Archer (Ciaran's granddaughter), who is SpaceCom's CEO, Louise Archer (Ciaran's wife), billionaire Bill Door (founder and current CEO of Banana Computer), and billionaire Stega Soros (an internationally renowned industrialist turned philanthropist).

Ciaran has been ill for some time. At the January 2008 SpaceCom board meeting Ciaran expressed his concern that upon his death, and/or the death of his wife and brother (also holders of large blocs of SpaceCom stock), federal estate taxes might force the family to sell significant amounts of SpaceCom stock, thereby losing voting control over the company. He further expressed his concern that if such loss of voting control occurred, SpaceCom would be a likely candidate for a hostile takeover, since its stock was so significantly undervalued by the market, and likely would remain so until the successful launch of its 100-passenger rocket ship, designed to provide two-week vacations in space for wealthy (risk-preferring) individuals.

Soros and Door were equally concerned. In their long tenures as the two outside directors of SpaceCom, they had come to appreciate that the Archer family was uniquely qualified to carry out SpaceCom's long-range plan. Soros and Door agree to serve as a special committee of the board, empowered to consider the problem and recommend a solution. The Special Committee immediately hired a top-notch law firm and investment banking firm to advise the Special Committee. After several weeks' deliberation and consideration of numerous plans, the Special Committee (and both of its advisors) recommended to the full board the adoption of a tenure voting plan to be implemented by an amendment to the SpaceCom certificate of incorporation. The effect of the amendment will be to provide for a form of "tenure voting" whereby holders of SpaceCom's common stock on the record date will receive ten votes per share. Upon sale or other transfer, however, each share would revert to one-vote-per-share status until that share is held by its owner for three years. This "recapitalization" will apply to every stockholder, whether a minority stockholder or part of the majority bloc. The full board adopted this recommendation, and resolved that the suggested amendment to the SpaceCom certificate of incorporation was in the best interest of the corporation. The amendment was then submitted to the shareholders for their approval. The proxy material notes that the Archer family will vote their shares in favor of the amendment, making its passage a certainty.

Sally Williams ("Williams"), an individual minority stockholder, brought suit in the Delaware Court of Chancery against SpaceCom and its directors, challenging the validity of the Amendment and Recapitalization bloc. Williams argues that the Recapitalization will disproportionately and invalidly favor stockholders who are part of the majority bloc and disfavor the minority stockholders. Williams further contends that the sole purpose of the Recapitalization is to entrench SpaceCom management in office and allow the majority bloc to sell a portion of its holdings while retaining control of the company.

You are clerking for the Court of Chancery, and have been asked by the chancellor to advise him on how he should rule on Williams's request for a preliminary injunction. What is your advice?

F. *State Anti-Takeover Statutes*

Delaware G.C.L. §203

From 1968 to 1982, 37 states adopted statutes regulating tender offers. Most followed the pattern of the Williams Act (enacted by Congress in 1968), but tilted the playing field in favor of target companies and their incumbent managers. These statutes often required even more disclosure than did the federal legislation and also required review by a state official or imposed other procedural requirements that could substantially delay a tender offer. In 1982, the Supreme Court's decision in Edgar v. MITE Corp., 457 U.S. 624, striking down the Illinois takeover statute as impermissible state interference with interstate commerce, seemingly sounded the death knell for most of these "first generation" statutes.

After *MITE*, state legislators desirous of slowing the rate of takeovers went back to the drawing board and developed new statutes responding to the concerns raised by the Court in *MITE*. These statutes focused not on bidder conduct but rather on empowering shareholders to approve changes in control or allowing directors to act as centralized agents for the corporation, matters that traditionally had been the concern of state corporation law. These statutes are sometimes referred to as second generation statutes, and one of them was upheld in CTS Corp. v. Dynamics Corp. of Am., 481 U.S. 69 (1987), against claims that it was preempted by the Williams Act and that it was impermissible state interference with interstate commerce. These claims are considered in more detail in Chapter 11.

The success of the Indiana statute in *CTS* spurred even greater state legislation, which can be grouped into the categories set out below. States have not limited themselves to just one statute; indeed, many have stockpiled several. In many cases these statutes were hastily passed in response to a takeover threat to a local corporation. See Romano, The Political Economy of State Takeover Statutes, 73 Va. L. Rev. 111 (1987) (describing the political climate in several states and suggesting that some corporations chose to seek protective state law instead of seeking shareholder approval of charter amendments).

1. Control share acquisition statutes.   The Indiana statute in *CTS* is an example. These statutes provide that when an acquiring shareholder crosses certain thresholds, such as 20 percent, 33 1/3 percent, or 50 percent, the acquired shares will lack voting rights unless voting power is reinstated by a majority vote of the disinterested shareholders. Encouraged by the Supreme Court's approval of the Indiana statute, many states enacted a similar statute. Proponents of control share acquisition statutes analogize the shareholder approval of tender offers to shareholder approval of mergers long required by state law (see Chapter 8 at page 689). However, the effect of these statutes often is to require an acquirer to launch two efforts—the acquisition of the shares and a proxy fight to persuade the remaining shareholders to give a vote to the acquired shares.

2. Business combination/moratorium statutes.   Originally pioneered by New York, moratorium statutes have become popular since the enactment of Delaware G.C.L. §203 and now exist in more than 30 states. Moratorium statutes prohibit business combinations between certain acquiring shareholders and the target corporation for a period of time (three years in Delaware, five years in New York) unless the acquirer gains the approval of Target's pre-acquisition board of directors or acquires a supermajority of the voting stock (85 percent in Delaware). A business combination is usually defined to include not just mergers and similar transactions, but any transaction that confers a financial benefit on the interested shareholder so that, absent compliance with the statute, the acquiror would have to operate the newly acquired corporation at arm's length for the moratorium period specified by the statute. A more specific description of moratorium statutes appears in the excerpt from the *Amanda* opinion following this discussion.

3. Supermajority/fair price statutes. These operate similarly to the moratorium statutes in that they condition completion of a second-step merger following a tender offer on the merger's receiving a supermajority vote or the remaining shareholders' receiving a statutorily defined fair price, often defined in a way that would provide remaining shareholders more than what had been initially offered in the tender offer.

4. Appraisal statutes. A few states provide that a tender offer triggers the right of any remaining shareholders to seek appraisal of their shares, but the definition of fair price is more like the fair price statutes than the merger appraisal statutes discussed in Chapter 8. Such statutes in effect prevent partial bids, a result that is also mandated by takeover rules in the United Kingdom.

5. Consideration of other constituencies. Recent statutes in more than half the states specifically authorize boards of directors to consider constituencies beyond shareholders in responding to tender offers. These other constituencies include bondholders, employees, neighbors, and the community. Such statutes seem designed to give directors substantial room to maneuver in response to an unwanted suitor, consistent with the approach of the Delaware court in Paramount Communications v. Time, Inc., supra. A 1990 Pennsylvania statute extends these statutes by stating that "directors shall not be required . . . to regard any corporate interest or the interest of any particular group affected by such action as a dominant or controlling interest or factor." Pennsylvania Stat. Ann. tit. 15, §1715(b) (Purdon). This direct affront to the primacy of director duty to shareholders has provoked substantial criticism of the Pennsylvania law. Critics argue that this break in accountability to shareholders leaves managers without sufficient constraint, absent the threat of being replaced at the next election. Proponents see the law as a way to change director focus on short-term share price maximization, a perception often linked with perceived social and economic injury to non-shareholder constituencies from takeovers.

6. Disgorgement. A 1990 Pennsylvania statute permits a target company to recover the profits made by an unwanted suitor on Target stock acquired within 24 months before or 18 months after the unwanted suitor becomes a controlling person or group. Pennsylvania Stat. Ann. tit. 15, §2575 (Purdon). The definition of controlling person or group is broadly defined to include (1) those acquiring, offering to acquire, or publicly disclosing or causing to be disclosed, directly or indirectly, an intent to acquire voting power over at least 20 percent of the votes that all shareholders would be entitled to cast in an election of directors; and (2) those who directly or indirectly publicly disclose or cause to be disclosed that they may seek to acquire control through any means. Pennsylvania Stat. Ann. tit. 15, §2573 (Purdon).

7. Severance compensation. Pennsylvania legislation provides for one-time lump sum severance payments to employees terminated within 24 months of a control share approval. The statute also protects labor contracts made with acquired companies. Pennsylvania Stat. Ann. tit. 15, §§2582, 2587 (Purdon). The severance payment statutes extend to a larger group of employees the benefit of "golden parachute" agreements that boards frequently give key management employees to protect them against loss of compensation after a takeover.

As you read the following case, consider what legislative judgments underlie the statutory provision at issue. Can you identify which constituencies the legislature is attempting to protect?

Amanda Acquisition Corp. v. Universal Foods Corp.
United States Court of Appeals, Seventh Circuit, 1989
877 F.2d 496, cert. denied 493 U.S. 955 (1989)

EASTERBROOK, CIRCUIT JUDGE: . . .

In mid-November 1988 Universal's stock was trading for about $25 per share. On December 1 Amanda commenced a tender offer at $30.50, to be effective if at least 75% of the stock should be tendered.[1] This all-cash, all-shares offer has been increased by stages to $38.00. Amanda's financing is contingent on a prompt merger with Universal if the offer succeeds, so the offer is conditional on a judicial declaration that [Wisconsin's moratorium] law is invalid. (It is also conditional on Universal's redemption of poison pill stock. For reasons that we discuss below, it is unnecessary to discuss the subject in detail.)

No firm incorporated in Wisconsin and having its headquarters, substantial operations, or 10% of its shares or shareholders there may "engage in a business combination with an interested stockholder . . . for 3 years after the interested stockholder's stock acquisition date unless the board of directors of the [Wisconsin] corporation has approved, before the interested stockholder's stock acquisition date, that business combination or the purchase of stock," Wis. Stat. §180.726(2). An "interested stockholder" is one owning 10% of the voting stock, directly or through associates (anyone acting in concert with it), §180.726(1)(e). A "business combination" is a merger with the bidder or any of its affiliates, sale of more than 5% of the assets to bidder or affiliate, liquidation of the target, or a transaction by which the target guarantees the bidder's or affiliates' debts or passes tax benefits to the bidder or affiliate, §180.726(1)(e). The law, in other words, provides for almost hermetic separation of bidder and target for three years after the bidder obtains 10% of the stock—unless the target's board consented before then. No matter how popular the offer, the ban applies: obtaining 85% (even 100%) of the stock held by non-management shareholders won't allow the bidder to engage in a business combination, as it would under Delaware law. Wisconsin firms cannot opt out of the law, as may corporations subject to almost all other state takeover statutes. In Wisconsin it is management's approval in advance, or wait three years. Even when the time is up, the bidder needs the approval of a majority of the remaining investors, without any provision disqualifying shares still held by

---

1. Wisconsin has, in addition to §180.726, a statute modeled on Indiana's, providing that an acquiring firm's shares lose their votes, which may be restored under specified circumstances. Wis. Stat. §180.25(9). That law accounts for the 75% condition, but it is not pertinent to the questions we resolve.

the managers who resisted the transaction, §180.726(3)(b).[3] The district court found that this statute "effectively eliminates hostile leveraged buyouts." As a practical matter, Wisconsin prohibits any offer contingent on a merger between bidder and target, a condition attached to about 90% of contemporary tender offers. . . .

If our views of the wisdom of state law mattered, Wisconsin's takeover statute would not survive. Like our colleagues who decided *MITE* and *CTS*, we believe that anti-takeover legislation injures shareholders.[5] *MITE*, 633 F.2d at 496-498 and 457 U.S. at 643-644; *CTS*, 794 F.2d at 253-255. Managers frequently realize gains for investors via voluntary combinations (mergers). If gains are to be had, but managers balk, tender offers are investors' way to go over managers' heads. If managers are not maximizing the firm's value—perhaps because they have missed the possibility of a synergistic combination, perhaps because they are clinging to divisions that could be better run in other hands, perhaps because they are just not the best persons for the job—a bidder that believes it can realize more of the firm's value will make investors a higher offer. . . .

Although a takeover-*proof* firm leaves investors at the mercy of incumbent managers (who may be mistaken about the wisdom of their business plan even when they act in the best of faith), a takeover-*resistant* firm may be able to assist its investors. An auction may run up the price, and delay may be essential to an auction. Auctions transfer money from bidders to targets, and diversified investors would not gain from them (their left pocket loses what the right pocket gains); diversified investors would lose from auctions if the lower returns to bidders discourage future bids. But from targets' perspectives, once a bid is on the table an auction may be the best strategy. The full effects of auctions are hard to unravel, sparking scholarly debate. Devices giving managers some ability to orchestrate investors' responses, in order to avoid panic tenders in response to front-end-loaded offers, also could be beneficial, as the Supreme Court emphasized in *CTS*, 481 U.S. at 92-93. ("Could be" is an important qualifier; even from a perspective limited to targets' shareholders given a bid on the table, it is important to know whether managers use this power to augment bids or to stifle them, and whether courts can tell the two apart.)

---

3. Acquirors can avoid this requirement by buying out the remaining shareholders at a price defined by §180.726(3)(c), but this is not a practical option.

5. Because both the district court and the parties—like the Williams Act—examine tender offers from the perspective of equity investors, we employ the same approach. States could choose to protect "constituencies" other than stockholders. Creditors, managers, and workers invest human rather than financial capital. But the limitation of our inquiry to equity investors does not affect the analysis, because no evidence of which we are aware suggests that bidders confiscate workers' and other participants' investments to any greater degree than do incumbents—who may (and frequently do) close or move plants to follow the prospect of profit. Joseph A. Grundfest, a Commissioner of the SEC, showed in Job Loss and Takeovers, address to University of Toledo College of Law, Mar. 11, 1988, that acquisitions have no logical (or demonstrable) effect on employment. See also Brown & Medoff, The Impact of Firm Acquisitions on Labor, in Corporate Takeovers: Causes and Consequences 9 (A. Auerbach ed. 1988); Roberta Romano, The Future of Hostile Takeovers: Legislation and Public Opinion, 57 U. Cin. L. Rev. 457 (1988); C. Steven Bradford, Protecting Shareholders from Themselves? A Policy and Constitutional Review of a State Takeover Statute, 67 Neb. L. Rev. 459, 529-534 (1988).

State anti-takeover laws do not serve these ends well, however. Investors who prefer to give managers the discretion to orchestrate responses to bids may do so through "fair-price" clauses in the articles of incorporation and other consensual devices. Other firms may choose different strategies. A law such as Wisconsin's does not add options to firms that would like to give more discretion to their managers; instead it destroys the possibility of divergent choices. Wisconsin's law applies even when the investors prefer to leave their managers under the gun, to allow the market full sway. Karpoff and Malatesta found that state anti-takeover laws have little or no effect on the price of shares if the firm already has poison pills (or related devices) in place, but strongly negative effects on price when firms have no such contractual devices. To put this differently, state laws have bite only when investors, given the choice, would deny managers the power to interfere with tender offers (maybe already *have* denied managers that power). See also Roberta Romano, The Political Economy of Takeover Statutes, 73 Va. L. Rev. 111, 128-131 (1987). . . .

[The court then ruled that "skepticism about the wisdom of a state's law does not lead to the conclusion that the law is beyond the state's power." See the *Amanda* excerpt and the Notes that follow in Chapter 11, page 1093, for a discussion of the federalism aspects of this question.]

NOTES AND QUESTIONS

1. Internal corporate defensive tactics—poison pills to block shareholder selling and staggered boards to block shareholder voting—muted the impact of state anti-takeover provisions for much of the past 20 years. Put simply, planners on the defense side obtained such sufficient protection from poison pills and staggered boards that they didn't need to aggressively pursue use of these state statutes. As poison pills and staggered boards have receded in recent years in the face of pressure from activist shareholders, the potential usefulness of these statutes has increased, requiring understanding as to how they might be used and how a court would approach a challenge to their use. These statutes operate similarly to the other defensive tactics already studied. They raise the costs to the bidder (for example, in the fair price, disgorgement, or severance pay statutes) or they narrow the space for shareholders to overcome a director decision not to pursue a takeover (by requiring such a high vote of shareholders that a minority can exercise a veto of the majority shareholder action).

2. Under §203(a)(1) if the directors approve of the transaction, the moratorium does not apply. Do directors have a fiduciary duty to remove this barrier to shareholder voting in the way that at times there has seemed to be a duty to redeem the poison pill barrier to shareholder selling? A 1988 Chancery Court decision denied this "novel request" as it would "usurp the managerial powers of the Board by forcing it to approve a Nomad offer which the Board has found to be inadequate." Nomad Acquisition Corp. v. Damon Corp., 1988 WL 383667 at *829. Reflecting that reasoning, a 2009 paper concludes that "it would seem unusual and unprecedented for a Delaware court to rule that a board's fiduciary duty prevented it from doing something that the Delaware legislature had explicitly authorized." Subramanian, Herscovici & Barbetta,

Is Delaware Antitakeover Statute Unconstitutional? Evidence from 1988-2008 (October 2009). In contrast, the law firm that popularized the poison pill has asserted, "It is clear that a board's decision whether to not to waive Section 203 is subject to fiduciary duty. In any situation where the fiduciary duties might compel a board to redeem a rights plan they would also likely compel a board to waive Section 203's waiting period." Wachtell, Lipton, Rosen & Katz Memorandum to Clients, Flawed Academic Challenge to Constitutionality of Delaware's Antitakeover Statute (September 29, 2009).

10 *Disclosure and Corporate Governance*

A. Introduction: Disclosure's Distinctive Role

Most of what you have studied so far in this book relates to corporate governance, the relative allocation of power within the corporate entity among shareholders, directors, and officers. By now the core of that allocation should be clear to you. Under state corporate law, all corporate power is exercised by or under the direction of the board, unless otherwise provided in the articles. That power, in turn, is balanced by several countervailing factors that we have studied: directors' fiduciary duties subject to after-the-fact judicial enforcement; shareholder voting; and the constraints from various markets, contracting, and other private ordering. Our focus here is how disclosure works as part of this menu of constraints.

For corporate governance, disclosure is primarily a methodology of federal law, derived from the federal legislation passed under President Franklin Roosevelt's New Deal in the midst of the Great Depression. For our purposes it is important to note what disclosure is not. In the midst of the financial calamity that followed the stock market crash of 1929, Congress chose not to pass a federal incorporation statute that specified the relative rights of shareholders and directors different from what was found at state law. Even though there was real concern that managers in many publicly held corporations were avoiding effective control by passive shareholders, Congress chose to focus on securities exchanges and to make more effective the shareholder role in some settings, such as when proxies are solicited.

Disclosure is the key methodology used in federal laws relating to corporate transactions. Professor Louis Loss described the recurrent theme in the federal securities statutes as "disclosure, again disclosure and still more disclosure." L. Loss and J. Seligman, Securities Regulation 27 (3d ed. 1989). The Securities Act of 1933 requires substantial disclosure before the initial issuance of securities, unless the transaction is exempt (a topic discussed in more detail in Chapter 3). The Securities Exchange Act of 1934 requires disclosure in quarterly and annual reports (§13); proxy solicitation (§14(a)); tender offers (§14(d)); when someone acquires more than 5 percent of a company's stock (§13(d) & (e)); or as to insider trading (§16 and Rule 10b-5).

Given its historical origins in an act referring to securities exchanges, these federal regulations are often framed as protecting the securities markets. Consider what effect disclosure will have on markets. Will markets or private ordering among market participants provide sufficient incentives for disclosure if the government does not? Note that, unlike most of state corporations law, federal securities law is mandatory; parties cannot choose an alternative rule. This mandatory nature of federal securities law is the focus of Part B in this chapter.

The emphasis and structure of the securities acts necessarily reflect their origins in the years after the great stock market crash of 1929, but current debate over the role of those statutes also reflects subsequent learning about markets, particularly the efficient capital market hypothesis discussed in Chapter 3 (see page 220). The weak, semi-strong, and strong versions of that hypothesis make corresponding claims about the ability of the market to reflect available information and the inability to develop a trading strategy to beat the market. While there is disagreement about how the hypothesis works in its strong form, there is widespread acceptance of the less strong versions of the hypothesis, which provide part of the foundation for the current debate over disclosure.

Theories supporting mandatory disclosure emphasize the law's ability to reduce the costs of trading. Absent mandatory disclosure, there may be a lack of incentives to produce information if securities information has the characteristics of a "public good" for which the person who incurs the costs of seeking or producing information cannot block the use of the information by others who do not contribute to the costs. At the same time that too little information is being produced, the absence of mandatory disclosure means there is the potential for waste as rival firms incur expenses to produce duplicative data banks. See Coffee, Market Failure and the Economic Case for a Mandatory Disclosure System, 70 Va. L. Rev. 717 (1984). Relying only on voluntary disclosure might lead to higher underwriting costs, excessive insider salaries and perquisites, and, generally, less public confidence in the securities markets. See Seligman, The Historical Need for a Mandatory Corporate Disclosure System, 9 J. Corp. L. 1 (1983).

Critics of the mandatory disclosure system emphasize the ability of markets and private ordering to protect investors. See, e.g., Stigler, Public Regulation of the Securities Markets, 37 J. Bus. 117 (1964); Benston, Required Disclosure and the Stock Market: An Evaluation of the Securities Exchange Act of 1934, 1973 Am. Econ. Rev. 132. Alternatively, securities regulation can be placed in a public choice model in which different interest groups seek to use the regulatory process for competitive advantage. Those who benefit from extensive disclosure because of preexisting investment or the ability to spread these costs over a larger base require rivals to meet the same standards and prevent competition by those offering differentiated products. See Easterbrook and Fischel, Mandatory Disclosure and the Protection of Investors, 70 Va. L. Rev. 669 (1984).

Parts C and D of this chapter present federal disclosure directed toward shareholder decisions—for example, their decisions to vote, sell, or sue that we have discussed in earlier chapters. What shareholders vote on is, of course, one of the key building blocks of state corporate law. As described in Part C, improving the shareholder voting process became one of the initial points of focus for the federal law. Part D focuses on the evolution of the implied private right of action under Rule 10b-5, which has become the dominant federal mechanism for protecting shareholders who buy and sell securities.

The federal statutes and rules are the principal vehicles requiring disclosure for publicly held corporations, but they are not the only sources of required disclosure. Stock exchanges have their own requirements, as seen in the discussion of confidential merger negotiations in Basic, Inc. v. Levinson in Part D of this chapter. State law, too, relies on disclosure. The statutory provisions, such as those found in Chapter 16 of the Model Business Corporation Act, are not that dramatic, but some states, such as California, have more extensive disclosure provisions. In addition, disclosure is an important part of fiduciary duty. Nondisclosure where the court finds a duty to speak is a violation of fiduciary duty; disclosure to an independent party capable of acting for the corporation can limit judicial review of claims alleging breach of fiduciary duty. See, e.g., Weinberger v. UOP, Inc. in Chapter 8 at page 728 and the fiduciary duty cases in Parts B and D of Chapter 4.

The federal law presented here has a strong disclosure component, but that is by no means its only focus. Parts of the federal securities laws not covered in this book provide substantive regulation of the securities market and the market professionals who trade in those markets. The securities provisions whose disclosure elements are emphasized in this presentation also have some substantive effects. For example, Rule 14a-8 (discussed in Chapter 3 at page 234) is ostensibly disclosure oriented, but it shapes the substantive role of shareholders vis-à-vis the directors. Sections of the Williams Act (discussed in Chapter 11) regulate the conduct of a tender offer as well as disclosure requirements. Concerns about the efficiency of markets, exacerbated by the financial meltdown of 2008, have led to increased substance regulation, such as shareholder access and executive compensation discussed in Chapter 3.

In addition to disclosure, a recurring theme in this chapter is the relationship of federal law to state law and the extent to which federal law should supplant existing state law rules. The initial focus of the 1933 Act on disclosure reflected a victory for arguments favoring a less intrusive federal role. The 1934 Act's use of proxy disclosure as a response to the ineffective role of shareholders in American corporations set the stage for a continuing struggle over the breadth of the federal role as subsequent courts and regulators have sometimes focused more on the ineffectiveness of the corporation's state-provided governance structure than on the disclosure mechanism for responding to those concerns. However, as we saw in Chapter 3 (see pages 232-234), in the years since the first enactment of the federal securities laws, the line between market regulation and corporate governance has become much more fuzzy. Not only has disclosure expanded dramatically, but also much of this additional disclosure relates to how a business is being managed; prominent examples of this new intrusiveness into the substantive regulation of corporate governance formerly left to the state are found in or required by the Sarbanes-Oxley Act of 2002 and Dodd-Frank in 2010.

In addition to changing concerns about federalism, you will also see expressed in this chapter differing views on the costs and benefits of representative litigation. The rights discussed in Parts C and D are usually brought as class actions, which means that, like derivative suits discussed in Chapter 4, one representative is seeking to represent an entire class, raising a concern that the attorney may have more to gain than the plaintiff and leading to the possibility of nuisance suits. The expansion of class actions, also discussed in Parts C and D of this chapter, has meant that federal class action disclosure suits have much broader effects than before and act as substitutes to state fiduciary duty suits regulating director conduct. This, too, constitutes an enhancement of the federal supervision of corporate governance.

B.   Mandatory Disclosure

Mandatory disclosure has increased dramatically, both in the information required and the events that trigger the obligation. The initial context that triggered congressional concern in 1933 was when an issuer seeks to persuade an investor to buy stock, as in an IPO, included in Chapter 3 of this book. A year later Congress addressed another shareholder decision: when shareholders are solicited by management to give their proxy in an action for which state law requires shareholder approval. In addition, the 1934 Act required certain periodic reports, either annually or quarterly (such as the 10-K disclosure in the case which follows). Initially, the companies subject to those obligations were limited to those traded on the national stock exchanges (e.g., the New York Stock Exchange), the amount of disclosure was much less than today, and the liability was much less severe than for the 1933 Act.

These disclosure obligations now apply to companies with shares traded on a national stock exchange or over a minimum size.[1] The expansion in the amount of disclosure is visible from a casual perusal of Regulation S-K, the SEC's integrated disclosure package that includes more than 60 items and takes up more than 100 pages of the federal rule book. For example, under Item 303 of Regulation S-K (a disclosure entitled "Management's Discussion and Analysis"), a company's annual report must include discussion of the registrant's financial condition, changes in those conditions, and results of operations. The specific categories of financial information required include explanations of liquidity, capital resources, and operational results. The case below illustrates how the SEC views the role of disclosure.

In the Matter of Informix Corp.
Securities and Exchange Commission Exchange Act Release #34-42326
January 11, 2000
http://www.sec.gov/litigation/admin/34-42326.htm

I.

The Securities and Exchange Commission ("Commission") deems it appropriate to institute public administrative proceedings pursuant to section 8A of the Securities Act of 1933 ("Securities Act") and section 21C of the Securities Exchange Act of 1934 ("Exchange Act") against Informix Corporation ("Respondent" or "Company").

---

1. As of 2012, the threshold is set at $10 million in assets and at least 2,000 shareholders of record or at least 500 "nonaccredited" shareholders of record (i.e., not an institution or not wealthy).

II.

In anticipation of the institution of these administrative proceedings, Respondent has submitted an Offer of Settlement ("Offer"), which the Commission has determined to accept. Solely for the purpose of these proceedings and any other proceedings brought by or on behalf of the Commission, or in which the Commission is a party, and without admitting or denying the findings, except as to the Commission's jurisdiction over it and over the subject matter of the proceedings, which are admitted, Respondent consents to the entry of this Order Instituting Public Administrative Proceedings Pursuant to Section 8A of the Securities Act of 1933 and Section 21C of the Securities Exchange Act of 1934, Making Findings, and Imposing a Cease-and-Desist Order ("Order").

III.   FINDINGS

A. RESPONDENT

Informix Corporation is a multinational database software company with its principal executive offices located in Menlo Park, California. Its common stock is registered pursuant to section 12(g) of the Exchange Act and is traded on NASDAQ. The Company's fiscal year ends on December 31.

B. INTRODUCTION

In November 1997, the Company restated its financial statements for fiscal years 1994 through 1996 and the fiscal quarter ended March 30, 1997. During the period covered by the restatements, former employees of the Company, including salespersons, members of management and others[,] engaged in a variety of fraudulent and other practices that inflated annual and quarterly revenues and earnings in violation of generally accepted accounting principles ("GAAP"). These practices included the following:

(1) backdating license sale agreements;
(2) entering into side agreements granting rights to refunds and other concessions to customers;
(3) recognizing revenue on transactions with reseller customers that were not creditworthy;
(4) recognizing amounts due under software maintenance agreements as software license revenues; and
(5) recognizing revenue on disputed claims against customers.

In numerous instances, revenue from software license purchase commitments by resellers was recognized improperly because the earnings process had not been completed due to the Company's obligations under side agreements to perform all, or substantially all, of the reselling effort. No disclosure of the fraudulent or other improper practices appeared in the Company's filings with the Commission. The filings also omitted or misrepresented information concerning the extent to which revenues were derived from nonmonetary exchanges and the extent to which revenues were derived from transactions with resellers that had not yet resold software licenses to end-users.

During 1997, after the Company filed its 1996 Form 10-K, former members of management, aware of evidence of material accounting irregularities, took actions to prevent the Company from restating its previously issued financial statements. They limited the scope of an internal investigation of 1995 and 1996 transactions with European resellers, concealed a side agreement with an Asian reseller given to obtain rescission of an earlier side agreement, and concealed other side agreements with a European reseller. In late July 1997, a former member of the Company's corporate finance staff learned of certain side agreements and informed the Company's auditors. The Company's new management then determined that its 1996 financial statements would need to be restated. On August 7, 1997, the Company publicly announced the need to restate those financial statements.

In the restatement process, the Company and its auditors identified $114 million of accounting irregularities in 1995 and 1996 involving more than a hundred transactions, mostly with resellers. Because the irregularities relating to reseller purchase commitments were so pervasive, the Company and its auditors determined that all such transactions for the three-year period ended in 1996 should be restated to defer revenue recognition until the resellers resold the licenses to end-users. After making this determination, the Company no longer attempted specifically to identify irregularities involving resellers, although additional irregularities subsequently were discovered. In November 1997, the Company filed restated annual financial statements for fiscal years 1994, 1995, and 1996 and restated quarterly financial statements for each interim quarter of 1996 and the first quarter of 1997. The restatements had a material effect on previously reported annual operating results. . . .

C. FACTS . . .

6. False and Misleading Books, Records, and Accounts and Insufficient Internal Accounting Controls

As a result of the fraudulent and other improper practices discussed supra at Part III(B) . . . the Company's books, records, and accounts were false and misleading. In addition, the Company failed to maintain a system of internal accounting controls that was sufficient to enable it to prepare financial statements in conformity with GAAP. The lack of sufficient internal accounting controls contributed directly to the fraud and resulted primarily from an organizational structure under which many key finance personnel responsible for revenue recognition reported directly to sales management rather than to senior finance executives. As a result of this organizational structure, finance personnel came under pressure from former sales management to recognize revenue from transactions that did not conform with GAAP, such as backdated transactions, transactions with customers whose creditworthiness had not been investigated, and transactions for future maintenance services that were treated as license transactions.

D. LEGAL CONCLUSIONS

The type of conduct that occurred in this matter strikes at the heart of the financial reporting system established by the federal securities laws. As we have emphasized in the past, "[c]omplete and accurate financial reporting by public companies is of paramount importance to the disclosure system underlying the stability and efficient operation of our capital markets. Investors need reliable financial information when making investment decisions." To achieve the objective of providing investors with complete and accurate financial information, it is essential that public companies maintain accurate books, records, and accounts and establish and maintain internal controls that serve to prevent and to detect fraudulent and other improper conduct. In addition, management, through its own conduct and through the policies and practices that it prescribes for others, must create an environment in which only the highest standards of integrity will be tolerated. Too often, accounting and disclosure rules are disregarded in order that revenues and earnings can be inflated improperly to meet earnings projections of analysts or others in the financial community or to achieve some other objective. The financial information that an issuer discloses simply should present completely and accurately the issuer's financial condition for the relevant reporting period. Without this information, investors are deprived of the opportunity to make informed investment decisions.

In this matter, through former members of management and others, the Company engaged in an accounting fraud that lasted more than two years and resulted in the preparation of numerous materially false and misleading financial statements and other disclosures that were included in filings with the Commission and disseminated to investors. As this fraud was being uncovered, certain of these individuals engaged in further fraudulent conduct that delayed the restatements of the Company's financial statements. In addition, as a result of the conduct of former management and others, the Company failed to maintain books, records, and accounts which, in reasonable detail, accurately and fairly reflected its transactions and dispositions of assets and failed to maintain a system of internal accounting controls sufficient to permit the preparation of financial statements in conformity with GAAP.

Based on the foregoing, the commission concludes that the Company violated section 17(a) of the Securities Act, sections 10(b), 13(a), and 13(b) of the Exchange Act, and Exchange Act rules 10b-5, 12b-20, 13a-1, 13a-13, and 13b2-1.

IV. ORDER

IT IS HEREBY ORDERED that, pursuant to section 8A of Securities Act and section 21C of the Exchange Act, Informix Corporation cease and desist from committing or causing any violation, and any future violation, of section 17(a) of the Securities Act, sections 10(b), 13(a), and 13(b) of the Exchange Act, and Exchange Act rules 10b-5, 12b-20, 13a-1, 13a-13, and 13b2-1; and

IT IS FURTHER ORDERED that Informix Corporation comply with its undertakings to do the following: (A) upon reasonable request by the Commission or its staff, and on reasonable notice and without service of a subpoena, it will provide documents or other information; (B) at the request of the Commission or its staff, it will appear and testify at any deposition, hearing, or trial in an action or administrative proceeding arising out of the matters described in the Order.

NOTES AND QUESTIONS

1. Disclosure, as discussed later in the chapter, provides a basis for shareholder lawsuits. This case illustrates an alternative source of enforcement, the professional staff of the Securities and Exchange Commission. But disclosure has an even broader set of users. When additional disclosure is required it permits directors to more accurately monitor officers, it permits auditors to more accurately perform their watchdog function, it permits self-regulatory organizations like the New York Stock Exchange to better implement its own listing requirements, and it permits civil or criminal enforcement where appropriate.

2. Another effect of the regulatory response in the wake of the Enron scandals was to give additional impetus to the move to "real time" disclosure. The periodic reports required by Section 13 of the 1934 Act must be made annually (on Form 10-K) or quarterly (on Form 10-Q). Disclosure in between quarterly reports is made as a "current report" on Form 8-K. Until Enron and Sarbanes-Oxley, the triggers for such disclosure were specific and relatively unusual (e.g., change in control or the company; filing for bankruptcy). After 2002, the number of items requiring 8-K disclosure tripled and covers more matters that relate to the ongoing business of the company. In addition, the time for filing an 8-K was shortened, with filing required in two days in many instances.

3. In the run-up to the enactment of Sarbanes-Oxley in 2002, then Federal Reserve Board chair Alan Greenspan noted that when "an infectious greed seemed to grip our business community, our historical guardians of financial information were overwhelmed." NY Times, July 17, 2002, at C8, col. 6. Sarbanes-Oxley responded to this perceived weakness by federalizing the regulation of auditors: the act created the Public Company Accounting Oversight Board (PCAOB) and mandated a complete overhaul of the auditing function. Key mandates now require audit partner rotation and restrict the ability of auditing firms to also provide consulting services. Sarbanes-Oxley and the PCAOB also increased the federal role in ensuring that public companies have adequate financial accounting and reporting systems in place.

The term "internal control over financial reporting" refers to a company's system of checks and processes designed to protect corporate assets, keep accurate records of those assets as well as its financial transactions and events, and prepare accurate periodic financial statements. Investors can have much more confidence in the reliability of a company's financial statements if management demonstrates that it maintains adequate internal control over bookkeeping, the sufficiency of books and records for the preparation of accurate financial statements, adherence to rules about the use of company assets, and the safeguarding of company assets. Indeed, research shows that disclosures about the reliability of internal control have a significant effect on companies' cost of capital.

Companies have been required to have internal control over their accounting since Congress enacted the Foreign Corrupt Practices Act in 1977. There is no doubt, however, that the Sarbanes-Oxley Act's requirement for annual assessments, and auditor attestations to those assessments, took corporate responsibilities for internal control over financial reporting to an entirely different level.

Mark W. Olson, "Testimony Concerning the Sarbanes-Oxley Act of 2002," U.S. Senate Committee on Small Business and Entrepreneurship (April 18, 2007).

4. Chairman Greenspan, in the opinion piece described above, put the fulcrum of corporate governance within the domain of the CEO, not the directors: "the state of corporate governance to a very large extent reflects the character of the CEO." NY Times, July 17, 2002, at C8, col. 6. Yet, as seen in Chapter 4, state corporate codes actually have very little to say about officer behavior, leaving it to directors to specify as they might wish. Federal law has stepped into that void. Much of modern disclosure relates to matters that reflect the performance of officers within the corporate governance structure, more so than directors. Sarbanes-Oxley §302 requires the chief executive officer and the chief financial officer personally to certify the company's quarterly results. Another section requires those two officers to disgorge certain bonuses and trading profits after accounting restatements.

5. How would the alleged misconduct in *Informix* be addressed under state law discussed in Chapter 4? Is it conduct that would be governed by the duty of care? If so, whose care? Directors? Officers? Other employees? Is the federal standard consistent with the business judgment rule application of state law? Arguably, federal law is filling some of the space left vacant in the care area by the business judgment rule and exculpation provisions discussed in Chapter 4. For example, §404 of Sarbanes-Oxley requires management to state that it is responsible for establishing and maintaining an adequate internal control structure and procedures for financial reporting and for assessing the effectiveness of the internal control structure. Other provisions illustrate the blurred lines between substance and disclosures. Section 406 of Sarbanes-Oxley, for example, requires a company to disclose "whether or not, and if not, the reasons therefore, such an issuer has adopted a code of ethics for senior financial officers." Is this effectively the same as a governance requirement that a corporation have a code of ethics or an effective internal control structure?

6. What liability will follow from this broadened federal role? Does the internal control structure mandate discussed in notes 3, 4, and 5 create a federal law counterpart to *Caremark* (page 361)? Could a state law complaint alleging a *Caremark* violation cite violations of the federal standard as giving rise to a state law cause of action? The *Informix* case itself illustrates the public side of securities enforcement in contrast to the private causes of action that appear in much of the remainder of this chapter. Sarbanes-Oxley gave the government broader civil and criminal penalties, including the ability to ban a person from serving as a director or officer of a public company.

PROBLEM 10-1

(a) Hitech Corporation has been developing a new health care procedure that has potential for wide use in addressing one of the major debilitating diseases present in this country. It has been beta testing the product and plans to go into production over the next six months with estimated sales that will equal about 40 percent of the company's current revenue. The company has just received informal word from the FDA that the procedure will not receive agency clearance, a setback that will delay the product's introduction for at least a year and possibly indefinitely. Must the company make immediate disclosure?

(b) Hitech's chief financial officer knows that the company's ability to meet the earnings estimates of financial analysts has been cited by the company's CEO and those outside the company as a benchmark of the company's performance. During the last four quarters, as it has become more and more difficult to deliver positive numbers, the CFO has engaged in a series of swap transactions at the end of the quarter with a company he has set up, which has the effect of transferring assets away from the company and providing it revenue that it can book as income for the quarter. This behavior is unknown to any of the directors. If the CFO's misconduct is later discovered, what legal problems might the company have?

C.   Disclosure Related to Shareholder Voting

1.   Coverage of §14(a)

Securities Exchange Act of 1934 §14(a)
SEC Rules 14a-1 through 14a-15 and Schedule 14A

Section 14(a) of the 1934 Act authorizes the Securities and Exchange Commission to regulate the process by which managers or others seek the proxies of shareholders. A frequent setting for proxy litigation is solicitation of shareholders to approve a merger pursuant to the requirements discussed in Chapter 8 at page 689. In large corporations where attendance of a significant number of shareholders at a shareholders' meeting is unlikely, management usually solicits proxies to gain the necessary quorum and shareholder votes required for approval under state law. The federal proxy rules seek to protect shareholders against unfair treatment in connection with voting, mostly by requiring disclosure but also by substantive regulation.

The federal purposes are achieved in several ways:

Required disclosure.   SEC Rule 14a-3 and Schedule 14A have extensive disclosure requirements as to matters on which shareholders will vote. The SEC has extended the disclosure required by the proxy provisions to include significant disclosure in the form of a company's annual report when management solicits proxies in connection with the company's annual meeting. This disclosure required by Rule 14a-3 to some extent has supplanted the other "annual report" on Form 10-K as required by §13 of the 1934 Act.

Procedural rules.   Rule 14a-4 and other rules specify the form of the proxy that may be solicited. (A sample proxy is reprinted in Chapter 3 at page 231.) There are also special regulations in Rule 14a-11 and elsewhere governing contested elections.

Antifraud rules.   The required disclosure is supplemented by a general provision in Rule 14a-9 prohibiting fraud in connection with the solicitation of a proxy. The SEC can bring suit for violations of §14 and a private right of action is available under §18 of the 1934 Act, but most of the judicial decisions for proxy questions arise under the implied private right of action derived from the antifraud provision, Rule 14a-9. The growth of this cause of action is examined later in this chapter.

Shareholder communication. Rule 14a-8 guarantees shareholders certain rights to include matters in the proxy solicitation sent out by management, a right that is attractive because it saves the proponents the cost of a solicitation and lets them avoid the regulation attendant to making their own solicitation. This topic is considered in Chapter 3 at page 234.

That earlier discussion and the material that follows illustrate two issues that recur throughout the chapter: (1) the federal effort to improve the place of shareholders in corporate governance without displacing state law and (2) the continuing desire to make corporations "socially responsible" in responding to issues of concern to society as a whole.

2. Rule 14a-9

Section 14(a) of the Securities Exchange Act of 1934 authorizes the SEC to regulate proxy solicitations "as necessary or appropriate in the public interest or for the protection of investors." Pursuant to this authority, the SEC has supplemented the express disclosure obligations found in Rule 14a-3 with a broad prohibition in Rule 14a-9 against any false or misleading statement of a material fact or any omission necessary to make an included statement not misleading or to correct a statement that has become misleading.

a. Implied Private Cause of Action

Securities Exchange Act of 1934 §§14(a), 27

In J.I. Case Co. v. Borak, the principal case below, the Supreme Court held that an implied private right of action exists under Rule 14a-9 for shareholders who believe they were misled by a federally regulated proxy statement. Since the elements of the private cause of action are not expressly set out as such in the statute or rule, the Court incorporated requirements drawn from the common law. Not surprisingly, courts have viewed Rule 14a-9 essentially as an antifraud provision and turned to the familiar law of common law fraud or the tort of deceit, a process you will see repeated in connection with Rule 10b-5 in Part D of this chapter. The black letter elements of common law fraud or deceit require a plaintiff to show misrepresentation or omission of a material fact made with scienter on which plaintiff relies, suffering damages as a consequence. Note that the first elements are drawn from the text of the rule itself. As you read the cases in the following sections, note the degree to which the interpretation of both the express and implied elements is affected by the court's changing view of the desirability of an implied private cause of action.

In reading J.I. Case Co. v. Borak, keep in mind alternative causes of action that would have been available to plaintiff:

Express federal cause of action. Section 21 of the 1934 Act permits the SEC to bring civil actions for violation of the act and §32 provides for criminal penalties. The 1934 Act provides express causes of action to private parties in §§9, 16, and 18. Section 18 covers false and misleading statements in any "application, report or document filed pursuant to this title or any rule or regulation thereunder." The proxy statement in *Borak* was filed with the Commission, so as to come under §18. The attractiveness of pursuing a cause of action under that section has been limited by courts requiring eyeball reliance on the misleading statement, and by other procedural restrictions, including a short statute of limitations.

State causes of action.   Note that the plaintiff shareholders in *Borak* couple their federal claims with a claim for relief based on state law of fiduciary duty. The basis for this relief is the substantive law presented in Chapters 4 and 8. Plaintiff sought to have this count heard in federal court based on diversity of jurisdiction.

J.I. Case Co. v. Borak presents two federalism questions. The more obvious one is the extent to which there should be a federal cause of action for corporate behavior already regulated by state law, here management pursuing a merger transaction in a context where breach of fiduciary duty was alleged. The less visible federalism question is the applicability in federal courts of state laws requiring plaintiffs in a derivative suit to post a bond or other security for the corporation's expenses in litigating the suit. These security for expenses statutes were an earlier manifestation of the continuing debate over the extent to which shareholders or directors can speak for the corporation. See Chapter 4. Security statutes were enacted to discourage frivolous suits but were seen by others as discouraging legitimate suits in which shareholders sought to constrain improper management conduct.

In this litigation, the courts had to decide whether state security for expense statutes would apply to claims brought under federal law. The district court held that the plaintiff was required to post security in seeking any relief other than prospective relief. The Seventh Circuit held that the plaintiff's claim was direct as well as derivative and therefore not subject to the security for expense statute, which only applied to derivative suits. The court also held that the federal claim provided relief beyond the prospective or declaratory relief found by the district court, and that state statutes, such as securities for expenses statutes, did not apply to these federal claims.

Be alert to both of these federalism issues as you read this case.

J.I. Case Co. v. Borak
United States Supreme Court, 1964
377 U.S. 426

Mr. JUSTICE CLARK delivered the opinion of the Court.

This is a civil action brought by respondent, a stockholder of petitioner J.I. Case Company, charging deprivation of the pre-emptive rights of respondent and other shareholders by reason of a merger between Case and the American Tractor Corporation. It is alleged that the merger was effected through the circulation of a false and misleading proxy statement by those proposing the merger. The complaint was in two counts, the first based on diversity and claiming a breach of the directors' fiduciary duty to the stockholders. The second count alleged a violation of §14(a) of the Securities Exchange Act of 1934 with reference to the proxy solicitation material. . . . We consider only the question of whether §27 of the Act authorizes a federal cause of action for rescission or damages to a corporate stockholder with respect to a consummated merger which was authorized pursuant to the use of a proxy statement alleged to contain false and misleading statements violative of §14(a) of the Act. . . .

I

Respondent, the owner of 2,000 shares of common stock of Case acquired prior to the merger, brought this suit based on diversity jurisdiction seeking to enjoin a proposed merger between Case and the American Tractor Corporation (ATC) on various grounds, including breach of the fiduciary duties of the Case directors, self-dealing among the management of Case and ATC and misrepresentations contained in the material circulated to obtain proxies. The injunction was denied and the merger was thereafter consummated. Subsequently successive amended complaints were filed and the case was heard on the aforesaid two-count complaint. The claims pertinent to the asserted violation of the Securities Exchange Act were predicated on diversity jurisdiction as well as on §27 of the Act. They alleged: that petitioners, or their predecessors, solicited or permitted their names to be used in the solicitation of proxies of Case stockholders for use at a special stockholders' meeting at which the proposed merger with ATC was to be voted upon; that the proxy solicitation material so circulated was false and misleading in violation of §14(a) of the Act and Rule 14a-9 which the Commission had promulgated thereunder; that the merger was approved at the meeting by a small margin of votes and was thereafter consummated; that the merger would not have been approved but for the false and misleading statements in the proxy solicitation material; and that Case stockholders were damaged thereby. The respondent sought judgment holding the merger void and damages for himself and all other stockholders similarly situated, as well as such further relief "as equity shall require." The District Court ruled that the Wisconsin security for expenses statute did not apply to Count 2 since it arose under federal law. However, the court found that its jurisdiction was limited to declaratory relief in a private, as opposed to a government, suit alleging violation of §14(a) of the Act. Since the additional equitable relief and damages prayed for by the respondent would, therefore, be available only under state law, it ruled those claims subject to the security for expenses statute. After setting the amount of security at $75,000 and upon the representation of counsel that the security would not be posted, the court dismissed the complaint, save that portion of Count 2 seeking a declaration that the proxy solicitation material was false and misleading and that the proxies and, hence, the merger were void.

II

It appears clear that private parties have a right under §27 to bring suit for violation of §14(a) of the Act. Indeed, this section specifically grants the appropriate District Courts jurisdiction over "all suits in equity and actions at law brought to enforce any liability or duty created" under the Act. The petitioners make no concessions, however, emphasizing that Congress made no specific reference to a private right of action in §14(a); that, in any event, the right would not extend to derivative suits and should be limited to prospective relief only. In addition, some of the petitioners argue that the merger can be dissolved only if it was fraudulent or non-beneficial, issues upon which the proxy material would not bear. But the causal relationship of the proxy material and the merger are questions of fact to be resolved at trial, not here. We therefore do not discuss this point further.

III

While the respondent contends that his Count 2 claim is not a derivative one, we need not embrace that view, for we believe that a right of action exists as to both derivative and direct causes.

The purpose of §14(a) is to prevent management or others from obtaining authorization for corporate action by means of deceptive or inadequate disclosure in proxy solicitation. The section stemmed from the congressional belief that "[fair] corporate suffrage is an important right that should attach to every equity security bought on a public exchange." H.R. Rep. No. 1383, 73d Cong., 2d Sess., 13. It was intended to "control the conditions under which proxies may be solicited with a view to preventing the recurrence of abuses which . . . [had] frustrated the free exercise of the voting rights of stockholders." Id., at 14. "Too often proxies are solicited without explanation to the stockholder of the real nature of the questions for which authority to cast his vote is sought." S. Rep. No. 792, 73d Cong., 2d Sess., 12. These broad remedial purposes are evidenced in the language of the section which makes it "unlawful for any person . . . to solicit or to permit the use of his name to solicit any proxy or consent or authorization in respect of any security . . . registered on any national securities exchange in contravention of such rules and regulations as the Commission may prescribe as necessary or appropriate in the public interest *or for the protection of investors*." (Italics supplied.) While this language makes no specific reference to a private right of action, among its chief purposes is "the protection of investors," which certainly implies the availability of judicial relief where necessary to achieve that result.

The injury which a stockholder suffers from corporate action pursuant to a deceptive proxy solicitation ordinarily flows from the damage done the corporation, rather than from the damage inflicted directly upon the stockholder. The damage suffered results not from the deceit practiced on him alone but rather from the deceit practiced on the stockholders as a group. To hold that derivative actions are not within the sweep of the section would therefore be tantamount to a denial of private relief. Private enforcement of the proxy rules provides a necessary supplement to Commission action. As in antitrust treble damage litigation, the possibility of civil damages or injunctive relief serves as a most effective weapon in the enforcement of the proxy requirements. The Commission advises that it examines over 2,000 proxy statements annually and each of them must necessarily be expedited. Time does not permit an independent examination of the facts set out in the proxy material and this results in the Commission's acceptance of the representations contained therein at their face value, unless contrary to other material on file with it. Indeed, on the allegations of respondent's complaint, the proxy material failed to disclose alleged unlawful market manipulation of the stock of ATC, and this unlawful manipulation would not have been apparent to the Commission until after the merger.

We, therefore, believe that under the circumstances here it is the duty of the courts to be alert to provide such remedies as are necessary to make effective the congressional purpose. As was said in Sola Electric Co. v. Jefferson Electric Co., 317 U.S. 173, 176 (1942):

> When a federal statute condemns an act as unlawful, the extent and nature of the legal consequences of the condemnation, though left by the statute to judicial determination, are nevertheless federal questions, the answers to which are to be derived from the statute and the federal policy which it has adopted.

It is for the federal courts "to adjust their remedies so as to grant the necessary relief" where federally secured rights are invaded. "And it is also well settled that where legal rights have been invaded, and a federal statute provides for a general right to sue for such invasion, federal courts may use any available remedy to make good the wrong done." Bell v. Hood, 327 U.S. 678, 684 (1946). Section 27 grants the District Courts jurisdiction "of all suits in equity and actions at law brought to enforce any liability or duty created by this title. . . ." In passing on almost identical language found in the Securities Act of 1933, the Court found the words entirely sufficient to fashion a remedy to rescind a fraudulent sale, secure restitution and even to enforce the right to restitution against a third party holding assets of the vendor. Deckert v. Independence Shares Corp., 311 U.S. 282 (1940). This significant language was used:

> The power to *enforce* implies the power to make effective the right of recovery afforded by the Act. And the power to make the right of recovery effective implies the power to utilize any of the procedures or actions normally available to the litigant according to the exigencies of the particular case.

At 288 of 311 U.S.

Nor do we find merit in the contention that such remedies are limited to prospective relief. This was the position taken in Dann v. Studebaker-Packard Corp., 288 F.2d 201, where it was held that the "preponderance of questions of state law which would have to be interpreted and applied in order to grant the relief sought . . . is so great that the federal question involved . . . is really negligible in comparison." But we believe that the overriding federal law applicable here would, where the facts required, control the appropriateness of redress despite the provisions of state corporation law, for it "is not uncommon for federal courts to fashion federal law where federal rights are concerned." Textile Workers v. Lincoln Mills, 353 U.S. 448, 457 (1957). In addition, the fact that questions of state law must be decided does not change the character of the right; it remains federal. As Chief Justice Marshall said in Osborn v. Bank of the United States, 9 Wheat. 738 (1824):

> If this were sufficient to withdraw a case from the jurisdiction of the federal Courts, almost every case, although involving the construction of a law, would be withdrawn. . . .

At 819-820 of 9 Wheat.

Moreover, if federal jurisdiction were limited to the granting of declaratory relief, victims of deceptive proxy statements would be obliged to go into state courts for remedial relief. And if the law of the State happened to attach no responsibility to the use of misleading proxy statements, the whole purpose of the section might be frustrated. Furthermore, the hurdles that the victim might face (such as separate suits, as contemplated by Dann v. Studebaker-Packard Corp., supra, security for expenses statutes, bringing in all parties necessary for complete relief, etc.) might well prove insuperable to effective relief.

IV

Our finding that federal courts have the power to grant all necessary remedial relief is not to be construed as any indication of what we believe to be the necessary and appropriate relief in this case. We are concerned here only with a determination that federal jurisdiction for this purpose does exist. Whatever remedy is necessary must await the trial on the merits.

NOTES

1. The Supreme Court's holding in *Borak* that private parties had a private cause of action for violations of Rule 14a-9 broadened the reach of that section and possibly other sections of the Securities Exchange Act of 1934 as well. The question of when a court should imply a private cause of action from a statute has arisen in other areas and other times with varying results. In 1979, in Touche Ross & Co. v. Redington, 442 U.S. 560, 576-578, the Supreme Court, with a substantially different composition than in 1964, refused to imply a private cause of action for a violation of §17 of the 1934 Act in language that discussed the *Borak* decision:

> In *Borak,* the Court found in §14(a) of the 1934 Act an implied cause of action for damages in favor of shareholders for losses resulting from deceptive proxy solicitations in violation of §14(a). [Plaintiffs] emphasize language in *Borak* that discusses the remedial purposes of the 1934 Act and §27 of the Act, which, inter alia, grants to federal district courts the exclusive jurisdiction of violations of the Act and suits to enforce any liability or duty created by the Act or the rules and regulations thereunder. . . . The reliance of [plaintiffs] on §27 is misplaced. Section 27 grants jurisdiction to the federal courts and provides for venue and service of process. It creates no cause of action of its own force and effect; it imposes no liabilities. The source of plaintiffs' rights must be found, if at all, in the substantive provisions of the 1934 Act which they seek to enforce, not in the jurisdictional provision. The Court in *Borak* found a private cause of action implicit in §14(a). We do not now question the actual holding of that case, but we decline to read the opinion so broadly that virtually every provision of the securities Acts gives rise to an implied private cause of action.
>
> The invocation of the "remedial purposes" of the 1934 Act is similarly unavailing. Only last Term, we emphasized that generalized references to the "remedial purposes" of the 1934 Act will not justify reading a provision "more broadly than its language and the statutory scheme reasonably permit." SEC v. Sloan, 436 U.S. 103, 116, (1978). Certainly, the mere fact that §17(a) was designed to provide protection for brokers' customers does not require the implication of a private damages action in their behalf. To the extent our analysis in today's decision differs from that of the Court in *Borak,* it suffices to say that in a series of cases since *Borak* we have adhered to a stricter standard for the implication of private causes of action, and we follow that stricter standard today. The ultimate question is one of congressional intent, not one of whether this Court thinks that it can improve upon the statutory scheme that Congress enacted into law.

2. The proxy provisions provide a cause of action if items relevant to a shareholder decision are not correctly disclosed. Possible federal claims often overlap with state law because a disclosure failing often accompanies unfairness that may be a violation of the fiduciary duty of those who manage and control the enterprise. Shareholders and their lawyers may prefer to argue over disclosure rather than substantive fairness because framing the issue as disclosure federalizes the controversy. As *Borak* illustrates, shareholders with a federal claim avoid procedural limitations like security for expense statutes. But compare a shareholder's inability to avoid restrictive state rules requiring demand on directors. See Kamen v. Kemper Financial Services, Inc., 500 U.S. 90 (1991). A federal claim has other procedural advantages such as nationwide service of process and liberalized venue rules. These federal benefits, though, are really only warm-ups for the main event, determining the degree to which the fraud requirements of the federal securities law cover misconduct by those in control of the corporation.

b. *Misrepresentations or Omissions of a Material Fact*

The Supreme Court defined materiality in TSC Industries, Inc. v. Northway, Inc. The lawsuit arose out of an individual shareholder's challenge to a proxy statement in advance of shareholder approval of a merger. The Court reversed summary judgment in favor of the shareholder, by which the lower court had ruled that certain omissions were material as a matter of law. In February 1969, National Industries acquired 34 percent of TSC's voting securities by purchase from the firm's founding family. Thereafter five National nominees were placed on TSC's ten-person board. In October, the TSC board, with the National nominees abstaining, approved a proposal to sell all of TSC's assets to National and then liquidate TSC, with TSC shareholders to receive preferred stock and warrants from National. Northway claimed that the proxy solicitation leading to the successful shareholder approval of the plan omitted material facts relating to the degree of National's control over TSC and the attractiveness of the terms of the proposal to TSC shareholders.

TSC Industries, Inc. v. Northway, Inc.
United States Supreme Court, 1976
426 U.S. 438

JUSTICE MARSHALL delivered the opinion of the Court. . . .

The question of materiality, it is universally agreed, is an objective one, involving the significance of an omitted or misrepresented fact to a reasonable investor. Variations in the formulation of a general test of materiality occur in the articulation of just how significant a fact must be or, put another way, how certain it must be that the fact would affect a reasonable investor's judgment.

The Court of Appeals in this case concluded that material facts include "all facts which a reasonable shareholder *might* consider important." 512 F.2d, at 330 (emphasis added). This formulation of the test of materiality has been explicitly rejected by at least two courts as setting too low a threshold for the imposition of liability under Rule 14a-9. Gerstle v. Gamble-Skogmo, Inc., 478 F.2d 1281, 1301-1302 (C.A.2 1973); Smallwood v. Pearl Brewing Co., 489 F.2d 579, 603-604 (C.A.5 1974). In these cases, panels of the Second and Fifth Circuits opted for the conventional tort test of materiality—whether a reasonable man *would* attach importance to the fact misrepresented or omitted in determining his course of action. See Restatement (Second) of Torts §538(2)(a) (Tent. Draft No. 10, Apr. 20, 1964). See also American Law Institute, Federal Securities Code §256(a) (Tent. Draft No. 2, 1973). Gerstle v. Gamble-Skogmo, supra, at 1302, also approved the following standard, which had been formulated with reference to statements issued in a contested election: "whether, taking a properly realistic view, there is a substantial likelihood that the misstatement or omission may have led a stockholder to grant a proxy to the solicitor or to withhold one from the other side, whereas in the absence of this he would have taken a contrary course." General Time Corp. v. Talley Industries, Inc., 403 F.2d 159, 162 (C.A.2 1968), cert. denied, 393 U.S. 1026 (1969). . . .

In formulating a standard of materiality under Rule 14a-9, we are guided, of course, by the recognition in *Borak* and [Mills v. Electric Auto-Lite Co., 396 U.S. 375 (1970)] of the Rule's broad remedial purpose. That purpose is not merely to ensure by judicial means that the transaction, when judged by its real terms, is fair and otherwise adequate, but to ensure disclosures by corporate management in order to enable the shareholders to make an informed choice. As an abstract proposition, the most desirable role for a court in a suit of this sort, coming after the consummation of the proposed transaction, would perhaps be to determine whether in fact the proposal would have been favored by the shareholders and consummated in the absence of any misstatement or omission. But as we recognized in *Mills*, such matters are not subject to determination with certainty. Doubts as to the critical nature of information misstated or omitted will be commonplace. And particularly in view of the prophylactic purpose of the Rule and the fact that the content of the proxy statement is within management's control, it is appropriate that these doubts be resolved in favor of those the statute is designed to protect. *Mills*, supra, at 385.

We are aware, however, that the disclosure policy embodied in the proxy regulations is not without limit. Some information is of such dubious significance that insistence on its disclosure may accomplish more harm than good. The potential liability for a Rule 14a-9 violation can be great indeed, and if the standard of materiality is unnecessarily low, not only may the corporation and its management be subjected to liability for insignificant omissions or misstatements, but also management's fear of exposing itself to substantial liability may cause it simply to bury the shareholders in an avalanche of trivial information—a result that is hardly conducive to informed decisionmaking. Precisely these dangers are presented, we think, by the definition of a material fact adopted by the Court of Appeals in this case—a fact which a reasonable shareholder *might* consider important. We agree with Judge Friendly, speaking for the Court of Appeals in *Gerstle*, that the "might" formulation is "too suggestive of mere possibility, however unlikely."

The general standard of materiality that we think best comports with the policies of Rule 14a-9 is as follows: An omitted fact is material if there is a substantial likelihood that a reasonable shareholder would consider it important in deciding how to vote. This standard is fully consistent with *Mills'* general description of materiality as a requirement that "the defect have a significant *propensity* to affect the voting process." It does not require proof of a substantial likelihood that disclosure of the omitted fact would have caused the reasonable investor to change his vote. What the standard does contemplate is a showing of a substantial likelihood that, under all the circumstances, the omitted fact would have assumed actual significance in the deliberations of the reasonable shareholder. Put another way, there must be a substantial likelihood that the disclosure of the omitted fact would have been viewed by the reasonable investor as having significantly altered the "total mix" of information made available.

The issue of materiality may be characterized as a mixed question of law and fact, involving as it does the application of a legal standard to a particular set of facts. In considering whether summary judgment on the issue is appropriate, we must bear in mind that the underlying objective facts, which will often be free from dispute, are merely the starting point for the ultimate determination of materiality. The determination requires delicate assessments of the inferences a "reasonable shareholder" would draw from a given set of facts and the significance of those inferences to him, and these assessments are peculiarly ones for the trier of fact. Only if the established omissions are "so obviously important to an investor, that reasonable minds cannot differ on the question of materiality" is the ultimate issue of materiality appropriately resolved "as a matter of law" by summary judgment. . . .

NOTES AND QUESTIONS

1. The Supreme Court's characterization of materiality suggests that resolving that issue by summary judgment without going to trial may be difficult. For example, the court of appeals found it a material omission not to include the facts that two of the National nominees were chairman of the TSC board of directors and chairman of the executive committee. The Supreme Court noted that the proxy statement prominently displayed the facts that National owned 34 percent of TSC and that no other person owned 10 percent and prominently revealed that five of ten TSC directors were National nominees, reciting the high positions of three nominees in the National hierarchy. The Court concluded that summary judgment was inappropriate:

> These disclosures clearly revealed the nature of National's relationship with TSC and alerted the reasonable shareholder to the fact that National exercised a degree of influence over TSC. In view of these disclosures we certainly cannot say that the additional facts that Yarmuth was chairman of the TSC board of directors and Simonelli chairman of its executive committee were, on this record, so obviously important that reasonable minds could not differ on materiality.

426 U.S. at 452-453.

2. The language of Rule 14a-9 (and Rule 10b-5, considered in the next part of this chapter) extends to misleading statements of material facts, which then requires, for example, distinguishing statements of fact from opinions. In Virginia Bankshares, Inc. v. Sandberg, 501 U.S. 1083 (1991), excerpted later in the chapter for its discussion of reliance and causation, the 85 percent shareholder implemented a cash-out merger of the minority public shareholders. Plaintiff brought a 14a-9 claim that, among other things, alleged that the directors had not believed that the price offered was high or

that the terms of the merger were fair, but had recommended the merger only because they believed they had no alternative if they wished to remain on the board. A jury found for Sandberg on both counts and awarded her $18 a share, having found that she would have received $60 if her stock had been valued adequately. The Court held Rule 14a-9 can cover a false or misleadingly incomplete statement of reasons, even when stated in conclusory terms.

> In reaching this conclusion we have considered statements of reasons of the sort exemplified here, which misstate the speaker's reasons and also mislead about the stated subject matter (e.g., the value of the shares). A statement of belief may be open to objection only in the former respect, however, solely as a misstatement of the psychological fact of the speaker's belief in what he says. In this case, for example, the Court of Appeals alluded to just such limited falsity in observing that "the jury was certainly justified in believing that the directors did not believe a merger at $42 per share was in the minority stockholders' interest but, rather, that they voted as they did for other reasons, e.g., retaining their seats on the board."
>
> The question arises, then, whether disbelief, or undisclosed belief or motivation, standing alone, should be a sufficient basis to sustain an action under §14(a), absent proof by the sort of objective evidence described above that the statement also expressly or impliedly asserted something false or misleading about its subject matter. We think that proof of mere disbelief or belief undisclosed should not suffice for liability under §14(a), and if nothing more had been required or proven in this case we would reverse for that reason.

How is a court to make such a distinction? In a case reconsidered after the Supreme Court opinion, the Second Circuit ruled:

> What the Court appears to require is "garden-variety evidence, subject neither to a plaintiff's control nor ready manufacture," with "no undue risk of open-ended liability or uncontrollable litigation," i.e., proof that the value of the company's stock "when assessed in accordance with recognized methods of valuation," was higher than the "fair" price stated by the directors.
>
> In the instant case, plaintiff has yet to produce any meaningful proof that the Loehmann stock was worth more than $31.30 a share. We believe that proof of this nature is required before the district court enters the morass of alleged motivation and knowing deception. Accordingly, we direct the district court upon remand to bifurcate the trial and to try first the issue of fair value. If plaintiff fails to establish that the fair value of the Loehmann stock, "when assessed in accordance with recognized methods of valuation," was materially in excess of $31.30 a share, that portion of plaintiff's complaint dealing with the alleged deception on this issue should be dismissed.

Mendell v. Greenberg, 938 F.2d 1528, 1529 (2d Cir. 1991).

c.   Scienter

The Supreme Court, in footnotes in *TSC* and again in *Virginia Bankshares,* deferred the issue of what showing of culpability is required to establish liability under §14(a). A leading Second Circuit case, Gerstle v. Gamble-Skogmo, Inc., 478 F.2d 1281 (2d Cir. 1973), written by Judge Henry Friendly, held that negligence was sufficient to establish liability under §14(a), distinguishing this section from §10b for which the Supreme Court later required a higher standard of culpability. See Ernst & Ernst v. Hochfelder, reprinted at page 1026. But see Adams v. Standard Knitting Mills, Inc., 623 F.2d 422 (6th Cir.), cert. denied, 449 U.S. 1067 (1980) (holding scienter should be an element of liability in private causes of action under §14(a)).

d. Reliance, Causation, and Remedy

Mills v. Electric Auto-Lite Co.
United States Supreme Court, 1970
396 U.S. 375

Mr. Justice Harlan delivered the opinion of the Court.

This case requires us to consider a basic aspect of the implied private right of action for violation of §14(a) of the Securities Exchange Act of 1934, recognized by this Court in J.I. Case Co. v. Borak, 377 U.S. 426 (1964). As in *Borak* the asserted wrong is that a corporate merger was accomplished through the use of a proxy statement that was materially false or misleading. The question with which we deal is what causal relationship must be shown between such a statement and the merger to establish a cause of action based on the violation of the Act.

I

Petitioners were shareholders of the Electric Auto-Lite Company until 1963, when it was merged into Mergenthaler Linotype Company. They brought suit on the day before the shareholders' meeting at which the vote was to take place on the merger, against Auto-Lite, Mergenthaler, and a third company, American Manufacturing Company, Inc. The complaint sought an injunction against the voting by Auto-Lite's management of all proxies obtained by means of an allegedly misleading proxy solicitation; however, it did not seek a temporary restraining order, and the voting went ahead as scheduled the following day. Several months later petitioners filed an amended complaint, seeking to have the merger set aside and to obtain such other relief as might be proper.

In Count II of the amended complaint, which is the only count before us, petitioners predicated jurisdiction on §27 of the 1934 Act. They alleged that the proxy statement sent out by the Auto-Lite management to solicit shareholders' votes in favor of the merger was misleading, in violation of §14(a) of the Act and SEC Rule 14a-9 thereunder. Petitioners recited that before the merger Mergenthaler owned over 50% of the outstanding shares of Auto-Lite common stock, and had been in control of Auto-Lite for two years. American Manufacturing in turn owned about one-third of the outstanding shares of Mergenthaler, and for two years had been in voting control of Mergenthaler and, through it, of Auto-Lite. Petitioners charged that in light of these circumstances the proxy statement was misleading in that it told Auto-Lite shareholders that their board of directors recommended approval of the merger without also informing them that all 11 of Auto-Lite's directors were nominees of Mergenthaler and were under the "control and domination of Mergenthaler." Petitioners asserted the right to complain of this alleged violation both derivatively on behalf of Auto-Lite and as representatives of the class of all its minority shareholders.

On petitioners' motion for summary judgment with respect to Count II, [both the district court and the court of appeals found that the claimed defects were material, but differed as to whether a sufficient causal relationship had been shown. The district court] found that under the terms of the merger agreement, an affirmative vote of two-thirds of the Auto-Lite shares was required for approval of the merger, and that the respondent companies owned and controlled about 54% of the outstanding shares. Therefore, to obtain authorization of the merger, respondents had to secure the approval of a substantial number of the minority shareholders. At the stockholders' meeting, approximately 950,000 shares, out of 1,160,000 shares outstanding, were voted in favor of the merger. This included 317,000 votes obtained by proxy from the minority shareholders, votes that were "necessary and indispensable to the approval of the merger." The District Court concluded that a causal relationship had thus been shown. [That ruling was reversed by the court of appeals. The appellate court] acknowledged that, if an injunction had been sought a sufficient time before the stockholders' meeting, "corrective measures would have been appropriate." However, since this suit was brought too late for preventive action, the courts had to determine "whether the misleading statement and omission caused the submission of sufficient proxies," as a prerequisite to a determination of liability under the Act. If the respondents could show, "by a preponderance of probabilities, that the merger would have received a sufficient vote even if the proxy statement had not been misleading in the respect found," petitioners would be entitled to no relief of any kind.

The Court of Appeals acknowledged that this test corresponds to the common-law fraud test of whether the injured party relied on the misrepresentation. However, rightly concluding that "[reliance] by thousands of individuals, as here, can scarcely be inquired into," the court ruled that the issue was to be determined by proof of the fairness of the terms of the merger. If respondents could show that the merger had merit and was fair to the minority shareholders, the trial court would be justified in concluding that a sufficient number of shareholders would have approved the merger had there been no deficiency in the proxy statement. In that case respondents would be entitled to a judgment in their favor. . . .

II

As we stressed in *Borak,* §14(a) stemmed from a congressional belief that "[fair] corporate suffrage is an important right that should attach to every equity security bought on a public exchange." H.R. Rep. No. 1383, 73d Cong., 2d Sess., 13. The provision was intended to promote "the free exercise of the voting rights of stockholders" by ensuring that proxies would be solicited with "explanation to the stockholder of the real nature of the questions for which authority to cast his vote is sought." Id., at 14; S. Rep. No. 792, 73d Cong., 2d Sess., 12; see 377 U.S., at 431. The decision below, by permitting all liability to be foreclosed on the basis of a finding that the merger was fair, would allow the stockholders to be bypassed, at least where the only legal challenge to the merger is a suit for retrospective relief after the meeting has been held. A judicial appraisal of the merger's merits could be substituted for the actual and informed vote of the stockholders.

The result would be to insulate from private redress an entire category of proxy violations—those relating to matters other than the terms of the merger. Even outrageous misrepresentations in a proxy solicitation, if they did not relate to the terms of the transaction, would give rise to no cause of action under §14(a). Particularly if carried over to enforcement actions by the Securities and Exchange Commission itself, such a result would subvert the congressional purpose of ensuring full and fair disclosure to shareholders.

Further, recognition of the fairness of the merger as a complete defense would confront small shareholders with an additional obstacle to making a successful challenge to a proposal recommended through a defective proxy statement. The risk that they would be unable to rebut the corporation's evidence of the fairness of the proposal, and thus to establish their cause of action, would be bound to discourage such shareholders from the private enforcement of the proxy rules that "provides a necessary supplement to Commission action." J.I. Case Co. v. Borak, 377 U.S., at 432.[5]

Such a frustration of the congressional policy is not required by anything in the wording of the statute or in our opinion in the *Borak* case. Section 14(a) declares it "unlawful" to solicit proxies in contravention of Commission rules, and SEC Rule 14a-9 prohibits solicitations "containing any statement which . . . is false or misleading with respect to any material fact, or which omits to state any material fact necessary in order to make the statements therein not false or misleading. . . ." Use of a solicitation that is materially misleading is itself a violation of law, as the Court of Appeals recognized in stating that injunctive relief would be available to remedy such a defect if sought prior to the stockholders' meeting. . . . In the present case there has been a hearing specifically directed to the causation problem. The question before the Court is whether the facts found on the basis of that hearing are sufficient in law to establish petitioners' cause of action, and we conclude that they are.

Where the misstatement or omission in a proxy statement has been shown to be "material," as it was found to be here, that determination itself indubitably embodies a conclusion that the defect was of such a character that it might have been considered important by a reasonable shareholder who was in the process of deciding how to vote.[6] This requirement that the defect have a significant *propensity* to affect the

---

5. The Court of Appeals' ruling that "causation" may be negated by proof of the fairness of the merger also rests on a dubious behavioral assumption. There is no justification for presuming that the shareholders of every corporation are willing to accept any and every fair merger offer put before them; yet such a presumption is implicit in the opinion of the Court of Appeals. That court gave no indication of what evidence petitioners might adduce, once respondents had established that the merger proposal was equitable, in order to show that the shareholders would nevertheless have rejected it if the solicitation had not been misleading. Proof of actual reliance by thousands of individuals would, as the court acknowledged, not be feasible, see R. Jennings & H. Marsh, Securities Regulation, Cases and Materials 1001 (2d ed. 1968); and reliance on the *nondisclosure* of a fact is a particularly difficult matter to define or prove, see 3 L. Loss, Securities Regulation 1766 (2d ed. 1961). In practice, therefore, the objective fairness of the proposal would seemingly be determinative of liability. But, in view of the many other factors that might lead shareholders to prefer their current position to that of owners of a larger, combined enterprise, it is pure conjecture to assume that the fairness of the proposal will always be determinative of their vote.

6. . . . In this case, where the misleading aspect of the solicitation involved failure to reveal a serious conflict of interest on the part of the directors, the Court of Appeals concluded that the crucial question in determining materiality was "whether the minority shareholders were sufficiently alerted to the board's relationship to their adversary to be on their guard." An adequate disclosure of this relationship would have warned the stockholders to give more careful scrutiny to the terms of the merger than they might to one recommended by an entirely disinterested board. Thus, the failure to make such a disclosure was found to be a material defect "as a matter of law," thwarting the informed decision at which the statute aims, regardless of whether the terms of the merger were such that a reasonable stockholder would have approved the transaction after more careful analysis.

voting process is found in the express terms of Rule 14a-9, and it adequately serves the purpose of ensuring that a cause of action cannot be established by proof of a defect so trivial, or so unrelated to the transaction for which approval is sought, that correction of the defect or imposition of liability would not further the interests protected by §14(a).

There is no need to supplement this requirement, as did the Court of Appeals with a requirement of proof of whether the defect actually had a decisive effect on the voting. Where there has been a finding of materiality, a shareholder has made a sufficient showing of causal relationship between the violation and the injury for which he seeks redress if, as here, he proves that the proxy solicitation itself, rather than the particular defect in the solicitation materials, was an essential link in the accomplishment of the transaction. This objective test will avoid the impracticalities of determining how many votes were affected, and, by resolving doubts in favor of those the statute is designed to protect, will effectuate the congressional policy of ensuring that the shareholders are able to make an informed choice when they are consulted on corporate transactions.[7] . . .

Virginia Bankshares, Inc. v. Sandberg
United States Supreme Court, 1991
501 U.S. 1083

JUSTICE SOUTER delivered the opinion of the Court.

I

In December 1986, First American Bankshares, Inc., (FABI), a bank holding company, began a "freeze-out" merger, in which the First American Bank of Virginia (Bank) eventually merged into Virginia Bankshares, Inc., (VBI), a wholly owned subsidiary of FABI. VBI owned 85% of the Bank's shares, the remaining 15% being in the hands of some 2,000 minority shareholders. FABI hired the investment banking firm of Keefe, Bruyette & Woods (KBW) to give an opinion on the appropriate price for shares of the minority holders, who would lose their interests in the Bank as a result of the merger. Based on market quotations and unverified information from FABI, KBW gave the Bank's executive committee an opinion that $42 a share would be a fair price for the minority stock. The executive committee approved the merger proposal at that price, and the full board followed suit.

---

7. We need not decide in this case whether causation could be shown where the management controls a sufficient number of shares to approve the transaction without any votes from the minority. Even in that situation, if the management finds it necessary for legal or practical reasons to solicit proxies from minority shareholders, at least one court has held that the proxy solicitation might be sufficiently related to the merger to satisfy the causation requirement, see Laurenzano v. Einbender, 264 F. Supp. 356 (D.C.E.D.N.Y. 1966). . . .

Although Virginia law required only that such a merger proposal be submitted to a vote at a shareholders' meeting, and that the meeting be preceded by circulation of a statement of information to the shareholders, the directors nevertheless solicited proxies for voting on the proposal at the annual meeting set for April 21, 1987. In their solicitation, the directors urged the proposal's adoption and stated they had approved the plan because of its opportunity for the minority shareholders to achieve a "high" value, which they elsewhere described as a "fair" price, for their stock. . . .

[After approval of the merger, Sandberg, a minority shareholder, brought suit alleging both misleading statements made in violation of §14(a) and Rule 14a-9 and breach of fiduciary duties owed to the minority shareholders under state law.] . . .

III

The second issue before us, left open in Mills v. Electric Auto-Lite Co., 396 U.S., at 385, n.7, is whether causation of damages compensable through the implied private right of action under §14(a) can be demonstrated by a member of a class of minority shareholders whose votes are not required by law or corporate bylaw to authorize the transaction giving rise to the claim. . . . The *Mills* Court avoided the evidentiary morass that would have followed from requiring individualized proof that enough minority shareholders had relied upon the misstatements to swing the vote. Instead, it held that causation of damages by a material proxy misstatement could be established by showing that minority proxies necessary and sufficient to authorize the corporate acts had been given in accordance with the tenor of the solicitation, and the Court described such a causal relationship by calling the proxy solicitation an "essential link in the accomplishment of the transaction." In the case before it, the Court found the solicitation essential, as contrasted with one addressed to a class of minority shareholders without votes required by law or by-law to authorize the action proposed, and left it for another day to decide whether such a minority shareholder could demonstrate causation. Id., at 385, n.7.

In this case, respondents address *Mills'* open question by proffering two theories that the proxy solicitation addressed to them was an "essential link" under the *Mills* causation test.[9] They argue, first, that a link existed and was essential simply because VBI and FABI would have been unwilling to proceed with the merger without the approval manifested by the minority shareholders' proxies, which would not have been obtained without the solicitation's express misstatements and misleading omissions.

---

9. Citing the decision in Schlick v. Penn-Dixie Cement Corp., 507 F.2d 374, 382-383 (C.A.2 1974), petitioners characterize respondents' proffered theories as examples of so-called "sue facts" and "shame facts" theories. "A 'sue fact' is, in general, a fact which is material to a sue decision. A 'sue decision' is a decision by a shareholder whether or not to institute a representative or derivative suit alleging a state-law cause of action." Gelb, Rule 10b-5 and *Santa Fe*—Herein of Sue Facts, Shame Facts, and Other Matters, 87 W. Va. L. Rev. 189, 198, and n.52 (1985), quoting Borden, "Sue Fact" Rule Mandates Disclosure to Avoid Litigation in State Courts, 10 SEC '82, pp. 201, 204-205 (1982). See also Note, Causation and Liability in Private Actions for Proxy Violations, 80 Yale L.J. 107, 116 (1970) (discussing theories of causation). "Shame facts" are said to be facts which, had they been disclosed, would have "shamed" management into abandoning a proposed transaction. See *Schlick*, supra, at 384. See also *Gelb*, supra, at 197.

On this reasoning, the causal connection would depend on a desire to avoid bad shareholder or public relations, and the essential character of the causal link would stem not from the enforceable terms of the parties' corporate relationship, but from one party's apprehension of the ill will of the other.

In the alternative, respondents argue that the proxy statement was an essential link between the directors' proposal and the merger because it was the means to satisfy a state statutory requirement of minority shareholder approval, as a condition for saving the merger from voidability resulting from a conflict of interest on the part of one of the Bank's directors, Jack Beddow, who voted in favor of the merger while also serving as a director of FABI. Under the terms of Va. Code §13.1-691(A) (1989), minority approval after disclosure of the material facts about the transaction and the director's interest was one of three avenues to insulate the merger from later attack for conflict, the two others being ratification by the Bank's directors after like disclosure, and proof that the merger was fair to the corporation. On this theory, causation would depend on the use of the proxy statement for the purpose of obtaining votes sufficient to bar a minority shareholder from commencing proceedings to declare the merger void.

Although respondents have proffered each of these theories as establishing a chain of causal connection in which the proxy statement is claimed to have been an "essential link," neither theory presents the proxy solicitation as essential in the sense of *Mills'* causal sequence, in which the solicitation links a directors' proposal with the votes legally required to authorize the action proposed. As a consequence, each theory would, if adopted, extend the scope of *Borak* actions beyond the ambit of *Mills,* and expand the class of plaintiffs entitled to bring *Borak* actions to include shareholders whose initial authorization of the transaction prompting the proxy solicitation is unnecessary.

Assessing the legitimacy of any such extension or expansion calls for the application of some fundamental principles governing recognition of a right of action implied by a federal statute, the first of which was not, in fact, the considered focus of the *Borak* opinion. The rule that has emerged in the years since *Borak* and *Mills* came down is that recognition of any private right of action for violating a federal statute must ultimately rest on congressional intent to provide a private remedy, Touche Ross & Co. v. Redington, 442 U.S. 560, 575 (1979). From this the corollary follows that the breadth of the right once recognized should not, as a general matter, grow beyond the scope congressionally intended.

This rule and corollary present respondents with a serious obstacle, for we can find no manifestation of intent to recognize a cause of action (or class of plaintiffs) as broad as respondents' theory of causation would entail. At first blush, it might seem otherwise, for the *Borak* Court certainly did not ignore the matter of intent. Its opinion adverted to the statutory object of "protection of investors" as animating Congress' intent to provide judicial relief where "necessary," and it quoted evidence for that intent from House and Senate Committee Reports. *Borak*'s probe of the congressional mind, however, never focused squarely on private rights of action, as distinct from the substantive objects of the legislation, and one member of the *Borak* Court later characterized the "implication" of the private right of action as resting modestly on the Act's "exclusively procedural provision affording access to a federal forum." Bivens v. Six Unknown Fed. Narcotics Agents, 403 U.S. 388, 403, n.4 (1971) (Harlan, J., concurring in judgment) (internal quotation marks omitted). In fact, the importance of enquiring specifically into intent to authorize a private cause of action became clear only later, see Cort v. Ash, 422 U.S., at 78, and only later still, in *Touche Ross,* was this intent accorded primacy among the considerations that might be thought to bear on any decision to recognize a private remedy. There, in dealing with a claimed private right under §17(a) of the Act, we explained that the "central inquiry remains whether Congress intended to create, either expressly or by implication, a private cause of action." 442 U.S., at 575-576.

Looking to the Act's text and legislative history mindful of this heightened concern reveals little that would help toward understanding the intended scope of any private right. According to the House report, Congress meant to promote the "free exercise" of stockholders' voting rights, H.R. Rep. No. 1383, 73d Cong., 2d Sess., 14 (1934), and protect "fair corporate suffrage," id., at 13, from abuses exemplified by proxy solicitations that concealed what the Senate report called the "real nature" of the issues to be settled by the subsequent votes, S. Rep. No. 792, 73d Cong., 2d Sess., 12 (1934). While it is true that these reports, like the language of the Act itself, carry the clear message that Congress meant to protect investors from misinformation that rendered them unwitting agents of self-inflicted damage, it is just as true that Congress was reticent with indications of how far this protection might depend on self-help by private action. The response to this reticence may be, of course, to claim that §14(a) cannot be enforced effectively for the sake of its intended beneficiaries without their participation as private litigants. *Borak,* supra, at 432. But the force of this argument for inferred congressional intent depends on the degree of need perceived by Congress, and we would have trouble inferring any congressional urgency to depend on implied private actions to deter violations of §14(a), when Congress expressly provided private rights of action in §§9(e), 16(b) and 18(a) of the same Act.[11]

The congressional silence that is thus a serious obstacle to the expansion of cognizable *Borak* causation is not, however, a necessarily insurmountable barrier. This is not the first effort in recent years to expand the scope of an action originally inferred from the Act without "conclusive guidance" from Congress, see Blue Chip Stamps v. Manor Drug Stores, 421 U.S., at 737, and we may look to that earlier case for the proper response to such a plea for expansion. There, we accepted the proposition that where a legal structure of private statutory rights has developed without clear indications of congressional intent, the contours of that structure need not be frozen absolutely when the result would be demonstrably inequitable to a class of would-be plaintiffs with claims comparable to those previously recognized. Faced in that case with such a claim for equality in rounding out the scope of an implied private statutory right of action, we looked to policy reasons for deciding where the outer limits of the right should lie. We may do no less here, in the face of respondents' pleas for a private

---

11. The object of our enquiry does not extend further to question the holding of either J.I. Case Co. v. Borak, 377 U.S. 426 (1964), or Mills v. Electric Auto-Lite Co., 396 U.S. 375 (1970), at this date, any more than we have done so in the past, see Touche Ross & Co. v. Redington, 442 U.S. 560, 577 (1979). Our point is simply to recognize the hurdle facing any litigant who urges us to enlarge the scope of the action beyond the point reached in *Mills.*

remedy to place them on the same footing as shareholders with votes necessary for initial corporate action.

A...

The same threats of speculative claims and procedural intractability [evidenced in *Blue Chip Stamps*] are inherent in respondents' theory of causation linked through the directors' desire for a cosmetic vote. Causation would turn on inferences about what the corporate directors would have thought and done without the minority share-holder approval unneeded to authorize action. A subsequently dissatisfied minority shareholder would have virtual license to allege that managerial timidity would have doomed corporate action but for the ostensible approval induced by a misleading statement, and opposing claims of hypothetical diffidence and hypothetical boldness on the part of directors would probably provide enough depositions in the usual case to preclude any judicial resolution short of the credibility judgments that can only come after trial. Reliable evidence would seldom exist. Directors would understand the prudence of making a few statements about plans to proceed even without minor-ity endorsement, and discovery would be a quest for recollections of oral conversations at odds with the official pronouncements, in hopes of finding support for ex post facto guesses about how much heat the directors would have stood in the absence of minor-ity approval. The issues would be hazy, their litigation protracted, and their resolution unreliable. Given a choice, we would reject any theory of causation that raised such prospects, and we reject this one.[12]

B

... [Respondent's] theory of causation [derived from Virginia law] rests upon the proposition of policy that §14(a) should provide a federal remedy whenever a false or misleading proxy statement results in the loss under state law of a shareholder plain-tiff's state remedy for the enforcement of a state right. Respondents agree with the sug-gestions of counsel for the SEC and FDIC that causation be recognized, for example, when a minority shareholder has been induced by a misleading proxy statement to forfeit a state-law right to an appraisal remedy by voting to approve a transaction, cf. Swanson v. American Consumers Industries, Inc., 475 F.2d 516, 520-521 (C.A.7 1973), or when such a shareholder has been deterred from obtaining an order enjoining a damaging transaction by a proxy solicitation that misrepresents the facts on which an injunction could properly have been issued. Cf. Healey v. Catalyst Recovery of

---

12. In parting company from us on this point, Justice Kennedy emphasizes that respondents in this particular case substantiated a plausible claim that petitioners would not have proceeded without minor-ity approval. ... The issue before us, however, is whether to recognize a theory of causation generally, and our decision against doing so rests on our apprehension that the ensuing litigation would be exemplified by cases far less tractable than this. Respondents' burden to justify recognition of causation beyond the scope of *Mills* must be addressed not by emphasizing the instant case but by confronting the risk inherent in the cases that could be expected to be characteristic if the causal theory were adopted.

Pennsylvania, Inc., 616 F.2d 641, 647-648 (C.A.3 1980); Alabama Farm Bureau Mutual Casualty Co. v. American Fidelity Life Ins. Co., 606 F.2d 602, 614 (C.A.5 1979), cert. denied, 449 U.S. 820 (1980). Respondents claim that in this case a predicate for recognizing just such a causal link exists in Va. Code §13.1-691(A)(2) (1989), which sets the conditions under which the merger may be insulated from suit by a minority shareholder seeking to void it on account of Beddow's conflict.

This case does not, however, require us to decide whether §14(a) provides a cause of action for lost state remedies, since there is no indication in the law or facts before us that the proxy solicitation resulted in any such loss. The contrary appears to be the case. Assuming the soundness of respondents' characterization of the proxy statement as materially misleading, the very terms of the Virginia statute indicate that a favorable minority vote induced by the solicitation would not suffice to render the merger invulnerable to later attack on the ground of the conflict. The statute bars a shareholder from seeking to avoid a transaction tainted by a director's conflict if, inter alia, the minority shareholders ratified the transaction following disclosure of the material facts of the transaction and the conflict. Va. Code §13.1-691(A)(2) (1989). Assuming that the material facts about the merger and Beddow's interests were not accurately disclosed, the minority votes were inadequate to ratify the merger under state law, and there was no loss of state remedy to connect the proxy solicitation with harm to minority shareholders irredressable under state law. Nor is there a claim here that the statement misled respondents into entertaining a false belief that they had no chance to upset the merger, until the time for bringing suit had run out.[14] . . .

JUSTICE KENNEDY dissented from this part of the Court's decision, in an opinion joined by JUSTICES MARSHALL, BLACKMUN and STEVENS:

II

A

The severe limits the Court places upon possible proof of nonvoting causation in a §14(a) private action are justified neither by our precedents nor any case in the courts of appeals. These limits are said to flow from a shift in our approach to implied causes of action that has occurred since we recognized the §14(a) implied private action in J.I. Case Co. v. Borak, 377 U.S. 426 (1964).

I acknowledge that we should exercise caution in creating implied private rights of action and that we must respect the primacy of congressional intent in that inquiry. Where an implied cause of action is well accepted by our own cases and has become an established part of the securities laws, however, we should enforce it as a meaningful remedy unless we are to eliminate it altogether. . . .

---

14. Respondents do not claim that any other application of a theory of lost state remedies would avail them here. It is clear, for example, that no state appraisal remedy was lost through a §14(a) violation in this case. . . . Va. Code §6.1-43 specifically excludes bank mergers from application of [the Virginia appraisal statute].

To the extent the Court's analysis considers the purposes underlying §14(a), it does so with the avowed aim to limit the cause of action and with undue emphasis upon fears of "speculative claims and procedural intractability." The result is a sort of guerrilla warfare to restrict a well-established implied right of action. If the analysis adopted by the Court today is any guide, Congress and those charged with enforcement of the securities laws stand forewarned that unresolved questions concerning the scope of those causes of action are likely to be answered by the Court in favor of defendants. . . .

III

Our decision in Mills v. Electric Auto-Lite Co., [396 U.S.] at 385, rested upon the impracticality of attempting to determine the extent of reliance by thousands of shareholders on alleged misrepresentations or omissions. . . . The merit of the essential link formulation is that it rests upon the likelihood of causation and eliminates the difficulty of proof. Even where a minority lacks votes to defeat a proposal, both these factors weigh in favor of finding causation so long as the solicitation of proxies is an essential link in the transaction.

A

The Court argues that a nonvoting causation theory would "turn on 'hazy' issues inviting self-serving testimony, strike suits, and protracted discovery, with little chance of reasonable resolution by pretrial process" (citing *Blue Chip Stamps,* 421 U.S. at 742-743 (1975)). The Court's description does not fit this case and is not a sound objection in any event. Any causation inquiry under §14(a) requires a court to consider a hypothetical universe in which adequate disclosure is made. Indeed, the analysis is inevitable in almost any suit when we are invited to compare what was with what ought to have been. The causation inquiry is not intractable. . . .

B

There is no authority whatsoever for limiting §14(a) to protecting those minority shareholders whose numerical strength could permit them to vote down a proposal. One of §14(a)'s "chief purposes is 'the protection of investors.'" J.I. Case Co. v. Borak, 377 U.S., at 432. Those who lack the strength to vote down a proposal have all the more need of disclosure. The voting process involves not only casting ballots but also the formulation and withdrawal of proposals, the minority's right to block a vote through court action or the threat of adverse consequences, or the negotiation of an increase in price. The proxy rules support this deliberative process. These practicalities can result in causation sufficient to support recovery.

The facts in the case before us prove this point. . . .

The theory that FABI would not have pursued the transaction if full disclosure had been provided and the shareholders had realized the inadequacy of the price is supported not only by the trial testimony but also by notes of the meeting of the

Bank's board which approved the merger. The inquiry into causation can proceed not by "opposing claims of hypothetical diffidence and hypothetical boldness," but through an examination of evidence of the same type the Court finds acceptable in its determination that directors' statements of reasons can lead to liability. Discussion at the board meeting focused upon matters such as "how to keep PR afloat" and "how to prevent adverse reaction/perception," demonstrating the directors' concern that an unpopular merger proposal could injure the Bank.

Only a year or so before the Virginia merger, FABI had failed in an almost identical transaction, an attempt to freeze out the minority shareholders of its Maryland subsidiary. FABI retained Keefe, Bruyette & Woods (KBW) for that transaction as well, and KBW had given an opinion that FABI's price was fair. The subsidiary's board of directors then retained its own adviser and concluded that the price offered by FABI was inadequate. The Maryland transaction failed when the directors of the Maryland bank refused to proceed; and this was despite the minority's inability to outvote FABI if it had pressed on with the deal.

In the Virginia transaction, FABI again decided to retain KBW. Beddow, who sat on the boards of both FABI and the Bank, discouraged the Bank from hiring its own financial adviser, out of fear that the Maryland experience would be repeated if the Bank received independent advice. Directors of the Bank testified they would not have voted to approve the transaction if the price had been demonstrated unfair to the minority. Further, approval by the Bank's board of directors was facilitated by FABI's representation that the transaction also would be approved by the minority shareholders. . . .

I conclude that causation is more than plausible; it is likely, even where the public shareholders cannot vote down management's proposal. Causation is established where the proxy statement is an essential link in completing the transaction, even if the minority lacks sufficient votes to defeat a proposal of management.

IV

The majority avoids the question whether a plaintiff may prove causation by demonstrating that the misrepresentation or omission deprived her of a state law remedy. I do not think the question difficult, as the whole point of federal proxy rules is to support state law principles of corporate governance. Nor do I think that the Court can avoid this issue if it orders judgment for petitioners. The majority asserts that respondents show no loss of a state law remedy, because if "the material facts of the transaction and Beddow's interest were not accurately disclosed, then the minority votes were inadequate to ratify the merger under Virginia law." This theory requires us to conclude that the Virginia statute governing director conflicts of interest, Va. Code §13.1-691(A)(2) (1989), incorporates the same definition of materiality as the federal proxy rules. I find no support for that proposition. If the definitions are not the same, then Sandberg may have lost her state law remedy. For all we know, disclosure to the minority shareholders that the price is $42 per share may satisfy Virginia's requirement. If that is the case, then approval by the minority without full disclosure may have deprived Sandberg of the ability to void the merger.

In all events, the theory that the merger would have been voidable absent minority shareholder approval is far more speculative than the theory that FABI and the Bank would have called off the transaction. Even so, this possibility would support a remand, as the lower courts have yet to consider the question. We are not well positioned as an institution to provide a definitive resolution to state law questions of this kind. Here again, the difficulty of knowing what would have happened in the hypothetical universe of full disclosure suggests that we should "resolve doubts in favor of those the statute is designed to protect" in order to "effectuate the congressional policy of ensuring that the shareholders are able to make an informed choice when they are consulted on corporate transactions." *Mills,* 396 U.S., at 385.

I would affirm the judgment of the Court of Appeals.

NOTES AND QUESTIONS

1. The *Mills* Court noted the impracticality of inquiring into the reliance of thousands of investors and resolved doubt in favor of those the statute is designed to protect. The *Virginia Bankshares* majority notes the threats of speculative claims and procedural intractability that raise prospects of protracted litigation and unreliable resolutions. Are claims that plaintiffs make about plaintiff conduct (that they actually voted because of the misrepresentation or omission) more speculative than claims plaintiffs make about defendants' conduct?

2. Justice Kennedy states that the whole point of federal proxy rules is to support state law principles of corporate governance. To what extent should federal disclosure support shareholders in deciding:

    a.   to vote their shares?
    b.   to sell their shares?
    c.   to seek appraisal rights?
    d.   to file suit against managers for breach of fiduciary duty?

Wilson v. Great American Industries, Inc.
United States Court of Appeals, Second Circuit, 1992
979 F.2d 924

CARDAMONE, CIRCUIT JUDGE: . . .

The thrust of plaintiffs' complaint is that the material misstatements induced them to exchange their shares of Chenango common stock for new preferred stock in Great American. [Defendants are Great American, Chenango, and various officers, directors, and attorneys connected with those two corporations.] Defendants at the time of the merger owned 73 percent of Chenango's stock, well over the two thirds necessary under New York law to approve a corporate merger. New York law only required that defendants hold a shareholders' meeting prior to which Chenango was required to give each shareholder notice of the meeting accompanied by a "copy of the plan of merger." N.Y. Bus. Corp. Law §903(a)(1). Because Chenango stock was registered under §12(g) of the [Securities Exchange Act of 1934], defendants were also required to provide shareholders with an "Information Statement" pursuant to §14(c) of the Act. Nonetheless, defendants mailed out joint proxy and registration statements seeking Chenango minority shareholders' approval of the merger.

The misrepresentations or omissions contained in the proxy created an unfair exchange ratio, plaintiffs assert, by overvaluing Great American's stock and undervaluing Chenango's stock. . . . [While an appeal of an award for plaintiff was pending, the Supreme Court decided Virginia Bankshares, Inc. v. Sandberg, 501 U.S. 1083 (1991), and defendants then sought a dismissal based on the holding in that case.]

A. INTERVENING SUPREME COURT DECISION

The Supreme Court in *Virginia Bankshares* did not hold that minority shareholders whose votes number too few to affect the outcome of a shareholder vote may *never* recover damages under §14(a) or that *no* implied private cause of action for such shareholders is provided under that section of the Act. And, it expressly declined to decide whether §14(a) provides an implied federal remedy for minority shareholders deprived of certain state remedies as a result of deceptive proxy solicitations. [501 U.S. at 1108 n.14.] To the extent that this Circuit recognizes such a remedy, defendants incorrectly contend therefore that *Virginia Bankshares* precludes plaintiffs from seeking such relief. . . .

One theory of causation advanced by the plaintiffs in *Virginia Bankshares* was that, but for the defective proxies, the minority shareholders would not have voted in favor of the merger. In that event, dissenting votes would have preserved their right to pursue under Virginia law avoidance of the merger based on an alleged conflict of interest on the part of one [of] the Bank's directors. Recognizing the possibility that a sufficient causal relationship might be established between a materially deceptive proxy and lost state remedies to support an implied right of recovery, the Court reasoned that causation under this theory could not be established because plaintiffs had not proved any loss.

Virginia law barred suits seeking to avoid a merger tainted by a director's conflict of interest only if the ratifying vote was procured pursuant to full disclosure of the material facts of the transaction, including the conflict of interest. Plaintiffs' contention that the proxy contained material misrepresentations necessarily prevented their loss of relief under this state law. Plaintiffs failed to allege any other lost state remedy. Hence, since plaintiffs failed to establish the necessary injury required under a theory of causation alleging lost state remedies, they could not succeed under such theory. The Supreme Court therefore found it unnecessary to decide whether §14(a) provided such implied relief.

B. PLAINTIFF'S THEORIES OF RECOVERY . . .

Plaintiffs set forth two theories of causation to support their claims. They assert first that an implied action under any of the four securities law provisions pleaded should be recognized because 85 percent of the voting shares, or 12 percent of the minority shareholders in addition to the controlling majority shareholders, had to approve the merger in order for the exchange of stock to take place without tax consequences. Although an opinion letter stated the merger might have tax-free consequences for the majority shareholders if 85 percent of the shareholders approved it, such an approval level was not a requirement of the merger. If it was not an express condition of the merger, the higher rate of dissenting voters could only prevent the merger were it to influence the controlling majority. Such a speculative and hypothetical causal connection would make liability "turn on 'hazy' issues [and invite] self-serving testimony, strike suits, and protracted discovery, with little chance of reasoned resolution by pretrial process." *Virginia Bankshares,* [501 U.S. at 1105] (rejecting causal theory [premised] on majority's desire for "cosmetic" vote and avoidance of minority shareholders' ill-will). Thus, we reject this theory of causation.

Plaintiffs' second theory of causation—one with more merit and upon which §14(a) causes of action have been sustained in the past—is that their deceptively procured vote in favor of the merger deprived them of their state appraisal rights under N.Y. Bus. Corp. Law §§623(a), (b); §910(a)(1). We and other courts have recognized that plaintiffs might prevail on such a §14(a) theory. . . .

As noted, *Virginia Bankshares* left open the possibility that §14(a) might include this type of implied right to recover and did not address whether the causal relationship between a deceptive proxy and lost state remedies was sufficient to support a federal remedy. Defendants, having failed to contest causation prior to the present appeal, . . . should hardly be allowed to argue the point now, especially when to permit such puts them in a better position than if they had made this objection earlier and lost. . . .

We continue to believe that a minority shareholder, who has lost his right to a state appraisal because of a materially deceptive proxy, may make "a sufficient showing of causal relationship between the violation and the injury for which he seeks redress." [Mills v. Electric Auto-Lite Co., 396 U.S. 375, 385 (1970).] The transaction effected by a proxy involves not only the merger of the corporate entities, and the attendant exchange of stock, but also the forfeiture of shareholders' appraisal rights. The injury sustained by a minority shareholder powerless to affect the outcome of the merger vote is not the merger but the loss of his appraisal right. The deceptive proxy plainly constitutes an "essential link" in accomplishing the forfeiture of this state right.

That the causal nexus between the merger and the proxy is absent when the minority stockholder's vote cannot affect the merger decision does not necessarily mean a causal link between the proxy and some other injury may not exist. We recognize that loss causation or economic harm to plaintiffs must be shown, as well as proof that the misrepresentations induced plaintiffs to engage in the subject transaction, that is, transaction causation. Here loss causation may be established when a proxy statement prompts a shareholder to accept an unfair exchange ratio for his shares rather than recoup a greater value through a state appraisal. And transaction causation may be shown when a proxy statement, because of material misrepresentations, causes a shareholder to forfeit his appraisal rights by voting in favor of the proposed corporate merger.

Even though the proxy was not legally required in this case, when defendants choose to issue a proxy plaintiffs have a right to a truthful one. With the Securities

Exchange Act of 1934, Congress sought to promote fair corporate suffrage with respect to "'every equity security'" by requiring an "'explanation to the stockholder of the real nature of the questions for which authority to cast his vote is sought.'" *Mills*, 396 U.S. at 381 (quoting H.R. Rep. No. 1383, 73d Cong., 2d Sess. 13-14 (1934)); see also J.I. Case Co. v. Borak, 377 U.S. 426, 431-32 (1964). Congress' interest in the protection of investors and the "'free exercise of [their] voting rights,'" *Borak*, 377 U.S. at 431 (quoting H.R. Rep. No. 1383, 73d Cong., 2d Sess. 14 (1934)), should not vary in degree according to the ability of the shareholder to affect the merger, if the vote nevertheless may result in a different sort of injury which full disclosure might have avoided. See Healey v. Catalyst Recovery of Pa., Inc., 616 F.2d 641, 646 (3d Cir. 1980) (that harm to plaintiff from violation of 10b-5 was deprivation of a state remedy in no way lessens federal interest in preventing the violation); Schlick [v. Penn-Dixie Cement Corp.,] 507 F. 2d [374] at 383 [2d Cir. 1974].

The statute does not suggest that the prohibition of material misrepresentation in a proxy extends only to necessary proxies that are mailed to shareholders the solicitation of whose votes may affect the outcome of the proposed corporate action. That a controlling group of shareholders may accomplish any corporate change they want does not insulate them from liability for injury occasioned when they commit the sort of fraud that §14(a) seeks to prevent. See Swanson v. American Consumer Indus., Inc., 415 F.2d 1326, 1331-1332 (7th Cir. 1969). To decline to extend the protection of §14(a) to plaintiffs, we think, might sanction overreaching by controlling shareholders when the minority shareholders most need §14(a)'s protection. See *Schlick*, 507 F.2d at 383. At the same time, allowing the action does not pose a threat of "speculative claims and procedural intractability," *Virginia Bankshares*, [501 U.S. at 1105], because the forfeiture of state appraisal rights is a question separate from the effectuation of the merger and does not require courts to guess how or whether the majority shareholders would have proceeded in the face of minority dissent. . . .

NOTES: REMEDIES

1. The Second Circuit in *Wilson* said plaintiffs "should be entitled to the profits attributable to the extra stock they would have received had the proxy provided a fair exchange ratio. Although the fraud may not be the proximate cause of the merger, it did cause a forfeiture of appraisal rights, which in turn prevented plaintiffs from realizing a fair exchange ratio." 979 F.2d at 932-933. Does that give plaintiff a better recovery under the federal rule than the plaintiff would have received at state law?

2. The Court's holding in *Mills*, to the extent that it survives *Virginia Bankshares*, requires consideration of remedy. Justice Harlan's opinion for the Court in *Mills* said:

> Our conclusion that petitioners have established their case by showing that proxies necessary to approval of the merger were obtained by means of a materially misleading solicitation implies nothing about the form of relief to which they may be entitled. We held in Borak that upon finding a violation the courts were "to be alert to provide such remedies as are necessary to make effective the congressional purpose," noting specifically that such remedies are not to be limited to prospective relief. In devising retrospective relief for violation of the proxy rules, the federal courts should consider the same factors that would govern the relief granted for any

similar illegality or fraud. One important factor may be the fairness of the terms of the merger. Possible forms of relief will include setting aside the merger or granting other equitable relief, but, as the Court of Appeals below noted, nothing in the statutory policy "requires the court to unscramble a corporate transaction merely because a violation occurred." In selecting a remedy the lower courts should exercise "'the sound discretion which guides the determinations of courts of equity,'" keeping in mind the role of equity as "the instrument for nice adjustment and reconciliation between the public interest and private needs as well as between competing private claims." Hecht Co. v. Bowles, 321 U.S. 321, 329-330 (1944), quoting from Meredith v. Winter Haven, 320 U.S. 228, 235 (1943). . . .

Monetary relief will, of course, also be a possibility. Where the defect in the proxy solicitation relates to the specific terms of the merger, the district court might appropriately order an accounting to ensure that the shareholders receive the value that was represented as coming to them. On the other hand, where, as here, the misleading aspect of the solicitation did not relate to terms of the merger, monetary relief might be afforded to the shareholders only if the merger resulted in a reduction of the earnings or earnings potential of their holdings. In short, damages should be recoverable only to the extent that they can be shown. If commingling of the assets and operations of the merged companies makes it impossible to establish direct injury from the merger, relief might be predicated on a determination of the fairness of the terms of the merger at the time it was approved. These questions, of course, are for decision in the first instance by the District Court on remand, and our singling out of some of the possibilities is not intended to exclude others.

396 U.S. at 386-389.

On remand, the trial court awarded damages of $1,233,918.35 plus interest. On appeal of that judgment, the Seventh Circuit concluded that the merger terms were fair and that the plaintiffs should recover nothing. 552 F.2d 1239 (7th Cir.), cert. denied, 434 U.S. 922 (1977). Who then benefits from the Supreme Court's ruling?

3. The Supreme Court in *Mills* left the question of relief to subsequent proceedings, but said that petitioners should be entitled to an interim award of litigation expenses and reasonable attorneys' fees:

While the general American rule is that attorneys' fees are not ordinarily recoverable as costs, both the courts and Congress have developed exceptions to this rule for situations in which overriding considerations indicate the need for such a recovery. A primary judge-created exception has been to award expenses where a plaintiff has successfully maintained a suit, usually on behalf of a class, that benefits a group of others in the same manner as himself. To allow the others to obtain full benefit from the plaintiff's efforts without contributing equally to the litigation expenses would be to enrich the others unjustly at the plaintiff's expense. This suit presents such a situation. The dissemination of misleading proxy solicitations was a "deceit practiced on the stockholders as a group," J.I. Case Co. v. Borak, 377 U.S., at 432, and the expenses of petitioners' lawsuit have been incurred for the benefit of the corporation and the other shareholders.

The fact that this suit has not yet produced, and may never produce, a monetary recovery from which the fees could be paid does not preclude an award based on this rationale. . . . [I]n shareholders' derivative actions, . . . the courts increasingly have recognized that the expenses incurred by one shareholder in the vindication of a corporate right of action can be spread among all shareholders through an award against the corporation, regardless of whether an actual money recovery has been obtained in the corporation's favor. For example, awards have been sustained in suits by stockholders complaining that shares of their corporation had been issued wrongfully for an inadequate consideration. A successful suit of this type, resulting in cancellation of the shares, does not bring a fund into court or add to the assets of the corporation, but it does benefit the holders of the remaining shares by enhancing their value. Similarly, holders of voting trust certificates have been allowed reimbursement of their expenses from the corporation where they succeeded in terminating the voting trust and obtaining for all certificate holders the right to vote their shares. In these cases there was a "common fund" only in the sense that the court's jurisdiction over the corporation as nominal defendant made it possible to assess fees against all of the shareholders through an award against the corporation.

In many of these instances the benefit conferred is capable of expression in monetary terms, if only by estimating the increase in market value of the shares attributable to the successful litigation. However, an increasing number of lower courts have acknowledged that a corporation may receive a "substantial benefit" from a derivative suit, justifying an award of counsel fees, regardless of whether the benefit is pecuniary in nature. A leading case is Bosch v. Meeker Cooperative Light & Power Assn., 257 Minn. 362, 101 N.W.2d 423 (1960), in which a stockholder was reimbursed for his expenses in obtaining a judicial declaration that the election of certain of the corporation's directors was invalid. . . .

In many suits under §14(a), particularly where the violation does not relate to the terms of the transaction for which proxies are solicited, it may be impossible to assign monetary value to the benefit. Nevertheless, the stress placed by Congress on the importance of fair and informed corporate suffrage leads to the conclusion that, in vindicating the statutory policy, petitioners have rendered a substantial service to the corporation and its shareholders. Whether petitioners are successful in showing a need for significant relief may be a factor in determining whether a further award should later be made. But regardless of the relief granted, private stockholders' actions of this sort "involve corporate therapeutics," and furnish a benefit to all shareholders by providing an important means of enforcement of the proxy statute. To award attorneys' fees in such a suit to a plaintiff who has succeeded in establishing a cause of action is not to saddle the unsuccessful party with the expenses but to impose them on the class that has benefited from them and that would have had to pay them had it brought the suit.

396 U.S. at 389-397.

In contrast to the award of attorneys' fees in *Mills,* a 1975 Supreme Court decision held it was improper to award attorneys' fees to several environmental organizations based on a theory that they were acting as private attorneys general. Alyeska Pipeline Serv. Co. v. Wilderness Society, 421 U.S. 240 (1975). On the basis of *Alyeska,* the Seventh Circuit's remand decision discussed in Note 2 held that plaintiffs in the *Mills* case were not entitled to compensation for fees and expenses for continuing in the case after their initial victory in the Supreme Court.

PROBLEM 10-2

Union, Inc., the owner of 55 percent of Subsidiary, Inc., decides it would be advantageous to purchase the remaining 45 percent of the shares of Subsidiary. Two Union directors, who also serve as Subsidiary directors, recommend to Union that it acquire Subsidiary at any price up to $25 per share, an amount that reflects expected synergy from the combination of Union and Subsidiary and savings from not having to make public filings and related matters for Subsidiary. Union decides to offer $21 per share, a premium over the $14 at which the shares have been traded. Union causes Subsidiary to retain an investment banker who opines that $21 is fair value, and the independent directors of Subsidiary approve the merger. Neither the investment banker nor the independent board members have access to the internal board report nor was it mentioned in the proxy solicitation that preceded the merger. Will minority shareholders be able to state a claim under §14a-9?

3. Disclosure Required by State Law

In re The Topps Company Shareholders Litigation
Delaware Court of Chancery, 2007
926 A.2d 58

STRINE, VICE CHANCELLOR.

I. INTRODUCTION

The Topps Company, Inc. is familiar to all sports-loving Americans. Topps makes baseball and other cards (think Pokemon), this is Topps's so-called "Entertainment Business." It also distributes Bazooka bubble gum and other old-style confections, this is Topps's "Confectionary Business." Arthur Shorin, the son of Joseph Shorin, one of the founders of Topps and the inspiration for "Bazooka Joe," is Topps's current Chairman and Chief Executive Officer. Shorin has served in those positions since 1980 and has worked for Topps for more than half a century, though he owns only about 7% of Topps's equity. Shorin's son-in-law, Scott Silverstein, is his second-in-command, serving as Topps's President and Chief Operating Officer.

. . . [I]ts financial performance has, as a general matter, flagged over the past five years. In 2005, Topps was threatened with a proxy contest. It settled that dispute by a promise to explore strategic options, including a sale of its Confectionary Business. Topps tried to auction off its Confectionary Business, but a serious buyer never came forward. Insurgents reemerged the next year, in a year when Shorin was among the three directors up for re-election to Topps's classified board. With the ballots about to be counted, and defeat a near certainty for the management nominees, Shorin cut a face-saving deal, which expanded the board to ten and involved his re-election along with the election of all of the insurgent nominees.

Before that happened, former Disney CEO and current private equity investor Michael Eisner had called Shorin and offered to be "helpful." Shorin understood Eisner to be proposing a going private transaction.

. . . Almost immediately, the insurgent directors and the incumbent directors began to split on substantive and, it is fair to say, stylistic grounds. The insurgents then became "Dissident Directors." . . . In particular, [an ad hoc committee of incumbent and dissident directors] divided on the issue of whether and how Topps should be sold. . . .

From the time the insurgents were seated, Eisner was on the scene, expressing an interest in making a bid. Two other financial buyers also made a pass. But Topps's public message was that it was not for sale.

Eventually, the other bidders dropped out after making disappointingly low value expressions of interest. Eisner was told by a key Incumbent Director that the Incumbent Directors might embrace a bid of $10 per share. Eisner later bid $9.24 in a proposal that envisioned his retention of existing management, including Shorin's son-in-law. Eisner was willing to tolerate a post-signing Go Shop process, but not a pre-signing auction.

The Ad Hoc Committee split 2-2 over whether to negotiate with Eisner. Although offered the opportunity to participate in the negotiation process, the apparent leader of the Dissidents refused, favoring a public auction. One of the Incumbent Directors who was an independent director took up the negotiating oar, and reached agreement with Eisner on a merger at $9.75 per share. The "Merger Agreement" gave Topps the chance to shop the bid for 40 days after signing, and the right to accept a "Superior Proposal" after that, subject only to Eisner's receipt of a termination fee and his match right.

The Topps board approved the Merger Agreement in a divided vote, with the Incumbent Directors all favoring the Merger, and the Dissidents all dissenting. . . .

Shortly before the Merger Agreement was approved, Topps's chief competitor in the sports cards business, plaintiff The Upper Deck Company, expressed a willingness to make a bid. That likely came as no surprise to Topps since Upper Deck had indicated its interest in Topps nearly a year and half earlier. In fact, Upper Deck had expressed an unrequited ardor for a friendly deal with Topps since 1999, and Shorin knew that. But Topps signed the Merger Agreement with Eisner without responding to Upper Deck's overture. Shortly after the Merger was approved, Topps's investment banker began the Go Shop process, contacting more than 100 potential strategic and financial bidders, including Upper Deck, who was the only serious bidder to emerge.

Suffice it to say that Upper Deck did not move with the clarity and assiduousness one would ideally expect from a competitive rival seeking to make a topping bid. Suffice it also to say that Topps's own reaction to Upper Deck's interest was less than welcoming. Instead of an aggressive bidder and a hungry seller tangling in a diligent, expedited way over key due diligence and deal term issues, the story that emerges from the record is of a slow-moving bidder unwilling to acknowledge Topps's legitimate proprietary concerns about turning over sensitive information to its main competitor and a seller happy to have a bid from an industry rival go away, even if that bid promised the Topps's stockholders better value.

By the end of the Go Shop period, Upper Deck had expressed a willingness to pay $10.75 per share in a friendly merger, subject to its receipt of additional due diligence and other conditions. Although having the option freely to continue negotiations to induce an even more favorable topping bid by finding that Upper Deck's interest was likely to result in a Superior Proposal, the Topps board, with one Dissident Director dissenting, one abstaining, and one absent, voted not to make such a finding.

After the end of the Go Shop period, Upper Deck made another unsolicited overture, expressing a willingness to buy Topps for $10.75 without a financing contingency and with a strong come hell or high water promise to deal with manageable (indeed, mostly cosmetic) antitrust issues. The bid, however, limited Topps to a remedy for failing to close limited to a reverse break-up fee in the same amount ($12 million) Eisner secured as the only recourse against him. Without ever seriously articulating why Upper Deck's proposal for addressing the antitrust issue was inadequate and without proposing a specific higher reverse break-up fee, the Topps Incumbent Directors have thus far refused to treat Upper Deck as having presented a Superior Proposal, a prerequisite to putting the onus on Eisner to match that price or step aside.

In fact, Topps went public with a disclosure about Upper Deck's bid, but in a form that did not accurately represent that expression of interest and disparaged Upper

Deck's seriousness. Topps did that knowing that it had required Upper Deck to agree to a contractual standstill (the "Standstill Agreement") prohibiting Upper Deck from making public any information about its discussions with Topps or proceeding with a tender offer for Topps shares without permission from the Topps board.

The Topps board has refused Upper Deck's request for relief from the Standstill Agreement in order to allow Upper Deck to make a tender offer and to tell its side of events. A vote on the Eisner Merger is scheduled to occur within a couple of weeks.

A group of "Stockholder Plaintiffs" and Upper Deck (collectively, the "moving parties") have moved for a preliminary injunction. They contend that the upcoming Merger vote will be tainted by Topps's failure to disclose material facts about the process that led to the Merger Agreement and about Topps's subsequent dealings with Upper Deck. Even more, they argue that Topps is denying its stockholders the chance to decide for themselves whether to forsake the lower-priced Eisner Merger in favor of the chance to accept a tender offer from Upper Deck at a higher price. Regardless of whether the Topps board prefers the Eisner Merger as lower risk, the moving parties contend that the principles animating Revlon, Inc. v. MacAndrews & Forbes Holdings, Inc. prevent the board from denying the stockholders the chance to make a mature, uncoerced decision for themselves.

In this decision, I conclude that a preliminary injunction against the procession of the Eisner Merger vote should issue until such time as: (1) the Topps board discloses several material facts not contained in the corporation's "Proxy Statement," including facts regarding Eisner's assurances that he would retain existing management after the Merger; and (2) Upper Deck is released from the standstill for purposes of: (a) publicly commenting on its negotiations with Topps; and (b) making a non-coercive tender offer on conditions as favorable or more favorable than those it has offered to the Topps board....

II.   A READER'S ROADMAP TO THE OPINION

.... When directors of a Delaware corporation seek approval for a merger, they have a duty to provide the stockholders with the material facts relevant to making an informed decision.[3] In that connection, the directors must also avoid making materially misleading disclosures, which tell a distorted rendition of events or obscure material facts.[4] In determining whether the directors have complied with their disclosure obligations, the court applies well-settled standards of materiality, familiar to practitioners of our law and federal securities law.[5]

---

3. E.g., Arnold v. Society for Savings Bancorp, Inc., 650 A.2d 1270, 1277 (Del. 1994).

4. E.g., Emerald Partners v. Berlin, 726 A.2d 1215, 1223 (Del. Supr. 1999) ("When stockholder action is requested, directors are required to provide shareholders with all information that is material to the action being requested and to provide a balanced truthful account of all matters disclosed in the communication with shareholders.") (quotation omitted).

5. See, e.g., Rosenblatt v. Getty Oil Co., 493 A.2d 929, 944 (Del. 1985) (explaining that information is material if "there is a substantial likelihood that a reasonable investor would consider it important in deciding how to vote") (citing TSC Industries, Inc. v. Northway, Inc., 426 U.S. 438, 449, 96 S. Ct. 2126, 48 L. Ed. 2d 757 (1976)).

The so-called *Revlon* standard is equally familiar. When directors propose to sell a company for cash or engage in a change of control transaction, they must take reasonable measures to ensure that the stockholders receive the highest value reasonably attainable. Of particular pertinence to this case, when directors have made the decision to sell the company, any favoritism they display toward particular bidders must be justified solely by reference to the objective of maximizing the price the stockholders receive for their shares. When directors bias the process against one bidder and toward another not in a reasoned effort to maximize advantage for the stockholders, but to tilt the process toward the bidder more likely to continue current management, they commit a breach of fiduciary duty.

III. FACTUAL BACKGROUND . . .

D. THE UNDISPUTED FACTS THAT ARE NOT
IN THE PROXY STATEMENT . . .

1. The Failure to Disclose Eisner's Assurances to Topps Management

The Stockholder Plaintiffs and Upper Deck believe that the Incumbent Directors, prefer a deal with Eisner that will enable the company's current managers to continue in their positions. More pointedly, they suggest that the Incumbent Directors want to help Shorin preserve his influence over the business his family started by perpetuating Silverstein in office.

In this respect, the Stockholder Plaintiffs and Upper Deck contend that the Proxy Statement obscures the extent of Eisner's assurances that a result of that type will obtain if the Eisner Merger is consummated. To that point, they note that the Proxy Statement goes out of its way to stress that the Topps board "instructed the Company's management not to have any discussions with [Eisner] . . . [before a merger agreement was signed] regarding any employment arrangements following the consummation of a transaction. Accordingly, no discussions regarding post-merger employment arrangements took place . . . prior to the execution of the merger agreement."

But that is true only in a misleadingly literal sense. The Proxy Statement does not disclose that both in Eisner's first indication of interest submitted on December 22, 2006 at $9.24 per share and his subsequent proposal at $9.75 per share, Eisner explicitly stated that his proposal was "designed to" retain "substantially all of [Topps's] existing senior management and key employees."

Nor does the Proxy Statement disclose that Eisner had continually communicated that intention and his high regard for Topps management to Feder and Greenberg during the course of the Merger Agreement negotiations. In fact, it is undisputed that before the signing of the Merger Agreement, Feder set up a conference call between Eisner, on the one side, and key Topps executives, including Silverstein, on the other. The purpose of that call was specifically to give Eisner the opportunity to personally reiterate the assurances about management's likely future that he had conveyed to Feder.

To be direct, the Proxy Statement should have disclosed these facts. As it currently stands, the Proxy Statement creates a misleading impression that Topps managers have been given no assurances about their future by Eisner.[12] In reality, Eisner has premised his bid all along as one that is friendly to management and that depends on their retention.

2.   *The Proxy Statement's Failure to Disclose a Lehman Brothers Valuation Presentation That Casts Doubt on the Fairness of the Merger*

The Proxy Statement has a detailed description of the financial analyses that Lehman Brothers undertook in connection with advising Topps. The Stockholder Plaintiffs raise several points about the valuation disclosure. But one point is a substantial one.

[The Proxy Statement disclosed the results of a Discounted Cash Flow (DCF) calculation done by Lehman Brothers, the firm's investment banker, on March 1, 2007, in connection with Lehman's ultimate fairness presentation and two sets of financial projections, one a very aggressive, very optimistic set, developed primarily as a selling tool and the other a more conservative, realistic projection of what Topps could achieve. That set also projected improved performance but at more modest levels than the selling projections. The range based on more realistic assumptions, but ones that Lehman still deemed "rather aggressive," indicated that Eisner was offering a very attractive price.]

The problem that the Stockholder Plaintiffs point out is that on January 25, 2007, a mere month or so beforehand, Lehman had made a detailed presentation to the Topps board containing similar analyses [of an aggressive case and a moderate case but producing a higher range of value in which Eisner's bid was in the low end of the moderate case. A discounted cash flow analysis projects estimated flow for each year of a specific period (often the next five years) and then computes a terminal value for cash flow beyond the specific period. The total cash flow is then discounted for the return that an investor would expect on that income stream given the risk of the enterprise as compared to other investments. Between the January 25 presentation and the March 1 opinion, Lehman raised this average cost of capital used to compute discounted cash flow and lowered the multiple used to compute the terminal value portion of the computation.] . . .

As anyone who performs valuations knows, raising discount rates and lowering terminal multiples drives down the resulting value range. Subjective judgments like these are, of course, not scientific, but highly-paid valuation advisors should be able to rationally explain them. In this case, one can accept the decrease that came from management changes that made the projections more realistic based on more current information; indeed, the very modest nature of those changes—reducing expected compound annual sales growth in the Moderate Case from 5.8% to 5.6%, and in the

---

12. By contrast, the Proxy Statement fairly discloses the agreement Shorin negotiated with Eisner over his own future.

Aggressive Case from 9.3% to 9.0% — inspires some confidence. What is not at all clear is why these modest changes were accompanied by major shifts in Lehman's analytical approach.

Candidly, the defendants have not made any confidence-inspiring explanations for Lehman's analytical changes. The record reflects what Dissident Director Ajdler feared — that Lehman would manipulate its analyses to try to make the Eisner offer look more attractive once it was clear Eisner would not budge on price. He sent an e-mail to Greenberg to that effect, and Greenberg's response seemed to agree that was a possibility.

In finding that the Proxy Statement does not fairly address this issue, I do not and need not make any finding that there was a purposeful intent on Lehman's part to generate a range of value that eased its ability to issue a fairness opinion. What I do find is that there is no evidence that the prior January 25 Moderate Case DCF analysis — which was based on five years of projections (and therefore involved less emphasis on a single terminal value estimate) and used a cost of capital that was rationally explained — was no longer reliable. That analysis cast the price Eisner was offering to pay in a quite different light than that which Lehman performed on March 1.

. . . Given the major subjective changes that Lehman made that were not explained, given that those changes made the Eisner bid look much more attractive, and given that those changes were made only after [an incumbent director's] attempts to negotiate a price higher than $9.75 had finally failed, the Proxy Statement is materially misleading for failing to discuss the advice given to the Board about valuation on January 25.

3. Alleged Omissions and Material Misstatements of Fact Bearing on Upper Deck's Credibility as a Bidder

. . . Upper Deck [argued] that the Proxy Statement and other public statements of Topps have misrepresented the two acquisition overtures Upper Deck has made to buy Topps following the execution of the Eisner Merger Agreement. As explained, Topps has publicly disclosed that it rejected Upper Deck's bid because of Upper Deck's failure to provide a firm debt financing commitment. The Proxy Statement fails to disclose, however, that Upper Deck's bid was not subject to a financing contingency. That is, Upper Deck was willing to enter into a merger agreement with Topps that would not let Upper Deck entirely off the hook in the event that it could not arrange financing. In that event, Upper Deck would be liable to Topps for the full amount of the $12 million reverse break-up fee that Upper Deck has proposed. That is the same remedy available to Topps if Eisner breaches. Topps did not make that clear. That was materially misleading. So was the failure to disclose the lack of a financing contingency.

Moreover, Upper Deck has now presented Topps with a letter from CIBC World Markets, a commercial lender, stating that CIBC is "highly confident" that it will be able to provide financing. Although Topps decries the contingent nature of that letter, it also does not explain that many of the conditions described in the letter relate to CIBC's desire to examine information that Topps was, at the time, refusing to provide to Upper Deck, or even CIBC (which promised not to share the information with Upper Deck).

Topps's Proxy Statement also cites antitrust concerns and Upper Deck's "unwillingness to sufficiently assume the risk associated with a failure to obtain the necessary antitrust approval." The Proxy Statement does not disclose, however, that in Upper Deck's revised unsolicited bid that it submitted after the close of the Go Shop Period, Upper Deck agreed to a strong "hell or high water" antitrust provision in which Upper Deck agreed to divest itself of any and all assets necessary to obtain regulatory approval. That is, if the antitrust regulators, or Major League Baseball for that matter, object to Upper Deck holding the only two existing licenses to print baseball cards, Upper Deck will divest itself of one of them. The only thing Upper Deck is unwilling to divest is its intellectual property, such as the Topps or Upper Deck name. Despite having every urgent reason to do so, Topps has identified no colorable argument as to why Upper Deck would or should be asked to do that. And Topps does not even fairly represent the substantial hell or high water provision offered by Upper Deck. In that respect, Topps also failed to disclose that Upper Deck presented Topps with an opinion from a reputable antitrust expert opining that there was no material antitrust risk. . . .

E. WHO'S TELLING THE TRUTH?: THE PARTIES' DEBATE ABOUT
HOW THINGS ACTUALLY WENT DOWN

In the preceding section, I described the disclosure arguments of the moving parties that were based on matters generally not in dispute. Most of the remaining disclosure arguments of the Stockholder Plaintiffs and Upper Deck fall into a different category. These are arguments premised on the notion that Proxy Statement has told only one version of a disputed version of events. [Dissident director Ajdler, who is soliciting proxies against the merger, has been telling his version of events, ensuring the Topps stockholders hear his version and that of the other dissident directors about a variety of issues.] The stockholders can hear out both sides on these issues, and there is no need to force Topps to disclose a version of events that they contend never happened.

The same, however, is not true about the matters of contention between the Topps Incumbent Directors and Upper Deck. Topps and Upper Deck also have many disagreements about the true course of events, but only Topps has been able to tell its story to the Topps stockholders.

For example, as indicated previously, the Proxy Statement notes that Lehman had advised Topps in 2005 that because of the divergent nature of Topps's Entertainment and Confectionary Businesses, there was no "logical strategic buyer for the company." But Upper Deck claims that it had indicated its interest in acquiring Topps on several occasions before Topps entered into negotiations with Eisner. And in fact, Topps does not dispute that Upper Deck has made overtures about acquiring Topps in the past. In fact, Topps has submitted communications between Topps and Upper Deck dating from the 1998-2000 era, in which Upper Deck stated that it wanted to buy Topps in a friendly deal. Upper Deck contends that it reiterated that desire in both 2003 and 2004, as well as in 2005. Topps denies that Upper Deck contacted it in 2003 and 2004. . . .

Likewise, Upper Deck believes that the Proxy Statement misrepresents the dynamics of the negotiations between Upper Deck and Topps during the Go Shop Period. . . .

Topps has reasonable responses. . . . This sort of "he said, she said" stuff between a bidder and a target cannot be rationally sorted out by a court in a preliminary injunction proceeding so as to permit the formulation of a judicial order requiring the target to disclose the bidder's preferred version of events. In the usual circumstances, that does not have a materially adverse effect on stockholders, because the bidder can tell its side of events and the stockholders therefore have an opportunity to make their own judgment about who is right. But in this case, the Topps Incumbent Directors have refused to release Upper Deck from the Standstill, even for the limited purpose of communicating with the Topps stockholders.

IV. THE ESSENCE OF THE *REVLON* CLAIMS

. . . [T]he Stockholder Plaintiffs' *Revlon* arguments . . . are premised on the notion that the Incumbent Directors who constitute a majority of the Topps board have been motivated by a desire to ensure that Topps remains under the control of someone friendly to the Shorin family and who will continue Shorin family members in the top leadership position. Since Shorin was forced into a face-saving settlement adding the Dissidents to the board, Shorin has known that time was running out on him. Therefore, he was motivated to find a buyer who was friendly to him and would guarantee that Shorin and Silverstein, his son-in-law, would continue to play leading roles at Topps. If Shorin didn't strike a deal to that effect before the 2007 annual meeting, he faced the prospect of having a new board majority oust him and his son-in-law from their managerial positions, and being relegated to a mere 7% stockholder of the company his father and uncles started, and that he has personally managed as CEO for more than a quarter century. According to the Stockholder Plaintiffs, Eisner was the answer to Shorin's dilemma, as he promised to be "helpful" by taking Topps private and retaining Silverstein as CEO.

To the supposed end of helping Shorin meet his personal objectives, the Topps board majority resisted the Dissidents' desire for a public auction of Topps, and signed up a deal with Eisner without any effort to shop the company beforehand. Not only that, the Stockholder Plaintiffs contend that defendant Greenberg capped the price that could be extracted from Eisner by making an ill-advised and unauthorized decision to mention to Eisner that a $10 per share bid was likely to command the support of the non-Dissident directors.

The Stockholder Plaintiffs also complain that the deal protection measures in the Merger Agreement precluded any effective post-signing market check. Although the Stockholder Plaintiffs admit the Merger Agreement contained a Go Shop provision allowing Topps to shop the company for forty days, the Stockholder Plaintiffs contend that that time period was too short and that the break-up fee and match right provided to Eisner were, in combination, too bid-chilling. Therefore, although Topps approached over 100 financial and strategic bidders to solicit their interest, the Stockholder Plaintiffs say that effort was bound to fail from the get-go, especially given the market's justifiable suspicions that Shorin and the board majority wanted to do a deal with Eisner to preserve the Shorin family's managerial influence. . . .

V.   RESOLUTION OF THE *REVLON* CLAIMS AND DECISION ON THE SCOPE OF THE INJUNCTION

. . . In the end, I perceive no unreasonable flaw in the approach that the Topps board took to negotiating the Merger Agreement with Eisner. I see no evidence that another bidder who expressed a serious interest to get in the game during 2006 was fended off. There is no suggestion by even the Stockholder Plaintiffs that the two other private equity firms who discussed making a bid with Topps were inappropriately treated.

Most important, I do not believe that the substantive terms of the Merger Agreement suggest an unreasonable approach to value maximization. The Topps board did not accept Eisner's $9.24 bid. They got him up to $9.75 per share — not their desired goal but a respectable price, especially given Topps's actual earnings history and the precarious nature of its business . . . .

For all these reasons, I cannot buttress the issuance of an injunction on the alleged unreasonableness of the Topps's board decision to sign up the Merger Agreement. I now turn to the more troubling claims raised, which are about the board's conduct after the Merger Agreement was consummated.

. . . Regardless of whose version of events is correct, the Topps board was hardly as receptive as one would expect in a situation where it received an unsolicited overture from a competitor who had long expressed interest in buying Topps in a friendly deal and who, given the likely synergies involved in a combination of the two businesses, might, if serious about doing a deal, be able to pay a materially higher price than a financial buyer like Eisner. And when Upper Deck actually suggested a price materially higher than Eisner, the Topps Incumbent Directors controlling the process did not evince enthusiasm about the possibilities for the stockholders; rather, they seemed more bent on coming up with obstacles to securing that higher value. This regrettably suggests that the Topps Incumbent Directors favored Eisner, who they perceived as a friendly suitor who had pledged to retain management and would continue Shorin and his family in an influential role.

At the same time, Upper Deck hardly moved with the speed expected of an interested buyer that has a limited time in which to secure a deal. Rather, Upper Deck initially acted in a manner that created rational questions about its seriousness and whether it was simply looking to poke around in Topps's files. . . . Although Shorin and the other defendants claim that they truly desire to get the highest value and want nothing more than to get a topping bid from Upper Deck that they can accept, their behavior belies those protestations. In reaching that conclusion, I rely not only on the defendants' apparent failure to undertake diligent good faith efforts at bargaining with Upper Deck, I also rely on the misrepresentations of fact about Upper Deck's offer that are contained in Topps's public statements.

This raises the related issue of how the defendants have used the Standstill. Standstills serve legitimate purposes. When a corporation is running a sale process, it is responsible, if not mandated, for the board to ensure that confidential information is not misused by bidders and advisors whose interests are not aligned with the corporation, to establish rules of the game that promote an orderly auction, and to give the corporation leverage to extract concessions from the parties who seek to make a bid.

But standstills are also subject to abuse. Parties like Eisner often, as was done here, insist on a standstill as a deal protection. Furthermore, a standstill can be used by a target improperly to favor one bidder over another, not for reasons consistent with stockholder interest, but because managers prefer one bidder for their own motives.

In this case, the Topps board reserved the right to waive the Standstill if its fiduciary duties required. That was an important thing to do, given that there was no shopping process before signing with Eisner.

The fiduciary out here also highlights a reality. Although the Standstill is a contract, the Topps board is bound to use its contractual power under that contract only for proper purposes. On this record, I am convinced that Upper Deck has shown a reasonable probability of success on its claim that the Topps board is misusing the Standstill. As I have indicated, I cannot read the record as indicating that the Topps board is using the Standstill to extract reasonable concessions from Upper Deck in order to unlock higher value. The Topps board's negotiating posture and factual misrepresentations are more redolent of pretext, than of a sincere desire to comply with their *Revlon* duties.

Frustrated with its attempt to negotiate with Topps, Upper Deck asked for a release from the Standstill to make a tender offer on the terms it offered to Topps and to communicate with Topps's stockholders. The Topps board refused. That refusal not only keeps the stockholders from having the chance to accept a potentially more attractive higher priced deal, it keeps them in the dark about Upper Deck's version of important events, and it keeps Upper Deck from obtaining antitrust clearance, because it cannot begin the process without either a signed merger agreement or a formal tender offer.

Because the Topps board is recommending that the stockholders cash out, its decision to foreclose its stockholders from receiving an offer from Upper Deck seems likely, after trial, to be found a breach of fiduciary duty. If Upper Deck makes a tender at $10.75 per share on the conditions it has outlined, the Topps stockholders will still be free to reject that offer if the Topps board convinces them it is too conditional. Indeed, Upper Deck is not even asking for some sort of prior restraint preventing the Topps board from implementing a rights plan in the event of a tender offer (although Upper Deck has indicated that will begin round two of this litigation if Topps does). What Upper Deck is asking for is release from the prior restraint on it, a prior restraint that prevents Topps's stockholders from choosing another higher-priced deal. Given that the Topps board has decided to sell the company, and is not using the Standstill Agreement for any apparent legitimate purpose, its refusal to release Upper Deck justifies an injunction. Otherwise, the Topps stockholders may be foreclosed from ever considering Upper Deck's offer, a result that, under our precedent, threatens irreparable injury.

Similarly, Topps went public with statements disparaging Upper Deck's bid and its seriousness but continues to use the Standstill to prevent Upper Deck from telling its own side of the story. The Topps board seeks to have the Topps stockholders accept Eisner's bid without hearing the full story. That is not a proper use of a standstill by a fiduciary given the circumstances presented here. Rather, it threatens the Topps stockholders with making an important decision on an uninformed basis, a threat that justifies injunctive relief.[30]

As this reasoning recognizes, one danger of an injunction based on the Topps board's refusal to waive the Standstill is that it will reduce the board's leverage to bargain with Upper Deck. Because this record suggests no genuine desire by the board to use the Standstill for that purpose, that danger is minimal. To address it, however, the injunction I will issue will not allow Upper Deck to go backwards as it were. The Merger vote will be enjoined until after Topps has granted Upper Deck a waiver of the Standstill to: (1) make an all shares, non-coercive tender offer of $10.75 cash or more per share, on conditions as to financing and antitrust no less favorable to Topps than contained in Upper Deck's most recent offer; and (2) communicate with Topps stockholders about its version of relevant events. The parties shall settle the order in good faith so as to avoid any timing inequities to either Eisner or Upper Deck, and therefore to the Topps stockholders. The injunction will not permit Upper Deck any relief from its obligations not to misuse Topps's confidential information. . . .

The other danger of an injunction of this kind is premised on a fear that stockholders will make an erroneous decision. In this regard, it is notable that nothing in this decision purports to compel the Topps board to enter a merger agreement with Upper Deck that it believes to be unduly conditional. What this decision does conclude is that, on this record, there is no reasonable basis for permitting the Topps board to deny its stockholders the chance to consider for themselves whether to prefer Upper Deck's higher-priced deal, taking into account its unique risks, over Eisner's lower-priced deal, which has its own risks. If the Topps board sees the Upper Deck tender offer and believes it should not be accepted, it can tell the stockholders why. It can even consider the use of a rights plan to prevent the tender offer's procession, if it can square use of such a plan with its obligations under *Revlon* and *Unocal*. But it cannot at this point avoid an injunction on the unsubstantiated premise that the Topps stockholders will be unable, after the provision of full information, rationally to decide for themselves between two competing, non-coercive offers.

Consistent with this reasoning, the vote on the Eisner Merger will also be enjoined until Topps issues corrective disclosures addressing the problems identified earlier in this decision.

NOTES AND QUESTIONS

1. As set out in the *Topps* opinion, above, disclosure obligations under Delaware law are drawn from the common law and judicial explications of directors' fiduciary duty. Under federal law, disclosure obligations are derived from federal statutes, SEC

---

30. See, e.g., Louisiana Municipal Police Employees' Retirement System v. Crawford, 918 A.2d 1172, 1192 (Del. Ch. 2007) ("Shareholders would suffer irreparable harm [if they] were . . . forced to vote without knowledge of . . . material facts."); ODS Technologies, L.P. v. Marshall, 832 A.2d 1254, 1262 (Del. Ch. 2003) ("The threat of an uninformed stockholder vote constitutes irreparable harm."); Pure Resources, 808 A.2d at 452 ("[I]rreparable injury is threatened when a stockholder might make a tender or voting decision on the basis of materially misleading or inadequate information.").

rule making, and judicial explications thereof. Although these sources are very different, the substance of disclosure obligations under state law is very similar to those arising under federal law. Delaware courts recognize and explicitly make use of federal judicial and regulatory expertise in setting disclosure standards. See, for example, the reference in Part II of the *Topps* opinion to materiality that incorporates the federal test established in TSC v. Northway (supra, page 963). Importantly, Delaware courts have followed the lead of federal lawmakers as to the specifics of what must be disclosed. See, for example, In re Netsmart Technologies, Inc. Shareholders Litigation, 924 A.2d 171, 206 (Del. Ch. 2007), where the Court of Chancery deferred to federal expertise in assessing the adequacy of disclosures related to directors' conflicting interests:

> Federal regulations and exchange rules address disclosure of this kind in a detailed manner that balances the cost of disclosing all past relationships against the need to give stockholders information about some prior relationship that, while not rendering directors non-independent of each other, are important enough to warrant disclosure. Those bodies of authority should not be lightly added to by our law.

2. The distinctive nature of Delaware disclosure law comes not in the substance of the obligation, but in the remedies that can be applied and the interaction of disclosure with the substantive duties of directors. While the court was willing to enjoin the shareholder vote until corrective disclosure had occurred, even more important was the court's invocation of the directors' substantive *Revlon* duty (addressed in Chapter 9) to get the best price for the shareholders. On the basis of *Revlon*, the court required the Topps board to release Upper Deck from the "Standstill Agreement" that the parties had signed earlier in the process.

D. Disclosure Related to Buying and Selling

Disclosure linked to proxy solicitations is necessarily sporadic and limited in scope to the relatively few things on which shareholders vote. In contrast, disclosure linked to shareholders' buying and selling can have a much larger effect. In larger enterprises where there is a developed market for shares, purchases and sales will be occurring almost continuously. Provisions based on such disclosure can have a much broader effect on the shareholder role in corporate governance and for constraining the actions of officers and directors. Rule 10b-5 has become the primary vehicle for this growth, although the scope of the rule is not obvious from reading its words.

1. Federal Law: Rule 10b-5

Securities Exchange Act of 1934 §§10(b), 18
SEC Rule 10b-5

Rule 10b-5 is a broad catchall that has become a key element in the federal regulation of corporations. It provides as follows:

Employment of manipulative and deceptive devices. It shall be unlawful for any person, directly or indirectly, by the use of any means or instrumentality of interstate commerce, or of the mails, or of any facility of any national securities exchange,

>   (a) To employ any device, scheme, or artifice to defraud,
>   (b) To make any untrue statement of a material fact or to omit to state a material fact necessary in order to make the statements made, in the light of the circumstances under which they were made, not misleading, or
>   (c) To engage in any act, practice, or course of business which operates or would operate as a fraud or deceit upon any person,

in connection with the purchase or sale of any security.

What Rule 10b-5 catches must be fraud, a term that we analyzed in connection with proxies in Part C. The various elements of fraud are considered further here in connection with Rule 10b-5. But fraud encompasses a broad variety of acts and Rule 10b-5 does not remedy all fraud, only that in connection with the purchase or sale of securities. This part begins with a focus on the jurisdictional and policy limitations on the fraud covered by Rule 10b-5 and then moves on to particular elements required for a fraud claim.

The origins of the rule in 1942 were described by Milton Freeman at a conference in the late 1960s:

> I was sitting in my office in the S.E.C. building in Philadelphia and I received a call from Jim Treanor who was then the Director of the Trading and Exchange Division. He said, "I have just been on the telephone with Paul Rowen," who was then the S.E.C. Regional Administrator in Boston, "and he has told me about the president of some company in Boston who is going around buying up the stock of his company from his own shareholders at $4.00 a share, and he has been telling them that the company is doing very badly, whereas, in fact, the earnings are going to be quadrupled and will be $2.00 a share for this coming year. Is there anything we can do about it?" So he came upstairs and I called in my secretary and I looked at Section 10(b) and I looked at Section 17, and I put them together, and the only discussion we had there was where "in connection with the purchase or sale" should be, and we decided it should be at the end.
>
>   We called the Commission and we got on the calendar, and I don't remember whether we got there that morning or after lunch. We passed a piece of paper around to all the commissioners. All the commissioners read the rule and they tossed it on the table, indicating approval. Nobody said anything except Sumner Pike who said, "Well," he said, "we are against fraud, aren't we?" That is how it happened.
>
>   . . . I never thought that twenty-odd years later it would be the biggest thing that had ever happened. It was intended to give the Commission power to deal with this problem. It had no relation in the Commission's contemplation to private proceedings.

22 Bus. Law. at 922 (1967).

2. The Reach of Rule 10b-5: Standing and in Connection with a Purchase or Sale

As Freeman's comments illustrate, Rule 10b-5 began as a tool for the government. Nongovernment lawyers, however, sought to make use of it in private suits. Beginning with Kardon v. National Gypsum Co., 69 F. Supp. 512 (E.D. Pa. 1946), federal courts implied a private cause of action. During the 1960s and early 1970s, federal courts extended Rule 10b-5 to cover a broad range of corporate activity, leading some to talk of a federalization of state corporation law. For example, in Supt. of Insurance v. Bankers Life and Casualty Co, 404 U.S. 6 (1971), the Supreme Court, in addition to affirming for the first time that an implied private right of action existed under Rule 10b-5, permitted it to cover an elaborate fraud in which a clever investor, with the help of a company insider, purchased an insurance company in effect with the company's own assets, thereby depleting the company of reserves needed to cover future insurance claims. The series of transactions used to accomplish this fraudulent purchase included a sale of bonds by Manhattan, the insurance company, which constituted the sale of a "security" sufficient to support a 10b-5 action. In the course of its opinion, the Supreme Court described the reach of Rule 10b-5 in broad strokes:

> There certainly was an "act" or "practice" within the meaning of Rule 10b-5 which operated as "a fraud or deceit" on Manhattan, the seller of the Government bonds. To be sure, the full market price was paid for those bonds; but the seller was duped into believing that it, the seller, would receive the proceeds. We cannot agree with the Court of Appeals that "no investor [was] injured" and that the "purity of the security transaction and the purity of the trading process were unsullied." . . .
>
> Section 10(b) outlaws the use "in connection with the purchase or sale" of any security of "any manipulative or deceptive device or contrivance." The Act protects corporations as well as individuals who are sellers of a security. Manhattan was injured as an investor through a deceptive device which deprived it of any compensation for the sale of its valuable block of securities.
>
> The fact that the fraud was perpetrated by an officer of Manhattan and his outside collaborators is irrelevant to our problem. For §10(b) bans the use of any deceptive device in the "sale" of any security by "any person." And the fact that the transaction is not conducted through a securities exchange or an organized over-the-counter market is irrelevant to the coverage of §10(b). Hooper v. Mountain States Securities Corp., 282 F.2d 195, 201. Likewise irrelevant is the fact that the proceeds of the sale that were due the seller were misappropriated. As the Court of Appeals for the Fifth Circuit said in the *Hooper* case, "Considering the purpose of this legislation, it would be unrealistic to say that a corporation having the capacity to acquire $700,000 worth of assets for its 700,000 shares of stock has suffered no loss if what it gave up was $700,000 but what it got was zero."
>
> The Congress made clear that "disregard of trust relationships by those whom the law should regard as fiduciaries are all a single seamless web" along with manipulation, investor's ignorance, and the like. H.R. Rep. No. 1383, 73d Cong., 2d Sess., 6. Since practices "constantly vary and where practices legitimate for some purposes may be turned to illegitimate and fraudulent means, broad discretionary powers" in the regulatory agency "have been found practically essential." Id., at 7. Hence we do not read §10(b) as narrowly as the Court of Appeals; it is not "limited to preserving the integrity of the securities markets" though that purpose is included. Section 10(b) must be read flexibly, not technically and restrictively. Since there was a "sale" of a security and since fraud was used "in connection with" it, there is redress under §10(b), whatever might be available as a remedy under state law.
>
> We agree that Congress by §10(b) did not seek to regulate transactions which constitute no more than internal corporate mismanagement. But we read §10(b) to mean that Congress meant to bar deceptive devices and contrivances in the purchase or sale of securities whether conducted in the organized markets or face to face. And the fact that creditors of the defrauded corporate buyer or seller of securities may be the ultimate victims does not warrant disregard of the corporate entity. The controlling stockholder owes the corporation a fiduciary obligation — one "designed for the protection of the entire community of interests in the corporation — creditors as well as stockholders." Pepper v. Litton, 308 U.S. 295, 307.

Supt. of Insurance v. Bankers Life and Casualty Co, 404 U.S. 6, at 9-12.

After several new appointments to the Supreme Court in the 1970s, the Court began sharply limiting the reach of Rule 10b-5, driven in part by a concern about vexatious litigation. During most of this period, Congress left the development of

Rule 10b-5 to the courts, but legislation passed in 1995, discussed in Section 4, reinforces the restrictive interpretation that the Supreme Court has given to Rule 10b-5 since the mid-1970s.

Blue Chip Stamps v. Manor Drug Stores
United States Supreme Court, 1975
421 U.S. 723

MR. JUSTICE REHNQUIST delivered the opinion of the Court.

This case requires us to consider whether the offerees of a stock offering, made pursuant to an antitrust consent decree and registered under the Securities Act of 1933, may maintain a private cause of action for money damages where they allege that the offeror has violated the provisions of Rule 10b-5 of the Securities and Exchange Commission, but where they have neither purchased nor sold any of the offered shares. See Birnbaum v. Newport Steel Corp., 193 F.2d 461 (C.A.2), cert. denied, 343 U.S. 956 (1952).

I

[As part of the settlement of a government antitrust action Blue Chip Stamp Co. (Old Blue Chip), a company in the business of providing trading stamps to retailers (perks akin to frequent flier miles of more recent years), agreed to widen its ownership base and to offer a substantial number of its shares of common stock to retailers who had used the stamp service in the past but who were not shareholders in the old company. The offering was registered with the SEC as required by the 1933 Act, and somewhat more than 50% of the offered units were actually purchased.] [T]wo years after the offering, respondent, a former user of the stamp service and therefore an offeree of the 1968 offering, filed this suit. . . . It alleged that Blue Chip intentionally made the prospectus overly pessimistic in order to discourage respondent and other members of the allegedly large class whom it represents from accepting what was intended to be a bargain offer, so that the rejected shares might later be offered to the public at a higher price. The complaint alleged that class members because of and in reliance on the false and misleading prospectus failed to purchase the offered units. Respondent therefore sought on behalf of the alleged class some $21,400,000 in damages representing the lost opportunity to purchase the units; the right to purchase the previously rejected units at the 1968 price; and in addition, it sought some $25,000,000 in exemplary damages. . . .

II . . .

Despite the contrast between the provisions of Rule 10b-5 and the numerous carefully drawn express civil remedies provided in the Acts of both 1933 and 1934, it was held in 1946 by the United States District Court for the Eastern District of Pennsylvania that there was an implied private right of action under the Rule. Kardon v. National

Gypsum Co., 69 F. Supp. 512. This Court had no occasion to deal with the subject until 25 years later, and at that time we confirmed with virtually no discussion the overwhelming consensus of the District Courts and Courts of Appeals that such a cause of action did exist. Superintendent of Insurance v. Bankers Life & Cas. Co., 404 U.S. 6, 13 n.9 (1971); Affiliated Ute Citizens v. United States, 406 U.S. 128, 150-154 (1972). Such a conclusion was, of course, entirely consistent with the Court's recognition of J.I. Case Co. v. Borak, 377 U.S. 426, 432 (1964), that private enforcement of Commission rules may "[provide] a necessary supplement to Commission action."

Within a few years after the seminal *Kardon* decision, the Court of Appeals for the Second Circuit concluded that the plaintiff class for purposes of a private damage action under §10(b) and Rule 10b-5 was limited to actual purchasers and sellers of securities. Birnbaum v. Newport Steel Corp., supra.

. . . For the reasons hereinafter stated, we are of the opinion that *Birnbaum* was rightly decided, and that it bars respondent from maintaining this suit under Rule 10b-5.

III

. . . Just as this Court had no occasion to consider the validity of the *Kardon* holding that there was a private cause of action under Rule 10b-5 until 20-odd years later, nearly the same period of time has gone by between the *Birnbaum* decision and our consideration of the case now before us. As with *Kardon,* virtually all lower federal courts facing the issue in the hundreds of reported cases presenting this question over the past quarter century have reaffirmed *Birnbaum*'s conclusion that the plaintiff class for purposes of §10(b) and Rule 10b-5 private damage actions is limited to purchasers and sellers of securities. . . .

[Congress did not adopt SEC proposals in 1957 and 1959 that would have added "any attempt to purchase or sell" to §10(b).] The longstanding acceptance by the courts, coupled with Congress' failure to reject *Birnbaum*'s reasonable interpretation of the wording of §10(b), wording which is directed toward injury suffered "in connection with the purchase or sale" of securities, argues significantly in favor of acceptance of the *Birnbaum* rule by this Court.

[The Court discusses §§17, 18, 28(a), and 29(b) of the 1934 Act and §§11 and 12 of the 1933 Act and concludes:] It would indeed be anomalous to impute to Congress an intention to expand the plaintiff class for a judicially implied cause of action beyond the bounds it delineated for comparable express causes of action.

Having said all this, we would by no means be understood as suggesting that we are able to divine from the language of §10(b) the express "intent of Congress" as to the contours of a private cause of action under Rule 10b-5. When we deal with private actions under Rule 10b-5, we deal with a judicial oak which has grown from little more than a legislative acorn. Such growth may be quite consistent with the congressional enactment and with the role of the federal judiciary in interpreting it, see J.I. Case Co. v. Borak, supra, but it would be disingenuous to suggest that either Congress in 1934 or the Securities and Exchange Commission in 1942 foreordained the present state of the law with respect to Rule 10b-5. It is therefore proper that we consider, in addition to the factors already discussed, what may be described as policy considerations when we come to flesh out the portions of the law with respect to which neither the congressional enactment nor the administrative regulations offer conclusive guidance.

Three principal classes of potential plaintiffs are presently barred by the *Birnbaum* rule. First are potential purchasers of shares, either in a new offering or on the Nation's post-distribution trading markets, who allege that they decided not to purchase because of an unduly gloomy representation or the omission of favorable material which made the issuer appear to be a less favorable investment vehicle than it actually was. Second are actual shareholders in the issuer who allege that they decided not to sell their shares because of an unduly rosy representation or a failure to disclose unfavorable material. Third are shareholders, creditors, and perhaps others related to an issuer who suffered loss in the value of their investment due to corporate or insider activities in connection with the purchase or sale of securities which violate Rule 10b-5. It has been held that shareholder members of the second and third of these classes may frequently be able to circumvent the *Birnbaum* limitation through bringing a derivative action on behalf of the corporate issuer if the latter is itself a purchaser or seller of securities. See, e.g., Schoenbaum v. Firstbrook, 405 F.2d 215, 219 (C.A.2 1968), cert. denied sub nom. Manley v. Schoenbaum, 395 U.S. 906 (1969). But the first of these classes, of which respondent is a member, cannot claim the benefit of such a rule.

A great majority of the many commentators on the issue before us have taken the view that the *Birnbaum* limitation on the plaintiff class in a Rule 10b-5 action for damages is an arbitrary restriction which unreasonably prevents some deserving plaintiffs from recovering damages which have in fact been caused by violations of Rule 10b-5. See, e.g., Lowenfels, The Demise of the *Birnbaum* Doctrine: A New Era for Rule 10b-5, 54 Va. L. Rev. 268 (1968). The Securities and Exchange Commission has filed an amicus brief in this case espousing that same view. We have no doubt that this is indeed a disadvantage of the *Birnbaum* rule,[9] and if it had no countervailing advantages it would be undesirable as a matter of policy, however much it might be supported by precedent and legislative history. But we are of the opinion that there are countervailing advantages to the *Birnbaum* rule, purely as a matter of policy, although those advantages are more difficult to articulate than is the disadvantage.

There has been widespread recognition that litigation under Rule 10b-5 presents a danger of vexatiousness different in degree and in kind from that which accompanies litigation in general. . . .

We believe that the concern expressed for the danger of vexatious litigation which could result from a widely expanded class of plaintiffs under Rule 10b-5 is founded in something more substantial than the common complaint of the many defendants who would prefer avoiding lawsuits entirely to either settling them or trying them. These concerns have two largely separate grounds.

---

9. Obviously this disadvantage is attenuated to the extent that remedies are available to nonpurchasers and nonsellers under state law. Cf. §28 of the 1934 Act, 15 U.S.C. 78bb. See Iroquois Industries, Inc. v. Syracuse China Corp., 417 F.2d 963, 969 (C.A.2 1969), cert. denied, 399 U.S. 909 (1970). Thus, for example, in *Birnbaum* itself, while the plaintiffs found themselves without federal remedies, the conduct alleged as the gravamen of the federal complaint later provided the basis for recovery in a cause of action based on state law. See 3 L. Loss, Securities Regulation 1469 (2d ed. 1961). And in the immediate case, respondent has filed a state-court class action held in abeyance pending the outcome of this suit. Manor Drug Stores v. Blue Chip Stamps, No. C-5652 Superior Court, County of Los Angeles, Cal.

The first of these concerns is that in the field of federal securities laws governing disclosure of information even a complaint which by objective standards may have very little chance of success at trial has a settlement value to the plaintiff out of any proportion to its prospect of success at trial so long as he may prevent the suit from being resolved against him by dismissal or summary judgment. The very pendency of the lawsuit may frustrate or delay normal business activity of the defendant which is totally unrelated to the lawsuit. See, e.g., Sargent, The SEC and the Individual Investor: Restoring His Confidence in the Market, 60 Va. L. Rev. 553, 562-572 (1974); Dooley, The Effects of Civil Liability on Investment Banking and the New Issues Market, 58 Va. L. Rev. 776, 822-843 (1972)....

Where Congress in those sections of the 1933 Act which expressly conferred a private cause of action for damages adopted a provision [§11, permitting courts to require a bond for expenses] uniformly regarded as designed to deter "strike" or nuisance actions, Cohen v. Beneficial Loan Corp., 337 U.S. 541, 548-549 (1949), that fact alone justifies our consideration of such potential in determining the limits of the class of plaintiffs who may sue in an action wholly implied from the language of the 1934 Act.

The potential for possible abuse of the liberal discovery provisions of the Federal Rules of Civil Procedure may likewise exist in this type of case to a greater extent than they do in other litigation. The prospect of extensive deposition of the defendant's officers and associates and the concomitant opportunity for extensive discovery of business documents, is a common occurrence in this and similar types of litigation. To the extent that this process eventually produces relevant evidence which is useful in determining the merits of the claim asserted by the parties, it bears the imprimatur of those Rules and of the many cases liberally interpreting them. But to the extent that it permits a plaintiff with a largely groundless claim to simply take up the time of a number of other people, with the right to do so representing an *in terrorem* increment of the settlement value, rather than reasonably founded hope that the process will reveal relevant evidence, it is a social cost rather than a benefit. Yet to broadly expand the class of plaintiffs who may sue under Rule 10b-5 would appear to encourage the least appealing aspect of the use of the discovery rules.

Without the *Birnbaum* rule, an action under Rule 10b-5 will turn largely on which oral version of a series of occurrences the jury may decide to credit, and therefore no matter how improbable the allegations of the plaintiff, the case will be virtually impossible to dispose of prior to trial other than by settlement....

The second ground for fear of vexatious litigation is based on the concern that, given the generalized contours of liability, the abolition of the *Birnbaum* rule would throw open to the trier of fact many rather hazy issues of historical fact the proof of which depended almost entirely on oral testimony. We in no way disparage the worth and frequent high value of oral testimony when we say that dangers of its abuse appear to exist in this type of action to a peculiarly high degree.... The virtue of the *Birnbaum* rule, simply stated, in this situation, is that it limits the class of plaintiffs to those who have at least dealt in the security to which the prospectus, representation, or omission relates. And their dealing in the security, whether by way of purchase or sale, will generally be an objectively demonstrable fact in an area of the law otherwise very much dependent upon oral testimony. In the absence of the *Birnbaum* doctrine, bystanders to the securities marketing process could await developments on the sidelines without risk, claiming that inaccuracies in disclosure caused nonselling in a falling market and that unduly pessimistic predictions by the issuer followed by a rising market caused them to allow retrospectively golden opportunities to pass. . . .

We quite agree that if Congress had legislated the elements of a private cause of action for damages, the duty of the Judicial branch would be to administer the law which Congress enacted; the Judiciary may not circumscribe a right which Congress has conferred because of any disagreement it might have with Congress about the wisdom of creating so expansive a liability. But as we have pointed out, we are not dealing here with any private right created by the express language of §10(b) or of Rule 10b-5. No language in either of those provisions speaks at all to the contours of a private cause of action for their violation. However flexibly we may construe the language of both provisions, nothing in such construction militates against the *Birnbaum* rule. We are dealing with a private cause of action which has been judicially found to exist, and which will have to be judicially delimited one way or another unless and until Congress addresses the question. Given the peculiar blend of legislative, administrative, and judicial history which now surrounds Rule 10b-5, we believe that practical factors to which we have adverted, and to which other courts have referred, are entitled to a good deal of weight.

Thus we conclude that what may be called considerations of policy, which we are free to weigh in deciding this case, are by no means entirely on one side of the scale. Taken together with the precedential support for the *Birnbaum* rule over a period of more than 20 years, and the consistency of that rule with what we can glean from the intent of Congress, they lead us to conclude that it is a sound rule and should be followed. . . .

Reversed.

[The concurring opinion of Justice Powell, joined by Justices Stewart and Marshall, is omitted.]

JUSTICE BLACKMUN, with whom JUSTICES DOUGLAS and BRENNAN join, dissenting:

. . . [T]he Court exhibits a preternatural solicitousness for corporate well-being and a seeming callousness toward the investing public, quite out of keeping . . . with our own traditions and the intent of the securities laws.

Santa Fe Industries, Inc. v. Green
United States Supreme Court, 1977
430 U.S. 462

MR. JUSTICE WHITE delivered the opinion of the Court.

The issue in this case involves the reach and coverage of §10(b) of the Securities Exchange Act of 1934 and Rule 10b-5 thereunder in the context of a Delaware short-form merger transaction used by the majority stockholder of a corporation to eliminate the minority interest.

I

In 1936, petitioner Santa Fe Industries, Inc. (Santa Fe) acquired control of 60% of the stock of Kirby Lumber Corp. (Kirby), a Delaware corporation. Through a series of purchases over the succeeding years, Santa Fe increased its control of Kirby's stock to 95%; the purchase prices during the period 1968-1973 ranged from $65 to $92.50 per share. In 1974, wishing to acquire 100% ownership of Kirby, Santa Fe availed itself of §253 of the Delaware Corporation Law, known as the "short-form merger" statute. Section 253 permits a parent corporation owning at least 90% of the stock of a subsidiary to merge with that subsidiary, upon approval by the parent's board of directors, and to make payment in cash for the shares of the minority stockholders. The statute does not require the consent of, or advance notice to, the minority stockholders. However, notice of the merger must be given within 10 days after its effective date, and any stockholder who is dissatisfied with the terms of the merger may petition the Delaware Court of Chancery for a decree ordering the surviving corporation to pay him the fair value of his shares, as determined by a court-appointed appraiser subject to review by the court.

Santa Fe obtained independent appraisals of the physical assets of Kirby—land, timber, buildings, and machinery—and of Kirby's oil, gas, and mineral interests. These appraisals, together with other financial information, were submitted to Morgan Stanley & Co. (Morgan Stanley), an investment banking firm retained to appraise the fair market value of Kirby stock. Kirby's physical assets were appraised at $320 million (amounting to $640 for each of the 500,000 shares); Kirby's stock was valued by Morgan Stanley at $125 per share. Under the terms of the merger, minority stockholders were offered $150 per share.

The provisions of the short-form merger statute were fully complied with.[3] The minority stockholders of Kirby were notified the day after the merger became effective and were advised of their right to obtain an appraisal in Delaware court if dissatisfied with the offer of $150 per share. They also received an information statement containing, in addition to the relevant financial data about Kirby, the appraisals of the value of Kirby's assets and the Morgan Stanley appraisal concluding that the fair market value of the stock was $125 per share.

Respondents, minority stockholders of Kirby, objected to the terms of the merger, but did not pursue their appraisal remedy in the Delaware Court of Chancery. Instead, they brought this action in federal court on behalf of the corporation and other minority stockholders, seeking to set aside the merger or to recover what they claimed to be the fair value of their shares. The amended complaint asserted that, based on the fair market value of Kirby's physical assets as revealed by the appraisal included in the information statement sent to minority shareholders, Kirby's stock was worth at least $772 per share.[5] The complaint alleged further that the merger took place without

---

3. The merger became effective on July 31, 1974, and was accomplished in the following way. A new corporation, Forest Products, Inc., was organized as a Delaware corporation. The Kirby stock, together with cash, was transferred . . . to Forest Products in exchange for all of the Forest Products stock. The new corporation was then merged into Kirby, with Kirby as the surviving corporation. The cash transferred to Forest Products was used to make the purchase offer for the Kirby shares not owned by [Santa Fe].

5. The figure of $772 per share was calculated as follows: "The difference of $311,000,000 ($622 per share) between the fair market value of Kirby's land and timber, alone, as per the defendants' own appraisal thereof at $320,000,000 and the $9,000,000 book value of said land and timber, added to the $150 per share, yields a pro rata share of the value of the physical assets of Kirby of at least $772 per share. The value of the stock was at least the pro rata value of the physical assets."

prior notice to minority stockholders; that the purpose of the merger was to appropriate the difference between the "conceded pro rata value of the physical assets," and the offer of $150 per share—to "freez[e] out the minority stockholders at a wholly inadequate price," and that Santa Fe, knowing the appraised value of the physical assets, obtained a "fraudulent appraisal" of the stock from Morgan Stanley and offered $25 above that appraisal "in order to lull the minority stockholders into erroneously believing that [Santa Fe was] generous." This course of conduct was alleged to be "a violation of Rule 10b-5 because defendants employed a 'device, scheme, or artifice to defraud' and engaged in an 'act, practice or course of business which operates or would operate as a fraud or deceit upon any person, in connection with the purchase or sale of any security.'" [The District Court refused to permit the use of Rule 10b-5 for either a low valuation or lack of business purpose and notice to the minority. The court said that federal law did not modify Delaware law and that if "full and fair disclosure is made, transactions eliminating minority interests are beyond the purview of Rule 10b-5."] The Court of Appeals' view was that, although the Rule plainly reached material misrepresentations and nondisclosures in connection with the purchase or sale of securities, neither misrepresentation nor nondisclosure was a necessary element of a Rule 10b-5 action; the Rule reached "breaches of fiduciary duty by a majority against minority shareholders without any charge of misrepresentation or lack of disclosure." The court went on to hold that the complaint, taken as a whole, stated a cause of action under the Rule:

> We hold that a complaint alleges a claim under Rule 10b-5 when it charges, in connection with a Delaware short-form merger, that the majority has committed a breach of its fiduciary duty to deal fairly with minority shareholders by effecting the merger without any justifiable business purpose. The minority shareholders are given no prior notice of the merger, thus having no opportunity to apply for injunctive relief, and the proposed price to be paid is substantially lower than the appraised value reflected in the Information Statement.

. . . We reverse.

II

. . . The court below construed the term "fraud" in Rule 10b-5 by adverting to the use of the term in several of this Court's decisions in contexts other than the 1934 Act and the related Securities Act of 1933. The Court of Appeals' approach to the interpretation of Rule 10b-5 is inconsistent with that taken by the Court last Term in Ernst & Ernst v. Hochfelder, 425 U.S. 185 (1976).

Ernst & Ernst makes clear that in deciding whether a complaint states a cause of action for "fraud" under Rule 10b-5, "we turn first to the language of §10(b), for '[t]he starting point in every case involving construction of a statute is the language itself.'" Id., at 197.

To the extent that the Court of Appeals would rely on the use of the term "fraud" in Rule 10b-5 to bring within the ambit of the Rule all breaches of fiduciary duty in connection with a securities transaction, its interpretation would, like the interpretation rejected by the Court in *Ernst & Ernst,* "add a gloss to the operative language of the statute quite different from its commonly accepted meaning." But, as the Court there held, the language of the statute must control the interpretation of the Rule:

> Rule 10b-5 was adopted pursuant to authority granted the [Securities and Exchange] Commission under §10(b). The rulemaking power granted to an administrative agency charged with the administration of a federal statute is not the power to make law. Rather, it is "the power to adopt regulations to carry into effect the will of Congress as expressed by the statute." . . . [The scope of the Rule] cannot exceed the power granted the Commission by Congress under §10(b).

The language of §10(b) gives no indication that Congress meant to prohibit any conduct not involving manipulation or deception. Nor have we been cited to any evidence in the legislative history that would support a departure from the language of the statute. "When a statute speaks so specifically in terms of manipulation and deception, . . . and when its history reflects no more expansive intent, we are quite unwilling to extend the scope of the statute. . . ." Thus the claim of fraud and fiduciary breach in this complaint states a cause of action under any part of Rule 10b-5 only if the conduct alleged can be fairly viewed as "manipulative or deceptive" within the meaning of the statute.

III

It is our judgment that the transaction, if carried out as alleged in the complaint, was neither deceptive nor manipulative and therefore did not violate either §10(b) of the Act or Rule 10b-5.

As we have indicated, the case comes to us on the premise that the complaint failed to allege a material misrepresentation or material failure to disclose. The finding of the District Court, undisturbed by the Court of Appeals, was that there was no "omission" or "misstatement" in the information statement accompanying the notice of merger. On the basis of the information provided, minority shareholders could either accept the price offered or reject it and seek an appraisal in the Delaware Court of Chancery. Their choice was fairly presented, and they were furnished with all relevant information on which to base their decision.

We therefore find inapposite the cases relied upon by respondents and the court below, in which the breaches of fiduciary duty held violative of Rule 10b-5 included some element of deception.[15] Those cases forcefully reflect the principle that "[§]10(b) must be read flexibly, not technically and restrictively" and that the statute provides a cause of action for any plaintiff who "suffer[s] an injury as a result of deceptive practices touching its sale [or purchase] of securities. . . ." Superintendent of Insurance v. Bankers Life & Cas. Co., 404 U.S. 6, 12-13 (1971). But the cases do not support the

---

15. The decisions of this Court relied upon by respondents all involved deceptive conduct as part of the Rule 10b-5 violation alleged. . . . We have been cited to a large number of cases in the Courts of Appeals, all of which involved an element of deception as part of the fiduciary misconduct held to violate Rule 10b-5. E.g., Schoenbaum v. Firstbrook, 405 F.2d 215, 220 (C.A.2 1968) (en banc), cert. denied, 395 U.S. 906 (1969) (majority stockholder and board of directors "were guilty of deceiving" the minority stockholders). . . .

proposition, adopted by the Court of Appeals below and urged by respondents here, that a breach of fiduciary duty by majority stockholders, without any deception, misrepresentation, or nondisclosure, violates the statute and the Rule.

It is also readily apparent that the conduct alleged in the complaint was not "manipulative" within the meaning of the statute. "Manipulation" is "virtually a term of art when used in connection with securities markets." *Ernst & Ernst*, 425 U.S., at 199. The term refers generally to practices, such as wash sales, matched orders, or rigged prices, that are intended to mislead investors by artificially affecting market activity. See, e.g., §9 of the 1934 Act, 15 U.S.C. §78i (prohibiting specific manipulative practices). Section 10(b)'s general prohibition of practices deemed by the SEC to be "manipulative"—in this technical sense of artificially affecting market activity in order to mislead investors—is fully consistent with the fundamental purpose of the 1934 Act "'to substitute a philosophy of full disclosure for the philosophy of caveat emptor. . . .'" Affiliated Ute Citizens v. United States, 406 U.S. 128, 151 (1972), quoting SEC v. Capital Gains Research Bureau, 375 U.S. 180, 186 (1963). Indeed, nondisclosure is usually essential to the success of a manipulative scheme. [3 L. Loss, Securities Regulation 1565 (2d ed. 1961).] No doubt Congress meant to prohibit the full range of ingenious devices that might be used to manipulate securities prices. But we do not think it would have chosen this "term of art" if it had meant to bring within the scope of §10(b) instances of corporate mismanagement such as this, in which the essence of the complaint is that shareholders were treated unfairly by a fiduciary.

IV

The language of the statute is, we think, "sufficiently clear in its context" to be dispositive here, *Ernst & Ernst*, supra, at 201; but even if it were not, there are additional considerations that weigh heavily against permitting a cause of action under Rule 10b-5 for the breach of corporate fiduciary duty alleged in this complaint. Congress did not expressly provide a private cause of action for violations of §10(b). Although we have recognized an implied cause of action under that section in some circumstances, Superintendent of Insurance v. Bankers Life & Cas. Co., supra, at 13 n.9, we have also recognized that a private cause of action under the antifraud provisions of the Securities Exchange Act should not be implied where it is "unnecessary to ensure the fulfillment of Congress' purposes" in adopting the Act. Piper v. Chris-Craft Industries [430 U.S. 1, 40 (1977)]. Cf. J.I. Case Co. v. Borak, 377 U.S. 426, 431-433 (1964). As we noted earlier, the Court repeatedly has described the "fundamental purpose" of the Act as implementing a "philosophy of full disclosure"; once full and fair disclosure has occurred, the fairness of the terms of the transaction is at most a tangential concern of the statute. Cf. Mills v. Electric Auto-Lite Co., 396 U.S. 375, 381-385 (1970). As in Cort v. Ash, 422 U.S. 66, 80 (1975), we are reluctant to recognize a cause of action here to serve what is "at best a subsidiary purpose" of the federal legislation.

A second factor in determining whether Congress intended to create a federal cause of action in these circumstances is "whether 'the cause of action [is] one traditionally relegated to state law. . . .'" Piper v. Chris-Craft Industries, Inc., at 40, quoting Cort v. Ash, supra, at 78. The Delaware Legislature has supplied minority shareholders with a cause of action in the Delaware Court of Chancery to recover the fair value of shares allegedly undervalued in a short-form merger. Of course, the existence of a particular state-law remedy is not dispositive of the question whether Congress meant to provide a similar federal remedy, but as in *Cort* and *Piper,* we conclude that "it is entirely appropriate in this instance to relegate respondent and others in his situation to whatever remedy is created by state law."

The reasoning behind a holding that the complaint in this case alleged fraud under Rule 10b-5 could not be easily contained. It is difficult to imagine how a court could distinguish, for purposes of Rule 10b-5 fraud, between a majority stockholder's use of a short-form merger to eliminate the minority at an unfair price and the use of some other device, such as a long-form merger, tender offer, or liquidation, to achieve the same result; or indeed how a court could distinguish the alleged abuses in these going private transactions from other types of fiduciary self-dealing involving transactions in securities. The result would be to bring within the Rule a wide variety of corporate conduct traditionally left to state regulation. In addition to posing a "danger of vexatious litigation which could result from a widely expanded class of plaintiffs under Rule 10b-5," Blue Chip Stamps v. Manor Drug Stores, 421 U.S., at 740, this extension of the federal securities laws would overlap and quite possibly interfere with state corporate law. Federal courts applying a "federal fiduciary principle" under Rule 10b-5 could be expected to depart from state fiduciary standards at least to the extent necessary to ensure uniformity within the federal system.[16] Absent a clear indication of congressional intent, we are reluctant to federalize the substantial portion of the law of corporations that deals with transactions in securities, particularly where established state policies of corporate regulation would be overridden. As the Court stated in Cort v. Ash, supra: "Corporations are creatures of state law, and investors commit their funds to corporate directors on the understanding that, except where federal law *expressly* requires certain responsibilities of directors with respect to stockholders, state law will govern the internal affairs of the corporation." 422 U.S., at 84 (emphasis added).

We thus adhere to the position that "Congress by §10(b) did not seek to regulate transactions which constitute no more than internal corporate mismanagement." Superintendent of Insurance v. Bankers Life & Cas. Co., 404 U.S., at 12. There may well be a need for uniform federal fiduciary standards to govern mergers such as that challenged in this complaint. But those standards should not be supplied by judicial extension of §10(b) and Rule 10b-5 to "cover the corporate universe."[17]

---

16. For example, some States apparently require a "valid corporate purpose" for the elimination of the minority interest through a short-form merger, whereas other States do not. Compare Bryan v. Brock & Blevins Co., 490 F.2d 563 (C.A.5), cert. denied, 419 U.S. 844 (1974) (merger arranged by controlling stockholder for no business purpose except to eliminate 15% minority stockholder violated Georgia short-form merger statute) with Stauffer v. Standard Brands, Inc., 41 Del. Ch. 7, 187 A.2d 78 (1962) (Delaware short-form merger statute allows majority stockholder to eliminate the minority interest without any corporate purpose and subject only to an appraisal remedy). Thus to the extent that Rule 10b-5 is interpreted to require a valid corporate purpose for elimination of minority shareholders as well as a fair price for their shares, it would impose a stricter standard of fiduciary duty than that required by the law of some States.

17. Cary, Federalism and Corporate Law: Reflections Upon Delaware, 83 Yale L.J. 663, 700 (1974) (footnote omitted). Professor Cary argues vigorously for comprehensive federal fiduciary standards, but

[The dissenting opinion of Justice Brennan and the separate concurring opinions of Justices Blackmun and Stevens, both of whom declined to join Part IV of the court's opinion, are omitted.]

NOTE: FEDERALISM CASE LAW SINCE SANTA FE

1. Part IV of the Court's opinion expresses a reluctance to see Rule 10b-5 take over questions of corporate mismanagement traditionally governed by state law, but the Court answered that question only on the facts of a case where it found no misrepresentation. Subsequent courts of appeals decisions have brought corporate mismanagement within Rule 10b-5 if there is also some deception. When a corporate transaction is involved, the issue arises as to how a corporation can be deceived. In Maldonado v. Flynn, 597 F.2d 789, 793 (2d Cir. 1979), a panel of the Second Circuit summarized the possibilities this way:

> When a corporate action requires shareholders' approval, full disclosure of material information must be made to them. Where approval by the shareholders is not necessary, however, full disclosure to a disinterested board of directors is equivalent to full disclosure to the shareholders. Even if some directors have an interest in the transaction, absent domination or control of a corporation or of its board by the officer-beneficiaries, approval of the transaction by a disinterested majority of the board possessing authority to act and fully informed of all relevant facts will suffice to bar a Rule 10b-5 claim that the corporation or its stockholders were deceived. See Goldberg v. Meridor; Schoenbaum v. Firstbrook. The knowledge of the disinterested majority must in such event be attributed to the corporation and its stockholders, precluding deception. For this purpose "disinterest" is defined as lack of any financial stake by a director in the transaction under consideration. Delaware law, although not controlling is to the same effect.

8 Del. Code Ann. §144.

The issue as discussed in *Maldonado* has some parallels to the issue discussed in Chapter 4 as to when directors may speak for the corporation in controlling derivative suits (and *Maldonado* itself arises from the same fact situation as Zapata Corp. v. Maldonado, Chapter 4 at page 435). As in Chapter 4, the crucial issue becomes: When will the court find that directors have a conflict such that they may not speak and act for the corporation?

2. If the deception is of the corporation by those who are fiduciaries, the overlap with state law comes front and center. In Goldberg v. Meridor, 567 F.2d 209 (2d Cir. 1977), cert. denied, 434 U.S. 1069 (1978), the Second Circuit permitted a Rule 10b-5 action by a shareholder of UGO Corporation who alleged that UGO's controlling shareholder (Maritimecor) caused UGO to acquire Maritimecor's assets and liabilities in exchange for UGO stock on terms unfair to UGO. The Second Circuit relied on a pre-*Santa Fe* case, Schoenbaum v. Firstbrook, 405 F.2d 215 (2d Cir. 1968) (en banc), cert. denied, 395 U.S. 906 (1969), which it distinguished from *Santa Fe*:

---

urges a "frontal" attack by a new federal statute rather than an extension of Rule 10b-5. He writes: "It seems anomalous to jig-saw every kind of corporate dispute into the federal courts through the securities acts as they are presently written." Ibid. See also Note, Going Private, 84 Yale L.J. 903 (1975) (proposing the application of traditional doctrines of substantive corporate law to problems of fairness raised by "going private" transactions such as short-form mergers).

Schoenbaum . . . can rest solidly on the now widely recognized ground that there is deception of the corporation (in effect, of its minority shareholders) when the corporation is influenced by its controlling shareholder to engage in a transaction adverse to the corporation's interests (in effect, the minority shareholders' interests) and there is nondisclosure or misleading disclosures as to the material facts of the transaction. . . . The Supreme Court noted in [*Santa Fe*] that the court of appeals "did not disturb the District Court's conclusion that the complaint did not allege a material misrepresentation or nondisclosure with respect to the value of the stock" of Kirby; the Court's quarrel was with this court's holding that "neither misrepresentation nor nondisclosure was a necessary element of a Rule 10b-5 action," and that a breach of fiduciary duty would alone suffice. It was because "the complaint failed to allege a material misrepresentation or material failure to disclose" that the Court found "inapposite the cases [including *Schoenbaum*] relied upon by respondents and the court below, in which the breaches of fiduciary duty held violative of Rule 10b-5 included some element of deception." . . .

Here the complaint alleged "deceit . . . upon UGO's minority shareholders." . . . The nub of the matter is that the conduct attacked in [*Santa Fe*] did not violate the "'fundamental purpose' of the Act as implementing a 'philosophy of full disclosure'"; the conduct here attacked does.

567 F.2d at 217-218.

Several Circuits followed Goldberg v. Meridor, often with dissents based on Santa Fe. See also LHLC Corp. v. Cluett, Peabody & Co., 842 F.2d 928, 931-932 (7th Cir. 1988) (limiting Rule 10b-5 to investment decisions not other decisions such as litigation). In the decades since, these kinds of cases have been less frequent.

PROBLEM 10-3

Hays, a minority shareholder of Hydro, Inc., seeks to challenge a transaction in which the board of directors sold certain shares it owned in a related business to a corporation owned by three of five members of the board. Hays believes that the purchase price was $500,000 less than fair value. Will Hays be able to state a cause of action under Rule 10b-5?

3. Elements of Common Law Fraud Applied to Rule 10b-5

Given the origins of the private cause of action under Rule 10b-5 as one implied by the courts, it should not be surprising if there were disagreement over the specific elements of the rule. As with the implied action under Rule 14a-9, courts often look to requirements of common law fraud as a touchstone, modifying the specifics to fit the perceived history and policy of the securities laws. Some of the elements of common law fraud are written into the rule; we begin with those specified in subparagraph (b) of Rule 10b-5.

a. Material Facts

Basic, Inc. v. Levinson
United States Supreme Court, 1988
485 U.S. 224

JUSTICE BLACKMUN delivered the opinion of the Court.

This case requires us to apply the materiality requirement of §10(b) of the Securities Exchange Act of 1934 and the Securities and Exchange Commission's

Rule 10b-5, promulgated thereunder, in the context of preliminary corporate merger discussions. . . .

I

Prior to December 20, 1978, Basic Incorporated was a publicly traded company primarily engaged in the business of manufacturing chemical refractories for the steel industry. As early as 1965 or 1966, Combustion Engineering, Inc., a company producing mostly alumina-based refractories, expressed some interest in acquiring Basic, but was deterred from pursuing this inclination seriously because of antitrust concerns it then entertained. In 1976, however, regulatory action opened the way to a renewal of Combustion's interest. The "Strategic Plan," dated October 25, 1976, for Combustion's Industrial Products Group included the objective: "Acquire Basic Inc. $30 million."

Beginning in September 1976, Combustion representatives had meetings and telephone conversations with Basic officers and directors, including petitioners here, concerning the possibility of a merger. During 1977 and 1978, Basic made three public statements denying that it was engaged in merger negotiations.[4] On December 18, 1978, Basic asked the New York Stock Exchange to suspend trading in its shares and issued a release stating that it had been "approached" by another company concerning a merger. On December 19, Basic's board endorsed Combustion's offer of $46 per share for its common stock, and on the following day publicly announced its approval of Combustion's tender offer for all outstanding shares.

Respondents are former Basic shareholders who sold their stock after Basic's first public statement of October 21, 1977, and before the suspension of trading in December 1978. Respondents brought a class action against Basic and its directors, asserting that the defendants issued three false or misleading public statements and thereby were in violation of §10(b) of the 1934 Act and of Rule 10b-5. Respondents alleged that they were injured by selling Basic shares at artificially depressed prices in a market affected by petitioners' misleading statements and in reliance thereon. . . .

II

The 1934 Act was designed to protect investors against manipulation of stock prices. See S. Rep. No. 792, 73d Cong., 2d Sess., 1-5 (1934). Underlying the adoption

---

4. On October 21, 1977, after heavy trading and a new high in Basic stock, the following news item appeared in the Cleveland Plain Dealer: "[Basic] President Max Muller said the company knew no reason for the stock's activity and that no negotiations were under way with any company for a merger. He said Flintkote recently denied Wall Street rumors that it would make a tender offer of $25 a share for control of the Cleveland-based maker of refractories for the steel industry." On September 25, 1978, in reply to an inquiry from the New York Stock Exchange, Basic issued a release concerning increased activity in its stock and stated that "management is unaware of any present or pending company development that would result in the abnormally heavy trading activity and price fluctuation in company shares that have been experienced in the past few days." On November 6, 1978, Basic issued to its shareholders a "Nine Months Report 1978." This Report stated: "With regard to the stock market activity in the Company's shares we remain unaware of any present or pending developments which would account for the high volume of trading and price fluctuations in recent months."

of extensive disclosure requirements was a legislative philosophy: "There cannot be honest markets without honest publicity. Manipulation and dishonest practices of the market place thrive upon mystery and secrecy." H.R. Rep. No. 1383, 73d Cong., 2d Sess., 11 (1934). This Court "repeatedly has described the 'fundamental purpose' of the Act as implementing a 'philosophy of full disclosure.'" Santa Fe Industries, Inc. v. Green, 430 U.S. 462, 477-478 (1977), quoting SEC v. Capital Gains Research Bureau, Inc., 375 U.S. 180, 186 (1963).

Pursuant to its authority under §10(b) of the 1934 Act, the Securities and Exchange Commission promulgated Rule 10b-5. Judicial interpretation and application, legislative acquiescence, and the passage of time have removed any doubt that a private cause of action exists for a violation of §10(b) and Rule 10b-5, and constitutes an essential tool for enforcement of the 1934 Act's requirements. See, e.g., Ernst & Ernst v. Hochfelder, 425 U.S. 185, 196 (1976); Blue Chip Stamps v. Manor Drug Stores, 421 U.S. 723, 730 (1975).

The Court previously has addressed various positive and common-law requirements for a violation of §10(b) or of Rule 10b-5. See, e.g., Santa Fe Industries, Inc. v. Green, supra ("manipulative or deceptive" requirement of the statute); Blue Chip Stamps v. Manor Drug Stores, supra ("in connection with the purchase or sale" requirement of the Rule); Dirks v. SEC, 463 U.S. 646 (1983) (duty to disclose); Chiarella v. United States, 445 U.S. 222 (1980) (same); Ernst & Ernst v. Hochfelder, supra (scienter). See also Carpenter v. United States, 484 U.S. 19 (1987) (confidentiality). The Court also explicitly has defined a standard of materiality under the securities laws, see TSC Industries, Inc. v. Northway, Inc., 426 U.S. 438 (1976), concluding in the proxy-solicitation context that "[a]n omitted fact is material if there is a substantial likelihood that a reasonable shareholder would consider it important in deciding how to vote." Acknowledging that certain information concerning corporate developments could well be of "dubious significance," the Court was careful not to set too low a standard of materiality; it was concerned that a minimal standard might bring an overabundance of information within its reach, and lead management "simply to bury the shareholders in an avalanche of trivial information—a result that is hardly conducive to informed decisionmaking." It further explained that to fulfill the materiality requirement "there must be a substantial likelihood that the disclosure of the omitted fact would have been viewed by the reasonable investor as having significantly altered the 'total mix' of information made available." We now expressly adopt the *TSC Industries* standard of materiality for the §10(b) and Rule 10b-5 context.

III

The application of this materiality standard to preliminary merger discussions is not self-evident. Where the impact of the corporate development on the target's fortune is certain and clear, the *TSC Industries* materiality definition admits straightforward application. Where, on the other hand, the event is contingent or speculative in nature, it is difficult to ascertain whether the "reasonable investor" would have considered the omitted information significant at the time. Merger negotiations, because of the ever-present possibility that the contemplated transaction will not be effectuated, fall into the latter category.[9]

A

Petitioners urge upon us a Third Circuit test for resolving this difficulty. Under this approach, preliminary merger discussions do not become material until "agreement-in-principle" as to the price and structure of the transaction has been reached between the would-be merger partners. See Greenfield v. Heublein, Inc., 742 F.2d 751, 757 (C.A.3 1984), cert. denied, 469 U.S. 1215 (1985). By definition, then, information concerning any negotiations not yet at the agreement-in-principle stage could be withheld or even misrepresented without a violation of Rule 10b-5.

Three rationales have been offered in support of the "agreement-in-principle" test. The first derives from the concern expressed in *TSC Industries* that an investor not be overwhelmed by excessively detailed and trivial information, and focuses on the substantial risk that preliminary merger discussions may collapse: because such discussions are inherently tentative, disclosure of their existence itself could mislead investors and foster false optimism. The other two justifications for the agreement-in-principle standard are based on management concerns: because the requirement of "agreement-in-principle" limits the scope of disclosure obligations, it helps preserve the confidentiality of merger discussions where earlier disclosure might prejudice the negotiations; and the test also provides a usable, bright-line rule for determining when disclosure must be made.

None of these policy-based rationales, however, purports to explain why drawing the line at agreement-in-principle reflects the significance of the information upon the investor's decision. The first rationale, and the only one connected to the concerns expressed in *TSC Industries,* stands soundly rejected, even by a Court of Appeals that otherwise has accepted the wisdom of the agreement-in-principle test. "It assumes that investors are nitwits, unable to appreciate—even when told—that mergers are risky propositions up until the closing." Flamm v. Eberstadt, [814 F.2d 1169, 1175 (C.A.7), cert. denied, 484 U.S. 853 (1987)]. Disclosure, and not paternalistic withholding of accurate information, is the policy chosen and expressed by Congress. We have recognized time and again, a "fundamental purpose" of the various securities acts, "was to substitute a philosophy of full disclosure for the philosophy of caveat emptor and thus to achieve a high standard of business ethics in the securities industry." SEC v. Capital Gains Research Bureau, Inc., 375 U.S. 180, 186 (1963). The role of the materiality requirement is not to "attribute to investors a child-like simplicity, an inability to grasp the probabilistic significance of negotiations," Flamm v. Eberstadt, 814 F.2d, at 1175, but to filter out essentially useless information that a reasonable investor would not consider significant, even as part of a larger "mix" of factors to consider in making his investment decision. TSC Industries, Inc. v. Northway, Inc., 426 U.S., at 448-449.

---

9. We do not address here any other kinds of contingent or speculative information, such as earnings forecasts or projections.

The second rationale, the importance of secrecy during the early stages of merger discussions, also seems irrelevant to an assessment whether their existence is significant to the trading decision of a reasonable investor. To avoid a "bidding war" over its target, an acquiring firm often will insist that negotiations remain confidential, see, e.g., In re Carnation Co., Exchange Act Release No. 22214, 33 SEC Docket 1025 (1985), and at least one Court of Appeals has stated that "silence pending settlement of the price and structure of a deal is beneficial to most investors, most of the time." Flamm v. Eberstadt, 814 F.2d, at 1177.

We need not ascertain, however, whether secrecy necessarily maximizes shareholder wealth—although we note that the proposition is at least disputed as a matter of theory and empirical research—for this case does not concern the *timing* of a disclosure; it concerns only its accuracy and completeness. We face here the narrow question whether information concerning the existence and status of preliminary merger discussions is significant to the reasonable investor's trading decision. Arguments based on the premise that some disclosure would be "premature" in a sense are more properly considered under the rubric of an issuer's duty to disclose. The "secrecy" rationale is simply inapposite to the definition of materiality.

The final justification offered in support of the agreement-in-principle test seems to be directed solely at the comfort of corporate managers. The bright-line rule indeed is easier to follow than a standard that requires the exercise of judgment in the light of all the circumstances. But ease of application alone is not an excuse for ignoring the purposes of the Securities Acts and Congress' policy decisions. Any approach that designates a single fact or occurrence as always determinative of an inherently fact-specific finding such as materiality, must necessarily be overinclusive or underinclusive. In *TSC Industries* this Court explained: "The determination [of materiality] requires delicate assessments of the inferences a 'reasonable shareholder' would draw from a given set of facts and the significance of those inferences to him. . . ." 426 U.S., at 450. After much study, the Advisory Committee on Corporate Disclosure cautioned the SEC against administratively confining materiality to a rigid formula. Courts also would do well to heed this advice.

We therefore find no valid justification for artificially excluding from the definition of materiality information concerning merger discussions, which would otherwise be considered significant to the trading decision of a reasonable investor, merely because agreement-in-principle as to price and structure has not yet been reached by the parties or their representatives.

B

The Sixth Circuit explicitly rejected the agreement-in-principle test, as we do today, but in its place adopted a rule that, if taken literally, would be equally insensitive, in our view, to the distinction between materiality and the other elements of an action under Rule 10b-5:

> When a company whose stock is publicly traded makes a statement, as Basic did, that "no negotiations" are underway, and that the corporation knows of "no reason for the stock's activity," and that "management is unaware of any present or pending corporate development that would result

in the abnormally heavy trading activity," information concerning ongoing acquisition discussions becomes material *by virtue of the statement denying their existence.* . . .

    . . . In analyzing whether information regarding merger discussions is material such that it must be affirmatively disclosed to avoid a violation of Rule 10b-5, the discussions and their progress are the primary considerations. However, once a statement is made denying the existence of any discussions, even discussions that might not have been material in absence of the denial are material because they make the statement made untrue. (786 F.2d, at 748-749 (emphasis in original).)

    This approach, however, fails to recognize that, in order to prevail on a Rule 10b-5 claim, a plaintiff must show that the statements were *misleading* as to *a material* fact. It is not enough that a statement is false or incomplete, if the misrepresented fact is otherwise insignificant.

C

    Even before this Court's decision in *TSC Industries,* the Second Circuit had explained the role of the materiality requirement of Rule 10b-5, with respect to contingent or speculative information or events, in a manner that gave that term meaning that is independent of the other provisions of the Rule. Under such circumstances, materiality "will depend at any given time upon a balancing of both the indicated probability that the event will occur and the anticipated magnitude of the event in light of the totality of the company activity." SEC v. Texas Gulf Sulphur Co., 401 F.2d, at 849. Interestingly, neither the Third Circuit decision adopting the agreement-in-principle test nor petitioners here take issue with this general standard. Rather, they suggest that with respect to preliminary merger discussions, there are good reasons to draw a line at agreement on price and structure.

    In a subsequent decision, the late Judge Friendly, writing for a Second Circuit panel, applied the *Texas Gulf Sulphur* probability/magnitude approach in the specific context of preliminary merger negotiations. After acknowledging that materiality is something to be determined on the basis of the particular facts of each case, he stated:

    Since a merger in which it is bought out is the most important event that can occur in a small corporation's life, to wit, its death, we think that inside information, as regards a merger of this sort, can become material at an earlier stage than would be the case as regards lesser transactions—and this even though the mortality rate of mergers in such formative stages is doubtless high. (SEC v. Geon Industries, Inc., 531 F.2d 39, 47-48 (CA2 1976).)

We agree with that analysis.

    Whether merger discussions in any particular case are material therefore depends on the facts. Generally, in order to assess the probability that the event will occur, a factfinder will need to look to indicia of interest in the transaction at the highest corporate levels. Without attempting to catalog all such possible factors, we note by way of example that board resolutions, instructions to investment bankers, and actual negotiations between principals or their intermediaries may serve as indicia of interest. To assess the magnitude of the transaction to the issuer of the securities allegedly manipulated, a factfinder will need to consider such facts as the size of the two corporate entities and of the potential premiums over market value. No particular event or factor short of closing the transaction need be either necessary or sufficient by itself to render merger discussions material.[17]

As we clarify today, materiality depends on the significance the reasonable investor would place on the withheld or misrepresented information.[18] The fact-specific inquiry we endorse here is consistent with the approach a number of courts have taken in assessing the materiality of merger negotiations. Because the standard of materiality we have adopted differs from that used by both courts below, we remand the case for reconsideration of the question whether a grant of summary judgment is appropriate on this record. . . .

NOTES AND QUESTIONS

1. The Supreme Court reaffirmed Basic's approach to materiality in Matrixx Initiatives, Inc. v. Siracusano, 131 S. Ct. 1309 (2011), in which a drug company argued that lack of scientific statistical significance should determine materiality when the company had not disclosed questions raised about possible linkage of loss of smell to a new product:

> As in *Basic,* Matrixx's categorical rule would "artificially exclud[e]" information that "would otherwise be considered significant to the trading decision of a reasonable investor." 485 U.S., at 236, 108 S. Ct. 978. Matrixx's argument rests on the premise that statistical significance is the only reliable indication of causation. This premise is flawed: As the SEC points out, "medical

---

17. To be actionable, of course, a statement must also be misleading. Silence, absent a duty to disclose, is not misleading under Rule 10b-5. "No comment" statements are generally the functional equivalent of silence. See In re Carnation Co., Exchange Act Release No. 22214, 33 S.E.C. Docket 1029 (1985). See also New York Stock Exchange Listed Company Manual §202.01, reprinted in 3 CCH Fed. Sec. L. Rep. ¶23,515 (1987) (premature public announcement may properly be delayed for valid business purpose and where adequate security can be maintained); American Stock Exchange Company Guide §§401-405, reprinted in 3 CCH Fed. Sec. L. Rep. ¶¶23,124 A-23, 124E (1985) (similar provisions). It has been suggested that given current market practices, a "no comment" statement is tantamount to an admission that merger discussions are underway. See Flamm v. Eberstadt, 814 F.2d, at 1178. That may well hold true to the extent that issuers adopt a policy of truthfully denying merger rumors when no discussions are underway, and of issuing "no comment" statements when they are in the midst of negotiations. There are, of course, other statement policies firms could adopt; we need not now advise issuers as to what kind of practice to follow, within the range permitted by law. Perhaps more importantly, we think that creating an exception to a regulatory scheme founded on a prodisclosure legislative philosophy, because complying with the regulation might be "bad for business," is a role for Congress, not this Court.

18. We find no authority in the statute, the legislative history, or our previous decisions, for varying the standard of materiality depending on who brings the action or whether insiders are alleged to have profited. . . . We recognize that trading (and profit making) by insiders can serve as an indication of materiality, see SEC v. Texas Gulf Sulphur Co., 401 F.2d, at 851; General Portland, Inc. v. LaFarge Coppee S.A., [1982-1983] CCH Fed. Sec. L. Rep. ¶99,148, p. 95,544 (N.D. Tex. 1981). We are not prepared to agree, however, that "[i]n cases of the disclosure of inside information to a favored few, determination of materiality has a different aspect than when the issue is, for example, an inaccuracy in a publicly disseminated press release." SEC v. Geon Industries, Inc., 531 F.2d 39, 48 (C.A.2 1976). Devising two different standards of materiality, one for situations where insiders have traded in abrogation of their duty to disclose or abstain (or for that matter when any disclosure duty has been breached), and another covering affirmative misrepresentations by those under no duty to disclose (but under the ever-present duty not to mislead), would effectively collapse the materiality requirement into the analysis of defendant's disclosure duties.

researchers . . . consider multiple factors in assessing causation. Statistically significant data are not always available. For example, when an adverse event is subtle or rare, "an inability to obtain a data set of appropriate quality or quantity may preclude a finding of statistical significance." Moreover, ethical considerations may prohibit researchers from conducting randomized clinical trials to confirm a suspected causal link for the purpose of obtaining statistically significant data.

A lack of statistically significant data does not mean that medical experts have no reliable basis for inferring a causal link between a drug and adverse events. As Matrixx itself concedes, medical experts rely on other evidence to establish an inference of causation. We note that courts frequently permit expert testimony on causation based on evidence other than statistical significance. We need not consider whether the expert testimony was properly admitted in those cases, and we do not attempt to define here what constitutes reliable evidence of causation. It suffices to note that, as these courts have recognized, "medical professionals and researchers do not limit the data they consider to the results of randomized clinical trials or to statistically significant evidence." Brief for Medical Researchers as *Amici Curiae* 31.

The FDA similarly does not limit the evidence it considers for purposes of assessing causation and taking regulatory action to statistically significant data. In assessing the safety risk posed by a product, the FDA considers factors such as "strength of the association," "temporal relationship of product use and the event," "consistency of findings across available data sources," "evidence of a dose-response for the effect," "biologic plausibility," "seriousness of the event relative to the disease being treated," "potential to mitigate the risk in the population," "feasibility of further study using observational or controlled clinical study designs," and "degree of benefit the product provides, including availability of other therapies." Not only does the FDA rely on a wide range of evidence of causation, it sometimes acts on the basis of evidence that suggests, but does not prove, causation. For example, the FDA requires manufacturers of over-the-counter drugs to revise their labeling "to include a warning as soon as there is reasonable evidence of an association of a serious hazard with a drug; a causal relationship need not have been proved." 21 CFR §201.80(e). More generally, the FDA may make regulatory decisions against drugs based on postmarketing evidence that gives rise to only a suspicion of causation. See FDA, The Clinical Impact of Adverse Event Reporting, *supra*, at 7 ("[A]chieving certain proof of causality through postmarketing surveillance is unusual. Attaining a prominent degree of suspicion is much more likely, and may be considered a sufficient basis for regulatory decisions" (footnote omitted)).

This case proves the point. In 2009, the FDA issued a warning letter to Matrixx stating that "[a] significant and growing body of evidence substantiates that the Zicam Cold Remedy intranasal products may pose a serious risk to consumers who use them." App. 270a. The letter cited as evidence 130 reports of anosmia the FDA had received, the fact that the FDA had received few reports of anosmia associated with other intranasal cold remedies, and "evidence in the published scientific literature that various salts of zinc can damage olfactory function in animals and humans." *Ibid.* It did not cite statistically significant data.

Given that medical professionals and regulators act on the basis of evidence of causation that is not statistically significant, it stands to reason that in certain cases reasonable investors would as well. As Matrixx acknowledges, adverse event reports "appear in many forms, including direct complaints by users to manufacturers, reports by doctors about reported or observed patient reactions, more detailed case reports published by doctors in medical journals, or larger scale published clinical studies." Brief for Petitioners 17. As a result, assessing the materiality of adverse event reports is a "fact-specific" inquiry, *Basic,* 485 U.S., at 236, 108 S. Ct. 978, that requires consideration of the source, content, and context of the reports. This is not to say that statistical significance (or the lack thereof) is irrelevant—only that it is not dispositive of every case.

Application of *Basic*'s "total mix" standard does not mean that pharmaceutical manufacturers must disclose all reports of adverse events. Adverse event reports are daily events in the pharmaceutical industry; in 2009, the FDA entered nearly 500,000 such reports into its reporting system, see FDA, Reports Received and Reports Entered in AERS by Year (as of Mar. 31, 2010), http://www.fda.gov/Drugs/GuidanceComplianceRegulatoryInformation/Surveillance/AdverseDrugEffects/ucm070434.htm. The fact that a user of a drug has suffered an adverse event, standing alone, does not mean that the drug caused that event. See FDA, Annual Adverse Drug Experience Report:

1996, p. 2 (1997), http://druganddevicelaw.net/Annual%20Adverse%20Drug%20Experience%20 Report%201996.pdf. The question remains whether a *reasonable* investor would have viewed the nondisclosed information "'as having *significantly* altered the "total mix" of information made available.'" *Basic*, 485 U.S., at 232, 108 S. Ct. 978 (quoting *TSC Industries*, 426 U.S., at 449, 96 S. Ct. 2126; emphasis added). For the reasons just stated, the mere existence of reports of adverse events—which says nothing in and of itself about whether the drug is causing the adverse events—will not satisfy this standard. Something more is needed, but that something more is not limited to statistical significance and can come from "the source, content, and context of the reports," *supra*, at 1321. This contextual inquiry may reveal in some cases that reasonable investors would have viewed reports of adverse events as material even though the reports did not provide statistically significant evidence of a causal link.

Moreover, it bears emphasis that §10(b) and Rule 10b–5(b) do not create an affirmative duty to disclose any and all material information. Disclosure is required under these provisions only when necessary "to make . . . statements made, in the light of the circumstances under which they were made, not misleading. 17 CFR §240.10b-5(b); see also *Basic*, 485 U.S., at 239, n. 17, 108 S. Ct. 978 ("Silence, absent a duty to disclose, is not misleading under Rule 10b-5"). Even with respect to information that a reasonable investor might consider material, companies can control what they have to disclose under these provisions by controlling what they say to the market.

131 S. Ct. 1319-1322.

2. The most significant limits on the breadth of materiality have arisen via judicial development of concepts like "truth on the market" and "puffery." Truth on the market builds on the fraud on the market concept introduced in Chapter 3 and discussed in more detail later in this chapter. If prompt incorporation of news into stock prices is the foundation for fraud on the market, the same reasoning can be used as to knowledge that counteracts the alleged misrepresentation. Thus in Wielgos v. Commonwealth Edison Co., 892 F.2d 509 (7th Cir. 1989), the court held that a utility's alleged misstatements in understating the costs of its nuclear power plant could not be the basis for liability: "Anyone who followed Commonwealth Edison's filings would have seen that each year the firm increased its estimated costs and delayed the estimated startup date of one or more of its reactors . . . Commonwealth Edison was estimating the costs it would experience *if nothing went wrong and nothing unexpected happened* . . . These were poor assumptions. Something always goes wrong, and in the nuclear power business the unexpected is the norm. . . . [P]rofessional investors and analysts surely deduced what was afoot. Once they did so, they supplied their own assumptions about the likelihood that the firm will encounter trouble or that the rules will change. . . . Knowledge abroad in the market moderated, likely eliminated the potential of a dated projection to mislead. It therefore cannot be the basis for liability." Id at 512, 515.

The Seventh Circuit has also found that "mere sales puffery is not actionable under Rule 10b-5." Eisenstadt v. Centel Corp., 113 F.3d 738, 746 (7th Cir, 1997). The court noted, "Where puffing is the order of the day, literal truth can be profoundly misleading, as senders and recipients of letters of recommendation well know." There, the alleged misstatement went to a company's characterization of efforts to arrange a competitive auction to sell itself. Despite disappointment as one prospective bidder after another informed the company that they were not interested in purchasing, the company's press releases continued to present the process as going smoothly. The court noted that "going smoothly" in this context may mean nothing more than going as distinguished from the company's lawyers having told management that encumbrances on assets would block the sale, in which case a "going smoothly" statement could have been materially deceptive.

b. Misleading Statements: Affirmative, Half-Truths and Omissions

Rule 10b-5(b) prohibits "untrue statements," the affirmative misstatements that are first likely to occur to you in thinking about fraud. The rule also prohibits "omissions," but the rule does not contain a period after that word. Rather, the long clause that follows effectively converts the prohibition to one simply against half-truths. Can fraud take in pure silence? Consistent with the common law, courts recognize that a pure omission can be fraud only when there is a duty to speak. Review the misstatements that gave rise to the fraud claim in *Basic* (contained in footnote 4). One was an affirmative misstatement in a periodic report. One was an affirmative misstatement required by stock exchange rules. (See NYSE Listed Company Manual §202.05: "A listed company is expected to release quickly to the public any news or information which reasonably might be expected to materially affect the market for its securities." The exchange relies on a continuous market surveillance program, looking for unusual price or volume changes or a large unexplained influx of buy-and-sell orders. Movement exceeding predetermined guidelines may trigger an inquiry to the company about developments that could explain unusual market activity, and the exchange could halt trading in a company's stock or impose other sanctions for failure to comply with exchange rules.) The third was a voluntary statement to a newspaper. What if the company had said nothing at all? Here is how the Supreme Court in *Basic* addressed that question from a fraud perspective, in a footnote no less (but do not let that placement lead you to overlook one of the most uncertain issues in Rule 10b-5 jurisprudence):

> To be actionable, of course, a statement must also be misleading. Silence, absent a duty to disclose, is not misleading under Rule 10b-5. "No comment" statements are generally the functional equivalent of silence. See In re Carnation Co., Exchange Act Release No. 22214, 33 S.E.C. Docket 1029 (1985). See also New York Stock Exchange Listed Company Manual §202.01, reprinted in 3 CCH Fed. Sec. L. Rep. ¶23,515 (1987) (premature public announcement may properly be delayed for valid business purpose and where adequate security can be maintained); American Stock Exchange Company Guide §§401-405, reprinted in 3 CCH Fed. Sec. L. Rep. ¶¶23,124 A-23, 124E (1985) (similar provisions). It has been suggested that given current market practices, a "no comment" statement is tantamount to an admission that merger discussions are underway. See Flamm v. Eberstadt, 814 F.2d, at 1178. That may well hold true to the extent that issuers adopt a policy of truthfully denying merger rumors when no discussions are underway, and of issuing "no comment" statements when they are in the midst of negotiations. There are, of course, other statement policies firms could adopt; we need not now advise issuers as to what kind of practice to follow, within the range permitted by law. Perhaps more importantly, we think that creating an exception to a regulatory scheme founded on a prodisclosure legislative philosophy, because complying with the regulation might be "bad for business," is a role for Congress, not this Court.

485 U.S. 224, 239 note 17.

As a thought experiment, play out what would happen next if the company had told the newspaper or stock exchange "no comment." What would be the next morning's headline or today's blog post a few minutes after the "no comment"? And then what would be the effect on the shareholders? How would you as a general counsel for Basic avoid being sued? After the decision in *Basic*, the SEC provided some relief from the need to disclose preliminary merger negotiations in annual 10-K reports if "disclosure is not otherwise required and has not otherwise been made . . . [and], in the registrant's view, inclusion of such information would jeopardize the completion of transaction." Securities Release No. 33-6835, Fed. Sec. L. Rep. (CCH) ¶72,439 (May 18, 1989)).

Other instances in which disclosure may be required are addressed in the case that follows.

In re Time Warner, Inc. Securities Litigation
United States Court of Appeals, Second Circuit, 1993
9 F.3d 259

NEWMAN, CHIEF JUDGE:

This appeal from the dismissal of a securities fraud complaint requires us to consider the recurring issue of whether stock fraud claims are sufficiently pleaded to warrant at least discovery and perhaps trial. [Issues presented include: (1) whether a corporation has a duty to update somewhat optimistic predictions about achieving a business plan when it appears that the plan might not be realized, and (2) whether a corporation has a duty to disclose a specific alternative to an announced business plan when that alternative is under active consideration.] . . .

Plaintiffs' complaint alleged that defendant Time Warner, Inc. and four of its officers had misled the investing public by statements and omissions made in the course of Time Warner's efforts to reduce its debt. The District Court dismissed the complaint with prejudice for failure to adequately plead material misrepresentations or omissions attributable to the defendants and for failure to adequately plead scienter. We hold that the complaint's allegations of scienter and certain of its allegations concerning omissions are adequate to survive a motion to dismiss, and we accordingly reverse the order of dismissal and remand.

BACKGROUND

On June 7, 1989, Time, Inc. received a surprise tender offer for its stock from Paramount Communications. Paramount's initial offer was $175 per share, in cash, and was eventually increased to $200 per share. See Paramount Communications, Inc. v. Time Inc., 571 A.2d 1140, 1147-49 (Del. 1989). Time's directors declined to submit this offer to the shareholders and continued discussions that had begun somewhat earlier concerning a merger with Warner Communications, Inc. Eventually, Time and Warner agreed that Time would acquire all of Warner's outstanding stock for $70 per share, even though this acquisition would cause Time to incur debt of over $10 billion. Time shareholders and Paramount were unsuccessful in their effort to enjoin the Warner acquisition, which was completed in July 1989.

Thus, in 1989, Time Warner Inc., the entity resulting from the merger, found itself saddled with over $10 billion in debt, an outcome that drew criticism from many shareholders. The company embarked on a highly publicized campaign to find international "strategic partners" who would infuse billions of dollars of capital into the company and who would help the company realize its dream of becoming a dominant worldwide entertainment conglomerate. Ultimately, Time Warner formed only two strategic partnerships, each on a much smaller scale than had been hoped for. Faced with a multi-billion dollar balloon payment on the debt, the company was forced to seek an alternative method of raising capital—a new stock offering that substantially diluted the rights of the existing shareholders. The company first proposed a variable price offering on June 6, 1991. This proposal was rejected by the SEC, but the SEC approved a second proposal announced on July 12, 1991. Announcement of the two offering proposals caused a substantial decline in the price of Time Warner stock. From June 5 to June 12, the share price fell from $117 to $94. By July 12, the price had fallen to $89.75.

The plaintiff class, which has not yet been certified, consists of persons who bought Time Warner stock between December 12, 1990, and June 7, 1991. Their complaint, containing causes of action under sections 10(b) and 20(a) of the Securities Exchange Act, and state law, alleges that a series of statements from Time Warner officials during the class period were materially misleading in that they misrepresented the status of the ongoing strategic partnership discussions and failed to disclose consideration of the stock offering alternative. . . . The statements, which we discuss in more detail below, consist of generally positive messages concerning the progress of the search for strategic partners, and imply to varying degrees that significant partnerships will be consummated and announced in the near future. None of the statements acknowledged that negotiations with prospective partners were going less well than expected or that an alternative method of raising capital was under consideration. . . .

DISCUSSION

Cases of this sort present an inevitable tension between two powerful interests. On the one hand, there is the interest in deterring fraud in the securities markets and remedying it when it occurs. That interest is served by recognizing that the victims of fraud often are unable to detail their allegations until they have had some opportunity to conduct discovery of those reasonably suspected of having perpetrated a fraud. Consistent with that interest, modern pleading rules usually permit a complaint to survive dismissal unless, in the familiar phrase, "it appears beyond doubt that the plaintiff can prove no set of facts in support of his claim which would entitle him to relief." See Conley v. Gibson, 355 U.S. 41, 45-46 (1957).

On the other hand, there is the interest in deterring the use of the litigation process as a device for extracting undeserved settlements as the price of avoiding the extensive discovery costs that frequently ensue once a complaint survives dismissal, even though no recovery would occur if the suit were litigated to completion. It has never been clear how these competing interests are to be accommodated, and the adjudication process is not well suited to the formulation of a universal resolution of the tensions between them. In the absence of a more refined statutory standard than the vague contours of section 10(b) or a more detailed attempt at rule-making than the SEC has managed in Rule 10b-5, despite 50 years of unavailed opportunity, courts must adjudicate the precise cases before them, striking the balance as best they can.

In doing so, we do well to recognize several consequences of this common law approach to what is supposed to be a statutory standard. First, our outcomes will not necessarily evolve a discernible pattern. Second, the absence of a clear pattern will inevitably create uncertainty in the fields of both securities and litigation. Third, however sensitively we strike the balance in a particular case, we will not avoid the risks of adverse consequences: in the aftermath of any ruling that upholds the dismissal of a 10b-5 suit, there will be some opportunity for unremedied fraud; in the aftermath of any ruling that permits a 10b-5 suit to progress beyond a motion to dismiss, there will be some opportunity to extract an undeserved settlement. Unattractive as those prospects are, they neither indicate a sound basis for decision nor permit avoidance of decision. . . .

I. EXISTENCE OF AN ACTIONABLE MISREPRESENTATION OR OMISSION

. . . B. *Attributed Statements and Corporate Press Releases*

. . . While plaintiffs claim [misleading statements that] exaggerated the likelihood that strategic alliances would be made, plaintiffs primarily fault these statements for what they did not disclose. The nondisclosure is of two types: failure to disclose problems in the strategic alliance negotiations, and failure to disclose the active consideration of an alternative method of raising capital. We have listed excerpts of the relevant statements in the margin.[3]

---

3. 1. "This company is worth a hell of a lot more than $200.00 a share. It was then. It is now." (Wall Street Journal, Feb. 7, 1990) (quoting defendant Levin). Third Amended Complaint, ¶41.

2. "There may be four big industrial partners with one in Europe and two in Japan, or two in Europe and two in Japan and [an] American company." (Wall Street Journal, Nov. 1990) (exact date unspecified) (quoting defendant Ross). Id. ¶51.

3. The company would seek foreign investors to take a minority interest in subsidiaries as a means of alleviating debt without selling off assets. (Time Warner announcement, Nov. 19, 1990) (no direct quotation provided). Id. ¶48.

4. The company "continues to have serious talks that could lead to the sale of five or six separate minority stakes in its entertainment subsidiaries next year." (Wall Street Journal, Nov. 30, 1990) (quoting defendant Ross). Id. ¶50.

5. The company "received and continue[s] to receive many expressions of interest in forming joint ventures of all of its businesses from all over the world." (Time Warner press release, Dec. 3, 1990). Id. ¶52.

6. "Management of Time Warner also has had discussions with potential partners on the mutual advantages of strategic alliances formed at the subsidiary level." (1990 SEC 10-K Statement). Id. ¶56.

7. Ross and Nicholas "are excited by the possibilities for growth that will increase shareholder value, especially through strategic partnerships." (1990 Annual Report). Id. ¶57.

8. The company "was in talks with possible buyers of stakes in some of its entertainment businesses." (Ross, March 7, 1991). Id. ¶63.

1. *Affirmative Misrepresentations*

We agree with the District Court that none of the statements constitutes an *affirmative* misrepresentation. Most of the statements reflect merely that talks are ongoing, and that Time Warner hopes that the talks will be successful. There is no suggestion that the factual assertions contained in any of these statements were false when the statements were made. As to the expressions of opinion and the projections contained in the statements, while not beyond the reach of the securities laws, see Virginia Bankshares, Inc. v. Sandberg, [501 U.S. 1083, 1090-1098] (1991) (proxy statements actionable under section 14(a)); Goldman v. Belden, 754 F.2d 1059, 1068-69 (2d Cir. 1985) (positive predictions actionable under section 10(b)), the complaint contains no allegations to support the inference that the defendants either did not have these favorable opinions on future prospects when they made the statements or that the favorable opinions were without a basis in fact.

2. *Nondisclosure of Problems in the Strategic Alliance Negotiations*

The allegations of nondisclosure are more serious. Plaintiffs' first theory of nondisclosure is that the defendants' statements hyping strategic alliances gave rise to a duty to disclose problems in the alliance negotiations as those problems developed. We agree that a duty to update opinions and projections may arise if the original opinions or projections have become misleading as the result of intervening events. See In re Gulf Oil/Cities Service Tender Offer Litigation, 725 F. Supp. 712, 745-49 (S.D.N.Y. 1989) (material misstatements or omissions adequately set forth alleging that defendants had expressed a strong interest in consummating a merger and had not disclosed a later "change of heart"). But, in this case, the attributed public statements lack the sort of definite positive projections that might require later correction. The statements suggest only the hope of any company, embarking on talks with multiple partners, that the talks would go well. No identified defendant stated that he thought deals would be struck by a certain date, or even that it was likely that deals would be struck at all. Cf. In re Apple Computer Securities Litigation, 886 F.2d 1109, 1118-1119 (9th Cir. 1989) (Chairman of the Board stated that new computer product would be "phenomenally successful the first year out of the chute," etc.), cert. denied, 496 U.S. 943 (1990). These statements did not become materially misleading when the talks did not proceed well.

3. *Nondisclosure of Alternative Methods of Raising Capital*

Still more serious is the allegation of a failure to disclose the simultaneous consideration of the rights offering as an alternative method of raising capital. As an

---

9. Time Warner "was continuing talks with potential foreign partners. . . . We're not selling or buying. . . . We're partnering." (Nicholas, March 15, 1991). Id.

10. Time Warner is "currently engaged in nearly two dozen discussions in Europe and Asia that could link most of the world's entertainment and media companies in a complex web of relationships. . . . We are making alliances at the subsidiary level with the partners keeping their national identities and bringing their respective strengths to bear." (Business Week, May 13, 1991) (quoting defendant Ross). Id. ¶66.

11. "[W]e are pursuing a number of innovative business ventures all over the world." (Time Warner public announcement, May 14, 1991). Id. ¶68.

initial matter, of course, a reasonable investor would probably have wanted to know of consideration of the rights offering. Though both the rights offering and strategic alliances would have brought capital into the corporation, the two acts would have directly opposite effects on the price of Time Warner stock. A successful strategic alliance, simultaneously opening new markets and reducing debt, would have improved the corporation's expected profit stream, and should have served to drive up the share price. An offering of new shares, in contrast, would dilute the ownership rights of existing shareholders, likely decrease dividends, and drive down the price of the stock.

But a corporation is not required to disclose a fact merely because a reasonable investor would very much like to know that fact. Rather, an omission is actionable under the securities laws only when the corporation is subject to a duty to disclose the omitted facts. See Basic Inc. v. Levinson, 485 U.S. 224, 239, n.17 (1988); Glazer v. Formica Corp., 964 F.2d 149, 157 (2d Cir. 1992). As Time Warner pointedly reminds us, we have not only emphasized the importance of ascertaining a duty to disclose when omissions are at issue but have also drawn a distinction between the concepts of a duty to disclose and materiality. See *Glazer*, 964 F.2d at 157. It appears, however, that the distinction has meaning only in certain contexts. For example, where the issue is whether an individual's relationship to information imposed upon him a duty to disclose, the inquiry as to his duty is quite distinct from the inquiry as to the information's materiality. See Dirks v. SEC, 463 U.S. 646 (1983). On the other hand, where the disclosure duty arises from the combination of a prior statement and a subsequent event, which, if not disclosed, renders the prior statement false or misleading, the inquiries as to duty and materiality coalesce. The undisclosed information is material if there is "a substantial likelihood that the disclosure of the omitted fact would have been viewed by the reasonable investor as having significantly altered the 'total mix' of information available." TSC Industries, Inc. v. Northway, Inc., 426 U.S. 438, 449 (1976). If a reasonable investor would so regard the omitted fact, it is difficult to imagine a circumstance where the prior statement would not be rendered misleading in the absence of the disclosure. As *Glazer* makes clear, one circumstance creating a duty to disclose arises when disclosure is necessary to make prior statements not misleading. *Glazer*, 964 F.2d at 157 (citing Roeder v. Alpha Industries, Inc., 814 F.2d 22, 26 (1st Cir. 1987)).

We have previously considered whether disclosure of one business plan required disclosure of considered alternatives in Kronfeld v. Trans World Airlines, Inc., 832 F.2d 726 (2d Cir. 1987), cert. denied, 485 U.S. 1007 (1988). In *Kronfeld,* the defendant, TWA's parent corporation, failed to disclose in the prospectus for a new issue of TWA stock that it was contemplating termination of its relationship with TWA. Because the prospectus discussed "in some detail the relationship between TWA" and the parent, 832 F.2d at 735, we held that a fact question was presented as to whether it was materially misleading not to disclose the possibility of termination, id. at 736-737. In effect, the alternative, if disclosed, would have suggested to investors that the various guarantees extended from the parent to TWA might be meaningless. In the pending case, the District Court understood the obligation to disclose alternate business plans to be limited to the context of mutually exclusive alternatives. It is true that *Kronfeld* involved such alternatives—the TWA parent could not both maintain and terminate its relations with TWA—and that this case does not. Time Warner potentially could have raised all its needed capital from either strategic alliances or a rights offering, or it could have raised some part of the necessary capital using each approach.

We believe, however, that a disclosure duty limited to mutually exclusive alternatives is too narrow. A duty to disclose arises whenever secret information renders prior public statements materially misleading, not merely when that information completely negates the public statements. Time Warner's public statements could have been understood by reasonable investors to mean that the company hoped to solve the entire debt problem through strategic alliances. Having publicly hyped strategic alliances, Time Warner may have come under a duty to disclose facts that would place the statements concerning strategic alliances in a materially different light.

It is important to appreciate the limits of our disagreement with the District Court. We do not hold that whenever a corporation speaks, it must disclose every piece of information in its possession that could affect the price of its stock. Rather, we hold that when a corporation is pursuing a specific business goal and announces that goal as well as an intended approach for reaching it, it may come under an obligation to disclose other approaches to reaching the goal when those approaches are under active and serious consideration. Whether consideration of the alternate approach constitutes material information, and whether nondisclosure of the alternate approach renders the original disclosure misleading, remain questions for the trier of fact, and may be resolved by summary judgment when there is no disputed issue of material fact. We conclude here only that the allegations in this complaint of nondisclosure of the rights offering are sufficient to survive a motion to dismiss.

NOTES AND QUESTIONS

1. Other appellate courts have expressed different views on the duty to update. Consider how the 7th Circuit distinguished duty to correct and duty to update in taking a narrower view of the later duty:

> Much of plaintiffs' argument reads as if firms have an absolute duty to disclose all information material to stock prices as soon as news comes into their possession. Yet that is not the way the securities laws work. We do not have a system of continuous disclosure. Instead firms are entitled to keep silent (about good news as well as bad news) unless positive law creates a duty to disclose. See, e.g., Basic, Inc. v. Levinson, 485 U.S. 224, 239 n. 17, 108 S. Ct. 978, 99 L. Ed. 2d 194 (1988); Dirks v. SEC, 463 U.S. 646, 653-54, 103 S. Ct. 3255, 77 L. Ed. 2d 911 (1983); Chiarella v. United States, 445 U.S. 222, 227-35, 100 S. Ct. 1108, 63 L. Ed. 2d 348 (1980); Stransky v. Cummins Engine Co., 51 F.3d 1329, 1331 (7th Cir. 1995); Backman v. Polaroid Corp., 910 F.2d 10, 16 (1st Cir. 1990) (en banc . . . . The 1933 Act requires firms to reveal information only when they issue securities, [which did not occur in the time frame in question] Section 13 of the Securities Exchange Act of 1934, 15 U.S.C. §78m, adds that the SEC may require issuers to file annual and other periodic reports—with the emphasis on *periodic* rather than continuous. Section 13 and the implementing regulations contemplate that these reports will be snapshots of the corporation's status on or near the filing date, with updates due not when something "material" happens, but on the next prescribed filing date.
>
> Regulations implementing §13 require a comprehensive annual filing, the Form 10-K report, and less extensive quarterly supplements on Form 10-Q. The supplements need not bring up to date everything contained in the annual 10-K report; counsel for the plaintiff classes conceded at oral argument that nothing in Regulation S-K (the SEC list of required disclosures) requires either an updating of Form 10-K reports more often than annually, or a disclosure in a quarterly Form

10-Q report of information about the firm's regulatory problems. The regulations that provide for disclosures on Form 10-Q tell us *which* items in the annual report must be updated (a subset of the full list), and how often (quarterly) . . . judges have no authority to scoop the political branches and adopt continuous disclosure under the banner of Rule 10b-5. *Especially* not under that banner, for Rule 10b-5 condemns only fraud, and a corporation does not commit fraud by standing on its rights under a periodic-disclosure system. . . .

[A] statement may be "corrected" only if it was *in*correct when made, and nothing said as of March 9 was incorrect. In order to maintain the difference between periodic-disclosure and continuous-disclosure systems, it is essential to draw a sharp line between duties to correct and duties to update. . . . If, for example, the 10-K report had said that Abbott's net income for 1998 was $500 million, and the actual income was $400 million, Abbott would have had to fix the error. But if the 10-K report had projected a net income of $125 million for the first quarter of 1999, and accountants determined in May that the actual profit was only $100 million, there would have been nothing to correct; a projection is not rendered false when the world turns out otherwise. See Wielgos v. Commonwealth Edison Co., 892 F.2d 509 (7th Cir. 1989). Amending the 10-K report to show the results for 1999 as they came in-or to supply a running narrative of the dispute between Abbott and the FDA-would *update* the report, not *correct* it to show Abbott's actual condition as of March 9.

Updating documents has its place in securities law. A registration statement and prospectus for a new issue of securities must be accurate when it is used to sell stock, and not just when it is filed. Section 12(a)(2) of the '33 Act, 15 U.S.C. §77*l*(a)(2); Regulation S-K, Item 512(a) . . . [But] Abbott did not sell any stock to the class members during the period from March 17 to November 2, 1999.

Gallagher v. Abbott Laboratories, Inc., 269 F. 3d 806, 808-811 (7th Cir. 2001).

2. Fear of litigation can make corporations and their executives unwilling to discuss the company's plans and expectations with analysts or the public, silence that can frustrate the disclosure aims of the securities laws. Legislation passed by Congress in 1995 was, in part, spurred by concerns that an unexpected change in a company's earnings triggered an instant lawsuit alleging fraud in prior statements. The high-tech ventures of Silicon Valley were cited as a prominent example where lawsuits were frequent and were seen by some as a drag on the growth of this industry. The 1995 legislation added a safe harbor (§21E of the 1934 Act and a parallel provision, §27A of the 1933 Act) that went beyond the language provided in prior SEC rules. The safe harbor seeks to protect projections of revenues, earnings, dividends, or similar items as well as statements of the plans and objectives of management for future operations, products, or services if the forward-looking statements are accompanied by "meaningful cautionary statements identifying important factors that could cause actual results to differ materially." The safe harbor does not protect statements made in an initial public offering, tender offers, going private transactions, and certain other transactions. Statements made with "actual knowledge" that the statement was false or misleading (or in the case of a business entity, made or approved by an executive officer with actual knowledge of falsity) are excluded, a limited reach that in part led to a presidential veto of the bill that later was overridden by Congress. Examine again the statements in footnote 3 of the *Time Warner* opinion. How many of those would be covered by the safe harbor of §21E and how many of the remaining could you modify to come within the safe harbor?

c. Defendant's Mental State—Scienter

Scienter is a Latin term used to refer to a defendant's knowing or intentional mental state regarding a proscribed act. You have probably addressed similar questions as to the required mental state for legal liability in your torts and criminal law courses. For courts implying a private cause of action, the required mental state remained a point to be filled in. Consider the possible range of responses: at one end of the spectrum, *strict liability* is the standard for some defendants under §11 of the Securities Act of 1933; *negligence* is a common standard; *recklessness* requires more than negligence, but its exact parameters are sometimes hazy; and at the other end of the spectrum *knowledge* or *intent* only leads to individual liability when conduct has crossed a higher threshold.

Ernst & Ernst v. Hochfelder
United States Supreme Court, 1976
425 U.S. 185

[The appellate court below had permitted continuation of a suit against Ernst & Ernst that had been based on the firm's alleged negligence in aiding and abetting the fraud committed by the president of a small brokerage firm whose books were audited by Ernst & Ernst. The president had induced plaintiffs to invest in "escrow" accounts represented as yielding a high rate of return, but in fact the accounts were spurious. After the president's suicide, the fraud came to light; plaintiff asserted that Ernst & Ernst had failed to discover the president's rule that only he could open mail addressed to him even if it came in his absence. The plaintiffs argued that the mail rule, once discovered, would have been disclosed to the stock exchange and the SEC as an irregular procedure that prevented an effective audit of the brokerage firm; this, in turn, would have led to an investigation that would have revealed the fraudulent scheme.]

MR. JUSTICE POWELL delivered the opinion of the Court:

We granted certiorari to resolve the question whether a private cause of action for damages will lie under §10(b) and Rule 10b-5 in the absence of any allegation of "scienter"—intent to deceive, manipulate, or defraud.[12]

. . . During the 30-year period since a private cause of action was first implied under §10(b) and Rule 10b-5, a substantial body of case law and commentary has developed as to its elements. Courts and commentators have differed with regard to whether scienter is a necessary element of such a cause of action, or whether negligent conduct alone is sufficient. In addressing this question, we turn first to the language of

---

12. Although the verbal formulations of the standard to be applied have varied, several Courts of Appeals have held in substance that negligence alone is sufficient for civil liability under §10(b) and Rule 10b-5. . . . But few of the decisions announcing that some form of negligence suffices for civil liability under §10(b) and Rule 10b-5 actually have involved only negligent conduct. In this opinion the term "scienter" refers to a mental state embracing intent to deceive, manipulate, or defraud. In certain areas of the law recklessness is considered to be a form of intentional conduct for purposes of imposing liability for some act. We need not address here the question whether, in some circumstances, reckless behavior is sufficient for civil liability under §10(b) and Rule 10b-5. Since this case concerns an action for damages we also need not consider the question whether scienter is a necessary element in an action for injunctive relief under §10(b) and Rule 10b-5. Cf. SEC v. Capital Gains Research Bureau, 375 U.S. 180 (1963).

§10(b), for "[t]he starting point in every case involving construction of a statute is the language itself." Blue Chip Stamps [v. Manor Drug Stores, 421 U.S. 723] 756 (Powell, J. concurring).

Section 10(b) makes unlawful the use or employment of "any manipulative or deceptive device or contrivance" in contravention of Commission rules. The words "manipulative or deceptive" used in conjunction with "device or contrivance" strongly suggest that §10 (b) was intended to proscribe knowing or intentional misconduct. . . .

. . . The Commission . . . reasons that since the "effect" upon investors of given conduct is the same regardless of whether the conduct is negligent or intentional, Congress must have intended to bar all such practices and not just those done knowingly or intentionally. The logic of this effect-oriented approach would impose liability for wholly faultless conduct where such conduct results in harm to investors, a result the Commission would be unlikely to support. But apart from where its logic might lead, the Commission would add a gloss to the operative language of the statute quite different from its commonly accepted meaning. The argument simply ignores the use of the words "manipulative," "device," and "contrivance" — terms that make unmistakable a congressional intent to proscribe a type of conduct quite different from negligence. Use of the word "manipulative" is especially significant. It is and was virtually a term of art when used in connection with securities markets. It connotes intentional or willful conduct designed to deceive or defraud investors by controlling or artificially affecting the price of securities.

In addition to relying upon the Commission's argument with respect to the operative language of the statute, respondents contend that since we are dealing with "remedial legislation," Tcherepnin v. Knight, 389 U.S. 332, 336 (1967), it must be construed "'not technically and restrictively, but flexibly to effectuate its remedial purposes.'" Affiliated Ute Citizens v. United States, 406 U.S., at 151, quoting SEC v. Capital Gains Research Bureau [375 U.S. 180], at 195. They argue that the "remedial purposes" of the Acts demand a construction of §10(b) that embraces negligence as a standard of liability. But in seeking to accomplish its broad remedial goals, Congress did not adopt uniformly a negligence standard even as to express civil remedies. . . .

It is . . . evident that Congress fashioned standards of fault in the express civil remedies in the 1933 and 1934 Acts on a particularized basis. Ascertainment of congressional intent with respect to the standard of liability created by a particular section of the Acts must therefore rest primarily on the language of that section. Where, as here, we deal with a judicially implied liability, the statutory language certainly is no less important. In view of the language of §10(b), which so clearly connotes intentional misconduct, and mindful that the language of a statute controls when sufficiently clear in its context, further inquiry may be unnecessary. We turn now, nevertheless, to the legislative history of the 1934 Act to ascertain whether there is support for the meaning attributed to §10(b) by the Commission and respondents. . . .

The most relevant exposition of the provision that was to become §10(b) was by Thomas G. Corcoran, a spokesman for the drafters. Corcoran indicated:

Subsection (c) [§9(c) of H.R. 7852—later §10(b)] says, "Thou shalt not devise any other cunning devices." . . .

Of course subsection (c) is a catch-all clause to prevent manipulative devices. I do not think there is any objection to that kind of clause. The Commission should have the authority to deal with new manipulative devices. (Hearings on H.R. 7852 and H.R. 8720 before the House Committee on Interstate and Foreign Commerce, 73d Cong., 2d Sess., 115 (1934).)

This brief explanation of §10(b) by a spokesman for its drafters is significant. The section was described rightly as a "catchall" clause to enable the Commission "to deal with new manipulative [or cunning] devices." It is difficult to believe that any lawyer, legislative draftsman, or legislator would use these words if the intent was to create liability for merely negligent acts or omissions. Neither the legislative history nor the briefs supporting respondents identify any usage or authority for construing "manipulative [or cunning] devices" to include negligence. . . .

We have addressed, to this point, primarily the language and history of §10(b). The Commission contends, however, that subsections (b) and (c) of Rule 10b-5 are cast in language which—if standing alone—could encompass both intentional and negligent behavior. These subsections respectively provide that it is unlawful "[t]o make any untrue statement of a material fact or to omit to state a material fact necessary in order to make the statements made, in the light of the circumstances under which they were made, not misleading . . ." and "[t]o engage in any act, practice, or course of business which operates or would operate as a fraud or deceit upon any person. . . ." Viewed in isolation the language of subsection (b), and arguably that of subsection (c), could be read as proscribing, respectively, any type of material misstatement or omission, and any course of conduct, that has the effect of defrauding investors, whether the wrongdoing was intentional or not.

We note first that such a reading cannot be harmonized with the administrative history of the Rule, a history making clear that when the Commission adopted the Rule it was intended to apply only to activities that involved scienter. More importantly, Rule 10b-5 was adopted pursuant to authority granted the Commission under §10(b). The rulemaking power granted to an administrative agency charged with the administration of a federal statute is not the power to make law. Rather, it is " 'the power to adopt regulations to carry into effect the will of Congress as expressed by the statute.'" Dixon v. United States, 381 U.S. 68, 74 (1965), quoting Manhattan General Equipment Co. v. Commissioner, 297 U.S. 129, 134 (1936). Thus, despite the broad view of the Rule advanced by the Commission in this case, its scope cannot exceed the power granted the Commission by Congress under §10(b). For the reasons stated above, we think the Commission's original interpretation of Rule 10b-5 was compelled by the language and history of §10(b) and related sections of the Acts. When a statute speaks so specifically in terms of manipulation and deception, and of implementing devices and contrivances—the commonly understood terminology of intentional wrongdoing—and when its history reflects no more expansive intent, we are quite unwilling to extend the scope of the statute to negligent conduct.

NOTES

1. Justice Blackmun dissented in Ernst & Ernst v. Hochfelder, as was his custom in many securities cases after 1971. His dissent again showed his focus on the effect on investors in contrast to the majority's focus on the wrongful conduct of the defendant.

Perhaps the Court is right, but I doubt it. The Government and the Commission doubt it too, as is evidenced by the thrust of the brief filed by the Solicitor General on behalf of the Commission as amicus curiae. The Court's opinion, to be sure, has a certain technical consistency about it. It seems to me, however, that an investor can be victimized just as much by negligent conduct as by positive deception, and that it is not logical to drive a wedge between the two, saying that Congress clearly intended the one but certainly not the other.

425 U.S. at 216.

2. The Court's opinion in *Ernst & Ernst* explicitly left undecided whether scienter is a necessary element for injunctive action as opposed to damages; and whether in some circumstances reckless behavior is sufficient for civil liability under Rule 10b-5. See footnote 12, supra page 1026. The Court answered the injunction question shortly thereafter in Aaron v. SEC, 446 U.S. 680 (1980). The Court repeated its discussion of the use of evil-sounding terms like "manipulative," "device," and "contrivance" and held that scienter is a required element for an injunctive action brought under Rule 10b-5.

3. In *Ernst & Ernst* the court left undecided whether civil liability for aiding and abetting is appropriate under Rule 10b-5. Eighteen years after *Ernst,* in Central Bank of Denver v. First Interstate Bank of Denver, 511 U.S. 164 (1994), the Court held that liability in a private cause of action cannot be imposed under Rule 10b-5 because a person aided and abetted a violation of the Rule. The ruling was very helpful to "deep pockets" like accounting firms, lawyers, or financial institutions who were sued along with primary action for furthering in some way the primary actor's fraud. The *Central Bank* opinion did not totally free the secondary actor.

> . . . The absence of §10(b) aiding and abetting liability does not mean that secondary actors in the securities markets are always free from liability under the Securities Acts. Any person or entity, including a lawyer, accountant, or bank, who employs a manipulative device or makes a material misstatement (or omission) on which a purchaser or seller of securities relies may be liable as a primary violator under 10b-5, assuming *all* of the requirements for primary liability under Rule 10b-5 are met. . . . In any complex securities fraud, moreover, there are likely to be multiple violators. (Emphasis by the Court.)

511 U.S. at 191.

4. In the absence of a Supreme Court decision on whether conduct short of intent could satisfy the scienter requirement, most federal appellate courts followed the path of the common law tort of deceit where recklessness was often sufficient for scienter. The 1995 securities reform legislation did not address the substantive standard of scienter that was worked out by the courts, but did require that a plaintiff's complaint must "state with particularity facts giving rise to a strong inference that the defendant acted with the required state of mind." See §21D(b)(2) of the 1934 Act.

Tellabs, Inc. v. Makor Issues & Rights, Ltd.
United States Supreme Court, 2007
551 U.S. 308

JUSTICE GINSBURG delivered the opinion of the Court.

This Court has long recognized that meritorious private actions to enforce federal antifraud securities laws are an essential supplement to criminal prosecutions and civil enforcement actions brought, respectively, by the Department of Justice and the Securities and Exchange Commission (SEC). See, e.g., Dura Pharmaceuticals, Inc. v. Broudo, 544 U.S. 336, 345 (2005); J.I. Case Co. v. Borak, 377 U.S. 426 (1964). Private securities fraud actions, however, if not adequately contained, can be employed abusively to impose substantial costs on companies and individuals whose conduct conforms to the law. See Merrill Lynch, Pierce, Fenner & Smith Inc. v. Dabit, 547 U.S. 71, 81 (2006). As a check against abusive litigation by private parties, Congress enacted the Private Securities Litigation Reform Act of 1995 (PSLRA).

Exacting pleading requirements are among the control measures Congress included in the PSLRA. The Act requires plaintiffs to state with particularity both the facts constituting the alleged violation, and the facts evidencing scienter, i.e., the defendant's intention "to deceive, manipulate, or defraud." Ernst & Ernst v. Hochfelder, 425 U.S. 185, 194, and n. 12 (1976); see 15 U.S.C. §78u-4(b)(1),(2). This case concerns the latter requirement. As set out in §21D(b)(2) of the PSLRA, plaintiffs must "state with particularity facts giving rise to a strong inference that the defendant acted with the required state of mind."

Congress left the key term "strong inference" undefined, and Courts of Appeals have divided on its meaning. In the case before us, the Court of Appeals for the Seventh Circuit held that the "strong inference" standard would be met if the complaint "allege[d] facts from which, if true, a reasonable person could infer that the defendant acted with the required intent." 437 F.3d 588, 602 (2006). That formulation, we conclude, does not capture the stricter demand Congress sought to convey in §21D(b)(2). It does not suffice that a reasonable factfinder plausibly could infer from the complaint's allegations the requisite state of mind. Rather, to determine whether a complaint's scienter allegations can survive threshold inspection for sufficiency, a court governed by §21D(b)(2) must engage in a comparative evaluation; it must consider, not only inferences urged by the plaintiff, as the Seventh Circuit did, but also competing inferences rationally drawn from the facts alleged. An inference of fraudulent intent may be plausible, yet less cogent than other, nonculpable explanations for the defendant's conduct. To qualify as "strong" within the intendment of §21D(b)(2), we hold, an inference of scienter must be more than merely plausible or reasonable—it must be cogent and at least as compelling as any opposing inference of nonfraudulent intent.

I.

Petitioner Tellabs, Inc., manufactures specialized equipment used in fiber optic networks. During the time period relevant to this case, petitioner Richard Notebaert was Tellabs' chief executive officer and president. Respondents (Shareholders) are persons who purchased Tellabs stock between December 11, 2000, and June 19, 2001. They accuse Tellabs and Notebaert (as well as several other Tellabs executives) of engaging in a scheme to deceive the investing public about the true value of Tellabs' stock.

Beginning on December 11, 2000, the Shareholders allege, Notebaert (and by imputation Tellabs) "falsely reassured public investors, in a series of statements, . . . that

Tellabs was continuing to enjoy strong demand for its products and earning record revenues," when, in fact, Notebaert knew the opposite was true. From December 2000 until the spring of 2001, the Shareholders claim, Notebaert knowingly misled the public in four ways. First, he made statements indicating that demand for Tellabs' flagship networking device, the TITAN 5500, was continuing to grow, when in fact demand for that product was waning. Second, Notebaert made statements indicating that the TITAN 6500, Tellabs' next-generation networking device, was available for delivery, and that demand for that product was strong and growing, when in truth the product was not ready for delivery and demand was weak. Third, he falsely represented Tellabs' financial results for the fourth quarter of 2000 (and, in connection with those results, condoned the practice of "channel stuffing," under which Tellabs flooded its customers with unwanted products). Fourth, Notebaert made a series of overstated revenue projections, when demand for the TITAN 5500 was drying up and production of the TITAN 6500 was behind schedule. Based on Notebaert's sunny assessments, the Shareholders contend, market analysts recommended that investors buy Tellabs' stock.

The first public glimmer that business was not so healthy came in March 2001 when Tellabs modestly reduced its first quarter sales projections. In the next months, Tellabs made progressively more cautious statements about its projected sales. On June 19, 2001, the last day of the class period, Tellabs disclosed that demand for the TITAN 5500 had significantly dropped. Simultaneously, the company substantially lowered its revenue projections for the second quarter of 2001. The next day, the price of Tellabs stock, which had reached a high of $67 during the period, plunged to a low of $15.87.

On December 3, 2002, the Shareholders filed a class action in the District Court for the Northern District of Illinois. Their complaint stated, *inter alia,* that Tellabs and Notebaert had engaged in securities fraud in violation of §10(b) of the Securities Exchange Act of 1934, and SEC Rule 10b-5, also that Notebaert was a "controlling person" under §20(a) of the 1934 Act, and therefore derivatively liable for the company's fraudulent acts. Tellabs moved to dismiss the complaint on the ground that the Shareholders had failed to plead their case with the particularity the PSLRA requires. The District Court agreed, and therefore dismissed the complaint without prejudice. [S]ee Johnson v. Tellabs, Inc., 303 F. Supp. 2d 941, 945 (N.D. Ill. 2004).

The Shareholders then amended their complaint, adding references to 27 confidential sources and making further, more specific, allegations concerning Notebaert's mental state. The District Court again dismissed, this time with prejudice. 303 F. Supp. 2d, at 971. The Shareholders had sufficiently pleaded that Notebaert's statements were misleading, the court determined, id., at 955-961, but they had insufficiently alleged that he acted with scienter.

The Court of Appeals for the Seventh Circuit reversed in relevant part. Like the District Court, the Court of Appeals found that the Shareholders had pleaded the misleading character of Notebaert's statements with sufficient particularity. Unlike the District Court, however, the Seventh Circuit concluded that the Shareholders had sufficiently alleged that Notebaert acted with the requisite state of mind.

The Court of Appeals recognized that the PSLRA "unequivocally raise[d] the bar for pleading scienter" by requiring plaintiffs to "plea[d] sufficient facts to create a strong inference of scienter" (internal quotation marks omitted). In evaluating whether that pleading standard is met, the Seventh Circuit said, "courts [should] examine all of the allegations in the complaint and then . . . decide whether collectively they establish such an inference." "[W]e will allow the complaint to survive," the court next and critically stated, "if it alleges facts from which, if true, a reasonable person could infer that the defendant acted with the required intent. . . . If a reasonable person could not draw such an inference from the alleged facts, the defendants are entitled to dismissal."

In adopting its standard for the survival of a complaint, the Seventh Circuit explicitly rejected a stiffer standard adopted by the Sixth Circuit, i.e., that "plaintiffs are entitled only to the most plausible of competing inferences" (quoting Fidel v. Farley, 392 F.3d 220, 227 (C.A.6 2004)). The Sixth Circuit's standard, the court observed, because it involved an assessment of competing inferences, "could potentially infringe upon plaintiffs' Seventh Amendment rights." We granted certiorari to resolve the disagreement among the Circuits on whether, and to what extent, a court must consider competing inferences in determining whether a securities fraud complaint gives rise to a "strong inference" of scienter.

II.

Section 10(b) of the Securities Exchange Act of 1934 forbids the "use or employ, in connection with the purchase or sale of any security . . . , [of] any manipulative or deceptive device or contrivance in contravention of such rules and regulations as the [SEC] may prescribe as necessary or appropriate in the public interest or for the protection of investors." SEC Rule 10b-5 implements §10(b). . . .

Section 10(b), this Court has implied from the statute's text and purpose, affords a right of action to purchasers or sellers of securities injured by its violation. See, e.g., Dura Pharmaceuticals, 544 U.S., at 341. See also id., at 345 ("The securities statutes seek to maintain public confidence in the marketplace . . . by deterring fraud, in part, through the availability of private securities fraud actions."); Borak, 377 U.S., at 432 (private securities fraud actions provide "a most effective weapon in the enforcement" of securities laws and are "a necessary supplement to Commission action"). To establish liability under §10(b) and Rule 10b-5, a private plaintiff must prove that the defendant acted with scienter, "a mental state embracing intent to deceive, manipulate, or defraud." Ernst & Ernst, 425 U.S., at 193-194, and n. 12.[3]

In an ordinary civil action, the Federal Rules of Civil Procedure require only "a short and plain statement of the claim showing that the pleader is entitled to relief." Fed. Rule Civ. Proc. 8(a)(2). Although the rule encourages brevity, the complaint must

---

3. We have previously reserved the question whether reckless behavior is sufficient for civil liability under §10(b) and Rule 10b-5. See Ernst & Ernst v. Hochfelder, 425 U.S. 185, 194, n. 12 (1976). Every Court of Appeals that has considered the issue has held that a plaintiff may meet the scienter requirement by showing that the defendant acted intentionally or recklessly, though the Circuits differ on the degree of recklessness required. See Ottmann [v. Hanger Orthopedic Group, Inc., 353 F.3d 338, 343 (8th Cir. 2003] (collecting cases). The question whether and when recklessness satisfies the scienter requirement is not presented in this case.

say enough to give the defendant "fair notice of what the plaintiff's claim is and the grounds upon which it rests." Prior to the enactment of the PSLRA, the sufficiency of a complaint for securities fraud was governed not by Rule 8, but by the heightened pleading standard set forth in Rule 9(b). See Greenstone v. Cambex Corp., 975 F.2d 22, 25 (C.A.1 1992) (Breyer, J.) (collecting cases). Rule 9(b) applies to "all averments of fraud or mistake"; it requires that "the circumstances constituting fraud . . . be stated with particularity" but provides that "[m]alice, intent, knowledge, and other condition of mind of a person, may be averred generally."

Courts of Appeals diverged on the character of the Rule 9(b) inquiry in §10(b) cases: Could securities fraud plaintiffs allege the requisite mental state "simply by stating that scienter existed," In re GlenFed, Inc. Securities Litigation, 42 F.3d 1541, 1546-1547 (C.A.9 1994) (en banc), or were they required to allege with particularity facts giving rise to an inference of scienter? Compare id., at 1546 ("We are not permitted to add new requirements to Rule 9(b) simply because we like the effects of doing so."), with, e.g., Greenstone, 975 F.2d, at 25 (were the law to permit a securities fraud complaint simply to allege scienter without supporting facts, "a complaint could evade too easily the 'particularity' requirement in Rule 9(b)'s first sentence"). Circuits requiring plaintiffs to allege specific facts indicating scienter expressed that requirement variously. See 5A C. Wright & A. Miller, Federal Practice and Procedure §1301.1, pp. 300-302 (3d ed. 2004) (hereinafter Wright & Miller). The Second Circuit's formulation was the most stringent. Securities fraud plaintiffs in that Circuit were required to "specifically plead those [facts] which they assert give rise to a *strong inference* that the defendants had" the requisite state of mind. Ross v. A.H. Robins Co., 607 F.2d 545, 558 (1979) (emphasis added). The "strong inference" formulation was appropriate, the Second Circuit said, to ward off allegations of "fraud by hindsight." See, e.g., Shields v. Citytrust Bancorp, Inc., 25 F.3d 1124, 1129 (1994) (quoting Denny v. Barber, 576 F.2d 465, 470 (C.A.2 1978) (Friendly, J.)).

Setting a uniform pleading standard for §10(b) actions was among Congress' objectives when it enacted the PSLRA. Designed to curb perceived abuses of the §10(b) private action—"nuisance filings, targeting of deep-pocket defendants, vexatious discovery requests and manipulation by class action lawyers," Dabit, 547 U.S., at 81 (quoting H. R. Conf. Rep. No. 104-369, p. 31 (1995) [U.S. Code Cong. & Admin. News 1995, p. 730] (hereinafter H. R. Conf. Rep.))—the PSLRA installed both substantive and procedural controls.[4] Notably, Congress prescribed new procedures for the appointment of lead plaintiffs and lead counsel. This innovation aimed to increase the likelihood that institutional investors—parties more likely to balance the interests of the class with the long-term interests of the company—would serve as lead plaintiffs. See id., at 33-34; S. Rep. No. 104-98, p. 11 (1995) [U.S. Code Cong. & Admin. News 1995, pp. 679, 690.] Congress also "limit[ed] recoverable damages and attorney's fees, provide[d] a 'safe harbor' for forward-looking statements, ... mandate[d] imposition of sanctions for frivolous litigation, and authorize[d] a stay of discovery pending

---

4. Nothing in the Act, we have previously noted, casts doubt on the conclusion "that private securities litigation [i]s an indispensable tool with which defrauded investors can recover their losses"—a matter crucial to the integrity of domestic capital markets. See Merrill Lynch, Pierce, Fenner & Smith Inc. v. Dabit, 547 U.S. 71, 81 (2006) (internal quotation marks omitted).

resolution of any motion to dismiss." *Dabit,* 547 U.S., at 81. And in §21D(b) of the PSLRA, Congress "impose[d] heightened pleading requirements in actions brought pursuant to §10(b) and Rule 10b-5." Ibid.

Under the PSLRA's heightened pleading instructions, any private securities complaint alleging that the defendant made a false or misleading statement must: (1) "specify each statement alleged to have been misleading [and] the reason or reasons why the statement is misleading," 15 U.S.C. §78u-4(b)(1); and (2) "state with particularity facts giving rise to a strong inference that the defendant acted with the required state of mind," §78u-4(b)(2). In the instant case, as earlier stated, see *supra,* at 2506, the District Court and the Seventh Circuit agreed that the Shareholders met the first of the two requirements: The complaint sufficiently specified Notebaert's alleged misleading statements and the reasons why the statements were misleading. 303 F. Supp. 2d, at 955-961, 437 F.3d, at 596-600. But those courts disagreed on whether the Shareholders, as required by §21D(b)(2), "state[d] with particularity facts giving rise to a strong inference that [Notebaert] acted with [scienter]," §78u-4(b)(2).

The "strong inference" standard "unequivocally raise[d] the bar for pleading scienter," 437 F.3d, at 601, and signaled Congress' purpose to promote greater uniformity among the Circuits, see H.R. Conf. Rep., p. 41. But "Congress did not . . . throw much light on what facts . . . suffice to create [a strong] inference," or on what "degree of imagination courts can use in divining whether" the requisite inference exists. 437 F.3d, at 601. While adopting the Second Circuit's "strong inference" standard, Congress did not codify that Circuit's case law interpreting the standard. See §78u-4(b)(2). With no clear guide from Congress other than its "inten[tion] to strengthen existing pleading requirements," H.R. Conf. Rep., p. 41, Courts of Appeals have diverged again, this time in construing the term "strong inference." Among the uncertainties, should courts consider competing inferences in determining whether an inference of scienter is "strong"? See 437 F.3d, at 601-602 (collecting cases). Our task is to prescribe a workable construction of the "strong inference" standard, a reading geared to the PSLRA's twin goals: to curb frivolous, lawyer-driven litigation, while preserving investors' ability to recover on meritorious claims.

III.

A.

We establish the following prescriptions: *First,* faced with a Rule 12(b)(6) motion to dismiss a §10(b) action, courts must, as with any motion to dismiss for failure to plead a claim on which relief can be granted, accept all factual allegations in the complaint as true. . . .

Second, courts must consider the complaint in its entirety, as well as other sources courts ordinarily examine when ruling on Rule 12(b)(6) motions to dismiss, in particular, documents incorporated into the complaint by reference, and matters of which a court may take judicial notice. See 5B Wright & Miller §1357 (3d ed. 2004 and Supp. 2007). The inquiry, as several Courts of Appeals have recognized, is whether *all* of the facts alleged, taken collectively, give rise to a strong inference of scienter, not whether any individual allegation, scrutinized in isolation, meets that standard.

Third, in determining whether the pleaded facts give rise to a "strong" inference of scienter, the court must take into account plausible opposing inferences. The Seventh Circuit expressly declined to engage in such a comparative inquiry. A complaint could survive, that court said, as long as it "alleges facts from which, if true, a reasonable person could infer that the defendant acted with the required intent"; in other words, only "[i]f a reasonable person could not draw such an inference from the alleged facts" would the defendant prevail on a motion to dismiss. 437 F.3d, at 602. But in §21D(b)(2), Congress did not merely require plaintiffs to "provide a factual basis for [their] scienter allegations," ibid. (quoting In re Cerner Corp. Securities Litigation, 425 F.3d 1079, 1084, 1085 (C.A.8 2005)), i.e., to allege facts from which an inference of scienter rationally *could* be drawn. Instead, Congress required plaintiffs to plead with particularity facts that give rise to a "strong"—i.e., a powerful or cogent—inference. See American Heritage Dictionary 1717 (4th ed. 2000) (defining "strong" as "[p]ersuasive, effective, and cogent"); 16 Oxford English Dictionary 949 (2d ed. 1989) (defining "strong" as "[p]owerful to demonstrate or convince" (definition 16b)); cf. 7 Id., at 924 (defining "inference" as "a conclusion [drawn] from known or assumed facts or statements"; "reasoning from something known or assumed to something else which follows from it").

The strength of an inference cannot be decided in a vacuum. The inquiry is inherently comparative: How likely is it that one conclusion, as compared to others, follows from the underlying facts? To determine whether the plaintiff has alleged facts that give rise to the requisite "strong inference" of scienter, a court must consider plausible nonculpable explanations for the defendant's conduct, as well as inferences favoring the plaintiff. The inference that the defendant acted with scienter need not be irrefutable, i.e., of the "smoking-gun" genre, or even the "most plausible of competing inferences," *Fidel,* 392 F.3d, at 227 (quoting Helwig v. Vencor, Inc., 251 F.3d 540, 553 (C.A.6 2001) (en banc)). Recall in this regard that §21D(b)'s pleading requirements are but one constraint among many the PSLRA installed to screen out frivolous suits, while allowing meritorious actions to move forward. See supra, and n. 4. Yet the inference of scienter must be more than merely "reasonable" or "permissible"—it must be cogent and compelling, thus strong in light of other explanations. A complaint will survive, we hold, only if a reasonable person would deem the inference of scienter cogent and at least as compelling as any opposing inference one could draw from the facts alleged.[5]

---

5. Justice Scalia objects to this standard on the ground that "[i]f a jade falcon were stolen from a room to which only A and B had access," it could not "*possibly* be said there was a 'strong inference' that B was the thief." (opinion concurring in judgment) (emphasis in original). I suspect, however, that law enforcement officials as well as the owner of the precious falcon would find the inference of guilt as to B quite strong—certainly strong enough to warrant further investigation. Indeed, an inference at least as likely as competing inferences can, in some cases, warrant recovery. See Summers v. Tice, 33 Cal.2d 80, 84-87, 199 P.2d 1, 3-5 (1948) (in bank) (plaintiff wounded by gunshot could recover from two defendants, even though the most he could prove was that each defendant was at least as likely to have injured him as the other); Restatement (Third) of Torts §28(b), Comment e, p. 504 (Proposed Final Draft No. 1, Apr. 6, 2005) ("Since the publication of the Second Restatement in 1965, courts have generally accepted the alternative-liability principle of [Summers v. Tice, adopted in] §433B(3), while fleshing out its limits."). In any event, we disagree with Justice Scalia that the hardly stock term "strong inference" has only one invariably right ("natural" or "normal") reading—his. . . .

B.

Tellabs contends that when competing inferences are considered, Notebaert's evident lack of pecuniary motive will be dispositive. The Shareholders, Tellabs stresses, did not allege that Notebaert sold any shares during the class period. See Brief for Petitioners 50 ("The absence of any allegations of motive color all the other allegations putatively giving rise to an inference of scienter."). While it is true that motive can be a relevant consideration, and personal financial gain may weigh heavily in favor of a scienter inference, we agree with the Seventh Circuit that the absence of a motive allegation is not fatal. See 437 F.3d, at 601. As earlier stated, allegations must be considered collectively; the significance that can be ascribed to an allegation of motive, or lack thereof, depends on the entirety of the complaint.

Tellabs also maintains that several of the Shareholders' allegations are too vague or ambiguous to contribute to a strong inference of scienter. For example, the Shareholders alleged that Tellabs flooded its customers with unwanted products, a practice known as "channel stuffing." But they failed, Tellabs argues, to specify whether the channel stuffing allegedly known to Notebaert was the illegitimate kind (e.g., writing orders for products customers had not requested) or the legitimate kind (e.g., offering customers discounts as an incentive to buy). Brief for Petitioners 44-46; Reply Brief 8. See also id., at 8-9 (complaint lacks precise dates of reports critical to distinguish legitimate conduct from culpable conduct). But see 437 F.3d, at 598, 603-604 (pointing to multiple particulars alleged by the Shareholders, including specifications as to timing). We agree that omissions and ambiguities count against inferring scienter, for plaintiffs must "state with particularity facts giving rise to a strong inference that the defendant acted with the required state of mind." §78u-4(b)(2). We reiterate, however, that the court's job is not to scrutinize each allegation in isolation but to assess all the allegations holistically. In sum, the reviewing court must ask: When the allegations are accepted as true and taken collectively, would a reasonable person deem the inference of scienter at least as strong as any opposing inference? . . .

JUSTICE SCALIA, concurring in the judgment.

I fail to see how an inference that is merely "at least as compelling as any opposing inference" can conceivably be called what the statute here at issue requires: a "strong inference." If a jade falcon were stolen from a room to which only A and B had access, could it *possibly* be said there was a "strong inference" that B was the thief? I think not, and I therefore think that the Court's test must fail. In my view, the test should be whether the inference of scienter (if any) is *more plausible* than the inference of innocence.

[The opinions of Justice Alito, concurring in the result, and Justice Stevens, dissenting, are omitted.]

On remand the Seventh Circuit considered whether the complaint satisfied the "strong inference" standard.

Makor Issues & Rights, Ltd. v. Tellabs, Inc.
United States Court of Appeals, Seventh Circuit, 2008
513 F.3d 702

POSNER, CIRCUIT JUDGE.

To judges raised on notice pleading, the idea of drawing a "strong inference" from factual allegations is mysterious. Even when a plaintiff is required by Rule 9(b) to plead facts (such as the when and where of an alleged fraudulent statement), the court must treat the pleaded facts as true and "draw all reasonable inferences in favor of the plaintiff."

To draw a "strong inference" in favor of the plaintiff might seem to imply that the defendant had pleaded facts or presented evidence that would, by comparison with the plaintiff's allegations, enable a conclusion that the plaintiff had the stronger case; and therefore that a judge could not draw a strong inference in the plaintiff's favor before hearing from the defendant. But comparison is not essential, and obviously is not contemplated by the Reform Act, which requires dismissal in advance of the defendant's answer unless the complaint itself gives rise to a strong inference of scienter. For a defendant will usually have evidence to present in his defense; and so a complaint that on its face, and without reference to the defendant's case, creates only a weak or bare inference of scienter, suggesting that the plaintiff would prevail only if there were no defense case at all, would be quite likely to fail eventually when the defendant had a chance to put on his case, which would normally be after pretrial discovery. Apparently Congress does not believe that weak complaints should put a defendant to the expense of discovery in a securities-fraud case, which is likely to be complex—as this case is. . . .

The company's statements that we have quoted or paraphrased were, we ruled in our previous opinion—and, to repeat, the ruling binds us as law of the case—adequately pleaded as materially false. But is an inference of scienter from these allegations cogent and at least as compelling as the contrary inference—that there was no scienter? . . .

There are two competing inferences (always assuming of course that the plaintiffs are able to prove the allegations of the complaint). One is that the company knew (or was reckless in failing to realize, but we shall not have to discuss that possibility separately) that the statements were false, and material to investors. The other is that although the statements were false and material, their falsity was the result of innocent, or at worst careless, mistakes at the executive level. Suppose a clerical worker in the company's finance department accidentally overstated the company's earnings and the erroneous figure got reported in good faith up the line to Notebaert or other senior management, who then included the figure in their public announcements. Even if senior management had been careless in failing to detect the error, there would be no corporate scienter. . . . To establish corporate liability for a violation of Rule 10b-5 requires "look[ing] to the state of mind of the individual corporate official or officials who make or issue the statement (or order or approve it or its making or issuance, or who furnish information or language for inclusion therein, or the like) rather than generally to the collective knowledge of all the corporation's officers and employees acquired in the course of their employment." . . . A corporation is liable for statements by employees who have apparent authority to make them. . . .

The Supreme Court has declined to incorporate common law principles root and branch into section 10(b) of the Securities Exchange Act (and hence into Rule 10b-5), and specifically has rejected aider and abettor liability. Central Bank of Denver, N.A. v. First Interstate Bank of Denver, N.A., 511 U.S. 164, 114 S. Ct. 1439, 128 L. Ed. 2d 119 (1994). But the doctrines of respondeat superior and apparent authority remain applicable to suits for securities fraud. AT&T v. Winback & Conserve Program, Inc., 42 F.3d 1421, 1429-33 (3d Cir. 1994). Tellabs does not argue the contrary.

The critical question, therefore, is how likely it is that the allegedly false statements that we quoted earlier in this opinion were the result of merely careless mistakes at the management level based on false information fed it from below, rather than of an intent to deceive or a reckless indifference to whether the statements were misleading. It is exceedingly unlikely. The 5500 and the 6500 were Tellabs's most important products. The 5500 was described by the company as its "flagship" product and the 6500 was the 5500's heralded successor. They were to Tellabs as Windows XP and Vista are to Microsoft. That no member of the company's senior management who was involved in authorizing or making public statements about the demand for the 5500 and 6500 knew that they were false is very hard to credit, and no plausible story has yet been told by the defendants that might dispel our incredulity. The closest is the suggestion that while "available" no doubt meant to most investors that the 6500 was ready to be shipped to customers rather than that the new product was having teething troubles that would keep it off the market for many months, this may have been a bit of corporate jargon innocently intended to indicate that the company was ready to take orders. If so, then while it was false as reasonably understood by investors the false impression was a result of mutual misunderstanding rather than of fraud. See Banque Arabe et Internationale D'Investissement v. Maryland National Bank, 57 F.3d 146, 153-54 (2d Cir. 1995). But this is highly implausible when "available" is set among the company's alleged lies about the 6500 — that "customers are embracing" the 6500, that "interest in and demand for the 6500 continues to grow," that "we are satisfying very strong demand and growing customer demand [for the 6500 and] we are as confident as ever — that may be an understatement — about the 6500," and that "we should hit our full manufacturing capacity in May or June to accommodate the demand [for the 6500] we are seeing. Everything we can build, we are building and shipping. The demand is very strong." . . .

Against all this the defendants argue that they could have had no motive to paint the prospects for the 5500 and 6500 systems in rosy hues because within months they acknowledged their mistakes and disclosed the true situation of the two products, and because there is no indication that Notebaert or anyone else who may have been in on the fraud profited from it financially. The argument confuses expected with realized benefits. Notebaert may have thought that there was a chance that the situation regarding the two key products would right itself. If so, the benefits of concealment might exceed the costs. Investors do not like to think they're riding a roller coaster. Prompt disclosure of the truth would have caused Tellabs's stock price to plummet, as it did when the truth came out a couple of months later. Suppose the situation had corrected itself. Still, investors would have discovered that the stock was more volatile than they thought, and risk-averse investors (who predominate) do not like volatility and so, unless it can be diversified away, demand compensation in the form of a lower price; consequently the stock might not recover to its previous level. The fact that a gamble—concealing bad news in the hope that it will be overtaken by good news—fails is not inconsistent with its having been a considered, though because of the risk a reckless, gamble. See First Commodity Corp. of Boston v. CFTC, 676 F.2d 1, 7-9 (1st Cir. 1982). It is like embezzling in the hope that winning at the track will enable the embezzled funds to be replaced before they are discovered to be missing.

So the inference of corporate scienter is not only as likely as its opposite, but more likely. And is it cogent? Well, if there are only two possible inferences, and one is much more likely than the other, it must be cogent. Suppose a person woke up one morning with a sharp pain in his abdomen. He thought it was due to a recent operation to remove his gall bladder, but realized it could equally well have been due to any number of other things. The inference that it was due to the operation could not be thought cogent. But suppose he went to a doctor who performed tests that ruled out any cause other than the operation or a duodenal ulcer and told the patient that he was 99 percent certain that it was the operation. The plausibility of an explanation depends on the plausibility of the alternative explanations. United States v. Beard, 354 F.3d 691, 692-93 (7th Cir. 2004); Ronald J. Allen, "Factual Ambiguity and a Theory of Evidence," 88 Nw. U. L. Rev. 604, 611 (1994). As more and more alternatives to a given explanation are ruled out, the probability of that explanation's being the correct one rises. "Events that have a very low antecedent probability of occurring nevertheless do sometimes occur (the Indian Ocean tsunami, for example); and if in a particular case all the alternatives are ruled out, we can be confident that the case presents one of those instances in which the rare event did occur." Anderson v. Griffin, 397 F.3d 515, 521 (7th Cir. 2005). Because in our abdominal-pain example all other inferences had been ruled out except the 1 percent one, the inference that the pain was due to the operation would be cogent. This case is similar. Because the alternative hypotheses—either a cascade of innocent mistakes, or acts of subordinate employees, either or both resulting in a series of false statements—are far less likely than the hypothesis of scienter at the corporate level at which the statements were approved, the latter hypothesis must be considered cogent.

And at the top of the corporate pyramid sat Notebaert, the CEO. The 5500 and the 6500 were his company's key products. Almost all the false statements that we quoted emanated directly from him. Is it conceivable that he was unaware of the problems of his company's two major products and merely repeating lies fed to him by other executives of the company? It is conceivable, yes, but it is exceedingly unlikely. . . .

The defendants complain, finally, about the complaint's dependence on "confidential sources." The 26 "confidential sources" referred to in the complaint are important sources for the allegations not only of falsity but also of scienter. Because the Reform Act requires detailed fact pleading of falsity, materiality, and scienter, the plaintiff's lawyers in securities-fraud litigation have to conduct elaborate pre-complaint investigations—and without the aid of discovery, which cannot be conducted until the complaint is filed. Unable to compel testimony from employees of the prospective defendant, the lawyers worry that they won't be able to get to first base without assuring confidentiality to the employees whom they interview, even though it is unlawful for an employer to retaliate against an employee who blows the whistle on a securities fraud, 18 U.S.C. §1514A, and even though, since informants have no evidentiary privilege, their identity will be revealed in pretrial discovery, though of course a suit might never be brought or if brought might be settled before any discovery was conducted. . . .

The confidential sources listed in the complaint in this case . . . are numerous and consist of persons who from the description of their jobs were in a position to know at first hand the facts to which they are prepared to testify, such as the returns of the 5500s, that sales of the 5500 were dropping off a cliff while the company pretended that demand was strong, that the 6500 was not approved by Regional Bell Operating Companies, that it was still in the beta stage and failing performance tests conducted by prospective customers, and that it was too bulky for customers' premises. The information that the confidential informants are reported to have obtained is set forth in convincing detail, with some of the information, moreover, corroborated by multiple sources. It would be better were the informants named in the complaint, because it would be easier to determine whether they had been in a good position to know the facts that the complaint says they learned. But the absence of proper names does not invalidate the drawing of a strong inference from informants' assertions.

We conclude that the plaintiffs have succeeded, with regard to the statements identified in our previous opinion as having been adequately alleged to be false and material, in pleading scienter in conformity with the requirements of the Private Securities Litigation Reform Act. . . .

d. Reliance and Causation

The precise connection required between defendant's misconduct and plaintiff's action has long been a source of confusion under Rule 10b-5. In the simple face-to-face transaction giving rise to a common law action in deceit, plaintiff would have to show reliance on defendant's misstatement that caused plaintiff's losses. When the alleged wrongdoing occurs in a market setting rather than face to face and is an omission rather than a misstatement, the difficulty of proving the common law elements increases and would act to exclude many securities claims. Courts developed alternative means of meeting this "connection" requirement in these settings. In Affiliated Ute Citizens v. United States, 406 U.S. 128 (1978), the Supreme Court observed the following:

> Under the circumstances of this case, involving primarily a failure to disclose, positive proof of reliance is not a prerequisite to recovery. All that is necessary is that the facts withheld be material in the sense that a reasonable investor might consider them important in the making of this decision. This obligation to disclose and the withholding of a material fact establishes the requisite element of causation in fact.

406 U.S. at 153-154.

After *Affiliated Ute*, some courts continued to require proof of actual reliance when the alleged misconduct involved an affirmative misrepresentation instead of an omission. See, e.g., Wilson v. Telecommunications Corp., 648 F.2d 88 (2d Cir. 1981). The fraud on the market doctrine discussed below in Basic Inc. v. Levinson opens up a broader range of cases in which reliance is presumed.

Basic, Inc. v. Levinson
United States Supreme Court, 1988
485 U.S. 224

JUSTICE BLACKMUN delivered the opinion of the Court.

[The facts of this case are contained in the portion of the opinion reprinted beginning at page 1009. Basic, Inc. made statements over a 14-month period denying it was engaged in merger negotiations that eventually led to a merger at a higher price.]

. . . We must also determine whether a person who traded a corporation's shares on a securities exchange after the issuance of a materially misleading statement by the corporation may invoke a rebuttable presumption that, in trading, he relied on the integrity of the price set by the market. . . .

IV

A

We turn to the question of reliance and the fraud-on-the-market theory. Succinctly put:

> The fraud on the market theory is based on the hypothesis that, in an open and developed securities market, the price of a company's stock is determined by the available material information regarding the company and its business. . . . Misleading statements will therefore defraud purchasers of stock even if the purchasers do not directly rely on the misstatements. . . . The causal connection between the defendants' fraud and the plaintiffs' purchase of stock in such a case is no less significant than in a case of direct reliance on misrepresentations. (Peil v. Speiser, 806 F.2d 1154, 1160-1161 (C.A.3 1986).)

Our task, of course, is not to assess the general validity of the theory, but to consider whether it was proper for the courts below to apply a rebuttable presumption of reliance, supported in part by the fraud-on-the-market theory. Cf. the comments of the dissent.

This case required resolution of several common questions of law and fact concerning the falsity or misleading nature of three public statements made by Basic, the presence or absence of scienter, and the materiality of the misrepresentations, if any. In their amended complaint, the named plaintiffs alleged that in reliance on Basic's statements they sold their shares of Basic stock in the depressed market created by petitioners. Requiring proof of individualized reliance from each member of the proposed plaintiff class effectively would have prevented respondents from proceeding with a class action, since individual issues then would have overwhelmed the common ones. . . .

Petitioners and their amici complain that the fraud-on-the-market theory effectively eliminates the requirement that a plaintiff asserting a claim under Rule 10b-5 prove reliance. They note that reliance is and long has been an element of common-law fraud, see e.g., Restatement (Second) of Torts §525 (1977); W. Keeton, D. Dobbs, R. Keeton & D. Owen, Prosser and Keeton on Law of Torts §108 (5th ed. 1984), and argue that because the analogous express right of action includes a reliance requirement, see, e.g., §18(a) of the 1934 Act, as amended, 15 U.S.C. §78r(a), so too must an action implied under §10(b).

We agree that reliance is an element of a Rule 10b-5 cause of action. See Ernst & Ernst v. Hochfelder [425 U.S. 185, 206 (1976)] (quoting Senate Report). Reliance provides the requisite causal connection between a defendant's misrepresentation and a plaintiff's injury. There is, however, more than one way to demonstrate the causal connection. Indeed, we previously have dispensed with a requirement of positive proof of reliance, where a duty to disclose material information had been breached, concluding that the necessary nexus between the plaintiffs' injury and the defendant's wrongful conduct had been established. See Affiliated Ute Citizens v. United States [406 U.S. 128, 153-154 (1978)]. Similarly, we did not require proof that material omissions or misstatements in a proxy statement decisively affected voting, because the proxy solicitation itself, rather than the defect in the solicitation materials, served as an essential link in the transaction. See Mills v. Electric Auto-Lite Co., 396 U.S. 375, 384-385 (1970).

The modern securities markets, literally involving millions of shares changing hands daily, differ from the face-to-face transactions contemplated by early fraud cases, and our understanding of Rule 10b-5's reliance requirement must encompass these differences.[22]

> In face-to-face transactions, the inquiry into an investor's reliance upon information is into the subjective pricing of that information by that investor. With the presence of a market, the market is interposed between seller and buyer and, ideally, transmits information to the investor in the processed form of a market price. Thus the market is performing a substantial part of the valuation process performed by the investor in a face-to-face transaction. The market is acting as the unpaid agent of the investor, informing him that given all the information available to it, the value of the stock is worth the market price. (In re LTV Securities Litigation, 88 F.R.D. 134, 143 (N.D. Tex. 1980).) . . .

B

Presumptions typically serve to assist courts in managing circumstances in which direct proof, for one reason or another, is rendered difficult. See, e.g., D. Louisell & C. Mueller, Federal Evidence 541-542 (1977). The courts below accepted a presumption, created by the fraud-on-the-market theory and subject to rebuttal by petitioners, that persons who had traded Basic shares had done so in reliance on the integrity of the price set by the market, but because of petitioners' material misrepresentations that price had been fraudulently depressed. Requiring a plaintiff to show a speculative state of facts, i.e., how he would have acted if omitted material information had been disclosed, see Affiliated Ute Citizens v. United States, 406 U.S., at 153-154, or if the misrepresentation had not been made, see Sharp v. Coopers & Lybrand, 649 F.2d 175, 188 (C.A.3 1981), cert. denied, 455 U.S. 938 (1982), would place an unnecessarily unrealistic evidentiary burden on the Rule 10b-5 plaintiff who has traded on an impersonal market. Cf. Mills v. Electric Auto-Lite Co., 396 U.S., at 385.

---

22. Actions under Rule 10b-5 are distinct from common-law deceit and misrepresentation claims, see Blue Chip Stamps v. Manor Drug Stores, 421 U.S. 723, 744-745 (1975), and are in part designed to add to the protections provided investors by the common law, see Herman & MacLean v. Huddleston, 459 U.S. 375, 388-389 (1983).

Arising out of considerations of fairness, public policy, and probability, as well as judicial economy, presumptions are also useful devices for allocating the burdens of proof between parties. See E. Cleary, McCormick on Evidence 968-969 (3d ed. 1984); see also Fed. Rule Evid. 301 and Advisory Committee Notes. The presumption of reliance employed in this case is consistent with, and, by facilitating Rule 10b-5 litigation, supports, the congressional policy embodied in the 1934 Act. In drafting that Act, Congress expressly relied on the premise that securities markets are affected by information, and enacted legislation to facilitate an investor's reliance on the integrity of those markets:

> No investor, no speculator, can safely buy and sell securities upon the exchanges without having an intelligent basis for forming his judgment as to the value of the securities he buys or sells. The idea of a free and open public market is built upon the theory that competing judgments of buyers and sellers as to the fair price of a security brings about a situation where the market price reflects as nearly as possible a just price. Just as artificial manipulation tends to upset the true function of an open market, so the hiding and secreting of important information obstructs the operation of the markets as indices of real value. (H.R. Rep. No. 1383, at 11.)

The presumption is also supported by common sense and probability. Recent empirical studies have tended to confirm Congress' premise that the market price of shares traded on well-developed markets reflects all publicly available information, and, hence, any material misrepresentations.[24] It has been noted that "it is hard to imagine that there ever is a buyer or seller who does not rely on market integrity. Who would knowingly roll the dice in a crooked crap game?" Schlanger v. Four-Phase Systems Inc., 555 F. Supp. 535, 538 (S.D.N.Y. 1982). Indeed, nearly every court that has considered the proposition has concluded that where materially misleading statements have been disseminated into an impersonal, well-developed market for securities, the reliance of individual plaintiffs on the integrity of the market price may be presumed. Commentators generally have applauded the adoption of one variation or another of the fraud-on-the-market theory. An investor who buys or sells stock at the price set by the market does so in reliance on the integrity of that price. Because most publicly available information is reflected in market price, an investor's reliance on any public material misrepresentations, therefore, may be presumed for purposes of a Rule 10b-5 action.

C

The Court of Appeals found that petitioners "made public material misrepresentations and [respondents] sold Basic stock in an impersonal, efficient market. Thus the class, as defined by the district court, has established the threshold facts for proving

---

24. See In re LTV Securities Litigation, 88 F.R.D. 134, 144 (N.D. Tex. 1980) (citing studies); Fischel, Use of Modern Finance Theory in Securities Fraud Cases Involving Actively Traded Securities, 38 Bus. Law. 1, 4, n.9 (1982) (citing literature on efficient-capital-market theory); Dennis, Materiality and the Efficient Capital Market Model: A Recipe for the Total Mix, 25 Wm. & Mary L. Rev. 373, 374-381, and n.1 (1984). We need not determine by adjudication what economists and social scientists have debated through the use of sophisticated statistical analysis and the application of economic theory. For purposes of accepting the presumption of reliance in this case, we need only believe that market professionals generally consider most publicly announced material statements about companies, thereby affecting stock market prices.

their loss." The court acknowledged that petitioners may rebut proof of the elements giving rise to the presumption, or show that the misrepresentation in fact did not lead to a distortion of price or that an individual plaintiff traded or would have traded despite his knowing the statement was false.

Any showing that severs the link between the alleged misrepresentation and either the price received (or paid) by the plaintiff, or his decision to trade at a fair market price, will be sufficient to rebut the presumption of reliance. For example, if petitioners could show that the "market makers" were privy to the truth about the merger discussions here with Combustion, and thus that the market price would not have been affected by their misrepresentations, the causal connection could be broken: the basis for finding that the fraud had been transmitted through market price would be gone. Similarly, if, despite petitioners' allegedly fraudulent attempt to manipulate market price, news of the merger discussions credibly entered the market and dissipated the effects of the misstatements, those who traded Basic shares after the corrective statements would have no direct or indirect connection with the fraud. Petitioners also could rebut the presumption of reliance as to plaintiffs who would have divested themselves of their Basic shares without relying on the integrity of the market. For example, a plaintiff who believed that Basic's statements were false and that Basic was indeed engaged in merger discussions, and who consequently believed that Basic stock was artificially underpriced, but sold his shares nevertheless because of other unrelated concerns, e.g., potential antitrust problems, or political pressures to divest from shares of certain businesses, could not be said to have relied on the integrity of a price he knew had been manipulated. . . .

THE CHIEF JUSTICE, JUSTICE SCALIA, and JUSTICE KENNEDY took no part in the consideration or decision of this case.

JUSTICE WHITE, with whom JUSTICE O'CONNOR joins, concurring in part and dissenting in part. . . .

I

Even when compared to the relatively youthful private cause-of-action under §10(b), see Kardon v. National Gypsum Co., 69 F. Supp. 512 (E.D. Pa. 1946), the fraud-on-the-market theory is a mere babe.[1] Yet today, the Court embraces this theory with the sweeping confidence usually reserved for more mature legal doctrines. In so doing, I fear that the Court's decision may have many adverse, unintended effects as it is applied and interpreted in the years to come. . . .

B

. . . [E]ven as the Court attempts to limit the fraud-on-the-market theory it endorses today, the pitfalls in its approach are revealed by previous uses by the lower courts of

---

1. The earliest Court of Appeals case adopting this theory cited by the Court is Blackie v. Barrack, 524 F.2d 891 (C.A.9 1975), cert. denied, 429 U.S. 816 (1976). Moreover, widespread acceptance of the fraud-on-the-market theory in the Courts of Appeals cannot be placed any earlier than five or six years ago.

the broader versions of the theory. Confusion and contradiction in court rulings are inevitable when traditional legal analysis is replaced with economic theorization by the federal courts.

In general, the case law developed in this Court with respect to §10(b) and Rule 10b-5 has been based on doctrines with which we, as judges, are familiar: common-law doctrines of fraud and deceit. See, e.g., Santa Fe Industries, Inc. v. Green, 430 U.S. 462, 471-477 (1977). Even when we have extended civil liability under Rule 10b-5 to a broader reach than the common law had previously permitted, we have retained familiar legal principles as our guideposts. See, e.g., Herman & MacLean v. Huddleston, 459 U.S. 375, 389-390 (1983). The federal courts have proved adept at developing an evolving jurisprudence of Rule 10b-5 in such a manner. But with no staff economists, no experts schooled in the "efficient-capital-market hypothesis," no ability to test the validity of empirical market studies, we are not well equipped to embrace novel constructions of a statute based on contemporary microeconomic theory.

. . . The Congress, with its superior resources and expertise, is far better equipped than the federal courts for the task of determining how modern economic theory and global financial markets require that established legal notions of fraud be modified. In choosing to make these decisions itself, the Court, I fear, embarks on a course that it does not genuinely understand, giving rise to consequences it cannot foresee.

For while the economists' theories which underpin the fraud-on-the-market presumption may have the appeal of mathematical exactitude and scientific certainty, they are — in the end — nothing more than theories which may or may not prove accurate upon further consideration. Even the most earnest advocates of economic analysis of the law recognize this. See, e.g., Easterbrook, Afterword: Knowledge and Answers, 85 Colum. L. Rev. 1117, 1118 (1985). . . .

Consequently, I cannot join the Court in its effort to reconfigure the securities laws, based on recent economic theories, to better fit what it perceives to be the new realities of financial markets. I would leave this task to others more equipped for the job than we.

c

. . . Even if I was prepared to accept (as a matter of common sense or general understanding) the assumption that most persons buying or selling stock do so in response to the market price, the fraud-on-the-market theory goes further. For in adopting a "presumption of reliance," the Court *also* assumes that buyers and sellers rely — not just on the market price — but on the *"integrity"* of that price. It is this aspect of the fraud-on-the-market hypothesis which most mystifies me.

To define the term "integrity of the market price," the majority quotes approvingly from cases which suggest that investors are entitled to " 'rely on the price of a stock as a reflection of its value.' " But the meaning of this phrase eludes me, for it implicitly suggests that stocks have some "true value" that is measurable by a standard other than their market price. While the Scholastics of Medieval times professed a means to make such a valuation of a commodity's "worth," I doubt that the federal courts of our day are similarly equipped.

Even if securities had some "value"—knowable and distinct from the market price of a stock—investors do not always share the Court's presumption that a stock's price is a "reflection of [this] value." Indeed, "many investors purchase or sell stock because they believe the price *inaccurately* reflects the corporation's worth." Black, Fraud on the Market: A Criticism of Dispensing with Reliance Requirements in Certain Open Market Transactions, 62 N.C. L. Rev. 435, 455 (1984) (emphasis added). . . . Yet today, the Court allows investors to recover who can show little more than that they sold stock at a lower price than what might have been.

I do not propose that the law retreat from the many protections that §10(b) and Rule 10b-5, as interpreted in our prior cases, provide to investors. But any extension of these laws, to approach something closer to an investor insurance scheme, should come from Congress, and not from the courts.

III . . .

And who will pay the judgments won in such actions? I suspect that all too often the majority's rule will "lead to large judgments, payable in the last analysis by innocent investors, for the benefit of speculators and their lawyers." Cf. SEC v. Texas Gulf Sulphur Co., 401 F.2d 833, 867 (C.A.2 1968) (en banc) (Friendly, J., concurring), cert. denied, 394 U.S. 976 (1969). This Court and others have previously recognized that "inexorably broadening . . . the class of plaintiff[s] who may sue in this area of the law will ultimately result in more harm than good." Blue Chip Stamps v. Manor Drug Stores, [421 U.S. 723, 747-748 (1975)]. See also Ernst & Ernst v. Hochfelder, 425 U.S., at 214; Ultramares Corp. v. Touche, 255 N.Y. 170, 179-180, 174 N.E. 441, 444-445 (1931) (Cardozo, C.J.). Yet such a bitter harvest is likely to be reaped from the seeds sown by the Court's decision today. . . .

NOTES AND QUESTIONS

1. *Basic*'s rebuttable presumption of reliance based on fraud on the market remains contentious well into the third decade after its decision as scholars, lawyers, and judges work through what it means for shares to trade in an efficient market. Four justices in Amgen, Inc. v. Connecticut Retirement Plans and Trust Funds, 133 S. Ct. 1184 (2013), encouraged reconsideration of its holding and the Erica P. John Fund v. Halliburton case to be argued in 2014 puts that issue before the Court. Part of the uncertainty derives from the *Basic* opinion's alternative phrasings of what is being relied on: is it that the price in the efficient market is accurate, or is it reliance on the price integrity of what is visible in the market? See Langevoort, *Basic* at Twenty: Rethinking Fraud on the Market, 2009 Wisc. L. Rev. 151, 161 (*Basic* creates an entitlement to an undistorted stock price). Index investors who do not necessarily rely on accurate pricing and principled investors may be committed to selling without regard to price. A discussion of these examples between Justices Blackmun and Brennan during the Court's deliberations in *Basic* is recounted in Langevoort, Judgment Day for Fraud-on-the-Market?: Reflections on *Amgen* and the Second Coming of *Halliburton* (working paper, 2013, available at http://ssrn.com/abstract=2281910).

Both the acceptance of the theory and the breadth of its application may turn on understanding and acceptance in legal circles of learning from financial economists.

> There are misunderstandings about what ECMH teaches about prices. The . . . opinion in *Basic* referred to legislative history suggesting that market processes lead to some kind of "fair" or "just" price. Justice White's dissent expressed doubts about expressions of reasonable reliance on the "integrity" of a market price and about statements that investors are entitled to "rely on the price of a stock as a reflection of its value." Justice White also expressed concern that questions of "true value" raise issues more suited to theologians than judges, noting that there are always individuals who decline to sell at the market price because they believe market prices are "inaccurate" reflections of value. The fact that sales occur at all in actively traded securities raises questions about the meaning of market prices. An understanding of what "value" means in this context is critical to understanding why it is reasonable for traders to rely on such prices. In this setting, it is fair to agree with the cynic who described an economist as one who knows the price of everything and the value of nothing, if by value something more than an individual's revealed reservation price is meant.
>
> To say that prices reflect a security's "value" in the context of modern financial economics only means that the price is set in an unbiased manner and reflects a consensus view of its value. If a stock is perceived to be a bargain by a sufficient number of traders, they will proceed to buy it and sell others, until its price is driven up to the point where it is no longer a bargain, relative to other stocks.
>
> Once this equilibrium is reached, a buyer ought to be able to sell any stock for exactly the price paid for it, if no changes take place. The number of traders who believe it is a bargain will be offset by those who think it is overpriced, so that for every willing buyer at that price there will always be a willing seller. Relative prices will change only upon the revelation of new information, which flows constantly and keeps stock prices in a state of flux. Thus a statement that price is "fair" is true at the moment of purchase but is no guarantee that a security will hold its value relative to the market as news about the issuer develops.
>
> While bargains may exist from time to time in efficient capital markets, on average all stocks will be fairly priced in relation to each other. Absent superior information a trader has little reason to believe she can beat the market and achieve above margin returns. Where stocks are efficiently priced, each bears a return that compensates for the risk assumed. The Capital Assets Pricing Model ("CAPM") provides a widely accepted method of describing the manner in which the values of securities bearing different risks can be equated by varying the returns. All stocks bearing the same amount of risk will be similarly priced in relation to expected earnings, and all riskier stocks will bear risk premiums in proportion to their expected risks. An investor can vary the risk of her portfolio by varying holdings of riskless government securities or the amount of leverage used to buy the stocks. As a result, any portfolio of stocks can produce any investor's desired mix of risk, and return, which explains the aphorism "seen one stock, seen them all."

Carney, The Limits of the Fraud on the Market Doctrine, 44 Bus. Law. 1259, 1272-1273 (1989).

2. The majority opinion applies the fraud on the market presumption in the context of an "impersonal efficient market." How would you determine if the presumption is appropriate for a stock traded over the counter or thinly traded, that is, relatively inactive? See, e.g., Cammer v. Bloom, 711 F. Supp. 1264 (D.N.J. 1989) (examining average weekly trading volume, number of securities analysts following the stock, number of market makers, eligibility to use SEC Form S-3).

Could the market for a new issuance of shares be efficient? In Shores v. Sklar, 647 F.2d 462 (5th Cir. 1981) (en banc), cert. denied, 459 U.S. 1102 (1983), the Fifth Circuit, by a 12-10 vote, extended the presumption to purchasers of a new issue of municipal bonds not traded in an efficient market on the theory that the bonds would have been unmarketable without the defendant's fraud.

Dura Pharmaceuticals, Inc. v. Broudo
United States Supreme Court, 2005
544 U.S. 336

JUSTICE BREYER delivered the opinion of the Court.

A private plaintiff who claims securities fraud must prove that the defendant's fraud caused an economic loss. 109 Stat. 747, 15 U.S.C. §78u-4(b)(4). We consider a Ninth Circuit holding that a plaintiff can satisfy this requirement—a requirement that courts call "loss causation"—simply by alleging in the complaint and subsequently establishing that "the price" of the security "*on the date of purchase* was inflated because of the misrepresentation." 339 F.3d 933, 938 (9th Cir. 2003) (internal quotation marks omitted). In our view, the Ninth Circuit is wrong, both in respect to what a plaintiff must prove and in respect to what the plaintiffs' complaint here must allege.

I

Respondents are individuals who bought stock in Dura Pharmaceuticals, Inc., on the public securities market between April 15, 1997, and February 24, 1998. They have brought this securities fraud class action against Dura and some of its managers and directors (hereinafter Dura) in federal court. In respect to the question before us, their detailed amended (181 paragraph) complaint makes substantially the following allegations:

(1) Before and during the purchase period, Dura (or its officials) made false statements concerning both Dura's drug profits and future Food and Drug Administration (FDA) approval of a new asthmatic spray device.

(2) In respect to drug profits, Dura falsely claimed that it expected that its drug sales would prove profitable.

(3) In respect to the asthmatic spray device, Dura falsely claimed that it expected the FDA would soon grant its approval.

(4) On the last day of the purchase period, February 24, 1998, Dura announced that its earnings would be lower than expected, principally due to slow drug sales.

(5) The next day Dura's shares lost almost half their value (falling from about $39 per share to about $21).

(6) About eight months later (in November 1998), Dura announced that the FDA would not approve Dura's new asthmatic spray device.

(7) The next day Dura's share price temporarily fell but almost fully recovered within one week.

Most importantly, the complaint says the following (and nothing significantly more than the following) about economic losses attributable to the spray device misstatement: "*In reliance on the integrity of the market, [the plaintiffs] . . . paid artificially inflated prices for Dura securities*" and the plaintiffs suffered "*damage[s]*" thereby. (emphasis added).

The District Court dismissed the complaint. In respect to the plaintiffs' drug-profitability claim, it held that the complaint failed adequately to allege an appropriate state of mind, i.e., that defendants had acted knowingly, or the like. In respect to the plaintiffs' spray device claim, it held that the complaint failed adequately to allege "loss causation."

The Court of Appeals for the Ninth Circuit reversed. In the portion of the court's decision now before us—the portion that concerns the spray device claim—the Circuit held that the complaint adequately alleged "loss causation" The Circuit wrote that "plaintiffs establish loss causation if they have shown that the price *on the date of purchase* was inflated because of the misrepresentation" 339 F.3d, at 938 (emphasis in original; internal quotation marks omitted). It added that "the injury occurs at the time of the transaction." Ibid. Since the complaint pleaded "that the price at the time of purchase was overstated" and it sufficiently identified the cause, its allegations were legally sufficient. Ibid.

Because the Ninth Circuit's views about loss causation differ from those of other Circuits that have considered this issue, we granted Dura's petition for certiorari. Compare ibid. with, e.g., Emergent Capital Investment Management, LLC v. Stonepath Group, Inc., 343 F.3d 189, 198 (C.A.2 2003); Semerenko v. Cendant Corp., 223 F.3d 165, 185 (C.A.3 2000); Robbins v. Koger Properties, Inc., 116 F.3d 1441, 1447-1448 (C.A.11 1997); cf. Bastian v. Petren Resources Corp., 892 F.2d 680, 685 (C.A.7 1990). We now reverse.

II

Private federal securities fraud actions are based upon federal securities statutes and their implementing regulations. Section 10(b) of the Securities Exchange Act of 1934 forbids (1) the "use or employ[ment] . . . of any . . . deceptive device" (2) "in connection with the purchase or sale of any security" and (3) "in contravention of" Securities and Exchange Commission "rules and regulations." Commission Rule, 10b-5 forbids, among other things, the making of any "untrue statement of material fact" or the omission of any material fact "necessary in order to make the statements made . . . not misleading."

The courts have implied from these statutes and Rule a private damages action, which resembles, but is not identical to, common-law tort actions for deceit and misrepresentation. See, e.g., Blue Chip Stamps v. Manor Drug Stores, 421 U.S. 723, 730, 744 (1975); Ernst & Ernst v. Hochfelder, 425 U.S. 185, 196. And Congress has imposed statutory requirements on that private action. E.g., 15 U.S.C. §78u-4(b)(4).

In cases involving publicly traded securities and purchases or sales in public securities markets, the action's basic elements include:

(1) *a material misrepresentation (or omission),* see Basic Inc. v. Levinson, 485 U.S. 224, 231-232 (1988);

(2) *scienter,* i.e., a wrongful state of mind, see *Ernst & Ernst,* supra, at 197,199;

(3) *a connection with the purchase or sale of a security,* see *Blue Chip Stamps, supra,* at 730-731;

(4)   *reliance,* often referred to in cases involving public securities markets (fraud-on-the-market cases) as "transaction causation" see *Basic,* supra, at 248-249 (nonconclusively presuming that the price of a publicly traded share reflects a material misrepresentation and that plaintiffs have relied upon that misrepresentation as long as they would not have bought the share in its absence);

(5)   *economic loss,* 15 U.S.C. §78u-4(b)(4); and

(6)   *"loss causation"* i.e., a causal connection between the material misrepresentation and the loss, ibid.; cf. T. Hazen, Law of Securities Regulation, §§12.11[1],[3] (5th ed. 2002).

Dura argues that the complaint's allegations are inadequate in respect to these last two elements.

A

We begin with the Ninth Circuit's basic reason for finding the complaint adequate, namely, that at the end of the day plaintiffs need only "establish" i.e., prove, that "the price *on the date of purchase* was inflated because of the misrepresentation." 339 F.3d, at 938 (internal quotation marks omitted). In our view, this statement of the law is wrong. Normally, in cases such as this one (i.e., fraud-on-the-market cases), an inflated purchase price will not itself constitute or proximately cause the relevant economic loss.

For one thing, as a matter of pure logic, at the moment the transaction takes place, the plaintiff has suffered no loss; the inflated purchase payment is offset by ownership of a share that *at that instant* possesses equivalent value. Moreover, the logical link between the inflated share purchase price and any later economic loss is not invariably strong. Shares are normally purchased with an eye toward a later sale. But if, say, the purchaser sells the shares quickly before the relevant truth begins to leak out, the misrepresentation will not have led to any loss. If the purchaser sells later after the truth makes its way into the market place, an initially inflated purchase price *might* mean a later loss. But that is far from inevitably so. When the purchaser subsequently resells such shares, even at a lower price, that lower price may reflect, not the earlier misrepresentation, but changed economic circumstances, changed investor expectations, new industry-specific or firm-specific facts, conditions, or other events, which taken separately or together account for some or all of that lower price. (The same is true in respect to a claim that a share's higher price is lower than it would otherwise have been—a claim we do not consider here.) Other things being equal, the longer the time between purchase and sale, the more likely that this is so, i.e., the more likely that other factors caused the loss.

Given the tangle of factors affecting price, the most logic alone permits us to say is that the higher purchase price will *sometimes* play a role in bringing about a future loss. It may prove to be a necessary condition of any such loss, and in that sense one might say that the inflated purchase price suggests that the misrepresentation (using language the Ninth Circuit used) "touches upon" a later economic loss. Ibid. But, even if that is so, it is insufficient. To "touch upon" a loss is not to *cause* a loss, and it is the latter that the law requires. 15 U.S.C. §78u-4(b)(4).

For another thing, the Ninth Circuit's holding lacks support in precedent. Judicially implied private securities-fraud actions resemble in many (but not all) respects common-law deceit and misrepresentation actions. See *Blue Chip Stamps*, supra, at 744; see also L. Loss & J. Seligman, Fundamentals of Securities Regulation, 910-918 (5th ed. 2004) (describing relationship to common-law deceit). The common law of deceit subjects a person who "fraudulently" makes a "misrepresentation" to liability "for pecuniary loss caused" to one who justifiably relies upon that misrepresentation. Restatement (Second) of Torts §525, p. 55 (1977) (hereinafter Restatement of Torts); see also Southern Development Co. v. Silva, 125 U.S. 247, (1888) (setting forth elements of fraudulent misrepresentation). And the common law has long insisted that a plaintiff in such a case show not only that had he known the truth he would not have acted but also that he suffered actual economic loss. See, e.g., Pasley v. Freeman, 3 T.R. 5:1, 100 Eng. Rep. 450, 457 (1789) (if "no injury is occasioned by the lie, it is not actionable: but if it be attended with a damage, it then becomes the subject of an action"); Freeman v. Venner, 120 Mass. 424, 426 (1876) (a mortgagee cannot bring a tort action for damages stemming from a fraudulent note that a misrepresentation led him to execute unless and until the note has to be paid); see also M. Bigelow, Law of Torts 101 (8th ed. 1907) (damage "must already have been suffered before the bringing of the suit"); 2 T. Cooley, Law of Torts §348, p. 551 (4th ed. 1932) (plaintiff must show that he "suffered damage" and that the "damage followed proximately the deception"); W. Keeton, D. Dobbs, R. Keeton, & D. Owen, Prosser and Keeton on Law of Torts §110, p. 765 (5th ed. 1984) (hereinafter Prosser and Keeton) (plaintiff "must have suffered substantial damage," not simply nominal damages, before the cause of action can arise").

Given the common-law roots of the securities fraud action (and the common-law requirement that a plaintiff show actual damages), it is not surprising that other courts of appeals have rejected the Ninth Circuit's "inflated purchase price" approach to proving causation and loss. See, e.g., *Emergent Capital*, 343 F.3d, at 198 (inflation of purchase price alone cannot satisfy loss causation); *Semerenko*, 223 F.3d. at 185 (same); *Robbins*, 116 F.3d., at 1448 (same); cf. *Bastian*, 892 F.2d. at 685. Indeed, the Restatement of Torts, in setting forth the judicial consensus, says that a person who "misrepresents the financial condition of a corporation in order to sell its stock" becomes liable to a relying purchaser "for the loss" the purchaser sustains "when the facts . . . become, generally known" and "as a result" share value "depreciate[s]." §548A, Comment *b*, at 107. Treatise writers, too, have emphasized the need to prove proximate causation. Prosser and Keeton §110, at 767 (losses do "not afford any basis for recovery" if "brought about by business conditions or other factors").

We cannot reconcile the Ninth Circuit's "inflated purchase price" approach with these views of other courts. And the uniqueness of its perspective argues against the validity of its approach in a case like this one where we consider the contours of a judicially implied cause of action with roots in the common law.

Finally, the Ninth Circuit's approach overlooks an important securities law objective. The securities statutes seek to maintain public confidence in the marketplace. See United States v. O'Hagan, 521 U.S. 642, 658 (1997). They do so by deterring fraud, in part, through the availability of private securities fraud actions. Randall v. Loftsgaarden, 478 U.S. 647, 664 (1986). But the statutes make these latter actions available, not to provide investors with broad insurance against market losses, but to protect them against those economic losses that misrepresentations actually cause. Cf. *Basic,* 485 U.S., at 252 (White. J., joined by O'Connor, J., concurring in part and dissenting in part) ("[A]llowing recovery in the face of affirmative evidence of non-reliance—would effectively convert Rule 10b-5 into a scheme of investor's insurance. There is no support in the Securities Exchange Act, the Rule, or our cases for such a result" (internal quotation marks and citations omitted)).

The statutory provision at issue here and the paragraphs that precede it emphasize this last mentioned objective. Private Securities Litigation Reform Act of 1995, The statute insists that securities fraud complaints "specify" each misleading statement; that they set forth the facts "on which [a], belief" that a statement is misleading was "formed"; and that they "state with particularity facts giving rise to a strong inference that the defendant acted with the required state of mind." 15 U.S.C. §§78u-4(b)(1), (2). And the statute expressly imposes on plaintiffs "the burden of proving" that the defendant's misrepresentations "caused the loss for which the plaintiff seeks to recover." §78u-4(b)(4).

The statute thereby makes clear Congress' intent to permit private securities fraud actions for recovery where, but only where, plaintiffs adequately allege and prove the traditional elements of causation and loss. By way of contrast, the Ninth Circuit's approach would allow recovery where a misrepresentation leads to an inflated purchase price but nonetheless does not proximately cause any economic loss. That is to say, it would permit recovery where these two traditional elements in fact are missing.

In sum, we find the Ninth Circuit's approach inconsistent with the law's requirement that a plaintiff prove that the defendant's misrepresentation (or other fraudulent conduct) proximately caused the plaintiff's economic loss. We need not, and do not, consider other proximate cause or loss-related questions.

B

Our holding about plaintiffs' need to *prove* proximate causation and economic loss leads us also to conclude that the plaintiffs' complaint here failed adequately to *allege* these requirements. We concede that the Federal Rules of Civil Procedure require only "a short and plain statement of the claim showing that the pleader is entitled to relief." Fed. Rule Civ. Proc. 8(a)(2). And we assume, at least for argument's sake, that neither the Rules nor the securities statutes impose any special further requirement in respect to the pleading of proximate causation or economic loss. But, even so, the "short and plain statement" must provide the defendant with "fair notice of what the plaintiff's claim is and the grounds upon which it rests." Conley v. Gibson, 355 U.S. 41, 47 (1957). The complaint before us fails this simple test.

As we have pointed out, the plaintiffs' lengthy complaint contains only one statement that we can fairly read, as describing the loss caused by the defendants' "spray device" misrepresentations. That statement says that the plaintiffs "paid artificially inflated prices for Dura's securities" and suffered, "damage[s]." The statement implies that the plaintiffs' loss consisted of the "artificially inflated" purchase "prices." The complaint's failure to claim that Dura's share price fell significantly after the truth became known suggests that the plaintiffs considered the allegation of purchase price inflation alone sufficient. The complaint contains nothing that suggests otherwise.

For reasons set forth in Part II-A, supra, however, the "artificially inflated purchase price" is not itself a relevant economic loss. And the complaint nowhere else provides the defendants with notice of what the relevant economic loss might be or of what the causal connection might be between that loss and the misrepresentation concerning Dura's "spray device."

We concede that ordinary pleading rules are not meant to impose a great burden upon a plaintiff. Swierkiewicz v. Sorema N. A., 534 U.S. 506, 513-515 (2002). But it should not prove burdensome for a plaintiff who has suffered an economic loss to provide a defendant with some indication of the loss and the causal connection that the plaintiff has in mind. At the same time, allowing a plaintiff to forgo giving any indication of the economic loss and proximate cause that the plaintiff has in mind would bring about harm of the very sort the statutes seek to avoid. Cf. H.R. Conf. Rep. No. 104-369, p. 31 (1995), U.S. Code Cong. & Admin. News 1995, pp. 679, 730 (criticizing "abusive" practices including "the routine filing of lawsuits . . . with only a faint hope that the discovery process might lead eventually to some plausible cause of action"). It would permit a plaintiff "with a largely groundless claim to simply take up the time of a number of other people, with the right to do so representing an in terrorem increment of the settlement value, rather than a reasonably founded hope that the [discovery] process will reveal relevant evidenced." *Blue Chip Stamps*, 421 U.S., at 741, 95 S. Ct. 1917. Such a rule would tend to transform a private securities action into a partial downside insurance policy. See H.R. Conf. Rep. No. 104-369, at 31, U.S. Code Cong. & Admin. News 1995, pp. 679, 730; see also *Basic*, 485 U.S., at 252, 108 S. Ct. 978 (White, J., joined by O'Connor, J., concurring in part and dissenting in part).

For these reasons, we find the plaintiffs' complaint legally insufficient. We reverse the judgment of the Ninth Circuit, and we remand the case for further proceedings consistent with this opinion.

NOTES AND QUESTIONS

1. Justice Breyer says the private damages action under rule 10b-5 "resembles but is not identical to, common law tort actions for deceit and misrepresentations." We have already seen that the implied private cause of action under Rule 10b-5 expressly refers to the traditional common law elements of materiality and misrepresentation and courts have incorporated scienter and reliance. The 1995 securities reform legislation added a statutory requirement for loss causation for private 10b-5 actions. Section 21D(b)(4) of the 1934 Act requires a plaintiff to prove that defendant's wrongful action "caused the loss for which the plaintiff seeks to recover." Courts use a variety of terms to refer to the connection between defendant's conduct and plaintiff's actions. You may have discussed some of the terms in your torts course. Reliance is a form of transaction causation, which can also be discussed as "but for" causation. Even if that element exists, courts considering fraud cases also require that there be loss causation, sometimes discussed as legal causation or proximate causation. Judicial discussion of these concepts is fluid. For example, discussion of loss causation also occurs within a

discussion of damages. Other courts introduce these causation discussions as a function of the Rule 10b-5 requirement that fraud be "in connection with" a purchase and sale of a security. Added to this surplus of terminology is a more substantive challenge arising from the effort to meld the traditional autonomy-based tort of deceit with an economic tort that vindicates a victim's loss when a market has been tainted by deliberate deception. Two leading tort scholars describe fraud on the market as "in reality the name for a distinct tort that allows redress for intentional misrepresentations that proximately cause a certain kind of economic loss, irrespective of whether the victim relied on the substance of the misrepresentation," Goldberg & Zipursky, The Fraud on the Market Tort, 66 Vand L. Rev. (2013) available at http://ssrn.com/abstract=2346315.

2. How similar is the securities fraud class action to the traditional tort cause of action for deceit that Justice Breyer uses as his template. In the typical common law action, a defendant misrepresents something about securities thereby getting plaintiff to pay defendant too much or receive too little money for the securities. In a typical securities class action, the company or its officers make misstatements to the entire market leading a class of investors to trade. However, the defendants are not on the other side of the transaction. Rather, the counterparties who gain at the plaintiff's expense are traders who disappear with their gains into the anonymity of the market. Often the company pays any damages such that it is ultimately a transfer of funds from one set of shareholders to another with a substantial amount being withdrawn for lawyers and other expenses of litigation. These differences mean the securities action is less oriented toward compensation than the typical common law action. To what extent can the securities claims effectively perform a deterrence function?

3. The presumption from *Basic* combined with the deep and developed market for the securities of many American public companies means that most Rule 10b-5 actions are brought as class actions covering all persons who bought or sold a particular security during the time an alleged misrepresentation or omission was affecting the market for a particular stock. See Stanford Clearing House for Securities Class Action Litigation at http://securities.stanford.edu (documenting class actions brought yearly since 1995). These class actions present incentive problems similar to what we examined in Chapter 4 regarding derivative suits. Few individual shareholders will have sufficient financial interests to incur the costs (including attorney's fees) to bring a suit. As with derivative suits, attorneys will have the greatest incentive to sue, but their weighing of costs and benefits may be too narrow. See generally, Coffee, The Unfaithful Champion: The Plaintiff as Monitor in Shareholder Litigation, 48 Law & Contemp. Probs. 1 (1985). As empirical studies have grown within legal scholarship, securities litigation has been the basis for many studies, many that question the effectiveness of recovery in class actions. See generally, Alexander, Do the Merits Matter? A Study of Settlements in Securities Class Actions, 43 Stan. L. Rev. 497 (1991) (survey of class actions brought against high-tech companies that had made initial public offerings during the first half of 1983 showed that all suits settled, most for approximately one-quarter of the face value of plaintiff's claim); Seligman, The Merits Do Matter, 108 Harv. L. Rev. 438 (1994).

Legislation passed by Congress in 1995 sought to dampen securities litigation. The heightened pleading standard for securities fraud suits and the safe harbor for forward-looking projections have already been discussed. Other provisions, directed more to the topic of this note, included:

- Permitting a court to appoint as lead counsel for plaintiff the party with the strongest economic interest in the case;
- Prohibiting bonus payments to plaintiffs and limiting attorneys' fees to reasonable percentages;
- Mandating judicial findings in a final adjudication as to attorney compliance with Rule 11 of the Federal Rules of Civil Procedure.

Class actions continued to be brought in similar numbers after enactment of the 1995 Act although empirical studies show shifts in the kinds of claims brought and there remains discussion over the relative extent to which its provisions discourage frivolous suits that should not be brought and meritorious suits that should be brought. See Pritchard & Sale, What Counts as Fraud? An Empirical Study of Motions to Dismiss Under the Private Securities Litigation Reform Act, 2 J. Empirical Legal Stud. 125 (2005); Choi, The Evidence on Securities Class Actions, 57 Vand. L. Rev. 1465 (2004).

The class action aspects of Rule 10b-5 litigation and particularly the pleading requirements added by the 1995 act as to scienter and misrepresentation have led to new cases arguing that other fraud elements should also have to be shown at the certification point of the litigation. The difference, of course, can shape settlement pressures given that litigation today seldom leads to trials. Supreme Court cases turned back efforts to advance loss causation to the certification point of decision and a subsequent effort arguing that materiality should be an issue at the certification phase of a fraud on the market case. See Erica P. John Fund, Inc. v. Halliburton Co., 131 S. Ct. 2179 (U.S. 2011); Amgen, Inc. v. Connecticut Retirement Plans and Trust Funds, 133 U.S. 1184 (U.S. 2013).

4. The roots of Rule 10b-5 in common law fraud have blurred the extent to which these class actions are performing a role that is more corporate governance oriented than fraud, with roots in fiduciary duty as well as deceit. The length of many class actions, the high percentage of shares that have turned over during such time, and the relatively small per share interest for each shareholder mean that these claims resemble corporate claims considered earlier in this book. Consider the behavior challenged in *Basic* (management dissembling about ongoing merger talks that if coming to fruition would benefit the entire body of shareholders) and Novak v. Kaskos, 216 F.3d 300 (2d Cir. 2000) (retailer's management failing to properly account for inventory). To what extent are these disclosure claims addressing what would be duty-of-care claims under state law? Is the federal law an indirect way of getting at bad management conduct that would be insulated from shareholder redress under state law doctrine? Is scienter under federal law doing the same work as the business judgment rule and exculpation under state law?

The disclosure orientation of the federal law also requires us to think about the extent to which there is a legal role for mandating truth-telling independent of its impact on the substance of a decision. Is it more like a dignitary tort than an economic tort? Does the widespread response of markets to any change in information regarding securities information mean that truth-telling can become the chief regulator of behavior for corporate managers?

5. The constant flow of new information into securities markets and the inevitable time that occurs between any fraud and its subsequent correction mean that there is always a need to separate any change in a stock price due to the fraud from change in a stock price due to changes in the market. That is a recurring challenge in almost any securities case and the basis for Justice Breyer's concern, expressed on two occasions in *Dura,* that the securities laws not become an insurance program against market losses. What it means in a case like *Dura* is that plaintiff must be able to show not only that the price was inflated because of the fraud, but that also some sort of correction occurred before the plaintiff traded leading to an economic loss for plaintiff. Plaintiffs likely could show that in *Dura* as to the profits claim (but were blocked by the scienter element) and plaintiffs have been able to show that in cases since *Dura.* See, e.g., In re Immune Response Securities Litig., 375 F. Supp. 2d 983 (S.D. Cal. 2005) (plaintiff's claim of inflation and the sharp stock price drop when the truth became known satisfy *Dura*). This focus on correction is a practical choice; ideally we would want to measure the harm at the time of fraud, but the nature of most misstatements is that they are designed to prevent any market reaction. In contrast, when truth is revealed, market changes occur that financial economists can capture in event studies. But buried facts, diffuse disclosures, and opportunistic bundling of fraud correction with offsetting good news can block the showing of economic loss that Dura seeks.

6. Recovery in a Rule 10b-5 suit reflects the shifting current of the discussion above. In 1995 Congress added a provision for damages, but that section—21D(e) of the 1934 act—only creates a cap not to exceed the difference between the purchase or sale price and "the mean trading price of that security during the 90 day period beginning on the date on which the information correcting the misstatement or omission that is the basis for the action is disseminated to the market."

Were it to be applied, it would permit defendants to avoid paying for fraud perpetrated in a rising market. The most common judicial approach, for those few cases that get to a damages consideration, has been to use the "out of pocket" measure from tort law, seeking to compensate plaintiffs for harm resulting from the misrepresentation. Out-of-pocket is usually (but certainly not always) described as the difference between the price paid for the security and the actual value received (measured at the time of the transaction). In practice, determining the price paid is relatively noncontroversial. The "value received" is more problematic since there is no certain measure for what the stock would have been worth absent the defendant's fraud. As discussed in the prior note, this leads to the use market value of the stock on the date after corrective information had been released because this sum was more readily available.

An alternative remedy is rescission, by which courts unwind the fraudulent transaction. This remedy typically would be available only when the plaintiff had transacted directly with the defendant (and not where defendant's misleading statements led plaintiff to trade on the market with an unrelated party). If a defendant through fraud purchased plaintiff's stock at too low a price and subsequently resold the shares at a much higher price (because of a takeover or a booming market or other reason), rescission permits a plaintiff to recover defendant's entire gain, which may be in excess of the out-of-pocket measure based on value at the date of the transaction. Courts frequently modified rescission or out-of-pocket or combined them in a sometimes confusing manner. The choices between the different measures make more sense if you focus on what risks are being allocated to each party:

> The primary practical difference among the measures of recovery in rule 10b-5 cases is how they allocate between the parties the post-transaction change in the value of the transferred securities. Securities by nature fluctuate in value; by the time a court decides that relief is appropriate in a fraud case the securities may be worth more or less than the amount paid for them in the transaction. Only part of this change in value may be due to the misrepresentations; other factors, such as general movement in the stock market since the transaction, also contribute to a fluctuation in value. Some remedies, like those termed "out of pocket," allow a plaintiff to recover only for the harm resulting from the misrepresentation itself and exclude any additional harm caused by a change in the market or some other factor that was not the proximate consequence of the fraud. In contrast, a remedy based on rescission allows the plaintiff to unwind the transaction and recover the entire purchase price, even though this may permit the plaintiff to escape a bargain that was bad independent of the fraud. . . .

Thompson, The Measure of Recovery Under Rule 10b-5: A Restitution Alternative to Tort Damages, 37 Vand. L. Rev. 349, 351-352 (1984).

To the extent that the theory of a Rule 10b-5 recovery is based on reliance on the integrity of the market price discussed above and not on a strict borrowing from the common law of deceit, an out of pocket measure might be appropriate.

PROBLEM 10-4

Sonic, Inc., a successful computer company that trades shares on the New York Stock Exchange, recently ran into its first rough spot. The company was unable to work out problems in making a new line of personal computers compatible with new industry software. In April 2013, Sonic announced that it was terminating the new line. The announcement confirmed what several industry publications had been saying for months, but it was a direct reversal of six different statements Sonic had made over the previous nine months, when Sonic had said that the new personal computer was on schedule and would be a success right out of the box. What reliance would plaintiffs have to show in a class action based on the alleged misstatements?

PROBLEM 10-5

Kramer, president of Palmer, Inc., sought to induce Sharp to invest in Palmer, an oil drilling concern. Kramer caused the corporation to issue a press release announcing a new oil discovery, leading to an increase in the price of Palmer's existing stock from $10 to $12. Sharp then purchased 100,000 newly issued shares from Palmer for $12 a share.

Six months later when the statement is found to be untrue, the price of Sharp stock drops, but because the price of oil has risen, it now sells for $11 a share. What liability does the company have to Sharp and to others who purchased stock in the stock market?

4. State Law

Malone v. Brincat

Supreme Court of Delaware (en banc), 1998
722 A.2d 5

HOLLAND, JUSTICE

FACTS

Mercury [Finance Company] is a publicly-traded company engaged primarily in purchasing installment sales contracts from automobile dealers and providing short-term installment loans directly to consumers. This action was filed on behalf of the named plaintiffs and all persons (excluding defendants) who owned common stock of Mercury from 1993 through the present and their successors in interest, heirs and assigns (the "putative class"). The complaint alleged that the directors "knowingly and intentionally breached their fiduciary duty of disclosure because the SEC filings made by the directors and every communication from the company to the shareholders since 1994 was materially false" and that "as a direct result of the false disclosures . . . the Company has lost all or virtually all of its value (about $2 billion)." The complaint also alleged that KPMG knowingly participated in the directors' breaches of their fiduciary duty of disclosure.

According to plaintiffs, since 1994, the director defendants caused Mercury to disseminate information containing overstatements of Mercury's earnings, financial performance and shareholders' equity. Mercury's earnings for 1996 were actually only $56.7 million, or $.33 a share, rather than the $120.7 million, or $.70 a share, as reported by the director defendants. Mercury's earnings in 1995 were actually $76.9 million, or $.44 a share, rather than $98.9 million, or $.57 a share, as reported by the director defendants. Mercury's earnings for 1994 were $83 million, or $.47 a share, rather than $86.5 million, or $.49 a share, as reported by the director defen-dants. Mercury's earnings for 1993 were $64.2 million, rather than $64.9 million, as reported by the director defendants. Shareholders' equity on December 31, 1996 was disclosed by the director defendants as $353 million, but was only $263 million or less. The complaint alleged that all of the foregoing inaccurate information was included or referenced in virtually every filing Mercury made with the SEC and every communication Mercury's directors made to the shareholders during this period of time.

Having alleged these violations of fiduciary duty, which (if true) are egregious, plaintiffs alleged that as "a direct result of [these] false disclosures . . . the company has lost all or virtually all its value (about $2 billion)," and seeks class action status to pursue damages against the directors and KPMG for the individual plaintiffs and common stockholders. The individual director defendants filed a motion to dismiss, contending that they owed no fiduciary duty of disclosure under the circumstances alleged in the complaint. KPMG also filed a motion to dismiss the aiding and abetting claim asserted against it.

After briefing and oral argument, the Court of Chancery granted both of the motions to dismiss with prejudice. The Court of Chancery held that directors have no fiduciary duty of disclosure under Delaware law in the absence of a request for shareholder action. In so holding, the Court stated:

> The federal securities laws ensure the timely release of accurate information into the marketplace. The federal power to regulate should not be duplicated or impliedly usurped by Delaware. When a shareholder is damaged merely as a result of the release of inaccurate information into the marketplace, unconnected with any Delaware corporate governance issue, that shareholder must seek a remedy under federal law.

We disagree, and although we hold that the Complaint as drafted should have been dismissed, our rationale is different.

ISSUE ON APPEAL

This Court has held that a board of directors is under a fiduciary duty to disclose material information when seeking shareholder action. . . .

It is well-established that the duty of disclosure "represents nothing more than the well-recognized proposition that directors of Delaware corporations are under a fiduciary duty to disclose fully and fairly all material information within the board's control *when it seeks shareholder action*." [1997 WL 697940 at *2]

The majority of opinions from the Court of Chancery have held that there may be a cause of action for disclosure violations only where directors seek shareholder action. The present appeal requires this Court to decide whether a director's fiduciary duty arising out of misdisclosure is implicated in the absence of a request for shareholder action. We hold that directors who knowingly disseminate false information that results in corporate injury or damage to an individual stockholder violate their fiduciary duty, and may be held accountable in a manner appropriate to the circumstances.

FIDUCIARY DUTY
DELAWARE CORPORATE DIRECTORS

The directors of Delaware corporations stand in a fiduciary relationship not only to the stockholders but also to the corporations upon whose boards they serve. . . .

DIRECTOR COMMUNICATIONS
SHAREHOLDER RELIANCE JUSTIFIED

The shareholder constituents of a Delaware corporation are entitled to rely upon their elected directors to discharge their fiduciary duties at all times. Whenever directors communicate publicly or directly with shareholders about the corporation's affairs, with or without a request for shareholder action, directors have a fiduciary duty to shareholders to exercise due care, good faith and loyalty. It follows *a fortiori* that when directors communicate publicly or directly with shareholders about corporate matters the *sine qua non* of directors' fiduciary duty to shareholders is honesty.

According to the appellants, the focus of the fiduciary duty of disclosure is to protect shareholders as the "beneficiaries" of all material information disseminated by the directors. The duty of disclosure is, and always has been, a specific application of the general fiduciary duty owed by directors. The duty of disclosure obligates directors to provide the stockholders with accurate and complete information material to a transaction or other corporate event that is being presented to them for action.

The issue in this case is not whether Mercury's directors breached their duty of disclosure. It is whether they breached their more general fiduciary duty of loyalty and good faith by knowingly disseminating to the stockholders false information about the financial condition of the company. The directors' fiduciary duties include the duty to deal with their stockholders honestly.

Shareholders are entitled to rely upon the truthfulness of all information disseminated to them by the directors they elect to manage the corporate enterprise. Delaware directors disseminate information in at least three contexts: public statements made to the market, including shareholders; statements informing shareholders about the affairs of the corporation without a request for shareholder action; and statements to shareholders in conjunction with a request for shareholder action. Inaccurate information in these contexts may be the result of a violation of the fiduciary duties of care, loyalty or good faith. We will examine the remedies that are available to shareholders for misrepresentations in each of these three contexts by the directors of a Delaware corporation.

STATE FIDUCIARY DISCLOSURE DUTY
SHAREHOLDER REMEDY IN ACTION REQUESTED CONTEXT

In the absence of a request for stockholder action, the Delaware General Corporation Law does not require directors to provide shareholders with information concerning the finances or affairs of the corporation. Even when shareholder action is sought, the provisions in the General Corporation Law requiring notice to the shareholders of the proposed action do not require the directors to convey substantive information beyond a statutory minimum. Consequently, in the context of a request for shareholder action, the protection afforded by Delaware law is a judicially recognized equitable cause of action by shareholders against directors.

The duty of directors to observe proper disclosure requirements derives from the combination of the fiduciary duties of care, loyalty and good faith. The plaintiffs contend that, because directors' fiduciary responsibilities are not "intermittent duties," there is no reason why the duty of disclosure should not be implicated in every public communication by a corporate board of directors. The directors of a Delaware corporation are required to disclose fully and fairly all material information within the board's control when it seeks shareholder action. When the directors disseminate information to stockholders when no stockholder action is sought, the fiduciary duties of care, loyalty and good faith apply. Dissemination of false information could violate one or more of those duties.

An action for a breach of fiduciary duty arising out of disclosure violations in connection with a request for stockholder action does not include the elements of reliance, causation and actual quantifiable monetary damages. Instead, such actions require the challenged disclosure to have a connection to the request for shareholder action. The essential inquiry in such an action is whether the alleged omission or misrepresentation is material. Materiality is determined with respect to the shareholder action being sought.[29]

The directors' duty to disclose all available material information in connection with a request for shareholder action must be balanced against its concomitant duty to protect the corporate enterprise, in particular, by keeping certain financial information confidential. Directors are required to provide shareholders with all information that is material to the action being requested and to provide a balanced, truthful account of all matters disclosed in the communications with shareholders. Accordingly, directors have definitive guidance in discharging their fiduciary duty by an analysis of the factual circumstances relating to the specific shareholder action being requested and an inquiry into the potential for deception or misinformation.

FRAUD ON MARKET REGULATED
BY FEDERAL LAW

When corporate directors impart information they must comport with the obligations imposed by both the Delaware law and the federal statutes and regulations of the United States Securities and Exchange Commission ("SEC"). Historically, federal law has regulated disclosures by corporate directors into the general interstate market. This Court has noted that "in observing its congressional mandate the SEC has adopted a 'basic philosophy of disclosure.'" Accordingly, this Court has held that there is "no legitimate basis to create a new cause of action which would replicate, by state decisional law, the provisions of . . . the 1934 Act." In deference to the panoply of federal protections that are available to investors in connection with the purchase or sale of securities of Delaware corporations, this Court has decided not to recognize a state common law cause of action against the directors of Delaware corporations for "fraud on the market." Here, it is to be noted, the claim appears to be made by those who did not sell and, therefore, would not implicate federal securities laws which relate to the purchase or sale of securities.

The historic roles played by state and federal law in regulating corporate disclosures have been not only compatible but complementary. That symbiotic relationship has been perpetuated by the recently enacted federal Securities Litigation Uniform Standards Act of 1998. Although that statute by its terms does not apply to this case, the new statute will require securities class actions involving the purchase or sale of nationally traded securities, based upon false or misleading statements, to be brought exclusively in federal court under federal law. The 1998 Act, however, contains two

---

29. In Rosenblatt v. Getty Oil Co., 493 A.2d at 944, this Court adopted the materiality standard set forth by the United States Supreme Court in TSC Industries, Inc. v. Northway, Inc., 426 U.S. 438, 449, 96 S. Ct. 2126, 48 L. Ed. 2d 757 (1976).

important exceptions: the first provides that an "exclusively derivative action brought by one or more shareholders on behalf of a corporation" is not preempted; the second preserves the availability of state court class actions, where state law already provides that corporate directors have fiduciary disclosure obligations to shareholders. These exceptions have become known as the "Delaware carve-outs."

STATE COMMON LAW
SHAREHOLDER REMEDY IN NONACTION CONTEXT

Delaware law also protects shareholders who receive false communications from directors even in the absence of a request for shareholder action. When the directors are not seeking shareholder action, but are deliberately misinforming shareholders about the business of the corporation, either directly or by a public statement, there is a violation of fiduciary duty. That violation may result in a derivative claim on behalf of the corporation or a cause of action for damages. There may also be a basis for equitable relief to remedy the violation.

COMPLAINT PROPERLY DISMISSED
NO SHAREHOLDER ACTION REQUESTED

Here the complaint alleges (if true) an egregious violation of fiduciary duty by the directors in knowingly disseminating materially false information. Then it alleges that the corporation lost about $2 billion in value as a result. Then it merely claims that the action is brought on behalf of the named plaintiffs and the putative class. It is a *non sequitur* rather than a syllogism.

The allegation in paragraph 3 that the false disclosures resulted in the corporation losing virtually all its equity seems obliquely to claim an injury to the corporation. The plaintiffs, however, never expressly assert a derivative claim on behalf of the corporation or allege compliance with Court of Chancery Rule 23.1, which requires pre-suit demand or cognizable and particularized allegations that demand is excused. If the plaintiffs intend to assert a derivative claim,[45] they should be permitted to replead to assert such a claim and any damage or equitable remedy sought on behalf of the corporation. Likewise, the plaintiffs should have the opportunity to replead to assert any individual cause of action and articulate a remedy that is appropriate on behalf of the named plaintiffs individually, or a properly recognizable class consistent with Court of Chancery Rule 23, and our decision in *Gaffin*.[47]

---

45. This will require an articulation of the classic "direct v. derivative" theory. See Grimes v. Donald, Del. Supr., 673 A.2d 1207 (1996) (distinguishing individual and derivative actions).

47. Gaffin v. Teledyne, Inc., 611 A.2d 467, 474 (1992) ("A class action may not be maintained in a purely common law or equitable fraud case since individual questions of law or fact, particularly as to the element of justifiable reliance, will inevitably predominate over common questions of law or fact."). See Barnes v. American Tobacco Co., 3rd Cir., 161 F.3d 127 (1998); Broussard v. Meineke Discount Muffler Shops, Inc., 4th Cir., 155 F.3d 331 (1998); Cimino v. Raymark Industries, Inc., 5th Cir., 151 F.3d 297 (1998); Amchem Products, Inc. v. Windsor, 521 U.S. 591, 117 S. Ct. 2231, 138 L. Ed. 2d 689 (1997). See also Donald J. Wolfe and Michael A. Pittenger, Corporate and Commercial Practice in the Delaware Court of Chancery §9-3 (1998).

The Court of Chancery properly dismissed the complaint before it against the individual director defendants, in the absence of well-pleaded allegations stating a derivative, class or individual cause of action and properly assertable remedy. Without a well-pleaded allegation in the complaint for a breach of fiduciary duty, there can be no claim for aiding and abetting such a breach. Accordingly, the plaintiffs' aiding and abetting claim against KPMG was also properly dismissed.

Nevertheless, we disagree with the Court of Chancery's holding that such a claim cannot be articulated on these facts. The plaintiffs should have been permitted to amend their complaint, if possible, to state a properly cognizable cause of action against the individual defendants and KPMG. . . .

NOTES AND QUESTIONS

1. Despite the broad pronouncements in *Malone,* any development of a Delaware state law remedy for disclosure not related to voting will be stunted by two limitations noted in the opinion. First Delaware refused to adopt the fraud on the market doctrine, a presumption of reliance discussed earlier in this chapter that has expanded the class of shareholders who may bring suit. Second, as described in footnote 47, it will be very difficult to bring a class action for disclosure violations in state court. The greater ability to bring federal class actions, including the fraud on the market presumption, means that federal law is likely to continue to dominate disclosure litigation based on purchases or sales, a conclusion that even the court in *Malone* seems to find comfortable. What about a derivative suit for harm to the corporation—what defenses would you expect a company defendant to raise?

2. Even if Delaware were to expand its remedies for disclosure, congressional action in 1998 will limit the space for state action. That legislation, as described in the opinion, did include an exception, or "Delaware carve-out," that preserves exclusively derivative actions or where state law already provides disclosure obligations. While the court in *Malone* does not decide this issue, a federal court might well find that class actions where shareholders are not asked to vote are not within the exception.

11 Federal Regulation of Tender Offers

A. The Williams Act

In a tender offer, an acquiring company offers to purchase part or all of a target company's shares directly from the shareholders of the target. Because the transaction does not involve any collective corporate action by the target corporation, state corporation codes initially had little impact. The acquiring company's purchase of target stock for cash is within the usual authority of its board of directors and requires no lengthy corporate proceedings by the acquiring company.

If an acquiring company issues its own stock as consideration for the shares to be acquired, that issuance is regulated by the Securities Act of 1933 (see Chapter 3); for cash consideration, however, no similar regulation existed prior to 1968. Furthermore, if control of the target corporation is sought by proxy solicitations, the target shareholders receive substantial disclosure as required by the rules and regulations under §14 of the Securities Exchange Act of 1934 (see Chapter 10, Part C). Yet prior to 1968, if control was sought by means of a cash tender offer, a target shareholder would have to decide whether to tender without similar information.

The Williams Act, passed in 1968, sought to respond to those perceived anomalies by adding §§13(d)-(e) and 14(d)-(f) to the 1934 Act. Two distinct events trigger disclosure obligations under the Williams Act. Section 13(d) requires certain disclosures if a person acquires more than 5 percent of the stock of a company whose stock is registered under the 1934 Act. Section 14(d) requires similar disclosure when a bidder makes a tender offer for the stock of such a company. Other provisions regulate the conduct of a tender offer, requiring, for example, that it remain open for a minimum period and specifying additional procedures to protect shareholders.

Tender offers involve several intersecting relationships among bidders, the target shareholders, and the target management. The dominant focus of the Williams Act is the target shareholders as they respond to the bidder's tender offer. However, that regulation necessarily affects the relationship between the bidder and the target management as two combatants for control of the corporation. In addition, the regulation also affects the relationship between target shareholders and their managers, which has been the traditional concern of state corporation law. One of the first Supreme Court cases to interpret the Williams Act described these complex and sometimes conflicting purposes this way:

The purpose of the Williams Act is to insure that public shareholders who are confronted by a cash tender offer for their stock will not be required to respond without adequate information regarding the qualifications and intentions of the offering party. By requiring disclosure of information to the target corporation as well as the Securities and Exchange Commission, Congress intended to do no more than give incumbent management an opportunity to express and explain its position. The Congress expressly disclaimed an intention to provide a weapon for management to discourage takeover bids or prevent large accumulations of stock which would create the potential for such attempts. Indeed, the Act's draftsmen commented upon the "extreme care" which was taken "to avoid tipping the balance of regulation either in favor of management or in favor of the person making the takeover bid."

Rondeau v. Mosinee Paper Corp., 422 U.S. 49, 58-59 (1975), quoting S. Rep. No. 550, 90th Cong., 1st Sess. 3 (1967); H.R. Rep. No. 1711, 90th Cong., 2d Sess. 4 (1968).

The difficulty in achieving the appropriate balance between regulation of bidders vs. target shareholders, target shareholders vs. target managers, and bidders vs. target managers is explored below, looking first at the disclosure and other requirements of the Williams Act and then in Part B addressing the relationship between state and federal law.

1. Disclosure

Securities Exchange Act of 1934 §§13(d), 14(d) and (e)
Schedules 13D and 14D
SEC Rule 13d-5

Should the disclosure required for a tender offer differ from that required for a proxy statement or an initial issuance of shares as discussed in earlier chapters? Section 14(d) requires that the tender offeror provide each security holder and the Securities and Exchange Commission with the information specified in §13(d) as well as any additional information required by the Commission. The §13(d) disclosure, which is made only to the SEC, includes information on the background and identity of the offeror or 5 percent owner, the source and amount of funds or other consideration used in making the purchase, and, if the purpose is to acquire control, any plans the purchaser has to liquidate, merge, or make other major changes.

Prudent Real Estate Trust v. Johncamp Realty, Inc.
United States Court of Appeals, Second Circuit, 1979
599 F.2d 1140

FRIENDLY, CIRCUIT JUDGE:

[Prudent Real Estate Trust (Prudent), the target of a tender offer by the defendant Johncamp Realty, Inc. (Johncamp), sought a temporary injunction against the continuation of a tender offer on the ground that the material filed with the Securities and Exchange Commission (SEC) pursuant to Schedule 14D implementing §14(d) of the Securities and Exchange Act was insufficient and that, because of certain statements and omissions, the offer violated §14(e) of the Act.]

. . . Defendant Johncamp is a Delaware close corporation which was founded by Johncamp Netherlands Antilles, N.V. (Johncamp N.V.) and The Pacific Company, a California corporation (Pacific). Johncamp N.V. owns 60% and Pacific 40% of the common shares of Johncamp. All of the stock of Johncamp N.V. is owned by Campeau Corporation (Campeau), a publicly held Ontario corporation; Robert Campeau, a resident of Canada, is chairman of its board and chief executive officer. John E. Wertin, a resident of California, is president, secretary and a director of Johncamp, president and a director and sole stockholder of Pacific, and president and director of John Wertin Development Corporation (JWDC), a California corporation, 95% of the stock of which is owned by Pacific. . . .

On March 12, 1979, Johncamp filed with the SEC a Schedule 14 D-1 as required for a tender offer by 17 C.F.R. §240.14d-100. The schedule contained the form of offer, which was advertised the following day in the New York Times. The offer, which was to expire on March 23 unless extended, was to purchase any and all of Prudent's outstanding shares at $7 net per share, as against the last available market price of 4, and was not conditioned upon any minimum number of shares being tendered. . . .

The offer went on to state that 80% of the required funds would be furnished by Johncamp N.V. which would obtain them from Campeau, out of the latter's own funds or from a $50,000,000 (Canadian) line of bank credit described in some detail, and that 20% would be supplied by Pacific which would obtain the funds from JWDC and Wertin. The purpose of the offer was to acquire all the shares of Prudent but if this did not occur pursuant to the offer, Johncamp, Campeau, Johncamp N.V. and Pacific desired to acquire enough shares to exercise control. The purchaser intended to reconstitute the board of trustees of Prudent as soon and as much as possible. Although no specific plans for Prudent's future had been formulated, Johncamp N.V. and Pacific had established a procedure to increase the likelihood that Campeau's investment in Johncamp would be fully recovered; pursuant to such procedure Johncamp N.V. could cause a liquidation of Prudent if Johncamp acquired at least two-thirds of the outstanding shares. . . .

The only other portion of the Schedule 14 D here relevant is *Item 9. Financial Statements of Certain Bidders.* This was answered: "Not applicable, but see Exhibit 1." Exhibit 1 consisted of the printed annual reports of Campeau for 1976 and 1977 and audited consolidated financial statements for 1978.

On March 16, 1979, Prudent initiated this action to enjoin the defendants from proceeding with the tender offer, and moved for a temporary restraining order and a preliminary injunction on various grounds. . . . [The ground discussed here is] the failure to disclose in the Offer or the Schedule any financial information about the Wertin interests, to wit, Pacific, JWDC, and Wertin himself, as 17 C.F.R. §240. 14d-100, Item 9, allegedly requires. . . .

The relevant sections of the Securities Exchange Act, §14(d)(1) and (e), added by the Williams Act of 1968, are too familiar to require extended exposition. . . . The House Interstate and Foreign Commerce Committee explained the need for the new legislation as follows:

> Where one company seeks control of another by means of a stock-for-stock exchange, the offer must be registered under the Securities Act of 1933. The shareholder gets a prospectus setting forth

all material facts about the offer. He knows who the purchaser is, and what plans have been made for the company. He is thus placed in a position to make an informed decision whether to hold his stock or to exchange it for the stock of the other company. . . .

In contrast when a cash tender offer is made, no information need be filed or disclosed to shareholders. Such an offer can be made on the most minimal disclosure; yet the investment decision—whether to retain the security or sell it—is in substance little different from the decision made on an original purchase of a security, or on an offer to exchange one security for another. . . .

The persons seeking control . . . have information about themselves and about their plans which, if known to investors, might substantially change the assumptions on which the market price is based. This bill is designed to make the relevant facts known so that shareholders have a fair opportunity to make their decision. (H. Rep. No. 1711, 90th Cong., 2d Sess., reprinted in 2 U.S. Code Cong. & Ad. News 2811, 2812-13 (1968).)

This discussion reflected views earlier expressed by the late Manuel F. Cohen, Chairman of the SEC, in A Note on Takeover Bids and Corporate Purchases of Stock, 22 Bus. Law. 149, 149-50 (1966). See also Sen. Rep. No. 539, 90th Cong., 1st Sess., at 2 and 3. . . .

[I]n a release appearing on July 28, 1977, 42 F.R. 38341-50 new regulations were issued, which for the first time adopted a schedule 14 D, specifically tailored to §14(d) of the Act. The schedule included as Item 9:

Item 9. Financial Statements of Certain Bidders. Where the bidder is other than a natural person and the bidder's financial condition is material to a decision by a security holder of the subject company whether to sell, tender or hold securities being sought in the tender offer, furnish current, adequate financial information concerning the bidder. . . .

Emphasizing that Item 9 retained the concept of materiality and that this was dependent on the facts and circumstances, the Commission said, 42 F.R. at 38346:

These may include, but are not limited to: (1) the terms of the tender offer, particularly those terms concerning the amount of securities being sought, such as any or all, a fixed minimum with the right to accept additional shares tendered, all or none, and a fixed percentage of the outstanding; (2) whether the purpose of the tender offer is for control of the subject company; (3) the plans or proposals of the bidder described in Item 5 of the Schedule; and (4) the ability of the bidder to pay for the securities sought in the tender offer and/or to repay any loans made by the bidder or its affiliates in connection with the tender offer or otherwise. It should be noted that the factors described above are not exclusive nor is it necessary that any or all such factors be present in order to trigger the materiality test. . . .

The parties accept that the test of materiality is that stated in TSC Industries, Inc. v. Northway, Inc., 426 U.S. 438, 449 (1976), although that case arose under Rule 14a-9 concerning proxy contests. . . . The Court's formulation was, 426 U.S. at 449:

An omitted fact is material if there is a substantial likelihood that a reasonable shareholder would consider it important in deciding how to vote. . . .

In applying this test to a cash tender offer, it is necessary to appreciate the problem faced by a stockholder of the target company in deciding whether to tender, to sell or to hold part or all of his securities. It is true that, in the case of an "any and all" offer such as that here at issue, a stockholder who has firmly decided to tender has no interest in the financial position of the offeror other than its ability to pay—a point not here at issue—since he will have severed all financial connections with the target. It is also true that in the case of such an offer, there is less reason for him to seek to eliminate the risk of being partly in and partly out by selling to arbitrageurs, usually at a price somewhere between the previous market and the offered price, than where the offer is for a stated number or percentage of the shares (with or without the right to accept additional shares) or is conditioned on a minimum number being obtained. Still, the shareholder of the target company faces a hard problem in determining the most advantageous course of action, a problem whose difficulty is enhanced by his usual ignorance of the course other shareholders are adopting. If the bidder is in a flourishing financial condition, the stockholder might decide to hold his shares in the hope that, if the offer was only partially successful, the bidder might raise its bid after termination of the offer or infuse new capital into the enterprise. *Per contra,* a poor financial condition of the bidder might cause the shareholder to accept for fear that control of the company would pass into irresponsible hands. The force of these considerations is diminished but not altogether removed in this case by the fact that the Wertin interests were supplying only 20% of the financing and that Campeau's annual reports for 1976 and 1977 and its financial statements for 1978, which were incorporated in the Schedule 14 D, showed it to be a company of substance. As against this, the stockholders' agreement gave Wertin the right to vote all acquired Prudent shares and the district court found that Wertin was to manage the properties. The case came within item (2) and possibly item (3) of the SEC's release, 42 F.R. 38346.

Johncamp relies on statements by SEC Chairman Cohen before the House Committee at the hearings that led to the Williams Act wherein he analogized the information required by the bill to be provided to stockholders with that required in proxy contests, where Regulation 14A does not require a challenger to file its financial statements unless it proposes a merger or consolidation or the issuance "of securities of another issuer," even if its objective is to gain control. Prudent counters with the language from the House Committee report quoted above, echoing Chairman Cohen's article, that in the case of a cash tender offer "the investment decision—whether to retain the security or sell it—is in substance little different from the decision made on an original purchase of a security, or on an offer to exchange one security for another." See to the same effect Sen. Rep. No. 550, 90th Cong., 1st Sess. at 3. In truth the situation is not precisely like any of these models. It differs from the proxy contest *simpliciter* in that an investment decision is being made; it differs from an original purchase of a security or an offer to exchange one security for another in that the stockholder does not have to appraise what he is buying. It differs also from an ordinary sale in that the investment decision is influenced not solely by general factors affecting the prospects of the economy, the market, or the company, but importantly by the particular proposal being made. In any event we must look to some extent to what the Congressional committees said rather than to what the facts are.

From the beginning of litigation under the Williams Act, this court has been conscious of its responsibility not to allow management to "resort to the courts on trumped-up or trivial grounds as a means for delaying and thereby defeating tender offers." Electronic Specialty Co. v. International Controls Corp., 409 F.2d 937, 947 (1969). . . . An important factor here is the impracticability of obtaining information about the Wertin interests from other sources. At the very least there is "fair ground for litigating" the issue of materiality and the balance of hardships tips heavily in Prudent's favor. Hamilton Watch Co. v. Benrus Watch Co., 206 F.2d 738, 740 (2 Cir. 1953). We are further influenced by the fact that our decision imposes no serious impediment to cash tender offers. Even in this case the omission can be readily corrected; in future cases presumably it will not be made. . . .

We therefore reverse the order under appeal and direct the district court to issue a temporary injunction. It will be sufficient if this extends only until Johncamp makes the necessary corrections and allows a reasonable period for withdrawal of stock already tendered; we see no need for the further cooling-off period that Prudent requests. . . . Since Prudent conceded that its only reason for declining to make its stockholder list available to Johncamp was the alleged defects in the offer and Schedule 14 D, the order should direct that this be done once the corrections are made if litigation in the New York courts has not yet produced that result. . . .

NOTES

1. The ability to pay, which Judge Friendly says would be the sole financial concern of a shareholder who had firmly decided to tender, was not an issue in Prudent Real Estate Trust v. Johncamp Realty. It was an issue in MAI Basic Four, Inc. v. Prime Computer, Inc., 871 F.2d 212 (1st Cir. 1989), however, where a trial and appeals court enjoined a tender offer pending disclosure of further information about the investment banking firm that was helping finance the bidders' acquisition. A group of firms, MAI Basic Four, Choice Corporation, and Brooke Partners, L.P., sought to take control of Prime Computer, Inc. A dispute arose as to the need for the bidders to make disclosures about their financial advisor, investor, and underwriter, Drexel Burnham Lambert, Inc. During the pendency of this tender offer, Drexel Burnham had agreed to plead guilty to six felony counts of mail, wire, and securities fraud as part of a plea bargain in which it agreed to pay $650 million in fines. The financing for the tender offer was to consist of $20 million in cash supplied by Brooke Partners, L.P., $650 million in bank financing, and $875 million in junk bonds. Drexel's links to the bidders came in at least three separate areas. First, it was entitled to 14 percent direct equity interest in MAI Basic Four, Inc. Second, Brooke Partners' sole general partner was L. Holdings, which in turn was wholly owned by LeBow, Inc. Drexel had a 17 percent equity interest in Brooke, a one-third equity interest in LeBow, and the right to name one of the three directors of LeBow, Inc. with veto powers over corporate action. During the litigation, Drexel gave up the right to a board member, but continued to have the right to attend board meetings and was guaranteed first refusal in future underwriting and placement. Third, Drexel was entitled to receive $65 million in fees upon successful placement of the junk bonds.

The court quoted with approval the dissent of an earlier decision: "In the event of doubt on a particular disclosure question, courts should exercise liberality in order to carry out the remedial purposes of the [Williams Act]. Excess information may well be harmless, but inadequate disclosure could be disastrous to the shareholder." 871 F.2d at 219, quoting City Capital Assoc. Ltd. Partnership v. Interco, Inc., 860 F.2d 60, 68 (3d Cir. 1988) (Weis, J., dissenting). The court held that Drexel was a bidder, pointing to "Drexel's early and pervasive role in the planning and execution of the present offer, its erstwhile board representation in the corporation controlling the sole equity participant in the bidder group, and record evidence sufficient to reasonably suggest an expectation though not a contractual obligation that Drexel would itself provide additional financing if it could not place the $875 (million) in junk bonds elsewhere." 871 F.2d at 219.

The court also determined that information about Drexel was material under Item 9 of Schedule 14D-1:

> It is not clear to us that the financial strength or vulnerability of Drexel, including the adverse impact of Drexel's plea bargain and other legal difficulties, is immaterial to Prime shareholders' deliberations. As opposed to the "highly confident" opinion of Drexel and the conclusory report that Drexel has over $2 billion of capital, and despite the argument that Drexel has recently financed far larger deals, the *Interco* submission indicated an equity of $1.4 billion as of June 24, 1988, *before* the $650 million plea bargain. . . .
>
> That shareholders might reasonably hold out for a higher offer is supported by the determination of the Delaware Chancery Court, rejecting Basic's challenge to the institution of takeover defenses by Prime directors, that the directors reasonably relied on independent investment bankers' valuation of Prime stock between $23 and $28 per share. MAI Basic Four, Inc. v. Prime Computer, No. 10428, slip op. at 11, 1988 WL 140221 (Del. Ch. Dec. 20, 1988). In turn, whether Drexel be seen as weak or strong is a legitimate datum for Prime stockholders.
>
> Nor can we discount the possible impact of Drexel's plea bargain and other legal difficulties as immaterial. This area of corporate cannibalism is not a neat and tidy one.

871 F.2d at 222.

2. The issue as to who must make disclosure under the Williams Act has arisen more frequently as to the definition of groups. The statutory definition in §13(d)(3) of a group as an aggregation of persons or entities who "act as a . . . group for the purpose of acquiring, holding or disposing of securities" has been given fairly broad interpretation by the courts. In Wellman v. Dickinson, 682 F.2d 355 (2d Cir. 1982), cert. denied, 460 U.S. 1069 (1983), Fairleigh S. Dickinson, Jr., the son of a founder of Becton, Dickinson & Co. and holder of more than 4 percent of the company's stock, lost an internal power struggle and was removed as chairman. Dickinson hired the investment banking firm of Salomon Brothers to assist him in locating a company that would be interested in purchasing his substantial holdings in Becton and those of his friends for a complete or partial takeover of the company. Dickinson and his friends could deliver 13 percent of the outstanding stock. The court of appeals supported the district court's findings that Dickinson and his friends "were all part of a group formed to dispose of their shares to aid a third party acquisition of a controlling interest in [Becton]," 682 F.2d at 363.

Rule 13d-5(b) adopts the holding of GAF Corp. v. Milstein, 453 F.2d 709 (2d Cir. 1971), cert. denied, 406 U.S. 910 (1972), that a group cannot wait until it makes its first concerted acquisition or disposition of shares but must file immediately upon formation of the group.

Securities and Exchange Commission v. Amster & Co.
United States District Court, S.D. New York, 1991
762 F. Supp. 604

HAIGHT, DISTRICT Judge: . . .

Defendant Amster & Co. is a New York limited partnership and the successor partnership of Lafer, Amster & Co. ("LACO"). The principal business of both Amster & Co. and LACO was and is risk arbitrage investing. . . .

Risk arbitrageurs do not purchase the shares of companies for long-term investment purposes. Rather, they purchase shares in the expectation or hope that some anticipated event occurring in the short term will drive the price of the shares up, setting the stage for resale and profit. Corporate mergers may have this happy effect; so may takeovers, friendly or hostile; so may the liquidation of the company. If arbitrageurs have reason to believe that a company will soon be liquidated, they are motivated to purchase its shares if their calculations indicate that the break-up value per share will exceed the then existing market price.

This last-described investment strategy brought a company called Graphic Scanning Corp. ("Graphic") to the attention of LACO in August 1984. At that time Graphic owned and operated radio paging and cellular telephone franchises throughout the United States. In August 1984 Graphic publicly announced a liquidation. LACO, anticipating the liquidation to occur within a year and a half of the announcement, began purchasing shares of Graphic. LACO made these investments on its own account, and also indirectly on behalf of its limited partners, the largest of which was the General Electric Pension Fund.

Eventually LACO's purchases of Graphic shares amounted to a 5% interest in Graphic. LACO was therefore required to comply with the disclosure provisions of §13(d) of the Securities Exchange Act. LACO's Schedule 13(D), dated August 18, 1985, described the purpose of its transactions in Graphic in part as follows:

> Each of LACO and the Other Filing Persons has acquired the shares of Common Stock which he owns for the purpose of making an investment in the Company and not with the present intention of acquiring control of the Company's business.
>
> The shares of the Common Stock reported as being owned by LACO were acquired in connection with arbitrage and other activities in the ordinary course of LACO's business. Certain general partners and employees of LACO have had telephone conversations with the Company. LACO does not believe that it received any material information during those conversations which had not then been publicly disseminated by the Company.
>
> Each of LACO and the Other Filing Persons supports the Company's public announcement on September 24, 1984 and February 15, 1985 regarding its intention to develop a plan of asset distribution to its stockholders complying with Section 337 of the Internal Revenue Code. LACO presently intends to continue to purchase shares of Common Stock in the over-the-counter market or in private transactions if appropriate opportunities to do so are available, on such terms and at such times as it considers desirable. If the Company abandons its intention referred to above, either by public announcement or through a course of action or inaction which leads LACO to believe that a distribution of the Company's assets to its stockholders will not be effected within a reasonable period of time, LACO intends to review its position and take any such action as it deems appropriate at the time.

On January 28, 1986, Graphic filed with the SEC a Form S-1 Registration statement in which Graphic indicated for the first time that the announced liquidation might not go forward. The Form S-1 stated in part: "Although the Company is currently considering the sale of all of its operations and assets, if appropriate offers are not received for all of the assets, it is possible that the Board may determine to sell only portions of the Company's operations and assets." The form also indicated that the Graphic Board was negotiating with the Company's founder and chairman, Barry Yampol, with respect to claims Yampol had against Graphic, one possible resolution being the transfer to Yampol of "certain cellular radio telephone properties and other assets of the Company."

These statements in Graphic's Form S-1 came as unwelcome news to LACO, which had invested in Graphic in anticipation of liquidation. On January 31, 1986, Lafer telephoned Graphic's general counsel, Jonathan Dodge, and asked what the Form S-1 meant. Lafer asked Dodge if the tax reform bill pending in Congress could impact upon the Section 337 liquidation originally contemplated by Graphic. Dodge replied that the tax bill could alter the liquidation plan, and added, in the context of Graphic's registration statement, that the use of the proceeds would be partially applied to assets acquisition. Lafer told Dodge that LACO and those associated with it were "unhappy shareholders."

There then ensued a series of meetings involving LACO officers, representatives of other Graphic shareholders, and various attorneys. . . .

For purposes of background, it is sufficient to say that on March 3, 1986, LACO and others affiliated with it filed Amendment 7 to their Schedule 13D with an effective date of February 28, 1986. Amendment 7 stated that defendants had decided to join a group to engage in a proxy contest to obtain control of Graphic. Amendment 7 had been preceded by Amendment 5, filed on or about February 10, 1986, and Amendment 6, filed on or about February 18. Amendment 5 made no changes in the description of defendants' purpose of their transactions in Graphic. Amendment 6 stated that the defendants had begun to consider "on a preliminary basis" waging a proxy contest for control of Graphic. . . .

The SEC's first claim alleges violations of §13(d) of the 1934 Act, a section of the statute popularly known as the Williams Act. . . .

The provision particularly applicable to the case at bar is found in §13(d)(1)(C), which, "if the purpose of the purchases or prospected purchases is to acquire control of the business of the issuer of the securities," requires the person holding more than 5% of the shares to disclose

> any plans or proposals which such persons may have to liquidate such issuer, to sell its assets to or merge it with any other persons, or to make any other major change in its business or corporate structure. . . .

Under the statutory scheme, these specific disclosures are required only if the purchaser's "purpose" is "to acquire control" of the insurer's business. In [GAF Corp. v. Milstein, 453 F.2d 709 (2d Cir. 1971)], the Second Circuit summarized §13(d)(1)(C) by saying that it "requires the person filing to disclose any intention to acquire control." 453 F.2d at 717. Thus *purpose* is equated with *intention*. . . .

It has been said generally of the securities laws that their "disclosure provisions are intended to protect investors and enable them to receive the facts necessary for informed investment decisions." Chromalloy American Corp. v. Sun Chemical Corp.,

611 F.2d 240, 248 (8th Cir. 1979). In *Chromalloy,* a case upon which the SEC at bar places particular reliance, the Eighth Circuit went on to say: "However, the objective of full and fair disclosure can be endangered as much by overstating the definiteness of plans as by understating them." . . . The danger inherent in overstating the definiteness of plans is that the overstatement "may cause the offeree or the public investor to rely on them unjustifiably." Susquehanna Corp. v. Pan American Sulfur Co., 423 F.2d 1075, 1085-86 (5th Cir. 1970), cited and quoted by the Second Circuit in Missouri Portland Cement Co. v. Cargill, Inc., 498 F.2d 854, 872 (2d Cir. 1974). Judge Pollack's careful analysis in Todd Shipyards Corp. v. Madison Fund, Inc., 547 F. Supp. 1383, 1387 (S.D.N.Y. 1982), deals with the pertinent distinction:

> The applicable rule in the disclosure laws is that disclosure is to be made of all definite plans and there is no requirement to make predictions, for example, of future behavior, or to disclose tentative plans, or inchoate plans. It is sufficient to merely identify those matters not fully determined.

While each case turns on its own facts, the language the Second Circuit uses in explaining its holdings in particular cases is instructive. Compare Gulf & Western Industries, Inc. v. Great [A.] & P. Tea Co., Inc., 476 F.2d 687, 696 (2d Cir. 1973) ("considerable evidence was adduced at the hearing which indicates that G&W purchased A&P stock not for the purpose of investment but with a view to exercising influence or control," and which "indicates that such intent was present"), and Gerstle v. Gamble-Skogmo, Inc., 478 F.2d 1281, 1295 (2d Cir. 1973) (approving the district court's findings that "Skogmo intended at least by and probably before July 19, 1963, to sell all the remaining outdoor advertising plants of General immediately after the merger"), with Missouri Portland Cement Co. v. Cargill, Inc., supra, at 872 ("But there is no evidence that any such plan was developed, much less adopted, or that the statement in the offer was anything but the truth."). . . .

Under the governing law, on its first claim the SEC bears the burden of proving the essential element that defendants failed to disclose in filings required by §13(d) a definitely formed intention to obtain control of Graphic by means of a proxy contest. To paraphrase Judge Pollack's formulation in *Todd Shipyards,* 547 F. Supp. at 1388, the SEC's burden at trial would be to prove by a preponderance of the credible evidence that at the time of defendants' filing of their Schedule 13D or at least one of its amendments, defendants had a "purpose or plans with respect to [Graphic] or their investment in [Graphic] other than as described in their Schedule 13D" or the amendments.

The SEC would derive from §13(d) a duty falling upon these defendants to report concerning a proxy contest before deciding to wage one. Its brief rejects as "plainly wrong" defendants' contention that to prevail the SEC must prove that defendants decided to launch a proxy contest before February 28, 1986. The SEC construes §13(d) to require the reporting of "any material change in purpose, not just a 'decision' on a particular course of action to effectuate a change." In a phrase that runs like a leitmotif throughout its brief, the SEC argues that §13(d) requires disclosure whenever "the securities purchaser has a perceptible desire to influence substantially the insurer's operations. . . ." Dan River, Inc. v. Unitex Ltd., 624 F.2d 1216, 1226 n.9 (4th Cir. 1980), cert. denied, 449 U.S. 1101 (1981), quoting Chromalloy American Corp. v.

Sun Chemical Corp., 611 F.2d 240, 246-47 (8th Cir. 1979). The SEC argues that "such a desire was manifested" by the defendants at bar not later than February 3, 1986, when they presented another Graphic shareholder with a scenario for a proxy contest for control of the company.

I consider that incident . . . together with the other evidence adduced during the investigation and discovery. However, it is useful to view that evidence through the prism of the governing law. In that regard, I reject the SEC's construction of §13(d) as applied to the facts of this case. I reject that construction because it is inconsistent with the cases previously cited, and stands upon fragile underpinnings. . . .

In the case at bar, the SEC gives the phrase "a perceptible desire to influence substantially the issuer's operations" an expansive reading requiring disclosure of desire before desire crystallizes into decision. The SEC is quite plain about that; its brief argues:

> a "decision" as to a particular course of action to effect a control purpose is not the event that triggers the obligation to amend the purpose section of a Section 13D. What triggers that obligation is the change from holding the securities for "investment only" to holding the securities with "a perceptible desire to influence substantially the insurer's operations."

Defendants, on the other hand, give the *Chromalloy* phrase a more narrow reading. Defendants stress that the *Dan River* footnote expresses the Fourth Circuit's belief that §13(d) "requires *disclosure of a control purpose* whenever 'the securities purchaser has a perceptible desire to influence substantially the insurer's operations,' . . . regardless of proof of a 'fixed plan' to acquire control." (emphasis added). Defendant Lafer argues in his reply brief:

> All that sentence means is that the decision to seek control requires a filing, even though the securities holder has not decided on the means to do it.

I agree. The facts in both *Chromalloy* and *Dan River* were sufficient to establish the defendants' formulation of a control *purpose,* that is to say, an *intent* to acquire control, prior to the filings at issue. Furthermore, those facts were central to the appellate decisions in *Chromalloy* and *Dan River*. Were it otherwise, the Eighth Circuit in *Chromalloy* would not have needed to quote the district court's finding that defendants "had the intent to control *Chromalloy* from the beginning," or to recite the various facts demonstrating that initial intent. Nor would the Fourth Circuit in *Dan River* have emphasized Unitex's "plan," logically consistent with gaining control, and pre-existing the challenged Schedule 13D amendments.

If the hot air balloon of desire is separated from the ballast of control purpose or intent, it is left free to soar wherever . . . an advocate's winds may blow. Shareholders subject to Williams Act reporting requirements will not know when initial itch matures into reportable "desire," and the reporting of desires not yet transformed into purpose or intent could mislead investors in manners contrary to the statute's purpose. To change the metaphor, the SEC argues for a §13(d) "Streetcar Named Desire." I do not think that streetcar runs. . . .

On this record, which is extensive, defendants are entitled to summary judgment dismissing the §13D claim. There is no evidence to support any of the SEC's criticisms of LACO's 13D amendments. LACO had not reached a decision to wage a proxy contest prior to the time they announced that intention in amendment 7. As for the earlier amendments, they gave timely advice of "those matters not fully determined," to use Judge Pollack's phrase in *Todd Shipyards,* supra. Those amendments were sufficient when viewed in the context of the original Schedule 13D and the disclosures it made with respect to LACO's status as an arbitrageur, the reason for its particular interest in Graphic, and the possibility of alternative steps if Graphic seemed to be backing away from its announced intention to liquidate. . . .

NOTES

1. The Williams Act provides no express private cause of action. Judicial decisions as to implied causes of action reflect the chilly reaction to that question that has overrun the more expansive view set out in J.I. Case Co. v. Borak (see Chapter 10 at page 958). In Piper v. Chris-Craft Industries, Inc., 430 U.S. 1 (1977), the Supreme Court ruled that a losing bidder did not have standing to sue under §14(e) to recover $27 million in damages allegedly caused when the competing bidder used misleading statements to acquire a majority of shares in a target company. The Court found that "the sole purpose of the Williams Act was the protection of investors who are confronted with a tender offer. . . . [There is] no hint in the legislative history . . . that Congress contemplated a private cause of action for damages by one of several contending offerors against a successful bidder or by a losing bidder against a target corporation." 430 U.S. at 35. Subsequently, lower courts have found that target companies can seek equitable relief such as corrective disclosure (see Florida Commercial Banks v. Culverhouse, 772 F.2d 1513 (11th Cir. 1985)), and that target shareholders can sue for an injunction or damages (see Plaine v. McCabe, 797 F.2d 713 (9th Cir. 1986)). Cf. In re Phillips Petroleum Securities Litigation, 881 F.2d 1236 (3d Cir. 1989) (false filing that bidder would not accept purchase of shares on terms different from those of other shareholders could justify an action under Rule 10b-5).

2. The disclosure obligations under §13(d) or §14(d) must be considered against the backdrop of remedies provided for a violation. Courts have often limited their orders to requiring corrective disclosures. See Rondeau v. Mosinee Paper Corp., 422 U.S. 49 (1975) (overturning court of appeals action that would have enjoined defendant from voting for two years any share acquired prior to correct filing of 13D statement); Chromalloy American Corp. v. Sun Chemical Corp., 611 F.2d 240 (8th Cir. 1979) (no cooling-off period required after bidder's correction). But see SEC v. First City Financial Corp., 890 F.2d 1215 (D.C. Cir. 1989) (upholding order requiring acquirer to disgorge $2.7 million from later resale of target stock). The court based its result on the assumption that if the Williams Act requirements had been met, the acquirer's purchase price "would have been affected by the disclosures that [the acquirer] had taken a greater than 5 percent stake in [the target] and would soon propose a tender offer." 890 F.2d at 1231.

In SEC v. Drexel Burnham Lambert Inc., 837 F. Supp. 587 (S.D.N.Y. 1993), a federal district court barred Victor Posner and his son Steven "from serving as officers and directors of any reporting company and [ordered] the stock they own in corporations under their control to be placed in voting trusts so as to divest them of control of those companies without divesting them of the economic value of the stock." 837 F. Supp. at 613. Victor Posner was held to have violated §13(d) by failing to amend Schedule 13D to disclose beneficial ownership of stock bought for his interests by Ivan Boesky, as part of transactions also involving Michael Milken. The court noted that a previous injunction entered against the Posners had been "notably ineffectual in preventing them from engaging in securities law violations. . . . [I]t would serve little purpose for the Court to issue yet another injunction against such recidivist violators without at the same time granting ancillary relief calculated to ensure that, this time, they comply with the Court's mandate." Id.

3. If courts are reluctant to enforce a remedy other than corrective disclosure, what effect does §14(d) have and, even more, what purpose is served by the early warning requirement of §13(d)? In one sense, disclosure gives the target a litigation opportunity to stall an unwanted tender offer while seeking out a white knight or implementing another defensive strategy. See Jarrell, The Wealth Effects of Litigation by Targets: Do Interests Diverge in a Merger?, 28 J.L. & Econ. 151 (1985). In a broader sense, the disclosure serves to encourage an auction, with the possible impact that tender offers that are undertaken will produce higher returns for target shareholders, but that fewer tender offers will occur as potential bidders find fewer incentives to seek out potential targets. See Macey and Netter, Regulation 13D and the Regulatory Process, 65 Wash. U. L.Q. 131 (1987).

PROBLEM 11-1

Bidder, Inc. is contemplating making a tender offer for all shares of Target, Inc. Target has been floundering in recent months because of a money-losing ancillary venture (the New Division). Bidder believes that shutting down the New Division would increase Target's value by 50 percent. If Bidder proceeds with the tender offer, must it disclose to Target's shareholders the potential value of jettisoning the New Division?

2. Substantive Regulation

Securities Exchange Act of 1934 §14(d)(5), (6), and (7)
SEC Rules 14d-2, 14d-7, 14d-10, and 14e-1

While many court opinions emphasize the disclosure orientation of the Williams Act, significant substantive regulation is also included. The clearest purpose of many of these rules is to limit the pressure on shareholders to tender quickly.

Under SEC Rule 14e-1 an offer must remain open for 20 business days. If a bidder seeks to buy less than all of a target's shares, §14(d)(6) requires that the purchases be pro rata from all those who tendered during the offering period. Thus a bidder cannot use a first-come, first-served limited time offer to force an immediate shareholder response. Section 14(d)(5), as supplemented by Rule 14d-7, permits a shareholder to withdraw tendered securities during the entire offer, thus freeing a shareholder from one peril of an immediate decision.

The "best-price rule" of §14(d)(7) and Rule 14d-10 requiring that the tender offer be open to all shareholders may reflect a concern for equal treatment of shareholders in a way that broadens federal law beyond its traditional disclosure focus.

Field v. Trump

United States Court of Appeals, Second Circuit, 1988
850 F.2d 938, cert. denied, 489 U.S. 1012 (1989)

WINTER, CIRCUIT Judge: . . .

Accepting the allegations of the complaint as true, this dispute arises from a leveraged buy-out in which defendants Julius and Eddie Trump, through corporations they owned and controlled, commenced a tender offer at a price of $22.50 per share for shares of defendant Pay'n Save Corporation, a Washington state corporation. Shortly after the market closed on the fourth business day after the announcement of the tender offer, the Trumps "withdrew" the offer in order to arrange a purchase of a bloc of shares from certain dissident directors. Later that night, after acquiring an option to purchase the dissidents' shares, the Trumps announced a "new" tender offer at $23.50 per share. When the price of the option and a side payment for "fees and expenses" is taken into account, the dissidents received $25.00 per share, a $1.50 premium over the price paid to the tendering shareholders. . . .

BACKGROUND

According to the amended complaint, the allegations of which we must accept as true, this dispute originates in Pay'n Save's acquisition of Schuck's Auto Supply, Inc. in January 1984. That transaction left the former owners of Schuck's, defendants Samuel N. Stroum and Stuart M. Sloan and members of their families ("Stroums" or "Stroum Group"), holding 18.4% of Pay'n Save's outstanding common stock. The Stroums were not happy shareholders, however, and had their own ideas about how to run Pay'n Save. Looking for ways to pacify the Stroums, Pay'n Save management sought and obtained a standstill agreement dated March 30, 1984. The Stroums agreed not to sell or otherwise dispose of their shares, or to offer to purchase Pay'n Save. In return, Stroum and Sloan received seats on the company's board.

Friction between the Stroums and management nevertheless continued. As a result, management retained Kidder Peabody and later Merrill Lynch Capital Markets to find a purchaser for the company. To the same end, defendant Calvin Hendricks, Pay'n Save's Chief Financial Officer and Vice-Chairman of its board, undertook discussions with Eddie Trump, President of the Trump Group, Ltd., about acquiring Pay'n Save. According to its subsequent Offer to Purchase, the Trump Group took the position that it "would only consider an acquisition of the company if management would participate in the equity of the resulting entity." Management agreed, and on August 31 the Trumps proposed to the Pay'n Save board a cash tender offer at $22.00 per share for two-thirds of the company's outstanding shares, to be followed by a cash-out merger at the same price. One week later, in the early morning hours of a late-night

Pay'n Save board meeting, the Trumps raised their offer to $22.50 but warned that it would be withdrawn if it were not approved. Merrill Lynch opined that $22.50 was a fair price, and a majority of Pay'n Save's board approved it. Stroum and Sloan dissented. That morning, September 7, 1984, Pay'n Save issued a press release announcing that it had reached a merger agreement with the Trumps and that the Trumps were initiating a tender offer at $22.50. In a statement of their own, the Stroums called the Trump offer "skimpy" and accused management of acting in "unseemly haste."

During the next few days, according to the Offer to Purchase, "Eddie Trump contacted Messrs. Stroum and Sloan and the parties had several conversations concerning the possibility of settling the objections of Messrs. Stroum and Sloan to the Transactions." At 5:10 P.M. on September 12, after a meeting between the Trumps, Stroum and Sloan, the Trumps told Pay'n Save's board that they were withdrawing their previously announced tender offer in order "to facilitate the negotiations with Messrs. Stroum and Sloan." The Trumps also issued a press release announcing both the withdrawal of their tender offer and their negotiations with the Stroums. These negotiations quickly bore fruit. Later that night, the Trumps and the Stroums entered into a Settlement Agreement under which the Trumps paid the Stroums $3,300,000 for an option to purchase the Stroums' shares at $23.50 per share. In addition, the Trumps paid the Stroums $900,000 for the Stroums' "fees and expenses." The Settlement Agreement was subject to the Pay'n Save board's approval of an amendment to the September 7 merger agreement that would provide for an increased price of $23.50 per share for the tender offer and merger. The $4,200,000 payment (option price plus "fees and expenses"), when added to the $23.50 per share purchase price, amounted to a price of $25.00 per share for the Stroums.

The next day, September 13, the Pay'n Save board approved the amendment to the merger agreement, and Pay'n Save issued a press release announcing that the Trumps would soon proceed with a tender offer at the new $23.50 price. According to the complaint, the press release announcing the new price and the September 12 press release announcing the "withdrawal" reached the public simultaneously.

Claiming to have been a Pay'n Save shareholder who tendered shares for $23.50, $1.50 less than the price paid to the Stroums, plaintiff brought this putative class action [against Pay'n Save, its officers, its pro-management directors, its dissident directors, and the Trump entities]. . . .

DISCUSSION

1. THE SECTION 14(d)(7) CLAIM

Plaintiff's principal claim arises under §14(d)(7) of the Williams Act, the so-called "best-price" provision, which states that:

> Where any person varies the terms of a tender offer or request or invitation for tenders before the expiration thereof by increasing the consideration offered to holders of such securities, such person shall pay the increased consideration to each security holder whose securities are taken up and paid for pursuant to tender offer or request or invitation for tenders whether or not such securities have been taken up by such person before the variation of the tender offer or request or invitation.

The purpose of this provision is to prevent a tender offeror from discriminating in price among tendering shareholders. The position taken by the SEC thus is that:

> (i) a tender offer must be extended to all holders of the class of securities which is the subject of the offer (the "all-holders requirement"); and (ii) all such holders must be paid the highest consideration offered under the tender offer (the "best-price rule").

Proposed Amendments to Tender Offer Rules, Securities Act Release No. 6595 [1984-1985 Transfer Binder] Fed. Sec. L. Rep. (CCH) ¶83,797 (July 1, 1985). To codify the "all-holders requirement" and "best-price rule," the SEC has adopted Rule 14d-10, which provides in pertinent part:

> (a) No bidder shall make a tender offer unless:
>> (1) The tender offer is open to all security holders of the class of securities subject to the tender offer; and
>> (2) The consideration paid to any security holder pursuant to the tender offer is the highest consideration paid to any other security holder during such tender offer.

To the same end, the SEC has promulgated a rule prohibiting side transactions involving purchases of securities subject to a tender offer. Rule 10b-13 thus provides in pertinent part:

> (a) No person who makes a cash tender offer or exchange offer for any equity security shall, directly or indirectly, purchase, or make any arrangement to purchase, any such security (or any other security which is immediately convertible into or exchangeable for such security), otherwise than pursuant to such tender offer or exchange offer, from the time such tender offer or exchange offer is publicly announced or otherwise made known by such person to holders of the security to be acquired until the expiration of the period, including any extensions thereof, during which securities tendered pursuant to such tender offer or exchange offer may by the terms of such offer be accepted or rejected.

The essence of plaintiff's claim is that the $4,200,000 paid to the Stroums during the brief "withdrawal" of the offer was in law and fact a payment of a $1.50 per share premium intended to induce the Stroums to accept the tender offer. The failure to pay this premium to the other tendering shareholders, plaintiff argues, violated the "best-price rule."

No party disputes the proposition that payment of a premium to one shareholder and not others during a tender offer is illegal. The issue rather is whether the purported withdrawal effectively ended the offer so that the $4,200,000 payment was not during or part of a tender offer. In dismissing the §14(d)(7) claim, the district court relied upon SEC rules governing the commencement of a tender offer, specifically Rule 14d-2(b), which provides that:

> [a] public announcement by a bidder through a press release, newspaper advertisement or public statement which includes the information in paragraph (c) of this section [namely, the identity of the bidder and the target, the amount and class of the securities sought, and the price to be paid] with respect to a tender offer . . . shall be deemed to constitute the commencement of a tender offer [for the purposes of §14(d) and rules promulgated thereunder] *except*, that such tender offer shall not be deemed to [have commenced under this section] on the date of such public announcement *if within five business days of such public announcement, the bidder . . . [m]akes a subsequent public announcement stating that the bidder has determined not to continue with such tender offer. . . .*

(emphasis added). Thus, while the public announcement of the essential terms of a tender offer results in the technical "commencement" of a tender offer, the offer will nevertheless be legally deemed not to have commenced if its withdrawal is announced within five business days. In the instant case, the initial announcement of the Trumps' tender offer came on the morning of Friday, September 7, 1984, and the purported withdrawal was announced on the afternoon of Wednesday, September 12, four business days later. Based on these facts, the district court concluded that, for purposes of §14(d)(7), "there was no tender offer in place at the time of the Settlement Agreement, and thus, as a matter of law, no violation of [that] Section." We disagree, however, and believe that the allegations of the complaint state a claim under the Williams Act. . . .

[G]iving effect to every purported withdrawal that allows a discriminatory premium to be paid to large shareholders would completely undermine the "best-price rule." For example, plaintiff has alleged that the purported withdrawal of the original tender offer was intended solely to allow the Trumps to pay a premium of $1.50 per share to the Stroums that was not offered to shareholders who tendered pursuant to the "new" tender offer announced immediately thereafter.[1] The "best-price rule" of §14(d)(7) and Rule 14d-10 is completely unenforceable if offerors may announce periodic "withdrawals" during which purchases at a premium are made and thereafter followed by "new" tender offers. Unless successive tender offers interrupted by withdrawals can in appropriate circumstances be viewed as a single tender offer for purposes of the Williams Act, the "best-price rule" is meaningless.

Whether the purchase of the Stroum shares was a private purchase or part of a continuing tender offer is not determined simply by the Trumps' use of the labels "withdrawal" and "new" offer. Cf. McDermott, Inc. v. Wheelabrator-Frye, Inc., 649 F.2d 489 (7th Cir. 1980) (announcement of increase in number of shares sought not new tender offer). Indeed, we have explicitly recognized that purchases after a purported withdrawal of a tender offer may constitute a continuation of the offer in light of the surrounding circumstances. [Hanson Trust PLC v. SCM Corp., 774 F.2d 47, 58-59 (2d Cir. 1985).] Finally, §14(d)(7) itself explicitly treats a material change in the terms of a tender offer in the form of an increased price as a continuation of the original offer rather than as a new tender offer. Clearly, therefore, purchases of shares by an offeror after a purported withdrawal of a tender offer may constitute a continuation of the original tender offer.

Rule 14d-2(b) is not to the contrary. That Rule merely creates a window of time during which a genuine withdrawal leaves matters for all legal purposes as though a tender offer had never been commenced. The Rule does nothing to alter the principle that the mere announcement of a withdrawal may not be effective if followed by purchases of shares and other conduct inconsistent with a genuine intent to withdraw. The Rule is also irrelevant because a bidder is always free to withdraw a tender offer. The

---

1. Whether the "fees and expenses" for which the Trumps paid $900,000 to the Stroums were actually incurred is irrelevant under the "best-price rule." Some or all of those sums were expended in order to obtain a premium for the Stroums, and it would thwart the purposes of §14(d)(7) to allow reimbursement. Moreover, we believe the "best-price rule" would be unworkable if offerors were permitted to discriminate among shareholders according to expenses that were not uniformly incurred, such as broker's or attorney's fees.

argument advanced by defendants, if correct, would thus apply even in cases in which the provisions of Rule 14d-2(b) governing withdrawal announcements did not.[2]

For purposes of the "best-price rule," therefore, an announcement of a withdrawal is effective when the offeror genuinely intends to abandon the goal of the original offer. The complaint here alleges that the Trumps' Offer to Purchase explicitly stated that the purported withdrawal was intended to allow negotiations with the Strouns. Such negotiations indicate a continuing intent to obtain control of Pay'n Save.

Moreover, the complaint alleges conduct from which inferences might be drawn that the Trumps had not abandoned the goal of the original offer. In determining the most appropriate analysis for evaluating the conduct of an offeror surrounding a purported withdrawal, we draw upon a suggestion of Professor Loss. He has noted that the determination of whether formally separate offerings of securities should be "integrated," and thus considered a single offering, for the purposes of the various registration exemptions, is closely analogous to the question of whether single or multiple tender offers have been made. L. Loss, Fundamentals of Securities Regulation 577 n.33 (1983) (suggesting comparison of "'integration' problem with respect to certain exemptions under the 1933 Act" with §202(166)(B) of the ALI's proposed Federal Securities Code, which "treats [tender] offers as separate if they are for different classes of securities or are 'substantially distinct on the basis of such factors as manner, time, purpose, price and kind of consideration'").

In establishing criteria to govern the integration of formally separate offerings, the SEC has identified the following factors, inter alia, as relevant: "(1) are the offerings part of a single [plan] of financing; (2) do the offerings involve issuance of the same class of security; (3) are the offerings made at or about the same time . . . ?" Section 3(a)(11) Exemption for Local Offerings, Securities Act Release No. 4434 (Dec. 6, 1961). Analogous factors may thus point to "integration" in the context of formally separate tender offers: (1) are the offers part of a single plan of acquisition; (2) do the offers involve the purchase of the same class of security; and (3) are the offers made at or about the same time? These factors are useful in determining the ultimate fact of whether an offeror has abandoned the goal of an initial tender offer in announcing a withdrawal of that offer. As previously noted, where the goal has not been abandoned, a purported withdrawal followed by a "new" offer must be treated as a single continuing offer for purposes of the "best-price rule."

Accepting as true the facts alleged in plaintiff's complaint, all of the listed factors weigh in favor of treating the Trumps' acquisition of Pay'n Save shares as a single tender offer. If the allegations are proven, the alleged $1.50 premium to the Strouns would violate §14(d)(7).

---

2. Defendants have emphasized that "the public shareholders of Pay'n Save ultimately received $23.50 per share, or approximately $5.00 per share in excess of the market value of their shares on the last full trading date prior to the announcement of the proposed tender offer and merger." They apparently wish to stress that application of the "best-price rule" where a payment of a premium above the offer to a large shareholder is necessary to consummate the transaction will ultimately work to the detriment of shareholders generally by decreasing such transactions. This point, however, can be made about the Williams Act generally, see, e.g., Dynamics Corp. of Am. v. CTS Corp., 794 F.2d 250, 262 (7th Cir. 1986) (citing Jarrell & Bradley, The Economic Effects of Federal and State Regulations of Cash Tender Offers, 23 J. Law & Econ. 371 (1980)), revd. on other grounds, 107 S. Ct. 1637 (1987), and thus must be addressed to Congress.

The parties and the district court have correctly assumed that §14(d)(7) impliedly affords a private right of action to shareholders. In Pryor v. United States Steel Corp., 794 F.2d 52, 57-58 (2d Cir.), cert. denied, 107 S. Ct. 445 (1986), we held that the best-price provision's statutory neighbor, §14(d)(6) of the '34 Act, 15 U.S.C. §78n(d)(6) (1982), which requires pro rata acceptance of tendered shares in oversubscribed offers, could be privately enforced. Section 14(d)(7) certainly provides at least as strong a basis for the implication of a private remedy as does §14(d)(6). As in Pryor, the plaintiff here is "surely [one of] the primary intended beneficiaries of [the statute], since 'the sole purpose of the Williams Act was the protection of investors who are confronted with a tender offer.'" 794 F.2d at 57 (quoting Piper v. Chris-Craft Indus., 430 U.S. 1, 35 (1977)). Moreover, §14(d)(7), like §14(d)(6) and "unlike the bulk of federal securities regulation, confers a substantive right on [its] beneficiaries," thereby "suggest[ing] that Congress intended to create a private right of action." Id. In addition, as is true of the proration provision, a private damage action provides a particularly effective means of enforcing the strictures of the "best-price rule." When a premium is paid to one shareholder in violation of §14(d)(7), "the injury is easy to calculate, the victims are easy to locate, and the likelihood of litigation by such victims is high if a private right of action exists." Id. at 58. Finally, a cause of action under §14(d)(7) is not one "traditionally relegated to state law." Id. (quoting Cort v. Ash, 422 U.S. 66, 78 (1975)). Accordingly, we hold that §14(d)(7) affords private plaintiffs an implied right of action, and we therefore reverse the dismissal of the §14(d)(7) claim. . . .

NOTES AND QUESTIONS

1. Rule 14d-10 was promulgated by the SEC in the aftermath of Unocal Corp. v. Mesa Petroleum Co. (see Chapter 9), where the target company used a discriminatory self-tender that excluded the raider T. Boone Pickens from participating in the target's offer. The Delaware Supreme Court upheld the target's use of this defensive tactic. As such, the rule illustrates a federal override of state law. The rule was upheld by a federal appellate court in Polaroid Corp. v. Disney, 862 F.2d 987 (3d Cir. 1988). Is the context of Field v. Trump a more defensible use of federal power than *Unocal*?

2. Field v. Trump dealt with payments made during a brief withdrawal of a tender offer. Similar issues have arisen as to whether certain payments made to insiders just before or just after a tender offer are covered by the rule. See In re Digital Island Securities Litigation, 357 F.3d 322 (3d Cir. 2004) where the appellate court recognized that a tender offeror cannot evade the requirements of the Williams Act simply by delaying the actual payment or by agreeing to an extra payment before hand, but found that an employment agreement for an ongoing business not deliberately inflated to offer a premium did not run afoul of the rule. Compare Epstein v. MCA, Inc., 50 F.3d 644 (9th Cir. 1995), rev'd on other grounds, Matsushita Elec. Indus. Co. Ltd. v. Epstein, 516 U.S. 367 (1996) (finding a violation), and Lerro v. Quaker Oats Co., 84 F.3d 239, 245 (9th Cir. 1996) (transactions before or after a tender offer are outside the scope of Rule 14d-10).

3. Rule 10b-13, mentioned in the *Field* case (and since redesignated as Rule 14e-5), was the principal federal law connection in the Texaco v. Pennzoil litigation that led

to the then largest damage judgment in American history. A Texas jury found that Texaco's $125 per share bid for Getty Oil Company, later accepted by the Getty board, tortiously interfered with Pennzoil's earlier "agreement in principle" with the Getty board and its major shareholders to acquire all Getty stock not owned by a family trust at $112.50 per share. Prior to reaching "agreement" with the Getty board, Pennzoil had launched a tender offer for 20 percent of Getty's shares at $100 per share. When reaching agreement at the $112.50 price, Pennzoil agreed to pay the corporation's largest shareholder, Getty Museum, $112.50 cash immediately, while other shareholders would receive their cash after the approval of the merger.

After Texaco's higher bid was accepted, Pennzoil sued and won a verdict for $10.5 billion. Texaco, having lost all the way through the state system on its argument that the Pennzoil-Getty agreement in principle was not a binding contract, needed a federal claim to get into federal court. A federal court found due process problems in the state procedure, but the U.S. Supreme Court later threw out this claim. Rule 10b-13 offered a possibility to get the case before the Supreme Court if the agreement to purchase from the Getty Museum on different terms from other shareholders violated Rule 10b-13's prohibition on purchasing shares outside of a tender offer during the pendency of an offer. How would you have ruled? The case was settled (for $3 billion) before the Supreme Court decided whether to hear the case.

4. Footnote 2 of the *Field* opinion contains a variation of an argument earlier considered in Chapter 8 that paying large shareholders a premium can benefit all shareholders. Why should the result here be different from the sale of control for a premium case in Part F of Chapter 8?

3. Definition of a Tender Offer

The procedural and substantive provisions discussed so far increase the costs of a tender offer, a term that is not defined in the statute. Obviously, stock acquirers would like to avoid part or all of these regulations. But when will a particular transaction be labeled a non-regulated purchase and not a regulated tender offer?

Courts often have used this eight-factor test to determine if a transaction is a tender offer:

(1) active and widespread solicitation of public shareholders for the shares of an issuer;

(2) solicitation made for a substantial percentage of the issuer's stock;

(3) offer to purchase made at a premium over the prevailing market price;

(4) terms of the offer are firm rather than negotiable;

(5) offer contingent on the tender of a fixed number of shares, often subject to a fixed maximum number to be purchased;

(6) offer open only for a limited period of time;

(7) offeree subjected to pressure to sell stock;

(8) public announcements of a purchasing program concerning the target company precede or accompany rapid accumulation of large amounts of the target company's securities.

See Wellman v. Dickinson, 475 F. Supp. 783, 823-824 (S.D.N.Y.), aff'd on other grounds, 682 F.2d 355 (2d Cir. 1982), and S.E.C. v. Carter Hawley Hale Stores, Inc., 760 F.2d 945 (9th Cir. 1985).

The test allows for flexible case-by-case adjudication to ensure that the purposes of the Williams Act are not circumvented, but makes it difficult for planners to determine the exact line between tender offers and non-regulated purchases. An illustrative case is Hanson Trust PLC v. SCM Corp., 774 F.2d 47 (2d Cir. 1985), which arose in the battle for control of a public corporation, SCM. Hanson Trust PLC (Hanson) began the contest with a publicly announced tender offer for control of SCM. Merrill Lynch emerged as a white knight to enable an insider group to make a counteroffer via a leveraged buyout at a higher price. To ensure the success of the insiders' bid, SCM granted lock-up options to Merrill Lynch triggered if Hanson successfully completed its tender offer. In response, Hanson terminated its tender offer and later that same day acquired 25 percent of SCM's stock via five privately negotiated cash transactions and one open-market purchase. These acquisitions gave Hanson sufficient voting power to prevent the insiders and Merrill Lynch from getting the two-thirds vote needed under state law to approve the leveraged buyout merger that the Merrill Lynch offer contemplated.

SCM sought injunctive relief preventing Hanson from voting the acquired shares or acquiring additional shares on the ground that Hanson's purchases constituted a "tender offer" that had not met the requirements of the Williams Act. The trial court ruled for SCM, but the Second Circuit reversed. Writing for the court, Judge Mansfield noted that the purpose of the Williams Act is to protect shareholders who are the object of entreaties to sell their stock, not the company whose stock is acquired, its management, or other parties interested in maintaining control. In holding that the Williams Act was not frustrated by Hanson's transactions, Judge Mansfield emphasized that:

> It may well be that Hanson's private acquisition of 25% of SCM's shares after termination of Hanson's tender offer was designed to block the SCM-Merrill leveraged buy-out group from acquiring the 66% of SCM's stock needed to effectuate a merger. It may be speculated that such a blocking move might induce SCM to buy Hanson's 25% at a premium or lead to negotiations between the parties designed to resolve their differences. But we know of no provision in the federal securities laws or elsewhere that prohibits such tactics in "hardball" market battles of the type encountered here. See Treadway Companies, Inc. v. Care Corp., 638 F.2d 357, 378-379 (2d Cir. 1980) ("We also see nothing wrong in Care's efforts to acquire one third of Treadway's outstanding stock, and thus to obtain a 'blocking position.'").

PROBLEM 11-2

Stores, Inc., faced with a hostile tender offer, seeks to acquire a large enough percentage of its shares to make the block held by insiders sufficient to defeat any acquisition. Stores announces its plan to buy 15 million shares and over the next week purchases on the market a total of 17.5 million shares (more than half of the stock outstanding). Has a tender offer taken place?

PROBLEM 11-3

Local Railroad, Inc. (Local) owns two major assets—a 100-mile rail line (the Middle Line) located between northern and southern lines owned by Continental Pacific, Inc. (Continental), and a large commercial office building (Building). Local's stock is divided among VRIP, the state employees' pension fund (35 percent), Continental (35 percent), and public shareholders (30 percent).

The boards of Local, Continental, and VRIP have been secretly negotiating a restructuring sought by Continental and VRIP. On May 1, the parties jointly issued a press release announcing an agreement to restructure Local via two separate transactions. First, VRIP would make a cash tender offer of $35 per share for all outstanding Local shares. Second, Local would exchange the Middle Line for all Local shares held by Continental. On May 2, VRIP formally announced the contemplated tender offer, and most publicly held shares were ultimately tendered. Later that week, Local and Continental concluded their contemplated exchange.

As a result of these transactions, Local is now a commercial real estate company, almost all of its shares are held by VRIP, and almost all of Local's former public shareholders have received $35 per share in the VRIP tender offer. One of the tendering shareholders has filed a class action seeking an increased price for all shares tendered to VRIP. The complaint alleges: (1) the Middle Line had a fair value of $75 million, double the value attributed to it in the agreement between Local and Continental; (2) as a result, Continental has received $70 per share for its Local stock; and (3) under Section 14(d)(7) of the Securities Exchange Act of 1934, plaintiffs are also entitled to receive $70 for each Local share tendered to VRIP.

What result?

4.   Antifraud Provisions of the Williams Act

Securities Exchange Act of 1934 §14(e)

Schreiber v. Burlington Northern, Inc.
United States Supreme Court, 1985
472 U.S. 1

CHIEF JUSTICE, BURGER delivered the opinion of the Court.

We granted certiorari to resolve a conflict in the Circuits over whether misrepresentation or nondisclosure is a necessary element of a violation of §14(e) of the Securities Exchange Act of 1934, 15 U.S.C. §78n(e).

I

On December 21, 1982, Burlington Northern, Inc., made a hostile tender offer for El Paso Gas Co. Through a wholly owned subsidiary, Burlington proposed to purchase 25.1 million El Paso shares at $24 per share. Burlington reserved the right to terminate the offer if any of several specified events occurred. El Paso management initially opposed the takeover, but its shareholders responded favorably, fully subscribing the offer by the December 30, 1982 deadline.

Burlington did not accept those tendered shares; instead, after negotiations with El Paso management, Burlington announced on January 10, 1983, the terms of a new and friendly takeover agreement. Pursuant to the new agreement, Burlington undertook, inter alia, to (1) rescind the December tender offer, (2) purchase 4,166,667 shares from El Paso at $24 per share, (3) substitute a new tender offer for only 21 million shares at $24 per share, (4) provide procedural protections against a squeeze-out[1] merger of the remaining El Paso shareholders, and (5) recognize "golden parachute" contracts between El Paso and four of its senior officers. By February 8, more than 40 million shares were tendered in response to Burlington's January offer, and the takeover was completed.

The rescission of the first tender offer caused a diminished payment to those shareholders who had tendered during the first offer. The January offer was greatly oversubscribed and consequently those shareholders who retendered were subject to substantial proration. Petitioner Barbara Schreiber filed suit on behalf of herself and similarly situated shareholders, alleging that Burlington, El Paso, and members of El Paso's board violated §14(e)'s prohibition of "fraudulent, deceptive or manipulative acts or practices . . . in connection with any tender offer." 15 U.S.C. §78n(e). She claimed that Burlington's withdrawal of the December tender offer coupled with the substitution of the January tender offer was a "manipulative" distortion of the market for El Paso stock. Schreiber also alleged that Burlington violated §14(e) by failing in the January offer to disclose the "golden parachutes" offered to four of El Paso's managers. She claims that this January nondisclosure was a deceptive act forbidden by §14(e).

The District Court dismissed the suit for failure to state a claim. The District Court reasoned that the alleged manipulation did not involve a misrepresentation, and so did not violate §14(e). The District Court relied on the fact that in cases involving alleged violations of §10(b) of the Securities Exchange Act, 15 U.S.C. §78j(b), this Court has required misrepresentation for there to be a "manipulative" violation of the section.

The Court of Appeals for the Third Circuit affirmed. The Court of Appeals held that the acts alleged did not violate the Williams Act, because "§14(e) was not intended to create a federal cause of action for all harms suffered because of the proffering or the withdrawal of tender offers." The Court of Appeals reasoned that §14(e) was "enacted principally as a disclosure statute, designed to insure that fully-informed

---

1. A "squeeze-out" merger occurs when Corporation A, which holds a controlling interest in Corporation B, uses its control to merge B into itself or into a wholly owned subsidiary. The minority shareholders in Corporation B are, in effect, forced to sell their stock. The procedural protection provided in the agreement between El Paso and Burlington required the approval of non-Burlington members of El Paso's board of directors before a squeeze-out merger could proceed. Burlington eventually purchased all the remaining shares of El Paso for $12 cash and one-quarter share of Burlington preferred stock per share. The parties dispute whether this consideration was equal to that paid to those tendering during the January tender offer.

investors could intelligently decide how to respond to tender offer." It concluded that the "arguable breach of contract" alleged by petitioner was not a "manipulative act" under §14(e).

We granted certiorari to resolve the conflict.[3] We affirm.

II

A

We are asked in this case to interpret §14(e) of the Securities Exchange Act, 48 Stat. 895, as amended, 15 U.S.C. §78n(e). The starting point is the language of the statute. Section 14(e) provides:

> It shall be unlawful for any person to make any untrue statement of a material fact or omit to state any material fact necessary in order to make the statements made, in the light of the circumstances under which they are made, not misleading, or to engage in any fraudulent, deceptive or manipulative acts or practices, in connection with any tender offer or request or invitation for tenders, or any solicitation of security holders in opposition to or in favor of any such offer, request, or invitation. The Commission shall, for the purposes of this subsection, by rules and regulations define, and prescribe means reasonably designed to prevent, such acts and practices as are fraudulent, deceptive, or manipulative. (15 U.S.C. §78n(e).)

Petitioner relies on a construction of the phrase, "fraudulent, deceptive or manipulative acts or practices." Petitioner reads the phrase "fraudulent, deceptive or manipulative acts or practices" to include acts which, although fully disclosed, "artificially" affected the price of the takeover target's stock. Petitioner's interpretation relies on the belief that §14(e) is directed at purposes broader than providing full and true information to investors.

Petitioner's reading of the term "manipulative" conflicts with the normal meaning of the term. We have held in the context of an alleged violation of §10(b) of the Securities Exchange Act:

> Use of the word "manipulative" is especially significant. It is and was virtually a term of art when used in connection with the securities markets. It connotes intentional or willful conduct *designed to deceive or defraud* investors by controlling or artificially affecting the price of securities." (Ernst & Ernst v. Hochfelder, 425 U.S. 185, 199 (1976) (emphasis added).)

Other cases interpreting the term reflect its use as a general term comprising a range of misleading practices:

> The term refers generally to practices, such as wash sales, matched orders, or rigged prices, that are intended to mislead investors by artificially affecting market activity. . . . Section 10(b)'s

---

3. The Court of Appeals for the Sixth Circuit has held that manipulation does not always require an element of misrepresentation or nondisclosure. Mobil Corp. v. Marathon Oil Co., 669 F.2d 366 (1981), cert. denied, 455 U.S. 982 (1982). The Court of Appeals for the Second and Eighth Circuits have applied an analysis consistent with the one we apply today. Feldbaum v. Avon Products, Inc., 741 F.2d 234 (C.A.8 1984); Buffalo Forge Co. v. Ogden Corp., 717 F.2d 757 (C.A.2), cert. denied, 464 U.S. 1018 (1983); Data Probe Acquisition Corp. v. Datalab, Inc., 722 F.2d 1 (C.A.2 1983), cert. denied, 465 U.S. 1052 (1984).

general prohibition of practices deemed by the SEC to be "manipulative"—in this technical sense of artificially affecting market activity in order to mislead investors—is fully consistent with the fundamental purpose of the 1934 Act "to substitute a philosophy of full disclosure for the philosophy of caveat emptor. . . ." . . . Indeed, nondisclosure is usually essential to the success of a manipulative scheme. . . . No doubt Congress meant to prohibit the full range of ingenious devices that might be used to manipulate securities prices. But we do not think it would have chosen this "term of art" if it had meant to bring within the scope of §10(b) instances of corporate mismanagement such as this, in which the essence of the complaint is that shareholders were treated unfairly by a fiduciary. (Santa Fe Industries, Inc. v. Green, 430 U.S. 462, 476-477 (1977).)

The meaning the Court has given the term "manipulative" is consistent with the use of the term at common law,[4] and with its traditional dictionary definition.[5]

She argues, however, that the term "manipulative" takes on a meaning in §14(e) that is different from the meaning it has in §10(b). Petitioner claims that the use of the disjunctive "or" in §14(e) implies that acts need not be deceptive or fraudulent to be manipulative. But Congress used the phrase "manipulative or deceptive" in §10(b) as well, and we have interpreted "manipulative" in that context to require misrepresentation.[6] Moreover, it is a " 'familiar principle of statutory construction that words grouped in a list should be given related meaning.' " Securities Indus. Assn. v. Board of Governors, 468 U.S. 207, 218 (1984). All three species of misconduct, i.e., "fraudulent, deceptive or manipulative," listed by Congress are directed at failures to disclose. The use of the term "manipulative" provides emphasis and guidance to those who must determine which types of acts are reached by the statute; it does not suggest a deviation from the section's facial and primary concern with disclosure or Congressional concern with disclosure which is the core of the Act.

B

Our conclusion that "manipulative" acts under §14(e) require misrepresentation or nondisclosure is buttressed by the purpose and legislative history of the provision. Section 14(e) was originally added to the Securities Exchange Act as part of the Williams Act, 82 Stat. 457. "The purpose of the Williams Act is to insure that public shareholders who are confronted by a cash tender offer for their stock will not be required to respond without adequate information." Rondeau v. Mosinee Paper Corp., 422 U.S. 49, 58 (1975).

---

4. See generally, L. Loss, Securities Regulation 984-989 (3d ed. 1983). For example, the seminal English case of Scott v. Brown, Doering, McNab & Co., [1982] 2 Q.B. 724, 724 (C.A.), which broke new ground in recognizing that manipulation could occur without the dissemination of false statements, nonetheless placed emphasis on the presence of deception. As Lord Lopes stated in that case, "I can see no substantial distinction between false rumors and false and fictitious acts." Id., at 730. See also, United States v. Brown, 5 F. Supp. 81, 85 (S.D.N.Y. 1933) ("[E]ven a speculator is entitled not to have any present fact involving the subject matter of his speculative purchase or the price thereof misrepresented by word or act").

5. See Webster's Third New International Dictionary 1376 (1971); (Manipulation is "management with use of unfair, scheming, or underhanded methods.").

6. Santa Fe Industries, Inc. v. Green, 430 U.S. 462, 476-477 (1977); Piper v. Chris-Craft Industries, 430 U.S. 1, 43 (1977); Ernst & Ernst v. Hochfelder, 425 U.S. 185, 199 (1976).

It is clear that Congress relied primarily on disclosure to implement the purpose of the Williams Act. Senator Williams, the bill's Senate sponsor, stated in the debate:

> Today, the public shareholder in deciding whether to accept or reject a tender offer possesses limited information. No matter what he does, he acts without adequate knowledge to enable him to decide rationally what is the best course of action. This is precisely the dilemma which our securities laws are designed to prevent. (113 Cong. Rec. 24664 (1967).)

The expressed legislative intent was to preserve a neutral setting in which the contenders could fully present their arguments.[8] The Senate sponsor went on to say:

> We have taken extreme care to avoid tipping the scales either in favor of management or in favor of the person making the takeover bids. S. 510 is designed solely to require full and fair disclosure for the benefit of investors. The bill will at the same time provide the offeror and management equal opportunity to present their case. (Ibid.)

To implement this objective, the Williams Act added §§13(d), 13(e), 14(d), 14(e), and 14(f) to the Securities Exchange Act. Some relate to disclosure; §§13(d), 14(d) and 14(f) all add specific registration and disclosure provisions. Others—§§13(e) and 14(d)—require or prohibit certain acts so that investors will possess additional time within which to take advantage of the disclosed information.

Section 14(e) adds a "broad antifraud prohibition," Piper v. Chris-Craft Industries, Inc., 430 U.S. 1, 24 (1977), modeled on the antifraud provisions of §10(b) of the Act and Rule 10b-5, 17 C.F.R. §240.10b-5 (1984). It supplements the more precise disclosure provisions found elsewhere in the Williams Act, while requiring disclosure more explicitly addressed to the tender offer context than that required by §10(b).

While legislative history specifically concerning §14(e) is sparse, the House and Senate Reports discuss the role of §14(e). Describing §14(e) as regulating "fraudulent transactions," and stating the thrust of the section:

> This provision would affirm the fact that persons engaged in making or opposing tender offers or otherwise seeking to influence the decision of investors or the outcome of the tender offer are under an obligation to make *full disclosure* of material information to those with whom they deal. (H.R. Rep. No. 1711, 90th Cong., 2d Sess., 11 (1968) (emphasis added); S. Rep. No. 550, 90th Cong., 1st Sess., 11 (1967) (emphasis added).)

Nowhere in the legislative history is there the slightest suggestion that §14(e) serves any purpose other than disclosure, or that the term "manipulative" should be read as

---

8. The process through which Congress developed the Williams Act also suggests a calculated reliance on disclosure, rather than court-imposed principles of "fairness" or "artificiality," as the preferred method of market regulation. For example, as the bill progressed through hearings, both Houses of Congress became concerned that corporate stock repurchases could be used to distort the market for corporate control. Congress addressed this problem with §13(e), which imposes specific disclosure duties on corporations purchasing stock and grants broad regulatory power to the Securities and Exchange Commission to regulate such repurchases. Congress stopped short, however, of imposing specific substantive requirements forbidding corporations to trade in their own stock for the purpose of maintaining its price. The specific regulatory scheme set forth in §13(e) would be unnecessary if Congress at the same time had endowed the term "manipulative" in §14(e) with broad substantive significance.

an invitation to the courts to oversee the substantive fairness of tender offers; the quality of any offer is a matter for the marketplace.

To adopt the reading of the term "manipulative" urged by petitioner would not only be unwarranted in light of the legislative purpose but would be at odds with it. Inviting judges to read the term "manipulative" with their own sense of what constitutes "unfair" or "artificial" conduct would inject uncertainty into the tender offer process. An essential piece of information—whether the court would deem the fully disclosed actions of one side or the other to be "manipulative"—would not be available until after the tender offer had closed. This uncertainty would directly contradict the expressed congressional desire to give investors full information.

Congress' consistent emphasis on disclosure persuades us that it intended takeover contests to be addressed to shareholders. In pursuit of this goal, Congress, consistent with the core mechanism of the Securities Exchange Act, created sweeping disclosure requirements and narrow substantive safeguards. The same Congress that placed such emphasis on shareholder choice would not at the same time have required judges to oversee tender offers for substantive fairness. It is even less likely that a Congress implementing that intention would express it only through the use of a single word placed in the middle of a provision otherwise devoted to disclosure.

C

We hold that the term "manipulative" as used in §14(e) requires misrepresentation or nondisclosure. It connotes "conduct designed to deceive or defraud investors by controlling or artificially affecting the price of securities." Ernst & Ernst v. Hochfelder, 425 U.S., at 199. Without misrepresentation or nondisclosure, §14(e) has not been violated.

Applying that definition to this case, we hold that the actions of respondents were not manipulative. The amended complaint fails to allege that the cancellation of the first tender offer was accompanied by any misrepresentation, nondisclosure or deception. The District Court correctly found, "All activity of the defendants that could have conceivably affected the price of El Paso shares was done openly." . . .

NOTE: DUTY TO DISCLOSE CORPORATE MISMANAGEMENT

Since §14(e) is an antifraud provision similar to Rule 10b-5, the allegation that failure to disclose corporate mismanagement is fraud actionable under §14(e) raises questions similar to those discussed in Santa Fe Indus., Inc. v. Green and Goldberg v. Meridor in Chapter 10. Note that §14(e)'s prohibition could be broader than §10(b)'s because of the inclusion of fraudulent acts as well as deceptive or manipulative acts. Chief Justice Burger suggests little sympathy for this argument without deciding it directly. We return to this issue in Chapter 12 as to the reach of the insider trading prohibitions under §14(e). See United States v. O'Hagan in Chapter 12.

Justice Winter, writing for a Second Circuit panel in Field v. Trump (excerpted earlier in this chapter) found the §14(e) issue in that case parallel to questions raised under §10(b):

> [A]s *Schreiber*'s reliance on *Santa Fe* suggests, the policy against overriding state corporate law absent a clear indication of contrary congressional intent applies with equal force to §14(e).

850 F.2d 938, 947 (2d Cir. 1988). Judge Winter then offered this summary of case law:

> We believe the following line to be drawn by our cases. Allegations that a defendant failed to disclose facts material only to support an action for breach of state-law fiduciary duties ordinarily do not state a claim under the federal securities laws. Certainly this is true of allegations of garden-variety mismanagement, such as managers failing to "maximiz[e] value for . . . shareholders," of directors failing "to adequately inform themselves," or of managers acting in a generally self-entrenching fashion. But where the remedy of an injunction is needed (and is available under state law) to prevent irreparable injury to the company from willful misconduct of a self-serving nature, disclosure of facts necessary to make other statements not misleading is required where the misleading statements will lull shareholders into forgoing the injunctive remedy.

850 F.2d at 948.

How much room do you think that leaves for federal action where there is corporate mismanagement?

B.   Intersection of Federal Regulation and State Anti-Takeover Statutes

U.S. Constitution art. I, §8, cl. 3
Securities Exchange Act of 1934 §28(a)

The various types of takeover statutes currently found in state law are described in Chapter 9 at pages 939-942. As that material states, a "first generation" state anti-takeover statute was declared unconstitutional by the Supreme Court in Edgar v. MITE Corp., 457 U.S. 624 (1982), as an indirect regulation of interstate commerce. Another part of the opinion, joined only by a plurality of the court, said an Illinois statute upset the balance between bidders and target managers and was preempted by the Williams Act. In response to *MITE,* state legislators took a different tack to slow down takeovers and sought to bring takeover regulation within the area of traditional state regulation of corporations. One method, a control share acquisition statute, permits a collective decision by target shareholders before a hostile change of control much like the shareholder approval that already occurs in a friendly change of control accomplished via a merger. The Supreme Court sustained such a statute against both preemption and interstate commerce challenges in CTS Corp. v. Dynamics Corp. of America, 481 U.S. 69 (1987). Still another approach, the business combination/moratorium statute, discussed in the case that follows, regulates corporate transactions occurring after a tender offer.

Amanda Acquisition Corp. v. Universal Foods Corp.
United States Court of Appeals, Seventh Circuit, 1989
877 F.2d 496, cert. denied, 493 U.S. 955 (1989)

EASTERBROOK, CIRCUIT JUDGE.

States have enacted three generations of takeover statutes in the last 20 years. . . .

Wisconsin has a third-generation takeover statute. Enacted after *CTS*, it postpones the kinds of transactions that often follow tender offers (and often are the reason for making the offers in the first place). Unless the target's board agrees to the transaction in advance, the bidder must wait three years after buying the shares to merge with the target or acquire more than 5% of its assets. We must decide whether this is consistent with the Williams Act and Commerce Clause.

I

Amanda Acquisition Corporation is a shell with a single purpose: to acquire Universal Foods Corporation, a diversified firm incorporated in Wisconsin and traded on the New York Stock Exchange. Universal is covered by Wisconsin's anti-takeover law. Amanda is a subsidiary of High Voltage Engineering Corp., a small electronics firm in Massachusetts. Most of High Voltage's equity capital comes from Berisford Capital PLC, a British venture capital firm, and Hyde Park Partners L.P., a partnership affiliated with the principals of Berisford. Chase Manhattan Bank has promised to lend Amanda 50% of the cost of the acquisition, secured by the stock of Universal.

In mid-November 1988 Universal's stock was trading for about $25 per share. On December 1 Amanda commenced a tender offer at $30.50, to be effective if at least 75% of the stock should be tendered.[1] This all-cash, all-shares offer has been increased by stages to $38.00. Amanda's financing is contingent on a prompt merger with Universal if the offer succeeds, so the offer is conditional on a judicial declaration that the law is invalid. . . .

No firm incorporated in Wisconsin and having its headquarters, substantial operations, or 10% of its shares or shareholders there may "engage in a business combination with an interested stockholder . . . for 3 years after the interested stockholder's stock acquisition date unless the board of directors of the [Wisconsin] corporation has approved, before the interested stockholder's stock acquisition date, that business combination or the purchase of stock," Wis. Stat. §180.726(2). An "interested stockholder" is one owning 10% of the voting stock, directly or through associates (anyone acting in concert with it), §180.726(1)(e). A "business combination" is a merger with the bidder or any of its affiliates, sale of more than 5% of the assets to bidder or affiliate, liquidation of the target, or a transaction by which the target guarantees the bidder's or affiliates debts or passes tax benefits to the bidder or affiliate, §180.726(1)(e). The law, in other words, provides for almost hermetic separation of bidder and target

---

1. Wisconsin has, in addition to §180.726, a statute modeled on Indiana's, providing that an acquiring firm's shares lose their votes, which may be restored under specified circumstances. Wis. Stat. §180.25(9). That law accounts for the 75% condition, but it is not pertinent to the questions we resolve.

for three years after the bidder obtains 10% of the stock—unless the target's board consented before then. No matter how popular the offer, the ban applies: obtaining 85% (even 100%) of the stock held by non-management shareholders won't allow the bidder to engage in a business combination, as it would under Delaware law. Wisconsin firms cannot opt out of the law, as may corporations subject to almost all other state takeover statutes. In Wisconsin it is management's approval in advance, or wait three years. Even when the time is up, the bidder needs the approval of a majority of the remaining investors, without any provision disqualifying shares still held by the managers who resisted the transaction, §180.726(3)(b).[3] The district court found that this statute "effectively eliminates hostile leveraged buyouts." As a practical matter, Wisconsin prohibits any offer contingent on a merger between bidder and target, a condition attached to about 90% of contemporary tender offers. . . .

II . . .

A

If our views of the wisdom of state law mattered, Wisconsin's takeover statute would not survive. Like our colleagues who decided *MITE* and *CTS,* we believe that antitakeover legislation injures shareholders. [This portion of the court's opinion appears in Chapter 9, page 942.]

B

Skepticism about the wisdom of a state's law does not lead to the conclusion that the law is beyond the state's power, however. We have not been elected custodians of investors' wealth. States need not treat investors' welfare as their summum bonum. Perhaps they choose to protect managers' welfare instead, or believe that the current economic literature reaches an incorrect conclusion and that despite appearances takeovers injure investors in the long run. Unless a federal statute or the Constitution bars the way, Wisconsin's choice must be respected.

Amanda relies on the Williams Act of 1968, incorporated into §§13(d), (e) and 14(d)-(f) of the Securities Exchange Act of 1934, 15 U.S.C. §§78m(d), (e), 78n(d)-(f). The Williams Act regulates the conduct of tender offers. Amanda believes that Congress created an entitlement for investors to receive the benefit of tender offers, and that because Wisconsin's law makes tender offers unattractive to many potential bidders, it is preempted. See *MITE,* 633 F.2d at 490-99, and Justice White's views, 457 U.S. at 630-640. . . .

There is a big difference between what Congress *enacts* and what it *supposes* will ensue. Expectations about the consequences of a law are not themselves law. To say that Congress wanted to be neutral between bidder and target—a conclusion reached

---

3. Acquirors can avoid this requirement by buying out the remaining shareholders at a price defined by §180.726(3)(c), but this is not a practical option.

in many of the Court's opinions, e.g., Piper v. Chris-Craft Industries, Inc., 430 U.S. 1 (1977) — is not to say that it also forbade the states to favor one of these sides. Every law has a stopping point, likely one selected because of a belief that it would be unwise (for now, maybe forever) to do more. Nothing in the Williams Act says that the federal compromise among bidders, targets' managers, and investors is the only permissible one. See Daniel R. Fischel, From *MITE* to *CTS:* State Anti-Takeover Statutes, the Williams Act, the Commerce Clause, and Insider Trading, 1987 Sup. Ct. Rev. 47, 71-74. Like the majority of the Court in *CTS,* however, we stop short of the precipice.

The Williams Act regulates the *process* of tender offers: timing, disclosure, proration if tenders exceed what the bidder is willing to buy, best-price rules. It slows things down, allowing investors to evaluate the offer and management's response. Best-price, proration, and short-tender rules ensure that investors who decide at the end of the offer get the same treatment as those who decide immediately, reducing pressure to leap before looking. After complying with the disclosure and delay requirements, the bidder is free to take the shares. *MITE* held invalid a state law that increased the delay and, by authorizing a regulator to nix the offer, created a distinct possibility that the bidder would be unable to buy the stock (and the holders to sell it) despite compliance with federal law. Illinois tried to regulate the process of tender offers, contradicting in some respects the federal rules. Indiana, by contrast, allowed the tender offer to take its course as the Williams Act specified but "sterilized" the acquired shares until the remaining investors restored their voting rights. Congress said nothing about the voting power of shares acquired in tender offers. Indiana's law reduced the benefits the bidder anticipated from the acquisition but left the process alone. So the Court, although accepting Justice White's views for the purpose of argument, held that Indiana's rules do not conflict with the federal norms.

CTS observed that laws affecting the voting power of acquired shares do not differ in principle from many other rules governing the internal affairs of corporations. Laws requiring staggered or classified boards of directors delay the transfer of control to the bidder; laws requiring supermajority vote for a merger may make a transaction less attractive or impossible. Yet these are not preempted by the Williams Act, any more than state laws concerning the *effect* of investors' votes are preempted by the portions of the Exchange Act, 15 U.S.C. §78n(a)-(c), regulating the process of soliciting proxies. Federal securities laws frequently regulate process while state corporate law regulates substance. Federal proxy rules demand that firms disclose many things, in order to promote informed voting. Yet states may permit or compel a supermajority rule (even a unanimity rule) rendering it all but impossible for a particular side to prevail in the voting. See Robert Charles Clark, Corporate Law §9.1.3 (1986). Are the state laws therefore preempted? How about state laws that allow many firms to organize without traded shares? Universities, hospitals, and other charities have self-perpetuating boards and cannot be acquired by tender offer. Insurance companies may be organized as mutuals, without traded shares; retailers often organize as cooperatives, without traded stock; some decently large companies (large enough to be "reporting companies" under the '34 Act) issue stock subject to buy-sell agreements under which the investors cannot sell to strangers without offering stock to the firm at a formula price; Ford Motor Co. issued non-voting stock to outside investors while reserving voting stock for the family, thus preventing outsiders from gaining control (dual-class stock is becoming more common); firms issue and state law enforces poison pills. All of these devices make tender offers unattractive (even impossible) and greatly diminish the power of proxy fights, success in which often depends on buying votes by acquiring the equity to which the vote is attached. See Douglas H. Blair, Devra L. Golbe & James M. Gerard, Unbundling the Voting Rights and Profit Claims of Common Shares, 97 J. Pol. Econ. 420 (1989). None of these devices could be thought preempted by the Williams Act or the proxy rules. If they are not preempted, neither is Wis. Stat. §180.726.

Any bidder complying with federal law is free to acquire shares of Wisconsin firms on schedule. Delay in completing a second-stage merger may make the target less attractive, and thus depress the price offered or even lead to an absence of bids; it does not, however, alter any of the procedures governed by federal regulation. Indeed Wisconsin's law does not depend in any way on how the acquiring firm came by its stock: open-market purchases, private acquisitions of blocs, and acquisitions via tender offers are treated identically. Wisconsin's law is no different in effect from one saying that for the three years after a person acquires 10% of a firm's stock, a unanimous vote is required to merge. Corporate law once had a generally-applicable unanimity rule in major transactions, a rule discarded because giving every investor the power to block every reorganization stopped many desirable changes. (Many investors could use their "hold-up" power to try to engross a larger portion of the gains, creating a complex bargaining problem that often could not be solved.) Wisconsin's more restrained version of unanimity also may block beneficial transactions, but not by tinkering with any of the procedures established in federal law.

Only if the Williams Act gives investors a right to be the beneficiary of offers could Wisconsin's law run afoul of the federal rule. No such entitlement can be mined out of the Williams Act, however. Schreiber v. Burlington Northern, Inc., 472 U.S. 1 (1985), holds that the cancellation of a pending offer because of machinations between bidder and target does not deprive investors of their due under the Williams Act. The Court treated §14(e) as a disclosure law, so that investors could make informed decisions; it follows that events leading bidders to cease their quest do not conflict with the Williams Act any more than a state law leading a firm not to issue new securities could conflict with the Securities Act of 1933. See also Panter v. Marshall Field & Co., 646 F.2d 271, 283-85 (7th Cir. 1981); Lewis v. McGraw, 619 F.2d 192 (2d Cir. 1980), both holding that the evaporation of an opportunity to tender one's shares when a defensive tactic leads the bidder to withdraw the invitation does not violate the Williams Act. Investors have no right to receive tender offers. More to the point — since Amanda sues as bidder rather than as investor seeking to sell — the Williams Act does not create a right to profit from the business of making tender offers. It is not attractive to put bids on the table for Wisconsin corporations, but because Wisconsin leaves the process alone once a bidder appears, its law may co-exist with the Williams Act.

C

The Commerce Clause, Art. I, §8, cl. 3 of the Constitution, grants Congress the power "[to] regulate Commerce . . . among the several States." . . .

Illinois's law, held invalid in *MITE*, regulated sales of stock elsewhere. Illinois tried to tell a Texas owner of stock in a Delaware corporation that he could not sell to a buyer in California. By contrast, Wisconsin's law, like the Indiana statute sustained by *CTS*, regulates the internal affairs of firms incorporated there. Investors may buy or sell stock as they please. . . .

Buyers of stock in Wisconsin firms may exercise full rights as investors, taking immediate control. No interstate transaction is regulated or forbidden. True, Wisconsin's law makes a potential buyer less willing to buy (or depresses the bid), but this is equally true of Indiana's rule. Many other rules of corporate law—supermajority voting requirements, staggered and classified boards, and so on—have similar or greater effects on some person's willingness to purchase stock. *CTS*, 481 U.S. at 89-90. States could ban mergers outright, with even more powerful consequences. Louisville & Nashville R.R. v. Kentucky, 161 U.S. 677, 701-04 (1896); see also Kansas City, Memphis & Birmingham R.R. v. Stiles, 242 U.S. 111, 117 (1916); Ashley v. Ryan, 153 U.S. 436, 443 (1894). Wisconsin did not allow mergers among firms chartered there until 1947. We doubt that it was violating the Commerce Clause all those years. Cf. Edmund W. Kitch, Regulation and the American Common Market, in Regulation, Federalism, and Interstate Commerce 7 (A. Dan Tarlock ed. 1981). Every rule of corporate law affects investors who live outside the state of incorporation, yet this has never been thought sufficient to authorize a form of cost-benefit inquiry through the medium of the Commerce Clause.

Wisconsin, like Indiana, is indifferent to the domicile of the bidder. A putative bidder located in Wisconsin enjoys no privilege over a firm located in New York. So too with investors: all are treated identically, regardless of residence. Doubtless most bidders (and investors) are located outside Wisconsin, but unless the law discriminates according to residence this alone does not matter. *CTS*, 481 U.S. at 87-88; Lewis v. BT Investment Managers, Inc., 447 U.S. 27, 36-37 (1980); Exxon Corp. v. Governor of Maryland, 437 U.S. 177 (1978). Every state's regulation of domestic trade (potentially) affects those who live elsewhere but wish to sell their wares within the state. A law making suppliers of drugs absolutely liable for defects will affect the conduct (and wealth) of Eli Lilly & Co., an Indiana firm, and the many other pharmaceutical houses, all located in other states, yet Wisconsin has no less power to set and change tort law than do states with domestic drug manufacturers. "Because nothing in the [Wisconsin] Act imposes a greater burden on out-of-state offerors than it does on similarly situated [Wisconsin] offerors, we reject the contention that the Act discriminates against interstate commerce." *CTS*, 481 U.S. at 88. For the same reason, the Court long ago held that state blue sky laws comport with the Commerce Clause. Hall v. Geiger-Jones Co., 242 U.S. 539 (1917); Caldwell v. Sioux Falls Stock Yards Co., 242 U.S. 559 (1917); Merrick v. N.W. Halsey & Co., 242 U.S. 568 (1917). Blue sky laws may bar Texans from selling stock in Wisconsin, but they apply equally to local residents' attempts to sell. That their application blocks a form of commerce altogether does not strip the states of power.

Wisconsin could exceed its powers by subjecting firms to inconsistent regulation. Because §180.726 applies only to a subset of firms incorporated in Wisconsin, however, there is no possibility of inconsistent regulation. Here, too, the Wisconsin law is materially identical to Indiana's. This leaves only the argument that Wisconsin's law hinders the flow of interstate trade "too much." *CTS* dispatched this concern by declaring it inapplicable to laws that apply only to the internal affairs of firms incorporated in the regulating state. States may regulate corporate transactions as they choose without having to demonstrate under an unfocused balancing test that the benefits are "enough" to justify the consequences.

To say that states have the power to enact laws whose costs exceed their benefits is not to say that investors should kiss their wallets goodbye. States compete to offer corporate codes attractive to firms. Managers who want to raise money incorporate their firms in the states that offer the combination of rules investors prefer. Ralph K. Winter, Jr., State Law, Shareholder Protection, and the Theory of the Corporation, 6 J. Legal Studies 251 (1977); Fischel, supra, 1987 Sup. Ct. Rev. at 74-84. Laws that in the short run injure investors and protect managers will in the longer run make the state less attractive to firms that need to raise new capital. If the law is "protectionist," the protected class is the existing body of managers (and other workers), suppliers, and so on, which bears no necessary relation to state boundaries. States regulating the affairs of domestic corporations cannot in the long run injure anyone but themselves. Professor Fischel makes the point, 1987 Sup. Ct. Rev. at 84:

> In the short run, states can enact welfare-decreasing legislation that imposes costs on residents of other states. State anti-takeover statutes . . . may be paradigm examples of cost-exporting legislation that is enacted in response to lobbying pressure by in-state constituents. [The managers who gain from the law live in-state; the investors who lose may live elsewhere.] In the long run, however, states have no ability to export costs to non-resident investors. When entrepreneurs want to raise capital for a corporate venture, they must decide where to incorporate. The choice of where to incorporate in turn affects the price investors are willing to pay for shares. And because shares of stock have many perfect substitutes which offer the same risk-return combinations, it is impossible for the entrepreneur to pass on the effects of the law to investors. . . . Nor can a state export costs to the founding entrepreneur since corporations can be incorporated anywhere, regardless of the firm's physical location. States that enact laws that are harmful to investors will cause entrepreneurs to incorporate elsewhere.

The long run takes time to arrive, and it is tempting to suppose that courts could contribute to investors' welfare by eliminating laws that impose costs in the short run. See Gregg A. Jarrell, State Anti-Takeover Laws and the Efficient Allocation of Corporate Control: An Economic Analysis of Edgar v. MITE Corp., 2 Sup. Ct. Econ. Rev. 111 (1983). The price of such warfare, however, is a reduction in the power of competition among states. Courts seeking to impose "good" rules on the states diminish the differences among corporate codes and dampen competitive forces. Too, courts may fail in their quest. How do judges know which rules are best? Often only the slow forces of competition reveal that information. Early economic studies may mislead, or judges (not trained as social scientists) may misinterpret the available data or act precipitously. Our Constitution allows the states to act as laboratories; slow migration (or national law on the authority of the Commerce Clause) grinds the failures under. No such process weeds out judicial errors, or decisions that, although astute when rendered, have become anachronistic in light of changes in the economy. Judges must hesitate for these practical reasons—and not only because of limits on their constitutional competence—before trying to "perfect" corporate codes.

The three district judges who have considered and sustained Delaware's law delaying mergers did so in large measure because they believed that the law left hostile offers "a meaningful opportunity for success." BNS, Inc. v. Koppers Co., [683 F. Supp. 458, 469 (D. Del. 1988)]. See also [RP Acquisition Corp. v. Staley Continental Inc., 686 F. Supp. 476, 482-484, 488 (D. Del. 1988); City Capital Associates L.P. v. Interco, Inc., 696 F. Supp. 1551, 1555 (D. Del. 1988)]. Delaware allows a merger to occur forthwith if the bidder obtains 85% of the shares other than those held by management and employee stock plans. If the bid is attractive to the bulk of the unaffiliated investors, it succeeds. Wisconsin offers no such opportunity, which Amanda believes is fatal.

Even in Wisconsin, though, options remain. Defenses impenetrable to the naked eye may have cracks. Poison pills are less fatal in practice than in name (some have been swallowed willingly), and corporate law contains self-defense mechanisms. Investors concerned about stock-watering often arranged for firms to issue pre-emptive rights, entitlements for existing investors to buy stock at the same price offered to newcomers (often before the newcomers had a chance to buy in). Poison pills are dilution devices, and so pre-emptive rights ought to be handy countermeasures.[11] So too there are countermeasures to statutes deferring mergers. The cheapest is to lower the bid to reflect the costs of delay. Because every potential bidder labors under the same drawback, the firm placing the highest value on the target still should win. Or a bidder might take down the stock and pledge it (or its dividends) as security for any loans. That is, the bidder could operate the target as a subsidiary for three years. The corporate world is full of partially owned subsidiaries. If there is gain to be had from changing the debt-equity ratio of the target, that can be done consistent with Wisconsin law. The prospect of being locked into place as holders of illiquid minority positions would cause many persons to sell out, and the threat of being locked in would cause many managers to give assent in advance, as Wisconsin allows. (Or bidders might demand that directors waive the protections of state law, just as Amanda believes that the directors' fiduciary duties compel them to redeem the poison pill rights.) Many bidders would find lock-in unattractive because of the potential for litigation by minority investors, and the need to operate the firm as a subsidiary might foreclose savings or synergies from merger. So none of these options is a perfect substitute for immediate merger, but each is a crack in the defensive wall allowing some value-increasing bids to proceed.

At the end of the day, however, it does not matter whether these countermeasures are "enough." The Commerce Clause does not demand that states leave bidders a "meaningful opportunity for success." Maryland enacted a law that absolutely banned vertical integration in the oil business. No opportunities, "meaningful" or otherwise, remained to firms wanting to own retail outlets. Exxon Corp. v. Governor of Maryland held that the law is consistent with the Commerce Clause, even on the assumption that it injures consumers and investors alike. A state with the power to forbid mergers

---

11. Imagine a series of Antidote rights, issued by would-be bidding firms, that detach if anyone exercises flip-over rights to purchase the bidder's stock at a discount. Antidote rights would entitle the bidder's investors, *other than those who exercise flip-over rights,* to purchase the bidder's stock at the same discount available to investors exercising flip-over rights. Antidotes for flip-in rights also could be issued. In general, whenever one firm can issue rights allowing the purchase of cheap stock, another firm can issue the equivalent series of contingent preemptive rights that offsets the dilution.

has the power to defer them for three years. Investors can turn to firms incorporated
in states committed to the dominance of market forces, or they can turn on legislators who enact unwise laws. The Constitution has room for many economic policies. "[A] law can be both economic folly and constitutional." *CTS*, 481 U.S. at 96-97
(Scalia, J., concurring). Wisconsin's law may well be folly; we are confident that it is
constitutional. . . .

NOTES AND QUESTIONS

1. Several federal district courts in Delaware (cited in the case above) upheld the
constitutionality of the Delaware statute. In upholding the statute against a claim that
it must yield to the federal law in this area, the courts noted that the state laws permitted a "meaningful opportunity for success." Judge Easterbrook in the case above moves
that reasoning to the commerce clause part of the case, but finds that the commerce
clause does not demand such an opportunity. How does this "meaningful opportunity
for success" compare to the space that must be left for shareholders under the *Unocal*
test applied in Chapter 9?

2. If Congress wanted to be neutral between bidder and target (see, e.g., Piper v.
Chris-Craft Industries, Inc., 430 U.S. 1 (1977)), do you think it contemplated states
trumping this neutrality by favoring target management over bidders? Is this another
way of asking why Congress protected shareholder voting if those votes were disem-
powered by management's use of discretion given by state law (see Chapter 10 at pages
978 and 1008)?

12 *Insider Trading*

A.   *The Common Law Foundation for Rule 10b-5*

Rule 10b-5, promulgated by the Securities and Exchange Commission pursuant to §10(b) of the Securities Exchange Act of 1934, is the primary regulator of insider trading today, but it is not the only legal source on this topic. Note that no specific reference to insider trading appears in the statute or the rule. Courts have construed a "deceptive device" and "fraud" as proscribed by the statute and rule to include insider trading in some circumstances, and those circumstances have changed over time.

Prior to Rule 10b-5 being adapted to the purpose of regulating insider trading, both federal statutes and the common law addressed this issue. Section 16(b) of the Securities Exchange Act of 1934 specifically regulates insider trading by requiring officers, directors, and 10 percent shareholders to disgorge any profits made on a purchase and sale during a six-month period. In addition, the common law in the various states has been interpreted to prohibit insider trading, although the law is not uniform. In the early part of the twentieth century, the "majority rule" held that directors purchasing stock from shareholders had no fiduciary duty to the shareholders. See Goodwin v. Agassiz, 283 Mass. 358, 186 N.E. 659 (1933) (in the context of a transaction on a stock exchange). A "minority rule" applied by some courts held that "a director negotiating with a shareholder for purchase of shares acts in a relation of scrupulous trust and confidence. . . . [S]uch transactions must be subjected to the closest scrutiny, and unless conducted with utmost fairness, the wronged shareholders may invoke proper remedy." Hotchkiss v. Fischer, 136 Kan. 530, 16 P.2d 531 (1932) (in the context of a face-to-face transaction).

Other decisions were interpreted as applying a "special facts doctrine": The ordinary relationship between a director and shareholder does not require disclosure of knowledge a director may possess, but, by reason of special facts, such duty exists. Strong v. Repide, 213 U.S. 419 (1909). In that case the majority shareholder was conducting negotiations to sell certain real estate owned by the corporation to the Philippine government. At the time of the defendant majority shareholder's purchase of shares from the plaintiff shareholder, a formal offer to purchase the assets had been made, but the majority shareholder was holding out for more money for the corporation. After purchase of the stock as described below, the real estate was sold to the

Philippine government and the shares were then worth about ten times the purchase price paid by the majority shareholder. The Court said:

> While this state of things existed, and before the final offer had been made by the governor, the defendant, although still holding out for a higher price for the lands, took steps, about the middle or latter part of September, 1903, to purchase the 800 shares of stock in his company owned by Mrs. Strong, which he knew were in the possession of F. Stuart Jones, as her agent. The defendant, having decided to obtain these shares, instead of seeing Jones, who had an office next door, employed one Kauffman, a connection of his by marriage, and Kauffman employed a Mr. Sloan, a broker, who had an office some distance away, to purchase the stock for him, and told Sloan that the stock was for a member of his wife's family. Sloan communicated with the husband of Mrs. Strong, and asked if she desired to sell her stock. The husband referred him to Mr. Jones for consultation, who had the stock in his possession. Sloan did not know who wanted to buy the shares, nor did Jones when he was spoken to. Jones would not have sold at the price he did had he known it was the defendant who was purchasing, because, as he said, it would show increased value, as the defendant would not be likely to purchase more stock unless the price was going up. As the articles of incorporation, by subdivision 20, required a resolution of the general meeting of stockholders for the purpose of selling more than one hacienda, and as no such general meeting had been called at the time of the sale of the stock, Mr. Jones might well have supposed there was no immediate prospect of a sale of the lands being made, while, at the same time, defendant had knowledge of the probabilities thereof, which he had acquired by his conduct of the negotiations for their sale, as agent of all the shareholders, and while acting specially for them and himself.

213 U.S. at 425-426.

An alternative common law approach has focused on fiduciary duty of trustees and agents owed to the corporation and the unjust enrichment of the insider. In Diamond v. Oreamuno, 24 N.Y.2d 494, 248 N.E.2d 910, 301 N.Y.S.2d 78 (1969), a shareholder challenged sales by insiders prior to the corporation's announcement of a sharp increase in charges from its principal supplier that led to a 75 percent decrease in earnings. After the disclosure of the information, the value of the corporation's stock immediately fell from $28 (the price at which defendants sold 56,500 shares) to $11. The court said:

> It is well established, as a general proposition, that a person who acquires special knowledge or information by virtue of a confidential or fiduciary relationship with another is not free to exploit that knowledge or information for his own personal benefit but must account to his principal for any profits derived therefrom. This, in turn, is merely a corollary of the broader principle, inherent in the nature of the fiduciary relationship, that prohibits a trustee or agent from extracting secret profits from his position of trust.
>
> In support of their claim that the complaint fails to state a cause of action, the defendants take the position that, although it is admittedly wrong for an officer or director to use his position to obtain trading profits for himself in the stock of his corporation, the action ascribed to them did not injure or damage [the corporation] in any way. Accordingly, the defendants continue, the corporation should not be permitted to recover the proceeds. They acknowledge that, by virtue of the exclusive access which officers and directors have to inside information, they possess an unfair advantage over other shareholders and, particularly, the persons who had purchased the stock from them but, they contend, the corporation itself was unaffected and, for that reason, a derivative action is an inappropriate remedy.
>
> It is true that the complaint before us does not contain any allegation of damages to the corporation but this has never been considered to be an essential requirement for a cause of action founded on a breach of fiduciary duty. This is because the function of such an action, unlike an ordinary tort or contract case, is not merely to compensate the plaintiff for wrongs committed by

the defendant but, as this court declared many years ago (Dutton v. Willner, 51 N.Y. 312, 319) "to *prevent* them, by removing from agents and trustees all inducement to attempt dealing for their own benefit in matters which they have undertaken for others, or to which their agency or trust relates" (emphasis supplied).

Just as a trustee has no right to retain for himself the profits yielded by property placed in his possession but must account to his beneficiaries, a corporate fiduciary, who is entrusted with potentially valuable information, may not appropriate that asset for his own use even though, in so doing, he causes no injury to the corporation. The primary concern, in a case such as this, is not to determine whether the corporation has been damaged but to decide, as between the corporation and the defendants, who has a higher claim to the proceeds derived from the exploitation of the information. In our opinion, there can be no justification for permitting officers and directors, such as the defendants, to retain for themselves profits which, it is alleged, they derived solely from exploiting information gained by virtue of their inside position as corporate officials.

In addition, it is pertinent to observe that, despite the lack of any specific allegation of damage, it may well be inferred that the defendants' actions might have caused some harm to the enterprise. Although the corporation may have little concern with the day-to-day transactions in its shares, it has a great interest in maintaining a reputation of integrity, an image of probity, for its management and in insuring the continued public acceptance and marketability of its stock. When officers and directors abuse their position in order to gain personal profits, the effect may be to cast a cloud on the corporation's name, injure stockholder relations and undermine public regard for the corporation's securities. As Presiding Justice Botein aptly put it, in the course of his opinion for the Appellate Division, "[t]he prestige and good will of a corporation, so vital to its prosperity, may be undermined by the revelation that its chief officers had been making personal profits out of corporate events which they had not disclosed to the community of stockholders."

The defendants maintain that extending the prohibition against personal exploitation of a fiduciary relationship to officers and directors of a corporation will discourage such officials from maintaining a stake in the success of the corporate venture through share ownership, which, they urge, is an important incentive to proper performance of their duties. There is, however, a considerable difference between corporate officers who assume the same risks and obtain the same benefits as other shareholders and those who use their privileged position to gain special advantages not available to others. The sale of shares by the defendants for the reasons charged was not merely a wise investment decision which any prudent investor might have made. Rather, they were assertedly able in this case to profit solely because they had information which was not available to any one else—including the other shareholders whose interests they, as corporate fiduciaries, were bound to protect.

24 N.Y.2d at 497-499, 248 N.E.2d at 912-913, 301 N.Y.S.2d at 80-82.

The theory of recovery in *Diamond* has received mixed reviews elsewhere. Compare Freeman v. Decio, 584 F.2d 186 (7th Cir. 1978) (concluding that Indiana would not follow New York, citing concern for lack of harm to corporation and possibility of double liability) and In re ORFA Securities Litigation, 654 F. Supp. 1449 (D.N.J. 1987).

Delaware law has recently revisited the *Diamond* issue. In the classic case of Brophy v. Cities Service Co., 70 A.2d 5 (Del. Ch. 1949), the Court of Chancery adopted the approach later taken in *Diamond*. However, in Pfeiffer v. Toll, 987 A.2d 683 (Del. Ch. 2010), Vice Chancellor Laster concluded that harm to the corporation was an essential element in a *Brophy* claim and that disgorgement was a theoretically possible remedy only in limited circumstances. Id. at 699-700. The Delaware Supreme Court rejected this revision and curtailment of *Brophy*.

In the venerable case of Brophy v. Cities Service Co., one of the defendants was an employee who had acquired inside information that the corporate plaintiff was about to enter the market and purchase its own shares. Using this confidential information, the employee, who was not an officer, bought a large block of shares and, after the corporation's purchases had caused the price to rise, resold them at a profit. Because the employee defendant occupied a position of trust and confidence within the plaintiff corporation, the court found his relationship analogous to that of a fiduciary. The employee defendant argued that the plaintiff had failed to state a claim because "it [did] not appear that the corporation suffered any loss through his purchase of its stock." The Court of Chancery expressly rejected that argument, stating that:

> In equity, when the breach of confidential relation by an employee is relied on and an accounting for any resulting profit is sought, loss to the corporation need not be charged in the complaint. . . . Public policy will not permit an employee occupying a position of trust and confidence toward his employer to abuse that relation to his own profit, regardless of whether his employer suffers a loss.

Thus, actual harm to the corporation is not required for a plaintiff to state a claim under *Brophy*. In *Brophy*, the court relied on the principles of restitution and equity, citing the Restatement of the Law of Restitution §200, comment a, for the proposition that a fiduciary cannot use confidential corporate information for his own benefit. As the court recognized in *Brophy*, it is inequitable to permit the fiduciary to profit from using confidential corporate information. Even if the corporation did not suffer actual harm, equity requires disgorgement of that profit.

This Court has cited *Brophy* approvingly when discussing how the duty of loyalty governs the misuse of confidential corporate information by fiduciaries. In In re Oracle Corp. Deriv. Litig., we affirmed the Court of Chancery's articulation of the elements essential for a plaintiff to prevail on a *Brophy* claim. The plaintiff must show that: "1) the corporate fiduciary possessed material, nonpublic company information; and 2) the corporate fiduciary used that information improperly by making trades because she was motivated, in whole or in part, by the substance of that information."

Kahn v. Kolberg Kravis Roberts & Co. L.P., 23 A.2d 831, 837-8 (Del. 2011) (internal citations omitted).

B. Rule 10b-5 as a Regulator of Insider Trading

The first important step in the use of Rule 10b-5 to regulate insider trading was the SEC's 1961 decision In re Cady, Roberts & Co., 40 S.E.C. 907 (1961). The Commission brought an action against the brokerage firm of Cady, Roberts & Company and one of its partners, Gintel, for actions arising out of a directors' meeting of the Curtiss-Wright Corporation at which the directors voted to cut the dividend. One of the directors, who was also an associate of Cady, Roberts, left the meeting after the dividend decision but prior to its public disclosure, which was inadvertently delayed. Gintel learned of the dividend decision from the director and immediately thereafter sold his customers' shares and those in a trust for his children and sold short for his own account.

The Commission held that Gintel violated Rule 10b-5 and announced the principle that a corporate insider who has material nonpublic information about the enterprise is under a duty either to abstain from trading or first to disclose the nonpublic information. In an opinion by Commission Chairman William Cary, the Commission developed the foundation for that obligation:

> Analytically, the obligation rests on two principal elements; first, the existence of a relationship giving access, directly or indirectly, to information intended to be available only for a corporate purpose and not for the personal benefit of anyone, and second, the inherent unfairness involved where a party takes advantage of such information knowing that it is unavailable to those with whom he is dealing.

40 S.E.C. at 912.

In the *Texas Gulf Sulphur* case below, the Second Circuit further refined this duty. The Supreme Court did not address insider trading and Rule 10b-5 until 1980 when its *Chiarella* decision (see page 1117) sent insider trading jurisprudence in a different direction.

1. Classic Insider Trading as Fraud

Securities and Exchange Commission v. Texas Gulf Sulphur Co.

United States Court of Appeals, Second Circuit (en banc), 1968
401 F.2d 833, cert. denied, 404 U.S. 1005 (1971)

WATERMAN, CIRCUIT JUDGE:

This action was commenced in the United States District Court for the Southern District of New York by the Securities and Exchange Commission (the SEC) pursuant to §21(e) of the Securities Exchange Act of 1934 (the Act) against Texas Gulf Sulphur Company (TGS) and several of its officers, directors and employees, to enjoin certain conduct by TGS and the individual defendants said to violate §10(b) of the Act, and Rule 10b-5 (the Rule), promulgated thereunder, and to compel the rescission by the individual defendants of securities transactions assertedly conducted contrary to law. The complaint alleged (1) that defendants Fogarty, Mollison, Darke, Murray, Huntington, O'Neill, Clayton, Crawford, and Coates had either personally or through agents purchased TGS stock or calls thereon from November 12, 1963 through April 16, 1964 on the basis of material inside information concerning the results of TGS drilling in Timmins, Ontario, while such information remained undisclosed to the investing public generally or to the particular sellers; (2) that defendants Darke and Coates had divulged such information to others for use in purchasing TGS stock or calls[3] or recommended its purchase while the information was undisclosed to the public or to the sellers....

THE FACTUAL SETTING

This action derives from the exploratory activities of TGS begun in 1957 on the Canadian Shield in eastern Canada. In March of 1959, aerial geophysical surveys were conducted over more than 15,000 square miles of this area by a group led by defendant Mollison, a mining engineer and a Vice President of TGS. The group included defendant Holyk, TGS's chief geologist, defendant Clayton, an electrical engineer and geophysicist, and defendant Darke, a geologist. These operations resulted in the

---

3. A "call" is a negotiable option contract by which the bearer has the right to buy from the writer of the contract a certain number of shares of a particular stock at a fixed price on or before a certain agreed-upon date.

detection of numerous anomalies, i.e., extraordinary variations in the conductivity of rocks, one of which was on the Kidd 55 segment of land located near Timmins, Ontario.

On October 29 and 30, 1963, Clayton conducted a ground geophysical survey on the northeast portion of the Kidd 55 segment which confirmed the presence of an anomaly and indicated the necessity of diamond core drilling for further evaluation. Drilling of the initial hole, K-55-1, at the strongest part of the anomaly was commenced on November 8 and terminated on November 12 at a depth of 655 feet. Visual estimates by Holyk of the core of K-55-1 . . . convinced TGS that it was desirable to acquire the remainder of the Kidd 55 segment, and in order to facilitate this acquisition TGS President Stephens instructed the exploration group to keep the results of K-55-1 confidential and undisclosed even as to other officers, directors, and employees of TGS. The hole was concealed and a barren core was intentionally drilled off the anomaly. Meanwhile, the core of K-55-1 had been shipped to Utah for chemical assay which, when received in early December, revealed [copper, zinc, and silver]. These results were so remarkable that neither Clayton, an experienced geophysicist, nor four other TGS expert witnesses, had ever seen or heard of a comparable initial exploratory drill hole in a base metal deposit. So, the trial court concluded, "There is no doubt that the drill core of K-55-1 was unusually good and that it excited the interest and speculation of those who knew about it." By March 27, 1964, TGS decided that the land acquisition program had advanced to such a point that the company might well resume drilling, and drilling was resumed on March 31.

During this period, from November 12, 1963 when K-55-1 was completed, to March 31, 1964 when drilling was resumed, certain of the individual defendants and persons said to have received "tips" from them, purchased TGS stock or calls thereon. Prior to these transactions these persons had owned 1135 shares of TGS stock and possessed no calls; thereafter they owned a total of 8235 shares and possessed 12,300 calls. [The defendants purchased at prices ranging from 17 on November 12 to 25 on March 31. In addition, during this period five defendants were among 26 officers and employees who received stock options from TGS.] . . .

When drilling was resumed on March 31, hole K-55-3 was commenced. . . . Daily progress reports of the drilling of this hole K-55-3 and of all subsequently drilled holes were sent to defendants Stephens and Fogarty (President and Executive Vice President of TGS) by Holyk and Mollison. . . . On April 7, drilling of a third hole, K-55-4 . . . was commenced and mineralization was encountered over 366 of its 579-foot length. . . . Like K-55-1, both K-55-3 and K-55-4 established substantial copper mineralization on the eastern edge of the anomaly. On the basis of these findings relative to the foregoing drilling results, the trial court concluded that . . . "There was real evidence that a body of commercially mineable ore might exist."

On April 8 TGS began with a second drill rig to drill another hole, K-55-6, to explore mineralization beneath K-55-1. . . . While no visual estimates of its core were immediately available, it was readily apparent by the evening of April 10 that substantial copper mineralization had been encountered over the last 127 feet of the hole's 569-foot length. On April 10, a third drill rig commenced drilling yet another hole, K-55-5. . . . By the evening of April 10 in this hole, too, substantial copper mineralization had been encountered over the last 42 feet of its 97-foot length.

Meanwhile, rumors that a major ore strike was in the making had been circulating throughout Canada. On the morning of Saturday, April 11, Stephens at his home in Greenwich, Conn., read in the New York Herald Tribune and in the New York Times unauthorized reports of the TGS drilling which seemed to infer a rich strike from the fact that the drill cores had been flown to the United States for chemical assay. Stephens immediately contacted Fogarty at his home in Rye, N.Y., who in turn telephoned and later that day visited Mollison at Mollison's home in Greenwich to obtain a current report and evaluation of the drilling progress. The following morning, Sunday, Fogarty again telephoned Mollison, inquiring whether Mollison had any further information and told him to return to Timmins with Holyk, the TGS Chief Geologist, as soon as possible "to move things along." With the aid of one Carroll, a public relations consultant, Fogarty drafted a press release designed to quell the rumors, which release, after having been channeled through Stephens and Huntington, a TGS attorney, was issued at 3:00 p.m. on Sunday, April 12, and which appeared in the morning newspapers of general circulation on Monday, April 13. It read in pertinent part as follows:

NEW YORK, April 12—The following statement was made today by Dr. Charles F. Fogarty, executive vice president of Texas Gulf Sulphur Company, in regard to the company's drilling operations near Timmins, Ontario, Canada. Dr. Fogarty said:

"During the past few days, the exploration activities of Texas Gulf Sulphur in the area of Timmins, Ontario, have been widely reported in the press, coupled with rumors of a substantial copper discovery there. These reports exaggerate the scale of operations, and mention plans and statistics of size and grade of ore that are without factual basis and have evidently originated by speculation of people not connected with TGS.

"The facts are as follows. TGS has been exploring in the Timmins area for six years as part of its overall search in Canada and elsewhere for various minerals—lead, copper, zinc, etc. During the course of this work, in Timmins as well as in Eastern Canada, TGS has conducted exploration entirely on its own, without the participation by others. Numerous prospects have been investigated by geophysical means and a large number of selected ones have been core-drilled. These cores are sent to the United States for assay and detailed examination as a matter of routine and on advice of expert Canadian legal counsel. No inferences as to grade can be drawn from this procedure.

"Most of the areas drilled in Eastern Canada have revealed either barren pyrite or graphite without value; a few have resulted in discoveries of small or marginal sulphide ore bodies.

"Recent drilling on one property near Timmins has led to preliminary indications that more drilling would be required for proper evaluation of this prospect. The drilling done to date has not been conclusive, but the statements made by many outside quarters are unreliable and include information and figures that are not available to TGS.

"The work done to date has not been sufficient to reach definite conclusions and any statement as to size and grade of ore would be premature and possibly misleading. When we have progressed to the point where reasonable and logical conclusions can be made, TGS will issue a definite statement to its stockholders and to the public in order to clarify the Timmins project."

The release purported to give the Timmins drilling results as of the release date, April 12. From Mollison Fogarty had been told of the developments through 7:00 p.m. on April 10, and of the remarkable discoveries made up to that time, detailed supra, which discoveries, according to the calculations of the experts who testified for the SEC at the hearing, demonstrated that TGS had already discovered 6.2 to 8.3 million tons of proven ore having gross assay values from $26 to $29 per ton. TGS experts, on the other hand, denied at the hearing that proven or probable ore could have been calculated on April 11 or 12 because there was then no assurance of continuity in the mineralized zone.

The evidence as to the effect of this release on the investing public was equivocal and less than abundant. On April 13 the New York Herald Tribune in an article head-noted "Copper Rumor Deflated" quoted from the TGS release of April 12 and back-tracked from its original April 11 report of a major strike but nevertheless inferred from the TGS release that "recent mineral exploratory activity near Timmins, Ontario, has provided preliminary favorable results, sufficient at least to require a step-up in drilling operations." Some witnesses who testified at the hearing stated that they found the release encouraging. On the other hand, a Canadian mining security specialist, Roche, stated that "earlier in the week [before April 16] we had a Dow Jones saying that they [TGS] didn't have anything basically" and a TGS stock specialist for the Midwest Stock Exchange became concerned about his long position in the stock after reading the release. The trial court stated only that "While, in retrospect, the press release may appear gloomy or incomplete, this does not make it misleading or decep-tive on the basis of the facts then known." . . .

While drilling activity ensued to completion, TGS officials were taking steps toward ultimate disclosure of the discovery. On April 13, a previously-invited reporter for The Northern Miner, a Canadian mining industry journal, visited the drillsite, interviewed Mollison, Holyk and Darke, and prepared an article which confirmed a 10 million ton ore strike. This report, after having been submitted to Mollison and returned to the reporter unamended on April 15, was published in the April 16 issue. A statement relative to the extent of the discovery, in substantial part drafted by Mollison, was given to the Ontario Minister of Mines for release to the Canadian media. Mollison and Holyk expected it to be released over the airways at 11 p.m. on April 15th, but, for undisclosed reasons, it was not released until 9:40 a.m. on the 16th. An official detailed statement, announcing a strike of at least 25 million tons of ore, based on the drilling data set forth above, was read to representatives of American financial media from 10:00 a.m. to 10:10 or 10:15 a.m. on April 16, and appeared over Merrill Lynch's pri-vate wire at 10:29 a.m. and, somewhat later than expected, over the Dow Jones ticker tape at 10:54 a.m.

Between the time the first press release was issued on April 12 and the dis-semination of the TGS official announcement on the morning of April 16, the only defendants before us on appeal who engaged in market activity were Clayton and Crawford and TGS director Coates. Clayton ordered 200 shares of TGS stock through his Canadian broker on April 15 and the order was executed that day over the Midwest Stock Exchange. Crawford ordered 300 shares at midnight on the 15th and another 300 shares at 8:30 a.m. the next day, and these orders were executed over the Midwest Exchange in Chicago at its opening on April 16. Coates left the TGS press conference and called his broker son-in-law Haemisegger shortly before 10:20 a.m. on the 16th and ordered 2,000 shares of TGS for family trust accounts of which Coates was a trustee but not a beneficiary; Haemisegger executed this order over the New York and Midwest Exchanges, and he and his customers purchased 1,500 additional shares.

During the period of drilling in Timmins, the market price of TGS stock fluctu-ated but steadily gained overall. On Friday, November 8, when the drilling began, the stock closed at 17; on Friday, November 15, after K-55-1 had been completed, it closed at 18. After a slight decline to 16 by Friday, November 22, the price rose to 20 by December 13, when the chemical assay results of K-55-1 were received, and closed at a high of 24 on February 21, the day after the stock options had been issued. It had reached a price of 26 by March 31, after the land acquisition program had been completed and drilling had been resumed, and continued to ascend to 30 by the close of trading on April 10, at which time the drilling progress up to then was evaluated for the April 12th press release. On April 13, the day on which the April 12 release was disseminated, TGS opened at 30, rose immediately to a high of 32 and gradually tapered off to close at 30. It closed at 30 the next day, and at 29 on April 15. On April 16, the day of the official announcement of the Timmins discovery, the price climbed to a high of 37 and closed at 36. By May 15, TGS stock was selling at 58.

I.   The Individual Defendants

A.   Introductory

. . . Rule 10b-5 was promulgated pursuant to the grant of authority given the SEC by Congress in §10(b) of the Securities Exchange Act of 1934. By that Act Congress purposed to prevent inequitable and unfair practices and to insure fairness in securities transactions generally, whether conducted face-to-face, over the counter, or on exchanges, see 3 Loss, Securities Regulation 1455-56 (2d ed. 1961). The Act and the Rule apply to the transactions here, all of which were consummated on exchanges. Whether predicated on traditional fiduciary concepts, see, e.g., Hotchkiss v. Fisher, 136 Kan. 530, 16 P.2d 531 (Kan. 1932), or on the "special facts" doctrine, see, e.g., Strong v. Repide, 213 U.S. 419 (1909), the Rule is based in policy on the justifiable expectation of the securities marketplace that all investors trading on impersonal exchanges have relatively equal access to material information, see Cary, Insider Trading in Stocks, 21 Bus. Law. 1009, 1010 (1966); Fleischer, Securities Trading and Corporation Information Practices: The Implications of the Texas Gulf Sulphur Proceeding, 51 Va. L. Rev. 1271, 1278-80 (1965). The essence of the Rule is that anyone who, trading for his own account in the securities of a corporation has "access, directly or indirectly, to information intended to be available only for a corporate purpose and not for the personal benefit of anyone" may not take "advantage of such information knowing it is unavailable to those with whom he is dealing," i.e., the investing public. Matter of Cady, Roberts & Co., 40 S.E.C. 907, 912 (1961). Insiders, as directors or management officers are, of course, by this Rule, precluded from so unfairly dealing, but the Rule is also applicable to one possessing the information who may not be strictly termed an "insider" within the meaning of §16(b) of the Act. *Cady, Roberts,* supra. Thus, anyone in possession of material inside information must either disclose it to the investing public, or, if he is disabled from disclosing it in order to protect a corporate confidence, or he chooses not to do so, must abstain from trading in or recommending the securities concerned while such inside information remains undisclosed. So, it is here no justification for insider activity that disclosure was forbidden by the legitimate corporate objective of acquiring options to purchase the land surrounding the exploration site;

if the information was, as the SEC contends, material,[9] its possessors should have kept out of the market until disclosure was accomplished. *Cady, Roberts,* supra at 911.

B. MATERIAL INSIDE INFORMATION

An insider is not, of course, always foreclosed from investing in his own company merely because he may be more familiar with company operations than are outside investors. An insider's duty to disclose information or his duty to abstain from dealing in his company's securities arises only in "those situations which are essentially extraordinary in nature and which are reasonably certain to have a substantial effect on the market price of the security if [the extraordinary situation is] disclosed." Fleischer, Securities Trading and Corporate Information Practices: The Implications of the Texas Gulf Sulphur Proceeding, 51 Va. L. Rev. 1271, 1289.

Nor is an insider obligated to confer upon outside investors the benefit of his superior financial or other expert analysis by disclosing his educated guesses or predictions. The only regulatory objective is that access to material information be enjoyed equally, but this objective requires nothing more than the disclosure of basic facts so that outsiders may draw upon their own evaluative expertise in reaching their own investment decisions with knowledge equal to that of the insiders.

This is not to suggest, however, as did the trial court, that "the test of materiality must necessarily be a conservative one, particularly since many actions under §10(b) are brought on the basis of hindsight," in the sense that the materiality of facts is to be assessed solely by measuring the effect the knowledge of the facts would have upon prudent or conservative investors. As we stated in List v. Fashion Park, Inc., 340 F.2d 457, 462 (1965)], "The basic test of materiality . . . is whether a *reasonable* man would attach importance . . . in determining his choice of action in the transaction in question. Restatement, Torts §538(2)(a); accord Prosser, Torts 554-55; I Harper & James, Torts 565-66." (Emphasis supplied.) This, of course, encompasses any fact ". . . which in reasonable and objective contemplation *might* affect the value of the corporation's stock or securities. . . ." List v. Fashion Park, Inc., supra at 462, quoting from Kohler v. Kohler Co., 319 F.2d 634, 642, 7 A.L.R.3d 486 (7 Cir. 1963). (Emphasis supplied.) Such a fact is a material fact and must be effectively disclosed to the investing public prior to the commencement of insider trading in the corporation's securities. The speculators and chartists of Wall and Bay Streets are also "reasonable" investors entitled to the same legal protection afforded conservative traders.[10] Thus, material facts include not only information disclosing the earnings and distributions of a company but also those facts which affect the probable future of the company and those which may affect the desire of investors to buy, sell, or hold the company's securities.

---

9. Congress intended by the Exchange Act to eliminate the idea that the use of inside information for personal advantage was a normal emolument of corporate office. See §§2 and 16 of the Act; H.R. Rep. No. 1383, 73rd Cong., 2d Sess. 13 (1934); S. Rep. No. 792, 73rd Cong., 2d Sess. 9 (1934); S.E.C., Tenth Annual Report 50 (1944). See *Cady, Roberts,* supra at 912.

10. The House of Representatives committee that reported out the bill which eventually became the Act did so with the observation that "no investor, *no speculator,* can safely buy and sell securities upon exchanges without having an intelligent basis for forming his judgment as to the value of the securities he buys or sells." H.R. Rep. No. 1383, 73d Cong., 2d Sess. (1934), p. 11. (Emphasis supplied.) . . .

In each case, then, whether facts are material within Rule 10b-5 when the facts relate to a particular event and are undisclosed by those persons who are knowledgeable thereof will depend at any given time upon a balancing of both the indicated probability that the event will occur and the anticipated magnitude of the event in light of the totality of the company activity. Here, notwithstanding the trial court's conclusion that the results of the first drill core, K-55-1, were "too 'remote' . . . to have had any significant impact on the market, i.e., to be deemed material," knowledge of the possibility, which surely was more than marginal, of the existence of a mine of the vast magnitude indicated by the remarkably rich drill core located rather close to the surface (suggesting mineability by the less expensive open-pit method) within the confines of a large anomaly (suggesting an extensive region of mineralization) might well have affected the price of TGS stock and would certainly have been an important fact to a reasonable, if speculative, investor in deciding whether he should buy, sell, or hold. After all, this first drill core was "unusually good and . . . excited the interest and speculation of those who knew about it."

Our disagreement with the district judge on the issue does not, then, go to his findings of basic fact, as to which the "clearly erroneous" rule would apply, but to his understanding of the legal standard applicable to them. Our survey of the facts found below conclusively establishes that knowledge of the results of the discovery hole, K-55-1, would have been important to a reasonable investor and might have affected the price of the stock.[12] On April 16, The Northern Miner, a trade publication in wide circulation among mining stock specialists, called K-55-1, the discovery hole, "one of the most impressive drill holes completed in modern times." Roche, a Canadian broker whose firm specialized in mining securities, characterized the importance to investors of the results of K-55-1. He stated that the completion of "the first drill hole" with "a 600 foot drill core is very very significant . . . anything over 200 feet is considered very significant and 600 feet is just beyond your wildest imagination." He added, however, that it "is a natural thing to buy more stock once they give you the first drill hole." Additional testimony revealed that the prices of stocks of other companies, albeit less diversified, smaller firms, had increased substantially solely on the basis of the discovery of good anomalies or even because of the proximity of their lands to the situs of a potentially major strike.

Finally, a major factor in determining whether the K-55-1 discovery was a material fact is the importance attached to the drilling results by those who knew about it. In view of other unrelated recent developments favorably affecting TGS, participation by an informed person in a regular stock-purchase program, or even sporadic trading by an informed person, might lend only nominal support to the inference of the materiality of the K-55-1 discovery; nevertheless, the timing by those who knew of it of

12. We do not suggest that material facts must be disclosed immediately; the timing of disclosure is a matter for the business judgment of the corporate officers entrusted with the management of the corporation within the affirmative disclosure requirements promulgated by the exchanges and by the SEC. Here, a valuable corporate purpose was served by delaying the publication of the K-55-1 discovery. We do intend to convey, however, that where a corporate purpose is thus served by withholding the news of a material fact, those persons who are thus quite properly true to their corporate trust must not during the period of non-disclosure deal personally in the corporation's securities or give to outsiders confidential information not generally available to all the corporations' stockholders and to the public at large.

their stock purchases and their purchases of *short-term* calls—purchases in some cases by individuals who had never before purchased calls or even TGS stock—virtually compels the inference that the insiders were influenced by the drilling results. This insider trading activity, which surely constitutes highly pertinent evidence and the only truly objective evidence of the materiality of the K-55-1 discovery, was apparently disregarded by the court below in favor of the testimony of defendants' expert witnesses, all of whom "agreed that one drill core does not establish an ore body, much less a mine." Significantly, however, the court below, while relying upon what these defense experts said the defendant insiders *ought* to have thought about the worth to TGS of the K-55-1 discovery, and finding that from November 12, 1963 to April 6, 1964 Fogarty, Murray, Holyk and Darke spent more than $100,000 in purchasing TGS stock and calls on that stock, made no finding that the insiders were motivated by any factor other than the extraordinary K-55-1 discovery when they bought their stock and their calls. No reason appears why outside investors, perhaps better acquainted with speculative modes of investment and with, in many cases, perhaps more capital at their disposal for intelligent speculation, would have been less influenced, and would not have been similarly motivated to invest if they had known what the insider investors knew about the K-55-1 discovery.

Our decision to expand the limited protection afforded outside investors by the trial court's narrow definition of materiality is not at all shaken by fears that the elimination of insider trading benefits will deplete the ranks of capable corporate managers by taking away an incentive to accept such employment. Such benefits, in essence, are forms of secret corporate compensation, see Cary, Corporate Standards and Legal Rules, 50 Calif. L. Rev. 408, 409-10 (1962), derived at the expense of the uninformed investing public and not at the expense of the corporation which receives the sole benefit from insider incentives. Moreover, adequate incentives for corporate officers may be provided by properly administered stock options and employee purchase plans of which there are many in existence. In any event, the normal motivation induced bystock ownership, i.e., the identification of an individual with corporate progress, is ill-promoted by condoning the sort of speculative insider activity which occurred here; for example, some of the corporation's stock was sold at market in order to purchase short-term calls upon that stock, calls which would never be exercised to increase a stockholder equity in TGS unless the market price of that stock rose sharply.

The core of Rule 10b-5 is the implementation of the Congressional purpose that all investors should have equal access to the rewards of participation in securities transactions. It was the intent of Congress that all members of the investing public should be subject to identical market risks,—which market risks include, of course the risk that one's evaluative capacity or one's capital available to put at risk may exceed another's capacity or capital. The insiders here were not trading on an equal footing with the outside investors. They alone were in a position to evaluate the probability and magnitude of what seemed from the outset to be a major ore strike; they alone could invest safely, secure in the expectation that the price of TGS stock would rise substantially in the event such a major strike should materialize, but would decline little, if at all, in the event of failure, for the public, ignorant at the outset of the favorable probabilities would likewise be unaware of the unproductive exploration, and the additional exploration costs would not significantly affect TGS market prices. Such inequities based upon unequal access to knowledge should not be shrugged off as inevitable in our way of life, or, in view of the congressional concern in the area, remain uncorrected.

We hold, therefore, that all transactions in TGS stock or calls by individuals apprised of the drilling results of K-55-1 were made in violation of Rule 10b-5. Inasmuch as the visual evaluation of that drill core (a generally reliable estimate though less accurate than a chemical assay) constituted material information, those advised of the results of the visual evaluation as well as those informed of the chemical assay traded in violation of law. The geologist Darke possessed undisclosed material information and traded in TGS securities. Therefore we reverse the dismissal of the action as to him and his personal transactions. The trial court also found that Darke, after the drilling of K-55-1 had been completed and with detailed knowledge of the results thereof, told certain outside individuals that TGS "was a good buy." These individuals thereafter acquired TGS stock and calls. . . . [We] hold that Darke violated Rule 10b-5(3) and §10(b) by "tipping" and we remand, pursuant to the agreement of the parties, for a determination of the appropriate remedy. As Darke's "tippees" are not defendants in this action, we need not decide whether, if they acted with actual or constructive knowledge that the material information was undisclosed, their conduct is as equally violative of the Rule as the conduct of their insider source, though we note that it certainly could be equally reprehensible.

With reference to Huntington, the trial court found that he "had no detailed knowledge as to the work" on the Kidd-55 segment. Nevertheless, the evidence shows that he knew about and participated in TGS's land acquisition program which followed the receipt of the K-55-1 drilling results, and that on February 26, 1964 he purchased 50 shares of TGS stock. Later, on March 16, he helped prepare a letter for Dr. Holyk's signature in which TGS made a substantial offer for lands near K-55-1, and on the same day he, who had never before purchased calls on any stock, purchased a call on 100 shares of TGS stock. We are satisfied that these purchases in February and March, coupled with his readily inferable and probably reliable, understanding of the highly favorable nature of preliminary operations on the Kidd segment, demonstrate that Huntington possessed material inside information such as to make his purchase violative of the Rule and the Act.

C. WHEN MAY INSIDERS ACT?

Appellant Crawford, who ordered[17] the purchase of TGS stock shortly before the TGS April 16 official announcement, and defendant Coates, who placed orders with and communicated the news to his broker immediately after the official

_____

17. The effective protection of the public from insider exploitation of advance notice of material information requires that the time that an insider places an order, rather than the time of its ultimate execution, be determinative for Rule 10b-5 purposes. Otherwise, insiders would be able to "beat the news," cf. Fleischer, supra, 51 Va. L. Rev. at 1291, by requesting in advance that their orders be executed immediately after the dissemination of a major news release but before outsiders could act on the release. Thus it is immaterial whether Crawford's orders were executed before or after the announcement was made in Canada (9:40 a.m., April 16) or in the United States (10:00 a.m.) or whether Coates's order was executed before or after the news appeared over the Merrill Lynch (10:29 a.m.) or Dow Jones (10:54 a.m.) wires.

announcement was read at the TGS-called press conference, concede that they were in possession of material information. They contend, however, that their purchases were not proscribed purchases for the news had already been effectively disclosed. We disagree.

Crawford telephoned his orders to his Chicago broker about midnight on April 15 and again at 8:30 in the morning of the 16th, with instructions to buy at the opening of the Midwest Stock Exchange that morning. The trial court's finding that "he sought to, and did, 'beat the news,'" is well documented by the record. The rumors of a major ore strike which had been circulated in Canada and, to a lesser extent, in New York, had been disclaimed by the TGS press release of April 12, which significantly promised the public an official detailed announcement when possibilities had ripened into actualities. The abbreviated announcement to the Canadian press at 9:40 a.m. on the 16th by the Ontario Minister of Mines and the report carried by The Northern Miner, parts of which had sporadically reached New York on the morning of the 16th through reports from Canadian affiliates to a few New York investment firms, are assuredly not the equivalent of the official 10-15 minute announcement which was not released to the American financial press until after 10:00 a.m. Crawford's orders had been placed before that. Before insiders may act upon material information, such information must have been effectively disclosed in a manner sufficient to insure its availability to the investing public. Particularly here, where a formal announcement to the entire financial news media had been promised in a prior official release known to the media, all insider activity must await dissemination of the promised official announcement.

Coates was absolved by the court below because his telephone order was placed shortly before 10:20 a.m. on April 16, which was after the announcement had been made even though the news could not be considered already a matter of public information. This result seems to have been predicated upon a misinterpretation of dicta in *Cady, Roberts*, where the SEC instructed insiders to "keep out of the market until the established procedures for public release of the information are *carried out* instead of hastening to execute transactions in advance of, and in frustration of, the objectives of the release," 40 SEC at 915 (emphasis supplied). The reading of a news release, which prompted Coates into action, is merely the first step in the process of dissemination required for compliance with the regulatory objective of providing all investors with an equal opportunity to make informed investment judgments. Assuming that the contents of the official release could instantaneously be acted upon,[18] at the minimum Coates should have waited until the news could reasonably have been expected to appear over the media of widest circulation, the Dow Jones

---

18. Although the only insider who acted after the news appeared over the Dow Jones broad tape is not an appellant and therefore we need not discuss the necessity of considering the advisability of a "reasonable waiting period" during which outsiders may absorb and evaluate disclosures, we note in passing that, where the news is of a sort which is not readily translatable into investment action, insiders may not take advantage of their advance opportunity to evaluate the information by acting immediately upon dissemination. In any event, the permissible timing of insider transactions after disclosures of various sorts is one of the many areas of expertise for appropriate exercise of the SEC's rule-making power, which we hope will be utilized in the future to provide some predictability of certainty for the business community.

broad tape, rather than hastening to insure an advantage to himself and his broker son-in-law.[19]

NOTES AND QUESTIONS

1. Why can the corporation buy the Kidd 55 tract of land without telling the sellers of the ore discovery, but purchasers of stock cannot act on the same information? Consider the court's explanation in Part I-A and the various policies that might support the rule announced in *Texas Gulf Sulphur:*

A general duty of disclosure in real estate or other areas is sometimes rejected because it would discourage productive activity.

> [T]he law cannot hope to put all parties to every contract on an equality as to knowledge, experience, skill, and shrewdness; even if it could, would such be a just and equitable law? It would certainly not be consistent with the present economic order. At one time, the Roman law taking the same high stand insisted upon a rigid equality between the parties contracting and demanded a full disclosure by each party of all the material facts known to him and equally accessible to the other. Bower quotes Cicero's case of conscience to this effect: a man takes corn from Alexandria to Rhodes where there is a famine and sells it to the Rhodians at famine prices keeping back from them the fact that on the voyage he had passed ships loaded with provisions making for the famished city, and then he sails away with the profits. But as Verplanck says in his essay on contracts: "It certainly cannot be essential to the making of a fair bargain, that before I can deal with my indolent neighbor, I should communicate to him all my private plans, my long sighted views of the future state of the market, my surmises—in short, all the results of that knowledge and address which have been the hard earned acquisitions of my own industry and activity. It is pointed out that it is neither just to the individual nor is it a wise social policy to follow because it tends to discourage industry and training."

Keeton, Fraud—Concealment and Nondisclosure, 15 Tex. L. Rev. 1, 22-23 (1936). See generally Kronman, Mistake, Disclosure, Information, and the Law of Contracts, 7 J. Legal Studies 1 (1978). See also United States v. Chestman, 947 F.2d 551 (2d Cir. en banc 1991) (Winter, J., dissenting) ("If the law fails to protect property rights in commercial information . . . less will be invested in generating such information.").

Insider trading as contributing to an efficient market. Consistent with the efficient market hypothesis discussed in Chapter 3, insider trading permits smoother changes in stock prices than would occur without insider trading. Stock trading by insiders, to the extent it affects stock prices, moves prices in the correct direction. In situations where information cannot credibly be disclosed to the market (because of competitive fears or because it is soft information), insider trading conveys some of this information

---

19. The record reveals that news usually appears on the Dow Jones broad tape 2-3 minutes after the reporter completes dictation. Here, assuming that the Dow Jones reporter left the press conference as early as possible, 10:10 a.m., the 10-15 minute release (which took at least that long to dictate) could not have appeared on the wire before 10:22, and for other reasons unknown to us did not appear until 10:54. Indeed, even the abbreviated version of the release reported by Merrill Lynch over its private wire did not appear until 10:29. Coates, however, placed his call no later than 10:20.

to the market. See Carlton and Fischel, The Regulation of Insider Trading, 35 Stan. L. Rev. 857, 879 (1983). But see Cox, Insider Trading and Contracting: A Critical Response to the "Chicago School," 1986 Duke L.J. 628, 648 ("If accepted this position justifies massive trading and tipping to ensure that sufficient trading occurs to propel the stock to the equilibrium price appropriate for the nondisclosed information. Such widespread trading, however, compromises the corporate interest that justifies nondisclosure in the first place.").

Insider trading as management compensation.   Henry Manne's 1966 book, Insider Trading and the Stock Market, launched the academic challenge to regulation of insider trading. Among the arguments Manne made was the use of insider trading as a legitimate form of management compensation. See Manne, supra, at 111-148. This part of the justification for insider trading has attracted strong opposition, in part, for reasons similar to that expressed in Diamond v. Oreamuno at the beginning of this chapter; insiders are able to benefit from bad news, which could be due to their own inefficient performance. Critics express concern that even for positive developments, insider trading gains may not correlate to executive contribution and that other forms of executive compensation can be more effectively provided by the corporation. See Cox, supra, at 657-658; Schotland, Unsafe at Any Price: A Reply to Manne, Insider Trading and the Stock Market, 53 Va. L. Rev. 1425 (1967).

Harms from permitting trading on inside information.   Part of the complexity surrounding the debate over insider trading is the uncertainty in identifying and measuring the harm caused by the activity. The possible harm derives from several sources:

Delayed disclosure.   There will be less information available to the market if insiders hold back in order to profit from trades, thus impairing the efficiency of the market, at least in a short-term time frame.

Corporate injury.   The trading will adversely affect a corporation producing the information if the inside information is used to purchase stock in a company that the first company is seeking to take over and the trading leads the price of the target to increase.

Investor injury.   Traders on the other side of the transaction will be harmed. This part is particularly tricky because insider trading normally occurs in open market transactions, and the "victim" will have been trading in the market anyway. See Wang, Trading on Material Non-Public Information on Impersonal Markets: Who Is Harmed and Who Can Sue Under SEC Rule 10b-5?, 54 S. Cal. L. Rev. 1217 (1981) (discussing harm to traders induced to buy/sell and those preempted from buying or selling). Professor Booth has argued that "making insider trading illegal means that someone other than the insider will get first crack at trading on it. It does not mean that the average small investor will get in on the action. In all likelihood, whatever benefit is shifted away from insiders will accrue to market professionals. There is nothing wrong with that necessarily. But is it worth the cost?" Booth, Insider Trading, Better Markets, Wall St. J., June 28, 1991, at A12. To the extent that market-makers or stock exchange specialists are on the opposite side of the transaction of those with the inside information, the market-makers will incorporate this risk into the price of shares through a larger "bid-asked" spread that will affect investors as a group.

Loss of public confidence in the markets. The Securities Exchange Act of 1934 is a product of the Great Depression that followed the stock market crash of 1929. Regulation of insider trading thus is often linked to restoring public confidence in the market. The *Texas Gulf Sulphur* court's emphasis on equal access probably reflects this broad equity argument. Another illustration comes from the committee report accompanying the Insider Trading and Securities Fraud Enforcement Act of 1988:

> [T]he far greater number of commentators support efforts to curb insider trading, viewing such efforts as crucial to the capital formation process that depends on investor confidence in the fairness and integrity of our securities markets. Insider trading damages the legitimacy of the capital market and diminishes the public's faith.

H.R. Rep. No. 910 (House Energy and Commerce Committee) to accompany H.R. 5133, 100th Cong., 2d Sess. 8 (1988).

2. Given the rules set out in *Texas Gulf Sulphur,* when would you advise insiders that they could buy or sell stock in their company:

- Never?
- After quarterly or annual reports are filed with the SEC?
- After any public announcement, as long as they are not the first (or second or third) person to trade?
- One day after a public announcement?
- One hour after a public announcement?

3. How does an insider's liability for trading without disclosure relate to potential liability if there has been no trading? Another part of the *Texas Gulf Sulphur* opinion, not reproduced here, held the corporation liable for the misleading press release as a misrepresentation in connection with the purchase or sale of stock by traders who sold. Basic, Inc. v. Levinson in Chapter 10 addresses this issue in more detail.

Chiarella v. United States
United States Supreme Court, 1980
445 U.S. 222

MR. JUSTICE POWELL delivered the opinion of the Court.

The question in this case is whether a person who learns from the confidential documents of one corporation that it is planning an attempt to secure control of a second corporation violates §10(b) of the Securities Exchange Act of 1934 if he fails to disclose the impending takeover before trading in the target company's securities.

I

Petitioner is a printer by trade. In 1975 and 1976, he worked as a "markup man" in the New York composing room of Pandick Press, a financial printer. Among documents that petitioner handled were five announcements of corporate takeover bids. When these documents were delivered to the printer, the identities of the acquiring and target corporations were concealed by blank spaces or false names. The true names were sent to the printer on the night of the final printing.

The petitioner, however, was able to deduce the names of the target companies before the final printing from other information contained in the documents. Without disclosing his knowledge, petitioner purchased stock in the target companies and sold the shares immediately after the takeover attempts were made public. By this method, petitioner realized a gain of slightly more than $30,000 in the course of 14 months. Subsequently, the Securities and Exchange Commission (Commission or SEC) began an investigation of his trading activities. In May 1977, petitioner entered into a consent decree with the Commission in which he agreed to return his profits to the sellers of the shares. On the same day, he was discharged by Pandick Press.

In January 1978, petitioner was indicted on 17 counts of violating §10(b) of the Securities Exchange Act of 1934 (1934 Act) and SEC Rule 10b-5. After petitioner unsuccessfully moved to dismiss the indictment, he was brought to trial and convicted on all counts.

The Court of Appeals for the Second Circuit affirmed petitioner's conviction. We granted certiorari, and we now reverse.

II . . .

This case concerns the legal effect of the petitioner's silence. The District Court's charge permitted the jury to convict the petitioner if it found that he willfully failed to inform sellers of target company securities that he knew of a forthcoming takeover bid that would make their shares more valuable. In order to decide whether silence in such circumstances violates §10(b), it is necessary to review the language and legislative history of that statute as well as its interpretation by the Commission and the federal courts.

Although the starting point of our inquiry is the language of the statute, Ernst & Ernst v. Hochfelder, 425 U.S. 185, 197 (1976), §10(b) does not state whether silence may constitute a manipulative or deceptive device. Section 10(b) was designed as a catchall clause to prevent fraudulent practices. But neither the legislative history nor the statute itself affords specific guidance for the resolution of this case. When Rule 10b-5 was promulgated in 1942, the SEC did not discuss the possibility that failure to provide information might run afoul of §10(b).

The SEC took an important step in the development of §10(b) when it held that a broker-dealer and his firm violated that section by selling securities on the basis of undisclosed information obtained from a director of the issuer corporation who was also a registered representative of the brokerage firm. In Cady, Roberts & Co, 40 S.E.C. 907 (1961), the Commission decided that a corporate insider must abstain from trading in the shares of his corporation unless he has first disclosed all material inside information known to him. The obligation to disclose or abstain derives from

> [a]n affirmative duty to disclose material information, [which] has been traditionally imposed on corporate "insiders," particularly officers, directors, or controlling stockholders. We, and the courts have consistently held that insiders must disclose material facts which are known to them by virtue of their position but which are not known to persons with whom they deal and which, if known, would affect their investment judgment. (Id., at 911.)

The Commission emphasized that the duty arose from (i) the existence of a relationship affording access to inside information intended to be available only for a corporate purpose, and (ii) the unfairness of allowing a corporate insider to take advantage of that information by trading without disclosure. Id., at 912, and n.15.[8]

That the relationship between a corporate insider and the stockholders of his corporation gives rise to a disclosure obligation is not a novel twist of the law. At common law, misrepresentation made for the purpose of inducing reliance upon the false statement is fraudulent. But one who fails to disclose material information prior to the consummation of a transaction commits fraud only when he is under a duty to do so. And the duty to disclose arises when one party has information "that the other [party] is entitled to know because of a fiduciary or other similar relation of trust and confidence between them."[9] In its Cady, Roberts decision, the Commission recognized a relationship of trust and confidence between the shareholders of a corporation and those insiders who have obtained confidential information by reason of their position with that corporation.[10] This relationship gives rise to a duty to disclose because of the "necessity of preventing a corporate insider from . . . tak[ing] unfair advantage of the uninformed minority stockholders." Speed v. Transamerica Corp., 99 F. Supp. 808, 829 (Del. 1951).

The federal courts have found violations of §10(b) where corporate insiders used undisclosed information for their own benefit. E.g., SEC v. Texas Gulf Sulphur Co., 401 F.2d 833 (C.A.2 1968), cert. denied, 404 U.S. 1005 (1971). The cases also have

---

8. In *Cady, Roberts*, the broker-dealer was liable under §10(b) because it received nonpublic information from a corporate insider of the issuer. Since the insider could not use the information, neither could the partners in the brokerage firm with which he was associated. The transaction in *Cady, Roberts* involved sale of stock to persons who previously may not have been shareholders in the corporation. 40 S.E.C., at 913, and n.21. The Commission embraced the reasoning of Judge Learned Hand that "the director or officer assumed a fiduciary relation to the buyer by the very sale; for it would be a sorry distinction to allow him to use the advantage of his position to induce the buyer into the position of a beneficiary although he was forbidden to do so once the buyer had become one." Id., at 914, n.23, quoting Gratz v. Claughton, 187 F.2d 46, 49 (C.A.2), cert. denied, 341 U.S. 920 (1951).

9. Restatement (Second) of Torts §551(2)(a)(1976). . . .

10. . . . The dissent of Mr. Justice Blackmun suggests that the "special facts" doctrine may be applied to find that silence constitutes fraud where one party has superior information to another. This Court has never so held. In Strong v. Repide, 213 U.S. 419, 431-434 (1909), this Court applied the special-facts doctrine to conclude that a corporate insider had a duty to disclose to a shareholder. In that case, the majority shareholder of a corporation secretly purchased the stock of another shareholder without revealing that the corporation, under the insider's direction, was about to sell corporate assets at a price that would greatly enhance the value of the stock. The decision in Strong v. Repide was premised upon the fiduciary duty between the corporate insider and the shareholder. See Pepper v. Litton, 308 U.S. 295, 307, n.15 (1939).

emphasized, in accordance with the common-law rule, that "[t]he party charged with failing to disclose market information must be under a duty to disclose it." *Frigitemp Corp. v. Financial Dynamics Fund, Inc.*, 524 F.2d 275, 282 (C.A.2 1975). Accordingly, a purchaser of stock who has no duty to a prospective seller because he is neither an insider nor a fiduciary has been held to have no obligation to reveal material facts. See *General Time Corp. v. Talley Industries, Inc.*, 403 F.2d 159, 164 (C.A.2 1968), cert. denied, 393 U.S. 1026 (1969).

Thus, administrative and judicial interpretations have established that silence in connection with the purchase or sale of securities may operate as a fraud actionable under §10(b) despite the absence of statutory language or legislative history specifically addressing the legality of nondisclosure. But such liability is premised upon a duty to disclose arising from a relationship of trust and confidence between parties to a transaction. Application of a duty to disclose prior to trading guarantees that corporate insiders, who have an obligation to place the shareholder's welfare before their own, will not benefit personally through fraudulent use of material, nonpublic information.[12]

III

In this case, the petitioner was convicted of violating §10(b) although he was not a corporate insider and he received no confidential information from the target company. Moreover, the "market information" upon which he relied did not concern the earning power or operations of the target company, but only the plans of the acquiring company. Petitioner's use of that information was not a fraud under §10(b) unless he was subject to an affirmative duty to disclose it before trading. In this case, the jury instructions failed to specify any such duty. In effect, the trial court instructed the jury that petitioner owed a duty to everyone; to all sellers, indeed, to the market as a whole. The jury simply was told to decide whether petitioner used material, nonpublic information at a time when "he knew other people trading in the securities market did not have access to the same information."

The Court of Appeals affirmed the conviction by holding that "[*a*]*nyone*—corporate insider or not—who regularly receives material nonpublic information may not use that information to trade in securities without incurring an affirmative duty to disclose." 588 F.2d, at 1365 (emphasis in original). Although the court said that its test would include only persons who regularly receive material, nonpublic information, its rationale for that limitation is unrelated to the existence of a duty to disclose. The Court of Appeals, like the trial court, failed to identify a relationship between petitioner and the sellers that could give rise to a duty. Its decision thus rested solely upon its belief that the federal securities laws have "created a system providing equal access

---

12. "Tippees" of corporate insiders have been held liable under §10(b) because they have a duty not to profit from the use of inside information that they know is confidential and know or should know came from a corporate insider, *Shapiro v. Merrill Lynch, Pierce, Fenner & Smith, Inc.*, 495 F.2d 228, 237-238 (C.A.2 1974). The tippee's obligation has been viewed as arising from his role as a participant after the fact in the insider's breach of a fiduciary duty. . . .

to information necessary for reasoned and intelligent investment decisions." The use by anyone of material information not generally available is fraudulent, this theory suggests, because such information gives certain buyers or sellers an unfair advantage over less informed buyers and sellers.

This reasoning suffers from two defects. First, not every instance of financial unfairness constitutes fraudulent activity under §10(b). See Santa Fe Industries, Inc. v. Green, 430 U.S. 462, 474-477 (1977). Second, the element required to make silence fraudulent—a duty to disclose—is absent in this case. No duty could arise from petitioner's relationship with the sellers of the target company's securities, for petitioner had no prior dealings with them. He was not their agent, he was not a fiduciary, he was not a person in whom the sellers had placed their trust and confidence. He was, in fact, a complete stranger who dealt with the sellers only through impersonal market transactions.

We cannot affirm petitioner's conviction without recognizing a general duty between all participants in market transactions to forgo actions based on material, nonpublic information. Formulation of such a broad duty, which departs radically from the established doctrine that duty arises from a specific relationship between two parties, should not be undertaken absent some explicit evidence of congressional intent.

As we have seen, no such evidence emerges from the language or legislative history of §10(b). Moreover, neither the Congress nor the Commission ever has adopted a parity-of-information rule. Instead the problems caused by misuse of market information have been addressed by detailed and sophisticated regulation that recognizes when use of market information may not harm operation of the securities markets. For example, the Williams Act[15] limits but does not completely prohibit a tender offeror's purchases of target corporation stock before public announcement of the offer. Congress' careful action in this and other areas contrasts, and is in some tension, with the broad rule of liability we are asked to adopt in this case.

Indeed, the theory upon which the petitioner was convicted is at odds with the Commission's view of §10(b) as applied to activity that has the same effect on sellers as the petitioner's purchases. "Warehousing" takes place when a corporation gives advance notice of its intention to launch a tender offer to institutional investors who then are able to purchase stock in the target company before the tender offer is made public and the price of shares rises. In this case, as in warehousing, a buyer of securities purchases stock in a target corporation on the basis of market information which is unknown to the seller. In both of these situations, the seller's behavior presumably would be altered if he had the nonpublic information. Significantly, however, the Commission has acted to bar warehousing under its authority to regulate tender offers after recognizing that action under §10(b) would rest on a "somewhat different theory" than that previously used to regulate insider trading as fraudulent activity.

We see no basis for applying such a new and different theory of liability in this case. As we have emphasized before, the 1934 Act cannot be read "'more broadly

---

15. Title 15 U.S.C. §78m(d)(1) (1976 ed., Supp. II) permits a tender offeror to purchase 5% of the target company's stock prior to disclosure of its plan for acquisition.

than its language and the statutory scheme reasonably permit.'" Touche Ross & Co. v. Redington, 442 U.S. 560, 578 (1979), quoting SEC v. Sloan, 436 U.S. 103, 116 (1978). Section 10(b) is aptly described as a catchall provision, but what it catches must be fraud. When an allegation of fraud is based upon nondisclosure, there can be no fraud absent a duty to speak. We hold that a duty to disclose under §10(b) does not arise from the mere possession of nonpublic market information. The contrary result is without support in the legislative history of §10(b) and would be inconsistent with the careful plan that Congress has enacted for regulation of the securities markets. Cf. Santa Fe Industries, Inc. v. Green, 430 U.S., at 479.[20]

[The concurring opinions of Justices Brennan and Stevens and the dissenting opinion of Chief Justice Burger are omitted. The last two are discussed in the next section.]

MR. JUSTICE BLACKMUN with whom MR. JUSTICE MARSHALL joins, dissenting: . . .

The Court continues to pursue a course, charted in certain recent decisions, designed to transform §10(b) from an intentionally elastic "catchall" provision to one that catches relatively little of the misbehavior that all too often makes investment in securities a needlessly risky business for the uninitiated investor. See, e.g., Ernst & Ernst v. Hochfelder, 425 U.S. 185 (1976); Blue Chip Stamps v. Manor Drug Stores, 421 U.S. 723 (1975). . . .

. . . [T]he Court's approach unduly minimizes the importance of petitioner's *access* to confidential information that the honest investor, no matter how diligently he tried, could not legally obtain. . . . Even at common law, . . . there has been a trend away from strict adherence to the harsh maxim caveat emptor and toward a more flexible, less formalistic understanding of the duty to disclose. . . .

By its narrow construction of §10(b) and Rule 10b-5, the Court places the federal securities laws in the rearguard of this movement, a position opposite to the expectations of Congress at the time the securities laws were enacted. . . .

NOTES

1. How does Justice Powell's approach in *Chiarella* differ from that of the Second Circuit in *Texas Gulf Sulphur* and in *Chiarella* and Justice Blackmun's dissent? The

---

20. Mr. Justice Blackmun's dissent would establish the following standard for imposing criminal and civil liability under §10(b) and Rule 10b-5: "[P]ersons having access to confidential material information that is not legally available to others generally are prohibited . . . from engaging in schemes to exploit their structural informational advantage through trading in affected securities." This view is not substantially different from the Court of Appeals' theory that anyone "who regularly receives material nonpublic information may not use that information to trade in securities without incurring an affirmative duty to disclose," and must be rejected for the reasons stated in Part III. Additionally, a judicial holding that certain undefined activities "generally are prohibited" by §10(b) would raise questions whether either criminal or civil defendants would be given fair notice that they have engaged in illegal activity. It is worth noting that this is apparently the first case in which criminal liability has been imposed upon a purchaser for §10(b) nondisclosure. Petitioner was sentenced to a year in prison, suspended except for one month, and a 5-year term of probation. 588 F.2d, at 1373, 1378 (Meskill, J., dissenting).

equal access approach of the latter necessarily focuses on plaintiffs. The fiduciary duty approach focuses on the defendant. Does that difference in focus explain the law that has developed?

2. Most of the legal debate about insider trading has focused on the duty aspect: when does silence become fraud? If that question is answered in the affirmative, there may be questions about other elements of a 10b-5 claim (discussed in more detail in Chapter 10) such as scienter or causation. For example, should "knowing possession" of material nonpublic information when trading be sufficient for liability or must there be a showing that the information was actually used in or has a causal connection to the trade? Two federal appellate courts in 1998 declined to apply a knowing possession standard. The Eleventh Circuit, in a civil case, was, however, willing to permit a strong inference: "[W]hen an insider trades while in possession of material nonpublic information, a strong inference arises that such information was used by the insider in trading. The insider can attempt to rebut the inference by adducing evidence that there was no causal connection between the information and the trade—i.e., that the information was not used." S.E.C. v. Adler, 137 F.3d 1325, 1337 (11th Cir. 1998). Suspicious timing of trades and evidence of phone calls with insiders were cited as factors that could raise a reasonable inference. The Ninth Circuit adopted a "use" requirement and gave an illustration of factors that might satisfy it: "Suppose, for instance, that an individual who has never before invested comes into possession of material nonpublic information and the very next day invests a significant sum of money in substantially out-of-the-money call options. We are confident that the government would have little trouble demonstrating "use" in such a situation, or in other situations in which unique trading patterns or unusually large trading quantities suggest that an investor had used inside information." United States v. Smith, 155 F.3d 1051 (9th Cir. 1998). How does Rule 10b5-1, promulgated after these cases, seek to resolve this issue?

2. Extensions of the Classic Theory

The defendants in *Texas Gulf Sulphur* were corporate officers, directors, and employees and thus were bound by state law fiduciary duty. In defining when insider trading is fraud prohibited by Rule 10b-5, the Supreme Court focused on silence by one who has such a state law duty. This liability is sometimes described as classic or traditional insider trading. This section describes extensions of that liability beyond the classic group, first addressing those who obtain information from the classic insider and are covered by the extension of that insider's duty. This group includes those who receive information from the insider or the corporation for an appropriate purpose (constructive or temporary insider) and those whom the insider tips for an improper purpose (tippee liability). The second category is somewhat broader, based either on the duty owed to a non-trading party (misappropriation) or one who receives information in the context of a tender offer (Rule 14e-3).

a.   Tippee Liability and Constructive Insiders

Dirks v. Securities and Exchange Commission
United States Supreme Court, 1983
463 U.S. 646

JUSTICE POWELL delivered the opinion of the Court.

Petitioner Raymond Dirks received material nonpublic information from "insiders" of a corporation with which he had no connection. He disclosed this information to investors who relied on it in trading in the shares of the corporation. The question is whether Dirks violated the antifraud provisions of the federal securities laws by this disclosure.

I

In 1973, Dirks was an officer of a New York broker-dealer firm who specialized in providing investment analysis of insurance company securities to institutional investors. On March 6, Dirks received information from Ronald Secrist, a former officer of Equity Funding of America. Secrist alleged that the assets of Equity Funding, a diversified corporation primarily engaged in selling life insurance and mutual funds, were vastly overstated as the result of fraudulent corporate practices. Secrist also stated that various regulatory agencies had failed to act on similar charges made by Equity Funding employees. He urged Dirks to verify the fraud and disclose it publicly.

Dirks decided to investigate the allegations. He visited Equity Funding's headquarters in Los Angeles and interviewed several officers and employees of the corporation. The senior management denied any wrongdoing, but certain corporation employees corroborated the charges of fraud. Neither Dirks nor his firm owned or traded any Equity Funding stock, but throughout his investigation he openly discussed the information he had obtained with a number of clients and investors. Some of these persons sold their holdings of Equity Funding securities, including five investment advisers who liquidated holdings of more than $16 million.[2]

While Dirks was in Los Angeles, he was in touch regularly with William Blundell, the Wall Street Journal's Los Angeles bureau chief. Dirks urged Blundell to write a story on the fraud allegations. Blundell did not believe, however, that such a massive fraud could go undetected and declined to write the story. He feared that publishing such damaging hearsay might be libelous.

During the 2-week period in which Dirks pursued his investigation and spread word of Secrist's charges, the price of Equity Funding stock fell from $26 per share to less than $15 per share. This led the New York Stock Exchange to halt trading

---

2. Dirks received from his firm a salary plus a commission for securities transactions above a certain amount that his clients directed through his firm. But "[i]t is not clear how many of those with whom Dirks spoke promised to direct some brokerage business through [Dirks' firm] to compensate Dirks, or how many actually did so." 681 F.2d, at 831. The Boston Company Institutional Investors, Inc., promised Dirks about $25,000 in commissions, but it is unclear whether Boston actually generated any brokerage business for his firm.

on March 27. Shortly thereafter California insurance authorities impounded Equity Funding's records and uncovered evidence of the fraud. Only then did the Securities and Exchange Commission (SEC) file a complaint against Equity Funding and only then, on April 2, did the Wall Street Journal publish a front-page story based largely on information assembled by Dirks. Equity Funding immediately went into receivership.[4]

The SEC began an investigation into Dirks' role in the exposure of the fraud. After a hearing by an Administrative Law Judge, the SEC found that Dirks had aided and abetted violations of §17(a) of the Securities Act of 1933, 48 Stat. 84, as amended, 15 U.S.C. §77q(a), §10(b) of the Securities Exchange Act of 1934, 48 Stat. 891, 15 U.S.C. §78j(b), and SEC Rule 10b-5, 17 C.F.R. §240.10b-5 (1983), by repeating the allegations of fraud to members of the investment community who later sold their Equity Funding stock. The SEC concluded: "Where 'tippees'—regardless of their motivation or occupation—come into possession of material 'corporate information that they know is confidential and know or should know came from a corporate insider,' they must either publicly disclose that information or refrain from trading." 21 S.E.C. Docket 1401, 1407 (1981) (footnote omitted) (quoting Chiarella v. United States, 445 U.S. 222, 230, n.12 (1980)). Recognizing, however, that Dirks "played an important role in bringing [Equity Funding's] massive fraud to light," 21 S.E.C. Docket, at 1412, the SEC only censured him.

Dirks sought review in the Court of Appeals for the District of Columbia Circuit. The court entered judgment against Dirks. . . .

III

We were explicit in *Chiarella* in saying that there can be no duty to disclose where the person who has traded on inside information "was not [the corporation's] agent, . . . was not a fiduciary, [or] was not a person in whom the sellers [of the securities] had placed their trust and confidence." Not to require such a fiduciary relationship, we recognized, would "depar[t] radically from the established doctrine that duty arises from a specific relationship between two parties" and would amount to "recognizing a general duty between all participants in market transactions to forgo actions based on material, nonpublic information." This requirement of a specific relationship between the shareholders and the individual trading on inside information has created analytical difficulties for the SEC and courts in policing tippees who trade on inside information. Unlike insiders who have independent fiduciary duties to both the corporation and its shareholders, the typical tippee has no such relationships.[14] In view of this absence, it has been unclear how a tippee acquires the *Cady, Roberts* duty to refrain from trading on inside information.

---

4. A federal grand jury in Los Angeles subsequently returned a 105-count indictment against 22 persons, including many of Equity Funding's officers and directors. All defendants were found guilty of one or more counts, either by a plea of guilty or a conviction after trial.

14. Under certain circumstances, such as where corporate information is revealed legitimately to an underwriter, accountant, lawyer, or consultant working for the corporation, these outsiders may become fiduciaries of the shareholders. The basis for recognizing this fiduciary duty is not simply that such

A

The SEC's position, as stated in its opinion in this case, is that a tippee "inherits" the *Cady, Roberts* obligation to shareholders whenever he receives inside information from an insider:

> In tipping potential traders, Dirks breached a duty which he had assumed as a result of knowingly receiving confidential information from [Equity Funding] insiders. Tippees such as Dirks who receive non-public, material information from insiders become "subject to the same duty as [the] insiders." Shapiro v. Merrill Lynch, Pierce, Fenner & Smith, Inc. [495 F.2d 228, 237 (C.A.2 1974) (quoting Ross v. Licht, 263 F. Supp. 395, 410 (S.D.N.Y. 1967))]. Such a tippee breaches the fiduciary duty which he assumes from the insider when the tippee knowingly transmits the information to someone who will probably trade on the basis thereof. . . . Presumably, Dirks' informants were entitled to disclose the [Equity Funding] fraud in order to bring it to light and its perpetrators to justice. However, Dirks—standing in their shoes—committed a breach of the fiduciary duty which he had assumed in dealing with them, when he passed the information on to traders. (21 S.E.C. Docket, at 1410, n.42.)

This view differs little from the view that we rejected as inconsistent with congressional intent in *Chiarella.* In that case, the Court of Appeals agreed with the SEC and affirmed Chiarella's conviction, holding that "[*a*]*nyone*—corporate insider or not—who regularly receives material nonpublic information may not use that information to trade in securities without incurring an affirmative duty to disclose." United States v. Chiarella, 588 F.2d 1358, 1365 (C.A.2 1978) (emphasis in original). Here, the SEC maintains that anyone who knowingly receives nonpublic material information from an insider has a fiduciary duty to disclose before trading.[15]

---

persons acquired nonpublic corporate information, but rather that they have entered into a special confidential relationship in the conduct of the business of the enterprise and are given access to information solely for corporate purposes. When such a person breaches his fiduciary relationship, he may be treated more properly as a tipper than a tippee. See Shapiro v. Merrill Lynch, Pierce, Fenner & Smith, Inc., 495 F.2d 228, 237 (C.A.2 1974) (investment banker had access to material information when working on a proposed public offering for the corporation). For such a duty to be imposed, however, the corporation must expect the outsider to keep the disclosed nonpublic information confidential, and the relationship at least must imply such a duty.

15. Apparently, the SEC believes this case differs from *Chiarella* in that Dirks' receipt of inside information from Secrist, an insider, carried Secrist's duties with it, while Chiarella received the information without the direct involvement of an insider and thus inherited no duty to disclose or abstain. The SEC fails to explain, however, why the receipt of nonpublic information from an insider automatically carries with it the fiduciary duty of the insider. As we emphasized in *Chiarella,* mere possession of nonpublic information does not give rise to a duty to disclose or abstain; only a specific relationship does that. And we do not believe that the mere receipt of information from an insider creates such a special relationship between the tippee and the corporation's shareholders.

Apparently recognizing the weakness of its argument in light of *Chiarella,* the SEC attempts to distinguish that case factually as involving not "inside" information, but rather "market" information, i.e., "information originating outside the company and usually about the supply and demand for the company's securities." This Court drew no such distinction in *Chiarella* and, as The Chief Justice noted, "[i]t is clear that §10(b) and Rule 10b-5 by their terms and by their history make no such distinction." 445 U.S., at 241, n.1 (dissenting opinion). See ALI, Federal Securities Code §1603, Comment (2)(j) (Prop. Off. Draft 1978).

In effect, the SEC's theory of tippee liability in both cases appears rooted in the idea that the antifraud provisions require equal information among all traders. This conflicts with the principle set forth in *Chiarella* that only some persons, under some circumstances, will be barred from trading while in possession of material nonpublic information. Judge Wright correctly read our opinion in *Chiarella* as repudiating any notion that all traders must enjoy equal information before trading: "[T]he 'information' theory is rejected. Because the disclose-or-refrain duty is extraordinary, it attaches only when a party has legal obligations other than a mere duty to comply with the general antifraud proscriptions in the federal securities laws." 681 F.2d, at 837. See *Chiarella*, 445 U.S., at 235, n.20. We reaffirm today that "[a] duty [to disclose] arises from the relationship between parties . . . and not merely from one's ability to acquire information because of his position in the market." Id., at 231-232, n.14.

Imposing a duty to disclosure or abstain solely because a person knowingly receives material nonpublic information from an insider and trades on it could have an inhibiting influence on the role of market analysts, which the SEC itself recognizes is necessary to the preservation of a healthy market.[17] It is commonplace for analysts to "ferret out and analyze information," 21 S.E.C. Docket, at 1406,[18] and this often is done by meeting with and questioning corporate officers and others who are insiders. And information that the analysts obtain normally may be the basis for judgments as to the market worth of a corporation's securities. The analyst's judgment in this respect is made available in market letters or otherwise to clients of the firm. It is the nature of this type of information, and indeed of the markets themselves, that such information cannot be made simultaneously available to all of the corporation's stockholders or the public generally.

B

The conclusion that recipients of inside information do not invariably acquire a duty to disclose or abstain does not mean that such tippees always are free to trade

---

17. The SEC expressly recognized that "[t]he value to the entire market of [analysts'] efforts cannot be gainsaid; market efficiency in pricing is significantly enhanced by [their] initiatives to ferret out and analyze information, and thus the analyst's work redounds to the benefit of all investors." 21 S.E.C. Docket, at 1406. The SEC asserts that analysts remain free to obtain from management corporate information for purposes of "filling in the 'interstices in analysis.' . . ." Brief for Respondent 42 (quoting Investors Management Co., 44 S.E.C., at 646). But this rule is inherently imprecise, and imprecision prevents parties from ordering their actions in accord with legal requirements. Unless the parties have some guidance as to where the line is between permissible and impermissible disclosures and uses, neither corporate insiders nor analysts can be sure when the line is crossed.

18. On its facts, this case is the unusual one. Dirks is an analyst in a broker-dealer firm, and he did interview management in the course of his investigation. He uncovered, however, startling information that required no analysis or exercise of judgment as to its market relevance. Nonetheless, the principle at issue here extends beyond these facts. The SEC's rule—applicable without regard to any breach by an insider—could have serious ramifications on reporting by analysts of investment views.

Despite the unusualness of Dirks' "find," the central role that he played in uncovering the fraud at Equity Funding, and that analysts in general can play in revealing information that corporations may have reason to withhold from the public, is an important one. Dirks' careful investigation brought to light a massive fraud at the corporation. And until the Equity Funding fraud was exposed, the information in the trading market was grossly inaccurate. But for Dirks' efforts, the fraud might well have gone undetected longer.

on the information. The need for a ban on some tippee trading is clear. Not only are insiders forbidden by their fiduciary relationship from personally using undisclosed corporate information to their advantage, but they also may not give such information to an outsider for the same improper purpose of exploiting the information for their personal gain. See 15 U.S.C. §78t(b) (making it unlawful to do indirectly "by means of any other person" any act made unlawful by the federal securities laws). Similarly, the transactions of those who knowingly participate with the fiduciary in such a breach are "as forbidden" as transactions "on behalf of the trustee himself." Mosser v. Darrow, 341 U.S. 267, 272 (1951). See Jackson v. Smith, 254 U.S. 586, 589 (1921); Jackson v. Ludeling, 21 Wall. 616, 631-632 (1874). As the Court explained in *Mosser*, a contrary rule "would open up opportunities for devious dealings in the name of others that the trustee could not conduct in his own." 341 U.S., at 271. See SEC v. Texas Gulf Sulphur Co., 446 F.2d 1301, 1308 (C.A.2), cert. denied, 404 U.S. 1005 (1971). Thus, the tippee's duty to disclose or abstain is derivative from that of the insider's duty. Cf. *Chiarella*, 445 U.S., at 246, n.1 (Blackmun, J., dissenting). As we noted in *Chiarella*, "[t]he tippee's obligation has been viewed as arising from his role as a participant after the fact in the insider's breach of a fiduciary duty." Id., at 230, n.12.

Thus, some tippees must assume an insider's duty to the shareholders not because they receive inside information, but rather because it has been made available to them *improperly*. And for Rule 10b-5 purposes, the insider's disclosure is improper only where it would violate his *Cady, Roberts* duty. Thus, a tippee assumes a fiduciary duty to the shareholders of a corporation not to trade on material nonpublic information only when the insider has breached his fiduciary duty to the shareholders by disclosing the information to the tippee and the tippee knows or should know that there has been a breach. As Commissioner Smith perceptively observed in In re Investors Management Co., 44 S.E.C. 633 (1971): "[T]ippee responsibility must be related back to insider responsibility by a necessary finding that the tippee knew the information was given to him in breach of a duty by a person having a special relationship to the issuer not to disclose the information. . . ." Id., at 651 (concurring in result). Tipping thus properly is viewed only as a means of indirectly violating the *Cady, Roberts* disclose-or-abstain rule.[21]

C

In determining whether a tippee is under an obligation to disclose or abstain, it thus is necessary to determine whether the insider's "tip" constituted a breach of the insider's fiduciary duty. All disclosures of confidential corporate information are not

---

21. We do not suggest that knowingly trading on inside information is ever "socially desirable or even that it is devoid of moral considerations." Dooley, Enforcement of Insider Trading Restrictions, 66 Va. L. Rev. 1, 55 (1980). Nor do we imply an absence of responsibility to disclose promptly indications of illegal actions by a corporation to the proper authorities—typically the SEC and exchange authorities in cases involving securities. Depending on the circumstances, and even where permitted by law, one's trading on material nonpublic information is behavior that may fall below ethical standards of conduct. But in a statutory area of the law such as securities regulation, where legal principles of general application must be applied, there may be "significant distinctions between actual legal obligations and ethical ideals."

inconsistent with the duty insiders owe to shareholders. In contrast to the extraordinary facts of this case, the more typical situation in which there will be a question whether disclosure violates the insider's *Cady, Roberts* duty is when insiders disclose information to analysts. In some situations, the insider will act consistently with his fiduciary duty to shareholders, and yet release of the information may affect the market. For example, it may not be clear — either to the corporate insider or to the recipient analyst — whether the information will be viewed as material nonpublic information. Corporate officials may mistakenly think the information already has been disclosed or that it is not material enough to affect the market. Whether disclosure is a breach of duty therefore depends in large part on the purpose of the disclosure. This standard was identified by the SEC itself in *Cady, Roberts:* a purpose of the securities laws was to eliminate "use of inside information for personal advantage." 40 S.E.C., at 912, n.15. Thus, the test is whether the insider personally will benefit, directly or indirectly, from his disclosure. Absent some personal gain, there has been no breach of duty to stockholders. And absent a breach by the insider, there is no derivative breach.[22] As Commissioner Smith stated in *Investors Management Co.:* "It is important in this type of case to focus on policing insiders and what they do . . . rather than on policing information per se and its possession. . . ." 44 S.E.C., at 648 (concurring in result).

The SEC argues that, if inside-trading liability does not exist when the information is transmitted for a proper purpose but is used for trading, it would be a rare situation when the parties could not fabricate some ostensibly legitimate business justification for transmitting the information. We think the SEC is unduly concerned. In determining whether the insider's purpose in making a particular disclosure is fraudulent, the SEC and the courts are not required to read the parties' minds. Scienter in some cases is relevant in determining whether the tipper has violated his *Cady, Roberts* duty.[23] But to determine whether the disclosure itself "deceive[s], manipulate[s], or defraud[s]" shareholders, Aaron v. SEC, 446 U.S. 680, 686 (1980), the initial inquiry is whether there has been a breach of duty by the insider. This requires courts to focus on

22. An example of a case turning on the court's determination that the disclosure did not impose any fiduciary duties on the recipient of the inside information is Walton v. Morgan Stanley & Co., 623 F.2d 796 (C.A.2 1980). There, the defendant investment banking firm, representing one of its own corporate clients, investigated another corporation that was a possible target of a takeover bid by its client. In the course of negotiations the investment banking firm was given, on a confidential basis, unpublished material information. Subsequently, after the proposed takeover was abandoned, the firm was charged with relying on the information when it traded in the target corporation's stock. For purposes of the decision, it was assumed that the firm knew the information was confidential, but that it had been received in arm's-length negotiations. In the absence of any fiduciary relationship, the Court of Appeals found no basis for imposing tippee liability on the investment firm.

23. Scienter — "A mental state embracing intent to deceive, manipulate, or defraud," Ernst & Ernst v. Hochfelder, 425 U.S. 185, 193-194, n.12 (1976) — is an independent element of a Rule 10b-5 violation. See Aaron v. SEC, 446 U.S. 680, 695 (1980). Contrary to the dissent's suggestion, motivation is not irrelevant to the issue of scienter. It is not enough that an insider's conduct results in harm to investors; rather, a violation may be found only where there is "intentional or willful conduct designed to deceive or defraud investors by controlling or artificially affecting the price of securities." Ernst & Ernst v. Hochfelder, supra, at 199. The issue in this case, however, is not whether Secrist or Dirks acted with scienter, but rather whether there was any deceptive or fraudulent conduct at all, i.e., whether Secrist's disclosure constituted a breach of his fiduciary duty and thereby caused injury to shareholders. Only if there was such a breach did Dirks, a tippee, acquire a fiduciary duty to disclose or abstain.

objective criteria, i.e., whether the insider receives a direct or indirect personal benefit from the disclosure, such as a pecuniary gain or a reputational benefit that will translate into future earnings. Cf. 40 S.E.C., at 912, n.15; Brudney, Insiders, Outsiders, and Informational Advantages Under the Federal Securities Laws, 93 Harv. L. Rev. 332, 348 (1979) ("The theory . . . is that the insider, by giving the information out selectively, is in effect selling the information to its recipient for cash, reciprocal information, or other things of value for himself . . ."). There are objective facts and circumstances that often justify such an inference. For example, there may be a relationship between the insider and the recipient that suggests a quid pro quo from the latter, or an intention to benefit the particular recipient. The elements of fiduciary duty and exploitation of nonpublic information also exist when an insider makes a gift of confidential information to a trading relative or friend. The tip and trade resemble trading by the insider himself followed by a gift of the profits to the recipient.

Determining whether an insider personally benefits from a particular disclosure, a question of fact, will not always be easy for courts. But it is essential, we think, to have a guiding principle for those whose daily activities must be limited and instructed by the SEC's inside-trading rules, and we believe that there must be a breach of the insider's fiduciary duty before the tippee inherits the duty to disclose or abstain. In contrast, the rule adopted by the SEC in this case would have no limiting principle.

IV

Under the inside-trading and tipping rules set forth above, we find that there was no actionable violation by Dirks. It is undisputed that Dirks himself was a stranger to Equity Funding, with no pre-existing fiduciary duty to its shareholders. He took no action, directly or indirectly, that induced the shareholders or officers of Equity Funding to repose trust or confidence in him. There was no expectation by Dirks' sources that he would keep their information in confidence. Nor did Dirks misappropriate or illegally obtain the information about Equity Funding. Unless the insiders breached their *Cady, Roberts* duty to shareholders in disclosing the nonpublic information to Dirks, he breached no duty when he passed it on to investors as well as to the Wall Street Journal.

It is clear that neither Secrist nor the other Equity Funding employees violated their *Cady, Roberts* duty to the corporation's shareholders by providing information to Dirks. The tippers received no monetary or personal benefit for revealing Equity Funding's secrets, nor was their purpose to make a gift of valuable information to Dirks. As the facts of this case clearly indicate, the tippers were motivated by a desire to expose the fraud. In the absence of a breach of duty to shareholders by the insiders, there was no derivative breach by Dirks. Dirks therefore could not have been "a participant after the fact in [an] insider's breach of a fiduciary duty." *Chiarella*, 445 U.S., at 230, n.12. . . .

JUSTICE BLACKMUN, with whom JUSTICE BRENNAN and JUSTICE MARSHALL join, dissenting. . . .

. . . The fact that the insider himself does not benefit from the breach does not eradicate the shareholder's injury. Cf. Restatement (Second) of Trusts §205, Comments c and d (1959) (trustee liable for acts causing diminution of value of trust); 3 A. Scott, Law of Trusts §205, p. 1665 (3d ed. 1967) (trustee liable for any losses to trust caused by his breach). It makes no difference to the shareholder whether the corporate insider gained or intended to gain personally from the transaction; the shareholder still has lost because of the insider's misuse of nonpublic information. The duty is addressed not to the insider's motives, but to his actions and their consequences on the shareholder. Personal gain is not an element of the breach of this duty. . . .

The improper-purpose requirement not only has no basis in law, but it also rests implicitly on a policy that I cannot accept. The Court justifies Secrist's and Dirks' action because the general benefit derived from the violation of Secrist's duty to shareholders outweighed the harm caused to those shareholders, see Heller, *Chiarella*, SEC Rule 14e-3 and *Dirks:* "Fairness" versus Economic Theory, 37 Bus. Lawyer 517, 550 (1982); Easterbrook, Insider Trading, Secret Agents, Evidentiary Privileges, and the Production of Information, 1981 S. Ct. Rev. 309, 338—in other words, because the end justified the means. Under this view, the benefit conferred on society by Secrist's and Dirks' activities may be paid for with the losses caused by shareholders trading with Dirks' clients.

Although Secrist's general motive to expose the Equity Funding fraud was laudable, the means he chose were not. Moreover, even assuming that Dirks played a substantial role in exposing the fraud, he and his clients should not profit from the information they obtained from Secrist. Misprision of a felony long has been against public policy. Branzburg v. Hayes, 408 U.S. 665, 696-697 (1972); see 18 U.S.C. §4. A person cannot condition his transmission of information of a crime on a financial award. As a citizen, Dirks had at least an ethical obligation to report the information to the proper authorities. The Court's holding is deficient in policy terms not because it fails to create a legal norm out of that ethical norm, but because it actually rewards Dirks for his aiding and abetting. . . .

In my view, Secrist violated his duty to Equity Funding shareholders by transmitting material nonpublic information to Dirks with the intention that Dirks would cause his clients to trade on that information. Dirks, therefore, was under a duty to make the information publicly available or to refrain from actions that he knew would lead to trading. Because Dirks caused his clients to trade, he violated §10(b) and Rule 10b-5. Any other result is a disservice to this country's attempt to provide fair and efficient capital markets. I dissent.

NOTE

Consider who benefits from the *Dirks* decision. In Regulation on Demand: A Private Interest Model with an Application to Insider Trading Regulation, 30 J.L. & Econ. 311 (1986), Professors Haddock and Macey suggest that the protection market professionals receive in *Chiarella/Dirks* and the fiduciary duty restrictions on insiders remove the market professionals' chief competition for information.

PROBLEM 12-1

A college football coach sitting in the bleachers while watching a high school track meet in which his son is participating overhears a corporate executive talking to the executive's spouse. The overheard information relates to a merger in which the executive's company will be taken over by a larger firm at a substantial premium. The executive is a member of the booster club for the college football program.

Is there liability under Rule 10b-5 if the coach purchases shares in the executive's company?

PROBLEM 12-2

A director of a corporation that is about to receive a tender offer from another corporation tells his adult son of the proposed takeover. The son thereupon buys an option in the target, which he sells three days later for a $400,000 profit.

Is there liability under Rule 10b-5 for the actions of the son?

PROBLEM 12-3

Royal is CEO of Card, Inc. and also a member of the board of directors of Video Corp. Royal approaches Bayly, the CEO of Video Corp., and asks if Video would be interested in providing $600,000 to finance a joint venture between Card, Inc. and a casino company. Video is unable to provide the financing, but Bayly buys 10,000 shares of Card, Inc. stock. After Card lines up a joint venture with another company, Card's stock rises and Bayly is able to sell her shares at a substantial profit.

Is there liability under Rule 10b-5 for Bayly's actions?

b.   Regulation FD

Justice Powell's opinion for the court in *Dirks* reflects concern for the role of securities analysts like Raymond Dirks who actively follow stocks and earn their livelihood by providing information to clients that others do not have. Often that information will come from insiders. In an environment where the market often punishes companies for missing earnings estimates, insiders will often want analysts to learn information. In such a setting the transfer of the information does not breach the insider's duty to the company that would trigger tippee liability nor has it been held to create liability under the constructive insider theory, but in 2000 the SEC promulgated Regulation FD to address such conduct.

Securities and Exchange Commission v. Siebel Systems, Inc.

United States District Court, S.D. New York, 2005

384 F. Supp. 2d 694

DANIELS, DISTRICT JUDGE.

Plaintiff, the Securities and Exchange Commission ("SEC"), commenced this action, against Siebel Systems, Inc. ("Siebel Systems"), Siebel Systems's Chief Financial

Officer, Kenneth Goldman, and one of Siebel System's Senior Vice Presidents, Mark Hanson. The SEC charges the defendants with, inter alia, violations of, or aiding and abetting in the violation of, Regulation FD ("Fair Disclosure"), 17 C.F.R. §243.100. In general terms, Regulation FD prohibits a company and its senior officials from privately disclosing any material nonpublic information regarding the company or its securities to certain persons such as analysts and institutional investors.

Defendants moved, pursuant to Fed. R. Civ. P. 12(b)(6), to dismiss the complaint for failure to state a claim upon which relief may be granted on the grounds that the statements disclosed were neither material nor nonpublic. Defendants' motion is granted. The nature and content of the statements that the SEC alleges violate Regulation FD do not support the Commission's claim that Siebel Systems or its senior officials privately disclosed material nonpublic information.

Regulation FD requires an issuer, to make public material information disclosed to security market professionals or holders of the issuer's securities who are reasonably likely to trade on the basis of that information. 17 C.F.R §§243.100; 242.101(c), (f). Where the issuer's selective disclosure of material nonpublic information is intentional, the issuer is to simultaneously make public disclosure. 17 C.F.R. §243.100(a)(1). In the case of non-intentional disclosure, public disclosure must be, promptly made. 17 C.F.R. §243(a)(2). "'Promptly' means as soon as reasonably practicable (but in no event after the later of 24 hours or the commencement of the next day's trading on the New York Stock Exchange) after a senior official of the issuer, . . . learns that there has been a non-intentional disclosure by the issuer or person acting on behalf of the issuer of information that the senior official knows, or is reckless in not knowing, is both material and nonpublic." 17 C.F.R. §243.101(d).

The gravamen of the complaint is that defendant Goldman made positive comments about the company's business activity levels and sales transaction pipeline at two private events on April 30th, 2003, attended by institutional investors and by defendant Hanson. The SEC alleges that, at these two events, Mr. Goldman privately disclosed material nonpublic information by stating that Siebel Systems's activity levels were "good" or "better," that new deals were coming back into the pipeline, that the pipeline was "building" and "growing" and that "there were some $5 million deals in Siebel's pipeline." The complaint alleges that immediately following the disclosure of this information or soon thereafter, certain attendants of the meetings and their associates made substantial purchases of shares of Siebel Systems's stock. The SEC alleges "by disclosing that Siebel's business activity levels were 'good' and 'better,' and that its sales transaction pipeline was 'growing' and 'building,' Goldman communicated to his private audiences that Siebel's business was improving as the result of new business, and that the increase in the Company's guidance for the second quarter was not simply because deals that had slipped from the first quarter were closing."

The SEC claims that these statements materially contrasted with public statements made by [founder and then CEO] Thomas Siebel during conference calls on April 4th and 23rd, and at an April 28th conference. In the complaint, the SEC sets forth, in great detail, the contents of Mr. Siebel's public statements of April 4th, April 23rd, and April 28th. Those statements provided information about the company's "performance in the first quarter of 2003 and its expected performance in the second quarter of 2003." The SEC alleges that in these statements it was reported that: (1) Siebel Systems's first quarter results were poor because the economy was poor and because some deals that were expected to close in the previous quarter did not, *i.e.*, deals had "slipped" into the second quarter; (2) Siebel Systems's software license revenues were expected to be higher in the second quarter than in the first quarter, but the company conditioned its estimate on the performance of the overall economy; and (3) there were no indications that the existing poor economic conditions were approving. "In each statement, the Company [allegedly] characterized the economy negatively (as not improved or not improving)." The complaint further states that, with regard to the guidance for the second quarter of fiscal year 2003, "[t]he Company conditioned its estimate on the performance of the overall economy. It said that if the economy improved, Siebel's business would improve, and that, conversely, if the economy did not improve," then Siebel's business would not improve." The SEC alleges that the public statements "linked the Company's prospective performance to the economy's performance — that is, if the economy improved, Siebel's business would improve."

The SEC contends that "[b]ased on these disclosures, the total mix of information available to investors was that Siebel's business had performed poorly in the first quarter and would improve in the second quarter only if the economy improved." Allegedly, Mr. Goldman's statements materially contrasted with the public statements that Thomas Siebel made during the April 4 and 23 conference calls and at the . . . conference on April 28. For example, in contrast to the apocalyptic economic environment that Thomas Siebel described at the [April 28th] conference, Goldman's disclosure at the April 30 [events] were significantly more positive and upbeat. Unlike the Company's prior public disclosure about its prospective performance in the second quarter, Goldman's statements about the Company's business were not linked to or conditioned upon the performance of the economy."

The complaint further alleges that analysts, who were participating in the April 23rd conference call and the April 28th conference, "wanted to know how much of the projected increase in software license revenues in the second quarter compared to the first quarter revenues was attributable to the deals that slipped from the first quarter as opposed to the Company's expectation that it would generate new business in the second quarter." The SEC alleges that when the analysts repeatedly inquired about the impact of the slipped deals on Siebel Systems's second quarter guidance, Mr. Siebel "avoided," "evaded," and "directly declined to answer the question." The SEC maintains that, publicly, "the total mix of information available to investors did not include information that would enable either analysts or investors to determine whether the increased guidance for the second quarter represented an improvement over the first quarter."

The complaint further alleges that Siebel Systems failed to file the requisite Form 8-K disclosing the material nonpublic information that Mr. Goldman had disclosed at the private meetings within the time frame specified by the SEC's rules, nor did it "disseminate that information through another method of disclosure reasonably designed to provide broad, non-exclusionary distribution of the information to the public." . . .

VIOLATION OF REGULATION FD

The complaint alleges four nonpublic material disclosures made by Mr. Goldman which are the basis for the SEC's claims for violations of Regulation FD: (1) that there were some *five million dollar deals* in the company's pipeline for the second quarter of 2003; (2) that *new deals* were coming into the sales pipeline; (3) that the company's sales pipeline was "*growing*" or "*building;*" and (4) that the company's sales or business activity levels were "*good*" or "*better.*" The complaint relies on no statements regarding specific earnings or sales figures. Defendants argue that dismissal of the complaint is warranted because the four statements at issue cannot support a conclusory allegation that these statements were either material or nonpublic.

Regulation FD does not contain definitions for the terms "material" or "nonpublic." In the SEC's release discussing the proposed adoption of the regulation ("Proposing Release"), the SEC "recognize[d] that materiality judgments can be difficult." Proposed Rule: Selective Disclosure and Insider Trading, 64 Fed. Reg. 72590, 72594 (Dec. 28. 1999) ("Proposing Release"). The SEC observed that the proposed regulation could have a "chilling effect" in that "[c]orporate officials [might] become more cautious in communicating with analysts or selected investors," especially since such communications may take the form of "unrehearsed question-and-answer sessions, and responses to unsolicited inquiries." Id. Thus, the SEC noted it was "mindful of the potential burdens of requiring instant materiality judgments to be made by those put in the position of responding immediately to questions." Id. Despite the SEC's concession that materiality determinations are difficult, the SEC nevertheless suggested that in most cases, the question of whether information was material will be reasonably clear. The SEC explained,

> Although materiality issues do not lend themselves to a bright-line test, we believe that the majority of cases are reasonably clear. At one end of the spectrum, we believe issuers should avoid giving guidance or express warnings to analysts or selected investors about important upcoming earnings or sales figures; such earnings or sales figures will frequently have a significant impact on the issuer's stock price. On the other end of the spectrum, more generalized background information is less likely to be material. Id. at 72595.

In the SEC's Adopting Release, the SEC again noted the frequently expressed concern that the regulation would not lead to broader dissemination of information, but would instead have a "chilling effect" on disclosure of information by the issuer. 65 Fed. Reg. 51716, 51718. The potential chilling effect could conceivably result in the issuers "speak[ing] less often out of fear of liability based on a post hoc assessment that disclosed information was material," and "such a chilling effect result[ing] from Regulation FD [] would be a cost to the overall market efficiency and capital formations." Id. at 51733.

In response to this concern and in recognizing that the market is best served by more, rather than less, disclosure of information by issuers, the SEC modified the proposed Regulation FD to include certain safeguards to narrow the applicability of Regulation FD so as not to diminish the flow of information.[7] Despite its previous

---

7. "In response to the comments [the SEC] received on the proposal, [the SEC has] made several modifications . . . in the final rules." Id. at 51716. "These modifications include narrowing the scope of the regulation so that it does not apply to all communications with persons outside the issuer, narrowing the types of issuer personnel covered by the regulation to senior officials and those who would normally be expected to communicate with securities market professionals or security holders, and clarifying that

acknowledgment, in the Proposing Release, that materiality judgments can be difficult, the SEC did not find that the "appropriate answer to this difficulty is to set forth a bright-line test, or an exclusive list of material items for purpose of Regulation FD." Id. at 51721. Although the SEC declined to set forth an all-inclusive list of what matters are to be deemed material, it did provide seven categories of information or events that have a higher probability of being considered material. The seven enumerated categories are:

> (1) Earnings information; (2) mergers, acquisitions, tender offers, joint ventures, or changes in assets; (3) new products or discoveries, or developments regarding customers or supplies (e.g., the acquisition or loss of a contract); (4) changes in control or in management; (5) change in auditors or auditor notification that the issuer may no longer rely on an auditor's audit report; (6) events regarding the issuer's securities—e.g., defaults on strict securities, calls of securities for redemption, repurchase plans, stock splits or changes in dividends, changes to rights of security holders, public or private sales of additional securities; and (7) bankruptcies and receiverships.

Id.

The specific matters included in the list, however, are not per se material.

Although Regulation FD does not contain definitions for the terms "material" or "nonpublic" the Adopting Release advises that those terms are to be defined as they have been in previous case law. Fed. Reg. 51716, 51721. With regard to the "nonpublic" element, the Adopting Release relied on the finding in SEC v. Texas Sulphur Co., 401 F.2d 833, 854 (2d Cir. 1968), that information is nonpublic if it has not been disseminated in a manner sufficient to ensure its availability to the investing public. Id. As the Second Circuit Court of Appeals explained, in SEC v. Mayhew, 121 F.3d 44 (2d Cir. 1997):

> Information becomes public when disclosed to achieve a broad dissemination to the investing public generally and without favoring any special person or group, or when, although known only by a few persons, their trading on it has caused the information to be fully impounded into the price of the particular stock. Mayhew, 121 F.3d at 50 (internal quotation marks and citations omitted).

With regard to the definition of "materiality," the Adopting Release embraced the definition set forth in TSC Indus., Inc. v. Northway, Inc., 426 U.S. 438 (1976), concluding that "[i]nformation is material if 'there is a substantial likelihood that a reasonable shareholder would consider it important' in making an investment decision." Fed. Reg. 51716, 51721 (quoting TSC Indus., Inc., 426 U.S. at 449 (1976)). To satisfy the materiality element, there must be a substantial likelihood that a reasonable investor would have considered the information as having significantly altered the 'total mix' of information made available. Id. (quoting TSC Indus., Inc., 426 U.S. at 449); see also Basic Inc. v. Levinson, 485 U.S. 224, 231-32, (1988); Mayhew, 121 F.3d at 52. The "total mix" of information includes all information that is reasonably available to the public.

---

where the regulation requires 'knowing or reckless' conduct, liability will attach only when the issuer's personnel know or are reckless in not knowing that the information selectively disclosed is both material and nonpublic. Additionally, . . . [the SEC] added an express provision in the regulation's text designed to remove any doubt that private liability will not result from a Regulation FD violation."

Id. at 51733, see also, Id. at 51719.

Starr v. Georgeson Shareholder, Inc., 412 F.3d 103, 110 (2d Cir. 2005) (quoting Press v. Quick & Reilly, Inc., 218 F.3d 121, 130 (2d Cir. 2000)). It is not a prerequisite to a finding of materiality that had a reasonable investor been privy to the information, the investor would necessarily have changed his or her investment decision as a result of that information. *TSC Indus., Inc.,* 426 U.S. at 449; *Mayhew,* 121 F.3d at 52 (citations omitted); see also, Falser Adam Co. v. PMI Indus., Inc., 938 F.2d 1529, 1533 (2d. Cir. 1991) (citation omitted) ("material fact need not be outcome-determinative," but rather it is sufficient that the information would assume actual significance to a reasonable investor). Information that would affect the probable future of the company and which may affect an investor's desire to buy, sell, or hold the company's securities is material. *Texas Gulf Sulphur Co.,* 401 F.2d at 849. "Some information is of such dubious significance that insistence on its disclosure may accomplish more harm than good. . . . [I]f the standard of materiality is unnecessary low, not only may the company and its management be subjected to liability for insignificant [nonpublic selective disclosure], but also management's fear of exposing itself to substantial liability may cause it simply to bury the shareholders in an avalanche of trivial information, a result that is hardly conducive to informed decisionmaking." *TSC Indus., Inc.,* 426 U.S. at 448-49.

The question of materiality generally presents a mixed question of law and fact, as it involves the application of a legal standard to a particular set of facts. *TSC Indus., Inc.,* 426 U.S. at 450; Ganino v. Citizens Utilities Co., 228 F.3d 154, 162 (2d Cir. 2000). The question of materiality is, however, an objective one, involving the significance of the information to a reasonable investor. *TSC Indus., Inc.,* 426 U.S. at 445 (1976). "[S]ince the importance of a particular piece of information depends on the context in which it is given, materiality has become one of the most unpredictable and elusive concepts of the federal securities laws." SEC v. Bausch & Lomb Inc., 565 F.2d 8, 10 (2d Cir. 1977). A determination with regard to materiality is a fact-specific inquiry to be determined on a case-by-case basis. *Basic,* 485 U.S., at 240, 250. A complaint may only be dismissed on the grounds that the alleged private disclosure of information was immaterial if the subject information is "so obviously unimportant to a reasonable investor that reasonable minds could not differ on the question of [its] importance." Goldman v. Belden, 754 F.2d 1059, 1067 (2d Cir. 1985). Hence, where the subject statements are so blatantly unimportant, it is appropriate for the Court to rule, as a matter of law, that the statements do not meet the materiality threshold, and to dismiss the complaint. See, Schoenhaut v. Am. Sensors, Inc., 986 F. Supp, 785, 790-91 (S.D.N.Y. 1997) (quoting In re Burlington Coat Factory Securities Litig., 114 F.3d at 1429).

In applying the aforementioned principles to the case at bar, the allegations in the complaint fail to demonstrate that Regulation FD was violated. Regulation FD was never intended to be utilized in the manner attempted by the SEC under these circumstances. The statements relied upon in the complaint cannot support a conclusion that material information privately provided by Mr. Goldman was unavailable to the public. Specifically, Mr. Goldman's private statement regarding the existence of five million dollar deals in the company's pipeline for the second quarter was equivalent in substance to the information previously disclosed by Mr. Siebel. With regard to the guidance for the second quarter, Mr. Siebel stated at the April 23rd conference call:

Our guidance and license revenue for the quarter is 120 to 140 million range. I think that we'll see lots of small deals. We'll see some medium deals. We'll see a number of deals over a million dollars. And I suspect we'll see some *greater than five*. And now that's what the mix will look like. (Dunning Decl., Ex. 2 at 7) (emphasis added).

The SEC argues that Mr. Goldman's statement, in contrast, was in the *present* tense, and hence constitutes a factually different material statement than that made by Mr. Siebel. The SEC contends that unlike Mr. Goldman's statement, Mr. Siebel's statement was in the *future* tense, and Mr. Siebel's use of the word "suspect" indicates his statement was not a present fact, but rather was forward looking.

It would appear that in examining publicly and privately disclosed information, the SEC has scrutinized, at an extremely heightened level, every particular word used in the statement, including the tense of verbs and the general syntax of each sentence. No support for such an approach can be found in Regulation FD itself, or in the Proposing and Adopting Releases. Such an approach places an unreasonable burden on a company's management and spokespersons to become linguistic experts, or otherwise live in fear of violating Regulation FD should the words they use later be interpreted by the SEC as connoting even the slightest variance from the company's public statements.

Regulation FD does not require that corporate officials only utter verbatim statements that were previously publicly made. In Kennecott Copper Corp. v. Curtiss-Wright Corp., 584 F.2d 1195 (2d Cir. 1978), which concerned the adequacy of a proxy disclosure, the Second Circuit advised that, in analyzing the disclosure of material statements, "nit-picking should not become the name of the game. . . . There is no requirement that a material fact be expressed in certain words or in a certain form of language. Fair accuracy, not perfection, is the appropriate standard." *Kennecott Copper Corp.*, 584 F.2d at 1200 (quotation marks and citations omitted). To require a more demanding standard, in the context of Regulation FD, could compel companies to discontinue any spontaneous communications so that the content of any intended communication may be examined by a lexicologist to ensure that the proposed statement discloses the exact information in the same form as was publicly disclosed. If Regulation FD is applied in such a manner, the very purpose of the regulation, i.e., to provide the public with a broad flow of relevant investment information, would be thwarted.

Mr. Goldman's private statement regarding the existence of five million dollars deals in the company's pipeline for the second quarter was equivalent in substance to the information publicly disclosed by the company in that it conveyed the same material information. As long as the private statement conveys the same material information that the public statement publicly conveyed, Regulation FD is not implicated, and hence no greater form of disclosure, pursuant to the regulation, is required. Although Mr. Goldman's statement was not literally a word for word recitation of Mr. Siebel's disclosure, both provided the same information, and Mr. Goldman's statement did not add, contradict, or significantly alter the material information available to the general public. It therefore cannot constitute a sufficient factual basis on which to allege a nonpublic disclosure of material information in violation of Regulation FD.

Similarly unavailing are the SEC's claims that Mr. Goldman's private statements regarding new business in the pipeline and that the pipeline was "growing" or "building" was information which was not previously disclosed to the public. The SEC argues that Mr. Siebel "did not describe the status of the Company's pipeline." However, at the April 23rd conference call, a question was posed regarding the makeup of the pipeline with respect to "new versus exist[ing] customers." The verbatim transcript on which the SEC relies indicates that in response thereto, Mr. Siebel publicly stated, "every quarter will be some place between 45 and 55 percent of our business with new customers." Such a statement clearly indicated that the second quarter pipeline would include new deals.

Mr. Goldman's private description of the pipeline as "growing" or "building" provides no additional material information that was not previously publicly disclosed by the company. The complaint acknowledges Siebel Systems's April 23rd and 28th public statements that "the Company projected that its software license revenues would be in the range of $120 to $140 million, which was more than the Company's reported revenues for the first quarter." Moreover, the company publicly disclosed that the projected total revenues for the second quarter appeared to be in the 340 to 360 million dollar range, which was greater than the reported total revenues for the first quarter. Additionally, at the April 23rd conference call, Mr. Siebel explained that the anticipated increase in the license revenues was based on an analysis of the pipeline. At the April 28th conference, Mr. Siebel again explained that the projected increase was Siebel Systems's "best professional judgment based upon the pipeline with the deals that we saw. . . ." Siebel Systems's public statements clearly disclosed that it was projecting an increase in revenues in the second quarter, and that this expectation was based, in part, upon an analysis of the pipeline. Based on this information, a reasonable investor would be aware that the sales pipeline was "growing" and "building." Hence Mr. Goldman's private wording, to that effect, added nothing to the total mix of information publicly available.

The SEC further alleges that Regulation ED was violated as a result of Mr. Goldman's private statements that Siebel Systems's sales or business activity levels were "good" or "better." Mr. Goldman's private statement that the activity levels were "good" or "better" was based on information available to the public since Siebel Systems publicly reported that it anticipated a future increase in the company's performance. The terms "better" and "good" are merely generalized descriptive labels based on the underlying quantitative information provided publicly by Siebel Systems. Given the detailed and specific information revealed in the company's public disclosures, Mr. Goldman's description of the company's performance and activity level as being "good" and "better" imparted no greater information to his private audiences than Siebel Systems had already disclosed to the public at large. Hence, the statements regarding the company's performance or activity levels being "good" or "better" did not alter the total mix of information already available to the reasonable investor.

The SEC maintains that Mr. Goldman's statements constituted nonpublic material information because his statements forecasted overall positive growth for the company, whereas the company's public statements avoided making such a positive affirmation.

Although the SEC is not disputing that the public information was that the second quarter guidance was higher than the first quarter's actual results, the SEC asserts that this is not dispositive of whether business was improving. However, the information available to the public provides a sufficient factual basis for a reasonable investor to conclude that business was improving.

The SEC places great emphasis on the alleged actions taken by certain individuals who were in attendance at Mr. Goldman's private speaking engagements. The complaint alleges that certain attendees, and other individuals with whom they communicated, purchased Siebel Systems stock almost immediately after Mr. Goldman's private statements or soon thereafter, causing the market for Siebel Systems stock to significantly rise and for trading to surge. The SEC argues that taking these allegations as true, and drawing all reasonable inferences in its favor, leads to the conclusion that Mr. Goldman disclosed information that was both new and material.

A major factor in determining whether information is material is the importance attached to it by those who were exposed to the information as may be expressed by their reaction to the information. *Mayhew,* 121 F.3d at 52 (citing *Texas Gulf Sulphur Co.,* 401 F.2d at 851); Elkind v. Liggett & Myers, Inc., 635 F.2d 156, 166-67 (2d Cir. 1980). Although stock movement is a relevant factor to be considered in making the determination as to materiality, it is not, however, a sufficient factor alone to establish materiality. United States v. Bilzerian, 926 F.2d 1285, 1298 (2d Cir. 1991).

An examination of the public and private statements do not support a conclusory allegation that Mr. Goldman's statements were the disclosure of nonpublic material information. The actions taken by those in attendance at Mr. Goldman's speaking engagements, although a relevant consideration, do not change the nature or content of Mr. Goldman's statements. Regulation FD deals exclusively with the disclosure of material information. The regulation does not prohibit persons speaking on behalf of an issuer, from providing mere positive or negative characterizations, or their optimistic or pessimistic subjective general impressions, based upon or drawn from the material information available to the public. The mere fact that analysts might have considered Mr. Goldman's private statements significant is not, standing alone, a basis to infer that Regulation FD was violated. See, 65 Fed. Reg. 51716, 51722 ("Regulation FD will not be implicated where an issuer discloses immaterial information whose significance is discerned by the analyst. . . . The focus of Regulation FD is on whether the issuer discloses material nonpublic information, not on whether an analyst, through some combination of persistence, knowledge, and insight, regards as material information whose significance is not apparent to the reasonable investor").

The SEC further argues that Mr. Goldman's statements "Constituted new information" because they were not "conditioned upon nor qualified by the performance of the economy," and therefore they "contrasted with the Company's prior statements and altered the total mix of information available to investors," which included, "that Siebel's business had performed poorly in the first quarter and would improve in the second quarter only if the economy improved."

It would be an unusual rule, indeed, to require that forecasts must repeatedly be accompanied by a warning that company performance might be affected by an improving or worsening economy. However, even if the potential effects of the economy constituted material information,[13] Siebel Systems had publicly disclosed that the performance of the company was linked to the performance of the economy. What Regulation FD does not require is that an individual, speaking privately on behalf of an issuer, repeat material information which has already been previously publicly proclaimed. See, Spielman v. Gen. Host Corp., 402 F. Supp. 190, 195 (S.D.N.Y. 1975). aff'd, 538 F.2d 39 (2d Cir. 1976). Mr. Goldman's alleged failure to qualify his private statement about the company's performance, by linking it to, or conditioning it upon, the performance of the economy, cannot be alleged as a private disclosure of non-public information. Regulation FD only pertains to the required public disclosure of information, not the failure to repeat a particular public statement in private.[14]

Significantly, none of the statements challenged by the SEC falls squarely within the seven enumerated categories listed by the SEC, in the Adopting Release, as being more likely to be considered material. Applying Regulation FD in an overly aggressive manner cannot effectively encourage full and complete public disclosure of facts reasonably deemed relevant to investment decisionmaking. It provides no clear guidance for companies to conform their conduct in compliance with Regulation FD. Instead, the enforcement of Regulation FD by excessively scrutinizing vague general comments has a potential chilling effect which can discourage, rather than, encourage public disclosure of material information.

In accepting the factual allegations in the complaint as true and drawing all reasonable inferences in the SEC's favor, the statements relied upon in the complaint fail to support its conclusory allegation that material information disclosed by Mr. Goldman in private, had not already been publicly disclosed by Siebel Systems. Accordingly, the complaint fails to sufficiently allege that Regulation FD was violated. Except with regard to the sixth cause of action against Siebel Systems for violation of its duty to maintain adequate disclosure controls and procedures to ensure compliance with Regulation FD, the SEC does not dispute that, absent a violation of Regulation [FD], its other remaining claims fail to state a viable cause of action. . . .

---

13. It is doubtful that a company's disclosure regarding its prospective performance being "linked to or conditioned upon the performance of the economy" would constitute material information. It is a fundamental and basic principle that the economy affects corporate America. Information which is so basic that a reasonable investor could be expected to know it does not constitute material facts. Levitin v. PaineWebber, Inc., 159 F.3d 698, 702 (2d Cir. 1998); see also, In re Northern Telecom Ltd. Sec. Litig., 42 F. Supp.2d 234, 236 (S.D.N.Y.1998) (statement that company would "be in good shape" if economy took an upward turn was merely an expression of corporate optimism which is too indefinite to be actionable under the securities laws.). "The role of the materiality requirement is not to 'attribute to investors a child-like simplicity' as it is unreasonable to assume investors are 'nitwits' unable to appreciate the fundamental risks associated with the stock market." See, Basic, 485 U.S. at 234, 108 S. Ct. 978 (quoting Flamm v. Eberstadt, 814 F.2d 1169, 1175 (7th Cir. 1987)); see also, Richland v. Crandalk 262 F. Supp. 538, 554 (S.D.N.Y. 1967) ("[C]orporations are not required to address their stockholder's as if they were children in kindergarten.").

14. Although Regulation FD pertains solely to disclosure of information, the challenged communication need not be an expressed verbal or written statement. Tacit communications, such as a wink, nod, or a thumbs up or down gesture, may give rise to a Regulation FD violation.

NOTES AND QUESTIONS

1. The *Dirks* opinion seeks to avoid inhibiting the role of market analysts who are "necessary to the preservation of a healthy market." To what extent is the SEC taking a different view in adopting Regulation FD? Does it matter, as set forth in Rule 102 of FD, that failing to meet the requirements of the rule does not create a violation of Rule 10b-5?

2. Regulation FD distinguishes intentional disclosure from unintentional disclosure. For example, in a case in 2002, a company had secured a contract to have its product bundled with a buyer's network system, but the buyer asked that the announcement be delayed pending testing with the buyer's customers. For that testing process, information was posted on the company's website, which led to questions during a conference call between the company's president and analysts, at which time the president discussed the sale, which had not otherwise been announced. While still on the call, a salesperson for a brokerage firm looked up the webpage on the company's site and mailed the webpage address to the brokerage firm's sales force. The SEC found the disclosure unintentional but found an announcement after the market closed on the second day following the disclosure was not prompt disclosure as required by Regulation FD. The only penalty was the company's agreeing to cease and desist from further violations. See In re Secure Computing Corporation, Exchange Act Release 46,895, November 23, 2002, at http://www.sec.gov/litigation/admin/34-46895.htm.

3. The court in *Siebel* dismissed an additional claim asserting that the company had failed to maintain disclosure controls and procedures designed to ensure the proper and timely handling of information required to be disclosed in the reports filed or submitted under the Exchange Act. It did not rule on claims that the regulation abridged freedom of speech or that the SEC exceeded its authority under Section 13 of the Exchange Act.

PROBLEM 12-4

Telecom Corp. is a large telecommunications firm that regularly holds a conference call with analysts following its stock; the calls are streamed online and widely available. At its most recent conference call, the company announced it was experiencing "significant weakness" and was likely to have minimal earnings for the quarter if the order pattern continued. Most analysts thereby lowered their earnings estimates for the company, but the company's investor relations (IR) director concluded the analysts were still likely overstating the company's quarterly results. Part of the problem was the variability or seasonality of earnings in the industry, where most of the earnings were in the first half of the year. In the prior year the company's seasonality slope was very steep (i.e., most of its earnings were going to be in the first half), and analysts were predicting that the current year would be more evenly distributed. Company estimates were that this year would match the prior year, with the result that first-quarter earnings were too high. Over a one-week period, the IR director directly contacted approximately 15 analysts to discuss their models. On these calls, the IR director reiterated particular statements from the earlier call, such as the term "significant." On most of these calls, the IR director specifically told analysts that when the company has in the past used "significant" or "significantly," it has intended a change of 25 percent or more. The IR director also told most of the analysts that the company would follow the same seasonality pattern as the previous year. Would these facts give the company a problem under Regulation FD?

c. Misappropriation and Rule 14e-3

Valuable information about a corporation's stock often comes from a source outside the corporation and thus from a source outside the group traditionally owing a fiduciary duty to the shareholders whose share value is affected by inside information. A prominent example is information from an acquiring company that is about to make a takeover bid for a target company at a price above current share value. Insider liability on this basis was argued in the *Chiarella* case (page 1117), but Justice Powell's majority opinion did not address this question because that theory was not presented to the jury that convicted Chiarella. In separate opinions, two justices suggested there could be liability. Chief Justice Burger's broad misappropriation theory would reach informational advantage obtained by an *unlawful* means. The focus was on the stealing, and not the fiduciary relationship to the person whose shares are traded. Justice Stevens defined misappropriation more narrowly, suggesting that actions, as in *Chiarella,* could constitute a fraud or deceit of the acquiring companies that had entrusted confidential information to Chiarella's employer. He noted, however, that the fraud on the source, who was neither a purchaser nor seller of securities, might negate a Rule 10b-5 claim because of *Blue Chip Stamps* (see page 998).

Several appellate courts upheld misappropriation liability on a similar theory, see United States v. Chestman, 947 F.2d 551 (2d Cir. en banc 1991); S.E.C. v. Cherif, 993 F.2d 403 (7th Cir. 1991). Prior to *O'Hagan* two circuit courts used *Blue Chip Stamps* and Santa Fe Industries, Inc. v. Green (page 1002) to assert that Section 10(b) is concerned with the deception of purchasers and sellers of securities and to extend it to breach of duty outside of that context would render meaningless the statutory requirement that the fraud be in connection with the purchase and sale of a security. See, e.g., United States v. Bryan, 58 F.3d 933 (4th Cir. 1995) (overturning the conviction of the former director of the West Virginia lottery for securities fraud arising from his trading on inside information as to companies that would receive state lottery contracts); United States v. O'Hagan, 92 F.3d 612 (8th Cir. 1996).

In the case that follows, the Supreme Court addressed that split and also liability based on SEC Rule 14e-3, which had been promulgated in the months after *Chiarella.* It derives its statutory authority not from §10(b), but §14(e), an antifraud provision regulating tender offers in which an acquiring company purchases shares directly from the shareholders of a target, in contrast to a merger (see Chapter 8) when the acquisition occurs by a vote of the directors and shareholders.

United States v. O'Hagan
United States Supreme Court 1997
521 U.S. 642

JUSTICE GINSBURG delivered the opinion of the Court.

This case concerns the interpretation and enforcement of §10(b) and §14(e) of the Securities Exchange Act of 1934, and rules made by the Securities and Exchange

Commission pursuant to these provisions, Rule 10b-5 and Rule 14e-3(a). Two prime questions are presented. . . . (1) Is a person who trades in securities for personal profit, using confidential information misappropriated in breach of a fiduciary duty to the source of the information, guilty of violating §10(b) and Rule 10b-5? (2) Did the Commission exceed its rulemaking authority by adopting Rule 14e-3(a), which proscribes trading on undisclosed information in the tender offer setting, even in the absence of a duty to disclose? Our answer to the first question is yes, and to the second question, viewed in the context of this case, no.

I

Respondent James Herman O'Hagan was a partner in the law firm of Dorsey & Whitney in Minneapolis, Minnesota. In July 1988, Grand Metropolitan PLC (Grand Met), a company based in London, England, retained Dorsey & Whitney as local counsel to represent Grand Met regarding a potential tender offer for the common stock of the Pillsbury Company, headquartered in Minneapolis. Both Grand Met and Dorsey & Whitney took precautions to protect the confidentiality of Grand Met's tender offer plans. O'Hagan did no work on the Grand Met representation. . . . By the end of September, [O'Hagan had purchased] 2,500 unexpired Pillsbury options, apparently more than any other individual investor. O'Hagan also purchased, in September 1988, some 5,000 shares of Pillsbury common stock, at a price just under $39 per share. When Grand Met announced its tender offer in October, the price of Pillsbury stock rose to nearly $60 per share. O'Hagan then sold his Pillsbury call options and common stock, making a profit of more than $4.3 million.

The Securities and Exchange Commission (SEC or Commission) initiated an investigation into O'Hagan's transactions, culminating in a 57-count indictment [for mail fraud, 10b-5 securities fraud, violating Rule 14e-3, and money laundering statutes]. The indictment alleged that O'Hagan defrauded his law firm and its client, Grand Met, by using for his own trading purposes material, nonpublic information regarding Grand Met's planned tender offer. According to the indictment, O'Hagan used the profits he gained through this trading to conceal his previous embezzlement and conversion of unrelated client trust funds.[1] . . . A jury convicted O'Hagan on all 57 counts, and he was sentenced to a 41-month term of imprisonment. . . .

II

We address first the Court of Appeals' reversal of O'Hagan's convictions under §10(b) and Rule 10b-5. . . .

---

1. O'Hagan was convicted of theft in state court, sentenced to 30 months imprisonment, and fined. See State v. O'Hagan, 474 N.W.2d 613, 615, 623 (Minn. App. 1991). The Supreme Court of Minnesota disbarred O'Hagan from the practice of law. See In re O'Hagan, 450 N.W.2d 571 (Minn. 1990).

A

[Section 10b] proscribes (1) using any deceptive device (2) in connection with the purchase or sale of securities, in contravention of rules prescribed by the Commission. The provision, as written, does not confine its coverage to deception of a purchaser or seller of securities, see United States v. Newman, 664 F.2d 12, 17 (CA2 1981); rather, the statute reaches any deceptive device used "in connection with the purchase or sale of any security." . . .

Under the "traditional" or "classical theory" of insider trading liability, §10(b) and Rule 10b-5 are violated when a corporate insider trades in the securities of his corporation on the basis of material, nonpublic information. Trading on such information qualifies as a "deceptive device" under §10(b), we have affirmed, because "a relationship of trust and confidence [exists] between the shareholders of a corporation and those insiders who have obtained confidential information by reason of their position with that corporation." Chiarella v. United States, 445 U.S. 222, 228 (1980). That relationship, we recognized, "gives rise to a duty to disclose [or to abstain from trading] because of the 'necessity of preventing a corporate insider from . . . tak[ing] unfair advantage of . . . uninformed . . . stockholders.'" (citation omitted). The classical theory applies not only to officers, directors, and other permanent insiders of a corporation, but also to attorneys, accountants, consultants, and others who temporarily become fiduciaries of a corporation. See Dirks v. SEC, 463 U.S. 646, 655, n.14 (1983).

The "misappropriation theory" holds that a person commits fraud "in connection with" a securities transaction, and thereby violates §10(b) and Rule 10b-5, when he misappropriates confidential information for securities trading purposes, in breach of a duty owed to the source of the information. See Brief for United States 14. Under this theory, a fiduciary's undisclosed, self-serving use of a principal's information to purchase or sell securities, in breach of a duty of loyalty and confidentiality, defrauds the principal of the exclusive use of that information. In lieu of premising liability on a fiduciary relationship between company insider and purchaser or seller of the company's stock, the misappropriation theory premises liability on a fiduciary-turned-trader's deception of those who entrusted him with access to confidential information.

The two theories are complementary, each addressing efforts to capitalize on nonpublic information through the purchase or sale of securities. The classical theory targets a corporate insider's breach of duty to shareholders with whom the insider transacts; the misappropriation theory outlaws trading on the basis of nonpublic information by a corporate "outsider" in breach of a duty owed not to a trading party, but to the source of the information. The misappropriation theory is thus designed to "protec[t] the integrity of the securities markets against abuses by 'outsiders' to a corporation who have access to confidential information that will affect th[e] corporation's security price when revealed, but who owe no fiduciary or other duty to that corporation's shareholders." Ibid.

In this case, the indictment alleged that O'Hagan, in breach of a duty of trust and confidence he owed to his law firm, Dorsey & Whitney, and to its client, Grand Met, traded on the basis of nonpublic information regarding Grand Met's planned tender offer for Pillsbury common stock. This conduct, the Government charged, constituted a fraudulent device in connection with the purchase and sale of securities.[5]

B

We agree with the Government that misappropriation, as just defined, satisfies §10(b)'s requirement that chargeable conduct involve a "deceptive device or contrivance" used "in connection with" the purchase or sale of securities. We observe, first, that misappropriators, as the Government describes them, deal in deception. A fiduciary who "[pretends] loyalty to the principal while secretly converting the principal's information for personal gain," Brief for United States 17, "dupes" or defrauds the principal. See Aldave, Misappropriation: A General Theory of Liability for Trading on Nonpublic Information, 13 Hofstra L. Rev. 101, 119 (1984).

We addressed fraud of the same species in Carpenter v. United States, 484 U.S. 19 (1987), which involved the mail fraud statute's proscription of "any scheme or artifice to defraud," 18 U.S.C. §1341. Affirming convictions under that statute, we said in *Carpenter* that an employee's undertaking not to reveal his employer's confidential information "became a sham" when the employee provided the information to his co-conspirators in a scheme to obtain trading profits. A company's confidential information, we recognized in *Carpenter,* qualifies as property to which the company has a right of exclusive use. The undisclosed misappropriation of such information, in violation of a fiduciary duty, the Court said in *Carpenter,* constitutes fraud akin to embezzlement—"'the fraudulent appropriation to one's own use of the money or goods entrusted to one's care by another.'" (quoting Grin v. Shine, 187 U.S. 181, 189 (1902)); see Aldave, 13 Hofstra L. Rev., at 119. Carpenter's discussion of the fraudulent misuse of confidential information, the Government notes, "is a particularly apt source of guidance here, because [the mail fraud statute] (like Section 10(b)) has long been held to require deception, not merely the breach of a fiduciary duty."

Deception through nondisclosure is central to the theory of liability for which the Government seeks recognition. As counsel for the Government stated in explanation of the theory at oral argument: "To satisfy the common law rule that a trustee may not use the property that [has] been entrusted [to] him, there would have to be consent. To satisfy the requirement of the Securities Act that there be no deception, there would

---

5. The Government could not have prosecuted O'Hagan under the classical theory, for O'Hagan was not an "insider" of Pillsbury, the corporation in whose stock he traded. Although an "outsider" with respect to Pillsbury, O'Hagan had an intimate association with, and was found to have traded on confidential information from, Dorsey & Whitney, counsel to tender offeror Grand Met. Under the misappropriation theory, O'Hagan's securities trading does not escape Exchange Act sanction, as it would under the dissent's reasoning, simply because he associated with, and gained nonpublic information from, the bidder, rather than the target.

only have to be disclosure." See generally Restatement (Second) of Agency §§390, 395 (1958) (agent's disclosure obligation regarding use of confidential information).[6]

The misappropriation theory advanced by the Government is consistent with Santa Fe Industries, Inc. v. Green, 430 U.S. 462 (1977), a decision underscoring that §10(b) is not an all-purpose breach of fiduciary duty ban; rather, it trains on conduct involving manipulation or deception. In contrast to the Government's allegations in this case, in *Santa Fe Industries,* all pertinent facts were disclosed by the persons charged with violating §10(b) and Rule 10b-5, therefore, there was no deception through nondisclosure to which liability under those provisions could attach. Similarly, full disclosure forecloses liability under the misappropriation theory: because the deception essential to the misappropriation theory involves feigning fidelity to the source of information, if the fiduciary discloses to the source that he plans to trade on the nonpublic information, there is no "deceptive device" and thus no §10(b) violation, although the fiduciary-turned-trader may remain liable under state law for breach of a duty of loyalty.[7]

We turn next to the §10(b) requirement that the misappropriator's deceptive use of information be "in connection with the purchase or sale of [a] security." This element is satisfied because the fiduciary's fraud is consummated, not when the fiduciary gains the confidential information, but when, without disclosure to his principal, he uses the information to purchase or sell securities. The securities transaction and the breach of duty thus coincide. This is so even though the person or entity defrauded is not the other party to the trade, but is, instead, the source of the nonpublic information. See Aldave, 13 Hofstra L. Rev., at 120 ("a fraud or deceit can be practiced on one person, with resultant harm to another person or group of persons"). A misappropriator who trades on the basis of material, nonpublic information, in short, gains his advantageous market position through deception; he deceives the source of the information and simultaneously harms members of the investing public.

The misappropriation theory targets information of a sort that misappropriators ordinarily capitalize upon to gain no-risk profits through the purchase or sale of securities. Should a misappropriator put such information to other use, the statute's prohibition would not be implicated. The theory does not catch all conceivable forms of fraud involving confidential information; rather, it catches fraudulent means of capitalizing on such information through securities transactions.

The Government notes another limitation on the forms of fraud §10(b) reaches: "The misappropriation theory would not . . . apply to a case in which a person defrauded a bank into giving him a loan or embezzled cash from another, and then used the proceeds of the misdeed to purchase securities." In such a case, the Government states, "the proceeds would have value to the malefactor apart from their use in a securities

---

6. Under the misappropriation theory urged in this case, the disclosure obligation runs to the source of the information, here, Dorsey & Whitney and Grand Met. Chief Justice Burger, dissenting in *Chiarella,* advanced a broader reading of §10(b) and Rule 10b-5; the disclosure obligation, as he envisioned it, ran to those with whom the misappropriator trades. 445 U.S., at 240 ("a person who has misappropriated nonpublic information has an absolute duty to disclose that information or to refrain from trading"). The Government does not propose that we adopt a misappropriation theory of that breadth.

7. Where, however, a person trading on the basis of material nonpublic information owes a duty of loyalty and confidentiality to two entities or persons—for example, a law firm and its clients—but makes disclosure to only one, the trader may still be liable under the misappropriation theory.

transaction, and the fraud would be complete as soon as the money was obtained." In other words, money can buy, if not anything, then at least many things; its misappropriation may thus be viewed as sufficiently detached from a subsequent securities transaction that §10(b)'s "in connection with" requirement would not be met.

The dissent's charge that the misappropriation theory is incoherent because information, like funds, can be put to multiple uses misses the point. The Exchange Act was enacted in part "to insure the maintenance of fair and honest markets," 15 U.S.C. §78b, and there is no question that fraudulent uses of confidential information fall within §10(b)'s prohibition if the fraud is "in connection with" a securities transaction. It is hardly remarkable that a rule suitably applied to the fraudulent uses of certain kinds of information would be stretched beyond reason were it applied to the fraudulent use of money. . . .

The dissent does catch the government in overstatement: Observing that money can be used for all manner of purposes and purchases, the Government urges that confidential information of the kind at issue here derives its value only from its utility in securities trading, substitute "ordinarily" for "only" and the Government is on the mark.

The misappropriation theory comports with §10(b)'s language, which requires deception "in connection with the purchase or sale of any security," not deception of an identifiable purchaser or seller. The theory is also well-tuned to an animating purpose of the Exchange Act: to insure honest securities markets and thereby promote investor confidence. See 45 Fed. Reg. 60412 (1980) (trading on misappropriated information "undermines the integrity of, and investor confidence in, the securities markets"). Although informational disparity is inevitable in the securities markets, investors likely would hesitate to venture their capital in a market where trading based on misappropriated nonpublic information is unchecked by law. An investor's informational disadvantage vis-à-vis a misappropriator with material, nonpublic information stems from contrivance, not luck; it is a disadvantage that cannot be overcome with research or skill. See Brudney, Insiders, Outsiders, and Informational Advantages Under the Federal Securities Laws, 93 Harv. L. Rev. 322, 356 (1979) ("If the market is thought to be systematically populated with . . . transactors [trading on the basis of misappropriated information] some investors will refrain from dealing altogether, and others will incur costs to avoid dealing with such transactors or corruptly to overcome their unerodable informational advantages.").

In sum, considering the inhibiting impact on market participation of trading on misappropriated information, and the congressional purposes underlying §10(b), it makes scant sense to hold a lawyer like O'Hagan a §10(b) violator if he works for a law firm representing the target of a tender offer, but not if he works for a law firm representing the bidder. The text of the statute requires no such result.[9] The misappropriation

---

9. As noted earlier, however, the textual requirement of deception precludes §10(b) liability when a person trading on the basis of nonpublic information has disclosed his trading plans to, or obtained authorization from, the principal, even though such conduct may affect the securities markets in the same manner as the conduct reached by the misappropriation theory. Contrary to the dissent's suggestion, the fact that §10(b) is only a partial antidote to the problems it was designed to alleviate does not call into question its prohibition of conduct that falls within its textual proscription. Moreover, once a disloyal agent discloses his imminent breach of duty, his principal may seek appropriate equitable relief under state law. Furthermore, in the context of a tender offer, the principal who authorizes an agent's trading on confidential information may, in the Commission's view, incur liability for an Exchange Act violation under Rule 14e-3(a).

at issue here was properly made the subject of a §10(b) charge because it meets the statutory requirement that there be "deceptive" conduct "in connection with" securities transactions. . . .

[T]he misappropriation theory, as we have examined and explained it in this opinion, is both consistent with the statute and with our precedent. Vital to our decision that criminal liability may be sustained under the misappropriation theory, we emphasize, are two sturdy safeguards Congress has provided regarding scienter. To establish a criminal violation of Rule 10b-5, the Government must prove that a person "willfully" violated the provision. See 15 U.S.C. §78ff(a). Furthermore, a defendant may not be imprisoned for violating Rule 10b-5 if he proves that he had no knowledge of the rule. See ibid. O'Hagan's charge that the misappropriation theory is too indefinite to permit the imposition of criminal liability thus fails not only because the theory is limited to those who breach a recognized duty. In addition, the statute's "requirement of the presence of culpable intent as a necessary element of the offense does much to destroy any force in the argument that application of the [statute]" in circumstances such as O'Hagan's is unjust. . . .

III

. . . Did the Commission, as the Court of Appeals held, exceed its rulemaking authority under §14(e) when it adopted Rule 14e-3(a) without requiring a showing that the trading at issue entailed a breach of fiduciary duty? We hold that the Commission, in this regard and to the extent relevant to this case, did not exceed its authority. . . .

Section 14(e)'s first sentence prohibits fraudulent acts in connection with a tender offer. This self-operating proscription was one of several provisions added to the Exchange Act in 1968 by the Williams Act. The section's second sentence delegates definitional and prophylactic rulemaking authority to the Commission. Congress added this rulemaking delegation to §14(e) in 1970 amendments to the Williams Act.

Through §14(e) and other provisions on disclosure in the Williams Act, Congress sought to ensure that shareholders "confronted by a cash tender offer for their stock [would] not be required to respond without adequate information," Rondeau v. Mosinee Paper Corp., 422 U.S. 49, 58 (1975) [see Lewis v. McGraw, 619 F.2d 192, 195 (CA2 1980) (per curiam) ("very purpose" of Williams Act was "informed decisionmaking by shareholders")]. As we recognized in Schreiber v. Burlington Northern, Inc., 472 U.S. 1 (1985), Congress designed the Williams Act to make "disclosure, rather than court-imposed principles of 'fairness' or 'artificiality,' . . . the preferred method of market regulation." Section 14(e), we explained, "supplements the more precise disclosure provisions found elsewhere in the Williams Act, while requiring disclosure more explicitly addressed to the tender offer context than that required by §10(b)." . . .

As characterized by the Commission, Rule 14e-3(a) is a "disclose or abstain from trading" requirement.[15] The Second Circuit concisely described the rule's thrust:

---

15. The rule thus adopts for the tender offer context a requirement resembling the one Chief Justice Burger would have adopted in *Chiarella* for misappropriators under §10(b). See supra, n.6.

One violates Rule 14e-3(a) if he trades on the basis of material nonpublic information concerning a pending tender offer that he knows or has reason to know has been acquired "directly or indirectly" from an insider of the offeror or issuer, or someone working on their behalf. Rule 14e-3(a) is a disclosure provision. It creates a duty in those traders who fall within its ambit to abstain or disclose, *without regard to whether the trader owes a pre-existing fiduciary duty* to respect the confidentiality of the information.

United States v. Chestman, 947 F.2d 551, 557 (1991) (en banc) (emphasis added), cert. denied, 503 U.S. 1004 (1992).

In the Eighth Circuit's view, because Rule 14e-3(a) applies whether or not the trading in question breaches a fiduciary duty, the regulation exceeds the SEC's §14(e) rulemaking authority. . . . [T]he SEC may "identify and regulate," in the tender offer context, "acts and practices" the law already defines as "fraudulent;" but, the Eighth Circuit maintained, the SEC may not "create its own definition of fraud." . . . Section 10(b) interpretations guide construction of §14(e), the Eighth Circuit added, citing this Court's acknowledgment in Schreiber that §14(e)'s "'broad antifraud prohibition' . . . [is] modeled on the antifraud provisions of §10(b) . . . and Rule 10b-5."

For the meaning of "fraudulent" under §10(b), the Eighth Circuit looked to *Chiarella*. In that case, the Eighth Circuit recounted, this Court held that a failure to disclose information could be "fraudulent" under §10(b) only when there was a duty to speak arising out of "'a fiduciary or other similar relationship of trust and confidence.'" *Chiarella*, 445 U.S., at 228 (quoting Restatement (Second) of Torts §551(2) (a) (1976)). Just as §10(b) demands a showing of a breach of fiduciary duty, so such a breach is necessary to make out a §14(e) violation, the Eighth Circuit concluded. . . .

We need not resolve in this case whether the Commission's authority under §14(e) to "define . . . such acts and practices as are fraudulent" is broader than the Commission's fraud-defining authority under §10(b), for we agree with the United States that Rule 14e-3(a), as applied to cases of this genre, qualifies under §14(e) as a "means reasonably designed to prevent" fraudulent trading on material, nonpublic information in the tender offer context.[17] A prophylactic measure, because its mission is to prevent, typically encompasses more than the core activity prohibited. . . . We hold, accordingly, that under §14(e), the Commission may prohibit acts, not themselves fraudulent under the common law or §10(b), if the prohibition is "reasonably designed to prevent . . . acts and practices [that] are fraudulent."[18]

Because Congress has authorized the Commission, in §14(e), to prescribe legislative rules, we owe the Commission's judgment "more than mere deference or weight."

---

17. We leave for another day, when the issue requires decision, the legitimacy of Rule 14e-3(a) as applied to "warehousing," which the Government describes as "the practice by which bidders leak advance information of a tender offer to allies and encourage them to purchase the target company's stock before the bid is announced." As we observed in *Chiarella*, one of the Commission's purposes in proposing Rule 14e-3(a) was "to bar warehousing under its authority to regulate tender offers." 445 U.S., at 234. The Government acknowledges that trading authorized by a principal breaches no fiduciary duty. The instant case, however, does not involve trading authorized by a principal; therefore, we need not here decide whether the Commission's proscription of warehousing falls within its §14(e) authority to define or prevent fraud.

18. The Commission's power under §10(b) is more limited. See supra (Rule 10b-5 may proscribe only conduct that §10(b) prohibits).

Batterton v. Francis, 432 U.S. 416, 424-426 (1977). Therefore, in determining whether Rule 14e-3(a)'s "disclose or abstain from trading" requirement is reasonably designed to prevent fraudulent acts, we must accord the Commission's assessment "controlling weight unless [it is] arbitrary, capricious, or manifestly contrary to the statute." Chevron U.S.A. Inc. v. Natural Resources Defense Council, Inc., 467 U.S. 837, 844 (1984). In this case, we conclude, the Commission's assessment is none of these.

In adopting the "disclose or abstain" rule, the SEC explained:

> The Commission has previously expressed and continues to have serious concerns about trading by persons in possession of material, nonpublic information relating to a tender offer. This practice results in unfair disparities in market information and market disruption. Security holders who purchase from or sell to such persons are effectively denied the benefits of disclosure and the substantive protections of the Williams Act. If furnished with the information, these security holders would be able to make an informed investment decision, which could involve deferring the purchase or sale of the securities until the material information had been disseminated or until the tender offer has been commenced or terminated.

45 Fed. Reg. 60412 (1980) (footnotes omitted).

The Commission thus justified Rule 14e-3(a) as a means necessary and proper to assure the efficacy of Williams Act protections.

The United States emphasizes that Rule 14e-3(a) reaches trading in which "a breach of duty is likely but difficult to prove." "Particularly in the context of a tender offer," as the Tenth Circuit recognized, "there is a fairly wide circle of people with confidential information," *Peters,* 978 F.2d, at 1167, notably, the attorneys, investment bankers, and accountants involved in structuring the transaction. The availability of that information may lead to abuse, for "even a hint of an upcoming tender offer may send the price of the target company's stock soaring." SEC v. Materia, 745 F.2d 197, 199 (CA2 1984). Individuals entrusted with nonpublic information, particularly if they have no long-term loyalty to the issuer, may find the temptation to trade on that information hard to resist in view of "the very large short-term profits potentially available [to them]." *Peters,* 978 F.2d, at 1167.

"[I]t may be possible to prove circumstantially that a person [traded on the basis of material, nonpublic information], but almost impossible to prove that the trader obtained such information in breach of a fiduciary duty owed either by the trader or by the ultimate insider source of the information." Ibid. The example of a "tippee" who trades on information received from an insider illustrates the problem. Under Rule 10b-5, "a tippee assumes a fiduciary duty to the shareholders of a corporation not to trade on material nonpublic information only when the insider has breached his fiduciary duty to the shareholders by disclosing the information to the tippee and the tippee knows or should know that there has been a breach." *Dirks,* 463 U.S., at 660. To show that a tippee who traded on nonpublic information about a tender offer had breached a fiduciary duty would require proof not only that the insider source breached a fiduciary duty, but that the tippee knew or should have known of that breach. "Yet, in most cases, the only parties to the [information transfer] will be the insider and the alleged tippee." *Peters,* 978 F.2d, at 1167.

In sum, it is a fair assumption that trading on the basis of material, nonpublic information will often involve a breach of a duty of confidentiality to the bidder or target company or their representatives. The SEC, cognizant of the proof problem that could enable sophisticated traders to escape responsibility, placed in Rule 14e-3(a) a "disclose or abstain from trading" command that does not require specific proof of a breach of fiduciary duty. That prescription, we are satisfied, applied to this case, is a "means reasonably designed to prevent" fraudulent trading on material, nonpublic information in the tender offer context. See *Chestman,* 947 F.2d, at 560 ("While dispensing with the subtle problems of proof associated with demonstrating fiduciary breach in the problematic area of tender offer insider trading, [Rule 14e-3(a)] retains a close nexus between the prohibited conduct and the statutory aims."); [accord, *Maio,* 51 F.3d, at 635, and n. 14; *Peters,* 978 F.2d, at 1167]. Therefore, insofar as it serves to prevent the type of misappropriation charged against O'Hagan, Rule 14e-3(a) is a proper exercise of the Commission's prophylactic power under §14(e). . . .

[The opinion of JUSTICE SCALIA, concurring in part and dissenting in part, is omitted.]

JUSTICE THOMAS, with whom THE CHIEF JUSTICE joins, concurring in the judgment in part and dissenting in part.

What the [majority's] embezzlement analogy does not do, however, is explain how the relevant fraud is "use[d] or employ[ed], in connection with" a securities transaction. And when the majority seeks to distinguish the embezzlement of funds from the embezzlement of information, it becomes clear that neither the Commission nor the majority has a coherent theory regarding §10(b)'s "in connection with" requirement.

Turning first to why embezzlement of information supposedly meets the "in connection with" requirement, the majority asserts that the requirement

is satisfied because the fiduciary's fraud is consummated, not when the fiduciary gains the confidential information, but when, without disclosure to his principal, he uses the information to purchase or sell securities. The securities transaction and the breach of duty thus coincide.

The majority later notes, with apparent approval, the Government's contention that the embezzlement of funds used to purchase securities would *not* fall within the misappropriation theory. The misappropriation of funds used for a securities transaction is not covered by its theory, the Government explains, because "the proceeds would have value to the malefactor apart from their use in a securities transaction, and the fraud would be complete as soon as the money was obtained."

Accepting the Government's description of the scope of its own theory, it becomes plain that the majority's explanation of how the misappropriation theory supposedly satisfies the "in connection with" requirement is incomplete. The touchstone required for an embezzlement to be "use[d] or employ[ed], in connection with" a securities transaction is not merely that it "coincide" with, or be consummated by, the transaction, but that it is *necessarily* and *only* consummated by the transaction. Where the property being embezzled has value "apart from [its] use in a securities transaction"—even though it is in fact being used in a securities transaction—the Government contends that there is no violation under the misappropriation theory. . . .

The Government's construction of the "in connection with" requirement—and its claim that such requirement precludes coverage of financial embezzlement—also demonstrates how the majority's described distinction of financial embezzlement is incomplete. Although the majority claims that the fraud in a financial embezzlement case is complete as soon as the money is obtained, and before the securities transaction is consummated, that is not uniformly true, and thus cannot be the Government's basis for claiming that such embezzlement does not violate the securities laws. It is not difficult to imagine an embezzlement of money that takes place via the mechanism of a securities transaction, for example where a broker is directed to purchase stock for a client and instead purchases such stock, using client funds, for his own account. The unauthorized (and presumably undisclosed) transaction is the very act that constitutes the embezzlement and the "securities transaction and the breach of duty thus coincide." What presumably distinguishes monetary embezzlement for the Government is thus that it is not necessarily coincident with a securities transaction, not that it never lacks such a "connection."

Once the Government's construction of the misappropriation theory is accurately described and accepted—along with its implied construction of §10(b)'s "in connection with" language—that theory should no longer cover cases, such as this one, involving fraud on the source of information where the source has no connection with the other participant in a securities transaction. It seems obvious that the undisclosed misappropriation of confidential information is not necessarily consummated by a securities transaction. In this case, for example, upon learning of Grand Met's confidential takeover plans, O'Hagan could have done any number of things with the information: He could have sold it to a newspaper for publication, he could have given or sold the information to Pillsbury itself, or he could even have kept the information and used it solely for his personal amusement, perhaps in a fantasy stock trading game.

Any of these activities would have deprived Grand Met of its right to "exclusive use," of the information and, if undisclosed, would constitute "embezzlement" of Grand Met's informational property. Under any theory of liability, however, these activities would not violate §10(b) and, according to the Commission's monetary embezzlement analogy, these possibilities are sufficient to preclude a violation under the misappropriation theory even where the informational property was used for securities trading. That O'Hagan actually did use the information to purchase securities is thus no more significant here than it is in the case of embezzling money used to purchase securities. In both cases the embezzler could have done something else with the property, and hence the Commission's necessary "connection" under the securities laws would not be met. If the relevant test under the "in connection with" language is whether the fraudulent act is necessarily tied to a securities transaction, then the misappropriation of confidential information used to trade no more violates §10(b) than does the misappropriation of funds used to trade. As the Commission concedes that the latter is not covered under its theory, I am at a loss to see how the same theory can coherently be applied to the former. . . .

NOTES AND QUESTIONS

1. The Court stated that the misappropriation theory applies to a person who "misappropriates confidential information for securities trading purposes, in breach of a

duty owed to the source of the information." Does the misappropriation theory have the breadth of the information theory rejected in *Chiarella* or does agency law act as a recognizable limit that prevents misappropriation from becoming a parity of information rule? Consider whether the following relationships would satisfy that duty (this list is drawn from appellate cases prior to *O'Hagan*):

- Between an employer and employee or former employee, see United States v. Newman, 664 F.2d 12 (2d Cir. 1981); United States v. Cherif, 933 F.2d 403 (7th Cir. 1991);
- Between a newspaper and its reporter, see United States v. Carpenter, 791 F.2d 1024 (2d Cir. 1986), aff'd (as to 10b-5 claims) by an equally divided court, 484 U.S. 19 (1987);
- Between a psychiatrist and patient, see United States v. Willis, 737 F. Supp. 269 (S.D.N.Y. 1990);
- Between a government official and his constituency, see United States v. Bryan, 58 F.3d 933 (4th Cir. 1995);
- Between a father and son, see United States v. Reed, 601 F. Supp. 685 (S.D.N.Y.), rev'd on other grounds, 773 F.2d 477 (2d Cir. 1985);
- Between a husband and wife, see United States v. Chestman, 947 F.2d 551 (2d Cir. en banc 1991).

United States v. Chestman, a pre-*O'Hagan* en banc decision of the Second Circuit, illustrates the difficulty of this line drawing. In that case, the relevant information could be traced to the founder of a business that was about to be sold who told his sister, who was a member of the board (so she might tender her shares with his), who in turn told her daughter (while warning her not to tell anyone but her husband because disclosure could ruin the sale), who told her husband (cautioning him not to tell anyone because "it could possibly ruin the sale"), who telephoned his stockbroker, who executed several trades. The question was whether misappropriation would cover the husband's receipt and use of information.

First, a fiduciary duty cannot be imposed unilaterally by entrusting a person with confidential information. . . .

Second, marriage does not, without more, create a fiduciary relationship. . . . [M]ore than the gratuitous reposal of a secret to another who happens to be a family member is required to establish a fiduciary or similar relationship of trust and confidence.

We take our cues as to what is required to create the requisite relationship from the securities fraud precedents and the common law. See *Chiarella*, 445 U.S. at 227-230. The common law has recognized that some associations are inherently fiduciary. Counted among these hornbook fiduciary relations are those existing between attorney and client, executor and heir, guardian and ward, principal and agent, trustee and trust beneficiary, and senior corporate official and shareholder . . .

That does not end our inquiry, however. The misappropriation theory requires us to consider not only whether there exists a fiduciary relationship but also whether there exists a "similar relationship of trust and confidence." As the term "similar" implies, a "relationship of trust and confidence" must share the essential characteristics of a fiduciary association. . . .

A fiduciary relationship involves discretionary authority and dependence: One person depends on another—the fiduciary—to serve his interests. In relying on a fiduciary to act for his benefit, the beneficiary of the relation may entrust the fiduciary with custody over property of one sort or another. Because the fiduciary obtains access to this property to serve the ends of the fiduciary relationship, he becomes duty-bound not to appropriate the property for his own use. What has been said of an agent's duty of confidentiality applies with equal force to other fiduciary relations: "an agent is subject to a duty to the principal not to use or to communicate information confidentially given him by the principal or acquired by him during the course of or on account of his agency." Restatement (Second) of Agency 395 (1958). These characteristics represent the measure of the paradigmatic fiduciary relationship. A similar relationship of trust and confidence consequently must share these qualities.

. . . . To remain consistent with our interpretation of a "similar relationship of trust and confidence," . . . we limit [*United States v.*] *Reed* to its essential holding: the repeated disclosure of business secrets between family members may substitute for a factual finding of dependence and influence and thereby sustain a finding of the functional equivalent of a fiduciary relationship. We note, in this regard, that *Reed* repeatedly emphasized that the father and son "frequently discussed business affairs." Id. at 690; see also id. at 705, 17-18.

Rule 10b5-2, promulgated subsequent to this case, creates a rebuttable presumption that a duty of trust or confidence exists whenever a person receives or obtains material nonpublic information from his or her spouse, child, or sibling.

2. Can tippee liability be combined with misappropriation liability? The federal appellate courts have said yes. See SEC v. Yun, 327 F.3d 1263, 1275-1276 (11th Cir. 2003) ("In either case the tippee is under notice that he received confidential information through an improper breach of a duty of loyalty and confidentiality"; but rejecting SEC's argument that the *Dirks* benefit requirement applied only to "classic" liability and not to misappropriation).

3. To what extent does misappropriation federalize a cause of action developed at state law? The Fourth Circuit in United States v. Bryan, 58 F.3d 933 (4th Cir. 1995), said, "The superimposition of a 'federal fiduciary principle,' *Santa Fe,* 430 U.S. at 479, however, would usurp the states' common law and statutory authority over fiduciary relationships, violating the Court's injunction in *Santa Fe* against the use of the federal securities laws to regulate areas of conduct 'traditionally relegated to state law.'" Wouldn't that argument apply equally to the classic insider trading liability sanctioned by the Court in *Chiarella* written not long after *Santa Fe,* which necessarily turns on federalizing the common law of deceit? Can the two cases be reconciled by *Santa Fe*'s focus on preempting established state policies of corporate regulation as opposed to the then relatively undeveloped law on insider trading at state law?

In any event, compare Justice Ginsburg's response (at page 1169), which echoes more the Second Circuit's artful distinction of *Santa Fe* in Goldberg v. Meridor in Chapter 10 (page 1008). The lower court in *Santa Fe* sought to use 10b-5 in a situation where all pertinent facts had been disclosed, and the Supreme Court held that it wentbeyond the bounds of the rule and statute to find fraud when there had been full disclosure; if as in *Goldberg* and *O'Hagan* there was not full disclosure, *Santa Fe* can be distinguished. Such reasoning makes both *Goldberg* and *O'Hagan* consistent with Part III of *Santa Fe,* but doesn't it duck the hard federalism question raised, but not answered, in Part IV of *Santa Fe?*

Federal law least displaces state law in the context where a fiduciary discloses to her principal her intent to trade, thereby avoiding 10b-5 liability, but opening herself up to a claim based on breach of fiduciary duty. In the more common situation where no disclosure takes place, the federal insider trading claim serves as a more effective substitute for the common law claim.

4. In the 17 years between *Chiarella* and *O'Hagan,* the Supreme Court's only decision on misappropriation, Carpenter v. United States, 484 U.S. 19 (1987), resulted in a 4-4 split and thus affirmance without discussion of a Second Circuit decision finding liability where a Wall Street Journal reporter had used information prior to its appearing in a popular column in the newspaper. The vacant seat on the court at the time was due to the retirement of Justice Powell, the author of *Chiarella* and *Dirks.* There is, however, evidence that Justice Powell almost certainly would have voted to reject misappropriation. The papers of Justice Thurgood Marshall include Powell's draft dissent to the court's initial refusal to grant certiorari of the lower court opinion approving misappropriation. Thereafter, two justices switched positions and agreed to hear the case, so the dissent was never published. Because of his retirement, Justice Powell did not participate when the case was heard, but his draft dissent clearly indicates his view that misappropriation could not come within the standard set in *Chiarella.* The draft opinion noted "such liability (failure to disclose) is premised upon a duty to disclose arising from a relationship of trust and confidence *between parties to a transaction.*" (Emphasis in the original.) See A.C. Pritchard, United States v. O'Hagan: Agency Law and Justice Powell's Legacy for the Law of Insider Trading, 78 Boston U. L. Rev. 13, 55 (1998). That view and the opinions in *Chiarella* and *Dirks* reflect the common law action of deceit and the torts concepts that it embodies. The Supreme Court's opinion in *O'Hagan* approves misappropriation using language from the common law of agency, also found in the state law material at the beginning of this chapter.

5. Rule 14e-3 was promulgated by the SEC shortly after *Chiarella* at a time when tender offers were a frequent source of information that created lucrative trading opportunities. Does it enact the parity of information standard rejected in *Chiarella?*

6. The *O'Hagan* majority opinion states, "[I]t would make scant sense to hold a lawyer like O'Hagan a §10(b) violator if he works for a law firm representing the target of a tender offer, but not if he works for a law firm representing the bidder." Does 14e-3 make someone like the husband in *Chestman* (Note 1) liable if he learns information about a tender offer, but not if he learns equivalent information from his wife about a takeover that is to take the form of a friendly merger as opposed to a tender offer?

PROBLEM 12-5

C arrives an hour late for a regular appointment with *H,* a local hairstylist, and is obviously distraught. *C* explains her delay as due to having just heard that *C*'s spouse, *S,* a well-known executive in the financial business, is about to announce a takeover of *X* Corp. that will cause *S* and *C* to move to a distant city. Can *H* buy shares in *X* without incurring liability under Rule 10b-5?

PROBLEM 12-6

Angela, an associate at a major New York law firm, has been working intensely on a merger in which her firm represents the acquiring company. The terms of the merger provide Target, Inc. shareholders with consideration that will be a 30 percent premium over the most recent market price. Angela tells the partner at the law firm with whom she has been working that she is resigning her job at the law firm and plans to buy shares in Target, Inc., and that she will be living on the proceeds at a faraway beach. Does she have any liability for insider trading?

PROBLEM 12-7

A director of a corporation that is about to make a tender offer to take over another corporation tells his adult son, who is a government official, of the proposed takeover. The son thereupon buys an option in the target, which he sells three days later for a $400,000 profit.

Would the son be liable for insider trading?

PROBLEM 12-8

Movie mogul Sid owns a Malibu beach house as a retreat from his Beverly Hills mansion and as a place where his wife and their two grown sons and their families can gather for quiet family weekends. On such a weekend, their son Jonathan, 33, arrived at a time when Sid was on the telephone in the next room, and Jonathan overheard Sid discussing secret negotiations for his company to be purchased by a Japanese conglomerate. After hanging up the phone and being informed by his wife that Jonathan overheard the conversation, Sid asked Jonathan to come along on his morning walk, during which he warned his son not to trade the corporation stock and not to do anything with the information. During the next few days Jonathan passed the word to his wife, from whom he was separated, and his wife's lover purchased the stock. He also told his business manager, "I can't purchase shares, but you should." The business manager then purchased shares. Jonathan also told his own lover, who told her mother, who told her father, who immediately called his broker, placing a large order on a Sunday evening, telling the broker, "I hear something is going on." The broker replied, "I hope you don't know anything." Can the SEC come after Jonathan for any or all of these trades?

PROBLEM 12-9

Martha Stewart sold shares of ImClone on December 27, 2001, just ahead of the company's public announcement that its lead pharmaceutical product would not receive government approval. The key parties for the discussion in this context included:

- Sam Waksal, then CEO of ImClone Systems, Inc.;
- Aliza Waksal, his daughter;
- Peter Baconovic, a stockbroker whose clients included both the Waksals and Martha Stewart;
- Martha Stewart, a friend of Sam Waksal and CEO of Martha Stewart Living Omnimedia, Inc.

Sam Waksal tried to sell his shares through Baconovic but was unsuccessful because the broker's firm declined to pursue the trade, citing SEC rules against insider trading. Aliza did sell shares that day through the brokerage firm. In addition, Baconovic sent word to Martha Stewart, en route to Mexico on a private plane, about the Waksal's selling and she had the broker sell her shares.

What is the theory by which each of the four could be liable for insider trading?

PROBLEM 12-10

Several months ago, Paula Poland purchased a substantial block of stock in Virtuoso, Inc. Recently, Virtuoso's CEO called Poland and disclosed the company's need to raise additional capital as rapidly as possible, its plans to do so via a private placement, and its hope that Poland would participate in the new round of financing. Poland reacted angrily. Not only did she not want to participate but worried about the dilution of her own shares. According to an SEC complaint brought against Poland alleging insider trading, she responded, "Well, now I'm screwed: I can't sell." In any event Poland did sell and avoided a loss of around $750,000 that she would have suffered had she held on to her stock until Virtuoso's public announcement of its plans and the fall in the price of the stock. What result under O'Hagan?

NOTE: ENFORCEMENT

Since misappropriation turns on the breach of a duty to the source of material nonpublic information, and not on the insider's fiduciary duty to the issuing company and its shareholders, who is the appropriate person to bring the suit? Judicial responses to these and other standing issues and several pieces of federal legislation have given enforcement of insider trading a more public bent with a large increase in both civil suits brought by the SEC and criminal prosecutions by the federal government.

Some courts held that investors could not recover from insider traders without proof that the trading had caused the investors' injury. See, e.g., Fridrich v. Bradford, 542 F.2d 307 (6th Cir. 1976), cert. denied, 429 U.S. 1053 (1977). For theories based on misappropriation, a duty to an employer does not translate into a duty to the shareholders of the unrelated company whose stock the defendant bought. See Moss v. Morgan Stanley, Inc., 719 F.2d 5 (2d Cir. 1983), cert. denied, 465 U.S. 1025 (1984).

In 1988 Congress added §20A to the 1934 Act, which provides an express cause of action to contemporaneous traders of "any person who violates any provisions of this chapter or the rules or regulations thereunder by purchasing or selling a security while in possession of material, nonpublic information." While creating an express cause of action, the statute does not define insider trading, leaving case law to provide the definition of the offense. The statute limits a defendant's total exposure to the amount of gain (or loss avoided).

The House committee report accompanying the 1988 legislation stated:

In particular, the codification of a right of action for contemporaneous traders is specifically intended to overturn court cases which have precluded recovery for plaintiffs where the defendant's violation is premised upon the misappropriation theory. See e.g., Moss v. Morgan Stanley, 719 F.2d 5 (2d Cir. 1983). The Committee believes that this result is inconsistent with the remedial purposes of the Exchange Act, and that the misappropriation theory fulfills appropriate regulatory objectives in determining when communicating or trading while in possession of material non-public information is unlawful. The bill does not define the term "contemporaneous" which has developed through case law.

H.R. Rep. No. 910 (House Energy and Commerce Committee) to accompany H.R. 5133, 100th Cong., 2d Sess. 26-27 (1988).

In the 1980s, the SEC's power to combat insider trading was considerably strengthened with provisions permitting the SEC to recover three times the amount of the trader's profits or loss avoided and to also recover from control persons of the violators. See Insider Trading Sanctions Act of 1984. In the Insider Trading and Securities Fraud Enforcement Act of 1988, Congress authorized civil penalties for controlling persons up to the greater of $1 million or three times the profit gained or loss avoided. These penalties are in addition to any disgorgement or criminal fine that may be ordered.

Criminal prosecutions have increased dramatically since *Chiarella*. In Carpenter v. United States, the Supreme Court split 4-4 on the misappropriation claim, but it unanimously affirmed the convictions based on mail and wire fraud statutes. This increased use of criminal law has sparked some criticism. See Coffee, Hush! The Criminal Status of Confidential Information After *McNalley* and *Carpenter* and the Enduring Problem of Overcriminalization, 26 Am. Crim. L. Rev. 121 (1988) (*Carpenter* overcriminalizes what should be a matter of civil law).

As the civil and criminal penalties and the number of insider trading cases have increased, the debate over the lack of a definition of insider trading in the statute or in an SEC rule has increased both in Congress and in academic commentary. See, e.g., Symposium: Defining Insider Trading, 39 Ala. L. Rev. 337 (1988). The House committee report accompanying the 1988 legislation explained the continued statutory silence on a definition of insider trading:

While cognizant of the importance of providing clear guidelines for behavior which may be subject to stiff criminal and civil penalties, the Committee nevertheless declined to include a statutory definition in this bill for several reasons. First, the Committee believed that the court-drawn parameters of insider trading have established clear guidelines for the vast majority of traditional insider trading cases, and that a statutory definition could potentially be narrowing, and in an unintended manner facilitate schemes to evade the law. Second, the Committee did not believe that the lack of consensus over the proper delineation of an insider trading definition should impede progress on the needed enforcement reforms encompassed within this legislation. Accordingly, the Committee does not intend to alter the substantive law with respect to insider trading with this legislation. The legal principles governing insider trading cases are well-established and widely-known.

H.R. Rep. No. 910 (House Energy and Commerce Committee) to accompany H.R. 5133, 100th Cong., 2d Sess. 11 (1988).

C. Regulation of Short-Swing Insider Trading Under §16 of the Securities Exchange Act of 1934

The increased attention paid to insider trading under §10(b), the antifraud section of the Securities Exchange Act of 1934, and to the more recent legislation that derives from §10(b) has obscured §16, the part of the 1934 Act that was originally intended to deal with insider trading. Section 16 takes a different approach by requiring disgorgement of profits of three named groups of defendants—directors, officers, and 10 percent shareholders—based on a purchase and sale occurring within six months of each other.

Since recovery is for the corporation, the question from Chapter 4 arises again—who may speak for the enterprise in this situation? Congress chose not to leave the corporate enforcement solely in the hands of the directors since they might be defendants, but authorized individual shareholders to bring a cause of action in the corporation's name. Section 16(b) violations are easier to discover than most law violations because of the public reporting of trading required by §16(a). Both parts of §16 apply to companies registered under Section 12 of the 1934 Act. In rules promulgated in 1991, the SEC requires corporations to state in their annual report any insiders who are not current with their §16(a) reporting.

The Supreme Court described the Congressional purpose of §16 this way:

> Prohibiting short-swing trading by insiders with nonpublic information was an important part of Congress' plan in the 1934 Act to "insure the maintenance of fair and honest markets," 15 U.S.C. §78b; and to eliminate such trading, Congress enacted a "flat rule [in §16(b)] taking the profits out of a class of transactions in which the possibility of abuse was believed to be intolerably great." Reliance Elec. Co. v. Emerson Elec. Co., 404 U.S. 418, 422 (1972). . . .
>
> The statute imposes a form of strict liability on "beneficial owners," as well as on the issuer's officers and directors, rendering them liable to suits requiring them to disgorge their profits even if they did not trade on inside information or intend to profit on the basis of such information. Because the statute imposes "liability without fault within its narrowly drawn limits," Foremost-McKesson, Inc. v. Provident Securities Co., supra, at 251, we have been reluctant to exceed a literal, "mechanical" application of the statutory text in determining who may be subject to liability, even though in some cases a broader view of statutory liability could work to eliminate an "evil that Congress sought to correct through §16(b)." Reliance Elec. Co. v. Emerson Elec. Co., supra, at 425.
>
> To enforce this strict liability rule on insider trading, Congress chose to rely solely on the issuers of stock and their security holders. Unlike most of the federal securities laws, §16(b) does not confer enforcement authority on the Securities and Exchange Commission. It is, rather, the security holders of an issuer who have the ultimate authority to sue for enforcement of §16(b). If the issuer declines to bring a §16(b) action within 60 days of a demand by a security holder, or fails to prosecute the action "diligently," 15 U.S.C. §78p(b), then the security holder may "institute" an action to recover insider short-swing profits for the issuer. Ibid.
>
> In contrast to the "narrowly drawn limits" on the class of corporate insiders who may be defendants under §16(b), the statutory definitions identifying the class of plaintiffs (other than the issuer) who may bring suit indicate that Congress intended to grant enforcement standing of considerable breadth. The only textual restrictions on the standing of a party to bring suit under §16(b) are that the plaintiff must be the "owner of [a] security" of the "issuer" at the time the suit is "instituted."

Gollust v. Mendell, 501 U.S. 115, 121-123 (1991).

The severity of §16(b) is heightened by the method commonly used to calculate damage, not "first in, first out," some tracing of actual shares, or averaging, but rather lowest price in, highest price out within six months. Smolowe v. Delendo Corp., 136 F.2d 231, 239 (2d Cir.), cert. denied, 320 U.S. 751 (1943) ("We must suppose that the statute was intended to be thorough going, to squeeze all possible profits out of stock transactions and thus to establish a standard so high as to prevent any conflict between the selfish interest of a fiduciary officer, director, or stockholder and the faithful performance of his duty. The only rule whereby all possible profits can be surely recovered is that of lowest price in, highest price out—within six months.").

PROBLEM 12-11

A director engaged in the following stock transactions of her company:

1. April 1, 2013, purchases 100 shares at $20.
2. May 1, 2013, sells 100 shares at $15.
3. October 15, 2013, purchases 100 shares at $10.
4. November 15, 2013, sells 100 shares at $5.

What would be the liability under §16(b)?

Table of Cases

Index